COMPETITION IN ENERGY MARKETS
Law and Regulation in the European Union

COMPETITION IN ENERGY MARKETS

Law and Regulation in the European Union

SECOND EDITION

Peter Duncanson Cameron

OXFORD
UNIVERSITY PRESS

OXFORD
UNIVERSITY PRESS

Great Clarendon Street, Oxford OX2 6DP

Oxford University Press is a department of the University of Oxford.
It furthers the University's objective of excellence in research, scholarship,
and education by publishing worldwide in

Oxford New York

Auckland Cape Town Dar es Salaam Hong Kong Karachi
Kuala Lumpur Madrid Melbourne Mexico City Nairobi
New Delhi Shanghai Taipei Toronto

With offices in

Argentina Austria Brazil Chile Czech Republic France Greece
Guatemala Hungary Italy Japan Poland Portugal Singapore
South Korea Switzerland Thailand Turkey Ukraine Vietnam

Oxford is a registered trade mark of Oxford University Press
in the UK and in certain other countries

Published in the United States
by Oxford University Press Inc., New York

© Peter Cameron, 2007

The moral rights of the author have been asserted
Database right Oxford University Press (maker)

First Edition published 2002
Second Edition 2007

All rights reserved. No part of this publication may be reproduced,
stored in a retrieval system, or transmitted, in any form or by any means,
without the prior permission in writing of Oxford University Press,
or as expressly permitted by law, or under terms agreed with the appropriate
reprographics rights organization. Enquiries concerning reproduction
outside the scope of the above should be sent to the Rights Department,
Oxford University Press, at the address above

You must not circulate this book in any other binding or cover
and you must impose this same condition on any acquirer

British Library Cataloguing in Publication Data
Data available

Library of Congress Cataloging in Publication Data

Cameron, Peter D.
  Competition in energy markets : law and regulation in the European Union / Peter
Duncanson Cameron.—2nd ed.
     p. cm.
  Includes bibliographical references and index.
  ISBN 978-0-19-928297-5 (hardback : alk. paper) 1. Energy industries—Law and
legislation—European Union countries. 2. Competition—European Union countries.
I. Title.
  KJE6698.C36 2007
  346.2404′679—dc22
                                                                    2007000870

Typeset by Cepha Imaging Pvt Ltd, Bangalore, India
Printed in Great Britain
on acid-free paper by
Biddles Ltd, King's Lynn

ISBN 978-0-19-928297-5 (Hbk.)

1 3 5 7 9 10 8 6 4 2

To my wife, Qiumin

ACKNOWLEDGEMENTS

The preparation of a second edition of this book required a sweeping review of the material in the original volume. Ultimately, the substantially expanded text has retained little of the first edition. For both academic and professional lawyers, the pressure to innovate on this scale is usually located in a change in the law itself. This was no exception. However, a considerable amount of rethinking was sparked by my participation in various workshops and seminars at the Robert Schuman Centre for Advanced Studies (RSCAS) at the European University Institute in Florence. The five annual workshops on EU energy law and policy which I have organized there between 2002 and 2006 have proved a rich source of ideas, and I wish to thank the many regulatory authorities, competition authorities, academics, companies, and law firms that have participated in these meetings for this stimulus. In particular, I want to thank Patrick McGovern (Arthur Cox), Vincent Aarts and Jolling de Pree (De Brauw Blackstone Westbroek), Peter Polak (Fiebinger, Polak, Leon and Partner), Kai Pritzsche (Linklaters), John Gulliver (Pierce Atwood) and György Antall (Réti, Antall and Madl Landwell). During the time when I was a professor at the RSCAS, the Florence School of Regulation was established, and I benefited from participation in a number of its meetings on regulation and competition in the energy sector. I am grateful to the director of the School, Pippo Ranci, as well as the directors of the RSCAS, first Helen Wallace and now Stefano Bartolini, for this opportunity.

A very striking difference between the preparation of the first and second editions is the degree to which information on EU energy law is now available on the internet. This surfeit of data presents challenges of interpretation as well as selection, however. I am particularly grateful that several officials at the European Commission Competition Directorate and Legal Services were able to comment on many of the chapters in this book. I wish to acknowledge the comments and suggestions of Michael Albers, Andre Bouquet, Leo Flynn, Dominik Schnichels and Walter Tretton. They bear no responsibility for the resulting text which is mine alone. In addition, specific subjects covered in the book have benefited from the comments and insights of a number of friends and colleagues. In this respect, I am grateful to Denis Cagney, David Halldearn, Sue Harrison, Margot Loudon, John Milligan, Jörg Spicker, Peter Styles and Jorge Vasconcelos. Michael Brothwood, who was consultant editor on the first edition, took time to read through the whole manuscript, and gave

Acknowledgements

valuable comments and suggestions on specific matters and also on the overall coherence of the study. Once again, responsibility for the final text lies with the author entirely.

Three final sources of support have to be acknowledged. At Oxford University Press, Chris Rycroft gave unflinching support to my idea that only a radical overhaul of the first edition, with a significant expansion of the treatment of competition law, would do justice to the subject matter at the present time. I am also grateful to Kirsty Asher, Faye Judges and Kate Bailey for their assistance in taking the manuscript through its various stages to the final form. At the Centre for Energy, Petroleum and Mineral Law and Policy at Dundee, I had continual support from my colleagues as well as challenging questions from my students, especially those from outside the EU, who compelled me to look at the subject matter from a less introspective point of view. Finally, the study benefited from the enthusiasm of my wife, Qiumin, who urged me to make the work as comprehensive as possible, and to keep at it until it was completed. Without her combination of roles as cheerleader and manager, it would have been a lesser work. As her pregnancy advanced, Nature too provided a gentle reminder of the need to bring the book to a timely conclusion.

Peter Duncanson Cameron
New Town, Edinburgh
January 2007

FOREWORD

My Foreword to the first edition of this book suggested that there was broad agreement that European energy markets should be liberalized and also that they need some degree of regulation. The question was how this should be achieved. Today the question remains, but is there still broad agreement about the need to liberalize and the need to regulate?

The problems of energy markets have evolved in an alarming way. The issue is no longer simply one of the availability of energy at competitive prices. It is now wider and more fundamental. For how long, from what sources, at what price, and at what cost to the environment and the future of the planet, will energy continue to be available to sustain the way of life to which we have become accustomed?

These questions cannot be detached from wider questions about 'security', using that phrase in a broad sense to cover the preoccupations of the Second Pillar (Foreign and Security Policy) including relations with Russia, China and the Middle East, and those of the Third Pillar (Freedom, Security and Justice), including terrorism, illegal immigration, people trafficking, international gangsterism, and money-laundering.

It seems clear that no European nation is in a position adequately to respond to these challenges by itself. Indeed, the attempts by some nations to secure their own energy supplies, apparently without regard to the interests of others, have led to protests that there must be a 'European' response. But the availability of a European response depends on there being a system of European government that is capable, not simply of taking decisions and enforcing them, but of the prior task of objective analysis and rational determination of priorities and methods.

On what basis of evidence and analysis should political choices about obtaining and sharing energy supplies be made? How should they be translated into legislative texts? Who should be responsible for their administration and enforcement? What should be the respective responsibilities of legislators, administrators and judges?

These questions have hardly been posed, far less answered, in the recent discussion of the European Constitution, its shipwreck on the shoals of French and Dutch public opinion, and the possibilities of refloating it with or without major repairs. Most of the discussion has been conducted in highly simplistic terms, centring either on rather woolly questions of governance ('overcoming the democratic deficit' and 'bringing Europe closer to the people') or on a false antithesis between a 'European social model' and an 'Anglo-Saxon free market model', both of which, in reality, form part of the programme of the EEC Treaty and the Single European Act.

It is even more remarkable that the urgent need to act together in response to common threats, and consequently to put in place institutional arrangements to enable this to be done effectively, has hardly, if at all, been prayed in aid as a reason for supporting a new constitutional dispensation. Part of the reason may be that little attention was given by the Constitutional Convention to the adequacy of the legal framework of the EC Treaties which reappears in truncated form in Part Three. There are even some enthusiasts who propose that we press ahead with Parts One and Two, leaving aside Part Three as deserving less attention from the European citizen and capable of being left to negotiation between the experts of the Member States. The potentially enormous significance of bringing the Inter-Governmental Third Pillar within the Community system has been downplayed.

The question needs to be faced whether the underlying economic assumptions of the EEC Treaty of 1957 are still valid at the beginning of the 21st century, and whether they are likely to remain so for the lifetime of the projected Constitution (50 years, according to the President of the Constitutional Convention). If the economic assumptions are no longer sound, then the method—the four freedoms strengthened by energetic enforcement of the competition rules—may prove to be inadequate, if not inappropriate and ultimately damaging.

It is worth remembering that the EEC Treaty was born, not in an atmosphere of Euro-enthusiasm, but against the background of Euro-scepticism following the failure of the European Defence and Political Communities. The supranational aims and methods of the ECSC were not to be reproduced in the Treaties of 1957. The aim was more limited and, in a sense, more precise—how to create an economy capable of competing effectively with that of the United States. The method was the creation of an internal market subject to the discipline of non-discrimination and open access binding on States and competition rules binding on undertakings.

The attraction of the Treaty system is that enforcement of the four freedoms and the competition rules is largely (though not wholly) assigned to the Commission, the Court of Justice, and the national courts and competition authorities. To that extent, the processes of enforcement are relatively immune to the vagaries of political opinion or the need to satisfy particularly clamant interest groups.

The Maastricht Treaty introduced a degree of uncertainty as to whether the four freedoms are still to be regarded as the 'foundations of the Community', so that they take precedence over other policies, especially in the energy sector, environmental protection and security of supply. Attempts by the Commission to use the courts to enforce its view of what the rules of the Treaty require have been met with only partial success.

To some extent this may be attributable to unwillingness on the part of judges to become involved in what they see as political choices, but such unwillingness reflects a deeper sense of the proper separation of powers, as does the tension as to aims and methods between the Commission, the Council and the Parliament.

Faced with today's problems, do we need to rethink the aims and methods of 1957? Are they still workable, particularly in a Community of 25 Member States (soon to be 27) of very different degrees of economic development? Has the 'heaviness' of the decision-making process, with its constant need to reconcile competing claims for relatively short-term political reasons, led to a situation in which it would be more honest, and in the long run more effective, to allow Member States to pursue their own policies, including energy policy, while facilitating but not enforcing co-operation?

These are 'hard' questions of governance that are not going to be solved by throwing *bonnes bouches* to the citizens. In order to assess whether the 'Community method' remains valid in a world that has changed out of all recognition, we need some points of reference.

Europe's energy industries, whose vigour and competitiveness are crucial to a successful economy, have to carry on their business according to the body of energy and competition laws as they are now. Quite independently of the policy debates and the latest legislative initiatives, people have to live day by day according to the current directives and regulations on liberalization and have to grapple with their various shortcomings and occasional lack of clarity. They need to be sure where they stand now.

Professor Cameron's book will be valuable as a guide to the existing system for those who work in the energy sector, whether as producers, administrators or enforcers. He explains the methods enjoined by the existing Treaties and how they have been deployed—on the one hand, through sectoral legislation and regulation and, on the other, through the administrative and judicial enforcement of competition law. He offers a fresh map of the landscape of EU energy law that will guide the reader through the lanes and the minor roads as well as the major routes and highways. Although the emphasis is mainly on the electricity and gas industries—the principal targets of liberalization so far—there is a new analysis of the emerging issues of competition and security of supply in the nuclear and 'renewables' sectors, as well as the problems of competing objectives.

Foreword

The book has a wider purpose. It illustrates the successes and inadequacies of the system we have and suggests a possible way of resolving the inadequacies without sacrificing the successes. The problems of the energy sector deserve to be studied for the insights they can offer to those who seek a wider view of where Europe is heading.

David Edward*

---

* The Rt Hon Sir David Edward KCMG QC is a former Judge of the European Court of Justice.

INTRODUCTION

Over the past decade a body of specialist 'energy law' has been adopted within the framework of EU law. Its raison d'être and programmatic intent has been to promote competition in the EU energy markets and ultimately to establish a single market in energy across Europe. In 2007 it has reached a turning point as the markets for electricity and gas become—by law—fully open to competition. Ironically, this peak in a ten-year process of legal innovation has coincided with mounting evidence of the very limited impact of competition across national borders and of a general weakness in the enforcement of the new rules. On 10 January 2007, the European Commissioner for Competition Policy presented the final report of an in-depth inquiry into the state of competition in EU energy markets.[1] In her words, 'the Report confirms that energy markets are not functioning properly. Its disappointing conclusion is that more than a decade after having launched the drive for liberalisation, we are still far from having a single, competitive and well-functioning European energy market . . . the historic incumbents remain dominant on their traditional markets throughout the supply chain'. As a result, the Commission's declared intention is to focus its future action on the more serious competition concerns, seeking tougher remedies in large merger cases, and considering the use of structural remedies such as divestiture in cases where companies are found to have violated competition rules. The report also underlines the importance of a strong regulatory framework for the enforcement of competition policy.

On exactly the same day, the Commission's Energy Directorate announced its annual benchmarking report on the implementation and practical results of the Directives on the internal gas and electricity market.[2] It concluded that 'meaningful competition does not exist in many Member States',[3] and noted that no less

---

[1] Commission of the European Communities, 'Inquiry pursuant to Article 17 of Regulation (EC) No 1/2003 into the European gas and electricity sectors (Final Report)', COM (2006) 851 final: <http://ec.europa.eu/comm/competition/antitrust/others/sector_inquiries/energy/#final>. The Commissioner's remarks are contained in her speech, 'Introductory Remarks on Final Report of Energy Sector Competition Inquiry', 10 January 2007, at this website.

[2] Commission of the European Communities, 'Prospects for the internal gas and electricity market', COM (2006) 841 final, and 'Implementation Report', SEC (2006) 1709, an accompanying document to the Communication: <http://ec.europa.eu/energy/energy_policy/doc/10_internal_market_country_reviews_en.pdf>.

[3] ibid at 2.

than 34 infringement procedures have been launched against 20 Member States for violation and non-transposition of the internal market legislation. Based on a detailed analysis of conditions in 25 of the 27 Member States, it concluded that 'the persistent nature of these infringements . . . clearly demonstrates the insufficiencies and shortcomings of the current EC legal framework arising from the directives'.[4] Worse still, the context for continuing market reform has sharply deteriorated in the face of rising concerns among Member States about its implications for their energy security, and a marked decline in their appetite for further integration following the stalled attempt to introduce a draft Constitution for Europe.

This book is a comprehensive examination of the legal architecture put in place to promote competition in markets that were in most cases characterized by monopoly and a strong government presence for a period of several decades. While the *first* edition of this book was concerned with how that architecture came to be put in place, this *second* edition is focused firmly on how it operates. The historical approach of the former is therefore replaced with one designed to capture its structure and its manner of operation. The larger Parts of this book are therefore concerned with the two bodies of legal rules that are relevant to the introduction of competition into the markets for electricity and gas: first, the sector-specific rules contained largely in two Directives and two regulations, and secondly, the body of rules in the growing number of decisions made by the Commission acting as a competition authority. The latter are designed to support the liberalization or market opening process which the sector-specific rules have triggered. The body of market opening rules—it might be called the 'new energy law'—sets the legal parameters for the operations and investments of companies and their bankers in one of the most strategically important sectors of the European economy.

However, the new energy law has to co-exist with three other sets of rules, made at different times and with different goals in mind. First, there are legislative measures on energy security introduced to mitigate potential threats including unintended effects of the market opening process. Secondly, there is a raft of legislative measures that are designed to achieve environmental policy objectives that impact directly or indirectly on the new energy law, and which have more or less potential for market distortion effects. Thirdly, there is a heterogeneous body of legal rules, both primary and secondary in character, which pre-dates the adoption of the new energy law but impacts upon it nonetheless. For the most part, the latter rules are directly concerned with energy sub-sectors such as nuclear energy, coal and oil. They reflect a different weighting of policy priorities, one which sometimes accords competition policy a lower priority than other goals such as security of supply or social and economic cohesion. This wider legal context for

---

[4] ibid, 6.

Introduction

the new energy law reveals the extent to which competition goals have usually had to be balanced against others in the energy sector, suggesting that the current uncertainties are—to some extent—due to pressures for a rebalancing of priorities in the internal energy market project in favour of security and environmental goals.

In this broad legal context, the book is concerned with the questions: *why has the new market-oriented energy law taken this particular form and what 'competition' is it seeking to achieve?* The book tackles these questions in two ways. First, it undertakes a comprehensive and detailed review of the body of law and regulation governing competition in the EU energy markets at the present time. Most of the existing studies have tended to limit themselves to one or other aspect of this legal and regulatory framework: for example, by emphasizing either the sector-specific law *or* the competition law developments; the electricity *or* the gas sector; the network aspects *or* the implications for 'upstream' activities. This study deliberately attempts to set the new energy law in the wider framework of rules of European law that are increasingly relevant to its application. In particular, this has involved a very detailed review of the extensive role now played by the Treaty rules on competition and the often neglected rules applicable to other energy sub-sectors such as nuclear energy, coal, and oil. There is now a significant body of case law, involving the Commission, national competition authorities and the courts, that is having a growing impact upon how the sector-specific rules operate in practice. The study draws this body of law together and analyzes its significance. It does, however, confine itself to the EU level, and does not include detailed case-studies of particular Member State experiences, since this would go beyond the projected scope of this volume.[5]

Secondly, the book advances an argument about the new energy law and the nature of the competition sought in this sector of the EU economy. Essentially, the development of market-oriented rules in this regional framework, in contrast to that of a Member State, has struggled to meet two requirements: on the one hand, the consent of all Member States to at least the core legal rules and principles, and, on the other, an increasingly detailed approach to implementation as competition and liberalization take hold in the energy markets. The form of the new energy law, as well as the procedures for its adoption, has been determined by these considerations. With respect to the first of these requirements, the difficulties in achieving a consensus on energy issues are well known: there is no common energy policy, no specific competence on energy matters set out in the EC Treaty, and no institution with special responsibility for energy at the EU level. All of these

---

[5] However, the reader is referred to another work edited by the author, which contains country studies: *Legal Aspects of EU Energy Markets: Implementing the New Directives on Electricity and Gas Across Europe* (Oxford University Press, 2005). A second edition is being planned.

matters have been discussed among Member States and the European institutions over several decades and to date have failed to achieve a result. It is therefore little short of remarkable that the EU has succeeded in adopting—through a highly consensual process—a body of law for important parts of this sector that is designed to sweep aside a multiplicity of anti-competitive practices in the face of strong vested interests.

The next question concerns the kind of competition that follows from this new body of law. What does 'competition', in contrast to 'competitiveness', mean in energy markets? Any answer to this question has to be provisional since the process of introducing competition still has far to go. However, some indications of the EU's approach to competition in this highly sensitive part of its economy are apparent. The goal of competition, however important, is one that has to co-exist in this sector with those of public service (including security of supply) and increasingly with the requirements of environmental sustainability. This entails a balancing of policies that is rooted in the Treaty itself, and presents enforcement bodies with a very considerable challenge. Given the diversity of energy conditions in the 27 Member States, it is clear that any such balancing at the EU level will be both difficult to achieve and will be prone to exceptions. At the present time, the weight given to the promotion of energy security relative to competition has increased considerably when compared to the climate in which the internal energy market project was initiated.

* * *

The structure of the book reflects the above considerations. It is divided into five Parts.

Part I comprises two chapters that provide an overview of the conceptual issues and the wider legal context for the developments in competition and energy law that form the core of this study. A further chapter provides an analysis of the EU system of energy regulation that has been emerging in recent years.

Part II examines in detail the legal regulation of each of the energy sub-sectors: electricity, gas, oil, coal, nuclear energy, and renewable energy.

Part III is concerned with the competition law relevant to the liberalization process, covering its application in upstream and downstream markets, but also with respect to cross-border mergers and acquisitions, state aid, and the role of special and exclusive rights.

Part IV analyzes the role of policies on environment and security in the introduction of competition into energy markets.

Part V contains a chapter that summarizes and concludes the study.

CONTENTS—SUMMARY

Table of Cases	xxix
Table of Legislation	xxxvi
Abbreviations	liii
Glossary	lix

PART I COMPETITION AND ENERGY LAW

1. The Competition Objective	3
2. The EU Legal Order and Energy	37
3. The EU System of Energy Regulation	95

PART II SECTOR REGULATION

4. Introduction to Part II: Sector Regulation	123
5. Electricity	125
6. Gas	173
7. Oil	221
8. Coal	231
9. Nuclear Energy	243
10. Renewable Energy	261

PART III COMPETITION LAW

11. The Application of Competition Law	279
12. Competition in Upstream Markets	303
13. Competition in Downstream Markets	323
14. Cross-Border Mergers and Acquisitions	367
15. State Aid	427
16. Special and Exclusive Rights	461

PART IV COMPETING OBJECTIVES

17. Environmental Protection — 495
18. Energy Security — 517

PART V THE FUTURE OF COMPETITION AND REGULATION IN ENERGY MARKETS

19. Conclusions — 557

APPENDICES

Appendix 1 Electricity Directive (2003/54/EC) — 579
Appendix 2 Electricity Regulation (1228/2003) — 603
Appendix 3 Gas Directive (2003/55/EC) — 615
Appendix 4 Gas Regulation (1775/2005) — 641
Appendix 5 New Annex to Electricity Regulation (Commission Decision 2006/770/EC) — 653

Select Bibliography — 661
Index — 673

CONTENTS

Table of Cases   xxix
Table of Legislation   xxxvi
Abbreviations   liii
Glossary   lix

PART I COMPETITION AND ENERGY LAW

1. The Competition Objective

    A. Introduction   1.01

    B. What is Competition?   1.05

    C. Energy Markets and Government Intervention: The Energy Paradigm
        (1) Historical Characteristics of the Electricity and Gas Industries   1.10
        (2) The Pre-Liberalization Paradigm   1.11
        (3) Beyond the Pre-Liberalization Paradigm   1.17
        (4) A Three-Stage Evolution   1.22
        (5) Crisis and the Shift Towards 'Energy Security'   1.45
        (6) Unfinished Business   1.47
        (7) A New Paradigm Emerging?   1.58

    D. Why is Energy Special?   1.60
        (1) Electricity   1.63
        (2) Gas   1.67

    E. The Requirements of Liberalization   1.75
        (1) Regulation and Access   1.76
        (2) Structure   1.83
        (3) Liberalization   1.90
        (4) Ownership   1.93

    F. Conclusions   1.95

2. The EU Legal Order and Energy

A.	Introduction	2.01
B.	The Origins of an EU *Acquis* in Energy	2.05
	(1) The Treaty Context	2.09
	(2) The Single European Act	2.36
	(3) Treaty on European Union (Maastricht)	2.46
	(4) Constitutional Fatigue: From Amsterdam to Nice and Beyond	2.55
	(5) The Proposed Energy Article and the Question of Competences	2.57
	(6) Conclusions on the Development of an Energy *Acquis*	2.61
C.	The European Commission in its Institutional Setting	2.64
	(1) The Commission and Commissioners: Functions and Powers	2.65
	(2) Commission and Council	2.76
	(3) Commission and Parliament	2.83
	(4) Commission and Court of Justice	2.93
	(5) Legislative Acts	2.110
D.	European Economic Area Agreement	2.115
	(1) EEA Agreement: Legally Binding	2.116
	(2) The Institutions	2.119
	(3) Impacts on Energy	2.123
E.	Energy Community Treaty	2.127
F.	Energy Charter Treaty	2.131
	(1) Main Treaty Provisions	2.134
	(2) The Charter Process: An Assessment	2.153
G.	The Wider Neighbourhood of the EU	2.160
	(1) Partnership and Co-operation Agreements	2.161
	(2) Euro-Mediterranean Association Agreements	2.168
H.	Conclusions	2.173

3. The EU System of Energy Regulation

A.	Introduction	3.01
B.	Establishing an EU Energy Regulatory Network	
	(1) The National Energy Regulator	3.05
	(2) Other Regulatory Bodies	3.07
	(3) The Role of the Commission	3.09
	(4) A Centralized Energy Regulator?	3.10
C.	The Florence and Madrid Forums	
	(1) The Regulators and Industry	3.12
	(2) The Florence Electricity Forum	3.18

Contents

(3) The Madrid Gas Forum		3.28
(4) ERGEG and the Forum Process		3.37
D. The Regional Energy Markets Initiative		3.40
E. Co-ordination and Co-operation among Regulators		3.44
(1) How the Role of the NRAs Grew		3.45
(2) Five Key Relationships		3.47
F. Assessing the EU System		3.59

PART II SECTOR REGULATION

4. Introduction to Part II: Sector Regulation

5. Electricity

A. Introduction	5.01
B. The Electricity Directive 2003	
(1) Aims and Scope	5.06
(2) General Rules	5.08
(3) Rules for Specific Activities	5.18
(4) Unbundling	5.38
(5) Access	5.44
(6) Market Opening and Reciprocity	5.48
(7) Direct Lines	5.51
(8) The Role of the Regulators	5.55
(9) Enforcement	5.69
C. The Electricity Regulation 2003	5.79
(1) The Inter-TSO Compensation Mechanism	5.84
(2) Charges for Network Access	5.86
(3) Congestion Management	5.90
(4) Exemptions for New Interconnectors	5.95
(5) Information Requirements	5.106
(6) Guidelines	5.113
(7) Enforcement	5.128
D. Conclusions	5.140

6. Gas

A. Introduction	6.01
B. The Gas Directive 2003	
(1) Aims and Scope	6.03
(2) General Rules	6.05

(3) Rules for Specific Activities	6.21
(4) Unbundling	6.36
(5) Access	6.38
(6) Market Opening and Reciprocity	6.63
(7) Direct Lines	6.65
(8) Regulation	6.68
(9) Enforcement	6.69
C. The Gas Regulation 2005	6.115
(1) Tariffs for Network Access	6.118
(2) Third Party Access Services	6.122
(3) Principles of Capacity Allocation and Congestion Management	6.125
(4) Transparency Requirements	6.128
(5) Balancing Rules and Imbalance Charges	6.129
(6) Trading of Capacity Rights	6.130
(7) Guidelines	6.132
(8) Enforcement	6.142
D. Conclusions	6.148

7. Oil

A. Introduction	7.01
B. Hydrocarbons Licensing	7.03
(1) Aims and Scope	7.04
(2) Common Rules	7.09
C. Conclusions	7.26

8. Coal

A. Introduction	8.01
B. Competition versus Intervention	8.05
C. The Post-ECSC Treaty Arrangements	
(1) Transition	8.10
(2) Key Features of the New Regime	8.12
(3) State Aids	8.18
(4) Decision-Making	8.22
D. Conclusion	8.27

9. Nuclear Energy

A. Introduction — 9.01

B. Euratom: A *Lex Specialis*
  (1) Purpose — 9.04
  (2) Objectives and Implementation — 9.07
  (3) Institutional Features — 9.12
  (4) Assessment — 9.14

C. Competition Issues — 9.16
  (1) Supplies — 9.17
  (2) State Aids — 9.29

D. Conclusions — 9.38

10. Renewable Energy

A. Introduction — 10.01

B. The Renewables Directive
  (1) Aims and Scope — 10.04
  (2) National Indicative Targets — 10.07
  (3) Support Schemes — 10.09
  (4) Guarantee of Electricity Origin — 10.21
  (5) Regulation — 10.24
  (6) Grid System Issues — 10.28
  (7) Reporting Requirements — 10.32
  (8) The Relevance of State Aid Control — 10.34
  (9) Implementation — 10.38

C. Conclusions — 10.39

PART III COMPETITION LAW

11. The Application of Competition Law

A. Introduction — 11.01

B. The 'Modernized' Legal Framework
  (1) Regulation 1/2003 — 11.06
  (2) The Competition Network — 11.19

C. Defining the Relevant Market
  (1) Market Definition in Energy — 11.21

D.	The Energy Sector Review	11.38
	(1) The Inquiry: Data Collection, Scope, and Compliance	11.42
	(2) Significance	11.47
	(3) The Results	11.48
E.	Conclusions	11.66

12. Competition in Upstream Markets

A.	Introduction	12.01
B.	Joint Marketing of Gas	12.04
	(1) The *GFU* Case	12.05
	(2) The *Corrib* Case	12.11
	(3) The *DUC/DONG* Case	12.14
C.	Joint Marketing of Electricity	12.30
D.	Territorial Sales Restrictions: 'Destination Clauses'	12.33
	(1) Norwegian Producers	12.38
	(2) The *NLNG* Case	12.39
	(3) The *Gazprom* Cases	12.42
	(4) *GDF/ENEL* and *GDF/ENI*	12.55
	(5) *Sonatrach*	12.58
E.	Conclusions	12.60

13. Competition in Downstream Markets

A.	Introduction	13.01
B.	Long-Term Agreements	
	(1) Long-Term Agreements: Gas	13.04
	(2) Long-Term Agreements: Electricity	13.15
C.	Transmission Pricing	13.31
	(1) Electricity Agreement: *Verbändevereinbarung*	13.34
	(2) Gas VV Agreement	13.40
	(3) Assessment	13.45
D.	Interconnector Use and Access	13.46
	(1) Methods of Allocating Available Capacity	13.49
	(2) Long-Term Capacity Reservations	13.52
	(3) Refusal to Build	13.87
E.	Refusal of Access	
	(1) The Issues	13.88
	(2) The *Marathon* Case	13.101
F.	Conclusions	13.139

14. Cross-Border Mergers and Acquisitions

A. Introduction — 14.01

B. The Rules
(1) The Merger Regulation — 14.07
(2) Jurisdiction over Mergers — 14.35

C. The Practice — 14.56
(1) Electricity — 14.62
(2) Gas — 14.74
(3) Convergence of Gas and Electricity — 14.85

D. Remedies
(1) General — 14.99
(2) Remedies used in the Energy Sector — 14.104
(3) Effectiveness of Energy Remedies — 14.120

E. Golden Shares as Barriers — 14.136
(1) The 2002 Judgments — 14.138
(2) The 2003 Judgments — 14.165

F. Conclusions — 14.168

15. State Aid

A. Introduction — 15.01

B. An Overview of the State Aid Rules — 15.04

C. Liberalization and State Aids — 15.10
(1) Stranded Costs — 15.12
(2) State Guarantees: the *EDF* Case — 15.56
(3) Public Service Obligations — 15.60

D. Environmental Aid — 15.62
(1) Promoting Renewable Energy — 15.63
(2) Promoting Biofuels and Wave Power — 15.73
(3) Climate Change — 15.75

E. Aid for Rescue and Restructuring — 15.79
(1) The *British Energy* Case 2004 — 15.81
(2) *BNFL* 2006 — 15.86

F. Conclusions — 15.90

16. Special and Exclusive Rights

- A. Introduction — 16.01
- B. Article 86 and its Context — 16.05
  - (1) Article 86 — 16.06
  - (2) The Context — 16.09
  - (3) Winds of Change — 16.11
- C. The Limits of Article 86(3) — 16.14
  - (1) The *Telecoms* Case — 16.18
  - (2) The Issues — 16.20
  - (3) Effects — 16.26
- D. Clarification of Monopoly Rights and their Limits — 16.31
  - (1) *Höfner v Macrotron* — 16.32
  - (2) *ERT* — 16.34
  - (3) *Port of Genoa* — 16.37
  - (4) The *RTT* Case — 16.40
  - (5) The *Corbeau* Case — 16.43
- E. Import and Export of Electricity and Gas — 16.46
  - (1) Early Enforcement in Energy — 16.48
  - (2) Electricity and Gas Import–Export Monopolies — 16.51
  - (3) Assessment — 16.81
- F. Conclusions — 16.87

PART IV COMPETING OBJECTIVES

17. Environmental Protection

- A. Introduction — 17.01
- B. Renewable Energy — 17.05
  - (1) Combining Internal Market and Renewables Regulation — 17.06
  - (2) Trade — 17.09
  - (3) State Aid — 17.10
- C. Energy Taxation — 17.17
  - (1) The Carbon Tax — 17.19
  - (2) The Energy Products Directive — 17.22
  - (3) National Measures and State Aid — 17.33
  - (4) Current Approaches to EU Carbon Taxation — 17.39
- D. The Emissions Trading Scheme — 17.42
  - (1) The Scheme — 17.43
  - (2) Implementation — 17.46
  - (3) Impacts on Competition and the Internal Energy Market — 17.49
- E. Conclusions — 17.51

18. Energy Security

A. Introduction	18.01
B. Secondary Legislation	18.07
(1) The Electricity Directive	18.11
(2) The Gas Directive	18.23
(3) Electricity Security	18.29
(4) Gas Security	18.49
(5) Oil Security	18.60
(6) Infrastructure	18.68
C. Treaty Provisions	18.81
(1) Import and Export	18.83
(2) Services of General Economic Interest	18.99
(3) Euratom	18.104
D. Conclusions	18.107

PART V THE FUTURE OF COMPETITION AND REGULATION IN ENERGY MARKETS

19. Conclusions

A. Introduction	19.01
B. The Sector-Specific Framework	
(1) The Regional Setting	19.06
(2) The Balancing of Objectives	19.13
(3) Relationship to the EC Treaty	19.17
C. The *Support* Role of Competition Law	
(1) An Interventionist Trend	19.20
(2) Cautionary Assessments of Instruments	19.23
D. Regulation by Co-operation	
(1) Who Regulates?	19.30
(2) The Management of Complexity	19.31
(3) The Potential for Regulatory Co-operation	19.35
E. Other Energy Sources	19.38
(1) Oil	19.39
(2) Coal	19.40
(3) Nuclear Energy	19.41
F. The Market Distorting Effects of Environmental Measures	19.42
G. Dealing with Non-Compliance	19.45
(1) A Stronger Network of Energy Regulators	19.47
(2) Stricter Competition Law Enforcement	19.48

(3) Regional Focus Not EU-Wide		19.49
(4) Improvement of Sector-Specific Legislation		19.50
H. A Strategy for Competition in EU Energy Markets		
(1) The Transition and Beyond		19.51
(2) Saving the Transition		19.53
(3) Post-Transition		19.57

APPENDICES

Appendix 1 Electricity Directive (2003/54/EC)	579
Appendix 2 Electricity Regulation (1228/2003)	603
Appendix 3 Gas Directive (2003/55/EC)	615
Appendix 4 Gas Regulation (1775/2005)	641
Appendix 5 New Annex to Electricity Regulation (Commission Decision 2006/770/EC)	653
Select Bibliography	661
Index	673

TABLE OF CASES

European Court of Justice and Court of First Instance	xxix
European Commission Decisions	xxxiii

EUROPEAN COURT OF JUSTICE AND COURT OF FIRST INSTANCE

Alphabetical

Adidas: C-223/98 [1999] ECR I-7081, ECJ 13.72
Adria Wien Pipeline GmbH v Finanzlandesdirektion für Karnten: C-143/99 [2001]
    ECR I-8365, ECJ 17.34
AEM SpA and AEM Torino SpA v Autorita per l'energia elettrica e per il gas: C-128 &
    129/03 [2005] ECR I-2861, ECJ 13.73
AES Drax Power Ltd v Commission: T-124/03 [2003] OJ C135/59, CFI 15.81
Aid in favour of British Energy plc: C-52/2003 [2005]
    OJ L142/26, ECJ 9.38, 15.81–15.83
Algemene Transport-en Expeditie Onderneming van Gend en Loos NV v Nederlandse
    Belastingadministratie: 26/62 [1963] ECR 1, ECJ 2.25, 2.106
Altmark Trans GmbH v Nahverkehrsgesellschaft Altmark GmbH: C-280/00 [2003]
    ECR I-7747, ECJ 2.93, 5.13, 5.14, 15.11, 15.60, 18.101, 18.103
Atlanta v European Community: C-104/97 P [1999] ECR I-6983, ECJ 13.78
Banks (HJ) & Co Ltd v British Coal Corporation: C-128/92 [1994]
    ECR I-1209, ECJ 9.01, 9.38
Belgische Radio en Televisie (BRT) v SV SABAM: 127/73 [1974]
    ECR 313, ECJ 16.45
Bronner (Oscar) GmbH & Co KG v Mediaprint Zeitings-und Zeitschriftenverlag
    GmbH & Co KG: C-7/97 [1998] ECR I-7791, [1999]
    4 CMLR 112, ECJ 13.99, 13.100
Campus Oil Ltd v Minister for Industry and Energy: 72/83 [1984]
    ECR 2727, ECJ 2.25, 14.152, 14.161, 18.85–18.89, 18.97, 18.98
Chemi-Con (Deutschland) v Council: C-422/02 P [2002] OJ C82/1, ECJ 13.74
Commercial Solvents: 6, 7/73. See Istituto Chemioterapico Italiano SpA and
    Commercial Solvents Corpn v Commission: 6, 7/73
Commission v Belgium: C-503/99 [2002] ECR I-4809, ECJ 14.138, 14.148, 18.100
Commission v Council: C-29/9, 10 December 2002, ECJ 9.03
Commission v France: 159/94 [1997] ECR I-5815, ECJ 16.70, 16.84
Commission v France: 160/94 [1997] ECR I-5699, ECJ 2.10
Commission v France: C-483/99 [2002] ECR I-4781, ECJ 14.138, 14.146
Commission v Greece: C-347/88 [1990] ECR I-4747, ECJ 2.25, 7.02, 12.01,
                                                           16.57, 18.85, 18.94–18.96
Commission v Italy: C-158/94 [1997] ECR I-5789, ECJ 2.10, 16.67, 16.84
Commission v Italy: C-58/99 [2000] ECR I-3811, ECJ 14.137
Commission v Netherlands: C-157/94 [1994] ECR I-1477, ECJ 2.10, 16.56, 16.84
Commission v Portugal: C-367/98 [2001] ECR I-4731, ECJ 14.138, 14.144
Commission v Spain: C-160/94 [1997] ECR I-5699, ECJ 2.10, 16.80

Table of Cases

Commission v Spain: C-463/00 [2003] ECR I-4581, ECJ 14.137, 18.100
Commission v Tetra Laval BV: C-12 & 13/03 P, 15 February 2005, ECJ 14.170
Commission v UK: C-98/01 [2003] ECR I-4641, ECJ 14.137
Corbeau (criminal proceedings against): C-320/91 [1993]
    ECR I-2533, ECJ 1.31, 2.26, 2.93, 13.19, 16.43, 16.61. 16.89
Costa v ENEL: 6/64 [1964] ECR 585, ECJ 2.10, 2.107, 16.68
Deutsche Babcock v Commission: 238/85 [1987] ECR 5131, ECJ 8.08
Deutsche Post: C-147 & 148/97 [2000] ECR I-825, ECJ 16.89
Di Lenardo and Dilexport: C-37 & 38/02 [2004] ECR I-6945, ECJ 13.78
Duff: C-63/93 [1996] ECR I-569, ECJ 13.79
EasyJet Airline v Commission: T-177/04 [2006] OJ C212/29 .... 14.105
Elliniki Radiophonia Tiléorassi AE and Panellinia Omospondia Syllogon
    Prossopikou v Dimotiki Etairia Pliroforissis: 260/89 [1991]
    ECR I-2951, ECJ 16.34, 16.69
Energias de Portugal (EDP) SA v Commission: T-87/05 [2005]
    5 CMLR 23, CFI 14.97
ENU v Commission: T-458 & 523/93 [1995] ECR II-2459, CFI 9.22, 9.25
ENU v Commission: C-357/95 [1997] ECR I-1329, ECJ 9.22
European Night Services v Commission: Joined Cases T-374, 375, 384, 388/94 [1998]
    ECR II-3141, CFI 13.99
EVN and Wienstrom v Austria: C-448/01 [2004] OJ C21/05, ECJ 15.70
France v Commission: C-202/88 [1991] ECR I-1223, ECJ 16.19
France v Commission (Stardust Marine): C-482/99 [2002] ECR I-4397, ECJ 15.68
France, Italy and United Kingdom v Commission: 188-190/80 [1982]
    ECR 2545, ECJ 16.10
Franz Grad v Finanzamt Traunstein: 9/70 [1974] 1970 ECR 825, ECJ 2.106
Franzen (Criminal proceedings against): C-189/95 [1997] ECR I-5909, ECJ 16.70
Gemeente Almelo v Energiebedrijf Ijssellmij NV: C-393/92 [1994] |
    ECR I-1477, ECJ 2.10, 13.16, 13.17, 14.152, 16.68, 16.76, 16.82, 18.99
Germany v Council: C-280/93 [1994] ECR I-4973, ECJ 13.74
Glöckner (Ambulanz) v Landkreis Südwestpfalz: C-475/99 [2001]
    ECR I-8089, ECJ 16.33, 16.40, 16.89
Greenpeace Ltd and Nexgen Group v Commission: T-121/03 [2003]
    OJ C184/83, CFI 15.81
HM Customs and Excise v Schindler: C-275/92 [1994] ECR I-1039, ECJ 16.69
Höfner (Klaus) and Elser (Fritz) v Macrotron GmbH: C-41/90 [1991]
    ECR I-1979, ECJ 2.26, 16.32, 16.33, 16.37, 16.39, 16.86
Impala v Commission: T-464/04, 13 July 2006, CFI 14.169
Industrias Nucleares do Brasil SA, Siemens AG v UBS AG and Texas Utilities Electric
    Corporation: C-123 & 124/04, 12 September 2006, ECJ 9.28, 9.39
Ireland v Commission: 325/85 [1987] ECR 5041, ECJ 13.79
Istituto Chemioterapico Italiano SpA and Commercial Solvents Corpn
    v Commission: 6, 7/73 [1974] ECR 223, ECJ 13.98
Italy v Saatchi: 155/73 [1994] ECR 409, ECJ 13.94, 16.26, 16.36, 16.45, 16.88
KLE v Commission: T-149 & 181/94 (First Chamber, extended composition),
    25 February 1997, CFI 9.25
KLE v Commission: C-161/97 [1999] ECR I-2057, ECJ 9.27, 9.28
Merci Convenzionali Porto di Genova SpA v Siderurgica Gabrielli SpA: C-179/90
    [1991] ECR I-1979, ECJ 2.26, 2.93, 13.96, 16.37
Merck: 292/82 [1983] ECR 3781, ECJ 13.72
Ministére Public de Luxembourg v Muller: 10/71 [1971] ECR 723, ECJ 16.45
Outokumpu: C-213/96 [1998] ECR I-1777, ECJ 17.09
Portugal v Commission: C-163/99 [2001] ECR I-2613, ECJ 16.84

Table of Cases

PreussenElektra AG v Schleswag AG (Windpark Reussenköge III GmbH intervening):
    C-379/98 [2001] ECR I-2099, ECJ 5.13, 10.36, 10.37, 15.55,
                                                                             15.64, 15.65, 15.67, 17.15
Procureur du Roi v Dassonville: 8/74 [1974] ECR 837, ECJ 2.24
Pubblico Ministero v Manghera: 59/75 [1976] ECR 91, ECJ 16.26, 16.50, 16.73
Pubblico Ministero v SAIL: 82/71 [1972] ECR 119, ECJ 16.45
Régie des télégraphes et des téléphones v GB-Inno-BM SA: C-18/88 [1991]
    ECR I-5973, ECJ 16.40
Rendo & Others v Commission: T-16/91 [1992] ECR II-1827, CFI 13.16
RJB Mining v Commission: T-156/98 [2001] ECR II-337, CFI 14.34
St Nikolaus Brennerei: 337/82 [1984] ECR 1501, ECJ 13.72
Société Civile Agricole du Centre d'Insémination de la Crespelle v Coopérative
    d'Elevage et d'Insémination Artificielle du Département de la Mayenne:
    C-323/93 [1994] ECR I-5077, ECJ 16.33
Spain, Belgium and Italy v Commission: C-271/90, 281/90 & 289/90 [1992]
    ECR I-5833, ECJ 16.26
Textilwerke Deggendorg GmbH (TWD) v Commission: C-355/95 P [1997]
    ECR I-2549, ECJ 15.43
UK v Commission: T-178/05 [2006]1 CMLR 33, CFI 17.47
Van Duyn v Home Office: 41/74 [1974] ECR 1337, ECJ 2.106
Van Es Douane Agenten: C-143/93 [1996] ECR I-431, ECJ 13.79
Vereniging voor Energie Milieu en Water v Directeur van de Dienst Uitvoering en
    Toezicht Energie: C-17/03 [2005] ECR I-4983, ECJ 2.93, 3.08,
                                                     5.141, 6.114, 13.59, 13.62, 16.94
Volkswagen AG v Commission: T-208/01 [2003] ECR II-5141, CFI 12.37
Walrave and Koch v Association Union Cycliste Internationale: 36/74 [1974]
    ECR 1405, ECJ 2.106
Wirtschaftskammer Kärnten and best connect Ampere Strompool v
    Commission: T-350/03 [2004] OJ C7/36, CFI 14.73

Numerical

26/62: Algemene Transport-en Expeditie Onderneming van Gend en Loos NV
    v Nederlandse Belastingadministratie [1963] ECR 1, ECJ 2.25, 2.106
6/64: Costa v ENEL [1964] ECR 585, ECJ 2.10, 2.107, 16.68
9/70: Franz Grad v Finanzamt Traunstein [1974] 1970 ECR 825, ECJ 2.106
10/71: Ministére Public de Luxembourg v Muller [1971] ECR 723, ECJ 16.45
82/71: Pubblico Ministero v SAIL [1972] ECR 119, ECJ 16.45
6, 7/73: Istituto Chemioterapico Italiano SpA and Commercial Solvents Corpn
    v Commission [1974] ECR 223, ECJ 13.98
127/73: Belgische Radio en Televisie (BRT) v SV SABAM [1974] ECR 313, ECJ 16.45
155/73: Italy v Saatchi [1994] ECR 409, ECJ 13.94, 16.26, 16.36, 16.45, 16.88
8/74: Procureur du Roi v Dassonville [1974] ECR 837, ECJ 2.24
36/74: Walrave and Koch v Association Union Cycliste Internationale [1974]
    ECR 1405, ECJ 2.106
41/74: Van Duyn v Home Office [1974] ECR 1337, ECJ 2.106
59/75: Pubblico Ministero v Manghera [1976] ECR 91, ECJ 16.26, 16.50, 16.73
188-190/80: France, Italy and United Kingdom v Commission [1982]
    ECR 2545, ECJ 16.10
292/82: Merck [1983] ECR 3781, ECJ 13.72
337/82: St Nikolaus Brennerei [1984] ECR 1501, ECJ 13.72
72/83: Campus Oil Ltd v Minister for Industry and Energy [1984]
    ECR 2727, ECJ 2.25, 14.152, 14.161, 18.85–18.89, 18.97, 18.98
238/85: Deutsche Babcock v Commission [1987] ECR 5131, ECJ 8.08
325/85: Ireland v Commission [1987] ECR 5041, ECJ 13.79

Table of Cases

C-18/88: Régie des télégraphes et des téléphones v GB-Inno-BM SA [1991]
ECR I-5973, ECJ 16.40
C-202/88: France v Commission [1991] ECR I-1223, ECJ 16.19
C-347/88: Commission v Greece [1990] ECR I-4747, ECJ 2.25, 7.02, 12.01,
16.57, 18.85, 18.94–18.96
C-260/89: Elliniki Radiophonia Tiléorassi AE and Panellinia Omospondia Syllogon
Prossopikou v Dimotiki Etairia Pliroforissis [1991] ECR I-2951, ECJ 16.34, 16.69
C-41/90: Höfner (Klaus) and Elser (Fritz) v Macrotron GmbH [1991]
ECR I-1979, ECJ 2.26, 16.32, 16.33, 16.37, 16.39, 16.86
C-179/90: Merci Convenzionali Porto di Genova SpA v Siderurgica Gabrielli SpA
[1991] ECR I-1979, ECJ 2.26, 2.93, 13.96, 16.37
C-271, 281 & 289/90: Spain, Belgium and Italy v Commission [1992]
ECR I-5833, ECJ 16.28
T-16/91: Rendo & Others v Commission [1992] ECR II-1827, CFI 13.16
C-320/91: Corbeau (criminal proceedings against) [1993]
ECR I-2533, ECJ 1.31, 2.26, 2.93, 13.19, 16.43, 16.61, 16.89
C-128/92: Banks (HJ) & Co Ltd v British Coal Corporation [1994]
ECR I-1209, ECJ 9.01, 9.38
C-275/92: HM Customs and Excise v Schindler [1994] ECR I-1039, ECJ 16.69
C-393/92: Gemeente Almelo v Energiebedrijf Ijsselmij NV [1994]
ECR I-1477, ECJ 2.10, 13.16, 13.17, 14.152, 16.68, 16.76, 16.82, 18.99
C-63/93: Duff [1996] ECR I-569, ECJ 13.79
C-143/93: Van Es Douane Agenten [1996] ECR I-431, ECJ 13.79
C-280/93: Germany v Council [1994] ECR I-4973, ECJ 13.74
C-323/93: Société Civile Agricole du Centre d'Insémination de la Crespelle v
Coopérative d'Elevage et d'Insémination Artificielle du Département de la
Mayenne [1994] ECR I-5077, ECJ 16.33
T-458 & 523/93: ENU v Commission [1995] ECR II-2459, CFI 9.22, 9.25
T-149 & 181/94: KLE v Commission, CFI (First Chamber, extended composition),
25 February 1997 .... 9.25
C-157/94: Commission v Netherlands [1994] ECR I-1477, ECJ 2.10, 16.56, 16.84
C-158/94: Commission v Italy [1997] ECR I-5789, ECJ 2.10, 16.67, 16.84
C-159/94: Commission v France [1997] ECR I-5815, ECJ 16.70, 16.84
C-160/94: Commission v Spain [1997] ECR I-5699, ECJ 2.10, 16.80
T-374, 375, 384, 388/94: European Night Services v Commission [1998]
ECR II-3141, CFI 13.99
C-189/95: Franzen (Criminal proceedings against) [1997] ECR I-5909, ECJ 16.70
C-355/95 P: Textilwerke Deggendorg GmbH (TWD) v Commission [1997]
ECR I-2549, ECJ 15.43
C-357/95: ENU v Commission [1997] ECR I-1329, ECJ 9.22
C-213/96: *Outokumpu* [1998] ECR I-1777, ECJ 17.09
C-7/97: Bronner (Oscar) GmbH & Co KG v Mediaprint Zeitings-und
Zeitschriftenverlag GmbH & Co KG [1998] ECR I-7791, [1999]
4 CMLR 112, ECJ 13.99, 13.100
C-104/97 P: Atlanta v European Community [1999] ECR I-6983, ECJ 13.78
C-147 & 148/97: Deutsche Post [2000] ECR I-825, ECJ 16.89
C-161/97: KLE v Commission [1999] ECR I-2057, ECJ 9.27, 9.28
T-156/98: RJB Mining v Commission [2001] ECR II-33, CFI7 .... 14.34
C-223/98: Adidas [1999] ECR I-7081, ECJ 13.72
C-367/98: Commission v Portugal [2001] ECR I-4731, ECJ 14.138, 14.144
C-379/98: PreussenElektra AG v Schleswag AG (Windpark Reussenköge III GmbH
intervening) [2001] ECR I-2099, ECJ 5.13, 10.36, 10.37, 15.55,
15.64, 15.65, 15.67, 17.15
C-29/99: Commission v Council, 10 December 2002, ECJ 9.03

C-58/99: Commission v Italy [2000] ECR I-3811, ECJ 14.137
C-143/99: Adria Wien Pipeline GmbH v Finanzlandesdirektion für Karnten [2001]
 ECR I-8365, ECJ 17.34
C-163/99: Portugal v Commission [2001] ECR I-2613, ECJ 16.84
C-475/99: Glöckner (Ambulanz) v Landkreis Südwestpfalz [2001]
 ECR I-8089, ECJ 16.33, 16.40, 16.89
C-482/99: France v Commission (Stardust Marine) [2002]
 ECR I-4397, ECJ 15.68
C-483/99: Commission v France [2002] ECR I-4781, ECJ 14.138, 14.146
C-503/99: Commission v Belgium [2002] ECR I-4809, ECJ 14.138, 14.148, 18.100
C-280/00: Altmark Trans GmbH v Nahverkehrsgesellschaft Altmark GmbH [2003]
 ECR I-7747, ECJ 2.93, 5.13, 5.14, 15.11, 15.60, 18.101, 18.103
C-463/00: Commission v Spain [2003] ECR I-4581, ECJ 14.137, 18.100
C-98/01: Commission v UK [2003] ECR I-4641, ECJ 14.137
T-208/01 Volkswagen AG v Commission [2003] ECR II-5141, CFI 12.37
C-448/01: EVN and Wienstrom v Austria [2004] OJ C21/05, ECJ 15.70
C-37 & 38/02: Di Lenardo and Dilexport [2004] ECR I-6945, ECJ 13.78
C-422/02 P: Chemi-Con (Deutschland) v Council [2002] OJ C82/1, ECJ 13.74
C-12 & 13/03 P: Commission v Tetra Laval BV, 15 February 2005, ECJ 14.170
C-17/03: Vereniging voor Energie Milieu en Water v Directeur van de Dienst
 Uitvoering en Toezicht Energie [2005] ECR I-4983, ECJ 2.93, 3.08, 5.141,
                                                                6.114, 13.59, 13.62, 16.94
C-52/03: Aid in favour of British Energy plc [2005] OJ L142/26, ECJ 9.38, 15.81–15.83
T-121/03: Greenpeace Ltd and Nexgen Group v Commission [2003]
 OJ C184/83, CFI 15.81
T-124/03: AES Drax Power Ltd v Commission [2003] OJ C135/59, CFI 15.81
C-128 & 129/03: AEM SpA and AEM Torino SpA v Autorita per l'energia elettrica e
 per il gas [2005] ECR I-2861, ECJ 13.73
T-350/03: Wirtschaftskammer Kärnten and best connect Ampere Strompool v
 Commission [2004] OJ C7/36, CFI 14.73
C-123 & 124/04: Industrias Nucleares do Brasil SA, Siemens AG v UBS AG and Texas
 Utilities Electric Corporation, 12 September 2006, ECJ 9.28, 9.29
T-464/04: Impala v Commission, 13 July 2006, CFI 14.169
T-87/05: Energias de Portugal (EDP) SA v Commission [2005] 5 CMLR 23, CFI 14.97
T-178/05: UK v Commission [2006]1 CMLR 33, CFI 17.47
T-177/04: EasyJet Airline v Commission [2006] OJ C212/29 .... 14.105

EUROPEAN COMMISSION DECISIONS

Airtours/First Choice (Case IV/M.1524) [2000] OJ L93/1 .... 14.170
Areva/Urenco (Case COMP/M.3099) of 6 October 2004 .... 11.22, 14.06
B&I Line plc/Sealink Harbours Ltd and Sealink Stena Ltd (Case IV/34.174) [1992]
 5 CMLR 255 11 .... 13.98
BP Amoco/Arco (Case IV/M.1532) 29 September 1999 .... 11.36, 14.61
BP/Sonatrach (Case COMP/M.672), 12 February 1996 .... 11.30
Britannia Case IP/96/1214 .... 12.12, 12.60
Corrib (Case COMP/E-3/37.708) IP/01/578 .... 12.04, 12.11, 12.12, 12.60
DONG/Elsam/E2 (Case COMP/M.3868), 14 March 2006 .... 11.31, 11.34, 12.04,
                                            12.14–12.29, 12.38, 14.03, 14.58, 14.89, 14.92,
                                                  14.107, 14.110, 14.111, 14.119, 14.135, 14.171
ECS/Sibelga (Case COMP/M.3318) 19 December 2003 .... 14.54
EDF/AEM/Edison (Case COMP/M.3729) 12 August 2005 .... 11.35
EDF/EnBW (Case COMP/M.1853) [2002] OJ L59/1 .... 14.68, 14.107, 14.110, 14.135
EDF/London Electricity (Case IV/M.1346) 27 January 1999 .... 14.58

Table of Cases

EDF/Louis Dreyfus (Case COMP/M.1557) 28 September 1999 .... 14.66
EDF/South Western Electricity (Case IV/M.1606) 19 July 1999 .... 14.58
EDP/ENI/GDP (Case COMP/M.3440) 9 December 2004 .... 1.66, 1.76, 11.22,
11.25–11.27, 11.31, 11.34, 11.35, 11.37, 14.03,
14.31, 14.34, 14.93, 14.95, 14.105, 14.170
Electricidade de Portugal/Pego project (Notice pursuant to Art 19(3) of
    Regulation 17/62) [1993] OJ C265/3 .... 13.24–13.26
EnBW/EDP/Cajastur/Hidrocantábrico (Case COMP/M.2684),
    19 March 2002 .... 1.66, 11.37, 14.70, 14.118
EnBW/ENI/GVS (Case COMP/M.2822) [2003] OJ C233/11 .... 11.31, 14.76, 14.119
ENI/GALP (Case COMP/M.1859) 29 June 2000 .... 14.93
E.ON/Endesa (Case COMP/M.4110) [2006] OJ C68/09 .... 14.36, 19.27
E.ON/MOL (Case COMP/M.3696) [2005] C140/05 .... 1.67, 5.79, 11.28, 11.30,
11.31, 14.79–14.85, 14.108–14.111, 14.115, 14.117,
14.121, 14.127, 14.135, 14.171, 19.26, 19.27
E.ON/Ruhrgas 14.41–14.45, 14.58, 14.107, 14.110, 14.111, 14.115,
14.116, 14.131, 14.169, 19.26, 19.56
E.ON/Sydkraft (Case COMP/M.2349), 9 April 2001 .... 11.34
Exxon/Mobil (Case COMP/M.1383), 19 September 1999 .... 7.02, 11.30, 11.31,
12.35, 14.04, 14.74, 14.75
Framatone/Siemens JV Case IP/00/1414 .... 14.06
Gas Natural/Endesa (Case COMP/M.3986), 15 November 2005 .... 3.49, 14.47, 14.169,
19.26, 19.27, 19.56
Gazprom Cases IP/03/1345 .... 12.42–12.54
GDF/Centrica/SPE (Case COMP/M.3883), 7 September 2005 .... 11.35
GDF/ENEL (Case COMP/38.662), 26 October 2004 .... 12.57, 12.60
GDF/ENI (Case COMP/38.662), 26 October 2004 .... 12.34, 12.57, 12.60
GFU (Case COMP/M.36.072) 2.124, 12.04, 12.08, 19.21, 19.54
Grupo VillarMir/EnBW/Hidroeléctrica del Cantábrico
    (Case COMP/M.2434)[2004] OJ C42/10 .... 11.34, 14.69, 14.70
Iberdrola/Scottish Power (Case COMP/M.4517) 14.53
Irish Synergen Case IP/02/792 .... 12.31
Ijsselcentrale (Case IV/32.732), 16 January 1991 .... 13.15, 13.16, 13.21, 13.30, 16.45
International Energy Agency (Case IV/30.525) 18.67
ISAB Energy (Notice pursuant to Art 19(3) of Regulation 17/62) [1996]
    OJ C138/3 .... 13.24, 13.27
Italy v Saatchi: 155/73 [1994] ECR 409 .... 13.94
Jahrhundertvertrag (Case IV/33.151) 13.21, 13.28
Marathon Case IP/01/1641 .... 13.101–13.138, 19.21, 19.25, 19.54
MAVEWA-ANSEAU, [1982] OJ L167/39 and [1982] 2 CML Rev 193 .... 16.45
Neste/Ivo (Case COMP/M.931), 2 June 1998 .... 14.88, 14.107
NLNG Case IP/02/1869 .... 12.38–12.41
N 661/1999, [1999] OJ L319/1 .... 15.55
NN 90/2000, [2001] OJ C333/8 .... 15.02
N 490/2000, [2005] OJ C250/10 .... 15.40
NN 3/A/2001 and NN 4/A/2001, [2003] OJ C104/10 .... 17.35
NN 3/B/2001, [2003] OJ C189/6 .... 17.35
N 133/2001, [2003] OJ C9/6 .... 15.34
N 90/2002, [2006] OJ C244/8 .... 15.77
NN 101/2002, [2003] OJ C39/15 .... 15.81
N 652/2002, [2003] OJ C104/9 .... 17.12
N 707/2002 MEP, [2003] OJ C148/11 .... 17.12
N 266/2003, [2003] OJ C266/2 .... 17.11
NN 12/2004, [2005] OJ C262/9 .... 15.76

Table of Cases

NN/43/2004, [2006] OJ C34/2 .... 15.73
N/187/2004, [2006] OJ C87/3 .... 15.73
N/206/2004, [2005] OJ C103/17 .... 15.73
N/427/2004, [2005] OJ C133/3 .... 15.73
N/582/2004, [2005] OJ C240/21 .... 15.73
N/599/2004, [2005] OJ C98/11 .... 15.73
N/44/2005, [2005] OJ C329/2 .... 15.73
NN 49/2005, [2005] OJ C324/12 .... 15.37, 15.90
N/223/2005, [2005] OJ C324/28 .... 15.73
N/314/2005, [2005] OJ C226/6 .... 15.73
N/318/2005, [2006] OJ C155/6 .... 15.74
N/334/2005, [2006] OJ C34/2 .... 15.73
N/570/2005, [2006] OJ C202/9 .... 15.73
Norsk Hydro/Saga (Case COMP/M.1573), 5 July 1999 .... 14.61
Opel Nederland BV/General Motors Nederland BV (Case COMP/36.653)
    [2001] OJ L39/1 .... 12.37
Port of Rodby Commission Decision 94/119/EC [1994] OJ L55/52 .... 13.98
PreussenElektra/EZH (Case No IV/M.1659), 30 September 1999 .... 14.58, 15.30
Promatech/Sulzer (Case COMP/M.2698) [2004] OJ C67/14 .... 14.22
REN/Turbogás (Notice pursuant to Art 19(3) of Regulation 17/62)
    [1996] OJ C118/7 .... 13.24, 13.26
RWE/VEW Case 14.62, 14.64
Sabena Case [1988] OJ L317/47 .... 13.96
Schneider/Legrand (Case COMP/M.2283) [2004] OJ C186/17 .... 14.170
Scottish Nuclear, Nuclear Energy Agreement (Case IV/33.473) 13.21, 13.28
Shell/Enterprise Oil (Case COMP/M.2745), 7 May 2002 .... 11.30
Statoil/BP/Sonatrach/In Salah (Case COMP/M.3230), 19 December 2003 .... 14.61
Sydkraft/Graninge (Case COMP/M.3268), 30 October 2003 .... 1.66, 11.24
Tetra Laval/Sidel (Case COMP/M.3255) [2005] OJ C92/31 .... 14.17
Tractebel/Distrigas (II) (Case IV/M.493), 1 September 1994 .... 11.22, 14.88
Unicredit/HVB (Case No COMP/M.3894) IP/06/277 .... 14.36
Vattenfall/Elsam & E2 Assets (Case COMP/M.3867),
    22 December 2005 .... 11.34, 14.03, 14.92
Vättenfall/Hamburgische Elektricitätswerke AG (HEW) (Case IV/M 1842),
    20 March 2000 .... 14.58
VEBA/VIAG (Case COMP/M.1673) [1999] OJ C371/8 .... 14.03, 14.04,
                                  14.62–14.64, 14.107, 14.111, 14.118
Verbund/EnergieAllianz (Case COMP/M.2947), 11 June 2003 .... 11.26, 14.72,
                                  14.107, 14.110, 14.111, 14.119, 14.135
VIK-GVSt (Case IV/33.997) 13.28
Viking Cable (Case COMP/E-3/37.921) [2001] OJ C247/11 .... 13.54
Volkswagen AG (Case IV/35.733) [1998] OJ L124/60 .... 12.37
Volkswagen (Case COMP/F-2/36.693) [2001] OJ L162/14 .... 12.37
WINGAS/EDF Trading (Case COMP/E-4/36.559),
    12 September 2002 .... 12.20, 12.24, 13.13

TABLE OF LEGISLATION

Agreements	xxxvi
Treaties	xxxvi
Regulations	xl
Directives	xliii
Decisions	xlix
Notices	l
Recommendations	li
Other Jurisdictions	li

AGREEMENTS

Agreement on Partnership and
  Co-operation between the EU
  and Russia [1997]
  OJ L327/3 .... 2.161–2.167
Art 65 .... 2.162
EEA Agreement 2.03, 2.115–2.126,
         2.157, 2.178, 10.06, 14.27
  Art 53(1) 2.125, 2.126, 12.05
  Art 57(2) 14.27
  Protocol 24, Art 6(5) 14.27
  Annex IV 2.117
  Annex XIV 14.27
European Convention on Human
  Rights 3.53
Framework Agreement Between UK and
  Norway, 4 April 2005 .... 7.25
General Agreement on Tariffs and
  Trade (GATT) 1.38, 2.140
Interstate Oil and Gas Transport to
  Europe Agreement
  (INOGATE) 2.172
Inter-institutional Agreement on
  Procedures for Implementing the
  Principle of Subsidiarity, concluded
  between the European Parliament,
  Council, and Commission,
  25 October 1993 [1993]
  OJ C329/135 .... 2.48
Partnership and Co-operation
  Agreement Between the EU and
  Russia (OJ 1997 L 327/3) 2.162
  Art 65 .... 2.162

Stockholm Agreement 2.116
Trade and Commercial Co-operation
  Agreement Between the EC and
  the former USSR 1989 .... 2.161

TREATIES

Energy Charter Treaty (Lisbon, 17
  December 1994) .... liv, 2.03,
         2.07, 2.08, 2.131–2.159,
         2.171, 2.172, 18.72
  Art 2 .... 2.131
  Art 3 .... 2.142
  Art 6 .... 2.157, 2.158
  Art 6(2) 2.158
  Art 7 .... 2.142, 2.143
  Art 7(2) 2.145, 2.146
  Art 7(4) 2.150
  Art 7(5) 2.151
  Art 7(6) 2.147
  Art 7(7) 2.149
  Art 10(4) 2.136
  Art 10(7) 2.135
  Art 14 .... 2.135
  Art 24 .... 2.147
  Art 27 .... 2.138
  Art 27(1) 2.158
  Art 29 .... 2.141
  Protocol on Transit 2.131, 2.142,
         2.144, 2.159
Energy Community Treaty (Athens,
  25 October 2005) 2.03, 2.07,
         2.127, 2.128–2.130, 2.157,
         2.167, 2.178

Table of Legislation

Euratom Treaty (Treaty establishing the
European Atomic Energy
Community) (Rome,
25 March 1957) 2.11,
2.17–2.21, 2.88, 9.01, 9.04–9.39,
15.02, 15.83, 15.88, 18.106, 19.41
Art 1 . . . . 2.17, 9.04
Art 2 . . . . 2.17, 9.01, 9.10
Art 2(b) 9.08
Art 2(c) 9.10, 9.18, 9.24
Art 2(d) 9.10, 9.18, 9.24, 9.25
Art 2(g) 9.10
Art 5(b) 9.23
Art 6 . . . . 9.11
Art 30 . . . . 9.08
Art 31 . . . . 9.08, 9.12
Art 33 . . . . 9.08
Art 34 . . . . 9.09
Art 38 . . . . 9.08
Art 47 . . . . 9.11
Art 52 . . . . 9.17, 9.23, 9.24
Art 52(2) 9.23, 9.26
Art 52(2)(a) 9.18, 9.23
Art 52(2)(b) 9.17, 9.22, 9.25
Art 53 . . . . 9.21
Art 57 . . . . 9.21, 9.22
Art 59(b) 9.22
Art 61 . . . . 9.26
Art 70 . . . . 18.106
Art 72 . . . . 9.11, 18.106
Art 75 . . . . 9.28
Title II
   Chapter III 9.08
   Chapter V 9.11
   Chapter VI 9.11, 9.18, 9.21
   Chapter VII 2.17
   Chapter IX 9.07, 9.11
Art 93 . . . . 9.07
Art 96 . . . . 9.07
Arts 171, 172 . . . . 9.11
Art 174 . . . . 9.11
Annex 3 . . . . 9.11
ECSC Treaty (Treaty establishing the
European Coal and Steel
Community) (Paris,
18 April 1951) 1.31, 2.11,
2.14, 2.15, 2.117, 2.128, 2.129,
8.01, 8.02, 8.05, 8.06–8.16, 8.24,
8.25, 8.27, 15.02, 15.09, 19.40
Art 2 . . . . 2.15
Art 3 . . . . 8.06
Art 4 . . . . 2.15, 8.06
Art 5 . . . . 8.06
Art 5(2) 8.07

Chapter 5 . . . . 8.08
Chapter 6 . . . . 8.08
Art 50 . . . . 2.14
Art 56 . . . . 8.09
Arts 58, 59 . . . . 8.07
Art 61 . . . . 8.07
Art 65 . . . . 8.10, 8.12
Art 66 . . . . 8.12
Art 66(1) 8.08, 8.14
Art 66(2) 8.08, 8.14, 8.16
Art 66(3)–(6) 8.08, 8.14
Art 66(7) 8.08, 8.10, 8.12, 8.15
Art 95 . . . . 8.08
Art 97 . . . . 9.04
EC Treaty (Treaty establishing the
European Economic Community)
(Rome, 25 March 1957) . . . . . . x, 1.08.
1.09, 1.31, 2.05, 2.06, 2.09, 2.11,
2.12, 2.14, 2.22–2.30, 2.35–2.37,
2.39, 2.46, 2.56, 2.69, 2.72, 2.74,
2.78, 2.86, 2.88, 2.97–2.100, 2.108,
2.110, 2.139, 2.157, 2.158, 2.174,
2.176, 3.06, 4.04, 8.01, 8.02, 8.12,
8.16, 8.27, 9.01, 9.06, 9.12, 9.14,
9.37, 9.38, 14.154, 14.161, 14.163,
14.166, 16.35, 17.01, 17.34, 17.49,
18.61, 18.69, 18.99, 19.02, 19.14,
19.16–19.18, 19.40
Art 2 (ex Art 2) 2.22, 17.01
Art 3 (ex Art 3) 17.01
Art 3(1)(g) 1.08
Art 3(1)(l) 17.01
Art 3(1)(u) 2.51
Art 5 (ex Art 3b) 2.47
Art 6 (ex Art 3c) 10.10, 17.01
Art 8 (ex Art 4a) 2.40
Art 8(A) 2.37, 2.39, 2.40
Art 10 (ex Art 5) 3.06
Art 12 (ex Art 6) 16.06, 16.25
Art 16 (ex Art 7d) 2.27, 16.01,
16.03, 16.45
Art 25 (ex Art 12) 15.72
Art 28 (ex Art 30) 2.23, 2.24, 13.69,
16.07, 16.11, 16.26, 16.34, 16.47,
16.54, 16.56, 16.66, 16.68–16.70,
16.82, 18.83, 18.89, 18.95
Art 29 (ex Art 34) 2.23, 2.24,
2.26, 16.07, 16.11, 16.34,
16.47, 16.68, 18.83, 18.89
Art 30 (ex Art 36) 2.23, 2.24, 2.26,
15.66, 16.11, 16.34, 16.47, 16.54,
16.56, 16.66, 16.68, 16.70, 18.81,
18.83, 18.85, 18.88–18.90,
18.93, 18.96–18.98

Table of Legislation

EC Treaty (Treaty establishing the
European Economic Community)
(Rome, 25 March 1957) (*cont.*)
Art 31 (ex Art 37) 2.23, 2.25, 2.26,
2.68, 2.117, 7.01, 12.01, 16.01,
16.06, 16.07, 16.11, 16.26,
16.46–16.51, 16.54, 16.56,
16.58–16.60, 16.68, 16.70,
16.81–16.85, 16.88
Art 31(1) 2.09, 16.50, 16.59,
16.73, 18.94
Art 32 (ex Art 38) 2.26
Art 34(2) 13.74
Art 36 (ex Art 42) 16.89
Art 37 (ex Art 43) 2.10
Art 37(1) 16.26
Art 43 (ex Art 52) 14.150
Art 46 (ex Art 56) 16.36
Art 49 (ex Art 59) 16.34,
16.36, 16.69
Art 50 (ex Art 60) 16.34
Art 51 (ex Art 61) 16.34
Art 52 (ex Art 63) 14.143,
14.145, 16.34
Art 53 (ex Art 64) 16.34
Art 54 (ex Art 65) 16.34
Art 55 (ex Art 66) 16.34, 16.36
Art 56 (ex Art 73b) 14.143, 14.145,
14.150, 14.151
Art 58 (ex Art 73d) 14.145, 14.152
Art 73(1)(b) 14.161
Art 81 (ex Art 85) 1.08, 2.26,
2.28, 2.72, 2.74, 2.117, 2.125,
2.126, 3.51, 8.10, 8.12, 8.14, 9.39,
11.02, 11.03, 11.06, 11.07,
11.12–11.14, 11.16–11.19, 11.21,
11.44, 11.45, 12.12, 12.37, 12.56,
13.01–13.03, 13.15, 13.18, 13.21,
13.28, 13.69, 13.95, 13.102, 16.06,
16.11, 16.17, 16.25, 18.99,
19.20, 19.24
Art 81(1) 2.126, 8.14,
11.10, 12.04, 12.05, 12.17, 12.36,
13.08, 13.23, 13.28, 13.30, 14.13
Art 81(2) 12.40
Art 81(3) 8.12, 11.08, 11.10,
11.12, 12.11, 12.17, 13.18, 13.23,
13.28, 18.67
Art 82 (ex Art 86) 2.26, 2.28,
2.30, 2.72, 2.74, 2.117, 3.51, 8.10,
8.12, 8.15, 9.39, 11.02, 11.03,
11.09, 11.10, 11.12–11.14,
11.17–11.19, 11.21, 11.44, 11.45,
13.01–13.03, 13.11, 13.28, 13.34,
13.55, 13.69, 13.87, 13.88, 13.91,
13.92, 13.94, 13.95, 13.97, 13.99,
13.102, 16.06, 16.11–16.13, 16.17,
16.25, 16.32, 16.33, 16.37, 16.38,
16.42, 16.42, 18.99, 19.20, 19.24
Art 82(b) 16.33
Art 82(1) 13.93, 13.94
Art 83 (ex Art 87) 16.06, 16.17
Art 84 (ex Art 88) 16.06
Art 85 (ex Art 89) 2.72, 16.06
Art 85(3) 2.32
Art 86 (ex Art 90) 1.31, 2.23,
2.26, 2.68, 2.70, 2.72, 2.117, 6.12,
6.70, 11.02, 11.19, 11.44, 13.68,
13.69, 13.94, 16.02–16.08, 16.25,
16.31, 16.46, 18.15
Art 86(1) 2.26, 2.30, 16.01,
16.06, 16.08, 16.11, 16.12, 16.23,
16.25, 16.33, 16.38, 16.42, 16.44.
16.45, 16.60
Art 86(2) 2.26, 2.27, 5.15, 6.13,
6.14, 13.16, 13.18–13.21, 13.28,
13.30, 13.62, 13.70, 13.93, 15.27,
16.07, 16.08, 16.13, 16.18, 16.32,
16.45, 16.60, 16.61, 16.64, 16.67,
16.75, 16.83–16.85, 18.81, 18.99,
18.100, 19.14
Art 86(3) 2.72, 2.110, 10.10,
16.04, 16.10, 16.12, 16.14–16.20,
16.22–16.30, 16.90, 16.93
Art 87 (ex Art 92) 2.29, 8.24,
10.09, 10.34, 11.02, 15.04, 16.06,
17.10, 17.49, 18.41
Art 87(1) 9.37, 10.37, 15.04,
15.06, 15.47, 15.66, 15.78, 17.12,
17.15, 17.38, 18.101
Art 87(2) 15.04, 15.06
Art 87(3) 15.06
Art 87(3)(a) 15.04, 15.06, 15.15
Art 87(3)(b) 15.04, 15.06
Art 87(3)(c) 15.04, 15.06, 15.15,
15.19, 15.24, 15.27, 15.47, 15.74
Art 87(3)(d), (e) 15.05, 15.06
Art 88 (ex Art 93) 2.29, 2.72,
10.09, 10.10, 10.34, 11.02, 15.04,
15.07, 16.06, 17.10, 17.49, 18.41
Art 88(1) 15.07
Art 88(2) 15.82
Art 88(3) 15.07, 17.30
Art 89 (ex Art 94) 2.29, 15.04,
15.07, 16.06
Art 90 (ex Art 95) 15.72,
16.17, 16.44
Art 90(2) 16.89

EC Treaty (Treaty establishing the
  European Economic Community)
  (Rome, 25 March 1957) (*cont.*)
Art 90(3) 16.28
Art 93 (ex Art 99) 17.18, 17.24
Art 94 (ex Art 100) 2.78
Art 95 (ex Art 100a) 2.11, 2.39,
  2.40, 2.78, 16.14–16.17, 16.19,
  16.22, 1016.29, 16.90, 16.91–16.93
Art 95(1) 16.22
Art 133 (ex Art 113) 2.11,
  2.161, 9.24
Art 149 (ex Art 126) 2.41
Art 154 (ex Art 129b) 18.69
Art 155 (ex Art 129c) 18.70
Art 155(3) 18.70
Art 156 (ex Art 129d) 18.69
Art 161 (ex Art 130d) 18.70
Title XVIII 2.11
Title XIX 2.11
Art 174 (ex Art 130r)) 2.43, 10.10,
  17.01, 17.42
Art 175 (ex Art 130s) 2.43
Art 175(1) 17.42
Art 176 (ex Art 130t) 17.01
Title XX 2.11
Art 189 (ex Art 137) 2.83, 2.113
Art 190 (ex Art 138) 2.83
Art 191 (ex Art 138a) 2.83
Art 192 (ex Art 138b) 2.83
Art 193 (ex Art 138c) 2.83
Art 194 (ex Art 138d) 2.83
Art 195 (ex Art 138e) 2.83
Art 196 (ex Art 139) 2.83
Art 197 (ex Art 140) 2.83
Art 198 (ex Art 141) 2.83
Art 199 (ex Art 142) 2.83
Art 200 (ex Art 143) 2.83
Art 201 (ex Art 144) 2.83
Part Five, Title I, Chapter 1,
  Section 2 (Arts 202–210
  (ex Arts 145–154)) 2.76
Art 202 (ex Art 145) 2.76
Art 203 (ex Art 146) 2.76
Art 203(1) 2.76
  ....
Art 204 (ex Art 148) 2.76
Art 205 (ex Art 149) 2.76, 2.79
Art 205(1) 2.78
Art 206 (ex Art 150) 2.76
Art 207 (ex Art 151) 2.76, 2.82
Art 208 (ex Art 152) 2.76
Art 209 (ex Art 153) 2.76
Art 210 (ex Art 154) 2.76

Art 211 (ex Art 155) 2.65
Art 211(1) 2.72
Art 212 (ex Art 156) 2.65
Art 213 (ex Art 157) 2.65
Art 214 (ex Art 158) 2.65
Art 215 (ex Art 159) 2.65
Art 216 (ex Art 160) 2.65
Art 217 (ex Art 161) 2.65
Art 218 (ex Art 162) 2.65
Art 219 (ex Art 163) 2.65
Part Five, Title I, Chapter 1,
  Section 4 (Arts 220–245
  (ex Arts 164–188)) 2.93
Art 221 (ex Art 165) 14.145
Art 222 (ex Art 166) 2.95
Art 223 (ex Art 167) 2.95
Art 226 (ex Art 169) 2.25, 2.74, 2.98,
  16.20, 16.23, 16.24, 16.29,
  16.47, 16.48, 16.51, 16.62,
  16.74, 16.84
Art 227 (ex Art 170) 2.98
Art 228 (ex Art 171) 2.98
Art 230 (ex Art 173) 2.48, 2.90, 2.99
Art 231 (ex Art 174) 2.99
Art 232 (ex Art 175) 2.100
Art 233 (ex Art 176) 2.99
Art 234 (ex Art 177) 13.62,
  16.13, 16.32
Art 235 (ex Art 178) 2.101
Art 238 (ex Art 181) 2.11
Part Five, Title I, Chapter 1,
  Section 5 (Arts 246–248
  (ex Arts 188a–188c)) 2.72
Art 249 (ex Art 189) 2.65, 2.76,
  2.83, 2.93, 2.110
Art 250 (ex Art 189a) 2.65, 2.76,
  2.83, 2.93
Art 251 (ex Art 189b) 2.65, 2.76,
  2.83, 2.87, 2.93
Art 252 (ex Art 189c) 2.65, 2.76,
  2.83, 2.93
Art 253 (ex Art 190) 2.65, 2.76,
  2.83, 2.93, 2.110
Art 254 (ex Art 191) 2.65, 2.76,
  2.83, 2.93
Art 255 (ex Art 191a) 2.65, 2.76,
  2.83, 2.93
Art 256 (ex Art 192) 2.65, 2.76,
  2.83, 2.93, 2.96
Art 257 (ex Art 193) 2.71
Art 258 (ex Art 194) 2.71
Art 259 (ex Art 195) 2.71
Art 260 (ex Art 196) 2.71
Art 261 (ex Art 197) 2.71, 2.96

Table of Legislation

EC Treaty (Treaty establishing the
European Economic Community)
(Rome, 25 March 1957) (*cont.*)
    Art 262 (ex Art 198) 2.71
    Part Five, Title I, Chapter 4
        (Arts 263–265
        (ex Arts 198a–198c)) 2.71
    Art 284 (ex Art 213) 2.70
    Art 288 (ex Art 215) 2.101
    Art 295 (ex Art 222) 5.02, 16.06
    Art 305(1) 9.01
    Art 305(2) 9.01, 9.24
    Art 308 (ex Art 235) 2.11, 2.58,
                            2.70, 2.161, 9.01
    Art 310 (ex Art 238) 2.161
Single European Act (Luxembourg
    and the Hague, 28 February
    1986) . . . . x, xxxiii, 2.36,
            2.44, 2.45, 2.47–2.53, 2.57, 2.78,
                  2.85, 17.22, 17.24, 19.11
    Art 129b 2.51
    Art 130r(4) 2.47
    Declaration 1 . . . . 2.51
    Declaration 3 . . . . 2.37, 2.39
Treaty Establishing a Constitution for
    Europe (Draft) 2.11, 2.59,
                      9.12, 19.08, 19.39
    Art I-12(2) 2.59
    Art II-96 . . . . 2.60, 16.01
    Art III-6 . . . . 5.15
    Art III-122 . . . . 2.60, 16.01
    Art III-234(2)(c) 2.59
    Art III-256 . . . . 2.59
Treaty of Accession (Denmark,
    Ireland and the United Kingdom,
    1972) 2.45
Treaty of Accession (Greece, 1979) 2.45
Treaty of Accession (Spain and Portugal,
    1985) 2.45
    Art 48 . . . . 7.02
    Art 208 . . . . 7.02
    Art 221 . . . . 14.145
    Art 231 . . . . 14.145
Treaty of Accession (Cyprus, Malta,
    Poland, the Czech Republic,
    Slovakia, Hungary, Estonia, Latvia,
    Lithuania and Slovenia
    2003) 2.55, 9.02, 10.08, 18.32
    Art 12(1)(a)(i) 2.79
    Annex IV.3 . . . . 15.49
Treaty on European Union (Amsterdam,
    June 1997) (Treaty
        of Amsterdam) . . . . xxxiii, 2.06,
                  2.55, 2.56, 2.66, 15.63

    Title XV 18.69
Treaty on European Union (Maastricht,
    7 February 1992; CM 1934)
    (Maastricht or TEU
    Treaty) . . . . xi, lvii, 2.06, 2.46,
                   2.50, 2.55, 2.57, 2.66,
                     2.87, 2.90, 7.23
    Art 3 . . . . 2.57
    Art 4 . . . . 2.76
    Titles II–IV 2.46
    Declaration No 1 . . . . 2.57
Treaty on European Union (Nice,
    December 2001) . . . . lvii, 2.06,
                     2.55, 2.58, 8.11

REGULATIONS

Regulation 17/62 implementing
    Articles 85 and 96 of the
    Treaty 11.06, 11.10, 11.12,
                     12.37, 13.94
    Art 1 . . . . 11.12
    Art 15 . . . . 12.37
    Art 19(3) 13.54
Regulation 4064/89/EEC on the
    control of concentrations
    between undertakings
    [1989] OJ L395/30
    (Merger Regulation) 5.01,
                  6.76, 14.05, 14.07,
                14.20, 14.22, 14.93
Regulation 2236/95/EC laying down
    general rules for the granting of
    Community financial aid in the
    field of trans-European networks
    [1995] OJ L228/1 . . . . 18.75
Regulation 1488/96/EC on financial
    and technical measures to
    accompany (MEDA) the reform
    of economic and social structures
    in the framework of the
    Euro-Mediterranean partnership
    [1998] OJ L187/01 . . . . 2.170
Regulation 1310/97/EC amending
    Regulation (EEC) No 4064/89 on
    the control of concentrations
    between undertakings [1997]
    OJ L180/1 . . . . 14.05, 14.07
Regulation 1655/1999/EC amending
    Regulation (EC) No 2236/95
    laying down general rules for the
    granting of Community financial
    aid in the field of trans-European
    networks [1999]

Table of Legislation

OJ L197/1 .... 18.75
Regulation 2790/99/EC on the application
   of Article 81(3) of the Treaty to
   categories of vertical agreements
   and concerted practices [1999]
   OJ L336/21 .... 12.37
   Art 2 .... 12.37
   Art 4(b) 12.36
Regulation 2658/2000/EC on the
   application of Article 81(3) of
   the Treaty to categories of
   specialisation agreements [2000]
   OJ L304/3 .... 12.18
   Recital 8 .... 12.18
   Art 3(b) 12.18
Regulation 2698/2000 amending
   Regulation 1488/96, adopted on
   23 July 1996 [2000]
   OJ L311/3 .... 2.170
Regulation 1407/2002/EC on state aid
   to the coal industry [2002]
   OJ L205/1 .... 8.04, 8.10,
                                     8.17–8.27
   Recital 7 .... 8.04
   Art 1 .... 8.04, 8.18
   Art 4 .... 8.19, 8.20
   Arts 5–7 .... 8.19
   Chapter 2 .... 8.19, 8.20
   Art 11(2) 8.21
   Art 13(1) 8.21
Regulation 1972/2002 amending
   Regulation 384/96 on the protection
   against dumped imports from
   countries not members of the
   European Community [2002]
   OJ L305/51 .... 2.166
Regulation 1973/2002 amending
   Regulation 2026/97 on the protection
   against subsidised imports from
   countries not members of the
   European Community [2002]
   OJ L305/4 .... 2.166
Regulation 1/2003 of 16 December 2002
   on the implementation of the rules
   on competition laid down in
   Articles 81 and 82 of the Treaty
   [2003] OJ L1/1 (Merger
   Regulation) 6.76, 8.12, 8.14,
                       8.16, 11.03–11.06, 11.10,
                 11.12–11.21, 11.38, 11.66, 12.62,
                   14.18, 15.91, 19.02, 19.21
   Recital 3 .... 11.10
   Recital 12 .... 11.15
   Recital 14 .... 11.15

Art 1 .... 11.12
Art 2 .... 8.16
Art 3 .... 11.13
Arts 7, 8 .... 11.15
Art 9 .... 11.15, 12.62
Art 10 .... 11.15
Art 11 .... 11.16
Art 11(1), (3), (4), (6) 11.16
Art 12 .... 11.16
Art 14 .... 11.16
Art 14(1) 8.15
Art 14(7) 11.16
Art 17 .... 11.03, 11.17, 11.18,
                  11.38, 11.42, 19.03
Art 18 .... 11.17, 11.42
Art 18(1) 11.17
Art 18(6) 11.17
Arts 19–24 .... 11.17
Regulation 1228/2003 on conditions
   for access to the network for
   cross-border exchanges in electricity
   [2003] OJ L176/37 (Electricity
   Regulation) .... **App 2**, 2.117,
            2.128, 3.13, 3.38, 3.52, 5.01,
            5.05, 5.47, 5.60, 5.63, 5.67,
           5.68, 5.79–5.123, 5.127–5.132,
           5.135–5.141, 6.19, 6.57, 6.68,
           6.115, 6.142, 6.146, 13.45, 13.81,
          14.73, 18.12, 18.39, 18.44, 19.13
Recitals 7, 8 .... 5.117
Recital 14 .... 5.86, 5.93
Recital 18 .... 5.130
Art 2(2)(b) 5.84
Art 2(2)(c) 5.90
Art 3 .... 5.81, 5.84
Art 3(1) 5.84
Art 3(6) 5.85
Art 4 .... 5.63, 5.81, 5.82
Art 4(1) 5.86
Art 4(3) 5.87
Art 4(4) 5.89
Art 4(5) 5.86
Art 5 .... 5.81, 5.106, 5.117
Art 5(1) 18.12
Art 5(2) 5.117, 18.12
Art 6 .... 5.81, 5.117,
                          5.126, 18.39
Art 6(1) 5.81, 5.90, 5.136
Art 6(2) 5.92, 5.137
Art 6(3) 5.93
Art 6(4) 5.64
Art 6(5) 5.93
Art 6(6) 5.96, 5.126
Art 7 .... 5.81, 5.96, 5.100, 5.101

Regulation 1228/2003 on conditions
for access to the network for
cross-border exchanges in electricity [2003]
OJ L176/37 (Electricity Regulation) (*cont.*)
Art 7(1) 5.104
Art 7(1)(a)–(e) 5.97
Art 7(1)(f) 5.97, 5.100
Art 7(3) 5.96
Art 7(4) 5.103
Art 7(4)(a) 5.98
Art 7(5) 5.99
Art 8 . . . . 5.83, 5.113, 5.115, 5.130
Art 8(2)(a)–(f) 5.114
Art 8(4) 5.115
Art 9 . . . . 3.52, 5.63, 5.130
Art 10 . . . . 5.106, 5.109
Art 10(1) 5.63
Art 10(2) 5.63, 5.110, 5.129
Art 10(3) 5.129
Art 10(5) 5.63, 5.129
Art 10(6) 5.106
Art 11 . . . . 5.140
Art 12(1) 5.128
Art 12(2) 5.110, 5.111
Art 13 . . . . 2.117, 5.67, 5.99
Art 13(2) 5.84, 5.117
Art 14 . . . . 5.131
Art 15 . . . . 2.117, 5.136
Art 21(2) 6.64
Art 23(5) 5.64
Art 23(6) 5.64
Art 23(8) 5.102
Art 95 . . . . 5.79
Annex 3.36, 5.63, 5.83,
5.119–5.121, 5.136, 5.140, 13.81
Guideline 1.5 . . . . 5.120
Guideline 1.6 . . . . 5.120
Guideline 1.9 . . . . 5.120
Guideline 2.6 . . . . 5.121
Guideline 2.10 . . . . 5.121
Guideline 2.13 . . . . 5.124
Guideline 3.4 . . . . 5.124
Guideline 5.4 . . . . 5.125
Guideline 5.5 . . . . 5.125
Guideline 6.2 . . . . 5.127
Regulation 139/2004 on the control of
concentrations between undertakings
[2004] OJ L24/1 . . . . 8.13, 11.03,
14.07–14.38, 14.40, 14.45, 14.170
Recital 3 . . . . 14.08
Recital 6 . . . . 14.08
Recital 8 . . . . 14.08
Recital 14 . . . . 14.35
Recital 18 . . . . 14.35
Art 1 . . . . 14.12, 14.20
Art 1(1)(a), (b) 14.33
Art 1(2) 14.12
Art 2 . . . . 14.32
Art 2(3) 14.10, 14.97
Art 2(4), (5) 14.13
Art 4 . . . . 14.46
Art 4(1) 14.14
Art 4(4) 14.14, 14.23, 14.25
Art 4(5) 14.14, 14.23, 14.25, 14.27
Art 5 . . . . 14.49
Art 6(1)(c) 14.14
Art 6(2) 14.15
Art 7 . . . . 14.14
Art 8(2) 14.15
Art 9 . . . . 14.21, 14.55
Art 10(1)–(3) 14.14
Arts 11–13 . . . . 14.17
Art 14 . . . . 14.17
Art 14(1)(b), (c) 14.17
Art 14(2) 14.14
Art 14(3) 14.17
Arts 15, 16 . . . . 14.17
Art 18(1)–(4) 14.17
Art 19(6) 14.17
Art 21 . . . . 14.37, 14.53
Art 21(1)–(3) 14.37
Art 21(4) 14.38, 14.39
Art 22 . . . . 14.22, 14.25, 14.52
Art 23(1)(a), (c) 14.18
Art 43 . . . . 14.53
Art 56 . . . . 14.25, 14.53
Regulation 411/2004/EC repealing
Regulation 3975/87/EC and
amending Regulations 3976/87/EC
and 1/2003/EC, in connection with
air transport between the
Community and third countries
[2004] OJ L68/1 . . . . 11.03, 12.62
Regulation 788/2004/EC amending
Council Regulation (EC)
No 2236/95 and Regulations (EC)
No 1655/2000 (EC) No 1382/2003
and (EC) No 2152/2003 with a view
to adapting the reference amounts to
take account of the enlargement of
the European Union [2004]
OJ L138/17 . . . . 18.75
Regulation 802/2004/EC of 7 April
2004 implementing Council
Regulation (EC) 139/2004 on
the control of concentrations
between undertakings [2004]
OJ L133/1 . . . . 14.07, 14.30

Table of Legislation

Annex 1 . . . . 14.30
Regulation 807/2004/EC amending
 Council Regulation (EC)
 No 2236/95 laying down general
 rules for the granting of Community
 financial aid in the field of
 trans-European networks [2004]
 OJ L143/46 . . . . 18.75
Regulation 1223/2004/EC amending
 Regulation 1228/2003 as
 regards the date of application
 of certain provisions to Slovenia
 [2004] OJ L233/3 . . . . 5.136
Regulation 1775/2005/EC on conditions
 for access to the natural gas
 transmission networks
 [2005] OJ L289/1 (Gas
 Regulation) . . . . **App 4**, 3.13, 6.01,
  6.43, 6.62, 6.115–6.149,
  12.48, 13.45
 Recital 2 . . . . 6.133
 Recital 7 . . . . 6.119
 Recital 8 . . . . 6.120
 Recitals 9, 10 . . . . 6.122
 Recital 11 . . . . 6.126
 Recital 18 . . . . 6.133
 Recital 19 . . . . 6.135
 Recital 20 . . . . 6.136
 Recital 21 . . . . 6.146
 Art 1(1) 6.117
 Art 3(1) 6.118
 Art 3(2) 6.121
 Art 4(1) 6.122
 Art 4(3) 6.124
 Art 5(1), (2) 6.125
 Art 5(3) 6.126
 Art 5(4), (5) 6.127
 Art 6 . . . . 6.128
 Art 7 . . . . 6.129
 Art 7(1)–(7) 6.129
 Art 8 . . . . 6.130
 Art 9 . . . . 6.136, 6.142
 Art 9(2) 6.147
 Art 9(3) 6.144
 Art 10 . . . . 6.143
 Art 11 . . . . 6.136
 Art 13 . . . . 6.142
 Art 14(2) 6.135
 Art 15 . . . . 6.145
 Art 16 . . . . 6.144
 Art 30 . . . . 6.135
 Annex 3.36, 6.116,
  6.125, 6.132, 6.134
 Guidelines 6.116, 6.132, 6.136

DIRECTIVES

Directive 68/414/EEC imposing an
 obligation on Member States
 of the EEC to maintain minimum
 stocks of crude oil and/or petroleum
 (OJ 1968 L308/4) 2.31,
  18.60–18.67
 Art 3 . . . . 18.67
 Art 103(a)(1) 18.61
Directive 72/425/EEC amending the
 Council Directive of 20 December
 1968 imposing an obligation on
 Member States of the EEC to
 maintain minimum stocks of crude
 oil and/or petroleum products
 [1972] OJ L291/154 . . . . 18.62
Directive 73/238/EEC on measures to
 mitigate the effects of difficulties
 in the supply of crude oil and
 petroleum products [1973]
 OJ L228/1 . . . . 18.60, 18.62, 18.65
Directive 73/278/EEC implementing the
 rules of the International Energy
 Agency 2.32
Directive 75/404/EEC on the restriction
 of the use of natural gas in power
 stations [1975]OJ L178/24 . . . . . . 1.33
Directive 76/579 (Euratom) laying down
 the revised basic safety standards
 for the health protection of the
 general public and workers [1976]
 OJ L187/1 . . . . 9.09
Directive 77/706/EEC on the setting of a
 Community target for a reduction
 in the consumption of primary
 sources of energy in the event of
 difficulties in the supply of crude
 oil and petroleum products [1977]
 OJ L292/9 . . . . 18.60
Directive 79/343 (Euratom) amending
 Directive 76/579/Euratom laying
 down the revised basic safety
 standards for the health protection
 of the general public and workers
 against the dangers of ionizing
 radiation [1979] OJ L83/18 . . . . . 9.09
Directive 80/836 (Euratom) amending
 the Directives laying down the basic
 safety standards for the health
 protection of the general public and
 workers against the dangers of
 ionizing radiation [1980]
 OJ L246/1 . . . . 9.09

Directive 83/189/EEC laying down a procedure for the provision of information in the field of technical standards and regulations [1983] OJ L109/8 .... 13.69
Directive 84/467 (Euratom) amending Directive 80/836/Euratom as regards the basic safety standards for the health protection of the general public and workers against the dangers of ionizing radiation [1984] OJ L265/4 .... 9.09
Directive 88/301/EEC Telecommunications Directive on the liberalization of terminal equipment [1988] OJ L131/73 ...... 16.18, 16.19
Directive 88/361/EEC for the implementation of Article 67 of the Treaty [1998] OJ L178/5 ...... 14.154
Annex I 14.154
Directive 90/388/EEC on competition in the markets for telecommunications services [1990] OJ L192/10 .... 16.19, 16.28
Recital 13 .... 16.36
Recital 16 .... 16.38
Recital 17 .... 16.38
Recital 21 .... 16.42
Recital 29 .... 16.33
Recital 33 .... 16.28
Directive 90/531/EEC on the procurement procedures of entities operating in the water, energy, transport and telecommunications sectors [1990] OJ L297/1
Art 3 .... 7.06, 7.20
Directive 90/547/EEC on the transit of electricity through transmission grids [1990] OJ L313/30
Directive 91/148/EEC on the restriction of the use of natural gas in power stations [1991] OJ L75/52 .... 1.33
Directive 91/296/EEC on the transit of natural gas through grids [1991] OJ L147/37 .... 6.61
Art 3(1) 6.61
Directive 92/12/EEC the movement and control of products subject to excise duties and other indirect taxes levied directly or indirectly on their consumption (except for VAT and taxes established by the EC) [1992] OJ L76/1 .... 17.22
Recitals 5, 8 .... 17.22

Art 3(2) 17.23
Directive 92/81/EEC on the harmonization of the structures of excise duties on mineral oils [1992] OJ L316/12 .... 17.23
Recitals 7, 12 .... 17.23
Directive 92/82/EEC on the approximation of the rates of excise duties on mineral oils [1992] OJ L316/19 .... 17.23
Recital 7 .... 17.23
Directive 92/108/EEC on the general arrangements for products subject to excise duty and on the holding, movement and monitoring of such products and amending Directive 92/81/EEC [1992] OJ L390/124 .... 17.22
Directive 93/38/EEC coordinating the procurement procedures of entities operating in the water, energy, transport and telecommunications sector [1993] OJ L199/9 .... 7.06, 7.20
Directive 94/22/EC on the conditions for granting and using authorizations for the prospection, exploration and production of hydrocarbons [1994] OJ L164/3 .... 2.123, 6.21, 6.51, 7.02, 7.03, 7.05–7.07, 7.11–7.22, 7.26, 19.39, 7.09
Art 3(2) 7.11
Art 3(2)(a) 7.11
Art 3(3) 7.11
Art 4 .... 7.09
Art 5 .... 7.12
Art 6 .... 7.13
Art 6(1) 7.15
Art 6(2) 7.07, 7.13
Art 6(3) 7.13, 7.14, 7.16
Art 6(4) 7.17
Art 7 .... 7.18
Art 7(a) 7.20
Art 8 .... 7.19
Art 12 .... 7.20
Art 13 .... 7.12
Art 14 .... 7.22
Annex VII 7.20
Directive 96/61/EC concerning integrated pollution prevention and control [1996] OJ L257/26 .... 17.45

Table of Legislation

Directive 96/92/EC on common rules for
the internal market in electricity
[1996] OJ L27/20 .... 2.06, 3.06,
3.14, 5.01, 5.03, 5.05, 5.08, 5.16,
5.38, 5.44, 5.45, 5.54, 5.70,
5.133–5.135, 5.140, 10.01, 13.59,
13.64, 13.65, 13.75, 13.79, 13.80,
13.83, 14.03, 15.10, 15.12,
15.15–15.18, 15.22, 15.66,
16.86, 17.01, 18.22
Recital 2 .... 17.01
Recital 18 .... 17.01
Recital 22 .... 17.01
Recital 25 .... 13.72, 17.01
Recital 26 .... 17.01
Recital 28 .... 15.66
Recital 39 .... 15.66
Art 3(1) 13.73
Art 3(2) 15.27, 15.53
Art 3(3) 13.76
Art 4 .... 10.24
Art 7 .... 13.63, 13.75, 13.76
Art 7(2) 13.72
Art 7(5) 13.60, 13.62,
13.69–13.72, 13.75–13.77,
13.79, 13.81, 13.82
Art 8(2) 13.76
Art 8(3) 10.01, 15.66
Art 8(4) 15.27, 15.53
Art 11(3) 15.66
Art 14(7) 10.01
Art 16 .... 13.60, 13.73,
13.75–13.77, 13.79,
13.81, 13.82
Art 17(5) 13.76
Art 19 .... 5.97
Art 24 .... 13.60, 13.75–13.77,
13.79, 13.82, 13.83, 15.10,
15.13, 15.47
Directive 97/11/EC on the promotion of
electricity produced from renewable
energy sources in the internal
electricity market [2001]
OJ L283/33 .... 7.25, 17.02
Annexes II, III 7.25
Directive 98/4/EC amending Directive
93/38/EEC coordinating the
procurement procedures of entities
operating in the water, energy,
transport and telecommunications
sectors [1998]
OJ L101/1 .... 7.06, 7.20
Directive 98/30/EC on common rules
for the internal market in natural gas
[1998] OJ L204/2 .... 1.73,
2.06, 3.06, 3.14, 6.01, 6.03, 6.05,
6.06, 6.15, 6.23, 6.48, 6.63, 6.71,
6.76, 7.23, 13.01, 13.101, 13.135,
15.10, 16.01, 18.59
Recital 24 .... 17.01
Recital 27 .... 17.01
Art 23 .... 6.47
Directive 98/93/EC imposing an
obligation on Member States of the
EEC to maintain minimum stocks
of crude oil and/or petroleum and
amending Directive 68/414/EC
[1998] OJ L358/100 .... 2.31,
18.60, 18.64, 18.65
Art 4 .... 18.64
Directive 2001/77/EC on the promotion
of electricity from renewable energy
sources in the internal electricity
market into the EEA Agreement
on 8 July 2005 [2001]
OJ L283/33 .... 2.117, 10.01,
10.03–10.40, 17.02, 17.04,
17.06–17.10, 18.32, 19.43, 19.44
Preamble 10.34
Recital 9 .... 10.03
Recital 11 .... 10.21
Recital 12 .... 10.34, 17.10
Recital 15 .... 10.09
Recital 16 .... 10.10
Recital 18 .... 10.40, 19.44
Recital 23 .... 10.04
Art 2(26) 2.117
Art 3 .... 17.05
Art 3(2) 10.07, 10.32
Art 3(3) 10.08, 10.23,
10.32, 10.38
Art 3(4) 10.08, 10.32
Art 4(1) 10.11
Art 4(2) 10.11, 10.32
Art 5 .... 17.09
Art 5(4) 10.23
Art 5(5) 10.26, 10.32
Art 5(6) 10.23, 10.32
Art 6(1) 10.33
Art 6(2) 10.32, 10.38
Art 6(3) 10.32, 10.33
Art 7(1), (2) 10.29
Art 7(4) 10.31
Art 7(5) 10.29
Art 7(6) 10.29, 10.31
Art 7(7) 10.32
Art 8 .... 10.23, 10.32, 10.33
Annex 10.07–10.09

Directive 2001/80/EC on the limitation
  of emissions of certain pollutants
  into the air from large combustion
  plants [2001] OJ L309/1
  Art 4.4(a) 8.03
Directive 2002/91/EC on the energy
  performance of buildings [2003]
  OJ L1/65 . . . . 17.02
Directive 2003/6/EC on insider dealing
  and market manipulation (market
  abuse) [2003]OJ L96/16 . . . . 11.63
Directive 2003/30/EC on the promotion
  of biofuels [2003] OJ L123/42 . . . 10.03
Directive 2003/54/EC concerning
  Common Rules for the Internal
  Market in Electricity [2003]
  OJ L176/37 . . . . . **App 1**, 2.117, 2.128,
    2.152, 3.01, 3.18, 3.21, 3.52, 3.62,
    5.01–5.64, 5.67, 5.69–5.78, 5.94,
    5.134, 5.135, 5.140, 5.141, 6.02, 6.05,
    6.06, 6.12, 6.13, 6.19, 6.21, 6.36, 6.39,
    6.65, 6.68, 6.74, 6.110, 7.06, 10.01,
    10.05, 11.01, 11.03, 11.50, 13.01,
    13.15, 13.63, 13.88, 13.92, 14.05,
    15.10, 15.21, 15.91, 16.01, 16.02,
    16.10, 16.83, 17.01, 18.08, 18.09,
    18.11–18.21, 18.23, 18.39, 19.14,
    19.15, 19.21, 19.35, 19.47, 19.50
  Recital 2 . . . . 5.06
  Recital 8 . . . . 5.39
  Recital 10 . . . . 5.02, 5.39
  Recital 11 . . . . 5.39
  Recital 15 . . . . 3.45, 5.56
  Recital 16 . . . . 3.46, 5.56
  Recital 18 . . . . 13.39A
  Recital 19 . . . . 5.11
  Recital 24 . . . . 5.10
  Recital 25 . . . . 5.12
  Recital 26 . . . . 5.09
  Recital 27 . . . . 5.10
  Chapter II 5.08
  Art 2(3) 5.27
  Art 2(15) 5.51
  Art 3 . . . . 5.11, 5.13, 5.19,
    5.34, 18.12, 18.16, 18.23
  Art 3(1) 5.09
  Art 3(2) 5.09, 5.10, 5.14, 5.31,
    18.13
  Art 3(3) 5.09, 5.10, 18.14
  Art 3(5) 5.09
  Art 3(6) 5.09, 5.12, 10.21, 17.09
  Art 3(7) 5.09
  Art 3(8) 5.72, 6.12, 18.15
  Art 3(9) 5.09, 5.13
  Art 4 . . . . 5.09, 5.16, 18.12, 18.17,
    18.23, 18.43, 18.46
  Art 5 . . . . 10.24
  Art 6 . . . . 5.18, 18.42
  Art 6(2) 5.19
  Art 6(3) 5.21
  Chapter IV 5.27, 5.28, 5.34
  Art 7 . . . . 18.12, 18.20, 18.23, 18.43
  Art 7(1) 5.22, 18.18, 18.41
  Art 7(2) 5.23
  Art 7(3) 5.24, 18.44
  Art 7(4) 5.25, 18.45
  Art 7(5) 5.26, 18.46
  Art 8 . . . . 5.28, 18.48
  Art 8(1) 5.39
  Art 9 . . . . 5.29, 18.47
  Art 10 . . . . 5.38
  Art 10(1) 5.38
  Art 10(2) 5.38, 5.39
  Art 10(2)(d) 5.40
  Art 11(1) 5.30
  Art 11(3) 5.31
  Art 12 . . . . 5.29
  Chapter V 5.34
  Art 13 . . . . 5.35
  Art 14 . . . . 5.35, 5.36
  Art 14(4) 5.37
  Art 14(7) 5.37
  Art 15 . . . . 5.35, 5.38, 5.39
  Art 15(2) . . . 5.38, 5.39, 5.72, 5.74, 16.02
  Art 15(2)(d) 5.40
  Art 16 . . . . 5.35, 5.36
  Art 17(d) 5.40
  Art 19(1)–(4) 5.38
  Chapter VII 5.27, 5.44
  Art 20 . . . . 5.96
  Art 20(1) 5.45
  Art 20(1)(b), (c) 5.49
  Art 20(2) 5.46
  Art 21 . . . . 5.48
  Art 21(2) 5.50
  Art 22 . . . . 5.54, 5.55
  Art 22(1) 5.51
  Art 23 . . . . . . 3.45, 5.52, 5.55, 6.68, 18.31
  Art 23(1) 18.17
  Art 23(2) 3.52, 5.96
  Art 23(3), (4) 5.62, 5.96
  Art 23(7) 3.45, 5.55
  Art 23(8) 5.55, 5.59
  Art 24 . . . . 5.09, 5.16,
    18.12, 18.23, 18.39
  Art 25 . . . . 5.77
  Art 26 . . . . 5.76
  Art 26(1) 5.71

Directive 2003/54/EC concerning
    Common Rules for the Internal
    Market in Electricity [2003]
    OJ L176/37 (cont.)
Art 28 .... 18.12
Art 28(1) 5.73, 18.21, 18.46
Art 28(2) 5.75
Art 28(3) 5.39, 5.73, 5.76
Art 29 .... 5.01
Art 30(2) 5.39
Annex A 5.09, 5.11, 6.10
Directive 2003/55/EC concerning
    Common Rules for the Internal
    Market in natural gas and repealing
    Directive 98/30/EC [2003]
    OJ 176/57 .... **App 3**, 1.73, 2.117,
        2.128, 2.152, 3.01, 3.35, 3.36, 3.39,
        3.52, 3.62, 5.03, 5.68, 6.01–6.115,
        6.118, 6.120, 6.144–6.149, 7.06,
        7.23–7.25, 11.01, 11.03, 11.37,
        11.57, 12.12, 12.57, 12.60, 12.63,
        13.01, 13.15, 13.88, 13.92, 13.101,
            13.136, 13.137, 13.138, 14.05,
            14.97, 15.10, 16.01, 16.02, 16.10,
            16.83, 17.01, 18.08, 18.09, 18.16,
            18.23–18.28, 18.55, 19.13–19.15,
                19.21, 19.35, 19.47, 19.50
Recital 2 .... 6.03
Recital 10 .... 6.49
Recital 13 .... 3.45
Recital 14 .... 3.46
Recital 16 .... 13.39A
Recital 20 .... 6.41
Recital 26 .... 6.07
Recital 27 .... 5.09, 6.06
Recital 30 .... 6.03
Art 2(2) 6.47
Art 2(3) 6.22
Art 2(5) 6.26
Art 2(17) 18.25
Art 2(18) 6.65
Art 2(31) 2.117, 6.99
Chapter II 6.05
Art 3 .... 6.88, 18.23
Art 3(1) 6.06
Art 3(2) 6.06, 6.11, 6.12, 6.88, 18.26
Art 3(3) 5.11, 6.06
Art 3(4) 6.06
Art 3(5) 6.11, 6.12, 6.71
Art 3(6) 5.13, 6.06
Art 4 .... 6.11, 6.15, 6.71, 6.101, 6.104
Art 4(4) 6.107
Art 5 .... 6.17, 18.23, 18.55
Art 6 .... 6.19
Chapter III 6.22, 6.24
Art 7 .... 6.24, 6.26, 6.40, 6.104
Art 8 .... 6.26, 6.104, 6.135
Art 8(1) 6.104
Art 8(1)(a) 6.25, 6.139
Art 8(2) 6.104
Art 9 .... 6.26, 6.101, 6.104, 6.136
Art 10 .... 6.25, 6.26
Art 11 .... 6.26, 6.104
Art 12 .... 6.26–6.28
Art 12(5) 6.104
Art 13 .... 6.26, 6.27, 6.104
Art 13(2) 6.71, 6.111, 16.02
Art 14 .... 6.26–6.28
Art 15 .... 6.26
Art 17 .... 6.104
Art 18 ...... 6.38, 6.74, 6.98, 6.104, 6.118
Art 18(2), (3) 6.39
Art 19 .... 6.29, 6.68
Art 19(1) 6.38, 6.40, 6.44
Art 19(2) 6.44
Art 20 .... 6.38, 6.47, 6.49, 18.28
Art 20(1) 6.44
Art 20(2) 6.49, 6.50
Art 20(3), (4) 6.52
Art 21 .... 1.73, 6.144, 18.26
Art 21(1) 6.12, 6.39, 6.88
Art 21(2) 6.39
Art 22 .... 3.54, 6.35, 6.38,
                    6.53, 18.23, 18.24, 18.55
Art 22(2) 6.53
Art 22(3) 6.54
Art 22(3)(c) 6.54
Art 22(4)(a)–(e) 6.55
Art 23 .... 6.63, 6.101
Art 23(1) 6.104
Art 23(2) 6.64
Art 24 .... 6.65, 6.101
Art 24(2), (3) 6.66
Art 25 .... 3.45, 6.66, 6.68, 6.122
Art 25(1) 6.68
Art 25(1)(f) 6.68
Art 25(2) 6.118
Art 25(3) 6.84
Art 25(7) 3.45
Art 25(8) 6.68
Art 25(12) 3.52
Art 26 .... 6.17, 18.23
Art 26(4) 6.107
Art 27 .... 6.39, 6.69, 6.71, 6.74,
                    6.80–6.82, 6.88, 6.98, 6.144
Art 27(1) 6.39, 6.76, 6.87
Art 27(2) 6.77
Art 27(3) 6.79, 6.82, 6.84

Table of Legislation

Directive 2003/55/EC concerning
  Common Rules for the Internal
  Market in natural gas and repealing
  Directive 98/30/EC [2003]
  OJ 176/57 (cont.)
  Art 27(3)(a) 6.83, 6.87, 6.94
  Art 27(3)(b) 6.83, 6.88, 18.27
  Art 27(3)(c) 6.83, 6.89
  Art 27(3)(e) 6.83, 6.85
  Art 27(3)(f) 6.83, 6.93
  Art 27(3)(g) 6.83, 6.92
  Art 27(3)(h) 6.83, 6.91
  Art 27(3)(i) 6.83, 6.95
  Art 28 . . . . 6.71, 6.100, 6.102, 6.144
  Art 28(1) 6.69, 6.101, 6.102
  Art 28(2) 2.117, 6.69, 14.95
  Art 28(3) 6.113, 14.95
  Art 28(4) 6.69
  Art 28(5) 6.106
  Art 28(5)(a), (b) 6.71
  Art 28(6) 6.109
  Art 28(8) 6.109
  Art 29 . . . . 6.113
  Art 30 . . . . 2.117, 6.68, 6.77
  Art 31 . . . . 6.110, 18.55
  Art 31(1) 6.110
  Art 31(1)(b) 6.71
  Art 31(1)(d) 18.23
  Art 31(2) 6.09, 6.112
  Art 31(3) 6.110, 6.145
  Art 32 . . . . 6.01, 6.38
  Art 32(1) 6.61
  Annex A 6.10, 6.98
Directive 2003/66/EC on energy
  labelling of household electric
  refrigerators, freezers and their
  combinations [2003]
  OJ L170/10 . . . . 17.02
Directive 2003/87/EC establishing a
  scheme for greenhouse gas emission
  allowance trading within the
  European Community and
  amending Directive 96/91/EC
  [2003] OJ L275/32 . . . . 17.02,
                                17.04, 17.42–17.54
  Art 1 . . . . 17.42
  Art 9 . . . . 17.44
  Art 14(1), (2) 17.45
  Art 15 . . . . 17.45
  Arts 19, 20 . . . . 17.45
  Art 26 . . . . 17.45
  Annex III 17.49
Directive 2003/96/EC restructuring the
  Community framework for the
  taxation of energy products
  and electricity [2003]
  OJ L283/51 . . . . 10.05, 17.04,
                                       17.23–17.34
  Art 2 . . . . 17.27
  Art 2(4)(b) 17.31
  Art 4 . . . . 17.27
  Art 7(2) 17.28
  Art 15 . . . . 17.29
  Art 15(1)(g) 17.29
  Art 16 . . . . 17.30
  Art 17(1)(b) 17.30
  Art 19(1) 17.30
  Art 25 . . . . 17.30
  Art 26 . . . . 17.30
  Art 26(2) 17.30
  Art 29 . . . . 17.28
  Annex II 17.30
Directive 2004/8/EC on the promotion
  of cogeneration based on a useful
  heat demand in the internal
  energy market [2004]
  OJ L52/50 . . . . 10.03, 17.02, 18.32
  Recitals 1, 2 . . . . 17.02
Directive 2004/17/EC co-ordinating the
  procurement procedures of entities
  operating in the water, energy,
  transport and postal services sectors
  [2004] OJ L134/1 . . . . 7.06, 7.21
  Recital 38 . . . . 7.21
  Art 27 . . . . 7.21
  Art 30 . . . . 7.20
  Art 30(3) 7.21
  Annex XI 7.21
Directive 2004/39/EC on markets in
  financial instruments [2004]
  OJ L145/1 . . . . 11.63
Directive (EC) 2004/67 concerning
  measures to safeguard security of
  natural gas supply[2004]
  OJ L127/92 . . . . 5.9, 18.49–18.59
  Recital 7 . . . . 18.52
  Recital 15 . . . . 18.54
  Recital 17 . . . . 18.53
  Recital 19 . . . . 18.49
  Art 1 . . . . 18.49
  Art 2(1) 18.55
  Art 2(2) 18.53
  Art 3 . . . . 18.50, 18.55, 18.57
  Art 4 . . . . 18.51, 18.52,
                                         18.55, 18.57
  Art 4(1) 18.51
  Art 4(6) 18.52
  Art 5 . . . . 18.55

Directive (EC) 2004/67 concerning
measures to safeguard security of
natural gas supply [2004]
OJ L127/92 (cont.)
  Art 5(a)–(d) 18.55
  Art 6 .... 18.56
  Art 6(3) 18.57
  Art 7 .... 18.53
  Art 8 .... 18.58
  Art 9 .... 18.53
  Art 9(1) 18.53
  Art 9(2) 18.54
  Art 9(4) 18.54
  Art 9(6) 18.54
  Art 10(1) 18.57
  Annex 18.51
Directive 2004/85/EC amending
Directive 2003/54 as regards
the application of certain
provisions to Estonia [2004]
OJ L236/10 .... 5.49
Directive 2004/101/EC establishing a
scheme for greenhouse gas emission
allowance trading within the
Community, in respect of the Kyoto
Protocol's project mechanisms
[2004] OJ L338/18 .... 17.45
Directive 2005/32/EC establishing a
framework for the setting of
ecodesign requirements for
energy-using products [2005]
OJ L191/29 .... 17.02
Directive 2005/89/EC concerning
measures to safeguard security of
electricity supply and infrastructure
investment [2006]
  OJ L33/22 .... 18.12,
            18.29–18.40, 18.43, 18.48
  Recital 3 .... 18.29
  Recital 7 .... 18.29
  Recital 18 .... 18.29
  Art 1 .... 18.30, 18.33
  Art 2(a) 18.31
  Art 2(c) 18.35
  Art 3(2), (3) 18.32
  Art 3(4) 18.34
  Art 4(1) 18.12, 18.16
  Art 4(1)(a) 18.36
  Art 4(2) 18.12, 18.16, 18.39
  Art 4(3), (4) 18.39
  Art 5(1)(a), (b) 18.40
  Art 5(2) 18.41
  Art 5(3) 18.40

Directive 2006/32/EC on the
promotion of end-use efficiency
and energy services [2006]
OJ L114/64 .... 17.02

DECISIONS

Decision 68/416/EEC [1968]
  OJ L308/19 .... 18.65
Decision of 1 January [1973]
  OJ L2/1 .... 2.45
Decision 77/706 [1977]
  OJ L292/9 .... 2.32, 18.65
Decision on British Telecommunications
(BT) [1982] OJ L360/36 .... 16.45
Decision 83/671 [1983]
  OJ L376/30 .... 2.32
Decision 91/50/EEC [1991]
  OJ L28/32 .... 13.15, 13.16,
                      13.21, 13.30, 16.45
Decision 91/329/EEC [1991]
  OJ L178/31 .... 13.21
Decision 93/126/EEC [1993]
  OJ L50/14 .... 13.21, 13.28
Decision 93/428/Euratom [1993]
  OJ L197/54 .... 9.21
Decision 93/676/EEC [1993]
  OJ L316/41 .... 7.21
Decision 3623/93/EC [1993]
  OJ L329/12 .... 8.17
Decision 94/119/EC [1994]
  OJ L15/80 .... 13.98
Decision of 21 February 1994 [1994]
  OJ L68/35 .... 18.67
Decision 94/153 [1994]
  OJ L68/35 .... 2.32
Decision 94/285/Euratom [1994]
  OJ L122/30 .... 9.23
Decision 97/367/EEC [1997]
  L156/55 .... 7.21
Decision 98/273/EC [1998]
  OJ L124/60 .... 12.37
Decision 1999/468 [1999]
  OJ L184/23 .... 3.38, 6.135
  Art 5 .... 6.135
  Art 5(6) 6.135
  Art 7 .... 6.135
Decision 1999/791/EC [1999]
  OJ L319/1 .... 15.55
Decision 1999/792/EC [1999]
  OJ L319/6 .... 15.33
Decision 1999/793/EC [1999]
  OJ L319/12 .... 15.44

Decision 1999/796/EC [1999]
    OJ L319/34 .... 13.75, 15.45
Decision 1999/797/EC [1999]
    OJ L319/41 .... 15.52
Decision 1999/798/EC [1999]
    OJ L319/47 .... 15.32
Decision 2000/45/EC [2001]
    OJ L18/1 .... 11.36
Decision 2000/276/EC [2000]
    OJ L93/1 .... 14.170
Decision 761/2000/EC [2000]
    OJ L305/8 .... 18.68
Decision 2001/146/EC [2001]
    OJ L59/1 .... 11.37
Decision 2001/519/EC [2001]
    OJ L188/1 .... 14.03, 14.04,
            14.62–14.64, 14.107,
            14.111, 14.118
Decision 2001/711/EC, [2001]
    OJ L262/14 .... 12.37
Decision 2002/164/EC, [2002]
    OJ L59/1 .... 14.68, 14.107,
            14.110, 14.135
Decision 2002/205/EC [2002]
    OJ L68/31 .... 7.21
Decision 2002/676/EC [2002]
    OJ L229/15 .... 17.31
Decision 2002/827/ECSC [2002]
    OJ L205/1 .... 8.25
Decision 1513/2002/EC [2002]
    OJ L232/13 .... 10.01
Decision of 1 February 2003 [2003]
    OJ L29/22 .... 8.11
Decision 2003/668/EC [2003]
    OJ L248/51 ..... 11.31, 14.76, 14.119
Decision 2003/796/EC [2003]
    OJ L296/34 .... 2.117, 3.02, 3.37,
            3.46, 3.52, 5.56, 5.67
    Recital 5 .... 3.37
    Recital 6 .... 3.52
    Recital 8 .... 5.68
    Art 3 .... 5.67
    Art 3(8) 3.02
    Art 4 .... 3.52
    Art 5(1) 5.67
    Art 7 .... 5.67
Decision 1229/2003/EC [2003]
    OJ L176/11 .... 18.44, 18.68
    Annex I 18.44
Decision 1230/2003/EC [2003]
    OJ L176/29 .... 10.01
Decision of 6 October 2004 [2006]
    OJ L61/11 .... 11.22, 14.06

Decision 2004/73/EC [2004]
    OJ L16/57 .... 7.21
Decision 2004/135/EC [2004]
    OJ L48/86 .... 11.34, 14.69, 14.70
Decision 2004/254/EC [2004]
    OJ L79/27 .... 14.22
Decision 2004/271/EC [2004]
    OJ L92/91 .... 11.26
Decision 2004/275/EC [2004]
    OJ L101/1 .... 14.170
Decision 2004/284/EC [2004]
    OJ L103/1 .... 7.92, 11.30, 11.31,
            12.35, 14.04, 14.74, 14.75
    Recital 111 .... 11.31
Decision 2005/15 [2005] OJ L7/7 ..... 7.20
Decision 2005/801/EC [2005]
    OJ L302/69 .... 1.66, 1.75, 11.22,
            11.25–11.27, 11.29, 11.31, 11.34,
            11.35, 11.37, 14.03, 14.31, 14.34,
            14.93, 14.95, 14.105, 14.170
    Recitals 52–54 .... 11.28
    Recitals 121–133 .... 14.97
Decision C 2005/1682/EC 11.38
    Recitals 5, 9 .... 11.44
Decision 2006/622/EC [2006]
    OJ L253/20 .... 1.67, 5.79, 11.28,
            11.30, 11.31, 14.79–14.85,
            14.108–14.111, 14.117, 14.127,
            14.135, 14.171
    Recitals 47, 478 .... 1.67
    Recitals 88–90 .... 11.30
    Recitals 219–221 .... 11.28
    Recital 286 .... 14.80
    Recital 314 .... 14.80
    Recitals 318, 319 .... 14.80
    Recitals 399, 400 .... 14.81
    Recital 729 .... 14.81
    Recitals 768–775 .... 14.121
    Recitals 776–785 .... 14.109, 14.121
    Recital 786 ...... 14.109, 14.121, 14.127
    Recitals 787–798 .... 14.109, 14.121
Decision 2006/770/EC [2006]
    OJ L 312................... App 5

NOTICES

Commission Notice on the definition of
    relevant market for the purposes of
    Community competition law,
    9 December 1997 [1997]
    OJ C372/3 .... 11.32, 11.37
Commission Notice on the definition of
    the Relevant Market for the purposes
    of Community competition law
    [1997] OJ C372/5 .... 14.29

Commission Notice on the concept of
full-function joint ventures under
Council Regulation 4064/89 on
the control of concentrations
between undertakings [1998]
OJ C66/1 .... 14.12
Commission Notice on the concept of
concentration under Council
Regulation 4064/89 on the control
of concentrations between
undertakings [1998]
OJ C66/5 .... 14.12
Commission Notice on the concept of
undertakings concerned under
Council Regulation 4064/89 on
the control of concentrations
between undertakings [1998]
OJ C66/14 .... 14.12
Commission Notice on calculation
of turnover under Council
Regulation 4064/89 on the control
of concentrations between
undertakings [1998]
OJ C66/25 .... 14.12
Commission Notice concerning
alignment of procedures for
processing mergers under the ECSC
and EC Treaties [1998]
OJ C66/36 .... 8.10
Commission Notice on Guidelines on
Vertical Restraints [2000]
OJ C291/1 .... 12.36
Commission Notice on remedies
acceptable under Council
Regulation 4064/89 and under
Council Regulation 447/98 [2001]
OJ C368/3 .... 14.15
Commission Notice on Agreements of
Minor Importance which do not
appreciably restrict competition
under Article 81(1) of the Treaty
establishing the European
Community (de minimis) [2001]
OJ C368/13 .... 8.14
Commission, Notice under Article 88(2)
EC [2003] OJ C180/5 .... 9.30
Commission Notice on co-operation
within the Network of Competition
Authorities [2004]
OJ C101/43 .... 11.19
Commission Notice on restrictions
directly related and necessary to
concentrations [2005]
OJ C56/24 .... 14.12

Commission Notice on a simplified
procedure for treatment of certain
concentrations under Council
Regulation (EC) No 139/2004
[2005] OJ C56/32 .... 14.12

RECOMMENDATIONS

Council Recommendation 88/611
[1988] OJ L335/29 .... 10.03

OTHER JURISDICTIONS

Austria

Green Electricity Act 2002 .... 15.71

Belgium

Royal Decrée of 8 August 1980
Art 181 .... 16.49
Royal Decree of 29 July 1983 .... 16.49
Royal Decree of 10 June 1994 ...... 14.148
Royal Decree of 16 June 1994 ...... 14.149

France

Law No 46–628 (1946) 16.50
Arts 36, 37 .... 16.76
Law No 93–1298 (1993) 14.146
Arts 1, 2 .... 14.146
Law No 97–1026 (1997) 15.59

Germany

Verbändevereinbarung
(VV-1 Electricity) Associations'
Agreement 13.35 13.36, 13.40
Verbändevereinbarung
(VV-2 Electricity) Associations'
Agreement 13.35, 13.36
Verbändevereinbarung (VV-2 Gas)
Associations' Agreement 13.40,
13.42, 13.43, 13.112, 14.64
Verbändevereinbarung (VV-2 Plus
Electricity) Associations'
Agreement 13.39
Energy Industry Act 13.43

Italy

Nationalization Law
No 1643 1962 .... 16.52
Decree No 342 of 1965 .... 16.52

Netherlands

Electricity Law 1989 .... 13.64,
13.65, 13.68, 16.52, 16.66
Art 2 .... 13.64, 13.66

Electricity Law 1989 (*cont.*)
    Art 24 . . . . 13.69
    Art 34 . . . . 13.64, 13.66
    Art 35 . . . . 13.64
    Art 26 . . . . 13.69
System Code, Chapter 5 . . . . 13.66,
    13.68, 13.74
Transition Act 2000 . . . . 13.67
    Art 13(1) 13.67, 13.74

Norway

Petroleum Act 1985 . . . . 2.123
    s 8(1), (7) 2.123
    s 23(1) 2.123
    s 26(1) 2.123
    s 54(1) 2.123

Portugal

Decree Law 11/90 . . . . 14.145
    Art 13(3) 14.144
Decree Law 65/90 . . . . 14.145
Decree Law 99/91 . . . . 13.25
Decree Law 380/93 . . . . 14.145
    Art 1 . . . . 14.145
Decree Law 65/94 . . . . 14.145

Spain

Law No 49/84 . . . . 16.52
Royal Decree
    Law 4/2006 . . . . 14.52, 14.53

United Kingdom

Competition Act 1998 . . . . 3.51
Competition Act 1998
    Concurrency Regulations 2004,
    (SI 2004/1077) 3.07
Energy Act 2004 . . . . 15.87, 15.88
    s 21 . . . . 15.87
    s 44 . . . . 15.87
Enterprise Act 2002 . . . . 3.51
Hydrocarbons Licensing
    Directive Regulations 1995
    (SI 1995/434) 7.11
Renewables Obligation Order 2006
    (SI 2006/1004) 10.20
    Arts 3, 4 . . . . 10.20
Sch 10.20

United States

Public Utilities Regulatory
    Policies Act 1978 . . . . 10.01

ABBREVIATIONS

AC	Alternating Current
ACQ	Annual Contract Quantity
AEM	Azienda Energetica Metropolitana (Italy)
AFX	news service
AGR	Advanced Gas-cooled Reactor
ALTENER	EU assistance programme for non-conventional energy
APC	Electricity utility (Austria)
ATC	Available Transmission Capacity
ATS	Austrian Schilling
BAFTA	Best Available Fair Trade Answer
BCM	Billion Cubic Metres
BDI	*Bundesverband der Deutschen Industrie*
BEB	German Gas company
BGE	Bord Gas Eireann
BGW	*Bundesverband der Deutschen Gas- und Wasserwirtschaft*
BNFL	British Nuclear Fuels Ltd
BV	Corporate legal status (Netherlands)
CADA	Capacity and Differences Agreements
CBB	*College van Beroep voor het bedrijfsleven*
CCGT	Combined Cycle Gas Turbine
CEGB	Central Electricity Generating Board
CEER	Council of European Energy Regulators
CEFIC	Council of European Chemical Industry
CER	Commission for Energy Regulation
CFI	Court of First Instance
CHP	Combined Heat and Power
CIS	Commonwealth of Independent States
CNIEG	National Fund for the Electricity and Gas Industries
CNR	Electricity generating company (France)
CO_2	Carbon Dioxide
COM	Commission (document)
COREPER	Committee of Permanent Representatives
CTC	Costs of Transition to Competition

DEM	Deutschmark
DEP	*Dimitoki Etairia Pliroforissis*
DG	Directorate General
DG COMP	Directorate General for Competition
DG TREN	Directorate General for Transport and Energy
DKK	Danish Kroner
DONG	*Dansk Olie og Naturgas*
DSB	Direct Supply to Business
DSO	Distribution System Operator
DTE	*Dienst uitvoering en toezicht energie*
DTI	Department of Trade and Industry
DUC	Danish Underground Consortium
EC	European Community
ECJ	European Court of Justice
ECN	European Competition Network
ECS	Electrabel Customer Solutions (Belgium)
ECSC	European Coal and Steel Community
ECR	European Court Reports
ECT	Energy Charter Treaty
EDF	*Electricité de France*
EDP	*Electricidade de Portugal*
EEA	European Economic Area
EEC	European Economic Community
EEG	*Gesetz über den Vorrang Erneuerbarer Energien*
EFET	European Federation of Energy Traders
EFTA	European Free Trade Association
EIA	Dutch tax relief scheme
EIB	European Investment Bank
ELR	European Law Review
EMA	Energy Markets Authority (Finland)
EMI	Energy Markets Inspectorate (Estonia)
EnBW	*Energiewerke Baden-Württemberg* (full name no longer used, only acronym)
ENEL	*Ente Nazionale per l'Energia Elletrica*
ENI	*Ente Nazionale Idrocarburi*
ENU	*Empresa Nacional de Uranio*
E.ON	German energy group (Acronym used only)
E.ON EK	trading subsidiary of E.ON in Hungary
EPD	Energy Products Directive
ERGEG	European Regulatory Group for Electricity and Gas
ERI	E.ON Ruhrgas International
ERSE	*Entidade Reguladora dos Serviços Energéticos*
ERT	*Elleniki Radiophonia Tileorassi*
ESA	Euratom Supply Agency

ETS	Emissions Trading Scheme
ETSO	European Transmission System Operators
EU	European Union
Euratom	European Atomic Energy Treaty
EURELECTRIC	Union of the (European) Electricity Industry
EUROPEX	Association of European Power Exchanges
EV	Economic Value
EZH	*Energie Zuid Holland*
FERC	Federal Energy Regulatory Commission
FCO	Federal Cartel Office
FF	French Francs
FSU	Former Soviet Union
GATT	General Agreement on Trade and Tariffs
GB	GB-Inno-BM (Belgian telephone sales company)
GCC	Gulf Co-operation Council
GDP	Gross Domestic Product
GDF	*Gaz de France*
GFU	*Gassforhandlings ut valget* (Norwegian Gas Negotiating Committee)
GGPSSO	Guidelines for Good (TPA) Practice for Storage System Operators
GIE	Gas Infrastructure Europe
GVS	Gasversorgung Süddeutschland GmbH (Germany)
GTE	Gas Transmission Europe
HC	House of Commons
HEW	*Hamburgische Elektricitätswerke AG*
HEO	Hungarian Energy Office
HHI	Herfindahl-Hirschmann Index (of market concentration)
HL	House of Lords
HLFA	Historic Liabilities Funding Agreement
IEA	International Energy Agency
IEM	Internal Energy Market
IFIEC	International Federation of Industrial Energy Consumers
IFRS	International Financial Reporting Standards
INOGATE	Interstate Oil and Gas Transport to Europe
INPC	Irish National Petroleum Company
IRC	Irish Refining Company
ISAB	Generating company (Italy)
IT	Information Technology
IVO	Imatran Volma Oy (Finland)

Abbreviations

KLE	*Kernkraftwerke Lippe-Ems*
kV	Kilovolt
kWh	Kilowatt-Hour
KWKG	*Gesetz zum Schutz der Stromerzeugung aus Kraft-Wärme-Kopplung*
LDC	Local Distribution Companies
LIC	Large Industrial Customer
LNG	Liquefied Natural Gas
M&A	Mergers & Acquisitions
MAQ	Minimum Annual Quantity
MEDA	EU instrument to assist non-EU Mediterranean countries
MEP	Member of the European Parliament
MFN	Most Favoured Nation
MOL	Hungarian energy company
MOL E&P	MOL's Exploration & Production subsidiary
MOL WMT	MOL's Wholesale Marketing & Trading subsidiary
MW	MegaWatt = one million watts
NAP	National Allocation Plan
NCA	National Competition Authority
NDA	Nuclear Decommissioning Authority
NEA	*Nederlands Elektriciteit Administratiekantoor*
NEL	Nordic (Electricity) Link
NESA	subsidiary of Elsam (Denmark)
NGO	Non-Governmental Organization
NIE	Northern Ireland Electricity
NLG	Netherlands Guilder
NLNG	Nigerian Liquefied Natural Gas (company)
NORDEL	Nordic Electricity Grid
Nordpool	Nordic Power Exchange
NRA	National Regulatory Agency
NT	National Treatment
OAPEC	Organisation of Arab Petroleum Exporting Countries
ODRC	Optimized Depreciated Replacement Cost
ODV	Optimized Deprival Value
OEW	*Zweckverband Oberschwäbische Elektrizitätswerke*
Ofgem	Office of Gas and Electricity Markets
OGP	Oil and Gas Producers
OJ	Official Journal
OMV	Austrian energy company
OPEC	Organization of Petroleum Exporting Countries
OSPAR	Oslo Paris (Convention)
OTC	Over the Counter Trading

Abbreviations

PCA	Partnership and Co-operation Agreement
PPA	Power Purchase Agreement
PPC	Permanent Partnership Council
PPC	Public Power Corporation
PSO	Public Service Obligation
QMV	Qualified Majority Voting
RDC	Retail Distribution Company
REB	Regulatory tax scheme (Netherlands)
Redesa	*Red Eléctrica de España*
REN	Transmission System Operator (Portugal)
RF	Russian Federation
RO	Renewables Obligation
ROC	Renewables Obligation Certificate
RP	Receipt Point
RTE	*Reseau de Transmission d'Electricité*
RTT	*Regie des Télégraphes et des Téléphones*
RWE	Formerly *Rheinisch-Westfälische Elektrizitätswerke AG* (now known only by its acronym)
SA	corporate legal status (Spain)
SAVE	Specific Actions for Vigorous Energy Efficiency
SEA	Single European Act
SEP	*Samenwerkende Elektriciteits-Productiebedrijven*
SGEI	Services of General Economic Interest
SMP	nuclear fuel production plant (UK)
SNAM	Subsidiary of ENI (acronym used only)
SPE	Belgian gas and electricity utility
SSNIP	small but significant and non-transitory increase in prices
TA	Treaty of Amsterdam
TAG	Trans-Austrian Gas (pipeline)
TENs	Trans-European Networks
TEU	Treaty of European Union
THERMIE	EU assistance programme for non-conventional energy
THORP	Thermal Oxide Reprocessing Plant (UK)
TN	Treaty of Nice
TPA	Third Party Access
TSA	Transmission Services Agreement
TSO	Transmission System Operator
UAG	Unaccounted-for Gas
UCTE	Union for the Co-ordination of the Transmission of Electricity
UK	United Kingdom

Abbreviations

UNMIK	United Nations Mission in Kosovo
USA	United States of America
VAMIL	Accelerated depreciation of environmental investments scheme (Netherlands)
VAT	Value Added Tax
VEBA	Former German utility (became part of E.ON)
VEMW	*Vereniging voor Energie, Milieu en Water*
VEAG	*Vereinigte Energiewerke AG*
VEW	Former German utility (merged into RWE)
VIAG	Former German utility (became part of E.ON)
VIK	*Verband der Industriellen Energie- und Kraftwirtschaft* (German Association of Industrial Energy and Power)
VKU	*Verband kommunaler Unternehmen*
VV	*Verbändevereinbarung* (Association Agreement)
WACOG	Weighted Average Cost of Gas
WTO	World Trade Organization

GLOSSARY

Access The ability to buy transportation service conditional only on a willingness and ability to subscribe to standard terms and conditions of service.

Allocative efficiency The act of setting the price for a commodity or service equal to its costs of production, including a normal rate of profit so that production occurs up to the point where the value of the commodity or service to the user is equal to the cost of producing it.

Alternating current Electricity current that moves forwards and backwards with a frequency measured in hertz units.

Ancillary services All services necessary for the operation of a transmission and/or a distribution system and in the case of gas, LNG facilities, and such storage facilities and equivalent instruments providing flexibility including load balancing and blending.

Applicant A person who has applied for a transmission service.

Asset sweating Cost cutting by promoting efficiencies from existing plant to avoid the need to build new infrastructure.

Auctions The base mechanism for several congestion management methods. In all cases, each market participant offers a price for use of the net transfer capacity. The bids of the participants are stacked with the highest bids first until the capacity is completely used.

Balancing A service provided by a party such as a TSO to ensure that supply and demand are matched by drawing upon the bids of generators willing to increase or decrease their generation at short notice, or consumers willing to increase or decrease consumption.

Base load The minimum continuous load on an operating electricity system.

Blackout A severe form of outage leading to a complete loss of electricity.

Brownout A form of outage in which the voltage level falls below the normal minimum level specified for the system; sometimes made intentionally to prevent a full power outage.

Bundled service The sale of a package consisting of transportation service and the natural gas commodity.

Capacity The ability of a pipeline or grid to transport gas or electricity between two locations under a particular set of operating conditions. The term is also used to refer to the proportion of the pipeline or grid system capacity that is reserved by an individual network user. Capacity is expressed in terms of the quantity of gas or electricity, which can be transported from one location (receipt point) and delivered to another (delivery point) in a specified time period, commonly a day.

Capacity reservation tariff The capacity reservation tariff is the price of reserved capacity. A different tariff may apply depending on where a customer wishes to put gas or electricity into the transmission network (receipt point) and where a customer wishes to take delivery of the gas or electricity following transportation (delivery point).

Capacity slicing Use of different market-based mechanisms in parallel to fill the interconnection capacity with layers allocated by means of different methods such as long term contracts, explicit and implicit auctions, or market splitting.

Glossary

Capital charge The return and depreciation on pipeline, compressor and station assets.

Chinese Wall A mechanism for the separation of transmission from supply and other functions within a vertically-integrated undertaking to preserve the confidentiality of commercially sensitive information obtained by a system operator when carrying out its business, especially with respect to taking decisions on network access.

Cogeneration Generation of electricity and steam simultaneously. The steam may be used locally and the electricity may be used by local customers, sold through a pool, or both.

Commodity tariff The price per unit of gas throughput on the transmission network.

Common carriage A process of selling transportation service in which users have no contractual obligation. New capacity is built on the basis of anticipated demand for the service.

Congestion A situation in which the transmission line linking transmission networks cannot accommodate all scheduled or intended transactions due to a lack of capacity.

Contract path A chain of contiguous transmission areas, identified without reference to the multitude of parallel flows which exist in practice on a meshed system.

Copperplating By analogy with the even movement of electrons across a copper plate, TSOs treat a network as open on all routes between generation and demand, thereby forcing congestion to the edges.

Cross-border transmission The transmission service provided by a TSO, resulting from all physical flows across borders, including imports, exports, and transits.

Daily quantity The actual energy value, in Gigajoules, of gas delivered on any day.[1]

Delivered quantity The quantity of gas delivered during a stated period of time, in Gigajoules.

Delivery point The point on the transmission network where a network user nominates to have gas delivered.

Derivatives market A market in which financial instruments are traded, the terms of which are derived from or linked to some underlying product or other extraneous matter.

Direct lines Electricity line or gas pipeline complementary to the interconnected system.

Distribution Transport of electricity or gas across the medium/low voltage integrated system or medium/low pressure pipeline network with a view to its delivery to final customers.

Distribution system A gas or electricity transportation system, operated between a city gate and final users of gas or electricity.

Dispatch Process by which the system operator instructs generators to operate their generating plant, or to stop doing so.

Downstream Those activities related to natural gas which involve transmission and distribution.

Economic value The value of an asset derived from a discounted cash flow analysis.

Economies of scale Reduced costs of producing a commodity or a service (such as gas transportation) as a result of producing very large quantities within a single producing unit (such as a transmission or distribution system).

---

[1] Natural gas may be measured in volume or energy terms. It is common to measure production gas (ex-field) in volume terms—cubic metres or cubic feet. However, once gas is treated/purified to meet a particular gas specification (see specification gas) it is more usual to measure it in energy terms (Gigajoules, MMBtu, or KCal).

Glossary

Economies of scope Reduced costs of producing a commodity or a service as a result of combining a number of complementary activities (such as gas storage, meter reading and management) within a single production unit.

Explicit auctions Capacity is auctioned for different time periods with bids accepted from the highest first. The price which all accepted bids have to pay is usually at the level of the bid that is required to fill the interconnector.

First come, first served A method of capacity reservation by request in which the first reservation made for a given period of time has priority over the subsequent reservations; leaves little room for short-term trading.

Gathering The act of moving raw gas to the purification plant.

Generation Production of electricity.

Grandfathering Future rights allocated according to historic usage. Essentially, it makes an allocation to mitigate risk and to recognize the reasonable expectations of investors in the face of major policy changes. It is used in some countries to allocate EU emissions allowances to mitigate the financial impact on participating installations of having to buy in emissions allowances.

Implicit auctions Capacity is allocated on the basis of generators' bids into the electricity spot market situated on the other side of the interconnector where they compete with local bids. Capacity is allocated to the cheapest bids until it is full. Any remaining price difference between these bids over the interconnector and the bids from the local generators is retained by the TSO as the profit made from its 'brokering' activities. This method requires at least one power exchange in the area importing from the interconnector.

Incumbent Company holding a monopolistic position by law prior to market liberalization.

In-plan gas prices Gas prices centrally determined for gas production set out in a Five Year Plan and allocated to a specific industrial sector—primarily fertilizer production. In general, these prices are considerably lower than the market value of gas as either fuel or feed-stock.

Interconnectors Equipment used to link electricity systems.

Interruptible Gas supply terms which include specific rights of curtailment of supply by vendor.

Line pack A form of storing natural gas using the pipeline to 'pack' it away.

Load factor Ratio of estimated average daily quantity of gas to be taken by a gas purchaser over a specified time period (eg, month, quarter, year) to the maximum permitted daily delivery schedule on any day in that period. The load factor cannot exceed one. The size of the load factor has an impact on the designed capacity of production and pipeline facilities.

Loop flow The unscheduled power that flows inadvertently across an electricity system caused by electricity taking the path of least resistance from generation to load instead of flowing across a particular schedule or contract transmission path.

Market power The ability of one company unilaterally to influence the terms and conditions of service, including price, on which a product is bought or sold.

Market splitting A system where optimal use of an interconnection is determined on the basis of a comparison of market prices prevailing in the relevant interconnected markets; encourages trading insofar as market participants receive *ex ante* information about the probability of congestion between some areas; works best when there is a common market structure and organization on both sides of a constrained border.

Maximum daily quantity The maximum energy value, in Gigajoules, of gas delivered on any day of the year. Where 'reserved MDQ' appears in the text, it means the same as 'reserved capacity'.

Merit order Ranking of capacity in ascending order of price together with amount of electricity that will be generated.

Natural monopoly Where average costs of the new entrant exceed the marginal costs of the existing supplier (ie, a situation where the market is most efficient economically if there is only one provider).

Negotiated TPA Third party access in which tariffs and conditions are the result of negotiations.

Network A network is a distinct unconnected part of the transmission system.

Network user A person who is either seeking, or has gained, access to the network.

Nodal pricing A method of electricity transmission pricing by location, where in the presence of competition the price at each location or node will be equal to marginal production and transportation cost.

Non-discriminatory Means to act impartially and not to distinguish between network users or to favour one network user over another in the terms and conditions and price for services offered or provided.

Non-specification gas Natural gas which is not specification gas (or is not pipeline marketable quality).

Open access Generally refers to a regime whereby a pipeline owner offers to transport gas for others, on a first come first served basis, under posted terms and conditions.

Optimized depreciated replacement cost The replacement cost of an optimized asset adjusted for depreciation.

Optimized deprival value This is the asset valuation methodology that has generally been adopted for the valuation of pipeline assets in the New Zealand gas industry but is rarely used elsewhere. The ODV of any asset is the lesser of its ODRC and its economic value.

Outage Withdrawal from service or non-availability of a generating set, or any part of a transmission or distribution system for a period of time, either scheduled or unscheduled.

Overrun Overrun means the quantity of gas delivered on any day in excess of a network user's reserved capacity. To incur an overrun means to use capacity in excess of reserved capacity.

Pancaking Accumulation of tariffs to be paid by a shipper on energy transactions between two locations using two or more TSOs with their own sets of tariffs. It discourages inter-system trade and usually fails to reflect transmission costs.

Performance-based regulation A method of setting the level of pipeline tariffs which breaks the link between the tariff level and the cost of providing transportation service, allowing the rate of profit to vary with the productive efficiency of the pipeline.

Pipeline marketable gas See Specification gas.

Pools Arrangements established to allow generating units to bid to the TSO (mainly a single buyer) to have their power dispatched, and where the TSO dispatches the generating units in the economic order of the bids.

Postage-stamp system A system of transmission pricing in which the same unit price is charged for transmission, irrespective of how far the energy is transported.

Power exchange An entity that will establish a competitive spot market for electricity through day- and/or hour-ahead auction of generation and demand bids.

Production The process of extracting natural gas from underground or undersea reservoirs.

Productive efficiency The act of producing a commodity or service of specified quality at the lowest possible cost.

Purification The process of extracting liquids, sulphur and impurities from raw gas.

Rate of return regulation A method for setting the level of pipeline tariffs by linking them directly and continuously to the cost of service, which includes an allowed rate of profit (rate of return).

Raw gas Natural gas in the state in which it exits the well at which point it contains liquids, sulphur and impurities.

Receipt point The point on the transmission network where a network user nominates to present gas for transportation.

Regulated TPA Third party access in which tariffs and conditions are approved or determined by the regulator.

Reserved capacity The amount of capacity a network user anticipates requiring and reserves in advance.

Retail competition A situation where all users of gas or electricity are able to buy gas or electricity directly from producers or marketers.

Secondary market A market in which rights are traded.

Shipper A company which contracts with a transmission/distribution company for the transportation of electricity or gas.

Single buyer Any legal person who, within the system where it is established, is responsible for the unified management of the transmission system and/or for centralized electricity purchase and sale.

Specification gas Gas which satisfies the physical and chemical composition criteria for gas entering a transmission network. This is also known as pipeline marketable gas.

Spot market The market (electricity or gas) in which contracts are struck for forward delivery, normally where delivery is to take place within a very short period after the contract is struck.

Spot price The price quoted on a given day for delivery of a product (electricity or gas) either on that day or normally within a very short period thereafter.

Stranded assets Past investments in plant, equipment, and/or power purchases made by utilities to meet customer (or governmental) needs, rendered uncommercial as a result of a liberalization of the market.

Stranded costs Synonymous with 'stranded assets'.

Supply Delivery and/or sale of electricity to customers.

Supply support services Services required to facilitate the progression of gas through the transportation system to final users, such as blending, back-up, gas storage and meter reading which may be unbundled from the transportation service and priced separately.

Swing Flexibility of gas contracts, allowing the buyer to vary daily take of gas up to a specified quantity. It is the quality (expressed as a percentage) by which maximum daily quantity exceeds the estimated average daily quantity (100% equals zero swing)

Take-or-pay In relation to gas contracts a provision which entitles the buyer either to pay for the quantity of gas contracted to be taken in a specified period (eg, day, month, quarter-year) or, if it does not take delivery of that quantity or only part of it, to pay for the quantity not taken.

Tariff The price charged by a transmission or distribution system for providing transportation services.

Transit A physical flow of electricity hosted on the transmission system of a Member State, which was neither produced nor is destined for consumption in this Member State; this definition includes transit flows which are commonly denominated as 'loop-flows'.

Transmission Transport of electricity or gas across the high-voltage interconnected system or high-pressure pipeline network (other than an upstream pipeline network) with a view to delivery to final customers or distributors.

Transmission network A transmission network is defined as an unconnected part of the current transmission system (see network).

Transmission services agreement The agreement signed by the transmission entity and a network user, setting out the respective rights and obligations in respect of the transportation of the network user's gas through the transmission entity's network.

Transmission system A system of high-pressure pipelines available for the transportation of specification gas (or pipeline marketable gas) between the purification plant and the receipt point of a large volume consumer and a city gate.

Transmission system operator One or more of the operators of the national transmission system in a Member State.

Unaccounted-for gas The difference between gas metered entering a pipeline system and gas metered leaving that system in a given period, after allowing for any change in the amount of gas contained in the system.

Unbundling The process of separating a service into its basic components and offering each segmented service for sale at separate rates: eg, generation, transmission, and distribution.

Upstream Those activities related to natural gas which involve exploration, development, production, gathering and purification.

Wheeling Transmission of electricity by an entity that does not own or directly use the power that it is transmitting.

Wholesale competition A situation in which large volume users of natural gas or electricity purchase their supplies directly from gas or electricity producers or marketers, other than transportation companies. Local distribution companies may participate in the wholesale market on behalf of their customers who do not have access to competing suppliers.

Part I

COMPETITION AND ENERGY LAW

1

THE COMPETITION OBJECTIVE

A. Introduction	1.01	D. Why is Energy Special?	1.60
B. What is Competition?	1.05	(1) Electricity	1.63
C. Energy Markets and Government Intervention: The Energy Paradigm		(a) The Europe Factor	1.66
		(2) Gas	1.67
		(a) The Europe Factor	1.68
		(b) The Impact of LNG	1.72
(1) Historical Characteristics of the Electricity and Gas Industries	1.10	E. The Requirements of Liberalization	1.75
(2) The Pre-Liberalization Paradigm	1.11	(1) Regulation and Access	1.76
(3) Beyond the Pre-Liberalization Paradigm	1.17	(a) An Independent Regulator	1.79
(4) A Three-Stage Evolution	1.22	(2) Structure	1.83
(a) Stage 1: Intervention	1.27	(a) Elements of Natural Monopoly in Supply Phases	1.84
(b) Stage 2: Uncertainty	1.32	(b) Solutions: 'Unbundling'	1.85
(c) Stage 3: Globalization	1.37	(3) Liberalization	1.90
(5) Crisis and the Shift Towards 'Energy Security'	1.45	(4) Ownership	1.93
(6) Unfinished Business	1.47	(a) Licensing and Concession Regimes	1.94
(a) Problems of Application	1.51	F. Conclusions	1.95
(b) Problems of Compatibility	1.55		
(7) A New Paradigm Emerging?	1.58		

(P)olitical and public opinion in the US is more ready to accept competition as a good in itself than opinion in most European countries.

David Edward[1]

A. Introduction

The goal of promoting competition in European energy markets has always had to jostle for policy space alongside two other important concerns: on the one hand, the provision of energy security in a region characterized by a high and growing **1.01**

---

[1] 'The Modernization of EC Antitrust Policy. Issues for Courts and Judges', paper presented at the Workshop on the Modernization of EC Antitrust Policy, European University Institute, Florence, 2000.

dependence on external sources for its primary energy consumption and, on the other, the achievement of environmental sustainability.[2] Their uneasy co-existence has been a much noted feature of European energy policy over the years, particularly since the competition goal acquired the status of *primus inter pares* with the internal market programme since the late 1980s. Very recently, the competition goal appears to have experienced a relative decline, even as the internal energy market programme has begun to make a real impact.

1.02 The manner in which competition is being introduced into EU energy markets is partly responsible for the emergence of doubts about the benefits. The first legal measures were finalized ten years ago after many years of controversy and set out a timetable for market opening or liberalization. This gradualist approach or 'managed liberalization' was designed to give energy companies time to adjust to a more competitive environment. Ultimately, energy consumers—that is, largely industrial consumers of energy—were expected to benefit from a greater choice of supplier and possibly from lower prices. By the end of the first decade of 'managed liberalization', consumer prices appeared to be volatile and lacking in transparency, markets for both electricity and gas remained segmented into national compartments, and there was a marked absence of new entrants. Even more challenging were a number of new problems that had appeared during the first decade: large investments were required in the ageing network infrastructures to modernize and expand them; dependence on non-EU imports of gas for power generation had grown continuously, and the introduction of a Europe-wide emissions trading scheme was beginning to impact upon electricity prices.

1.03 A consequence of these developments was to underline—if that were necessary—how sensitive and strategic the energy sector remains for the economy of the nation-state, and in this case the Member States of the EU. For a number of participants it appeared to confirm their perception of energy as, essentially, a service of general economic interest, which should not be entrusted to the care of the market, at least not entirely. The notion of energy as a *service public*, guaranteeing reliability and continuity of supply, preferably entrusted to the care of a privately or publicly owned national champion, has become again an influential idea in some parts of the EU, even if it lacks a coherent ideological framework. It is a challenge to the competition objective that has been the ultimate, if not the only, objective of the internal energy market programme over the past decade. All the more ironic then, that the key idea of *service public* has already been incorporated into the EU model for liberalized energy markets.

---

[2] The co-existence of these goals is vividly illustrated in the European Commission's Green Paper, *A European Strategy for Sustainable, Competitive and Secure Energy*, COM (2006) 105 final, 8 March 2006, and in the Strategic European Energy Review document: *An Energy Policy for Europe*, COM (2007)1 final, 10 January 2007.

In this chapter a number of issues are addressed that are preparatory to the examination of EU energy and competition law that follows. First, the issue is examined of what competition means in the energy sector and why the goal of competition appears to have a particular sensitivity (section B). Next, the wider historical and intellectual changes that drove forward the idea of energy market reform are described by reference to the notion of a changing 'energy paradigm' (section C). Some of the specific reasons why electricity and gas present special challenges for the introduction of competition are then explained (section D). The 'nodal points' of liberalization, that is, the sensitive areas that must be operated on for a programme of market opening to succeed, whether in the EU or elsewhere, are also analyzed (section E).

B. What is Competition?

There are many ways of answering the question of what 'competition' really means. From an essentially economic point of view, a leading competition lawyer, the late Daniel Goyder, offered a convenient definition:

> Competition is basically the relationship between a number of undertakings which sell goods or services of the same kind at the same time to an identifiable group of customers. Each undertaking having made a commercial decision to place its goods and services on the market, utilizing its production and distribution facilities, will by that act necessarily bring itself into a relationship of potential contention and rivalry with the other undertakings in the same geographic market . . .[3]

The advantages often attributed to the operation of competition include:[4]

- *Allocative efficiency*: the part that competition plays in allocating resources in the direction preferred by consumers. This has the benefit of reducing the risk that goods or services produced will not be wanted, or not wanted at the price at which they are offered.
- *Innovation*: the constant process of dynamic adjustment to continual changes in consumer preferences is an incentive for producers to invest in research and development and to innovate, leading to the survival and growth of those companies which make the necessary changes in good time, whilst those that fail to do so inevitably fall behind.
- *Cost reduction*: the continual pressure on all producers and sellers in the market to keep down costs, and therefore prices, for fear of losing custom to other sellers who find ways to attract business either by general price cuts or by special discounts to favoured buyers.

---

[3] *EC Competition Law* (4th edn, 2003) 8.
[4] For a fuller discussion of this, see Prosser, T, *The Limits of Competition Law: Markets and Public Services* (2005) ch 2.

- *Progress*: the likelihood that a country whose economy is committed to the competitive process will enjoy greater advances in productive efficiency and in utilization of its resources of raw material and human capital.

1.07 All of these prospective benefits from competition could be said to lie behind the EU programme for energy market reform in recent years. The frequent linkage of energy market reform to the so-called Lisbon Agenda of growth and competitiveness testifies to the influence of the fourth item on the EU thinking about competition in this area.

1.08 If one seeks to rely upon a definition in the EC Treaty, there is a reference to 'competition' as a concept in both Articles 3(1)(g) and 81, but a proper definition is not offered. Article 81 has no application unless the agreement, decision or practice concerned has either the object or the effect of preventing, restricting or distorting competition, but the concept itself is not defined. At the same time, a perusal of the Treaty framework quickly reveals that competition is a *policy* with equivalent status to other *policies*, such as environmental or social policy. In the event of any actual or potential conflict there is a need to establish some balancing of the policies concerned.

1.09 This co-existence of competition policy with other policies in the framework of the EC Treaty is the key to how competition in the context of energy markets should be approached if not necessarily defined. The EC Treaty gives a particular importance to the notion of services of general economic interest (in which electricity and probably gas are included) and to notions of public service. By contrast, there is almost no mention of 'energy' in the EC Treaty at all. A balancing of the competition objective with the many possible interpretations of service public and all that it implies is rooted in the Treaty itself. It makes a social interpretation of 'competition' inescapable. Given the crucially important role that electricity and gas supply play in modern life in the EU as in most other parts of the world, this means that the scope for an unfettered form of competition is—at least within this legal framework—non-existent, and the way that competition in energy markets is introduced and promoted has to take fully into account the role of non-economic goals and values, not least those affecting the public service character of this sector.

C. Energy Markets and Government Intervention: The Energy Paradigm

(1) Historical Characteristics of the Electricity and Gas Industries

1.10 In every industrialized country it has been normal practice for governments to involve themselves in the energy business, and especially in the activities of the

C. Energy Markets and Government Intervention: The Energy Paradigm

electricity and gas industries. This has been encouraged by at least five principal characteristics of these industries:

(1) They necessarily involve activities that develop in successive phases (generation or production; followed by transmission, distribution and supply/retailing).[5] There are elements of *natural monopoly* in transmission and distribution activities which stimulate vertical integration of the above activities within a single company. Those integrated companies have traditionally been obliged by governments to provide and supply electricity and gas, and have in return been granted exclusive rights of supply over a specific area or territory (see below).

(2) The services provided by these companies have traditionally been seen as *essential* for communities, and an obligation to supply has often been imposed by governments on the companies—electricity prices normally being controlled by government and based on costs.

(3) The electricity and gas sectors are *strategic* for the overall economy and for the military capability of the nation-state.

(4) They are capital-intensive industries with a high degree of technical complexity, which creates entry barriers and necessitates technical co-ordination in their operation. This has led to a structure of regulation that places strong emphasis on reliability of transmission and delivery. This has been particularly evident in the electricity sector, because electricity cannot be stored; rapid changes in demand can occur throughout any given day, and each request must be linked with supply.

(5) There is a measure of *integration* between the various energy sub-sectors, so the regulatory status of one influences the other. Electricity is a secondary form of energy that derives from various primary natural sources such as gas, oil, coal, water or uranium. Gas is commonly found in conjunction with oil. But both electricity and gas can be substituted for each other and so compete for end-use in consumer markets.

(2) The Pre-Liberalization Paradigm

These characteristics contributed to a specific model or pattern of government– energy industry relations that, with some variations, was dominant in all the industrialized countries for several decades. Its wide acceptance over a long period of time and its impact on the policies of governments suggest that it may be described as the 'traditional paradigm' of energy network regulation. By this it is intended to refer not only to certain ways of organizing government relations with the

1.11

---

[5] Other phases can be distinguished, eg system operation and dispatch, 'spot' and contractual markets and, for gas, storage and possibly liquefaction and re-gasification. These, however, have different functional and cost characteristics and are less fundamental to the industries concerned.

electricity and gas industries, but also to a set of ideas about the scope of competition and the appropriate legal and institutional methods to achieve public policy aims. Such ideas have had both a prescriptive and a constraining effect on choices in policy. These ideas were dominant in the period before the current liberalization of electricity and gas markets began.

1.12 The concept of 'paradigm' has been defined in the context of the natural sciences as comprising 'universally recognised scientific achievements that for a time provide model problems and solutions to a community of practitioners'.[6] In the electricity and gas sectors the traditional paradigm comprised a wide variety of legal and institutional arrangements that were predicated on *a model of technical organization involving central control over a synchronized network*. It was assumed that these network-bound systems were strategic assets for a national economy and that the nature of their production made it economic to have a single entity construct the system facilities and operate the transmission grids. It emphasized stability, reliability of supply, and public service. This model of centrally-controlled and vertically-integrated monopoly is still to be found in various forms in some OECD countries, and in many developing countries as well as the emerging markets.

1.13 For many years most countries favoured a common technical model of an electricity system, based on central station synchronized 'AC' (alternating current). However, each system evolved its own structures for planning, decision-making, and other aspects of management. The technical feature was common, but the legal and institutional arrangements varied widely according to local history, politics, and culture.

1.14 The principal regulatory characteristics included:

- exclusive rights to build and operate networks, granted under concessions or licences;
- closure to competition;
- detailed regulation;
- vertically-integrated operations;
- remuneration on the basis of historical costs; and
- a high degree of planning with tight, centralized control.

1.15 They had another common feature: they did not allow the ultimate beneficiary—the electricity consumer—to participate in decision-making. The electricity user had 'almost no role in this process except to switch things on and off'.[7] The legal and financial arrangements were set up and supervised by governments, generally

---

[6] Kuhn, T, *The Structure of Scientific Revolutions* (1970) viii. Although Kuhn's work is primarily concerned with the natural sciences, the paradigm concept that he used has gained a wide currency in law and the social sciences, even if not always acknowledged.

[7] Patterson, W, *Transforming Electricity* (1999) 5.

C. Energy Markets and Government Intervention: The Energy Paradigm

national governments. Technical arrangements were designed, manufactured, and installed by engineering companies. Electricity systems were operated by companies that had grown up with the systems—such as Électricité de France (EDF), Ontario Hydro, and Tokyo Electric Power.

The activities of all of these participants were guided by a single basic idea: large power stations generate electricity in large quantities and deliver it by wire to every user in the area, continuously adjusting the total amount being generated to match the total amount being used at any instant. A serious shortcoming of this approach was that those who planned, managed, and operated the system did not bear any of the risk, and did not suffer if it failed. The costs of incompetence or bad judgment were passed on to customers and sometimes to taxpayers. A similar approach was adopted in the transmission and supply activities of the natural gas industry. 1.16

(3) Beyond the Pre-Liberalization Paradigm

The basic relationship between government and the electricity and gas industries has for some time been undergoing a radical, and seemingly irreversible, change. With respect to electricity markets, the current state of change has been characterized as one in which the 'comfortable old certainties have evaporated'. Indeed, the 'basic premises that everyone involved accepted without thought, which guided the evolution of electricity systems worldwide throughout the 20th Century, suddenly no longer apply'.[8] Throughout the 1990s, governments in countries around the world began to change the ground rules. This change may be characterized as a movement from 'traditional regulation' to 'regulation for competition'.[9] 1.17

The new idea behind this movement was that the institutional configuration of a system based on the technically-centralized model can be restructured, and monopoly rights withdrawn to permit different suppliers to compete for customers. The technical reasons for this have been discussed in the literature,[10] and include 1.18

---

[8] ibid 3.
[9] Ariño, GO, *Principios de Derecho Público Económico* (1999) 605–55, and see Newbery, DM, *Privatization, Restructuring, and Regulation of Network Utilities* (1999) ch 1. There is a considerable body of literature on economic regulation and on theories such as those of the public choice and public interest schools: see Newbery, ibid 133–69. An early overview of the arguments of the latter two schools is provided in Ogus, A, *Legal Form and Economic Theory* (1994) ch 4. An introduction to the various meanings of the concept of regulation is provided by Daintith, T, 'Regulation: Legal Form and Economic Theory' in *International Encyclopedia of Comparative Law*, vol XVII (State and Economy) ch 10. For an overview of UK experiences in energy and non-energy sectors of the economy, see Robinson, C, (ed), *Regulating Utilities and Promoting Competition* (2006) and for an earlier period, Prosser, T, *Law and the Regulators* (1997). For a contrasting but highly stimulating view of national energy policy changes during this period, see De Jong, J, Weeda, E, Westerwoudt, T and Correlje, A, *Dertig Jaar Nederlands Energiebelied* (Clingendael International Energy Programme, 2005).
[10] eg, OECD/IEA study, *Electricity Market Reform* (1999) 23–4; this should also be read in the light of the more recent assessment in OECD/IEA, *Lessons from Liberalised Electricity Markets* (2005).

particularly the development of the combined cycle gas turbine. As a result, a new paradigm in government–energy industry relations has emerged, based on a greater reliance on markets. It has sought to introduce competition whenever possible, encouraging openness, decentralized production with network access, and remuneration on the basis of market prices, not costs. If an activity has the potential for competition, the kind of regulation implied by the new paradigm facilitates competition by (inter alia) encouraging and supporting new market entrants. If an activity is a natural monopoly, then regulation provides a substitute for the competitive market by introducing measures which act as a surrogate for competition (eg, publication of tariffs for transmission and distribution). Many diverse approaches result from this. Several basic characteristics of this new kind of regulation may be identified as follows:[11]

- separation of activities in order to facilitate the introduction of competition wherever possible;
- freedom of entry and freedom of investment in competitive activities, instead of a centrally-planned approach;
- freedom of contract and competitive formation of prices;
- access to networks and infrastructure;
- supervision of the model by an independent regulator; and
- adaptation to the use of information technology.

1.19 For effective regulatory oversight it is necessary that the regulators understand how the energy businesses work and how the various elements in them combine. In systems organized according to the traditional paradigm, where public sector monopolies predominated in the energy sector of many economies, problems of co-ordination and cost allocation among the elements of an electricity or gas network were concealed. And in the reformed electricity markets in particular it has become of critical importance to understand how the different components work and *must work* together. New rules (including those on cost allocation) must be designed to promote the economic benefits that liberalization is supposed to bring. Some co-ordination by a regulator is necessary to support competition. However, the profile of other government bodies should decline through arrangements set up under the new paradigm, except in relation to social and environmental matters.

1.20 The new energy paradigm has emerged in a context that displays some of the familiar characteristics of paradigm change noted by Thomas Kuhn.[12] A radical shift involves the successful challenge by a competitor theory of the practice carried out within the traditional paradigm, and leads to a redefinition of the problems suitable

---

[11] Ariño, GO, *Principios de Derecho Público Económico* (1999) 608–09.
[12] Kuhn, T, *The Structure of Scientific Revolutions* (1970).

C. Energy Markets and Government Intervention: The Energy Paradigm

for research and a change in world view. To promote this change, he notes, the proponents of a new paradigm will claim that they can solve the problems that have led the old one into its condition of crisis. In energy regulation, the advocates of the new market-oriented paradigm have successfully challenged the idea that network-bound energy industries defy the introduction of competition because of their natural monopoly characteristics. A new consensus emerged that was organized around a belief in markets. However, its supporters have not for the most part been proponents of some form of market fundamentalism in which all key issues are settled by way of reference to market principles. In challenging the traditional paradigm, it may well appear that this is being argued, but it is by no means inevitable and is expressly contradicted in some cases.[13] It is not necessarily being argued that energy should be treated as just another commodity.

On the contrary, in at least two ways the new paradigm's supporters acknowledge flexibility and open-endedness. First, the way in which governments introduce and promote competition has been and will remain highly diverse. Secondly, no one knows much at all as yet about the medium to long-term effects of liberalization (particularly on security and continuity of supply) because experience in most cases is still too recent.   **1.21**

(4) A Three-Stage Evolution

The reasons for this paradigmatic shift are economic, ideological, and legal. They can perhaps best be understood in an historical context since much of the power of the new paradigm comes from its claim that the traditional paradigm in the electricity and gas industries had—because of technological advances and globalization of trade—outlived its usefulness. A number of recent studies of energy market reform have been at pains to explain the historical developments that have led to the present market-oriented reforms and to claim their superiority. For convenience, *three* broad stages in the evolution of government relations with the energy sector may be distinguished.   **1.22**

The first began with the reconstruction and expansion after the Second World War. In Europe it saw the nationalization of energy companies (electricity, gas, town gas, coal, and, to a limited extent, oil companies) and the establishment of very close relationships between government and the state-owned (or controlled) energy companies. A characteristic of this stage was the consolidation of a highly fragmented electricity industry and, in Western Europe following the introduction of natural gas, the creation of state-owned monopoly suppliers.   **1.23**

---

[13] OECD/IEA, *Electricity Market Reform* (1999); Hogan, WF, 'Making Markets in Power' (London, 2000) <http://ksghome.harvard.edu/~whogan/index.htm>; Helm, D, *Energy, the State, and the Market: British Energy Policy since 1979* (2nd edn, 2004).

1.24 A second stage can be seen as commencing with the energy crises in the 1970s and is characterized by first an intensification and then a critical reassessment of the government–energy relations that had been built up during the previous stage, particularly those that had been built up in relation to security of supply in the oil industry and the construction of nuclear power stations. The tentative beginnings of a new market-based approach to energy policy emerged during this stage, especially in the USA.

1.25 A third stage began from around 1985 onwards. Governments loosened the ties that bound them to their energy companies, whether through strategies of commercialization or privatization or both, and moved to set up independent regulators. Despite many national variations, a clear market orientation has now become evident in the energy affairs of most industrialized countries.

1.26 This three-stage scheme provides a useful framework for a brief review of the principal linkages between governments and the energy industry over these decades.

(a) Stage 1: Intervention

1.27 The dominant view of governments in Western Europe in 1945 was that the control by the state of the commanding heights of the economy (which included the coal, electricity, and gas industries) was essential to the reconstruction of Western Europe and the creation of the new post-War society. Accordingly, those industries were nationalized and their assets vested in state agencies or state-owned companies which were responsible, subject to tight governmental control, for running them. In this way the high cost of investment incurred in production and infrastructure could be made to meet rising demand. Abuse of this concentrated power was to be avoided in most cases by public ownership or significant public control. Examples of this approach are to be found in France with the creation of EDF and GDF (Gaz de France) in 1946 and 1949, in Italy with the creation of ENEL in 1962, and in the UK with the establishment in the late 1940s of the Central Electricity Generating Board (CEGB), the Electricity Council and the regional Electricity Boards, and the establishment of the Gas Council and the area gas boards that were superseded by the state-owned British Gas Corporation in 1972.[14] So close was the relationship between government and industry in these cases that the term 'regulation' seems inappropriate to describe the kind of government supervision it entailed.[15]

1.28 Further consequences of this assumption were that the operations of the industries were usually exempted from the scope of national competition law, and entry of

---

[14] This even extended into the oil sector with the establishment of a state oil corporation which operated—successfully—for several years: see Cameron, P, *Property Rights and Sovereign Rights: the Case of North Sea Oil* (1983) 138–171.

[15] Well-illustrated by the use in the UK in the 1970s and 1980s of the term 'lunch-time Directive' to describe the means by which the minister responsible for a particular nationalized undertaking communicated his requirements to the Chairman of the undertaking.

C. Energy Markets and Government Intervention: The Energy Paradigm

new players into the market was excluded or strictly limited by statute. Public service obligations were imposed on the industry with respect to equality of treatment and continuity of service. In return, these industries obtained exclusive rights that amounted to, in practice, a monopoly, although the exact form differed from one country to another according to institutional structure, cultural background, political style, economic policy, and of course, the energy resource base.

1.29 In the USA, a different model was in operation: that of the private monopoly regulated by a publicly-appointed state or federal regulatory commission. There were a number of federal or municipally-owned power companies in business. The nearest counterpart to this in Europe was found in West Germany, where large, privately owned electricity and gas (and oil) companies constituted the dominant force in the energy sector. There too, many smaller energy distribution companies were in municipal or mixed ownership.

1.30 The highly interventionist role of the state during this time appeared to be vindicated by the rapid economic growth in which the energy industry played a major part by supplying increasing quantities of energy at affordable prices. It was also promoting the investment in networks that established the modern electricity and gas businesses.

1.31 This extensive and overt role of the state in national energy management had a considerable impact on the first efforts at European integration. The EC Treaty addressed issues of economic integration, but energy was not expressly mentioned. Although nuclear energy and coal were treated in some detail in the two other Treaties of the period (ECSC and Euratom), the network-related barriers to competition in the electricity and gas sectors were not addressed. In practice, even the antitrust provisions of the EC Treaty were not applied to these sectors, allowing various kinds of exclusive rights to be exercised by monopolies in most of the Member States. Indeed, it was not until the judgments of the ECJ in the *Genoa* and *Corbeau* cases (see paras 16.37–16.39 and 16.43–16.45) that it was established that holders of exclusive or special rights could be challenged under Article 86.

(b) Stage 2: Uncertainty

1.32 The energy crises of the 1970s led to the high watermark of government intervention in the energy sector in the industrialized economies. This was a period in which the goal of security of supply figured largely in public policy. For oil supply, this was a matter of particular concern due to the dependence of most of the industrialized countries on imports from the OPEC countries. The energy crises called into question the reliability of that oil supply—at that time the principal input fuel to electricity generation after coal.

1.33 There were many specific government interventions in energy markets. Some of these were concerned to avoid possible politically-inspired disruptions to supply, but others were aimed at encouraging fuel diversification to reduce dependence on imported oil supplies and avoid a possible future scarcity of fossil fuels. Very expensive programmes were introduced to fund the construction of nuclear power plants and subsidies made available for alternative forms of energy generation. At intergovernmental level, the International Energy Agency was established to supervise an emergency allocation scheme and encourage fuel diversification. The European Community took related measures, including the adoption of a new Directive restricting the use of gas for electricity generation.[16] A proliferation of national energy policies and plans emerged, as well as energy departments and agencies to implement them.

1.34 The results of these market-distorting interventions were on the whole mixed. On the positive side, there was reduced dependency on imported fuels, greater efficiency in oil production, and use of alternative fuels, especially nuclear energy. Indeed, much of the French nuclear energy programme resulted from policy decisions taken as a result of these interventions. However, in the USA, federal capping of wellhead gas prices had adverse and unexpected results. Moreover, the government-inspired investment in new power plant capacity subsequently proved in a number of cases to have been very costly and unnecessary. Examples of this were particularly evident in the nuclear energy sector in several countries.

1.35 The negative effects of such attempts at government direction of the energy economy led to a severe questioning of the assumptions on which the interventions had been made. This climate of doubt about the role of government in the energy sector in the face of considerable evidence of malfunctioning did not by itself bring about a change in thinking about the adequacy of the prevailing paradigm for government–energy industry relations. That change required another very important development—a synergy between advocates of an alternative, pro-market approach and decision-makers who were able to put their ideas into practice. Such pioneers were beginning to emerge in the UK and the USA by the end of the 1970s.

1.36 Those pioneers were encouraged by several developments that occurred from the 1970s. Alternatives to vertically-integrated electricity systems appeared possible from the experience of independent generators operating on existing grids without seeing any decline in the quality of service provided through the system. Technical progress was also shifting the minimum efficient scale in power generation away from the large fossil fuel consuming units towards smaller ones, creating the possibility of easier entry for new players into energy markets. These developments were seized upon to challenge the traditional mode of thinking and replace

---

[16] Directive (EEC) 75/404 on the restriction of the use of natural gas in power stations [1975] OJ L178/24 (since repealed by Directive (EEC) 91/148 revoking Directive 75/404/EEC on the restriction of the use of natural gas in power stations [1991] OJ L75/52).

C. Energy Markets and Government Intervention: The Energy Paradigm

it with the idea that some competition in energy networks was both possible and desirable. It was argued that the activities of generation/exploration, end-use supply, marketing, and billing could be unbundled and opened to competition without significant adverse effects. This laid the basis for an alternative paradigm.

(c) Stage 3: Globalization

From the mid-1980s onwards, the traditional paradigm of government–energy industry relations was challenged again. There were two principal sources of this challenge. The first lies outside the energy sector—the complex of processes commonly referred to as 'globalization'. The second came from within—specific initiatives taken by states to liberalize their energy markets. 1.37

'Globalization' refers to processes that promote economic interdependence and cut across the borders of nation-states, seeming to threaten the sovereignty of those states. These processes were greatly assisted by changes to the GATT agreed in the Uruguay Round (1994) bringing about both the creation of the WTO and increased opportunities for international trade. One of globalization's most striking features has been the expanded role of world financial markets which increasingly operate on a real-time basis on a global scale. Another has been its relationship to the spread of information technology and transformation of everyday notions of time and space. Support for globalization has come from corporations, states, and many NGOs. Its effects have been most visible in the OECD countries. 1.38

Economic globalization triggered a debate on the future of the nation-state. With a few notable exceptions,[17] most writers have seemed to agree that there has been no decline in the nation-state but rather a transformation in its functions, some powers transferred away from nations and into a depoliticized global space or to supra-national entities.[18] At the same time, there has been a trend for some decision-making to move from the centre of nation-states to sub-national level. However, the scope of government, taken overall, has appeared to expand rather than diminish as globalization proceeds.[19] Nation-states remain the most important agents on the international scene. 1.39

Although the phenomenon of economic globalization is not entirely new, the current globalization processes have been occurring hand-in-hand with a widespread economic liberalization in which many functions associated with the state have been transferred to the private sector and made subject to different and often unfamiliar forms of regulation, either by the state or its agencies. There has also 1.40

---

[17] Stiglitz, J, *Globalization and its Discontents* (2002); Ohmae, K, *The End of the Nation State: The Rise of Regional Economies* (1996).
[18] Sassen, S, *Losing Control? Sovereignty in an Age of Globalization* (1996) xii–xiii.
[19] See, eg, Giddens, A, *The Third Way: the Renewal of Social Democracy* (1998) 32; *The Third Way and its Critics* (2000) 122; Stiglitz, J, *Making Globalization Work* (2006).

been a change in the role of supra-national institutions in promoting and facilitating these economic reforms. The nation-state has become more and more involved in the implementation of those laws necessary for economic liberalization and globalization, especially those concerning deregulation and the formation of legal regimes that favour the free circulation of capital, goods, information, and services.

1.41 The second and most significant challenge of all became from the actions taken by advocates of a new market-oriented approach to energy market organization. Their early experiments in liberalizing the electricity and gas markets first of the USA, the UK, and farther afield in Latin America showed that positive results could follow from the process, and went some way to confounding predictions of inefficiency and even system collapse. Amid much debate about the virtues and shortcomings of traditional regulation, a number of experiments were initiated in the liberalization of national energy markets. The significance of these early—and in retrospect rather primitive—experiments in market reform is that they had sufficient success to persuade others that there were hard-headed arguments in favour of this paradigm. As the arguments multiplied, with the growing number of experiments, the converts grew. There was a basis in the real world for faith in the new paradigm.

1.42 Other countries soon followed this route. In doing so they showed that there was no single model to be replicated but rather a set of ideas that could be adapted to permit a liberalization tailor-made to each specific setting. In the Nordic countries, for example, an electricity pooling system was established but without the privatization that had been chosen in the UK and in Chile. Australia and New Zealand also favoured approaches that suited their own special circumstances. The new paradigm became associated with 'progress', even if some stocktaking has taken place as a result of the concerns over various forms of energy security in recent years.

1.43 Differences between the two industries (electricity and gas) did present liberalizers with serious challenges. Take the USA for example. There the transition to greater reliance on competition to govern the performance of the natural gas market did not raise many important structural issues[20] (in contrast to the UK). Essentially, the network of gas pipelines had reached a mature stage, and when access provisions were introduced in the legal regime a very large geographic market was created. After the elimination of west-to-east constraints in transportation capacity, a continental market was created making it virtually impossible for a single seller or a combination of a few sellers to exercise market power. By contrast, the transition to competition in electricity markets has raised a host of structural questions. As one commentator observed, 'depending on the locations and effects

---

[20] Pierce Jr, RJ, 'The Antitrust Implications of Energy Restructuring' in *Natural Resources & Environment* (1998) 269.

of transmission capacity constraints, and depending on the way transmission is priced, the geographic market for electricity can be as large as a region of the country or as small as part of a single state'.[21] As a result, the idea took root in the USA that it is technically possible and economically desirable to develop a model of regulation based on market principles. There was a growing pressure for reduction in gas and electricity prices, particularly from major energy users. In addition, somewhat fortuitously, this pressure coincided with a period in which oil and gas were available at historically low prices. Moreover, as consumer benefits of competition in other sectors such as telecommunications became clear, similar benefits were sought in electricity and gas.

At a wider international level, there has been a growing acceptance of policies aimed at generating revenues for state finances from privatizations and of the benefits of international trade. An effect of globalization has been to encourage governments to accelerate experimentation in market reform at national level. The various experiences of governments committed to energy market reform showed too that the chaos predicted by some critics was avoidable. As a result of all this, the mindset of most governments to competition in network-bound energy markets changed fundamentally. **1.44**

(5) Crisis and the Shift Towards 'Energy Security'

Against the trend described in the preceding paragraphs it may be argued that the energy crisis in California in 2000 triggered conceins about the security risks of energy market liberalization. The California crisis comprised a lack of supply and artificially escalating prices resulting in the largest utility filing for bankruptcy. A combination of factors led to this situation including: **1.45**

- lack of new generation capacity due to an uncertain regulatory environment and unusually strict planning controls;
- rapidly increasing demand due to Silicon Valley (high-tech industry) consumption;
- existence of an obligatory pool leading to anti-competitive, oligopolistic pricing practices;
- the impossibility of off-setting risk through long-term supply agreements;
- locked retail prices and exposure to spot prices;
- impossibility of TSO launching tenders for the construction of new capacity combined with power purchase agreements;
- lack of interconnection capacity and supply arrangements with neighbouring states;
- external factors, eg drought; and
- lack of appropriate inter-state trading arrangements.

---

[21] ibid.

The result of this unusual combination of adverse conditions was a kind of 'perfect storm' that few, if any, systems could have survived intact, unless heavily protected by state subsidies and bail-outs funded by taxpayers. Nevertheless, the fact that interruptions to the power supply have occurred in many EU countries (and North America) from 2003 onwards has been sufficient to foster a sense of vulnerability about electricity supply in liberalizing markets that has required some adaptation of the market paradigm, if only in emphasis. Uncertainties in gas supply and external dependence have only served to underscore this factor. The legal measures taken are discussed in Chapter 18.

1.46 However, several of these factors could have been anticipated when designing the legal and technical structure of the liberalized regime. If new generation capacity is an objective, then incentives for new investment should be included and unduly restrictive planning or environmental laws should be either modifed prior to implementation or taken into account in the regime's design. In the EU, the Commission has been keen to emphasize that the EU internal energy market regime allows Member States to take emergency action at an early stage if faced with an imbalance between demand and supply—notably by launching tenders for new capacity backed up by fixed price power purchase agreements.[22] In addition, most EU Member States have an excess of capacity that could, if necessary, provide a cushion to any disruptive effects of liberalization.

(6) Unfinished Business

1.47 In spite of the continued existence of systems organized according to the traditional paradigm, by the late 1990s the contest appeared to have been decisively won by the new market-oriented paradigm: 'regulation for competition' (see below) had become at least an organizing principle to which most governments aspired in those sectors of the economy characterized by networks.

1.48 However, a paradigm is more like an open-ended framework than a model, and the triumph of the market-oriented paradigm leaves a great many issues open for development by its supporters (and its converts). These may be divided into two categories.

1.49 First, there are problems that must be addressed that arise from the introduction of competition into network-bound energy sectors, such as the so-called 'stranded asset problem' (problems of *application*). They do not involve questioning the basic assumptions of the new paradigm but lead instead to the analysis and attempted solution of what might be called 'micro problems', using techniques compatible with the basic assumptions of the new paradigm.

---

[22] European Commission, 'Communication on Completing the Internal Energy Market' (2001) 46; Commission Press Release MEMO/01/174, 'The California Power Crisis', 11 May 2001.

C. Energy Markets and Government Intervention: The Energy Paradigm

Secondly, there are problems that are not directly connected with the new paradigm but which impact on it and present a possible threat to its implementation (problems of *compatibility*). They include the many environmental and public service issues that affect the energy sector and the issues concerned with the sustainable development debate. **1.50**

(a) Problems of Application

Problems of application are already apparent and are certain to increase. Three sets of problems may be noted. First, there are those concerning the transition to a liberalized market. As the IEA has noted, 'given that no competitive power market has operated for more than a few years, none has yet completed the stage of transition'.[23] Indeed, '[t]he impact of market liberalization on investments in long-term generating capacity and diversity of fuel inputs to power generators is not yet fully clear'.[24] The problem of stranded costs, or remuneration for sunk costs incurred in a regulated regime but not recoverable after the market has been opened to competition is only one example of such a problem of mopping-up after the basics of the new paradigm have been accepted. It has sparked off a very lively debate and interesting research into the possible solutions.[25] **1.51**

More fundamentally however, it appears that the transitional period may be a very lengthy one, involving periodic reviews by government and regulatory authorities and further legislation. In other words, the role of government may well have changed but the electricity and gas industries will probably remain subject to a high degree of government interference for the foreseeable future. **1.52**

Another set of problems concerns the application of competition law in the context of liberalized energy markets. Many established notions about energy markets became open to question because of the spread of liberalization. This is especially so when the actions of market incumbents are such as to anticipate and undermine the effects of liberalization while it is being introduced (through mergers and acquisitions, for example). **1.53**

Finally, outside the mature energy markets there are problems that affect those developing countries in seeking to liberalize their energy markets and at the same time increase investment in new networks and plant. In a number of such cases, this has led to a rejection of the energy market paradigan itself (in Russia, for example). **1.54**

---

[23] OECD/IEA, *Electricity Market Reform* (1999) 93.
[24] ibid 98.
[25] See, eg, Sidak, G and Spulber, D, *Deregulatory Takings and the Regulatory Contract: the Competitive Transformation of Network Industries in the US* (1998).

(b) Problems of Compatibility

1.55 Problems of compatibility primarily involve potentially market-distorting initiatives taken by governments. In particular they could involve measures to promote policies of sustainable development. It is early days for trying to discern how such problems will be addressed in ways that are compatible with the promotion of competitive markets. This is something of a 'black box'. The increasingly central position taken by environmental and social questions in energy law and policy is a powerful trend that is beginning to test the market orientation that developed in the 1990s. The new paradigm emerged during a period of abundant supply of electricity and gas but has increasingly had to concern itself with issues of security of supply.

1.56 The significance of these historically specific conditions for its long-term continuation is not yet clear: the complex relationships between markets, regulation, and investment behaviour (often cyclical in character when left to the market) are indeed 'not properly understood'.[26]

1.57 Paradigm changes also affect the method of inquiry in problem-solving. They will have a significant impact on the way in which a problem is defined and the way in which problems are prioritized.[27] A paradigm shift will ensure that some problems are not placed on the agenda for solution, as they would have been under the preceding paradigm.

(7) A New Paradigm Emerging?

1.58 In the pre-liberalization paradigm, a near absolute security of energy supply was provided but at unknown and inherently high cost. As liberalization has proceeded, the excess capacity built up during these early years has been reduced by companies that are unwilling to pay the high costs of such reserve capacity, with a corresponding reduction in security of supply. In the UK this has triggered a fairly new emphasis by policy-makers on the need for investment in additional capacity to combat what is known as 'asset-sweating'. In itself, this is not an argument against market reform since there are many ways of providing incentives to investors to make the large investments that may be required. As Chapters 5 and 6 show, this has been done within the framework of the pro-competition legal framework.

1.59 Other developments have been identified by observers as indicative of a new paradigm shift: the various changes taking place in international gas markets[28]

---

[26] Perceptive remarks by Robert Mabro underline this point: Oxford Institute for Energy Studies News, May 2001. For an assessment of the potential impact on energy of legal developments in combating climate change, see the contributions in Cameron, PD and Zillman, D, (eds), *Kyoto: From Principles to Practice* (2002), and Helm, D, (ed), *Climate Change Policy* (2005).

[27] Kuhn, T, *The Structure of Scientific Revolutions* (1970) 110.

[28] Clingendael Institute, 'The paradigm change in international natural gas markets and the impact on regulation', 2006.

and the advent of a low-carbon economy[29] are two examples. From a legal point of view, neither of these developments has yet generated the kind of sweeping changes that the market-driven paradigm initiated and effected over the past decade or more. The key to the success of this paradigm is the balance that it achieves with respect to three potentially divisive elements: market, security and sustainability. The weight given to each may change over time but they are always present. As we shall see, they have always been present in EU law, and have deep and surely long-lasting roots. What is very striking in the European context is the extent to which the new market-orientated approach has made extensive efforts to incorporate the other objectives in the formulation of specific legal measures. On the environmental side, it is perhaps equally striking that efforts have been made to achieve sustainability goals through the adoption of market mechanisms. This does not lead us to the conclusion that at this stage a further paradigm shift is taking place.

D. Why is Energy Special?

The dependence of electricity and gas supply on fixed networks to transport and deliver energy to users is a serious complication for any policy of market opening. In practice, the transmission system is almost always a national monopoly. By contrast, the supply of oil and coal are not affected by such transportation bottlenecks. The physical characteristics of coal and oil have led to international trade and free market practices, with a declining government role except in fiscal matters. Customers can readily negotiate with competing suppliers to obtain the best deal for oil or coal purchase. The price obtained by the customer may be influenced by product quality and by differing levels and structures of taxation or subsidies. However, transportation and distribution constraints in a network will not create problems of access for customers and producers in the way that they readily do in the gas and electricity sectors. **1.60**

A further characteristic of both sectors, linked to the above, is the high cost of infrastructure and the element of sunk costs. This has often been used to justify anti-competitive features. Exclusive rights over a determinate period have been sought by investors to permit financing of these projects, with long-term contractual obligations, such as those involving 'take-or-pay' obligations. The rights granted may include an exclusive right to own and operate a transmission system over a specified period and an exclusive right to import gas or electricity. **1.61**

---

[29] Helm, D, 'The Assessment: the New Energy Paradigm' (2005) 21 Oxford Rev of Economic Policy 1–18. The investment argument and the end of a long period of low energy prices are also used to suggest a paradigm shift.

1.62 As the sections below illustrate, there are different obstacles to competition presented by the specific features of the gas and electricity sectors. For example, in the European context the production structures in each case are quite different and gas is obtained from a limited number of sources, many of which are located outside the EU. The markets are not however capable of being treated as *entirely* separate since a large part of the electricity generation market uses gas as a fuel: problems in the wholesale markets for gas can therefore impact upon electricity markets and upon the suppliers that make dual fuel offers.

(1) Electricity

1.63 Electricity has a number of characteristics that are specific to it and impact on the design of any regulatory regime.

(1) *Lack of storage potential* Electricity may not be stored in large amounts and at low cost, with the consequence that power at any point in time is not a good substitute for power at another point in time (except possibly in the case of small consumers of electricity). Power production and supply may therefore be seen as 'multiple time-differentiated products'.[30]

(2) *High cost of outages* There is a high cost involved when load exceeds supply, or when there are so-called 'brownouts' or blackouts.

(3) *Fluctuation* The above features, when taken together with a third feature, one which electricity shares with gas—that demand fluctuates throughout the day and also differs according to the season (with random variations superimposed, in large part due to the fact that much of it is used in weather-related uses such as heating and cooling)—create what is known as a 'peak-demand problem'. Essentially, if the entire load has to be supplied, capacity has to equal or exceed the load at all times. If not, there will be random supply interruptions in the form of brownouts or blackouts, leading to considerable economic damage. Demand for electricity can be subdivided into base-load power—electricity that is required seven days a week 24 hours a day—and flexible power—electricity required to absorb demand during peak hours.

(4) *Transformation* Electricity demand requires transformation of electricity into some final form before it may be met. This form may be light, heat, and cooling- or motion-power. It means that some of the input energies to electricity such as natural gas are also its competitors in final energy markets. Moreover, demand is not very 'price-elastic' in the short term since a customer's transformation equipment is generally long-lasting. Electricity supply assets such as generating capacity have an even longer working life.

---

[30] IEA, *Electricity Market Reform: An IEA Handbook* (1999) 11.

D. Why is Energy Special?

(5) *Technical specifications* Further, technical and financial specifications of power stations differ considerably due to the fact that electricity can be generated using different technologies and different raw materials (gas, coal, nuclear energy and hydro-power). The degree of flexibility of the generating units determines their ability to respond to changes in demand.

1.64 The impact of these characteristics is that the cost structures of power stations lead to the deployment of a 'merit order' or order of capacity based on the short-term marginal cost of a power station. Those power stations with relatively low marginal costs and/or which lack the capacity to generate electricity more or less quickly and on demand operate almost continuously and generate base load power. Those power stations that can increase or decrease production on demand and/or which have higher marginal costs operate mainly during peak hours. During the latter periods, when most facilities are fully utilized and cannot increase their generation further to meet peak demand, the number of effective competitors declines.[31]

1.65 Finally, there is another consequence that has relevance for competition policy. Some of the characteristics of electricity mean that abuse of market power is fairly easy and therefore likely. Due to the fact that short-run demand elasticities are very low, the supply cannot be stored and wholesale markets (even competitive ones) are highly volatile. Companies with small market shares 'have both the ability and incentive to raise prices when markets are tight and suppliers pivotal, rendering standard tests of market power (HHI or market shares) less effective'.[32] Among the consequences is a more complicated approach to the analysis of mergers. Moreover, where vertical mergers are planned between electricity and gas companies with market power in the gas market, this has the potential to increase the incentive to raise gas prices by the merged entity through ownership of power generation.

(a) The Europe Factor

1.66 In the European context two features of electricity supply organization may be noted.

(1) *Lack of import dependence* Import dependence is practically zero. Self-sufficiency is very high as electricity companies have been able to locate generation close to where electricity is needed. Cross-border trade represents about six to eight per cent of total UCTE electricity consumption.[33] Electricity is generated to

---

[31] Netherlands Competition Authority, Consultation Document on Mergers on the Energy Markets in the Netherlands and a Possible North-East European Market, June 2006, paras 53–5.
[32] Gilbert, R and Newbery, R, *Electricity Merger Policy in the Shadow of Regulation* (2006) EPRG 06/27:<http://www.electricitypolicy.org.uk/pubs/wp/eprg0628.pdf>.
[33] European Commission, 'Communication on Completing the Internal Market in Energy', COM (2001) 125 final, 13 March 2001.

meet immediate demand and usually travels much shorter distances, requiring closer co-ordination between generation, transmission, and distribution elements of the industry, encouraging the creation of vertically-integrated monopolies. Where issues of cross-border trade have arisen, their focus has largely been on how to improve the efficiency, depth, and interconnected character of the existing transmission grids to promote exchanges between incumbent players. Consumer choice across borders has arguably been less important as a result. In this context, it is unsurprising that a major objective of the European Commission has been to identify and remove obstacles to cross-border trade in electricity (see Chapter 5).

(2) *Interconnections are poor* A second notable feature of the European scene is that interconnections are poor. There are serious congestion problems, occurring when the state of the electricity networks and the transport capacities are such that the electricity that was planned to be transported from one point to another cannot be entirely physically transported. The levels of congestion can be serious: between Spain and Portugal they are almost permanent, and 'are not due to exceptional circumstances and are likely to keep occurring in the near future'.[34] These levels of congestion are much higher than those observed on the Nordic electricity pool, which are in the range of 0 per cent to 7 per cent of the time.[35] The limited interconnection capacity depends on the progressive implementation of a number of successive steps including not only technical measures on the electrical grids but also the elimination of regulatory and administrative barriers and the harmonization of the functioning and management methods of the systems' operators.[36]

(2) Gas

1.67 Gas[37] has seven principal contrasting characteristics that impact significantly on the design and pricing of transmission services.

(1) *Geopolitics* Gas supply has an international character with the bulk of supplies coming from non-EU countries on the basis of long-term contracts, but is

---

[34] *EDP/ENI/GDP* (Case COMP/M.3440) Commission Decision 2005/801/EC, [2005] OJ L302/69, para 83.

[35] In its decision *Sydkraft/Graninge* (Case COMP/M.3268) of 30 October 2003, the Commission found (p 26) that Sweden was isolated from all other areas in the Nordpool area only 5.5% (2000), 0.0% (2001), 0.1% (2002) and 0.0% (Jan–Sept 2003) of the time. Isolation percentages between individual neighbouring territories and Sweden were rather higher but also generally low (eg on average 7% between Sweden and Denmark East in the same period).

[36] *EnBW/EDP/Cajastur/Hidrocantabrico* (Case COMP/M.2684) Commission Decision of 19 March 2002, para 25.

[37] 'Gas' means here natural gas and not so-called 'town gas', which is manufactured from coal or oil at gasworks located very near consumption areas. It includes liquefied natural gas (LNG) but not liquefied petroleum gas (LPG).

D. Why is Energy Special?

much less exposed to competition in pricing than the oil sector. Its organization usually reflects this separation of the sources of production from the consumption markets. In Europe natural gas frequently travels very long distances and crosses many inter-state borders to reach its users. For many gas-consuming countries in Europe a dependence on external (non-EU) suppliers has been a fact of life for decades. More than 40 per cent of EU gas supply originated from non-EU sources such as Algeria, Norway, and Russia.[38] Even with respect to the EU's own gas production, the element of cross-border trade is considerable, one in every five cubic metres of gas produced in EU countries being exported. Just as non-EU gas from Norway is transported across the Netherlands to Belgium and France, gas produced from the Netherlands crosses Germany and Switzerland to reach Italy. About 50 per cent of all internationally-traded gas in the world is imported into the EU. This geopolitical element makes energy policy links with Russia, Algeria, and Norway of great importance. At the same time, such cross-border transactions normally take the form of transit and/or supply agreements between incumbent major gas wholesalers. There are few competition implications and it is misleading to describe it as 'trade' in the generally accepted sense of the term.

(2) *The gas chain* Gas operations have a vertically integrated character from production to consumption (the so-called *gas chain*). This means that regulatory action in one segment of the chain can easily impact on other segments. When the internal energy market programme began in 1988, the gas sector came under scrutiny by the Commission mainly because of the exercise of monopoly power in the transmission and distribution segments of its operations. However, legislation designed to liberalize these segments has usually had significant implications for the 'upstream' activities of exploration and production as well.

(3) *Storage and timing of actions* Gas can be stored in underground facilities, in transmission or distribution pipelines, in above-ground LNG facilities or by means of a technique known as 'line-pack'. The result is to provide gas system operators with a considerable degree of flexibility in balancing their systems over time. This contrasts quite starkly with the lot of electricity system operators who must manage the stability and reliability of the grid according to a time-frame of a few seconds. Pressure and flow management in gas pipelines may occur over much longer intervals, perhaps hours or days. This presents a rather different situation on harmonization requirements between the respective systems. In gas there is more flexibility, since the task is only to manage the balancing protocols between systems to ensure that there is adequate gas quality and timing consistency to permit each operator to maintain

---

[38] European Commission, *Next Steps Towards Completion of the Internal Market in Gas: draft strategy paper for discussion* (2000) 2.

its system flexibility.[39] Customers have in principle more discretion in exercising their rights to utilize various receipt and delivery points. To be active on the gas retail markets a gas supplier needs to have access to storage facilities. This allows it to manage the seasonal fluctuations in the demand of its customers. The supplier will have to manage daily, weekly and seasonal fluctuations according to the type and the number of its customers. Access to storage facilities is therefore 'an absolutely necessary condition' for any supplier. It may be noted that gas suppliers with a large and diversified customer base are subject to a lower overall variation in demand than suppliers with a limited number of customers and a fluctuating demand, limiting their storage requirements and giving them a competitive advantage over smaller competitors.[40]

(4) *Technical ('loop-flows' and 'wheeling')* Electricity and gas share the characteristic, being network-bound energy sources. The network effects have different characteristics in each case however. The flow of electricity over wires follows different physical laws to that of gas, giving rise to 'loop-flows'. These are intrinsic to electricity transmission and affect the way that access to transmission capacity is made available to buyers and the way it is controlled by the system operator. So-called 'wheeling' transactions along one part of the path can have an effect on the availability of transmission capacity along an interconnected path. In the EU context, 'transit' has recently been defined as a physical flow of electricity hosted on the transmission system of a Member State, neither produced nor destined for consumption in this Member State, and including transit flows commonly denominated as loop-flows.[41] Although there are no 'loop-flows' in gas transmission, there are network effects nevertheless. The use by a consumer or third-party supplier of a receipt point into a gas network, or a delivery point out, will affect the ability of another shipper to utilize other receipt and delivery points on the network. As a result, the amount of transmission capacity that may be made available at any given time is a function of the planned utilization of the network. In electricity, however, the determination of available capacity is made considerably more difficult by the existence of loop-flows.

(5) *Energy quality* Gas produced from different fields and wells can have a very different energy content and may contain variable contaminants and water in the gas stream. A number of issues of supply quality must therefore be addressed

---

[39] 'Methodologies for Establishing National and Cross-Border Systems of Pricing of Access to the Gas System in Europe', report for the European Commission prepared by the Brattle Group (February 2000) Appendix 2, 96.

[40] *E.On/MOL* (Case COMP/M.3696) Commission Decision 2006/622/EC, [2006] OJ L253/20, Recitals 477–8.

[41] European Commission, 'Proposal for a Regulation of the European Parliament and Council on Conditions for Access to the Network for Cross-Border Exchanges in Electricity in the Internal Electricity Market', 2001.

through physical specification standards or accounting treatment (calorific value). In electricity, by contrast, the supply is generated to meet very specific characteristics.

(6) *Safety* If electricity is temporarily interrupted, it can be restored without risk to the consumer at a later date. This is not possible with the supply of gas. If non-interruptible gas consumers have their gas supplies unexpectedly terminated, supply cannot be resumed until safety checks have been carried out on every appliance to make sure they are switched off. This process may be costly and time-consuming, especially if it involves residential consumers. In terms of operational security of supply, it is not 'fail safe'.

(7) *Size of provider* Historically, the players have been different between gas and electricity, with large international companies involved in gas and often also the oil business, directly or indirectly. They are often vertically integrated too. This situation arose from the fact that gas was usually found in association with oil or as an indirect result of exploration originally directed at finding oil. Conveniently, the price of gas is linked to oil in much of continental Europe, reflecting the high degree of substitutability between them. In recent years there has been a trend towards convergence of gas and electricity supply by companies that have become increasingly focused on the provision of several kinds of energy. In some cases, such companies have also been involved in the provision of water or telecommunications services as well, creating a so-called 'multi-utility'.

(a) The Europe Factor

At an early stage, analysis of the European gas market by the European Commission reached negative conclusions about the potential for competition: 'the structure of the European gas markets is currently not favourable to competition'.[42] Essentially, the gas markets are characterized by horizontal and vertical demarcation. This situation is brought about by the long-term supply contracts concluded by incumbents which are part of a well-established vertical supply chain, extending from gas producers to end-users.

'Vertical demarcation' means that each operator has its well-defined function and position in the supply chain and usually refrains from entering the markets of its customers and/or suppliers (eg, there will be no direct sales by producers to end-users). 'Horizontal demarcation' means that each importer or wholesaler and/or regional or local distributor has its traditional supply area and usually does not enter the neighbouring supply area.

1.68

1.69

---

[42] European Commission, *XXXth Report on Competition Policy 2000*, 35; Commission Press Release IP/99/708, 'Commission clears merger between Exxon and Mobil (both USA) subject to conditions', 29 September 1999.

Chapter 1: The Competition Objective

Table 1.1 Gas Constraints on competition (a) Downstream market segment

Product markets	Corresponding geographic markets
Onshore transmission	National markets and potentially markets smaller than national
Sales to regional wholesale and/or local distribution companies, power plants and other industrial users	National markets and potentially markets smaller than national
Sales to private users by local distribution companies	Regional/local markets
Storage	National markets and potentially smaller than national ones

Note: The competition characteristics of these markets is as follows: network-bound industry; number of players limited; few new market entrants.

1.70 The Commission also found that the upstream markets were for the most part characterized by various forms of co-operation between competitors. This included the activities of exploration, production, and sales to wholesalers. Downstream markets, covering transportation, distribution, and storage, are at most only national in scope and are dominated by former monopolists. The latter are usually vertically-integrated and control the pipeline network. These pipeline networks are usually, and will probably remain, natural monopolies.

Table 1.2 Gas Constraints on competition (b) Upstream market segment

Product markets	Corresponding geographic markets
Exploration and development	Gas fields in EEA plus potentially Russian Federation and Algeria
Offshore transmission processing	Region in which the pipelines are located. Depends on geographic market defined for the offshore transmission.
Production and sales to wholesale companies	Gas fields in EEA plus potential RF and Algerian sources

Source: European Commission Competition Directorate.

1.71 A similar situation prevails today as can be seen from paras 11.48–11.64.

(b) The Impact of LNG

1.72 The prospect of increased supplies of gas becoming available from Liquefied Natural Gas (LNG) may seem to offer a way of limiting this external dependence and facilitating competition among suppliers to consumer benefit. However, there are competition issues here arising from the LNG business itself.

1.73 LNG terminals are very capital intensive. For this investment to be recouped, capacity is usually booked well in advance before the terminal is constructed.

If this capacity is already booked it will not be available for third parties under the TPA rules of the Gas Directive.[43] Even if there is capacity available for competitors, it is possible for the terminal owner to make access difficult for them. This can be explained as follows:[44] the regasification activity of an LNG terminal is composed of three main parts which are all inter-dependent and constitute as many bottlenecks:

(1) LNG carrier ships have to be unloaded; time slots have to be booked; arbitrage between ships and priority rules are then crucial;
(2) LNG can be stored in a storage facility; storage capacity may be limited, thereby preventing a competitor from unloading or forcing him to inject the gas in the network very rapidly; and
(3) the LNG has to be regasified before being injected. There again, the regasification plant has limited capacity which has to be booked in advance.

Technical rules may also act as a restriction of the market. An LNG carrier may set technical constraints that can prevent certain LNG carriers unloading.

TPA rules are not sufficient to guarantee a satisfactory level of access to third parties. There are too many factors that can be manipulated to prevent effective use by third parties. Most of the LNG terminals are operated by their main user. Even when spare capacity is available, terms have to be negotiated, including pricing mechanisms, overall flexibility and allocation. Consequently, additional rules to TPA have been adopted by regulators on a case-by-case basis to help improve the way that competitors can use LNG terminals (such as paying for the booked capacity and/or use-it-or-lose-it rules).

1.74

E. The Requirements of Liberalization

There are a number of prerequisites for the introduction of competition into the gas and electricity markets. They include changes in the legal and institutional framework of regulation, particularly to ensure access by third parties, as well as liberalization, industry restructuring, and (possibly) ownership changes. Such changes are usually linked and are especially necessary where the industry has been vertically integrated or highly concentrated horizontally. Both of these characteristics were familiar in the pre-liberalization paradigm and have therefore had to be redesigned with the introduction of competition. Various national programmes of energy reform have yielded examples of the practical mechanisms required to support change, but diverse approaches to the introduction of competition have resulted.

1.75

---

[43] Art 21: 'Natural gas undertakings may refuse undertakings access to the system on the basis of a lack of capacity'.
[44] *EDP/ENI/GDP* (Case COMP/M.3440) Commission Decision 2005/801/EC, [2005] OJ L302/69, paras 397–9; see para 14.93 below.

Chapter 1: The Competition Objective

(1) Regulation and Access

1.76 The idea of 'regulation for competition' may seem perverse. After all, the aim of liberalization and deregulation is to allow competition to do the work of regulating rather than to leave it to a regulator. However, as competition will not naturally occur in markets where natural monopolies of transportation exist, it is necessary for regulation to provide a surrogate for competition. Essentially, a dominant network owner will control access to consumers and network access will quickly become the principal but not the sole barrier to entry. The core aim of most market reform programmes is the creation of enforceable rights of access for third parties to the transmission and distribution networks. Experience shows that some form of regulation will be required to prevent the owner and operator of the networks from extracting monopoly rents at the expense of other parties in the supply chain. One of the tasks of a regulator will be to define and prioritize rights of access to the network. Another task will be to address the pricing of these rights.

1.77 The various regulatory tasks may be conveniently classified according to:

- structure (concerning unbundling and prevention of cross subsidies);
- conduct (organization of regulation and the control of market behaviour through licensing, price-capping and non-discriminatory access); and
- transitional problems (so-called 'stranded investments' and environmental matters).

1.78 Tasks affecting conduct, for example, would include the regulation of quality through safety standards and safety margins to ensure security of supply. Transitional issues have focused principally on 'stranded' investments. These can be unamortized costs of prior investments that would have been recovered through the continued charging of monopoly prices had liberalization of the market not taken place. They may include generation and transmission facilities, nuclear plant maintenance, and decommissioning costs as well as conservation measures. Other forms of stranded cost include contracts to purchase power from alternative energy sources and 'take-or-pay' obligations in long-term gas contracts. The latter impose an obligation on the buyer to pay for a percentage of the annual off-take volume even if he is unable to use or re-sell the gas.

(a) An Independent Regulator

1.79 Experience has shown that a prerequisite to a successful programme of liberalization in the network-bound sector of the energy market is the establishment of an independent regulator charged with taking actions to promote competition. Independence in this context means independence of the regulator from the companies being regulated and from day-to-day interference from the government authorities. This autonomy will provide assurance to market participants and especially to potential new market entrants that the rules of the game will be

E. The Requirements of Liberalization

applied in a non-discriminatory, stable, and transparent manner. This facilitates the creation of a 'level playing field'. The question of independence does however raise issues about accountability of the regulatory body. It has been addressed differently by various governments.

1.80 There has been much debate about the organization of regulation and especially about the horizontal and vertical allocation of authority.[45] Not surprisingly, such debates have been particularly intense in countries with federal systems of government. However, in the context of the EU, the interplay between the centre and Member State levels with respect to energy regulation is particularly complex, as will be seen in the following chapters.

1.81 In the network-bound energy sector, there is now a widespread acceptance that a single regulator to monitor the electricity and gas industries jointly is the most efficient solution, although more wide-ranging options are possible (eg Germany). There is a broad consensus too that a regulatory commission is preferable to regulation by an individual since it helps to avoid a personalization of the process. A separate issue concerns the relationship to be established between the regulatory body and the competition authority, where separate institutions are normally in operation. The important issue is which body is to be responsible in cases where both have jurisdiction. The regulation involved in each case is quite different—that of a competition authority typically being *post facto* in character. A sector-specific regulator will be charged with applying rules irrespective of actual conduct. Key differences will turn on the specificity of the rules, the burden of proof, and the penalties for violating the rules.

1.82 The procedures established for regulation are of great importance. Decision-making has to be transparent and the reasons should be published. The procedures should also be detailed and set out in advance.

(2) Structure

1.83 It has been said that 'structure forms the context within which regulation takes place'.[46] If an industry is structured in such a way as to give market power to a single producer or consumer, choice for other producers and consumers must inevitably be limited and regulation has to be strongly interventionist. In recent years, an appreciation of the importance of industry structure for market reform has made restructuring central to most programmes of energy market reform and at the EU level has underlined the importance of 'ownership unbundling'. The aim has usually been to dismantle the monopoly positions that were common for many years

---

[45] Some examples are: McCahery, J, Bratton, WW, Picciotto, S and Scott, C, *International Regulatory Competition and Coordination: Perspectives on Economic Regulation in Europe and the US* (1996); the various contributions in (2000) 3 J International Economic L.

[46] Helm, D and Yarrow, G, 'Regulation and Utilities' (1988) 4 Oxford Rev of Economic Policy vii.

Chapter 1: The Competition Objective

and to introduce competition. However, the natural monopoly elements in transmission and distribution networks present a challenge to such efforts.

(a) Elements of Natural Monopoly in Supply Phases

1.84 A network owner and operator is likely to have a conflict of interest if also involved in generation or supply phases. Both the latter stages in the supply chain are actually or potentially competitive, while the transmission and distribution phases are natural monopolies, allowing the owner and operator to extract monopoly rents. In the electricity chain this also applies to dispatch and real-time balancing. There is ample evidence that, if unchecked, the exercise of such monopoly rights will lead to abuses.[47] The customer could be charged anything the monopolist wishes for network access up to the cost of building an alternative system (or switching to another fuel). A policy objective is therefore to establish arm's length relationships between the owner and operator of the natural monopoly phases and the parties in the other phases of the supply chain.

(b) Solutions: 'Unbundling'

1.85 Various techniques have been developed to deal with this among countries engaged in market reform. The solutions have to take into account the continuing inter-relationship between the generation or production phases with the transmission network, and between the distribution network and sales within vertically-integrated energy companies. They will involve a form of vertical separation of activities by incumbent companies known as 'unbundling', aimed at eliminating incentives or abilities to discriminate against competitors by means of their control of assets up- or downstream from the transmission network. This may take one of three forms:

(1) full structural separation by law;
(2) functional separation; or
(3) separation for accounting purposes.

1.86 **Full structural separation by law**   A full legal separation of the various operations is one possibility. This can take the form of 'ownership' unbundling or a 'legal' separation as required in the EU (see paras 5.38–5.43 and 6.36–6.37). In the electricity sector, for example, a separation of supply or retailing from distribution is likely to encourage competition to develop in supply. Assets from the integrated company would be divided up among several newly-formed legal entities that have no common ownership, management, control, or operations. However, vertical separation may also be effected by means of a form of corporatization rather than formal legal separation. This has been the approach favoured in Norway, Sweden, and New Zealand.

---

[47] Kahn, AE, *The Economics of Regulation: Principles and Institutions* (1998) 118–20.

E. The Requirements of Liberalization

Functional separation Alternatively, there may be an unbundling according to functions. Functional unbundling allows for the same ownership of the elements that may be subject to competition and the monopoly infrastructure elements, but their operation is placed in the hands of separate management structures. The disaggregated entities will be managed independently but will not be legally separate companies. This kind of unbundling is designed to prevent discrimination against competitors who do not have a direct financial interest in the physical infrastructure.[48] In California an entity has been established in the electricity sector called an Independent System Operator. It has responsibility for short-term co-ordination, prices for use of the transmission grid, and administers a system of tradable congestion contracts.[49] 1.87

Separation for accounting purposes Finally, there is the option of arranging unbundling by ring-fencing the accounts of the different types of businesses in the entity. The idea is that this promotes transparency and in so doing it will expose cross-subsidies and so prevent an entity from discriminating in favour of itself and against competitors. However, in practice it is hard to ensure that commercially sensitive information is not being transferred between the business units. This is probably the weakest form of unbundling and requires detailed regulation if it is to have any chance of being effective. 1.88

So far, experience in market reform suggests that the unbundling of transportation networks from the activities that can be subjected to competition is a structural change of major importance. The means by which it is achieved and the extent to which it is adopted have, however, differed widely (see Chapters 5 and 6). 1.89

(3) Liberalization

'Liberalization' refers to a process of market opening which at a minimum removes legal barriers to trade but in the EU context involves creation of an industrial structure in which competitive forces can work and a competive ethos can be stimulated. Some of the general conditions for liberalization are obvious. If customers are to be able to choose suppliers, any statutory restrictions that limit their freedom to a particular supplier must be removed. Entry of new suppliers and producers should be possible, and the normal commercial consequences should apply to those companies which are unsuccessful in the market. In the EU entry barriers have often taken the form of exemptions from general competition law, frequently involving the grant of special or exclusive rights. However, competition is unlikely to develop if governments dismantle entry barriers and do little else. A level playing 1.90

---

[48] In the USA a definition of functional unbundling is in FERC Order 888 (1996).
[49] IEA, *Electricity Market Reform: An IEA Handbook* (1999) 40–1. Australia and Canada have similar ISOs, while the USA has moved toward Regional Transmission Organizations.

field for information is also important to establish. All market participants should have simultaneous and equal access to information on the price of a commodity, whether it is gas or electricity, and for capacity.

1.91 Since transmission and distribution networks are likely to remain natural monopolies in most cases, the creation of non-discriminatory access rights to the networks is one of the most important conditions for liberalization. However, the tariffs and conditions of such access need to be transparent if competition is to develop in activities such as generation or production and supply. There are two regimes to facilitate the exercise of such rights: (i) regulated and (ii) negotiated access. In practice, the latter has proved less effective and usually involves an element of regulation too.

1.92 The methods of opening up gas and electricity markets have not been uniform but they opt for opening markets usually in a staggered manner, the large industrial customers being included in the first phase. Among the reasons for the popularity of this phased approach is that the liberalization process creates problems as it develops, and a staged approach allows adaptation to incorporate the lessons of previous stages. It also allows for the incorporation of lessons from the experiences of other countries with market reform (and also allows incumbents time to adjust). Some of the specific problems of transition that have arisen in the European setting are considered later in this book (see Chapters 5 and 6).

(4) Ownership

1.93 The importance of ownership for the introduction of competition is complex.[50] Early experience of privatization showed that the transfer of a publicly-owned monopoly into private ownership did not produce the expected benefits in competitiveness. Other structures are possible and perhaps inevitable when one considers the range of forms of public ownership: national, federal, provincial, cantonal, or municipal ownership. Nonetheless, substantial public ownership in energy companies is likely to impede the operation of competition by encouraging their protection from adverse market developments. They will not in all probability have the 'freedom to fail'. Changes in ownership have therefore been encouraged as part of an overall reform programme, involving an unbundling of industry elements. Usually, they involve a minimum of corporatization, where a government continues to hold a substantial shareholding but ceases to have any direct control of management. A financial separation will ensure that financial and asset transfers

---

[50] An IEA review has noted that ownership alone is not of overwhelming importance for power sector performance *in the short term*. Instead, key factors are subjecting potentially competitive parts to more competition and increasing the quality of regulation: *Electricity Market Reform: An IEA Handbook* (1999).

between government and the corporatized entity are at arm's length and transparent. This is intended to facilitate a degree of competition.

(a) Licensing and Concession Regimes

However, a key element in any regulatory system will be the establishment of a license or concession regime. This instrument will set down obligations with respect to the operation, maintenance, and development of transmission or distribution systems, as well as obligations to supply gas or electricity—the 'public service obligations'. With this instrument it is possible for the authorities to exercise a potentially large measure of control over the natural monopoly elements of an industry—irrespective of the form and pattern of ownership that is chosen.   **1.94**

F. Conclusions

This chapter has attempted to sketch out the wider context in which a liberalization of EU energy markets was launched. It has emphasized the importance of the 'ideas' factor in energy market regulation by reference to a paradigmatic shift from a monopolist and state-interventionist approach to one in which market mechanisms are given a wide rein, checked mainly by independent regulation. The idea has taken firm root in public policy that the natural monopoly element in network industries is not a barrier to the creation of the internal market in electricity and gas as was asserted by the opponents of liberalization. It was accepted that the natural monopoly element could be dealt with by using regulation as a surrogate for competition and that the physical and technological problems of mass third-party access could be overcome.   **1.95**

Key features of the new context such as the emphasis on markets and their creation and the impacts of globalization are not absolutely new. However, the extent of their acceptance and their effects is unprecedented. In this sense it is justified to utilize the concept of a paradigm shift. The rejection of many of the features associated with the pre-liberalization paradigm is now widespread, most evidently in the developed countries but also in a growing number of developing countries and economies in transition.   **1.96**

Recent doubts about the priority given to the competition objective have been kindled by a variety of relatively new challenges faced by this paradigm, principally in the provision of energy security. This has required adaptation to promote new investment in infrastructure and to manage the growing import dependence. In addition, the development of a low-carbon economy is a challenge that will make significant impacts on the energy sector. The energy law framework that is the subject of this book is however based on a balancing of the competition goal with other aims, including those of security and sustainability.   **1.97**

1.98 Nevertheless, it is important to note how recent this consensus is and how open-ended the new paradigm is. Reformers face challenges in applying its framework character and in dealing with some issues that are potentially incompatible with it, such as those concerning environmental protection and sustainability. Many questions about energy market reform remain to be answered including questions that are being generated by the reform process itself. These include the new concerns about investment in additional capacity for security of supply purposes and the growing impact of climate change measures on energy markets. If one recalls the words of Thomas Kuhn about the victory of a new paradigm, he notes that its success depends 'less on past achievement than on future promise'. That promise is increasingly being questioned.

1.99 In practice, whoever embraces a new paradigm at an early stage must 'have faith that the new paradigm will succeed with the many large problems that confront it, knowing only that the older paradigm has failed with a few'.[51]

---

[51] Kuhn, T, *The Structure of Scientific Revolutions* (1970) 158.

2

THE EU LEGAL ORDER AND ENERGY

A. Introduction	2.01	(b) Executive Function	2.72
B. The Origins of an EU *Acquis* in Energy	2.05	(2) Commission and Council	2.76
		(a) QMV	2.79
(1) The Treaty Context		(b) New Co-operation Procedure	2.81
(a) Should Energy be Afforded a Special Status in the Treaty?	2.09	(c) Coreper	2.82
		(3) Commission and Parliament	2.83
(b) Coal	2.14	(a) Co-operation Procedure and Power of Veto	2.85
(c) Nuclear Energy	2.17	
(d) EEC Treaty	2.22	(b) Which Procedure?	2.88
(e) A European Energy Policy: First Steps	2.31	(c) Committees	2.91
		(d) Procedure for Adopting Legislation	2.92
(2) The Single European Act	2.36	
(a) An Internal Market by the End of 1992 (Article 8A)	2.37	(4) Commission and Court of Justice	
		(a) Emergence of an ECJ Energy Jurisprudence	2.93
(b) Streamlining Decision-making Procedures	2.39	
		(b) Composition of the Court	2.94
(c) Predecessor to Co-decision: the Co-operation Procedure	2.41	(c) Advocate-General's role	2.95
		(d) ECJ Procedure	2.96
(3) Treaty on European Union (Maastricht)	2.46	(e) Jurisdiction of the ECJ	2.97
		(f) Preliminary Rulings	2.103
(a) Subsidiarity	2.49	(g) Court of First Instance	2.108
(4) Constitutional Fatigue: From Amsterdam to Nice and Beyond	2.55	(5) Legislative Acts	2.110
		(a) Directives	2.111
(5) The Proposed Energy Article and the Question of Competences	2.57	(b) Regulations	2.112
		(c) Decisions	2.113
(6) Conclusions on the Development of an Energy *Acquis*	2.61	(d) Recommendations and Opinions	2.114
		D. European Economic Area Agreement	2.115
C. The European Commission in its Institutional Setting	2.64	
		(1) EEA Agreement: Legally Binding	2.116
(1) The Commission and Commissioners: Functions and Powers	2.65	
		(2) The Institutions	2.119
(a) Legislative Role	2.69	(3) Impacts on Energy	2.123

E. Energy Community Treaty	2.127	G. The Wider Neighbourhood of the EU	2.160
F. Energy Charter Treaty	2.131	(1) Partnership and Co-operation Agreements	2.161
(1) Main Treaty Provisions			
(a) Investment	2.134	(a) Russia and the EU	2.165
(b) Trade	2.140	(2) Euro-Mediterranean Association Agreements	2.168
(c) Transit	2.142		
(2) The Charter Process: An Assessment	2.153	H. Conclusions	2.173

Europe has entered into a new energy era.

European Commission[1]

A. Introduction

2.01 The steps taken by the EU towards the creation of an internal market in energy over the past decade have marked a watershed in Community energy law and policy. Never before has there been such a deliberate and comprehensive attempt to link energy specifically to the body of Community law and to the integration process. It marked the beginning of a determined—and so far quite successful—attempt to put an end to the 'special' or de facto exempted status of the energy sector in the process of European integration.

2.02 Ironically, in putting an end to this special status, the EU has found it necessary to design an increasingly comprehensive legal regime specifically for the electricity and gas sectors, which supplements and co-exists with the main body of European law. Moreover, it has created a European network of enforcers with specialist expertise and powers to supplement the existing institutional framework for enforcement of EU law. This approach perpetuates the sense that competition problems in energy require a special treatment. In practice, there are now two bodies of legal rules, one that is sector-oriented and the other that comprises the general rules of competition law. They are discussed in detail in Parts II and III of this book. However, they exist within a wider framework of European law and institutions. Indeed, given the pan-European character of energy issues, a comprehensive approach to the legal setting would require consideration of a variety of international treaties, to which the EC and its Members are parties, and the various 'external relations' initiatives that the EU takes vis-à-vis its neighbours. Such a broad approach goes beyond the scope of this book, however.

---

[1] Green Paper, *A European Strategy for Sustainable, Competitive and Secure Energy*, COM (2006) 105 final, 8 March 2006, 3.

B. The Origins of an EU *Acquis* in Energy

2.03 The purpose of this chapter is to provide a review of the principal legal and institutional contours of the European energy scene that establish the broader foundations for the legal measures specifically aimed at promoting competition in energy markets. These foundations and the legal framework they establish have influenced, on the one hand, the design and the operation of the sector-specific legal regime and, on the other hand, the application of the competition rules of the EC Treaty. A familiarity with this context is therefore necessary to fully appreciate the following Parts of the book. The chapter is divided into six parts:

(1) origins of an EU *acquis* in energy;
(2) the European Commission and its institutional setting;
(3) the European Economic Area Agreement;
(4) the Energy Community Treaty;
(5) the Energy Charter Treaty;
(6) the Wider Neighbourhood and the energy *acquis*.

2.04 Two aspects of the subject matter require comment. First, the legal order discussed in sections B and C has been in the throes of constant change during the decade over which the sector-specific 'energy' law has come into being. The institutions of the EU have had to adapt to this process of rapid change. As Part III of this book demonstrates, the process of legal innovation in competition law has been rapid in recent years and reflection on its key concepts continues, with consequences for the application of competition law in the energy sector. Secondly, the pan-European legal arrangements discussed in sections D and E have essentially involved an export of the sector-specific energy law, either by incorporating it into the domestic legal regimes of the countries concerned or by reaching transition agreements to do so. Institutional co-operation has also been part of these relationships. This process largely reflects the increasing inter-dependence of the countries concerned in their energy relations, and especially the economic and technical imperatives arising from the expansion of grid and pipeline connections across Europe. However, it contrasts sharply with the policy-based arrangements that characterize energy relations with the EU's 'neighbourhood' to the East and the South.

B. The Origins of an EU *Acquis* in Energy

2.05 The adoption of a body of rules specifically designed to promote competition in the energy markets was clearly intended to strengthen the existing framework of EU law as it applied to those markets, and particularly the network-bound sectors of electricity and gas. At first, this may seem a little puzzling. Much of the law in the EC Treaty already granted the Community institutions extensive powers to achieve the objectives of market reform, especially with respect to competition matters— such as an abuse of dominant positions by the operators of energy networks.

In principle, further legislation was not a prerequisite for a liberalization of the energy sector. But it was quite clear that if the Commission were to rely on EC competition law to deal with individual cases of abuse of a dominant position by system network owners, it would take many years of litigation before a body of case law could be built up which could clarify the basic legal principles to be applied in cases of abuse of dominant position in relation to networks. There was also uncertainty about the legal position in relation to abuse of a dominant position where the network owner had been granted exclusive or special rights in respect of the network. In these circumstances, and having regard to the need to establish common rules applicable throughout the Community, the Commission decided to tackle the removal of obstacles to an internal energy market by applying the existing law and also submitting specific initiatives in the form of proposals for Directives. The Council of Ministers supported this approach (see below). Changes made in the law-making process under the EC Treaty including the introduction of qualified majority voting in the Council and a greater involvement of the European Parliament in the law-making process were greatly to enhance the possibility that such Directives would be adopted and be transposed into law.

2.06 By 2003 a distinct framework of rules of EC energy law had emerged, the most important elements of which were measures providing common rules for the electricity and gas industries. An earlier set of directives, Directives (EC) 96/92 and (EC) 98/30, had been quickly rendered obsolete by events. They had taken no less than five and seven years respectively to go from initial proposal stages to adoption by the Member States and the European Parliament.[2] During that time, the context of European integration had changed dramatically. A Treaty establishing the European Union and amending (inter alia) the EC Treaty—the Treaty on European Union (TEU)—was concluded at Maastricht in 1992, and, after a review of its operation at an Inter-Governmental Conference in 1997, further amendments were subsequently included in the Treaty of Amsterdam (TA). Among the many changes were procedural ones that extended the influence of the European Parliament over a wide range of matters including energy harmonization proposals. The European Union acquired three new members from the European Economic Area (EEA). A further ten new members joined in 2003, mostly from Central and North-East Europe.

2.07 Further, the collapse of the Soviet Union triggered a pan-European approach to energy policy that reflected the importance of non-EU suppliers and transit countries to the EU energy market. From the early 1990s the EU gave support to the development of international agreements to promote stability in the East and

---

[2] For a detailed account of these events, see the 1st edition of this book, *Competition in Energy Markets: Law and Regulation in the European Union* (2002).

B. The Origins of an EU Acquis in Energy

to ensure the continuation of the oil and gas supplies that many Member States relied on. These included the use of bilateral association agreements on co-operation between the EU and the countries of post-Communist Central and East Europe, as well as looser forms of partnership agreement between East and West. The EU also played a leading role in the negotiation and conclusion of another, more ambitious legal instrument, the Energy Charter Treaty, signed and ratified by more than 50 nation-states from East and West. In South-East Europe, the EU participated in the reconstruction of the energy economies of the Balkans by negotiating a treaty establishing a European Energy Community. All such instruments have, in addition to their political objectives, the goal of economic liberalization in which energy market reform plays a more or less important part. As EU energy law and policy was re-moulded in the 1990s and early 21st century, these instruments have functioned as channels for the export of ideas and techniques that were being developed within the EU internal energy market programme.

2.08 In aggregate, the various legal and policy instruments constitute a pan-European legal order for the energy sector, sometimes called an '*acquis communautaire*' or EU *acquis* for energy.[3] Essentially, this comprises all of the rights and obligations, actual and potential, which result from EC legislation and case law. Much of it is of very recent origin, dating from long after the first period of European integration. It has been constructed or has become operational during the last decade. Although some of the instruments have a distinctly 'soft' legal character, they act as a channel for a Europe-wide dissemination of the ideas of energy market liberalization and create a system of peer group pressure among the many countries that act within this framework. To the extent that liberalization is an ongoing—and distinctly unfinished—process, they facilitate the rapid transmission of ideas and experiences around Europe. Although the instruments have diverse goals, including integration and economic co-operation, they all share, to a greater or lesser degree, a commitment to the introduction of competition in energy markets, and to the use of 'regulation for competition'.

(1) The Treaty Context

(a) Should Energy be Afforded a Special Status in the Treaty?

2.09 Since the inception of what is now the EU, there has been no explicit grant of a 'special' status to the energy sector under the EC Treaty (formerly EEC Treaty; see paras 2.22–2.30 below), exempting it from the ambit of some or all of its provisions.

---

[3] For discussion of this concept see Gialdino, C, 'Some Reflections on the *Acquis Communautaire*' (1995) 32 CML Rev 1089 and Delcourt, C, 'The *acquis communautaire*: Has the concept had its day?' (2000) 38 CML Rev 829. More recently, the abbreviated term has been preferred to reflect Treaty changes that make energy an *acquis* of the EU. Parts of the Energy Charter Treaty go beyond the competence of the European Community and are based on the prerogatives of the Member States.

There are at least two possible interpretations of this lacuna. First, it may be argued that the intention was to treat energy no differently from any other economic sector in the integration process. Had the authors of the Treaty establishing the European Economic Community sought to set the industry apart in any way, they would have been well aware of the means by which this could have been done—but they did not.[4] After all, explicit provisions were inserted into the Treaty, especially Article 33(1), at a time when, with the aim of stabilizing markets, actions were envisaged to ensure security of supplies (including energy products) or to guarantee access to the market to consumers at reasonable prices).

2.10 For example, production of and trade in agricultural products was excluded from the application of the competition rules under Article 37 to the extent determined by the Council. Where special circumstances were deemed to exist—as in the sub-sectors of coal and nuclear energy—legal instruments had already been concluded and were in force. Moreover, the European Court of Justice (ECJ) has expressly ruled that electricity is a 'good' and falls within the scope of the competition rules.[5] And there was no doubt about the status of other sources of energy—such as oil and gas—which were classifiable as goods.

2.11 An alternative view is that the energy sector has unique characteristics and a special importance in the EU so that provision for it should be made in the primary law itself. The absence of a systematic provision in the EC Treaty was therefore a mistake. To a large extent, this lay behind the design of a new Energy Chapter in the proposed Constitution for Europe (see paras 2.57–2.60). Indeed, the most important sources of energy in the EU today—oil, natural gas, and electricity—received little or no express treatment in the original three founding legal instruments: the European Coal and Steel Community Treaty (now expired), the Euratom Treaty, and the Treaty of the European Economic Community. The only energy subjects expressly covered by law were coal, nuclear energy and, at a time of emergency in supply, oil.[6] One commentator has concluded that this situation was 'a serious flaw in the vision' of the progenitors of the Community.[7] Another has described the patchwork treatment of energy policy in the EC Treaty

---

[4] This view is expressed in Ehlermann, CD, 'The Role of the European Commission as Regards National Energy Policies' (1994) 12 J Energy Natural Resources L 342. For a historical review of the early period, see Daintith, T and Hancher, L, *Energy Strategy in Europe: The Legal Framework* (1986).

[5] Case 6/64 *Costa v Enel* [1964] ECR 1251. At a later date, this was reinforced by Case C-393/92 *Almelo Gemeente v NV Energiebedrijf Ijsselmij* [1994] ECR I-1477, and Cases C-157/94 *Commission v Netherlands*, C-158/94 *Commission v Italy* [1997] ECR I-5789, C-159/94 *Commission v France*, C-160/94 *Commission v Spain* [1997] ECR I-5699 et seq.

[6] There have been attempts to enlarge Community competences during crises in oil supply in the 1970s and during the Gulf War: see *Security of Supply, the Internal Market and Energy Policy*, Working Paper of the Commission of the EC, 1990, SEC (90) 1248; and later in the definition of common energy objectives.

[7] Green, N, 'The Legal Basis of a Community Energy Policy' (1983) 8 ELR 52–57, 52.

B. The Origins of an EU Acquis in Energy

as 'astonishing'.[8] The effect of this lacuna has been that for many years measures on energy have been adopted on the basis of powers conferred for other purposes, such as the internal market, competition matters, the environment or external relations.[9]

2.12 Whatever assessment one may make of the treatment of energy in the primary legislation of the EC Treaty, it is certainly true to say that for many years the application of those provisions relevant to the network-bound energy sector was virtually non-existent. Even for the European Commission, state monopolies of a commercial character 'were not perceived as an obstacle to the establishment of the first stages of the Common Market'.[10]

2.13 A key factor behind this state of affairs was the close relationship between Member State governments on the one hand and public undertakings in energy networks on the other. Throughout the Community's history, Member States have been reluctant to cede control over energy policy to the European institutions. If the absence of a systematic approach to energy constituted a flaw, it nevertheless received tacit approval from the majority of Member States, wishing to retain maximum control over their national energy regimes.[11] Moreover, given the diversity of aims of national energy policies, the instruments designed to achieve them, the industry structure as well as the resource base of each Member State, and not least, the strategic character of energy supplies for any modern state, this resistance to a centralized approach to energy policy was understandable.

(b) Coal

2.14 The first source of Community interest in energy matters can be found in the— now expired—European Coal and Steel Community Treaty 1951 (ECSC Treaty).[12]

---

[8] Schwarze, J, 'European Energy Policy in Community Law' in Mestmäker, EJ, (ed), *Natural Gas in the Internal Market* (1992) 155.

[9] The main powers are to: adopt measures for the approximation of provisions concerned with the establishment and functioning of the internal market (Art 95); establish a common commercial policy (if the measure relates to trade in raw materials, eg oil or coal; Art 133 EC); adopt research and development programmes and agreements (Title XVIII EC); adopt measures relating to the environment (Title XIX EC); take measures or conclude agreements in the area of development co-operation policy (Title XX EC), if they are part of the Community's co-operation with less developed countries; encourage the establishment and development of trans-European networks, if measure concerns energy infrastructures (Title XV EC); conclude association agreements under Art 238 EC, that provide inter alia for energy co-operation. Also relevant is Art 308 EC, where no other powers can be found and where the proposed measure meets the criteria in this article.

[10] Ehlermann, CD, 'The Role of the European Commission as Regards National Energy Policies' (1994) 12 J Energy Natural Resources L342.

[11] The close connection between energy policies and national interests as a limit to integration in the EU energy sector at the time is explored in Daintith, T, and Williams, S, *The Legal Integration of Energy Markets* (1987).

[12] ECSC Treaty (Treaty of Paris), Paris, 18 April 1951, UKTS 2 (1973); Cmnd 5189. Signed in Paris on 18 April 1951, entering into force on 25 July 1952, and expiring 50 years later, it is sometimes known as the Treaty of Paris. The Contracting Parties were also the six original Member States of the EEC: Belgium, France, Germany, Italy, Luxembourg, and the Netherlands (see Chapter 8).

The aim of the ECSC was to transfer control of national coal and steel industries from national authorities, particularly those of Germany and France, to a supranational authority (the High Authority). The Treaty provided far-reaching competences on market organization and some horizontal policies, such as research and development, as well as restructuring of the coal and steel industries. For example, Article 50 allowed the High Authority (now the European Commission) to raise levies on coal and steel production. The Treaty expired in July 2002 at which time the provisions of the Treaty lapsed and the coal industry became subject to the general provisions of the EC Treaty including those relating to competition (with a specific regime in respect of state aids) (see Chapter 8).

2.15 The Treaty did not seek to establish full competition in the EC coal industry. It created a system of regulated competition under which the Commission could intervene in the market in specific circumstances. However, the Treaty did contain specific regimes relating to anti-competitive agreements, abuse of a dominant position and also merger control.[13] It also contained social provisions on employment, cost of living, and supply[14] (and reconversion). The ECSC Treaty was in fact the only one of the original three Treaties to deal expressly with the social aspects of energy industry activity.

2.16 This early attempt at integration of the two key industrial sectors of continental Europe's most powerful states clearly accorded great weight to energy issues. Coal was at that time responsible for about 90 per cent of all energy consumed in the countries concerned. However, the provisions lost much of their significance when cheap oil imports supplanted the pre-eminence of coal in the ECSC countries. When demand exceeded supply it could be argued that a complex and quite sophisticated body of regulation was justified, allowing the High Authority to intervene in matters of pricing policy, competition policy, commercial policy, crisis management, and matters of financial and social concern. Once the hegemonic role of coal in the energy sector had disappeared, the Treaty provisions lost their justification in economic reality. In practice, the development of the coal market was influenced more and more by competition from other energy sources such as oil, natural gas, and nuclear power. However, it is certainly true to say that with a liberal interpretation of its state aid rules the Treaty enabled an orderly rundown of unprofitable national coal production.

(c) Nuclear Energy

2.17 The second instrument of integration to be aimed at the energy sector was the European Atomic Energy Community Treaty (Euratom) concluded in 1957.[15]

---

[13] ibid, Art 4.
[14] ibid, Arts 2 and 3.
[15] Euratom Treaty (Rome, 25 March 1957), UKTS 1 (1973) Pt II; Cmnd 5179–II. Signed at Rome on 25 March 1957. Entered into force on 1 January 1958. The Contracting Parties were the six Member States of the ECSC. The Treaty was concluded for an unlimited period.

B. The Origins of an EU Acquis in Energy

The task of Euratom was to create the conditions 'necessary for the speedy establishment and growth of nuclear industries' among the Member States (see paras 9.04–9.11).[16] To carry out its task the Community is required to act in areas specified in Article 2. They include the establishment of a nuclear common market as provided in the Treaty and the promotion of uniform health and safety standards to protect workers and the general public. Safeguards provisions—dealing with transfers of fissile materials—were intended as a contribution to non-proliferation.[17]

The Euratom Treaty had its origins in the Suez Crisis of 1956 in the Middle East. **2.18** It aimed at reducing energy import dependence upon that region and at countering the nuclear power dominance of the USA and USSR that had been established at that time. Its success turned on the willingness of key Member States to relinquish control over their national nuclear programmes.

However, in the event, a failure by Member States to agree on a common nuclear **2.19** policy left important gaps in the operation of the Treaty. The establishment of a centralized monopoly agency, charged with relating user needs to producer capacities and the availability of non-EC supplies, was fundamental to the Treaty. It was given the exclusive right to import nuclear materials into the Community and an exclusive right of purchase from producers within it. It was also given responsibility for the conclusion of contracts for the provision of such supplies. This centralized supply agency only became partly operational. The driving force behind such a body was clearly not the idea of an internal or common market but rather the idea that users could only receive a regular supply of ores and nuclear fuels by the establishment of a centralized monopoly supply agency.[18] Two further omissions may be noted.

First, the Euratom Treaty does not confer on the Community powers of jurisdiction **2.20** with respect to the use of nuclear fuels or nuclear installations for military purposes, nor powers over the safe design, construction, or operation of Member States' nuclear facilities and installations. It confers powers only over a quite narrow sector of activity. Its 'centre of gravity' has been in practice the development of research and the dissemination of technical knowledge.[19]

Secondly, a further limit on the operation of the Treaty arose from the adverse **2.21** fortunes of the commercial nuclear industry itself three decades after the Treaty

---

[16] ibid, Art 1.
[17] ibid, Title II, ch 7. Their success in implementation was limited, however.
[18] For background, see Grünwald, J, 'The Role of Euratom' in Cameron, P, Hancher, L, and Kühn, W, (eds), *Nuclear Energy Law After Chernobyl* (1988) 32 and Allen, D, 'The Euratom Treaty, Chapter IV: New Hope or False Dawn?' (1983) 20 CML Rev 473; Daintith, T, and Hancher, L, *Energy Strategy in Europe: The Legal Framework* (1986) 15.
[19] Kapteyn, PJG and VerLoren van Themaat, P, (eds), *Introduction to the Law of the European Communities: From Maastricht to Amsterdam* (1998) 1218.

was concluded. After a period of rapid expansion, public opinion in the EU moved against the use of nuclear power after the nuclear accident at Chernobyl in 1986, and the economics of nuclear power appeared increasingly unattractive during a long period of low energy prices which lasted until quite recently.

(d) EEC Treaty

2.22 Of the three treaties the more general instrument of integration was the Treaty establishing the European Economic Community. It was entered into between the six original Member States in 1957 (the EEC Treaty), and subsequently renamed the European Community Treaty (EC Treaty). The scope of the EEC Treaty was much broader than the other two treaties. Article 2 described the task of the Community as one in which, by establishing a common market and 'progressively approximating the economic policies of the Member States', it would:

> ... promote throughout the Community a harmonious development of economic activities, a continuous and balanced expansion, an increase in stability, an accelerated raising of the standard of living, and closer relationships between the States belonging to it.

2.23 The EEC Treaty contained specific provisions dealing with the establishment of the common market, although none specifically providing for a common energy policy.[20] Some provisions of the EC Treaty are highly relevant to energy activities, and especially to the electricity and gas businesses. The rules falling under Articles 28 to 31 and those falling under Article 86 are of particular relevance.

2.24 Articles 28 and 29 prohibit quantitative restrictions on imports and exports and all measures with an equivalent effect. The ECJ has held that 'quantitative restrictions' includes all national measures and rules capable of hindering trade, no matter what their intended result.[21] There are however two sources of exceptions, deriving from Article 30 and in particular the 'public security' exemption and the 'rule of reason' exception which has been developed in the case law for the application of Article 28.

2.25 **Article 31** Article 31 requires Member States progressively to adjust state monopolies of a commercial character through which a Member State supervises, determines, or appreciably influences imports or exports between Member States.

---

[20] cf *Rapport des Chefs de Délégations aux Ministères des Affaires Étrangères* (Secretariat of the Inter-Governmental Conference, Brussels, 21 April 1956 (the Spaak Report)). The Report had identified energy and especially oil as an area for urgent attention but this was not taken further. A widely held view at the time, which led to non-action in this area, was that oil companies were well-equipped to deal with issues in this sector.

[21] Case 8/74 *Procureur du Roi v Dassonville* [1974] ECR 837.

B. The Origins of an EU Acquis in Energy

The enforcement of this requirement is a matter for the Commission.[22] It may use its powers under Article 226 to bring a case against a Member State before the ECJ for breach of obligations under the Treaty, subject to the Member State first being given an opportunity to submit its observations on the complaint to the Commission. In the early days, the Commission used its powers under Article 31 to pursue the dismantling of 'oil products monopolies' in France and Greece— successfully, albeit over a very long period of time.[23] It also had success in using Article 31 to persuade the Belgian Government to remove the statutory exclusive right of the then state-owned gas utility, Distrigas, to import gas. In 2006 it opened an infringement procedure against Malta for a failure to comply with Article 31 and abolish its monopoly for the import, storage, and wholesale of petroleum products.

Article 86 and public service obligations Under Article 86 the Commission is required (inter alia) to ensure that the rules of the Treaty (including, inter alia, Articles 31, 81, and 82) are complied with. Article 86(1) imposes upon Member States the obligation not to enact or maintain in force any measures contrary to Treaty rules with respect to public undertakings or undertakings to which they have granted special or exclusive rights. Article 86(1) acknowledges that Member States may create public undertakings (ie state owned/controlled companies) and also grant to such undertakings or private undertakings special or exclusive rights (eg, in transmission and/or distribution) subject to the proviso that the legal measures by which they create these undertakings or grant special or exclusive rights do not contain any provisions contrary to the rules of the EC Treaty. It was not until the early 1990s that a number of cases came before the ECJ which provided it with the opportunity to clarify the relationship between the provisions of Article 86(1), the provisions of Article 82, and Articles 29 to 32. Also the ECJ assisted in the clarification of exemptions under Article 86(2)—see Chapter 16 for analyses of a number of these cases, including *Höfner, Port of Genoa* and *Corbeau (Belgian Postal Monopoly)*.[24] Essentially, these judgments opened up to legal challenge

2.26

---

[22] Note that individuals may invoke their rights independently in national courts where the provisions of the Treaty have direct effect: *Allgemene Transport en Expedetie Onderneming Van Gend en Loos v Nederlandse Administratie der Belastingen* [1963] ECR 1; for a discussion of the doctrine of direct effect in relation to this case see Chalmers, D, Hadjiemmanuil, C, Monti, G, and Tomkins, A, *European Union Law* (2006) 365–81.

[23] Sixth Report on Competition Policy (1977), points 268–9 (France); Case C-347/88 *Commission v Greece* [1990] ECR 4747. In this context see also the judgment in Case 72/83 *Campus Oil Ltd v Minister for Industry and Energy* [1984] ECR 277.

[24] Case C-41/90 *Klaus Höfner and Fritz Elser v Macrotron GmbH* [1991] ECR I-1979; Case C-320/91 *Corbeau* [1993] ECR I-2533; Case C-179/90 *Merci Convenzionali Porto di Genova SpA v Siderurgica Gabriella SpA* [1991] ECR I-1979. The ECJ ruled that the grant of a special or exclusive right was lawful even if it gave the undertaking concerned a dominant position in the relevant market, but that the exercise of that right was subject to the provisions of Art 82 and that the exercise of that right could in itself be held to be unlawful.

under the competition rules of the EC Treaty any exclusive generating, transportation, distribution, and supply rights—and made it possible to begin the opening up of the electricity and gas markets to new entrants.

2.27 Article 86(2) provides an exemption, narrowly drawn, from the reach of the Treaty (particularly competition) for undertakings entrusted with the operation of services of general economic interest. Services of a general economic interest include essential services provided for the public at large. They include the provision of water, electricity, and gas. Special obligations ('public service obligations') are frequently placed on the providers of such services. Such obligations include security, including security of supply, regularity, quality and price of supplies, and environmental protection. They may also include specific obligations relating to the supply of electricity and gas to householders, the poor, and disabled people. In return for the acceptance of such obligations, Member States have granted special or exclusive rights.[25] The undertakings which accept such public service obligations may be able to obtain an exemption from the application of the competition rules under the provisions of Article 86(2). It is worth emphasizing how fundamental the idea of services of general economic interest is to the EU.[26] Article 16 EC states that they have a place in the shared values of the EU and in the promotion of social and economic cohesion, and the Commission has produced a package of documents on this subject.[27]

2.28 **Articles 81 and 82** There are two other articles of the EC Treaty which have been relevant to liberalization. These are: Article 82, which prohibits companies in a dominant position from abusing that position and is therefore also relevant to the energy sector (applicable to refusals of access to networks); and Article 81 which prohibits anti-competitive agreements. Both articles apply to public and private undertakings equally. A number of Commission decisions applying these articles are discussed in Chapters 12 and 13.

2.29 **Articles 87 to 89** Finally, mention should be made of the articles on state aids. These have become increasingly relevant to energy. They prohibit the provision of state aids where they threaten to distort trade, but create exceptions and are subject to EC policing.

2.30 However, despite the existence of these provisions of the EC Treaty, it was not until the decisions of the ECJ interpreting Article 86(1) in conjunction with

---

[25] See generally, Buendia Sierra, JL, *Exclusive Rights and State Monopolies under EC Law* (1999).
[26] European Commission, *Communication on Services of General Interest in Europe* [2001] OJ C17/4.
[27] Commission Press Release IP/04/235, 'Commission proposes new rules to increase legal certainty for services of general economic interest', 18 February 2004; COM (2003) 270, 21 May 2003; COM (2004) 374, 12 May 2004, and see generally <http://ec.europa.eu/services_general_interest/index_en.htm>.

B. The Origins of an EU Acquis in Energy

Article 82, that action was taken against exclusive rights of transmission, distribution, and supply existing in the Member States that had made it impossible or futile for potential applicants to try to gain access to networks (see para 2.26). Prior to this, the Commission responded to the lacuna in the Treaty by making several efforts to develop a Community energy policy.

(e) A European Energy Policy: First Steps

The 1960s As early as 1964, a Protocol of Agreement between the Member States on energy problems was drawn up.[28] This resulted from a growing awareness that the global character of energy issues was covered by no less than three different Treaties and three different bodies of institutions with no provision for co-ordination. It comprised a statement of objectives and principles, an agenda, and a procedural agreement. In 1967 the Council took a decision on Community policy concerning oil and gas.[29] In 1968, the Commission outlined the first guidelines of a Community energy policy in a Communication to the Council, noting that '[t]here are still considerable barriers in trade in energy products within the Community'.[30] If this state of affairs did not alter, it argued, and if a common energy market were not achieved in the near future, 'the degree of integration achieved in this sector may well be jeopardised'.[31] In contrast to Community policy on coal and nuclear energy, the Commission assigned considerable weight to the market mechanism as a co-ordinating instrument. Further, in 1968 an obligation was imposed upon Member States to maintain a minimum level of stocks of oil and/or petroleum products.[32]

2.31

1980s: good intentions overtaken by oil price collapse After several failed attempts, and in spite of various emergency measures taken during and after the energy crises of the 1970s,[33] the idea of a Community energy policy gave way to a new approach to energy strategy in 1981.[34] This abandoned any attempt at a transfer of

2.32

---

[28] [1964] OJ 1009.

[29] Council doc 1014/67.

[30] *First orientation for a common energy policy*, Communication from the Commission to the Council, 18 December 1968, p 9, para 4.

[31] ibid.

[32] Directive (EEC) 68/414 imposing an obligation on Member States of the EEC to maintain minimum stocks of crude oil and/or petroleum products [1968] OJ L308/14, as amended by Directive (EC) 98/93 [1998] OJ L358/100.

[33] The Community measures focused on crisis management and energy saving. In the former case, Directive 73/278 was adopted, implementing the rules of the International Energy Agency. They are supplemented by an agreement between the major oil companies, exempted under Art 85(3): *International Energy Agency* Decision 83/671 [1983] OJ L376/30, renewed by Decision 94/153 [1994] OJ L68/35. Energy savings measures were included in Decision 77/706 [1977] OJ L292/9. Other measures restricting the use of natural gas and petroleum products in power stations have since been repealed.

[34] *Development of an Energy Strategy for the Community*, COM (1981) 540 final.

competence, a centralized decision-making process, or the creation of EC rules on a common policy. A leading EC official at the time put it in this way: 'The strategy ... accepts more that action is better taken at national level, subject always to the constraint that it contributes to a common effort but Community initiatives are advantageous ... whenever and wherever it seems necessary or more effective'.[35] A common policy would therefore be justified only in those areas where the Community possessed specific or exclusive powers.

2.33 In 1983 the Council made a formal declaration that there was a need to identify common energy objectives to be co-ordinated across the Community and at the same time to strengthen national measures.[36] In 1986 a Council Resolution set out various energy policy objectives to be achieved by 1995.[37] Principal features were security of supply and price stability. A convergence of the energy policies of the Member States was envisaged.

2.34 However, this strategy-oriented approach was overtaken by events. In particular, the precipitous fall in oil prices in 1986 led Member States to abandon their agreed targets to achieve energy efficiency and common goals. It also underlined the vulnerability of European economies to outside forces in the supply of their energy. This generated efforts by the Commission to secure agreement with important external suppliers, including attempts to establish a general free trade and co-operation agreement with members of the Gulf Co-operation Council (GCC—a group of countries ranking among the main suppliers of oil to the Community). These proved unsuccessful due to the inability of GCC members to agree on certain prerequisites, such as the establishment of a common customs tariff. Links were in fact established with institutions grouping various oil producing countries: OAPEC and subsequently OPEC. These led to exchanges of information but not to agreements or arrangements of a legal character.

2.35 Throughout this period the energy sector had proved resistant to the integration process. However, it was not unique in this respect. Progress towards the removal of barriers to trade in other sectors of industry and commerce was also slow. The legislation and practices of Member States displayed a very considerable number of barriers to the 'four freedoms': free movement of goods, persons, services, and capital—cornerstones of the common market. This situation had improved slightly during the 1970s but it became increasingly apparent that without a new impetus the level of integration implied by the idea of a common market as envisaged by the architects of the EEC Treaty would not come into existence.

---

[35] De Bauw, R, *Legal Implementation of Energy Policy*, paper presented to EU Colloquium, European University Institute, Florence, Italy, September 1982.
[36] The Declaration was made in November 1983. Council Resolutions on energy objectives were made earlier in 1974 and 1980 ([1975] OJ C153/1 and [1980] OJ C149/1, respectively).
[37] [1986] OJ C241/1.

B. The Origins of an EU Acquis in Energy

(2) The Single European Act

2.36 To make further progress in integration, modifications in the Treaty framework were required. These were made through a Treaty known as the Single European Act (SEA),[38] which amended all three Treaties establishing the European Communities. The most significant of the changes were those made to the EEC Treaty to enable the internal market to be completed by removing the remaining barriers to trade within the Community before the end of December 1992. Amendments affecting the energy sector in particular were:

(1) those on the establishment of the objective of an internal market by the end of 1992;
(2) a streamlining of Council decision-making procedures on internal market matters; and
(3) the enforcement of the role of the European Parliament in the review of legislation.

(a) An Internal Market by the End of 1992 (Article 8A)

2.37 A new article was added to the Treaty, providing that the Community adopt measures to establish the internal market progressively over a period expiring on 31 December 1992. It defined the concept of the internal market as comprising 'an area without internal frontiers in which the free movement of goods, persons, services and capital is ensured' in accordance with the EC Treaty.[39] Implications were elucidated by a Declaration on the article.[40] Through this the Inter-Governmental Conference expressed its 'firm political will' to take prior to 1 January 1993 'the decisions necessary to complete the internal market defined in those provisions'. This extended to the implementation of the Commission's programme described in the White Paper on the Internal Market.[41] In fact, the idea of an internal (or common) market was not at all novel, but the setting of a deadline was, and the improvement of harmonization procedures was a positive development for policy co-ordination.

2.38 The White Paper referred to in the Declaration is the Commission's White Paper to the Council of Ministers on 'Completing the Internal Market',[42] submitted in 1985. It set out the tasks that the Commission saw as being necessary for the completion of the internal market. Among its general provisions, several were of

---

[38] [1987] OJ L169/1. It was signed by the 12 Member States at Luxembourg on 17 February 1986 and The Hague on 28 February 1986, and entered into force on 1 July 1987.
[39] Art 8(A), second para.
[40] Declaration 3, contained in the Final Act, a document forming part of the SEA.
[41] The Declaration concludes with the words: 'Setting the date of 31 December 1992 does not create an automatic legal effect'.
[42] COM (1985) 310 final, Brussels, 14 June 1985.

Chapter 2: The EU Legal Order and Energy

importance to the energy industry, although energy as such was omitted from the White Paper. These included the application of the Community Law[43] and the removal of territorial barriers—in particular the approximation of indirect taxation.[44]

(b) Streamlining Decision-making Procedures

2.39 The second change introduced by the SEA concerned voting procedures within the Council of Ministers. A qualified majority system of voting was to apply in relation to measures involving the achievement of the objectives of the new Article 8(A). The existing system of voting that imposed a formal requirement of unanimity remained in effect with respect to many but not all other decisions of the Council. The relevant provisions were contained in a new Article 100A (now Article 95) of the EC Treaty providing that:

> The Council shall acting by way of a qualified majority on a proposal from the Commission in co-operation with the European Parliament and after consulting with the Economic and Social Committee, adopt the measures for the approximation of the provisions laid down by law, regulation, or administrative action in Member States which have as their object the establishment and functioning of the internal market.

2.40 The effect of the additions to Articles 8 and 100 was to enhance the possibility of taking legislative steps to break up the existing compartmentalized energy market. It was now only necessary to obtain a qualified majority in the Council of Ministers in relation to harmonization measures proposed under Article 8A. This supplemented the legislative routes open to the Commission under existing Treaty rules that might have provided a basis for abolishing the segmented character of the energy markets. In this context, it may be noted that the weighting of votes had changed as a result of the accession of Spain and Portugal, with the effect that whereas before 1986 only one of the larger Member States could be outvoted, afterwards two could be outvoted.

(c) Predecessor to Co-decision: the Co-operation Procedure

2.41 Finally, it may be noted that the role of the Parliament in the legislative process expanded as a result of a new co-operation procedure, introduced through an amendment of Article 149 of the EEC Treaty and applied to almost all internal market legislation. This was to prove an important first step in securing additional legitimacy for the Commission's proposals for completion of the internal market in energy.

2.42 Under the co-operation procedure, a Commission proposal for legislation is sent to Parliament as well as the Council. Parliament, after a first reading, notifies the Council of its opinion. The Council then adopts a common position—taking

---

[43] ibid, paras 152–9.
[44] ibid, paras 185 et seq.

B. The Origins of an EU Acquis in Energy

into account the Commission's proposal, Parliament's opinion and its own deliberations—which is sent to Parliament for a second reading. Within a three-month period, Parliament may accept the common position, refrain from acting, reject it, or propose amendments to the common position. If the Commission accepts those amendments, the Council can accept them by a qualified majority vote. If Parliament rejects the common position, the Council can only adopt the instrument unanimously. This procedure was, in relation to many measures including internal energy market ones, replaced in 1993 by the co-decision procedure, which for the first time gave Parliament the right to block measures approved in Council.

Articles 174 and 175 Further changes were made within the framework of environmental policy that had a bearing on the energy sector. Article 174 referred to the 'prudent and rational utilisation of natural resources', while Article 175 concerned the adoption of 'measures significantly affecting a Member State's choice between different energy sources and the general structure of its energy supply'. However, in a Declaration on this Article, the Inter-Governmental Conference noted that the Community's activities in environmental matters may not interfere with national policies on the exploitation of energy resources. **2.43**

1988 inventory of obstacles to an internal energy market The Single European Act was to prove a turning point in the integration process, especially with respect to energy. The Commission took it as a green light to initiate a study of the EU energy sector in the context of the proposed completion of the single market by 1992. The Energy Council of June 1987 authorized the Commission's proposal to draw up an inventory of existing obstacles to an internal energy market, and to submit recommendations for their progressive elimination. Extensive consultations were held. Contributions were submitted to the Commission by 'a hundred or so organizations and enterprises representing all the Member States, all the energy sources and both energy producers and energy users'.[45] The result, published the following year, was a report based on a comprehensive inventory outlining the expected results of an internal energy market and the main priorities to be addressed to remove the obstacles to its creation.[46] It favoured a parallel approach to the removal of the obstacles, applying the existing rules of EC law and submitting specific initiatives in the form of Directives. The Council gave its support to this approach.[47] **2.44**

This development of primary legislation in the SEA was to have an effect in a very different context from those in which the three treaties had been concluded. **2.45**

---

[45] European Commission, *Energy in Europe: Special Issue on the Internal Energy Market*, 6.
[46] *The Internal Energy Market*, COM (1988) 238 final, 2 May 1988.
[47] *Energy in Europe*, Presidency Conclusions, 59, point 4.

The European entity to which the new provisions were to apply was much enlarged. The first enlargement saw the accession of the UK, Denmark, and Ireland on 1 January 1973,[48] Greece subsequently on 1 January 1981,[49] and Spain and Portugal on 1 January 1986.[50] The diversity of energy policies and practices within the EC grew correspondingly. In this context it would prove harder to sustain the tacit consensus among the Member States that energy matters should be kept out of the integration process.

(3) Treaty on European Union (Maastricht)

2.46 The Treaty on European Union (TEU) made further important changes to the Treaties especially through Titles II, III, and IV.[51] It was signed in Maastricht in the Netherlands on 7 February 1992 and entered into force on 1 November 1993. It established the European Union. The EEC Treaty (as amended) became the EC Treaty.

2.47 Among the various changes made by the Treaty, one deserves particular emphasis in the context of the Internal Energy Market programme. The notion of 'subsidiarity' was introduced as a principle of general application instead of being restricted to environmental matters as it had appeared in the SEA.[52] In Article 3B (now Article 5), it is stated that:

> In areas which do not fall within its exclusive competence, the Community shall take action, in accordance with the principle of subsidiarity, only if and in so far as the objectives of the proposed action cannot be sufficiently achieved by the Member States and can therefore, by reason of the scale or effects of the proposed action, be better achieved by the Community.

2.48 The application of this principle requires a delicate and case-by-case balancing of central and national authority in the law-making process. In areas where the Community does not have exclusive competence, the principle must be applied to decide whether in a given case it is appropriate for the Community (and its

---

[48] Treaty concerning the Accession of the Kingdom of Denmark, Ireland, the Kingdom of Norway, and the United Kingdom of Great Britain and Northern Ireland to the European Economic Community and the European Atomic Energy Community, Brussels, 22 January 1972 (UKTS 18 (1979); Cmnd 7463; [1972] OJ L73/5), and Declaration of Accession to the European Coal and Steel Community, ibid. Following a negative result in a referendum, Norway did not ratify the Treaty and the instruments of accession were amended accordingly: see Council Decision of 1 January 1973 [1973] OJ L2/1.
[49] Treaty of Accession 1979 (EC 18) (1979); Cmnd 7650; [1979] OJ L291/9.
[50] Treaty of Accession 1985 (EC 27) (1985); Cmnd 9634; [1985] OJ L302/9.
[51] UKTS 12 (1994); Cmnd 2485; [1992] OJ C191/1. Signed by the 12 Member States at Maastricht on 12 February 1992, it came into force on 1 November 1993.
[52] Art 130r(4) provided that 'the Community shall take action relating to the environment to the extent to which the objectives . . . can be attained better at Community level than at the level of the individual Member States'.

B. The Origins of an EU Acquis in Energy

institutions) to take action. It may be invoked to justify Community action but also to oppose it. Since it appears in the body of the Treaty, it binds the Community institutions and can give rise to annulment under Article 230 if it is disregarded. Indeed, the Commission is obliged to provide a justification for a proposed legislative measure in terms of subsidiarity in the explanatory memorandum.[53] However, its exact scope is unclear and the ECJ has yet to provide a detailed exposition of its flexibility and meaning. In the meantime, the principle has also been the subject of criticism from various legal authorities.[54]

(a) Subsidiarity

For the energy sector subsidiarity is a principle that has had particular significance. **2.49** It has both contributed to and constrained the Commission in its attempts to promote a single market in energy. While it has facilitated the making of proposals to act in this field with respect to the distribution of powers between Member States and Community institutions, it has also made their relations more complex and open-ended by encouraging a reliance on framework Directives as the favoured instrument for change. For example, the explanatory memorandum to the proposals for the first Directives on common rules for electricity and gas interpreted subsidiarity to mean that:

> The Community must not impose rigid mechanisms, but rather should define a framework enabling Member States to opt for the system best suited to their natural resources, the state of their industry and their energy policies.[55]

This leaves much scope to national authorities when incorporating the provisions of the Directives into national law.

In addition, the TEU brought about an increase in the subjects on which legislative **2.50** decisions could be taken by qualified majority voting in the Council.

No specific provisions on energy were added—with the exception of Article 3(1)(u), **2.51** which lists measures in the 'spheres of energy, civil protection and tourism' as one of the Community's common policies or activities; and Declaration No 1 annexed to the new Treaty which referred to 'the question of introducing into the Treaty Titles relating to the spheres referred to in Article 3(1)(u) . . . on the basis of a report which

---

[53] Inter-institutional Agreement on Procedures for Implementing the Principle of Subsidiarity, concluded between the European Parliament, Council, and Commission, 25 October 1993, [1993] OJ C329/135.

[54] Toth, A, 'A Legal Analysis of Subsidiarity' in O'Keeffe, D, (ed), *Legal Issues of the Maastricht Treaty* (1994) 37; Steiner, J, 'Subsidiarity under the Maastricht Treaty' in ibid, 49; Lenaerts, K, 'The Principle of Subsidiarity and the Environment in the European Union: Keeping the Balance of Federalism' (1994) 17 Fordham Intl LJ 846; Brinkhorst, L, 'Subsidiarity and EC Environmental Policy' (1993) 8 European Environmental L Rev 20.

[55] Amended Proposals for a European Parliament and Council Directive on common rules for the internal market in electricity, COM (1993) 643 final, [1993] OJ C123/1.

the Commission will submit to the Council by 1996 at the latest'. Article 129b on Trans-European Networks also included a reference to energy.

2.52 This was rather modest progress given the original proposals to include a separate chapter on energy in the Treaty negotiations—caused by failure of the Member States to agree on further EU competences going beyond those already existing in the Treaties.

2.53 **Enhanced role for Parliament: the co-decision procedure** Importantly, the Treaty further enhanced the role of the Parliament in the legislative process with respect to internal market legislation, especially vis-à-vis the Commission. At the second reading stage, Parliament and the Council are required to proceed in co-decision. Parliament has three months in which to agree with the Council's common position, refrain from reacting to it, make amendments to it, or reject it. In the latter two cases, a Conciliation Committee is set up comprising representatives of the Council and Parliament in equal proportions with the task of negotiating a compromise. This requirement to hold a direct dialogue between the two institutions to secure an agreement contrasts with the SEA regime, under which only those Parliamentary amendments supported by the Commission could be adopted by a majority in the Council.

2.54 This co-decision procedure with the Council was applied to all Internal Market legislation and some other areas.

(4) Constitutional Fatigue: From Amsterdam to Nice and Beyond

2.55 The impending enlargement to include ten countries from the eastern parts of Europe by 2004 provided an incentive to streamline decision-making through the extension of co-decision and majority voting. After a further Inter-Governmental conference, the Treaty of Amsterdam came into force in 1997. Twenty-four areas moved to QMV from unanimity. Many other changes were introduced but they are less relevant to the subject of this book, such as the idea of an Area of Freedom, Security and Justice. Soon afterwards, a further Treaty—the Treaty of Nice—continued the 'managerial' process of preparing the EU for enlargement that had started at Amsterdam.[56] Among the matters dealt with were the size and composition of the Commission, the re-weighting of votes in the Council and the possible extension of QMV. It extended QMV to 31 new areas, but most of these were procedural in character. The result of these latest and not very successful conferences was that, as one writer comments:

> The Union now had a bewildering and confusing gamut of competences, governed by an array of legislative procedures, producing a range of legal instruments, many with very different legal effects.[57]

---

[56] Treaty of Nice, Amending the Treaty on European Union, The Treaties Establishing the European Communities, and certain Related Acts [2001] OJ C80/1. All references to the Treaty are to this version as amended by the Accession Act 2003.

[57] Chalmers, D, Hadjiemmanuil, C, Monti, G, and Tomkins, A, *European Union Law*, 42.

B. The Origins of an EU Acquis in Energy

The outcome was a revival of the idea of a Constitution that would among other things prepare and re-design the European institutions for enlargement and codify and consolidate the various parts of the European legislation into a single document, including the TEU, the EC Treaty and the various Accession Treaties.[58] Following two negative referendum results, this Treaty has been shelved. Its content is not without interest however, and the fact that a large number of Member States have in fact ratified it, indicates that for many Member States the central ideas that it contains are at least satisfactory. In particular, it is worth noting two aspects of the draft Constitution that are relevant to this book: the proposed chapter on energy and the various provisions on services of general economic interest. 2.56

(5) The Proposed Energy Article and the Question of Competences

The idea that energy should have express recognition in the founding documents of the EU has a long history. Looking back to the Single European Act of 1986 or the Treaty on European Union, it is notable that there is no reference to an energy policy or other energy provision in spite of the fact that there were proposals for their inclusion—which were rejected. This underlined the Member States' wish to retain their competence over energy. Article 3 of the Maastricht Treaty had introduced a specific competence, albeit in rather vague terms: 'the activities of the Community shall include... measures in the spheres of energy, civil protection and tourism'. Subsequently, the Commission carried out its task according to Declaration No 1 of the Maastricht Treaty, producing a proposal for an energy chapter which would either have consolidated the provisions of the three Treaties or have introduced a new chapter pursuing the completion of the single market, environmental protection, and measures to improve security of supply.[59] Although the proposal was noted by the Council of Ministers in May 1996, no action was taken or encouraged. Two months prior to the Amsterdam Inter-Governmental Conference, the Commission issued a further document.[60] It also had no effect. 2.57

An alternative approach adopted by the Commission was to advocate a greater co-ordination of existing EU competences.[61] The impetus to both of these initiatives was the absence of a clear competence on energy matters which led to a dependence upon a number of EU competences that have a bearing upon energy policy: for example, the single market rules including technical and tax harmonization and 2.58

---

[58] British Management Data Foundation, *The European Constitution in Perspective: Analysis and Review of The Treaty Establishing a Constitution for Europe* (2004).

[59] COM (1996) 496 final, 3 April 1996. There was an earlier report by the Commission for the Reflection Group chaired by Carlos Westendorp in May 1995 prior to the EC Inter-Governmental Conference in 1996.

[60] European Commission, *An Overall View of Energy Policy and Actions*, COM (1997) 167, 23 April 1997.

[61] *Towards an EU Energy Policy*, COM (1995) 682 final, 13 December 1995 (the White Paper).

public procurement; environment, regional, and competition policy; and the TENs policy. However, it is questionable whether these are so inadequate that a new chapter is required. At a later date, during the discussions on the Treaty of Nice text, the Portuguese Presidency noted that an 'issue to be addressed' was whether the repeated use of Article 308 in areas such as energy, external competence, and the establishment of decentralized agencies justified the creation in the EC Treaty of a specific legal basis requiring a qualified majority.[62] However, the proposal was dropped.

2.59 The draft Constitution took a bolder step in this direction, and declared that energy is a 'shared competence' between the Union and the Member States. This means that under Article I-12(2) the Union and the Member States may legislate and adopt legally binding acts in that area. The Member States are to exercise their competence to the extent that the Union has not exercised or has decided to cease exercising its competence. The provision in Section 10, Article III-256 falls within Chapter III concerned with 'Policies in Other Areas' (than say economic or monetary policy), and reads as follows:

> 1. In the context of the establishment and functioning of the internal market and with regard for the need to preserve and improve the environment, Union policy on energy shall aim to:
> (a) ensure the functioning of the energy market;
> (b) ensure security of energy supply in the Union, and
> (c) promote energy efficiency and energy saving and the development of new and renewable forms of energy.
> 2. Without prejudice to the application of other provisions of the Constitution, the objectives of paragraph 1 shall be achieved by measures enacted in European laws or framework laws. Such laws or framework laws shall be adopted after consultation of the Committee of the Regions and the Economic and Social Committee.
>
> Such European laws or framework laws shall not affect a Member State's right to determine the conditions for exploiting its energy resources, its choice between different energy sources and the general structure of its energy supply, without prejudice to Article III-234(2)(c).
> 3. By way of derogation from paragraph 2, a European law or framework law of the Council shall establish the measures referred to therein when they are primarily of a fiscal nature. The Council shall act unanimously after consulting the European Parliament.

2.60 The short provision would have made energy a 'policy' alongside existing policies such as 'environment', 'social policy', 'agriculture and fisheries' and 'trans-European networks'. It would have given formal recognition to a situation that had already emerged in practice, with the adoption of a comprehensive sector-specific energy

---

[62] Conference of the Representatives of the Governments of the Member States, 22 February 2000, CONFER 4711/00.

law regime and specialist regulatory institutions. However, in dealing with the long-standing question of competence, it would also have placed energy into a horizontal zone of policies in which no clear priority exists, and in dealing with any particular issue a balancing of policy priorities is required: a situation that has already occurred with respect to competition and environmental policies. This point is underlined by the Constitution's efforts to initiate a proactive policy to ensure that the citizens of Europe have access to the best service. Under Article III-122 the Union and the Member States 'shall take care that such services (of general economic interest) operate on the basis of principles and conditions, in particular economic and financial conditions, which allow them to fulfil their missions. European laws shall establish these principles and set these conditions . . . to provide, to commission and to fund such services'. Elsewhere, in Article II-96, it is stated that 'the Union recognizes and respects access to services of general economic interest as provided for in national laws and practices . . . in order to promote the social and territorial cohesion of the Union'. It would be very hard not to see the provision of electricity and probably gas too as falling within the scope of these provisions, with all the potential for tensions arising from the exercise of 'constitutional rights' to energy services and decision-making by suppliers on more or less economic grounds.[63]

(6) Conclusions on the Development of an Energy *Acquis*

2.61 For many years the growing importance of energy law in the EU has made no impact on the various high-level schemes to modify and expand the scope of primary legislation, even if it has benefited from their more consensual orientation. Ironically, amidst the turmoil of the debate on the Constitution, a formal recognition emerged of the current importance of energy in the EU legal order—only to disappear very soon after. As a result, the growing body of EU energy law and de facto if not *de jure* energy policy continues to develop on the back of other, more established, legal and policy competences.

2.62 The Constitutional episode highlighted the real tensions that exist between energy as de facto a policy and other undisputed policies of the EU: in particular, the relationship between competition and public service or services of a general interest, and, perhaps to a lesser extent but still of importance, between competition policy and environmental policy. Energy issues intrude into all of these established policy areas, each of which will from time to time claim energy as their own.

2.63 The institution that has the principal responsibility for ensuring that the result of this is an orderly and effective balancing of priorities is the European Commission.

---

[63] There have been a number of critical commentaries on the energy article in the draft Constitution: see eg, Rashbrooke, G, 'Clarification or Complication: The New Energy Title in the Draft Constitution for Europe' (2004) 22 J Energy Natural Resources L373–87.

Since it is the lead—if not at all the only—actor in the legal processes that are the subject of this book, it merits some extended introduction of its role.

C. The European Commission in its Institutional Setting

2.64 The motor driving liberalization in the EU energy sector has been and remains the European Commission. It has been the key European institution behind the adoption and promotion of the internal energy market programme—frequently in the face of strong opposition from individual Member States and incumbent market players.[64] It remains in a central, leading role with respect to energy market developments in spite of the growing importance of specialist national regulators and competition authorities in the enforcement of EU law. It is therefore important to have some understanding of how the Commission acts within the broad institutional framework and the law-making process of the EU, and how its role has developed over the period since the sector-specific legislation was first put in place.[65]

(1) The Commission and Commissioners: Functions and Powers

2.65 The Commission[66] is composed of 27 members known as Commissioners, one of whom is nominated as President by the Heads of State or governments of the Member States. This choice is made prior to the appointment of the other Commissioners. The governments of the Member States nominate the other persons whom they intend to appoint as Members of the Commission in agreement with the nominee for Commission President. Both the nominee President and the members-designate are subject to a collective vote of approval by Parliament. After such approval, they are appointed by common accord of the governments of the Member States. The Members of the Commission are appointed for a five-year term, which may be renewed. Currently, each Member State has one Commissioner. A maximum of two Vice Presidents may be appointed by the Commissioners themselves from among their number.

2.66 Each Commissioner is required to be independent in the exercise of his or her duties. The Commission bears collective responsibility for its acts. It takes decisions by simple majority vote. Under the Treaties of Maastricht and Amsterdam the powers of Parliamentary scrutiny of the Commission and its legislative proposals were enhanced. Previously, its powers were limited to the power to force the resignation of the entire Commission through a vote of censure or no confidence.

---

[64] This view of the Commission is based on that argued for by Usher, J, in 'The Commission and the Law' in Edwards, G, and Spence, D, (eds), *The European Commission* (1994) 212.
[65] For a recent overview of the various institutions, see Chalmers, D, et al, *European Union Law* (2006) ch 3.
[66] See generally, Arts 211–19 and 249–56 EC.

C. The European Commission in its Institutional Setting

The Commissioners are supported by 26 Directorates-General (DGs) and a body of specialized services, including a Legal Service. Each DG is headed by a Director-General, with rank equivalent to the top civil servant in a government ministry. Political and operational responsibility for one or more DGs is allocated to a Commissioner, who also has a private office or 'cabinet'. The latter consists of six officials who act as the channel between the Commissioner and the DGs. The overall work of the Commission is managed by a secretary-general. **2.67**

The principal functions of the Commission are threefold. It: **2.68**

(1) is the main initiator of EC policy;
(2) has a wide range of executive and regulatory functions and a limited law-making role; and
(3) acts as the guardian of the Treaties (ensuring that Treaty obligations are observed).[67]

(a) Legislative Role

This is an important role since the Council of Ministers, in exercising its legislative powers under the EC Treaty, can normally only act on proposals submitted to it by the Commission. However, it is the Council that makes the principal decisions on EU policies and priorities and decides on major legislation in co-decision or consultation with the Parliament. The Commission is also limited by the principle of subsidiarity, which it is obliged to take into account. It may initiate legislation only in those areas where the EU is better placed than individual Member States to take effective action. **2.69**

The Commission can act, basing itself on the EC Treaty, either: **2.70**

- where the power is specifically granted as in Article 86 (where a Member State is making improper use of the powers provided to it by this Article); or
- under the more general power in Article 308 (to propose action to the Council to attain Community objectives; matters not specifically identified in the EC Treaty).

In addition, under Article 284 of the Treaty, the Commission may collect any information and carry out any checks required for the performance of its tasks. It can also initiate White Papers, covering matters such as energy and competition,[68] and Green Papers, such as that on Energy Policy issued in 2006.[69]

---

[67] eg, the Commission's powers under Arts 31 and 86 EC.
[68] European Commission, *An Energy Policy for the European Union*, COM (95) 682 final, 13 December 1995; *White Paper on Modernisation of the Rules Implementing Articles 85 and 86 of the EC Treaty*, COM (1999) 101, 28 April 1999.
[69] European Commission, *A European Strategy for Sustainable, Competitive and Secure Energy*, COM (2006) 105 final, 8 March 2006.

2.71 When preparing draft legislation, the Commission consults widely with interested parties from all sectors and attempts to take their views into account in formulating its legislative proposals. This has been very evident in the development of legislation to promote integration in energy markets. In drawing up the proposals for the internal energy market Directives, several of the 26 DGs were involved: in particular, those for Energy and Transport, Competition, and the Internal Market. Once the final proposal is formulated, the document is sent to the Council where it is discussed by the Energy Experts' Group, composed of experts from the Member States and by the High-Level Energy Group. The latter is composed of Directors General of the Member States, who have responsibility for energy. The Committee of Permanent Representatives (Coreper) will also play a role at this stage. The difference between the Energy Experts' Group and Coreper is that the former is predominantly technical, while Coreper is expected to submit political dossiers to Ministers. The document is simultaneously under consideration by the Parliament and the appropriate Parliamentary Committees. In this process, two consultative bodies—the Economic and Social Committee and the Committee of the Regions[70]—provide opinions on the Commission's proposals either on an *ex officio* or voluntary basis.

(b) Executive Function

2.72 As the executive body of the EU the Commission has a duty to ensure that the rules of the Treaties are applied to the conduct of Member States and also to the conduct of undertakings and individuals. Under Article 211(1) of the EC Treaty, the Commission has a duty to ensure the application of that Treaty and the measures taken by its institutions. The EC Treaty also contains specific expressions of this duty, including those contained in Article 85 (duty to ensure the application of Articles 81 and 82), and in Article 86(3) by which the Commission has a duty to ensure the application of the provisions of Article 86. Also, Article 88 imposes a duty on the Commission to keep under strict review the application of the provisions relating to state aids. Other executive functions include the management of the EU annual budget and its Structural Funds (aimed at levelling out economic disparities between the richer and the poorer parts of the EU). Its management of the budget is monitored by a body called the Court of Auditors, whose reports are reviewed by the Parliament.[71]

2.73 The regulatory functions relate to the making of secondary legislation, particularly in relation to competition matters. The *formal* law-making powers are limited but, in the context of the internal energy market, there are many delegated powers,

---

[70] Respectively, Arts 257–62 and Arts 263–5 EC.
[71] Arts 246–8 EC.

C. The European Commission in its Institutional Setting

exercisable through 'comitology' procedures, where laws on matters of detail are adopted by the Commission in conjunction with a group of national representatives in a committee. As the Guidelines discussed in Chapters 5 and 6 demonstrate, the subject matter of such law-making is far from trivial.[72]

The role of the Commission as guardian of the EC Treaty is, in respect of Member States, derived primarily from the duty imposed on it by Article 226 to initiate a proceeding against a Member State that it considers to have failed to fulfil an obligation under the EC Treaty. The Commission is required to draw the attention of the Member State to the alleged breach and give it an opportunity to submit its observations. If the matter is not satisfactorily resolved, the Commission is to deliver a reasoned opinion on the matter to the Member State. If the State concerned does not comply with the opinion within the period specified by the Commission, the latter may bring the matter before the ECJ (Article 226). The Commission also has powers to ensure the compliance of undertakings and individuals in the public or private sectors with their EC Treaty obligations and the provisions of secondary legislation made under the Treaty. These powers are particularly important in the context of the application of the articles of the EC Treaty relating to competition, particularly Articles 81 and 82. It may decide, for example, that an unauthorized aid is incompatible with the EC Treaty and in these circumstances, the Commission can require the Member State concerned to secure repayment of the aid. 2.74

The Commission's responsibilities have expanded through the provisions of the various treaties discussed in the preceding section. Areas where new responsibilities have been added in this way include the environment, economic and monetary union, the development of trans-European networks, and consumer affairs. 2.75

(2) Commission and Council

The relationship between the Commission and the Council[73] of the EU (the Council) is probably the most important of all relations between the Community institutions.[74] The sensitivity of energy matters to the economic well-being of Member States has given this relationship a decisive role in energy market liberalization. In connection with the internal energy market the Council shares the role 2.76

---

[72] See generally, Chalmers, D, et al, *European Union Law*, 159–67, and Hayes-Renshaw, F and Wallace, H, *The Council of Ministers* (2nd edn, 2006) 196–7.
[73] See generally, Arts 202–10 and 249–56 EC. For a comprehensive overview of the work of the Council, see Hayes-Renshaw and Wallace, ibid.
[74] This is not to be confused with the European Council, a political body comprising Heads of State or governments of the 15 Member States and the President of the European Commission. It is charged by Art 4 TEU with providing the EU with 'the necessary impetus for its development' and with defining 'the general political guidelines thereof'.

of law-making body of the EC with the Parliament. This partnership is exercised in the co-decision procedure for legislation.

2.77 All 27 Member States are represented at ministerial level at meetings of the Council. Each Minister is authorized to commit its own government. In practice, there are specialist meetings of Council Ministers, such as that for energy, which meets normally twice a year (the Energy Council). The Presidency of the Council is held in turn by each Member State for a term of six months in an order decided upon by the Council. The Presidency chairs meetings but also has some limited power to set priorities during its tenure. Apart from this, it plays a key role in establishing a consensus among the various Member States on issues facing the EU and has responsibility for liaison with the Parliament, usually in conjunction with the Commission to form a 'trilogue'.

2.78 Decisions are taken by simple majority voting except for those cases specifically provided for elsewhere in the EC Treaty.[75] The exceptions to this rule are requirements for unanimity or a qualified majority. As mentioned, the SEA contained provisions that amended the EEC Treaty by replacing in a number of articles a requirement for a unanimous vote or a simple majority with a requirement for a qualified majority. The purpose of the amendment was to facilitate the creation of an internal market. Among the amendments was the requirement of unanimity in relation to proposals relating to the approximation of legislation. The SEA added to the EC Treaty a new article which became Article 95. More than two-thirds of the legislation required to complete the internal market was eligible for a qualified majority under this Article. Article 95 states that the Council shall, acting by a qualified majority on a proposal from the Commission in co-operation with the European Parliament, and after consulting the Economic and Social Committee, adopt the measures for the approximation of the provisions laid down by law, regulation, or administrative action in the Member States which have as their object the establishment and functioning of the internal market. Fiscal provisions, measures relating to free movement of persons, or rights or interests of employed persons are excluded from the scope of Article 95 and require approval by unanimous vote under Article 94.

(a) QMV

2.79 Voting by qualified majority is a system of weighted voting.[76] Acts of the Council require for their adoption at least 232 votes in favour cast by a majority of the members.[77]

---

[75] Art 205(1) EC.
[76] Art 205 EC, as modified by the Act of Accession 2003, Art 12(1)(a)(i).
[77] ibid.

C. The European Commission in its Institutional Setting

Table 2.1 Qualified Majority Voting

Member States	No of votes
France, Italy, UK, Germany*	29
Spain, Poland	27
Romania	14
The Netherlands	13
Belgium, Greece, Portugal, Czech Republic, Hungary	12
Austria, Bulgaria, Sweden	10
Denmark, Ireland, Finland, Lithuania, Slovakia	7
Luxembourg, Estonia, Cyprus, Latvia, Slovenia	4
Malta	3†

Note: * The four largest States; † least populous Member State.

2.80 The system of qualified majority voting (QMV) makes for a more rapid and effective system of decision-making than a system based upon unanimity. The application of the QMV system to the internal market measures has emboldened the Commission to perform, with remarkable zeal, its role as policy initiator in the context of the internal market, not only in the energy sector. It has also led to considerable bargaining between Member States to pass measures through the Council. If the Commission agrees, a proposal may be modified by the Council by a qualified majority, but if the Commission does not agree any modification requires unanimity. For decisions on Treaty reform and enlargement of the EU, it is the Member States that decide.

(b) New Co-operation Procedure

2.81 Significant changes in the exercise of the Council's powers in the law-making process, accompanied by an enhancement of Parliament's role, initially created a new co-operation procedure involving the Parliament—used primarily in cases where Council legislation concerning harmonization measures for the establishment and functioning of the internal market is proposed. Subsequently, the co-decision procedure was established between Council and Parliament (see paras 2.53–2.54, 2.87).

(c) Coreper

2.82 Although it does not take decisions itself, Coreper plays an important part in the decision-making process.[78] Its main responsibility is to prepare the work of the Council and to carry out tasks assigned to it by the Council. It is composed of civil servants: senior ones supported by more junior ones, and meets on a weekly basis. It must ensure that only the most difficult and sensitive issues are dealt with at ministerial level. It co-ordinates closely with the many Council working groups of national experts.

---

[78] Art 207 EC.

Chapter 2: The EU Legal Order and Energy

(3) Commission and Parliament

2.83 A significant factor in the making of legislation on energy (as in many other areas) is the active role of the European Parliament.[79] Not only has the Commission been required to consult and co-operate with the Parliament on a wider range of issues under the amended primary law of the EC, but it also has an interest in acquiring the support of the Parliament for its proposals in its discussions with the Member States.

2.84 The citizens of the Member States directly elect their national members of the Parliament for a five-year term under a system of proportional representation. Until 1975, however, they were nominated from among members of the Parliaments of the Member States. In 1976 the Member States agreed in a Decision and Act relating to direct elections,[80] that direct elections should be held. The first direct elections were held in Member States in 1979. There are 732 members at present.

Table 2.2 Members of the European Parliament

Member State	No of members*
Germany	99
France, Italy, UK	78
Spain, Poland	54
The Netherlands	27
Belgium, Czech Republic, Greece, Hungary, Portugal	24
Sweden	19
Austria	18
Denmark, Finland, Slovakia	14
Ireland	13
Slovenia	7
Cyprus, Estonia, Luxembourg	6
Malta	5
Lithuania	13
Latvia	9

* Roughly reflecting the population of the Member States.

Note: The turn-out in the elections remains low and there is no common electoral system.

(a) Co-operation Procedure and Power of Veto

2.85 Although called a 'Parliament', the institution is not the legislature of the Community in the normally accepted sense of the term.[81] Initially, the Parliament

---

[79] See generally, Arts 189–201 and 249–56 EC.
[80] [1976] OJ L278/1.
[81] It may be argued that no institution can be identified as the legislature of the EC or the EU as a whole. The primary powers conferred by the Treaties are exercised in accordance with a set of procedures under which the Parliament, Council, and Commission interact with each other in prescribed ways: Dashwood, A, 'The Constitution of the European Union after Nice: law-making procedures' (2001) 26 ELR 215–38, 218.

C. The European Commission in its Institutional Setting

was called the Assembly of the European Communities and was merely consulted on the proposed legislation of the Council. However, the part played by the Parliament in the legislative process was enlarged by the introduction of the *co-operation* procedure through the SEA in 1987 and applied to almost all internal market legislation.

2.86 The introduction of the co-operation procedure encouraged the Parliament to take a much more active and critical interest in proposed legislation affecting rights that, under the EC Treaty, the Commission is entitled to make without the need to consult or co-operate with the Parliament.

2.87 This legislative role was further enhanced by changes in procedure introduced under the Maastricht Treaty. In most cases, including all internal market legislation, the Parliament has acquired a power of *co-decision* with the Council in the adoption of legislation[82] and has the right to be consulted in other areas. The key point is that legislation introduced under the co-decision procedure cannot be adopted against the will of Parliament. In the last resort, the Parliament can veto the proposal.

(b) Which Procedure?

2.88 The way to determine which procedure is applicable is to examine the Treaty article or the 'legal basis' for the particular measures that are to be presented to Parliament. Under the Euratom Treaty (and some areas of policy under the EC Treaty), the procedure is different again, requiring the Council to consult Parliament before adopting a legislative act. Essentially, the opinion of Parliament must be sought on most important legislation.

2.89 At present, the Commission attends all sessions of the Parliament and must explain and justify its policies if requested to do so by members of the Parliament. It is required to reply to written and oral questions put to it by members of the Parliament.

2.90 In addition, the Parliament's financial control includes the right to make alterations to certain aspects of the Community's budget. The Parliament formally adopts the budget and the Commission is charged with its implementation. In terms of democratic supervision, it holds hearings for nominee Commissioners and approves the Commission by a vote of confidence. It may also dismiss the members of the Commission as a body on a vote of censure with a two-thirds majority of votes cast—although this power has never been exercised (see paras 2.65–2.66). Finally, it has the right to bring actions for judicial review of Community acts by the ECJ, under Article 230 EC 'for the purpose of protecting their prerogatives'. The origins of this power lie in the TEU but it has been enlarged by the TN.

---

[82] Art 251 EC.

(c) Committees

2.91 Much of the Parliament's legislative work takes place in specialist committees. Seventeen standing committees prepare the work of the Parliament's plenary sessions, corresponding closely to the work of the Commission's DGs. Energy matters are covered by the Committee on Industry, External Trade, Research, and Energy. Initially, the function of these committees was to prepare reports that were used by members for information purposes in connection with general debates. While the Committees do perform this function, they also act to maintain contact with the Council and the Commission and with industry and consumer bodies.

(d) Procedure for Adopting Legislation

2.92 There are four principal stages for the adoption of resolutions by Parliament:

(1) The relevant committee appoints an MEP as Rapporteur to draft a report on the Commission proposal under consideration.
(2) The Rapporteur delivers his or her draft report to the committee after discussions.
(3) The draft report is considered by the committee and then put to the vote and perhaps amended.
(4) The report is discussed in a plenary session, amended and put to a vote.

(4) Commission and Court of Justice

(a) Emergence of an ECJ Energy Jurisprudence

2.93 If the Commission has been the catalyst for the internal energy market legislation, the ECJ[83] is the body that it has looked to as the ultimate interpreter and enforcer of the legal measures adopted under the programme. The ECJ is of the greatest importance to the implementation of the internal energy market. For many years, its role in energy matters was almost non-existent. The advent of the Commission's proposals on energy market reform in the mid-1980s led to a re-assessment of the energy sector's status in European law, and during the 1990s the case law of the ECJ began to reflect this. Particularly significant are the judgments of the ECJ in the *Corbeau* and *Port of Genoa* cases.[84] These established that while the Treaty did not prohibit grants of exclusive or special rights, the exercise of those rights can constitute an abuse of a dominant position. More recently, the ECJ has handed down important rulings for the energy sector in the *Dutch Interconnector* case and *Altmark* (see paras 13.59–13.86 and 15.60).[85]

---

[83] See generally, Arts 220–45 and 249–56 EC; also <http://curia.eu.int>. For a recent scholarly overview of the ECJ, see Arnull, A, *The European Court of Justice* (2nd edn, 2006).
[84] Case C-320/91 *Corbeau* [1993] ECR I-2533; Case C-179/90 *Merci Convenzionali Porto di Genova SpA v Siderurgica Gabriella SpA* [1991] ECR I-1979.
[85] Case C-17/03 *Vereniging voor Energie Milieu en Water v Directeur van de Dienst Uitvoering en Toezicht Energie* [2005] ECR I-4983; Case C-280/00 *Altmark Trans GmbH v Nahverkehrsgesellschaft Altmark GmbH* [2003] ECR I-7747.

(b) Composition of the Court

2.94 The ECJ is composed of 27 judges—one national from each of the Member States. Appointments are made by common agreement of Member State governments. The judges hold office for a renewable term of six years. Every three years there is a partial replacement of the judges. They select one of their number to act as President of the ECJ for a renewable term of three years. The ECJ may sit in plenary session or in chambers of three, five, or seven judges. It may sit in plenary session when a Member State or a Community institution that is a party to the proceedings requests it, or when the proceedings have a character that is especially complex or important.

(c) Advocate-General's role

2.95 The Treaty provides that Advocates-General should assist the ECJ in the performance of its tasks.[86] Eight Advocates-General must be appointed. Every three years there is a partial replacement of the Advocates-General, four replaced on each occasion. The function of the Advocate-General as described in Article 222 is, in respect of hearings before the ECJ, to make reasoned submissions in open court, acting with complete impartiality and independence. An Advocate-General is appointed in respect of each case to be heard before the ECJ. He or she is required to analyse to the ECJ the relevant Community law and to propose a solution to the case. Advocate-Generals' submissions are not binding on the ECJ—although the ECJ usually follows the Advocate-General's submission. Even if the ECJ does not follow the Advocate-General's submission, it may nevertheless be useful as a dissenting view.

(d) ECJ Procedure

2.96 The procedure of the ECJ is divided into a written stage and an oral stage. During the written stage pleadings are exchanged in which the arguments are set out in full. In the oral stage, at which the parties must be legally represented, the legal representatives put the arguments forward to the ECJ, and questions may be asked by the ECJ and by the Advocate-General. Subsequently, the Advocate-General delivers his or her Opinion in open court, proposing a solution to the problem. After deliberations, the judgment of the ECJ is then delivered. It is taken by majority vote and no dissenting or separate judgements are published. There is no appeal against a judgment of the ECJ. Member States are required to comply with an order of the ECJ;[87] in cases where fines are imposed against undertakings or individuals, the courts of the relevant Member State may recover such fines without any further formalities.[88]

---

[86] Arts 222–3 EC.
[87] Art 261 EC.
[88] Art 256 EC.

(e) Jurisdiction of the ECJ

2.97 The ECJ has jurisdiction under the EC Treaty to hear five principal kinds of action and may also give preliminary rulings.

2.98 **Failure to fulfil an obligation**[89]   The ECJ will be asked to decide on whether a Member State has fulfilled its obligations under Community law. Such actions are usually brought by the Commission, but they may also be brought by another Member State. The State is first given the opportunity by the Commission to comply with a reasoned opinion on the matter within a certain period after it has had the opportunity to submit its observations. If the ECJ finds against the Member State, then it must take measures to comply without delay. Further non-compliance may result in a fixed or periodic penalty. If the action is initiated by another Member State, it must do so through the Commission.

2.99 **Proceedings for annulment**[90]   The ECJ may review the legality of a variety of measures by Community institutions in actions brought by a Member State, the Commission, the Council and in certain circumstances the Parliament. The action may be brought on grounds of lack of competence, infringement of an essential procedural requirement, infringement of the EC Treaty or of any rule relating to its application, or misuse of powers. The result may be an annulment of all or part of a measure of Community legislation. A natural or legal person may institute proceedings to annul a legal measure that is of direct and individual concern to them. If the action is well founded, the ECJ will declare the contested act or part of the act void.

2.100 **Failure to act**[91]   The ECJ may review the legality of a failure to act by a Community institution, in infringement of the EC Treaty. An action may be brought before the ECJ by a Community institution or a Member State to have the infringement established. A natural or legal person may also complain to the ECJ about inaction by a Community institution. A failure to act will be penalized by the ECJ.

2.101 **Actions for damages**[92]   The ECJ may rule on the liability of the Community in an action for damages based on non-contractual liability. The ruling will apply to damage caused by its institutions or servants in the performance of their duties.

2.102 **Appeals**   The ECJ may hear appeals on points of law against judgments given by the Court of First Instance in cases within its jurisdiction.

---

[89] Arts 226–8 EC.
[90] Arts 230–31, 233 EC.
[91] Art 232 EC.
[92] Arts 235 and 288 EC.

C. The European Commission in its Institutional Setting

(f) Preliminary Rulings

Many disputes involving Community law are commenced in the courts and tribunals of the Member States. They have jurisdiction to review the administrative implementation of Community law and many provisions of the Treaties and of secondary legislation which confer rights on nationals and which national courts must uphold. If doubt arises about the interpretation and validity of such law, the national court or tribunal may seek a preliminary ruling from the ECJ on the relevant question. Within two months the parties, the Member States, and the Community institutions must submit their written observations to the ECJ. After this, the procedure is the same as that applicable to direct action. The ruling by the ECJ is sent back to the national court or tribunal, which is bound by the result in deciding the case in which the question has arisen (see eg paras 13.59–13.86). 2.103

The procedure for a preliminary ruling may also be activated when citizens seek clarification of the Community rules that affect them. Such a ruling may only be sought by a national court, which will also decide if this is the appropriate course of action. All parties involved in the proceedings may participate in the proceedings before the ECJ. 2.104

Preliminary rulings have played an important role in the development of Community law, particularly because of two rulings on Community law made by the ECJ. The ECJ has ruled in landmark cases that primary Community law has: 2.105

(1) direct effect in the Member States; and
(2) primacy over national law.

Direct effect   A provision of the Treaty or of Community legislation was held to confer rights on individuals that they may enforce before a national court, provided that certain conditions are fulfilled (the legal norm must be clear, precise, and unconditional).[93] These rights flow directly from primary Community law and are independent of national law. This is not the same as the requirement that regulations are 'directly applicable', which means that the regulations have legal effect in Member States without any national implementing legislation or similar action. 2.106

Primacy   A large number of preliminary rulings have affirmed the principle of supremacy of Community law over the national law of the Member States since it was first established in the 1964 case of *Costa v ENEL*.[94] This has the effect that no rule of national law can be invoked to prevent the grant of a remedy to protect a Community right. 2.107

---

[93] Case 26/62 *Van Gend en Loos* [1963] ECR 1, brought to the ECJ on a preliminary ruling; further developed in, eg, Case 36/74 *Walrave and Koch v Association Union Cycliste Internationale* [1974] ECR 1405; Case 9/70 *Franz Grad v Finanzamt Traunstein* [1970] ECR 825; Case 41/74 *Van Duyn v Home Office* [1974] ECR 1337.
[94] Case 6/64 *Costa v ENEL* [1964] ECR 585.

(g) Court of First Instance

2.108 In 1989 a new court was established to assist the ECJ in handling the growing volume of cases that came before it.[95] The CFI[96] was created by the Council with the aim of strengthening the judicial safeguards available to individuals by introducing a second tier of judicial authority and so enabling the ECJ to concentrate on its basic task—the uniform interpretation of Community law. It has authority to hear and determine certain classes of action or proceeding at first instance. It is not competent to hear and determine certain questions (eg, those concerning the interpretation of the EC Treaty).

2.109 The CFI is made up of one judge from each Member State selected on similar terms and conditions as those appointed to the ECJ. No permanent Advocates-General are appointed to the CFI, but judges may serve in this function from time to time. The Members of the CFI select one of their own number as President and the CFI appoints its own registrar. Its administrative needs are met by the services of the ECJ. It sits in chambers of three or five judges and may sit in plenary session in cases of particular importance. Its decisions have contributed to the discussion of the doctrine of 'essential facilities' (see paras 13.97–13.99).

(5) Legislative Acts

2.110 The institutions share various law-making powers under the EC Treaty. Legislative acts may take three principal forms: Directives, Decisions, and Regulations. Provision is also made for recommendations and opinions. These are provided for in Article 249. For the purposes of bringing about the internal market in energy, Directives have proved to be the more influential instruments so far.[97] The power to issue these instruments is almost always given to the Council, acting in co-operation with the Parliament. In some cases, however, the EC Treaty gives such power to the European Commission.[98] Regulations, Directives, and Decisions must state the reasons on which they are based and refer to any proposals or opinions which may have had to have been obtained before their adoption.[99]

(a) Directives

2.111 A Directive is binding with respect to ends but not the choice of form or methods. It has usually been adopted to require Member States to harmonize national law

---

[95] Between 1978–85 the number of new cases brought before the ECJ in a single year increased from 200 to more than 400. By the end of 2005, the CFI had ruled on more than 4,700 cases: <http://curia.europa.eu/en/instit/presentationfr/index_tpi.htm>.
[96] Art 225 EC.
[97] eg, Prechal, S, *Directives in Community Law: A Study of Directives and their Enforcement in National Courts* (2nd edn, 2005).
[98] eg Art 86(3) EC.
[99] Art 253 EC.

D. European Economic Area Agreement

in certain areas. A deadline for implementation will always be provided, usually of one or two years from the date of adoption by the EC to implementation by the Member State. This allows a Member State to consider and decide upon the manner of implementation. Such measures usually have a framework character and have tended to leave Member States with more or less scope in implementing their provisions. This element of subsidiarity has been especially apparent in the Directives setting out common rules for the electricity and gas sectors. In the absence of direct effect, national courts have a duty to interpret national law, as much as possible, in conformity with EC law. Where there is a failure of this duty, an individual may be able to seek damages against the Member State.

(b) Regulations

2.112 Regulations are applied directly in all the Member States without necessarily requiring national implementing measures to bring them into force. This characteristic of direct applicability once made and published is unique to regulations. They are issued by the Commission, the Council, and the Parliament and are sources of Community law in the national legal order. In this respect they contrast with the legislative character of Directives. In practice, most Regulations require some implementing action by the Member States (eg, the Regulation on the introduction of the euro). Recently, Regulations have been adopted for the electricity and gas sectors which address matters of detail anticipated in the respective framework Directives (see paras 5.79–5.139 and 6.115–6.147).

(c) Decisions

2.113 A decision does not normally have general application, being instead restricted to a single Member State, undertaking or individual.[100] It is binding on those to whom it is addressed (see paras 3.37, 5.83, and 11.15).

(d) Recommendations and Opinions

2.114 Recommendations and opinions are not binding. However, despite their 'soft law' character, they may prove influential in interpreting the national law at which the recommendation is directed.[101]

D. European Economic Area Agreement

2.115 Although not a Member of the European Union, Norway is linked to the corpus of EC law by an international instrument known as the EEA Agreement, which

---

[100] Art 189 EC.
[101] See the discussion in Weatherill, S, *Law and Integration in the European Union* (1995) 83–4.

entered into force on 1 January 1994, and to which Norway is a party.[102] As a key supplier of gas and oil to the EU and an essential player in the Nordic electricity market, the Norway–EU energy link is an important element in the pan-European energy scene. In practice, the Agreement has functioned as a channel for the internal energy market legislation into Norway, albeit with some minor adaptations.

(1) EEA Agreement: Legally Binding

2.116 The Agreement was concluded between the EEC, the ECSC, their Member States, and what were at that time the seven Member States of the European Free Trade Association (EFTA).[103] Its basic aim was to extend the single market to the EFTA countries. Originally, it was to include Switzerland but a negative result in the Swiss referendum in 1992 led to the withdrawal of both Switzerland and Liechtenstein (which had a customs union with Switzerland; Liechtenstein joined the EEA in 1995). Following the rejection of membership of the EU by Norway, the EEA remains a forum for co-operation between Norway, Iceland, Liechtenstein, and the EU.

2.117 The Agreement extends many of the rights and obligations of the EU Member States to the EFTA States that participate in the EEA. It includes the four basic freedoms of the single market but also the 'flanking policies' such as co-operation on research and environmental protection. A list of legislative acts affecting the energy sector is contained in Annex IV to the Agreement.[104] It is updated from time to time. A number of internal market measures on energy were incorporated into the Agreement on 2 December 2005. They included Directives (EC) 2003/54 and (EC) 2003/55, as well as the Electricity Regulation and Commission Decision 2003/796/EC on the establishment of the European Regulators Group for Electricity and Gas (see Chapters 5 and 6, and on the ERGEG, para 5.66). An EEA Joint Committee Decision incorporated Directive (EC) 2001/77 on the promotion of electricity from renewable energy sources in the internal electricity market into the EEA Agreement on 8 July 2005 (see Chapter 10). This decision

---

[102] The text of the Agreement can be found at <http://secretariat.efta.int/Web/EuropeanEconomicArea/EEAAgreement/EEAAgreement>.
[103] These were Austria, Finland, Iceland, Liechtenstein, Norway, Sweden, and Switzerland. EFTA was created through the Stockholm Convention in 1960 and entered into operation in the same year.
[104] Annex IV lists the legal measures that are part of the EEA Agreement. The only major piece of legislation in the energy sector to be excluded is that on mandatory oil stocks. There are three principal reasons for this: EFTA countries have already made the same commitments as the EC concerning stockpiling within the framework of the IEA; this legislation does not have any great importance for the normal movement of goods; although the joint decision-making system in the EC is stricter relative to that of the IEA, the EEA does not give EFTA countries any formal say in internal EC decision-making. Moreover, the European Atomic Energy Community is not a signatory to the EEA, and hence nuclear legislation is not covered by the Agreement.

set indicative targets for Norway and Iceland on renewable energy production and allowed for a derogation from the Directive for Liechtenstein. The list of measures in Annex IV also includes acts on energy consumption of certain equipment and rules on labelling of energy consumption of household equipment. Acts concerning the safety of goods and 'technical' barriers to trade have a bearing on energy policy and are also included. These may concern exhaust emissions from vehicles, safety of equipment using gas or electricity, as well as sulphur and lead content in fuels. In some cases, the Agreement is subject to adaptations, transitional periods or limited derogation. Three examples relevant to the EU are:

(1) Within the meaning of Article 2(31) of the Gas Directive, Norway is to be considered as an emergent market from 10 April 2004, and the derogation set out in Article 28(2) applies accordingly.
(2) The EFTA States are permitted to send observers to the Committee meetings under Article 13 of the Electricity Regulation and Article 30 of the Gas Directive. While they may participate fully in the Committee work, they do not have the right to vote. Within the meaning of Article 2(26) of the Electricity Directive, Iceland is to be considered as a small isolated system and the derogation set out in Article 15 therefore applies accordingly.
(3) The Agreement includes rules on competition, state aids, and state monopolies—very similar to those of the EC Treaty. With respect to state monopolies, it follows the wording of Article 31. The rules on competition follow very closely those of the EC Treaty to ensure equal conditions of competition for economic operators throughout the Area. The central provisions in the main Agreement are therefore identical to those of Articles 81, 82, and 86. Provisions in the ECSC as well as secondary legislation were integrated into the Agreement through Protocols and an Annex.

The Agreement has a dynamic character. A central feature is that its common rules are continuously updated through the incorporation of subsequent measures of EU law in the EEA. Each month new legislation is incorporated into the Agreement by a decision of the EEA Joint Committee. Adaptations may be negotiated in the application of EU legislation to the EEA when this appears appropriate and when agreement can be reached by both sides. The idea here is to have a parallel development of new EU rules and new EEA rules. 2.118

(2) The Institutions

The institutional structures follow a two-pillar model, with strong co-operation between the Brussels-based EFTA Surveillance Authority and the European Commission. The first pillar comprises joint bodies for decision-shaping, decision-making, and dispute settlement. The EEA States have not accepted direct decision-making by the European Commission or the ECJ. 2.119

2.120 The ongoing management of the Agreement is the responsibility of the EEA Joint Committee. It comprises ambassadors of the EFTA–EEA States and representatives of the European Commission and EU Member States. Decisions are made by consensus to incorporate EC legislation into the Agreement. Decisions adopted by the Joint Committee must in principle be transposed into national legislation, in accordance with the national system in the EEA country—since there is no transfer of legislative power to the EEA institutions. Another body, the EEA Council, provides political impetus for the development of the Agreement and guidelines for the Joint Committee. It is composed of foreign ministers of the EU and EFTA–EEA countries. There is also a Joint Parliamentary Committee and an EEA Consultative Committee.

2.121 The other pillar comprises the EFTA bodies. The Surveillance Authority is responsible for implementation and enforcement of the competition rules in EFTA States. It has the same powers as the Commission in dealing with those competition matters that fall within its competence. This means that the Surveillance Authority can issue negative clearance, individual exemptions and comfort letters, and can undertake investigations and impose fines for infringements. However, it does not have a legislative power, so block exemptions are adopted through the normal EEA decision-making rules. A system for allocation of cases between the two surveillance authorities (ie, the Surveillance Authority and the European Commission) has been created which is based upon objective criteria. Decisions by either body are valid throughout the EEA.

2.122 There is also an EFTA Court operating in parallel to the ECJ in matters relating to the EFTA–EEA states. It deals with infringement actions raised against EFTA States by the Surveillance Authority concerning implementation, application or interpretation of EEA rules, and the settlement of disputes between two or more EFTA States. There is also a Standing Committee of EFTA States that has a co-ordinating role in preparing for meetings of the EEA Joint Committee.

(3) Impacts on Energy

2.123 Since the Agreement came into force, the EEA States have adopted that part of the EU *acquis communautaire* that falls within the scope of the Agreement. The EEA States (primarily Norway) have also provided regular input into the shaping of such EC legislation. An example of the effects of transposition is Norway's petroleum legislation. Substantial changes were made to align it with the requirements of the EC Hydrocarbons Directive within the framework of its obligations under the EEA. Changes to the 1985 Petroleum Act included amendments to its provisions on establishment (s 8(1)), procurement (ss 8(7)), 23(1), and 54(1)), landing requirements (s 26(1)), and the power to make regulations relating to the duty of information under the EEA.

An important point about the Agreement lies in *legal enforceability* on the parties. **2.124**
The judicial enforcement of the EEA Agreement is very specific. An example of
joint enforcement in the energy sector is the co-operation in the *GFU* case.

GFU/Norwegian Gas Sales Consortium[105] The competition provisions (Article 81 **2.125**
EC and Article 53(1) EEA) were applied in connection with the joint negotiation
of all sales of Norwegian gas by the Gas Sales Consortium or GFU (originally
comprising the three Norwegian oil and gas producers, Statoil, Norske Hydro,
and Saga Petroleum. The latter company was subsequently taken over by Norske
Hydro and disappeared from the consortium.). These companies hold very substantial licence interests in the Norwegian oil and gas reserves, but non-Norwegian
companies (including TotalElf and ExxonMobil) also have significant interests.
The GFU was a creation of the Norwegian Government. The consequence of the
exclusive negotiating right granted to the members of the GFU for all sales of
Norwegian gas automatically precluded the non-Norwegian licence interest holders from negotiating or participating in negotiation of their own sales. In spite of
this, they were entitled to refuse to accept the terms negotiated for them by the
GFU, if they could obtain better terms from the buyers. In practice, the negotiations were with Statoil, the most important member of the GFU and until
recently a wholly-owned state entity. The European gas buyers were effectively
negotiating with the Norwegian Government.

These arrangements became the subject of an investigation that commenced in **2.126**
1996, initiated jointly by the EFTA Surveillance Authority and the European
Commission. The joint negotiation of natural gas sales contracts, by fixing the
price, volumes, and all other trading conditions, was alleged to be contrary to
Article 81(1) EC and Article 53(1) EEA. For EU consumers their choice between
Norwegian producers was reduced artificially from about 30 to effectively one. The
Norwegian Government contended that Norway (and the GFU members) was
entitled to spread the benefits of sales of Norwegian oil and gas because of their economic implications to Norway. They claimed that Article 81 EC and Article 53(1)
EEA should not apply to them. However, finally on 29 May 2001, Norway agreed
to disband the GFU, with effect from 1 June 2001 (see paras 12.05–12.10).

E. Energy Community Treaty

This Treaty establishing an Energy Community for South-East Europe was signed **2.127**
on 25 October 2005 in Athens.[106] Initially, it was designed to establish a regional

---

[105] Case COMP/36.072.
[106] <http://ec.europa.eu/energy/electricity/south_east/treaty_en.htm>. It entered into force in 2006.

Chapter 2: The EU Legal Order and Energy

electricity market in South-East Europe. However, from the end of 2005 it was charged with assisting in the creation of a regional gas market as well. The 34 signatory states are: the 25 EU Member States and the Balkan States of Albania, Bosnia and Herzegovina, Bulgaria, Croatia, the Former Yugoslav Republic of Macedonia, Montenegro, Romania, Serbia and UNMIK Kosovo. Moldova, Ukraine, Turkey, and Norway have observer status.

2.128 The basis for the structure of the Energy Community Treaty was the European Coal and Steel Community (ECSC) Treaty.[107] Like the ECSC Treaty, it has its origins in post-war reconstruction and the identification of a key economic sector on which to base a legally binding scheme for co-operation. Although these countries are not members of the EU, the Treaty will act as a vehicle for the gradual transfer to these countries of the *acquis communautaire* in key areas: not only energy but also competition and environmental matters. The Treaty is also designed to create regional mechanisms that extend into the EU to allow for a deeper integration of local energy markets, especially by means of accelerated infrastructure development. In particular, the Treaty provides that the States Parties will do the following:

- implement electricity and gas tariff reform plans;
- implement all necessary technical standards, such as grid codes, accounting systems and information exchange for grid operation;
- implement effective third party access to infrastructure;
- create National Regulatory Authorities and transmission system operators;
- develop local solutions to pressing problems of regulation, energy poverty and social equity; and
- implement the Electricity and Gas Directives,[108] and the Electricity Regulation.

2.129 The instruments established to achieve these goals reflect the origins in the ECSC Treaty. There are four distinct institutions: a ministerial council, a permanent high level group, a treaty secretariat and an energy community regulatory board. First, there is a Ministerial Council which comprises the energy ministers of the member countries and the EU Energy Commissioner. It takes strategic decisions and gives directions to the Treaty and formally adopts or endorses secondary legislation. The Presidency rotates on a six-monthly basis. Secondly, there is a Permanent High Level Group, which is composed of representatives of the energy ministers of the member countries and the European Commission. The group is

---

[107] 'The Energy Community Treaty was consciously modelled on the European Coal and Steel Community that is the basis of the European Union': Commission Press Release MEMO/05/397, 'An integrated market for electricity and gas across 34 European Countries', 25 October 2005, 2.

[108] Each Contracting Party to the Treaty has to ensure that eligible customers within the meaning of the Electricity and Gas Directives comprise from 1 January 2008 all non-household customers and from 1 January 2015 all customers (Annex I).

convened on an ad hoc basis on the initiative of either the Commission or the country that holds the Presidency at the time. The aim of its meetings is to prepare the Ministerial Council and to ensure the follow-up of its decisions. The Commission co-chairs this group along with the President in Office. Thirdly, there is a Treaty Secretariat, based in Vienna, which will act as the central co-ordinating body for the Treaty. It has the right to initiate in developing the Treaty and to make use of the secondary law provisions of the Treaty. It has responsibility for the co-ordination of international donors, validating work and proposing technical, legal and regulatory developments. Finally, there is an Energy Community Regulatory Board, based in Athens. This body is charged with considering issues of regulatory co-operation and may develop into a regulatory decision-making body and/or a dispute settlement mechanism.

A Forum mechanism is set up under the Treaty called the Electricity and Gas Forum. This comprises representatives of the European Commission, governments, regulators and TSOs from the countries of SE Europe, the CEER, ETSO, UCTE, representatives of donors, electricity producing companies and consumers. It is co-chaired by the Commission and a representative of the president in office. It meets in Athens. In practice, this has been an Electricity Forum in the first stage but a Gas Forum is envisaged. However, the gas market is relatively undeveloped at present and is likely to be small, even if supplies of Caspian and Middle East gas are delivered by pipeline.

2.130

F. Energy Charter Treaty

The overall dependence of EU countries on energy imports from third countries has made it important for the EU to create formal links with producers and transmitters of energy to contribute to the long-term stability that energy supply contracts typically require—especially in the case of supplies of natural gas. This reality has encouraged an orientation not only to the Gulf region but also to the East. The collapse of the Soviet Union set off a chain of events that led to the creation of new states including the Caspian Sea oil and gas producing states and more independently-minded governments along the established energy transit routes from the East to the EU—raising questions about the security of future energy supplies. The EU therefore threw its weight behind the development of a legal instrument for co-operation between East and West Europe called the Energy Charter Treaty (the Treaty).[109]

2.131

---

[109] [1998] OJ L69/1. Final Act of the European Energy Charter Conference: 69/5–69/114. The Treaty and related Protocol on Energy Efficiency and Environmental Relations entered into force on 16 April 1998, following the deposit of the 30th instrument of ratification on 16 January 1998; see *The Energy Charter Treaty and Related Documents* (1996). The initiative behind the Treaty lay originally with the 'Lubbers Declaration' of June 1990: see n 110 below.

This multilateral treaty was signed by some 50 states and the European Communities on 17 December 1994. Its purpose is:

> to establish a legal framework in order to promote long-term co-operation in the energy field, based on complementaries and mutual benefits, in accordance with the objectives and principles of the [European Energy] Charter.[110]

2.132 The Treaty's scope is wide: in a geographic sense, it is essentially pan-European; in an economic sense, it includes different kinds of market or market-oriented systems; and in a legal sense, it incorporates a wide range of legal commitments, both of the 'hard' and the 'soft' law variety. It entered into force in April 1998, three months after ratification by the required number of 30 states. It has been ratified by all of the EU States and may be seen as part of the *acquis communautaire* or legal order in energy. It has also been ratified by all the CIS countries (except Russia), the Central Asian Republics, Azerbaijan, Georgia, and Turkey.

2.133 The Treaty creates rights and obligations in international law for all of its contracting parties.[111] It applies both to East–West transactions and West–East transactions. Its scope comprises 'energy materials and products'. It is principally concerned with the promotion and protection of investment, trade, and the transit of energy goods. Other subjects covered by the Treaty are either supportive of the provisions on these matters or have a lesser significance. The provisions on competition in energy could be placed in the latter category.

(1) Main Treaty Provisions

(a) Investment

2.134 The Treaty distinguishes between two stages in the investment process: the 'pre-investment' stage, involving the making of investments and setting of access conditions; and the 'post-investment' stage, concerning investments already in place. It is the latter stage that is subject to a legal regime of 'hard law' obligations, similar to those common to bilateral investment treaties and enforceable by international arbitration.

---

[110] Art 2 ECT. The Treaty is only one of many initiatives to promote stability in long-term investment. For an overview of these efforts, see Cameron, PD, 'Stabilization in Investment Contracts and Changes of Rules in Host Countries: Tools for Oil and Gas Investors' (2006) at <http://www.aipn.org/modelagreements/research.asp>.

[111] The origin of the Treaty lies in a non-binding Declaration signed by 50 states and the European Community three years earlier on 17 December 1991, called the European Energy Charter, based on an initiative of Prime Minister Ruud Lubbers of the Netherlands in 1990. The primary aim of the project was 'to give political support to the democratic process in the former centrally-planned economies. The welfare of these countries' population would benefit from a properly managed supply and from an influx of Western investment attracted by a stable free market system. The resulting improvement in conditions of life would underpin the evolution towards a democratic society': Dore, J, and De Bauw, R, *The Energy Charter Treaty: Origins, Aims and Prospects* (1995) 2. The aims of the Charter Declaration were to: improve security of supply; maximize efficiency of production, conversion, transport, distribution, and use of energy; enhance safety; and

F. Energy Charter Treaty

Post-investment stage For the post-investment stage, contracting parties are obliged to encourage and create stable, equitable, favourable, and transparent conditions for foreign investors to make investments in their areas. The standard of treatment to be accorded to foreign investors is the better of national (NT) or Most Favoured Nation (MFN) treatment.[112] From the date of signature, each contracting party agrees to treat foreign investors at least as well as it treats its national or domestic companies or investors. The exceptions to the NT and the MFN clauses are limited in scope, number, and time while being clearly known and transparent at the time of signature. In practice, the exceptions actually claimed by economies in transition were far fewer than initially expected and most of these have since been phased out. Compensation for losses is provided for under the NT and MFN clauses and fair conditions in the event of expropriation are also provided for. This means that, for instance, freely convertible currencies will be used in designing compensation arrangements. Free movement of capital and repatriation of profits are also provided for.[113] There are no NT provisions on taxes on income or on capital. **2.135**

Pre-investment phase For the pre-investment phase, the NT principle is to be implemented in two stages: **2.136**

(1) investments are to receive either NT or MFN treatment on a voluntary basis (best efforts)—whichever is the most advantageous; and
(2) all signatories are committed to work towards extending the provisions on NT to the pre-investment stage, on a legally-binding basis.[114]

Supplementary treaty negotiations Negotiations on a 'second-phase' investment treaty were to be concluded by 1 January 1998. However, although the commitment to negotiate was fulfilled it did not result in agreement on the resulting draft instrument, the 'Supplementary Treaty'. **2.137**

The Treaty contains provisions on the settlement of any investment disputes that may arise. They provide for the use of compulsory arbitration against governments at the option of foreign investors for alleged breaches of the investment agreements, without the need first to exhaust local remedies. Moreover, binding state-to-state arbitration is provided for in Article 27. This involves the use of an ad hoc tribunal for disputes between states concerning the application or interpretation of the Treaty. It is not restricted to the resolution of disputes arising from investment issues. The dispute settlement procedures may in fact be diverse, including international arbitration, and provide for final and binding solutions to many disputes. The rules and procedures governing transit disputes in particular **2.138**

---

minimize environmental problems. For a comprehensive collection of materials on the Charter see Waelde, TW, (ed), *The Energy Charter Treaty: An East-West Gateway for Investment and Trade* (1996).

[112] Art 10(7) ECT.
[113] Art 14 ECT.
[114] Art 10(4) ECT.

have been enhanced since ratification to minimize disruption when a dispute is taking place.[115]

2.139 As a general comment, the sector specific character of the Treaty provisions may weaken the legal protection it offers relative to many of the investment protection treaties in force, or indeed the EC Treaty. However, the special importance of the energy sector in the economies of many Eastern European countries may justify the treatment of investment issues in a separate legal instrument focused exclusively on this sector.

(b) Trade

2.140 A second major feature of the Treaty is that it subjects trade in energy materials and products between contracting parties to the provisions of the GATT and its related instruments, even where those contracting parties to the Treaty are not yet parties to the GATT (eg some of the FSU republics). The aim is to promote access to international markets for non-GATT parties on commercial terms. A weakness here is the failure to treat the link between trade and competition—the latter being relegated to the status of a second order issue. As in the investment provisions, there was also a Treaty provision for 'second stage' negotiations on trade matters.

2.141 In April 1998 a trade amendment was adopted following a meeting of the Energy Charter Conference. A new Article 29 dealt with each of the three issues on which negotiations were mandated. It included several understandings and declarations, one in relation to trade-related intellectual property rights. This brought the Treaty into line with current World Trade Organization (WTO) rules on multilateral agreements on trade in goods. It was also aimed at encouraging the introduction of WTO-compatible rules in non-WTO countries that are parties to the Treaty. In addition, it allowed the inclusion of more than 70 categories of energy-related equipment—eg pipelines, power masts, furnaces, and transformers—into the extended WTO-based regime, and opened the way for future legally-binding tariff commitments for energy materials and products, and for energy-related equipment. The amendment is provisionally applied by signatories to the Treaty and contracting parties until it enters into force. Until then the trade regime in the Treaty will continue to be more relevant.

(c) Transit

2.142 The third major feature of the Treaty is the provision it makes for the transit of energy goods through a state that is a party to it. Article 7 establishes a legal framework for relationships between governments in relation to transit. It is to be supplemented

---

[115] Rules Concerning the Adoption of Transit Disputes ('Rules'), adopted December 1998.

by a Protocol on transit which is under negotiation.[116] Article 7 sets out rules on the following:

- non-discriminatory passage with no distinction allowed as to origin, destination, or ownership of products or materials;
- non-discriminatory pricing;
- absence of unreasonable delays, restrictions, or charges;
- modernization of infrastructure;
- offer of possible new-build infrastructure;
- non-interruption of transit in case of dispute, and clear dispute and conciliation procedures.

Article 7 requires each contracting state to take: 2.143

> ... necessary measures to facilitate the transit of Energy Materials and Products consistent with the principle of freedom of transit and without distinction as to the origin, destination or ownership of such Energy Materials or Products or discrimination as to pricing on the basis of such distinctions, and without imposing any unreasonable delays, restrictions or charges.

An obligation is therefore imposed on the parties to facilitate transit. However, the choice of the word 'facilitate' over alternatives such as 'ensure' or 'encourage' guarantees a weaker formulation. It does not require the transit states to adopt specific legislation to improve transit access, although by implementing Treaty provisions in domestic legislation a state may include provisions on access.

'Freedom of transit' The principle of 'freedom of transit' is referred to without 2.144 any apparent legal basis for such a principle. However, the obligation of non-discrimination in transit relates to both the terms of access to the energy transport facilities and to the terms and conditions of carriage. Transit is also to be allowed 'without unreasonable delays, restrictions or charges'. The contracting parties must also secure existing flows of transit energy even in circumstances where such transit would endanger the security of supply. The proposed Transit Protocol contains provisions which would greatly clarify the rights and obligations of transit states.

Soft law obligations Other transit requirements include an obligation to encourage the relevant entities to co-operate in the following: 2.145

- modernizing energy transport facilities which are necessary for transit;
- developing and operating energy transport facilities which serve more than one contracting party;

---

[116] Energy Charter Secretariat, Final Act of the Energy Charter Conference with Respect to the Energy Charter Protocol on Transit, 31 October 2003 (draft text). Art 3 states that the Protocol shall complement, supplement, extend, or amplify the Treaty provisions but not derogate from them.

- taking 'measures to mitigate supply interruptions';[117] and
- facilitating interconnection.

It is unclear how a state might seek to encourage a relevant entity that is in private ownership.

2.146 The transit state is also required to transit energy 'in no less favourable a manner than its provisions treat such materials and products originating in or destined for its own Area'.[118] It must therefore apply the more favourable of NT or MFN treatment in its approach to goods in transit.

2.147 **Dispute resolution** In the event of a dispute over transit, the contracting parties must not interrupt or reduce the existing flow of energy materials and products and not permit the introduction or reduction of transit flows by any entity subject to its control or require any entity subject to its jurisdiction to interrupt or reduce a transit flow.[119] However, this is subject to an exception in Article 24.

2.148 An important qualification to the above obligation is that contracting parties are not precluded from adopting or enforcing any measure in relation to transit as is essential to the acquisition or distribution of energy materials and products 'in conditions of short supply arising from causes outside the control of that Contracting Party'.

2.149 The dispute resolution mechanism is important since, if it is successfully applied, it could function as a means of securing the continuity of transit flows when transit disputes occur between contracting parties.[120] It is governed by a set of Rules and Procedures issued by the Secretariat in 1998.[121] These include the provision of guidance to its secretary-general on how to appoint conciliators, guidance for conciliators conducting proceedings with a view to seeking agreements between parties, and the imposition of interim tariffs for one year if agreement is not reached.

2.150 If negotiations for access to existing facilities fail, provision is made to facilitate the construction of new transit facilities. In cases where transit 'cannot be achieved on commercial terms' by means of energy transport facilities, a contracting party 'shall not place obstacles in the way of new capacity being established, except as may be otherwise provided in applicable legislation'.[122] Although the 'commercial terms' are not defined, this is a matter that could be addressed by a court in terms of the aims of the Treaty.

---

[117] Art 7(2) ECT.
[118] ibid.
[119] Art 7(6) ECT. For comparative experiences see Stevens, P, 'Pipelines or Pipe Dreams? Lessons from the history of Arab Transit Pipelines' (2000) 54 Middle East J 224–41.
[120] This seems to have been the idea behind an early threat to invoke the transit dispute settlement provisions by a Russian Deputy Prime Minister over charges being levied by the Ukraine for oil transited through the Druzhba pipeline: *BBC Monitoring Survey of World Broadcasts*, 19 February 1996. But note the different approach adopted in 2006 (see para 18.10).
[121] Rules (n 115 above); Art 7(7) ECT.
[122] Art 7(4) ECT.

2.151 This provision should be read alongside the provisions of Article 7(5), which contains a number of exceptions to the obligations of transit states. For example, the transit states are required not:

- to construct or modify existing energy transport facilities; or
- to permit new or additional transit through existing energy transport facilities.

They may do so if it can be demonstrated to the other contracting parties concerned that the granting of such permissions would 'endanger the security or efficiency of its energy systems, including the security of supply'. In practice, the burden of proof would be difficult to discharge.

2.152 **Treaty transit provisions as a 'Trojan horse'** From the foregoing, it should not be assumed that the definition of transit is so broad as to impose an obligation on states to introduce third party access. In the Understandings that are included in the Final Act of the Conference on the Charter, it is clearly stated that '[t]he provisions of the Treaty do not ... oblige any Contracting Party to introduce mandatory third party access'.[123] This provision has its origins in the discussions within the EU at the time of the Treaty negotiations on the introduction of third party access by means of new legislation, which subsequently became the Electricity and Gas Directives. The transit provision in the Treaty was seen as a potential 'Trojan horse' for the introduction of such access into the EU to circumvent the difficulties that the European Commission was experiencing in securing the passage of the proposed Directives. The incumbent players were successful in persuading their governments to support the inclusion of this restrictive interpretation.

(2) The Charter Process: An Assessment

2.153 The developmental character of the Treaty may be grasped by the notion of the 'Charter process'. This can be divided into three stages,[124] with different implications for the Treaty's relationship to the EU arising from each one.

2.154 The first stage was the difficult one of negotiating a text that could secure agreement among a very diverse group of countries. This was completed by December 1994 when the Treaty was signed in Lisbon. The second stage was characterized mainly by the efforts to encourage signatories to ratify the Treaty so it might enter into force, on the one hand, and on the other, the conclusion of 'second stage' negotiations as envisaged in the Treaty. This was concluded in April 1998. The third and most recent stage involves an emphasis upon the removal of obstacles to the transit of energy materials and products and attempts to secure Russian ratification of the Treaty.

---

[123] Final Act of the European Energy Charter Conference, Understanding 1(b)(i).
[124] See discussions by Bamberger, CS, Linehan, J, and Waelde, T, 'Energy Charter Treaty in 2000: in a New Phase' (2000) 18 J Energy Natural Resources L 331–52; and Cameron, P, 'Het Verdrag inzake het Energiehandvest: een beoordeling na zes jaar' (2001) SEW 139–148.

2.155 **Soft law 'too soft'?** The Treaty that was concluded in the first stage is a combination of hard and soft law commitments—the latter made up of aspirations or statements of legal intention. It would be unwise to restrict an assessment purely to the former provisions. Many of its concepts were and in some cases still are new to the countries with emerging markets. The Treaty therefore has value as an educational device, although it is still open to differences in interpretation. It may help to break with the prevailing case-by-case approach to negotiations on these matters. However, the abundance of soft law commitments such as 'shall work to promote', 'shall encourage', and 'shall agree to promote' is not likely to inspire confidence in its relevance to large-scale investment in energy infrastructure since such assurances are unenforceable in a court of law.

2.156 **East–West exchange** The prevailing assumption behind the Treaty's inception was that there are complementary interests which permit a kind of exchange between East and West: Russia and the FSU countries have gas and oil reserves which can be developed with Western technology and capital, to restore declining production, and to provide markets for its energy production. This requires investment protection, trade, and guarantees about energy transit. To a large extent this approach has been overtaken by events, as many Central European countries have since joined the EU and Russia no longer has difficulty in securing investment on favourable terms. However, EU dependence on imports of gas and oil from the East remains and will increase.

2.157 **Competition provisions** Competition is not a central feature of the Treaty, in contrast to the EC Treaty, the EEA Agreement, or even the Energy Community Treaty. Article 6 is characterized by a procedural approach to anti-competitive conduct in which states may take steps to address the consequences of such actions.

2.158 Two obligations are imposed: each state must work towards (i) alleviating market distortions and (ii) removing barriers to competition in energy. Article 6(2) requires states to establish and enforce laws to deal with unilateral and concerted anti-competitive conduct in energy. However, Understanding No 7 to the Treaty states that what is to be included in such laws is up to each of the contracting parties. Complaints to the competition authorities of the state concerned may include a request that they take appropriate enforcement action, but they cannot compel them to do so. The kind of action taken is also a matter for the state concerned. There is no requirement that reasons be given for the action taken or failure to take action. This is the only means available to advance complaints, apart from the diplomatic means of dispute settlement in Article 27(1). Article 6 does not give rights to firms or individuals who are injured by anti-competitive conduct in other states parties to the Treaty. This missing element is a stark contrast to the EC Treaty that confers rights on individuals and the means by which they can enforce these rights. The Treaty's approach is explicable, however, in terms of the Treaty's aims, which do not include that of removing barriers to competition.

Future credibility of the Charter Despite the failure to secure Russian ratification after more than a decade, the Charter process will continue to matter to the EU in future years, not least because its other attempts to establish 'bridges' on energy issues with Russia have proved no more successful. The Treaty established a framework within which multilateral discussions could take place among all stakeholders but especially governments. It has established a Working Group on transit, substantially completed negotiations on a legally-binding Protocol on Transit, and developed non-binding model host government and intergovernmental agreements on cross-border energy flows—including transit. If they become effective, these instruments will constitute a significant elaboration of the Treaty's provisions on transit of energy. In addition, the Treaty has been used in an increasing number of investor–state disputes, which suggests that it will have a practical relevance for some time to come. The Charter process will therefore continue to be highly relevant to all the countries involved, whether the EU grouping, or both the European and Asian states of the FSU. Most of these countries lack indigenous supplies of gas and oil and are highly dependent on imports, while all of them are more or less dependent upon the Russian Federation for a transportation system that is controlled by it. Nonetheless, the continued absence of Russian ratification is a significant challenge for its future credibility. 2.159

G. The Wider Neighbourhood of the EU

Both the enlargement to the East and the increasing concerns about security of energy supply in the EU have triggered a rethinking of the EU's external relations in the field of energy. The old programmes of trade and co-operation with countries to the East were superseded by arrangements designed to bring many of these countries into the EU itself. These accession strategies included an important element of approximation of laws, especially with respect to internal market legislation. They have given the energy *acquis* a genuine pan-European reach, confirmed by eventual membership. While the energy links with many of the non-member countries to the East and the south are more evident than ever, the legal bases for such relations remain weak and the policies insubstantial. At a policy level, they are described as being part of a 'European Neighbourhood Policy'.[125] The following section assesses the significance of these relationships. 2.160

---

[125] European Commission, *European Neighbourhood Policy: Strategy Paper*, COM (2004) 373 final, 12 May 2004. It offers a closer relationship to the EU to those countries that do not have formal candidate status. The EU offers privileged access to its single market provided that they can make progress with economic and political reform, in an attempt to replicate the leverage the EU has over policy developments in candidate countries without having to offer the prospect of membership.

(1) Partnership and Co-operation Agreements

2.161 A distinct form of agreement developed between the EU and the countries that were formerly part of the Soviet Union, excluding the Baltic States. A Partnership and Co-operation Agreement (PCA) is a bilateral agreement with fairly general terms that in no way implies future membership of the EU. It is a mixed agreement based on Articles 133 and 308 of the EC Treaty. It establishes an institutional, political, and administrative framework. These agreements have their roots in the 1989 Trade and Commercial Co-operation Agreement between the European Community and the former Union of Soviet Socialist Republics. They can be distinguished into two groups: those signed with the European states of the USSR (Russia, Ukraine, Moldova, and Belarus)—and the rest. The latter have usually been less detailed than the former. Neither category of PCA can be compared with the terms of an association agreement, which is a form of mixed agreement concluded under Article 310 EC and aimed at possible integration into the EU.

2.162 A PCA typically includes provisions on energy and the environmental impact of energy production, covering matters such as:

- environmental impact of energy production, supply, and consumption;
- improvement of security of supply;
- formulation of energy policy;
- improvement of the management and regulation of the energy sector in line with a market economy;
- promotion of energy saving;
- modernization of energy infrastructure including interconnection of gas supply and electricity networks; and
- introduction of the institutional, legal, and fiscal conditions necessary to increase trade and investment.[126]

In terms of substance and the dispute settlement mechanism, the PCA is significantly weaker than most association agreements.

2.163 The most significant of the PCAs in every sense is the one concluded between the EU and the Russian Federation. It establishes three institutional mechanisms:

- a Co-operation Council that meets at least annually at the ministerial level and monitors implementation of the PCA;
- a Co-operation Committee that brings together senior civil servants; and

---

[126] eg, Agreement on Partnership and Co-operation between the EU and Russia [1997] OJ L327/3, Art 65. The PCAs concluded between the EU and Armenia, Azerbaijan, Georgia and Uzbekistan contain a paragraph on the exchange of information regarding investment projects in energy, especially those that concern energy production and the construction and refurbishment of oil and gas pipelines.

G. The Wider Neighbourhood of the EU

- a Parliamentary Co-operation Committee, composed of representatives from the European Parliament and the Federal Assembly of the Russian Federation.

2.164 It has a ten-year duration and entered into force on 1 December 1997. Renewal at the end of this period is automatic on an annual basis. Sectoral agreements are envisaged and are part of the overall PCA framework. The PCA was strengthened by the adoption of a Common Strategy in 1999. Among its 'principal objectives', it refers to the integration of Russia into 'a common economic and social space in Europe'—not least because Russia 'provides a significant part of the Union's energy supplies'. The language remains fairly general, although both parties commit to continue consultations on a multilateral transit framework that is designed to enhance co-operation between Russia and its neighbours over access to the Russian pipeline system.

(a) Russia and the EU

2.165 The principal forum for discussing EU–Russia affairs is the Permanent Partnership Council (PPC). It comprises Ministers from Russia, the EU Presidency, the incoming EU Presidency and a European Commissioner. Where there is a shared competence on a specific matter, such as foreign affairs or justice, it is thought that such a small forum can contribute positively to its discussion. Its first meeting on energy was held in October 2005. The agenda included a wide range of issues, from security of energy supply and energy investment to trade and climate change. The PPC has no legal authority but gives political direction to the work of experts in the four Thematic Groups established within the framework of a policy-based arrangement known as the EU–Russia Energy Dialogue.

2.166 An early result of the Dialogue was an EU declaration that Russia is a market economy in the context of trade protection leading to amendment of EU anti-dumping and anti-subsidy laws.[127] In practical terms, this means that Russian companies' own costs and prices will be used instead of taking proxy costs and prices from a third country for the purpose of calculating and 'dumping' margins.

2.167 Despite the considerable importance of many of the above countries for the pan-European energy scene, the legal frameworks established by the EU are of a different order of significance from those established with the countries seeking membership. As one commentator has observed, the PCAs 'establish and consolidate in reality a new dividing line in Europe'.[128] They express a policy of differentiated treatment

---

[127] Regulation (EC) 1972/2002 amending Regulation (EC) 384/96 on the protection against dumped imports from countries not members of the European Community [2002] OJ L305/51 and Regulation (EC) 1973/2002 amending Regulation (EC) 2026/97 on the protection against subsidised imports from countries not members of the European Community [2002] OJ L305/4.
[128] Maresceau, M, 'Association, Partnership, Pre-Accession and Accession' in Maresceau, M, (ed), *Enlarging the EU: Relations between Central and Eastern Europe* (1997) 12.

from that accorded to candidate countries and therefore have a quite different relationship to the EU energy *acquis*. This applies to a much lesser degree to the countries involved in the EU's Stabilization and Association process, the framework for the EU's policy in South-East Europe, including the Western Balkans, to the extent that they are now members of the Energy Community Treaty.[129]

(2) Euro-Mediterranean Association Agreements

2.168 While the 1990s were dominated by questions of enlargement to the East and the creation of links with former Soviet states, another region has since received a greater attention than before in external policy development in energy. This is the so-called 'southern' or Mediterranean dimension of the EU. For the Member States in the northern parts of the EU with their relatively secure supplies of energy from the North Sea, it is easy to forget that some of the largest primary fuel suppliers to the EU are located in the Mediterranean region. This reality has helped to give momentum to the establishment of a Euro–Mediterranean Partnership,[130] involving the Mahgreb (Algeria, Morocco, and Tunisia) and Mashrak (Egypt, Jordan, Syria, and Lebanon) countries, as well as Libya, Israel and the Palestinian Authority. It also includes Turkey, which is pursuing its relations with the EU in a pre-accession framework. The EU and the 12 parties above signed a Declaration on 28 November 1995 to achieve, inter alia, a free trade zone among themselves, setting a target date of 2010 for the removal of all tariff and non-tariff barriers to trade in manufactured goods. Trade in services is to be progressively liberalized, including the right of establishment, based on WTO principles. The parties agreed to adopt measures regarding rules of origin, certification, protection of intellectual property rights, and competition.

2.169 For the EU the energy objectives of such a Partnership are principally justified on security of supply grounds. A number of these countries play, or in the medium-term could play, an important role in the transit of energy from neighbouring regions such as the Gulf and the Caspian Sea and Central Asian Republics. In addition, the volume of oil and gas reserves in these countries is an important guarantee of supplies to the EU. However, their links to the EU in terms of external trade in energy are so diverse that a programme of common interests in this sector is difficult to define. Some of the countries, such as Algeria and Egypt, are net exporters; others, like Syria and Tunisia, are in balance; the rest are net importers of energy (Israel, Jordan, Lebanon, Morocco, Palestinian Territories, and Turkey).

---

[129] Stabilization and Association Agreements are being negotiated with Albania, Bosnia and Herzegovina, Croatia, FYROM, and the Federal Republic of Yugoslavia. Integration of energy networks with the EU is a priority in this process.

[130] European Commission, *Strengthening the Mediterranean Policy of the European Union: Establishing a Euro-Mediterranean Partnership*, COM (1994) 427.

G. The Wider Neighbourhood of the EU

In most cases, they are characterized by a growing energy consumption, especially in electricity, which will require additional financing in the future. It is in the latter area that the linkage with the EU is most likely to lead to substantive results (see paras 18.68–18.80).

Given the differences of interest, it is hardly surprising that there have been lengthy discussions as to the appropriate instruments for developing co-operation. The principal instruments are Euro–Mediterranean Association Agreements concluded between the EU and the Mediterranean countries individually. These are free trade agreements but also aim at the greatest possible harmonization on economic issues, including competition, state aids, and monopolies, and also at economic co-operation in the field of energy, for example. They are of unlimited duration and may be denounced with a six-month notification period.[131] There is also a multilateral dimension to this co-operation, with funding from the MEDA programme.[132] **2.170**

A possible model for regional co-operation that has been considered by the European Commission in this context is the Energy Charter Treaty.[133] However, such an instrument is unlikely to prove suitable to the task for at least three reasons. First, the ECT has been tailored to the situation of the former communist states and to the role played by many Central and East European countries as transit routes for gas and oil to the consumer countries; most of the Mediterranean countries lack this kind of energy interdependence. Secondly, one of the fundamental components of the ECT, transit, is limited in the Mediterranean region by the underdevelopment of the network infrastructure. Finally, the ECT was negotiated in response to an absence of a framework for co-operation and of legal frameworks for trade, but for the Mediterranean countries accession to the ECT is unlikely to make much difference to their legal situation, since their starting point is quite different.[134] **2.171**

The agenda of energy issues to be addressed in this context has been defined by the principal organ for multilateral consultation, the Euro–Mediterranean Forum, **2.172**

---

[131] European Commission, 'Information Notes on the Euro–Mediterranean Partnership', January 2001, 6.
[132] MEDA refers to the financial and technical flanking measures for the reform of the economic and social structures within the framework of the Euro–Mediterranean Partnership: Council Regulation (EC) 1488/96, adopted on 23 July 1996, as amended by Council Regulation (EC) 2698/2000, [2000] OJ L311/3.
[133] Communication from the Commission to the European Parliament and Council on the Euro–Mediterranean Partnership in the Energy Sector, COM (1996) 149 final, 3 April 1996; see also the Ministerial Declaration by the Euro–Mediterranean Energy Forum, 1–2 December 2003, point 8: 'The possible extension of the Energy Charter Treaty towards non-Member countries in the Euro–Mediterranean area will aid energy market reforms' (Euromed Report No 72, 8 December 2003), and Conclusions of the Council of the European Union, 19 December 2003 (16099/03), point 6: 'transit and supplier countries in the Mahgreb should be encouraged to follow the principles of the Energy Charter Treaty'.
[134] ibid 11–12. Turkey ratified the ECT in May 2001.

set up in 1997 as the reference body for Euro–Mediterranean co-operation. There are four priority areas:[135]

- Reform of the legislative and regulatory framework, including a restructuring of the energy industry of the Mediterranean Partners. To attract the foreign direct investment they need, a reform process is required, taking into account the EU's experience in reforming the energy sector.
- Convergence of the energy policies of the EU and the Mediterranean Partners. Part of this is an encouragement by the EU that the Partners accede to the ECT as a reference framework for the promotion of investment and security of supply.
- Integration of the Mediterranean markets and the development of interconnections. This aim is directly linked to the EU aim of security of supply, and would involve their inclusion in an enlarged INOGATE agreement.[136]
- Sustainable development of the Mediterranean Partners and use of renewable energy.

The common thread that runs through all of these priorities is a concern by the EU to promote security of energy supply. Since the establishment of the Forum, this goal has been supplemented by ones concerned to achieve market access and equivalent environmental and safety standards but the goal of energy security remains the dominant one.

H. Conclusions

2.173 The development of a body of pro-competitive energy law in the EU over the past decade has benefited, at least initially, from the climate—or 'atmosphere'—of continual constitutional reform over almost two decades. However, that wider programme of reform has for the moment lost its momentum, as the EU pauses for breath after its largest intake of new members in 2004, and since the referendum results in two of the founding Member States have indicated some dissatisfaction with its achievements. Arguably, the energy *acquis* or legal order that has emerged and which continues to develop rapidly no longer needs that broader support—never given in an explicit manner in any case—since it has a momentum of its own.

2.174 Basing itself upon the ideas implicit or explicit in the primary law of the EC, a new legal order for energy has been developed over the past decade—slowly and with

---

[135] European Commission, 'Enhancing Euro-Mediterranean Co-operation on Transport and Energy', Euromed Report, Issue No 26, 22 March 2001.

[136] INOGATE is the Interstate Oil and Gas Transport to Europe, an EU programme to promote the construction and interconnection of oil and gas transport infrastructures between the EU and the regions of the Caspian Sea, Black Sea, Mediterranean and South-East Europe. It has given rise to a multilateral agreement, signed by 17 countries of south-east Europe, and covering the operation, maintenance and safety of the above infrastructures.

H. Conclusions

much controversy. It is characterized principally by an elaboration of existing EC primary rules in the form of secondary legislation (see Part II of this book). Its driving purpose has been to enhance the *integration* aspects of the EC Treaty with respect to the energy sector, rather than, say, security of supply. Efforts to amend or elaborate the primary law itself by adding a chapter on energy have proved in the event unnecessary to the achievement of these objectives so far and, almost certainly, in the foreseeable future.

However, the tensions over competing policies, priorities and competences are as evident in that body of new energy law as they are at the higher level of EU law-making. The notions of public service, services of general economic interest, security and sustainability and other environmental policy concerns, all figure largely in the debates on competition in EU energy markets as sources of constraint on its scope. **2.175**

To resolve the tensions that result, and to promote a form of balancing of interests and priorities that achieves fairness, while promoting the aims of the new, pro-competitive energy law, the EU has increasingly relied upon a less formally constituted institutional network than that described in section C of this chapter. While the Commission retains the undisputed role of promoter of the single energy market programme, whether through sector-specific legislation or the application of competition law, this has been supplemented by a secondary level of rule-making, albeit one which in many respects is still *in statu nascendi*. Essentially, this is based on the co-operative efforts of specialist national regulators and competition authorities, with consultation procedures applied for market players and consumers. The importance of this development lies in the liberalization process itself. Even though far from complete, its initial impacts have already imposed strains upon the institutional framework based on the EC Treaty. The increasing complexity of EU electricity and gas markets and the new problems that they give rise to require a constant flow of expertise into the traditional legislative and enforcement framework to ensure co-ordination and coherence along the road to further integration. The emergence of this energy regulatory network, and its significance, is the subject of the following chapter. **2.176**

Some of the long-standing areas of difficulty in energy policy discussed in section B are being modified by the increasing energy inter-dependence of EU Member States—not entirely the result of energy market liberalization—leading to a change of policy by individual Member States. Most notably, with respect to the notion of a common EU energy policy, open support was given by the Council in March 2006, even if the content contains little that is new.[137] It is also notable that **2.177**

---

[137] Council of the European Union, 18 May 2006, Presidency Conclusions of the European Council, 23/24 March 2006, 13–17 (Part 2: Energy Policy for Europe). This gave a boost to the Commission's own plans for a Strategic European Energy Review: see *An Energy Policy for Europe*, COM (2007)1 final, 10 January 2007.

all Member States were able to agree on a text for a new energy chapter in the draft Constitution, where again the UK reversed a long-standing policy of trying to limit the competence of the Commission over energy matters. This suggests that the initial impacts of liberalization, combined with other developments, may be creating a new context for resolving the tensions between competing policy priorities in this area.

2.178 Finally, some comments may be made on the wider legal context that has been sketched out in this chapter (sections D to G). There are two conclusions that may be drawn. First, the 'reach' of EU energy, environment, and competition law and its market-based concepts has been continually extended in recent years, becoming for the first time genuinely pan-European. As a result, the framework of sector-specific energy law has come to correspond more closely with the energy resource map of Europe. The EEA Agreement brings Norway (and others) into an area in which this body of primary and secondary law is applied in 27 countries. The European Energy Community Treaty has increased this reach further. Even if some of the countries involved in this European bloc are, with the exception of Norway, not important producers of energy, in some cases they are important as carriers of transit energy to the main centres of consumption in the EU.

2.179 A second conclusion, the countries that are a part of the looser legal arrangements examined in sections F and G may indeed have become more estranged from this process in recent years than a part of it. A *differentiation* in energy law and policy has been the characteristic feature in recent years. Russia has shown little interest in energy market liberalization. In other countries to the East where it has been attempted, it is clear that the benefits will emerge only after a very long time. The interest of the EU has also become clearer: it is driven by strategic concerns about security of supply, and little else.

3

THE EU SYSTEM OF ENERGY REGULATION

A. Introduction	3.01	(3) The Madrid Gas Forum	3.28
B. Establishing an EU Energy Regulatory Network		(a) Purpose	3.29
		(b) Composition	3.30
(1) The National Energy Regulator	3.05	(c) Assessment	3.31
(2) Other Regulatory Bodies	3.07	(4) ERGEG and the Forum Process	3.37
(3) The Role of the Commission	3.09	D. The Regional Energy Markets Initiative	3.40
(4) A Centralized Energy Regulator?	3.10	E. Co-ordination and Co-operation among Regulators	3.44
C. The Florence and Madrid Forums		(1) How the Role of the NRAs Grew	3.45
(1) The Regulators and Industry	3.12	(2) Five Key Relationships	3.47
(a) The Forum Concept	3.14	(a) The NRAs and the Competition Authorities	3.48
(b) Legal Status of the Forums	3.17		
(2) The Florence Electricity Forum		(b) Co-ordination among the NRAs	3.52
(a) Purpose	3.18		
(b) Composition	3.20	(c) The NRAs and the Judiciary	3.53
(c) Creation of a European TSO Association	3.21	(d) The NRAs and the Regulated Energy Industry	3.54
(d) Council of European Energy Regulators	3.25	(e) The NRAs and the European Commission	3.56
(e) Trading in Electricity	3.26	F. Assessing the EU System	3.59
(f) Assessment	3.27		

Our findings suggest that purely voluntary cooperation schemes of regulators do not provide the investment certainty and regulatory coherence necessary to develop international pipelines and interconnectors.

Commissioner N Kroes[1]

---

[1] *Towards an Efficient and Integrated European Energy Market—First Findings and Next Steps*, 16 February 2006.

A. Introduction

3.01 One of the most striking innovations in the body of sector specific energy law is the requirement that each Member State establish *ex ante* regulation of networks by means of a specialist energy authority. The minimum functions and responsibilities for such regulators are set out in the Electricity and Gas Directives. In each of the 27 Member States there is now such a regulatory authority. It is tempting to focus on this innovation—which is undoubtedly significant for the promotion of competition—and infer from subsequent or related regulatory actions that a trend is at work towards the kind of 'regulation for competition' that one finds in some liberalizing nation-states.

3.02 Indeed, there is plenty of evidence of an emerging *network* of energy regulators in the EU. The various national regulatory authorities (NRAs), responsible for energy matters, have taken steps to co-ordinate and to co-operate in, for example, a voluntary association of European regulators called the Council of European Energy Regulators (CEER). They are also part of another body called the European Regulatory Group for Electricity and Gas (ERGEG), which carries out an advisory role vis-à-vis the European Commission and is established in the EU by means of a Commission Decision.[2] All of the regulators play a role in various informal discussions that take place in the so-called Florence Regulatory Forum on Electricity and the Madrid Regulatory Forum on Gas, along with a very wide range of other governmental and industry players. Moreover, their interaction with national competition authorities (NCAs) separately or through their European Competition Network (ECN) has grown recently. The inputs into legislation from these Forum meetings and other network-based debates can be influential and are actively sought by the Commission when developing its proposals for legislation on the internal market. This growth of regulation has been the subject of much study and comment.[3]

3.03 However, if the emergence of this network is seen as the basis for a European energy regulator, this is at best premature and at worst misleading. The current 'system' is one that fits together very loosely and is voluntary in character. There are limits to the

---

[2] Commission Decision 2003/796/EC on establishing the European Regulators Group for Electricity and Gas [2003] OJ L296/34. It is required to submit a report to the Commission, Parliament and Council on an annual basis under Art 3(8) of the Commission Decision.

[3] eg, Vasconcelos, J, 'Towards the internal energy market: how to bridge a regulatory gap and build a regulatory framework' [2005] European Rev of Energy Markets 81–103; Eberlein, B, 'Regulation by Cooperation: The "Third Way" in Making Rules for the Internal Energy Market' in Cameron, PD, *Legal Aspects of EU Energy Regulation: Implementing the New Directives on Electricity and Gas across Europe* (2005) 59–88; Eurelectric, *Report on Regulatory Models in a Liberalized European Electricity Market* (2004); Centre for European Policy Studies, *Rethinking the EU Regulatory Strategy for the Internal Energy Market* (2004).

ability of regulators to co-operate since their powers on, say, cross-border trade do not allow them to act collectively and secure a modification of access terms and conditions, enforcing the necessary modifications at EU level. At the national level, the Directives may be interpreted in ways that in effect give most of the regulatory power to a government department or ministry, with the energy regulator confined to an advisory role.[4] The NRAs are statutory bodies and therefore are more constrained in their actions than companies such as TSOs. They may only act within the powers conferred on them by their founding statute, whereas companies enjoy a broad freedom to act so long as it is not prohibited by law. To this extent, the conclusion of a 'co-operative agreement' between individual regulators about common action on the European stage is of little practical significance. The NRAs can only work together to the extent that their Member States allow them to do so. There are other public authorities with overlapping competences such as the NCAs, with which they need to co-operate, or at least co-exist. In this context, there is a need for co-ordination of regulatory activity at EU level, but the current arrangements are incomplete, creating 'regulatory gaps' and therefore are unable to provide it.

3.04 This chapter describes and assesses the system of energy regulation that has developed in recent years, comprising a variety of different institutions and procedures, both formal and informal, aimed at ensuring the implementation of the sector-specific legislation and, where necessary, clarifying and supplementing it.

B. Establishing an EU Energy Regulatory Network

(1) The National Energy Regulator

3.05 The key regulatory innovation of the 2003 legislation has been the generalization of national regulatory authorities (NRAs) for electricity and gas, with a minimum set of powers, across the EU. In many cases, these had already been established,[5] but they are now mandatory in each Member State, as is the grant of a minimum set of competences. The Directives expressly require a co-ordination of NRA activity inter se and, importantly, between NRAs and competition bodies. It may be inferred that they aim to establish, albeit implicitly, nothing less than a 'regulatory culture' in the EU energy sector. These changes serve to underpin the emerging EU regulatory architecture.

3.06 While the first Directives (1997–98) approached the establishment of a co-ordinated EU regulatory framework in a way that was both hesitant and imprecise, the second

---

[4] European Commission, *Report on Progress in Creating the Internal Gas and Electricity Market: Technical Annex*, 85.
[5] By 2002 they were present in all Member States, except one (Germany), and in almost all of the then candidate countries from central and eastern Europe: see Second Commission Benchmarking Report, 7 April 2003, SEC (2003) 448.

Directives try to compensate for this unpromising start by setting out minimum requirements for the functions and competences of sector regulatory bodies charged by the Member States with supervising the electricity and gas sectors (see paras 5.55–5.68). Their independence from the electricity and gas industries has also to be guaranteed by the Member States.[6] More than this, they require the NRAs to co-ordinate with each other and to liaise with the Commission from time to time. While Member States have discretion at many points about how exactly they meet the requirements (such as over the choice of competent body and its legal status), the outcome has the potential to function as a very different, more pervasive and significantly less politicized regulatory environment—if the Member States permit such a loosening of state control.

(2) Other Regulatory Bodies

3.07 However, the NRA represents only one layer in a governance scheme that includes a number of other important bodies. In each Member State there exists a 'holy trinity' of enforcement agencies, comprising a lead ministry, a sector regulatory agency (the NRA) and a competition authority (and sometimes a competition court). The differences in the development of their relationships inter se and the relative independence of the NRAs from political control may vary considerably from one Member State to another. Indeed, there is no requirement to limit the number of energy regulatory agencies to one in each Member State; more may be established if it is considered appropriate for reasons of regional policy, for example. In some cases, administrative instruments such as guidelines and concordat-style agreements have been developed in the Member States themselves to avoid duplication of effort between the respective authorities and to minimize conflicts over jurisdiction.[7] In other cases, however, the relationships within government appear to be at an early stage of development. For example, in two very different regimes, Germany and Greece, the regulatory authority is in need of considerable development vis-à-vis the Member State ministries to comply with the minimum conditions of powers and independence that are required by the Directives. Yet, in spite of the foregoing remarks, the sector regulator has, in a number of countries, already laid down sufficient roots for the proper exercise of its regulatory powers and, as a result of its published decisions, a distinct body of jurisprudence has begun to build up (Austria, Italy and Spain are examples, in addition to the Netherlands and the UK).[8]

---

[6] There are no specific provisions against interference by government but the EC Treaty requires Member States to abstain from any measure which could jeopardize the attainment of the objectives of the Treaty (Art 10): in this case, this would be the creation of the internal market in energy.

[7] An example is the UK: see the Competition Act 1998 Concurrency Regulations, SI 2004/1077, and the competition law guideline for the Concurrent Application to Regulated Industries (OFT 405).

[8] See, eg, Cameron, PD, *Legal Aspects of EU Energy Regulation: Implementing the New Directives on Electricity and Gas across Europe* (2005) chs 6, 11, 12, 14 and 15.

B. Establishing an EU Energy Regulatory Network

A final layer in the levels of public sector governance comprises the role of the courts in reviewing exercises of regulatory authority. In a number of Member States the NRAs' decisions have been challenged by private parties in the courts, most notably in the *VEMW* case in the Netherlands (see paras 13.59 et seq).[9] In Germany too there is a practice of challenging decisions by government bodies including the NRA in the courts. This role can be expected to increase.

3.08

(3) The Role of the Commission

The role of the Commission in the regulatory framework for electricity and gas is discussed in detail elsewhere (Chapters 5 and 6). However, at this stage a distinction may be drawn between the various activities that usually fall under the heading of regulation and the function of *oversight* of the liberalization process itself. The latter may include the former but is distinct from it. The European Commission has important oversight functions and a few regulatory ones under the Treaty and secondary legislation. The oversight functions may be variously described as 'monitoring', 'impact assessment', 'benchmarking', and 'reform' or 'proactive policy development', and may result from responsibilities to 'harmonize' or ensure the 'co-ordination' of national practices. However, they are distinct from regulatory functions in the usual sense of that term. They are essential functions in a context in which the market is characterized by a pre-liberalization legacy, and has yet to satisfy the basic requirements of a liberalized market. Such a distinction between regulation and oversight contrasts with any similar distinction in a purely national setting in one important sense. The liberalization process is accompanied by an explicit programme for the creation of a single market that transcends national boundaries, and therefore has an element that creates additional challenges and levels of complexity than would be found within a nation-state.

3.09

(4) A Centralized Energy Regulator?

The goal of a single integrated European market would seem to imply that ultimately this would involve the establishment of a European energy regulatory body. At the present time the market is very far from being European in character, however. The existing legal framework under the Directives sets conditions *within* national borders, while a single market has to operate *across* them. The ability of the current co-operative arrangements of the NRAs to regulate the industry and particularly the network industry is limited. In fact, much is currently not being regulated at all. The main elements in this 'regulatory gap' are: the absence of cross-border enforcement; the uneven implementation of existing Directives

3.10

---

[9] The case was referred by a Dutch court to the ECJ, which resulted in a defeat by the Dutch government; analyzed in detail in Cameron, P, 'The Consumer and the Internal Market in Energy: Who Benefits?' (2006) 31 ELR 114–24.

and both Regulations; the absence of effective unbundling in many cases; the use of wholesale or retail price controls; the varied powers of the NRAs themselves; and the prevalence of long-term contracts including grandfathering rights (carried over from the pre-liberalization days). An additional source of tension is that accountability for security of supply currently lies at the national level (see Chapter 18), raising issues about how this might be accommodated in a more co-ordinated European approach. In any case, some form of European regulation seems essential if the consequences of this 'regulatory gap' are to be remedied. At a minimum, it would include a role in compliance and monitoring of cross-border transactions by the NRAs.

3.11 If there is a strong case for a supra-national or European form of regulation, the question arises as to which institutional actor is best able to perform it. There are three principal options: the Commission, a European energy regulator, or an enhancement of the current regulatory arrangements, probably with a new legal basis. The Commission appears to be the obvious candidate for such a role but is largely restricted to an oversight function, with some policing powers vis-à-vis the progress of liberalization and, under the Treaty, with respect to certain competition matters.[10] Indeed, if one were asked to identify a single factor responsible for shaping the current EU regulatory framework for the electricity and gas industries, it has been the determination of the Member States to resist any attempt to create within the Commission a centralized energy regulatory authority. The heterogeneity of NRAs and the creation of regulatory associations with important co-ordinating roles has been the result of this resounding '*non*' to the idea of a centralized federal-style regulatory body. It is hardly an exaggeration to claim that the entire multi-level construction that has been developed gives the lie to any suggestion that a single energy regulator might emerge in the EU in the foreseeable future. However, the Member States and all of the parties to that structure of governance have a strong interest in encouraging cohesion and co-ordination among the diverse elements that make up the complex EU regulatory structure. There are two quite different issues here: the suitability of the Commission for the role and the need for a new, centralized energy regulator distinct from the Commission itself. Given the current stage of market development (especially the absence of an integrated European grid), it seems premature and perhaps a distraction to embark upon the design of an entirely new institution. There is a third option, however. By building on the existing co-ordinating functions of the NRAs, a number of tasks might be carried out by a more streamlined association.

---

[10] The idea that a European energy regulator could be established to regulate cross-border issues is being examined by the Commission, but it is doubtful whether the new concerns about collective energy security are yet strong enough to mobilize support for such a major policy departure: see European Commission, *A European Strategy for Sustainable, Competitive and Secure Energy*, COM (2006) 105 final, 8 March 2006, 6.

They could include market surveillance and the making of recommendations on cross-border issues of access and infrastructure investment. Of the three options available, this is the least controversial and probably the easiest to implement. As markets become more integrated, however, the case for a new regulatory agency will become stronger so it is an option that should be kept under review.

C. The Florence and Madrid Forums

(1) The Regulators and Industry

3.12 For some parts of the energy industry, this emerging regulatory structure is a development that has been viewed with some apprehension. An authoritative electricity industry report declared:

> Regulation is the single most important factor facing electricity utilities in the foreseeable future. The action and decisions of these sector specific regulatory authorities affects core company revenue, business processes, customer service, company structure and the nature of competition for most utilities.[11]

There is a genuine issue here of whether the expansion of regulatory powers will lead to companies becoming over-burdened with regulation and creating disincentives to the kind of large-scale investment that is increasingly viewed as essential for new interconnectors, LNG facilities and replacement of ageing infrastructure.

3.13 To address concerns such as these, mechanisms have been developed to permit and indeed encourage industry input into the legal architecture. The Regulations on electricity and gas include Guidelines in Annexes covering very specific matters such as the management and allocation of available transmission capacity of interconnections, congestion management and the provision of third party access services (see Appendices 2, 4, and 5). These instruments have relied on input from the so-called Florence and Madrid Regulatory Forums on respectively, electricity and gas.[12] For some years this was the only formal means by which stakeholders in industry could influence the shape of legislative proposals or supplementary measures for their implementation. Increasingly, they have been side-lined by the extensive use of formal consultation procedures established by ERGEG, and NRAs separately, and by the many opportunities for contact at an informal level between stakeholders and governments, agencies and the Commission itself.

---

[11] Eurelectric Report, *Regulatory Models in a Liberalized European Electricity Market* (January 2004) 2.
[12] For a detailed assessment of the Florence Electricity Regulatory Forum see Eberlein (n 3 above); the origins and early meetings of both gas and electricity regulatory forums are examined in Cameron, PD, *Legal Aspects of EU Energy Regulation: Implementing the New Directives on Electricity and Gas across Europe* (2005) 283–311.

(a) The Forum Concept

3.14 The Forum concept developed soon after the first electricity and gas Directives were adopted in 1997–98. It has therefore been operational throughout the period in which the EU regulatory system has been established. It has been the principal means through which the market participants, including the associations of transmission network operators (TSOs), producers, consumers, network users, traders, and energy exchanges meet the NRAs, Member States and the Commission at roughly twice-yearly intervals to shape measures aimed at deepening the impact of the EU legislation and taking the internal market process forward. The concept was expanded in 2004–05 to permit the holding of small-scale, regional forums on electricity in various parts of the EU on the assumption that progress in certain areas of market reform might be faster if approached from a regional rather than a Europe-wide view, at least in the first instance.[13]

3.15 The agreements reached by the diverse participants in the Forum process have seemed to justify the term 'regulation by co-operation'.[14] In this voluntary process, an agenda is set by the Commission and the CEER and discussions with all the parties lead to the allocation of tasks for the following meeting where progress is monitored.

3.16 Many specific and often highly technical issues had to be addressed in order to make the Directives effective. If left entirely to the national authorities, the mixture of separate national solutions to these specific issues which would emerge—(eg, rules for tarification and allocation of transmission capacity)—would undermine the overall goal of the creation of a level playing field in the EU. The Forum concept, with its wide-ranging participation and consensus approach to the development of common principles and rules, therefore appeared to present an ideal solution to the problem of harmonization in this context. It seemed to offer a form of 'regulation by co-operation'.

(b) Legal Status of the Forums

3.17 Each Forum has been accorded a status greater than that of a working group but has no law-making powers. It initiates and considers proposals made by participants on the basis of information provided on a voluntary basis. Information flow has been crucial since the movement towards an integrated market has given rise to new problems, many of which have a significant technical aspect, requiring both additional data and reflection to develop possible solutions. The widening range of participants in the successive meetings of the Forums illustrates how

---

[13] A second attempt at a regional approach was announced by the ERGEG on 27 February 2006 (see paras 3.40–3.43).
[14] Vasconcelos, J, (2001), 'Co-operation between Energy Regulators in the European Union' in Henry, C, Matheu, M, and Jeunemaitre, A, (eds), *Regulation of Network Utilities* (2001) 284–9.

(2) The Florence Electricity Forum

(a) Purpose

3.18 The Florence Electricity Regulatory Forum (Florence Forum) was initially convened by the European Commission to monitor and discuss implementation of the Electricity Directive. It met for the first time in autumn 1998 in Florence, Italy, and has been convened at intervals of between six months to a year since then.

3.19 The matters discussed in the meetings have included guidelines on congestion management, transparency and information disclosure, cross-border tarification, allocation of capacity, and secure network operation. An important objective of the Forum in its early days was to encourage the formation of a Europe-wide association of TSOs to receive and channel views, proposals, and recommendations made in the Forum meetings.

(b) Composition

3.20 The participants comprise not only independent regulators from the Member States, government representatives of the Member States, the European Commission, and the EU TSOs' association (ETSO), but also representatives of the European Parliament, the network users (Eurelectric), traders (EFET), consumers (IFIEC and CEFIC), and exchanges (Europex). The establishment of ETSO was an early result and the association has played an important role in all of the meetings. The NRAs developed the CEER, which has also had an important voice in the initiation and co-ordination of proposals for change. Finally, the role of energy traders should be noted since they represent a new group of market players that have grown in importance as liberalization takes hold.

(c) Creation of a European TSO Association

3.21 There were several reasons why the European Commission sought to have a single partner in its discussions with the TSOs. The independence of TSOs was a requirement of the first Electricity Directive, and it made sense to establish an association to reflect their views. The Commission sought an independent body for four reasons:[15]

(1) There was an expectation of increased cross-border trade in electricity in future. Work was required to facilitate this process to make such trade cost-reflective and efficient. This implied a close and long-term collaboration between the TSOs.

---

[15] European Commission, Steering Brief: Meeting of Transmission System Operators, 21 January 1999 (unpublished).

(2) This work would require an exchange of confidential and commercial information, so the independence of the TSOs from other sectors of the electricity industry would have to be assured. Without independence, significant regulatory problems were likely.

(3) No body existed that met this requirement (described at point 2), nor which was representative of all EU transmission systems, nor which possessed the infrastructure and resources necessary to carry out required functions, eg development of payment/settlement and flow-management systems.

(4) The TSOs have an obligation in the internal energy market to provide their services in a non-discriminatory manner to all customers. An association that is independent of any particular group of customers is an important element in ensuring this.

3.22 The TSOs established an association in 1999 in response to the European Commission's request for a single partner in its dialogue on cross-border electricity issues. Members of ETSO include:

- the Western European TSOs association;
- Union for the Coordination of the Transmission of Electricity (UCTE);
- NORDEL (Scandinavian grid operators); and
- British and Irish power grid owners.

3.23 ETSO had as its first task the development of proposals for pricing of electricity transits across Europe, which included total transparency of transactions. Proposals were circulated by the newly-named European Transmission System Operators[16] and by several of the national regulators in a joint document, *Transmission and Trade of Electricity in Europe*.[17]

3.24 The formation of ETSO was an important step. In effect, it established a form of unbundling at the European level, by separating out the TSOs from companies involved in other activities in the electricity business. This was done irrespective of what happened at the national level. As a result, the Commission was able to conduct a dialogue about the rules on transmission and transmission services. ETSO could be relied on to draft the operational rules to implement the principles developed in the Forum. A major task carried out by the TSOs has been the rewriting of rules in the UCTE Operational Handbook to promote system security in the light of system disturbances in 2003.

---

[16] International Exchanges of Electricity: Rules proposed by the European Transmission System Operators, 23 March 1999.

[17] *Transmission and Trade of Electricity in Europe: Position Paper on Recent Developments in the Proposal of Rules*, 5 March 1999. The authors were the offices of the Italian, Portuguese, and Spanish regulators: *Autorità per l'energia elettrica e il gas* (Italy), *Entidade Reguladora do Sector Electrico* (Portugal), and *Comisión Nacional del Sistema Eléctrico* (Spain).

C. The Florence and Madrid Forums

(d) Council of European Energy Regulators

3.25 A further development in terms of articulating group interests within the Forum was the establishment of the CEER in March 2000.[18] It comprises the national independent regulators with responsibility for electricity and/or natural gas. Initially, it had ten members, comprising the regulators of Belgium, Finland, Ireland, Italy, the Netherlands, Portugal, Spain, Sweden, and the UK. Among its stated objectives are: co-operation to achieve competitive European markets in electricity and gas; the provision of the necessary elements for the development of regulation in electricity and gas; the development of joint approaches with respect to transnational energy utilities and companies that operate in separated regulated utility markets; and the establishment of common policies among members[19] on important issues based on common regulatory principles. It provides a forum in which the national regulators can co-ordinate their work for the Florence and Madrid Processes. However, it should not be seen as a kind of supranational regulator. It is a kind of regulators' club, and carries out no public consultations nor does it have any *formal* obligation to tender advice to the European Commission (unlike the ERGEG[20]). Regulatory policy in each Member State remains a matter for national regulators and their respective governments.

(e) Trading in Electricity

3.26 The development of energy trading in Europe had long been considered a probable (and desirable) consequence of the liberalization process. In other liberalized markets, so-called 'hubs' had been set up to facilitate spot trading. Trading on power exchanges plays an important role in promoting price transparency where such exchanges operate as a secondary market in tandem with bilateral contracts.[21] Exchanges have begun to develop on which electricity, and ultimately gas, could be bought and sold like any other commodity. Evidence of this is present in the Forum's composition, with the participation of the European Federation of Energy Traders (EFET) and Europex, a body set up to co-ordinate the interests of power exchanges. Some of these exchanges are established by law (as in Spain) but in most cases they are private initiatives. They are expected to play an important role in harmonizing trading arrangements to facilitate the single market objective.

---

[18] For details of CEER activities see <http://www.ceer-eu.org>.
[19] CEER, *Practical Steps for Developing a Competitive European Gas Market* (October 2000).
[20] For details of ERGEG activities, their procedures for consultation and annual reports, see <http://www.ergeg.org>; also paras 3.36–3.38, 3.51 below.
[21] For a useful and very comprehensive overview of power exchanges with case studies, see Roggenkamp, MM and Boisseleau, F, *The Regulation of Power Exchanges* (2005). See also EFET, *The Past and Future of European Energy Trading* (June 2005): <http://www.efet.org>.

(f) Assessment

3.27 The Florence Forum has proved a useful means of exchanging information, but early attempts to achieve more from this instrument encountered four specific shortcomings:

(1) in-depth discussion of highly detailed issues is limited by the informal character of the process, based on (usually) bi-annual meetings lasting less than two days;
(2) the consensus requirement makes it difficult to make progress on controversial issues;
(3) the absence of enforcement procedures means that any decisions reached can be implemented only to the extent that all parties respect them; and
(4) certain issues such as the calculation of the correct level of inter-TSO payments necessitate regular detailed decisions, which the Forum process is unable to accommodate.

As a result, the Forum has settled into the limited role of a discussion forum in which presentations are made by ERGEG, the Commission and other parties, and information is exchanged among the participants. Other channels now exist in which to tackle more ambitious goals.

(3) The Madrid Gas Forum

3.28 Taking the Florence Forum as a model, a Gas Regulatory Forum was established in Madrid in 1999. At the initiative of the Commission, the Forum meets at intervals of between 6 and 12 months.[22]

(a) Purpose

3.29 The broad aim of the Forum is to encourage a greater convergence of views, regulatory practices, and actions among participants as the liberalization process gains momentum. Basing itself on the experience with ETSO, the Commission sought to encourage a separation of transmission operation from other services and to establish a gas TSOs association. In addition, the external dimension of EU gas—its dependence on non-EU suppliers for a significant proportion of gas—introduced a number of elements that were absent in the electricity sector: the EEA Member States were invited to the meetings as well as the EFTA Surveillance Authority, and indeed Norway requested via the Forum that it be granted full membership status in the ERGEG Gas Regional Initiative.[23] The oil and gas producers were also active in the Forum through the OGP. At recent meetings, draft Guidance Notes, prepared by the Commission, on the Gas Regulation have been presented and discussed.[24]

---

[22] See <http://ec.europa.eu/energy/gas/madrid/index_en.htm>.
[23] Conclusions of the 11th Meeting of the European Gas Regulatory Forum, 18–19 May 2006.
[24] ibid.

(b) Composition

3.30 The participants in the Forum are similar to those in the Florence Forum, and include representatives designated by Member State governments as having regulatory authority over the gas sector; the European Commission; representatives of the Council Presidency; Member State government representatives; the European Parliament; and representatives from all sections of the gas industry and consumer associations. The EEA is also represented. The ERGEG has played a role of growing importance in its activities.

(c) Assessment

3.31 The same comments apply to the development of the Madrid Forum as to the Florence Forum.

3.32 **Successes** There have been two notable successes in the Madrid Process to date.

3.33 The first is the establishment of a group of TSOs that is—more or less—independent from the association that represents the other business interests of the gas industry. This was announced at the second meeting of the Forum and the body has been developing further in a constructive way since then. Given the diverse composition of the Gas Transmission Infrastructure (GTI), and the continuing close involvement of Member States and international oil companies in the EU gas business, the evolution of the GTI may be expected to be slower than its counterpart in the electricity sector.

3.34 A second achievement is the Forum's encouragement to market participants to prepare for a fully functioning internal market in gas by means of strategy papers and plans, even if not all participants have agreed upon their content. This has involved an (ongoing) process of data gathering, identification of the specifics of the EU gas industry, setting of priorities, and some preliminary examination of possible ways of overcoming obstacles to liberalization present in this particular industry. While a less tangible achievement than the establishment of a group of TSOs, the start made on this complex process also represents an achievement. It has proved essential to gather and analyse data on the different systems in the EU for transmission tarification, capacity allocation, and balancing, gas quality and network inter-operability, with a view to ensuring their convergence.

3.35 **Failures** The voluntary and informal character of the process has made it vulnerable in the face of intransigence on the part of incumbent market players. If the latter insist on proceeding no farther than the minimum requirements of the Gas Directive, the Forum mechanism has no legal authority to compel them to do otherwise. In such circumstances, further legislation becomes the only alternative.

3.36 The limitations of the Forum process have shown themselves in different ways in the two sectors. In the gas sector, the reluctance of the industry to make adaptations to the climate created by the first Gas Directive drew attention to the absence of teeth in the Forum process. Later on, there were similar difficulties in making progress with the establishment of guidelines on access to gas storage facilities (but these were eventually overcome). In the electricity sector, the impasse reached in 2002 over a set of common rules on cross-border tarification highlighted the difficulties in making progress on an issue when a very few parties were not prepared to make concessions.[25] Although the issue was subsequently resolved, it was done so largely by the introduction of draft legislation. There are other shortcomings in the Forum process as an alternative to legislation. Most importantly, it is slow, with consensus being built up only gradually among the various participants. However, if the electricity or gas industry and/or other parties do not agree with a proposal for market reform, there is always the threat that legislation may be introduced to resolve the deadlock. If they do agree, there is the possibility that the resulting codes of practice or guidelines will in any case be given legislative form by incorporation in an Annex to the Electricity or Gas Regulation to 'consolidate' the regime and to harmonize with existing legislation.

(4) ERGEG and the Forum Process

3.37 The establishment of a new European regulators' body, the ERGEG, in 2003 raised a question about the continued need for the Forum process.[26] It was specifically established by law to advise the Commission and consult with industry and other parties on matters relating to the achievement of the internal energy market, including legislative proposals, on the basis of a clear set of rules (see para 3.52). Historically, the Forum process has been extremely useful and has constituted an important initiative of the Commission immediately after the first liberalization Directives. However, the decline in the number of meetings of both of the Forums in the past couple of years (and subtle shifts in their operating procedures) might also suggest that their relevance has already been undermined by this further development of the NRAs' network. This should not suggest a corresponding decline in the role of guidelines and codes of practice (and the need for extensive discussions of them with interested parties at the draft stage) but rather that the leading role in their development lies now with the ERGEG as co-ordinator of the process of drafting, developing and ultimately presenting them to the Commission for discussion in the comitology procedure. In this process a formal consultative role for the Forum is but one part (of several).

3.38 The shift is evident from the recent practice with respect to the development of three important Guidelines on cross-border trade. ERGEG developed Guidelines

---

[25] See Conclusions from the Florence Regulatory Forum meetings, 2002: <http://ec.europa.eu/energy/electricity/florence/index_en.htm>.

[26] But see Commission Decision 2003/796/EC on establishing the European Regulators Group for Electricity and Gas [2003] OJ L296/34, Recital 5: the Forums 'will remain important as comprehensive discussion platforms involving all players from government, regulators, and industry'.

on Congestion Management at electricity interconnectors that were adopted in 2006 by means of the comitology[27] process under Regulation 1228/2003. It has also been requested by the Commission to develop Guidelines on Transmission Tarification and on Inter-TSO Mechanisms. In the course of doing so, the ERGEG has engaged in a very thorough and transparent process of consultation, which included as one part of that process of preparation work a presentation and discussion at the Florence Forum. This process seems likely to continue. ERGEG has taken on the preparation of another set of Guidelines, this time to cover Good Practice in Electricity Balancing, which is expected to result in the establishment of a more formal framework on balancing markets and especially on the interdependencies between balancing and congestion management.[28]

3.39 A similar pattern is evident with respect to the development of Guidelines with respect to gas. First of all, at the request of the Commission, the ERGEG developed a set of Guidelines for Good TPA Practice for Storage System Operators (GGPSSO) which is aimed at setting out minimum requirements for non-discriminatory and transparent access conditions to storage facilities, in line with the Gas Directive (see paras 6.137–6.141). These have since been adopted. A set of Guidelines for Good Practice for Gas Balancing is also under development.[29]

D. The Regional Energy Markets Initiative

3.40 The idea has developed that progress in making energy markets more competitive could be faster if it targets regional units within the EU and makes intensive efforts at promoting competition and integration. This was first launched by the Commission at the tenth meeting of the Florence Forum and subsequently followed through by the ERGEG.[30] The guiding thread seems to be as follows: since some Member States have already adopted common harmonized rules, the development of a number of regional markets between them may be a necessary

---

[27] There are three distinct comitology procedures, using an Advisory, Management or Regulatory Committee, with varying degrees of control over the Commission's power to adopt new rules: Council Decision of 28 June 1999 laying down the procedures for the exercise of implementing powers conferred on the Commission, [1999] OJ L184/23.

[28] ERGEG, *Annual Report 2005*, 7.

[29] ibid. ERGEG has also been active in streamlining the reporting process from the NRAs so that the Commission can draw on the data more efficiently, as well as assisting the Commission in the interpretation and analysis of the national data: ibid 11.

[30] European Commission, DG TREN and Transport Working Paper; Strategy Paper: 'Medium Term Vision for the Internal Electricity Market', <http://ec.europa.eu/energy/electricity/florence/doc/florence_10/strategy_paper/strategy_paper_march_2004.pdf>; Eurelectric produced a Road Map document on regional electricity markets with a generally positive view on its harmonization potential: *Integrating Electricity Markets through Wholesale Markets: Eurelectric Road Map to a Pan-European Market*, June 2005, <http://www.eurelectric.org>; for a comparative discussion of the US and EU approaches to electricity market integration, see De Jong, J, 'The 'Regional Approach' in Clingendael International Energy Programme, *Establishing the Internal EU Electricity Market* (2004).

Chapter 3: The EU System of Energy Regulation

interim stage before an integrated single market is attained. Within regions, market arrangements tend to show a greater degree of harmonization and to reflect strong, underlying physical, institutional and political links. The Nordic region is one example of this, with its regional electricity market. A greater degree of harmonization of regulation could therefore be achieved on a regional basis for key issues such as the determination of transmission tariffs, rules for bilateral trading and congestion management methodologies. However, the ERGEG has noted that, on the basis of experience, 'it is not necessary for the establishment of the single electricity market that full harmonization of national and regional arrangements must occur'.[31] Differences arising from taxation, environmental and social measures that reflect national priorities will remain and may affect the market, but need not lead to inefficient trade. An important caveat about this regional approach is that its justification can only be that it permits a faster degree of integration than that required at EU level.[32]

3.41 It may well be asked what a regional market is. The CEER has stated that a regional market exists where the following conditions are found:[33]

- sufficient transmission capacity exists between the markets within the region and is made available to market participants;
- there are no distortions within the local markets which significantly affect the functioning of the regional market;
- an appropriate legal and regulatory framework is in place which allows for action across a regional market; and
- national institutions within the regional market co-ordinate and co-operate closely with each other within an appropriate legal framework. Examples of this include the co-operation of TSOs to ensure that interconnector capacity is optimized and allocated efficiently, and regulators working together and exchanging information to ensure proper monitoring and regulation of both national and regional markets.

3.42 A regional market may be defined therefore as a market comprising at least two Member States with arrangements in place to minimize barriers to trade within the region and with market rules that take account of interactions with, and which require compatibility with, other areas within that region. It may be limited to segments of the supply chain such as wholesale markets and not retail ones.

3.43 The support of Member State governments for this initiative was crucial,[34] and in fact the role of regulators in enhancing co-operation and co-ordination with

---

[31] ERGEG, *Discussion Paper: the Creation of Regional Electricity Markets* (June 2005).
[32] It may be noted that a number of Member States have, independent of this development, taken their own initiatives: the Spanish and Portuguese authorities have committed themselves to creating a single Iberian market for electricity. Great Britain has had a single market in electricity from 1 April 2005.
[33] CEER Working Paper, *Key interactions and potential trade distortions between electricity markets* (September 2004).
[34] ERGEG, *Annual Report 2005*, 7.

E. Co-ordination and Co-operation among Regulators

TSOs on a regional basis has been encouraged by the Council.[35] It expressly noted that such co-operation and co-ordination could be enhanced by 'building on already existing administrative bodies like the... [ERGEG]'. In fact, ERGEG's initial efforts in this respect—its consultation paper on the creation of regional electricity markets—received a very favourable response from market participants and led to the launch of a major initiative in spring 2006, called the Electricity Regional Initiative.[36] This created seven electricity Regional Energy Market blocks, each of which has to tackle the key cross-border obstacles within its region through concrete action plans, which would involve all of the major stakeholders and lead to full integration by 2012. A separate initiative was launched in April 2006 called the Gas Regional Initiative, following a separate process of consultation on a Roadmap for a Competitive Single Gas Market in Europe. The Gas Initiative comprises four regional energy market blocks. In both Initiatives, a national regulator chairs a co-ordination committee of regulators and it defines, inter alia, the geographic scope of the regional market, the working groups comprising gas hub operators, TSOs and network users, and the stakeholder consultation. In each case, ERGEG is to report on progress to the Florence and Madrid Forums.

E. Co-ordination and Co-operation among Regulators

The network of governance mechanisms described in the previous sections is still one *in statu nascendi*. The large number of government agencies in the 27 Member States with competence in energy matters,[37] and the diverse formal structures chosen by Member States for their NRAs, means that there is a complex array of (largely untested) enforcement mechanisms in the EU. In each of the two main networks (the NRAs and the competition authorities) the European Commission plays a key role, although it shares this with the ERGEG among the NRAs. For the consumers of regulation, the energy companies, and the judiciary, this regulatory regime presents an important—and still quite new—challenge. For the regulatory authorities themselves, it presents a challenge of co-ordination and co-operation.   **3.44**

(1) How the Role of the NRAs Grew

As the new kids on the block, the role of the NRAs requires some comment. Compared with the national competition authorities, they are almost all of very recent origin and are developing their rules and practices for the first time.   **3.45**

---

[35] European Council, Presidency Conclusions, 23/24 March 2006, <http://europa.eu/european_council/conclusions/index_en.htm>.
[36] ERGEG, *Annual Report 2005*, 5.
[37] Of course, environmental authorities have a role in many energy issues; this is likely to increase with the impact of the EU Emissions Trading Scheme and legislation on renewable energy.

In Germany's case, the energy regulator or *Bundesnetzagentur* (BnetzA) only became operational in 2005. Prior to that, regulatory competence was divided between the *Bundeskartellamt* and the Ministry at the federal level. The 2003 Directives have significantly enhanced the legal status of the NRAs in two ways[38](see paras 5.55–5.68): there is an obligation on Member States to charge one or more competent bodies with the function of regulatory authorities, and a minimum set of functions and competences is set out in the Directives in the interests of harmonization.[39] In addition, Member States are required to take measures to ensure that the NRAs are able to carry out their duties in an efficient and expeditious manner.[40] Their supervisory role over network access and tariff setting or approval has been given a basis in European law. These tariffs, or the methodologies underlying their calculation, are to allow the necessary investments in the networks to be carried out in a manner so that these investments ensure the viability of the networks.[41]

3.46 While both of these developments enhance the potential impact of the NRAs on the liberalization process, nationally and potentially on a European scale, they also increase the risk of failure in co-ordination and co-operation. This is fuelled by the potential for divergence that the operation of subsidiarity entails. In many cases, the NRAs sprang up in response to specific national circumstances. The resulting diversity created a patchwork of regulatory entities with widely differing powers. It is hardly surprising then to note that the Directives and Regulations seek to avert this.[42] As a result, they may rein in this heterogeneous regulatory development, with Member States such as Finland, Greece, Germany, and Sweden being required to abandon their preference for *ex post* regulation. However, this is likely to prove a temporary brake, as some Member States and NRAs design a national regime that goes beyond the minimum competences in the Directives, and as both Member States and NRAs interpret the provisions differently. Pressure on the design and operation of regulatory regimes can also be expected to come from the enhanced co-operation between NRAs and the Commission through the ERGEG. This will be in the direction not only of harmonization but also of strengthening the NRAs' role vis-à-vis Member State governments. At the same

---

[38] Electricity Directive, Art 23 and Gas Directive, Art 25.

[39] Electricity Directive, Recital 15; Gas Directive, Recital 13. There are also some requirements imposed by the Directives on Member States that they may elect to devolve to NRAs, such as those on providing tendering procedures for additional capacity in the interest of security of supply and ensuring that reliable information is provided to customers about the energy sources for the electricity supplied.

[40] Electricity Directive, Art 23(7); Gas Directive, Art 25(7).

[41] See generally in this context, the DG TREN Interpretation Note, 'The Role of the Regulatory Authorities', 14 January 2004. However, note the many criticisms about the actual operation of the NRAs in some Member States, where their independence is minimal: European Commission, *Benchmarking Report 2005*, 85–86; ERGEG, *Annual Report 2005*, 12.

[42] Electricity Directive, Recital 16; Gas Directive, Recital 14. Commission Decision 2003/796/EC on establishing the European Regulators Group for Electricity and Gas [2003] OJ L296/34.

E. Co-ordination and Co-operation among Regulators

time, the relationship between the NRAs and the ministries in their respective countries that have competence for energy matters can be expected to produce some frictions. A 'regulatory culture' is still a recent phenomenon in most Member States, so it is unlikely that the inter-relationship between these two partners will be free from tensions.

(2) Five Key Relationships

3.47 Indeed, if a regulatory culture is to take root, there are at least five key relationships that will have to be managed so as to encourage co-ordination or at least a peaceful co-existence. They are the relationships between (1) the NRAs and the national competition authorities within each Member State; (2) the NRAs themselves, to ensure that their actions are not contradictory from one Member State to the next; (3) the NRAs and the judiciary, more relevant in some Member States than others; (4) the NRAs and the entities they regulate; and (5) the NRAs and the Commission.

(a) The NRAs and the Competition Authorities

3.48 A measure of overlap between competition law and sector regulation is in several respects inevitable. The owners of networks have a natural monopoly and therefore a dominant position on the market. A refusal to grant access may be seen as a regulatory matter but it can also be viewed as an abuse of a dominant position on the market and therefore a matter best left to the competition authorities. There are many other areas in which competence may overlap. The question arises as to how best to deal with this. Several Member States have already taken steps to demarcate the competence of the various authorities and to require them to consult with each other in specified areas. Under the new German legislation, the regulator for energy has a strong position vis-à-vis the competition authorities.[43] However, there is an argument in favour of flexibility rather than the demarcation of competence according to strict rules, which may slow down the regulation process and make it more complex.

3.49 Since much of competition law has an *ex post* character in contrast to sector regulation, it may seem that avoidance of overlapping competence is primarily a matter of setting out procedural guidelines and requiring consultation among the relevant authorities. With respect of issues concerning merger control, this does not apply, however. In Spain this is exactly the field in which the lack of harmony between the two sets of authorities has been most pronounced.[44]

---

[43] For a detailed discussion of this issue, see Pritzsche, K, and Klauer, S, 'Germany' in Cameron, PD, *Legal Aspects of EU Energy Regulation: Implementing the New Directives on Electricity and Gas across Europe* (2005) 145–71.
[44] Garayar, E, 'Spain' in Cameron, ibid 315–44; see the highly politicized role of the NRA in the *Endesa/E.ON* takeover case in 2006: Commission Press Release IP/06/1265, 'Mergers: Commission rules against Spanish Energy Regulator's measures concerning E.ON's bid for Endesa', 26 September 2006.

3.50 In Portugal procedural requirements have been introduced to address this issue. In a large number of situations, both ERSE and the Competition Authority can claim jurisdiction over the same facts. A typical example is a refusal to grant access where access is required by sector specific legislation. The competition law regime established in 2003 took this into account and adopted specific rules on co-ordination between the two bodies. With respect to anti-competitive agreements or practices, in cases where there are facts subject to specific regulation and which may be categorized as restrictive practices, the competition law requires the competition authority to inform the sector authority immediately and give the latter time to consider the issue prior to delivering its own opinion. This applies *mutatis mutandis*, with the sector regulator giving the competition authority an opportunity to have a prior hearing on an issue that has a restriction of competition as one of its elements. In spite of this, potential conflict cannot be ruled out over jurisdiction and indeed such conflict has been a feature of other sectors, such as telecommunications, where the liberalization process has proceeded further.[45]

3.51 In the UK an attempt to demarcate the competence of the NRA, Ofgem, from the competition authority, has been made by giving Ofgem concurrent power with the Director General of Fair Trading to apply the Competition Act and Enterprise Act prohibitions in the gas and electricity sectors. These concurrent powers also apply with respect to the application and enforcement of Articles 81 and 82 EC.[46] However, some areas such as exploration and production of gas and matters related to offshore waters remain the exclusive preserve of the competition body.

(b) Co-ordination among the NRAs

3.52 Under the Electricity and Gas Directives, the NRAs are required to contribute to the development of the internal market and a level playing field by co-operating with each other and with the Commission in a transparent manner.[47] To facilitate this, the Commission established the ERGEG as an independent advisory group in November 2003. Its membership comprises the heads of the competent NRAs in the Member States, with the EEA countries participating as observers. Its aim is to facilitate consultation, co-ordination, and co-operation between the regulatory bodies in Member States and between these bodies and the Commission, to consolidate the internal market and to ensure the consistent application in all the Member States of the two Directives and the Electricity Regulation.[48] It tenders advice to the Commission and assists it in the preparation of draft implementing measures in electricity and gas. It acts either at its own initiative or at the request

---

[45] Protasio, M and Pinto Correia, C, 'Portugal' in Cameron, ibid 287–313.
[46] UK Office of Fair Trading, *Application in the Energy Sector: Understanding Competition Law* (2005).
[47] Electricity Directive, Art 23(12); Gas Directive, Art 25(12); Electricity Regulation, Art 9.
[48] Commission Decision 2003/796/EC on establishing the European Regulators Group for Electricity and Gas [2003] OJ L296/34, Recital 6.

E. Co-ordination and Co-operation among Regulators

of the Commission. Under Article 4 of the Decision establishing it, the ERGEG is required to 'consult extensively and at an early stage with market participants, consumers and end-users'. The establishment of this advisory body was strongly supported by the European Parliament during the debates on the Directives. It mirrors the roles of similar bodies already established in the telecommunications and financial services sectors.[49] According to its Rules of Procedure, the ERGEG will submit an annual report to the Commission, which will then be transmitted to the Parliament and Council.[50] The Chair must report to the Parliament when requested to do so (and did so for the first time in autumn 2004). The success of this co-ordination mechanism is likely to be driven by the more independent NRAs and the Commission, since a number of them have less secure bases of support from their respective governments.

(c) The NRAs and the Judiciary

3.53 The role of the courts in reviewing exercises of regulatory authority should not be neglected. In some Member States (the Netherlands, for example) this has already played a role in constraining the scope of the regulatory bodies. Where a written constitution provides protection for private property there may be a basis for challenging the more ambitious attempts to tackle market structure by rigorous unbundling requirements. The European Convention on Human Rights may be noted as an influence on the administrative law framework in which regulators operate. This factor is significant in the UK, for example, where it represents a very recent addition to the regulatory landscape. The Charter of Human Rights contained in the draft Treaty on a Constitution for Europe could (if revived) also be expected to enhance the legal basis for private actions through the courts. As the powers of regulators expand with the implementation of the new Directives, it can only be expected that their actions will increasingly become subject to scrutiny by the courts with respect to their operation and scope. As they explore their new powers, the NRAs will find themselves in new territory such as this.

(d) The NRAs and the Regulated Energy Industry

3.54 A key issue for the EU is the management of this relationship. The market structure has remained highly resistant to the introduction of competition that the legal framework is designed to promote, and new efforts are being made to

---

[49] [2002] OJ L200/38 (ERG—telecommunications); COM (2001) 1501 (CESR—financial services). The ERGEG is in practice, if not formally, an offshoot of the CEER. It shares a common chairperson and members, and ERGEG relies on the CEER for funding and expertise. The CEER is a voluntary association that includes most of the EU energy regulators, and has been highly active in the Electricity and Gas Forums since its establishment in March 2000. It has a number of working groups: <http://www.ceer-eu.org>.

[50] Rules of Procedure, Art 9 (Accountability): <http://www.ergeg.org>.

address this.[51] However, at the same time there is a new appreciation among the regulatory authorities that incentives have to be provided to investors if the large investments in new energy infrastructure are to be met. To encourage this, the 2003 legislation allowed exemptions to be granted from the mandatory requirement for third party access.[52] Regulators have been pro-active in their implementation in both the electricity and gas sectors.

3.55 Elsewhere, there is evidence that industry concerns about rates of return are being treated seriously by the Commission in its internal debates on the quality of regulation ('better regulation').[53] Moreover, the Forum process has shown that the various sides of industry are welcomed by both the Commission and the NRAs to contribute to the development of proposals for detailed rules, regulations and guidelines for electricity and gas that are essential if the liberalized electricity and gas markets are to work well. The consultation procedures agreed by the ERGEG (and practice to date) also support this conclusion that industry input is actively sought by the NRAs.[54]

(e) The NRAs and the European Commission

3.56 To a large extent the new European role of the NRAs is a creation of the Commission itself, through progressive support for the development of, first, an association of NRAs (the CEER) by involving it in the Forum process, and secondly, the establishment by law of the explicitly European body, the ERGEG. The relationship can be expected to remain a close one. It is however an odd one: the Commission encourages and formalizes the establishment of networks but the Member States establish the NRAs themselves. The networks can be seen as instruments for the management of the inevitable tensions that will appear from time to time in such a relationship.

3.57 There is however ample evidence that, no matter how successful the Commission's relations with NRAs are through the ERGEG, the Commission is highly dissatisfied with the way in which some Member States have implemented the Directives with respect to the establishment and functioning of NRAs. In its 2005 benchmarking report, it noted the 'high degree of variability' that exists in the manner

---

[51] European Commission, Communication from the Commission to the Council and the European Parliament: 'Report on progress in creating the internal gas and electricity market', COM (2005) 568 final, 15 November 2005.

[52] Gas Directive, Art 22.

[53] See Communication of the Commission to the European Parliament, the Council, the Economic and Social Committee and the Committee of the Regions, 'Implementing the Community Lisbon Programme—A Strategy for the simplification of the regulatory environment', COM (2005) 535 final, 25 October 2005.

[54] 'Public Guidelines on ERGEG's Consultation Practices', 10 August 2004.

in which regulatory functions are exercised. Among the shortcomings in effective regulation it identified are the following:[55]

- regulators do not directly set tariffs or tariff methodologies and instead only have an advisory role to the Ministry;
- regulators are not responsible for control of access to gas storage;
- regulators do not have responsibilities for the surveillance of wholesale electricity markets in terms of transparency and disclosure for producers and TSOs and/or market operators/power exchanges;
- regulators have no input into conditions applied to companies seeking to merge;
- regulators may have insufficient ability to enforce their decisions through sanctions.

3.58 The possibility of a lack of consistency in regulation is raised by a combination of these shortcomings. The Commission also notes that in some Member States the fact that two authorities are monitoring and controlling parts of the market might lead to regulatory gaps. It appears likely that proposals to remedy such shortcomings will appear in the future.

F. Assessing the EU System

3.59 The approach adopted by the EU towards the creation of an internal energy market has been shaped by a dilemma: a single market is to be created but there is considerable reluctance by Member States to address the question of how it is to be governed. For a long time, it has been clear that the establishment of a single market is not to entail the creation of a single, centralized regulatory authority for the sector. The choice of instruments and the way they have been used—with a heavy emphasis upon consensus-building and avoidance of the blunter legal instruments available—illustrate vividly the extent to which Member States have had to be persuaded of the lack of governance implications of the single market programme so far. A slow, complex, and highly politicized result has followed. It has emerged as much by default as by design.

3.60 What is new in this is the emergence of a multi-level structure of regulatory authorities, wearing a cloak of governance. The material is thin, but it is there nonetheless. The network of energy sector regulators have to co-ordinate with each other, with their respective governments and with the Commission, or the

---

[55] European Commission, *Benchmarking Report 2005*, 85–6; ERGEG, 'Assessment of the Development of the European Energy Markets 2006' and 'Compatibility of National Legal Conditions Concerning Regulatory Competences' at <http://www.ergeg.org/portal/page/portal/ERGEG_HOME/ERGEG_DOCS/NATIONAL_REPORTS/2006>. This critical line of analysis was continued in the 2006 Benchmarking Report: European Commission, 'Prospects for the internal gas and electricity markets,' COM (2006) 841 final, 10 January 2007, 12–15.

EU legal regime for energy will not work. The network of competition authorities that has come into being must, to the extent that it becomes involved in energy matters, co-ordinate with the NRAs and their association, with their respective governments and with the Commission itself. This complex of regulatory bodies has every incentive to co-operate, comparing notes on solutions to similar problems and discussing common approaches to cross-border issues. The manner of such co-operation and the subjects on which co-operation occurs may still be determined on a pragmatic, case-by-case basis rather than a rule-based system. The alternative is that the new regulatory 'system' will rapidly become a source of regulatory uncertainty on an unprecedented scale, with considerable costs imposed on the achievement of competitiveness. Moreover, to the extent that such co-operation *does* succeed, it will become a new driver in the single market process. In terms of institutional design, this is a high-risk model of regulation. It contains few clear divisions of competence among the players,[56] it is complex and untested, it has little ability to reach or adopt European objectives over national ones, and it relies upon voluntary mechanisms to succeed.

3.61 This is not the only liberalizing sector of the EU economy in which these trends can be observed. Others have commented on trends of 'new governance'.[57] However, the evidence from the energy sector suggests that the EU remains a very long way from becoming a 'regulatory state'. Indeed, the multi-level form of governance outlined here may prove attractive to other parts of the world with federal structures such as Canada or which have strong incentives to engage in energy co-operation (North-East Asian states, for example). If optimism about a positive outcome in the EU is justified, that a 'regulatory culture' may indeed develop, and that Member States may let it grow, this is perhaps more soundly based on the parties' awareness that effective competition will require a significant further development of this regulatory structure. The need for a more co-ordinated approach to investment in the EU's ageing and increasingly inadequate energy infrastructure—and the growing concerns about energy security—should provide a momentum for the co-operation and co-ordination among the various regulatory actors that this model of governance implicitly supports. This is rooted in the dynamic of liberalization itself, which is forcing Member States to consider

---

[56] In some Member States the lines of demarcation between the NRAs and NCAs are quite clearly distinguished: the Netherlands and the UK are two examples.

[57] Of course, the use of the Forum process and indeed the way in which the energy regulators' network has been developed provide some evidence for 'new governance' arguments, even if this not explicit. However, they co-exist with more traditional instruments of law and regulation. For an interesting discussion of this combination of new and traditional instruments (but not in energy) see de Burca, G, 'The Constitutional Challenge of New Governance in the European Union' (2003) 28 ELR 814–39.

F. Assessing the EU System

institutional reform on a European scale in a sector not normally associated with co-operation among the EU Member States.

The Electricity and Gas Directives have initiated a very different regulatory environment in the EU from the one that existed before their adoption. Their provisions have had far-reaching institutional consequences for the supervision of the electricity and gas sectors, leading to a proliferation of regulatory authorities in the Member States—and raising questions about the interaction between these new institutions and the EU authorities. However, if one notes the considerable progress being made by the ERGEG in combining several different roles—and not least keeping the support of the Member States—it suggests that a basis already exists for a further stage in regulatory development without which an internal energy market will not happen.

3.62

Part II

SECTOR REGULATION

4

INTRODUCTION TO PART II: SECTOR REGULATION

The purpose of this second part of the book is to examine the rules of European law that are applicable to the various energy sub-sectors: electricity, gas, oil, coal, nuclear energy, and renewable energy. The scope of competition in these sub-sectors varies considerably at the European level according to the legal frameworks, policy priorities, and the need to accommodate national initiatives, sometimes pre-existing and often pursued at different levels of intensity. They represent a mix of the new energy law, in which the competition objective is the dominant policy aim, and an earlier approach, which has usually given at least co-equal status to the goal of energy security. In four of these sub-sectors, the principal rules are laid down by means of secondary legislation, and are of fairly recent origin. In the other two cases, the rules on coal and nuclear energy have their roots in treaty instruments adopted at an earlier stage in European legal history, driven by different policy concerns. In the first group, the competition goal is strongly evident and linked to the goal of achieving an internal market. In the second, the competition objective is usually subordinate to other concerns. This contrast is less marked however when it is noted that the rules on coal have acquired a more conventional legal basis from 2002, when the relevant treaty instrument expired. **4.01**

The policy objectives driving the various laws have been present for many years. In brief terms, these can be summarized as: energy security, competition, and environmental sustainability. However, the balance between them differs considerably between the current 'liberalization' phase of the EU economy and the period when the foundations of nuclear energy law were laid in the late 1950s. In terms of the paradigm shift discussed in Chapter 1, the latter were put in place long before the current paradigm in energy markets took root in European law. **4.02**

Given this background, the treatment of energy law in some chapters of this Part differs significantly from that in others. The EU has made extensive efforts to tackle both monopoly elements and distortions of competition in the electricity and gas sub-sectors, and this is apparent from the number and variety of legislative **4.03** instruments that have been developed to achieve these aims. In addition to Directives, Decisions and Regulations, this includes legally enforceable Guidelines, and non-binding Guidance Notes issued by the Commission. In terms of the law-making process, it includes a 'parallel' legislative process, through the Florence and Madrid Forums, comitology, and the ERGEG drafting and consultative role. In the case of renewable energy, the balance between market and environmental sustainability goals is stronger than in any of the other chapters. The enforcement provisions are correspondingly weaker. In the chapter on coal, the present legal basis subjects it more closely to the ambit of the competition law, but there remains a delicate balance between the application of these rules and the elements of 'social regulation' that have always been important in this sector. The chapter on nuclear energy stands out in offering little by way of evidence of competitive goals, and only indirectly an emphasis on sustainability. In this field, the law-making is heavily biased towards national measures, with some influence from the Community institutions, and the dominant policy objective is one of energy security.

4.04 Inevitably, there are some legislative measures that apply to a particular sub-sector that are not treated in the relevant chapter. Measures concerning renewable energy clearly impinge greatly on electricity, but they are treated in a separate chapter. Where there is an element of overlap between the subject of one chapter and that of another, this has been addressed by the use of cross-referencing to avoid duplication of treatment. Although this means that each chapter is not entirely a 'stand-alone' work, the cross-referencing mechanism should ensure that a full comprehension of the issues discussed can nonetheless be gained. Finally, it should be emphasized that the impact of the competition law as set out in the EC Treaty is treated in the next Part of this book. For that reason, important subjects that touch on the subject matter of a particular chapter, such as state aid rules in relation to nuclear energy or antitrust rules in relation to network access, are given only a brief mention or are omitted entirely. This is an artificial device, adopted for purposes of exposition in this volume, and designed to provide a deeper insight into each of the component parts. The reality is of course that both sector-specific legislation and competition rules interact.

5

ELECTRICITY

A. Introduction	5.01	(e) Dispute Settlement	5.64
B. The Electricity Directive 2003		(f) Co-ordination Among Regulators	5.66
(1) Aims and Scope	5.06	(9) Enforcement	5.69
(2) General Rules	5.08	(a) Derogations	5.70
(a) Public Service Obligations	5.09	(b) Reporting Requirements	5.73
(b) Security of Supply	5.16	(c) Infringement	5.78
(c) Technical Rules	5.17	C. The Electricity Regulation 2003	5.79
(3) Rules for Specific Activities		(1) The Inter-TSO Compensation Mechanism	5.84
(a) Generation	5.18	(2) Charges for Network Access	5.86
(b) Transmission	5.27	(3) Congestion Management	5.90
(c) Distribution	5.34	(4) Exemptions for New Interconnectors	5.95
(4) Unbundling		(a) The Estlink Interconnector	5.100
(a) The Approach	5.38	(5) Information Requirements	5.106
(b) Legal Unbundling	5.39	(6) Guidelines	
(c) Compliance	5.40	(a) Article 8	5.113
(d) Interpretation	5.43	(b) The New Guidelines on Congestion Management	5.119
(5) Access	5.44	(7) Enforcement	5.128
(6) Market Opening and Reciprocity	5.48	(a) Preferential Access Ruling by the ECJ	5.132
(7) Direct Lines	5.51	(b) Slovenian Derogation	5.136
(8) The Role of the Regulators		D. Conclusions	5.140
(a) The Framework	5.55		
(b) The Obligations of the NRA	5.57		
(c) Tariff Supervision	5.61		
(d) Cross-Border Issues	5.63		

For electricity the main problems can mostly be traced to the failure to create an integrated market . . . This is the single most important issue for the electricity market.

European Commission[1]

---

[1] *Report on Progress in Creating the Internal Gas and Electricity Market: Technical Annex*, COM (2005) 568 final, 15 November 2005, 9.

A. Introduction

5.01 The principal legislation applicable to the EU electricity sector is Directive (EC) 2003/54 ('the Electricity Directive'),[2] adopted on 26 June 2003, and the Regulation on conditions for access to the network for cross-border exchanges in electricity ('the Regulation'),[3] adopted on the same date. This body of legislation has its origins in the limited success of the first electricity liberalization Directive.[4] This first measure[5] proved to be too modest in its ambitions and scope, and proposals were tabled by the Commission in 2001 for a successor. In addition, a new approach was proposed to implementation of the 'common rules' it was to contain. Its successor would be accompanied by other instruments, which would allow for regulation to evolve once the Directive and Regulation were in place. In this manner, the Commission and those Member States most ardently supporting market reform sought to bring within the scope of the new legislation a more detailed subject matter.

5.02 Four features of the Electricity Directive are especially noteworthy. First, there are strengthened provisions on unbundling. Such rules are required to ensure that network access charges are cost reflective and do not contain hidden cross-subsidies. These provisions represent a major step forward in the Commission's efforts to address structural constraints on the creation of an internal market in energy. They apply to network businesses if these are part of a 'vertically integrated undertaking'.[6] However, the shift towards only *legal* unbundling (as distinct from the stronger form, ownership unbundling) shows the limits imposed on these efforts by the Treaty provisions guaranteeing non-interference in property ownership under Member State law.[7]

---

[2] Directive (EC) 2003/54 concerning common rules for the internal market in electricity and repealing Directive (EC) 96/92 [2003] OJ L176/37.

[3] Regulation (EC) 1228/2003 of 26 June 2003 on conditions for access to the network for cross-border exchanges in electricity [2003] OJ L176/1. The set of guidelines are already being further developed to provide more detail on the general provisions of the Regulation on co-ordination between TSOs, transparency and maximizing available capacity, and the treatment of congestion rents.

[4] Directive (EC) 96/92 concerning common rules for the internal market in electricity [1997] OJ L27/20.

[5] Directive (EC) 96/92 was repealed by Art 29 of the Electricity Directive.

[6] Discussion of how the terms 'vertically integrated undertaking' and 'control' are understood by the Commission in relation to Council Regulation (EEC) 4064/89 (merger control), is contained in the DG TREN Interpretation Note, 'The Unbundling Regime', 16 January 2004, <http://ec.europa.eu/dgs/energy_transport/index_en.html>.

[7] Art 295 EC states: 'This Treaty shall in no way prejudice the rules in Member States governing the system of property ownership'. Recital (10) notes that 'this Directive is not addressing ownership issues'.

B. The Electricity Directive 2003

A major obstacle to the completion of the internal market has been the shortcomings of the regime in some continental countries for network access. Under the first Directive, a choice had been given to the Member States between negotiated and regulated third party access (TPA). The results from the operation of the negotiated option, as well as the experience of some countries where the regulatory intervention in grid access was in effect weak, proved unsatisfactory. The new Directive seeks to address these shortcomings in its second notable feature, the inclusion of TPA provisions that are clearer and are based largely on a commitment to regulated TPA. These provisions vary in significant ways from the TPA provisions included in Directive (EC) 2003/55 for the gas sector, even though it was adopted at the same time (see paras 6.38–6.60). **5.03**

A third feature of the Directive that is innovative and practically very important is the extended and reinforced role accorded to the national regulatory authorities (NRAs). The Directive attempts to establish a minimum set of competences for the NRAs in all Member States, and to ensure their role in the further development of the internal market in electricity. **5.04**

There is another notable feature of the sector legislation. Surprisingly, the first Directive on electricity had almost nothing to say about cross-border trade. Neither does the second one. Instead, the legislation tackles cross-border trade in a different way, by establishing the principle that an internal market directive may be elaborated by means of a regulation. The text proposed by the Commission in 2001 set out in detail the basic principles and some rules for access to high voltage transmission infrastructure spanning national boundaries within the EU, for the purpose of exports and imports of electricity ('cross-border exchanges in electricity'). The main articles of the Regulation are supplemented by sets of guidelines, most notably on congestion management (the preliminary version of these guidelines was set out in an annex to the Regulation as adopted in 2003, and a new version was adopted in 2006 (see Appendix 5). **5.05**

B. The Electricity Directive 2003

(1) Aims and Scope

The Directive has six principal aims,[8] all designed to remedy shortcomings which were identified in the period after the adoption of the first Directive, and to bring about potential improvements to the functioning of the internal market in electricity. The first of these aims is to ensure a level playing field in generation. The second **5.06**

---

[8] Electricity Directive, Recital 2.

is to reduce the risks of market dominance and predatory behaviour. The third is to ensure non-discriminatory transmission and distribution tariffs, and to do so by means of network access on the basis of tariffs published prior to their entry into force. Fourthly, the Directive aims at ensuring that the rights of small and vulnerable customers are protected. Fifthly, it aims to ensure that information on energy sources for electricity generation is disclosed, and, finally, linked to this aim, but distinct from it, that reference be made to sources of electricity generation, where this is available, giving information on their environmental impact.

5.07 To achieve these aims, the Directive establishes common rules for the generation, transmission, distribution and supply of electricity. The rules cover the organization and functioning of the electricity sector, access to the market, the criteria and procedures applicable to calls for tenders and the granting of authorizations, and the operation of systems.

(2) General Rules

5.08 It is significant in terms of the Directive's priorities that, at the very beginning of the Directive, and ranked as first of all of the general rules in Chapter II, are the rules applicable to 'public service' obligations and consumer protection. They include a requirement that electricity be provided to certain categories of customer as a 'universal service'. By comparison, the other general rules, covering the monitoring of security of supply issues and technical matters, are relatively short, comprising a single paragraph each. The former represent a significant strengthening and expansion of such provisions when compared with the first Electricity Directive.

(a) Public Service Obligations

5.09 The Directive declares that 'respect of the public service requirements is a fundamental requirement'.[9] The provisions on 'public service' obligations (PSOs) and consumer protection measures may be distinguished into three broad groupings. First, there are obligations imposed upon the Member States. These include the obligation to guarantee universal service in electricity;[10] to ensure that electricity undertakings respect the Directives' requirements and do not discriminate between these undertakings in terms of rights or obligations;[11] to protect customers in various ways;[12] to notify measures taken to achieve universal service and PSOs;[13] to publish PSOs;[14] and to ensure that eligible customers can easily switch supplier.[15]

---

[9] Electricity Directive, Recital 26; Gas Directive, Recital 27.
[10] Electricity Directive, Art 3(3).
[11] ibid, Art 3(1).
[12] ibid, Art 3(5) and (6), and Annex A.
[13] ibid, Art 3(9).
[14] ibid, Art 3(2).
[15] ibid, Art 3(5).

B. The Electricity Directive 2003

There is also a positive duty to protect final customers, especially vulnerable customers.[16] Secondly, there are objectives to be pursued by the Member States: environmental protection, security of supply, and social and economic cohesion.[17] Member States may also monitor and if necessary intervene in markets in the interests of security of supply.[18] Finally, there are options available to Member States, such as the establishment of a supplier of last resort,[19] the protection of remote customers, and the extension of universal service to small enterprises.[20]

Universal service A significant innovation is the concept of 'universal service'. This is defined as the right to be supplied with electricity of a specified quantity within their territory at reasonable, easily and clearly comparable and transparent prices.[21] It is extended to all household customers and, if Member States so decide, all small enterprises.[22] This is a new concept borrowed from the telecommunications sector, and is intended to set the 'price to beat' for electricity suppliers, putting competitive pressure on pricing supply offers. To make it work, Member States have the option of appointing a supplier of last resort (also in the gas sector).[23] This supplier may be a sales division of a vertically integrated undertaking, which also performs the functions of distribution, provided that it meets the unbundling requirements of the Directive.[24] However, the term 'reasonable' with respect to prices is not defined in the Directive. It seems to be designed to reassure customers that a competitive market will benefit them and appears to be linked to the notion of 'vulnerable customer' (also undefined). However, the manner in which a 'reasonable prices' regime for household customers and small enterprises would operate is unclear. Who is to fix the prices? Presumably, it would be the State. The Directive does not grant non-household customers a right to be supplied at reasonable prices. However, if a Member State imposes on a supplier a PSO relating to the price of supplies (see Article 3(2)), then considerations of state aid would apply. 5.10

Consumer protection There is a marked emphasis upon consumer protection in the Directive. All Community industry and commerce, the Directive states, and all Community citizens should be able to enjoy high levels of consumer protection.[25] 5.11

---

[16] ibid, Art 3(5).
[17] ibid, Art 3(5) and (7).
[18] ibid, Arts 3(7), 4, 24; see also DG TREN Interpretation Note, 'Measures to Secure Electricity Supply', 16 January 2004, and the discussion of the Security of Electricity Supply Directive at paras 18.29–18.48.
[19] For an interesting discussion of this potentially controversial concept see the Eurelectric Report on Public Service Obligations, February 2004, 15–18, <http://public.eurelectric.org>.
[20] Electricity Directive, Art 3(3) and (5).
[21] ibid, Art 3(3). This does not apply to gas.
[22] Variation in the form of universal service provided between the two is permitted (ibid, Recital 24).
[23] Gas Directive, Art 3(3).
[24] Electricity Directive, Recital 27.
[25] ibid, Recital 19.

Households in particular, and small enterprises where Member States consider appropriate, should be able to enjoy public service guarantees, especially with respect to security of supply and reasonable tariffs. This is justified in terms of fairness, competitiveness, and as an indirect source of employment. A considerable degree of detail about consumer protection measures is contained in Annex A of the Directive.[26] It notes that the measures referred to in Article 3 are to ensure that customers are, among other things, granted a right to a contract with their electricity service provider that specifies the services provided, quality levels offered, and similar conditions. Customers are also to be given adequate notice of any intention to modify contractual conditions; to receive transparent information on applicable prices and tariffs and on standard terms and conditions in terms of access to and use of electricity services; to be offered a wide choice of payment methods; not to be charged for changing supplier; to benefit from transparent, simple and inexpensive procedures for dealing with complaints, and when having access to universal service are to be informed about their rights regarding that service.

5.12 Consumers will also benefit from information on the generation characteristics of the electricity supplied, a factor that may influence their choice of supplier. Under a 'labelling' requirement, every electricity supplier must specify in or with invoices sent to, and in any promotional materials directed at, final customers details of the fuel mix of the generation sources from which that supplier purchases (either directly or indirectly, at the wholesale level). They are also obliged to give an assessment of the related environmental impact of the relevant sources, including mention of any radioactive waste resulting from the electricity produced.[27] Member State authorities will be obliged to ensure that the information provided by suppliers is reliable.[28]

5.13 **Potential abuse of PSOs** The familiar concern about distortions of competition arising from the operation of PSOs remains. It has provoked some cautionary remarks from the Commission on the operation of Article 3.[29] In general, PSOs are regarded as necessary and their achievement cannot be left to the operation of the market. Such PSO requirements may be interpreted by the Member States

---

[26] Relevant also in this context is the DG TREN Interpretation Note, 'Practical Measures for Distribution Resulting from the Opening Up to Competition', 16 January 2004, which treats among other things the metering of consumption.
[27] Electricity Directive, Art 3(6) and Recital 25.
[28] DG TREN Interpretation Note, 'Labelling Provision in Directive 2003/54/EC', 2004.
[29] DG TREN Interpretation Note, 'Public Service Obligations', 16 January 2004. Among other things, the Note deals with the important issue of compensation for the costs relating to carrying out PSOs and the *Altmark* case (Case C-280/00 *Altmark Trans GmbH v Nahverkehrsgesellschaft Altmark GmbH* [2003] ECR I-7747). For rather different circumstances in which financial compensation to companies may be permissible, see the ECJ's ruling in Case C-379/98 *PreussenElektra AG v Schleswag AG* [2000] ECR I-2099.

B. The Electricity Directive 2003

themselves, taking into account national circumstances. However, this discretionary aspect raises the spectre that Member States, especially those with state-owned utilities, might rely on them to limit competition or slow down market opening. To combat this, Member States are now under a general obligation to notify *all* measures taken to fulfil the universal service and public service objectives, including measures on consumer and environmental protection, to the Commission, with details of their possible effects on national and international competition.[30] In contrast to the similar provisions in previous Directives on electricity and gas, the provision in the new legislation is not limited to measures that relate to a request for a derogation. There is therefore a more onerous informational requirement imposed on Member States in the present Directive. Benchmarking may be used by the Commission to ascertain whether a Member State has been able to achieve the same result as another but in a less restrictive manner. The onus is on the Member State to prove that a particular approach to a PSO is necessary.

There is a wider context for the Commission's interest in this area. This interest arises from the statement in Article 3(2) that 'Member States may impose on undertakings operating in the electricity sector, in the general economic interest, public service obligations'. PSOs have been the subject of scrutiny in the context of the Commission's ongoing review of 'services of general economic interest' (SGEI) and its assessment of the ruling by the ECJ in the *Altmark* case. In the latter, the ECJ ruled that financial compensation for the costs of carrying out PSOs is not a form of state aid, as long as it meets four conditions. The conditions are: **5.14**

- the recipient undertaking must actually have PSOs to discharge, and those obligations must be clearly defined;
- the parameters on the basis of which the compensation is calculated must be established in advance and done so in an objective and transparent manner;
- the compensation cannot exceed what is necessary to cover all or part of the costs incurred in the discharge of the PSOs, taking into account the relevant receipts and a reasonable profit for discharging those obligations;
- finally, where the undertaking is not chosen pursuant to a public procurement procedure, the level of compensation needed must be determined on the basis of an analysis of the costs which a typical undertaking would incur.

This ruling has not been viewed by the Commission as providing all the necessary clarification on the definition of SGEI, and so several measures have been proposed by it to provide further legal certainty on the issue of when compensation **5.15**

---

[30] Electricity Directive, Art 3(9); compare Gas Directive, Art 3(6).

for SGEI is permissible.[31] It may be noted that Article III-6 of the draft European Constitution was seen as a potential additional legal basis for Community action in this area.[32]

(b) Security of Supply

5.16 Member States are required to monitor security of supply issues, either directly or indirectly through the NRA.[33] A report on the monitoring is to be submitted to the Commission every two years, which summarizes the findings, as well as measures taken or envisaged. The activities that are to be included in the monitoring exercise include the supply/demand balance on the national market, the level of expected future demand and envisaged additional capacity planned or under construction, the quality and level of maintenance of the networks, measures to cover peak demand and to deal with shortfalls by one or more suppliers. The subject of security of supply is discussed in more detail in Chapter 18 in relation to the Electricity Directive. It is also covered by the provisions of a separate Directive, which imposes a number of important obligations on Member States, and is discussed further in Chapter 18 (see paras 18.29–18.48).

(c) Technical Rules

5.17 Member States are required to ensure that a variety of technical rules and standards are operational, and to notify the Commission of this. Essentially, this involves the definition of technical safety criteria, and rules developed and published for the establishment of minimum technical design and operational requirements for system connection, with respect to generating installations, distribution systems, directly connected consumers' equipment, interconnector circuits and direct lines. The aim is to ensure interoperability.

(3) Rules for Specific Activities

(a) Generation

5.18 The aim of the provisions on generation is to completely open up investment in, and the construction and operation of generating capacity to competition. The significance of this lies in the assumption that independent (or at least non-indigenous) generators will play an important part in stimulating competition in future years. To achieve this aim, the Directive restricts the procedures available to

---

[31] *White Paper on Services of General Interest*, COM (2004) 374 final, 12 May 2004, 13–14; in this context see the draft Commission Decision on the application of Art 86(2) of the Treaty to state aid in the form of public service compensation granted to certain undertakings entrusted with the operation of services of general economic interest: <http://ec.europa.eu/comm/competition/state_aid/others/action_plan/sgei_art86_en.pdf>.
[32] COM (2004) 374, ibid 6.
[33] Electricity Directive, Art 4; see also Art 24.

B. The Electricity Directive 2003

Member States under Article 6 to an authorization procedure, in preference to the dual approach of the first Electricity Directive, which offered Member States a choice between this procedure and a tendering procedure. This must be carried out in accordance with objective, transparent, and non-discriminatory criteria. Only in specially—but not very restrictively—defined circumstances may the tendering procedure be used.[34]

Member States are required to establish criteria for the grant of authorizations for the construction of generating capacity in their territory.[35] These criteria are to be made public and may relate to: 5.19

- the safety and security of the electricity system, installations, and associated equipment;
- protection of public health and safety;
- protection of the environment;
- land-use and siting;
- use of public ground;
- energy efficiency;
- the nature of the primary sources;
- characteristics particular to the applicant, such as technical, economic, and financial capabilities; or
- compliance with measures adopted pursuant to Article 3 (public service obligations and consumer protection).

Applications that fit the criteria for granting an authorization must be approved. In the event of a refusal to grant an authorization, the applicant must be informed of the reasons, which must be objective, non-discriminatory, well-founded and duly substantiated. Such data must be forwarded to the Commission for information purposes. Lack of demand is not a valid reason for a refusal. Appeal procedures must be made available to the applicant. 5.20

With respect to small and/or distributed generation, Member States are required to ensure that authorization procedures take into account their limited size and potential impact.[36] 5.21

Member States are also required to ensure the possibility of a tendering procedure or 'equivalent' for new capacity, in the interests of security of supply.[37] This also 5.22

---

[34] Arguably, the combination of powers and discretion that is left to Member States with respect to security of supply, the environmental and PSO provisions of the Directive may be deemed sufficient for a Member State to organize tenders for a particular type of generating capacity, such as nuclear generation, in the event of a deemed lack of interest from the private sector.
[35] Electricity Directive, Art 6(2).
[36] ibid, Art 6(3).
[37] ibid, Art 7(1).

applies to energy efficiency and demand-side management measures. An equivalent procedure is defined as one that is equivalent in terms of transparency and non-discrimination. Such procedures must be based on published criteria. They may only be launched if, on the basis of the authorization procedure, the generating capacity being built or the energy efficiency or demand-side management measures being taken are not sufficient to ensure security of supply. The tender specifications have to be made available to any interested undertaking.

5.23 Member States may also provide for the option of a tendering procedure for new capacity in the interests of environmental protection and the promotion of infant new technologies.[38] New capacity includes renewables and combined heat and power. This has to be based on published criteria and may relate to either new capacity or energy efficiency/demand-side management measures. The caveat is that such a procedure may only be launched if the generation capacity being built or the measures being taken on the basis of the authorization procedure proves to be insufficient to achieve these objectives.

5.24 Details of the tendering procedure are to be published in the Official Journal six months prior to the closing date for tenders.[39] Tender specifications must contain a detailed description of the contract specifications, of the procedure to be followed by all tenderers, and an exhaustive list of criteria governing the selection of tenderers and the award of the contract, including incentives, such as subsidies, that the tender covers. The tender specifications are required to be made available to any interested undertaking that is established in the territory of a Member State to ensure that it has sufficient time to submit a tender.

5.25 When invitations to tender for the requisite generating capacity are made, there is a requirement that consideration be given to such electricity supply offers as have long term guarantees from *existing* generating units, on condition that additional requirements can be met in this manner.[40] This aims to catch potential bids that involve increasing the capacity from existing units, or re-activating dormant plants and long-term supply contracts from generators established in other Member States.

5.26 Responsibility for organizing, monitoring, and controlling the tendering procedure must be vested in an authority designated by the Member State or in a public or private body independent of the generation, transmission, distribution and supply activities.[41] This may be an NRA. The transmission system operator (TSO) may be designated as the body responsible for these tasks, but only where it is

---

[38] ibid, Art 7(2).
[39] ibid, Art 7(3).
[40] ibid, Art 7(4).
[41] ibid, Art 7(5).

wholly independent from other activities not relating to the transmission system in ownership terms. The authority or body must take all necessary steps to ensure confidentiality of the information contained in the tenders. This is intended to encourage objective and non-discriminatory decision-making. However, there is no specific regime to provide remedies in the event of a breach.

(b) Transmission

5.27 Chapter IV concerns the operation of the transmission system. 'Transmission' is defined as the transport of electricity on the extra high-voltage and high-voltage interconnected system with a view to its delivery to final customers or to distributors, but not including supply.[42] The focus of its five articles is the designation of TSOs, their tasks, unbundling requirements, technical issues (such as dispatching and balancing)[43] and confidentiality requirements for TSOs. The unbundling requirements are discussed in section 4 below (see paras 5.38–5.43). Organization of access to the system is dealt with separately in Chapter VII of the Directive (see paras 5.44–5.47).

5.28 Member States are required to designate, or require undertakings which own transmission systems to designate, one or more TSOs.[44] They are also required to ensure that the TSOs act in accordance with the provisions of Chapter IV. The appointment of the TSO must be for a period of time to be determined by the Member State, taking into account considerations of efficiency and economic balance.

5.29 The responsibilities of each TSO are set out in Article 9. The primary task is to ensure the long-term ability of the system to meet reasonable demands for electricity transmission. The TSO must also manage energy flows on the system, taking into account exchanges with other interconnected systems. The TSO is therefore to have responsibility for ensuring a system that is secure, reliable and efficient. This extends to the availability of ancillary services to the extent that this is independent from any other transmission system to which the system has an interconnection. Additionally, the TSO is responsible for contributing to security of supply by means of adequate transmission capacity and system reliability. The TSO has to provide information to other TSOs with which it has an interconnection that is sufficient to ensure the secure and efficient operation, co-ordinated development and interoperability of the interconnected system, and to system users to the extent they need information for system access. Finally, the TSO is responsible for ensuring non-discrimination between system users or classes of users, especially

---

[42] ibid, Art 2.3.
[43] Such 'technical' issues as the provision of ancillary services such as balancing and reserve to network users, as well as the elaboration of rules for their nominations and for scheduling of power, can have adverse commercial consequences for grid customers if the relevant rules are not objectively written.
[44] Electricity Directive, Art 8.

with respect to its related undertakings. Confidentiality of commercially sensitive information is treated separately in Article 12. Where this is obtained by the TSO in the course of carrying out its business, the TSO has an obligation to preserve its confidentiality.

5.30 The important tasks of dispatching the generating installations and determining the use of interconnectors with other systems are also the responsibilities of the TSO.[45] Criteria for dispatching and use of interconnectors must be objective, published, and applied in a non-discriminatory manner. They may also be subject to the approval of the Member State. In other words, the TSO is not allowed to favour those generating facilities or distribution and supply entities belonging to the same company or to shareholders of the company, in cases where ownership of the TSO is not totally separated from ownership of such facilities or entities. The criteria also have to take into account the economic precedence (that is, offered price) of electricity from available generating installations within the TSO territory, as well as of potentially competing transfers of electricity over interconnections to neighbouring networks; the observation of such economic criteria may be conditional upon technical constraints on the system. These rules entail, in effect, the application of a merit order to national and international supplies—but not solely on a pricing basis—which means, for instance, that plant could be dispatched or constrained off, or an interconnection point declared congested, for reasons of system security. Member States may also impose requirements on TSOs with respect to compliance with minimum standards for system maintenance and development, including interconnection capacity.

5.31 In pursuit of an environmental policy, Member States may require the TSO to give priority in dispatching electricity to those generating installations producing electricity from renewable energy sources or waste or producing combined heat and power (CHP).[46] It is permissible to design an environmental policy so as to assist these forms of electricity despite their (generally) higher cost than electricity produced from traditional sources. This is the only express mechanism in the Directive for the favourable treatment of electricity from renewable energy sources, waste, or CHP. Most Member States already used such a mechanism. Essentially, a TSO will purchase electricity from renewable energy or the other sources, and will pass the cost on to its customers (that is, those grid users liable to pay transmission charges, either at a point of production or a point of consumption), such costs thereby being distributed over the total consumer base. On its own, favourable dispatching of this type is unlikely to support a policy for promoting renewables. The Directive does not cover schemes that provide direct or indirect support to renewable energy

---

[45] ibid, Art 11(1).
[46] ibid, Art 11(3).

B. The Electricity Directive 2003

sources nor does it allow Member States to authorize a TSO to oblige eligible customers to purchase its share of renewable energy directly or via green certificates or the imposition of levies. However, the Renewables Directive (discussed in Chapter 10) does provide for such subsidies and schemes. For Member States seeking to go further than the favourable dispatching mechanism, the provisions of Article 3(2) may assist in so doing.

5.32 A Member State may order priority to be given in dispatching to electricity generated from indigenous primary fuel sources. This may reach up to 15 per cent in any calendar year of the overall primary energy that is required to generate all of the electricity consumed in the Member State concerned. The aim is to meet concerns about security of supply.

5.33 There are several additional requirements on the rules and procedures used by TSOs with respect to procurement of energy to cover their losses and reserve capacity and in system balancing. They have to conform to the usual criteria of transparency, non-discrimination, and objectivity. Terms and conditions for the provision of balancing services by TSOs are to be set according to a methodology fixed or approved by the NRAs.

(c) Distribution

5.34 'Distribution' is defined as the transport of electricity on high-voltage, medium-voltage and low-voltage distribution systems with a view to its delivery to customers, but not including supply. It is the subject of Chapter V of the Directive, and follows closely the order of Chapter IV on transmission. Its operation has attracted attention from the Commission because of the impact of the timetable for market opening. By July 2004 this had to extend to all non-domestic customers, but by July 2007 to all consumers. The concern has been to ensure that this becomes more than a formal opening and has the intended practical consequences.[47] However, many of these matters are addressed in Article 3 or the recitals, rather than in Chapter V, which is concerned with organizational issues.

5.35 In most Member States there is a single TSO but there are several distribution system operators (DSOs). The Directive requires Member States to designate, or to require undertakings that own or are responsible for distribution systems to designate, one or more system operators.[48] They are also required to ensure that the DSOs act in accordance with the provisions of Articles 14 to 16 of the Directive. The appointment of the TSO is to be for a period of time to be determined by the

---

[47] DG TREN Interpretation Note, 'Practical Measures for Distribution Resulting from the Opening Up to Competition', 16 January 2004.
[48] Electricity Directive, Art 13.

Member State, taking into account considerations of efficiency and economic balance. The unbundling requirements are examined in section 4 below.

5.36 The responsibilities of each DSO are set out in Article 14. As is the case with TSOs, the primary task of a DSO is to maintain a secure, reliable and efficient system in its area. Due regard has to be taken of the environment. Other requirements include the provision of information to system users such as they require for access to the system. DSOs' procedures with respect to procurement of energy to cover losses and reserve capacity have to conform to the criteria of transparency and non-discrimination, and be market-based. Similar requirements apply where DSOs are responsible for balancing the system; the rules are to be objective, transparent and non-discriminatory, including rules for charging system users for energy imbalance. The NRAs may fix or approve the terms and conditions for the provision of such services by DSOs. The Directive expressly prohibits DSOs from discriminating between system users or classes of system users, especially in favour of its related undertakings. Confidentiality of commercially sensitive information is treated separately in Article 16. Where the DSO obtains such information in the course of carrying out its business, the DSO has an obligation to preserve its confidentiality.

5.37 A Member State may require the DSO to give priority to generating installations using renewable energy sources or waste or producing CHP, when dispatching generating installations.[49] In practice, this policy concern for CHP will prove more significant at this than at the transmission level. Measures such as energy efficiency and demand-side management and also distributed electricity may be considered by DSOs when they are planning further development of the network. The idea is that this might render an upgrade or replacement of capacity unnecessary.[50]

(4) Unbundling

(a) The Approach

5.38 There are three kinds of unbundling envisaged in the Directive: legal, management, and accounting unbundling. The essential aim of these provisions is to establish the pre-conditions for non-discriminatory treatment of a request for access to the network. With respect to the first, it should be distinguished from ownership unbundling since Member States failed to agree on common rules on this, including any move towards financial ring-fencing of grid management. Legal unbundling would separate the TSO and DSO from other activities not related to transmission and distribution. Transmission and distribution would be carried out by a

---

[49] ibid, Art 14(4).
[50] ibid, Art 14(7).

separate 'network' company, with a legal form chosen by the vertically integrated company.[51] The second—functional or management unbundling—permits the retention of the assets of the TSO and DSO but involves a separation of the TSO and DSO to ensure its functional/management independence from the vertically integrated undertaking.[52] This provision is greatly strengthened compared with the preceding Directive, which did not specify what management unbundling entailed. Article 10(1) requires the TSOs and DSOs to be separate in terms of their 'organisation and decision-making'. The third form of unbundling focuses on company accounts.[53] The guiding principle is that separate accounts have to be maintained for network activities relating to electricity and gas. These provisions are largely unchanged from those in the first Directive but the companies affected by them are far fewer. Under the new regime they affect mainly those DSOs that are not legally unbundled. Accounting unbundling is the minimum separation requirement to be observed by every network operator. No derogations are possible from this requirement, unlike the other forms of unbundling. NRAs are expected to monitor this form of unbundling by ensuring that there is an accurate application of accounting principles, and therefore no cross-subsidies between generation and supply on the one hand and transmission and distribution on the other.[54] Irrespective of the form of unbundling adopted, the raison d'être of the system operator is the same: to have the principal responsibility for the safe and efficient operation, maintenance, and development of its network, and to be able to meet all reasonable demands made upon it by current and future network users.

(b) Legal Unbundling

The most radical shift in this Directive is the emphasis on *legal* unbundling. For electricity TSOs and DSOs that are part of a vertically integrated undertaking, they are to be independent at least in terms of their legal form, organization, and decision-making from other activities not related to transmission or distribution (that is, generation and supply).[55] The Directive is however careful to distinguish between this and ownership unbundling.[56] No change of ownership of assets is required, so no company will have to sell off its transmission and distribution arms. It is also limited to the network business as a natural monopoly; all other activities may continue to be operated in a single company or group of companies. The caution here reflects amendments made during the debates on the draft Directives, but **5.39**

---

[51] For TSOs: ibid, Art 10; for DSOs: ibid, Art 15.
[52] ibid, Arts 10(2) and 15(2).
[53] ibid, Art 19(1)–(4).
[54] DG TREN Interpretation Note, 'The Unbundling Regime', 16 January 2004, 20. Incentive-based regulation of network access charges is expressly encouraged to reduce the risk of cross-subsidization.
[55] Electricity Directive, Art 10(2) and see Art 15.
[56] ibid, Art 8(1), Recital 8, and Recital 10: 'this Directive is not addressing ownership issues'.

the provisions are to be revisited for the distribution sector in 2007. Nonetheless, the independence of decision-making by the TSOs and DSOs over assets necessary to maintain, operate and develop networks has to be guaranteed when those assets are owned and operated by vertically integrated entities. Independent management structures have to be put in place. Member States may in national legislation provide for exemptions for DSOs from the legal unbundling requirements if they might lead to a disproportionate financial and administrative burden on small distribution companies.[57] The exemptions for smaller DSOs are not limited in time but for larger ones (those serving more than 100,000 customers) the requirement for legal unbundling may only be postponed until 1 July 2007.[58] An analysis of the functioning of legal unbundling has been included in the progress report produced by the Commission.[59]

(c) Compliance

5.40 In the Directive there is provision for a compliance programme, to be established by the TSO, the DSO and/or a combined system operator.[60] This is to include details of measures taken to ensure that discriminatory conduct is excluded and that observance of the unbundling requirements is properly monitored. It has to set out specific obligations of employees in this respect. The person or body responsible for monitoring this programme is required to submit an annual report to the NRA and ensure it is published. This report will set out the measures taken.

5.41 Separately from the above, a study was carried out in 2005–06 for the Commission on the practical implementation of unbundling.[61] This concluded that ownership unbundling remained an unusual choice. However, there are some examples of its adoption or consideration:

- In Belgium there is a plan to make the DSOs completely owned by municipalities by 2018.
- In the Netherlands, there have been discussions about statutorily enforceable ownership unbundling of local supply and distribution entities.
- In Italy, there has been a debate about the ownership of HV TSO which led to the transfer of HV grid assets out of an ENEL subsidiary to Terna.
- In Hungary the grid operator Mavir has been merged back into the main generator, MVM.

---

[57] ibid, Art 15 and Recital 11.
[58] ibid, Art 30(2).
[59] ibid, Art 28(3). European Commission, *Report on Progress in Creating the Internal Gas and Electricity Market: Technical Annex*, COM (2005) 568 final, 15 November 2005, 78–84.
[60] ibid Arts 10(2)(d) (TSOs), 15(2)(d) (DSOs) and 17(d)(combined operators).
[61] *Unbundling of Electricity and Gas Transmission and Distribution System Operators, Final Report*, 1 December 2005, <http://ec.europa.eu/energy/electricity/publications/doc/2006_03_08_final_common_report.pdf>.

B. The Electricity Directive 2003

By contrast, the number of countries that require *legal* unbundling for TSOs is considerable, including Denmark, Finland, France, Germany, Ireland, Italy, Poland, Slovenia and Sweden. Others require legal unbundling by a later date. For DSOs the number was less but many Member States require it at a later date. Functional unbundling also remains a popular option for both TSOs and DSOs.

5.42

(d) Interpretation

In a subsequent publication the Commission has clarified a number of issues arising from the Directives' provisions on unbundling.[62] For example, if the national law that governs the legal form of the unbundled network company does not match the requirements of functional unbundling, it has to be modified through a specific contractual arrangement in the company statutes to ensure that the company management has sufficient independence from the parent company. Other matters covered are those concerning combined network operators, the minimum criteria for functional unbundling, and the ways in which the rules on functional unbundling will be set out in detail at Member State level to be operational in practice (in legislation, guidelines, or network operator licences).

5.43

(5) Access

The Chapter of the Directive that deals with 'Organisation of Access to the System' contains a short provision on access but, significantly, a long article addressing the role of the regulatory authorities. The balance in the first Electricity Directive was entirely in the opposite direction, with several kinds of access regime offered to the Member States. In the present Directive the choice of access regime is limited to one, and the minimum oversight capability of the NRAs is made more explicit.

5.44

A fundamental characteristic of competition in networks is the operation of non-discriminatory and transparent TPA to the networks with *ex ante* supervision by the NRAs. In this way, network users can accurately predict the exact costs that would be incurred from using the system. Without this, competition will fail to develop. Member States therefore are required to ensure that the system of TPA that they implement is based on published tariffs, is applicable to all eligible customers and is applied objectively and without discrimination between system users.[63] It applies to both transmission and distribution. The role of the NRAs is underlined by the requirement that tariffs or the methodologies underlying their calculation are approved prior to their entry into force. These tariffs or the methodologies, once approved by the NRAs, are to be published prior to their entry into force. The rationale behind this promotion of the regulated TPA option

5.45

---

[62] DG TREN Interpretation Note, 'The Unbundling Regime', 6–15.
[63] Electricity Directive, Art 20(1).

is to secure competition in the wholesale market, rather than in the retail market. This represents a change of emphasis from the first Directive.

5.46 Refusal of access by a TSO or DSO is still possible where there is no available capacity.[64] The reasons for this refusal have to be substantiated, taking any public service obligations into account. Where appropriate and where there has been a refusal, Member States are obliged to ensure that the TSO or DSO provides relevant information on measures that would be necessary to reinforce the network.

5.47 Access to interconnection capacity for wholesale exporters and importers is provided for in detail in the Regulation rather than in the Directive (see paras 5.95–5.105). The former is concerned with the provision of adequate access, in the sense that market participants should not face cross-border artificial congestion, discriminatory charges for overcoming that congestion, nor should they face uncertainty about being scheduled across borders over given time-frames.

(6) Market Opening and Reciprocity

5.48 Since full market opening is scheduled for July 2007 and most Member States are already required to have large segments of their markets open to competition, the provisions in the Directive on this topic are significantly shorter than those in the first Electricity Directive. At its simplest, Article 21 requires Member States to ensure that all non-household customers are eligible from 1 July 2004 at the latest and, from 1 July 2007, all customers are to be eligible. This means that they are to be free to purchase electricity from a supplier of their choice.

5.49 The special circumstances of Estonia were recognized in this respect by the grant of a temporary derogation from the application of Article 21(1)(b) and (c) until 31 December 2012.[65] This grant was based on submission of a restructuring plan for the country's oil shale sector (the only indigenous energy resource in the country, which generates 90 per cent of its electricity). The derogation was designed to guarantee investments in generating plants and security of supply while allowing the serious environmental problems created by these plants to be resolved. Market opening is to be carried out gradually over the reference period to lead to complete market opening by 1 January 2013. On 1 January 2009 market opening must reach at least 35 per cent of consumption. Estonia is required to communicate annually to the Commission the consumption thresholds that extend eligibility to final customers.

5.50 A transitional mechanism is provided for in Article 21(2). To avoid an imbalance in the opening of the markets, contracts for electricity supply with an eligible customer

---

[64] ibid, Art 20(2).
[65] Directive (EC) 2004/85 of 28 June 2004 amending Directive (EC) 2003/54 as regards the application of certain provisions to Estonia [2004] OJ L236/10.

in the system of another Member State are not to be prohibited if the customer is considered as eligible in both systems involved. Where a transaction is refused because of the customer being eligible in only one of the two systems, the Commission may require the refusing party to execute the requested supply at the request of the Member State where the eligible customer is located. In doing so, the Commission is required to take into account the market situation and the common interest.

(7) Direct Lines

5.51 All electricity generators and suppliers have a right to supply their own premises, subsidiaries, and eligible customers through a direct line once the generators and suppliers have the necessary authorization from the Member State.[66] A 'direct line' is defined as either an electricity line linking an isolated production site with an isolated customer or an electricity line linking an electricity generator and an electricity supply undertaking to supply directly their own premises, subsidiaries and eligible customers.[67]

5.52 Any eligible customer within the territory of a Member State may be supplied through a direct line by a generator and supply undertakings, where they have been authorized by the Member States to do so. However, the Directive qualifies the freedom to construct a direct line. The criteria for the grant of an authorization for constructing a direct line must be objective and non-discriminatory. Member States may nevertheless make the grant of such authorizations subject to conditions. These may include the refusal of system access on grounds of a lack of transmission or distribution network capacity, or the opening of a dispute settlement procedure under Article 23. In practice, this means a complaint made to the NRA. Moreover, Member States may refuse to authorize the construction of a new direct line if it might obstruct the performance of PSOs (in which case, duly substantiated reasons must be given).

5.53 This provision is unlikely to prove of much practical significance. The definition of 'direct line' is narrow, meaning only that it would connect producers or suppliers with subsidiaries or eligible customers. Such a line would normally have only one connection point to the interconnected system, with the second point being a power plant or a consumer. The definition of 'direct line' here means that third parties cannot use the line for purposes other than direct supply contracts with the owner of the direct line. Issues of network access and remuneration are therefore of little consequence. This conclusion does not apply, however, if a direct line connects two distinct TSO systems.

---

[66] Electricity Directive, Art 22(1).
[67] ibid, Art 2(15).

5.54 An example of a situation that might arise was given in one of the Commission's early reports on the first Directive.[68] The generation or sales arm of a vertically-integrated company might build a direct line to a distribution company within another TSO area. This distributor might be a subsidiary of the vertically-integrated company but still be a purchaser under Article 22 of the Electricity Directive, with a right to build a direct line. Such a line would be connected at both ends to two interconnected systems and could be used by third parties.

(8) The Role of the Regulators

(a) The Framework

5.55 The legal status of NRAs has been significantly enhanced in two ways.[69] First, there is an obligation on Member States to charge one or more competent bodies with the function of regulatory authorities. The requirement is more precise than in the previous Directives.[70] However, it may be noted that regulatory functions may be spread over several authorities if that is deemed appropriate by the Member State, permitting, say, local or regional regulatory bodies, but also a combination of NRA, ministry and, say, a competition authority. The independence of the regulatory authority (or authorities) is obligatory but is defined in relation to the interests of the electricity and gas *industries* rather than in relation to existing government structures. Nonetheless, those Member States with state-owned utilities may have to develop mechanisms to separate the regulatory authority from the ministerial body that supervises the state-owned energy utility. In addition, Member States are required to take measures to ensure that the regulatory authorities are able to carry out their duties in an efficient and expeditious manner.[71]

5.56 Secondly, while Member States continue to set out the functions, competences and administrative powers of the regulatory authorities, a minimum set of functions and competences is set out in the Directive in the interests of harmonization.[72] In particular, their supervisory role over network access and the setting or approval

---

[68] European Commission, *Second Report to the Council and the European Parliament on Harmonisation Requirements*, SEC (1999) 470, 13–4.
[69] Electricity Directive, Art 23.
[70] Compare the wording in Art 22 of the first Electricity Directive: 'Member States shall create appropriate and efficient mechanisms for regulation, control and transparency so as to avoid any abuse of a dominant position.' In practice, however, the regulatory competences of national authorities have usually gone far beyond this. This wording reappears in the new Directive as Art 23(8), first paragraph.
[71] Electricity Directive, Art 23(7).
[72] ibid, Recital 15. There are also some requirements imposed by the Directive on Member States that they may elect to devolve to NRAs, such as those on providing tendering procedures for additional capacity in the interest of security of supply and ensuring that reliable information is provided to customers about the energy sources for the electricity supplied.

B. The Electricity Directive 2003

of network tariffs (or at least the methodologies underlying the calculation of the tariffs) has been given a basis in European law. An additional development of importance is the enhanced European co-operation and co-ordination that the Directives and supporting measures provide.[73] In practice, however, these have been found to contain 'regulatory gaps' (see generally Chapter 3).

(b) The Obligations of the NRA

5.57 The Directive sets out three general responsibilities for the NRAs: to ensure non-discrimination, effective competition, and the efficient functioning of the market.

5.58 More specifically, eight activities are listed that constitute the minimum that the NRAs shall monitor. Each item listed has to be included in an annual report on the outcome of monitoring. The activities are:

- the rules on the management and allocation of interconnection capacity (in conjunction with the regulatory authority or authorities of those Member States with which interconnection exists);
- any mechanisms to deal with congestion on the national electricity or gas network;
- the time taken by TSOs and DSOs to make connections and carry out repairs;
- the publication of appropriate information by TSOs and DSOs concerning interconnectors, grid usage and capacity allocation to interested parties, taking into account the need to treat non-aggregated information as commercially confidential;
- the effective unbundling of accounts to ensure that there are no cross-subsidies between generation, transmission, distribution and supply activities (and in the case of gas, storage and LNG);
- the terms, conditions and tariffs for connecting new producers of electricity to guarantee that these are objective, transparent and non-discriminatory, in particular taking full account of the costs and benefits of the various renewable energy sources technologies, distributed generation and combined heat and power; in the case of gas, this activity is defined as the access conditions to storage, line pack and other ancillary services;
- the extent to which TSOs and DSOs fulfil their tasks in accordance with the Directive's provisions; and
- the level of transparency and competition.

5.59 A reporting requirement is imposed in Article 23(8) with respect to changing patterns of ownership and their impact upon new market entry. Until 2010, 'the relevant authorities of the Member States' are to provide a report on market dominance, predatory and anti-competitive behaviour on an annual basis. This report has to

---

[73] ibid, Recital 16; Commission Decision 2003/796/EC on establishing the European Regulators Group for Electricity and Gas [2003] OJ L296/34.

be submitted to the Commission before 31 July. In addition, the report has to review the changing ownership patterns and any practical measures taken at national level 'to ensure a sufficient variety of market actors or practical measures taken to enhance interconnection and competition'. After 2010, this report is to be provided every two years by the relevant authorities.

5.60 An absence in the Directive is that it does not provide for incentive-based regulation. This would have been advantageous in enabling a harmonized and co-ordinated enforcement of the Regulation.

(c) Tariff Supervision

5.61 In addition to the monitoring functions, the Directive charges the NRAs to be responsible for fixing or approving, prior to their entry into force (*ex ante*), at least the methodologies used to calculate or establish the terms and conditions for the connection and access to national networks, including transmission and distribution tariffs.[74] These tariffs, or methodologies, are to allow the necessary investments in the networks to be carried out in a manner that allows these investments to ensure the viability of the networks. In addition, the NRAs are to be responsible for fixing or approving the methodologies used to calculate or establish the terms and conditions for the provision of balancing services.

5.62 This regulatory power on the fixing or approving of tariff methodologies may be limited, since Article 23(3) provides that Member States may require the NRAs to submit for formal decision to the relevant body in the Member State the tariffs or at least the methodologies. In such cases, the relevant body may have the power either to approve or reject a draft decision submitted by the regulatory authority. These tariffs or methodologies or modifications relating to them are to be published together with the decision on formal adoption. Any formal rejection of a draft decision is also to be published together with the reasons for its decision. Both TSOs and DSOs may be required to modify their terms and conditions, tariffs, rules, mechanisms and methodologies by the NRAs to ensure that they are proportionate and applied in a non-discriminatory manner.[75]

(d) Cross-Border Issues

5.63 On issues arising from cross-border electricity exchanges, the NRAs are required to:

- approve operational and planning standards of the TSOs, including schemes for the calculation of the total transfer capacity;[76]

---

[74] See generally in this context, the DG TREN Interpretation Note, 'The Role of the Regulatory Authorities', 14 January 2004.
[75] Electricity Directive, Art 23(4).
[76] Electricity Regulation, Annex to the Guidelines.

B. The Electricity Directive 2003

- decide on exemptions to normal access rules for new investments;[77]
- ensure compliance with all guidelines adopted under the Regulation, and impose fines, where necessary, for a failure to respect the requirements of the Regulation or the Guidelines;[78]
- provide information to the Commission to carry out its duties under the Regulation (such as adopting or amending guidelines).[79] If the NRA does not provide this information within the given time-limit, the Commission may request the information directly from the undertakings concerned. Failure by them to comply may result in the imposition of penalties.

(e) Dispute Settlement

5.64 Any party with a complaint against a TSO or a DSO on the matters set out in the preceding sections may refer the complaint to the regulatory authority.[80] In such circumstances, the NRA will act as a dispute settlement authority and issue a decision within two months after receipt of the complaint. Extensions to this deadline of a further two months (and longer with the consent of the complainant) may be granted where additional information is sought by the NRA.[81] The final decision is binding unless and until overruled on appeal. Appeals may also be made against certain decisions by the NRAs and against a decision to refuse to grant an authorization.[82] This does not preclude any complaint under rights of appeal according to Community and national law. The procedure is deliberately intended to facilitate speedy decision-making when a complaint is made, in contrast to the approach in cases brought under competition law.

5.65 With respect to cross-border disputes, the deciding regulatory authority is to be that authority that has jurisdiction in respect of the system operator which refuses use of, or access to, the system.

(f) Co-ordination Among Regulators

5.66 **ERGEG as advisor** The role of the ERGEG as advisor to the Commission and as co-ordinator of a number of tasks and initiatives on behalf of the NRAs has been discussed elsewhere (see paras 3.37–3.38, 3.52). Its activities in this respect have

---

[77] ibid, Art 4.
[78] ibid, Art 9. It is not necessarily the energy regulator that is the administrative body with the power to impose the fine. The Member States have discretion in this area.
[79] ibid, Art 10(1), (2) and (5).
[80] ibid, Art 23(5). This includes the possibility of appeals against decisions or proposed decisions by the NRA on the methodology.
[81] The deadlines may be extended by the NRA beyond the two-month period for an indefinite period where the complaint is concerned with 'connection tariffs for major new generation facilities', which may take considerably longer to settle: ibid, Art 23(5).
[82] Respectively: ibid, Arts 23(6) and 6(4).

quickly acquired a place among those that are central to the further development of the internal energy market and appear likely to remain so.

5.67 **The Regulatory Committee** The ERGEG should not be confused with the Regulatory Committee established by Article 13 of the Electricity Regulation, and governed by the so-called comitology procedure. The Regulatory Committee is to assist the Commission with the taking of measures necessary for the implementation of the Regulation and Directive. Such Committees are composed of Member State representatives, not NRAs, and are chaired by the Commission representative.[83] The Regulation specifically refers to Articles 3 and 7 of the Decision on comitology. The former article sets out a 'regulatory procedure'. The general idea is to allow the Commission the power to propose rules on very specific implementation matters that will be subject to the advice or approval of the Council through an ad hoc Committee set up for the purpose. In this instance, Commission officials have been at pains to emphasize that their role in such Committees is weaker than in comparable Committees in say the telecoms sector. In electricity and gas, the Commission may submit proposals to the Committees which can oppose them; in contrast to the Committee procedure in the telecoms sector where the Member States notify proposals and the Commission may veto them.

5.68 In Recital 8 of the Decision establishing ERGEG, it is expressly enjoined to 'maintain close co-operation with the Committees established' under the Regulation and also under the Gas Directive: 'its work should not interfere with the work of those Committees'. The ERGEG chairperson is obliged, according to its Rules of Procedure, to report to these Committees when requested to do so. In application of the Regulation, DG TREN had already issued draft guidelines on congestion management, tarification, and inter-TSO compensation by May 2004. Such proposals are first prepared with key players, further developed in the Regulatory Forum, and then sent to the Committee under the comitology procedure (see paras 5.119–5.127).

(9) Enforcement

5.69 The enforcement mechanisms of the Directive are much more tightly drawn than in its predecessor. There are fewer derogations, more extensive reporting requirements, and a review procedure by the Commission. Above all, there is an important role accorded to the NRAs in the enforcement of the Directive. However, the complexity of the issues it raises and the diverse circumstances of the Member States' electricity practices are likely to lead to difficulties in interpretation of its provisions, suggesting that the Commission will continue to have an important role as both arbiter and enforcer. This is confirmed by the proliferation of

---

[83] Commission Decision 2003/796/EC on establishing the European Regulators Group for Electricity and Gas [2003] OJ L296/34, Art 5(1).

B. The Electricity Directive 2003

'interpretative notes' published on the Commission's website which, while prima facie non-legally binding, will undoubtedly exercise a persuasive influence on the actions of market players.

(a) Derogations

5.70 The Directive continues the practice of allowing Member States to apply for derogations in a number of highly specific circumstances. However, their scope is considerably reduced from the previous Directive. Indeed, the idea that transitional arrangements may be required is not present in the Directive, largely because of the stage which market opening had reached by the time of its adoption.

5.71 For the electricity sector, the scope for derogations applies mainly to cases of small or micro-isolated systems. If they are likely to experience substantial problems in their operation or, in the latter case, problems in upgrading of existing capacity and expansion of existing capacity, Member States have to be able to demonstrate this in their applications to the Commission for a derogation.[84] Similarly, if a Member State has substantial problems due to technical reasons in opening its market for certain limited groups of non-household customers, it may apply to the Commission for a temporary derogation from this provision on market opening. Such derogations have to end no later than 1 July 2007.

5.72 Other potential derogations are the exemption from unbundling of integrated distribution companies serving fewer than 100,000 connected customers or serving small isolated systems (Article 15(2)), and the possible non-application of several provisions (including TPA) under Article 3(8).

(b) Reporting Requirements

5.73 The Directive imposes two principal requirements on the Commission to undertake monitoring and review of the Directive and its effects. The first report is an annual progress report to be submitted to the Parliament and Council.[85] Focusing on the Directive, the first of these was submitted in 2005 and is due annually after that date. The second report had a wider scope, covering progress in creating the internal electricity market.[86] It was presented at the end of 2005.

5.74 The Report on the Directive is required to cover a wide range of issues, including the following:

- experience gained and progress made in creating a complete and fully operational internal market and the obstacles that remain; this is to include issues of

---

[84] Electricity Directive, Art 26(1).
[85] ibid, Art 28(1); *Report on Progress in Creating the Internal Gas and Electricity Market*, COM (2005) 568 final, 15 November 2005.
[86] ibid, Art 28(3); *Report on Progress*, ibid.

market dominance, concentration in the market, predatory or anti-competitive behaviour and its effects in terms of market distortion;
- unbundling and tarification requirements in terms of providing access to the EU electricity system and equivalent levels of competition, and economic, environmental and social consequences of market opening for customers;
- system capacity and security of supply issues;
- measures taken by Member States covering peak demand and shortfalls by one or more suppliers;
- implementation of the unbundling derogation in Article 15(2), with a view to revising the threshold;
- bilateral relations with third countries that generate and export or transport electricity: the assessment is to include the social and environmental consequences of the electricity trade and network access of such third countries;
- possible harmonization requirements not linked to the Directive;
- energy labelling implementation practices.

5.75 The report may include recommendations, especially with respect to labelling provisions and particularly the way in which information is provided on environmental impact in terms of CO_2 emissions and radioactive waste resulting from electricity generation, and also with respect to measures that might counteract negative effects of market dominance and market concentration. Every two years it has to include an analysis of PSOs in the Member States and 'in particular, their effects on competition in the electricity market'.[87] Recommendations may be made on measures to improve the level of public service standards or to prevent market foreclosure.

5.76 The second report was a once-only progress report aimed at reviewing matters relevant to the progress in creating an internal electricity market rather than the Directive itself. It was submitted at the end of 2005.[88] The final paragraphs of Article 28(3) require the Commission (where this is appropriate) to submit proposals with this report 'to guarantee high public service standards'. These proposals could also include measures to address issues of market dominance, market concentration or anti-competitive behaviour, and were to be made 'in conformity with competition law'. Article 26 sets out a review procedure in the event that the above report concludes that certain obligations imposed by the Directive on undertakings are not proportionate to the objective pursued. The Member State may submit a request to the Commission for exemption from the requirement.

5.77 A different kind of reporting requirement is imposed upon Member States with respect to electricity imports.[89] They are to inform the Commission every three months

---

[87] ibid, Art 28(2).
[88] *Report on Progress in Creating the Internal Gas and Electricity Market*, COM (2005) 568 final, 15 November 2005.

C. The Electricity Regulation 2003

of imports, in terms of physical flows, that have taken place during the previous three months from third countries.

(c) Infringement

Infringement proceedings against Greece At the end of 2004 the Commission referred a case to the ECJ concerning a lack of compliance by Greece with unbundling requirements in the Electricity Directive.[90] Although Greece has transposed the Electricity Directive, the practice of the Public Power Corporation (PPC) of not publishing separate (unbundled) accounts for lignite extraction and electricity generation may have the effect of facilitating cross-subsidies between different sections of PPC and may distort competition on the electricity market in Greece. Currently, no new entrants have access to lignite deposits for electricity generation. In the absence of action by PPC to make available consolidated group accounts and balance sheets, or explanations from the Greek authorities, the Commission referred the case to the ECJ. The threat of legal action had the desired effect, however, and the case was removed from the register in July 2006.

C. The Electricity Regulation 2003

The general aim of the Electricity Regulation is to contribute to an intensification of trade in electricity which has been historically quite low in the EU. At the high end is Hungary with 18.1 per cent of electricity used met through imports, with Italy close behind at 15.9 per cent, and Austria, Belgium, and Portugal with more typical rates of 11 per cent, 7.3 per cent, and 6.5 per cent respectively.[91] The specific aims of the Regulation are to improve conditions for cross-border trade through increased harmonization of tariffs and charges for access, as well as the allocation of available interconnection capacities and through regulatory measures. It builds on work carried out by the Florence Electricity Regulatory Forum (see paras 3.18–3.27). The instrument chosen—the Regulation—is one that does not require implementation in the same way as the Directives do. Instead of a transposition period of one or two years, this measure is directly applicable and in this case it entered into force on 1 July 2004. The regime is based on the EC's competence to adopt measures for the harmonization of national standards to complete the single market (Article 95).

---

[89] Electricity Directive, Art 25.
[90] Commission Press Release IP/04/1498, 'Internal Electricity Market: European Commission decides to take Greece to the Court of Justice', 16 December 2004. A wide-ranging set of infringement procedures was commenced by the Commission against 16 Member States including Greece in December 2006: MEMO/06/481, 'The Commission to act over EU energy markets', 12 December 2006.
[91] Figures from 2003: *E.On/MOL* (Case COMP/M.3696) Commission Decision 2006/622/EC, [2006] OJ L253/20, para 258. Hungary is an important transit country, however.

5.80 The Regulation sets out to lay down rules for cross-border flows of electricity, intended to be 'fair, cost-reflective, transparent and directly applicable'. However, the use of the term 'cross-border flows' is misleading. Except to the extent that it envisages security guidelines, the Regulation is not really about flows at all but rather about the scheduling of commercial transactions across borders, irrespective of where power actually flows on the interconnected HV systems. From the above statement it is clear that the rules under consideration are actually the rules of access for cross-border nominators of power.

5.81 The Regulation aims to enhance competition in the internal electricity market by means of three core-concepts.

(1) It introduces an inter-TSO compensation mechanism to compensate for costs incurred as a result of hosting cross-border flows of electricity on their networks by TSOs from which those flows originate and the systems where they end (Article 3).
(2) It sets down harmonized principles for cross-border transmission charges, encouraging consistency in charges for network access by outlawing so-called pancaking (see Glossary) and distance related-charges, and thereby avoiding distortions of trade (Article 4).
(3) It sets out measures to improve capacity allocation including congestion management (Articles 5, 6, and 7).[92]

5.82 With respect to the first, it may be noted that the compensation mechanism does not of itself help competition at all. It is the rules about TSOs not being allowed to charge transaction-based fees to exporters and importers, standing behind their wish for mutual compensation, which really count. Those rules derive from normal EU legal principles of not permitting artificial barriers to trade. With respect to the second, it should be noted that no fees are permitted to be charged to exporters or importers. The effect of Article 4 is to oblige TSOs to charge grid fees only at the point of generation or at the point of consumption of electricity across the internal market, unless the NRA or government department of the Member State clears with the Commission a non-discriminatory injection fee for a particular interconnection point.

5.83 These are developed in detail in Guidelines that are contained in an Annex to the Regulation. In 2006 the Commission introduced a Decision which repealed the Annex,[93] following the procedure for amendment of Guidelines in Article 8. This New Annex (see Appendix 5 of this book) introduced methods of congestion management for cross-border electricity interconnection capacities.

---

[92] A derogation was granted to Slovenia in 2004 from the application of Art 6(1) of the Regulation and the related provisions in the Guidelines (see paras 5.135–5.136).
[93] Commission Decision 2006/770/EC amending the Annex to Regulation (EC) No 1228/2003 on conditions for access to the network for cross-border exchanges in electricity [2006] OJ L 312/59.

C. The Electricity Regulation 2003

(1) The Inter-TSO Compensation Mechanism

Article 3 provides for a compensation mechanism for TSOs which host cross-border flows of electricity on their networks. In an open, competitive market, TSOs should be compensated for costs incurred in this way and Article 3(1) states this principle clearly. A cross-border flow is defined as a physical flow of electricity on a transmission network of a Member State that results from the impact of the activity of generators and/or consumers outside that Member State on its transmission network.[94] This compensation is to be paid by the national transmission systems from which cross-border flows originate and the systems where those flows end. The payments are to be made on a regular basis with respect to a given period of time in the past. Adjustments are to be made *ex post* if this is necessary to reflect costs actually incurred. The amounts of compensation payable are to be set by the Commission according to the committee procedure in Article 13(2). 5.84

The Regulation lays down rules for the assessment of both the amounts of cross-border flows and the costs incurred as a result of hosting them. The amounts of flows hosted and those designated as originating and/or ending in national transmission systems are to be set on the basis of the physical flows of electricity actually measured in a given period of time. The costs are to be set on the basis of forward-looking, long-run average incremental costs, taking into account losses, investment in new infrastructure, and an appropriate proportion of the cost of existing infrastructure, to the extent that such infrastructure is used for the transmission of cross-border flows. With respect to the latter point, the Regulation adds: 'in particular taking into account the need to guarantee security of supply'.[95] Recognized standard-costing methodologies are to be used when establishing the costs incurred. However, if a network incurs benefits as a result of hosting cross-border flows, these are to be taken into account to reduce the amount of compensation to be paid. 5.85

(2) Charges for Network Access

A pre-condition for effective competition in the internal electricity market is the operation by TSOs of non-discriminatory and transparent charges for network use. This includes interconnecting lines in the transmission system.[96] According to Article 4(1), the charges must take into account the need for network security and reflect the actual costs incurred, to the extent that they correspond to those of an efficient and structurally comparable network operator. The charges must not 5.86

---

[94] Electricity Regulation, Art 2(2)(b).
[95] ibid, Art 3(6).
[96] ibid, Recital 14, Art 4(1).

be distance-related. No specific network charge is be made on individual transactions for declared transits of electricity.[97]

5.87 When TSOs are setting national charges for network access they are required to take into account the following two considerations: payments and receipts resulting from the inter-TSO compensation mechanism, and actual payments made and received as well as payments expected for future periods of time, estimated on the basis of past periods.[98]

5.88 The Regulation addresses the balance of charges between generation and consumption in the region concerned. Both producers and consumers may be charged for network access but some differentiation of charges is required. The proportion of the total amount of the network charges that producers bear is to be lower than the proportion which consumers bear. This is subject to the need to provide appropriate and efficient long-term locational signals. Where appropriate, the level of tariffs applied to generators and/or consumers is to provide locational signals at the European level, and also take into account the amount of network losses and congestion caused, as well as investment costs for infrastructure. Member States are not prevented from providing locational signals within their territory or from applying mechanisms to ensure that network access charges that consumers bear are uniform throughout their territory.

5.89 The Regulation attempts through Article 4(4) a measure of harmonization of charges to avoid distortions of trade. Given that the actual amount payable can vary considerably according to the TSOs involved and the differences in the structure of the tarification systems applied in the Member States, the Regulation requires charges applied to generators and consumers to be applied irrespective of the countries of destination and origin respectively, of the electricity that is the subject of the underlying commercial arrangement. The condition for this is that appropriate and efficient locational signals are in place.[99] This requirement does not prevent special charges being made on 'declared exports' and 'declared imports' if they face system congestion, declared in advance by the TSOs to apply at borders. The former term ('declared export') applies to the dispatch of electricity in one Member State on the basis of an underlying contractual arrangement to the effect that the simultaneous corresponding take-up ('declared import') of electricity will take place in another Member State or a third country.

---

[97] ibid, Art 4(5).
[98] ibid, Art 4(3).
[99] Between 2003 and mid-2006 neither the Commission nor the ERGEG had taken any steps to initiate a harmonization of tariffs nor to create a pan-European system of locational signals.

C. The Electricity Regulation 2003

(3) Congestion Management

5.90 Congestion is defined as a situation in which an interconnection linking national transmission networks cannot accommodate all physical flows resulting from international trade that are requested by market participants. This arises because of a lack of capacity of the interconnectors and/or the national transmission systems concerned.[100] Diverse solutions to congestion problems are possible but subject to certain conditions. The methods used must provide efficient economic signals to the market participants and the TSOs involved and must be based on non-discriminatory market mechanisms. The congestion problems are required to be solved 'preferentially' with non-transaction based methods.[101] The latter means those methods that do not involve a selection between the contracts of individual market participants. In practice, the only market mechanisms that will comply with the Regulation and the Guidelines are explicit and implicit auctions.

5.91 Several capacity allocation methods are available for cross-border trade in electricity. Under an explicit auction, the capacity is auctioned for different time periods (by the week, month, hour, or the year). Bids are accepted commencing with the highest, and the price which all accepted bids have to pay is usually at the level of the bid that will fill the interconnector. The method has been used at the German/Belgian/Netherlands borders and at the France/UK DC link, for example. An implicit auction would, by contrast, award capacity on the basis of bids from generators into the electricity spot market on the other side of the interconnector where they compete with the local bids. The capacity is allocated with the cheapest bids until the interconnector is full. Implicit auctioning requires at least one power exchange in the area importing from the interconnector in question. A version of this is in use at the Portugal/Spain border.[102] In this context, the non-compliant means of allocation of some capacity at Dutch borders were commented on by the ECJ (see paras 5.132–5.135 and 13.59–13.86).

5.92 The use by TSOs of transaction curtailment procedures is expressly limited.[103] They may only be used in emergency situations where the TSO has to act in an expeditious manner and where re-dispatching or counter-trading is not possible. If used, such procedures have to be applied in a non-discriminatory manner. Unless the case is one in which *force majeure* is operative, market participants who have been allocated capacity are to be compensated for any curtailment. This suggests

---

[100] Electricity Regulation, Art 2(2)(c).
[101] ibid, Art 6(1).
[102] For further explanation of these methods, see the study for the European Commission carried out by Consentec/Frontier Economics, 'Analysis of Cross-Border Congestion Management Methods for the EU Internal Electricity Market', June 2004.
[103] Electricity Regulation, Art 6(2).

that a robust debate about the meaning of *force majeure* will result, and about how the compensation due can be quantified.

5.93 The capacity available for market participants is to be set at the maximum level of the interconnections and/or transmission networks which is consistent with safety standards for secure network operation.[104] Market participants are to inform the TSOs concerned a reasonable time ahead of the relevant operational period whether they intend to use allocated capacity. If such capacity is not to be used, it is required to be re-attributed to the market in an open, transparent, and non-discriminatory manner. As far as it is technically possible, TSOs are to net the capacity requirements of any power flows in the opposite direction over the congested interconnection line in order to use this line to its maximum capacity. Transactions that relieve the congestion are never to be denied, subject only to the TSO 'having full regard to network security'.[105]

5.94 Rules are laid down for the use of revenues that result from congestion management procedures. Exceptions to this may be justified in the case of interconnectors. The rules are to be used for one or more of the following purposes:

- to guarantee the actual availability of the allocated capacity;
- network investments that maintain or increase interconnection capacities;
- for income to be taken into account by NRAs when approving the methodology for calculating network tariffs, and/or in assessing whether tariffs should be modified.

(4) Exemptions for New Interconnectors

5.95 The importance of interconnections for the enhancement of competition has been emphasized by the Commission in a number of different communications and statements.[106] Interconnectors can expose generators and suppliers on both sides of a border to competition, and are essential for market integration. Moreover, their role has changed substantially since the pre-liberalization period. Formerly, they were constructed principally for security of supply reasons by the integrated incumbents. Now, access to interconnector capacity is a means by which market participants can trade on wholesale markets and benefit from price differentials between regions. However, the need for interconnector capacity has increased substantially. Without additional interconnectors 'the principles of market opening may become

---

[104] ibid, Art 6(3), Recital 14.
[105] ibid, Art 6(5).
[106] See, for example, the Commission's Communication on European Energy Infrastructure, COM (2001) 775; *Report on Progress in Creating the Internal Gas and Electricity Market*, COM (2005) 568 final, 15 November 2005, 23–25; Energy Sector Inquiry Preliminary Report (2006), 150–166; Green Paper, *A European Strategy for Sustainable, Competitive and Secure Energy*, COM (2006) 105 final, 6.

C. The Electricity Regulation 2003

meaningless as companies consolidate their position in particular regions of the European Union and the market becomes segmented'.[107] Nevertheless, the Directive does not provide any comprehensive measure on this, leaving it to be regulated by the Member States.

The Regulation does make provision for the exemption of new interconnectors from Article 6(6) of the Regulation (allocation of revenues from interconnection) and also Articles 20 and 23(2), (3), and (4) of the Electricity Directive (TPA, regulation of tariffs).[108] These must be direct current interconnectors that are not completed at the date of entry into force of the Regulation. However, in exceptional cases, exemptions may be provided to alternating current (AC) interconnectors. In such cases, the costs and risks of the investment must be especially high in comparison with the costs and risks normally incurred when connecting two neighbouring national transmission systems by an AC interconnector. This possibility of exemption also applies to significant increases in the capacity of existing interconnectors.[109]   **5.96**

The Regulation sets out in Article 7(1)(a) to (f) the conditions that need to be met before an exemption may be granted. There are six tests that have to be satisfied for an exemption to be granted: **5.97**

(a)   the investment must enhance competition in electricity supply;

(b)   the level of risk attached to the investment is such that the investment would not take place unless an exemption is granted;

(c)   the interconnector must be owned by a natural or legal person which is separate at least in terms of its legal form from the system operators in whose systems that interconnector will be built;

(d)   charges are levied on users of that interconnector;

(e)   . . . no part of the capital or operating costs of the interconnector has been recovered from any component of charges made for the use of transmission or distribution systems linked by the interconnector;[110]

(f)   the exemption is not to the detriment of competition or the effective functioning of the internal electricity market, or the efficient functioning of the regulated system to which the interconnector is linked.

---

[107] European Commission, CADA Decision, 'State aid N 475/2003—Ireland; Public Service Obligation in respect of new electricity generation capacity for security of supply', C(2003) 4488fin, 16 December 2003. For a recent discussion of these and other interconnector issues, see Talus, K and Wälde, T, 'Electricity Interconnectors—A Serious Challenge for EC Competition Law' (2006) 1 *Competition and Regulation in Network Industries* 353–88.

[108] Electricity Regulation, Art 7.

[109] ibid, Art 7(3).

[110] The starting point for calculation of this is the commencement of the partial market opening referred to in Art 19 of the first Electricity Directive.

5.98 The first stage in the procedure for requesting and granting an exemption involves a key role for the national authority. If it is the NRA that is vested with the granting power, it may decide on the request on a case-by-case basis. However, a Member State may prefer that the NRA submits its opinion on the request for a formal decision to 'the relevant body in the Member State'.[111] If so, this opinion must be published along with the decision (and any conditions attached to it). The exemption may cover all or part of the capacity of the new or existing interconnector (where significantly increased capacity is requested). Conditions may be imposed with respect to the duration of the exemption and non-discriminatory access to the interconnector. Both of these conditions are to be considered in the light of the additional capacity to be built, the expected time horizon of the project, and national circumstances. The NRA or 'relevant authority' may approve or fix the rules and/or mechanisms on the management and allocation of capacity. Consultation with other Member States or NRAs concerned is required before an exemption decision may be taken.

5.99 The second stage in the exemption process is triggered by notification of the decision to the Commission. This has to be done without delay and has to include all the information relevant to the decision, preferably submitted in aggregate form. Such information has to include the analysis of the effect on competition and the effective functioning of the internal electricity market which results from the grant of an exemption.[112] Where the information has a commercially sensitive character, the Commission is obliged to preserve its confidentiality. The Commission has a maximum of two months in which to request that the NRA or the Member State concerned either amend or withdraw the decision to grant an exemption. If additional information is sought by the Commission, an extension of one month is possible. Failure to comply with a request for additional information within a period of four weeks means that a final decision will be taken by the Commission under the committee procedure set up by Article 13.

(a) The Estlink Interconnector

5.100 The first formal decision relating to Article 7 of the Regulation was made with respect to the Estlink project for the construction of an electricity interconnector between the national grids of Finland and Estonia. The decision to grant a full exemption was made by the national authorities and de facto approved by the Commission on 23 April 2005.[113] The case provides a useful illustration of how

---

[111] Electricity Regulation, Art 7(4)(a).
[112] ibid, Art 7(5).
[113] See the decisions made by the Estonian and Finnish energy regulatory authorities: respectively, Estonian Decree No 52, 9 February 2005, and Energy Market Authority Decision RNo 195/429/2004, 2 February 2005 at <http://ec.europa.eu/energy/electricity/infrastructure/exemptions_en.htm>. For an extended discussion of these decisions, see Talus, K, 'First Experience under the Exemption Regime of EC Regulation 1228/2003 on Conditions for Access to the Network of Cross-Border Exchanges in Electricity' (2005) 23 J Energy and Natural Resources L266–81.

C. The Electricity Regulation 2003

the exemption procedure will work in practice and how the relevant authorities will approach their task. It also provides some insight into the application of Article 7(f)—the exemption is not to be to the detriment of competition—and is therefore worthy of an extended review. However, an important caveat should be made at the outset. The Estlink case has limited internal market implications. Estonia, like other Baltic States, is still linked to the Russian electricity system, and therefore on a different frequency to UCTE and Nordel; for practical commercial purposes, it is not directly connected to either of these systems at the present time.

AS Nordic Link (NEL) requested the energy regulatory authorities of Estonia and Finland to grant an exemption under Article 7 of the Electricity Regulation. The DC submarine cable between the two countries is to have a capacity of 350 MW and would be the first interconnector between the Baltic and Nordic power systems. Estlink was to be built as a commercial project with the return deriving from electricity exports from the Baltic countries to the Nordic area and vice versa. The exemption was requested until the end of the year 2013, but with the condition that the exemption would expire if the interconnector is sold to the TSOs earlier than that date. **5.101**

While the Estonian Energy Markets Inspectorate (EMI) adopted the opinion that the request be approved, and submitted their opinion to the Estonian Ministry, the latter questioned one of the clauses in the NEL transmission capacity purchase agreement. It appeared to be in conflict with the TPA principles of the Electricity Directive, especially Article 23(8). NEL abandoned the relevant clause of the agreement and accepted the Ministry's proposal to limit the initial auction price to avoid a situation where the user of the cable could restrict TPA to the cable's available capacity by setting a high initial price at the auction. **5.102**

Following the requirements of Article 7(4) of the Regulation, the relevant Member States and regulatory authorities concerned entered into consultations prior to a decision on the grant of the exemption. Several meetings followed between the Estonian Ministry responsible for commercial matters and communications, and the EMI, on the one hand, and the Energy Markets Authority of Finland (EMA) about the exemption application, as well as with officials from DG TREN of the Commission. They discussed issues such as the TPA arrangements within the Nordic electricity exchange Nordpool, preferential rights of the parties to the project as set out in the initial contracts with respect to TPA, and the terms and conditions of holding auctions. The intention was to avoid any conflict in the terms of the separate decisions made by the respective authorities, and to ensure that their simultaneous application would not be unreasonable from the applicant's point of view. **5.103**

In their assessment of the application, the respective authorities considered the six criteria set out in Article 7(1) of the Regulation one by one to assess compliance. The submarine cable would strengthen competition between electricity generators in **5.104**

Chapter 5: Electricity

the region and, since both the Finnish and Baltic power companies were parties to the project, no single company has a dominant position in the project. The investment could also be classified as a 'major investment' for Estonia, within the terms of the Regulation, the costs of which could not be covered by the national grid tariffs due to their large effect on the end consumer prices. The level of risk was deemed to be high and, following a risk assessment, was in line with the conditions set out in the DG TREN Note 2003/54-55[114] and the Regulation, and all the investors were, in the opinion of EMI and the investors, unwilling to proceed without the grant of an exemption for the project. Ownership of the interconnector would vest in NEL, a distinct legal person with no part ownership by TSOs in whose systems Estlink is to be built. The return on the investment is to be covered by the parties from the charges levied for the rights to use the capacity. The tariffs have been developed according to the principle that they include only the networks' justified operating costs and profitability on the regulated assets. The cost of the interconnector would not be included in the prices of the services provided by the national grid and the distribution networks. Finally, the exemption was deemed not to be detrimental to competition or the effective functioning of the internal electricity market, or the effective functioning of the regulated system to which the interconnector is linked. On the latter point, the Finnish authority conducted an analysis based on the relevant product and geographic markets, noting Commission precedents in various merger decisions, prior to analyzing market shares in electricity generation and procurement. The Estonian energy authority noted NEL's plan to auction available unused capacity to all market players, demonstrating the operation of the 'use-it-or-lose-it' principle in operating the cable to ensure TPA in its use.

5.105 The co-operation between the regulatory authorities, and their respective ministries, also involved the European Commission. The sources drawn on to develop the decisions included the relevant market definitions provided in Commission Decisions as well as the DG TREN Guidance Note (see para 5.104 above), as well as the Regulation and the relevant national legislation. Differences of perspective on the project did exist between the relevant authorities, and much effort was made to ensure that the final decision was one that was harmonious with respect to future NRA working relations and workable for the parties which made the application. The interconnector became operational in December 2006.

(5) Information Requirements

5.106 The requirements to provide information fall on both TSOs (Article 5) and Member States and NRAs (Article 10). They are concerned with information relevant to

---

[114] Exemptions from Certain Provisions of the Third Party Access Regime, 30 January 2004, <http://ec.europa.eu/energy/electricity/legislation/doc/notes_for_implementation_2004/exemptions_tpa_en.pdf>.

C. The Electricity Regulation 2003

the inter-TSO compensation mechanism and the adoption and/or amendment of guidelines.[115] These information gathering powers significantly enhance the regulatory power of the Commission.

5.107 The TSOs are required to provide information on interconnection capacities. They have therefore to publish estimates of available transfer capacity for each day, indicating any available transfer capacity that is already reserved. These publications of estimates are to be made at specified intervals before the day of transport and are to include week-ahead and month-ahead estimates. They are also to include a quantitative indication of the expected reliability of the available capacity.

5.108 Safety and security measures are also the subject of information requirements. TSOs are to put into place co-ordination and information exchange mechanisms to ensure the security of the networks in situations of congestion management. The safety standards—and also the operational and planning standards—used by TSOs are to be published. This information is to include a general scheme for the calculation of the total transfer capacity and the transmission reliability margin based upon the electrical and physical features of the network. Such schemes are subject to the approval of the NRAs.

5.109 Article 10 imposes obligations upon Member States and the NRAs to provide information to the Commission for purposes of calculating the amounts of compensation payable under the inter-TSO mechanism and of adopting and/or amending guidelines. In connection with the former, the NRAs are to provide information on a regular basis that covers costs actually incurred by national TSOs, as well as data and other relevant information that relates to the physical flows in TSOs' networks and the cost of the network. The Commission must set a time-limit for the submission of such data, and in doing so it must take into account the complexity of the information required and the urgency with which it is needed.

5.110 A failure by the NRA or Member State concerned to provide the information requested within the time-limit set means that the Commission may then approach the undertakings concerned directly.[116] When doing so, the Commission is required to forward a copy of the request to the NRA (or NRAs) of the Member State in whose territory the undertaking is based. Procedural requirements are imposed on the Commission if it is to request information directly in this way. It has to state the legal basis for its request, the time-limit for submission of the requested information, the purpose of the request and the penalties provided for in Article 12(2) of the Regulation (see paras 5.128–5.129) for supplying incorrect, incomplete, or misleading information. In setting the time-limit for a response, the Commission

---

[115] Electricity Regulation, Art 10(6).
[116] ibid, Art 10(2).

has to take into account the complexity of the information sought and the urgency with which it is needed. On the other hand, the owners of the undertakings or their representatives are subjected to an obligation to supply the information requested. This may be done through a legal representative on behalf of its client but the client has full responsibility for ensuring that the information supplied meets the required tests.

5.111 If the undertaking fails to supply the information requested within the time-limit, or if it is incomplete, the Commission may require the information by means of a decision. This instrument has to set out the information required and fix an appropriate time-limit for its provision, as well as indicating the penalties applicable through Article 12(2) and the undertaking's right to have the decision reviewed by the ECJ. A copy of the decision has to be sent by the Commission to the NRAs of the Member State in which the undertaking is based.

5.112 For information collected under the Regulation that is of a confidential character, the Commission is under an obligation not to disclose it.

(6) Guidelines

(a) Article 8

5.113 The adoption of Guidelines by the Commission is envisaged under the Regulation as are the issues that they may address. This is an important implementing mechanism for the achievement of the Regulation's aims. The Commission may amend such guidelines and did in fact amend the first (that is, 2003) set of guidelines in 2006. Member States may maintain or introduce measures that contain more detailed measures than those set out in the guidelines.

5.114 The guidelines are required to provide details on six key matters:[117]

(1) The procedure for determining which TSOs are liable to pay compensation for cross-border flows, including details about the split between the operators of national transmission systems from which cross-border flows originate and the systems where those flows end.
(2) The payment procedure to be followed, including the determination of the first period of time for which compensation is to be paid.
(3) Methodologies for determining the cross-border flows hosted for which compensation is to be paid, in terms of both quantity and type of flows and the designation of the magnitudes of such flows as originating and/or ending in transmission systems of individual Member States.
(4) The methodology for determining the costs and benefits incurred as a result of hosting cross-border flows.

---

[117] ibid, Art 8(2)(a)–(f).

C. The Electricity Regulation 2003

(5) The treatment in the context of the inter-TSO compensation mechanism of electricity flows originating or ending in countries outside the EEA.
(6) The participation of national systems which are interconnected through DC lines.

While all of the above points relate to the ITC mechanism, Article 8 also refers to further guidelines which arguably have much greater importance for the internal market than those relating to the making of rather modest compensation payments between TSOs. These guidelines concern congestion management and security in Article 8(4) and are to ensure that congestion management mechanisms evolve in a manner compatible with the aims of the internal market, supplemented (where appropriate) by common rules on minimum safety and operational standards for the use and operation of the network. **5.115**

Additionally, the guidelines are required to set out appropriate rules that lead to a progressive harmonization of the underlying principles for the setting of charges applied to producers and consumers under national tariff systems, including the reflection of the inter-TSO compensation mechanism in national network charges and the provision of appropriate and efficient locational signals. The latter are to be provided at the European level, but this is not to prevent Member States from applying mechanisms to ensure that the network access charges that consumers bear are comparable throughout their territory. **5.116**

The Guidelines may be amended from time to time in accordance with principles set out in Articles 5 and 6 of the Regulation and the committee procedure set out in Article 13(2). The aim of this is to ensure that the guidelines are able to be adapted rapidly to meet changed circumstances.[118] Five considerations play a part in any such amendment. First, amendment should be aimed at ensuring that the guidelines include all capacity allocation methodologies that are *applied in practice*. Secondly, it should ensure that congestion management mechanisms evolve in a manner that is compatible with the objectives of the internal market. Thirdly, such amendments should include, where appropriate, common rules on minimum safety and operational standards for the use and operation of a network.[119] Fourthly, adoption or amendment requires the Commission to ensure that the guidelines provide the minimum degree of harmonization to achieve the Regulation's aims and not to go beyond what is necessary for that purpose. Finally, the Commission is required to indicate what actions it has taken regarding the conformity of rules in third countries which are part of the European electricity system with the guidelines or amendments it proposes.[120] **5.117**

---

[118] ibid, Recital 8.
[119] ibid, Art 5(2).
[120] This also applies to the rules in the Regulation itself: Recital 7. The aim is to increase the effective functioning of the internal market.

5.118 The procedure for comitology is as follows (see para 5.38). First, the draft Guidelines are presented to a committee of representatives from the Member States. A positive vote is required in this committee by qualified majority. If this is not obtainable, the matter is referred to the Council, which requires a qualified majority vote to prevent the Commission from adopting the Guidelines. The European Parliament has a *droit de regard* in this process, and may therefore examine whether the Commission has exceeded its implementing powers. However, the opinion expressed by the Parliament has no binding force on the Commission.

(b) The New Guidelines on Congestion Management

5.119 The Annex to the Regulation contains a set of Guidelines on the management and allocation of available transfer capacity of interconnections between national systems. The first version of these Guidelines was replaced in 2006 by a New Annex that is substantially longer and more detailed (see para 5.83 and Appendix 5). It covers congestion management methods; co-ordination of congestion management methods and procedures; timetable for market operation, transparency and use of congestion income. It grants a substantial number of additional powers to NRAs. There are 15 such powers in the New Annex, in contrast to three in the previous (2003) Annex. Often the power granted is one of review, in contrast to the power of approval that was proposed in earlier drafts of the New Annex.

5.120 Under the General Provisions of the New Annex, it is stated in Guideline 1.5 that the methods for management of congestion are intended to give efficient economic signals to market participants and TSOs, to promote competition, and also to be suitable for regional and community-wide application. In Guideline 1.6 grounds for denial of a particular request for transmission service are given. This may happen only when two conditions are jointly fulfilled: first, the incremental physical power flows resulting from the acceptance of this request imply that secure operation of the power system may no longer be guaranteed, and the value in monetary amount attached to the request in the congestion management procedure is lower than all other requests intended to be accepted for the same service and conditions. Further, a deadline is set for the establishment of mechanisms for intra-day congestion management of interconnector capacity. By 1 January 2008 these are to be established in a co-ordinated way and under secure operational conditions to maximize opportunities for trade and to provide for cross-border balancing.[121]

5.121 The section on methods of congestion management comprises 13 paragraphs to the former Annex's three. Methods are to be market-based, and so capacity is to be allocated only by means of explicit (capacity) or implicit (capacity and energy) auctions. There is no section on explicit auctions in the New Annex. Access rights

---

[121] Guideline 1.9; see n 93 above.

C. The Electricity Regulation 2003

for long- and medium-term allocations are to be firm transmission capacity rights, subject to both use-it-or-lose-it and use-it-or-sell-it principles at the time of nomination. The TSOs are charged with the design of a structure for capacity allocation between different time-frames. This allocation structure is subject to a review by the respective NRAs.[122] All market participants are permitted to participate in the allocation process without restriction. However, the relevant NRAs or competition authorities may impose restrictions in general or on an individual company on account of market dominance.[123]

Firm transmission capacity rights are of considerable importance and differ from non-firm rights. TSOs are under an obligation to maximize the amount of capacity they allocate to market participants at international borders. This crucial provision of the Regulation is not yet effectively enforced. There is an interesting dynamic in the trade-off between desired, and apparently compulsory firmness on the one hand and *ex ante* maximization on the other (that is, minimization of declared congestion in advance). In this respect the Regulation sets up the potential for long-running future disputes about who can get transmission capacity, when, and at what price, in particular, compared with normally guaranteed access inside national boundaries.   **5.122**

In a case where a secondary trade is refused by a TSO, this must be clearly and transparently communicated and explained to all the market participants by that TSO and notified to the NRA. In addition, liabilities that accrue on failure to honour obligations associated with the allocation of capacity are to be set according to key concepts and methods which are to be made available and reviewed by the NRA or NRAs.[124]   **5.123**

A common co-ordinated congestion management method and procedure for capacity allocation is to be applied from 1 January 2007 at the latest. This involves seven regions: Northern Europe; North-West Europe; Italy; Central Eastern Europe; South-West Europe; UK, Ireland and France, and finally the Baltic states. This is to be on a yearly, monthly and day-ahead basis. This is an important matter since 'compatible congestion management procedures shall be defined in all these seven regions with a view to forming a truly integrated Internal European Electricity Market'.[125] Market participants are not to be confronted with incompatible regional systems.   **5.124**

The transparency requirements on TSOs are increased, and each TSO is required to publish a general scheme for the calculation of interconnection capacity for   **5.125**

---

[122] Guideline 2.6.
[123] Guideline 2.10.
[124] Guideline 2.13.
[125] Guideline 3.4.

different time-frames, which is subject to the review of the NRAs concerned. Also subject to NRA review is the set of operational and planning security standards.[126] TSOs are required to provide all relevant data on cross-border trade in a published form. To do this, the market participants concerned are required to provide the TSOs with the relevant data. The minimum set of data to be published is itemized in Guideline 5.5. Once again, there is a provision for review by the NRAs, this time concerning the way in which such information is published. Data on network and load flow is to be made available to the NRAs and the European Commission on request, and is to be treated in confidence.

5.126 The Regulation's provisions on use of congestion income in Article 6 are supplemented by a Guideline on this matter. The procedure for distribution of the revenue is subject to review by the NRAs. Moreover, the congestion income to be shared among the TSOs involved is subject to review by the respective NRAs. TSOs are required to 'clearly establish beforehand the use they will make of any congestion income they may obtain' and to report on the actual use of this income. The NRAs are to verify that this use complies with the Regulation and Guidelines, and that the total amount of congestion income is devoted to one or more of the three purposes set out in Article 6(6) of the Regulation (see para 5.94).

5.127 No hierarchy for the three permitted uses is given, which may be storing up potential for disputes in the future. Annually, the NRAs are required to publish a report on the amount of revenue collected for the 12 month period up to 30 June of the same year and the use made of the revenues in question, together with a 'verification' that this use is in compliance with the Regulation and the Guidelines. The NRAs are required to be transparent in the use of revenues from the allocation of interconnection capacity.[127]

(7) **Enforcement**

5.128 The Member States are required to lay down rules on penalties applicable to infringements of the provisions of the Regulation and to take all the measures necessary to ensure that they are implemented.[128] These penalties must be effective, proportionate and dissuasive. These provisions have to be notified to the Commission by 1 July 2004 at the latest. These penalties are not to have the character of measures of criminal law.

5.129 The Commission may impose financial penalties upon undertakings by means of a Decision.[129] If an undertaking supplies incorrect, incomplete, or misleading

---

[126] Guideline 5.4.
[127] Guideline 6.2.
[128] Electricity Regulation, Art 12(1).
[129] ibid, Art 10(2).

C. The Electricity Regulation 2003

information in response to a request made for data under Article 10(3), the fine imposed may not exceed 1 per cent of the total turnover in the preceding business year. Similarly, a failure to provide information within the time-limit fixed by a decision adopted further to Article 10(5), first sub-paragraph, may lead to an imposition of a fine of up to the same amount. The Commission is obliged when setting the amount of the fine to take into account the gravity of the failure to comply.

The NRAs are expressly charged with ensuring compliance with the Regulation and the Guidelines adopted under Article 8. This is in addition to other responsibilities they have under the Regulation. If this requires co-operation with each other and with the Commission, they are required to do so.[130] Recital (18) makes it clearer how this role fits into the overall enforcement strategy. It states that: 5.130

> To ensure the smooth functioning of the internal market, provision should be made for procedures which allow the adoption of decisions and guidelines with regard to among other things tarification and capacity allocation by the Commission whilst ensuring the involvement of Member States' regulatory authorities in this process; where appropriate through their European association. Regulatory authorities, together with their relevant authorities in the Member States, have an important role to play in contributing to the proper functioning of the internal electricity market.

Implementation of the Regulation is to be monitored by the Commission.[131] The Commission is required to report to the European Parliament and the Council on the experience gained in the application of the Regulation no more than three years after its entry into force (that is, before 1 July 2007). The report must pay special attention to the extent to which the Regulation has been successful in ensuring non-discriminatory and cost-reflective network access conditions for cross-border exchanges of electricity 'in order to contribute to customer choice in a well functioning internal market and to long-term security of supply, as well as to what extent effective locational signals are in place'.[132] If the Commission considers it necessary, proposals and/or recommendations may be included in this report. 5.131

(a) Preferential Access Ruling by the ECJ

The ECJ became involved in enforcement, in a matter concerning access. Although this did not directly concern the Regulation, it was an issue related to scheduling of export/import transactions across borders and so is considered below. 5.132

---

[130] ibid, Art 9.
[131] ibid, Art 14.
[132] ibid, Art 14.

5.133 The ECJ ruled on preferential access to networks in June 2005. Although the ruling concerned Directive (EC) 96/92 (the first Electricity Directive, now repealed), it is an important one nevertheless. It is discussed at paras 13.59–13.86 in some detail but a few remarks are appropriate at this stage. In the ECJ's opinion, the non-discrimination rules that the Directive provided for have the effect of precluding national measures that grant an undertaking preferential capacity for the cross-border transmission of electricity. This applies even in cases where this preferential capacity is conferred on an operator by reason of commitments assumed before the Directive entered into force. This includes long-term electricity supply contracts made within the framework of the performance of a task of general economic interest.

5.134 The ECJ considered that the existence of the contracts (in the Netherlands) did not justify any preferential treatment, even though they were concluded before the entry into force of the Directive. The latter provided Member States with the option to grant transitional derogations for commitments given before the entry into force of the Directive, if those commitments appeared to be incompatible with the Directive. The ECJ also concluded that the principles of the protection of legitimate expectations and of legal certainty could not be used to justify a derogation from the non-discriminatory rules of the Directive.

5.135 There were a number of specific consequences of the judgment. First, it seems to follow that the existence of long-term supply and capacity reservation contracts prior to the entry into force of the Directive does not justify the grant of priority allocation of transmission capacity. This interpretation lay behind the Commission's decision in April 2006 to send infringement letters to all Member States where issues were outstanding on the priority allocation of cross-border network in favour of pre-liberalization contracts. Several Member States have already taken steps to remove priority access rights.[133] Secondly, the relevant principles on non-discriminatory access to electricity transmission and distribution networks contained in the first Electricity Directive are provided for in the current Electricity Directive and Regulation. So, the Commission has concluded that 'the grant to an undertaking of preferential transmission or distribution capacities must be considered as being discriminatory and is precluded by Directive 2003/54/EC and Regulation (EC) No 1228/2003'.[134] Thirdly, the derogations provided for under the first Electricity Directive were of a transitional character and a limited duration (applying to commitments taken before 19 February 1997). There is no comparable provision in

---

[133] Conclusions of the 13th Meeting of the European Electricity Regulatory Forum, Florence, 7–8 September 2006, para 6.

[134] European Commission, 'Commission Staff Working Document on the decision C-17/03 of 7 June 2005 of the Court of Justice of the European Communities: Preferential Access to Transport Networks under the Electricity and Gas Internal Market Directives', 26 April 2006.

the 2003 Electricity Directive concerning the grant of derogations from the application of non-discriminatory rules to historical long-term supply and capacity reservation contracts. At present, only the priority allocation of transmission and distribution capacities is incompatible with EC rules. Long-term supply contracts cannot be subject to preferential treatment but are not in themselves invalid under the ECJ judgment.

(b) Slovenian Derogation

5.136 As a contrast to the above case concerning electricity crossing Dutch borders, the derogation granted to Slovenia by means of a Regulation in 2004 merits some comment. Following a request from Slovenia for a transitional period and a proposal from the Commission, a sub-paragraph was added to Article 15 of the Electricity Regulation 2003.[135] It reads:

> As regards interconnectors between Slovenia and neighbouring Member States, Article 6(1), as well as rules 1 to 4 contained in the chapter entitled 'General' of the Annex, shall apply from 1 July 2007. This paragraph shall apply only to the interconnection capacity which is allocated by the Slovenian transmission system operator and only insofar as such capacity does not exceed half of the total available interconnection capacity.

5.137 Slovenia argued for a transitional period for the application of Article 6(1) (which requires network management problems to be addressed by means of non-discriminatory market-based solutions) and related provisions in the Guidelines (which contain rules directly linked to the general principle in the Regulation). Its justification was that certain energy-intensive industries would be adversely affected by higher prices for electricity imported from Austria and certain electricity generators by lower incomes from export sales to Italy. This situation would impede ongoing restructuring efforts by the industries and therefore their efforts to comply with the requirements of the *acquis* applicable to electricity generation. The derogation was justified on the ground that the interconnection capacity of the two interconnectors was small, the situation was unlikely to change before July 2007, and hence the practical impact on the internal market of the derogation would be small. The derogation was to cover only the part of the interconnection capacity allocated by the Slovenian TSO and to apply only insofar as the capacity does not exceed half of the total capacity available.

5.138 The derogation is notable since the capacity may be small but it lies at the heart of the UCTE system and affects the severely constrained Italian borders. It is therefore a potentially greater practical hindrance to the internal electricity market

---

[135] Council Regulation (EC) 1223/2004 of 28 June 2004 amending Regulation (EC) 1228/2003 of the European Parliament and of the Council as regards the date of application of certain provisions to Slovenia [2004] OJ L233/3.

5.139 The Electricity Regulation entered into force on 1 July 2004. It is directly applicable in all the Member States from that date. However, there appears to be a growing body of evidence of non-compliance, which raises questions about the adequacy of the enforcement mechanisms. For example, there has been an increase in declared congestion at borders across Europe in the last three years, often well rewarded (for the TSOs) by heavy congestion rents through auctions, contrasted with national systems or regional high-voltage networks as 'copperplates' for national generators and consumers. In other words, these networks are treated by the TSOs as open on all routes between generation and demand rather than sometimes constraining off some sources of generation, forcing congestion to the edges. The Commission's Sector Inquiry report reveals a catalogue of problems with the operation of competition in the electricity markets, including serious transparency issues, a highly concentrated market structure, and uneven regulatory enforcement. It confirms the rather negative assessment of these markets in the 'benchmarking' reports issued by DG TREN.

D. Conclusions

5.140 Both the Electricity Directive and its predecessor have been legal instruments designed for a specific phase in the transition to an internal market in electricity. Each represented a specific 'bargain' struck between the Member States and the Community in terms of sharing competences over the reform of a strategic economic sector. Each contained mechanisms that were designed to achieve a balance between the objectives of competition, environment and various public service goals. In this sense the Electricity Directive provides simultaneously a 'constitution' and a 'road map' for the liberalizing electricity market in the EU. The more ambitious provisions can be seen in the sections on TPA, unbundling, and regulation, which contrast markedly with comparable provisions in the first Directive. From a legal point of view, the provisions in the Regulation and attached Guidelines are interesting since they are an attempt to move from the level of 'common rules' to that of regulation aimed at tackling specific—and often highly complex—problems that need to be addressed for competition to be effective. It may be noted that the provisions of the Regulation do not preclude the rights of Member States to maintain or introduce measures that contain more detailed measures than those set out in the Regulation or the guidelines in the Annex.[136] The New Annex to the Regulation is instructive because of the shift it demonstrates towards more detailed regulation,

---

[136] Electricity Regulation, Art 11.

D. Conclusions

greater powers to NRAs and an orientation towards not only the achievement of an internal market but also towards those initiatives that aim to establish competitive *regional* electricity markets as intermediate steps.

The 'vision' guiding the Directive and Regulation is that of a single market in electricity. However, the Regulation already hints in its revised Annex on congestion management guidelines at a different perspective: an interim stage in which energy markets are connected on a regional basis. This regional approach has already been discussed by the Commission[137] and is now part of the strategy of the ERGEG (see paras 3.40–3.43). The shift of focus is indicative of a much larger problem, however. The introduction of competition has proved more difficult than had been foreseen, raising questions about the adequacy of the measures in the Directive (in particular, the absence of ownership unbundling and the minimum powers of the NRAs) and the level of detail provided for in the Regulation and related Guidelines. To some extent, these shortcomings, highlighted by the transition process, are remediable by introducing new legislation or rules through the procedures set up under the Regulation. However, they also highlight the apparent limits of these sector-specific instruments to address issues of enforcement and the anti-competitive elements in the market structure. The former may be addressed both by the Commission and by the actions of private parties as happened in the *VEMW* case. The latter set of issues may require the additional use of other legal powers such as those examined in Part III.

5.141

---

[137] DG Energy and Transport Working Paper, 'Strategy Paper: Medium Term Vision for the Internal Electricity Market', 1 March 2004.

6

GAS

A. Introduction	6.01	(6) Market Opening and Reciprocity	6.63
B. The Gas Directive 2003		(7) Direct Lines	6.65
(1) Aims and Scope	6.03	(8) Regulation	6.68
(2) General Rules	6.05	(9) Enforcement	
(a) Public Service Obligations	6.06	(a) Derogations	6.69
(b) Authorization Procedure	6.15	(b) Take-or-Pay Commitments	6.72
(c) Security of Supply	6.17	(c) Emergent and Isolated	
(d) Technical Rules	6.19	Markets	6.99
(3) Rules for Specific Activities		(d) Reporting	6.110
(a) Production	6.21	(e) Enforcement by the ECJ	6.114
(b) Transmission	6.22	C. The Gas Regulation 2005	6.115
(c) Distribution and Supply	6.26	(1) Tariffs for Network Access	6.118
(d) Storage	6.29	(2) Third Party Access Services	6.122
(e) Liquefied Natural Gas	6.35	(3) Principles of Capacity	
(4) Unbundling	6.36	Allocation and Congestion	
(a) Compliance	6.37	Management	6.125
(5) Access	6.38	(4) Transparency Requirements	6.128
(a) Regulated TPA in Gas	6.39	(5) Balancing Rules and Imbalance	
(b) Access to Storage	6.40	Charges	6.129
(c) Access to Upstream Pipeline		(6) Trading of Capacity Rights	6.130
Networks	6.47	(7) Guidelines	6.132
(d) Exemptions for New		(a) Guidelines on Storage	6.137
Infrastructure	6.53	(8) Enforcement	6.142
(e) Access to Transit Pipelines	6.61	D. Conclusions	6.148

The Community legislation does not include measures that directly address the concentrated market structure inherited from the monopoly era, which remains a key problem of the internal gas market.

Energy Sector Inquiry Report[1]

---

[1] European Commission DG COMP, *Report on Energy Sector Inquiry*, SEC (2006) 1724, 10 January 2007, p 30 (para 48).

A. Introduction

6.01 The principal legislation applicable to the EU gas sector is Directive (EC) 2003/55 ('the Gas Directive'),[2] and the Regulation on conditions for access to the natural gas transmission networks ('the Regulation').[3] Like the Electricity Directive, the Gas Directive has its origins in the shortcomings of its predecessor, the first Gas Directive,[4] which it repealed.[5] Although parts of the first Directive are essentially taken over by its successor, there are significant differences in content and approach. Moreover, it forms part of a package of legal instruments that are intended to provide both common rules for the gas sector and specific regulations and guidelines for its *continuing liberalization*. This chapter will review and assess the legal framework for the introduction of competition into the gas sector, which the Directive and Regulation provide.

6.02 In general, the approach in the Gas Directive is less interventionist than that of the Electricity Directive with fewer monitoring and reporting requirements, relying on further input from the discussions in the Madrid Forum and from the European Regulatory Group for Electricity and Gas (ERGEG). Some differences between the two Directives, such as the provisions on storage, take-or-pay commitments, the absence of a 'universal service' provision, the approach to third party access (TPA) and unbundling, are in large part the result of differences between the gas and electricity sectors themselves. Gas is, of course, a primary and not a secondary energy source, capable of being stored for long periods, unlike electricity, with different market shares in the Member States, and dependent on large-scale front-end investments in fixed infrastructure and long-term supply contracts. The gas market structure is heavily influenced by the role of a few large non-EU suppliers, with contract prices for wholesale gas almost always linked to those for oil and oil derivatives. Where the provisions in the Gas Directive are essentially the same as those in the Electricity Directive, the text below will indicate this and the relevant sections of Chapter 5 will be referred to. Where there are contrasts, these are noted.

---

[2] Directive (EC) 2003/55 concerning common rules for the internal market in natural gas and repealing Directive (EC) 98/30 [2003] OJ L176/57.
[3] Regulation (EC) 1775/2005 of 28 September 2005 on conditions for access to the natural gas transmission networks [2005] OJ L289/1.
[4] Directive (EC) 98/30 concerning common rules for the internal market in natural gas [1998] OJ L204/1.
[5] Gas Directive, Art 32.

B. The Gas Directive 2003

(1) Aims and Scope

The overall aim of the Directive is stated in Recital 30 as 'the creation of a fully operational internal gas market, in which fair competition prevails'. There are four subordinate goals,[6] all designed to remedy shortcomings and bring about potential improvements to the market which were identified in the period after the adoption of the first Directive. The first of these is to ensure a level playing field. The second is to reduce the risks of market dominance and predatory behaviour. The third is to ensure non-discriminatory transmission and distribution tariffs, through access to the network on the basis of tariffs published prior to their entry into force. Fourthly, the Directive aims at ensuring that the rights of small and vulnerable customers are protected. **6.03**

To achieve these various aims, the Directive establishes common rules for the transmission, distribution, supply and storage of natural gas. These rules concern the organization and functioning of the natural gas sector, access to the market, the criteria and procedures applicable to the granting of authorizations for transmission, distribution, supply and storage of natural gas, and the operation of systems. In terms of scope, they apply not only to natural gas and liquefied natural gas (LNG) but also to biogas and gas from biomass and other types of gas which can be technically and safely injected into and transported through the natural gas system. **6.04**

(2) General Rules

Similar to the Electricity Directive, there is a high priority given to 'public service' in the provisions of the Gas Directive. The obligations on Member States with respect to public service and the protection of consumers are set out first of all of the general rules in Chapter II. There are some differences however, such as the absence of a requirement for a universal service. Indeed, in one of the Commission's Guidance Notes, it is expressly stated that 'contrary to electricity, gas supply cannot be considered a universal service'.[7] The provisions represent a reinforcement and expansion of the provisions on public service contained in the first Gas Directive. **6.05**

(a) Public Service Obligations

The scope of PSOs The Directive states that respect of the public service requirements is 'a fundamental objective'.[8] The provisions on public service obligations **6.06**

---

[6] ibid, Recital 2.
[7] DG TREN Guidance Note, 'Security of Supply Provisions for Gas', 16 January 2004, 3.
[8] Gas Directive, Recital 27.

(PSOs) and consumer protection measures may be distinguished into three broad groupings. First, there are obligations imposed upon the Member States. They are similar to those set out in the Electricity Directive. They include the obligations to ensure that gas undertakings respect the Directive's requirements and not to discriminate between undertakings as regards either rights or obligations;[9] to protect final customers;[10] to ensure that there are adequate safeguards to protect vulnerable customers, including measures to help them to avoid disconnection;[11] to ensure high levels of consumer protection, especially with respect to transparency regarding general contractual terms and conditions, general information, and dispute settlement mechanisms;[12] to ensure that the eligible customer is effectively able to switch to a new supplier;[13] and to notify the Commission of all measures taken to fulfil PSOs, and their possible effect on national and international competition.[14] Secondly, there are objectives to be pursued by the Member States, such as social and economic cohesion, environmental protection and security of supply.[15] Member States may also introduce the implementation of long-term planning in pursuit of security of supply, environmental protection, and demand-side management or energy efficiency.[16] Finally, there are options available to Member States, such as the establishment of a supplier of last resort for customers connected to the gas network and the protection of customers in remote areas who are connected to the gas system.[17]

6.07 In the absence of an equivalent provision to that of 'universal service' in the Gas Directive, the only comparable provision is the requirement that Member States should ensure that when customers are connected to the gas system, they are informed about their rights to be supplied with natural gas of a specified quality 'at reasonable prices'.[18] The absence of universal service reflects an important difference between gas and electricity. Gas is a substitutable primary source of energy. It can be replaced by alternative sources such as coal, oil, or nuclear energy. The dependence of final consumers on it is therefore less acute than on electricity supply, which is used by virtually all households.

---

[9] ibid, Art 3(1).
[10] ibid, Art 3(3).
[11] ibid, Art 3(3).
[12] ibid, Art 3(3).
[13] ibid, Art 3(3).
[14] ibid, Art 3(6). The notification requirement in the first Directive was limited to those PSOs relating to a request for a derogation (in practice there were no notifications), but the requirement is now for *all* measures taken to be notified to the Commission, irrespective of whether they require a derogation from the Directive or not.
[15] ibid, Art 3(4).
[16] ibid, Art 3(2).
[17] ibid, Art 3(3).
[18] ibid, Recital 26.

B. The Gas Directive 2003

The specific obligations that a Member State may impose on a natural gas undertaking relate to: **6.08**

(1) security, including security of supply;
(2) regularity;
(3) quality of supplies;
(4) price of supplies;
(5) environmental protection, including energy efficiency and climate protection; and
(6) the implementation of long-term planning (in relation to security of supply, energy efficiency/demand-side management and the fulfilment of environmental goals, as defined under point 5).

PSOs must be clearly-defined, transparent, non-discriminatory and verifiable. The transparency requirement is interpreted by the Commission as requiring publication.[19] The aim is to enable all or several operators to make a bid to carry out the PSO. The notification to the Commission is to be updated every two years and the information feeds into the Commission's report published according to Article 31(2). **6.09**

A considerable degree of detail about consumer protection measures is contained in Annex A to the Directive. The content is almost identical to that in Annex A of the Electricity Directive, except that, under para (g), customers who are connected to the gas system are to be informed about their rights to be supplied with natural gas 'of a specified quality at reasonable prices'. **6.10**

Exemptions Member States may in limited circumstances decide not to apply the provisions of Article 4 (authorization procedure) to distribution (Article 3(5)). There must first be obligations in the general economic interest imposed on natural gas undertakings within the framework of PSOs in Article 3(2), and a clear risk that the application of Article 4 will obstruct in law or in fact the performance of those PSOs. It is also a requirement for the non-application of Article 4 that the development of trade must not be affected to such an extent as would be contrary to the interests of the Community, including competition with respect to eligible customers within the terms of the Gas Directive and Article 86 EC. The overall aim of Article 4 is relevant: to ensure that eligible customers benefit from a competitive framework, the provision is designed to give gas undertakings the possibility of establishing a distribution network on the basis of Article 4. Not every customer has the right to be supplied with natural gas since there is no universal obligation to supply gas. **6.11**

The narrow scope of Article 3(5) of the Gas Directive can be contrasted with the much wider scope of the corresponding Article 3(8) of the Electricity Directive, **6.12**

---

[19] DG TREN Guidance Note, 'Public Service Obligations', 16 January 2004, 5.

which provided that Member States could decide in specific circumstances not to apply the provisions of the Directive relating to competition in generation, access to networks, and direct lines. In addition, by contrast to the powers granted to Member States not to apply the access provisions in the Electricity Directive, Article 21(1) of the Gas Directive allows a natural gas undertaking to refuse access to its transmission/distribution system if the granting of access would prevent it from carrying out its PSOs referred to in Article 3(2). However, in that event, duly substantiated reasons must be given for such a refusal (Article 21(1)).

6.13 As in the case of the Electricity Directive, Member States may apply for an exemption under Article 86(2) from the application of the Directive on the grounds of PSOs. The burden of proof lies upon the Member State concerned to show that a derogation is required. Exemption applications are considered on a case-by-case basis. However, the intention is not to allow Member States to apply PSOs to such an extent that the market would in effect be closed indefinitely. (The potential for abuse of PSOs was discussed at para 5.13.)

6.14 The procedure for assessing an application for an exemption under Article 86(2) is two-stage. Stage one addresses the issue of whether the exemption is justified; stage two addresses the issue of whether the proposed measure is the least restrictive one reasonably available to achieve the objective in question. A proportionality test will be applied to both and the Commission will benchmark an application against the best practice. The provisions on derogations will be applied in a restrictive manner in order to prevent a widespread proliferation of derogations. In sum, the proportionality test has at least three principal elements, comprising examinations of the:

(1) legitimacy of the purpose of the exemption;
(2) adequacy of the measure proposed to meet the objective; and
(3) necessity of the measure proposed and its scope by comparison with other possible alternative measures which might have a less distortive effect on the internal gas market.

In procedure (3) there is a benchmarking of best practice and of the least distortive measure necessary to meet the objective.

(b) Authorization Procedure

6.15 Article 4 lays down general rules for the granting of authorizations such as licences, permissions, concessions, consents, or approvals for the construction or operation of natural gas facilities and pipelines, for the supply of natural gas, and for wholesale customers. The text is unchanged from the first Directive. The authorizations are to be granted by Member States or competent bodies they authorize to do so, according to objective, non-discriminatory criteria that are published. Reasons for refusals have to be given, and communicated to the Commission, with provision

B. The Gas Directive 2003

for appeals by the applicants. Member States are exempted from the obligation to grant authorizations in relation to distribution systems in an area where such a system has already been or is proposed to be built in the area concerned or if existing or proposed capacity is still available. Two conditions apply here:

(1) distribution pipelines should already exist in the area or are scheduled to be built on the basis of an authorization granted and work commenced; and
(2) spare capacity in existing pipelines should exist.

In the Commission's view,[20] a Member State may only utilize the latter exemption when it is pursuing two objectives at the same time: development of newly-supplied areas and efficient operation. Any such exemption is likely to be limited in time to the period covered by the term 'newly supplied areas', which is undefined in the Directive's definitions section. **6.16**

(c) Security of Supply

Member States are required to monitor security of supply issues, either directly or indirectly through the national regulatory agency (NRA).[21] A report on the monitoring is to be published annually and submitted to the Commission, summarizing the findings from the monitoring exercise, as well as measures taken or envisaged. The activities that are to be included in the monitoring exercise include the supply/demand balance on the national market, the level of expected future demand and available supplies, envisaged additional capacity planned or under construction, the quality and level of maintenance of the networks, measures to cover peak demand and to deal with shortfalls by one or more suppliers. **6.17**

The subject of security of supply appears in the Directive text in relation to PSOs; monitoring and reporting duties of the Commission and the Member States; TPA to upstream pipelines; justifications for exemption from TPA rules for new major gas infrastructure; refusal of network access; and derogations with respect to take-or-pay commitments. These measures are discussed further in Chapter 18 on energy security. **6.18**

(d) Technical Rules

As in the Electricity Directive, Member States are required to ensure that a variety of technical rules and standards are operational, and to notify the Commission of this. This is not, however, a matter of ensuring that market participants are subject to binding rules as is the implication in the Electricity Regulation. The requirement in Article 6 involves the definition of technical safety criteria, and rules developed and published for the establishment of minimum technical design and operational **6.19**

---

[20] European Commission, DGXVII/A3/B3, 'Authorisations for New Distribution Pipelines' (Discussion Note prepared for the Follow-up Meeting, 22 October 1998).
[21] Gas Directive, Art 5; see also Art 26.

requirements for system connection, with respect to LNG and storage facilities, other transmission and distribution systems, and direct lines. The overall aim is to ensure interoperability. However, the rules and standards should also address the chemical characteristics of gases such as biogas and gas from biomass or other types of gas, and ensure that they can be technically and safely injected into and transported through the natural gas system.

6.20 The higher level of flexibility with respect to levels of pressure in gas networks means that the perceived need for binding guidelines is much reduced. The gas industry has however established a voluntary body, EASEE gas, to provide advice on flow management between TSOs.[22]

(3) Rules for Specific Activities

(a) Production

6.21 Unlike the Electricity Directive, the Gas Directive is not concerned to provide common rules with respect to production operations. For natural gas this had already been done through the Hydrocarbons Licensing Directive as early as 1994.[23] The only exception to this is the provision in the Directive concerning access to pipeline facilities linked to offshore installations for network access purposes (see paras 6.47–6.52). Otherwise, the provisions of the Hydrocarbons Licensing Directive should be referred to, since they concern similar subject matter to that of the generation-related provisions of the Electricity Directive, covering authorization procedures, non-discrimination including the abolition of exclusive rights and tendering criteria.

(b) Transmission

6.22 'Transmission' is defined as the transport of natural gas through a high-pressure pipeline network other than an upstream pipeline network with a view to its delivery to customers, but not including supply.[24] It is covered in Chapter III of the Directive, along with the specific rules applicable to gas storage and LNG. In contrast to the electricity industry, the storage of gas plays an important role in system organization and access.

6.23 The provisions on the designation of transmission system operators (TSOs) and their tasks in transmission operation are much more elaborate than those contained in the previous Directive. So too are the unbundling requirements (discussed below at paras 6.36–6.37).

---

[22] <http://www.easee-gas.org>.
[23] Directive (EC) 94/22 on the conditions for granting and using authorisations for the prospection, exploration and production of hydrocarbons [1994] OJ L164/3; see Chapter 7.
[24] Gas Directive, Art 2(3).

Member States are required to designate, or require natural gas undertakings which **6.24** own transmission, storage, or LNG systems to designate, one or more TSOs.[25] They are also required to ensure that the TSOs act in accordance with the provisions of Chapter III. The appointment of the TSO must be for a period of time to be determined by the Member State, taking into account considerations of efficiency and economic balance.

A general duty is imposed on transmission, storage, and LNG system operators to **6.25** operate, maintain, and develop under economic conditions the secure, reliable, and efficient transmission, storage, and/or LNG facilities, with due regard to the environment.[26] They must not discriminate between system users or classes of system users, especially in favour of their related undertakings. They are placed under an obligation to provide any other transmission, storage, or distribution undertaking with sufficient information to ensure that the transport and storage of natural gas takes place in a manner compatible with the secure and efficient operation of the interconnected system. System users have to be provided with the information they need for efficient access to the system. Rules for balancing the transmission system are to be objective, transparent, and non-discriminatory, including rules for charging system users for network imbalance. The NRAs are to fix or approve the methodology for the terms and conditions, including rules and tariffs, applicable to these services. The confidentiality of commercially sensitive information obtained in the process of carrying out the business must be preserved.[27] In particular, transmission undertakings must not abuse commercially sensitive information obtained from third parties in the context of providing or negotiating access to the system. This is especially relevant in cases of sales or purchases of natural gas by the transmission undertakings or related undertakings. This does not imply, however, that a company is under any obligation to modify its legal structure or create new companies.

(c) Distribution and Supply

The provisions on distribution and supply as set out in Articles 11–15 of the **6.26** Directive are almost identical to those applicable to Articles 7–10 on transmission, storage, and LNG. The definition of 'distribution' provided in Article 2(5) is given as the transport of natural gas through local or regional pipeline networks with a view to its delivery to customers, but not including supply. 'Supply' is defined as the sale, including resale, of natural gas, including LNG, to customers.

The Directive requires Member States to designate, or to require undertakings **6.27** that own or are responsible for distribution systems to designate, one or more

---

[25] ibid, Art 7.
[26] ibid, Art 8(1)(a).
[27] ibid, Art 10.

distribution system operators (DSOs).[28] They are also required to ensure that the DSOs act in accordance with the provisions of Articles 12–14 of the Directive. The appointment of the TSO is to be for a period of time to be determined by the Member State, taking into account considerations of efficiency and economic balance. The unbundling requirements are examined at paras 6.36 et seq below.

6.28 The responsibilities of each DSO are set out in Article 12. As is the case with TSOs, the primary task of a DSO is to operate, maintain, and develop under economic conditions a secure, reliable, and efficient system. Due regard has to be taken of the environment. Other requirements include the provision of information to system users such as they require for access to the system. The Directive expressly prohibits DSOs from discriminating between system users or classes of system users, especially in favour of related undertakings. Each DSO must provide any other DSO and/or TSO and/or LNG system operator and/or storage system operator with sufficient information to ensure that the transport of gas may take place in a manner compatible with the secure and efficient operation of the interconnected system. Similar requirements apply where DSOs are responsible for balancing the system: the rules they adopt are to be objective, transparent, and non-discriminatory, including rules for charging system users for energy imbalance. The NRAs may fix or approve the terms and conditions for the provision of such services by DSOs. Confidentiality of commercially sensitive information is treated separately in Article 14. Where this is obtained by the DSO in the course of carrying out its business, the DSO has an obligation to preserve its confidentiality. Further, distribution undertakings are prohibited from abusing commercially sensitive information obtained from third parties in the course of providing or negotiating access to the system.

(d) Storage

6.29 Gas storage is treated together with the provisions on transmission and LNG. It is also treated in Article 19 with respect to access to storage facilities and is the subject of a distinct set of guidelines that have been developed in the Madrid Forum in 2005 and 2006 (discussed at paras 6.137 et seq below). Some words on the function of storage in the gas business are appropriate since they are peculiar to this energy sub-sector.

6.30 Storage plays an important role in optimizing the operations of a pipeline network and in overcoming constraints in system capacity. It helps to match gas supply and demand at seasonal and daily level so that the utilization of capital-intensive gas production and transport infrastructure improves and the unit costs of gas supply decline. Without this storage capacity, production and transportation capacity

---

[28] ibid, Art 13.

would have to be built to meet the peak day demand and so have a significant overcapacity for much of the time. Availability of storage facilities (eg, underground salt caverns or aquifers) or similar alternative flexibility mechanisms (eg, gas production and supplies with a high 'swing factor', coming from fields close to the market or interruptibility of supplies to customers) is essential to the smooth operation of a gas system. It has been a common feature in the gas supply activities of integrated gas companies. It is also important in connection with the provision of security of supply. As a capital-intensive activity, it is normally carried out by a few TSOs as part of their bundled gas supply activities. They have taken decisions as to the amount of storage that needs to be constructed and the storage service is then offered as part of a bundled sales service. This has the potential to act as a barrier to entry for new market players and as a limit to competition.

6.31 In contrast to electricity systems, the optimal functioning of a gas system is therefore heavily dependent on the existence and use of storage facilities. Storage provides a series of services to the gas network: load balancing, grid optimization and flexibility security.

6.32 In this context, the Directive inevitably had to include provisions that address the issue of access to storage facilities. These apply when such access is technically necessary to provide efficient access to transmission and/or distribution networks. They are examined at para 6.40 below.

6.33 In practice, the provision of storage facilities varies widely across the EU. Six Member States have no storage of any kind. In Finland and Sweden, the geology is unsuitable for storage construction, while in Greece, Ireland, and Portugal there are sites that have potential for storage but as yet no facilities have been built. In contrast, a number of Member States, such as Austria, Denmark, France, Germany, Italy, and Spain, have significant levels of strategic storage over and above that required for normal seasonal use.

6.34 Experience of market liberalization in the UK and the USA shows that the availability of storage or similar services may prove very important to a new market entrant as part of the system to which it is seeking access.

(e) Liquefied Natural Gas

6.35 The Directive differs from its predecessor in paying attention to the role of LNG in European gas markets, a role that has grown rapidly in recent years.[29] The advantages in terms of security of supply are considerable: among other factors, it encourages a diversification of supply and avoids transit-related issues. There are also some destination flexibility and re-sale opportunities. However, these are

---

[29] For an overview see Jensen, JT, *The Development of a Global LNG Market: Is it likely? If so, when?* (2004).

capital intensive projects that require a stable and financially capable long-term off-taker, which used to mean a publicly owned electricity or gas utility. A new LNG carrier alone has a cost that is about twice as much to construct as an oil tanker and carries only a quarter of the energy, making it almost eight times more expensive to transport than oil. The number and variety of participants in this market have expanded, and the new buyers and sellers have developed new forms of contract. Nonetheless, the treatment of LNG import terminals in the Directive has had to provide flexibility to investors in the form of an exemption regime in Article 22.[30] This is discussed at paras 6.53 et seq below.

(4) Unbundling

6.36 The provisions on unbundling are identical in approach to those of the Electricity Directive, distinguishing between legal, management, and accounts unbundling, and taking care not to require ownership unbundling (see paras 5.38–5.43). The provisions in the Directive are therefore not repeated here.

(a) Compliance

6.37 A study was carried out in 2005–06 for the Commission on the practical implementation of unbundling.[31] This concluded that only in a few cases was ownership unbundling identified, where the TSO is not a vertically integrated company: Denmark, Great Britain, Spain, Sweden, and the Netherlands. By contrast, the number of countries that require compulsory legal unbundling for TSOs is considerable, including Austria, Belgium, Denmark, France, Germany, Great Britain, Hungary, Italy, Poland, Slovakia, Slovenia, Spain, and Sweden. For DSOs the number was less but many require it by 1 July 2007. Management unbundling also remains a popular option for both TSOs and DSOs.

(5) Access

6.38 TPA to transmission and distribution networks is to be provided on the basis of published and regulated tariffs,[32] but this regulated TPA regime has a number of exceptions. For storage facilities (including line pack, a means of gas storage that relies on compression of the gas in the transmission and distribution systems), Member States may choose either access on a negotiated or regulated basis or both.[33]

---

[30] For an analysis of the contrasting approaches of the EU and the USA in this respect, see Trischmann, H, 'LNG into Europe: regulation—American style?' [2004] Intl Energy L & Taxation Rev 233–243.

[31] *Unbundling of Electricity and Gas Transmission and Distribution System Operators, Final Report*, 1 December 2005, <http://ec.europa.eu/energy/electricity/publications/doc/2006_03_08_final_common_report.pdf>.

[32] Gas Directive, Art 18.

[33] ibid, Art 19(1).

B. The Gas Directive 2003

For access to upstream pipeline networks the regime continues to be separated out to give Member States discretion over the arrangements adopted.[34] Thirdly, exemptions from TPA may be granted for major new gas infrastructure investments such as international interconnectors, LNG, and storage facilities.[35] Finally, transit pipelines are governed by different access conditions than those applying to gas transmission within Member States due to the operation of Article 32.

(a) Regulated TPA in Gas

6.39 The provisions follow closely those in the Electricity Directive, including those on refusals of access. Three differences can be found in the Gas Directive's treatment of long-term transportation contracts and cross-border transmission. First, the implementation of the TPA provisions should not prevent the conclusion of long-term contracts in so far as these comply with EC competition rules.[36] Secondly, a refusal of TPA may be made on the ground that it would give rise to serious economic and financial difficulties with take-or-pay contracts.[37] In such (and other) cases of refusal, the Member State may however take the necessary measures to ensure that the natural gas undertaking refusing access makes the necessary enhancements to the pipeline network as far as it is economic to do so or when a potential customer is willing to pay for them.[38] By contrast, in the Electricity Directive the refusing party is only required to provide information on measures that would be necessary to reinforce the network. A final difference arose partly in order to facilitate cross-border transmission of gas: those TSOs that need to transmit across borders are to have access to the network of other TSOs.[39]

(b) Access to Storage

6.40 Member States have a choice with respect to the access regime for gas storage facilities, line pack, and ancillary services. It may be either negotiated or regulated TPA or both.[40] Irrespective of the system chosen, it has to be operated in accordance with objective, transparent and non-discriminatory criteria. Such access is important for

---

[34] ibid, Art 20.
[35] ibid, Art 22.
[36] ibid, Art 18(3).
[37] ibid, Art 21(1). The provisions of Art 27 (derogations in relation to take-or-pay commitments) and the alternative chosen by the Member State according to Art 27(1) have to be taken into account here. Refusals of access to storage facilities on grounds of lack of capacity must satisfy certain preconditions: refusal due to a need to meet take-or-pay obligations is not regarded by the Commission as one of these (DG TREN Interpretation Note, 'Third Party Access to Storage Facilities', 16 January 2004).
[38] ibid, Art 21(2).
[39] ibid, Art 18(2).
[40] ibid, Art 19(1). Member States are also allowed to designate a separate system operator for storage (Art 7).

new market entrants since storage is an important flexibility tool. It may assist market actors in using the opportunities of spot markets to reduce the price of electricity and gas, and for power generators access to storage may enhance continuity of supply.

6.41 The differences between this provision and its predecessor may seem insignificant, but the definitions are wider and the goal is more ambitious. The guiding principle is that experience gained with the first Gas Directive in developing an internal market requires the Directive to act as a step towards *clarification* of the provisions for access to storage and ancillary services.[41] This idea is less evident in the Directive itself than in the Interpretation Note issued subsequently by the Commission.[42]

6.42 The thrust of the Commission's interpretation (which is neither legally binding nor considered to be binding on the Commission itself) is to limit exemption from the Directive's access provisions to those storage facilities that are exclusively reserved to TSOs for carrying out their functions and the portion of storage facilities used for production operations. TSOs should be required to provide a justification to the national authorities for their exclusion of facilities from the scope of the Directive's access provisions. This may be done by the use of historical data. Moreover, since the Directive requires the establishment of storage system operators, they will have to act in accordance with the Directive's provisions on system operators, which include a requirement to provide information to system users for efficient access to the system. The latter would in the Commission's view include the following:

(1) information on available firm and interruptible capacities in relevant storage facilities over a specific time period;
(2) information on access conditions including tariffs; and
(3) information on services available.

For the operation of storage access, the criteria in point 1 above are relevant, but so is the criterion in the Directive that access is restricted to circumstances when it is technically and economically necessary for the supply of customers. When it cannot be proved that a request for access is linked to the supply of customers, it is not to be treated as justified.

6.43 There was sufficient agreement that the Gas Directive needed to be supplemented in this area for action to be taken within the framework of the Madrid Forum.

---

[41] ibid, Recital 20. Long-term LNG storage can be included within its scope as a means of transmission support as well as linepack.
[42] DG TREN Interpretation Note, 'Third Party Access to Storage Facilities', 16 January 2004. The following paragraphs relate to the text in this document.

B. The Gas Directive 2003

A set of detailed and clear rules was developed with a similar level of detail as that in the Good Practice Guidelines for Third Party Access, subsequently incorporated into the Gas Regulation (see paras 6.132–6.135). The guidelines will be binding on the storage operators and will apply to both regulated and negotiated access.

6.44 Two exceptions to the scope of Article 19(1) may be noted. First, storage facilities used in connection with local production operations at the site of a gas field are excluded from the access provisions relating to upstream pipeline networks in Article 20(1) ('facilities supplying technical services incidental to such access'). The storage requirements of these production operations are therefore excluded from the access rights of third parties to storage facilities. Secondly, there is an exclusion provided for ancillary services and temporary storage related to LNG facilities, which are necessary for the re-gasification process and subsequent delivery to the transmission system.[43]

6.45 Tariffs for the use of storage services must be published if a Member State chooses a system of regulated access, while, under negotiated access systems, information on the main commercial conditions for the use of the storage, linepack, and other ancillary services must be made available. This should include information on the commercial conditions for access to storage or similar services to allow customers and new players to assess the total costs of the gas supply prior to making their business decisions.

6.46 Since storage may be an important contributor to a country's strategy for security of supply, the Directive is not designed to operate in a way that limits this security— one of the main pillars of EU energy policy. Access to storage, when necessary for system use, is only to be available to the extent that storage capacity is available.

(c) Access to Upstream Pipeline Networks

6.47 The Gas Directive continues the special access regime for upstream pipeline networks.[44] Such networks are defined as 'any pipeline or network of pipelines operated and/or constructed as part of an oil or gas production project, or used to convey natural gas from one or more such projects to a processing plant or terminal or final coastal landing terminal'.[45] They constitute an important part of the gas chain and are therefore relevant to the general aim of achieving a competitive market in natural gas.

6.48 Upstream pipeline networks were originally included in the scope of the first Gas Directive only after much controversy, and remain a sensitive issue. The text of the Directive reflects the need to meet the concerns of Member States with significant

---

[43] Gas Directive, Art 19(2).
[44] ibid, Art 20. Compare Art 23 of the first Gas Directive, which has wording that is identical.
[45] ibid, Art 2(2).

gas production and the gas producing companies themselves, which had originally sought to limit the Directive's scope to downstream pipeline networks. Considerable scope for interpretation by Member States has been left to Member States at the implementation stage. In effect, a negotiated access regime is retained for these networks.

6.49 Article 20 sets out the general principles that Member States must follow when making specific rules for access to upstream pipeline networks and related facilities. Member States are required to take measures to ensure that natural gas undertakings and eligible customers can access the networks, but the form of such access is to be determined by the Member State itself. Access has to be 'provided in a manner determined by the Member State in accordance with the relevant legal instruments'.[46] In doing so, Member States are required to apply the overall objectives of the Directive, namely: fair and open access; achieving a competitive market in natural gas; and avoiding any abuse of a dominant position—while taking into account security and regularity of supplies; capacity which is or can reasonably be made available; and environmental protection. In this respect, those other provisions of the Directive relevant to upstream pipeline networks (eg, unbundling rules specifically mentioned in Recital 10) are applicable. Other areas in which the Directive's provisions may be relevant to implementation measures for upstream operations include the establishment of technical rules to ensure inter-operability and interconnections in relation to upstream gas facilities, as well as rules on information exchange and the publication of technical rules for access to these pipelines. The measures taken by the Member State are to be notified to the Commission. Exempted from these requirements are those parts of networks and facilities used for local production operations at the site of a field where the gas is produced.

6.50 When establishing the detailed rules, Member States may take into account several considerations that give some protection to the interests of the owner or operator of the upstream pipeline. The Directive itemizes four considerations:[47]

(a) the need to refuse access where there is an incompatibility of technical specifications which cannot be reasonably overcome;
(b) the need to avoid difficulties which cannot be reasonably overcome and could prejudice the efficient, current and planned future production of hydrocarbons, including that from fields of marginal economic viability;
(c) the need to respect the duly substantiated reasonable needs of the owner or operator of the upstream pipeline network for the transport and processing of gas and the interests of all other users of the upstream pipeline network or relevant processing or handling facilities who may be affected; and

---

[46] ibid, Art 20(2).
[47] ibid, Art 20(2).

(d) the need to apply their laws and administrative procedures, in conformity with Community law, for the grant of authorization for production or upstream development.

These considerations will be of more relevance to gas producing companies than to eligible customers. Most of them relate to the capacity available in the upstream pipeline networks and related facilities. The first consideration (a) relates to the refusal of access if it would be technically impossible; it might, for example, create serious technical problems due to incompatibility of gas qualities; (b) is designed to safeguard current and planned production against serious difficulties that could have been caused by the implementation of the Directive; operational considerations such as those that may act to hamper access to upstream pipeline networks must be fully substantiated and justified; (c) refers to existing commitments and needs of current users that must be respected in the same way as with downstream pipeline networks; the assumption here is that access must be provided only to the extent that uncommitted capacity is available; (d) refers to the need for balance between national laws and EU legislation and the interface between the Gas Directive and other legislation such as the Hydrocarbons Licensing Directive.

6.51

To deal with any possible disputes, an independent authority has to be designated by the Member States and arrangements for dispute settlement put in place.[48] The Directive requires such arrangements to enable disputes to be settled expeditiously, taking the above criteria into account and the number of parties that may be involved in negotiating access to such networks. Where the disputes have a cross-border character, the arrangements for settlement for the Member State with jurisdiction over the upstream pipeline network that refuses access must be applied.[49] Consultation between Member States is necessary where more than one Member State has jurisdiction over a network and a cross-border dispute arises. The aim is to ensure that the provisions of the Directive are applied consistently.

6.52

(d) Exemptions for New Infrastructure

The provisions for the exemption from the general rules of TPA for electricity in specific cases involving new interconnectors (see paras 5.95 et seq) are substantially repeated in relation to TPA for gas in specific cases involving new major infrastructure projects (that is, interconnectors between Member States, LNG, and storage facilities).[50] The exemption procedure also applies to significant increases in the capacity of existing infrastructures and to modifications in such infrastructures that allow for the development of new sources of gas supply.[51] There are detailed

6.53

---

[48] ibid, Art 20(3).
[49] ibid, Art 20(4).
[50] ibid, Art 22.
[51] ibid, Art 22(2).

criteria for grant of an exemption: the investment proposed for an exemption must contribute to competition in gas supply, and must enhance security of supply, and not be detrimental to competition or the effective functioning of the internal gas market or the effective functioning of the regulated system to which the infrastructure is connected. Importantly, the level of risk attached to the investment must be such that investment would not take place unless an exemption is granted.

6.54 Applications for exemptions are made to the NRA but Member States may elect to require the NRA to submit an opinion on the application to the relevant body in the Member State for formal decision.[52] The decision taken has to be duly reasoned, published, and communicated to the Commission with all the relevant information. The exemption may cover all or parts of the infrastructure involved. On a case-by-case basis, conditions may be added regarding its duration and non-discriminatory access to the interconnector. Other considerations to be taken into account include: the duration of the contracts; additional capacity to be built or the modification of existing capacity; the time horizon of the project; and national circumstances. Rules and mechanisms for management and allocation of capacity may also be decided upon when granting an exemption 'insofar as this does not prevent the implementation of long-term contracts'.[53] Where the infrastructure is an interconnector, no exemption decision may be taken without consultation with the other Member States or NRAs concerned.

6.55 The submission of a decision to the Commission has to be accompanied by data. The data requirements are listed in the Directive and include the analysis undertaken of the effect on competition and the effective functioning of the internal gas market that results from the grant of the exemption.[54] The Commission has a period of two months in which to request that the NRA or Member State concerned amend or withdraw the decision to grant an exemption. This may be extended by one month if further information is required by the Commission. The absence of express criteria by which the Commission might reject the NRA decision is a potential source of uncertainty, compensated only slightly by the publication of information in an Interpretation Note.[55] It appears that DG Competition would also be 'closely involved' in a Commission decision to accept an exemption in this context. Nonetheless, the grant of an exemption 'does not give an exemption of any type from competition law and the possibility of intervention from competition authorities, including the Commission, will always exist'.[56]

---

[52] ibid, Art 22(3).
[53] ibid, Art 22(3)(c).
[54] ibid, Art 22(4)(a)–(e).
[55] DG TREN Interpretation Note, 'Exemptions from Certain Provisions of the Third Party Access Regime', 30 January 2004; 'Security of Supply Provisions for Gas', 16 January 2004, 5–7.
[56] ibid 7.

B. The Gas Directive 2003

6.56 It may be noted that none of the above prejudices the power of the NRA to choose specific rules for specific pieces of infrastructure, both existing and new, including the grant of incentives to develop specific types of investment. Nor does it prevent an NRA from policing the operations carried out under an exemption.[57]

6.57 The rules on exemptions are to be applied (and monitored) very carefully.[58] They do not apply to existing infrastructure (that is, where the main financial commitment to construction was taken before 15 July 2003, the date of publication of the Gas Directive and Electricity Regulation). No block exemptions may be applied for specific types of infrastructure, and exemptions are to be granted on a case-by-case basis, with applications assessed on their merits. Exemptions cannot apply where the result would be to create or reinforce a dominant position or where it would reduce the scope for diluting existing dominant positions.

6.58 A number of decisions have been taken on exemptions, mainly for LNG facilities, since the adoption of the Directive concerning new infrastructure projects in the UK, the Netherlands, and Italy.[59] Experience so far with the operation of the exemption provisions has been uneventful and for potential investors reassuring.

6.59 **The Hackberry decision: 'managed access'** A contrasting approach to essentially the same problem—securing investment in costly new infrastructure—is provided by the US experience with authorization of LNG terminals. For many years, terminal capacity had to be made available by means of an open season with terms and tariffs of the resulting access contract negotiated with the US regulatory body, the Federal Energy Regulatory Agency (FERC). Construction permits were difficult to obtain because of local opposition. This context made investment in new capacity unattractive to investors. Due largely to concerns about security of supply, Congress passed new legislation to establish a regulatory programme for LNG terminals to encourage their development *offshore*. A new provision was that offshore LNG terminals could be operated on a 'managed access' basis, as distinct from a TPA basis which applied to onshore LNG terminals. Under this regime, a terminal owner, or its affiliate, may use all or a portion of the terminal's capacity without first having to make such capacity available to the market. Terminal owners are also entitled to negotiate the applicable rates and the terms and conditions of their services, which must be reasonable.

6.60 Subsequently, the FERC elected to change its policy as well. It issued a preliminary determination on an application made by Hackberry LNG to construct and

---

[57] House of Lords European Union Committee, *The Commission's Green Paper, 'A European Strategy for Sustainable, Competitive and Secure Energy': Evidence* (2005–06, HL 224) Reply to Q193 by Ofgem: 'If we think that the company is not using it properly, we can actually withdraw an exemption and introduce formal regulation and use that quite effectively' (64).
[58] ibid 4–7.
[59] <http://ec.europa.eu/energy/gas/infrastructure/exemptions_en.htm>.

operate a new LNG terminal at the Gulf of Mexico (that is, *onshore*).[60] FERC granted an authorization to Hackberry to provide services and all of the available terminal capacity on freely negotiable terms to one of its marketing affiliates (no requirement to offer access first) and to charge market-based rates. The reasoning provided by FERC was that, on the basis of the new legislation which allowed 'managed access' for offshore terminals, Hackberry should be treated in a similar way as a new entrant into the LNG terminal business bearing the entire project risk; onshore and offshore terminals should enjoy a 'competitive parity'; the fixed costs of the project could only be recovered through downstream sales of re-gasified LNG at competitive prices; and the project would bring new supplies into the region. The light-handed regulation was successful in encouraging in excess of 40 applications for new LNG terminals. It was further streamlined by FERC in 2003 and 2004 when, among other things, it removed the requirement to publish the subsequently concluded access agreement.

(e) Access to Transit Pipelines

6.61 Article 32(1) of the Directive states that 'contracts concluded pursuant to Article 3(1) of Directive 91/296/EEC (that is, the now repealed Transit Directive)... shall continue to be valid and to be implemented under the terms of the said Directive'. As a result of this transitional regime, transit contracts within the meaning of Article 3(1) and concluded before the entry into force of the Gas Directive remain valid, and are to be implemented under the terms applicable at the time of their conclusion. Although these terms include non-discriminatory conditions of transit, transmission under these contracts will (until they expire in, on average, 2022) be carried out under negotiated rather than regulated conditions.

6.62 The significance of this provision was underlined in the Energy Sector Inquiry[61] which noted that potential new entrants encountered obstacles in their attempts to secure capacity on transit pipelines. The pipelines concerned are often cross-border pipelines, controlled by TSOs and large holders of capacity which claim either that the 'use-it-or-lose-it' principle does not apply to pipelines at all, or that it cannot be effectively applied to transit. These historic incumbents argue that the 'ship-or-pay' transport contracts allow the capacity holder to renominate usually until two hours before the effective gas flows. Capacity not used is therefore likely to be released on to the secondary market on a very short-term and interruptible basis only, offering potential users of the unused capacity few opportunities to secure gas. Primary cross-border capacity appears to be fully booked over

---

[60] *Hackberry LNG Terminal LLC*, 101 FERC 61, 294 (18 December 2002); see analysis in Trischmann, H, 'LNG into Europe: regulation—American style?' [2004] Intl Energy L & Taxation Rev 233–243, 238.
[61] Preliminary Report, February 2006, 58–81.

the long term and current holders have in a significant number of cases preferential rights to prolong capacity reservations beyond the originally foreseen end-date. Moreover, incumbents have argued that a full application of transparency requirements would damage their commercial wholesale interests. At an early stage in its inquiry the Commission concluded that 'this treatment of pre-liberalisation contracts is a major obstacle for access to cross-border infrastructure' and that such legacy contracts 'are the main reason why primary capacity is booked long-term by historical incumbents'.[62] It may be noted that such contracts are nonetheless subject to the relevant provisions of the Gas Regulation (discussed in section C below).

(6) Market Opening and Reciprocity

6.63 Since full market opening is scheduled for 2007 and most Member States are already required to have large segments of their markets open to competition, the provisions on this topic are significantly shorter than those in the first Gas Directive. At its simplest, Article 23 requires Member States to ensure that all non-household customers are eligible from 1 July 2004, at the latest and, from 1 July 2007, all customers are to be eligible. This means that they are to be free to purchase gas from a supplier of their choice.

6.64 A transitional mechanism is provided for in Article 23(2) that is identical to that in Article 21(2) of the Electricity Directive. To avoid an imbalance in the opening of the markets, contracts for gas supply with an eligible customer in the system of another Member State are not to be prohibited if the customer is considered as eligible in both systems involved. Where a transaction is refused because of the customer being eligible in only one of the two systems, the Commission may require the refusing party to execute the requested supply at the request of the Member State where the eligible customer is located. In doing so, the Commission is required to take into account the market situation and the common interest.

(7) Direct Lines

6.65 The Directive facilitates the construction of direct lines. It is essentially the same as the provision in the first Gas Directive and very similar (but shorter) than the equivalent provision in the Electricity Directive. A 'direct line' is defined as a natural gas pipeline complementary to the interconnected system.[63] Article 24 requires Member States to take measures necessary to enable natural gas undertakings established within their territory to supply eligible customers by means of a direct line and to ensure that any such eligible customers may be supplied through a direct line by natural gas undertakings.

---

[62] Issues Paper, 15 November 2005, 18.
[63] Gas Directive, Art 2(18).

6.66 Where an authorization is required for construction or operation of direct lines, the Member State or competent authority it designates must lay down the criteria for the grant of authorizations for the construction or operation of such lines in their territory. These criteria must be objective, transparent, and non-discriminatory.[64] The authorizations for pipeline construction may be made subject to either the refusal of pipeline system access provisions or to the opening of a dispute settlement procedure under Article 25.[65] Member States may also refuse to authorize the construction of a new direct line if it might obstruct the performance of PSOs (in which case, duly substantiated reasons must be given).

6.67 As with the comparable provision in the Electricity Directive, this provision is unlikely to prove of much practical significance. The definition of 'direct line' is narrow, meaning only that it would connect producers or suppliers with subsidiaries or eligible customers. The definition means that third parties cannot use the line for purposes other than direct supply contracts with the owner of the direct line. Issues of network access and remuneration are therefore of little consequence. This conclusion does not apply if a direct line connects two distinct TSO systems.

(8) Regulation

6.68 The provisions of Article 25 on regulatory authorities are almost identical to the provisions in Article 23 of the Electricity Directive (see the discussion at paras 5.55 et seq). There are several minor differences between the provisions. For example, among the subjects which an NRA has to monitor in the list in Article 25(1) are access conditions to storage, linepack, and to other ancillary services as provided for under Article 19 (access to storage).[66] The reporting requirement differs in Article 25(8) with a less extensive obligation imposed upon the regulatory authorities with respect to monitoring market dominance, predatory, and anti-competitive behaviour (see para 5.59). Finally, the provision on an advisory committee is contained in Article 30 of the Gas Directive while it is included in the Electricity Regulation, and omitted from the Electricity Directive.

(9) Enforcement

(a) Derogations

6.69 In the Directive the term 'derogation' is used in two senses, describing either *an act of the Commission* which grants to a Member State a right not to comply with its obligations under specific provisions of the Directive (eg, Article 28(4)), or a unilateral *act by a Member State* made under specific provisions of the Directive by

---

[64] ibid, Art 24(2).
[65] ibid, Art 24(3).
[66] ibid, Art 25(1)(f).

B. The Gas Directive 2003

which it states that specific provisions will not be applied (eg, Article 28(1) and (2), and Article 27 (access/take-or-pay)). Derogation decisions taken under Article 28(2) and (4) could be challenged by the Commission on the grounds that conditions for making the derogation were not satisfied.

More general rules applicable to the award of derogations include the following: **6.70**

- the derogation sought should not be wider in extent than is strictly necessary for the ends sought;
- the party applying for the derogation (and refusing access) has the burden of proof to demonstrate that a derogation is necessary;
- it must also establish that it is subject to a specific PSO that has been imposed on it by a public authority and that the performance of that obligation would be obstructed if the access applied for were granted;
- applicants for a derogation are limited to the possibilities for derogations arising from the Directive; and
- further derogations than these are not granted by Article 86 of the Treaty.

There are several derogation possibilities in the Directive that Member States may have recourse to. In particular, they include cases arising from take-or-pay commitments, and where the systems are either emerging or are relatively isolated.[67] While the provisions on the former are virtually identical to those in the first Gas Directive, those in Article 28 differ slightly. For gas transmission infrastructure, a derogation may only be granted if no gas infrastructure has been established or if it has been established for less than ten years.[68] The temporary derogation may not be granted for longer than ten years from the date at which gas is first supplied in the area. However, for distribution infrastructure, the duration of any derogation may be longer: a maximum of 20 years from the time that gas is first supplied through the system in the area.[69] Other potential derogations are the exemption of integrated undertakings serving fewer than 100,000 connected customers,[70] and the non-application of Article 4 with respect to distribution companies through Article 3(5) on PSOs. **6.71**

(b) Take-or-Pay Commitments

The bulk of European gas supplies remain contracted under long-term contracts that contain so-called 'take-or-pay' clauses. Under such arrangements, gas buyers will agree to take delivery of not less than a minimum quantity over a specified period (such as a year), or, if they do not, pay for the shortfall from the agreed minimum. **6.72**

---

[67] ibid, Arts 27 and 28 respectively.
[68] ibid, Art 28(5)(a).
[69] ibid, Art 28(5)(b).
[70] ibid, Art 13(2). This threshold is subject to review under Art 31(1)(b).

In this way, the buyer bears the market risk, while the gas producer takes the production risk. By assuring a regular cash-flow over a period of many years, such contracts reduce the risk for producers and facilitate their ability to finance the infrastructure of their projects.

6.73 The duration of such contracts has typically been for between 15 and 25 years, and could cover the life of the project. They have played a fundamental role in bringing the European gas market into existence. However, many of the existing long-term take-or-pay contracts were concluded at a time when the Member State gas markets were organized around national and regional monopolies of supply and distribution and an absence of competition in supply.[71]

6.74 A transitional regime is therefore included in Article 27 to mitigate the effects of the transition to a liberalized gas market on the performance of take-or-pay contracts entered into by transmission or distribution system companies. If a natural gas undertaking encounters, or considers it will encounter, serious economic and financial difficulties because of the take-or-pay commitments it has accepted in one or more of its gas purchase contracts, an application may be made for a *temporary* derogation from the access provisions of Article 18. This is intended as a last resort measure for exceptional cases in which a company may face the prospect of bankruptcy. However, it may be noted that in principle an undertaking may refuse access to an applicant company before it has experienced serious economic and financial difficulties and before it has applied for a derogation. This system of derogations in the Directive is important due to its potential for delay and frustration of the objectives of the Directive, even though the article has to date not been applied. The system is essentially equivalent to the transitional regime established for stranded assets under the first Electricity Directive. However, the treatment of criteria for the grant of derogations is more detailed than its counterpart in that Directive.

---

[71] The benefits of long-term contracts to buyers diminish with the growth of a competitive market in gas unless the contract provides for some price adjustment to reflect market changes. Specifically, natural gas purchased under existing contracts will not always be able to compete on price with gas that becomes available in the competitive gas market that develops from the impact of the Gas Directive. Such contracts incorporate provisions the purpose of which is to protect both the seller and the buyer from the consequences of fluctuations in gas prices. There are two different types of protection clause: the price adjustment clause, which applies at agreed intervals (three, six or 12 months), has the primary purpose of ensuring for the seller that it is entitled to benefit from an increased market value of gas arising from increases in prices of specified competing fuels (typically gas oil and fuel oil and sometimes coal and electricity), and for the buyer to enable its selling prices to remain competitive if prices of competing fuels (established from reliable published indices) fall; the price adjustment clause, the primary purpose of which is to establish a contractual mechanism whereby, at agreed intervals (three to five years), either party may request that the price provisions of the contract be adjusted, where as a result of changed circumstances affecting the buyer's gas market the price provisions do not reflect the changed market circumstances. It is quite clear that neither of these provisions could be applicable in a fully liberalized European gas market.

B. The Gas Directive 2003

Procedures for granting a take-or-pay derogation Applications for derogations are made on a case-by-case basis. There is a two-stage procedure for dealing with applications which involves: **6.75**

(1) submission of an application to the Member State of the applicant or to its designated competent authority; and
(2) notification and review by the Commission of any decision by a Member State or its designated competent authority to grant a derogation. The Commission has the final say.

Member States are allowed, under Article 27(1), to give the natural gas undertaking the choice of presenting its application either before or after refusal of access to the system. In cases where a natural gas undertaking has refused access to the system, the application for a derogation must be presented 'without delay'. The Commission has stated that the maximum delay in this respect is one week, corresponding to the delay allowed for notification under the EU Merger Regulation.[72] All applications must be accompanied with information relevant to the nature and extent of the problem and also the efforts undertaken by the gas undertaking to solve the problem. If there are no reasonable alternatives available to the company, a derogation may be granted by the Member State or the designated competent authority.   **6.76**

Once a derogation has been granted, either by the Member State or by its designated competent authority, the Commission must be notified, without delay, of the decision. All relevant information must be submitted to the Commission, if appropriate in an aggregated form, so that the Commission may reach a 'well-founded decision'.[73] Within four weeks of receiving notification, the Commission may request that the Member State or designated competent authority amend or withdraw the decision to grant a derogation. Failure to comply with the Commission's request for amendment or withdrawal within a period of four weeks will lead to a final decision being taken 'expeditiously' under the procedure established by Article 30 (the advisory committee). Throughout, the Commission must preserve the confidentiality of commercially sensitive information. Derogations granted must be properly substantiated and published in the Official Journal.   **6.77**

In circumstances where the Commission requests the Member State to withdraw a decision and the Member State fails to do so, a consultative committee will advise the Commission on next steps. This committee will be composed of representatives   **6.78**

---

[72] 'Take-or-Pay Contracts', Discussion Note, 22 October 1998 (prepared in connection with the first Gas Directive). The Note refers to the old Merger Regulation (see paras 14.07–14.34).
[73] Gas Directive, Art 27(2).

of the Member States and will be chaired by a representative of the Commission. Three steps follow from this:

- The Commission representative submits to the Commission a draft of the measures to be taken.
- The committee delivers its opinion on this draft within a time-limit set by the chair. That opinion is recorded in the minutes. Each Member State is entitled to ask to have its position recorded in the minutes.
- The Commission takes its decision, drawing on the opinion and informing the committee of the decision, and how the opinion has informed it.

6.79 Decisions on requests for derogations concerning contracts concluded *before* the Directive entered into force should not create a situation in which it is not possible to identify alternative outlets that are economically viable. The Commission will not consider problems as 'serious difficulties' unless sales of natural gas fall below the level of minimum off-take guarantees contained in gas purchase take-or-pay contracts or if the relevant gas purchase take-or-pay contract can be adapted, or the gas undertaking is able to identify alternative outlets for the gas.[74] This provision appears to enhance the possibility of obtaining derogations in respect of contracts in existence before the Directive entered into force, but also sets criteria which must be satisfied to obtain a derogation for such a contract.

6.80 In cases where a gas undertaking has not been granted a derogation by the Member State under Article 27 of the Directive, the company can no longer refuse access to the system because of take-or-pay commitments that have been accepted in a gas purchase contract. Member States must ensure that the provisions on system access are then complied with. The unsuccessful applicant may then rely on the mechanisms for appeal in the Member State.

6.81 The operation of Article 27 is subject to a review to be carried out within five years of the Directive entering into force (that is, by July 2008). The findings of this review are to be reported to the Parliament and Council, which will then consider whether amendments are needed.

6.82 **Criteria for the grant of derogations**   Derogations may not be granted unless and until nine criteria listed in Article 27 are considered by the Member State and the Commission[75]. These are as follows:

(a) the objective of achieving a competitive gas market;
(b) the need to fulfil public service obligations and to ensure security of supply;

---

[74] ibid, Art 27(3).
[75] ibid, Art 27(3).

B. The Gas Directive 2003

(c) the position of the natural gas undertaking in the gas market and the actual state of competition in this market;
(d) the seriousness of the economic and financial difficulties encountered by natural gas undertakings and transmission undertakings or eligible customers;
(e) the dates of signature and terms of the contract or contracts in question, including the extent to which they allow for market changes;
(f) the efforts made to find a solution to the problem;
(g) the extent to which, when accepting the take-or-pay commitments in question, the undertaking could reasonably have foreseen, having regard to the provisions of this Directive, that serious difficulties were likely to arise;
(h) the level of connection of the system with other systems and the degree of interoperability of these systems; and
(i) the effects the granting of a derogation would have on the correct application of this Directive as regards the smooth functioning of the internal natural gas market.

6.83 This is not an exhaustive list and may therefore be supplemented by criteria relevant to the specific case in question. More importantly, the criteria are not necessarily listed in order of importance (and do not indicate the weight a court might give them in the event of a dispute). A different order of priority would probably be adopted by an applicant for a derogation.[76] Such a 'practice' order of the nine criteria would probably take the following form (retaining the above numbering): beginning with criterion Article 27(3)(e), then (a), (b), (c), (h), (g), (f), (a), and finally (i).

6.84 Irrespective of their order of priority, the individual criteria require some comment, given their broad formulation in the Directive itself. They are considered below in the 'practice' order and *not* in the order presented in Article 27(3) of the Directive text.[77]

6.85 *Dates of signature and terms of contract(s), including the extent to which they allow for market changes: Article 27(3)(e)*   From a practical point of view the most important criterion will concern the dates when the contract or contracts were signed. This allows for distinctions to be made between existing and future contracts. This was designed to give market operators a clear signal that prudence should be exercised when signing future take-or-pay contracts to take account of the changing market circumstances. It was also designed to ensure that any take-or-pay contracts entered into or renewed after the entry into force of the Directive would make a prudent allowance for changes resulting from a more competitive gas market so as not to hamper a significant opening of the market.

6.86 The relevance of the date of signature is that it gives an indication of the extent to which legislative changes could and should have been taken into account when

---

[76] Brothwood, M, 'The EU Gas Directive and Take or Pay Contracts' [1998] Oil & Gas L & Taxation Rev 318.
[77] The order specified in Art 25(3) is noted in brackets after the practice order numbering; see also DG XVII Discussion Note, 'Take-or-Pay Contracts' (1998).

signing a contract. However, no date is expressly mentioned in the Directive. In the original proposal submitted by the Commission in February 1992, only contracts signed before 1 July 1991 were covered. This date was retained in the amended proposal of early 1994 but prior to the conclusion of the first Directive, it seems that a possible cut-off date was 25 July 1996. For contracts signed after the adoption of the Gas Directive (15 July 2004) the matter is easier.

6.87 *Seriousness of economic and financial difficulties encountered by natural gas undertakings and transmission undertakings or eligible customers: Article 27(3)(a)* This criterion concerns the economic and financial difficulties faced by the players. Since Article 27(1) expressly refers to derogations being considered if a company encounters 'or considers it would encounter' serious difficulties, this criterion implies that preventive action may be considered before the serious problems have in practice occurred. Such problems must of course have their origins in the entry into force of the Gas Directive and not in any other cause. The economic and financial implications for the eligible customers should be taken into account since they face their request for access being denied as a result of the grant of a derogation. The seriousness of the problem should be reflected in a proportionate manner with access refusal tailored according to a percentage of the requested TPA volumes. It appears that the Commission would take the view that a serious economic and financial difficulty would imply a major loss caused by a greater than normal business risk.[78] It seems that a comparative analysis would be carried out between the Member States when analyzing a request for derogation to obtain input from concrete examples and actual experiences, if available, where serious economic and financial problems have in fact faced gas companies in take-or-pay situations.

6.88 *Need to fulfil public service obligations and ensure security of supply: Article 27(3)(b)* Although this criterion concerns PSOs and security of supply, the main provision for the protection of PSOs is in fact Article 3, not Article 27. Article 21(1) takes Article 3(2) into account and should therefore be seen as the principal vehicle for protection of PSOs rather than Article 27.

6.89 *Position of natural gas undertaking in the gas market and actual state of competition in the market: Article 27(3)(c)* This criterion refers to the position of the natural gas undertaking in the gas market and the actual size of competition in this market. It should be kept in mind here that the Council and the Commission have declared that this criterion must be applied equally to all natural gas undertakings.[79] The 'position' of the gas undertaking can be taken to include inter alia:

- size of the company, including area of operation, balance sheet, assets, market share, and turnover;

---

[78] Discussion Note, ibid 7.
[79] Statement 93/98 to the Minutes of the Council Meeting, May 1998.

B. The Gas Directive 2003

- role of the company in international gas trade;
- supply and sales portfolio of the company;
- extent of infrastructure owned, including storage; ownership in other energy/gas companies, whether upstream or downstream; and
- rights and obligations of the company, including PSOs.

6.90 The market conditions referred to in the criterion are also open to interpretation. They could be regional, national, or wider within the EU. An analysis of the state of competition would include an assessment of the level of market-opening in the area concerned in terms of both the eligible share of the market and the share of the market that actually benefits from competition. It would also include a consideration of the number of suppliers competing in the market and the impact of competition on market shares, prices, and profits. The general level of competition in the market may also be considered, not only the level of gas-to-gas competition.

6.91 *Level of connection of the system with other systems and degree of inter-operability: Article 27(3)(h)* An important criterion concerns the level of connection of the system with other systems and the extent of their inter-operability. Although the pace of network integration is rapid, there remain regional and national gas networks that are not well-integrated into the European gas grid. Technical aspects may hamper inter-operability with other systems and in such areas gas companies may face difficulties to sell gas outside their traditional supply area in the event of serious take-or-pay problems.

6.92 *Extent to which, when accepting take-or-pay commitments, the undertaking could reasonably have foreseen, having regard to the provisions of the Gas Directive, that serious difficulties were likely to arise: Article 27(3)(g)* This applies to take-or-pay contracts signed after the entry into force of the Directive. It turns on the prudence that an undertaking has shown when taking on the take-or-pay commitments at issue and whether the resulting difficulties could reasonably have been foreseen. If they could have been foreseen or were in fact foreseen, there is no basis for an expectation that a grant of derogation may be made to solve the difficulties that have followed.

6.93 *Efforts to find a solution: Article 27(3)(f)* This criterion for derogation from the access provisions of the Directive is focused on the efforts made to find a solution to the problem. Derogation should be adopted only as a last resort when all other attempts by the operators involved have failed to identify an alternative solution to the problem. Such efforts may include efforts to sell the gas elsewhere or attempts to re-negotiate the contract or to increase company efficiency.

6.94 *Achieving a competitive gas market: Article 27(3)(a)* This criterion is likely to be influential at the Commission stage. It relates to the overall objective of the Directive: market-opening, largely by means of TPA. Whatever decision is taken with respect to refusal of access must be balanced and justified against this principal objective of the Directive, which is to provide for the opposite.

6.95 *Effects the grant of a derogation would have on achieving smooth functioning of the internal natural gas market: Article 27(3)(i)*   Finally, there is the criterion that is based on the effects of a grant of derogation on the smooth functioning of the internal gas market. By implication, this emphasizes that any grant of a derogation would have a restrictive effect on the operation of an internal gas market in the EU. The criteria should therefore be applied by Member States and the Commission in a cautious manner and balance any derogations against the overall objective of a smooth-functioning internal gas market and a significant degree of market-opening.

6.96 **'Ship-or-pay' contracts**   An issue arose after the Directive's adoption in the context of accession negotiations between the EU and Slovenia concerning the relationship between possible derogations from take-or-pay commitments and 'ship-or-pay' contracts, which are not expressly referred to nor recognized in the Gas Directive, despite being widely used within the EU.[80] These contracts are transportation contracts that contain commercial commitments for the reservation of capacity through a pipeline. Their principal feature is the obligation on the gas purchasing company to pay for the capacity contracted even if that capacity is not used. They may be used, for example, when the gas buyer is neither owner nor co-owner of the transportation system up to its national border. The buyer therefore needs to conclude commercial contracts for gas transportation with the owners of these pipelines. This transportation cost may represent a significant share of the total gas supply costs since the distance between the national border of a buyer and the delivery point of the gas producer (or supplier) is often long, and in general gas transportation costs are high.

6.97   Such agreements are essentially complementary to take-or-pay agreements. They are concluded by gas companies when the delivery point for gas in a supply contract is further upstream than the national border of the buyer. However, they may also be concluded with a view to reserving transportation capacity to ensure transit through the pipeline of gas supplied on a different contractual basis or as part of the company's general business operations. Since they are not expressly mentioned in the Directive, they fall under the general rules of the Treaty and in particular the competition rules. In the unlikely event of a challenge under EU law, these rules would provide the basis for an evaluation of any legal issues or disputes that may arise concerning the compatibility of ship-or-pay commitments with the *acquis communautaire*.

6.98   Given the Directive's silence on this matter, there is no legal ground for justifying a specific derogation on the basis of ship-or-pay obligations, but it appeared to the Commission that an economic evaluation of 'serious economic and financial

---

[80] DG XVII Discussion Note, 'Ship-or-Pay Contracts', 29 April 1999.

B. The Gas Directive 2003

difficulties' arising under Article 27 of the Directive could lead to unequal treatment.[81] It could also lead to potential discrimination between different arrangements for gas supply according to the ship-or-pay provisions on transportation services. To resolve this, the Commission has proposed that when assessing a request for a derogation on the basis of Article 27 a separate analysis of the ship-or-pay component should be carried out to avoid derogation becoming necessary. This suggests that the Commission prefers to exclude ship-or-pay liabilities from its calculation of 'serious difficulties'. The introduction of published tariffs for transmission and distribution pipelines (Article 18) and the Guidelines on Third Party Access in the Annex to the Regulation (particularly the 'use-it-or-lose-it' provision) should remove this problem in time.

(c) Emergent and Isolated Markets

6.99 The wide differences in the penetration of gas in the energy markets of Member States are taken into account in several places in the Directive. In particular, it makes special provision for Member States that are not yet fully linked to the European gas system and have a high degree of dependence on a single external supplier. Special provisions also apply to those Member States classified as 'emergent markets', and for those areas or regions within certain Member States that are seeking to encourage investment in transmission infrastructure. The term 'emergent market' means 'a Member State in which the first commercial supply of its first long-term natural gas supply contract was made not more than 10 years earlier'.[82] It therefore applied initially to Greece and Portugal, where the first supply commenced in 1996 to 1997.

6.100 Article 28 provides for the grant of derogations to Member States that experience the effects of one of three categories of uneven market development.

6.101 **Lack of system connection (isolated markets)**   The Directive provides for derogation for those Member States that are not directly connected to the interconnected system of any other Member State and have only one main external supplier. A supplier should have a market share of more than 75 per cent to be considered a main supplier. In such cases, Article 28(1) permits those Member States to derogate from Articles 4, 9, 23, and/or 24 of the Directive. However, such derogations expire automatically from the moment that at least one of these conditions is no longer fulfilled. This provision in Article 28(1) would at present appear to apply to Finland and Greece only.

6.102 **Emergent markets**   The second paragraph of Article 28 provides for a similar derogation for those Member States that are 'emergent markets' and which would

---

[81] ibid.
[82] Gas Directive, Art 2(31). Cyprus and Malta do not at present have a gas market.

experience 'substantial problems' as a result of the implementation of the Directive. The term 'substantial problems' may not be associated with the performance of take-or-pay commitments in this case. They may derogate from the same provisions of the Directive as Member States in the first category but such derogations expire once they cease to be classifiable as 'emergent markets'. At that point of expiry, the definition of eligible customers is to result in a market opening equal to at least 33 per cent of the total annual gas consumption of the national gas market. Paragraph 3 of Article 28(1) provides for the timetable for full market opening.

6.103 In both categories above (paras 6.101 and 6.102) such derogations must be notified to the Commission. It may be noted that under the terms of the Decision incorporating the Gas Directive into the EEA Agreement, Norway is classified as an emergent market.

6.104 **Risk to investment in infrastructure** The third category is the most complex. It concerns the interplay between investment in new transmission capacity and implementation of the Directive. For a Member State that foresees that implementation of the Directive would cause substantial problems in a geographically-limited area of its territory, an application for a temporary derogation is possible. This applies especially where the development of transmission infrastructure is involved and where a competitive market as envisaged by the Directive might inhibit new large-scale investment or undermine recent investment. In other words, the infrastructure investments will or would not be economically viable within the area in question without the grant of a derogation. Temporary derogations may be granted by the Commission for developments within such an area. The derogation may be from Articles 4, 7, 8(1) and (2), 9, 11, 12(5), 13, 17, 18, 23(1), and/or 24 for developments in this area. However, such derogations may only be granted if no gas infrastructure (other than distribution infrastructure) has yet been established in the area or where it has been in operation for less than ten years. The temporary derogation may not exceed a period of ten years from the time that gas is first supplied in the area concerned. For distribution infrastructure a derogation may be granted for up to 20 years from the time the gas is first supplied through the system in the area.

6.105 The procedure for grant of derogations in this category is different from that in the other two cases. Once an application for a temporary derogation has been submitted to the Commission by a Member State, it may grant a derogation only after taking into account at least six criteria.

6.106 The list in Article 28(5) is not exhaustive but includes the following:

- the need for infrastructure investments, which would not be economical to operate in a competitive market environment;
- the level and pay-back prospects of investments required;
- the size and maturity of gas system in the area concerned;

B. The Gas Directive 2003

- the prospects for gas market concerned;
- the geographic size and characteristics of the area or region concerned, and socio-economic and demographic factors.

6.107 It is very probable that the Commission will seek to apply the above criteria in a restrictive manner, and that derogations for investments in the transport of gas through local or regional pipeline networks to final consumers are unlikely to be accepted. Indeed, it has stated 'in principle, there will be no need to grant derogations under Article 26(4) in order to facilitate investment in distribution systems, in view of the provisions in Article 4(4)'. (Article 4(4) has already established a procedure for exemptions for areas of recent supply by distribution undertakings in a particular area.)

6.108 In designing specific tests for assessing rates of return on investments with or without a derogation some reference may be made to experience gained under the Trans-European Networks programme, which allows for a grant of limited investment subsidies in exceptional circumstances (see paras 18.68–18.80).

6.109 Specific mention is made of both Luxembourg and Greece as being potential beneficiaries of derogations under this article.[83] However, the conditions are also set out, with a period of review at the end of five years in Luxembourg's case and limitations on the extent of areas and durations to be included in the case of Greece.

(d) Reporting

6.110 The Directive imposes very similar reporting requirements under Article 31 to those in the Electricity Directive. There are two principal requirements imposed on the Commission to undertake monitoring and review of the Directive and its effects. The first report is an annual progress report to be submitted to the Parliament and Council.[84] Focusing on the Directive, the first of these was due before the end of July 2005 and annually after that date. The second report had a wider scope, covering progress in creating the internal gas market.[85] A combined report to meet both of these requirements was presented at the end of 2005.

6.111 The Report on the Directive is required to cover a wide range of issues, including the following:

- Experience gained and progress made in creating a complete and fully operational internal market and the obstacles that remain. This is to include issues of

---

[83] ibid, Art 28(6) and (8) respectively.
[84] ibid, Art 31(1).
[85] ibid, Art 31(3); European Commission, *Report on Progress in Creating the Internal Gas and Electricity Market*, COM (2005) 568 final, 15 November 2005.

market dominance, concentration in the market, predatory or anti-competitive behaviour and its effects in terms of market distortion.
- The derogations granted under the Directive, including a possible revision of the threshold for the derogation granted under Article 13(2).
- Extent to which the unbundling and tarification requirements have been successful in providing access to the EU gas system and equivalent levels of competition, and economic, environmental, and social consequences of market opening for customers.
- System capacity and security of supply issues.
- Measures taken by Member States covering peak demand and shortfalls by one or more suppliers.
- Bilateral relations with third countries that produce and export or transport natural gas: the assessment is to include the social and environmental consequences of the gas trade and network access of such third countries.
- Possible harmonization requirements not linked to the Directive.

6.112 The report may include recommendations, especially with respect to measures that might counteract negative effects of market dominance and market concentration. Every two years it has to include an analysis of PSOs in the Member States and 'in particular, their effects on competition in the gas market'.[86] Recommendations may be made on measures to improve the level of public service standards or to prevent market foreclosure.

6.113 The second report was a once-only progress report aimed at reviewing matters relevant to the progress in creating an internal electricity market rather than the Directive itself. It was submitted at the end of 2005.[87] The final paragraphs of Article 28(3) require the Commission (where this is appropriate) to submit proposals with this report to address issues of market dominance, market concentration or anti-competitive behaviour, and were to be made 'in conformity with competition law'. Article 29 sets out a review procedure in the event that the above report concludes that certain obligations imposed by the Directive on undertakings are not proportionate to the objective pursued. The Member State may submit a request to the Commission for exemption from the requirement.

(e) Enforcement by the ECJ

6.114 The judgment of the ECJ in Case C-17/03 of 7 June 2005[88] was interpreted by the Commission as having relevance for network access in the gas sector, even though

---

[86] ibid, Art 31(2).
[87] European Commission, *Report on Progress in Creating the Internal Gas and Electricity Market*, COM (2005) 568 final, 15 November 2005.
[88] Case C-17/03 *Vereniging voor Energie Milieu en Water v Directeur van de Dienst Uitvoering en Toezicht Energie* [2005] ECR I-4983.

it concerned non-discriminatory access to electricity transmission capacity. The ECJ's argument that a grant of preferential treatment would create risks for the transition from monopolistic and compartmentalized markets to open and competitive ones is applicable to the gas sector. According to the Commission, 'in substance and spirit, the Court ruling is therefore applicable to the grant of preferential transmission and distribution capacities of natural gas'.[89] This is only subject to caveats concerning the continuing validity of transit gas contracts and the right of operators to refuse network access on the basis of serious economic and financial difficulties with take-or-pay contracts under the Gas Directive. The decision did not challenge the validity of long-term gas supply contracts and no suggestion was made by the Commission that it had any bearing upon the operation of such contracts in the gas industry.

C. The Gas Regulation 2005

The principal aim of the Gas Regulation is the establishment of non-discriminatory rules for access conditions to gas transmission systems. Like its sister Regulation in the electricity sector, it is designed to complete the provisions of the main legislation, embodied in this case in the Gas Directive. In spite of the parallels, the focus of this Regulation is different, and turns on one assumption in particular: that the internal market cannot work effectively in the gas sector if access conditions to the networks do not correspond to certain minimum standards. However, the procedural origins of this Regulation are similar to the Electricity Regulation, in the sense that they both arise from a Forum context (see paras 3.28–3.36). The content of the Gas Regulation is expressly built upon a set of guidelines for good practice developed in discussions with industry, regulators, and Member State government representatives in the context of the Madrid Gas Regulatory Forum.[90] The Regulation makes these guidelines legally enforceable.   **6.115**

The Regulation is to be equivalent to and procedurally the same as the one already adopted for cross-border exchanges in electricity. Similarly, these rules are viewed as having an evolutionary character, requiring supplementary rules on issues such as the alleviation of contractual congestion. The Regulation therefore provides that the implementing rules in the Annex may be modified according to the comitology   **6.116**

---

[89] Commission Staff Working Document on the decision C-17 of 7 June 2005 of the Court of Justice of the European Communities, 'Preferential Access to Transport Networks under the Electricity and Gas Internal Market Directives', SEC (2006) 547, 26 April 2006, 4.

[90] Madrid Forum, 24–25 September 2003: Second Guidelines on Good Practice. Indeed, discussions took place in the Forum during 2005 and 2006 on draft explanatory notes to accompany the Regulation. They cover tariffs, a capacity allocation mechanism, and congestion management procedures.

Chapter 6: Gas

procedure for the exercise of implementing powers granted to the Commission. It may be noted that Member States are expressly recognized as having the right to maintain or introduce measures that contain more detailed provisions than those set out in the Regulation and Guidelines.

6.117 The overall objective of the Regulation comprises a set of specific goals:

(1) setting harmonized principles for tariffs, or the methodologies underlying their calculation, for network access;
(2) the establishment of TPA services;
(3) harmonized principles for capacity allocation and congestion management;
(4) the determination of transparency requirements;
(5) balancing rules and imbalance charges; and
(6) the facilitation of capacity trading.[91]

(1) Tariffs for Network Access

6.118 Tariffs (or the methodologies used to calculate them), as applied by TSOs and approved by the NRAs according to Article 25(2) of the Gas Directive, as well as tariffs published according to Article 18 of the Gas Directive, must be set according to five criteria:[92]

(1) they must be transparent;
(2) they must take into account the need for system integrity and its improvement;
(3) they must reflect the actual costs incurred;
(4) they must be applied in a non-discriminatory manner; and
(5) they must facilitate efficient gas trade and competition.

6.119 With respect to the costs in item 3, such costs have to correspond to those of an efficient and structurally comparable network operator and be transparent, as well as including an appropriate return on investments and incentives to construct new infrastructure. Where appropriate, eg if effective pipeline-to-pipeline competition exists, the benchmarking of tariffs by the NRAs will be a relevant consideration, complementary in the Commission's view to the cost-based tariff-setting approach.[93] With respect to item 5, this requirement should avoid cross-subsidies between network users and provide incentives for investment as well as maintaining or creating interoperability for transmission networks.

6.120 Member States are given the option to have tariffs set through market-based arrangements, such as auctions. Nevertheless, such arrangements and the revenues

---

[91] Gas Regulation, Art 1(1).
[92] ibid, Art 3(1).
[93] ibid, Recital 7.

C. The Gas Regulation 2005

they generate as well as the use of such revenues have to be approved by the NRA. In general, they have to be compatible with the provisions of the Gas Directive.[94]

The impact of tariffs on market liquidity and cross-border trade is also considered. Tariffs for network access must not restrict liquidity or distort trade across borders of different transmission systems. In cases where it appears that tariff structures or balancing mechanisms are likely to restrict trade across transmission systems, TSOs are to 'actively pursue convergence of tariff structures and charging principles including in relation to balancing'.[95] This requirement is, however, of no practical relevance if the NRAs have exclusive responsibility for tariff setting. They are to do so in close co-operation with the relevant national authorities. The wording makes it clear that the search for a solution to a possible restriction of trade across systems by TSOs is a priority objective. **6.121**

(2) Third Party Access Services

The services offered by TSOs are required to conform to a common minimum to ensure that a minimum standard applies throughout the EU, to ensure that TPA services are sufficiently compatible and to allow for the benefits accruing from a well-functioning internal gas market to be felt.[96] The common minimum set of practices contains the following three elements:[97] **6.122**

(1) Services are to be offered on a non-discriminatory basis to all network users. Where a TSO offers the same service to different customers, it has to do so under equivalent contractual terms and conditions. This may be achieved either by using harmonized transportation contracts[98] or a common network code approved by the competent authority in line with the procedure set out in Article 25 of the Gas Directive.
(2) Both firm and interruptible TPA services must be provided. The price of the interruptible capacity has to reflect the probability of interruption.
(3) Network users must be offered both long and short-term services.

Transportation contracts concluded with non-standard start dates or with a shorter duration than a standard annual transportation contract must not lead to **6.123**

---

[94] ibid, Recital 8.
[95] ibid, Art 3(2).
[96] ibid, Recital 9.
[97] ibid, Art 4(1).
[98] ibid, Recital 10 is careful to note that 'harmonized transportation contracts' in this context does not mean that the terms and conditions of the transportation contracts of a particular system operator in a Member State must be the same as those of another TSO in that Member State or in another Member State, unless minimum requirements are set which must be met by all transportation contracts.

arbitrarily higher or lower tariffs which do not reflect the market value of the service. This is to be organized according to the principles set out in the previous section on tariffs.

6.124 An option is for TPA services to be granted subject to appropriate guarantees from network users regarding the creditworthiness of such users. These guarantees are not to function as 'undue market entry barriers'[99] and must be non-discriminatory, transparent, and proportionate.

(3) Principles of Capacity Allocation and Congestion Management

6.125 The principles of capacity allocation are contained in Article 5(1) and (2). The basic principle is that the maximum capacity at all relevant points (including entry and exit points) is to be made available to market participants.[100] This has to take into account system integrity and efficient network operation. TSOs must implement and publish non-discriminatory and transparent capacity allocation mechanisms, which are to:

- provide appropriate economic signals for efficient and maximum use of technical capacity and facilitate investment in new infrastructure;
- be compatible with the market mechanisms including spot markets and trading hubs, while being flexible and capable of adapting to evolving market circumstances;
- be compatible with the network access systems of the Member States.

6.126 With respect to congestion management, in the event of contractual congestion, the challenge is to develop common rules that balance the need to free up unused capacity in accordance with the principle of 'use-it-or-lose-it' with the rights of holders of the capacity to use it when necessary, and at the same time enhancing the liquidity of capacity.[101] Under Article 5(3) TSOs are required to take into account two principles when they conclude new transportation contracts or renegotiate existing transportation contracts. These principles are:

- in the event of contractual congestion, the TSO is to offer unused capacity on the primary market at least on a day-ahead and interruptible basis;
- network users who wish to re-sell or sub-let their unused contracted capacity on the secondary market are to be entitled to do so. In addition, Member States may require that network users provide notification or information to the TSO.

6.127 If capacity that is contracted under existing transportation contracts remains unused and contractual congestion occurs, TSOs are to apply the above principles

---
[99] ibid, Art 4(3).
[100] See ibid, Annex, 3.2: 'Definition of all relevant points for transparency requirements'.
[101] ibid, Recital 11.

C. The Gas Regulation 2005

unless this would infringe the requirements of the existing contracts.[102] If it would lead to an infringement of the existing contracts, TSOs must submit a request to the network user for the use on the secondary market of unused capacity in line with the above principles. The submission of such a request follows consultation with the competent authorities. In the event that physical congestion occurs, that is, a situation in which the capacity of the pipeline concerned is fully used (in other words, nominated for use) and incremental capacity is needed to accommodate actual or forecast flows, the governing principle is that non-discriminatory, transparent capacity allocation mechanisms are to be applied by the TSO or by the regulatory authorities, if the latter is appropriate.[103]

(4) Transparency Requirements

Article 6 sets out six common minimum standards on transparency requirements. The aim is to ensure that network users gain effective access to gas networks by having information available on technical requirements and available capacity. **6.128**

(1) TSOs are required to make public detailed information regarding the services they offer and the conditions on which they are offered. Technical information has to be supplied that a network user would need to gain effective network access.
(2) TSOs or relevant national authorities are also required to publish reasonably and sufficiently detailed information on tariff derivation, methodology and structure.
(3) For TPA services, each TSO has to publish information on technical, contracted and available capacities on a numerical basis for all relevant points on a regular and rolling basis and in a user-friendly standardized manner.
(4) The relevant points of a transmission system on which information has to be published are to be approved by the competent authorities after consultation with network users.
(5) In cases where a TSO takes the view that confidentiality reasons preclude the publication of all of the data required, the TSO must seek the authorization of the competent authorities to limit publication with respect to the point or points at issue. The competent authorities are to review such requests on a case-by-case basis, assessing them according to (inter alia) the need to respect legitimate commercial confidentiality and the goal of creating a competitive internal gas market. Where it decides to grant an authorization, details of the available capacity are to be published without indicating the numerical data that would contravene confidentiality. Where three or more network users

---

[102] ibid, Art 5(4).
[103] ibid, Art 5(5).

have contracted capacity at the same point, no such authorization is to be granted.

(6) Information to be disclosed by TSOs under the Regulation is to be done 'in a meaningful, quantifiably clear and easily accessible way and on a non-discriminatory basis'.

(5) Balancing Rules and Imbalance Charges

6.129 For new market entrants that may have difficulty in balancing their overall sales portfolio, a non-discriminatory and transparent balancing system is an important mechanism. The Regulation seeks therefore to lay down rules according to which TSOs will operate such mechanisms in ways compatible with non-discriminatory, transparent, and effective access to the network. It contains seven rules:[104]

(1) Balancing rules are to be designed in a fair, non-discriminatory, and transparent manner and are to be based on objective criteria. They must reflect genuine system needs which take into account the resources available to the TSO.
(2) Where a balancing system is not market-based, tolerance levels are to be designed in a way that either reflects seasonality or results in a tolerance level higher than that which results from seasonality, and which reflects the actual technical capabilities of the transmission system. Tolerance levels are to reflect genuine system needs and take into account the resources available to the TSO.
(3) Imbalance charges are to be cost-reflective as far as possible, while providing appropriate incentives on network users to balance their input and off-take of gas. They are to avoid cross-subsidization between network users and are not to create obstacles for potential new market entrants. Any calculation methodology for imbalance charges as well as the final tariffs is to be made public by the competent authorities or the TSO as appropriate.
(4) TSOs may impose penalty charges on network users whose input into and off-take from the transmission system is not in balance according to the balancing rules in Article 7(1).
(5) Penalty charges which exceed the actual balancing costs incurred, defined as costs that an efficient and structurally comparable network operator would incur and which are transparent, are to be taken into account when calculating tariffs. This is to be done in such a way that does not reduce the interest in balancing and is to be approved by the competent authorities.

---

[104] ibid, Art 7(1)–(7). The ERGEG has published a consultation document on its interpretation of Art 7, aimed at guiding both TSOs and NRAs in the design of gas balancing mechanisms. It is not legally binding but compliance of both of these groups is expected by the ERGEG: *Guidelines for Good Practice for Gas Balancing: An ERGEG Public Consultation Paper*, 20 April 2006 <http://ec.europa.eu/energy/gas/madrid/doc_11/documents/9_eregeg.pdf>.

(6) TSOs are to provide sufficient, well-timed, and reliable online-based information on the balancing status of network users. This will enable network users to take timely corrective action. The level of information provided must reflect the level of information available to the TSO. Charges for the provision of such information (where they exist) are to be approved by the competent authorities and are to be made public by the TSO.

(7) Member States are required to ensure that TSOs 'endeavour to harmonise' balancing regimes and streamline structures and levels of balancing charges in order to facilitate trade in gas.[105]

(6) Trading of Capacity Rights

6.130 The development of a competitive market has as one of its central components the trading of primary capacity rights. It plays an important part in the creation of liquidity. The Regulation therefore lays down fundamental rules for this form of trading.[106] These are brief, however.

6.131 Each TSO has to take reasonable steps to allow capacity rights to be freely tradable and to facilitate such trade. It also has to develop harmonized transportation contracts and procedures on the primary market to facilitate secondary trade of capacity and to recognize the transfer of primary capacity rights where notified by network users. The harmonized transportation contracts and procedures are to be notified to the NRAs.

(7) Guidelines

6.132 The Regulation envisages the adoption of Guidelines to provide the minimum degree of harmonization required to achieve its aim of laying down rules for access conditions to gas networks. Such Guidelines are to provide the detail of TPA services, including the character, duration, and other requirements of these services. These are provided for in the set of Guidelines attached to the Regulation in the form of an Annex. Details are also to be provided in the Guidelines of the principles underlying capacity allocation mechanisms and on the application of capacity management procedures in the event of contractual congestion, and finally details are to be provided on the definition of the technical information necessary for network users to gain effective access to the system and the definition of all relevant points for transparency requirements. The latter includes the information to be published at all relevant points and the time schedule according to which this information is to be published.

---

[105] ibid, Art 7(7).
[106] ibid, Art 8.

Chapter 6: Gas

6.133 It is important to understand that the meaning of 'guidelines' in the context of the Regulation is not the same as that usually understood by the term: a directing principle with no binding legal force. Recital 2 of the Regulation is explicit about the purpose and the reasons for the drafters' approach. The origins of the Guidelines lie in discussions in the Madrid Gas Regulatory Forum, where a first set of Guidelines for Good Practice was adopted in 2002, with unsatisfactory results. Experience gained in the implementation and monitoring of these Guidelines demonstrated that in order to ensure the full implementation of the rules set out in the first set of Guidelines in all the Member States, and in order to provide a minimum guarantee of equal market access conditions in practice, 'it is necessary to provide for them to become legally enforceable'. This point is crucial. Although a second set of common rules was adopted at the meeting of the Madrid Gas Regulatory Forum on 24–25 September 2003, the purpose of the Gas Regulation was to treat these Guidelines as no more than a basis for a legally binding instrument.[107] What is called 'Guidelines' in the Annex to the Regulation is in fact a set of 'specific detailed implementing rules',[108] which are legally binding and legally enforceable. Moreover, these rules are designed to evolve over time. They are therefore of greater legal significance than might appear on a cursory review.

6.134 This view of the Guidelines is further reinforced when it is appreciated that the rules and principles contained in the Annex are essentially a reprise, albeit in more detail, of rules, principles, and standards contained in the body of the Regulation itself. Presumably, the aim is to secure a more robust legal basis and ensure the highest level of compliance. The Annex covers six main areas:

- the criteria according to which charges for access to the network are determined, to ensure that they take fully into account the need for system integrity and reflect effectively incurred costs;
- a common minimum set of TPA services—concerning for example the duration of transportation contracts offered and on an interruptible basis;
- common rules regarding contractual congestion of networks that balance the need to free up unused capacity with the rights of the holders of the capacity to use it when necessary;
- information on technical requirements and available capacity;
- rules ensuring that TSOs operate balancing systems in a manner compatible with the internal market; and
- common basic requirements regarding the trading of primary rights to capacity.

6.135 The amendment of these Guidelines may be made by the Commission, in accordance with the procedure provided for in Article 14(2). This is the committee

---

[107] ibid, Recital 3.
[108] ibid, Recital 18.

C. The Gas Regulation 2005

procedure known as 'comitology'. This means that the Commission is to be assisted by the committee established under Article 30 of the Gas Directive. It follows the procedure set out in Articles 5 and 7 of Decision 1999/468/EC,[109] taking into account Article 8. The period laid down in Article 5(6) of that Decision is set at three months. The Regulation adds some details about the procedure by which the Commission will proceed if it seeks an amendment to the Guidelines. In Recital 19 it notes that the Commission should ensure prior consultation of all relevant parties concerned, represented by the professional organizations, and the Member States within the Madrid Forum. It should also request the input of the ERGEG in such consultations.

If the Commission requires information for purposes linked to the Guidelines in Article 9, both Member States and NRAs are required to provide all information at its request.[110] The time-limit for Member States and NRAs to respond to the Commission's request is to be fixed by the Commission itself. This has to meet the tests of reasonableness, and be proportionate to the complexity of the information required and the urgency with which the information is needed. The Commission has to treat such information confidentially.[111] **6.136**

(a) Guidelines on Storage

A diversity of practices on gas storage emerged across the EU which meant that, although storage is not a natural monopoly, its crucial role in providing customers with supply flexibility was far from optimal. To overcome this, discussions commenced within the framework of the Madrid Regulatory Forum to establish minimum requirements for storage access which the NRAs would implement. The Guidelines for Good TPA for Storage System Operators (Guidelines) were the result.[112] **6.137**

The Guidelines were based on a proposal from ERGEG, and were discussed with storage operators in the Forum during 2004 and 2005. The association of TSOs for gas, the GTE, reorganized itself into a wider group called Gas Infrastructure Europe, which established a group of storage system operators. The voluntary guidelines that resulted were adopted on 23 March 2005. **6.138**

The Guidelines are addressed to all Storage System Operators (SSOs) as well as storage users and relate to the implementation of the Gas Directive. However, this does not include storage systems that are not available for TPA within the meaning of the Gas Directive, such as temporary storage related to the LNG regasification process. The Guidelines do not go beyond the Directive by creating or restricting **6.139**

---

[109] Council Decision 1999/468/EC [1999] OJ L184/23.
[110] Gas Regulation, Art 11.
[111] ibid, Recital 20.
[112] <http://ec.europa.eu/energy/gas/madrid/jwg/ggpsso_23.3.2005.pdf>.

TPA rights to any storage facility or part of one. Their broad aim is to provide the services needed on a fair and non-discriminatory basis. However, an 'overriding principle' is that storage systems and processes that are implemented by the SSOs should be secure, reliable, and operated efficiently, under Article 8(1)(a) of the Directive. The scope of the Guidelines covers:

(1) roles and responsibilities of SSOs;
(2) role of storage users;
(3) necessary TPA services;
(4) storage capacity allocation and congestion management;
(5) confidentiality and transparency requirements;
(6) tariff structure and derivation;
(7) storage penalties;
(8) secondary market;
(9) co-operation with TSOs.

6.140 With respect to the various subjects, the following points may be noted. In line with the overall tendency of sector-specific rule-making, item 1 identifies who does what in the liberalizing market for gas storage. The SSOs are defined and are declared to be 'responsible for the provision and management of technical storage capacity, storage services and information as well as technical integrity and safety of storage facilities'. They are required to offer TPA services to all storage users on a non-discriminatory basis and establish rules on capacity use aimed at facilitating competitive and efficient use of that storage facility. Any capacity reservations linked to PSO obligations which the SSO is responsible for are to be demonstrated to the NRA on request as being no more than what is required to satisfy the relevant PSO.[113] If there is evidence of capacity being unused in circumstances of significant and prolonged contractual congestion, in spite of measures to prevent capacity hoarding, the relevant NRA may introduce measures to ensure the efficient functioning of the market, including the efficient use of storage capacity.[114]

6.141 Monitoring the operation of the Guidelines is a primary responsibility of the NRAs. It is incumbent on the SSOs to demonstrate to the NRA at its request that it meets the Guidelines. The NRA is required to ensure that results in both negotiated and regulated TPA regimes are equivalent in terms of non-discrimination, transparency, and competition. In pursuance of this monitoring role, the ERGEG has published several reports on the performance of SSOs in meeting the guidelines. Compliance with the Guidelines has initially proved to be, in the view of the ERGEG, 'insufficient'.[115]

---

[113] ibid 3.2.
[114] ibid 4.5.
[115] <http://www.ergeg.org>. See 'ERGEG Final 2006 Report on Monitoring the Implementation of the Guidelines for Good TPA Practice for Gas Storage System Operators'.

C. The Gas Regulation 2005

(8) Enforcement

6.142 The Member States are required to lay down rules on penalties applicable to infringements of the provisions of the Regulation and to take all the measures necessary to ensure that they are implemented.[116] These penalties must be effective, proportionate, and dissuasive. These provisions had to be notified to the Commission by 1 July 2006 at the latest. These penalties are not to be of a criminal nature. The power given to the Commission in the Electricity Regulation to impose fines on undertakings for the supply of incorrect, incomplete, or misleading information is missing from the Gas Regulation (see paras 5.128–5.129).

6.143 The NRAs are expressly charged with ensuring compliance with the Regulation and the Guidelines adopted under Article 9. This is in addition to other responsibilities they have under the Regulation. If this requires co-operation with each other and with the Commission, they are required to do so.[117]

6.144 Enforcement is qualified, however, by a number of derogations and exemptions contained in Article 16. These interface with those of the Gas Directive. For example, the Regulation is not to apply to gas transmission systems in those Member States for the duration of derogations granted under Article 28. Moreover, Member States that have been granted derogations under Article 28 may apply to the Commission for a temporary derogation from the application of the Regulation. This may be for a period of up to two years from the date at which the derogation granted under Article 28 expires. Efforts are made to harmonize the Regulation with the derogation provisions in Articles 21 and 27 of the Gas Directive. However, the Regulation states in Article 9(3) that the application and amendment of Guidelines adopted under the Regulation 'shall reflect differences between national gas systems, and shall not therefore require uniform detailed terms and conditions of third party access at Community level'. This offers scope for variable interpretation of the Regulation's requirements.

6.145 Implementation of the Regulation is to be monitored by the Commission. In its report under Article 31(3) of the Gas Directive, the Commission is required also to report on the experience gained in the application of the Regulation. The report must pay special attention to the extent to which the Regulation has been successful in ensuring non-discriminatory and cost-reflective network access conditions for gas transmission networks 'in order to contribute to customer choice in a well functioning internal market and to long-term security of supply'.[118] If the Commission

---

[116] Gas Regulation, Art 13.
[117] ibid, Art 10.
[118] ibid, Art 15.

considers it necessary, proposals and/or recommendations may be included in this report.

6.146 It may also be noted that Recital 21 states that the Regulation and the guidelines adopted under it are without prejudice to the application of the Community rules on competition. There is no comparable provision in the Electricity Regulation.

6.147 The Regulation entered into force on 1 July 2006 with the exception of Article 9(2) (amendments to the Guidelines) which applies from 1 January 2007. It is directly applicable in all the Member States.

D. Conclusions

6.148 The body of 'European gas law' that is examined in this chapter has deliberately been worked out to apply a pro-competitive policy to a sector long characterized by monopoly and segmentation into national markets, and to stimulate the transitional process itself. It has been structured around a timetable for so-called 'market opening' or liberalization and therefore contains an in-built dynamic for change. Evidence of that dynamic is clear from the body of law that has already emerged. Prior to 2003, it comprised only a single Directive, but the current legal regime comprises not only a Directive and a Regulation, but also a growing body of legally binding, second-order rules made in the form of 'guidelines'.

6.149 The shape of the law is increasingly being determined by a tension between the transitional process and the pro-competitive aims that have initiated it. This is evident in at least four ways. First, in order to make competition effective and address issues that arise from the transition to competitive markets, the legal framework is required to be increasingly detailed, fixing the roles and responsibilities of the market participants, including some that have come into being as a result of competition, and redefining the relationship between Community and Member State bodies. The proliferation of Guidelines is a vivid illustration of this process. At the EU level, it represents an expression of 'regulation for competition'. Secondly, the design and administration of these second-order rules has required a greater use of mechanisms to ensure that the balance of power between Member States and the Community is maintained. The use of comitology as a way of reviewing new proposals for rules on highly specific matters is one instance of this. Thirdly, as competition begins to take root in the gas market, the limits imposed by pre-liberalization practices and legal arrangements such as transit contracts are increasingly apparent. The inclusion of special transitional regimes within the current legal framework appears less necessary as the timetable advances. The maintenance of such legal enclaves for potentially long periods becomes harder to justify. Finally, the Directive and Regulation both provide ample evidence of the balance that is being

D. Conclusions

struck between the competitive goal on the one hand and public service and environmental goals on the other. Considerable care has been taken to ensure that while the latter goals are more evident in the current legal regime than in its predecessor, they are not likely to undermine the creation of competition. It is still too early to say whether the balance struck is one that will withstand the pressures created by the continuing transition.

7

OIL

A. Introduction	7.01	(c) Links to Other Legislation:	
B. Hydrocarbons Licensing	7.03	Procurement	7.20
(1) Aims and Scope	7.04	(d) Implementation	7.22
(2) Common Rules		(e) Concluding Remarks	7.23
(a) Award of Licences	7.09	C. Conclusions	7.26
(b) State Participation	7.13		

A. Introduction

The internal market programme has had little direct impact on the oil industry within the EU.[1] In part this is the result of the relatively small (and declining) quantities of oil produced from within the EU itself. This condition of relative dependence upon imports, together with the international—as distinct from national or regional—character of the oil industry has meant that EU energy policy has been focused largely on security of supply concerns. Several legal measures have been adopted to give Member States an added measure of protection in the event of a crisis of oil supply (see paras 18.60–18.67), but action to promote liberalization in EU oil markets has been deemed largely unnecessary, since the oil sector has long been subject to competition. There are two exceptions to this, however. The first is the dismantling of the oil products monopolies in France and Greece in the 1980s, and the second was the intervention in the licensing of hydrocarbons by Member States in the 1990s. The first represented a targeted use of existing legal powers to tackle abuses resulting from exclusive rights over import and export. In the market for petroleum products, the European Commission acted under Article 31[2] to pursue

7.01

---

[1] Of course, to the extent that many oil companies are also gas companies, the extensive changes made in the competitive environment for gas in the EU have affected these companies' operations.
[2] Art 31 EC requires Member States to adjust any state monopolies of a commercial character through which a Member State supervises, determines, or appreciably influences imports or exports between Member States so as to ensure that there is no discrimination regarding the conditions under which goods are procured and marketed between nationals of Member States. This is enforced by the Commission.

the dismantling of 'oil products monopolies' in France and Greece during the 1980s.[3] This pre-dated the drive for an internal market in energy that commenced with the White Paper of 1988,[4] and, though taking a very long period of time, was largely successful. The second was an attempt to impose a regime of common rules on administrative practices in all Member States to counter practices in some cases that were deemed incompatible with the internal market in energy.

7.02 This chapter is concerned largely with the second of these initiatives, the EU Hydrocarbons Licensing Directive. The measure formed part of the internal market programme initiated in the late 1980s and was one of the first legal measures adopted under its auspices. It has remained the only measure taken by the EU as part of that programme that is directed at the oil sector. However, if oil is understood more widely as petroleum, the exploration and production segment of this sector has attracted a growing interest from a competition perspective in recent years as the Commission has acted to remove restrictions on the supply of gas (discussed in Chapters 12 and 13). The proposed mergers of petroleum companies have also attracted the scrutiny of the Commission.[5] This combination of targeted measures and exercise of oversight has played an important complementary role to the various directives in the liberalization process.

B. Hydrocarbons Licensing

7.03 The conditions for access to hydrocarbons and their management are governed by Directive (EC) 94/22 (the 'Hydrocarbons Licensing Directive' or 'Directive').[6] This framework Directive has its roots in two sets of practices identifiable at that time: on the one hand, there was a widespread use of discriminatory provisions by Member States to limit access by foreign companies and, on the other, there was a lack of transparency in hydrocarbons licensing procedures. For many years there had been mandatory landing obligations and rights of first refusal to produced hydrocarbons, which were frequently enjoyed by state monopolies in exploration and production. However, the uneven distribution of hydrocarbons in the EU

---

[3] Sixth Report on Competition Policy (1977), points 268–9 (France); Case C-347/88 *Commission v Greece* [1990] ECR 4747. These difficulties in adjusting a state trading monopoly in petroleum products encouraged a different approach in dealing with the adjustment of Spanish and Portuguese monopolies. In the Acts of Accession provision was made for a stricter timetable for adjustment: see respectively Art 48 and Art 208 of the Acts of Accession.

[4] *The Internal Energy Market*, COM (1988) 238 final, 2 May 1988.

[5] *Exxon/Mobil* (Case COMP/M.1383) Commission Decision 2004/284/EC, [2004] OJ L103/1; see paras 14.74–14.75.

[6] Directive (EC) 94/22 on conditions for granting and using authorizations for the prospection, exploration and production of hydrocarbons [1994] OJ L164/3.

meant that these practices were evident in only a few of the Member States, usually those with offshore petroleum deposits. The principal Member States concerned were the UK, the Netherlands, Denmark, Ireland, and Italy, although France, Germany, and Greece also had (and have) some petroleum deposits. Although this use of discriminatory provisions appeared to be in decline by the late 1980s, it was nevertheless clearly inconsistent with the framework of rules being developed for the internal energy market. The Directive was adopted on 30 May 1994.

(1) Aims and Scope

The objectives of the Directive are to set up common rules to ensure that: 7.04

- procedures for granting authorizations to prospect or explore for and produce hydrocarbons are open to all entities that possess the necessary capabilities;
- authorizations are granted on the basis of objective, published criteria; and
- the conditions under which authorizations are granted are known in advance by all entities taking part in the procedure.

Transparency and non-discrimination are central to the achievement of these objectives.

The Directive rests on a careful balance between respect for the rights of Member States based on sovereignty over natural resources and the Community interest in the way in which those rights are exercised. It avoids the path of detailed regulation in favour of establishing a framework of general principles to which the rules made by Member States have to conform. In line with the principle of subsidiarity, each Member State remains free to choose or to maintain the rules that it considers most appropriate to its natural and operational circumstances, as well as its national policies on resource management. 7.05

The approach taken by the Directive involves the establishment of common rules but it carries out this task in a way that is quite different from that taken in the Electricity and Gas Directives (discussed in Chapters 5 and 6). It resembles the focused approach followed by the Directives on public procurement contracts rather than the broader approach of the latter two Directives. This reflects the Directive's origins in an earlier attempt to achieve its aims through the public procurement arrangements provided for under Article 3 of Utilities Directive (EEC) 90/531, now codified as Directive (EC) 2004/17.[7] The latter Directive provided that there would be an exemption from the tendering procedures for upstream activities in Member States which had implemented the Hydrocarbons Licensing Directive. 7.06

---

[7] Directive (EC) 2004/17 of the European Parliament and of the Council of 31 March 2004 co-ordinating the procurement procedures of entities operating in the water, energy, transport and postal services sectors [2004] OJ L134/1. This repealed Directive (EEC) 93/38, as amended by Directive (EEC) 94/22 [1994] OJ L164/3, and Directive (EC) 98/4 [1998] OJ L101/1.

7.07 The issue of sovereignty was approached with some delicacy. The provisions of the Directive do not directly affect the sovereignty or sovereign rights of Member States over hydrocarbon resources within their territory. Member States retain their rights and responsibilities with respect to the management of hydrocarbons, including revenues that arise from their development. In particular, they retain the right to decide:

- which areas must be opened for exploration and production;
- the level and the rates of tax, royalties, and other revenues such as those arising from state participation;
- who the licensees will be; and
- how their activities are to be monitored.

The Directive expressly gives Member States the right to be involved both in areas of public policy, including the central one of depletion policy (affecting tax revenues), and the protection of the Member State's financial interest.[8]

7.08 The measure applies to all Member States but in practice this excludes Finland and Luxembourg, which have no commercial petroleum deposits. Norway has adopted the Directive under the EEA procedure.

(2) Common Rules

(a) Award of Licences

7.09 The procedures for applications for authorizations have to be publicized. Three conditions are set out to ensure that the procedures are transparent and objective:[9]

- decisions are to be based on objective, pre-established criteria, published in advance;
- all general conditions and obligations imposed on undertakings are to be established and made available to entities before applications are submitted; and
- criteria, conditions, and obligations are to be applied in a non-discriminatory way.

7.10 The kind of procedures that are permitted include the 'concession' or licensing system (where authorizations are granted administratively or by auction after the Member State has published a notice in the Official Journal), and the 'open door' system (where authorizations are granted on a permanent basis for a pre-declared territory). Individual awards are also possible.

7.11 Some recent examples of Member States' efforts to comply with these provisions may serve to illustrate the diversity and number of notifications that publicize licensing as a result of the Directive's requirements. The following notifications have been published on the Commission's website:[10]

---

[8] Hydrocarbons Licensing Directive, Art 6(2).
[9] ibid, Arts 3 and 4.
[10] <http://ec.europa.eu/energy/oil/upstream_licensing/index_en.htm>.

B. Hydrocarbons Licensing

- The *UK* submitted a notice under the Directive which comprised an announcement of its 24th offshore oil and gas licensing round in 2006. It stated that all applications would be judged in accordance with the terms of the Hydrocarbons Licensing Directive Regulations 1995 (SI 1995/1434);[11]
- *Norway* submitted an announcement of its 19th round of licensing on its continental shelf, inviting applications for petroleum production licences, in accordance with the Hydrocarbons Licensing Directive, Article 3(2)(a);[12]
- *The Netherlands* has submitted a number of communications inviting applications for authorizations to prospect for hydrocarbons in specific blocks on the Dutch continental shelf, according to Article 3(2);[13]
- *Ireland* published a notice announcing its 2006 licensing round, covering the Slyne, Erris, and Donegal Basins, in line with Article 3(2)(a);[14]
- *Italy* issued a notice of a request for a licence to explore for geothermal resources in Sicily, allowing interested parties to submit a licence for the same area within 90 days of the date of publication of this notice in the Official Journal;[15]
- *France* has issued several communications under the Directive of applications for licences to prospect for oil and gas. Interested companies may then submit competing applications in accordance with a published procedure;[16]
- *Poland* issued a communication that gave notice of the procedures governing award of authorizations for prospection and exploration pursuant to Article 3(3) of the Directive, including a map showing the areas on offer.[17]

The principles of transparency, objectivity, and non-discrimination must be met in the criteria on which decisions on applications for authorizations are made.[18] The criteria are to be based on the financial and technical capability of entities and on the manner in which they propose to prospect, explore, and bring into operation the area in question. They must be published in the Official Journal. Denmark obtained a derogation from this provision, in connection with an authorization with a 50-year term that had been granted in 1962.[19] 7.12

(b) State Participation

The aim of the detailed provisions on state participation is to ensure that if a Member State wishes to link the grant of a licence to State participation, it may do so and may manage such participation, directly or indirectly. However, it is required 7.13

---

[11] [2006] OJ C63/35.
[12] [2005] OJ C304/37.
[13] eg, [2006] OJ C92/11.
[14] [2005] OJ C309/9.
[15] [2006] OJ C46/31.
[16] eg, the notification of an application for a licence in the department of Marne: [2006] OJ C56/6.
[17] [2006] OJ C98/22.
[18] Hydrocarbons Licensing Directive, Art 5.
[19] ibid, Art 13.

to ensure that the principles set out in the Directive, especially those of transparency, non-discrimination, and equality of treatment, are respected.[20] Participants other than the State should not be subject to undue pressure. The State is required not to be party to information nor exercise any voting rights on decisions regarding sources of procurement for entities; nor shall it exercise majority voting rights on other decisions; nor shall the State or its legal representative prevent the management decisions of the licensee company from being taken on the basis of normal commercial principles. Voting by the State or its legal representative must also be based on transparent, non-discriminatory, and objective principles. Much of the above, set out in Article 6(3), sub-paragraph 2, was designed to meet the Danish insistence on a continued State presence in the exploration and production of hydrocarbons while ensuring that the Directive's principles are respected. By contrast, an earlier, ambitious UK experiment with State participation had been abandoned by this time.[21]

7.14 Another Member State, the Netherlands, had concerns that the Directive might threaten the State's ability to influence depletion policy and to take actions to protect its financial interests. This led to the third sub-paragraph of Article 6(3).[22] It provides that the State or its legal representative may oppose a decision by the licence holders if such a decision would not respect the conditions and requirements on these matters as they are set out in the licence.

7.15 The State as the public authority may also impose conditions and requirements on the exercise of licence activities based on specific public interest reasons such as national security, public safety, public health, security of transport, protection of the environment, protection of biological resources and of national treasures possessing artistic, historic, or archaeological value, safety of installations and of workers, planned management of hydrocarbons resources (depletion rates or optimizing recovery), or the need to secure tax revenues.[23]

7.16 The final sub-paragraph of Article 6(3) concerns the situation where the State company is also a licence holder. It was developed to meet the demands of Norway, which was present as an observer in the discussions on the Directive text in anticipation of its future accession to the EU (subsequently its application was withdrawn following a negative domestic referendum result in 1994). While rejecting a proposal to divide the state hydrocarbons company, Statoil, into two separate parts, it accepted a provision to create a division or 'Chinese Wall' between its business activities, and its role as manager of the State's participation interest. In particular, this arrangement required that no information should flow from the part responsible

---

[20] ibid, Art 6.
[21] Cameron, P, *Property Rights and Sovereign Rights: The Case of North Sea Oil* (1983) 138–71.
[22] In fact, the Dutch State participation share was reduced in 1995 from 50% to 40%.
[23] Hydrocarbons Licensing Directive, Art 6(1).

B. Hydrocarbons Licensing

for the management of the State's participation share to the part that holds licences in its own right. This could in principle be circumvented, however, if the manager of the State participation share were to engage the part of the licence holder as a consultant. In such cases, information necessary to carry out such consultancy activities might be handed over.

Article 6(4) imposes a general constraint upon the monitoring of licensees by the Member States. Such monitoring is limited to that which is necessary to ensure compliance with the conditions, requirements, and obligations following upon the grant of a licence. The thrust of this provision, however, is to avoid any requirement to provide information on actual or intended sources of procurement.   7.17

Article 7 requires Member States to abrogate legal, regulatory, and administrative provisions reserving the right to obtain authorizations in a specific geographic area within the territory of a Member State to a single entity. Such exclusive rights conflict with the principle of equal access to resources and were to be abolished by 1 January 1997. Essentially, this article addresses a specific problem faced by Italy over authorizations held by the then State-owned entity, ENI, in the Po Valley, the Venetian plains (and territorial waters), and the Northern Apennine hills.[24]   7.18

The Commission is required to monitor the treatment of EU entities in third countries to ascertain whether they receive treatment comparable to the treatment granted to entities from the same third countries in the EU.[25] The Directive lays down a procedure for evaluating this situation and, if the need arises, for initiating negotiations with third countries to establish reciprocal rights.   7.19

(c) Links to Other Legislation: Procurement

The Directive establishes a link in Article 12 with the relevant public procurement legislation. A Member State is allowed to utilize the alternative regime in relation to upstream activities in that legislation automatically once it has implemented the Hydrocarbons Licensing Directive in its national law (that is, by 1 July 1995). The relevant legislation has been modified several times during the life of the Hydrocarbons Directive.[26]   7.20

---

[24] The measures taken to adapt Italian law to the Directive are discussed by Nocera, F and Roggenkamp, MM, in *Energy Law in Europe* (2001) 598–9.

[25] Hydrocarbons Licensing Directive, Art 8.

[26] Originally, this was Art 3 of Directive (EEC) 90/531, then Directive (EEC) 93/38, as amended by Directive (EEC) 94/22 [1994] OJ L164/3, and Directive (EC) 98/4 [1998] OJ L101/1. This has been repealed by Directive (EC) 2004/17 of the European Parliament and of the Council of 31 March 2004 co-ordinating the procurement procedures of entities operating in the water, energy, transport, and postal services sectors [2004] OJ L134/1. This applies to the exploration and exploitation of both oil and gas: see Art 7(a) and Annex VII. Also relevant is Commission Decision 2005/15 on the detailed rules for the application of the procedure provided for in Article 30 of Directive (EC) 2004/17 of the European Parliament and of the Council co-ordinating the procurement procedures of entities operating in the water, energy, transport, and postal services sectors [2005] OJ L7/7.

7.21 Under the current arrangements brought in by Directive 2004/17 there is a general procedure allowing for exemption of sectors directly exposed to competition. This has to be without prejudice to the four Commission Decisions that grant special exempted status to the exploitation of geographic areas in the Netherlands, the UK, Austria, and Germany.[27] If a Member State has implemented and applied the Hydrocarbons Directive, access to a market is not deemed to be restricted,[28] and contracts in the hydrocarbons sector may be subject to special arrangements. However, Member States are required to ensure that any entity operating in the hydrocarbons sector observes the principle of non-discrimination and competitive procurement in respect of the award of supplies, works and service contracts, especially with regard to the information which an entity makes available to economic operators concerning its procurement intentions. These are admittedly vague notions and there is no definition in the Directives or other guidance of what exactly they should entail. Such entities also have to communicate to the Commission information relating to the contracts that they award.

(d) Implementation

7.22 Member States were required by Article 14 of the Directive to adopt the necessary legal, regulatory or administrative measures to comply with it by 1 July 1995, and to inform the Commission of the fact. The Directive's operation was the subject of some scrutiny in 1998.[29] The conclusion of the Commission report was that its provisions were being implemented correctly. No reciprocity problem had been detected, not least because the Directive was operating in a context of progressive international opening-up of hydrocarbons exploration and production. Neither the oil companies nor the entities in the Member States reported any discriminatory treatment and no entity had complained directly to the Commission. All of the Member States—except Finland and Luxembourg—had transposed the Directive into national law.

(e) Concluding Remarks

7.23 The Directive was adopted after the Treaty of European Union entered into force and was therefore made subject to the new co-decision procedure with Parliament for the last stages of its passage. The inclusion of natural gas in this Directive (being subject to similar physical, technical, and legal conditions as oil) ensured that the first Gas Directive (EC) 98/30 on common rules for the natural gas sector (under discussion at that time) would be limited in scope and would exclude

---

[27] Commission Decisions 93/676/EEC, 97/367/EEC, 2002/205/EC and 2004/73/EC. See Directive (EC) 2004/17, Art 27 and Recital 38.
[28] Directive (EC) 2004/17, Art 30(3) and Annex XI. For gas transport and distribution see Annex I.
[29] *Report from the Commission to the Council on Directive 94/22/EC on the conditions for granting and using authorisations for the prospection, exploration and production of hydrocarbons*, COM (1998) 447 final.

production of gas. This approach was continued with Directive (EC) 2003/55, its successor, but provisions on access to upstream facilities in the latter Directive have had practical significance.

The Directive was an early example of pan-European co-operation on energy legislation as countries linked to the EU by means of the EEA participated in its development. In particular, the involvement of Norway was of great importance to the long-term credibility of the final result. 7.24

In the event, liberalization of hydrocarbons licensing has proved relatively painless to all entities established in the EU, including subsidiaries of non-EU companies. Since the Directive was adopted, the Commission has taken several highly specific measures with respect to competition issues such as joint marketing of gas (discussed in Chapter 12), energy taxation (see paras 17.22–17.32), oil stocks (see paras 18.61–18.66), and to promote certain environmental goals in areas of environmental management, such as the decommissioning of oil and gas installations[30] and impact assessment.[31] Member States have also taken steps to anticipate EU obligations and thereby to ensure that such involvement by the Commission remains minimal.[32] 7.25

C. Conclusions

In contrast to the expansion of EU oversight and regulatory intervention in the gas sector, there has been relatively little effort to become involved in the oil sector. The Hydrocarbons Licensing Directive remains a notable exception to this. It is the only instance of a sustained legislative attempt to enforce internal market principles in the exploration and production of oil. The extent to which Member States with commercial petroleum deposits have observed its provisions is considerable, with gains in transparency and potential for new market players as a result. 7.26

---

[30] *Communication on the Removal and Disposal of Disused Oil and Gas Installations*, COM (1998) 49 final.
[31] Directive (EC) 97/11, Annexes II and III. In this respect, the Convention for the Protection of the Environment of the North-East Atlantic 1992 (the OSPAR Convention) is relevant. No fewer than 12 Member States are parties to it and the European Community has also acceded to it; OSPAR has been a focus for initiatives on environmental clean-up for some years: see OSPAR Decision 98/3 on the Disposal of Disused Offshore Installations <http://www.ospar.org>.
[32] An example is Art 2.4(1) of the Framework Agreement between the Government of the United Kingdom of Great Britain and Northern Ireland and the Government of the Kingdom of Norway Concerning Cross-Boundary Petroleum Co-operation, 4 April 2005. It reads: 'The terms and conditions for access to a Cross-Boundary Pipeline, including the setting of entry and exit tariffs, shall be in accordance with applicable European Union law. The principles of fairness, non-discrimination, transparency and open access to spare capacity and avoidance of any abuse of a dominant position or other anti-competitive behaviour shall apply.' <http://www.og.dti.gov.uk/upstream/infrastructure/nfa_2005.doc> (see Cameron, PD, 'The Rules of Engagement: Developing Cross-Border Petroleum Deposits in the North Sea and the Caribbean' (2006) 55 ICLQ 559–86).

8

COAL

A. Introduction	8.01
B. Competition versus Intervention	8.05
C. The Post-ECSC Treaty Arrangements	
(1) Transition	8.10
(2) Key Features of the New Regime	8.12
(3) State Aids	8.18
(4) Decision-Making	8.22
D. Conclusion	8.27

A. Introduction

The legal framework that applies to the coal sector is that of the EC Treaty as well as the procedural rules and other secondary legislation derived from it. However, this dates only from 24 July 2002. For a period of 50 years previous to that date, the principal rules of European law applicable to the coal sector were those set down in the Treaty establishing the European Coal and Steel Community (ECSC), signed on 18 April 1951 by six States (Belgium, France, Germany, Italy, Luxembourg, and the Netherlands). **8.01**

This chapter will examine the market orientation of the current legal regime under the EC Treaty, noting also the principal features of the previous regime under the ECSC Treaty. A longer discussion of state aid controls is to be found in Chapter 15. **8.02**

The driver of legal development in this area has been the long-term decline in overall coal production within the EU.[1] There are now only a few Member States that have significant production from indigenous sources of hard coal: Germany, **8.03**

---

[1] There are a variety of reasons behind the high costs of production in EU Member States. The reserves nearest the surface have been depleted so that if mining is to continue it must be done at greater depths and requires more costly infrastructure. In some cases, this is compounded by the poor quality of the deposits that result from complex, irregular, geological structures and a low density of reserves compared with those of the main non-EU coal exporters: see Piper, J, 'State Aid to the European Union coal industry' (1994) 23 Energy in Europe 22.

Spain, the UK, Poland, and the Czech Republic and, to a lesser extent, Hungary.[2] Large quantities of brown coal or lignite are also produced, mostly from Germany, Greece, and Spain, but also from the Czech Republic, Hungary, Poland, Slovakia, and Slovenia. The majority of the remaining coal mines are not competitive against imported coal. Consumption of coal has also been in decline. The driver for change has been competition from other sources of energy, particularly oil products, natural gas, and to some extent from nuclear power. The impact of liberalization in electricity markets has accelerated a shift from coal to gas for electricity generation. Gas is also significantly less environmentally damaging than coal. Nonetheless, the picture is not uniformly bleak for coal. Virtually all of the Member States consume coal as part of their energy mix, a rising gas price can create advantages for coal in power generation, and coal's advantages in terms of security of supply have been acknowledged by the EC.[3] Moreover, the operation of the ETS scheme may work to the advantage of the coal sector by allowing coal plants to purchase emissions allowances, and continue to operate.

8.04 A major task for the current legal regime is nevertheless to continue the social and economic adaptation of the EU coal sector to this long-term trend towards decline, and to ensure that the resulting grant of state aids is subject to strict control. What may be a new element in EU policy towards the coal sector is the notion that a minimum level of coal production is a significant contributor to energy security in the EU. This security consideration has been used to justify the maintenance of a coal-producing capability supported by state aid.[4] As the Commission has stated in a decision allowing the grant of aid to the coal sector of a Member State:[5]

> The world political situation brings an entirely new dimension to the assessment of geopolitical risks and security risks in the energy sector and gives a wider meaning to the concept of security of supplies... It is therefore necessary, on the basis of the current energy situation, to take measures which will make it possible to guarantee access

---

[2] IEA Clean Coal Centre, 'Profiles: Coal in an Enlarged European Union', June 2004.
[3] Green Paper, *Towards a European Strategy for the Security of Supply*, COM (2000) 0769 final: 'The production of coal on the basis of economic criteria has no prospect... in the European Union ... Its future can only be maintained within the framework of the European Union's security of supply' (at II.B(d)). However, environmental pressures on coal use are considerable: the Large Combustion Plant Directive, for example, requires that any coal-fired power stations not equipped to extract SOx emissions from flue gases by 2008 face a maximum operational life of 20,000 hours until 2015, after which compulsory closure occurs (Art 4.4(a), Directive (EC) 2001/80 on the limitation of emissions of certain pollutants into the air from large combustion plants [2001] OJ L309/1. See also the Commission follow-up to the Green Paper: *Sustainable power generation from fossil fuels: aiming at near-zero emissions from coal after 2020*, COM (2006) 843 final, 10 January 2007.
[4] Council Regulation (EC) 1407/2002 of 23 July 2002 on state aid to the coal industry [2002] OJ L205/1, Recital 7 and Art 1.
[5] Commission Decision on grant of aid to Hungary, State aid N 92/2005, point 40: <http://ec.europa.eu/dgs/energy_transport/state_aid/doc/decisions/2005/2005_0092_hu_n.pdf>; similar wording was used in the grant of aid to Poland on 22 June 2005, N 571/2004: <http://ec.europa.eu/dgs/energy_transport/state_aid/doc/decisions/2004/2004_0517_po_n1.pdf>.

to coal reserves and hence a potential availability of Community coal. Strengthening the European Union's energy security therefore justifies the maintenance of coal-producing capability supported by State aid.

B. Competition versus Intervention

The general aim of the ECSC Treaty was to establish a common market with common institutions. It placed the production of coal and steel in six signatory States under a common authority within the framework of an organization. The Treaty provided a framework of production and distribution arrangements for coal and steel and set up an autonomous institutional system to manage it. It entered into force on 23 July 1952 and expired on 23 July 2002. **8.05**

The principles of a market economy were accorded a central role in the ECSC treaty (Article 4) but the potential for regulatory intervention in cases of need such as crisis or shortage was extensive.[6] The declared objectives were revealing in this respect. Under Article 3, the ECSC institutions were charged with the following tasks in the common interest: ensuring an orderly supply to the common market; ensuring to all consumers in comparable positions in the common market equal access to the sources of production; ensuring the establishment of the lowest prices; ensuring conditions which will encourage undertakings to expand and improve their potential to produce, and to promote a policy of using natural resources rationally and avoiding their unconsidered exhaustion; promoting the improvement of the living and working conditions of the labour force and their gradual equalization; promoting the growth of international trade; and promoting the orderly expansion and the modernization of production. Article 4 lays down the principles of the market economy and requires the abolition or prohibition of import and export duties and quantitative restrictions on the movement of products; measures and practices that discriminate between producers, between purchasers or between consumers; and measures or practices that interfere with the purchaser's free choice of supplier; subsidies or aids granted by States 'in any form whatsoever'; and restrictive practices which tend towards the sharing or exploiting of markets. Article 5 permits a limited degree of intervention and sets out the principles on which the ECSC was to base its intervention policy. The powers to intervene in cases of crisis or shortage were considerable—allowing intervention in production, distribution, and prices. The principles set out in these articles played a considerable role as co-ordinating principles for interpretation of other parts of the Treaty by the Court. **8.06**

---

[6] For an overview of the ECSC Treaty provisions with respect to competition, see Bellamy, C, and Child, G, *European Community Law of Competition* (5th edn, Roth, P (ed), 2001) 1176–99.

8.07 Whilst the exercise of the restructuring and contracting provisions might be said to blunt the competitive thrust of the Treaty (Article 5(2), third indent), that is, to ensure the establishment, maintenance, and observance of normal competitive conditions, the exercise of direct influence upon production or upon the market is permitted only when circumstances so require. The main circumstances are set out in Article 58 (intervention in times of decline in demand—the establishment of production quotas); Article 59 (intervention in times of serious shortage of product or products—establishment of consumption priorities), and Article 61 (intervention in time of market disorder—fixing of maximum or minimum prices). These measures, if used, had the effect of establishing a 'managed competition' for limited periods.

8.08 The general objectives were further developed in the sections on competition and pricing in Chapters 5 and 6 of the Treaty. Among the notable provisions were the prohibition on restrictive agreements within the common market under Article 65; the prohibition of certain concentrations without prior authorization from the Commission under Article 66(1) to (6); the prohibition of abuse of a dominant position under Article 66(7), and the rules on state aids in the coal and steel sector. Where matters relating to the coal sector were not dealt with by the ECSC Treaty or in the rules made under it, the provisions of the EC Treaty applied.[7] In the case of state aids, the blanket prohibition on subsidies or aids granted by Member States through Article 4(c) proved unsustainable in the face of a need for restructuring. The Commission exercised its residual powers under Article 95 and introduced temporary rules for state aids to the coal industry as early as 1965. The article allowed the Commission to make a decision where such action was necessary to attain the objectives of the Treaty, subject to the unanimous approval of the Member States for such a measure. This route was taken because, unlike the EC Treaty, there was no provision in the ECSC regime for exemptions for state aid. The rules proved to be the first of several similar frameworks for direct and indirect forms of state aid. In these circumstances, the challenge was then to ensure that such aid was compatible with the common market in coal and in later years with the completion of the internal energy market.

8.09 The principal success of the ECSC was in managing the contraction of the European coal industry and to a lesser extent the steel industries during the 1970s and 1980s, when it assisted in industrial restructuring, placing a particular emphasis on the protection of workers' rights. Between 1953 and the end of 2001 output of coal declined from 485 million tonnes to 83 million tonnes in the 15 EU Member States.[8]

---

[7] Case 238/85 *Deutsche Babcock v Commission* [1987] ECR 5131.
[8] Commission Press Release IP/02/898, 'Fifty years at the service of peace and prosperity: the European Coal and Steel Community (ECSC) treaty expires', 19 June 2002.

During the same period, the number of people working in the coal sector in the same countries fell from 1,860,000 to 87,000. The social impacts of this transformation were cushioned by a re-adaptation scheme, set up under Article 56 ECSC.

C. The Post-ECSC Treaty Arrangements

(1) Transition

8.10 The regulation of the coal sector is now governed by EC rules and, until 2010, by a new scheme for state aids, Council Regulation (EC) 1407/2002 on state aid to the coal industry.[9] The principles underlying the competition rules of both EC and ECSC Treaties are similar, with Articles 81 and 82 EC as the clear successors of Articles 65 and 66(7) ECSC. Although the wording of the latter article differs slightly from Article 82 EC, the substantive application is similar, with the Commission making a similar analysis of geographic and product markets to determine the existence of a dominant position. In fact, the application of the competition rules under the two Treaties had been converging for many years prior to 2002. It was signalled in the Commission's Twentieth Report on Competition Policy in 1990,[10] when the Commission stated that it was time to align enforcement of ECSC competition rules as much as possible with the practice under the EC Treaty. Several years later, it published a notice on the alignment of procedures for processing mergers under both Treaties.[11] As a result of this convergence, the changes in procedure and in substance that arise from the expiry of the ECSC Treaty have proved to be minimal. Further clarification was made by the Commission in 2002 in a Communication which summarized the most important changes in the applicable substantive and procedural law that arose from the transition to the EC regime.[12] It also explained to market players and Member States how the Commission proposed to address specific issues raised by the transition from the ECSC regime to the EC regime in the areas of antitrust, merger control, and state aid control. This included the statement that the Commission does not intend to initiate proceedings under Article 81 EC regarding agreements previously authorized under the ECSC regime.

8.11 Separately, measures were taken for the ECSC net assets and liabilities (€1.6 billion) to be transferred to the overall EU budget, and to fund research activities within

---

[9] [2002] OJ L205/1.
[10] European Commission, *XXth Report on Competition Policy 1990*, para 122.
[11] Commission Notice concerning alignment of procedures for processing mergers under the ECSC and EC Treaties [1998] OJ C66/36.
[12] Communication from the European Commission concerning certain aspects of the treatment of competition cases resulting from the expiry of the ECSC Treaty [2002] OJ C152/5.

the coal and steel sectors. The instrument for this was a Protocol on the financial consequences of the Treaty's expiry and on the establishment of a Research Fund for Coal and Steel annexed to the Treaty of Nice. The financial Protocol was endorsed in February 2002 by EU Member States as an Inter-Governmental agreement.[13]

(2) Key Features of the New Regime

8.12 There are several areas of competition law in which changes have occurred. The three key areas are in the fields of antitrust, merger control, and state aids. In both antitrust and merger control, there are notable changes in jurisdiction, since the requirements of the EC Treaty and the ECSC differed. For antitrust, the Commission had exclusive jurisdiction under the ECSC regime, which meant that national authorities and national courts could not apply either Article 65 and 66 ECSC or their own national competition rules to deal with coal cases. This ceased to apply once the transition to the EC regime had been effected. The national authorities and courts responsible for competition are now competent to apply EC competition rules in the coal sector since they have direct effect. The Commission and the national authorities and courts therefore have parallel powers to apply EC competition law.[14] In cases where agreements or practices restricting competition or an abuse of a dominant position do *not* affect trade between Member States, Articles 81 and 82 will not apply and as a result only the relevant national law will be applied. By contrast, under Articles 65 and 66(7) ECSC, there were no conditions relating to effect on trade that would have the effect of limiting the Commission's jurisdiction.

8.13 With respect to merger control, there is a different jurisdictional change. The ECSC Treaty gave the Commission exclusive jurisdiction over all concentrations involving coal and steel undertakings. However, the EC Merger Regulation[15] gives the Commission a more limited jurisdiction: it is restricted to concentrations involving undertakings with a turnover that exceeds certain thresholds. As a result, some concentrations that would have required prior authorization from the Commission under the ECSC rules, but which do not meet the thresholds of the EC Merger Regulation, now fall outside the Commission's jurisdiction and are to be examined by the national authorities under whatever national merger rules apply.

---

[13] The measures for the implementation of the Protocol are set out in Council Decision of 1 February 2003, [2003] OJ L29/22.

[14] The only exception is Art 81(3) for which the Commission retains the sole competence (but note the impact of Council Regulation (EC) 1/2003 of 16 December 2002 on the implementation of the rules on competition laid down in Articles 81 and 82 of the Treaty [2003] OJ L1/1; see paras 11.06–11.20).

[15] Council Regulation (EC) 139/2004 of 20 January 2004 on the control of concentrations between undertakings [2004] OJ L24/1.

C. The Post-ECSC Treaty Arrangements

With respect to the substantive and procedural rules on antitrust, there are a number of differences. There are at least three substantive changes. First, the notion of an appreciable restriction of competition under Article 81(1) EC will be shaped by the Commission's policy concerning agreements of minor importance in terms of market share[16] (that is, agreements that are not therefore covered by Article 81(1)). This policy is now applied in full to the coal sector. Secondly, under the ECSC regime, joint ventures were usually covered by the provisions on concentrations under Article 66(1) to (6) ECSC. However, joint ventures notified after 23 July 2002 that lack the characteristics of a 'full-function' joint venture within the meaning of the EC Merger Regulation are to be regarded as agreements within the meaning of Article 81 EC. Where these undertakings conclude agreements, the latter are to be covered by the relevant provisions of Regulation (EC) 1/2003.[17] Finally, the system under the ECSC that required price lists and conditions of sale to be notified to the Commission and made public has been abolished. This means that undertakings wishing to make use of such data are no longer required to communicate it to the Commission before doing so.

8.14

There are a further three procedural changes. The first of these concerns transparency and is of relatively minor importance. As already mentioned, the Commission's efforts at promoting convergence of practice in the application of ECSC and EC rules date back many years. Procedural features such as access to the file, hearings, or the closing of a case with a comfort letter were introduced into ECSC practice on the basis of EC practice. The Commission expected the transparency of these practices to be enhanced as a result of the transition to the EC regime.[18] Secondly, two innovative factors are introduced into the coal sector with respect to agreements restricting competition. Where parties apply to the Commission for negative clearance or exemption, there is a requirement that the agreements as notified on form A/B are officially introduced. Secondly, prior consultation with an Advisory Committee is required before the adoption of any Commission decision that is mentioned in Article 14(1) of Regulation 1/2003. This will lead to the involvement of national competition authorities in the decision-making process. The third and final change in the procedural rules affecting antitrust is that the provisions implementing the ban on abuse of a dominant position are more straightforward under the EC regime than under the ECSC. Under the Article 66(7) ECSC procedure, the Commission had first to send the undertaking concerned

8.15

---

[16] Commission Notice on Agreements of Minor Importance which do not appreciably restrict competition under Article 81(1) of the Treaty establishing the European Community (de minimis) [2001] OJ C368/13.

[17] See n 14 above.

[18] Communication from the European Commission concerning certain aspects of the treatment of competition cases resulting from the expiry of the ECSC Treaty [2002] OJ C152/5, para 2.1.3.

a recommendation and only at that point was able to take a decision in consultation with the Member State concerned; under Article 82 EC the Commission is able to adopt directly applicable decisions. This is likely to prove considerably more onerous for dominant companies.

8.16 On merger control, there are few changes involved with respect to substantive and procedural law relating to concentrations. The substantive tests under Article 66(2) ECSC and Article 2 of the EC Merger Regulation are similar. The procedures for the treatment of concentrations were already aligned from March 1998 when the Commission applied the provisions of its Notice concerning alignment of procedures for processing mergers under the ECSC and EC Treaties.[19] One difference lies in the timing of notifications. The ECSC rules permitted notification of a proposed concentration at any time, although the legal completion of the proposal required the prior authorization of the Commission. The EC Merger Regulation requires the parties to notify within one week of the so-called triggering event, defined as the moment when the contractual agreement becomes irrevocable. After that event, the Commission is required to adopt its decision within the time-limits prescribed by the EC Merger Regulation. If it fails to do so, the proposal is authorized automatically.

8.17 In the final area of importance here, that of state aid control, the Commission introduced new rules in Regulation 1407/2002 with effect from 24 July 2002.[20] It expressly provided that aid covering costs for the period of 2002 prior to its entry into force may continue to be subject to the rules and principles laid down in Decision 3632/93/EC,[21] with the exception of rules on deadlines and procedures. This is activated by a request by a Member State. In terms of procedure, aid to the coal industry is now subject to special rules of notification, appraisal, and authorization as set out in the state aid regime under the Regulation.

(3) State Aids

8.18 Regulation 1407/2002 (the Coal Regulation) aims to make coal respond to the energy and sustainable development needs of the EU in the 21st century. In Article 1 it emphasizes that the rules for the grant of state aid to the coal industry have the aim of contributing to the restructuring process, but will also take into account the social and regional aspects of this process and the need to maintain—as a precautionary measure—a minimum quantity of indigenous coal production for security of supply purposes.

---

[19] [1998] OJ C66/36.
[20] [2002] OJ L205/1.
[21] [1993] OJ L329/12.

8.19 The Coal Regulation requires any grant of aid to comply with the provisions of Chapter 2, without prejudice to aid schemes concerning research and technological development or the environment or training. Aid is to be restricted to costs of coal for the generation of electricity, the combined generation of heat and electricity, the production of coke, and the fuelling of blast furnaces in the steel industry. Three kinds of aid are compatible with the proper functioning of the common market: aid that is granted for the reduction of activity (Article 4); aid granted for accessing of coal reserves (Article 5); and aid that is granted to cover exceptional costs (Article 7). The overall amount of aid to the coal industry that is granted in accordance with Articles 4 and 5 is required to follow a downward trend so that a significant reduction results (Article 6). No aid for the reduction of activity may be granted under Article 4 beyond 21 December 2007.

8.20 Among the specific requirements of Chapter 2, there are some worthy of note. The conditions for the grant of aid for the reduction of activity under Article 4 include the requirements that aid must not lead to any distortion of competition on the electricity market, or the market for combined heat and electricity generation, nor to the distortion of competition between coal buyers and users in the EU, nor may aid lead to delivered prices for coal to be lower than those for coal of a similar quality from third countries. Where aid is granted for accessing coal reserves, this may be for initial investment or for current production.

8.21 The Commission is required to report on the operation of the Coal Regulation to the Parliament, the Council, the Economic and Social Committee, and the Committee of the Regions. The deadline for this was 31 December 2006. The report has to cover its experience and any problems encountered in its application of the Regulation, and to evaluate the results of coal industry restructuring and its effects on the internal market, in the light of measures taken by Member States. This report also has to evaluate the contribution of indigenous coal to long-term energy security in the EU, taking into account developments in renewable energy.[22] This is to be part of a strategy of sustainable development and include an assessment of how much coal the EU needs to achieve that end. Further proposals may be included in the report for the amendment of the Coal Regulation with respect to its application to aid beyond 1 January 2008.[23]

(4) Decision-Making

8.22 A number of decisions have been taken by the Commission under the Coal Regulation since it entered into force. They have concerned several countries that joined the EU in 2003, but also France, Germany, Spain, and the UK.

---

[22] Coal Regulation, Art 11(2).
[23] ibid, Art 13(1).

Chapter 8: Coal

8.23 Several of the new member countries submitted restructuring plans to the Commission. The Commission approved plans by Poland and Hungary covering the years 2004 to 2006 and 2004 to 2010 respectively. Slovakia received authorization for aid to one of its three mining companies, HBP, in the years 2005 to 2010 to cover initial investments.[24] The aid measure does not exceed 30 per cent of the foreseen investment costs, and was therefore deemed to be compatible with the proper functioning of the common market.

8.24 Decisions have also been taken under the Regulation with respect to Member States whose coal industries were until 2002 subject to the legal regime of the ECSC. The Commission reviewed a restructuring plan and in approving it, commented on its forward-looking approach to the years 2011 and 2012.[25] A decision on aid for those years was only possible once a follow-up regulation to the Coal Regulation had been decided upon. If no such regulation was made, the aid for the years 2011 and 2012 would have to be assessed under Article 87 EC, the Commission observed. The Spanish coal industry has figured in a number of cases. These include grants of aid approved for the improvement of working safety and environmental protection in private coal mines in the Asturias;[26] an investigation into the grant of aid to a mining company that was originally subject to the ECSC Treaty;[27] and, at the end of 2005, a review of aid for restructuring measures to support the Spanish coal industry.[28]

8.25 The case involving the ECSC Treaty merits some comment. It turned on Decision 2002/827/ECSC which had been adopted on 2 July 2002 on the basis of the ECSC Treaty.[29] The Commission had ordered Spain to take all necessary measures to recover the aid granted in 1998 and 2000 to a mining company, González y Díez SA. The decision was challenged before the Court of First Instance. In order to overcome possible transitional problems and to respect the procedural rules that applied after the expiry of the ECSC Treaty, the Commission decided to reopen the investigation on the possible abuse of the aid and requested Spain to submit its comments on the aid which the Commission considered unlawful.[30]

---

[24] Commission Press Release IP/06/76, 'The Commission authorises Slovakia's investment plan for the coal industry for the years 2005 to 2010', 25 January 2006.
[25] State aid N 320/2004, 'Restructuring plan for the German coal industry 2006–2010', paras 129–31.
[26] Commission Press Release IP/03/95, 'Commission authorises the Principality of Asturias to grant aid to the coal industry', 21 January 2003.
[27] See para 8.10 above.
[28] Commission Press Release IP/05/1676, 'European Commission authorises restructuring measures to support the Spanish coal industry', 21 December 2005; Commission Press Release IP/04/413, 'Commission investigates new aid scheme for Spanish coal-mining companies', 30 March 2004.
[29] Commission Press Release IP/02/979, 'Commission approves aid to the Spanish coal industry for 2001 but calls for the reimbursement of aid granted in 1998, 2000 and 2001', 2 July 2002.
[30] Commission Press Release IP/03/251, 'Commission reopens procedure against coal mining company Gonzalez y Diez SA', 19 February 2003.

D. Conclusion

The Commission subsequently affirmed its earlier decision, concluding that the aid granted was unlawful.[31]

The Spanish case on restructuring aid was approved in 2005 after an investigation procedure started on 30 March 2004 in which the Commission assessed whether the notified restructuring measures could be legally justified. The measures covered the years 2003 to 2005, and involved a grant of approximately one billion Euros annually to its coal industry during this period. The Commission considered the plan to be insufficiently detailed. The Spanish Government provided additional information to the Commission, making it clear that the proposed restructuring measures would continue to reduce significantly the scale of state subsidies for the coal industry in Spain, while taking into account the social and regional importance of the industry. It was also seen to be reducing its mining capacity under the plan. As a result, the proposed aid was found to respect the provisions of the Coal Regulation and was therefore compatible with the proper functioning of the common market. Aid schemes have also been approved for France and the UK.[32] **8.26**

D. Conclusion

The driver for competition in the coal sector has been de facto the state aid controls since a measure of cushioning of the sector from the full blast of market forces has long been considered essential for reasons of social policy. The legal mechanism for achieving this has shifted from being largely the special sector treaty instrument of the ECSC to one of a general treaty instrument, the EC Treaty. An interesting new source of constraint on the operation of the market mechanism is the security of supply consideration which is explicitly recognized in the Coal Regulation. Nonetheless, the long-term aim of the legal regime for this sector is clearly one of normalization of the regulation of the sector in line with the EC Treaty rules. **8.27**

---

[31] Commission Press Release IP/03/1502, 'Commission decides aid to Spanish coal mining company has to be recovered', 5 November 2003.

[32] Commission Press Release IP/03/759, 'Commission authorises the United Kingdom to grant aid in respect of the closure of coal mines', 27 May 2003; Commission Press Release IP/03/881, United Kingdom authorised to grant investment aid to the coal industry', 24 June 2003.

9

NUCLEAR ENERGY

A. Introduction	9.01	(a) The Context	9.18
B. Euratom: A *Lex Specialis*		(b) The ENU Case	9.21
(1) Purpose	9.04	(c) The KLE Case	9.23
(2) Objectives and Implementation	9.07	(2) State Aids	9.29
(3) Institutional Features	9.12	(a) Restructuring	9.30
(4) Assessment	9.14	(b) Decommissioning	9.37
C. Competition Issues	9.16	D. Conclusions	9.38
(1) Supplies	9.17		

A. Introduction

Issues of competition in the nuclear sector have arisen in recent years more in relation to the operation of general rules on state aids than to the sector-specific law. Indeed, the framework of European law for this sector contrasts with that of all other energy sectors, since nuclear energy has its own special legal base in EC primary law, with a Treaty all to itself. There are differences of opinion about the applicability of general rules of EC law.[1] As a *lex specialis*, the applicable legal principle is that a specific law takes precedence over a general law (*lex specialis derogat legi generali*).[2] The relationship between the two Treaties is governed by Article 305(2) of the EC Treaty.[3] It is probably correct to state that where the European Atomic

9.01

---

[1] The various positions are summarized in a report produced by the International Nuclear Law Association Working Group on International Nuclear Trade, *Legal Certainty in International Nuclear Trade* (2001).

[2] Advocate General van Gerven, Conclusions of 27 October 1993, Case C-128/92 *HJ Banks & Co Ltd v British Coal Corporation* [1994] ECR I-1209, point 8.

[3] Art 305(2) EC states: 'The provisions of this Treaty shall not derogate from those of the Treaty Establishing the European Atomic Energy Community'. In the field of competition, there are some matters which are regulated such as supplies, investments, and joint undertakings, which suggests that competition rules are only partly applicable in the nuclear sector. In general, where Treaty rules do not regulate a specific matter, the EC Treaty rules will apply, including areas such as

Energy Community (Euratom) does not regulate a matter in detail, that matter is subject to EC rules. In this chapter, the relevant provisions of the primary and secondary legislation are considered, and then instances of interface between the competition law and sector rules. First, however, it is appropriate to summarize the main lines of policy that influence the nuclear sector and its immediate prospects.

9.02 The nuclear policy of the EU has been shaped in recent years by three key events. The first of these is the Chernobyl accident that occurred in 1987 in what is now the Ukraine. It illustrated dramatically the trans-boundary potential of nuclear accidents, and effectively brought to an end a long period of expansion in nuclear power. It triggered wide-ranging efforts to improve the health and safety environment for nuclear energy, which continue to this day.[4] The second was the enlargement of the EU in May 2004 which expanded significantly the number of Member States in the EU nuclear club. Among the new Member States, those with a heavy reliance upon nuclear energy include Lithuania, the Czech Republic, Hungary, and the Slovak Republic (and to a limited extent Slovenia). They also include countries that have nuclear power plants located close to their borders with neighbouring states, and the only remaining uranium mine in the EU, in the Czech Republic.[5] For the first time in five waves of accession since 1957, nuclear power played a significant role in the enlargement negotiations. Five of the ten countries entering in 2004 had between them a total of 19 reactors. They could be expected to have a relatively benign view of nuclear power in contrast to the negative view found among some of the 'older' Member States. In that sense, their views on nuclear power ensure that there is a greater balance of opinion among Member States.[6] A third event did not directly concern nuclear power at all. It was the interruption to EU gas supply from Russia via the Ukraine in January 2006. Although a very brief interruption to the gas flow to the eastern part of the EU, it provided Member States with a vivid reminder of the dangers of relying heavily upon

---

the harmonization of laws, the right of establishment, the free movement of capital, common commercial policy, and the power in Art 308 to deal with unexpected problems. Presumably, this would also include internal energy market measures.

[4] For an assessment of Euratom at the time of Chernobyl, see Grunwald, J, 'The Role of Euratom' in Cameron, P, et al (eds), *Nuclear Energy Law After Chernobyl* (1989) 33–48.

[5] Romania also has mines under production. The Czech mine operation was recently extended, and uranium exploration is ongoing in Finland, Sweden, and Slovakia: *ESA Annual Report 2005*, <http://ec.europa.eu/euratom/ar/ar2005.pdf> 4.

[6] However, the Accession Treaties included commitments to close down eight nuclear reactors in three of the new Member States, and specific provisions on nuclear safety. The three Member States were Lithuania, Slovakia, and Bulgaria. In each case, EU financial assistance was provided. For a discussion of the safety considerations, see European Commission, 'Communication from the Commission to the Council and the European Parliament: Nuclear Safety in the European Union', COM (2002) 605 final, 6 November 2002. An overview of the various concerns at the time by many of the key participants is contained in Horbach, NLJT, *Contemporary Developments in Nuclear Energy Law: Harmonising Legislation in CEEC/NIS* (1999).

imported gas from the East, and supported arguments in favour of diversification of sources of primary energy for electricity generation. In the background to this event was a slow but steady process of rethinking about energy security that had its roots in the 9/11 terrorist attack in the USA in 2001, but which has never been far from the surface in the European context.

Recent policy orientations on nuclear energy in the EU emphasize what might be called the 'public service' tasks:[7] the promotion of research and the dissemination of technical knowledge; implementing nuclear safeguards to ensure that nuclear materials are not diverted from their intended peaceful uses (non-proliferation); and protection of the health and safety of EU citizens. The concern over health protection has been interpreted by the Commission as encompassing radiation protection and nuclear safety, an interpretation that has been supported by ECJ.[8] There are current efforts to expand it further to include the management of radioactive waste.[9] Another objective of current nuclear policy is a continuation of the long-term commitment to increasing security of energy supply through a greater diversification of sources. Finally, mention should be made of the claims made for nuclear energy as a contributor to meeting climate change targets and reducing the impact of greenhouse gases on the atmosphere. Against that possible benefit in terms of sustainability, there are the long-term consequences of radioactive waste that arise from nuclear energy use. 9.03

B. Euratom: A *Lex Specialis*

(1) Purpose

The principal source of European law on the nuclear energy sector is the Treaty Establishing the European Atomic Energy Community (hereafter either Euratom or Community), which was signed on 17 April 1957.[10] Since its adoption, it has been supplemented by a variety of Directives, Regulations, and Decisions on nuclear energy matters. However, in contrast to Article 97 of the former ECSC Treaty, 9.04

---

[7] See, eg, De Esteban, F, 'The Future of Nuclear Energy in the European Union', Background Paper, 23 May 2002 (personal views of Deputy DG of DG TREN, European Commission).
[8] Case C-29/99 *Commission v Council*, 10 December 2002; see also the Opinion of Advocate-General Jacobs delivered on 13 December 2001.
[9] European Commission, Amended Proposal for a Council Directive (Euratom) laying down basic obligations and general principles on the safety of nuclear installations, and on the safe management of the spent fuel and radioactive waste, COM (2004) 526. A further proposal for a Directive was made in December 2005, concerning the supervision and control of shipments of radioactive waste and spent nuclear fuel (that is, nuclear fuel that has been removed from a nuclear reactor after use).
[10] For a comprehensive overview of the Treaty, see Grunwald, J, *Das Energierecht der Europäischen Gemeinschaften* (2003) 193–308.

it has no built-in time-limit. Its overall aim was to act both as a vehicle for the promotion of nuclear energy for civil purposes and as a means of regulating the emerging nuclear industry. This goal of promotion is spelled out in Article 1 of the Treaty, which states that:

> It shall be the task of the [Atomic Energy] Community to contribute to the raising of the standard of living in the Member States and to the development of relations with the other countries by creating the conditions necessary for the speedy establishment and growth of nuclear industries.

9.05 The origins of this goal lay in the perception of nuclear energy as an alternative safe source of energy for European countries. At the time it was drafted, the growing dependence upon imported sources of oil from the Middle East, and the uncertainties following the Suez crisis, plus the limited growth potential of coal and geographic constraints on hydro-power, all combined to reinforce that perception. At the same time, the very considerable investment that would be required to fund the development of the nuclear fuel cycle was beyond the financial means of individual European countries and this too provided an impetus to co-operation in a Community structure. The latter goal has since fallen into abeyance, partly due to the lack of consensus on nuclear energy among the Member States, and partly because the nuclear industry is well established and needs little of this kind of support from the EU. Perceptions of nuclear energy have also become somewhat more complex.

9.06 With respect to competition matters, a key difference between the two Treaties was evident at the outset. The Euratom Treaty was designed to promote a highly specialized industry which at the time of signature was virtually non-existent in Europe. The EC Treaty had as its main aim a general economic integration by means of fairly strict legal rules. The aim of those rules was to ensure competition in all of the industrial and economic sectors of the signatory States, which were deemed to have already reached a level of maturity.

(2) Objectives and Implementation

9.07 Euratom has various tasks, including the promotion of research, establishment of safety standards, facilitation of investment, ensuring all users receive a regular and equitable supply of ores and nuclear fuels, and ensuring that nuclear materials are not diverted to purposes other than the peaceful ones they were intended for (non-proliferation).[11] Among the stated goals of the Treaty was the creation of a nuclear common market in the goods and products involved in the use of nuclear energy.[12] To this end, Article 93 provides for an abolition of all customs duties on imports and exports, charges with equivalent effect, and all quantitative restrictions

---

[11] Art 2 Euratom.
[12] ibid, Art 2 and Ch IX.

B. Euratom: A Lex Specialis

in imports and exports in internal trade. Article 96 provides for free movement of workers with specialist skills in the nuclear energy sector.

Significant efforts have been made by the Community to achieve the task of establishing uniform safety standards to protect the health of workers and the general public and ensuring that they are applied.[13] The Commission (the implementing agency under the Treaty) has the power to require Member States to implement safety directives and to ensure that they are enforced.[14] Some Member States have been reluctant to allow the Commission to regulate nuclear power in a comprehensive way. Health and safety are covered only to a very limited extent under Euratom, but efforts have been made to use Chapter III as a legal base for a number of measures and proposals on basic safety standards by the Commission. 9.08

Directives have been made under the Treaty to lay down radiation standards for health protection.[15] The aim of these Directives has been to ensure that Community citizens are adequately protected to internationally agreed levels, and that all exposures are adequately regulated and kept as low as is reasonably achievable (the ALARA principle). Radioactivity levels are monitored by the EC through national reporting.[16] These measures should not be confused with the more recent package of safety measures that are intended to provide a more comprehensive regulation. These include measures taken and/or proposed in the setting of standards for operational safety, radioactive waste management, and rules on the funding of decommissioning.[17] 9.09

Safety is, however, only one of the eight tasks listed in Article 2 Euratom. Other tasks that are more relevant to this chapter are in Article 2(c), (d) and (g). They state that the Community shall: 9.10

(c) facilitate investment and ensure, particularly by encouraging ventures on the part of undertakings, the establishment of the basic installations necessary for the development of nuclear energy in the Community;
(d) ensure that all users in the Community receive a regular and equitable supply of ores and nuclear fuels, and . . .
(g) ensure wide commercial outlets and access to the best technical facilities by the creation of a common market in specialised materials and equipment, by the free movement of capital for investment in the field of nuclear energy and by freedom of employment for specialists within the Community.

The second of the above objectives, (d), is concerned with security of supply, and relates mainly to Chapter VI (Supplies). Objective (c) relates mainly to Chapter V 9.11

---

[13] ibid, Arts 2(b), 30, 31.
[14] ibid, Arts 33, 38.
[15] Directive (Euratom) 76/579 [1976] OJ L187/1; Directive (Euratom) 79/343 [1979] OJ L83/18; Directive (Euratom) 80/836 [1980] OJ L246/1; Directive (Euratom) 84/467 [1984] OJ L265/4.
[16] Art 34 Euratom.
[17] See n 6 above.

(Investment) but has some influence on Chapter VI. Their practical implementation is elaborated in these Chapters and also Chapter IX (The nuclear common market). A number of potentially market distorting features are evident, however. These include:

- The operation of the Euratom Loan Facility. By virtue of Articles 6, 47, 72, 171, 172, and 174 Euratom, the Community may participate directly in investments. Since 1977 the Commission has been empowered to issue loans to contribute to the financing of nuclear power stations. About a hundred loans have been awarded by Euratom for the construction of nuclear power plants and facilities inside and outside the EU, which has the potential to give a market advantage to nuclear energy in the internal electricity market.
- Tax exemptions that may be enjoyed by joint undertakings which receive a special status under the Treaty (Chapter V and Annex III). The name is misleading since the Treaty does not require that these are to be 'joint ventures' involving two or more Member States.
- The interventionist role of the ESA in pursuit of security of supply (Chapter VI).

(3) Institutional Features

9.12 There are a number of institutional features that also require comment. A key feature of the Treaty is the degree of control in law-making that is exercised by the Council and the Commission in relation to the Parliament. There is no co-decision procedure for its operational functions. Under Article 31 Euratom the Council only has to request the opinion of the Parliament. In this sense, the competence structure is very different from that of the EC Treaty where Parliament and the Council have the leading role in law-making, with the Commission taking the role as initiator of legislation. When the European Convention was discussing the draft Treaty establishing a Constitution for Europe, there was a proposal to incorporate the Euratom Treaty into the new structure (see para 9.14, and paras 2.56–2.63). Such a change would have increased the scope for Parliamentary scrutiny of Euratom, in line with the competence of Parliament over environmental issues that has grown in recent years. This was unsuccessful and the Treaty remained outside the proposed framework. The institution that has the key decision-making role remains the Council of Ministers.

9.13 Another notable feature is the establishment of a Euratom Supply Agency (ESA) under the Treaty, supervised by the Commission. Its task is to ensure a regular and equitable supply of ores and nuclear fuels for all EU users. It has a combination of market and planned economy characteristics, and is required to pursue the aim of long-term security of supply through a diversification of supply sources and avoidance of excessive dependence upon any one source. In a context of liberalized electricity markets and fair trade, it is required to ensure that the viability of the

European nuclear industry is maintained.[18] At the time of its creation, the US government had ownership of fissile material and a monopoly on the offer of nuclear materials and services, and there was strict governmental control over the nuclear industry with few commercial applications. In this context of perceived scarcity of source material, the ESA was to be the European 'owner' and supplier to EU users, as a counterweight to US dominance. Now, however, there is a relatively open commercial market for the European nuclear industry, with support and monitoring by the ESA over the contractual landscape of the fuel cycle operations.

(4) **Assessment**

The Treaty remains the primary source of competence for the Commission in this area. Given the considerable changes that have taken place since the Treaty was drawn up, both in terms of attitudes to nuclear energy and in terms of EU membership, it is not surprising that there should have been questions about its continued relevance, at least in its present form. Many of the doubts coalesced at the time when the proposal was under discussion to introduce a draft Constitution. Various arguments were advanced to have the Euratom Treaty abolished or absorbed into the new draft Treaty or into the existing EC Treaty,[19] but ultimately, it was decided to retain the separate treaty instrument for the nuclear sector (see para 9.12, and paras 2.56–2.63). 9.14

The interaction between the Treaty support for nuclear energy and the trends in energy law and policy in the EU generally does give rise to some issues. Three deserve particular mention. First, the absence of provision for decommissioning under the Treaty or for the management of high-level radioactive waste means that there are important—and costly—subjects to be tackled by Member States in a way that avoids the market distorting impacts of subsidies or other support schemes. In the context of the EU's ongoing programme of market liberalization, this is an issue that will have to be addressed in a way that contributes to a pro-competitive solution. Secondly, the considerable importance played by environmental and sustainability considerations in all EC policy-making, including energy, raises questions about the legal framework for the long-term management of high-level radioactive waste,[20] a matter that will require at least some elaboration 9.15

---

[18] ESA, Advisory Committee Task Force on Security of Supply, *Analysis of the Nuclear Field Availability at EU*, Final Report of the Task Force, June 2005, 6.

[19] See, eg, the contribution to the European Convention by Ms Marie Nagy, Ms Renee Wagner and Sir Neil MacCormick, alternate members of the Convention: 'The Future of the Euratom Treaty in the Framework of the European Constitution', CONV 563/03, 18 February 2003.

[20] This has however been addressed at the multilateral level in the Joint Convention to which the EC and its Member States are parties: see Cameron, P, 'Joint Convention on the Safety of Spent Fuel Management and on the Safety of Radioactive Waste Management' in Horbach, NLJT, *Contemporary Developments in Nuclear Energy Law: Harmonising Legislation in CEEC/NIS* (1999) 117–28.

of the current Treaty provisions. Finally, the issue of security of supply that has played such an important part in the Treaty from its origins has developed—in large part—independently from the role of such concerns in the EC Treaty. In the current climate, and in the context of the liberalizing energy markets, some greater connection between the two seems appropriate.

C. Competition Issues

9.16 In the following sections three issues concerning competition and nuclear energy are discussed. They involve, first, the interventionist consequences of the common supply policy, and then, two instances of state aids granted by Member States.

(1) Supplies

9.17 The ESA is established by Article 52 Euratom and operates under the supervision of the Commission.[21] It exercises its powers within the framework of a common supply policy, and under Article 52(2)(b) has two fundamental rights: a right of option on ores, source materials, and special fissile materials produced in the Community; and an exclusive right to conclude contracts relating to the supply of ores, source materials, and special fissile materials coming from inside or outside the Community. In practice, Community users negotiate supply contracts for ores and raw materials (mainly natural uranium) directly with the suppliers of their choice and then they submit these contracts for co-signature by the ESA. The ESA takes a decision and delivers reasons in the event of a refusal within ten working days. The same procedure applies to contracts relating to special fissile materials such as contracts for enrichment and for the supply of enriched uranium or plutonium. In the 1990s it developed a new policy with respect to imports of materials from Russia and other countries of the former Soviet Union. This operated to restrict such imports into the Community, and was the subject of challenge before the ECJ and the Court of First Instance (CFI). The two judgments are notable in confirming the wide discretionary powers of the ESA.

(a) The Context

9.18 The former Soviet Union (FSU) had been a supplier of enrichment services under long-term contracts and at prices comparable to those in the EU. Between 1990 and 1992 it expanded this role to include that of supplier of uranium. The countries of the FSU increased their share of the market in natural uranium from zero in 1989 to about 25 per cent in 1992 and 1993. The increase in market share was

---

[21] For an authoritative examination of the subject see Bouquet, A, 'The Euratom provisions on nuclear supply and ownership' (2001) 68 Nuclear Law Bulletin 1–32.

C. Competition Issues

achieved largely by the very low prices charged, well below production costs in Europe and other Western countries. Following a number of requests for protection by EU suppliers and concerned about the continuation of this upward trend, the ESA devised a policy on acquisitions originating from Russia and other FSU producers. This was based on two objectives contained in the Euratom Treaty: those of industry viability and long-term security of supply contained in Article 2(c) and (d) and the instruments described in Chapter VI (the exclusive right to conclude contracts and in some cases to refuse to conclude them or to impose certain conditions). This new policy was publicized in the EU[22] and mentioned in the ESA's annual reports. The policy contains two elements: a limitation of the FSU supplies which Community users may acquire and a recommendation to apply market-related prices. The restriction on supplies is applied to users in such a way as to avoid the rigidities of a quota system, but also to prevent certain users from obtaining a privileged access to the FSU source.[23] Adopting a flexible procedure to meet users' requests, the ESA took each decision according to the circumstances of the case made to it (taking into account the contract portfolio, long-term strategy, and diversification aspects). The effect was that some users had their opportunities to purchase FSU materials considerably reduced. The policy was defended by the then Competition Commissioner Sir Leon Brittan:

> Massive imports at extremely low prices coming from the CIS republics risk endangering the diversification of the Community's supply sources and hence its long-term security of supply and the viability of its production industries. That is why the Supply Agency, in exercising its right to conclude contracts, is ensuring that the Community does not become overdependent beyond reasonable limits on any single source of supply and that the acquisition of nuclear materials from CIS republics takes place at prices related to those on the market: that is to say prices that reflect cost of production and are compatible with prices of producers in market economy countries.[24]

A little later, the policy was given support in the 1995 White Paper on Energy Policy: 'With these factors in mind, the Euratom Supply Agency and the Commission are applying a policy which aims at diversification of sources'.[25]

9.19 This policy was challenged directly or indirectly in two separate cases: the first involved the Empresa Nacional de Uranio (ENU), a small-scale producer of natural

---

[22] Lennartz, R and Bouquet, A, 'The Legal Framework of the EAEC Common Supply Policy in Nuclear Materials in the Light of the "ENU" and "KLE" Cases' (1996) 27 Energy in Europe 21–27, 22.
[23] Privileged access would be contrary to Art 52(2)(a).
[24] Statement in the European Parliament by Sir Leon Brittan on behalf of the Commission, Oral question H-1087, OJ Annex Proceedings of the European Parliament, No 424, 18 November 1992, 227, and Reply by Sir Leon Brittan on behalf of the Commission to Written question E-2042/93, [1994] OJ C219/58.
[25] *White Paper: An Energy Policy for the European Union*, COM (95) 682, December 1995, para 79.

uranium in Portugal; the second involved a German company called Kernkraftwerke Lippe-Ems (KLE), the operator of a uranium plant and a uranium user. In the first case, ENU challenged the ESA and the Commission for failing to guarantee the sale of its production of uranium (not the policy itself). In the second case, the policy was challenged by a user who maintained that the ESA had no right to refuse or to impose conditions on the conclusion of contracts, even if the contracts were, in the ESA's view, contrary to the Treaty.

9.20 It should be noted, however, that the context in which this policy was developed was overtaken by events during the later 1990s. The operating environment for the market in nuclear materials changed dramatically with the impending enlargement of the EU and the impact of nuclear disarmament agreements. The enlargement to the East meant that countries became members which used Soviet-made reactors for electricity generation and for which Russia was in practice the only fuel supplier. In addition, the prices for natural uranium increased dramatically.[26]

(b) The ENU Case

9.21 ENU was a small-scale producer of natural uranium in Portugal, which was unable to sell its production locally and so had to find other markets. Facing increasing difficulties in the late 1980s, it requested the ESA for assistance in selling its production, offering all of its stocks and future production to the ESA. On 21 December 1990 it submitted a request to the Commission, based on Article 53 Euratom. It argued that the Treaty provides for a Community preference prohibiting imports as long as Community production is available at 'normal' prices. The ESA should be directed to implement the mechanisms of Chapter VI (that is, to exercise its right of option under Article 57 Euratom and purchase ENU's output) and undertake an investigation into the provision of supplies to users from outside the Community, discuss compensation and adopt a 'special course of action' to solve the problem forthwith. In its decision the Commission stated that the Treaty and the ESA implementing rules provided a mechanism for balancing supply and demand, taking into account the prevailing conditions of supply, and allowing the ESA to exercise its rights to conclude contracts and its right of option by signing contracts negotiated directly between users and producers. Further, there was no such Community preference in either the Treaty or the secondary legislation, so the ESA was not required to impose on Community users an obligation to give preference to Community producers for their supplies.[27]

---

[26] For background to this, see the *ESA Annual Report 2005*.
[27] Commission Decision 93/428/Euratom of 19 July 1993 on a procedure for the application of the second paragraph of Article 53 of the EAEC Treaty [1993] OJ L197/54.

C. Competition Issues

The matter was appealed to the CFI by ENU. The Court held that the Treaty contains no provisions for ensuring preferential treatment with respect to the sale of Community production, in contrast to the preference in favour of Community users, as shown in the right of option in Article 52(2)(b), in Article 57, and in the export scheme provided for in Article 59(b).[28] The Court therefore concluded that 'the Agency would not be able therefore to oppose imports . . . at prices lower than those asked for by Community producers, unless such imports threatened to jeopardise attaining the Treaty's objectives, notably by their impact on supply sources'.[29] In this case, the threat to ENU's production, which amounted to no more than 1.5 per cent of Community consumption, did not jeopardize security of supplies. The proposed interpretation of the Treaty provisions was rejected by the Court, and this decision was subsequently endorsed by the ECJ in an appeal.[30]

9.22

(c) The KLE Case

KLE submitted a supply contract to the ESA for 400 tonnes of uranium between itself and British Nuclear Fuels Limited plc, under Article 52 Euratom. Since the price level was unusually low, the ESA asked the parties to provide additional information on the origin of the uranium. BNFL disclosed that it would be sourced from the FSU, probably Russia. KLE had already contracted large quantities of uranium from this source and so, in the ESA's view, had no right to enjoy a privileged position in relation to other users (Article 52(2)(a)), and so decided that the contract could be concluded but only on condition that the uranium did not come from the FSU countries. KLE referred the matter to the Commission, arguing that the attachment of conditions to the conclusion of a contract constituted the application of an interventionist policy that was not provided for under the Treaty. It requested the Commission to order the ESA to compensate it for the loss that it would incur by being obliged to conclude a replacement contract at a higher price for uranium sourced from an alternative area. The Commission rejected KLE's requests,[31] arguing that the ESA is not under an obligation to meet orders when there are legal and material obstacles to their execution. If the ESA were to meet the order and so provide a privileged position for certain users it would contravene Article 52(2) of the Treaty. Moreover, under the ESA's Regulation, Article 5(b), it is entitled to refuse to conclude a contract.

9.23

Three other claims made by KLE were rebutted by the Commission in its decision of 21 February 1994. The first concerned diversification of sources of supply.

9.24

---

[28] Joined Cases T 458 & 523/93 *ENU v Commission* [1995] ECR II-2459.
[29] ibid, para 64.
[30] Case C-357/95 *ENU v Commission* [1997] ECR I-1329.
[31] Commission Decision 94/285/Euratom of 21 February 1994 relating to a procedure in application of the second paragraph of Article 53 of the Euratom Treaty [1994] OJ L122/30.

In KLE's view, the ESA was not empowered to take interventionist measures on the market or to impose price controls, thereby establishing a policy of diversifying sources of supply. The Commission took the view that the common supply policy in Article 52 had to be directed to the security of supply objective in Article 2(d) and (c) which requires the Commission to ensure the establishment of the basic installations necessary for the development of nuclear energy in the Community. The legal instruments for implementing this diversification policy included the right of the ESA to decide whether and with which partners it concludes contracts for the supply of ores, source materials, or special fissile materials from outside the Community. It may also determine the ways and means that such supplies are delivered. Where supplies are available at prices that are unrelated to market conditions, the Commission must take that into account when exercising its exclusive right to conclude contracts. A second line of argument concerned the ESA's competence to take commercial policy measures. These could only be adopted on the basis of Article 133 EC. The Commission's view was that the Euratom Treaty takes precedence over the provisions of the EC Treaty since it is a sectoral treaty which contains special rules on a common supply policy that also extends to supplies from outside the Community. It argued that this precedence derives both from Article 305(2) EC and from the fact that both Communities were established, from a legal, organizational, and institutional viewpoint, as two mutually independent Communities. Finally, KLE argued that by limiting imports from the former Soviet Union, the ESA forced users to purchase uranium at excessively high prices. The Commission noted that the ESA's decision referred to market-related prices, which means prices that reflect production costs and are consistent with the prices charged in market-based economies. In addition, the common supply policy had also to take into account the long-term supply contracts which the Community had concluded with a number of third countries.

9.25 The case was appealed by KLE to the CFI. In its judgment, the Court held that the operation of the supply system had to be considered in the light of the objectives of the Community. The ESA has the task of guaranteeing 'one of the essential aims which the Treaty assigns to the Community, in Article 2(d), namely reliability of supplies'.[32] Article 52(2)(b) Euratom establishes the ESA expressly for that purpose and confers on it in principle exclusive rights to ensure that Community users receive regular and equitable supplies of nuclear materials both from Community and non-member countries. To perform its task, the ESA has the exclusive right to conclude contracts for the supply of those products from inside and outside the Community. While the ESA must in general observe the principle

---

[32] Joined Cases T 149 & 181/94 *KLE v Commission*, CFI (First Chamber, extended composition), 25 February 1997, para 85.

C. Competition Issues

of balancing supply and demand in exercising its exclusive right to conclude supply contracts, it also has to ascertain on a case-by-case basis whether there are any legal or material obstacles to meeting the order. In this respect, where decisions concerning its economic and commercial policy and nuclear policy are concerned, the ESA has a broad discretion when exercising its powers. This factor limits the scope of any review by the CFI to that of identifying any manifestly wrong assessment or misuse of power.[33]

The CFI held that the ESA may lawfully bar imports of nuclear materials if those imports are liable to jeopardize the achievement of aims of the Treaty, 'in particular by their effect on sources of supply'.[34] This risk may be classified as a legal obstacle to meeting an order within the meaning of Article 61 Euratom. It added: 9.26

> in order to ensure geographic diversification of external sources of supply, the Agency has a discretion—exercising its exclusive right to conclude contracts for the supply of ores and other nuclear fuels so as to ensure reliability of supplies in accordance with the principle of equal access to resources, in conformity with the task conferred on it by the Treaty—to bar certain imports of uranium which would reduce such diversification.[35]

This is further justified by the fact that the materials are not being imported at market-related prices and they give one user a privileged position in relation to competitors. The application by the ESA of a permissible threshold of dependence, set by reference to the state of the market at a maximum percentage of individual users' consumption, is a legitimate means of guaranteeing equal access to resources, in line with Article 52(2) Euratom.

The case was subsequently appealed to the ECJ but the appeal was rejected.[36] 9.27

In 2006, the ECJ handed down a judgment which by an indirect effect qualified the *KLE* decision. In *INB*,[37] the ECJ limited the categories of contracts that the ESA has responsibility for. A contract for the enrichment of uranium does not qualify as an operation for the supply and production of nuclear fuels (as in the *KLE* case). Instead, it falls within the exceptions listed in Article 75 Euratom, first paragraph. The Treaty itself does not provide a classification of uranium enrichment activities 9.28

---

[33] ibid, para 90; citing Joined Cases T 458 & 523/93 *ENU v Commission* [1995] ECR II-2459, para 67.
[34] ibid, para 92.
[35] ibid, para 92. This is elaborated in para 112: 'the Community cannot afford to give some non-member countries, to the detriment of all others, privileged access in the short term to the Community market and thereby enable those non-member countries to acquire a dominant position and eject from the market partners who have been operating there for a long time, including developing countries'. At the time, demand far exceeded production capacity.
[36] Case C-161/97 *KLE v Commission* [1999] ECR I-2057.
[37] Joined Cases C 123 & 124/04 *Industrias Nucleares do Brasil SA, Siemens AG v UBS AG and Texas Utilities Electric Corporation*, 12 September 2006.

since, at the time it was drafted, such activities had not been developed on a commercial scale.[38] However, the ECJ followed the Advocate General's opinion that enrichment consists in the provision of a service carried out on materials delivered by a third party and placed at that party's disposal. To the extent that the aim is to process goods in transit, on behalf of a foreign national, and not to supply the Community with nuclear materials, the supply and ownership rules of the Euratom Treaty should not be applied to it. Essentially, there are commercial relations that are outside the Community's control. The purpose of the exceptions set out in Article 75 is to ensure that the Euratom supply system does not extend to technical operations or commercial relationships which have no direct effect on supplies to users in the Community. The key to this provision is the idea that commitments which do not entail a transfer affecting Community users are removed from the scope of Community rights, even if they involve a movement of nuclear materials in the Community.

(2) State Aids

9.29 The interplay between Euratom and issues concerning state aids is illustrated below by two instances where the rules interfaced. The outcomes are unfortunately not very clear. The subject of state aids is discussed in greater detail in Chapter 15.

(a) Restructuring

9.30 The UK Government granted restructuring aid to British Energy in 2003 after the company experienced severe financial difficulties. Several of the measures proposed concerned issues covered by the Euratom Treaty, as well as the EC Treaty rules on state aids. The Commission analyzed the restructuring plan which confers a selective competitive advantage in a sector in which there is intra-Community trade, and opened procedures against the package.[39]

9.31 In 2004 the Commission decided on a wide-ranging restructuring plan that was submitted by British Energy.[40] The company is the operator of eight nuclear power stations in the UK, and was the only private operator of nuclear power stations. It supplied electricity on the UK wholesale market and is a supplier of large and commercial enterprises, but not retail customers. The need for a restructuring plan (supported by the State) arose from a significant fall in electricity prices in 2002. The revenue loss could not be offset by electricity trading nor by direct sales to large business customers, also known as Direct Supply to Business (DSB).

---

[38] Opinion of AG Maduro, 6 April 2006, para 42.
[39] Commission, Notice under Article 88(2) EC [2003] OJ C180/5.
[40] Commission Press Release IP/04/1125, 'Commission approves restructuring of British Energy', 22 September 2004.

C. Competition Issues

The Commission's approval was given subject to certain conditions. British Energy had to ring-fence the nuclear generation branch of its activities that are entitled to receive state aid. This aid is destined for decommissioning the nuclear power plants in the future. Such aid may not be used to subsidize competitive activities, such as the operation of a fossil fuel power plant or energy trading with large business customers. 9.32

Three conditions were attached to the grant in all. The ring-fencing requirement means that British Energy will create three separate businesses which each have their own separate accounts. These are to comprise the business concerned with nuclear generation, which will operate the company's eight nuclear power plants in the UK, the unit concerned with non-nuclear generation, and finally a unit concerned with DSB. 9.33

The other two conditions were that British Energy had to cap its production capacity, including nuclear capacity, for a period of six years. British Energy was required not to extend its activities in fossil fuels outside the UK and is prevented from acquiring large hydro-power plants from its competitors in the UK. This prohibition does not apply, however, to investments in renewable energy sources, since fostering renewable energy sources is a stated objective of EU environmental policy. Finally, British Energy was not allowed to undercut prices that its non-aided competitors are unable to afford in the DSB market. For a period of five years the company may not set its DSB prices below the prices that prevail in the wholesale part of the market. 9.34

There is to be monitoring of adherence to this condition by an independent entity, which the UK Government is to designate through a transparent tendering procedure under the auspices of the DTI. 9.35

In the Commission's press release there is no information about how the Euratom issues were resolved before reaching this decision.[41] 9.36

(b) Decommissioning

In December 2004 the Commission announced its intention to investigate the UK Government's plans to establish a Nuclear Decommissioning Fund (NDA).[42] A number of nuclear sites were to be transferred to the NDA as would a number of nuclear power stations. Liabilities of commercial companies were to be taken over to the amount of up to two billion pounds for decommissioning purposes. The UK argued that decommissioning activities and their treatment, reprocessing, and 9.37

---

[41] But see the summary in the Offer for Sale, British Energy Group plc, 2005, 353–7.
[42] [2004] OJ C315/4. In this context, note the adoption of a recommendation on the use of decommissioning funds: Commission Press Release IP/06/1466: 'Commission adopts a recommendation on the efficient use of nuclear decommissioning funds', 24 October 2006.

disposal of nuclear waste are not activities within competitive markets. The financial support will not then affect competition and intra-Community trade. The Commission considered that the measure fell within the scope of Article 87(1) EC. However, the UK argued that the restructuring measures contribute to the attainment of Euratom objectives and especially to safe and effective waste management. The Commission nonetheless took the view that, to the extent that the measure is not necessary for or goes beyond the objectives of the Euratom Treaty or distorts or threatens to distort competition in the internal market, it has to be assessed under the EC Treaty. The Commission therefore asked for detailed information on the markets served by the entities that are the primary beneficiaries of the measure. There appeared to be some doubt in the Commission's thinking as to whether the positive elements in the package could outweigh the impact on trading conditions.

D. Conclusions

9.38 In this overview of the legal framework applicable to competition issues in the nuclear sector, the key role is clearly played by the *lex specialis*, the Euratom Treaty. The impact of the change in circumstances of the nuclear industry from the time when it was drafted and its contemporary application is illustrated by the state aid cases considered in section C. Not only do they reveal an interplay between the rules of the EC Treaty and Euratom which is less than satisfactory, but in the *British Energy* case the problem to be addressed is one that arises from a process that was inconceivable at the time that the Euratom Treaty was signed: the liberalization of electricity markets. While much of the debate in the context of the draft Constitution for Europe focused on the alleged redundancy of a *lex specialis* or the lack of scrutiny it entailed, a more powerful argument might have been that the impact of market liberalization is already undermining the separateness of the EU nuclear industry from other parts of the energy economy, even if this is more apparent in some Member States than in others. From an international perspective, nuclear markets have become increasingly subject to competition, the once-pervasive state influence on those markets through publicly-owned companies has declined, and the monitoring of abuse of dominant positions or monopolies is increasing. Among the many consequences of liberalization, nuclear power generators have to compete with non-nuclear generators in the sale price of their electricity. An increasingly fluid pattern of demand also works against the construction of nuclear power stations (slow and expensive) in favour of power stations requiring less investment which can follow demand more closely and adapt to it. The circumstances of the *British Energy* case underline the new economic context for nuclear power and at the same time raise questions about the appropriateness of state intervention to address the effects of the market.

D. Conclusions

The legal order for EU nuclear energy has yet to adapt to this new context. Increasingly, the rules of EC competition law are becoming relevant to its operations. The rules of Articles 81 and 82 do not provide for exclusions for the nuclear industry in their scope of application. Merger control too is applicable and has indeed been applied to the nuclear sector (see paras 11.22 and 14.01). The position with respect to state aids is less clear.[43] The interface between the rules in both treaties is likely to become a matter that will arise with greater frequency as the wider impact of electricity market reform is felt and the more integrated character of the nuclear industry becomes more evident. The only exception to this concerns security of supply (see Chapter 18). The increased concerns of Member States about this are likely to guarantee a minimum level of intervention in the nuclear sector for some time to come. In this respect, as the *INB* case shows, Member States are keen to limit any further centralization of power in the ESA. Oversight of activities not deemed to fall within the scope of its monitoring mandate is to remain at Member State level, in line with a familiar pattern in EU energy law and policy.

9.39

---

[43] See n 1 above. However, see the positive note struck by the Commission in its *Nuclear Illustrative Programme*, COM (2006) 844 final, 10 January 2007, 12–13.

10

RENEWABLE ENERGY

A. Introduction	10.01	(4) Guarantee of Electricity Origin	10.21
B. The Renewables Directive		(5) Regulation	10.24
(1) Aims and Scope	10.04	(6) Grid System Issues	10.28
(2) National Indicative Targets	10.07	(7) Reporting Requirements	10.32
(3) Support Schemes	10.09	(8) The Relevance of State Aid Control	10.34
(a) The Renewables Obligation		(9) Implementation	10.38
in the UK	10.20	C. Conclusions	10.39

A. Introduction

The promotion of renewable energy has become an important plank in EU energy policy, in line with its strategic role in most Member States' energy and environmental policies. This commitment is evident in a number of EU documents, from the Green Paper on Energy Policy[1] to the title of the principal legal measure applicable to the renewable energy sector, Directive (EC) 2001/77:[2] 'the *promotion* of electricity from renewable energy sources in the internal electricity market' ('the Renewables Directive'). The principal drivers behind it are its contribution to

10.01

---

[1] European Commission, *A European Strategy for Sustainable, Competitive and Secure Energy*, COM (2006) 105 final, 8 March 2006. For a long-term vision, see the Commission's *Renewable Energy Road Map*, COM (2006) 848 final, 10 January 2007.

[2] Directive (EC) 2001/77 on the promotion of electricity produced from renewable energy sources in the internal electricity market [2001] OJ L283/33. Other documents in which its importance is emphasized include: *Energy for the Future: Renewable Sources of Energy*, COM (1997) 599 final; *Towards a European Strategy for the Security of Energy Supply*, COM (2000) 769 final; *On energy efficiency or doing more with less*, COM (2005) 265 final; Directive (EC) 96/92 concerning common rules for the internal market in electricity [1997] OJ L27/20, Art 8(3); Directive (EC) 2003/54 concerning common rules for the internal market in electricity and repealing Directive (EC) 96/92 [2003] OJ L176/37, Art 14(7); Decision 1230/2003/EC of the European Parliament and the Council of 26 June 2003 concerning a multi-annual programme for action in the field of energy [2003] OJ L176/29; Decision 1513/2002/EC of the European Parliament and the Council of 29 August 2002 concerning the Sixth Framework Programme of the European Community for research, technological development and demonstration activities (2002–2006) [2002] OJ L232/13.

security and diversification of energy supply within the EU and its role in meeting the EU targets with respect to climate change by substituting for fossil fuels. Other benefits include the creation of employment, positive impacts on social cohesion, and improvements to air quality. The EU renewable energy market now has an annual turnover of €15 billion, equivalent to half the global market, and is a major exporter.[3] By the year 2010, the EU hopes to meet as much as 21 per cent of its electricity requirement from renewable sources of energy, although this target is likely to be missed by several percentage points.[4]

10.02 The significant role that renewable energy has acquired in the EU energy mix would not have been possible without the use of various support schemes to build up a position of growing competitiveness with fossil fuels. This has raised issues about the compatibility of such measures with the rules of competition law and particularly those applicable to state aids. Moreover, the express linkage of legal measures aimed at promoting various forms of renewable energy to the liberalizing thrust of internal market policy raises other, different issues about their compatibility and potential conflict in European law. In particular, the impact of a legal framework that *positively* encourages green electricity within the framework of the still developing internal market in energy is a source of potential constraint on the progress of competition.

10.03 The general commitment of the Community to the promotion of renewable sources of energy is not at all new. It dates from at least 1988,[5] but the approach and the use of legal instruments changed radically between the adoption of the first and second Directives on electricity. The first evidence of a new approach came in the Renewables Directive in 2001, but is evident in other legal instruments such as Directive (EC) 2003/30 on the promotion of biofuels[6] and Directive (EC) 2004/8 on the promotion of cogeneration.[7] In these cases important sources of justification were that the measures contributed to the internal market programme, to the fulfilment of the EU Kyoto targets, and to an enhancement of security of supply. In this chapter the first of these legal measures is considered. Renewable energy is also considered in Chapter 17 which addresses a number of issues concerning the energy-environment interface. The Directives on the promotion of biofuels and cogeneration have at the present time few implications for the development of competition in the EU energy market, the theme of this book.

---

[3] European Commission, *A European Strategy for Sustainable, Competitive and Secure Energy*, COM (2006) 105 final, 8 March 2006, 11.
[4] ibid. By contrast, the expansion of renewable energy in the US has proceeded at considerable speed, partly due to the extension of the 'production tax credit' in 2004 and to an earlier start made with the Public Utilities Regulatory Policies Act 1978, and its implementing regulations.
[5] Council Recommendation 88/611, [1988] OJ L335/29.
[6] [2003] OJ L123/42.
[7] [2004] OJ L52/50.

B. The Renewables Directive

(1) Aims and Scope

The two aims of the Renewables Directive are to promote an increase in the contribution of renewable energy sources to electricity generation in the internal market for electricity, and to establish a basis for a future Community framework for this. However, the detailed implementation of these general objectives is expressly left to the Member States, allowing each Member State to choose the regime that corresponds best to its particular situation.[8] **10.04**

Renewable energy sources[9] are defined as renewable non-fossil energy sources such as wind, solar, geothermal, wave, tidal, hydro-power, biomass, landfill gas, sewage treatment plant gas, and biogases. Biomass is further defined in the Directive as the biodegradable fraction of products, waste and residues from agriculture (including vegetal and animal substances), forestry and related industries, and includes the biodegradable fraction of industrial and municipal waste.[10] In connection with the internal energy market, it may be noted that the definitions in the first Electricity Directive are applicable. **10.05**

The scope of the Directive extends to the EEA countries of Norway and Iceland through Decision No 102/2005 taken by the EEA Joint Committee to amend Annex IV (Energy) of the EEA Agreement. **10.06**

(2) National Indicative Targets

Member States are required to take 'appropriate steps' to encourage greater consumption of electricity that is generated from renewable sources in line with a set of national indicative targets. The steps they take are required to be in proportion to the objective to be attained. A key feature of this is the setting of national indicative targets for future consumption of electricity generated from renewable sources of energy in terms of a percentage of electricity consumption for the next ten years. These targets are to be included in a report adopted and published by the Member State no later than 27 October 2002 and every five years afterwards. In addition, the report is to outline the measures taken or planned at national level **10.07**

---

[8] Renewables Directive, Recital 23.
[9] It may be noted that Directive (EC) 2003/54 also contains a definition of renewable energy sources, although its predecessor did not; see also the definition provided in Directive (EC) 2003/96 restructuring the Community framework for the taxation of energy products and electricity [2003] L283/51 (see paras 17.22–17.32).
[10] But note that Recital 9 allows the use of a different definition in national legislation for purposes other than those set out in this Directive.

to achieve these targets. A framework for the setting of targets until 2010 is provided in Article 3(2). It requires Member States to take account of the reference values in the Annex to the Directive. They must also ensure that the targets are compatible with any national obligations undertaken in the context of climate change commitments accepted by the EC under the Kyoto Protocol.

10.08 Two further reporting requirements are laid down in Article 3(3) and (4). Member States are to publish a report that includes an analysis of their 'success in meeting the national indicative targets' (see para 10.32 below). The targets of the ten accession countries joining in 2004 were agreed bilaterally before the Accession and are set out in the Act of Accession. The first reports on national targets were published by all of the Member States in 2002, and the progress reports on the success in meeting those targets were submitted to the Commission in the course of 2003. The second reporting requirement was imposed upon the Commission in Article 3(4). Drawing on the Member States' reports on national indicative targets, the Commission is to make an assessment of Member States' progress towards achieving those targets and of the extent to which the targets are consistent with the global indicative target of 12 per cent of gross national energy consumption by 2010. In particular, the Commission is to assess whether the national target is consistent with the 22.1 per cent indicative share of electricity generated from renewable energy sources in total Community electricity consumption by 2010. The first such report was published in May 2004, and the subsequent reports are to be published every two years. The report is to be accompanied by proposals to the European Parliament and the Council for further measures if that appears necessary. Indeed, the final paragraph in Article 3(4) makes express reference to the inclusion of possible mandatory targets in the proposals. In the 2004 report, *The Share of Renewable Energy in the European Union*,[11] the Commission concluded that while the targets adopted by the Member States were consistent with the national reference values in the Directive's Annex I, the policies and measures adopted by Member States were not likely to lead to the achievement of the 2010 target. It was instead likely to fall 3 to 4 per cent below that figure. A major contributory factor was found to be the lower than expected generation of electricity from biomass.

(3) Support Schemes

10.09 The need for schemes of public support for renewable sources of energy is assumed in the Directive,[12] but the long-term objective is clearly one of establishing a

---

[11] COM (2004) 366 final.
[12] eg, see the sentence in the Annex to the Directive under footnote (*): 'In taking into account the reference values set out in this Annex, Member States make the necessary assumption that the State aid guidelines for environmental protection allow for the existence of national support schemes for the promotion of electricity produced from renewable energy sources'.

B. The Renewables Directive

Community framework for support schemes. At present, a Community-wide framework for support schemes is premature 'in view of the limited experience with national schemes and the current relatively low share of price supported electricity produced from renewables energy sources in the Community'.[13] Importantly, it then adds that it is necessary to adapt support schemes to the developing internal electricity market, albeit 'after a sufficient transitional period'.[14] The Commission should monitor the national support schemes and if necessary make a proposal for a Community framework, which has to be compatible with the principles of the internal electricity market. It notes that the need for public support schemes is also recognized in the Community guidelines for state aid for environmental protection.[15] The Treaty rules apply to such public support, and especially Articles 87 and 88.

The Directive requires the Commission to conduct an evaluation of the operation of mechanisms used in the Member States which provide direct or indirect support to electricity generators.[16] The support given to generators has to be such as is based on regulations issued by the public authorities and which could have the effect of restricting trade. The measures are to be evaluated according to their contribution to the objectives set out in Articles 6 and 174 EC without prejudice to Articles 87 and 88 EC. **10.10**

The Commission is required to 'present a well-documented report' on experience gained from the application and co-existence of the different support mechanisms.[17] The report is required to evaluate the success of the support systems, including their cost-effectiveness, in promoting the consumption of electricity from renewable energy sources in line with the national indicative targets. A large measure of autonomy is given to each Member State. The Commission is to monitor progress and assess measures in the Member States. It is to present (to the Parliament and Council) a report on experience gained with the application and co-existence of the different mechanisms used in Member States after four years, that is, not later than 27 October 2005. This report may also be accompanied by a proposal for a Community framework with regard to support schemes, if that is appropriate. Requirements are set out for such a framework proposal. These require it to: **10.11**

- contribute to the achievement of the national indicative targets;
- be compatible with the principles of the internal electricity market;

---

[13] Renewables Directive, Recital 15.
[14] ibid, Recital 16.
[15] [2001] OJ C37/3.
[16] Renewables Directive, Art 4(1).
[17] ibid, Art 4(2).

Chapter 10: Renewable Energy

- take into account the characteristics of different sources of renewable energy, together with their different technologies and geographic differences;
- promote the use of renewable energy sources in an effective way, be simple and simultaneously as efficient as possible, especially with respect to cost; and
- include sufficient transitional periods for national support schemes of at least seven years in order to maintain investor confidence.

10.12 In the first of the Commission's reports on the operation of the Directive, it made a number of observations on the operation of support schemes in the EU.

10.13 There are four main groups of support schemes in operation:[18] those with feed-in tariffs, green certificate systems, tendering systems, and tax incentives. Most of the Member States use schemes with feed-in tariffs. They use a specific price which is usually set for a period of several years, and which must be paid for by electricity companies, usually distribution companies, to domestic producers of 'green electricity'. Additional costs incurred by these schemes are usually paid for by the suppliers in proportion to the sales volume and are passed through to the power consumers by way of a premium on the kilowatt per hour end-user price.

10.14 In favour of such schemes, they provide investment security, as well as the possibility of fine tuning and the promotion of mid- to long-term technologies. On the other hand, they are difficult to harmonize at the EU level, they may be challenged in relation to internal market principles, and involve a risk of over-funding. A variation of this scheme is called the fixed premium mechanism, used in Denmark and to some extent in Spain. It involves a fixed premium or environmental bonus set by the government and paid above the normal or spot electricity price to generators of electricity from renewable energy sources.

10.15 The second of these schemes in popularity was found to be the green certificate system. This involves the sale of renewables at conventional power market prices. To finance the additional cost of producing green electricity and to ensure that the desired green electricity is in fact generated, all consumers (or in some countries producers) are obliged to purchase a certain number of green certificates from generators of renewable electricity according to a fixed percentage or quota of their total electricity consumption (or generation). Penalty payments for non-compliance are imposed: these are transferred either to a fund for renewables research, development, and demonstration or to the general government budget.

---

[18] This classification follows that of the European Commission in its report, *The Support of Electricity from Renewable Energy Sources*, COM (2005) 627 final, 7 December 2005. However, an alternative approach is adopted by Eurelectric in its report, *A Quantitative Assessment of Direct Support Schemes for Renewables*, January 2004. It distinguishes between direct price support schemes; capital investment aid; tax measures; R&D support; and support for the enhancement of sources, meaning biomass incentives. Included in the first category are quota-based systems such as green certificates and tendering procedures, and fixed price schemes such as feed-in tariffs and straight subsidies.

B. The Renewables Directive

Under this system a secondary market will develop, since generators and consumers will seek to buy these certificates as cheaply as possible. Generators of renewables will compete with each other to sell green certificates. Green certificates are therefore market-based instruments and could provide the basis for a Community-wide regime. However, they pose a higher risk for investors and, moreover, a more uncertain basis for the development of long-term, high-cost technologies. They also carry with them higher administrative costs. **10.16**

Tendering procedures are in operation in only two Member States (Ireland and France). The tendering procedure involves the state placing a series of tenders for the supply of renewable-sourced electricity. This is then supplied on a contract basis at the price resulting from the tender. The additional costs generated by the purchase of the electricity are then passed on to the end-consumer of electricity through a special levy. These procedures do not appear to have a long-term future. France has already changed its tendering system to one based on a feed-in tariff combined with a tendering system in some cases. Ireland is taking steps in a similar direction. Although tendering systems make optimum use of market forces, they have a stop-and-go character that is not conducive to stable conditions. This type of scheme also carries the risk that low bids may result in projects not being implemented. **10.17**

The final kind of support system that is in operation is the use of tax incentives. These are applied in Malta and Finland. For the most part, however, this is used as an additional policy tool, rather than a separate scheme. **10.18**

In its 2005 report on the Directive, the Commission announced that no major regulatory change at Community level was required in the short term.[19] The Commission would continue to monitor the state of play and make a further report no later than December 2007. It left open the possibility of adopting a different approach and framework for schemes to support electricity produced from renewables. An element of this that is likely to be included is possible harmonization of incentive schemes, following a Resolution on Renewable Energies adopted by the European Parliament.[20] **10.19**

(a) The Renewables Obligation in the UK

There have been various schemes in Britain to support renewables since 1989. A legally binding 'UK Renewables Obligation' (RO) was introduced in 2002 as a market-based support mechanism for auctions of contracts for renewables. It obliges electricity suppliers to source a rising percentage of electricity from **10.20**

---

[19] *The Support of Electricity from Renewable Energy Sources*, ibid.
[20] EP Resolution, 28 September 2005 (Turmes report on the share of renewable energy sources).

renewable sources. In 2006–07 the level of the obligation was 6.7 per cent. Article 3 of the Renewables Obligation Order 2006[21] defines the RO as an obligation whereby each designated electricity supplier produces evidence demonstrating that it has supplied to customers in Great Britain during the obligation period a determined amount of electricity generated from renewable sources or that another supplier has done so. The amount of electricity is established in accordance with Article 4 of the Order, and is an amount that equals the relevant percentage set out in a Schedule. The evidence has the form of a certificate (ROC), and the competent authorities are to establish and maintain a register of ROCs. The aim of the scheme is to incentivize the most economic forms of renewable generation. So far, it has favoured onshore wind, co-generation, and landfill gas.

(4) **Guarantee of Electricity Origin**

10.21 Member States are required to ensure that the origin of electricity generated from renewable sources in the internal electricity market can be guaranteed as such, according to objective, transparent, and non-discriminatory criteria laid down by each Member State. The aims behind this requirement are to facilitate trade in electricity from renewable sources and to increase transparency for the consumer's choice between renewable and non-renewable sources of power. It should be clear that such a guarantee of origin is not the same as a *certificate* of origin. This is emphasized in Recital 11 which notes the difference between such guarantees and 'exchangeable green certificates'. The latter is possible only on the basis of a specific, market-based regime of public support for trade in electricity generated from renewable sources. At the time the Directive was drafted there was insufficient support for a Community-wide harmonized public support system for green electricity trading. The Directive therefore requires something less. Subsequently, in Article 3(6) of the Electricity Directive, a requirement was introduced that Member States implement a scheme for the disclosure of the fuel mix, and the guarantee of origin could be used as a basis for this information.

10.22 Each Member State has discretion with respect to the issuing of guarantees to renewable energy generators within its own territory. The task may be delegated to one or more competent bodies which must be independent of generation and distribution activities.

10.23 The guarantee of origin has to specify the energy source from which the electricity was generated, the dates and places of generation, and (in the case of hydro-electric installations) the capacity. It also has to allow generators of renewable electricity to show that the electricity they sell is in fact generated from renewable

---

[21] SI 2006/1004.

B. The Renewables Directive

sources of energy. Measures have to be taken to ensure that the guarantees are accurate and reliable; there is a requirement that the measures taken to ensure the reliability of the system are reported along with other data under Article 3(3). Each Member State has to recognize guarantees issued by other Member States as proof of these elements. If a Member State refuses to do so, the refusal has to be based on objective, transparent and non-discriminatory criteria. The Commission may also 'compel the refusing party to recognise it'.[22] This hint of a stronger response from the Commission in the event of a failure to comply is also present in Article 5(6). The Commission is required to consider the form and methods that Member States could follow to guarantee the origin of electricity generated from renewables in its summary report submitted under Article 8. This has to be preceded by a consultation process with the Member States but the Commission may nonetheless propose to the Parliament and Council that common rules be adopted in this area if other methods appear not to be working.

(5) Regulation

There are a number of oversight tasks in the Directive. The most wide-ranging is the requirement that Member States or the competent authorities appointed by them conduct an evaluation of the existing legislative and regulatory framework on authorization procedures or other procedures laid down in the Electricity Directive applicable to generating plants for electricity from renewables.[23] The three goals of such an evaluation are quite specific: **10.24**

- to reduce the regulatory and non-regulatory barriers to the increase in electricity generation from renewable energy sources;
- to streamline and expedite procedures at the appropriate administrative level; and
- to ensure that the rules are objective, transparent and non-discriminatory, and fully take into account the particular features of the various renewable energy technologies.

A reporting requirement is imposed on the Member States with respect to this evaluation, and the actions taken as a result of it. It has to indicate the stage that the Member State has reached in co-ordinating between the different bodies with respect to deadlines, reception, and treatment of applications for authorizations; in drawing up possible guidelines for the activities concerned and the feasibility of a fast-track planning procedure for generators of renewable energy; and in designating authorities to act as mediators in disputes between the authorities responsible for issuing authorizations and the applicants for those authorizations. Furthermore, these **10.25**

---

[22] Renewables Directive, Art 5(4).
[23] The Directive refers to Art 4 of the first Electricity Directive; presumably this is now taken over by Art 5 of Directive (EC) 2003/54.

reports will provide the basis for an assessment by the Commission on best practices in achieving the three goals listed above, to be included in the Commission's summary report that Article 8 requires it to present to the Parliament and Council.

10.26 With respect to guarantees of origin, the Member State or competent authorities have to put in place mechanisms to ensure that guarantees of origin are both accurate and reliable.[24] They have to report on the measures taken to ensure the reliability of the guarantee system in the progress report submitted on the national indicative targets.

10.27 To date, several kinds of administrative barriers have been identified.[25] First, the existence of several layers of competence for the authorization of generating units can (and does) lead to delays, investment uncertainty, a multiplication of efforts, and increased demands for incentives from developers. The latter is aimed at offsetting investment risks or the initial capital intensity of the project. As a solution, the Commission recommends the creation of one-stop authorization agencies charged with the co-ordination of the different administrative procedures, and the adoption of standard forms and requirements by the different authorities. Secondly, the long lead times required to obtain the necessary permits are an obstacle in many countries. This has impacted negatively on onshore and especially offshore wind projects. To address this, obligatory response times could be introduced for the authorities involved, and clear guidelines established. Finally, the future development of renewable energy projects is often not anticipated in designing spatial plans, which requires additional plans to be adopted at a later stage, causing delays. This affects wind and biomass projects in particular. Authorities could be encouraged to anticipate the development of future renewable energy projects by allocating suitable areas, and adopting 'pre-planning mechanisms' (regions and local authorities would be required to assign locations for the different forms of renewable energy).

(6) Grid System Issues

10.28 The promotion of renewables raises a number of issues about the operation and adaptation of electricity grids that need to be addressed by Member States. Most of the current grid infrastructure was constructed before liberalization began and was designed with large power plants in mind, often located near the main centres of consumption. The normal scale of renewable power plants is smaller and their location different. Often they are connected to the distribution grid and require not only connection but also grid extensions and reinforcements. The thrust of the Directive's provisions in this respect is to ensure that Member States and TSOs and DSOs provide the conditions for access to the transmission and distribution

---

[24] Renewables Directive, Art 5(5).
[25] *The Support of Electricity from Renewable Energy Sources*, 12–14.

B. The Renewables Directive

grids by generators of renewable energy. However, in certain circumstances it may not be possible to transmit and distribute electricity from renewable sources without incurring consequences for the reliability and safety of the grid system.

Member States are obliged to take measures to ensure that TSOs and DSOs in their territory guarantee the transmission and distribution of electricity generated from renewable sources. They may also provide for priority access to the grid system for renewable sourced electricity. When dispatching generating installations, TSOs are required to give priority to those generating installations that use renewables in so far as the system operation permits.[26] This entails the establishment of a legal framework for three consequences of grid access to generators of electricity from renewable sources:[27]   **10.29**

(1) to provide for the costs of making technical adaptations, since grid connections and reinforcements will be required to permit new generators to feed electricity into the interconnected grid;
(2) to provide for sharing the costs of system installations between all generators that benefit from them; and
(3) to ensure that fees charged for transmission and distribution from plants using renewable sources of electricity reflect realizable cost benefits arising from the plant's connection to the network.

This legal framework may be put into place for these operations by the Member State directly or, alternatively, it must require the TSOs and DSOs to set up and publish their standard rules on these matters. Irrespective of how the rules are established, they must meet the usual tests of objectivity, transparency, and non-discrimination. Cost-sharing is to be enforced by a mechanism that takes into account the benefits which existing and new generators derive from the grid connections as well as the TSOs and DSOs. The latter may be required by Member States to bear the costs, in whole or in part, of technical adaptations to the grid to allow access to renewable sources of electricity. Different types of grid connection are permitted.   **10.30**

New generators seeking grid access are given some protection by the requirement on TSOs and DSOs to provide any new generator with a 'comprehensive and detailed estimate of the costs associated with the connection'.[28] Moreover, Member States are required to ensure that charges of transmission and distribution fees do not discriminate against such sources of electricity, especially if it is sourced from peripheral regions such as islands or areas of low population density.[29] The reporting requirements include an obligation on Member States to comment on the measures   **10.31**

---

[26] ibid, Art 7(1).
[27] ibid, Art 7(2), (5) and (6).
[28] ibid, Art 7(4).
[29] ibid, Art 7(6).

taken to facilitate access to the grid system of electricity generated from renewable sources, which is to include the feasibility of introducing two-way metering.

(7) Reporting Requirements

10.32 The Directive imposes a considerable number of reporting requirements on the Member States and on the Commission: in total, there are ten.[30] It is not surprising then that several reporting requirements are sometimes bundled into a single report. In addition to the report setting out national indicative targets which Member States are required to adopt and publish, Article 3(3) requires Member States to publish every two years a report on the progress made in reaching these targets. Publication of such reports commenced no later than 27 October 2003, and in preparing them they are to take into account climatic factors that are likely to affect the achievement of those targets. They are also to indicate to what extent the measures taken are consistent with the national climate change commitment. Further, in Article 6(2) Member States are required to publish a report on the evaluation of the existing legislative and regulatory framework, indicating the actions that have been taken. The aim of this report is to provide an indication of the stage specifically reached in three areas, where this is appropriate in the context of national legislation. These are:

(1) co-ordination between the different administrative bodies as regards deadlines, reception, and treatment of applications for authorizations;
(2) drawing up possible guidelines for the activities referred to in point 1, and the feasibility of a fast-track planning procedure for electricity generators relying on renewable energy sources; and
(3) the designation of authorities to act as mediators in disputes between authorities responsible for issuing authorizations and applicants for authorizations.

A report is required under Article 8 on administrative barriers and grid issues, as well as the implementation of the guarantee of origin on renewable electricity.

10.33 The above reports are to furnish the basis for the Commission to draw up a summary report on the implementation of the Directive. This report is to be presented to the European Parliament and the Council no later than 31 December 2005 and every five years after.[31] The report is to consider the progress made in reflecting the external costs of electricity generated from non-renewable energy sources and the impact of public support that is granted to electricity generation. Of equal importance, the report must take into account the possibility for Member States to meet

---

[30] ibid, Arts 3(2), (3) and (4); 4(2); 5(5) and (6); 6(2) and (3); 7(7) and 8.
[31] ibid, Art 8. See, for example, the progress report made under Art 3(4) in 2007: European Commission, *Green Paper Follow-up Action; Report on Progress in Renewable Electricity*, COM (2006) 849 final, 10 January 2007.

B. The Renewables Directive

the national indicative target, the global indicative target, and the existence of discrimination between different energy sources. In addition, the Commission is required to include an assessment of the best practices with respect to authorization or other administrative procedures in relation to the objectives set out in Article 6(1).[32] If it appears appropriate to do so, the Commission is required to submit with the report further proposals to the European Parliament and the Council.

(8) The Relevance of State Aid Control[33]

The support schemes offered by Member States to renewable energy are potentially open to challenge under Articles 87 and 88 EC. Support schemes can inevitably have a distorting effect on the workings of the market. In the Preamble of the 2001 Directive, Recital 12, it is clearly stated that the Treaty rules, including Articles 87 and 88, apply to public support. Such support might be economically justified on various grounds if the beneficial effects of such measures on the environment outweigh the distorting effects on competition. First, it has to be decided whether the support constitutes an aid within the meaning of Article 87. If so, it has then to be decided if the aid is compatible with the internal market. In many cases, support schemes applicable to renewable energy are state aids within the meaning of Article 87 and so are covered by the Community guidelines on state aid for environmental protection (see paras 15.62–15.78).[34] These Guidelines provide for an assessment of whether the aid administered by Member States is compatible with the internal market. They contain a number of relevant considerations for renewable sources of electricity. For example, point 5 states that the beneficial effects of such aid must outweigh the distorting effects on competition. They also make express reference in point 24 to the possibility that state aid may be used for the promotion of the use of renewables and cogeneration by means of tax exemptions or reductions. Where it can be shown to be necessary, investment grants of the eligible costs (extra investment costs required to meet environmental objectives) in support of renewable energy up to 100 per cent are permitted (point 32). Operating aid may be justified to cover a difference between the cost of generating energy sources and the market price for energy (point 56). Finally, the Guidelines note that state aid based on avoided external costs is allowed but should not exceed €0.05/kWh.

10.34

Since the use of renewable sources of energy is a policy priority, the Guidelines have been interpreted in a way that is quite positive towards the various support schemes (see paras 15.62–15.74). During the period 2001–04, the Commission approved no fewer than 60 state aid schemes which supported renewable energy sources.[35]

10.35

---

[32] ibid, Art 6(3).
[33] The subject of state aids is dealt with in detail in Chapter 15.
[34] [2001] OJ C37/3. These Guidelines expire on 31 December 2007.
[35] *The Support of Electricity from Renewable Energy Sources*, 10.

10.36 The subject of state aid in relation to renewable sources of energy was addressed in a case before the ECJ which arose from the operation of the German feed-in support system.[36] The *PreussenElektra* case is examined elsewhere (see paras 15.64–15.67).

10.37 A consequence of the decision was that feed-in schemes were not seen to involve any direct or indirect transfer of state resources to undertakings and not to constitute state aid within the meaning of Article 87(1) EC. A Member State is therefore able to apply such a scheme without notification. Another consequence is that the Commission agreed that two German laws designed to support electricity from renewable sources and from combined heat and power did not constitute state aid.[37] These laws required public and private network operators to connect installations that generated renewables to the grid, to give a priority to the purchase of renewables and to pay a minimum price for such energy above the market price and under the same conditions. Referring to the *PreussenElektra* case, it held that the two laws did not amount to aid.

(9) Implementation

10.38 The Directive requires Member States to implement legislation, and take administrative measures with respect to grid access and a guarantee of origin inter alia within two years of entering into force. It entered into force on 27 October 2001. For the countries acceding to the EU in 2003 the deadline was set at 1 May 2004. However, in a significant number of cases, the transposition process was delayed. In April 2006 the Commission commenced infringement proceedings against eight Member States which had still failed to meet the deadline of October 2003.[38] Four of these had failed to report on their progress on the use of electricity from renewable sources to the Commission (Article 3(3)): Italy, Poland, Czech Republic, and the UK. Five had taken insufficient measures to enable an adequate promotion of renewable energy (Article 6(2)): Italy, Latvia, Cyprus, Greece, and Ireland.

C. Conclusions

10.39 The regime established by the Renewables Directive is one in which Member States are required to set indicative targets but have a wide discretion in taking measures to meet them. The enforcement method employed by the Directive is of the soft kind, relying heavily upon information transparency and publicity through a system of

---

[36] Case C-379/98 *PreussenElektra AG v Schleswag AG* [2001] ECR I-2099.
[37] Commission Press Release IP/02/739, 'Commission raises no objections to German feed-in laws for electricity from renewable sources and combined heat and power', 22 May 2002.
[38] Commission Press Release IP/06/429, 'Eight Member States still not in compliance with Community legislation promoting renewable electricity', 4 April 2006. Separately, infringement

C. Conclusions

reporting requirements, which the Commission has to monitor and enforce. The sheer number of reporting requirements and different timetables has the effect of establishing a process of continuous review. However, it is clear that the EU is still in a transitional phase with respect to the development of renewable energy. The uneven pattern of implementation of the Directive's requirements among the Member States, and very modest progress of some underlines the importance of the monitoring process and the extent to which the EU has to travel to reach a stage in which a Community-wide harmonized regime becomes possible.

While the market orientation of the Directive's measures is clear enough,[39] it is equally clear that a principal goal of the legislation has been to limit the impact of competitive forces on this segment of the EU energy market in order to let it grow and take root. Member States have been encouraged to allow a priority access to generators of renewables, to remove administrative obstacles, and to streamline procedures so that investment will flow into this sector. The application of EC law has also been relatively benign, allowing a variety of support schemes to flourish. It may therefore be thought that as renewable energy takes root in many Member States it is appropriate that this approach to enforcement will be reviewed and perhaps replaced with a more constraining application of the Treaty rules on state aid, free movement of goods, and anti-trust law in the medium term.[40] On the basis of its 2005 review, the Commission has clearly decided that the market remains in a state of development, and that investment will benefit from regulatory stability in terms of a continuation of the legal status quo. At the same time, it is clear that as some forms of renewable energy become competitive, there will be a shift of emphasis towards greater support for those forms of renewable energy that have failed to attract significant amounts of investment.[41]

10.40

---

proceedings were opened against Italy and Greece in relation to the biofuels directive: Commission Press Release IP/06/862: 'Biofuels: European Commission launches infringement procedures against Italy and Greece', 28 June 2006.

[39] Renewables Directive, Recital 18.

[40] See Gunst, A, 'Impact of European Law on the Validity and Tenure of National Support Schemes for Power Generation from Renewable Energy Sources' (2005) 23 J Energy Natural Resources L95–119.

[41] As is evident by the Commission's subsequent initiatives; eg, the biomass action plan: COM (2005) 628 final, 7 December 2005; *An EU strategy for Biofuels*, COM (2006) 34 final, and especially the *Biofuels Progress Report*, COM (2006) 845 final, 10 January 2007, in which the Commission argues for legally binding targets and signals its intention to table legislation in 2007 to revise the Biofuels Directive.

Part III

COMPETITION LAW

11

THE APPLICATION OF COMPETITION LAW

A. Introduction	11.01	D. The Energy Sector Review	11.38
B. The 'Modernized' Legal Framework		(1) The Inquiry: Data Collection, Scope and Compliance	11.42
(1) Regulation 1/2003	11.06	(2) Significance	11.47
(a) Articles 81 and 82	11.07	(3) The Results	11.48
(b) Implementation	11.10	(a) Electricity	11.49
(c) The New Approach	11.12	(b) Gas	11.54
(2) The Competition Network	11.19	(c) Supplementary Issues	11.59
C. Defining the Relevant Market		(d) Remedies	11.60
(1) Market Definition in Energy	11.21	E. Conclusions	11.66
(a) Product Market	11.22		
(b) Geographic Market	11.32		
(c) Market Integration	11.37		

From 1991 to 2003 the Commission accepted settlements in all of the cases that came before it. There were no infringement procedures commenced. By 2004 there was a sense that something had changed, and that this practice would not continue.

Schnichels and Nyssens[1]

A. Introduction

The application of competition law in the energy sector has been largely shaped by the sector-specific legislation adopted between 1997 and 2003. Prior to the adoption of the first Electricity and Gas Directives, there were relatively few instances of competition law being actively applied in the energy sector. Once the first Directives were adopted, competition policy had to be adapted to meet the

11.01

---

[1] For an extended discussion of this point by Schnichels and Nyssens, see Faull, J and Nikpay, A, *The EC Law of Competition* (2nd edn, 2007) at paras 12.116–12.118.

specific challenges presented by the initial phase of a long-term transition to a liberalized market in energy. It became important to identify the precise areas in which competition law could be used to greatest effect in support of this process, and tested in specific cases.

11.02 The Commission's strategy during this time comprised *three* distinct strands. The first was an attempt at increasing supply competition in a context in which supply was structured in a predominantly monopolistic way. The second was to ensure effective access to energy networks (which remain natural monopolies even after liberalization). The third was to guarantee free consumer choice by challenging consumer lock-in.[2] The principal instruments used were the competition rules in Articles 81, 82, and 86 of the EC Treaty, merger control, and the state aid rules in Articles 87 and 88 EC.

11.03 The adoption of a second generation of more comprehensive Directives on electricity and gas in 2003 marked the end of this initial phase. By the time they had entered into force one year later, a new phase in the application of competition law had begun, in which a variety of actions were planned and launched. The acceleration of energy market liberalization had in fact coincided with several changes in the competition law itself, which had developed independently. Among these changes were the introduction of Regulation 1/2003,[3] which 'modernized' the application of Articles 81 and 82, and introduced a new form of co-operation in enforcement between the Commission and the national competition authorities (the European Competition Network). Article 17 of the new Regulation allowed the Commission to engage in comprehensive reviews of sectors that appeared resistant to competition. In 2005 a review was launched into the operation of the competition law in the liberalizing sectors of electricity and gas.[4] In addition, a new Merger Regulation[5] offered further possibilities of scrutiny of anti-competitive developments in the energy sector. In the field of state aid, an Action Plan was followed by a package of measures that would lead to a stricter and more focused approach to enforcement.

11.04 In this context, a new approach to the application of competition law has begun to emerge, one that is increasingly focused on reaching *formal* decisions after investigations, instead of concluding a case with an amicable settlement with the parties

---

[2] For statements of this view by Commission officials, see Albers, M, 'The New EU Directives on Energy Liberalization from a Competition Point of View' in Cameron, PD, (ed), *Legal Aspects of EU Energy Regulation: Implementing the New Directives on Electricity and Gas across Europe* (2005) 41–58; Schaub, A, 'Competition Policy and Liberalization of Energy Markets', paper presented at the European Utilities Circle 2000 conference, 23 November 2000.

[3] Regulation (EC) 1/2003 of 16 December 2002 on the implementation of the rules on competition laid down in Articles 81 and 82 of the Treaty [2003] OJ L1/1, as amended by Regulation (EC) 411/2004 [2004] OJ L68/1.

[4] Commission Press Release IP/05/716, 'Competition: Commission opens sector inquiry into gas and electricity', 13 June 2005.

[5] Regulation (EC) 139/2004 on the control of concentrations between undertakings [2004] OJ L24/1.

A. Introduction

involved. The reasons for this lie elsewhere than in Regulation 1/2003. By 2003 evidence had accumulated of the very considerable obstacles that remained to be overcome before a liberalized energy market could become a reality in the EU. The markets in electricity and gas had been developing in the direction of oligopoly while the Directives were predicated on assumptions about competition. The absence of new market entrants and the clear segmentation of electricity and gas markets along national lines in the overwhelming majority of cases raised questions about the credibility of an internal energy market. From the outset, a characteristic of the Directive-based approach to liberalization had been the inclusion of a timetable as one of its central elements. Within the time-frame envisaged, and enshrined in European law, the completion of an internal market appeared impossible. Yet the entry into force of the second generation Directives had given all market players a clear signal that a new stage in the process had begun. The clear legislative support they gave to the NRAs left no room for doubt about the intention with respect to enforcement. In this context, it could hardly be argued that a gentle approach should still be taken towards violations of competition law, coaxing the parties into making concessions, with a summary of the details available only in the form of a Commission press release, because the commercial participants had to make 'difficult' adjustments to a more demanding market environment. The fresh legal capacity given to the competition authorities presented an opportunity for a new approach, based on identifying the most serious antitrust violations and imposing penalties.

This chapter examines the new *context* of competition law. It covers, first, Regulation 1/2003 and the enforcement mechanisms envisaged under the Competition Network. Secondly, it reviews the growing challenges of defining the relevant product and geographic markets in electricity and gas, as these are affected by the liberalization process. Thirdly, it considers the Energy Sector Review, carried out by the Commission in conjunction with the national competition authorities, and the various anti-competitive practices which the Review has identified. Subsequent chapters in this Part of the book examine the practice of applying competition law in the upstream (exploration and production) area (Chapter 12), in networks (Chapter 13), in mergers and acquisitions (Chapter 14), in state aids (Chapter 15), and with respect to special and exclusive rights (Chapter 16). In these chapters, the emphasis is very much upon the practice of competition law in energy markets as a support to the sector-specific regime rather than as, say, an expression of the general principles of competition law. **11.05**

B. The 'Modernized' Legal Framework

(1) Regulation 1/2003

On 1 May 2004 new rules governing the application of EC competition law came into force. Council Regulation 1/2003 repealed its predecessor, Regulation **11.06**

17/62, which had been adopted as far back as 1962, and in so doing claimed to be effecting a 'modernization' of the application of Articles 81 and 82 EC. In particular, it set up a system of parallel competences in which the Commission and Member State National Competition Authorities (NCAs) can apply these articles. Both the NCAs and the Commission are to form a network of public authorities called the European Competition Network (ECN). This approach was designed to achieve a more effective enforcement of these articles. For the energy sector they have considerable implications and began to make an impact almost immediately in the form of a Sector Review, discussed below. Before examining the reforms brought about by Regulation 1/2003 and the reasons why they were considered necessary, it is useful to recall the content of Articles 81 and 82, with which the Regulation is directly concerned.

(a) Articles 81 and 82

11.07 Article 81 EC expressly prohibits the following as incompatible with the common market: agreements between undertakings, and decisions by associations of undertakings and concerted practices that may affect trade between Member States and which have as their object or effect the prevention, restriction, or distortion of competition within the common market. In particular, those agreements, decisions, and concerted practices are prohibited which involve the following: price-fixing; limiting or controlling production, markets, technical development, or investment; sharing markets or sources of supply; applying dissimilar conditions to equivalent transactions with other trading parties; and tying (making the conclusion of contracts subject to acceptance by the other parties of supplementary obligations). Any agreements or decisions which are prohibited by this Article are automatically void.

11.08 The prohibition system envisages exemptions, however, in Article 81(3). This is a provision for individual exemptions, although block exemptions may be (and are) granted by the Commission. The exemptions may be granted to an agreement, decision or concerted practice (or categories thereof) between undertakings if four cumulative conditions are met:

- it contributes to improving the production or distribution of goods or to promoting technical or economic progress;
- it allows consumers a fair share of the resulting benefit;
- it does *not* impose on the undertakings concerned restrictions which are not indispensable to the attainment of these objectives; and
- it does *not* afford such undertakings the possibility of eliminating competition in respect of a substantial part of the products in question.

11.09 A different form of competition distortion can arise through an abuse of dominant market positions. Article 82 is an attempt to tackle this problem. It prohibits abuse by one or more undertakings of a dominant position within the common

B. The 'Modernized' Legal Framework

market or in a substantial part of it. Such an abuse is incompatible with the common market in so far as it may affect trade between Member States. It is not the *fact* of a dominant position that is the problem; it is the abuse of it. Article 82 provides several examples of what an abuse might consist of. This is not an exclusive list but includes: directly or indirectly imposing unfair purchase or selling prices; limiting production, markets, or technical development to the detriment of consumers; applying dissimilar conditions to equivalent transactions with other trading parties; and tying.

(b) Implementation

The preceding Regulation, 17/62, took effect on 13 March 1962,[6] and was highly influential over the next 40 years, doing much to disseminate a competition culture within the EU. However, it envisaged a very modest role for the NCAs. This became increasingly inappropriate as competition law in the Member States matured, and the willingness of NCAs to participate in the enforcement of competition law increased.[7] Moreover, with the expansion of competition cases the Commission's own resources became more stretched, a problem that further enlargement was expected to worsen. In particular, the centralized approach to the application of Article 81(3) EC (the exception from the prohibition on agreements) appeared in need of reform. In the Commission's view, the centralized approach had come to hinder application of the competition rules by the courts and competition authorities of the Member States, and its system of notification prevented the Commission from concentrating its resources on the most serious infringements, as well as imposing considerable costs on undertakings.[8] Following a period of discussion, there was widespread support for the idea that NCAs should be empowered to apply Article 81(3) in addition to Articles 81(1) and 82 which are directly applicable.

11.10

The idea of a competition network also gained ground. To some extent this reflected the practice of working relationships, both in the vertical sense of Commission–NCA relationships and in the horizontal sense of NCA relationships inter se. It appeared timely and appropriate to give the network concept a structure and provide in law a set of rules that would govern its operation.

11.11

(c) The New Approach

Under Regulation 1/2003 the Commission sought to focus its attention on more serious cases and to have powers of investigation that would support this direction.

11.12

---

[6] Regulation (EEC) 17/62 [1962] OJ L13/204.
[7] For background to these developments see Goyder, DG, *EC Competition Law* (4th edn, 2003) 445–55; also Tesauro, G, 'Modernization and Decentralisation of EC Competition Law' and Temple-Lang, J, 'Decentralised Application of Community Competition Law' in Rivas, J and Horspool, M, (eds), *Modernization and Decentralisation of EC Competition Law* (2000) 1–12 and 13–29.
[8] Regulation 1/2003, Recital 3.

In this respect, Article 1 replaces Article 1 of the old Regulation 17 but *importantly* it provides that the whole of Article 81 as well as Article 82 becomes of direct effect, and that no prior decision of the Commission is necessary for the application of Article 81(3). This abolishes the *ex ante* authorization system under the previous regime so that parties to an agreement may no longer apply to the Commission to obtain an individual exemption. Assessment of the legality of agreements is left to the undertakings themselves.

11.13 Article 3 provides for the supremacy of EC competition law while permitting a measure of freedom to NCAs in the application of their national law. The NCAs are allowed to apply national law of a stricter or different character in cases of control of unilateral conduct by undertakings, merger control, and when applying national law that has a predominantly different objective from that pursued by Articles 81 and 82 (such as laws concerning environmental or consumer protection).

11.14 The Regulation made it compulsory for NCAs:

(1) to apply Article 81 EC where they apply national competition law to agreements or concerted practices which may affect trade between Member States; and
(2) to apply Article 82 EC where they apply national competition law to any abuse prohibited by Article 82.

11.15 The provisions on 'Commission Decisions' in Articles 7 to 10 are interesting in two respects. Under Article 7 the Commission may impose on undertakings behavioural or structural remedies which are proportionate to the infringement committed. The preference is clearly for the former, since the latter are only to be imposed if there is no equally effective behavioural remedy available or where that remedy would be more burdensome for the undertaking concerned than the structural remedy. This limit is underlined by Recital 12 which states: 'Changes to the structure of an undertaking as it existed before the infringement was committed would only be proportionate where there is a substantial risk of a lasting or repeated infringement that derives from the very structure of the undertaking.' Under Article 9 the commitments offered by undertakings to meet Commission concerns expressed in a preliminary assessment of a case may be made binding on the undertakings. The use of a published decision would be a more formal approach than has been the Commission's practice in many cases to date (such as those examined in Chapters 12 and 13). Where there is a public interest involved, Article 10 allows the Commission to adopt a decision of a declaratory character finding that a prohibition does not apply 'with a view to clarifying the law and ensuring its consistent application throughout the Community'.[9]

---

[9] ibid, Recital 14.

B. The 'Modernized' Legal Framework

11.16 Articles 11 and 12 provide the rules for co-operation between the Commission and the NCAs. Notable among these are a duty to co-operate,[10] an obligation on the NCAs to inform the Commission at the outset of proceedings under Article 81,[11] an obligation on the NCAs to consult the Commission prior to adopting a prohibition decision or accepting commitments or withdrawing the benefit of a group exemption,[12] the right of any member of the network to provide another member with evidence in any matter of fact or of law,[13] and, in Article 14, the use of an Advisory Committee to discuss a case pending before the NCA before a final decision is taken.[14] Article 11(6) allows the Commission to take over a case, relieving the NCA, but this is likely to be a power used in unusual circumstances (for instance, where it appears likely to be in conflict with existing case law of the Commission or the courts), and only after full consultation.

11.17 The Commission's powers to carry out its own investigations have been extended. This is evident in Articles 17 to 21 which provide for powers of investigation. Under Article 17 the Commission may conduct general inquiries into a particular sector of the economy or a particular type of agreement across various sectors where a trend of trade between Member States, price rigidity or other circumstances suggest that competition may be restricted or distorted within the common market. The Commission does not require indications that specific undertakings have infringed the relevant Treaty provisions. It may publish a report on the results of a sector inquiry and invite comments from interested parties. Once a decision has been adopted by the Commission under Article 17, it has investigative powers to obtain all necessary information from undertakings and associations of undertakings. The powers available are those pursuant to Articles 18, 19, 20, and 22 of the Regulation. Article 18(1) allows the Commission to request, or to require by decision, all the necessary information from undertakings and associations of undertakings, with the possibility of fines under Articles 23 and 24 where information is misleading or incorrect, or where—following a decision that requires the provision of information—responses are incomplete or absent. Article 18(6) also allows the Commission to request all necessary information from governments and NCAs. The latter may be required to assist it with the execution of dawn raids, for example, or obtaining the required court orders from national courts on its behalf. Under Article 19, the Commission can take oral statements from natural or legal persons that consent to do so. The Commission also has the power under Article 20 to undertake inspections in the framework of the inquiry or, basing itself on Article 22, to ask a competition authority to carry out such an

---

[10] ibid, Art 11(1).
[11] ibid, Art 11(3).
[12] ibid, Art 11(4).
[13] ibid, Art 12(1).
[14] ibid, Art 14(7).

inspection on its behalf, to establish whether there has been an infringement of Article 81 or 82.

11.18 Information can only be collected for the purposes of Article 17, giving effect to Articles 81 and 82 EC, either on their own or in conjunction with Article 86 EC. However, guarantees are to be provided to undertakings that confidential information and business secrets will be protected.

(2) The Competition Network

11.19 Regulation 1/2003 creates a system of parallel competences in which all of the competition authorities will co-operate closely in the application of Articles 81 and 82. The NCAs and the Commission are to act as a network of European competition authorities—the ECN—in the public interest and in order to protect competition. The operation of this network is set out in the Regulation and is supplemented by a Notice on Co-operation[15] and a Joint Declaration of the Council and Commission[16] that was adopted at the same time as the Regulation. Among the principles established are the following:

- the Commission has the ultimate but not the sole responsibility for developing policy and safeguarding efficiency and consistency;
- additional powers have been granted to the Commission but these must be exercised with the utmost regard for the co-operative nature of the ECN;
- cases will be dealt with by a single competition authority as often as possible;
- where more than three Member States are involved, the Commission is best placed to deal with the case;
- case allocation is to be completed as quickly as possible and normally the competition authority that has notified the case to the ECN will remain the responsible competition authority;
- in cases where an agreement or practice affects competition in more than one Member State, the ECN members will agree on who is best placed to deal with the case. This may involve joint action and if so, one competition authority may be designated as lead authority; and
- the ECN members should assist in the exchange of information and best practices and ensure a coherent application of EC competition law in cases with a cross-border dimension where Articles 81 and 82 EC apply.

11.20 The ECN itself is not a distinct institution and has no autonomous powers or competences. It is rather a framework in which the independent competition

---

[15] Commission Notice on co-operation within the Network of Competition Authorities [2004] OJ C101/43.
[16] Joint Statement of the Council and the Commission on the Functioning of the Network of Competition Authorities: <http://ec.europa.eu/comm/competition/antitrust/ecn/joint_statement_en.pdf>.

C. Defining the Relevant Market

authorities of the EU Member States and the Commission co-operate with each other with respect to the application of competition rules on restrictive business practices and abuses of dominant positions.[17] In this respect, companies and individuals enter into contact with one or more of the competition authorities rather than with the ECN itself.

C. Defining the Relevant Market

(1) Market Definition in Energy

For the competition rules to be applied, an essential first step is to define the relevant market. However, the process differs from that under the Merger Regulation. Under the competition rules, the establishment that under Article 82 a dominant position exists will require an examination of the relevant product and geographic markets.[18] The process of market definition will determine whether other firms in the market can resist successfully the behaviour of firms whose conduct is in question. In merger cases the assessment of 'market power' is equally important and, given the limited number of antitrust cases in the energy sector to date, it is in the merger cases that most of the discussion has taken place of the relevant product and geographic markets for electricity and gas. This is usually a very fact-specific kind of analysis, which turns on the interpretation of a variety of data such as consumer preferences, taxation levels, transmission costs, the use of cross-border transit fees, special and exclusive rights and so on. In energy cases, it is complicated by the fact that the markets have changed under the impact of liberalization and continue to do so. For an *ex post* analysis of an abuse, this is clearly less of a challenge than for the kind of *ex ante* analysis that is required in a merger investigation. After the markets are defined, the market shares can be assessed.

11.21

(a) Product Market

All Commission decisions on product market definitions in the energy sector have concluded that gas and electricity do *not* belong to the same product market[19] and

11.22

---

[17] The website is <http://ec.europa.eu/comm/competition/antitrust/ecn/ecn_home.html>.

[18] The concept of 'dominant position' in Art 82 EC has a controversial history. Among recent critical writings on this subject, see Sharpe, T, '*Trying* to Make Sense of Abuse of a Dominant Position' in *Regulating Utilities and Promoting Competition* (2006) 138–55.

[19] *Tractebel/Distrigas (II)* (Case IV/M.493) Commission Decision of 1 September 1994; *EDP/ENI/GDP* (Case COMP/M.3440) Commission Decision 2005/801/EC, [2005] OJ L302/69. In the following paras only electricity and gas are considered. There have of course been cases in which product and geographic market definitions have been considered in other sectors such as nuclear energy. A recent example is *Areva/Urenco* (Case COMP/M.3099) Commission Decision of 6 October 2004, [2006] OJ L61/11, in which the product market was held to comprise enriched natural uranium, enriched deleted uranium, and down-blended highly enriched uranium. The geographic market appeared to be Europe-wide and possibly wider, but the Commission decided to leave this issue open: paras 8–13.

should therefore be treated as distinct product markets. This arises from the high switching costs between the two forms of energy, which require large investments in applications geared to processing one form of energy or the other. Most customers would not consider switching from gas to electricity or vice versa in the event of even a significant increase in price of one of the two forms of energy. However, a company able to offer customers both electricity and gas has a competitive advantage over one that does not.[20]

11.23 A word of caution may be entered at the outset. The definitions provided with respect to both product and geographic markets will vary to some extent from one Member State to another, given the different degrees of liberalization that have taken place. They should not be taken as of uniform application across all the 27 Member States.

11.24 Electricity   The Commission has distinguished the following product markets in various merger decisions:

- generation and wholesale supply of electricity:
  — generation in power plants;
  — physical import of electricity through interconnectors;
  — its sale on the wholesale market to traders, distribution companies, or large industrial end-users;
- transmission via the high-voltage grid (220 kV and above);[21]
- distribution via the low-voltage grids;
- (retail) supply to large industrial users;
- possibly, (retail) supply to commercial and small industrial users;[22]
- (retail) supply to residential customers; and possibly also
- the provision of regulating/balancing power services.[23]

11.25 Within the wholesale category, the Commission has considered whether separate trading markets exist for over-the-counter trading (OTC), trade with physical products at stock exchanges, and trade with non-physical financial derivatives. It has refrained from taking a decision as to whether they are separate markets or part of the wholesale market, however.[24]

---

[20] *EDP/ENI/GDP*, ibid, para 15.
[21] Medium voltage grids (not less than 20 kV) may constitute a separate market if they do not overlap with the other grids: see ibid, para 34.
[22] This 'middle area' is sometimes considered to be part of the large industrial users' market, and sometimes considered to be part of the residential customers' market. The separateness of such a market has also been considered possible. A definitive view on this issue has so far not been necessary in the relevant decisions.
[23] *Sydkraft/Graninge* (Case COMP/M.3268) Commission Decision of 30 October 2003.
[24] ibid, para 14; *EDP/ENI/GDP* (Case COMP/M.3440) Commission Decision 2005/801/EC, [2005] OJ L302/69, paras 37 et seq.

C. Defining the Relevant Market

11.26 In the category of 'retail supply' the Commission has distinguished separate product markets as between large (that is, industrial and commercial) customers and small (household and small business) customers.[25] In the *EDP/ENI/GDP* case, the Commission distinguished large industrial customers which are connected to the high-voltage and medium voltage grid from smaller, industrial, commercial, and domestic customers which are connected to the low voltage grid.[26]

11.27 With respect to interconnectors that link two Member States, there is a question about whether they constitute a separate product and/or geographic market. This has not been the subject of a Commission decision as yet.[27]

11.28 Previous decisions have assumed a separate product market for *balancing* power, since this is not easily substitutable with other electricity supply at wholesale level. The Commission's reasoning is as follows.[28] Supply services may be required to overcome network congestion but there may also be a need for suppliers to adjust the electricity they are supplying to the actual (as opposed to the expected) demand of their customers. If demand from a customer exceeds the supplier's planning (and therefore exceeds the amount of energy that it has bought on the wholesale market or that it can generate itself), it has two options. The supplier may be able to correct the deviation itself or it must procure the balancing services from another party, such as the transmission system operator (TSO), which in turn procures the energy needed to perform this service either from the pool or through other contracts with producers who need to be on 'stand-by duty'. For the TSO there is a technical necessity for such a service as it is responsible for maintaining the tension in the grid within a very narrow bandwidth. In the event of over-consumption, the tension in the grid will drop, causing network stability problems at some point. A problem also arises if there is under-consumption since the tension in the grid rises above an acceptable tolerance level and the TSO must make sure that either some generation capacity is switched off or that some consumption is added. This service needs to be paid for and there will normally be a 'penalty' for deviation if demand of a customer exceeds, or falls below, the expected level which corresponds to the amount that each supplier purchases from the wholesale level or plans to produce himself and which he has to communicate in advance to the TSO.

---

[25] *Verbund/EnergieAllianz* (Case COMP/M.2947) Commission Decision 2004/271/EC, [2004] OJ L92/91.

[26] *EDP/ENI/GDP* (Case COMP/M.3440) Commission Decision 2005/801/EC, [2005] OJ L302/69, Recital 64. For a comprehensive discussion of the relevant product market in relation to electricity, see Netherlands Competition Authority, 'Consultation Document on Mergers on the Energy Markets in the Netherlands and a Possible North-West European Market', June 2006, 19–27.

[27] Nyssens and Schnichels argue that in certain circumstances they do constitute a separate product and geographic market: in Faull, J and Nikpay, A, *The EC Law of Competition* (2nd edn, 2007), ch 12.

[28] *EDP/ENI/GDP* (Case COMP/M.3440) Commission Decision 2005/801/EC, [2005] OJ L302/69, Recitals 52–4; *E.ON/MOL* (Case COMP/M.3696) Commission Decision 2006/622/EC, [2006] OJ L253/20, Recitals 219–21.

11.29 The wholesale service that approximates most closely to balancing power services is the so-called 'intra-day' trading opportunities.[29] In this situation, the companies that are in actual under- or over-supply can trade their surpluses or purchase their extra needs. If there is no continuous intra-day trading, with immediate delivery, this trading system is in itself not sufficient to match supply and demand at any time. Alternative ways of managing it are through the conclusion of interruptible contracts that allow customers no advance warning and customers who are prepared to increase their demand at any time.

11.30 **Gas** The Commission distinguishes the following product activities as distinct product markets in the natural gas sector:[30]

(1) upstream (all activities until gas is sold to wholesalers):
  - exploration;[31]
  - development, production, and sale (usually to wholesalers);[32]
  - transmission through upstream gas pipelines or LNG ships;[33]
  - processing of gas;[34]

(2) Downstream (all activities after gas is sold to wholesaler):
  - transmission (via the high-pressure pipeline grid);
  - distribution (via the low-pressure pipeline grids);
  - storage; and
  - trading and supply.

11.31 The Commission has also drawn distinctions in the category of 'gas supply' between eligible and non-eligible customers and between customers according to their annual gas consumption and type of activity.[35] The latter include:

- supply of gas to power producers (CCGTs);
- supply of gas to local distribution companies (LDCs);
- supply of gas to large industrial customers (LICs);

---

[29] *EDP/ENI/GDP* (Case COMP/M.3440) Commission Decision 2005/801/EC, [2005] OJ L302/69, n 29.

[30] *E.ON/MOL* (Case COMP/M.3696) Commission Decision 2006/622/EC, [2006] OJ L253/20, Recitals 88–90.

[31] *Exxon/Mobil* (Case COMP/M.1383) Commission Decision 2004/284/EC, [2004] OJ L103/1, paras 15 et seq.

[32] ibid.

[33] *Shell/Enterprise Oil* (Case COMP/M.2745) Commission Decision of 7 May 2002, paras 10 et seq; on LNG as part of the same market as pipeline gas see *BP/Sonatrach* (Case COMP/M.672) Commission Decision of 12 February 1996, para 17.

[34] ibid.

[35] *Exxon/Mobil* (Case COMP/M.1383) Commission Decision 2004/284/EC, [2004] OJ L103/1; *EDP/ENI/GDP* (Case COMP/M.3440) Commission Decision 2005/801/EC, [2005] OJ L302/69; *E.ON/MOL* (Case COMP/M.3696) Commission Decision 2006/622/EC, [2006] OJ L253/20.

- traders (all classifiable as 'wholesale supply'[36]); and
- retail supply of gas to small industrial, commercial, and household customers.[37]

In addition, the Commission has found that the German long-distance and short-distance wholesale transmission markets constitute distinct product markets for natural gas.[38]

(b) Geographic Market

The relevant geographic market has been defined by the Commission as follows: 11.32

> ... the area in which the undertakings concerned are involved in the supply and demand of products or services, in which the conditions of competition are sufficiently homogeneous and which can be distinguished from the neighbouring area because the conditions of competition are appreciably different in those areas.[39]

To reach a geographic definition of the relevant markets, the Commission has based its findings on statistical analyses of historical price differences between regions or countries. This data may point to the existence of a separate geographic market. In the energy sector the Commission has, in general, taken the view that the relevant market is the national market. However, there are some instances in which it may be more or less than the national market. In reaching a decision about this, the Commission will, with respect to electricity, take into account elements such as system designs, the existence of congestion at points in the grid, the existence of price correlations and price differentials, and the differing nature of supply and demand on both sides of the congestion points.[40] 11.33

Electricity The relevant geographic market for the wholesale supply of electricity has usually been—for example, in Commission decisions such as *Grupo Villar*[41] and 11.34

---

[36] It may be noted that the issue of the scope of the terms 'wholesale' or 'wholesale supply' is particularly complex in the definition of natural gas markets. Sometimes notifying parties propose all supplies to large users (regional distributors, power plants, and large industrial users) to be part of one 'wholesale market' whereas the Commission separates these markets further per customer group (eg *EDP/ENI/GDP* (Case COMP/M.3440) Commission Decision 2005/801/EC, [2005] OJ L302/69). In the Commission's definitions usually only sales to resellers are conceptually accepted as one or more 'wholesale' markets. Similarly, the expression of 'retail' supply can be ambiguous, sometimes being limited to small end-customers, sometimes being applied to all end-customer markets.

[37] As with electricity, the existence of separate markets for, on the one hand, commercial and small industrial customers and, on the other hand, household customers was repeatedly considered but it has not so far been necessary to decide on the issue (cf, eg, *DONG/Elsam/E2* (Case COMP/ M.3868) Commission Decision of 14 March 2006).

[38] *Exxon/Mobil* (Case COMP/M.1383) Commission Decision 2004/284/EC, [2004] OJ L103/1, Recital 111; *EnBW/ENI/GVS* (Case COMP/M.2822) Commission Decision 2003/668/EC, [2003] OJ L248/51.

[39] Commission Notice on the definition of relevant market for the purposes of Community competition law, 9 December 1997 [1997] OJ C372/03, para 7.

[40] Energy Sector Review, *Preliminary Report*, 16 February 2006, Annex B (Electricity), 195.

[41] *Grupo VillarMir/EnBW/Hidroeléctrica del Cantábrico* (Case COMP/M.2434) Commission Decision 2004/135/EC, [2004] OJ L48/86.

EDP/ENI/GDP—considered to be no wider than national borders. Even with respect to the Nordic countries where the integration of electricity markets seems to be the most advanced within the EU, the Commission has expressed doubts as to whether wider than national markets can be assumed.[42] This hesitation is supported by a decision by the NCA in Denmark, which assumed two relevant electricity wholesale markets no wider than Denmark.[43]

11.35 In the *EDP/ENI/GDP* case, contrary to the claims of the parties, the Commission's analysis confirmed that the relevant electricity wholesale market is currently national in scope and is highly unlikely to become Iberian in the near future.[44] Therefore, the Commission has generally considered that wholesale electricity markets are national in scope. However, in the *EDF/AEM* case,[45] the Commission noted that the Italian market was in practice segmented into seven geographic zones. It did not reach a conclusion as to whether the Italian market could be described as national or zone-based. Similarly, it has always considered that ancillary services are no wider than national in scope. There has been evidence that (narrower) balancing zone-based markets exist, but the question was ultimately left open. The retail electricity markets (final customer markets) are regarded as national, but narrower than national zone-based markets are not excluded, in particular for residential customers.[46] Subsequently, the Italian Energy Authority and the Competition Authority have both supported the view that the Italian market is segmented. The segmentation corresponds to the links which are by far the most congested ones and aggregates the zones which have prices that are almost perfectly correlated.[47]

11.36 **Gas** For gas, the relevant geographic markets are no wider than national, with one exception. For upstream product markets such as exploration and production,

---

[42] cf *E.ON/Sydkraft* (Case COMP/M.2349) Commission Decision of 9 April 2001; *Vattenfall/Elsam & E2 Assets* (Case COMP/M.3867) Commission Decision of 22 December 2005; *DONG/Elsam/E2* (Case COMP/M.3868) Commission Decision of 14 March 2006. In these decisions there was a remarkable tendency to assess the cases on all potential geographic wholesale markets, some of those options being wider than national. The existence of 'variable' geographic markets according to congestion level, a concept which is quite new in merger control, is not excluded. No definitive view was necessary, however.

[43] *Elsam/NESA* press release, <http://www.ks.dk/english/competition/national/2004/elsam>; see the discussion in Pedersen, TT, Smidt, C, and Christiansen, PK, 'Topics in Merger Control—Experiences from a Recent Merger in the Danish Electricity Sector' (2004) 27 World Competition 595–612. Within the Nordpool area itself, there may be three distinct markets: South Norway, West and East Denmark: see Energy Sector Review, *Preliminary Report*, 16 February 2006, Annex B (Electricity), 195–6.

[44] *EDP/ENI/GDP* (Case COMP/M.3440) Commission Decision 2005/801/EC, [2005] OJ L302/69, Recital 77.

[45] *EDF/AEM/Edison* (Case COMP/M.3729) Commission Decision of 12 August 2005.

[46] *EDP/ENI/GDP* (Case COMP/M.3440) Commission Decision 2005/801/EC, [2005] OJ L302/69; *GdF/Centrica/SPE* (Case COMP/M.3883) Commission Decision of 7 September 2005.

[47] Energy Sector Review, *Preliminary Report*, 16 February 2006, Annex B (Electricity), 195.

offshore transmission processing and production and sales to wholesale companies, the corresponding geographic markets have been distinguished by the Commission into, respectively: gas fields in the EEA plus potentially Russian Federation (RF) and Algeria; the region in which the pipelines are located (for the offshore transmission);[48] gas fields in the EEA plus potential RF and Algerian sources. For oil, the Commission has accepted that the relevant geographic markets are world-wide in scope for the development, production, and sale of crude oil.

(c) Market Integration

The Commission takes into account the continuing process of market integration when defining geographic markets. Any specific measures that have been adopted as part of the energy market liberalization process have therefore to be considered. An example of this is the special provision made by the Gas Directive for the stage of development of Portugal's gas market. In the *EDP/ENI/GDP* case, it was noted that the definition of the relevant product market has to take into account the existing and foreseen degree of opening of that market.[49] According to the Commission Notice on the definition of the Relevant Market, for the purposes of EC competition law: 'A process of market integration that would, in the short term, lead to wider geographic markets may be taken into consideration when defining the geographic market for the purposes of assessing concentrations and joint ventures.' In particular, 'a situation where national markets have been artificially isolated from each other because of the existence of legislative barriers that have now been removed will generally lead to a cautious assessment of past evidence regarding prices, market shares or trade patterns'[50] (this might be called a transitional market approach). Commission decisions have supported the idea that the definition of the relevant product market must normally be viewed in the context of the opened segment of the market, but some decisions have taken into account the existing and foreseen degree of opening of the market.[51]

11.37

D. The Energy Sector Review

As a senior Commission official observed, the new Regulation 'changed the way the Commission is enforcing the EC competition rules, by moving its culture

11.38

---

[48] *BP Amoco/Arco* (Case IV/M.1532) Commission Decision 2000/45/EC, [2001] OJ L18/1 in which a southern North Sea gas transportation market was assumed.
[49] See *EnBW/EDP/Cajastur/Hidrocantábrico* (Case COMP/M.2684) Commission Decision of 19 March 2002.
[50] Commission Notice on the definition of relevant market for the purposes of Community competition law, 9 December 1997 [1997] OJ C372/03, 6.
[51] *EnBW/EDP/Cajastur/Hidrocantábrico* (Case COMP/M.2684) Commission Decision of 19 March 2002 23; *EDP/ENI/GDP* (Case COMP/M.3440) Commission Decision 2005/801/EC, [2005] OJ L302/69, Recital 16.

from re-active to pro-active enforcement'.[52] Evidence of this change emerged soon after the Regulation entered into force. On 13 June 2005 the European Commission announced an investigation into the operation of competition in the EU electricity and gas markets,[53] using its powers under Article 17 of Regulation 1/2003. The justification for the inquiry was set out in a communication issued jointly with the Competition and Energy Commissioners.[54] The action was part of a wider agenda by the Commission to pursue a more proactive application of the competition rules and thereby ensure open and competitive markets in the EU, especially in the energy sector.[55]

11.39 The inquiry in electricity had a different focus from that on gas. Competition in the sectors is at different stages of development and the structures of production are very different. However, the links between the two sectors are important, such as the increasing use of gas as a primary fuel for electricity generation. In electricity the competition concerns were focused more on the price formation mechanisms in the wholesale markets, in generation and supply and the factors that determine the generators' dispatching and bidding strategies. Three issues were of particular concern: whether generators have significant market power and can therefore influence wholesale prices; barriers to entry and cross-border flows that arise from long-term supply agreements in certain Member States; and finally, the legal and operational regimes for the interconnectors that link national electricity grids. In the gas sector—which at the earliest planning stages had not been targeted for an inquiry—the focus was to be on the long-term import contracts, swap agreements and barriers to cross-border flows, but also balancing requirements for network users and gas storage. The inquiry also extended to downstream long-term contracts and the effects they might have on switching costs and market entry.

11.40 The announcement followed an earlier announcement of a review into the operation of competition in the retail banking sector. Prior to this, there had been a sector review into telecommunications, but almost no other use of this policy instrument over a 20-year period. It was indicative of a wider change in thinking about enforcement.

11.41 The lead institution in the energy review was the Competition Directorate, but the tasks were carried out in close co-operation with the Energy Directorate (DG TREN),

---

[52] Lowe, P, 'Anti-Trust Reform in Europe: A Year In Practice', paper delivered at International Bar Association/European Commission Conference, Brussels, 11 March 2005, 4.
[53] Commission Decision (EC) C(2005)1682 of 13 June 2005 initiating an inquiry into the gas and electricity sectors pursuant to Article 17 of Council Regulation (EC) 1/2003. See Commission Press Release IP/05/716, 'Competition: Commission opens sector inquiry into gas and electricity', 13 June 2005.
[54] See <http://europa.eu.int/comm/competition/antitrust/others/sector_inquiries/energy/communication_en.pdf>.
[55] The strategy was intended to revive the so-called Lisbon Agenda of economic reform: *Communication to the Spring European Council—Working together for growth and jobs—A new start for the Lisbon Agenda*, COM (2005) 24, 2 February 2005, 8 and 19.

D. The Energy Sector Review

the national regulatory authorities, and the NCAs. The CEER had asked the Commission for such a review some time earlier and had strongly supported it since it began. The main driver for the inquiry was the rising wholesale prices for electricity and gas in 2004–05, combined with customers' lack of trust in the mechanisms by which the prices are formed. Other drivers were the persistent complaints about barriers to entry and limited consumer choice, the effects of a high level of market concentration, and a limited development of cross-border trade in electricity.

(1) The Inquiry: Data Collection, Scope, and Compliance

The scale of the investigation was considerable. The first phase began with the design and sending of questionnaires to all the major companies during the summer of 2005—more than 3,000 of them, split unevenly between electricity (about 1,900) and gas (about 1,300), and translated into all of the EU languages—as a data-collection exercise. This data covered the years 2003–05. The recipients of questionnaires were producers, generators, suppliers, traders, importers, power exchanges, brokers, storage operators, transmission and distribution system operators, customers, and regulatory authorities. Failure to complete this form could have resulted in the imposition of a legal penalty (fines), but in fact the compliance was so high that this was not necessary. Articles 17 and 18 of the Regulation allow the Commission to ask for confidential documents since they require facts. There are confidentiality obligations upon the Commission about the use of the data. This large quantity of data was then analyzed at the Commission's Competition Directorate to provide the basis for the findings in the final report. An interim report—called an Issues Paper[56]—was presented for discussion with national regulators and NCAs in November 2005, and subsequently was discussed by the Energy Council on 1 December 2005.   **11.42**

This was only phase 1 of the investigation, however. A second, more detailed phase commenced in 2006 with further questionnaires sent to and interviews held with selected companies. Even before the publication of the final report, its effects were being felt. While the investigation was ongoing, the Commission could—and did—launch antitrust actions against specific companies.   **11.43**

What kind of legal actions might the Commission initiate? The aim was to identify whether there had been any infringements of Articles 81, 82, or 86 EC that have resulted in a malfunctioning of the electricity and gas markets. In such circumstances, the Commission could take 'proactive corrective action'[57] to restore competition in the relevant markets, by 'addressing individual decisions to the entities con-   **11.44**

---

[56] European Commission, Competition DG, *Energy Sector Inquiry—Issues Paper*, 15 November 2005 <http://ec.europa.eu/comm/competition/antitrust/others/sector_inquiries/energy/issues_paper 15112005.pdf>.
[57] European Commission, *Report on Competition Policy 2005*, 24, point 41.

cerned, based on Article 81 and Article 82 of the Treaty, on their own or, for the Commission, in conjunction with Article 86 of the EC Treaty'.[58] There were three kinds of possible actions that could arise from the investigation:

(1) actions against companies refusing to co-operate properly (an unwillingness to answer questionnaires or giving inappropriate or late answers);
(2) formal proceedings against individual companies (based on information gathered in sector inquiries or by the Commission or NCAs); and
(3) further legislative initiatives of the Commission.

11.45 The timing of actions based on the facts collected in the inquiry and the analysis thereof did not depend on the conclusion of the report. From the outset, the intention was to take up cases as soon as they emerged. Indeed, on-site inspections were carried out on the premises of several energy groups in April and May 2006, including RWE, E.ON and Gaz de France. The raids included more than 20 sites in Austria, Belgium, France, Germany, Hungary, and Italy. In Hungary the inspection concerned several electricity companies which were suspected of excluding competitors from the wholesale electricity market by entering into long-term power purchase agreements and import contracts underpinned by long-term capacity reservation on interconnectors.[59]

11.46 The first output of the inquiry was an Issues Paper, published in November 2005, which provided the basis for the final report. It concerned the identification of problems rather than the proposal of specific remedies. There were separate chapters on electricity and gas. In each chapter, there was a description of the markets, followed by a review of the five main themes based on perceived impediments to competition. These were: market concentration; vertical foreclosure; market integration; transparency and the price formation mechanism. It formed the basis for the subsequent report, which is discussed below.

(2) Significance

11.47 Why does the sector inquiry matter? The answer lies in both content and context.

- **Content** The inquiry focuses on the core problem facing the establishment of a liberalized energy market in the EU: the *structure* of the market that has emerged from the pre-liberalization period, in which incumbents have retained a dominant role. In the past ten years the incumbents have become stronger and more consolidated than before liberalization was started. A more consistent and

---

[58] Commission Decision (EC) C(2005)1682, Recitals 5 and 9.
[59] Commission Press Releases MEMO/06/203 and MEMO/06/205, 17 May 2006, but in a later Press Release, MEMO/06/220, 'Competition: Commission confirms inspections in the energy sector', 30 May 2006, it stated that these 'surprise inspections' were not a part of the energy sector inquiry but arose from evidence that the companies concerned may have violated Arts 81 and 82.

D. The Energy Sector Review

rigorous application of competition law is the main instrument to deal with the barriers to competition that result.

- **Context** This is one of two reports that will be presented to the EU energy ministers. The other report is being produced by the Commission's energy directorate, DG TREN, and is a progress report on the functioning of legislation introduced in 2003 to accelerate liberalization. The main source of data for this is derived from the national energy regulators, but it will also benefit from information sharing with the Commission's competition arm. It is likely to be highly critical of the current market structure and set the scene for further proposals for legislation.

- **Policy-making** The sector inquiry is a proactive tool to identify barriers to competition and how to remove them, but the tool is also designed to ensure that internal market and competition policies develop in harmony, contributing to 'better regulation'. Since it is intended to contribute to laying down a new basis for competition and energy policy, it is the first explicit example of such 'joined-up policy-making' in the energy sector.

(3) The Results

11.48 In its final report[60] the Commission built on the analysis in the Issues Paper and examined the five main categories of barrier to a fully functioning internal energy market: market concentration; vertical foreclosure; lack of market integration; lack of transparency; and price formation. These findings differ with respect to electricity and gas markets. The overall picture presented by the findings is, in the words of the Competition Commissioner, 'rather gloomy'.[61]

(a) Electricity

11.49 **Market concentration** For the most part, the wholesale markets remain national in scope and exhibit high levels of concentration in generation, giving scope for the exercise of market power by incumbents. The sales in spot markets reflect the level of concentration in generation, whereas those for trading in forward markets show less concentration. However, market shares do not provide an entirely reliable indicator of market power in electricity markets. Analysis of trading in power exchanges shows that generators have in some cases the scope to raise prices, which has been a matter of concern for many customers. Similarly, analysis of generation portfolios shows that the main generators have the ability to withdraw capacities to raise prices.

11.50 **Vertical foreclosure** A dominant feature of many electricity markets is the vertical integration of generation, supply, and network activities. The effect of this

---

[60] European Commission, 'Inquiry pursuant to Article 17 of Regulation (EC) No 1/2003 into the European gas and electricity sectors (Final Report)', COM (2006) 851 final; an earlier draft, *Preliminary Report*, was published on 16 February 2006.

[61] Kroes, N, *Towards an Efficient and Integrated European Energy Market—First Findings and Next Steps*, 16 February 2006.

vertical integration in generation and retail is to stifle the incentive to trade on wholesale markets. An entry barrier is established by low levels of liquidity. Where there are strong links between supply and network companies, this reduces the economic incentives for network operators to grant access to third parties. In this context, the solution provided by existing unbundling provisions in the second Electricity Directive is deemed to be inadequate.

11.51 **Market integration** The low level of cross-border trade means that there is little pressure exerted on the dominant generators in national markets. There are also barriers to integration created by inadequate interconnector capacity or long-term capacity reservations predating the implementation of liberalization measures. If access to such interconnectors is to be improved, this requires better methods of congestion management. Investment in additional capacity to eliminate long-established bottlenecks is not likely to be made without greater incentives for this. Finally, there are different market designs which have the effect of hampering market integration.

11.52 **Transparency** The Commission's finding is that there is a serious lack of transparency in the electricity wholesale markets and that this is widely recognized by the sector. If there was an improvement in transparency this would minimize the risks for market players and so reduce entry barriers to generation and supply markets, as well as providing a level playing field and improving trust in the wholesale markets and confidence in its price signals. At present, users are in need of greater information on technical availability of interconnectors and transmission networks, on generation, on balancing and reserve power, and on load. Finally, there are significant differences between Member States with respect to proper market conduct and supervision, as well as little harmonization at the EU level of the transparency requirements in electricity markets.

11.53 **Price formation** The evidence gathered by the Commission suggested strongly that many users have limited trust in the price formation mechanisms. This is a complex area, however, in which there is a growing impact from the EU emissions trading system. It appears that fuel price rises have an impact on electricity price developments (fuel oil is a competing source of fuel for generation). There appears to be little agreement between experts in this area. Where a Member State seeks to introduce a scheme for the reduction of electricity costs for large energy intensive users, this is limited by the state aid and antitrust rules.

(b) Gas

11.54 **Market concentration** The high level of concentration evident in the pre-liberalization period is largely maintained in the wholesale markets. Wholesale trade has been slow to develop, while the incumbents remain dominant in their traditional (that is, national) markets. This is secured largely by control of

D. The Energy Sector Review

upstream gas imports and/or EU gas production. Only a very small proportion of gas is traded on hubs by incumbents. Since there is little new entry in retail markets, the scope for customer choice is limited and competitive pressure is reduced accordingly. The overall picture for potential new entrants is therefore one in which they are dependent upon vertically integrated incumbents for services throughout the supply chain.

Vertical foreclosure New market entrant suppliers are prevented from offering their services to consumers by the lack of liquidity and limited access to infrastructure. The existence of a network of long-term supply contracts between gas producers and incumbent importers makes it very difficult for new entrants to obtain access to gas on the upstream markets. Moreover, the contracts themselves contain features that limit incentives to incumbents to provide liquidity on traded markets. The network and storage infrastructure is to a large extent owned by the incumbent gas importers, and the inadequate separation of this infrastructure from supply functions has the effect that market opening is insufficient. There are of course rules on third party access (TPA) and legal and functional unbundling, but new entrants still lack effective access to networks, and operators are alleged to favour their own affiliates. **11.55**

Market integration Cross-border sales do not at present exert any significant competitive pressure. In contrast to electricity, there is considerable trade in gas across frontiers but this has few competitive effects. Incumbents rarely enter other national gas markets as competitors, and available capacity on cross-border import pipelines is limited. On key routes, new entrants are unable to secure transit capacity. The primary capacity on transit pipelines is controlled by the incumbents by means of legacy contracts that derogate from normal TPA rules. This is reinforced by ineffective congestion management mechanisms. The result is that it is hard to secure even small volumes of short-term, interruptible capacity on the secondary market. In the majority of cases, new entrants do not have the secured capacity even if there have been expansions of the transit pipeline capacity. **11.56**

Transparency Reliable and timely information is missing from the markets. Network users are keen to have more transparency on access to networks, transit capacity, and storage, going beyond the current minimum requirements set by the Gas Directive. To ensure a level playing field, information would be required to be made available on an equal footing. The rules on confidentiality also work to undermine effective transparency when they are interpreted too widely. **11.57**

Price formation A more effective and transparent price formation is required to deliver the full advantages of market opening to consumers. Gas import contracts use price indices that are oil-indexed and have therefore tracked the price increases in the oil markets. The prices fail to react to changes in the supply and demand for gas. It was noted that even in circumstances where different producers are selling **11.58**

from the same gas field, the contracts usually contain the same price index and often the same price.

(c) Supplementary Issues

11.59 Several issues were identified during the first phase of the inquiry as worthy of further study: competition in downstream (ie, retail) markets; balancing in electricity and gas markets, and the role of LNG. The results are included in the final report. In retail markets competition was found to be limited in most cases. Features such as long contract duration, contracts with indefinite duration, tacit renewal clauses, and long termination periods were found to have negative cumulative effects. Balancing markets show a tendency to favour incumbents and to create obstacles for newcomers. Indeed, the small size of current balancing zones leads to increased costs and protects the incumbents' market power. The report's assessment of LNG was positive as a contributor to competition between upstream suppliers and EU security of supply.

(d) Remedies

11.60 The remedies for this situation may be of structural, regulatory, or competition law varieties. With respect to *competition law* remedies, the Commission is pursuing infringements in close co-operation with the NCAs. Three areas in particular appear to be problems for the competition law: market concentration, vertical foreclosure, and market integration. These are not the sole areas for attention, only the priority ones. Other cases of anti-competitive and exclusionary conduct that are to be examined include the inhibiting of customers from switching suppliers.

11.61 With respect to market concentration, this is the major problem and requires action under the Merger Regulation. Although the normal practice is for each merger case to be assessed according to its specific characteristics, the sector inquiry will help to identify the most relevant criteria and the most efficient remedies in the given market environment. With respect to vertical foreclosure and the tying of downstream markets, the sector inquiry has confirmed that foreclosure of the market by long-term downstream contracts is an immediate priority for the review of case situations under competition law. Market integration raises particular issues with respect to access to capacity on pipelines, gas storage, and on interconnectors. This has been found to be a major stumbling block towards more market integration, and so should be an immediate priority for review in terms of anti-competitive conduct.

11.62 *Regulatory* actions may be addressed to three principal areas, such as transparency, grandfather rights, and interconnectors. Transparency is insufficient in both electricity and gas. This may be corrected by strengthening transparency obligations, whether under regulation or competition law. The remaining grandfather rights (capacity rights arising from pre-liberalization monopoly contracts) are regarded by many as presenting a serious obstacle to the effective entry of competitors. They undermine the pro-competitive operation of the market. Finally, more

D. The Energy Sector Review

needs to be done to fix common rules regarding the interconnectors between national grids. There are a number of schemes between national regulators in place or being set up concerning co-ordination but it appears that purely voluntary schemes for co-operation between regulators are unlikely to provide the investment certainty and the regulatory protection needed to develop international pipelines and interconnectors in a stable environment and to keep them open. The report concludes that a substantial strengthening of the powers of NRAs and reinforced co-ordination are essential.

11.63 It might be expected that improved transparency obligations could be rooted in the requirements of the financial services Directives. The two Directives that are relevant are the Directive on Markets in Financial Instruments[62] and the Market Abuse Directive.[63] The purpose of these Directives is to regulate the trade of securities, including derivatives of commodity markets and related financial services. Their aim does not include the regulation of commodity trading itself. While they do impose various transparency obligations on financial markets, some of their provisions are applied under national implementing legislation to some but not all electricity wholesale markets. Member States are allowed considerable discretion in their implementation so the result is that they impose only limited transparency obligations on electricity wholesale markets or their participants.

11.64 *Structural* actions are required in parallel with regulatory ones. The report states that 'it is essential to resolve the systemic conflict of interest inherent in the vertical integration of supply and network activities'.[64] This has its roots in the pre-liberalization period and acts as a brake on the development of an efficient competitive market. One further consequence is that it makes the EU energy market less receptive to the introduction of new forms of energy such as renewables due to the vested interests of stakeholders at all three levels of the value chain. It also prevents an effective diversification of supply, which has security implications. A decisive reinforcement of the current levels of unbundling is therefore necessary.

11.65 One of the remedies that may be included in a Regulation is a requirement for gas release and contract release programmes (discussed at paras 14.108–14.118). The aim of these would be to ensure that new suppliers can buy enough gas to build a supply business. There are examples of these being imposed by national authorities in the UK and Italy. In other cases, these have been imposed by the Commission in the context of approvals for mergers. The programmes require incumbents to sell a defined volume of gas. Their effectiveness will be enhanced if they are operated over

---

[62] Directive (EC) 2004/39 on markets in financial instruments [2004] OJ L145/1. See discussion in the Report at 194–197.
[63] Directive (EC) 2003/6 on insider dealing and market manipulation (market abuse) [2003] OJ L96/16.
[64] p 325.

a number of years and in conjunction with a release of network capacity. A contract release is a different matter, involving a transfer of some of the incumbent's existing gas purchase contracts to new buyers. This will be effective if there are entrant suppliers which are able to assume the risks involved in traditional gas purchase contracts.

E. Conclusions

11.66 The overhaul of competition law and policy in recent years is designed to place the consumer interest at the heart of competition policy, although the motivation behind the new Merger Regulation may be rather different. Cases that directly affect the consumer interest have acquired a priority status. In addition, competition policy has been identified as an instrument for structural reform and promotion of the Lisbon strategy. Both of these objectives are evident behind the use of the sector review instrument discussed in this chapter. Faced with a high volume of consumer complaints in 2004–05 about energy prices, the Commission has chosen to ratchet up its support for energy market liberalization by the use of competition policy. As an information-gathering exercise, the Energy Sector Review reveals few surprises about the current operation of the electricity and gas markets. Their complexity and the dynamics will undoubtedly be better understood by the Commission with respect to, inter alia, the definition of product and geographic markets. However, as an evidence-gathering exercise to justify the launch of specific actions against individual companies or groups of companies in national or regional settings, it has been a bold first step towards the development of the new, more assertive competition policy that the 'modernized' legal framework makes possible. The next steps will determine whether consumers will benefit from the new proactive approach to these markets which the Commission has acquired, and whether competition policy can complement energy policy to achieve a break-through in this area.

11.67 Whatever steps are taken to develop the 'new direction' in competition policy, it will draw on the Commission's experience with competition problems in the electricity and gas sectors in the recent past. The following chapters review this experience of enforcing competition law in the energy sector, beginning with the use of antitrust rules in the upstream sector (Chapter 12) before turning to the various actions concerning networks (Chapter 13). However, an important new dimension to enforcement is the increased weight given to the role of NCAs and to close co-operation within the Network. Where information is available on such co-operation, the following chapters attempt to take it into account.

12

COMPETITION IN UPSTREAM MARKETS

A. Introduction	12.01	D. Territorial Sales Restrictions:	
B. Joint Marketing of Gas	12.04	'Destination Clauses'	12.33
(1) The *GFU* Case	12.05	(1) Norwegian Producers	12.38
(2) The *Corrib* Case	12.11	(2) The *NLNG* Case	12.39
(3) The *DUC/DONG* Case	12.14	(3) The *Gazprom* Cases	12.42
(a) Joint Marketing	12.17	(a) ENI and Russian Gas	12.44
(b) The Reduction Clauses	12.20	(b) OMV and Russian Gas	12.49
		(c) Ruhrgas and Russian Gas	12.51
(c) Restrictions on Use	12.25	(d) Gasunie and Gazprom	12.53
(d) Access	12.27	(e) Conclusion	12.54
(e) Monitoring	12.28	(4) *GDF/ENEL* and *GDF/ENI*	12.55
C. Joint Marketing of Electricity	12.30	(5) *Sonatrach*	12.58
		E. Conclusions	12.60

> For gas, competition is only really active in the North Sea region and to a lesser extent in Spain.
>
> European Commission[1]

A. Introduction

The impact of EU law on the hydrocarbons sector has differed considerably between oil and gas. The oil market is global in character, and effective commodity markets in crude oil and petroleum products have existed for some time. Legal action to promote liberalization has therefore been deemed largely unnecessary. However, there are two exceptions to this. First, in the market for petroleum products, the Commission used its powers under Article 31 EC to pursue the dismantling of

12.01

---

[1] *Report on Progress in Creating the Internal Gas and Electricity Market: Technical Annex*, COM (2005) 568 final, 15 November 2005, 9.

'oil products monopolies' in France and Greece during the 1980s.[2] The second exception was the hydrocarbons licensing legislation (see Chapter 7). This formed part of the liberalization programme and was one of the first legal measures it introduced.

12.02 For the gas sector the situation is more complex. First, it has an international character with the bulk of supplies coming from non-EU countries on the basis of long-term contracts, but is much less exposed to competition in pricing than the oil sector. Secondly, there are elements of natural monopoly in the high-pressure pipeline network that impose limits on the scope of competition. Finally, gas operations have a vertically integrated character from production to consumption (the so-called *gas chain* or *gas column*). This means that regulatory action in one segment can easily impact on other segments. With the design of sector-specific legislation, the gas sector came under scrutiny by the Commission mainly because of the exercise of monopoly power in the transmission and distribution segments of its operations. In a separate development, competition policy has been increasingly applied in the 'upstream' gas sector to complement the liberalization process stimulated by the internal market legislation.

12.03 The focus of competition policy has been in three areas: first, the anti-competitive barriers to competition between suppliers, such as the joint marketing arrangements of gas producers; secondly, the anti-competitive obstacles for effective and non-discriminatory third party access; and thirdly, the anti-competitive behaviour of suppliers by imposing so-called 'destination clauses' in their contracts with EU wholesalers. The latter clauses are usually found in transit contracts and prevent the gas purchasers from reselling the gas outside the territories where they are traditionally established. The scope of these investigations has drawn in third countries since it has included the content of transactions between non-EU suppliers of gas and EU-based purchasers. The procedure adopted by the Commission is striking in the sense that *in every case except one* it agreed to conclude the proceedings with a negotiated settlement with the parties rather than taking formal action.

B. Joint Marketing of Gas

12.04 Gas producers sometimes venture beyond joint production of gas into its sale. Their practice of using joint arrangements to sell gas has attracted scrutiny from the Commission. These horizontal arrangements have been a traditional practice on the part of gas producers but could be viewed as a way of artificially reducing the

---

[2] Sixth Report on Competition Policy (1977), points 268–9 (France); Case C-347/88 *Commission v Greece* [1990] ECR 4747.

number of independent players. Although this practice had been tacitly permitted for some time, it came under new scrutiny in the late 1990s[3] and was deemed to be in breach of Article 81(1) EC. However, there have been *two* kinds of joint marketing of gas by producers that have caused concerns to the Commission. The first is the joint marketing arrangements for a single country and the second is the joint marketing arrangements concerning a single gas field. The sections below examine each of these in the context of the *GFU* case (paras 12.05–12.10) and the cases on *Corrib* and the *DUC/DONG* (paras 12.11–12.29).

(1) The *GFU* Case

12.05 The Commission began investigations in 1996 into the joint selling arrangements used in the supply of gas from Norway to EU gas companies, as a possible infringement of Article 81(1) EC and Article 53(1) of the EEA Agreement (to which Norway is a party). The central body in this selling arrangement was the GFU or Gas Sales Consortium, a statutory body established in Norway. It comprised two permanent members, Statoil and Norsk Hydro, Norway's largest gas producers, and sometimes included other Norwegian gas producers.

12.06 The GFU had an exclusive negotiating right for all sales of Norwegian gas. Its principal task was to negotiate the terms of all the supply contracts with buyers located for the most part in the EU on behalf of all of the natural gas producers in Norway. The status of single seller automatically precluded the non-Norwegian licence interest holders from negotiating or participating in the negotiation of sales of their own gas to buyers in the EU. The GFU fixed the price, volumes, and all other trading conditions. As a result, it severely limited the choice of EU consumers to negotiate with Norwegian gas producers.

12.07 The Commission initiated proceedings against about 30 Norwegian gas companies, and argued that the selling scheme was incompatible with EC competition law.[4] The scheme led to rigidity in the markets and a lack of liquidity. This followed an announcement from the Government of Norway that it would suspend the sale of Norwegian natural gas through the GFU from 1 June 2001 and abolish it entirely as of 1 January 2002. However, the effects of this measure were unlikely to be felt for many years due to the fact that most of the gas sold by the GFU was already contracted under arrangements that had up to 25 years to run. The Commission called upon national energy regulators and competition authorities to assist it by pursuing 'with vigour' any violations of the internal market and competition rules

---

[3] Dinnage, J, 'Competition in Gas Supply: The Competition Man Cometh' (1998) 16 J Energy Natural Resources L249–85.
[4] Commission Press Release IP/01/830, 'Commission objects to GFU joint gas sales in Norway', 13 June 2001.

regarding access of Norwegian gas to European pipelines.[5] In this respect, the Commission would focus on cross-border cases while the national authorities would be best placed to deal with cases that have a national dimension.

12.08 In the next steps, the parties explored the basis for a settlement. The gas companies argued that EC competition law should not be applied since the selling scheme had been discontinued as of June 2001.[6] Moreover, it *could* not be applied since the Norwegian gas producers had been compelled to sell gas by the Norwegian Government through the GFU which had been established by the Norwegian Government itself, as long ago as 1989. However, most of the gas companies were willing to provide commitments to settle the case. Two categories of company could be distinguished among them.[7] The first group comprised the permanent members of the GFU, Statoil, and Norsk Hydro. The second group comprised six groups of companies which sold Norwegian gas through contracts negotiated by the GFU: ExxonMobil, Shell, TotalFinaElf, Conoco, Fortum, and Agip. The commitments made by these two groups were such that the Commission decided to accept them and close the case.

12.09 The commitments made by Statoil and Norsk Hydro were followed by the six groups in the second category. Essentially, there were two principal commitments made in the settlement:

- the discontinuation of all joint marketing and sales activities unless these are compatible with EC competition law; and
- the reservation of certain gas volumes for new customers which have in the past not purchased gas from Norwegian gas producers.

12.10 The first commitment meant that when existing supply contracts came up for review, there would be individual negotiations. Under the second commitment, Statoil undertook to make available 13 billion cubic metres (BCM) of gas to new customers on commercially competitive terms. Norsk Hydro gave an undertaking to do the same for 2.2 BCM. On an annual basis this corresponds to more than 5 per cent of the total sales volumes of Norwegian gas.[8] This quantity of gas had to be offered for sale during the commitment period from June 2001 to September 2005. The performance of the commitments was to be monitored by external auditors.

---

[5] Commission Press Release IP/01/1170, 'Commission Insists on Effective Access to European Pipelines for Norwegian Gas', 2 August 2001.
[6] Lindroos, M, Schnichels, D, Svane, LP, 'Liberalization of European Gas Markets—Commission settles GFU case with Norwegian gas producers' (2002) 3 Competition Policy Newsletter 50–52.
[7] A third group comprised all the other Norwegian gas producers which had been involved in the proceedings by the Commission. The Commission closed its case with them on the understanding that they would sell Norwegian gas individually in the future.
[8] Commission Press Release IP/02/1084, 'Commission successfully settles GFU case with Norwegian gas producers', 17 July 2002.

B. Joint Marketing of Gas

(2) The *Corrib* Case

12.11 Another case in which joint marketing arrangements were reviewed turned on plans for the marketing of gas from a newly discovered gas field in Ireland called Corrib.[9] The licensee companies, Enterprise Energy Ireland Limited, Statoil, and Marathon, applied to the Commission for an exemption under Article 81(3) EC to market the gas jointly for the first five years of production. They argued that joint marketing was necessary to balance the countervailing purchasing power of the incumbent Irish energy companies, Bord Gáis Eireann, the state-owned gas company, and the Electricity Supply Board, the state-owned electricity company. The companies withdrew their application after the Commission raised objections on competition grounds, and instead they agreed to market their gas individually. The Commission argued that the ongoing liberalization process would create an increasing number of 'eligible' customers, including power generators and energy-intensive industrial consumers. The net effect would be to expand the customer-base in the power market and offer potential sales outlets to gas suppliers. The case confirmed that there is now a policy of not tolerating joint selling of gas, unless compelling reasons are provided as a justification.

12.12 The outcome of the *Corrib* case provides an interesting contrast to the *Britannia* case of only a few years earlier.[10] In that case, the Commission cleared an agreement notified to it by the companies participating in the development of the Britannia gas field in the UK. The agreement affected joint selling operations between February 1992 and the end of 1994. In the absence of a gas interconnector between the UK and continental Europe, the agreement did not affect trade between Member States to an appreciable extent and so did not fall within the prohibition of Article 81. However, this conclusion was based on the absence of any pipeline system between the UK and any other Member State that could have managed the volumes of gas to be produced by this field. By 1998 the UK-Belgium gas interconnector entered into operation, and this argument in support of joint selling was no longer justified. That appears to have triggered a change in the Commission's response when it was subsequently presented with the proposal of the gas producers to market jointly the Corrib gas. However, an influential development was surely the adoption of the first Gas Directive in 1998, which marked the beginning of the first phase of gas market liberalization.

12.13 The Commission has kept under review the horizontal arrangements concluded among gas producers, on the ground that this traditional practice—where gas

---

[9] Commission Press Release IP/01/578, 'Enterprise Oil, Statoil and Marathon to market Irish Corrib gas separately', 20 April 2001.
[10] [1996] OJ C291/10; Commission Press Release IP/96/1214, 'The Commission Clears a Notified Agreement Concerning the Britannia Gas Field', 19 December 1996.

producers co-operate closely with each other in both production and marketing in order to minimize risk and to ensure maximum revenues from sales—has artificially reduced the number of independent players. In the Commissioner's view, the case confirmed the Commission's general policy 'not to tolerate joint selling, unless compelling reasons are provided as a justification'.[11]

(3) The *DUC/DONG* Case

12.14   An investigation of joint marketing of gas in Denmark was concluded in April 2003.[12] It concerned not only the joint marketing activities of the gas producers concerned but also involved certain restrictive provisions contained in the gas supply contracts they had concluded with the Danish incumbent gas supplier, DONG. It differed from the GFU case in being limited to gas produced from one or more fields, rather than all gas produced in a single country.

12.15   The partners in the DUC (Danish Underground Consortium) accounted for 90 per cent of the production on the Danish continental shelf. The gas was produced by the three partners, Shell, AP Moller/Maersk, and Chevron/Texaco, with 46 per cent, 39 per cent, and 15 per cent shares respectively, under three large gas supply agreements, and sold exclusively to DONG. A significant proportion of the gas was consumed in Denmark while the rest was exported to Sweden and Germany.

12.16   The gas supply agreements between the DUC partners and DONG were negotiated jointly by the DUC partners and DONG, but they were subsequently entered into separately by each of the DUC partners and by DONG. The contracts contained a number of notable provisions. First, the partners granted DONG certain priority rights over the sale of 'additional' or newly discovered gas volumes. Secondly, price formulae were included and varied according to the customer to whom DONG resold the gas. Thirdly, they contained a mechanism that became operational if the parties commenced sales in Denmark itself. This mechanism was understood as providing the right to ask for, among other things, adjustments to the gas volumes which were purchased from the DUC partners. The Commission's approach differed according to whether the restraints were horizontal (joint marketing) or vertical (concerning the supply relationship between the DUC partners and DONG). The vertical restraints could be distinguished into the restraints imposed on the DUC partners in their function as suppliers (the reduction clause) and the restraints imposed on DONG in its function as buyer/customer (restrictions on use). These three elements are discussed separately below.

---

[11] Commission Press Release IP/01/578, 'Enterprise Oil, Statoil and Marathon to market Irish Corrib gas separately', 20 April 2001.
[12] Commission Press Release IP/03/566, 'Commission and Danish competition authorities jointly open up Danish gas market', 24 April 2003.

B. Joint Marketing of Gas

(a) Joint Marketing

12.17 The DUC partners had negotiated their gas supply agreements with DONG jointly but had signed separate contracts with DONG. However, this had occurred only at the end of the negotiations with DONG. The Commission took the view that the joint marketing activities reduced the options of customers to choose between suppliers or producers, and in this way competition was restricted contrary to Article 81(1) EC. An exemption was not appropriate since joint marketing does not usually improve the production or distribution of goods within the meaning of Article 81(3).

12.18 The gas producers argued that their joint production and marketing arrangements were covered by Regulation (EC) 2658/2000 (the Specialization Block Exemption).[13] Under this Regulation, Article 3(b) allows for 'joint distribution' of goods that were produced jointly, in certain circumstances. However, in the Commission's view, the joint marketing provided by the contracts amounted to a mere 'joint coordination of sales' between independent gas operators relating to the conclusion of a few long-term gas contracts covering essentially all of the gas available to the producers. This was quite different from the 'joint distribution' envisaged by the Regulation. Moreover, according to Recital 8 of the Regulation, one of the effects of specialization should be that 'the undertakings concerned can concentrate on the manufacture of certain products and thus operate more efficiently and supply the products more cheaply'. This is hardly applicable to the forms of joint production in the gas industry.

12.19 The arguments of both sides were inconclusive, but the DUC offered commitments which brought the investigation to a conclusion. First, they agreed to discontinue joint marketing activities for as yet non-contracted gas produced from the Danish continental shelf. In particular, they agreed to market all new gas individually in the future. Secondly, they undertook to carry out negotiations individually on existing contracts when prices were to be renegotiated. Thirdly, they promised to offer for sale 7 BCM of gas to new customers over a period of five years commencing 1 January 2005, when new gas volumes would be available. On an annual basis, this amounted to 17 per cent of the total production of the DUC parties. Since DONG promised not to buy such volumes, this undertaking was considered by the Commission to be sufficient to close the investigation of joint marketing in past years.

(b) The Reduction Clauses

12.20 In another investigation the Commission identified a mechanism which it referred to as a 'reduction clause', and which raised competition concerns. The case concerned

---

[13] Commission Regulation (EC) 2658/2000 of 29 November 2000 on the application of Article 81(3) of the Treaty to categories of specialisation agreements [2000] OJ L304/3.

German gas wholesaler Wingas and the UK-based EDF Trading.[14] Two contracts were notified to the Commission which provided for the delivery to Wingas of 2 BCM of gas per annum over a period of ten years commencing in 1998/99, which could be extended by a further five years. The clause that concerned the Commission foresaw a reduction of the volumes bought by Wingas, if EDF Trading were to sell gas into Wingas' main supply territory. The mechanism would not apply to sales of EDF Trading to German incumbent operators such as Ruhrgas that operated in Wingas' supply area, but sales of EDF Trading to new market participants in the German market were not adequately exempted. The parties proposed amendments to the contracts which would redefine the mechanism. The effect of the amended version was that EDF Trading could sell to all wholesalers, whether incumbents or new entrants, on the German border and so create a level playing field. As a result, the contracts were cleared by the Commission.

12.21 A mechanism included in the gas supply agreement between the DUC partners and DONG bore some similarity to the above 'reduction clause' and was deemed likely to have the same anti-competitive effect.[15] It was called the 'necessary adjustment mechanism'. This provided that—if the DUC partners commenced sales of gas into Denmark—the DUC partners and DONG had to agree on adjustments to the gas supply agreements such as the take-or-pay obligations of DONG.

12.22 The argument advanced in defence of the reduction clause was that it was necessary to counterbalance the take-or-pay obligations imposed on the buyer by giving DONG the protection of the Danish market in order to respect the take-or-pay obligations. If it were not included, the producer could sell its gas twice: once to the buyer, even if that gas were not taken, and again to former customers of the buyer. If the reduction clause were not included, the commercial equilibrium of the contracts would be impaired. This would be the result even after new gas pipelines to neighbouring countries are in place, providing for new marketing outlets. However, in the Commission's view, reduction clauses have the same effects as exclusivity clauses: they prevent the supplier (the DUC partners) from entering the downstream markets or at least create disincentives for direct sales to that market by the supplier. Since the buyer (DONG) has a dominant position on the Danish markets concerned, the effect of the clause was to support a protection of DONG's home markets.

12.23 The different interpretations of the clause were resolved when DONG agreed to modify it. There were two principal commitments made by DONG. First, it undertook to limit the scope of the clause by not invoking it for gas originating

---

[14] Commission Press Release IP/02/1293, 'Commission clears gas supply contracts between German gas wholesaler WINGAS and EDF-Trading', 12 September 2002.
[15] See the account by Schnichels, D and Valli, F, 'Vertical and horizontal restraints in the European gas sector—lessons learnt from the DONG/DUC case' (2003) 2 Competition Policy Newsletter 60–3, 61.

B. Joint Marketing of Gas

from sources other than the DUC fields. This means that gas imports from Germany are permitted without triggering the clause. Secondly, DONG undertook to waive the clause at such time as a new pipeline is commissioned which links the gas fields on the Danish continental shelf with other continental European countries. A six months' transition period was accepted by the Commission in such an event. As a result of this, the DUC partners are free to sell DUC gas into the Danish market six months after the commissioning of a new pipeline (one was already planned and entered into operation in 2005) without the risk that the clause would be invoked.

The outcome of the decision is similar to that in the *EDF Trading/Wingas* case above. There, Wingas agreed in its amendments to the supply contracts not to invoke the reduction clause in its contracts with EDF Trading to the extent that the latter sells gas to other wholesalers in Germany. The undertakings given by DONG also allow sales to customers other than wholesalers such as industrial users. 12.24

(c) Restrictions on Use

In the supply contracts DONG was required to report to the DUC partners the volumes of gas sold to certain categories of consumers in order to benefit from special price formulae for these customers. This was identified by the Commission as a specific form of use restriction. DONG was not free to sell the gas to whichever customer it chose without running the risk that it would lose the benefit of the specific price formula. In the context of gas sales, use restrictions which relate to the territory into which the buyer may sell the contractual goods or the customers to whom it may sell, will lead to a partitioning of the market. This outcome was clearly at odds with the aim of creating an internal gas market, and incompatible with competition law. 12.25

The parties gave undertakings to amend their supply contracts to meet this objection. DONG undertook to refrain from buying the volumes dedicated by the DUC partners to new customers. It also undertook not to buy any new gas from DUC partners during the time period from the settlement to three years after the commissioning of the new pipeline.[16] The effect of the amendment was to permit DONG to sell the gas wherever it deems appropriate and to whomever it wishes. There would be no need to report to the DUC partners about any such sales. 12.26

(d) Access

A further undertaking that was given in the settlement concerned access. To facilitate market entry of the DUC partners and potentially other suppliers into Denmark, 12.27

---

[16] DONG had a right of first refusal, whereby the DUC partners had to offer all their future gas finds to it first: Commission Press Release IP/03/566, 'Commission and Danish competition authorities jointly open up Danish gas market', 24 April 2003.

DONG gave an undertaking to introduce an improved access regime for its offshore gas pipelines that link Danish gas fields to the Danish mainland. DONG undertook to increase the transparency of the system by publishing information on available capacity, to allow short-term trading in line with the access regime that applied to its onshore pipelines, and also to introduce interruptible transmission contracts.

(e) Monitoring

12.28 The investigation was carried out jointly between the Commission and the Danish Competition Authority. The latter was charged with monitoring the performance of the commitments by the DUC partners and DONG. These commitments were also published on the companies' websites.

12.29 The case underlined again the Commission's view that joint marketing of gas by gas producers was not to be regarded as acceptable in the context of an ongoing EU energy market liberalization. However, it also gave a clear message that certain forms of vertical restraint such as reduction clauses and use restrictions are no longer acceptable either. The close co-operation with the national competition authority throughout the investigation and its involvement in monitoring underlined the partnership approach that has become common practice.

C. Joint Marketing of Electricity

12.30 It may be noted that the Commission has also examined cases of joint marketing in the electricity industry. By comparison with the gas industry, joint marketing of electricity by generators is unusual. Smaller generators have tended to sell their entire output to the incumbent. Where there was a legal monopoly on supply this practice was not controversial.

12.31 In the *Irish Synergen* case[17] the Commission took a different view. In this case ESB, the dominant electricity company in Ireland, and the Norwegian gas company Statoil notified four agreements relating to the construction and operation of the Synergen power plant, a 400 MW gas-fired plant in Dublin. Under the Partnership Deed establishing the joint venture, ESB would hold a 70 per cent stake in the company while Statoil would hold the remaining 30 per cent. Under a separate agreement, the Supply Agreement, ESB was to market the power generated by Synergen for 15 years, while under a Gas Supply Agreement, Statoil would supply Synergen with gas for 15 years. Under the Operation and Maintenance Agreement, ESB would provide operation and maintenance services to Synergen for 15 years.

---

[17] Commission Press Release IP/02/792, 'Commission clears Irish Synergen venture between ESB and Statoil following strict commitments', 31 May 2002; *Report on Competition Policy 2002*, 192–3.

The Commission investigated the agreements in close co-operation with the Irish energy regulator, the Commission for Electricity Regulation, which conducted the settlement negotiations. It analyzed in particular whether the creation of the joint venture would remove Statoil as a potential competitor from the highly concentrated Irish electricity market. The joint venture agreement would prevent Statoil from participating in competing power projects or from entering the market independently.

The companies offered commitments to address the Commission's concerns. There were two components to this. First, ESB and Synergen would make available 600 MW of electricity per year, mostly under an auction system, until additional volumes of 400 MW became available on the market. Secondly, the non-compete obligation imposed on Statoil with respect to competing power projects was removed. These commitments were designed to compensate for the probable elimination of a potential competitor from the Irish electricity market and to facilitate market entry for new suppliers which would have access to gas from Synergen as well as from the ESB auction, and from a new power plant that was being commissioned. **12.32**

D. Territorial Sales Restrictions: 'Destination Clauses'

Between 2001 and 2003 a shift in the Commission's focus of antitrust enforcement was noticeable. Instead of cases related mostly to gas production, the trend was to identify and analyze cases involving long-term exclusive supply contracts, which had potential foreclosure effects for new market participants or territorial sales restrictions in transport contracts reached with EU companies. This section is concerned with the latter. **12.33**

In 2001 the Commission began a series of investigations into territorial sales restrictions in gas supply contracts between non-EU gas producers and EU gas wholesalers/importers. These so-called 'destination clauses' in long-term gas supply contracts in continental Europe prohibit the resale of purchased gas to consumers outside the traditional supply area of the importer, usually the Member State in which the importer is located. These were included in contracts made between the Russian gas utility, Gazprom, and Italian companies, SNAM (at the time the gas distribution unit of ENI and now the network operator), ENEL, and Edison, involving some 20 BCM of gas a year. They were also found in contracts involving Sonatrach of Algeria and the Nigerian national LNG supplier. In the former case, they also prohibited Gazprom from selling to other companies in Italy. Such clauses were deemed by the Commission to hinder the creation of an internal energy market. Within the EU they are evident in transit contracts, as the *GDF* case below illustrates (see paras 12.55–12.57). **12.34**

12.35 The origin of this form of restraint appears to lie in an attempt to protect the 'market value principle' in the pricing of gas. In this way, gas is priced differently according to the alternative energy sources that are available to gas buyers in each Member State.[18] The practice is for the producers to discount from the market value price the costs of transporting their gas to the country of consumption (the 'net-back' principle); the producers therefore have an interest in maintaining the market value principle.

12.36 The Commission's approach was to deal with all of the territorial restrictions cases as vertical agreements.[19] The destination clauses were treated as hardcore restrictions in vertical agreements concluded between the wholesaler and the producer. A vertical agreement is an agreement entered into by two or more companies that, for the purposes of that agreement, operate at a different level of the production or distribution chain. Provided that a vertical agreement does not contain any hardcore restrictions and where the supplier's market share is below 30 per cent, the Block Exemption provides an umbrella that protects it from the application of Article 81(1). However, Article 4(b) of the Block Exemption is clear that it does not apply to agreements or concerted practices that directly or indirectly restrict sales by the buyer in terms of the territory into which, or the customers to whom, it may sell the contract goods. This applies to direct restrictions, such as the obligation not to sell in certain territories or indirect ones, such as profit-splitting mechanisms. Both are considered to be classifiable as hardcore restrictions.

12.37 The procedure adopted by the Commission did not involve the notification of formal charges (with one exception), but rather the negotiation of solutions with the parties concerned. The initial step of the Commission was to send a statement of objections to the parties, including the non-EU parties, noting the incompatibility of the destination clause with Article 81 EC. A contrasting approach was adopted in the automobile industry, where the practice has been to impose fines on companies that have attempted the same practices, in accordance with Article 15 of Regulation 17.[20] The cases involving automobile distributors Volkswagen and Opel and Daimler-Chrysler are illustrative of this approach.[21] Ultimately, the Commission may impose the sanction of a fine amounting to 10 per cent of the

---

[18] *Exxon/Mobil* (Case COMP/M.1383) Commission Decision 2004/284/EC, [2004] OJ L103/1, paras 52, 62.

[19] See Commission Notice, 'Guidelines on Vertical Restraints' [2000] OJ C291/1; and Commission Regulation (EC) 2790/99 on the application of Article 81(3) of the Treaty to categories of vertical agreements and concerted practices [1999] OJ L336/21, Art 2.

[20] Regulation (EEC) 17/62 [1962] OJ L13/204.

[21] Commission Press Release IP/01/1394, 'Commission imposes fine of nearly 72 million on Daimler-Chrysler for infringing the EC competition rules in the area of car distribution', 10 October 2001; *Volkswagen AG* (Case IV/35.733) Commission Decision 98/273/EC, [1998] OJ L124/60; *Opel Nederland BV/General Motors Nederland BV* (Case COMP/36.653) Commission Decision 2001/146/EC, [2001] OJ L59/1; *Volkswagen* (Case COMP/F-2/36.693) Commission Decision 2001/711/EC, [2001] OJ L262/14.

D. Territorial Sales Restrictions: 'Destination Clauses'

companies' global revenues. In this context it may be noted that indirect measures such as the refusal or reduction of bonuses or discounts are prohibited, if the aim is to induce a gas purchaser not to resell to customers outside his traditional supply territory. However, the fact that the Court of First Instance annulled a Commission decision to impose a fine on Volkswagen in 2003 suggests that the Commission's 'negotiated' approach contained some practical wisdom.[22] The following cases are illustrative of this preference for 'walking softly, while carrying a big stick'.

(1) Norwegian Producers

12.38 In the course of reaching a settlement in the GFU case, the Commission secured commitments from Statoil and Norsk Hydro that they would not introduce any territorial sales restrictions into their gas supply contracts. The companies also agreed not to introduce any use restrictions in their contracts (such as those that arose in the *DONG/DUC* case and the *NLNG* case below).[23]

(2) The *NLNG* Case

12.39 The Commission conducted an investigation into the use of territorial sales restrictions involving the Nigerian gas company, NLNG.[24] The company is the second largest supplier of LNG in the EU with about 5 BCM of gas shipped every year to customers in Italy, Spain, France and Portugal. While NLNG has concluded a number of contracts with European buyers, only one of these contained a territorial sales restriction. The company agreed to release its customer from this obligation. It also undertook not to introduce a number of clauses, with a potentially restrictive effect, into the future gas supply contracts it concluded with EU buyers.

12.40 A concern of the Commission was that the supply contracts might contain 'profit splitting' mechanisms affecting the EU markets.[25] These are clauses which oblige the buyer to pass over to the producer a share of the profits made when reselling the gas outside the territory agreed upon (say, Italy) or when the gas is re-sold to a customer using the gas for a different purpose than that which has been agreed upon. The concern with such clauses is that they have a similar aim and/or effect as territorial sales restrictions.[26] They are therefore void in accordance with Article 81(2) EC.

---

[22] Case T-208/01 *Volkswagen AG v Commission* [2003] ECR II-5141.
[23] Lindroos, M, Schnichels, D, Svane, LP, 'Liberalization of European Gas Markets—Commission settles GFU case with Norwegian gas producers' (2002) 3 Competition Policy Newsletter 50–2 at 51.
[24] Commission Press Release IP/02/1869, 'Commission settles investigation into territorial sales restrictions with Nigerian gas company NLNG', 12 December 2002.
[25] See the account in Nyssens, H, Cultrera, C and Schnichels, D, 'The territorial restrictions case in the gas sector: a state of play' (2004) 1 Competition Policy Newsletter 48–51.
[26] This subject is discussed by Commission officials in Nyssens, H, Osbourne, I, 'Profit splitting mechanisms in a liberalized gas market: the devil lies in the detail' (2005) 1 Competition Policy Newsletter 25–8.

None of the existing NLNG contracts contained such clauses and the company gave an undertaking not to introduce any into its future contracts.

12.41 NLNG also gave an undertaking not to introduce use restrictions into its future gas supply contracts, which might prevent the buyer from using the gas for other purposes than those agreed upon in the contract. On the basis of these undertakings, the Commission closed its investigation into the company's European gas supply contracts.

(3) The *Gazprom* Cases

12.42 Several cases involving the supply of Russian gas from Gazprom to ENI/SNAM (Italy), OMV (Austria), and E.ON/Ruhrgas (Germany) were settled after the companies deleted the restrictive clause from their existing gas supply contracts. ENI and OMV also committed themselves to taking a number of pro-competitive measures that promoted gas-to-gas competition in the EU, including an offer to sell significant gas volumes of Russian gas in Italy or elsewhere in the EU and to further development of the Trans-Austrian Gas (TAG) pipeline. Gazprom is no longer contractually prevented from selling its gas to competitors of ENI or even from entering the Italian gas market itself.[27] It has also agreed not to introduce new destination clauses or similar contractual mechanisms in the future.

12.43 The wider policy context of this investigation is that there are already very few suppliers of gas on the market so that efforts should be made by the Commission to ensure that the suppliers are not further reduced.[28] Such actions therefore fit with the overall aim of increasing the amount of gas available on the EU market. If SNAM, for example, is prevented by a non-EU supplier from exporting the gas it purchases, then a consumer based in another EU Member State cannot approach SNAM as a potential supplier. Such practices are targeted for removal. The fact that the Commission chose to raise this matter with non-EU and non-EEA suppliers is a novel development in the application of EU law in the energy sector.

(a) *ENI and Russian Gas*

12.44 There were two principal sets of undertakings in the settlement reached with ENI, distinguishable into contractual matters and accompanying measures.

12.45 **The contractual issues** The parties undertook to delete the destination clause imposed on ENI from all of their existing gas supply contracts. As a consequence,

---

[27] Commission Press Release IP/03/1345, 'Commission reaches breakthrough with Gazprom and ENI on territorial restriction clauses', 6 October 2003.
[28] For further discussion of this, see Albers, M, 'The New EU Directives on Energy Liberalization from a Competition Point of View' in Cameron, PD, (ed), *Legal Aspects of EU Energy Regulation: Implementing the New Directives on Electricity and Gas Across Europe* (2005) 41–58.

D. Territorial Sales Restrictions: 'Destination Clauses'

two delivery points are provided for Russian gas, instead of one as before. ENI has the right to take the gas to destinations of its choice from these two delivery points.

12.46 The parties undertook to refrain from introducing the contested clauses into new gas supply contracts. ENI undertook not to accept any such clauses or any provision with similar effects such as use restrictions or profit-splitting mechanisms in all its future purchase contracts with any gas producer. This applied to both pipeline gas and LNG.

12.47 The parties deleted a provision in the existing contracts that obliged Gazprom to obtain ENI's consent when selling gas to other customers in Italy. The removal of such 'consent clauses' had already been effected and, as a result, Gazprom was now allowed to commence sales of gas to ENI's competitors in Italy.

12.48 **Accompanying measures** ENI gave three undertakings that were designed to facilitate a settlement and thereby a closure of the case. These were undertakings:

- To release significant quantities of gas to customers outside Italy over a five year period. The Member States most likely to benefit were Austria and Germany.
- To promote an increase of the capacity in its majority-controlled TAG pipeline (which runs through Austria to Italy and carries gas from Russia and other states to the Italian market).
- To promote an improved third party access (TPA) regime, which would facilitate the use of TAG as a transit pipeline. This includes the introduction of one-month transport contracts, an effective congestion management system, the introduction of a secondary market, and the regular publication on the internet of available capacity. This will be modelled on the Good Practice Guidelines for TPA, contained in the Gas Regulation 2005.[29]

(b) OMV and Russian Gas

12.49 The bulk of Austrian gas is imported from Russia, and Austria is an important transit route for Russian gas exports to the French, German, and Italian gas markets. The restrictions on reselling imported gas outside of Austria were therefore an important constraint on OMV, the principal Austrian oil and gas operator. The wholesaling of such gas could contribute to the creation of a more integrated gas market, promoting both competition and security of supply.

12.50 The case was closed in 2005 after the Commission had secured undertakings from the parties.[30] There were four principal undertakings given:

- The companies agreed to delete the territorial sales restrictions from their existing gas supply contracts.

---

[29] Regulation (EC) 1775/2005 of 28 September 2005 on conditions for access to the natural gas transmission networks [2005] OJ L289/1.
[30] Commission Press Release IP/05/195, 'Competition: Commission secures improvements to gas supply contracts between OMV and Gazprom', 17 February 2005.

- They agreed to delete contractual provisions that obliged Gazprom to offer any gas destined for Austria first to OMV (a right of first refusal).
- OMV as a shareholder of the TAG pipeline undertook to promote an increase in capacity in that pipeline, which runs through Austria and transports Russian gas to the Italian market.
- OMV offered to promote improved TPA on the TAG pipeline based on the Guidelines for Good Practice.

(c) Ruhrgas and Russian Gas

12.51 The Commission's interest in the contracts for imported gas into Germany lay partly in the size of the German market and partly in its role as a transit country for Russian (and Norwegian) gas into neighbouring countries. The identification of Ruhrgas in this context lay in its role as one of Gazprom's most important customers.

12.52 The Commission reached a settlement with Ruhrgas and Gazprom in 2005.[31] There were two principal undertakings given by the two companies. They agreed:

- To delete the territorial sales restrictions from the contracts under investigation.
- To delete the 'most favoured customer' clauses from their agreements (that obliged Gazprom to offer similar conditions to Ruhrgas as it would have offered Ruhrgas' competitors on the wholesale market in Germany).

(d) Gasunie and Gazprom

12.53 The Commission also conducted an investigation into contracts involving Gazprom and Gasunie. This failed to identify any territorial sales restrictions. Gasunie expressly confirmed that it was free to sell the gas delivered by Gazprom wherever it considered appropriate. The gas delivered to Gasunie was delivered at the German/Dutch border.[32]

(e) Conclusion

12.54 The closure of the cases with OMV and Ruhrgas brought to an end all of the Commission investigations that had been opened in 2001 into export restrictions on Russian gas. They had covered imports into Austria, France, Germany, Italy, and the Netherlands.[33] Apart from the deletion of territorial sales restrictions in existing contracts, the undertakings given by ENI and OMV required each company to increase pipeline capacity and adhere to the Guidelines for improved TPA.

---

[31] Commission Press Release IP/05/710, 'Competition: Commission secures changes to gas supply contracts between E.ON Ruhrgas and Gazprom', 10 June 2005.

[32] Nyssens, H, Cultrera, C, and Schnichels, D, 'The territorial restrictions case in the gas sector: a state of play' (2004) 1 Competition Policy Newsletter 48–51, at 51.

[33] European Commission, *Report on Competition Policy* 2005, 26.

D. Territorial Sales Restrictions: 'Destination Clauses'

(4) *GDF/ENEL* and *GDF/ENI*

The Commission investigated two contracts concluded by GDF with two Italian companies in 1997.[34] The first was with the oil and gas company, ENI, while the second was with the electricity utility, ENEL. Each was found to contain a territorial restriction clause and constituted a restriction of competition. The companies agreed to remove them.

12.55

The contract between GDF and ENI concerned the transportation of natural gas purchased by ENI in northern Europe.[35] GDF would transport the gas across French territory to the border with Switzerland. ENI was obliged to market the gas exclusively 'downstream of the delivery point'; in other words, only after the gas had left France. The contract between GDF and ENEL concerned the swap of LNG purchased by ENEL in Nigeria. It contained a clause which required ENEL to use the gas only in Italy. Both of these clauses were introduced at the request of GDF. The Commission's assessment of these two clauses was that they were designed to partition the national markets and prevent consumers of natural gas established in France from obtaining supplies from ENEL and ENI. They were therefore in contravention of Article 81 EC.

12.56

The Commission's approach to the matter is interesting in the sense that it is more formal than in previous cases. Although the parties had already terminated the infringement, the Commission published two formal decisions on the matter.[36] Its intention was not only to clarify the law on this matter for the benefit of the parties but also for all other firms operating in this sector. In its public statement, the Commission added that 'if, having adopted these decisions, it [ie the Commission] should find restrictions of the same type in other gas contracts, it will show much less clemency'.[37] However, no fines were imposed on the companies concerned. The Commission justified this by reference to the stage reached by the liberalization process: from the conclusion of the contracts to the conclusion of the investigation

12.57

---

[34] Commission Press Release IP/04/1310, 'Commission confirms that territorial restriction clauses in the gas sector restrict competition', 26 October 2004.

[35] The circumstances behind the contract signature were unusual. ENEL had been unable to construct a re-gasification terminal in Italy due to local opposition but had signed the contract for gas supplies after obtaining the necessary government approvals. Unable to take the contracted gas in Italy, it reached an agreement with NLNG—following an arbitration proceeding—that GDF re-gasify the LNG in France, but the condition which GDF attached was that the gas should not be used inside France.

[36] *GDF/ENI* (Case COMP/38.662) 26 October 2004 (French and Italian language text only) <http://ec.europa.eu/comm/competition/antitrust/cases/decisions/38662/eni_fr.pdf>; *GDF/ENEL* (Case COMP/38.662) 26 October 2004 <http://ec.europa.eu/comm/competition/antitrust/cases/decisions/38662/enel_fr.pdf>; see the discussion by Cultrera, C, 'Les décisions GDF: La Commission est formelle: les clauses de restriction territoriale dans les contrats de gaz violent l' article 81' (2005) 1 Competition Policy Newsletter 45–8.

[37] Commission Press Release IP/04/1310, 'Commission confirms that territorial restriction clauses in the gas sector restrict competition', 26 October 2004.

the liberalization process has 'involved a profound change in the commercial practices of the operators present on the market'. Tellingly, it added that this stage had ended with the entry into force of the Gas Directive in 2004.

(5) *Sonatrach*

12.58 The Commission has also been in discussions with the Algerian gas supplier, Sonatrach, and its principal EU customers, which are operating companies in Italy and Spain, about a possible use of destination clauses in its contracts. The investigations opened in 2001. The Algerian Energy Ministry and Sonatrach informed the Commission in 2002 that Sonatrach will no longer introduce any provisions that limit cross-border sales into its future gas supply contracts with EU importing companies.[38]

12.59 Subsequently, negotiations commenced to discuss the modification of existing contracts for the import of Algerian gas, particularly LNG contracts, which contain restrictive clauses, with a view to reaching a settlement. The restrictions in current contracts are thought to prevent wholesaling and arbitrage of the contracted gas into neighbouring territories; in the case of LNG, into terminals located in a different Member State. These negotiations appear to be ongoing.[39]

E. Conclusions

12.60 Most of the Commission's actions reviewed in this chapter pre-date the entry into force of Directive (EC) 2003/55 (the Gas Directive) in 2004. All of them contain a justification that such actions were aimed at providing constructive support to the ongoing liberalization process in the EU gas markets. It is less surprising therefore that the later decisions demonstrate a firmness that appears to be absent from the earlier ones. The contrast between the *Britannia* decision and the Corrib case is only one illustration of this. The *GDF/ENI* and *GDF/ENEL* decisions in relation to earlier decisions on use restrictions are another. Once the Gas Directive had entered into force, the kind of support from the competition law that the liberalization process required simply had to adapt.

12.61 The approach adopted by the Commission in almost every case considered here was one in which it sought to persuade the parties to reach a settlement. This 'amicable'

---

[38] Nyssens, H, Cultrera, C, and Schnichels, D, 'The territorial restrictions case in the gas sector: a state of play' (2004) 1 Competition Policy Newsletter 48–51, 51.
[39] European Commission, *Report on Competition Policy 2005*, 26; Commission Press Release IP/05/710, 'Competition: Commission secures changes to gas supply contracts between E.ON Ruhrgas and Gazprom', 10 June 2005, in which the Competition Commissioner is quoted as saying: 'The Commission will now focus its attention on the gas import contracts from Algeria and more particularly the LNG contracts'.

E. Conclusions

procedure was designed, in the words of the then Competition Commissioner, to allow 'the companies concerned to find a commercial solution for the competition problem we identified'.[40] The justification for this negotiated approach was summed up succinctly by the Commissioner himself when he said:

> [D]uring the initial delicate transition phase from monopolised to liberalised energy markets, the focus should lie, in some occasions, on Commission's interventions improving effectively the market structure, rather than on formal procedures imposing fines.[41]

There is some evidence that the Commission itself was not entirely satisfied with the results of this approach.[42] In its Report on Competition Policy for 2003, it stated that 'in future more formal decisions will be taken. This will provide additional legal certainty and allow the Commission to clarify its policy formally.'[43] Now that the 'initial delicate transition phase' has ended, and the legal framework for settlements has been modified in Article 9 of Regulation 1/2003,[44] there appears to be no obstacle to a more robust approach in applying the competition rules in future.[45]

12.62

It may also be noted that some principles are now settled. The principle is now established that joint selling of gas by producers is not permitted unless in very exceptional circumstances. Marketing has to be conducted individually by gas producers. The territorial and other restrictions on gas-to-gas supply competition are not in line with EC law, and will be the subject of formal action where they are identified. On several occasions in the above cases, the Commission also made it clear that none of its actions were targeted against the use of long-term contracts per se. This is in line with the approach taken in the Gas Directive.

12.63

---

[40] Monti, M, 'Applying EU competition law to the newly liberalized energy markets', World Forum on Energy Regulation, Rome, 6 October 2003.
[41] ibid.
[42] See remarks by Albers, M, in *EU Energy Law*, Vol II, 129–130.
[43] European Commission, *Report on Competition Policy 2003*, 39, point 97. The use of a formal decision would make it easier to render commitments legally binding and more enforceable in the event of non-compliance.
[44] Regulation (EC) 1/2003 of 16 December 2002 on the implementation of the rules on competition laid down in Articles 81 and 82 of the Treaty [2003] OJ L1/1, (as amended by Regulation (EC) 411/2004 [2004] OJ L68/1.
[45] Because almost all of the decisions were reached informally, the details of the settlements have to be gleaned from press releases and published articles by Commission officials.

13

COMPETITION IN DOWNSTREAM MARKETS

A. Introduction	13.01	(c) The UK/Belgium Interconnector	13.57
B. Long-Term Agreements		(d) The Dutch/German Interconnector	13.59
(1) Long-Term Agreements: Gas	13.04		
(a) The German FCO's Actions	13.07	(3) Refusal to Build	13.87
(b) The Belgian *Distrigas* Case	13.11	E. Refusal of Access	
(c) *Gas Natural/Endesa*	13.12	(1) The Issues	13.88
(d) Exclusive Supply Agreements	13.13	(a) Cases on Refusals of Access	13.96
(2) Long-Term Agreements: Electricity		(b) Essential Facilities	13.98
(a) Network Access	13.15	(2) The *Marathon* Case	13.101
(b) Contract Duration	13.21	(a) Transparency	13.104
C. Transmission Pricing	13.31	(b) Balancing	13.109
(1) Electricity Agreement: *Verbändevereinbarung*	13.34	(c) Handling of Access Requests	13.114
		(d) Trade in Capacity Rights	13.118
(2) Gas VV Agreement	13.40	(e) Congestion Management	13.119
(3) Assessment	13.45	(f) Entry-Exit Regime	13.123
D. Interconnector Use and Access	13.46	(g) Tarification	13.127
(1) Methods of Allocating Available Capacity	13.49	(h) Gas Release	13.129
		(i) Conversion of Gas	13.130
(2) Long-Term Capacity Reservations	13.52	(j) Monitoring	13.131
(a) The Skaggerak Cable	13.53	(k) Assessment	13.135
(b) The UK/French Interconnector	13.55	F. Conclusions	13.139

Articles 81 and 82 EC have been conceived largely to operate as guarantees that competitive markets will not become less competitive, rather than to function as instruments to force monopolised industries into a more competitive structure.

M Monti, then Commissioner for Competition[1]

---

[1] Monti, M, 'Applying EU competition law to the newly liberalized energy markets', World Forum on Energy Regulation, Rome, 6 October 2003.

A. Introduction

13.01 While competition law has a complementary role vis-à-vis the Electricity and Gas Directives,[2] interventions by the Commission only allow it to take action where it has detected a violation of the competition rules, such as restrictive agreements or abuses of a dominant position. Certain tasks such as the development and introduction of competitive network charges and congestion management methods are challenges that lie primarily within the competence of the national regulatory agencies (NRAs) and, perhaps to a lesser extent, with the national competition authorities (NCAs). Indeed, the Directives and Regulations have gone a long way towards fixing responsibility for the operation of third party access (TPA) in the NRAs, so that they have a priority 'not only in developing pro-competitive network access regimes, but also in taking action in access disputes in the interest of preventing parallel actions by the Commission'.[3]

13.02 However, there are many matters involving the use of long-term contracts and the management of transmission and distribution networks that raise questions about restraints on competition or potential abuse of dominant positions.[4] In the past, the Commission has taken action to challenge long-term agreements and to tackle barriers to network access, such as those arising from excessive pricing, refusals of access, and the lack of interconnector access. In all of these areas the role of its *ex post* interventions has delivered results on a case-by-case basis. Often they have been carried out in close co-operation with the relevant NCAs, whose role will be of growing importance in applying Articles 81 and 82 of the EC Treaty, in consultation or co-operation with the Commission.

13.03 This chapter examines two broad areas in which Articles 81 and 82 have been used to promote the liberalization process: long-term agreements and barriers to network access. It is important to keep in mind, however, that the dynamic of the liberalization process means that decisions taken in specific circumstances—especially ones taken before that process began—may not be influential, still less binding, on the competition authorities at the present stage of liberalization.

---

[2] Directive (EC) 2003/54 concerning common rules for the internal market in electricity and repealing Directive (EC) 96/92 [2003] OJ L176/37; Directive (EC) 2003/55 concerning common rules for the internal market in natural gas and repealing Directive (EC) 98/30 [2003] OJ L176/57.

[3] Albers, M, 'The New EU Directives on Energy Liberalization from a Competition Point of View' in Cameron, PD, (ed), *Legal Aspects of EU Energy Regulation: Implementing the New Directives on Electricity and Gas across Europe* (2005) 49.

[4] In this context, see the Commission Guidelines on the applicability of Article 81 of the EC Treaty to horizontal cooperation agreements [2001] OJ C3/2, and the extensive discussion on this by Albers, M, in Jones, C (ed), *Competition Law and Energy Markets* (2005) 113 et seq; Nyssens, H and Schnichels, D, 'Energy' in Faull, J and Nikpay, A, *The EC Law of Competition* (2nd edn, 2007) Ch 12.

B. Long-Term Agreements

(1) Long-Term Agreements: Gas

Despite the opening up of the gas sector to competition in 2004, it became clear that there were instances of possible foreclosure of the downstream market by means of long-term gas supply contracts made between traditional suppliers (wholesalers) and two kinds of customer: distribution companies, and industrial and commercial users. The issue was discussed within the framework of the European Competition Network (ECN) Energy Subgroup on two occasions in 2005.[5] 13.04

The problem arises in the following manner. Contracts for gas supply have been concluded on terms which provide incentives to consumers not to switch to alternative suppliers. These are long-term contracts with many years to run and which therefore lock in consumers who might otherwise seek to benefit from competition developing in the sector. Such contracts can also delay the ability of alternative suppliers to build up their market share to compete effectively, allowing incumbents to benefit from economies of scale in the gas supply market (the high cost of balancing and flexibility declines as supplied gas volumes increase). These contracts may therefore have the effect of foreclosing the markets to would-be market entrants. If the contracts are not indispensable to generate countervailing benefits to consumers, they may give rise to competition concerns. 13.05

In this area there have been three notable developments in clarifying the appropriate steps for a competition authority to take. The first is the report published on this issue by the German Federal Cartel Office (FCO) (*Bundeskartellamt*) in January 2005, with reference to the role of such contracts in the market for gas supply to local distributors in Germany (municipal utilities or *Stadtwerke*). The second is an ongoing case involving long-term gas supply contracts in the Belgian market. The third is an investigation into a long-term supply agreement in Spain. 13.06

(a) The German FCO's Actions

The FCO report is called *Principles of Evaluation of Long-term Gas Supply Contracts under Competition Law*.[6] It is a consultative document. The thrust of the report is that the long-term, commonly used commitments entered into by distribution companies are a major impediment to competition. The duration and the supply volumes in the agreements would have to be reduced so that third party suppliers could take a role in supplying gas to free customers. Two kinds of contract represented 13.07

---

[5] European Commission, *Report on Competition Policy 2005*, 25–26 at point 46.
[6] Bundeskartellamt, 8th Decision Division, B8-113/03, Bonn, 28 January 2005, <http://www.bundeskartellamt.de/wDeutsch/download/pdf/Diskussionsbeitraege/050125_Diskussionspapier Gasvertraege.pdf>.

a particular problem: exclusive supply contracts with volumes of between 80 and 100 per cent with a duration of two years, and contracts that supply between 50 and 80 per cent of a customer's requirements for more than four years. The FCO then sets out draft terms or guidelines that could be adopted by the parties to alleviate their competition concerns. These are quite innovative and merit some review.

13.08 In the FCO's view, the long-term commitment of a local gas distributor to obtain its total requirement or at least a very high proportion of this from a single gas transmission company is incompatible with EC and German competition law. Yet, its investigation of a large sample of contracts showed that this was common practice. The vertical agreements between established gas suppliers and local gas distributors constitute a foreclosure of the market which is incompatible with Article 81(1) EC. Customers are tied to suppliers in terms of contract periods and quantities so that third companies seeking to enter the market cannot acquire them as customers. It should be emphasized, however, that these are not import contracts concluded by the gas transmission companies but rather concern the next level of business; that is, gas that can be supplied by domestic importers to domestic purchasers. There is therefore no direct security of supply link in this debate.

13.09 There are five guidelines offered by the FCO:

- Free volumes must correspond with the actual demand. In other words, if the main supplier seeks to conclude a contract for a period of two to four years, the secondary supplier must have the opportunity *effectively* to obtain a 20 per cent share of the customer's actual needs.
- The share of financial risk held by a secondary supplier must not exceed his share of the total contracted supply quantity. The larger the share of the main supplier, approaching the 80 per cent threshold, the greater the share of the risk of incurring losses due to the divergence between the amount of gas reserved and the actual requirement.
- Multiple supply contracts with the same supplier are considered to be one agreement. An artificial splitting of a contract to circumvent thresholds by 'stapling' different contracts together is not allowed.
- Clauses in supply contracts that allow the customer to inform the supplier of rival offers below their respective contract price and leave it to the supplier to respond, perhaps with a price reduction, are not permitted (so-called 'English clauses').
- Clauses that permit a tacit extension after the set contract period has expired are deemed to be contracts concluded for an indefinite period of time.

13.10 Subsequently, the FCO entered into negotiations with the 15 largest suppliers on the market to introduce clear limits on the duration of their supply contracts. When these proved unsuccessful, the FCO initiated formal prohibition proceedings against E.ON/Ruhrgas as the major and representative gas supplier in Germany.[7] The FCO requested the company to stop writing new contracts covering more than four years for more than 50 per cent of its customers' annual demand, or contracts covering more than two years for more than 80 per cent of annual demand. The company will not be allowed to offer additional volumes under short-term contracts for the second 50 per cent of customers' needs. In June 2006 the Higher Regional Court of Düsseldorf (Oberlandsgericht) supported the FCO's claim that E.ON/Ruhrgas should no longer have long-term sales contracts with its distribution companies. The FCO decision was to forbid the stapling of several contracts with different durations to ensure that E.On could not circumvent the prohibition. The court also accepted the FCO's regional approach: ie, that there is no integrated German gas market, only regional markets, as a national TPA does not work in practice. On this assessment the FCO will prohibit the long-term contracts of other gas companies. It may be noted that in the current circumstances non-German suppliers have no opportunity to provide gas to the municipal utilities.

(b) The Belgian Distrigas Case

In this case the Commission is the lead competition authority and has taken the view that Distrigas, the Belgian gas supplier, is preventing new suppliers from entering the Belgian gas market contrary to Article 82 EC.[8] As a result of the contracts it has concluded with many industrial customers, significant parts of the country's gas market are not available for competition for long periods. A significant part of other gas sales are intra-group sales within the Suez Group (eg, Distrigas sales to Electrabel) and are therefore not accessible to new market entrants. The problem at issue here is one that has also arisen in the Energy Sector Inquiry (see paras 11.38 et seq), whereby long term gas supply contracts between wholesalers and industrial customers have the effect of excluding would-be market entrants.

13.11

(c) Gas Natural/Endesa

Somewhat earlier, an investigation into a long-term supply agreement in Spain was carried out by the Commission in 1999–2000. The exclusive supply agreement was between the Spanish gas utility, Gas Natural, and Endesa, an electricity generator.[9] Under the agreement, Endesa was required to purchase its entire gas demand for new gas-fired power plants from Gas Natural for a period of more than 20 years. The interest of the Commission lay in ensuring that the supply contract did not allow the dominant gas supplier, Gas Natural, to prolong a de facto

13.12

---

[7] Bundeskartellamt, 8th Decision Division, B8–113/03, Bonn, 13 January 2006, <http://www.bundeskartellamt.de/wDeutsch/entscheidungen/Kartellrecht/EntschKartell.shtml>.

[8] Commission Press Release MEMO/06/197, 'Competition: Commission confirms sending Statement of Objections to Distrigas concerning Belgian gas supply market', 16 May 2006.

[9] Fernandez Salas, M, 'Long-term supply agreements in the context of gas market liberalization: Commission closes investigation of Gas Natural' (2000) 2 Competition Policy Newsletter 55.

monopoly for many years and thus block new entrants into the gas market in Spain, then in the process of being liberalized. After the Commission had expressed its concerns in a warning letter,[10] the companies proposed some amendments to the contract. Essentially, the amendments proposed by the parties were to:

- substantially reduce the gas volumes covered by the contract (around 25 per cent) in order to free a part of Endesa's purchasing capacity and thereby ensure that it continued to exist as a customer that could attract new market entry. De facto exclusivity would disappear from the contract;
- reduce the long-term duration of the supply contract by one-third to avoid an excessively long period of dependence of the customer on the supplier. The maximum duration would therefore be 12 years during the plateau period;
- allow Endesa to resell the gas after a start-up period;[11] and
- modify other clauses of the contract that might have the effect of discriminating in favour of Endesa vis-à-vis other gas customers.

The Commission closed its investigation as a result of these commitments made by the parties.

(d) Exclusive Supply Agreements

13.13 There have been other cases involving exclusive purchase obligations in the gas sector, considered either by the Commission or by NCAs.[12] The potential foreclosure effects of two supply agreements were a concern of the Commission in a case involving the sale of gas by EDF-Trading to the German wholesale gas company, Wingas, for a ten-year period, extendable for a further five years.[13] The companies agreed to modify the agreements so that other wholesalers (incumbents and new entrants) would not be impaired from being supplied by EDF-Trading at the German border. The contracts which were notified to the Commission had included a mechanism leading to a reduction of the volumes bought by Wingas if EDF-Trading were to sell the gas into Wingas' main supply territory, especially to new market participants (see paras 12.20–12.24). Notably, when clearing the amended contracts, the Competition Commissioner added: 'The decision demonstrates that the Commission does not oppose long term gas supply contracts as such.'[14] However, those contracts are not to include significant market foreclosure effects.

---

[10] Commission Press Release IP/00/297, 'Commission closes investigation on Spanish company GAS NATURAL', 27 March 2000.
[11] The Commission has previously accepted that a resale prohibition could be imposed on an electricity generator, as long as it is limited in time: Transgas-Turbogas case, *Report on Competition Policy 1996*, 48 and 135.
[12] See, eg, the decision of the Danish NCA in December 2005: Press release, 'Natural gas agreement approved with commitments' at <http://www.ks.dk/english/competition/national/2005/dong>.
[13] Commission Press Release IP/02/1293, 'Commission clears gas supply contracts between German gas wholesaler WINGAS and EDF-Trading', 12 September 2002.
[14] ibid.

B. Long-Term Agreements

In the same year, another gas supply agreement was cleared as part of the Irish Synergen project. Statoil, the Norwegian oil and gas company, agreed to deliver gas to Synergen for 15 years on an exclusive basis. On this occasion the Commission cleared it, taking into account that the Synergen contract is for the first large-scale gas supply contract for Statoil in Ireland, where the market is dominated by the incumbent gas supplier, BGE. Statoil also offered a special price formula for its gas, which would not have been possible if there had been no long-term exclusivity. The guidance which this case offers on the application of EC competition rules is weakened by the existence of special circumstances: as in the *Gas Natural/Endesa* case above, it concerned the construction of new gas-fired power plants. Moreover, the market share of the gas supplier in this case was close to the *de minimis* threshold.[15] **13.14**

(2) Long-Term Agreements: Electricity

(a) Network Access

In the period before the first Electricity and Gas Directives, a number of issues of network access came to the fore. Indeed, in a line of cases involving Dutch electricity companies, the European Court of Justice (ECJ) examined the applicability of Article 81 EC to the electricity industry, which for long had been treated as excluded from the scope of these provisions. Certain agreements were common in the electricity sector that raised competition issues under that article. There were two principal cases: *Ijsselcentrale* and *Almelo*. The *Almelo* case was the more important of a number of Dutch electricity restructuring disputes at the time. **13.15**

In the *Ijsselcentrale* case[16] the Commission prohibited an agreement concluded by electricity generating companies in the Netherlands, preventing both distribution companies and, indirectly, private industrial consumers from using imported electricity and from exporting electricity. Although Article 86(2) EC applied (the companies involved were indeed engaged in the operation of services of general economic interest), it was decided that this did not justify a monopolization of imports and exports. Also, at that time the Competition Directorate of the Commission was looking at vertical agreements between coal producers and electricity generators and horizontal agreements between electricity producers. **13.16**

The *Almelo* case[17] brought before the ECJ served to highlight some of the frustrations felt by those in favour of liberalizing energy markets. It arose from proceedings **13.17**

---

[15] See Nyssens, H and Schnichels, D, 'Energy' in Faull, J and Nikpay, A, *The EC Law of Competition* (2nd edn, 2007) ch 12, para 41.
[16] *Ijsselcentrale* (Case IV/32.732) Commission Decision 91/50/EEC, [1991] OJ L 28/32. See also the long-running *Rendo* case concerning import restrictions on electricity: Case T-16/91 RV *Rendo v Commission* [1996] ECR II-1827.
[17] Case C-393/92 *Gemeente Almelo v Energiebedrijf Ijssellmij NV* [1994] ECR I-1477.

brought by the Municipality of Almelo and other electricity distributors against the Ijsselmij (formerly Ijsselcentrale), an undertaking engaged in the regional distribution of electricity, concerning the interpretation of an agreement on the public supply of electricity, its conditions and especially an 'equalization supplement', charged by Ijsselcentrale to the local distributors. The distributors argued that the exclusive purchasing obligation imposed upon them was an infringement of the Treaty since it prevented them from importing electricity. The national court referred the matter to the ECJ.

13.18 The ECJ held that the use of an exclusive purchasing obligation by the regional electricity undertaking contained in the general conditions of sale restricted competition and also had effects on inter-state trade because the regional distributor belongs to a group of undertakings that occupy a collective dominant position in a substantial part of the common market. The competition rules in Articles 81 and 82 precluded this, and therefore were shown to be applicable to the electricity sector. Any special characteristics would have to be considered in relation to Articles 81(3) and 86(2). There were high expectations at the time that the ECJ's ruling would cast fresh light on the interpretation of Article 86(2).

13.19 The Commission argued that Article 86(2) could not justify an exclusive purchasing agreement, but Ijsselmij claimed that the agreements were necessary to guarantee the security of the electricity supply. The ECJ did not rule on these legal arguments. It held that restrictions on competition might be justified under Article 86(2) if they were necessary for the performance of tasks of general interest. This followed the line established in *Corbeau* (see paras 16.43–16.45).[18] The task of determining whether or not such restrictions were necessary was entrusted to the national courts by the ECJ.

13.20 In practice, this interpretation of Article 86(2) was a cautious one, and omitted any consideration of the meaning of *service public*. By permitting entry barriers to the market and cross-subsidization to remain in place, based on technical considerations and the general economic interest, the ECJ 'confirmed more or less in *Almelo* the status quo with regard to the electricity market'.[19] The result was therefore a disappointing one to those who had been seeking from the ECJ evidence of support for the Commission's programme of liberalization of the electricity sector.

(b) Contract Duration

13.21 There have been several cases which illustrated Commission policy on the permissible duration of long-term exclusive contracts and market foreclosure. These include

---

[18] Case C-320/91 *Corbeau* [1993] ECR I-2533.
[19] Pfrang, E, *Towards Liberalization of the European Energy Markets* (1999) 41.

B. Long-Term Agreements

the *Scottish Nuclear* case,[20] three cases involving power purchase agreements with exclusive terms, the case of the *Jahrhundertvertrag*,[21] and the *Ijsselcentrale* case.[22] They show that the Commission was willing to apply the exemption clause in Article 86(2) on a case-by-case basis. It also took particular care to limit the use of the security of supply argument by parties seeking an exemption from the application of the competition rules.

Contract duration: *Scottish Nuclear* Two supply contracts were notified to the Commission in 1990 and the Commission adopted a Decision in 1991 that authorized the contracts for a period of 15 years. They were concluded between Scottish Nuclear Ltd and Scottish Power and Scottish Hydroelectric, two vertically-integrated electricity utilities that had been created at the time of electricity privatization in Scotland. The British Government wished to provide the newly privatized companies with a diversified generating capacity portfolio and include access to power generated by Scottish Nuclear, which was to remain in the public sector. The contracts had four main characteristics: 13.22

- Scottish Nuclear was not allowed to supply electricity to any other party without the consent of both electricity companies;
- a take-or-pay obligation was imposed on Scottish Power and Scottish Hydroelectric for, respectively, 74.9 per cent and 25.1 per cent of Scottish Nuclear's production;
- the price at which the two companies purchased nuclear-generated electricity was fixed under the agreements; and
- the contracts had an initial duration of 30 years.

The Commission found that the agreements restricted competition and (surprisingly) affected trade between Member States. Although it was held to infringe Article 81(1), the Commission decided that an exemption under Article 81(3) was justified due to the need for long-term planning for production purposes, the need to guarantee security of supply, and the need for an independent electricity market. It did however insist on a reduction of the duration of the contracts from 30 years (which corresponded to the expected lifetime of the power stations concerned) to 15. No reasoning was provided for this choice of number, but the aim seems to have been to free up the market while not imposing obstacles to the domestic liberalization programme.   13.23

Contract duration and market foreclosure The duration of contracts figured prominently in three cases decided by the Commission between 1993 and 1996. The investigations occurred in the context of restrictions arising from market foreclosure and led the Commission to limit the contract periods. The cases were   13.24

---

[20] *Scottish Nuclear, Nuclear Energy Agreement* (Case IV/33.473) Commission Decision 91/329/EEC, [1991] OJ L178/31 relating to a proceeding under Art 85 of the EEC Treaty (now Art 81 EC).
[21] *Jahrhundertvertrag* (Case IV/33.151) Commission Decision 93/126/EEC, [1993] OJ L50/14.
[22] *Ijsselcentrale* (Case IV/32.732) Commission Decision 91/50/EEC, [1991] OJ L28/32.

Electricidade de Portugal/Pego,[23] *REN/Turbogás*,[24] and *ISAB Energy*.[25] There were four principal similarities in the cases:

- in each case a power purchase agreement had been concluded between a new electricity generator and the incumbent monopoly;
- the agreement notified to the Commission had a long duration;
- the duration was rejected by the Commission, partly because of the exclusivity of supply involved and the restriction on the generator from supplying consumers other than the incumbent monopoly; and
- Commission approval in each case was conditional on a reduction of the duration to 15 years. This period has therefore acquired the status of a 'standard' term, providing investors with sufficient security for a long-term commitment.[26]

13.25 *Pego* In the *Pego* case the result was to reserve the capacity and output of the coal-fired power station exclusively to Electricidade de Portugal for 15 years instead of the original 28 years. A so-called 'first option' system was put in place for the remaining 13 years of the project, which allowed the generator to sell to third parties should there be surplus capacity not required by the grid. Under this system the generator would compete with the grid to find an outside market for its capacity, either in Portugal or in another Member State. The favourable view taken by the Commission was influenced by 'the expected development of electricity supply conditions in Portugal stemming from Decree Law 99/91 [the pro-competition law for the electricity sector]'.[27]

13.26 *REN/Turbogás* The *REN/Turbogás* case concerned a power purchase agreement for the supply of electricity from a combined cycle gas turbine power station in Portugal by Turbogás to REN, the Portuguese system manager and operator of the national grid. It involved the same 'first option' clause but this time the Commission did not accept it. Three years after *Pego*, its thinking on market liberalization had developed further. It asked the parties to allow the generator to opt to sell the capacity and the electricity to third parties after 15 years. In practice, the contract design left this possibility open. The generator received a high price for electricity generated during the first 15 years and a lower price for the remaining period. However, if the generator wished to sell to a third party after the 15-year period had elapsed, the contract provided for the provision of compensation to the incumbent

---

[23] *Electricidade de Portugal/Pego project* (Notice pursuant to Art 19(3) of Regulation 17/62) [1993] OJ C265/3.
[24] *REN/Turbogás* (Notice pursuant to Art 19(3) of Regulation 17/62) [1996] OJ C118/7.
[25] *ISAB Energy* (Notice pursuant to Art 19(3) of Regulation 17/62) [1996] OJ C138/3.
[26] There is no apparent objective legal or economic justification for the choice of the 15-year term: see Devlin, B and Levasseur, C, 'Energy' in Faull, J and Nikpay, A, *The EC Law of Competition* (1st edn, 2000) 711.
[27] *Electricidade de Portugal/Pego project* (Notice pursuant to Art 19(3) of Regulation 17/62) [1993] OJ C265/3, para 20. This implied that any future notification would be scrutinized more critically.

B. Long-Term Agreements

monopoly for the loss of its low-cost supply during that period covered by the contract.

13.27 *ISAB Energy* The *ISAB Energy* case involved a notification of a contract that had a 20-year duration. The new generator was based in Sicily and under the agreement would supply renewable sourced energy exclusively to ENEL. The generator was prevented from supplying electricity to consumers other than ENEL and in return ENEL agreed to purchase the entire output. The Commission concluded that the case should be re-examined after the first 15 years of commercial operation.

13.28 *Jahrhundertvertrag* The agreement in question was one between the German mining industry and the German public electricity supply industry, and concerned annual sales of fixed quotas of German coal to the electricity companies. Under the agreement exclusive long-term purchasing obligations were imposed on the companies. These were deemed by the Commission to be in breach of Article 81(1). The undertakings argued that they were part of the German strategy of ensuring security of supply. The application of Articles 81 and 82 was therefore precluded by Article 86(2). The Commission also held that the agreement was concluded to share markets and affected trade between Member States, even though it was an arrangement involving only parties from a single Member State. The Commission adopted a similar approach to that in the *Scottish Nuclear* decision and held that the *Jahrhundertvertrag* qualified for an exemption under Article 81(3).[28] It took the view that the agreement improved coal production and electricity generation in an area where production and demand had to be in constant balance, since electricity cannot be stored. The Commission refused, however, to apply Article 86(2) on the ground that it was not evident that the security of supply could only be maintained through this particular agreement.

13.29 However, care should be exercised in interpreting this case. The exemption reasoning adopted here would be hard to apply to joint purchases made by large electricity utilities since market opening has occurred.[29]

13.30 *Ijsselcentrale* This involved a demarcation agreement between SEP, a joint venture company entrusted with the planning of electricity supply and generation in the Netherlands at the time, and various generating companies. It imposed an import/export ban through the co-operation agreements. The Commission held that the agreement constituted an infringement of Article 81(1) in so far as it had as its object or effect the restriction of imports by private industrial consumers and

---

[28] *Jahrhundertvertrag* (Case IV/33.151), *VIK-GVSt* (Case IV/33.997) Commission Decision 93/126/EEC, [1993] OJ L50/14.
[29] See Nyssens, H and Schnichels, D, 'Energy' in Faull, J and Nikpay, A, *The EC Law of Competition* (2nd edn, 2007) ch 12, para 169.

of exports of production outside the field of public supply.[30] The Commission also examined the possibility and scope of a public security exemption under Article 86(2). It took the view that the performance of the service did not require an absolute control over exports and imports, with respect to non-public supply of electricity. With respect to electricity imports destined for and exports from the public supply, the Commission refused even to consider the application of Article 86(2).

C. Transmission Pricing

13.31 For competition to be effective, a transmission price has to emerge, and rules of access to the network are required—in particular to those parts of the infrastructure that are subject to congestion. The powers required to deal with this are available through the Directives and Regulations. Network operators usually have a dominant position in the geographic area covered by the grid.

13.32 In competition law it is clearly prohibited to impose unfair selling prices or other unfair trading conditions. An 'unfair' price could be either predatory or excessive. Prices must also be non-discriminatory. If prices appear to be unfairly high, there are three tests that may be applied:[31]

- Do the prices reflect costs related to the product sold or the service provided (test for excessive pricing)?
- Do prices charged to different customers deviate between each other without sufficient justification (discrimination)?
- Do operators' prices deviate from each other without sufficient justification (benchmarking)?

13.33 The first case in which the Commission was able to consider the calculation of transmission prices in the energy industry arose in the German electricity sector.

(1) Electricity Agreement: *Verbändevereinbarung*

13.34 Access to both the electricity and gas networks in Germany was largely governed by a system of negotiated TPA. The Government had no formal role in the system's initial design or implementation, but encouraged the associations that represented the several hundred network operators to reach a framework agreement that would formalize common access conditions. The TSOs and market entrants had to agree on the price and non-price terms of each request for access. To simplify

---

[30] *Ijsselcentrale* (Case IV/32.732) Commission Decision 91/50/EEC, [1991] OJ L28/32.
[31] Schaub, A, 'Competition Policy and Liberalization of Energy Markets', paper presented at the European Utilities Circle 2000 conference, 23 November 2000.

C. Transmission Pricing

matters, the German industry associations concluded a framework agreement on 22 May 1998 setting out joint principles for the calculation of prices, known as the *Verbändevereinbarung* (VV-1 Electricity) or Associations' Agreement.[32] This non-legally binding framework agreement had to be approved by the Ministry of Economics, FCO, and the European Commission. It failed to obtain Commission support largely because it envisaged a transaction and distance-based price model. The Commission preferred to see transmission pricing based on the costs of actual physical flows rather than the individual generator–customer contract path. The former method reflected specific physical characteristics of the electricity flows (which do not travel like other goods but follow the route of 'least resistance') (see paras 1.64–1.67). A TSO that charges its tariff on the basis of an erroneous parallel with other goods is not a price within the meaning of Article 82 EC since this is not related to the actual cost incurred. Another criticism of the system was that it was discriminatory in favour of generators in the vicinity of consumers.[33] A serious deficiency was identified in its lack of rules to ensure transparent and non-discriminatory access, such as rules to require the publication of available capacity and underlying transmission costs. Incumbents were granted discretion to make exceptions or depart from the guidelines of the VV-1.

13.35 As a result of these concerns, the industry associations produced a second framework agreement in December 1999. The second agreement (VV-2 Electricity), included an important step in the development of the kind of transmission pricing system appropriate to an internal market in energy. It provided for a non-transaction based ('stamp') tariff for the consumer's total use of the system, without any distance (point-to-point) component. This provided third party network users with greater freedom in selecting suppliers and delivery points, and making changes to these choices as the need arose. This emphasis on network service removed the discrimination identified in the point-to-point charges in VV-1.

13.36 Unfortunately, VV-2 introduced a new form of discrimination. Its transmission tariffs included a supplementary 'T' component tariff (see below) for the transportation of gas between the two trading zones, one covering the North and the other covering the South of the country. These borders were artificially drawn so that the supra-regional incumbents could cross the zones without paying the 'T' tariff as long as they stayed within their traditional demarcation areas.

---

[32] Levasseur, C, (1998) 3 Competition Policy Newsletter 43. See generally Boerner, AR, 'Negotiated Third Party Access in Germany: Electricity and Gas' (2001) 19 J Energy Natural Resources L 32 and Albers, M, 'Energy Liberalization and EC Competition Law', paper presented to 28th Annual Fordham Conference of Antitrust Law and Policy, 26 October 2001, 16–18.

[33] Many criticisms are summarized in Lapuerta, C, Pfaffenberger, W, and Pfeifenberger, J, 'Netzzugang in Deutschland: ein Laendervergleich (Tiel I & II)', *Energiewirtschaft*, March/April 1999.

13.37 The special fee called the 'T' component would be levied on each occasion when the parties to a transaction were located in different zones or when one party operated in another Member State. It also included a balancing mechanism to allow companies to compensate their flows in opposite directions crossing those borders.

13.38 The Commission regarded this approach as incompatible with competition law and sent a warning letter to the associations concerned. There were three principal objections to the system.

(1) The 'T' component did not provide for cost-reflexivity in transactions over a short distance, but had the effect of imposing an additional fee in cross-border transactions, while transmissions over long distances within a single trading zone were free of additional charges. It is a principle of EC competition law that prices lacking cost-reflexivity may be abusive.
(2) The 'T' component was discriminatory because it would give large German electricity suppliers the option to balance counter-directed flows and so avoid payment of the 'T' component, even though this option was not in practice available to smaller market actors or to foreign suppliers.
(3) Transmission costs were significantly higher than in Scandinavia.

13.39 The outcome was that the 'T' component ceased to be applied to transactions in Germany—but not before the Commission insisted that a merger between VEBA and VIAG could not proceed without the abandonment of the internal 'T' component (see para 14.64). Finally, in December 2001 a further version was concluded called VV-2 plus.[34] It stipulated that the system operator must grant access to the grid to suppliers without requiring the suppliers' customers to conclude a grid usage agreement. It also prohibited system operators from charging customers for switching suppliers.[35]

13.39A The German experience with association agreements was reflected in Recital 18 of the Electricity Directive (and Recital 16 of the Gas Directive). NRAs may draw upon such agreements in the calculation of network charges, so long as all legal requirements are met. However, these agreements and the system of negotiated TPA were replaced as a result of the Energy Industry Act (Energiewirtschaftsgesetz: EnWG), which entered into force on 13 July 2005.[34] Regulated TPA and an independent regulatory authority were introduced, with the latter responsible for the supervision of network operators and network charges. Consequently, the Associations Agreement became redundant. Some of its principles were adopted in Ordinances of the Federal Government.[35] However, the new legal framework goes beyond its scope and imposes stricter obligations on network operators. The principles and methods are set down in law and applied by the NRA. The competition

---

[34] Federal Law Gazette (Bundesgesetzblatt), Part 1, No 42 of 12 July 2005, p 1970.
[35] Law Gazette Part 1, No 46 of 28 July 2005, p 2210 (electricity) and p 2243 (gas) (on grid access); p 2197 (electricity) and p 2225 (gas) (charges for network access).

C. Transmission Pricing

authorities no longer have the authority to review individual network charges but remain competent for non-regulated parts of the energy industry, especially power generators and suppliers to end consumers, which includes control of final energy prices (although here they are bound to the network charges that the NRA approves).

(2) Gas VV Agreement

13.40 Similar developments occurred in the German gas sector. To develop and apply the system of negotiated TPA, an agreement on transmission charges and conditions of access was concluded in July 2000. This was complicated by the fact that the gas business is split into three levels: national, regional, and local—with responsibilities divided across all three. The agreement was concluded by the associations of consumers and suppliers. The consumers' associations were the *Bundesverband der Deutschen Industrie* (BDI) and the *Verband der Industriellen Energie- und Kraftwirtschaft* (VIK). The suppliers' associations were the *Bundesverband der Deutschen Gas- und Wasserwirtschaft* (BGW) and *Verband kommunaler Unternehmen* (VKU). Like the electricity VV-1, the Gas VV agreement encountered problems.

13.41 The arrangements attracted widespread criticism from energy traders and consumers. Tariffs appeared not to be cost-related, terms for various services did not appear to be available, and there was a lack of transparency regarding standard conditions and capacity availability.[36] In March 2001 a supplement to the existing agreement was signed by the four participating associations. Its aim was to improve the basis for competition in the gas sector. It attempted to improve transparency, guarantee non-discriminatory treatment in transport and storage, and improve congestion management. However, there were few details available as to how these aspirations were to be made operational. The amendment contained no binding legal rules and no sanctions were provided if the principles were breached. Above all, the tariff and contract arrangements remained both complex and expensive. Given the layered system that operates in Germany, the costs of gas transport when added up created an environment in which Germany had some of the highest transport costs in the EU.

13.42 There was a further amendment in September 2001, followed by the conclusion of a new agreement in May 2002 (VV-2 Gas). This amended the method of tariff calculation. Under this method, the supra-regional and regional suppliers were to base integrated tariffs on a system of points. The VV-2 Gas was intended to function as an interim solution, but no further agreement was concluded.

---

[36] European Federation of Energy Traders (EFET), 'Open Letter on Gas VV', 8 August 2000.

13.43 A fundamental change was only brought about when the VV-2 was replaced by the regulated TPA regime under the Energy Industry Act and Ordinances in 2005. As with electricity, network tariffs have to be introduced ex ante by the NRA. Initially a cost-based form of regulation has been introduced for a transitional period, to be replaced by one of incentive regulation, based on caps and efficiency guidelines for the network operators (ss 21, 21a and 23a of the Act). Instead of the restrictive contract path (or point-to-point) approach to network access under the VV-2 gas agreement, the Act requires an entry-exit model from February 2006.[37] However, a working entry-exit model requires a high level of co-operation between the many gas network operators (more than 700). Again, industry associations were invited to develop a co-operation agreement between network operators, albeit under the supervision of the NRA. In July 2006 the so-called Co-operation Agreement (Kooperationsvereinbarung) resulted. This is a multilateral agreement that applies only to network operators which sign it. Attached to the Agreement are several model contracts necessary for network access. Given the large number of networks, the differing gas qualities, and congestion, Germany remains split into 19 distinct market areas, complicating network access considerably. Since new market entrants complained that the Agreement set stricter conditions for network access than the Act itself, the NRA investigated and, in a special procedure for control of abusive behaviour by network operators, for which the NRA is exclusively competent, decided in November 2006 that this part of the Agreement was not compatible with the Act.[38]

13.44 Germany provides an illustration of the importance of technical considerations in the liberalization equation. Two gas qualities are supplied: low calorie or 'L' gas and high calorie or 'H' gas. The grid operators import or produce various types of gas. They then manage the qualities to ensure that customers consistently receive the gas quality they need. Competition and especially trading are difficult if there is no blending service provided by a transportation company in accordance with predefined and transparent rules. 'L' gas can be delivered to customers consistently by blending 'L gas with 'H' gas, or by adding nitrogen to 'H' gas. A blending service allows customers to have a gas that corresponds to the 'L' or 'H' limits, but transportation companies would have to provide all relevant information about blending facilities, and charges for conversion would have to be reasonable and efficiently allocated.

---

[37] Energy Industry Act, s 20, para 1b; in an entry-exit model the network user no longer has to book the actual transport route through all networks which he has to cross to reach his customer. He only books capacities at the feed-in and off-take points and hence has to conclude only two contracts. The network operators are responsible for organizing the transport between these two points. Feed-in and off-take capacities can be reserved, used, and traded independently from one another. Gas can be traded at virtual trading points, which leads to increased liquidity in the market.
[38] Bundesnetzagentur, 7th Decision Division, BK-06-074, Bonn, 17 November 2006.

(3) Assessment

13.45 The above German cases suggest—prima facie—that EC competition law is flexible about the particular method adopted to calculate transmission prices, leaving this to be set by sector-specific law or by the regulatory authorities in a way that reflects the specific circumstances. The principal aim is only to set out the parameters for the pricing conduct of the dominant network operators in individual cases. This would appear to rule out the use of competition law to promote a pan-European tarification system aimed at promoting trade in electricity.[39] However, such an interpretation would have to be accompanied by several caveats. The VV agreements were concluded at a relatively early stage in the European liberalization process and have been largely but not entirely sidelined by the new law and the establishment of a German NRA, and the Commission would make any current assessment in the light of progress made through application of the Electricity and Gas Regulations[40] and developments within the context of the Florence and Madrid Electricity Regulatory Forums.

D. Interconnector Use and Access

13.46 The lack of market integration in the EU is linked to the absence of sufficient interconnections, so the development of competition in this area has for some time been seen as strategically important for the internal market (see paras 5.95–5.105, 6.53–6.58, 18.68–18.80). In the pre-liberalization period, the electricity interconnectors were used mainly for reasons of security of supply and not, unlike the gas sector, for large-scale commercial export or import. The expansion of both electricity and gas interconnector capacity is a priority for the EU through the encouragement of investment in major new infrastructure.

13.47 As far as *existing* infrastructure is concerned, the competition problems will usually take the form of capacity hoarding and reservation. A distinction may be made between interconnectors built before liberalization commenced, usually by the dominant vertically integrated players of the time, and merchant interconnectors that are of more recent origin and have been constructed jointly by several suppliers. Where investments have taken place a long time ago and are amortized already, it may be appropriate to review capacity reservations that are no longer linked to the provision of legal certainty to high risk investments.

---

[39] Schaub, A, 'Competition Policy and Liberalization of Energy Markets', paper presented at the European Utilities Circle 2000 conference, 23 November 2000, 6.
[40] Regulation (EC) 1228/2003 of 26 June 2003 on conditions for access to the network for cross-border exchanges in electricity [2003] OJ L176/1; Regulation (EC) 1775/2005 of 28 September 2005 on condition for access to the natural gas transmission networks [2005] OJ L289/1.

13.48 Access to interconnector capacity is of crucial importance. It has become a priority area for competition policy.[41] For both electricity and gas markets, interconnectors are crucial to the functioning of the pan-European energy network. They include not only lines that cross national land borders but also undersea lines that connect different countries such as the UK–Belgium gas interconnector and Estlink. Access to these lines is essential if importers are to enter the markets of other Member States. They are also the only source of competition in the short term in those Member States that have a monopolistic supply structure. However, in many cases they lack sufficient capacity to transmit all of the electricity and gas that producers, traders, and large consumers wish to import or export in a liberalizing market. In this context, two questions in particular have proved to be important to competition policy: 'how is scarce transmission capacity to be allocated in a manner compatible with the aims of the internal energy market?' (the method); and 'where capacity is reserved through long-term capacity reservation agreements, are these reservations compatible with EC competition law?'.

(1) Methods of Allocating Available Capacity

13.49 Questions of capacity allocation are of great importance to the competition authorities since they are usually raised by potential new market entrants. In practice, there is no requirement in competition law to adopt a particular method of allocation of transmission rights. The aim is only to set down the parameters for dominant network operators.

13.50 The need for a method of allocation arises when demand exceeds supply. The TSOs usually choose to apply pro-rata rationing and/or auctions to deal with this. If demand does not exceed available capacity to a large extent, pro-rata rationing works well at border points and bottlenecks in some Member States. However, it may lead to the allocation of very little capacity in situations where demand greatly exceeds available capacity. The individual transaction will then lose its commercial value. This can be avoided by choosing the auction method.

13.51 In addressing this question of allocation methods and their compatibility with competition law, there have been questions about the 'first-come, first-served' method and about auctions. The problem with the 'first-come, first-served' approach is that it can favour former monopolists over new market entrants. This may occur if a dominant firm has concluded long-term capacity reservation contracts before liberalization. It may also facilitate discrimination by a TSO in favour of its vertically-integrated supply business, foreclosing other traders from entering the downstream supply markets.

---

[41] European Commission, Energy Sector Inquiry Report, February 2006, 58–74, 150–66; Commission of the European Communities, 'Inquiry pursuant to Article 17 of Regulation (EC) No 1/2003 in to the European gas and electricity sectors (Final Report)', COM (2006) 851 final, 10 January 2007, 8, 16, 17, 172–186.

D. Interconnector Use and Access

(2) Long-Term Capacity Reservations

For some time agreements that reserve capacity to parties over a long period have come under the scrutiny of the Commission with respect to their validity and their exclusion from normal allocation procedures.[42] The issue is whether a long-term reservation agreement is incompatible with competition law—an important question because in the event of incompatibility, this capacity would become available for reallocation. The Commission therefore launched a number of investigations into these contracts, not least because the beneficiaries of long-term capacity reservation agreements are usually former monopolists.

13.52

(a) The Skaggerak Cable

An early example of capacity booking on an electricity interconnector leading to distortions of trade was identified by the Commission at the Norwegian/Danish and Danish/German borders. Various agreements on transmission capacity had the effect of blocking off all of the interconnector capacity at the Norwegian/Danish end and about one-third of the capacity at the Danish/German border. This led to trade distortions between Norway, Western Denmark, and Germany. The congestion on these lines was partly the result of a long-term reservation agreement for 60 per cent of the total capacity of the only cable connecting Western Denmark and Norway, called the 'Skagerrak cable'. This had a duration of around 20 years and benefited largely the dominant producers in Norway and Western Denmark, Statkraft, and Elsam. The remaining 40 per cent of the capacity on the cable was subject to a long-term reservation agreement between Statkraft and E.ON, with a duration of 25 years from 1998. It included a reservation of transit capacity through the Western Danish network and about 34 per cent of the capacity of the Danish/German interconnector towards Germany. The two purchasing parties, E.ON and Elsam, each enjoyed dominant positions in their respective markets.

13.53

Following serious doubts expressed by the Commission about the compatibility of the reservation agreements with competition law, the Statkraft/Elsam agreement was amended to free up capacity in its entirety from 1 January 2001.[43] The German company E.ON also yielded its capacity on the Skagerrak cable and on the Danish/German interconnector.

13.54

---

[42] Commission Press Release MEMO/01/76, 'Role of interconnectors in the electricity market. A competition perspective', 12 March 2001; the Commission's competition concerns about capacity reservation on the interconnectors of VEBA and VIAG led to their abandonment by the merging entity during the merger procedure: Commission Press Release IP/00/613, 'Commission allows merger of VEBA and VIAG subject to stringent conditions', 13 June 2000.

[43] Commission Press Release IP/01/30, 'Increased Scope for Electricity Imports Competition in Northern Europe: a step forward towards an internal market in electricity', 11 January 2001; note also the Commission decision at about the same time with respect to the construction of a sub-sea cable between Norway and Germany for the transmission of high-voltage electricity: Notice pursuant to Article 19(3) of Council Regulation No 17 concerning case COMP/E-3/37.921—Viking Cable [2001] OJ C247/11.

(b) The UK/French Interconnector

13.55 A second case involving access to electricity interconnectors concerned the UK–French submarine interconnector.[44] Its use had been reserved exclusively for EDF exports into the UK under an agreement on management of the interconnector. Prior to the introduction of new rules on allocation of capacity, the owners sought the Commission's views. Since the TSOs are in a dominant position in the market for transmission of electricity between the continent and the UK, any restriction on the attribution of transmission rights or discriminatory treatment would have been contrary to EC competition law, under Article 82. If a priority right had been granted in favour of a particular company, this would have allowed it to circumvent the rules for capacity allocation that apply to other companies, constituting discriminatory treatment.

13.56 As a result of the Commission's observations, the two companies opened up access to the interconnector without any reserve being made in favour of any particular company, with capacity being tendered in specific blocks over the next few years. The French network operator, RTE (*Reseau de Transmission d'Electricité*) also made changes to procedures and duration of transit rights in France to ensure compatibility with the transmission rights in the UK–French interconnector.

(c) The UK/Belgium Interconnector

13.57 The operation of the gas interconnector between Bacton in the UK and Zeebrugge in Belgium has raised competition concerns on several occasions. In the mid-1990s the Commission expressly stated[45] that it considered the entire project to be pro-competitive, since it created the possibility of competition between two formerly segmented markets and because third parties had opportunities to acquire capacity. However, in 2001 the UK Department of Trade and Industry expressed concerns about the interconnector's functioning.[46] In January 2001 the gas flows changed from reverse flow (or imports into the UK) to forward flow (exports to the Continent) and did not reverse back before 24 January, even though UK prices were higher than those on the continent. The question arose as to whether there was any anti-competitive practice involved in this situation that might help to explain the UK price increases.

13.58 The investigation did not yield any evidence of collusion among UK shippers which are also major gas producers, to influence the flow direction of the interconnector. Nor was there any evidence of antitrust infringements involving the Belgian utility, Distrigas. The principal reason for the increases appeared to arise from the

---

[44] Commission Press Release IP/01/341, 'UK-French electricity interconnector opens up, increasing scope for competition', 12 March 2001.
[45] European Commission, *Report on Competition Policy 1995*, 39–40.
[46] Commission Press Release IP/02/401, 'Commission closes investigation into UK/Belgium gas interconnector', 13 March 2002. A similar incident about use of the interconnector arose in March 2006.

D. Interconnector Use and Access

disparity between a liberalized market in the UK and a liberalizing market on the continent, which linked its gas price to that of oil. There were nonetheless rigidities in the Standard Transportation Agreement governing the interconnector, through which the companies owning and controlling it jointly decided, in a uniform manner, to make capacity available to third parties. This procedure had the effect of restricting shippers in their capacity to transfer capacity to third parties. These included the long minimal duration of assignment and sub-lease contracts and the high minimal amounts due to be delivered by means of such contracts. The UK shippers agreed to adopt more flexible rules to include swifter flow transition rules and less stringent sublease conditions for interested third parties. They also introduced greater transparency by announcing flow reversals in advance. These features contributed to a more level playing field.

(d) The Dutch/German Interconnector

An important case concerning interconnector capacity and legacy contracts was decided by the ECJ in 2005.[47] The implications of the ECJ's judgment have been much discussed within the Commission and both electricity and gas industries. The Commission has even issued a paper in which it sets out its understanding of the decision and its implications for the internal energy market[48] (see paras 5.131–5.134, 6.114). Given the significance attached to the case it is worth giving it an extended consideration and analysis.   **13.59**

In a reference from a Dutch court for a preliminary ruling, the ECJ ruled that: **13.60**

- a prohibition of discrimination under Articles 7(5) and 16 of Directive (EC) 96/92 concerning common rules for the internal market in electricity[49] is not limited to technical rules but must apply to all forms of discrimination, and
- these articles preclude national measures that grant an undertaking preferential capacity for the cross-border transmission of electricity, whether those measures derive from the system operator, the controller of system management, or the legislature, in the case where such measures have not been authorized within the framework of the procedure set out in Article 24 of Directive (EC) 96/92 (Member States can apply for derogations from the prohibition of discrimination).

---

[47] Case C-17/03 *Vereniging voor Energie, Milieu en Water, Amsterdam Power Exchange Spotmarket BV, Eneco NV v Directeur van de Dienst uitvoering en toezicht energie* [2005] ECR I-4983.
[48] *Commission Staff Working Paper on the decision C-17/03 of 7 June 2005 of the Court of Justice of the European Communities*, SEC (2006) 547, 26 April 2006; see also *Report on Competition Policy 2005*, 27: 'although the case specifically concerned long-term capacity reservations of interconnector capacity into the Netherlands, it has important implications for many historic long-term capacity reservations on interconnectors that continued to exist after the entry into force of the First Electricity Directive . . . [T]he judgment opens the door for possible cases to be brought by the Competition DG even though the Court's judgment did not explicitly address competition issues.'
[49] [1997] OJ L27/20.

13.61 Essentially, the preferential treatment for the electricity generating firms concerned had to be terminated but the long-term take-or-pay contracts for electricity imports had to be honoured.[50] In September the preferential treatment was terminated by the TSO. In a wider context, the case is significant in being initiated by a consumers' association (and not the Commission) with the aim, inter alia, of lowering energy prices. However, the length of time that the case has taken from its initiation in the Netherlands suggests that the direct benefits to consumers from pursuing change through the courts are likely to be small. The immediate beneficiaries from this case are likely to be the companies engaged in electricity trading on the EU market.

13.62 **The facts**   The case was brought by a Netherlands consumers' group, the *Vereniging voor Energie, Milieu en Water* (VEMW) against a preferential arrangement for several Dutch electricity generators that reserved to them a large portion of the cross-border capacity for electricity imports. The case arose from actions taken by the Netherlands Government at a time of liberalization of its electricity sector in compliance with EC legislation, and it concerned in particular a decision of the NRA, the *Directeur van de Dienst uitvoering en toezicht energie* (DTE) (see para 13.66). The case was also supported by the Amsterdam Power Exchange Spot Market and Eneco. A reference was made by the Dutch court, the *College van Beroep voor het bedrijfsleven* (Administrative Court for Trade and Industry; hereinafter 'CBB') to the ECJ for a preliminary ruling under Article 234 EC. The reference concerned two matters: first, the interpretation of Article 86(2) EC (the nature and role of public service obligations as a justification for the allocation of exclusive access rights), and secondly, the interpretation of Article 7(5) of Directive (EC) 96/92 (the scope of the prohibition of discrimination and the allocation of cross-border capacity).

13.63 Under Article 7 of Directive (EC) 96/92, since replaced by the Electricity Directive,[51] a TSO was to be designated by Member States and charged with responsibility for operating, ensuring the maintenance of and, if necessary, developing the electricity transmission system in a given area and its interconnectors with other systems, in order to guarantee security of supply. Member States had also to ensure that technical rules were developed and published on matters such as the minimum technical design and operational requirements for the connection to the system

---

[50] This conclusion was different from the one that followed from the opinion of Advocate-General Stix-Hackl, delivered on 28 October 2004.

[51] Directive (EC) 2003/54 concerning common rules for the internal market in electricity and repealing Directive (EC) 96/92 [2003] OJ L176/37. For discussion of this Directive's provisions, and those of the related Gas Directive, see paras 5.06–5.78 and 6.03–6.114; also, Cameron, PD, 'Completing the Internal Market in Energy: An Introduction to the New Legislation' in Cameron, PD, (ed), *Legal Aspects of EU Energy Regulation: Implementing the New Directives on Electricity and Gas across Europe* (2005) 7–39.

D. Interconnector Use and Access

of generating installations, distribution systems, directly connected consumers' equipment, interconnector circuits and direct lines. The Member State has to ensure that these requirements bring about the inter-operability of electricity systems and are objective and non-discriminatory. The TSO is responsible for ensuring a secure, reliable, and efficient electricity system, as well as the availability of the necessary ancillary services. It is also responsible for managing energy flows on the system, taking into account exchanges with other interconnected systems. The system operator is required not to discriminate between system users or classes of system users, particularly in favour of its subsidiaries or shareholders.

The context of market liberalization The origins of the case lay some years prior to Directive (EC) 96/92, when a company was charged by the Netherlands Electricity Law 1989[52] with the task of ensuring the reliable and efficient public distribution of electricity at the lowest possible cost and in the public interest. This company, called the SEP (Samenwerkende Elekriciteits-Productiebedrijven), was the only designated company authorized to import electricity into the Netherlands when such electricity was intended for public distribution.[53] However, it was not authorized to enter into any import contracts without the approval of the competent minister.[54] The rights of this designated company were taken over by the NEA (Nederlands Elektriciteit Administratiekantoor) from 1 January 2001. **13.64**

In 1998 a further Electricity Law transposed Directive (EC) 96/92 and repealed the 1989 Act. It initiated two changes relevant to this case. First, the SEP transferred the operation of the high-voltage network to its subsidiary, TenneT BV. Ownership of that network was subsequently transferred to a subsidiary of SEP, called Saranne (in 2001). In the same year the State acquired ownership first of TenneT and then of Saranne. One of the tasks of TenneT is to establish and maintain the network, ensuring that it is reliable and secure, guaranteeing a sufficient reserve capacity and supplying to third parties electricity imported into the Netherlands and exported to other countries. **13.65**

Secondly, supervision of the operation of the network and of the network operator is entrusted to the DTE. The latter is subject to the Minister for Economic Affairs, who may issue both individual and general instructions, a power that was to become highly relevant for this case. The DTE is also required to determine, on a proposal of the network operator, the conditions governing access to the network. To that end, it adopted a System Code in a decision of 12 November 1999. This Code set out the conditions governing operation of the system for the cross-border transmission of electricity. Under Chapter 5 of the Code, an electricity import **13.66**

---

[52] Art 2 (*Elekriciteitswet*), Staatsblad 1989, 535.
[53] ibid, Art 34.
[54] ibid, Art 35.

capacity of 1,500 Megawatts (MW) of the 3,200 MW available on cross-border lines was reserved on a preferential basis for the SEP for the transmission of electricity that was the subject of purchase contracts signed by the SEP at an earlier stage under Article 35 of the 1989 Act. Three 'international contracts' for the purchase of electricity had been concluded by the SEP in 1989–90 to fulfil its task under Article 2 of the 1989 Electricity Act (to ensure a reliable and efficient public distribution of electricity). The contracts were concluded with Electricité de France, Preussen Elektra and the Vereinigte Elektrizitätswerke Westfalen for a total of 1,500 MW.

13.67 After 2000, the preferential allocation of annual capacity to the SEP for the cross-border transmission of electricity was regulated by another law, the Transition Act on Electricity Generation.[55] Article 13(1) of this law required the system operator of the national high-voltage grid to allocate (on request) to the designated company a maximum of 900 MW until 31 March 2005 and a maximum of 750 MW from 1 April 2005 to 31 March 2009 for the transmission of electricity where such transmission serves to implement these three international contracts.

13.68 **The dispute** The claimants lodged an administrative objection to the adoption of Chapter 5 of the System Code by the DTE. The latter considered the matter before dismissing the objection in its decision of 17 July 2000, following an instruction from the Minister of Economic Affairs. The DTE recognized that the preferences granted to the SEP constituted obstacles to the proper functioning of the electricity market, and that meaningful competition on the market for generation of electricity in the Netherlands was still extensively limited, to the extent that competition could only operate in practice by means of electricity generated outside the Netherlands. To increase the available capacity for cross-border transmission from the current level of 3,200 MW would be expensive. The reservation under the international contracts would therefore involve a serious restriction on import possibilities and on intra-Community electricity trade. However, in rejecting the complaint, the DTE argued that the international contracts were long-term ongoing contracts concluded by the SEP pursuant to a service of general economic interest within the terms of Article 86 EC. The 1998 Electricity Law did not contain any provision capable of casting doubt on the validity of those contracts, with the result that those contracts had in principle to be performed. If the existing contracts were not to be honoured, this would in the DTE's view amount to an unacceptable interference with the legal certainty of the parties and would constitute a significant financial loss. Further, performance of those contracts would not take up all of the international transmission capacity.

13.69 The claimants brought an action against the decision of the DTE, arguing that his decision was in breach of Articles 28, 81, 82, and 86 EC and was also contrary to

---

[55] *Overgangswet elektriciteitsproducktiesektor* of 21 December 2000, Staatsblad 2000, 607.

D. Interconnector Use and Access

the principle of non-discrimination laid down in Article 7(5) of Directive (EC) 96/92 and Article 24 of the 1998 Electricity Act, and further was contrary to the principles of non-discrimination and objectivity. The decision by the DTE ignored the interest in promoting the development of trade on the market in electricity within the terms of Article 36 of the 1998 Act. Finally, the claimants submitted that the method for attribution of the System Code had to be classified as a 'technical regulation' and ought for that reason to have been brought to the attention of the European Commission, in line with Council Directive (EEC) 83/189 laying down a procedure for the provision of information in the field of technical standards and regulation.[56]

This action was brought in the CBB, which decided to stay the proceedings and refer certain questions to the ECJ for a preliminary ruling. There were two principal questions referred to the ECJ: **13.70**

(1) (a) Can Article 86(2) EC be invoked to justify continuing to grant a company which was formerly entrusted with the operation of services of general economic interest and which entered into certain commitments in connection with such operation a special right to enable it to honour those commitments after the particular task assigned to it has been completed?
 (b) If this question is answered in the affirmative, is a rule which provides for the preferential allocation over a period of ten years of half to a quarter (declining over time) of the cross-border transmission capacity for electricity to the undertaking concerned nevertheless invalid because it:
  (i) is not proportionate in relation to the (public) interest served thereby;
  (ii) affects trade to such an extent as would be contrary to the interests of the Community?
(2) (a) Is Article 7(5) of Directive (EC) 96/92 to be interpreted as meaning that the prohibition of discrimination it contains is restricted to the requirement that the system operator must not draw any distinction in granting access to the system by means of technical rules?
 If so, is an allocation method relating to the cross-border transmission capacity of electricity to be regarded as a technical rule within the meaning of the above provision?
 (b) In the event that the allocation method must be regarded as a technical rule or in the event that Article 7(5) of Directive (EC) 96/92 is not limited to technical rules, is a rule under which preferential cross-border transmission capacity is made available for contracts concluded in connection with a particular public task compatible with the prohibition of discrimination contained in that article?

---

[56] [1983] OJ L109/8.

13.71 **The ECJ's ruling** The ECJ chose to examine the second question first and, in the light of its decision, found that an answer to the first question was unnecessary. Essentially, it focused on the issue of whether the prohibition of discrimination laid down by Article 7(5) of Directive (EC) 96/92 precluded national measures which allocated to the SEP a preferential capacity for the cross-border transmission of electricity.

13.72 In interpreting Article 7(5), the ECJ considered not only its wording but also the context in which it occurred and the objects of the rules of which it is part.[57] In this instance, Article 7(5) is couched in general terms which prohibit all discrimination 'between system users or classes of system users'. There is no indication from that wording that supports a restrictive interpretation limited to technical rules. Further, from the context of Article 7, para (5) cannot be limited to technical rules. Article 7(2) already provides that technical rules must not be discriminatory. If the rule on non-discrimination which is set out in Article 7(5) were limited to technical rules, the rule provided for in Article 7(2) would serve no purpose. Finally, with regard to the objectives of the Directive, Recital 25 states, without setting out any limitation in regard of technical rules, that a system operator must behave 'in an objective, transparent and non-discriminatory manner'. From the above three considerations, the ECJ concluded that Article 7(5) is not limited to covering technical rules but must be interpreted as applying to all discrimination.[58]

13.73 The same conclusion was drawn with respect to Article 16 of Directive (EC) 96/92 (since the dispute relates to state measures that are not attributable to the system operator). This article allows Member States to choose between the negotiated access procedure and the single buyer procedure for the organization of access to the system. Both sets of procedure must be operated in accordance with objective, transparent, and non-discriminatory criteria.[59] The rule on non-discrimination laid down in that Article is couched in general terms and has to be read in the light of Article 3(1) of Directive (EC) 96/92, under which Member States are required to refrain from all discrimination in regard to the rights and obligations of electricity undertakings.

13.74 Next, the ECJ addressed the question of whether the national measures such as Article 5 of the System Code and Article 13(1) of the Transition Law amounted to discrimination contrary to the Directive. It noted that the provisions of the Directive—requiring non-discrimination on the part of the system operator and the Member State in creating access to the system—are specific expressions of the

---

[57] Following inter alia Case 292/82 *Merck* [1983] ECR 3781, para 12; Case 337/82 *St Nikolaus Brennerei* [1984] ECR 1501, para 10; and Case C-223/98 *Adidas* [1999] ECR I-7081, para 23.
[58] [2005] ECR I-4983, para 45.
[59] Joined Cases C 128 & 129/03 *AEM SpA and AEM Torino SpA v Autorita per l'energia elettrica e per il gas* [2005] ECR I-2861, para 57.

D. Interconnector Use and Access

general principle of equality.[60] Further, it noted that the prohibition of discrimination, as one of the fundamental principles of Community law, requires that comparable situations are not treated differently unless such difference in treatment is objectively justified.[61] In this case there was common ground among the parties that the priority access to the network for the cross-border transmission of electricity, granted originally to the SEP and subsequently to the NEA, amounts to differential treatment.[62] The NEA argued, however, that the differential treatment granted to it in the form of priority access was justified by the fact that the NEA was in a situation not comparable to that of other operators. The international, long-term contracts concluded by the SEP prior to liberalization (and taken over by the NEA) were necessary for the performance of its tasks. If the NEA were not able to import the quantities of electricity contemplated in these contracts, which were characterized by a high fixed cost and relatively low price per MW, performance of those contracts would severely penalize it, in view of the absence of adequate capacity on the network for cross-border transmission. This situation justified the reservation for the NEA of a certain capacity on the network on a priority basis. This argument was rejected by the ECJ in the light of the Directive's provisions.

The ECJ noted that Directive (EC) 96/92 provides for a transitional regime in Article 24 to 'tone down' some of the consequences of liberalization. Member States may seek derogations from certain provisions in the Directive, including Articles 7 and 16, in cases where commitments or guarantees of operation given before the entry into force of the Directive may not be honoured on account of its provisions. The existence of this provision to deal with individual situations arising out of the legal context existing before the Directive entered into force means that the existence or otherwise of discrimination within the terms of Articles 7(5) and 16 has to be appraised without regard being had to those individual situations. Article 24 of the Directive contained a deadline for submission of applications for a derogation, gave the decision-making power to the Commission, set out a procedure which the Commission had to follow, and required such derogations to be of limited duration and be linked to the expiry of the commitments or guarantees in question. The Netherlands Government could have had recourse to Article 24 to request a temporary derogation from Articles 7(5) and 16 in favour of the SEP in the form of a request to be allowed to allocate to it on a priority basis a part of the capacity for the cross-border transmission of electricity. It did not do so. Instead, it submitted only a request for compensation for a portion of the financial losses which would be incurred by the SEP by virtue

13.75

---

[60] ibid, para 58; by analogy, see also in regard to the second subparagraph of Art 40(3) EEC (now, of Art 34(2) EC), Case C-280/93 *Germany v Council* [1994] ECR I-4973, para 67 and Case C-422/02 P *Chemi-Con (Deutschland) v Council*, para 33.
[61] See *Germany v Council* [1994] ECR I-4973, para 33.
[62] [2005] ECR I-4983, para 50.

of its performance of the international contracts concluded for its previous public service task.⁶³ The Article 24 transitional regime, with its procedure, the criteria and limits set out in it, would be rendered meaningless if a Member State were able to apply unilaterally, and without complying with that procedure, differential treatment to electricity importers on grounds that are capable of justifying, under Article 24, a derogation from Articles 7(5) and 16. The aim behind the design of a system of derogations was to ensure, among other things, that there should be equal treatment for undertakings which previously held a national monopoly and which found themselves in situations such as that of the NEA.

13.76 The Netherlands Government, however, tried to argue that a refusal of access to the system by the system operator under Articles 3(3) and 17(5) of Directive (EC) 96/92 showed that some reservation of cross-border transmission capacity is not necessarily at variance with the principle of non-discrimination. However, Article 3(3), which allows Member States to derogate from certain provisions of the Directive, does not apply to Article 7 or to Article 16. It cannot therefore be relied upon to justify a derogation from Articles 7(5) and 16. The provisions of Article 17(5) provide that the system operator may refuse access to the system where it lacks the necessary capacity and requires duly substantiated reasons to be given for such a refusal. However, the ECJ's reasoning about the transitional regime of the Directive means that priority access based on the existence of contracts concluded before the Directive entered into force and granted outside the procedure provided for in Article 24 cannot be regarded as justified.⁶⁴

13.77 The ECJ concluded by stating that:

> ... priority access to a portion of the capacity for the cross-border transmission of electricity conferred on an operator by reason of commitments assumed before the Directive entered into force, but without compliance with the procedure set out in Article 24 of the Directive, must be regarded as being discriminatory within the terms of Article 7(5) and 16 of the Directive and as therefore being contrary to those articles.⁶⁵

13.78 A further argument based on the principle of protection of legitimate expectations received short shrift.⁶⁶ This was designed to support the view that an operator such as the NEA is entitled to perform the international contracts of the SEP.

---

[63] Commission Decision 1999/796/EC concerning the application of the Netherlands for a transitional regime under Art 24 of Directive (EC) 96/92 [1999] OJ L319/34, point 44.

[64] The ECJ also dismissed certain arguments made by the NEA and the Commission based on recitals of the Directive, and a line of reasoning developed by the Finnish Government based on Arts 8(2) and 17(5): see [2005] ECR I-4983, paras 66–70.

[65] ibid, para 71. Note the contrasting view of Advocate-General Stix-Hackl in his opinion of 28 October 2004, available on the website at <http://www.curia.eu.int> (in Dutch).

[66] ibid, paras 73–9.

D. Interconnector Use and Access

While the principle is one of the fundamental principles of the Community,[67] the ECJ argued that it may not be relied upon if a prudent and circumspect trader could have foreseen that the adoption of a Community measure is likely to affect his interests. Looking at the history of Community actions in this area in the 1990s it could not be concluded that the Community institutions had created any well-founded expectations on the part of SEP that an import monopoly would be maintained or that preferential rights for network use for cross-border transmission of electricity could continue until the expiry of the international contracts.

13.79 With respect to the principle of legal certainty, the requirement is that rules involving negative consequences for individuals should be clear and precise and their application predictable for those subject to them.[68] It allows an individual to call into question the arrangements made for the implementation of a legislative amendment. It also requires that the legislature take account of the particular situations of traders and provide, where appropriate, adaptations to the application of the new legal rules. In this case, Directive (EC) 96/92 allows for account to be taken of the special situations of traders such as the SEP in the context of the liberalization of the electricity market. In particular, the ECJ pointed out, the Directive offers Member States the possibility of applying, through Article 24, for a derogation from Articles 7(5) and 16 with respect to operating commitments or guarantees that were granted before the Directive entered into force. The Netherlands Government did not take advantage of this possibility.

13.80 The *long-term* character of the international contracts came under the scrutiny of the ECJ and gave rise to some remarks in the context of this discussion of the impact of the two principles. The Court stated that while there was no obligation in the Directive to revoke contracts such as those made by the SEP, this did not authorize a breach of the Directive's rules on the ground that such a breach is necessary to honour those contracts. Moreover, revocation of those contracts would be merely an indirect and potential consequence of the Directive. The SEP (and after 2001 the NEA) is not in principle prevented from selling outside the Netherlands the electricity that it has agreed to purchase under those international contracts.

13.81 The NEA also invoked the Electricity Regulation,[69] and especially point 2 in the annex to that Regulation, which provides that 'existing long term contracts shall have no pre-emption rights when they come up for renewal'. On the basis of this provision, the NEA argued that it must be possible to honour contracts concluded

---

[67] See inter alia Case C-104/97 P *Atlanta v European Community* [1999] ECR I-6983, para 52; and Joined Cases C 37 & 38/02 *Di Lenardo and Dilexport* [2004] ECR I-6945, para 70.
[68] Case 325/85 *Ireland v Commission* [1987] ECR 5041; Case C-143/93 *Van Es Douane Agenten* [1996] ECR I-431, para 27; and Case C-63/93 *Duff* [1996] ECR I-569, para 20.
[69] Regulation (EC) 1228/2003 of 26 June 2003 on conditions for access to the network for cross-border exchanges in electricity [2003] OJ L176/1.

before that Regulation entered into force. The ECJ did not accept this argument. The provision was consistent with the Court's interpretation of Articles 7(5) and 16 of the Directive. Reliance on these two principles—the protection of legitimate expectations and legal certainty—was therefore not possible in these circumstances.

13.82 The ECJ's conclusion was that Articles 7(5) and 16 of the Directive are not limited to covering technical rules but must be construed as applying to all discrimination, and that those articles preclude national measures that grant an undertaking preferential capacity for the cross-border transmission of electricity, whether those measures derive from the system operator, the controller of system management, or the legislature, in cases where such measures have not been authorized within the framework of the procedure set out in Article 24 of the Directive. The first question referred to the Court (public service obligations as a justification for the allocation of exclusive access rights) no longer required an answer, given its reply to the second question. The case returned to the CBB in the Netherlands. On 24 May 2006 the CBB annulled the NRA's decision to give priority to the old SEP contracts. The decision is final.

13.83 *Assessment* In ruling against the grant of preferential treatment to cross-border transmission capacity, the ECJ was careful to take into account the fact of an ongoing process of market liberalization, both in the Netherlands and in the EU generally. It gave considerable weight to the 'transitional regime' introduced by Directive 96/92/EC, which offered Member States an opportunity to apply for exemptions from some aspects of the liberalization process that the Directive initiated, according to a timetable set by the Directive. The failure of the Dutch Government to take advantage of that opportunity by seeking an exemption for the long-term contracts at issue was crucial in the Court's rejection of its case. Indeed, it provided the basis for remarks made by the Court[70] that the incumbent companies might seek to recover compensation for losses incurred by virtue of the fact that the Dutch Government had failed to seek a derogation under Article 24 in respect of the measures at issue. However, the Court left open the possibility that there may be a public interest justification in the preferential allocation of transmission capacity, but in the absence of an attempt to trigger the mechanism provided by the Directive, this consideration was not relevant.

13.84 Since the ECJ's decision affects long-term contracts that have a take-or-pay character (described in the case as 'import contracts'), it may be thought that this decision has wider implications for network owners of facilities such as LNG terminals or gas pipelines and such facilities. In many cases, such facilities have been constructed and operated on the basis of preferential arrangements secured by long-term contracts as a condition for making large investments. It is far from clear that it has

---

[70] [2005] ECR I-4983, para 86.

D. Interconnector Use and Access

such relevance, however, since the issue here, as seen by the ECJ, is one concerned with market power rather than one concerned with infrastructure. The generating companies that have inherited the contracts from the pre-liberalized regime are not seen as having as their main goal competition with each other but rather the maximization of profit from their assets. Moreover, the ECJ in its judgment[71] has emphasized its support for the performance of the long-term contracts at issue.

13.85 The case raises a wider issue about the enforcement of EC legislation on the liberalization of the electricity and gas markets. The framework character of such legislation means that it has placed a heavy reliance upon the Member States and especially the recently established NRAs for enforcement. In the background, the European Commission is charged with the responsibility for monitoring and reporting on progress in implementing the legislation. Yet, this case contains a number of role-reversals or at best ambiguities in the positions taken by the enforcement authorities vis-à-vis liberalization. To begin with, the party that was the subject of the complaint was in fact the NRA, even though the material beneficiaries of the system of preferential treatment were in fact the incumbent electricity generating companies. The regulator's decision in support of the incumbent companies was in fact taken following an instruction from the Minister of Economic Affairs, using powers given to the Minister under the then Dutch law (it has since been changed to provide the regulator with greater independence). Rather than suggesting some possible inconsistency on the part of the NRA, the decision it took in this case underlines the limits to the powers currently enjoyed by 'independent' regulators vis-à-vis Member State governments. The European Commission also played an unexpected role, rejecting the consumers' association requests to support its case. This has little, if anything, to do with the merits of the complaint. It reflects the highly politicized character of the liberalization process: the Dutch Government's support was important for the Commission's proposals for a wider liberalization of the gas sector, and action on behalf of the consumers in this case might have jeopardized that support.

13.86 Another feature of the case requires some comment. It concerns the consumer interests which constituted the driver in the main proceedings. The length of time taken from the commencement of the case in the Netherlands to its current stage is likely to prove daunting to many consumer interests. Before the referral for a preliminary ruling reached the ECJ, it had already taken three years in the Netherlands from the initiation of the complaint. The time taken by the ECJ to reach its judgment added a further two years, and afterwards, the case continued in the Netherlands for almost a year. Even for large industrial consumers, to commit to such long periods of time to remove a barrier to trade is a major disincentive, not

---

[71] ibid, para 83.

only due to the costs involved. Moreover, the direct benefits of pursuing change through the courts are likely to be small in this case. The immediate beneficiaries are likely to be companies engaged in electricity trading on the EU market. At the same time, an increase in competition resulting from greater opportunities for traders to gain access to cross-border capacity may bring some benefits to consumers, even if they do not benefit directly from equal treatment in the allocation of such capacity.

(3) Refusal to Build

13.87 In a case decided by the Italian Competition Authority in February 2006, a very robust approach was taken against ENI's cancellation of construction of additional capacity on the Tunisian interconnector. Various competing shippers had already signed 'ship-or-pay' transport contracts for that capacity, but the company discontinued work on upgrades which had begun some time before. The NCA decided that ENI had abused its dominant market position by hindering the entry of independent operators into the national market for the wholesale supply of natural gas. It imposed a very large fine amounting to €290 million and ordered ENI to desist from its anti-competitive conduct which was in breach of Article 82 EC. ENI was ordered to provide non-discriminatory access to third parties through its subsidiary, the Trans Tunisian Pipeline Company, by increasing capacity and allocating tranches of the additional capacity during 2008.[72]

E. Refusal of Access

(1) The Issues

13.88 Although the Electricity and Gas Directives and their respective Regulations provide for TPA for interested parties, this is not unconditional. If a TSO wishes to refuse such access requests, it may do so, subject to certain requirements being met (see paras 5.46 and 6.39). The interpretation of 'refusal of access' and its operation will ultimately depend on how this is dealt with by the TSOs on a daily basis, monitored by the NRAs and the NCAs. There will be some scope for application of Article 82 EC.

13.89 There is some evidence that a 'refusal of access' will be interpreted broadly by the Commission, including not only a straight refusal of access to a network by a

---

[72] Italian Competition Authority Press Release, 'ENI fined €290m for abuse of dominant market position in wholesale supply of natural gas', 20 February 2006 <http://www.agcm.it.agcm_eng/COSTAMPA/E_PRESS.NSF>.

E. Refusal of Access

TSO but also the imposition of excessive transmission fees or of discriminatory technical requirements.[73] The concept of available transmission capacity (ATC) will be examined not only as a technical issue but as a contractual one. In this way refusals of access motivated by a lack of transmission capacity because that capacity is reserved in the first place to another party would lead to such a reservation clause being examined by the Commission.

An issue that arises here is whether access rights apply when capacity contracted by the network owner(s) has been contracted but is in the event not used. This issue is tackled by the application of the principle of 'use-it-or-lose-it'. In this way, unused capacity may be made available to third parties. **13.90**

If one considers the abuse provisions in Article 82, an undertaking in a dominant position as network operator is limited in its freedom to restrict access to a third party. Specifically, it is limited when: **13.91**

- the requesting party is willing to provide reasonable remuneration;
- there is capacity available;
- there are no technical obstacles which would make this access impossible;
- the construction of a direct line would not be an economically viable alternative; and
- the supply is carried out under a programme that permits proper planning on the part of the network operator.

On this view,[74] the transmission or distribution undertaking has an obligation to open the network to third parties and third parties have a right to obtain access to a network as a result of Article 82 EC. The only remaining condition to be fulfilled is that a possible refusal would affect trade between the Member States. The provisions on TPA in the Electricity and Gas Directives can therefore be seen less as creating a new right of access, and more *as defining and clarifying the extent of a right that already exists*. However, it is acknowledged that the practical application of such a right is likely to be the source of some considerable legal uncertainty since there is difficulty in defining *a priori* all the hypotheses of 'justified refusals'. **13.92**

Although the prohibitions of Article 82(1) are designed to apply to all undertakings which hold or enjoy a dominant position, some of them may be exempted from it by the provisions of Article 86(2), which exempts from the scope of the competition articles those undertakings entrusted with the provision of services of general economic interest. This is especially relevant in the electricity and gas sectors. **13.93**

---

[73] Tradacete, A, 'Role of EC Competition Policy in the Liberalization of EU Energy Markets', April 2000.
[74] Ehlermann, CD, 'The Role of the European Commission as regards National Energy Policies' (1994) 12 J Energy Natural Resources L342, 343.

13.94 The provisions of Article 82 have been held by the ECJ to be directly applicable[75] and therefore individual undertakings have the right to bring proceedings before national courts alleging abuse of a dominant position by undertakings. Individual undertakings that consider themselves to have been damaged by an abuse of a dominant position as defined by Article 82(1) may also complain of the conduct to the Commission. If the Commission finds evidence of an abuse, it may impose fines on the undertaking concerned.[76]

13.95 Article 82 contrasts with the provisions of Article 81, which prohibits anti-competitive agreements. These are agreements between undertakings that may affect trade between Member States and that have as their object or effect the prevention or restriction or distortion of competition within the common market. In the context of TPA the conduct of individual grid or pipeline owners that contravenes the prohibition in Article 82 is more important, since Article 81 would be limited more to cases of anti-competitive conduct of joint owners of pipelines to which third parties seek access.

(a) Cases on Refusals of Access

13.96 Case law supports the principle that a refusal to allow access may amount to an abuse of a dominant position. The first notable case is *Port of Genoa*,[77] but a further decision of note is *Sabena*.[78] The Commission had imposed a fine on the former Belgian airline on the ground that its conduct was intended to prevent a privately-owned airline from continuing its flights on the route between Brussels and Luton (UK). Sabena had refused to provide access to its computerized reservation system called 'Saphir' when this company requested it. The latter had quoted tariffs at half the standard IATA tariffs, undercutting Sabena, and had not assigned the ground handling of its tariffs to Sabena.

13.97 The Commission took the view that the computerized reservation system was an *essential facility* that air carriers required if they were to compete on this particular route. Sabena's position made it the dominant player on the route. Without access to this system a company could not compete. This use of the notion of 'essential facilities' appears to enhance the potential for use of Article 82 to establish a right to TPA.

---

[75] See Case 155/73 *Italy v Saatchi* [1994] ECR 409, where the ECJ ruled that '[e]ven within the framework of Article 90 [now Art 86], therefore, the prohibitions of Article 86 [now Art 82] have a direct effect and confer on interested parties rights which the national courts must safeguard' (point 18.a).

[76] Regulation (EEC) 17/62 [1962] OJ L13/204.

[77] Case C-179/90 *Merci Convenzionali Porto di Genova SpA v Siderurgica Gabriella SpA Porto di Genova* [1991] ECR I-1979.

[78] [1988] OJ L317/47. See also *Report on Competition Policy* (1996), paras 83–5 where a national rail network was considered to be an essential facility by the Commission. By refusing to deal with an applicant's requests for access to the railway infrastructure it had denied access to the network which was considered to be an essential facility.

E. Refusal of Access

(b) Essential Facilities

13.98 The doctrine of 'essential facilities' has provoked considerable discussion and controversy[79] since it was first used.[80] It was taken from American jurisprudence and applied by the Commission in the European setting. It has appeared in a number of Commission decisions on access, commencing with two interim decisions on access to the port of Holyhead in the UK,[81] where the Commission found that there was a duty to assist competitors in certain circumstances.[82] In a robust statement, the Commission declared that:

> ... the owner of the essential facility, which also uses the essential facility, may not impose a competitive disadvantage on its competitor, also a user of the essential facility, by altering its own schedule to the detriment of the competitor's service, where, as in this case the construction or the features of the facility are such that it is not possible to alter one competitor's service in a way chosen without harming the others.[83]

13.99 However, this view has attracted considerable criticism and has not yet found favour with the ECJ in its jurisprudence.[84] It is not a separate rule, apart from Article 82, and it is possible to decide most cases involving a refusal to sell (or deny access) without necessarily invoking this doctrine. It is unclear what added value lies in the use of the term since it is still necessary to show a breach of EC law.

13.100 The ECJ has never applied the doctrine and indeed neither has the US Supreme Court.[85]

(2) The *Marathon* Case

13.101 While the Gas Directive includes a regime for TPA and for dealing with unjustified refusals of access, as did the first Gas Directive of 1998, there are other legal

---

[79] eg Stothers, C, 'The Role of the Essential Facilities Doctrine in the Regulated Sectors in the United Kingdom' (2001/02) 12 Utilities L Rev 5; Doherty, B, 'Just What are Essential Facilities?' (2001) 38 CML Rev 397–436; Temple-Lang, J, 'Defining Legitimate Competition: companies' duties to supply competitors and access to essential facilities' (1994) 18 Fordham Intl LJ 437; Stothers, C, 'Refusal to Supply as Abuse of a Dominant Position: Essential Facilities in the European Union' [2001] ECLR 256–62.

[80] Although the term was not used explicitly, an early example is Joined Cases 6 & 7/73 *Commercial Solvents v Commission* [1974] ECR 223.

[81] *B&I Line plc/Sealink Harbours Ltd and Sealink Stena Ltd* (Case IV/34.174) Commission Decision 94/19/EC, [1994] OJ L15/80; see also *Port of Rodby*, Commission Decision 94/119/EC, [1994] OJ L55/52.

[82] *B&I Line*, ibid.

[83] ibid.

[84] eg, Case C-7/97 *Bronner (Oscar) v Mediaprint* [1998] ECR I-7791, and the discussion of this in Doherty, B, 'Just What are Essential Facilities?' (2001) 38 CML Rev 397–436. Also, the similar approach taken by the CFI in Joined Cases T 374, 375, 384 & 388/94 *European Nightservices v Commission* [1998] ECR II-3141.

[85] eg, the much-discussed *Bronner* case, ibid. Several illuminating contributions are to be found in Ehlermann, CD, and Gosling, L, (eds), *Regulating Communications Markets* (2000) 1–237; see also Flynn, L, 'Access to the Postal Networks: the Situation after Bronner' in Geradin, G and Humpe, C, *Postal Services, Liberalization and EC Competition Law* (2002).

instruments available to the Commission to address such refusals: it may be tackled as a potential abuse or a restricted concerted practice, if the refusal is carried out jointly. The most dramatic example of the use of these alternative legal powers is provided by the *Marathon* case, which commenced before the adoption of the Gas Directive and provided an opportunity for the Commission to persuade several leading German companies to adopt practices in line with the internal energy market. The results offer examples of how competition law may be used positively to improve TPA but the settlements also merit some cautionary remarks.

13.102 The case arose from a complaint made against five EU gas companies by the Norwegian subsidiary of Marathon, a US-based oil and gas producer, about an alleged joint refusal of access to gas pipelines. The complaint alleged that the companies had unreasonably refused access to their pipelines in Emden in 1989 and 1995 individually, a potential abuse of their dominant position in violation of Article 82 EC, but in addition they colluded to refuse access to Marathon in violation of Article 81 EC. The Commission began an investigation into access to gas pipelines upon Marathon's intervention in 1996. Marathon withdrew its intervention in 2000 after settling the case out of court. The Commission pursued the case on its own in 2001 and offered a settlement in exchange for improvement in access conditions. The last case was concluded in 2004.[86] The five companies concerned were Thyssengas GmbH[87] (a joint venture between the German electricity utility, RWE, and Shell), NV Nederlandse Gasunie,[88] BEB[89] (a joint venture between ExxonMobil and Shell), Gaz de France (GDF),[90] and Ruhrgas.

13.103 The settlements reached with the individual companies (all concluded at different times) bore similarities but also contained some differences, reflecting inter alia the market situation in each country. The undertakings given by the five companies are very comprehensive and are reviewed in detail below.

---

[86] Marathon also began an arbitration against two of the companies, and requested damages. After the case concluded with a settlement, Marathon withdrew its complaint. The Commission pursued the case on an *ex officio* basis in the Community interest since the settlement did not remove the suspected infringements: Commission Press Release IP/03/547, 'Commission's competition services settle Marathon case with Gasunie', 16 April 2003.

[87] Commission Press Release IP/01/1641, 'Commission settles Marathon case with Thyssengas', 23 November 2001.

[88] In addition to these main commitments, Gasunie undertook to offer the possibility of linking other pipelines with its own pipeline system: Commission Press Release IP/03/547, 'Commission's competition services settle Marathon case with Gasunie', 16 April 2003.

[89] Commission Press Release IP/03/1129, 'Commission settles Marathon case with German Gas Company BEB', 29 July 2003.

[90] Commission Press Release IP/04/573, 'Commission settles Marathon case with Gaz de France and Ruhrgas', 30 April 2004.

E. Refusal of Access

(a) Transparency

13.104 Thyssengas undertook to publish a detailed map on its website which would show the available capacity at the main entry points of Thyssengas' pipeline system through a traffic light system. It also agreed to establish a computer system which would allow shippers to obtain information on the Company's transmission tariffs in a simplified manner.

13.105 Gasunie undertook to improve the transparency of its access regime by publishing on its website the contracted transport capacity at all entry and all major exit points of its gas network (all in absolute figures). It also undertook to provide information about the capacity still available. This commitment relates not only to cross-border points, but also to domestic/national entry/exit points so that shippers would find it easier to obtain information about available transmission capacity.

13.106 BEB agreed to publish and update regularly on its website the available transport capacity at all entry and all major exit points of its transmission network. It agreed to do the same with respect to its storage facilities. The result would be to make it easier for shippers to obtain information about available transmission and storage capacity.

13.107 Ruhrgas agreed to publish on its website a list of all entry and exit points, as well as the capacities and quality of gas available.

13.108 GDF agreed to make improvements in its transparency arrangements.

(b) Balancing

13.109 Thyssengas undertook to assist shippers in avoiding high imbalancing charges by introducing a free of charge online balancing system avoiding imbalances of nominated and actual deliveries. The company also agreed to offer an 'extended balancing regime' which would increase shippers' flexibility from 15 to 25 per cent, though at a price. Shippers would also be allowed to compensate imbalances within the following month either by means of extra deliveries of gas or by swapping imbalances with other customers or by paying for the imbalance.

13.110 Gasunie undertook to assist shippers with a flexible source of supply to avoid a situation developing of imbalances. These can occur if the input and withdrawal of gas into the system are not identical or deviate from the forecasted volumes. In particular, Gasunie undertook to introduce an online balancing system to avoid situations where suppliers and shippers are charged very high prices for the gas supplied by Gasunie following an unexpected increase or decrease in consumption by one of their customers.

13.111 BEB agreed first to assist those shippers with a flexible supply source to avoid getting into a situation of imbalances. This involved the introduction of a regime of 'online balancing' at no cost to them, which would ensure that input and output of gas in the BEB system would remain in balance at all times. Secondly, BEB also agreed to introduce a bulletin board which would allow shippers to get into contact with each other to optimize their transport and storage requirements. Finally, BEB agreed to let companies use its storage facilities even if the technical minimum flow requirements are not fulfilled. The sole condition attached to this was the 'back-pack' principle: at the same time other shippers, either individually or jointly, may fulfil the minimum flow requirements.

13.112 Ruhrgas agreed to maintain free of charge balancing services for its transport customers until 1 November 2008 (beyond the duration of the VV-2 Gas Agreement). It agreed to offer online balancing services which would allow transport customers to have a fully balanced injection and withdrawal of gas in the Ruhrgas network. The only requirement faced by the customer to whom the gas is delivered is that it has the appropriate technical equipment to measure the gas flows. For flexible supply sources, the user of the Ruhrgas network may apply flexible supply contracts or gas stored in Ruhrgas' virtual gas storage. Customers are allowed to create balancing areas, which would help suppliers to avoid situations of imbalances, that can result in large financial penalties, and will allow shippers to be more competitive in the Ruhrgas transmission area.

13.113 GDF undertook to put in place an optional daily balancing service which would even out all or most of the customer's imbalance that results from its transport contract as part of its offer of access to storage for third parties. It agreed to offer the possibility of booking daily transport capacity and to develop the secondary market in transport capacity.

(c) Handling of Access Requests

13.114 Thyssengas undertook to improve its handling of access requests. The company agreed to develop standard access forms and contracts (to be published on the internet) and to limit the reasons which would justify refusals to grant access to its pipelines. This would increase planning security and reduce transaction costs, preventing cases of refusal to grant access to the network.

13.115 Gasunie gave an undertaking to improve its handling of access requests and to do so by introducing online screen-based booking procedures. This was intended to eliminate the sometimes lengthy response times. Online bookings have particular value for short-term trading. During the conduct of the investigation, Gasunie had already taken steps to improve its access regime. These included the introduction of short-term transmission contracts for one day; the introduction of interruptible transmission contracts for congestion scenarios; and the introduction of a bulletin board which allowed traders to bundle their access requests and balancing requirements.

E. Refusal of Access

BEB agreed to introduce online screen-based booking procedures to eliminate the response times (sometimes lengthy). It agreed to shorten its maximum response time when replying to access requests. **13.116**

Ruhrgas and GDF separately agreed to improve their handling of network access requests. In the latter case, there had already been improvements made following requests from the French regulator, the CRE. **13.117**

(d) Trade in Capacity Rights

Thyssengas made commitments on trading of capacity rights which the Commission considered to be the first steps in the development of a secondary market, in which capacity holders could trade capacity rights acquired from pipeline owners. The company also indicated a willingness to offer transport contracts with a short duration and to allow several shippers to bundle transportation contracts in order to reduce costs. **13.118**

(e) Congestion Management

Thyssengas undertook to introduce a 'use-it-or-lose-it' principle for capacity reservations of its own gas trading department. This had the effect that third parties would be entitled to use, on request, unused transmission capacity that was originally booked by the company's trading branch. The 'use-it-or-lose-it' principle was not strict, however, in being offered only if the company's gas trading department was not interested in using the capacity, rather than not used. The company also undertook to offer interruptible contracts, which generally lead to a continuous transport, unless an interrupting event occurs such as a reduction in temperature. **13.119**

BEB undertook to introduce a 'use-it-or-lose-it' principle for capacity reservations of its own gas trading branch. Third parties are therefore able to use on request unused transport capacity that had been originally booked by the BEB trading branch. BEB also undertook to facilitate the creation of a secondary market by permitting customers to sell or sub-lease capacity booked from BEB. **13.120**

Ruhrgas promised to introduce a 'use-it-or-lose-it' principle into all of its transport contracts, including the contracts with its trading branch. This would oblige the capacity holder to make the booked capacity available to the market if the capacity remains unused. However, clear commitments regarding the transfer of capacity from 'old' contracts and the availability of interruptible contracts were not provided. **13.121**

GDF undertook to reduce the capacity reservations made by the trading division of GDF. **13.122**

(f) Entry-Exit Regime

13.123 Thyssengas did not offer any entry-exit regime, but rather confirmed the point-to-point system then in use in Germany's negotiated TPA regime.

13.124 Gasunie gave a commitment to maintain an entry-exit system for its access regime. This has the advantage that shippers are only obliged to book capacity at the relevant entry and exit points and do not have to pay for gas contracts along contractual transmission paths which are often fictitious, and do not coincide with the physical gas flows.

13.125 BEB undertook to introduce an 'entry-exit' regime, under which shippers book capacity at the relevant entry and exit points separately. The basis for the fees paid for transport is one of entry charges and exit charges, instead of one based on the 'contractual path': the distance between the entry and exit points. This system facilitates booking procedures as it no longer requires a capacity reservation for each pipeline section notionally used for the fulfilment of the transport contracts. BEB expressed a willingness to extend this regime to larger territories in Germany. It therefore had possible benefits for cross-border transmission as well as domestic transmission, an outcome that never materialized due to lack of co-operation between the TSOs.

13.126 Ruhrgas agreed to replace its current regime linking capacity reservations to a fictitious contract path with a new regime that would allow customers to book transport capacity separately at entry and exit points. Customers would also be able to book across tariff and quality zones throughout Germany (this applied to H and L calorific gas respectively). No quality adaptation fees were to be charged except for conversion between H and L gas, to the extent that flexibility in the system allowed it to do so. The entry-exit regime was to be extended beyond the company's own network, to include Ferngas Nordbayern in its entry/exit system (in which it owns a majority share) and to offer the same to other regional transmission companies in which it holds a minority stake. In practice, the system turned out to be more complex and more expensive than the 'old' one. Entry and exit points were still linked through virtual paths for every transaction, and subscripts were introduced arbitrarily and without apparent justification.

(g) Tarification

13.127 Ruhrgas agreed to introduce a system of six tariff zones, comprising four H-gas zones and two L-gas zones. For transport across several tariff zones, Ruhrgas is to charge a fee on a causation basis, ruling out any 'pancaking' of rates. This initial differentiation of zones was reduced from six to four by May 2006. Total tariffs to be paid by users, however, ended up being higher than in the traditional model.

13.128 GDF agreed to a gradual reduction in the number of tariff and balancing zones on which the entry-exit transport system is based in France. The number would be reduced from seven to four. GDF offered to implement an investment programme to reduce congestion which could make a further reduction to two possible, and facilitate access for new entrants by reducing the cost of transport connected with the crossing of several zones.

(h) Gas Release

For a three-year period from January 2005 GDF agreed to implement a gas release programme in southern France, a region where there was at that time no competition. The duration of the commitment took into account plans for new infrastructure which would lead to a reduction in entry barriers in that part of the French market. The details of this were negotiated with the French regulator, the CRE, which was also responsible for supervising the implementation of the programme. **13.129**

(i) Conversion of Gas

GDF agreed to offer operators the possibility of converting from H gas to L gas. This would be done on a transparent and non-discriminatory basis for operators. L gas users constitute a large part of the French market and would in this way be given access to competing gas. Previously, the principal beneficiaries of liberalization had been the H gas customers located close to the northern and eastern borders of France. **13.130**

(j) Monitoring

Most of the commitments made by Thyssengas entered into force in November 2001, some changes occurred in 2002 and were to last until July 2005. They were to be monitored by a trustee, who was charged with reporting regularly to the Commission. **13.131**

The commitments made by Gasunie entered into force on 21 April 2003 and were to remain in place until January 2007. Compliance was monitored by a trustee, who was charged with reporting regularly to the Commission. Meanwhile, the Dutch regulator (at that time the DTE), which had been actively involved in the investigation, would continue to monitor the operation of the access regime in the Netherlands (and Gasunie's role in it) as part of its duties. **13.132**

Most of BEB's commitments were to enter into force immediately, and remain in place until January 2007. An independent auditor is to monitor compliance, and to report regularly to the Commission. **13.133**

The commitments made by GDF and Ruhrgas remain in force 'for several years' and are to be monitored by a trustee who will report regularly to the Commission Competition Directorate. In the former case, the negotiations on a settlement were carried out closely with the CRE which would continue to monitor the access regime after these commitments had been made. **13.134**

(k) Assessment

13.135 The very detailed commitments on TPA obtained by the Commission are an excellent illustration of what can be achieved by the application of competition law when the Commission has evidence of a clear violation and has the will to pursue the matter. The commitments are extensive and the level of detail involved led, not surprisingly, to the extensive involvement of the NRAs, and particularly the French and Dutch NRAs. However, it was the Commission that appreciated the opportunity which the case presented.[91] The parties' principal defence was that access had been refused because they themselves wished to use the applicant's gas supplies; the alleged infringement had gone on over some time and a repetition could not be ruled out if no action were taken. In this context, and noting that the first Gas Directive had been adopted, the Commission drew up a list of the areas in which access could be improved, after consultations with a variety of market participants. This list was the basis of the negotiations with the parties for a settlement.

13.136 The case contains a number of elements that would seem to be essential for such a strong support role by the Commission competition authorities for the liberalization process. First, the Commission perceived that the offer of a settlement might act as an incentive to the parties to make commitments with results that had a greater practical impact than a formal prohibition. Secondly, it chose to consult with market participants to identify the goals that such negotiations should seek to achieve. Thirdly, it co-operated closely with the relevant national authorities throughout. Fourthly, it defined its support role in a positive manner, by seeking to obtain commitments which, where possible, went beyond the minimum requirements in the (first) Gas Directive. Fifthly, it avoided any hint of dogmatism by a willingness to accept commitments that took into account the particular features of each of the gas transmission markets concerned. Sixthly, it did not take a final decision on commitments offered by the parties until it had carried out a market test with market participants and associations representing the interests of gas consumers and traders. Finally, it set up a supervisory mechanism to monitor the performance of the commitments.

13.137 However, the results might be criticized on several grounds. First, some of the commitments on transparency, balancing, booking procedures, congestion management, and unbundling were rendered superfluous when the (second) Gas Directive entered into force in July 2004. Of even more questionable significance was BEB's commitment to an entry/exit system, which came more than a year

---

[91] This is clear from the account given by Fernandez Salas, M, Klotz, R, Moonen, S, and Schnichels, D, 'Access to gas pipelines: lessons learnt from the Marathon case' (2004) 2 Competition Policy Newsletter 41–3.

F. Conclusions

after the Madrid Forum had concluded that these systems would be the preferred choice throughout the EU. Secondly, while the principal achievement of the settlements with the German companies was an acceptance of the entry-exit model, more could have been done to incorporate details of the entry-exit regime design into the settlement, particularly with respect to the methods of capacity allocation and tariff calculation. Some areas that were important for market development were left completely untouched. The resulting different access terms for the major German pipeline systems created a greater degree of complexity for the users through the years 2003 and 2004, resulting in a declining number of grid access cases. Important aspects such as the lack of enforceability of co-ordination among TSOs were not on the Commission's agenda, apparently, with considerable consequences for the behaviour of the TSOs that were still being felt some time later. Thirdly, many of the commitments were designed to accelerate the opening of the German gas market but the delay in reaching agreement with the German companies (the last was with Ruhrgas in 2004) meant that the original 'wish-list' of outcomes looked increasingly unambitious. The settlement with Ruhrgas is illustrative in this respect. By the time it was achieved, some remedies had been achieved in the E.ON takeover, a German sector regulator was about to be established, and a new pro-competitive energy law (including an entry-exit model) was at an advanced stage of discussion. The concessions offered by Ruhrgas appeared in this new context to be less than modest and were unlikely to contribute to an improvement in access conditions. The potential for a quite remarkable success was present in this case, but the Commission failed to press its advantage through to the end, and a slower introduction of competition into the German market was the result.

13.138 In the Commission's defence, a strategic aspect of the case may be emphasized: the case was driven very much as a form of support for the ongoing liberalization process. At the time the case unfolded, the discussion both at Community level and in Germany was very heated. When the Commission was discussing its commitments with these companies, it was far from clear what the final form of legislation would be, either in the EU (the proposal for a second Gas Directive was under discussion) or in Germany. The aim was therefore to ensure that future law and regulatory practice could not fall behind what had already been achieved in this case.

F. Conclusions

13.139 This chapter has examined a wide range of cases in which the competition authorities or courts have become involved in the promotion of competition in downstream markets. A key feature that affects all of these often very diverse investigations and settlements is their relation to points in an ongoing process of liberalization. The driver has been and remains the adoption and implementation of secondary legislation with the approval of the Member States acting through the Council and the Parliament. Into that process, the competition authorities and especially the Commission have made selective interventions through specific cases that appeared at the time to offer the prospect of contributing positively to the wider process.

13.140 In this context, it is hardly surprising that the development of liberalization should have had a significant impact on the kind of cases and the approach that the Commission considers appropriate for investigation. The growth of experience of both NRAs and NCAs among the Member States mean that some kinds of energy cases are best led by them, either individually, through the NRA association (the ERGEG) or by means of the ECN. The cases themselves are affected by this process, with a current shift in focus towards interconnector issues and transit lines, and new infrastructure projects. The Marathon case is, however, an example of what a determined focus on outcomes might achieve, and how valuable the application of the competition law could be in the ongoing liberalization process.

14

CROSS-BORDER MERGERS AND ACQUISITIONS

A. Introduction	14.01	D. Remedies		
B. The Rules		(1) General	14.99	
(1) The Merger Regulation	14.07	(2) Remedies used in the Energy Sector	14.104	
(a) The New Test of Dominance	14.09	(a) Divestiture	14.107	
(b) Appraisal of Concentrations	14.12	(b) Energy Release Programmes	14.108	
(c) Procedure	14.14	(c) Interconnection/Infrastructure Release	14.118	
(d) Jurisdictional Issues	14.19	(d) Customer Release/Termination of Customer Contracts	14.119	
(e) Criteria for Assessment	14.28	(3) Effectiveness of Energy Remedies		
(2) Jurisdiction over Mergers		(a) Divestiture	14.120	
(a) Enforcement	14.35	(b) Release Programmes	14.121	
(b) The Two-Thirds Rule	14.40	(c) Capacity Auctions	14.135	
C. The Practice	14.56	E. Golden Shares as Barriers	14.136	
(1) Electricity		(1) The 2002 Judgments	14.138	
(a) *VEBA/VIAG*	14.62	(a) The Context: General	14.142	
(b) *EDF/Louis Dreyfus*	14.66	(b) The Context: the Member States Concerned	14.144	
(c) *EDF/EnBW*	14.68	(c) The Public Security Argument	14.151	
(d) *EnBW/Hidrocantábrico*	14.69	(d) The Judgments	14.154	
(e) *Verbund/EnergieAllianz*	14.72	(2) The 2003 Judgments	14.165	
(2) Gas		F. Conclusions	14.168	
(a) *Exxon/Mobil*	14.74			
(b) *EnBW/ENI/GVS*	14.76			
(c) *E.ON/MOL*	14.79			
(3) Convergence of Gas and Electricity	14.85			
(a) *Dong/Elsam/Energi E2*	14.89			
(b) *ENI/EDP/GDP*	14.93			
(c) *Gaz de France/Suez*	14.98			

Persistent concentration is a core problem in the markets. So there can be no alternative to meticulous scrutiny of future merger operations . . . The rules of the EU Merger Regulation may have to be reviewed and amended.

Mrs N Kroes, Commissioner for Competition[1]

---

[1] 'Towards an Efficient and Integrated European Energy Market—First Findings and Next Steps', speech given on 16 February 2006.

A. Introduction

14.01 The internal market legislation has triggered a significant increase in cross-border M&A over the last decade. Between 1998 and 2003 there were about 135 merger and acquisition transactions in the EU electricity and gas sector, of which about one-third was cross-border and two-thirds had a national dimension.[2] This figure has continued to increase since then (see Table 14.1). Indeed, between 2000 and 2005 there was a 75 per cent increase in the number of cross-border mergers in the energy sector which fell within the Commission's merger control jurisdiction. In the first half of 2006 there were ten alone, three more than in the whole of 2005.[3] Table 14.1 provides an overview of the 'problematic' cases that had a Community dimension in the two 'waves' of merger activity that followed the adoption of the Directives. Some were gas-to-gas and others were electricity-to-electricity but a few of them were gas-to-power or convergence mergers, which raise particular competition concerns. The nuclear sector was also affected. Much of this cross-border corporate restructuring represents healthy commercial activity, and enhances the competitiveness of EU firms by equipping them to succeed in global markets. In the context of the EU's growing import dependency for primary energy sources, this

Table 14.1 Change of Energy Mergers

Wave 1: 1998–2003	
Neste/Ivo (1998)	Gas
BP/Amoco and Exxon/Mobil (both 1999)	Gas/Oil
EDF/Louis Dreyfus (1999)	Electricity
VEBA/VIAG (2000)	Electricity
Framatome/Siemens/Cosema/JV	Nuclear
Grupo Vilar MIR/EnBW (2001)	Electricity
EDF/EnBW (2001)	Electricity
ENI/EnBW/GVS (2002)	Gas
ECS/Sibelga and Intercommunales (2003)	Gas/Electricity
VERBUND/EnergieAllianz (2003)	Electricity
Wave 2: 2004–	
Total/GDF (GSO) (2004)	Gas
EDP/ENI/GDP (2004)	Gas/Electricity
Areva/Urenco (2004)	Nuclear
E.ON/MOL (2005)	Gas
DONG/Elsam/E2 (2006)	Gas/Electricity
GDF/Suez (2006)	Gas/Electricity

---

[2] Codognet, M-K, Glachant, JM, Leveque, F, and Plagnet, M-A, 'Mergers and Acquisitions in the European Electricity Sector—Cases and Patterns' (2003); <http://www.cerna.ensmp.fr/Documents/FL-MA-MAsEu-Cases-2003.pdf>.

[3] Kroes, N, 'Cross-Border Mergers and Energy Markets', speech delivered at conference at Cernobbia, Italy, 2 September 2006.

A. Introduction

factor—improved competitiveness—is an important one. Moreover, some parts of the EU such as Eastern Europe and the Iberian Peninsula are less 'saturated' than the markets of Western and Central Europe, offering a growth potential for new entrants. Nor are the high levels of merger activity in the energy sector unique. They mirror similar increases in M&A in the telecoms and air transport industries as liberalization has taken hold.

However, there are cases in which proposed M&A transactions could have negative consequences for the development of competition in the internal energy market, especially when a merger is between existing incumbents or when it appears designed to foster the creation of a 'national champion' rather than a European one. The risks have been underlined in studies undertaken by both the energy and the competition directorates of the Commission, pointing to the highly concentrated character of national electricity and gas markets at the present time and the lack of liquidity in these markets.[4] Further concentration is expected to lead to between five and eight big players emerging in the medium term.[5] The high level of concentration and trend towards its increase compel a sobering appreciation of market realities on those who may have viewed the internal market through the legislative lens of pro-competitive Directives and Regulations. They emphasize the risks that further concentration presents, even after full market opening by the middle of 2007. **14.02**

The rules of merger control are an important means of tackling this issue. They cannot per se act as an instrument of liberalization policy, but they can be applied *in support of* the liberalization process. In the EU context, this has been complicated by the choice of a phased approach to market opening between 1997 (the entry into force of the first Electricity Directive[6]) and 2007 (full market opening across the EU). Decision-making on a proposed merger is therefore wedded to an assessment of the specific stage of liberalization in a specific setting, and an assessment of its potential impact on the liberalization process, both in the geographic location and more widely in the common market. It should not create barriers to a restructuring but it should prevent the establishment of monopolies and oligopolies. In a liberalizing sector such as energy, the prospective and dynamic aspects of merger control are particularly evident. Moreover, as liberalization takes hold, the **14.03**

---

[4] European Commission (DG TREN), *Report on Progress in Creating the Internal Gas and Electricity Market*, COM (2005) 568 final, 15 November 2005; European Commission (DG COMP), *Energy Sector Inquiry—Preliminary Report*, 16 February 2006.

[5] The principal players that might be expected to dominate the electricity market would be EDF (France), ENEL (Italy), E.ON and RWE (Germany), and Vattenfall (Sweden). For gas the dominant players in the medium to long term might be expected to be E.ON (Germany), ENI (Italy), Suez/GDF (France/Belgium), and Statoil (Norway).

[6] Directive (EC) 96/92 concerning common rules for the internal market in electricity [1997] OJ L27/20.

application of merger control can be expected to change: for example, with respect to the definition of the relevant market, an increasingly complex approach will become necessary both in terms of product and geography.[7] In this respect, the regional markets approach that is currently being adopted by the ERGEG in both electricity and gas markets may generate additional questions (see paras 3.40–3.43).

14.04 The initial application of merger control in the energy sector was controversial. In the first wave of M&A activity, a number of significant concentrations were allowed to proceed subject to conditions that were designed to contribute to the ongoing liberalization programme.[8] Most of these concentrations were in the electricity sector. The practice adopted—clearances of notifications subject to remedies—has been criticized, as the number of market players was reduced and incumbents appeared to gain advantages in new markets; indeed, the Commission initiated a comprehensive study into the operation of remedies. Subsequently, the approach to proposed concentrations has become more exacting, but at the dawn of full market opening there is a large body of evidence (see paras 11.48–11.65) to support concerns about the high level of market concentration in the electricity and gas sectors at a relatively late stage in the liberalization timetable.

14.05 Experience has been one catalyst for a change in the way that proposed concentrations are now being viewed. Another has been the introduction of a revised set of merger control rules. Independently of the liberalization programme for the energy sector, the rules applicable to merger control have undergone important changes from 2004 onwards. This followed a widespread perception that the rules under Merger Regulation (EEC) 4064/89[9] were unsatisfactory.[10] To some extent, the resulting overhaul of merger control has permitted EC competition authorities to make a fresh start, meeting criticisms about its operation in the first phase of liberalization from 1997 to 2003, when the present Electricity and Gas Directives were adopted.[11]

14.06 This chapter examines the contribution of merger control to the promotion of competition in energy markets, mainly understood as the markets for electricity

---

[7] cf the approach towards market definition taken in the *VEBA/VIAG* decision (and only one product market considered in electricity) and the more complex approach in newer decisions such as *EDP/ENI/GDP*, *Vattenfall/Elsam & E2 Assets*, or *DONG/Elsam/E2* (multiple electricity product markets considered both at wholesale and retail levels).
[8] eg, *Exxon/Mobil* (Case COMP/M.1383) Commission Decision 2004/284/EC, [2004] OJ L103/1, and *VEBA/VIAG* (Case COMP/M.1673) Commission Decision 2001/519/EC, [2001] OJ L188/1.
[9] [1989] OJ L395/1. Corrected version in [1990] OJ L257/13. Regulation as last amended by Regulation (EC) 1310/97 [1997] OJ L180/1. Corrigendum in [1998] OJ L40/17.
[10] See European Commission, *Report on Competition Policy 2002*, 82–9.
[11] Directive (EC) 2003/54 concerning common rules for the internal market in electricity and repealing Directive (EC) 96/92 [2003] OJ L176/37; Directive (EC) 2003/55 concerning common rules for the internal market in natural gas and repealing Directive (EC) 98/30 [2003] OJ L176/57.

and gas, since these have generated the precedents so far.[12] The focus is upon those concentrations that have a Community dimension (although the manner in which that has been defined has sometimes been controversial), and particularly those that have raised serious concerns about competition *in the context of a liberalizing market*. The chapter summarizes first the rules applicable to merger control, noting the differences between the current and the pre-2004 regime;[13] secondly, it examines the practice of the Commission in dealing with energy cases that have given rise to serious concerns about competition, including their willingness to grant clearance, subject to remedies; next, the chapter reviews how barriers to M&A presented by so-called 'golden shares' have been tested in a number of cases before the courts; and finally, it offers some comments on future developments in this area. Two themes are notable: first, there is a continuing pressure on the part of Member States to promote certain mergers for essentially non-competitive reasons ('the public interest'); and secondly, co-operation in the enforcement of merger control between the Commission and national competition authorities (NCAs) is growing and appears to be very constructive in designing practical solutions.

B. The Rules

(1) The Merger Regulation

14.07   The legal regime for merger control is established by the Merger Regulation,[14] as well as its implementing Regulation and several interpretative notices.[15] While there

---

[12] There have of course been merger cases in the nuclear, coal, and oil sectors: eg, *Areva/Urenco* (Case COMP/M.3099) Commission Decision of 6 October 2004; Commission Press Release IP/06/1215, 'Mergers: Commission clears Toshiba's planned acquisition of Westinghouse Electric UK and BNFL USA Group subject to conditions', 19 September 2006 and earlier Framatome/Siemens JV, which led to the creation of Areva: IP/oc/1414, 'Commission clears joint venture between Framatome and Siemens, after modification of the operation', 6 December 2000. Since the focus of this book is on mergers in relation to the single energy market process or 'liberalization', the selection of cases has been limited to ones concerning electricity and gas mergers where the impact of liberalization has been significant.

[13] What follows is inevitably a cursory review of a complex subject, and is limited to features that are particularly important for the discussions of mergers in the context of the electricity and gas sectors. For a full account, see Navarro, E, Font, A, Folguera, J, and Briones, J, *Merger Control in the EU: Law, Economics and Practice* (2nd edn, 2005).

[14] Council Regulation (EC) 139/2004 of 20 January 2004 on the control of concentrations between undertakings [2004] OJ L24/1. It applies from 1 May 2004, and repeals Regulation (EEC) 4064/89 and Regulation (EC) 1310/97 from the same date.

[15] Commission Regulation (EC) 802/2004 of 7 April 2004 implementing Council Regulation (EC) 139/2004 on the control of concentrations between undertakings [2004] OJ L133/1; DG COMP, *Best Practices on the conduct of EC Merger Control Proceedings* <http://ec.europa.eu/comm/competition/mergers/legislation/regulation/best_practices.pdf>; Commission Notice on the definition of the relevant market for the purposes of Community competition law, PJ C 372, 9 December 1997.

are similarities between the Merger Regulation and its predecessor, Regulation (EEC) 4064/89 as amended, there are several important differences. There is, for example, a new substantive test of dominance and a new approach to jurisdictional allocation between the Commission and the NCAs by means of a new referral system.

14.08 The Merger Regulation was introduced to meet the challenges of a more integrated market and the effects of enlargement, both of which were thought likely to lead to major corporate reorganizations, particularly in the form of concentrations.[16] Its provisions are to apply to 'significant structural changes, the impact of which goes beyond the national borders of any one Member State'.[17] This includes not only mergers, but also acquisitions of shares or assets, and some kinds of joint venture, that have a Community dimension. Such concentrations have to be notified to and cleared by the Commission before being put into effect. As a general rule, they are to be reviewed at Community level according to a 'one-stop shop' principle.

(a) The New Test of Dominance

14.09 Under the pre-2004 merger control, the method of competitive assessment used by the Commission was to identify whether a dominant position would arise from the merger or be strengthened as a result of it, which would lead to a restriction of competition on the markets involved. That test has been reworded. Now, the test is whether a merger restricts de facto competition appreciably, so that the creation or strengthening of a dominant position is still an important, but no longer the only possible cause of this restriction.

14.10 The text of Article 2(3) of the Merger Regulation reads: 'A concentration which would significantly impede effective competition, in the common market or in a substantial part of it, in particular as a result of the creation or strengthening of a dominant position, shall be declared incompatible with the common market'.

14.11 The emphasis of the material assessment has shifted from the effects on market structure to an unambiguous concern with the direct effects of a merger on competition. There are two implications of this change to the test. First, it has become clearer as a result of this change that mergers which do not result in market shares that exceed 40 to 50 per cent but which are nonetheless damaging to competition because it is rational for the merging undertakings and their competitors to increase their prices appreciably to a supra-competitive level (a non-collusive oligopoly), can also be prohibited. The economic incentives of the merged firm (and its rivals) are to be taken into account. A merger on a concentrated market may also appreciably restrict de facto competition by giving rise to or strengthening a joint dominant

---

[16] Merger Regulation, Recitals 6 and 3.
[17] ibid, Recital 8.

position, because it increases the likelihood that undertakings can co-ordinate their behaviour in this way and can increase their prices, even without entering into an agreement or becoming involved in concerted practices. Secondly, the new test offers the merging undertakings a clearer basis on which to raise the efficiency advantages which arise as a result of the merger. For a merger with a Community dimension, the Commission must first consider the effect on competition, and assess the advantages raised by the parties to ascertain whether these outweigh the negative effects of the merger on competition. The undertakings involved also have an onerous burden of proof in that they have to present a plausible case that the advantages will in fact occur and will be passed on to the end-user, and could not have been otherwise achieved by less far-reaching means.

(b) Appraisal of Concentrations

The Merger Regulation applies to all concentrations that have a Community dimension.[18] Article 1 provides that when all the undertakings concerned by a concentration have more than two-thirds of their Community-wide turnover in one and the same Member State, the concentration does not have a Community dimension and falls outside the Commission's competence. The Commission has competence in cases where (i) the undertakings involved in the merger have realized a combined global turnover exceeding €5 billion and (ii) at least two of the undertakings have each separately realized a turnover within the EU exceeding €250 million.[19] Where these thresholds are not met, there is still a Community dimension where (i) the combined aggregate global turnover of all of the undertakings is more than €2.5 billion; (ii) in each of at least three Member States, the combined aggregate turnover of all the undertakings involved is more than €100 million; (iii) in each of at least three Member States included for the purpose of (ii), the aggregate turnover of each of at least two of the undertakings involved is more than €25 million; and (iv) the aggregate global turnover of at least two of the undertakings involved is more than €100 million. These thresholds may be revised by the Council acting on a proposal from the Commission.

14.12

---

[18] See also Commission Notice on the concept of concentration under Council Regulation 4064/89 on the control of concentrations between undertakings [1998] OJ C66/5; Commission Notice on the concept of full-function joint ventures under Council Regulation 4064/89 on the control of concentrations between undertakings [1998] OJ C66/1; Commission Notice on the concept of undertakings concerned under Council Regulation 4064/89 on the control of concentrations between undertakings [1998] OJ C66/14; Commission Notice on a simplified procedure for treatment of certain concentrations under Council Regulation (EC) No 139/2004 [2005] OJ C56/32; Commission Notice on restrictions directly related and necessary to concentrations [2005] OJ C56/24.

[19] Merger Regulation, Art 1(2); see also Commission Notice on calculation of turnover under Council Regulation 4064/89 on the control of concentrations between undertakings [1998] OJ C66/25.

14.13 The criteria for appraisal of the concentrations notified include the objectives of the Regulation and the following:[20]

- the need to maintain and develop effective competition within the common market in view of the structure of all of the markets concerned and the actual or potential competition from undertakings located either within or outside the Community;
- the market position of the undertakings concerned and their economic and financial power;
- the alternatives available to suppliers and users;
- their access to supplies or markets;
- any legal or other barriers to entry;
- supply and demand trends for the relevant goods and services;
- the interests of the intermediate and ultimate consumers; and
- the development of technical and economic progress provided that it is to consumers' advantage and does not form an obstacle to competition.

(c) Procedure

14.14 Concentrations with a Community dimension must be notified to the Commission prior to their implementation and following the conclusion of the agreement, the announcement of a public bid, or the acquisition of a controlling interest.[21] Failure to do so will result in the imposition of a fine.[22] While the proceedings are under way, the concentration has to be suspended.[23] In defined circumstances, the notified concentration may be examined by the Member State[24] (or Member States where a Community dimension is lacking[25]). Where it is to be handled by the Commission, the absence of any serious doubts about its compatibility with the common market has to lead to a declaration of compatibility with the common market in the initial 'Phase I' investigation period. If there are serious doubts however, the Commission can either accept initial 'Phase I' remedies which it finds to be adequate to eliminate these serious doubts or, in the absence of such remedies, it is required to 'initiate proceedings',[26] that is, to open an in-depth 'Phase II' investigation. Phase I and Phase II proceedings have different time-limits

---

[20] Additional considerations are to be taken into account in cases where joint ventures are to be created that would constitute a concentration and which are to be appraised in accordance with Art 81(1) EC: see Merger Regulation, Art 2(4) and (5).

[21] Merger Regulation, Art 4(1). These circumstances are supplemented in the second paragraph to include inter alia notification following a good faith intention to conclude an agreement.

[22] ibid, Art 14(2).

[23] ibid, Art 7.

[24] ibid, Art 4(4).

[25] ibid, Art 4(5). Both paras (4) and (5) are subject to review by the Commission in a report to be submitted to the Council before 1 July 2009.

[26] ibid, Art 6(1)(c).

B. The Rules

involved for investigation. The Phase I deadline is 25 working days, extendable to 35 days in cases where commitments have been offered or where a request for referral has been received. Where an in-depth investigation is required, this Phase II involves a period of no more than 90 days from the initiation of (Phase II) proceedings extendable to 105 working days where the parties have offered commitments with a view to making the proposed concentration compatible with the common market.[27] Phase I and Phase II deadlines are cumulative.

In both stages of the proceedings, remedies proposed by the undertakings may remove doubts, leading to a declaration of compatibility by the Commission. Such remedies will usually seek to reduce the market power of the merging companies. The Commission's decision will normally have conditions and obligations attached to it to ensure that the undertakings concerned comply with the commitments they have entered into vis-à-vis the Commission.[28] Failure to fulfil such obligations can lead to a revocation of the decision. Examples of remedies in the energy sector include: divestments of subsidiaries or participations, which can have the effect of reducing or removing horizontal and vertical links; and divestment of energy capacity, transmission capacity, and customers. Other remedies have been proposed to facilitate entry and to foster competition, such as the improvement of access and entry conditions by increasing liquidity, de-bottlenecking transmission or interconnection, stimulation of demand (perhaps by terminating contracts), and lowering the cost of balancing energy.

14.15

The operation of remedies has been a source of controversy since the perception grew that the first wave of mergers in electricity and gas (between 1997 and 2003) were approved with conditions that were not subject to a rigorous monitoring by the Commission or by the NCAs. The Commission carried out an internal study of merger remedies which produced results that were critical of previous practices[29] (see para 14.101 below).

14.16

The Commission has extensive powers of inspection under Article 13 of the Merger Regulation to require national authorities to assist with the inspection tasks, to impose fines and periodic penalty payments.[30] The latter decisions may be reviewed by the ECJ.[31] However, the Commission will use those powers only in exceptional circumstances, and so far, they do not appear to have been used. The Commission's main tool of investigation is information requests under Article 11. Wrong or

14.17

---

[27] ibid, Art 10(1)–(3).
[28] ibid, Art 6(2) para 2; Art 8(2) para 2; Commission Notice on remedies acceptable under Council Regulation 4064/89 and under Council Regulation 447/98 [2001] OJ C68/3.
[29] DG COMP, European Commission, *Merger Remedies Study* (October 2005) <http://ec.europa.eu/comm/competition/mergers/others/remedies_study.pdf>.
[30] Respectively Merger Regulation, Arts 12, 14, and 15.
[31] ibid, Art 16.

misleading answers to such requests are severely sanctioned.[32] Where the Commission decides to issue such a request not only by simple request by letter but by formal decision, its powers are increased. It can then enforce the respect of deadlines for reply since it can adopt fines decisions.[33] As a milder form of sanction, late or incomplete replies by the notifying parties can also stop the clock. The parties involved have a right to be heard at every stage of the procedure, and third parties may also be heard by the Commission or the competent authorities of the Member States.[34] Respect of this right to be heard during the Commission proceedings is to be safeguarded by a Hearing Officer who is directly responsible to the Commissioner for Competition and is therefore placed outside DG Competition's internal hierarchy. An Advisory Committee on concentrations has a consultative role in the key decisions made by the Commission. It comprises representatives from each Member State's competent authority.[35] The Commission convenes and chairs the joint meetings. The Commission is required to 'take the utmost account of the opinion delivered by the Committee' and 'to inform the Committee of the manner in which its opinion has been taken into account'.[36] Decisions made under the Merger Regulation are to be published in the Official Journal together with the opinion of the Advisory Committee.

14.18 The Merger Regulation grants the Commission the power to lay down implementing provisions on diverse matters such as the form, content, and other details of notifications, the procedure and time-limits for the submission and implementation of commitments.[37] Examples are the Guidelines on the assessment of horizontal mergers[38] and the Best Practice Guidelines,[39] which codify informal practices that the Commission has found to be effective in the conduct of investigations under Regulation 4064/89 in the past. It has also provided Standard Models for Divestiture Commitments and for Trustee Mandates, both developed after consultation periods with interested parties, and intended to serve as best practice guidelines.[40]

---

[32] *Tetra Laval/Sidel* (Case COMP/M.3255), Art 14(1)(b), (c) and (3) provided the basis for imposition of a fine by the Commission.

[33] An example of such a fines decision would be the one imposed on Mitsubishi Heavy Industries for failure to respond to an information request by decision.

[34] Merger Regulation, Art 18(1)–(4).

[35] A few Member States can send representatives from two national authorities (eg, from Germany there can be a delegate from the *Bundeswirtschaftsministerium* and one from the Federal Cartel Office). However, each Member State has only one vote.

[36] Merger Regulation, Art 19(6).

[37] ibid, Art 23(1)(a) and (c).

[38] [2004] OJ C31/5.

[39] DG COMP, *Best Practices on the Conduct of EC Merger Control Proceedings* <http:ec.europa.eu/comm/competition/mergers/legislation/regulation/best_practices.pdf>.

[40] <http://ec.europa.eu/comm/competition/mergers/legislation>.

(d) Jurisdictional Issues

The referral system One of the principal aims of the Merger Regulation was to 'optimize the allocation of cases between the Commission and NCAs in the light of the principle of subsidiarity'.[41] The referral system is therefore streamlined.

14.19

As under Regulation 4064/89, Article 1 of the Merger Regulation sets out the cases, defined by turnover thresholds, for which the Commission has exclusive competence. Below these thresholds, or if the two-thirds rule applies (both parties to the concentration having more than two-thirds of their turnover in one and the same Member State), a case falls under national jurisdiction.

14.20

In its essence unchanged, Article 9 provides for a possibility for a Member State to ask for referral—to the Member State—of a case after its notification to the Commission, if the concentration significantly affects competition in a market within that Member State. If the Commission finds that such a threat exists, it has discretion whether to refer the case (or part of the case) to this national authority. However, the Commission has no discretion where a Member State asks for a referral of a case that affects competition in this Member State on a market that does not form 'a substantial part of the Common Market'. In these circumstances, if it indeed agrees that that market, in its geographic dimension, is not a substantial part of the common market, the Commission must refer the case for such a market to the Member State.

14.21

Conversely, since the entry into force of Regulation 4064/89, Member States have had the possibility to ask for a referral—to the Commission—of a case for which the Commission lacks competence because the turnover thresholds are not met. Member States can do this on the basis of Article 22 of the Merger Regulation if a case affects trade between Member States and threatens significantly to impede competition within the territory of the country making the request. This provision had its main application during the early phase of EC merger control, at a moment when not all Member States had their own national systems of merger control in place.[42] However, it has also been used for other circumstances in which Member States felt they were not well placed to assess a concentration.[43]

14.22

The new elements of case allocation are laid down in Article 4(4), for re-allocation towards a Member State, and Article 4(5), for re-allocation towards the Commission.

14.23

---

[41] European Commission, *Report on Competition Policy 2005*, 64.
[42] This is the reason why some referrals occurred on this legal basis from the Netherlands to the Commission.
[43] eg, if the affected market is wider than national, for the assessment of which national authorities are obviously not ideally placed, or even in case of national markets if the proper assessment needed to take into account the interplay of various national markets. (Cf *Promatech/Sulzer* (Case COMP/M.2698) Commission Decision 2004/254/EC, [2004] OJ L79/27.)

14.24 The important new element is that it is the parties to the concentration themselves which can trigger such a re-allocation process by means of a reasoned submission to the Commission. The Commission must then consult Member States, who have a veto right for any re-allocation concerning them. The Commission has a veto right for re-allocation, to a national authority, of a case for which it is competent. However, it cannot oppose re-allocation of a case to the Commission if the Member States concerned have not expressed any opposition to such wish by the parties to the concentration. In this pre-notification re-allocation procedure, each side has to respect tight deadlines. For re-allocation of a case to the Commission, an important requirement is that three or more Member States have competence to review such a concentration on the basis of their national provisions. It was exactly this aspect of an increasing number of cases not meeting Community turnover thresholds but triggering burdensome 'multiple filing' requirements in several Member States (likely to be aggravated by enlargement) which prompted this new system of increased flexibility of case allocation rules in the new Merger Regulation. In the same logic of subsidiarity, the new possibility of re-allocation of multiple-filing cases to the Commission needed to be counterbalanced by the possibility of re-allocation of cases in the opposite direction, namely to Member States. Enlargement and inflation were likely to push an ever increasing number of cases above non-indexed Community thresholds, although their competition impact would be strictly limited to one Member State. The Commission is to report to the Council on the operation of these new rules by July 2009. The Council can then, by qualified majority, adapt them.

14.25 **Referrals in practice**   Recent evidence suggests that referral mechanisms are working, both by companies at the pre-notification stage and by competition authorities at the post-notification stage.[44] In the first two years of operation (May 2004 to May 2006), there were ten referrals to Member States via Article 4(4), four referrals to the Commission via Article 22, and 56 referrals to the Commission via Article 4(5).[45] By contrast, between 1997 and 2003 there were only 47 referrals. Examples of referrals in energy cases, all on the basis of the old rules, include German regional and local energy mergers (1997), an Italian energy merger (2001), and acquisitions by the Belgian company Electrabel (2002–03). It is perhaps interesting to note that in the energy area the new re-allocation system has so far not had a decisive impact. The first example of a re-allocation occurred in September 2006 and concerned RWE/SaarFerngas. The latter is a regional supply company in the west of Germany. The case clearly had little in the way of a potentially European-wide impact.

---

[44] Ryan, SA, 'The revised system of case referral under the Merger Regulation: experiences to date' (2005) 3 Competition Policy Newsletter 38–42.
[45] See Lowe, P, 'EC Merger Regulation: Is there really a new approach?', presentation at EC Competition Day, 19 June 2006.

B. The Rules

With respect to referrals to national authorities, there may be disadvantages for companies in terms of delay, an unclear timetable, language problems (especially in cases where there is a partial referral), and possibly in terms of the cost of co-ordinating multiple proceedings. For the Commission, the balance between risks and disadvantages is different: the Commission loses control of the case, and inter alia there are different levels of competence and experience among the NCAs; the NCAs may be under pressure to protect their own industry or otherwise have their own agenda; and even NCAs can be overruled for non-competition reasons (as has happened in Spain, the Netherlands, France, and Germany). The pressure upon NCAs to protect their dominant energy utilities is likely to be substantial in some Member States. This does not undermine the case for referrals but it does suggest some caution in its application to the energy sector.

14.26

The EEA When the Commission has competence to deal with a case under the Merger Regulation, it is also the sole authority in the EEA.[46] It therefore exercises its powers with respect to the territories of the EFTA States (Norway, Iceland, and Lichtenstein). The rules on referral are contained in Protocol 24 of the EEA Agreement, and are based on the Merger Regulation's system of referral. Many of the new rules on referral have been incorporated into the EEA Agreement.[47] These are sometimes in an adapted form. For example, the EEA Agreement provides for pre-notification referrals from the EFTA States to the Commission: parties to a concentration are allowed to request the Commission to examine a concentration which is 'capable of being reviewed under the national competition laws of at least three EC Member States and at least one EFTA State'.[48] Within the Nordic area there has been much discussion of merger issues with a view to promoting a more coherent competition policy between Norway and the EU Member States in that area.[49]

14.27

(e) Criteria for Assessment

Market definition In taking a decision on whether a concentration significantly impedes competition, the Commission, as a first step in its assessment, has to decide on the scope of the relevant reference markets which are to be defined both in a product dimension and in a geographic dimension. For this, it will consider the nature and characteristics of the products or services concerned, the existence of entry barriers or of consumer preferences, appreciable differences of the undertakings' market shares between the area concerned and neighbouring areas, and substantial price differences. It will also, in a test which is difficult to apply in practice but

14.28

---

[46] EEA Agreement, Art 57(2) and Annex XIV.
[47] Decision Nos 78/2004 and 79/2004 of the EEA Joint Committee of 8 June 2004.
[48] EEA Agreement, Protocol 24, Art 6(5); compare Merger Regulation, Art 4(5).
[49] See, in particular, the report from the Nordic competition authorities, *A Powerful Competition Policy: Towards a more coherent competition policy in the Nordic market for electric power*, 1/2003, June 2003.

nevertheless has a substantial disciplining importance, consider the effect of a small but significant and non-transitory increase in prices (SSNIP) on the sales of one product in a specific area, assuming the existence of a hypothetical monopolist who could enforce such a price increase. If the likely response of the buyers of that product is such as to defeat the benefit of the price increase for the hypothetical monopolist, then a wider product and/or geographic market needs to be assumed.

14.29 The definition of the relevant market in terms of product and geographic dimensions is a crucial element in the Commission's assessment.[50] Nor is it a simple matter in a liberalizing sector. It is necessary to determine the products and services with which, and the geographic areas in which, the merging parties will compete with each other, as well as which other parties exercise competitive pressure on the merging undertakings, and what the competitive strength is of the merging undertakings and their competitors after the merger. Where it is possible to determine which products and services constitute a market on the basis of their substitutability, the market position of the parties and their competitors can be determined in more detail within the framework of the material assessment of the effects of the merger.

14.30 The Implementing Regulation provides the following definitions for relevant product markets and relevant geographic markets:[51]

Relevant product markets:

A relevant product market comprises all those products and/or services which are regarded as interchangeable or substitutable by the consumer, by reason of the products' characteristics, their prices and their intended use. A relevant product market may in some cases be composed of a number of individual products and/or services which present largely identical physical or technical characteristics and are interchangeable.

Factors relevant to the assessment of the relevant product market include the analysis of why the products or services in these markets are included and why others are excluded by using the above definition, and having regard to, for example, substitutability, conditions of competition, prices, cross-price elasticity of demand or other factors relevant for the definition of the product markets (for example, supply-side substitutability in appropriate cases).

Relevant geographic markets:

The relevant geographic market comprises the area in which the undertakings concerned are involved in the supply and demand of relevant products or services, in which the

---

[50] See Commission Notice on the definition of the Relevant Market for the purposes of Community competition law [1997] OJ C372/5.
[51] Commission Regulation (EC) 802/2004 of 7 April 2004 implementing Council Regulation (EC) 139/2004 on the control of concentrations between undertakings [2004] OJ L133/1, Annex I (Form CO), Section 6: 'Market Definitions' I and II.

B. The Rules

conditions of competition are sufficiently homogeneous and which can be distinguished from neighbouring geographic areas because, in particular, conditions of competition are appreciably different in those areas.

Factors relevant to the assessment of the relevant geographic market include inter alia the nature and characteristics of the products or services concerned, the existence of entry barriers, consumer preferences, appreciable differences in the undertakings' market shares between neighbouring geographic areas or substantial price differences.

14.31 In the Commission's view, 'the perception of parties and of competitors on how they group the market in commercial terms very well influences competition between firms on these markets or market segments, especially if parties' and competitors' perceptions converge to a significant degree. Prospective growth rates and achievable/achieved margins are an important element of commercial decisions to be active or not on a specific market.'[52] This is an area of some complexity in which the role of economic analysis has been increasingly applied.[53] For further discussion of this subject, the reader is referred to paras 11.21–11.37.

14.32 **Substantive test** Article 2 of the Merger Regulation lays down the substantive test applicable to the appraisal of concentrations by the Commission. A merger must be 'compatible with the common market'. It will be compatible if it does not 'significantly impede effective competition, in the common market or in a substantial part of it, in particular as a result of the creation or strengthening of a dominant position'. (For comments on the evolution of this test, see para 14.09 above.)

14.33 In such an appraisal, the Commission must take account in general of the following: the need to maintain and develop effective competition, and more particularly of the structure of the markets concerned and the actual or potential competition from undertakings located within or outside the EC; the market position of the undertakings concerned and their economic and financial power; the alternatives available to suppliers and users; their access to supplies or markets; legal or other barriers to entry,[54] supply and demand trends; the interests of the intermediate and ultimate consumers; and 'the development of technical and economic progress provided that it is to the consumers' advantage and does not form an obstacle to competition'.[55]

---

[52] *EDP/ENI/GDP* (Case COMP/M.3440) Commission Decision 2005/801/EC, [2005] OJ L302/69, para 267.

[53] Fingleton, J, 'The Role of Economics in Merger Review' in *Regulating Utilities and Promoting Competition* (2006) 161–83. For its role in the context of national merger policy development, see the final report of the Brattle Group/University of Cambridge, *Factors Affecting Geographic Market Definition and Merger Control for the Dutch Electricity Sector* (June 2006) especially 15–8.

[54] Barriers to entry are thus considered twice. On a preliminary basis for the purposes of market definition and then finally, more definitively, in the framework of application of the substantive test.

[55] This latter provision opens the door to a so-called 'efficiency defence' which may rescue a merger which may otherwise be found to be incompatible with the common market. The Commission's Horizontal Merger Guidelines elaborate on this aspect, whose practical importance due to the strict criteria attached to its application has so far remained marginal. Cf Merger Regulation, Art 1(1)(a) and (b).

14.34   It may also be noted that, mainly in application of the assessment of the financial power of the undertakings concerned, the Commission has a duty in its substantive assessment to take account of the effects of state aids for the purpose of the assessment of a concentration. In the *RJB Mining* case, it was held by the Court of First Instance (CFI) that 'in adopting a decision on the compatibility of a concentration between undertakings with the common market the Commission cannot ignore the consequences which the grant of State aid to those undertakings has on the maintenance of effective competition in the relevant market'.[56] In the *ENI/EDP/GDP* case (see paras 14.93–14.97 below), it was noted by the Commission that it had by decision of 22 September 2004 authorized a state aid scheme to be compatible with the common market, which would award compensation to power generators for the abolition of Power Purchase Agreements.

(2) Jurisdiction over Mergers

(a) Enforcement

14.35   An important element in the new enforcement regime is the Competition Network of public authorities. This co-operative network is designed to ensure that each case is dealt with by the most appropriate authority and has its main importance in the merger area in the practical application of the new case allocation system of Article 4(4) and (5). As indicated above (para 14.24), this is largely to ensure that multiple notifications of a given concentration are avoided to the greatest extent possible.[57] However, the Commission is the body that has the exclusive competence to apply the Merger Regulation and Member States are not permitted to apply their national legislation on competition to concentrations that have a Community dimension, unless the Regulation provides for it.[58]

14.36   An important limit on the scope of the Merger Regulation is that it does not, within quite strict limits and subject to the observance of rules, prevent Member States from taking appropriate measures to protect legitimate interests other than those pursued in the Regulation. This delimitation of Member States' room for manoeuvre can be a source of discussion or even pre-contention between the Commission and Member States, as happened recently in the banking sector between the Commission and Poland (*Unicredit/HVB* merger) and in the energy sector between the Commission and Spain (*E.ON/Endesa* merger).[59]

---

[56] Case T-156/98 *RJB Mining v Commission* [2001] ECR II-337.
[57] Merger Regulation, Recital 14.
[58] ibid, Recital 18.
[59] No final decision on Commission intervention has been taken. However, the Commission has clearly indicated to both Member States that it is closely monitoring the application of any exceptions. For the Polish case the Commission has taken an official preliminary view: cf Commission Press Release IP/06/277, 'Mergers: Commission launches procedure against Poland for preventing Unicredit/HVB merger', 8 March 2006.

B. The Rules

Article 21 provides, on the one hand, that '(t)his regulation alone shall apply' to mergers where the Commission has jurisdiction in the application of the rules of the Merger Regulation.[60] Further provisions in this sense in Article 21 are that '[s]ubject to review by the Court of Justice, the Commission shall have sole jurisdiction to take the decisions provided for in this Regulation' and that '[n]o Member State shall apply its national legislation on competition to any concentration that has a Community dimension'.[61]

14.37

However, Article 21(4) addresses certain exceptions according to which Member States may take appropriate measures to protect legitimate interests other than those taken into consideration by the Merger Regulation as long as they are compatible with the general principles and other provisions of Community law. Three areas are explicitly addressed which are to be regarded as such legitimate interests, namely public security, plurality of the media, and prudential rules.[62] The Commission will, however, closely monitor whether these exceptions can indeed be invoked and whether the measures are proportionate to the legitimate interest pursued. Also the ECJ will apply, in its review, the test of whether the measures in question comply with the proportionality principle which is one of the general principles of Community law.

14.38

For energy, the question naturally arises to what extent 'security of energy supply' can be regarded as an element of 'public security' (which is, however, likely following the jurisprudence on golden shares, see paras 14.136 et seq below) or as 'any other public interest' for which stricter rules apply. Intended actions by a Member State based on 'any other public interest' must be communicated to the Commission by the Member State concerned and needs to be recognized by the Commission only after an explicit assessment of their compatibility with the general principles and other provisions of Community law. Only then can measures based upon such public interest be adopted by the Member State. [63]

14.39

(b) The Two-Thirds Rule

The adequacy of the two-thirds rule as a factor in determining the appropriate jurisdiction for deciding on a particular merger proposal has been criticized and is currently under review by the Commission itself.[64] In some Member States, especially the larger ones, a proposed merger may have implications beyond the national borders, and therefore have a Community dimension, especially in a

14.40

---

[60] Merger Regulation, Art 21(1).
[61] ibid, Art 21(2) and (3).
[62] ibid, Art 21(4), subpara 2.
[63] ibid, Art 21(4), subpara 3.
[64] Lowe, P, 'EC Merger Regulation: Is there really a new approach?', presentation at EC Competition Day, 19 June 2006.

liberalizing market where concentration levels are already very high in most countries. However, the manner in which this dimension is calculated under the Merger Regulation imposes quite strict limits on the Commission's right to intervene. These limits have been the source of controversy in several cases involving proposed mergers in the electricity and gas sector. Usually there has been a context of suspicion that the government of the Member State concerned was tacitly in favour of the proposed merger as a way of creating a 'national champion' to fight on the European stage. In this situation, the Commission has an important role as a potential counterweight to this tendency: hence, the importance of the jurisdictional issue. The following sections review controversies involving two proposed mergers in, respectively, Germany and Spain and another less controversial instance of a jurisdictional issue in a merger case in the energy sector.

14.41 *E.ON/Ruhrgas* A merger was proposed between the largest German electricity utility, E.ON, and Ruhrgas, the dominant German importer and transporter of natural gas, in early 2002. Since more than two-thirds of the parties' aggregate turnover derived from operations in Germany, the case lacked a Community dimension. This is in spite of the fact that Germany is the EU's largest energy market and its central location gives the country a strategic significance for any company seeking to engage in EU-wide energy trading. The proposed merger also had the appearance of the creation of a 'national champion'. The proposal represented a significant challenge to competition in Germany's energy markets and was investigated by the federal competition authority, the *Bundeskartellamt*. It led to the *Bundeskartellamt*'s first formal prohibition of a concentration in the network-based energy sector since liberalization commenced in 1999.[65]

14.42 In its analysis the German competition authority assumed a dominant duopoly of RWE and E.ON in the national markets for the supply of electricity distributors and major industrial and commercial customers, and a single firm-dominance by Ruhrgas in the natural gas markets. The proposed merger was expected to strengthen existing dominant positions in both the electricity and gas sales markets. As the proposed remedies were found to be insufficient, it had therefore to be prohibited. The prohibition was intended to prevent a further concentration in these markets and the restraints on competition that could be expected to result from this.

14.43 Subsequently, the competition authority was overruled by the Government, which cleared the proposal by means of a ministerial authorization, subject to certain requirements on divestiture (especially in the water sector) and gas release

---

[65] Bundeskartellamt, 8. Beschlussabteilung, B8-4000-U-109/01, 21 January 2002. A negative evaluation was also given by the Monopolies Commission: Zusammenschlussvorhaben der E.ON AG mit der Gelsenberg AG und der E.ON AG mit der Bergemann GmbH, Sondergutachten der Monopolkommission. The case is available on the website in the archives for the year 2002: <http://www.bundeskartellamt.de>.

B. The Rules

(see para 14.113).[66] The Minister of Economic Affairs attached greater weight to general welfare considerations than to the restraint of competition.[67] These considerations included international competitiveness and the security of national gas supplies. Even though the negative competition effects of the merger were likely to be immediate, the public interest arguments relating to future problems in the above areas were to take priority. Moreover, if the majority shareholding ownership of the merged company is acquired by another company 'to the detriment of the German market', the Minister of Economics may require all E.ON shares in Ruhrgas to be sold to a third party under a clause that is valid until 2012. The German Government has stated that the formula created (for a possible sale) 'will be considered only in the event that E.ON can be acquired by a company that would want to hand over or sell its gas assets, one quarter or one fifth at a time. This would endanger Germany's access to gas pipelines and, as a result, its access to gas supplies. Only in such a case would we make use of this clause.'[68] The ministerial authorization was challenged in the courts, however, and the merger procedure was suspended. A second authorization was issued shortly afterwards which upheld the first but provided for stricter conditions in the merger. The court case only ended when the plaintiffs withdrew their complaint following an out-of-court settlement with E.ON, which included elements of network access, share swaps, and energy supply.

The use of a ministerial authorization is unusual in German competition law and some remarks about this instrument are therefore in order. While the examination by the Bundeskartellamt is based exclusively on competition criteria, a ministerial authorization can be issued if the merger leads to advantages in the overall economy or is justified by overriding public interests which outweigh the restraint of competition resulting from the merger. This means that the relevant considerations in this case are the non-competition related considerations. Since merger control was first introduced in 1973, a ministerial authorization has only been applied for in 17 cases, in which seven were granted and five of those were granted subject to conditions.[69] In contrast, the number of mergers examined by the

14.44

---

[66] Decision of the Ministry of Economics of 5 July 2002, WuW/E DE-V 573, and 18 September 2002, WuW/E DE-V 643. The decision is available on the website under press releases: <http://www.bmwa.bund.de>.

[67] Der Bundesminister für Wirtschaft und Technologie, Gesch.-Z: IB 1-220840/129, 84–5.

[68] Cited in Estrategia, 'Revolution in the European Energy Market', 22 March 2006. For a fuller account of this case, see Pritzsche, K, and Klauer, S, 'Germany' in Cameron, PD, (ed), *Legal Aspects of EU Energy Regulation* (2005) 167–8. The German Government's rights were the subject of criticism by a European Commissioner in October 2006: 'Germany urged to end Eon golden share', Financial Times, 22 October 2006.

[69] Böge, U, 'Merger Control and Regulation of the Energy Sector: Contradiction or Complement?', paper presented at the Second Annual EU Energy Law and Policy Workshop, European University Institute, Florence, 25 September 2003 (author's copy), 7.

Bundeskartellamt was about 30,000, of which about 135 were prohibited. In terms of actual use in practice, the ministerial authorization is indeed special, but not to the extent that it affects the substantive weighing-up of competition and general political objectives. Other countries such as the UK, France, and Italy provide for the use of non-competitive criteria in their merger control regimes when considering cases of justified exceptions. It could be argued that the device of a ministerial authorization has at least the virtue of transparency to the public since it constitutes a distinct procedure.

14.45 Nonetheless, the perception that a European interest was involved in this case gave rise to questions about the lack of any intervention by the European Commission. There were attempts to involve the Commission because of the acquisition's considerable potential for the development of competition outside Germany. These were unsuccessful, since the Commission lacked the powers under the Merger Regulation to intervene. Subsequently, the British energy regulator expressed public concerns that the merger created a major obstacle to the development of effective competition, arguing that 'deals such as the one between E.ON and Ruhrgas are against the spirit of competition and serve to slow down the liberalization process'.[70] In his view, E.ON had side-stepped the EC competition rules on market concentration by not announcing its merger with Powergen (which might possibly have shifted the jurisdiction to Community competence by lowering the percentage of E.ON intra-sales below the two-thirds threshold) until after it had announced to the national authority that it was acquiring Ruhrgas.

14.46 *Gas Natural/Endesa* On 5 September 2005 the Spanish energy company Gas Natural announced its intention to bid for the entire share capital of Endesa, another Spanish energy company. Gas Natural is the incumbent natural gas company in Spain, where it also generates and sells electricity. Endesa is one of the two main electricity operators in Spain and is also active in the gas sector. Endesa is active in the electricity sector in other countries, especially in Portugal, France, and Italy. Several days later, Gas Natural notified the bid to the Spanish competition authority. The Minister of Economy, on request from the Competition Service, referred the case to the Competition Court for investigation. Endesa had meanwhile approached the Commission and submitted that this proposed concentration had a Community dimension and should therefore be notified to the Commission under Article 4 of the Merger Regulation. Essentially, Endesa argued that in 2004 it did not achieve more than two-thirds of its Community-wide turnover in Spain. Therefore, Gas Natural's bid gives rise to a concentration with a Community dimension.

---

[70] Ofgem Press Release R/14, 'Deal Means Serious Consequences for Energy Liberalization in Europe', 18 February 2003.

B. The Rules

14.47 Gas Natural maintained that the concentration lacked a Community dimension, since Gas Natural had more than two-thirds of its Community-wide turnover in Spain, and Endesa's audited accounts showed that it also had more than two-thirds of its Community-wide turnover in Spain. In 2004 both Gas Natural and Endesa achieved at least 75 per cent of their Community-wide turnover within Spain. The Commission examined the issues to ascertain if it had competence to intervene.[71]

14.48 The Commission's conclusion was that the complaint by Endesa concerning Gas Natural's failure to notify its proposed takeover of Endesa to the Commission had to be rejected. On its analysis the proposed deal fell outside the Commission's jurisdiction.[72]

14.49 Endesa made two submissions:

- the analysis of the 2004 turnover figures should be based on the new International Financial Reporting Standards (IFRS) rather than Endesa's accounts audited on the basis of the Spanish rules then in force; and
- a number of adjustments should be made to these IFRS accounts in order to comply with the requirements of Article 5 of the Merger Regulation, as interpreted by the Commission Notice on the calculation of turnover.

On the basis of these calculations, Endesa argued that less than two-thirds of its Community-wide turnover was in Spain in 2004. The adjustments proposed by Endesa would have led to a total deduction of more than €4.5 billion from its 2004 turnover in Spain and an addition of more than €0.7 billion to its audited turnover in other EU countries.

14.50 The Commission sought additional information from Gas Natural, Endesa, and the Spanish competition authority, who were also given an opportunity to express their views on relevant matters. After having considered all the arguments put forward, the Commission concluded that Endesa's audited accounts were the starting point for the application of the turnover criteria, and several adjustments proposed by Endesa were not justified under the provisions of the Merger Regulation and of the Commission Notice on the calculation of turnover. These proposed adjustments included:

- the elimination of revenue of the distribution companies from allegedly representing a mere 'pass through' (eg, a proportion of retail tariffs paid to the transmission operator and generators);
- the elimination of revenue from gas swaps;

---

[71] *Gas Natural/Endesa* (Case COMP/M.3986) Commission Decision of 15 November 2005.
[72] Commission Press Release IP/05/1425, 'Mergers: Commission rejects Endesa's complaint; declares proposed Gas Natural takeover of Endesa falls outside Commission's competence', 15 November 2005.

- the elimination of the alleged state aid to indigenous coal producers, external costs and security and diversification costs;
- the elimination of revenue from assets assigned to Endesa;
- the elimination of additional compensation for extra costs for non-mainland systems allegedly relating to previous years;
- recording of additional revenues at Endesa Italia; and
- the elimination of revenue from discounts, taxes, and levies.

14.51 Endesa also proposed other adjustments to its 2004 legally audited accounts concerning capitalized expenses of in-house work, alleged intra-group sales of electricity, jointly controlled companies and corrections related to the purchase or sale of companies after the end of the 2004 financial year. It was not necessary for the Commission to reach a conclusion on these points because, even if accepted, they would not have reduced Endesa's Spanish turnover to less than two-thirds of its Community-wide turnover. Endesa subsequently appealed this finding by the Commission of lack of competence at the CFI. However, the Court found that the Commission had correctly assessed the jurisdictional issue and consequently rejected Endesa's appeal. The case continued, however, in the Spanish courts, as Endesa appealed for cautionary measures to be taken, leading to the suspension of the bid until January 2007.

14.52 The absence of a role for the Commission[73] appeared to remove any serious obstacle to the proposed takeover by Gas Natural, which had tacit government support. It suggested, however, that the method of calculating the two-thirds amount could lead to an outcome that was not in line with the spirit of the rule, and had implications for competition in Spain that were unwelcome from an EU point of view. However, the case is notable not only for the jurisdictional issue but for the fact that it was overtaken by events which raised different but equally important issues. In February 2006 E.ON submitted a bid for Endesa, which was significantly higher than the amount bid by Gas Natural. E.ON notified the proposed transaction to the Commission under the Merger Regulation. The Commission examined the proposed acquisition and concluded that the proposed transaction would not significantly impede effective competition in the EEA or any substantial part of it, and therefore approved it.[74] In the meantime, the Spanish Government had introduced a special legal instrument, Royal Decree-Law 4/2006, which increased the supervisory powers of the energy regulator, the CNE. Subsequently,

---

[73] Italy and Portugal asked the Commission under the Art 22 referral provision (see paras 14.24–14.25 above) to assess the case for their countries. However, as the main impact of the concentration was obviously not on Portugal and Italy but on Spain, and as Spain had not asked for such a referral, the Commission rejected the requests of Portugal and Italy (both decisions adopted on 27 October 2005).

[74] Commission Press Release IP/06/528, 'Mergers: Commission approves acquisition by E.ON of Endesa', 25 April 2006.

B. The Rules

CNE approved the bid but subject to severe conditions including the divestiture of important assets of Endesa that made the transaction less attractive to E.ON.

14.53 The energy regulator's decision to impose such conditions was declared unlawful by the Commission in September 2006.[75] On the basis of Article 21 of the Merger Regulation, the Commission may in such a case appeal a national measure which unjustly encroaches upon the Commission's prerogative to assess mergers with a Community dimension. In this case, the Commission concluded that there was a violation of Article 21 due to the adoption of CNE's decision without prior communication or approval of the Commission and the submission of E.ON's acquisition of control over Endesa to a number of conditions that were contrary to Articles 43 and 56 on, respectively, freedom of establishment and free movement of capital. On the latter issue, the Royal Decree required authorization by the CNE for the acquisition of more than 10 per cent of the share capital, or any percentage giving significant influence in a company that engages, either directly or indirectly, in regulated activities or activities that are subject to special administrative control, as well as any direct acquisition of assets to carry out these activities. Under the Decree, the CNE may grant or refuse such acquisitions for the following reasons: the existence of risks in relation to the above activities; the inability to perform them as a consequence of other activities carried out by the acquiring or acquired company; and the protection of the general interest and reasons of public security. The Commission considered that the authorization procedure went beyond what is necessary to safeguard the minimum supply of essential energy products and services and might indeed have the effect of deterring investment from other Member States. It required the Spanish Government to withdraw the conditions imposed by CNE's decision without delay.

14.54 *ECS/Sibelga* Another case decided ultimately by a national authority but in a less controversial manner than the preceding cases was the *ECS/Sibelga* case. ECS, a subsidiary of Electrabel in Belgium, sought to acquire some of the assets of Sibelga, a semi-public distribution company which supplied electricity and gas to customers in Brussels. ECS was responsible for sales to final customers.[76] In its investigation the Commission found that the relevant geographic market for all of the electricity and gas markets concerned was no larger than Belgium. Electrabel was considered to be dominant on both markets due to its market share and the significant economies of scale it enjoyed, the impact on its dominance of virtual power plant auctions ordered by the Belgian authorities was likely to be minimal,

---

[75] Commission Press Release IP/06/1265, 'Mergers: Commission rules against Spanish Energy Regulator's measures concerning E.ON's bid for Endesa', 26 September 2006; Commission Press Release IP/06/1264, 'Free movement of capital: Commission calls on Spain to modify the law amending the functions of the Spanish electricity and gas regulator', 26 September 2006. A similar cross-border acquisition arose in the UK at the end of 2006 involving a Spanish company, but in contrast contained no national protectionism: *Iberdrola/Scottish Power* (Case COMP/M.4517).

[76] *ECS/Sibelga* (Case COMP/M.3318) Commission Decision of 19 December 2003.

and the entry barriers to competitors were considerable. The proposed merger would reinforce Electrabel's existing dominant position, and would also reinforce existing links between Electrabel and Sibelga by means of a profit-sharing clause that was an integral part of the consideration that Electrabel was to pay for the retail assets. The Commission therefore had competition concerns.

14.55 The Belgian competition authorities requested that the case be referred back to them under Article 9 of the Merger Regulation. The Belgian authorities argued that they had already dealt with five similar cases and wished 'to avoid contradictory decisions, or decisions difficult to reconcile with one another taken by different authorities in question'. The Commission acceded to this request on the ground that it was consistent with the 'principle of good administration' that the various cases should be assessed by the same authority and in the same manner. The Belgian competition authority subsequently approved the merger, subject to certain commitments. These included: termination possibilities of one month; ending a cartel; a promise of 100 MW for exchange; 1,200 MW in blocks of 25 MW until 2008; and Chinese walls and logos.

C. The Practice

14.56 The various published decisions of the Commission are an important source of insight into the application of the rules in contexts in which markets are still in the process of liberalizing. In such cases, the Commission has to ask what kind of concentration would significantly impede effective competition. If it has serious concerns in this respect, is the appropriate response to prohibit the proposed merger or to seek remedies? If the latter, which remedies are acceptable in the light of experience with remedies in liberalizing markets so far?

14.57 This section examines a number of electricity and gas merger cases in which the Commission has had to address the above questions. In almost every case, where the Commission has had concerns about the effects of a proposed concentration, it has chosen to seek remedies from the notifying parties rather than to prohibit the transaction. However, as its experience with remedies in this sector has grown, and the difficulties in achieving competition have become apparent, the Commission's approach to its assessment has become more rigorous and critical.

14.58 In practice, mergers in the energy industry have tended to be driven by economies of scale or by economies of scope. In the first case, companies attempt to extend their customer base by acquiring companies that operate in a different geographic market, particularly ones that are highly concentrated. Examples of these are the Wave 1 mergers involving EDF and London Electricity, EDF and South Western Electricity (UK), PreussenElektra and the Dutch company EZH, and Vattenfall

C. The Practice

and HEW.[77] In the second category, the acquisition is directed at companies active in other energy markets. Examples of such mergers are *E.ON/Ruhrgas* and *DONG/Elsam/E2* (involving gas and electricity).

It may be noted that, for many years, the compartmentalization of national markets and the use of closed supply areas, with the consequent protection of energy utilities from competition, acted as a disincentive to the strengthening of a corporate position through mergers. Immediately prior to and after the adoption of the first Electricity and Gas Directives, this changed, and the trend towards M&A activity has been almost uninterrupted since then.   14.59

In cases where liberalization has compelled former monopolists to become direct competitors and as a result they propose to merge, there is a risk of consolidating the strong market position of the parties in their former exclusive supply area. The Commission has in circumstances like these adopted a 'dynamic' approach, taking into account the actual and future conditions for supply competition. Factors to be taken into account include the degree of market-opening, the economic independence of transmission system operators (TSOs), and the actual conditions for third party access (TPA). If entry into the supply area of former monopolists becomes more difficult as a result of a proposed merger, it is unlikely to be approved. Substantial remedies offered by the merger parties either to eliminate or to reduce the negative effects on competition are taken into account and may lead to approvals that would, on a 'static' view of existing market conditions, not have been approved.   14.60

The following distinguishes between notifications that are primarily, if not always exclusively, made by undertakings that operate either predominantly in the electricity or in the gas sector, before moving on to examine proposed cross-energy mergers between electricity and gas utilities (that is, mergers between competing or potentially competing firms). The latter can generate particularly acute concerns about their impacts on competition. It is important to emphasize however, that not all proposed mergers in the electricity or gas (or oil) markets have the effect of triggering in-depth investigations or are cleared only subject to conditions. A significant number of them are not contested and are cleared with no further consequences.[78] Mergers in the upstream gas markets have not given rise to major   14.61

---

[77] *EDF/London Electricity* (Case IV/M.1346) Commission Decision of 27 January 1999; *EDF/South Western Electricity* (Case IV/M.1606) Commission Decision of 19 July 1999; *PreussenElektra/EZH* (Case IV/M.1659) Commission Decision of 30 September 1999; and *Vattenfall/Hamburgische Elektricitaetswerke AG* (Case IV/M.1842) Commission Decision of 20 March 2000.

[78] eg, Gaz de France and Ruhrgas acquired joint control over SPP in 2002, giving them control of the Slovakian part of the transit gas pipeline from Russia to Germany and Austria, accounting for about 75% of Russian gas sales to the EU. There were no competition concerns: Commission Press Release IP/02/834, 'Commission clears acquisition of joint control of Gaz de France and Ruhrgas over Slovakian gas supplier', 7 June 2002. E.ON's acquisition of sole control over Sydkraft was cleared due to the absence of any overlap in their activities and the presence of other competitors: Commission Press Release IP/01/531, 'Commission authorises acquisition of sole control over Sydkraft by E.ON', 10 April 2001.

concerns, for example.[79] The following cases fall into the category of notifications that were 'problematic'.

(1) Electricity

(a) VEBA/VIAG

14.62   A proposal to merge two German electricity companies, VEBA and VIAG, was notified to the Commission in 2000.[80] VEBA and VIAG proposed to merge to create what would eventually become E.ON. Taken together with the dominant role of *RWE/VEW* in the other principal region of Germany (which was under investigation at the same time by the Bundeskartellamt[81]), this would have had the effect of creating a dominant duopoly in the wholesale market for electricity throughout Germany. A combination of factors would have established a market structure conducive to co-ordinated effects. Treating the entire territory of Germany as the relevant market, the Commission noted these factors:

- a total homogeneity of product;
- market transparency;
- similar cost structures due to a similarly composed stock of power stations and a few jointly-operated large power stations; plus
- various interrelationships between *VEBA/VIAG* and *RWE/VEW*;
- the expected modest increase in demand; and
- the low price elasticity of electricity as a product.[82]

14.63   The Commission took a dynamic view of market development since a number of key requirements for the nationwide sale of electricity were already in place such as framework rules for TPA. It gave its approval when the parties provided undertakings to the respective authorities to remedy the competition problems. These consisted mainly in divestments affecting various joint holdings, particularly in the eastern part of Germany, thereby cutting important links between the two new groups and transforming VEAG, a major electricity generator jointly controlled by the two duopolists, into an independent competitor. The undertakings also

---

[79] eg, *Statoil/BP/Sonatrach/In Salah* (Case COMP/M.3230) Commission Decision of 19 December 2003; *Norsk Hydro/Saga* (Case COMP/M.1573) Commission Decision of 5 July 1999. The only, partial, exemption being *BP Amoco/Atlantic Richfield (Arco)* (Case COMP/M.1532) Commission Decision of 29 September 1999 which gave rise to a competition problem in offshore pipelines.
[80] *VEBA/VIAG* (Case COMP/M.1673) Commission Decision 2001/519/EC, [2001] OJ L188/1.
[81] The *RWE/VEW* case was the first in which the Bundeskartellamt defined all of the relevant product markets in the electricity sector as national markets. The assumption at the time was that competition in the country would be strengthened in the short to medium term following further liberalization of EU energy markets, including market entry by foreign suppliers such as EDF and Vattenfall and with the impact of non-discriminatory transmission. This would be the basis for the emergence of competition at the national level.
[82] European Commission, *Annual Competition Law Report 2000*, 63.

included various improvements to the basic rules governing transmission through the network operated by the two leading interconnected entities. As a result, the incentive to peaceful parallel behaviour by the market leaders was removed and the likelihood of privileged access to information about the strategy of the other party to the duopoly was reduced.

14.64 An interesting element of the agreement was the willingness of both *VEBA/VIAG* and *RWE/VEW* to abandon the tariff for transmission known as the 'T-component', which was payable where a supplier of energy between the two German trading zones was unable to balance or 'net out' the quantities they supply against equivalent quantities in the opposite direction. This would have adversely affected competition from traders and small generators. In principle they accepted the agreement on cross-border tarification that had been worked out in the Florence Regulatory Forum in March 2000 (but which was not put into effect) in preference to the intra-German VV-2 Agreement, which had entered into force on 1 February 2000.[83]

14.65 The Commission also linked its competition concerns in this case to its action on the Skagerrak interconnector cable. As a result, E.ON abandoned its reservation of capacity on that cable and also on the Danish/German interconnector. Finally, the parties undertook to issue in future separate bills for network charges and energy prices to promote price transparency for their customers and to limit cross-subsidies by the TSO in favour of the electricity sales units.

(b) EDF/Louis Dreyfus

14.66 EDF proposed to set up a joint venture in electricity trade with the firm of Louis Dreyfus. The Commission had concerns about the proposed merger since EDF would have become the only trader on the French market and so able to gain a competitive advantage over its competitors which were barred from entry as the French market lagged behind in terms of liberalization.[84] Contrary to France's obligations under Community law at the time of notification, the French market had not been liberalized and the conditions for TPA were unknown, as was the definition of eligible customers in France. During the period from the creation of EDF Trading, the joint venture, and the opening of the French market, EDF could in principle use the joint venture to provide the technical expertise and cover the risks involved in order to conclude complex structured contracts with eligible customers. It could also take advantage of this opportunity to enter into new contracts with the eligible customers and in this way delay or reduce the entry of competing suppliers.

---

[83] See paras 3.18–3.27 and 13.34–13.39A.
[84] *EDF/Louis Dreyfus* (Case COMP/M.1557) Commission Decision of 28 September 1999.

14.67 Subsequently, approval was granted subject to undertakings by the parties to:

> ... implement measures to prevent the joint venture from assisting EDF in establishing prices, structuring offers or by assuming risks associated with such contracts in relation to eligible customers until the French market is legally and effectively open; ensure that there is no transfer of know-how or relevant information from EDF Trading to the departments of EDF which deal with eligible customers in France during this period.[85]

An independent observer was charged with monitoring the performance of the undertakings.[86] However, enforcement was made more difficult by the uncertainty surrounding the entry into force of the new legal framework.

(c) EDF/EnBW

14.68 A further investigation took place with respect to EDF in relation to a proposal to take a 34 per cent stake in an electricity distributor, EnBW, the third largest in Germany.[87] It would then share control jointly with OEW (Zweckverband Oberschwäbische Elektrizitätswerke), an association of nine municipalities in the south-west of Germany. The supply area of EnBW ran along the border between France and Germany, and it could be considered a potential supplier to eligible customers in the French electricity market. The acquisition could have led to the removal of a potential competitor in the French market. In the event, approval was given subject to certain conditions. EDF undertook to make available to competitors 6,000 MW of generating capacity located in France. Access to this capacity was to be granted through auctions, prepared and operated by EDF under the supervision of a trustee, appointed by EDF but approved by the Commission. The aim was to open up one-third of the liberalized electricity market (measured by the liberalization obligation at the time of assessment) in France through 'virtual power plant' auctions of slices of capacity (see paras 14.108–14.109). This and other undertakings, such as the severance of its connection with the French electricity generator, CNR, to make it an independent generator, have a five-year term, at the conclusion of which the Commission would review their effects and then terminate or extend EDF's obligation to grant access to generation capacities. This was the first example of a virtual power plant auction in which it was agreed to sell off generating capacity temporarily through an auction. The idea is to enable new players or smaller competitors to have access to a dominant or jointly dominant incumbent's output over a specific period of time. Typically, power is offered at a fixed price per MWh. In this case there were criticisms

---

[85] ibid.
[86] Commission Press Release IP/99/711, 'Commission authorises EDF and Louis Dreyfus joint venture in energy trading, subject to conditions', 29 September 1999.
[87] *EDF/EnBW* (Case COMP/M.1853) Commission Decision 2002/164/EC, [2002] OJ L59/1.

C. The Practice

about the initial auction methods but it appears that subsequent efforts in this respect have been considerably more successful, involving the French regulatory agency, the CRE, in their organization. In the absence of divestiture this option provides a way of giving new entrants or smaller competitors opportunities to secure electricity (or gas through a release programme) at competitive terms.

(d) EnBW/Hidrocantábrico

A bid was notified to the Commission for control of Hidroelectrica del Cantábrico (Hidrocantábrico) by EnBW and a Spanish group, Villar Mir, in 2001.[88] Given the ownership links between EnBW and EDF, the Commission was concerned about the elimination of potential competitors to EDF. In particular, there was the possibility that the existing collective dominant position of Iberdrola and Endesa on the Spanish wholesale market for electricity would be strengthened. The French–Spanish interconnector had little free capacity for commercial use, creating a barrier to imports into Spain, contributing to the market's isolation from other Member States' electricity markets. To address the Commission's competition concerns, EDF and EDF-RTE, the TSO, undertook to take the necessary steps to increase the commercial capacity on this interconnector by almost four times.

14.69

In a subsequent case, involving a bid for joint control of Hidrocantábrico by EnBW, EDP and Cajastur, the Commission cleared the agreement, subject to conditions.[89] The transaction would have led to the strengthening of the existing collective dominant position on the Spanish wholesale market for electricity. To meet the Commission's concerns, EDF (which jointly controls EnBW) and the operator of the French electricity grid, EDF-RTE, agreed to increase to about 4,000 MW the commercial capacity on the interconnector between France and Spain. As in the previous examination of the *Villar Mir/EnBW* bid, the main competition concern was with the scarce commercial capacity on the French-Spanish interconnector, which creates a barrier to electricity imports into Spain. If the merger were to be approved, EDF might resist any substantial increase in the capacity of the interconnector. To resolve these concerns, EDF and the French grid operator resubmitted the same commitments proposed in the *Villar Mir* case.

14.70

However, due to EnBW's later exit from Hidrocantábrico (which is currently controlled by EDP), and the interim (environmental) obstacles of implementing this commitment rapidly, it was never fully implemented.

14.71

---

[88] *Grupo Villar Mir/ENBW/Hidroelectrica del Cantabrico* (Case COMP/M.2434, Commission Decision 2004/135/EC [2004] OJ L48/86.
[89] *EnBW/EDP/Cajastur/Hidrocantábrico* (Case IV/M.2684) Commission Decision of 19 March 2002.

(e) Verbund/EnergieAllianz

14.72 In 2003, a proposed concentration was notified to the Commission between the Austrian electricity generator, Österreichische Elektrizitätswirtschafts-AG (Verbund), and five Austrian regional electricity supply companies operating under the name of EnergieAllianz.[90] The parties sought to form two joint ventures in which they would combine their respective activities in electricity trade and supply to large industrial customers. The Commission conducted an investigation and concluded that the transaction would have created or strengthened dominant positions held by both groups in the markets for supply of electricity to large customers, small distributors, and small customers in Austria. Their combined share on these markets amounted to between 50 and 75 per cent. Since Verbund was the most important existing and potential competitor to EnergieAllianz, its absence would have contributed further to this concentration.

14.73 The parties made commitments which resolved the Commission's concerns. For example, they agreed to the sale of Verbund's controlling stake in APC, its distributor for large customers, which was to be completed before the merger took place; to transfer existing contracts with final consumers, held by APC on behalf of Verbund; to sell 20 per cent holdings in two other companies; and to make available through APT an amount of 450 MWh of electricity for auction per year to be supplied through Austria's high-voltage grid until 30 June 2008 for the supply of final consumers. The Commission was influenced by three significant factors. First, there is the impact of liberalization on the Austrian market. The entry into force of the Electricity Directive and related Regulation was expected to lead to a reduction of barriers to entry. Secondly, at the time there was an adequate interconnection capacity to and from Germany and a high degree of market liberalization in Austria itself. Moreover, the Austrian Minister responsible for energy indicated his intention to implement the unbundling provisions to ensure that legal unbundling took effect immediately. A third consideration was the close involvement of the Austrian regulatory authorities in the case (both the NRA and the NCA). The NRA was to supervise the implementation of sections of the commitment package. The Commission cleared the merger after the companies agreed to assist in the creation of a stronger competitor in the Austrian market and after they offered to make certain amounts of electricity available for sale by auction to smaller competitors. However, although the concentration, due to intra-Austrian obstacles (both sides were under various forms of public ownership and found it difficult to agree on implementation provisions) never took effect,[91] this decision was challenged (unsuccessfully) before the CFI.[92]

---

[90] *Verbund/EnergieAllianz* (Case COMP/M.2947) Commission Decision of 11 June 2003.
[91] However, the, 'upfront' sale of APC by Verbund was implemented.
[92] Case T-350/03 *Wirtschaftskammer Kärnten and best connect Ampere Strompool v Commission* [2004] OJ C7/36; dismissed as inadmissible: [2006] OJ C294/100.

C. The Practice

(2) Gas

(a) Exxon/Mobil

On 3 May 1999 Exxon and Mobil notified a proposed merger to the Commission. Like VEBA and VIAG, Exxon and Mobil were active in the same product markets. The main impact was on oil markets but gas markets were also affected. This raised certain competition concerns, partly motivated by Exxon's shareholding in Ruhrgas (which it later sold in a separate transaction unrelated to this case) and partly motivated by Exxon's and Mobil's own overlapping activities. However, the Commission was willing to declare the concentration compatible with the common market once the parties delivered certain undertakings.[93] The areas of concern, with respect to gas, lay in the likely creation or strengthening of a dominant position in certain markets: wholesale and long-distance transmission of natural gas and underground storage, in specific geographic markets, such as Germany and the Netherlands.

14.74

The commitments offered by Exxon and Mobil with respect to gas included a divestment of some upstream ('small fields') activities in the Netherlands (Mobil's Dutch gas business), commitments relating to shareholdings or voting rights in German long-distance transmission companies (Thyssengas and Erdgas Münster), and a commitment to offer to sell Mobil's rights in one or more depleted reservoirs suitable for conversion into natural gas underground storage facilities in Bavaria.

14.75

(b) EnBW/ENI/GVS

On 14 August 2002 the Commission was notified of a proposed acquisition by EnBW and ENI of a 50 per cent share of GVS, a German regional gas wholesaler.[94] This would result in the parties taking joint control of the company from the State of Baden Württemberg and several local distribution companies. The Commission commenced an in-depth investigation to assess the impact of the proposed transaction.

14.76

EnBW and GVS are both companies located in Baden-Württemberg in South-West Germany. EnBW is active in electricity generation, transmission, distribution, supply, and trading as well as in the supply of gas and district heating. GVS operates a gas transmission system in the region through which it supplies gas to local distribution companies and to a few industrial customers. ENI is active in all activities connected with oil and gas operations. About 90 per cent of the market

14.77

---

[93] *Exxon/Mobil* (Case COMP/M.1383) Commission Decision 2004/284/EC, [2004] OJ L103/1.
[94] *EnBW/ENI/GVS* (Case COMP/M.2822) Commission Decision 2003/668/EC, [2003] OJ L248/51.

for regional gas wholesale supply in the area was controlled by GVS, but appeared likely to be challenged by Wingas.

14.78 The Commission was concerned with the long-term supply contracts which GVS had with customers in the region. Some of these supply contracts were with EnBW affiliates. After the operation, these EnBW affiliates would become inaccessible to competitors of GVS such as Wingas. The operation would thereby increase barriers to entry through customer foreclosure. To remedy these concerns, EnBW and ENI submitted a proposal to grant early termination rights for all long-term supply contracts concluded between local gas distributors and either GVS or EnBW's subsidiaries. The right could be exercised once on two possible dates at six months' notice. The commitments would free up a substantial demand and would coincide with increased competition through the completion of the Wingas pipeline.

(c) E.ON/MOL

14.79 **The facts** The German-based utility, E.ON Ruhrgas International AG (ERI) made a proposal to acquire control of two subsidiaries of the established Hungarian oil and gas producer and supplier, MOL Hungarian Oil and Gas Rt by way of a purchase of shares. ERI also proposed to acquire MOL's shareholdings in Panrusgaz, a joint venture company between OAO Gazprom and MOL. The proposed concentration was notified to the Commission on 2 June 2005.[95] ERI is a solely controlled subsidiary of E.ON Ruhrgas AG, which is in turn an indirect subsidiary of E.ON AG. All three companies are members of the E.ON group of companies, a privately owned group with a focus on the supply of electricity and gas. MOL is an integrated oil and gas group, active mainly in Hungary, in markets for natural gas, oils, fuels and chemicals. It is 12 per cent owned by the Hungarian State which also has a golden share. The core of the proposed transaction was the acquisition by E.ON of sole control over MOL WMT (an acronym for Wholesale, Marketing and Trading), which supplies natural gas to regional gas distributors, industrial customers and large power plants in Hungary, and MOL Storage, which operates five storage facilities in Hungary. The notified operation had a Community dimension since the parties do not achieve more than two-thirds of their aggregate Community-wide turnover within one and the same Member State.

14.80 **The concerns** The notified operation gave rise to competition concerns. They related to the market position of the parties and the supply of gas to third parties. E.ON had strong market positions in Hungary in the retail supply of gas through

---

[95] *E.ON/MOL* (Case COMP/M.3696) Commission Decision 2006/622/EC, [2006] OJ L253/20. The case is discussed by Bartok, C, Moonen, S, Lahbabi, P, Paolicchi, A, and De la Mano, M, 'A combination of gas release programmes and ownership unbundling as remedy to a problematic energy merger: E.ON/MOL' (2006) 1 Competition Policy Newsletter 73–83.

C. The Practice

its majority and minority ownership in three regional gas distribution companies, as well as in the generation of electricity, and in the retail supply of electricity through its majority ownership in three electricity regional distributors and its trading subsidiary E.ON EK. The proposed concentration would therefore create a fully integrated entity along both the gas and electricity supply chains. Such integration would directly result in the new entity having the ability and the incentive to impede competition significantly on the downstream gas and electricity markets by raising rivals' costs or by foreclosing their access to gas resources. Competition concerns were expected to arise immediately after the transaction, under the existing regulatory framework, but would become even greater when the framework was modified to complete gas and electricity market liberalization in Hungary. One of the most important concerns revealed by the market investigation was the existence of significant barriers to entry on the gas market: new entrants would have difficulties in accessing competitive sources of gas and would face a lack of liquidity on the wholesale markets (due to a lack of market players and of offers on the gas 'secondary market' or the sale of gas between gas traders).[96] The new entity, like MOL WMT prior to the transaction, would enjoy a dominant position in the upstream markets for gas supply. The 'essential change' which the transaction would bring about is that:

> E.ON, unlike MOL, is active in the retail supply of gas, through the two RDCs it controls and its participation in a third one. Thus, the proposed merger will result in a vertically integrated company active across all stages of the gas supply chain and controlling access to gas volumes and part of the infrastructure . . . [T]he vertical integration created by the transaction is likely to result in the new entity having the ability *and* the incentive to foreclose its actual and potential competitors on the downstream markets for the supply of gas so as to significantly impede competition thereon.[97]

The remedies A package of remedies was proposed by MOL and E.ON, which in a modified form was accepted by the Commission. It comprised both structural and behavioural remedies. The structural remedies included the complete unbundling of ownership of the gas production and transmission activities (remaining with MOL) and the wholesale and storage activities (acquired by E.ON). While ownership unbundling of the gas production and transmission activities on the one hand and the wholesale activities on the other hand was part of the notified concentration, there would have remained ownership links, notably through joint ownership

14.81

---

[96] ibid, Recital 286; see further Recitals 314 and 318–9.
[97] ibid, Recitals 399–400. The merged entity would also have had the ability and incentive to foreclose access to its competitors' new gas-fired power plants and/or discriminate in its supply to competitors' new gas-fired power plants, deterring competition from rivals in replacement and expansion of generation capacity (Recital 729).

of the storage activities. This was resolved through MOL's agreement to relinquish its remaining shareholding in storage which thus came entirely under E.ON's control.

14.82 The remedies further included the obligatory sale of 1 billion cubic metres of gas per year during the period 2006–13 and the divestiture of one-half of its ten-year gas supply contract with MOL E&P (a subsidiary of MOL not acquired by E.ON active in the production of gas in Hungary) through a contract release. This represented the most significant gas release ever achieved in the EU in terms of volume and duration (if measured by the affected country's consumption of gas).

14.83 The Commission—which co-operated closely with the Hungarian authorities, in particular the energy regulator, the Hungarian Energy Office—accepted that the remedies were adequate to remove the competition concerns that it had. In particular, it considered that the combination of a gas release with a contract release would ensure that gas end-users and wholesalers will have the ability to source their gas needs under competitive and non-discriminatory conditions, independently from the merged entity. The volumes offered in the gas release programme would be able to create sufficient liquidity in the gas markets (and through de-blocking gas as a fuel to electricity generation also in electricity) so that effective competition could develop and be sustainable. In comparison with other existing gas release programmes, the Commission found—through an international benchmarking exercise—that the total quantities to be released through both remedies are significant. The contract release would be to a third party assignee, which would purchase significant quantities of gas from MOL E&P starting in July 2007 until 2013/14, giving it sufficient long-term gas resources to develop a position on the Hungarian gas markets and to introduce liquidity on these markets. The regulatory framework was thought robust enough to ensure that sufficient transmission and distribution capacities would be made available to the third party assignee to transport the acquired gas within Hungary. The parties also made commitments to grant access to storage for the successful bidders of the gas release programme and the assignee of the contract release at regulated prices. For the task of monitoring the commitments, the Hungarian Energy Office was responsible, with the assistance of the Commission's Trustee.

14.84 It should also be noted that E.ON and Gazprom have, in July 2006, announced an asset swap agreement under which Gazprom will acquire 50 per cent minus one share in E.ON's Hungarian storage and trading activities and 25 per cent plus one share in E.ON's Hungarian regional gas and power company in exchange for E.ON's participation in upstream activities in Russia. The acquisition of the shareholdings in Hungary by Gazprom is likely to constitute a concentration with a Community dimension which will need to be assessed by the European Commission.

(3) Convergence of Gas and Electricity

14.85 There have also been cases before the Commission in which companies providing different forms of energy have sought to combine into a single unit.[98] If a new market entry (or rather the strengthening of a small challenger to the incumbent) is likely to be the result of such convergence, the merger proposal will be viewed as pro-competitive. However, this will be different if it is a merger between the dominant electricity undertaking and the dominant gas supplier. At the academic level too, there has been considerable debate about the risks of concentrations between gas and electricity companies, with a number of leading economists concluding that convergent mergers of such utilities can have considerable anti-competitive effects. In particular, they cite removal of a potential competitor and market foreclosure.[99] This view has also been taken by the Commission.

14.86 With regard to the market foreclosure aspect, there is a risk that the combined electricity and gas incumbent will take control of the cost of production of its competitors in the electricity market. In such an event, if competing electricity generators active in other European markets then sought to enter this geographic market on the basis of a gas-fired plant, they would probably have to purchase the fuel from the incumbent electricity supplier (having merged with the dominant gas supplier). A combined dominant electricity and gas supplier would also have reduced incentives to support the choice of industrial customers as to whether they should engage in auto-generation of power via gas-fired plants rather than a pure gas supplier.

14.87 Furthermore, an important concern in convergence mergers between incumbents is the elimination of potential competition. Undoubtedly, electricity incumbents are well placed to enter gas markets and gas incumbents are well placed to enter electricity markets. In a situation in which the incumbent generally experiences little actual competition, such elimination of potential competition will likely be seen as highly problematic.

14.88 Early examples of convergence gas/electricity cases are the *Tractebel/Distrigaz*[100] and *Neste/IVO*[101] mergers. In the case of *Neste/IVO*, the solution proposed by the

---

[98] Among the cases discussed above, in particular *E.ON/MOL*, in addition to its intra-gas dimension, also had a cross-energy dimension (existing E.ON gas and electricity activities were complemented by gas activities). It may therefore be classified in both groups.
[99] Barquin, J, et al, 'Brief Academic Opinion of Economics Professors and Scholars on the Project of Acquisition of Endesa by Gas Natural', 26 October 2005, published as 'The Acquisition of Endesa by Gas Natural: Why the Antitrust Authorities Are Right to be Cautious' (2006) 19 Electricity Journal 62–8; see also Gilbert, R, and Newbery, R, 'Electricity Merger Policy in the Shadow of Regulation', 2006 (unpublished conference paper) (see Ch 1, n 32).
[100] *Tractebel/Distrigaz* (Case COMP/M.493) Commission Decision of 1 September 1994.
[101] *Neste/Ivo* (Case COMP/M.931) Commission Decision of 2 June 1998.

parties and accepted by the Commission was to require (partial) divestiture: the companies and the Finnish Government (which held controlling stakes in both companies) agreed to sell the controlling stake in Neste's subsidiary, Gasum, the dominant operator on the gas supply markets. The cases discussed in more detail below are more recent and thereby provide a good overview of the Commission's current approach to this type of merger.

(a) Dong/Elsam/Energi E2

14.89 In 2006 the Commission approved the acquisition by DONG, the state-owned gas incumbent in Denmark, of sole control over Elsam and Energi E2, two regional electricity generation incumbents and two suppliers, Kobenhavns Energi Holding and Frederiksberg Elnet, subject to certain conditions and undertakings.[102] The Commission's initial conclusion was that the deal would have anti-competitive effects in several markets along the gas supply chain in Denmark. These effects would have resulted from the combination of DONG's dominant position and the removal of actual and potential competition from the above four companies (including NESA, Elsam's subsidiary for electricity retailing), along with the fact that DONG would acquire the ability to weaken its remaining competitors on the market (by raising competitors' costs for storage and flexibility). Entry barriers would have been raised on these markets and an important segment of Danish demand for natural gas would have been foreclosed.

14.90 The response of DONG to these concerns was to offer a structural remedy by divesting the larger of its two Danish gas storage facilities, along with a gas release programme. The programme is to include six annual auctions of 400 million cubic metres for a total duration of seven years, releasing volumes equivalent to 10 per cent of annual Danish demand. The auction is to have two stages, whereby the primary auction will involve swapping the auctioned lots between the Danish hub and any of four northern hubs in the UK, the Netherlands, Belgium, and Germany. If all lots are not disposed of in the course of the primary auction, any remaining volumes will be sold against cash settlement in a secondary auction. The Commission took into account the pre-existing level of liberalization in Denmark in its assessment: in particular, the storage remedy will reinforce the effect of the full unbundling of gas transmission which has already taken place in Denmark and create conditions for competition in the provision of gas storage services. The gas release remedy was thought likely by the Commission to improve the liquidity of the Danish gas market and ensure that gas users will not face less choice than before the merger. The divestiture was expected to establish a second, independent player on the Danish storage market. It would also act to encourage new entry onto the Danish

---

[102] Commission Press Release IP/06/313, 'Mergers: Commission approves acquisition by DONG of Danish electricity generators and suppliers, subject to conditions', 14 March 2006.

C. The Practice

natural gas market and increase the flexible liquidity of the wholesale market as well as free up contractually locked-in customers.

In its press release the Commission stressed the close co-operation which it had with the Danish authorities; they are also given a special role in overseeing the implementation of the commitments. **14.91**

In a parallel operation, some of the generation assets of Elsam and E2 were also to be acquired by Vattenfall, the Swedish state-owned electricity incumbent,[103] which would also contribute to promoting competition in both West and East Denmark. This circumstance can be considered a 'prior remedy' to the *DONG/Elsam/E2* case, ie an inbuilt remedy avoiding the finding of a competition problem for wholesale electricity markets, which would otherwise have been likely. **14.92**

(b) ENI/EDP/GDP

In July 2004 a proposed concentration was notified by Energias de Portugal (EDP), the incumbent electricity supplier in Portugal, and Eni, an Italian energy company, whereby they would obtain joint control of GDP, the incumbent gas company in Portugal.[104] EDP is active in the generation, distribution, and supply of electricity in Portugal. It also had joint control over the Spanish company, Hidrocantábrico. ENI is active at all levels of the energy supply and distribution chain. GDP and its subsidiaries cover all levels of the gas chain and had already acquired joint control (with the Portuguese State) of GDP in a previous operation.[105] GDP and its subsidiaries cover all levels of the gas chain in Portugal. Through its subsidiary, Transgas, GDP imports natural gas into Portugal, through pipelines and an LNG terminal, and is responsible for the transportation, storage, transport, and supply through the high-pressure natural gas network. It also supplies natural gas to large industrial customers and controls five of the country's six local distribution companies. **14.93**

The Commission concluded that the operation raised serious doubts as to its compatibility with the common market and so initiated an in-depth investigation of the case. Despite commitments given by the notifying parties, it concluded that the proposed operation would lead to the strengthening of EDP's and GDP's respective dominant positions on the electricity and gas markets in Portugal, as from when these markets were opened to competition, as a result of which effective competition would be significantly impeded in a substantial part of the common market. **14.94**

---

[103] cf *Vattenfall/ Elsam & E2 Assets* (Case COMP/M.3867) Commission Decision of 22 December 2005.
[104] *EDP/ENI/GDP* (Case COMP/M.3440) Commission Decision 2005/801/EC, [2005] OJ L302/69, adopted under Council Regulation (EC) 4064/89. The case is summarized and discussed by Conte, G, Loriot, G, Rouxel, F-X, and Tretton, W, 'EDP/ENI/GDP: the Commission prohibits a merger between gas and electricity national incumbents' (2005) 1 Competition Policy Newsletter 84–7.
[105] *ENI/GALP* (Case COMP/M.1859) Commission Decision of 29 June 2000.

14.95 Portugal has its electricity markets open to competition but the gas markets are being opened progressively in accordance with a derogation under Article 28(2) and (3) of the Gas Directive from its full operation until 2007 (see para 6.99). As a result, a legal monopoly is held by GDP, which is present at all levels in the gas supply chain in Portugal. The competition concerns related to the market position of the parties, the elimination of EDP of an important potential competitor (GDP), and the effects on supply to third parties. Both EDP and GDP have a dominant position in the various electricity and gas markets. The dominant positions of EDP in the electricity markets (the wholesale supply of electricity, ancillary services and retail supply of electricity) would be strengthened by the removal of a potential entrant. The dominant positions of GDP in the gas markets (the supply of gas to combined cycle gas turbines, local distribution companies, large industrial customers, and small customers) would also be strengthened at a time when these markets are being opened up in stages up to 2010.[106] In response, the parties offered to make temporarily accessible some of their generation capacity to third parties through a toll-manufacturing or lease agreement, to sell minority shareholdings and reduce their interest in a third party generator, and not to construct any new generation capacity until 2010. With respect to the production and sale of gas, the parties offered to guarantee access to the infrastructure in various ways, and to divest two distribution undertakings.

14.96 The above-mentioned remedies were considered by the Commission to be insufficient to remove the competition concerns in relation to the market position of the parties on the wholesale market and on the resale market for electricity. The proposed concentration was declared incompatible with the common market. Their view was that it was uncertain whether refraining from the construction of new capacity and leasing part of the capacity would have the same effects as a structural remedy which would make possible effective and timely entry to the market. The remedy that was proposed was also insufficient to remove the concerns in relation to the supply of gas to competing electricity producers. Finally, the Commission stated that there was insufficient certainty that the proposed remedies could solve the competition concerns with regard to the market position of the parties on the wholesale market for the supply of gas to various groups of buyers.

14.97 Subsequently, EDP brought an action for annulment of the Commission's decision before the CFI, which confirmed the Commission's decision.[107] The Court criticized the Commission's decision to base its prohibition of the concentration on the strengthening of dominant positions giving rise to a significant impediment to

---

[106] *EDP/ENI/GDP* (Case COMP/M.3440) Commission Decision 2005/801/EC, [2005] OJ L302/69, para 609.
[107] Case T-87/05 *Energias de Portugal (EDP) SA v Commission* [2005] 5 CMLR 23.

C. The Practice

competition on the gas markets.[108] These were, by virtue of the derogation, not open to competition. The Commission had disregarded the effects and therefore the scope of the derogation. Essentially, GDP held a monopoly on virtually all of the gas markets since they were not open to competition. A monopoly represents the ultimate dominant position which cannot be strengthened. There was therefore no effective competition which could be impeded by the concentration.[109] The error is however limited to one group of relevant markets, the gas markets, in Portugal and does not affect the competitive assessments made by the Commission with respect to the electricity markets. The conclusion that the concentration would cause an important potential competitor to disappear from all the electricity markets is correct. This would lead to an important strengthening of EDP's position on each of these markets, with the result that effective competition would be significantly impeded. It may be noted that the case was heard by the CFI under the 'fast-track' procedure[110] and the judgment was delivered within seven months, the shortest period ever achieved for a case of this kind. Another feature was extra-legal in character. Essentially, in terms of the Commission's strategy it was important to give a signal to other market participants of what the limits were to its policy on mergers. Had a prohibition not been made in this case, it is not difficult to conceive of leading players such as EDF taking it as a signal to pursue a more active policy in M&A.

(c) Gaz de France/Suez

14.98 In 2006 the Commission opened an investigation into a proposed merger between Gaz de France (GDF) and the Suez Group.[111] Its initial investigation generated concerns that the planned merger between two companies, active in both the gas and electricity sectors in France and Belgium, would result in a significant impediment to competition. This would arise at all levels of the gas and electricity supply chain in Belgium and at all levels of the gas chain in France, in the light of the horizontal overlaps and the vertical relationships between the two companies' activities. The combination would include the supply activities of the two main gas and electricity operators in Belgium and two of the three main gas operators

---

[108] ibid, Recitals 121–33: 'The absence of competition on the gas markets under the derogation granted in accordance with the Second Gas Directive precludes the application of Art 2(3) of the Merger Regulation. Undertakings cannot be criticised for significantly impeding effective competition where that competition does not exist as a result of national and Community legislation' (para 126).

[109] The CFI's position, requiring the demonstration of an immediate effect, implicitly considered as not sufficient certain announcements made by the Portuguese Government to advance the liberalization of the Portuguese gas markets, in particular the market for supply of gas to power plants.

[110] For a description of this procedure, see Fountoukakos, K, 'Judicial Review and Merger Control: The CFI's Expedited Procedure' (2002) 3 Competition Policy Newsletter 7–12.

[111] Commission Press Release IP/06/802, 'Mergers: Commission opens in-depth investigation into merger between Gaz de France and Suez Group', 19 June 2006.

in France. The new entity would have control over most gas imports into both Belgium and France. This would incur the risk of excluding competitors from the downstream gas and electricity markets as little gas liquidity would exist independently of the new entity. The Commission also identified potential vertical problems arising from the parties' control over essential infrastructure such as transmission networks and storage facilities. The merger could therefore remove competitive constraints that the two companies currently exert on each other, and may create or strengthen barriers for third parties to enter the market, and in this way undermine the benefits of the ongoing liberalization process in France and Belgium. On 18 August 2006, the Commission issued a statement of objections, a procedural document preceding the Commission's final decision, in which it set out its in-depth but still preliminary finding of competition problems created by the proposed merger.[112] Shortly afterwards, remedies were proposed by the parties. They included, among other things, the divestiture of the Suez group's holding in Distrigaz and GDF's holding in SPE, a restructuring of Fluxys and relinquishing of all control of that company. The Commission's response was positive, emphasizing that structural remedies such as ownership unbundling and the separation of supply and infrastructure to create pro-competitive conditions were consistent with the findings of the Energy Sector Inquiry. An interesting element in the case was the apparent willingness of the Commission to allow the French Government to retain a golden share in GDF after the proposed merger with Suez.

D. Remedies

(1) General

14.99 In the event of competition concerns being raised by a proposed merger, the parties may propose 'remedies' or measures that are designed to remove these competition concerns. Remedies must meet substantive requirements and be submitted and implemented in certain ways. Three kinds of remedies may be distinguished: structural, behavioural, and quasi-structural remedies. The first category comprises remedies that affect the control relationships and bring about a structural change on the market. Usually, this involves divestments of one or more of the undertakings to be merged. The second category comprises remedies that imply that the undertaking that results from the merger will behave in a particular way

---

[112] Commission Press Release IP/06/1109, 'Merger: The European Commission adopted a "Statement of Objections" regarding the merger project between Suez and Gaz de France', 19 August 2006; Commission Press Release IP/06/1558, 'Mergers: Commission approves merger of Gaz de France and Suez, subject to conditions', 14 November 2006 and MEMO/06/424, 'Mergers: summary of the remedies offered by GDF and Suez', 14 November 2006. The golden share issue is reported in the *Financial Times*, 'Brusssels backs GDF golden share plan', 7 September 2006.

D. Remedies

or will refrain from certain behaviour. These remedies require continuous monitoring of the behaviour of undertakings. Finally, there are quasi-structural remedies that do not have a structural character but have permanent and therefore more or less structural effects on the market.

Remedies may also have a temporary character. This may apply to markets which are in transition from strong price regulation to a market orientation. In such situations, markets may experience strong development, also in geographic terms. In this case, when assessing the merger it is necessary to consider what the market and market relationships will be in a number of years' time and how the expected market developments will be taken into account in the assessment. **14.100**

The remedies may also be organized so as to address different types of competition concerns. For example, they may be concerned with the market position of the parties. Given the potential for a creation or strengthening of market power due to parties to a merger combining their strength on a market, the typical remedy is to require part of the undertaking on the market to be divested. However, a study by the Commission into the operation of remedies between 1996 and 2000 has shown that approximately 30 per cent of remedies involving the divestiture of a subsidiary were only partially effective or were not affected at all in the period following the merger.[113] The weaknesses of this approach appear to lie mainly in the inadequate scope of the parts of undertakings to be divested. Moreover, factors such as finding a suitable buyer, the disintegration of the part of the company to be divested from the remaining parts of the company, and the actual transfer all play a part in the effectiveness of the remedies. **14.101**

Other remedies may focus on barriers to entry. Competition concerns can arise from the creation of an increase in the barriers to entry. The vertical integration of two parties active at various levels in the product chain may result in a situation where one entrant would have to enter at both levels to compete effectively. Another case would be where the merged undertaking acquires control of important infrastructure which may create barriers to entry. Remedies to address this kind of problem include the stimulation of new entry (by granting access to infrastructure or making technologies compatible), and removing contractual agreements which obstruct entry, such as exclusive contracts and the purchase or supply of bundled products. Other sets of remedies may focus on deliveries to third parties and procurement from third parties. In the first case, vertical integration of two parties, active at various levels in the product chain, delivery to third parties and/or procurement from third parties may be restricted if the merged parties trade more internally and consequently deliver less to third parties and/or procure less from **14.102**

---

[113] DG COMP, European Commission, *Merger Remedies Study* (October 2005) <http://ec.europa.eu/ comm/competition/mergers/others/remedies_study.pdf>.

third parties. Competition concerns in relation to deliveries to third parties may be solved by divesting parts of the undertaking, but in some cases also they may be resolved by means of behavioural remedies, such as granting access to infrastructure and granting licences. Competition concerns in relation to procurement from third parties can be solved by means of procurement guarantees.

14.103 However, it should be noted that remedies are quite different from the regulatory actions taken by an NRA in which rules are established for an industry or substantial business segment (as are the common rules established by an EC legislative measure): the remedies accepted in the context of merger proceedings are designed to address specific competition concerns identified by the competition authority and are directed only at the parties to the merger decision.

(2) Remedies used in the Energy Sector

14.104 Typically, remedies accepted in merger conditional clearances have attempted to address one or both of two questions: how to reduce the market power of the merging companies, and how to facilitate entry? With respect to the first of these questions, the principal method adopted has been to require divestments. These may be divestments of subsidiaries or participating shares, carried out with a view to reducing or removing horizontal or vertical links. Alternatively, they may involve a divestment of energy capacity, transmission capacity, or of customers. With respect to stimulation of entry and fostering competition in this way, the general aim is to improve access and entry conditions by, for example, increasing liquidity, de-bottlenecking transmission and interconnection, stimulating demand and lowering or preventing the rise of costs of balancing energy.

14.105 There is a body of recent case law that may be drawn upon in considering merger remedies. In the *Easyjet* case, the principle of proportionality was established. If the merger is viable, no remedies should go beyond what is needed. In the *Cementbouw* case, the principle was established that if remedies offered went beyond the restoration of the pre-merger situation, the Commission can accept them. In the *EDP* case, it was established that the burden of proof lay upon the Commission and the parties have to provide an explanation.[113a] The remedies must be 'clear-cut' (that is, there is no market test).

14.106 An important contextual factor has been the ongoing liberalization process. In the past, the choice of remedies has been made with a view to contributing to the process positively.

[113a] 'Commission Press Release IP/03/1308, 'Commission clears Cementbouw acquisition of CRH and JV between CRH and CVC Capital Partners', 30 September 2003; Case T-177/04, *EasyJet Airline v Commission* [2006] OJ C212/29.

D. Remedies

(a) Divestiture

The most often used remedy in merger proceedings has been the structural one of divestiture. It has figured in the cases involving *VEBA/VIAG*, *EDF/EnBW*, *E.ON/Ruhrgas*, *Neste/IVO*, and *Verbund/EnergieAllianz*, all discussed in the preceding section. This can take various forms however, all designed to achieve a reduction in market power. It may consist in:

14.107

- divestiture of interests in market participants in the markets concerned, or subsidiaries (*VEBA/VIAG*; *Verbund/EnergieAllianz* and *IVO/Neste*);
- divestiture of infrastructure assets, notably storage assets (*DONG/Elsam/E2*); or
- divestiture of customers (*Verbund/EnergieAllianz*, via a subsidiary).

(b) Energy Release Programmes

Release programmes may be designed to overcome the problem of inadequate access to supplies or to capacity. They have an advantage in not requiring any divestment of assets. So far they have been little used, but they offer considerable potential and have figured prominently in the remedies adopted in the *E.ON/MOL* and *DONG/Elsam/E2* cases. Their increasing importance, combined with their particular suitability for gas supply, merit extended consideration.

14.108

There are only two principal forms of release programme that have been implemented in the EU:[114] energy (gas or electricity) release (which can itself be implemented through bilateral contracts or through auctions (see para 14.68)) and contract release (implemented through bilateral negotiations). An example of a case where both forms were employed is the *E.ON/MOL* merger case, in which the parties chose to submit remedies that included both a gas release through auctions and a contract release through bilateral negotiations.

14.109

In a gas release programme, the incumbent offers for sale to its competitors/customers certain quantities of gas/electricity from its overall gas sourcing portfolio or electricity generation portfolio. A purchaser will enter into a contract with the incumbent for these quantities. The aim is to make gas or electricity available to wholesalers and end-users at the wholesale level. There are two principal ways of effecting gas or electricity release: either by means of auctions or bilateral contracts. Under the former, the gas or electricity quantities may be sold through public auctions where companies are selected according to the highest bid. In the

14.110

---

[114] See generally, EFET, 'Implementation of Gas Release Programmes for European Gas Market Development' at <http://www.efet.org>, and *E.ON/MOL* (Case COMP/M.3696) Commission Decision 2006/622/EC, [2006] OJ L253/20, Recitals 776–98; summary details of various Member State initiatives in France (generation capacity), Ireland (generation capacity), Italy (gas and generation capacity), Spain (gas), and the UK (gas) are included in *Discussion Document on Long-term Contracts, Gas Release Programmes and the Availability of Multiple Gas Suppliers*, for discussion at the 5th Meeting of the Gas Regulatory Forum, Madrid.

latter case, the incumbent negotiates with interested parties and gas or electricity sales are concluded based on mutual agreement. At EC level, the auction approach has generally been the preferred solution (*EDF/EnBW*; *Verbund/EnergieAllianz*; *E.ON/MOL*; *DONG/Elsam/E2*) which is also true for national merger procedures (*E.ON/Ruhrgas*; *OMV/Econgas*[115]). This may be due to the fact that bilateral negotiations risk giving the incumbents too much leeway in selecting 'preferred competitors'. However, in some gas release programmes, bilateral negotiations were allowed for part of the capacity (GDF and Total/GSO gas release for the south of France).

14.111 Moreover, the behavioural or quasi-structural, remedy of auctions has been used as a remedy in energy sector merger proceedings. It may concern the auctioning of energy and/or transmission capacity to facilitate market entry by increasing liquidity. It has been evident in the cases involving *VEBA/VIAG* (transmission capacity); *EDF/EnBW* (electricity); *Verbund/EnergieAllianz* (electricity); *E.ON/MOL* (gas); *DONG/Elsam/E2* (gas); and *E.ON/Ruhrgas* (gas).

14.112 The purpose of the auction may be to encourage purchase of energy by traders to resell in the market. They may build up a customer base without having to make large investments at the outset, such as in infrastructure or concluding a long-term gas supply contract.

14.113 In a contract release programme, so far only applied in the gas markets, the gas incumbent assigns part of its gas supply contracts with gas producers. Purchasers will enter into a supply contract directly with the gas producers, without the intermediary role of the incumbent, and the assigned parts of the gas supply contract (or contracts) of the incumbent is (or are) terminated or reduced according to whatever quantity has been assigned to the third party. By contrast with a gas release programme (in which the incumbent's supply portfolio remains the same), the incumbent's supply portfolio is partly transferred to competitors or customers in a contract release programme. This may seem a preferable solution, as it is closer to a structural remedy. However, there are some limits to the applicability of such a solution as assignments of (parts) of contracts with third parties (producers) usually require the assent of those third parties, which may be difficult to obtain, especially within the tight temporal framework of merger proceedings.[116]

---

[115] Following the combination of gas activities between Austrian regional suppliers and Austria's incumbent wholesaler OMV in 2002, leading to the creation of the Econgas JV, the Austrian authorities imposed, conditional to their clearance, a gas release programme amounting to 250 million cubic metres per year.

[116] The contact release in *E.ON/MOL* was possible due to the fact that both the contract parties were parties to the merger, namely purchaser (MOL WMT being purchased by E.ON) and seller (MOL E&P retained by MOL).

D. Remedies

Both release programmes (gas/electricity release and contract release) have as their aim the improvement of liquidity of gas markets and an enabling of competing traders and customers to acquire gas (or electricity) for their own use or for resale. **14.114**

Experience of the two release programmes varies, since contract release has been tried only occasionally whereas gas/electricity release has been implemented in several EU countries, usually as part of a broader action plan required under national law or designed by NRAs to open the wholesale markets to competition or implemented as commitments undertaken in merger or antitrust procedures (for example, France, Germany, and Austria). Below are two examples of gas release programmes that emerged from M&A cases. They are contrasting examples since the requirements of the German Government in the *E.ON/Ruhrgas* case were deemed to have failed, while those adopted by the Commission in the later case of *E.ON/MOL* were developed on the basis of that earlier negative experience. **14.115**

E.ON/Ruhrgas In this acquisition of Ruhrgas by E.ON the approval of the German Government was conditional on a number of undertakings. One of these was that a gas release programme be established to release 200 billion kWh from its long-term import contracts. A summary of the main commitments is provided below. **14.116**

- 200 billion kWh of gas to be sold in six separate annual auctions, with the first tranche of gas offered at the end of July 2003 for a start date of 1 October 2003;
- a summary information memorandum has to be published in English (and in German) on the Ruhrgas website at <http://grp.ruhrgas.de/englisch/grp>;
- 33.33 billion kWh over three years (11.11 billion kWh/year) to be offered in the first auction in 33 lots;
- no single bidder may bid for more than 11 lots;
- delivery period is three years starting from 1 October 2003;
- minimum annual quantity 80 per cent, minimum daily quantity 60 per cent daily contract quantity (DCQ);
- gas to be delivered at the flange near the Emden-Bunde Hub where the Norpipe Terminal joins the Ruhrgas pipeline system;
- nominations to be made D-1 at 11.00 hours;
- the starting price for the auction is 95 per cent of the published average border price (by the best available fair trade answer (BAFTA)) for the delivery month concerned plus the premium set by the auction;
- monthly payment to be made 10 days after delivery, with a later adjustment payment based on the average gas import price;
- *force majeure* provisions apply;
- companies wishing to bid must provide a bank guarantee for €1 million per lot being bid for and a higher guarantee if their bid is successful; and
- companies with more than a 10 per cent holding in E.ON and Ruhrgas are excluded from the auction.

14.117 *E.ON/MOL* Eight-year release programme with 1 billion cubic metres per annum for release:

- sale to be organized by way of a business-to-business internet auction, to be carried out by an international IT service provider;
- sales contract to provide for an annual minimum off-take obligation of 85 per cent to the effect that the purchaser will only have to purchase and pay 85 per cent of the annual contract quantity;
- each tranche to be offered at the auction for 80 per cent gas delivery at the Hungarian side of the Eastern entry point into Hungary and 20 per cent at the Hungarian side of the Western entry point into Hungary;
- a Monitoring Trustee to supervise the auction process;
- seller undertakes to modify and/or improve the implementing programme on the basis of experience gained from the annual auctions.

(c) Interconnection/Infrastructure Release

14.118 A different kind of auction occurs when the transmission capacity of interconnectors is offered for sale as a result of commitments made in merger proceedings. It is a remedy that is designed to achieve similar results. It has been evident in the *Hidrocantábrico* cases and in *VEBA/VIAG*. The aim is to de-bottleneck the interconnector. In the case of the French-Spanish interconnection, import capacities were reserved on a long-term basis to the incumbent operators and so preventing others from entering the Iberian markets. If long-term capacity reservation can be discontinued, alternative users may be able to acquire transport rights and so enter the markets.

(d) Customer Release/Termination of Customer Contracts

14.119 In several merger cases another behavioural remedy has been tried: the introduction of termination rights for (long-term) supply contracts. For example, this has figured in the *ENI/EnBW/GVS* and *Verbund/EnergieAllianz* cases. In the former case, GVS offered the following remedy to the Commission. The customers of GVS would have the option of terminating their contracts at six months' notice. In this way, the market was opened to new entrants such as Wingas. Termination rights for customers, as an element supporting the gas auction, is also an element in the *DONG/Elsam/E2* commitments.

(3) Effectiveness of Energy Remedies

(a) Divestiture

14.120 The manner of implementation of divestiture commitments, and indeed the implementation of such commitments at all, was the subject of some criticism in the Commission's internal study of remedies in 2005. There is clearly room for improvement in the design of divestment remedies.

D. Remedies

(b) Release Programmes

14.121 In a survey of the experience of NRAs with gas release programmes, the Commission found that there were 12 key requirements for an effective gas release programme amounting to 'Best Practice'.[117] These are commented on below:

14.122 **Volumes** In a merger case, the volumes to be released in a programme have to be sufficient to remove competition concerns. They will be determined by the number and size of the markets in which competition concerns arise. The volumes released have to be sufficient to ensure that the incumbent supplier is not able to foresee that all or most of the released volumes will be acquired by certain consumer categories. The volumes released have to be sufficient to permit eligible customers in all of the affected markets to benefit from the programme if the programme is to offset an incumbent's ability and incentive to engage in anti-competitive behaviour and so remove the negative impact on competition. Provision has to be made for offered but unsold gas quantities in a given year to be added to the quantities to be released in subsequent years.

14.123 **Duration** The general aim is to increase liquidity on gas wholesale markets and to facilitate new entrants. In merger cases, the aim should be to reduce or eliminate the parties' ability and incentives to engage in behaviour that would significantly impede effective competition. To do this, the programme has to remain in place for a sufficient duration to ensure that both the market structure and the competitive conditions have changed significantly, and that the level of competition achieved by means of the programme is one that is sustainable.

14.124 **Price and costs** The price at which gas is made available through the release programme has to be low enough for the wholesalers to compete with the supplier on wholesale and retail markets. On one view:

> . . . the price must not be higher than the average price paid by the incumbent (including contractual discounts), nor must it be higher than the average netback from the incumbent's eligible customers. If a release programme is also used as a remedy to balance the incumbent's market power, the price must not be higher than that offered in the wholesale market, even if this implies a financial loss to the incumbent.[118]

14.125 The auction mechanism is a common method for the allocation of gas quantities in a release programme. In this way, the final price results from competitive bids, and represents the price that bidders are willing to pay for the gas made available under the programme, in the prevailing market conditions. It will tend to be around the lower of the WACOG (meaning the weighted average cost of gas) or the average netback from the incumbents' eligible customers. In its paper on release programmes, the European Federation of Energy Traders (EFET) argues that use

---

[117] *E.ON/Mol*, Recitals 768–98.
[118] EFET, 'Implementation of Gas Release Programmes for European Gas Market Development', 2.

of WACOG for benchmarking purposes in an auction requires account to be taken of the financial discounts that most long-term contracts include and which may not be reflected in published border prices.[119] The WACOG calculation should be confirmed by an independent audit. Where the aim is to compensate for incumbents' market power, as in a merger remedy, the price should at least reflect the wholesale market price, if this is lower than the incumbents' WACOG. All costs incurred by participants in auctions and by successful bidders should be clearly defined, and additional costs avoided as much as possible.

14.126 **Gas supply duration and lot size** Both the duration of the supply contract and the size of the lots of gas made available in a release programme should be designed to meet the needs of the various categories of bidders in the relevant markets.

14.127 **Flexibility** A crucial role is played by the flexibility provisions for the gas supplied through the programme. These are normally divided into daily, quarterly, and yearly flexibility provisions. The buyer, whether it is a wholesaler or industrial customer, should have the ability to structure the gas quantities purchased according to its own or its customers' profiles. The requirements for the flexibility of the gas supplied will differ according to the conditions of storage access. With respect to annual flexibility (swing and take-or-pay levels), this should reflect the incumbent's average annual flexibility. With respect to quarterly flexibility, this is linked to the provision by the seller of storage access in the programme. If access to storage or other flexibility tools is difficult or available only at punitive prices, competition in supply will not develop from the programme. With respect to daily flexibility, some buyers will have higher flexibility requirements than others. Large importers such as the seller will have lower flexibility needs than the wholesalers, especially small ones, and end-users. The provision of a daily flexibility that is similar to the seller's gas portfolio's average daily flexibility or a base-load gas supply may not be adequate. The Commission's survey of NRA experiences revealed that 'particularly in Germany ... the attractiveness of a gas release programme for small wholesalers and industrial customers strongly depends on the flexibility provisions of the gas supply'.[120]

14.128 **Gas delivery points** The release programme will be made more attractive to prospective buyers if there is some flexibility provided in the choice of delivery point. It should be at a point from which wholesalers can easily transport and store the gas, such as a gas hub or a cross-border entry point. In certain circumstances, the delivery point location is particularly important: when ownership of the transmission network is shared, when the level of free capacity is low in the transmission or storage system, and when entry-exit tariffs are applicable. Where gas is available at more than one delivery point, the risk is reduced that the transmission regime

---

[119] ibid 4.
[120] *E.ON/MOL*, Recital 786.

D. The Remedies

will constrain competition in any particular area or market segment. New entrants (the purchasers) will also find themselves facing the same physical and operational risks as the incumbent (the seller) by sharing the same entry points. Where a release programme is being designed, the delivery point should be selected to enable wholesalers and end-users to source gas from the gas release programme for resale or for their own use in the geographic market where competition concerns have been identified.

Security of supply Following the standard practice in the relevant markets, gas supply conditions should include provisions on security of supply issues (maintenance, *force majeure*, interruptibility, for example). There should be a balance between the rights and obligations of the purchasers and the seller. 14.129

Auction design and guarantees Experience suggests that the 'ascending clock' form of auction is the most appropriate way of allocating gas quantities. The design has to ensure that the seller does not gain information on its competitors. Payment of deposits and guarantees should be proportionate and not constitute a disincentive to potential bidders. Payment terms should reflect standard market practices, especially those of the seller's upstream supply contracts. 14.130

Access to transmission An essential feature is access to transmission capacities, as without this the programme will not work since the wholesalers and end-users which purchase gas cannot transport gas to the place where the programme is intended to solve the competition concerns. Where capacity has been booked by the company that organizes the release programme, it should be released to the TSO to the extent of the gas quantities released. It appears that difficulties in obtaining sufficient capacity to transport the acquired gas were one of the principal reasons behind the lack of success of the first auctions in the German release programme of E.ON/Ruhrgas. 14.131

Access to storage In the absence of sufficient flexibility in the programme for the needs of the wholesaler and end-user, access to sufficient storage capacities is necessary. In this respect, marginal storage capacity has to be available in the storage system. If it is booked by the company that is organizing the release programme, then it should release capacity to the storage system operator to the extent of the gas quantities released. 14.132

Access to customers Customers purchasing gas in the release programme or indirectly from a trader purchasing gas in the programme need to have the opportunity to terminate their existing gas supply contracts or to reduce their obligation to purchase gas. This is needed to counter the likelihood that the majority of customers are bound to their gas suppliers under long-term supply contracts. The release programme will have no effect if customers are not able to switch suppliers. 14.133

Monitoring and review provision Given the high degree of complexity involved in a programme of gas release and the specific features of the market conditions, 14.134

a provision should be made to review the conditions for implementation to address any difficulties encountered in practice. Flexibility has to be provided for modification of the auction and supply rules to take into account the needs of third parties. Close monitoring has to be provided by the competent national authorities. There is an important dimension to this, however. Since this programme is imposed by way of undertakings arising from a merger case, and not directly imposed by a national authority, the parties should be limited in the freedom to set the terms and conditions of the programme to ensure the effectiveness of the remedy. Most practical or technical rules for the programme's implementation should not be part of the undertakings attached to a decision. Instead, they should be defined at a later stage under the supervision of the relevant competition authority.

(c) Capacity Auctions

14.135 Auctions have nevertheless attracted considerable criticism,[121] on the grounds of being overly complex, too slow, and offering inferior flexibility to the capacity retained by the seller. Critics also focus on the means by which the selling price is determined (if it is set too high it may not facilitate market entry), and the destination of the energy once auctioned (it may be exported to other markets where the price is higher, so not achieving liquidity where it is intended). However, at the EC level there is as yet quite limited experience in energy auctions apart from those gained in *EDF/EnBW* (see para 14.68).[122] Despite strong initial criticism, the auctions of generation capacity in *EDF/EnBW* have been successful and it may be questioned whether potential entry of EnBW in France (the elimination of which these auctions were designed to offset) would have had a bigger impact on the French market. In addition the Commission has accepted energy auctions in two recent gas cases (*E.ON/MOL* and *DONG/Elsam/E2*), where the observation period for assessing their effectiveness is still too short.[123]

E. Golden Shares as Barriers

14.136 The possibility that a significant cross-border merger or acquisition may be blocked by a political intervention is always present in an industry as strategically sensitive as the energy industry. This is illustrated in a particularly vivid manner by the existence

---

[121] EFET, 'Public Consultation on VPP; Letter to CRE' (in French), 13 January 2006; <http://www.efet.org>.

[122] The auctions in *Verbund/EnergieAllianz* were never implemented as the merger itself was not implemented. Other merger case-induced auctions fall under the responsibility of national authorities such as in Germany (Ruhrgas auction) and in Austria (OMV/Econgas auction). A further group of auctions was induced by regulators, such as the one in Spain at the beginning of its gas market opening.

[123] The first auction in *E.ON/MOL* in 2006 was partly successful. The first auction in *DONG/Elsam/E2* took place in August and October 2006.

E. Golden Shares as Barriers

of so called golden shares, or special rights vested in the State or other public entities which grant control over privatized companies.[124] As recently as 2006, the Spanish Government found it necessary to deny that it would use its golden share in Endesa to block a takeover bid from E.ON.[125] The Commission also intervened with the statement that it 'would very much like to remind the Spanish authorities not to use any constructions or any special rights in this particular situation which are already declared not in compliance with the relevant rules'.[126] In fact, further to an adverse judgment of the ECJ in 2003, Spain had agreed to remove the golden shares from four privatized companies, including Endesa.

14.137 The ECJ has delivered judgments on golden shares on several occasions, starting from 2000 with its decision in C-58/99 against the Government of Italy and most recently, in 2003 in Cases C-463/00 and C-98/01, involving Spain and the UK.[127] The Commission had brought actions against the respective governments on the ground that the shares constituted an infringement of the principle of free movement of capital. Essentially, it set out criteria of legality that the golden shares must satisfy. If a golden share can be justified on specified grounds or by overriding requirements of the general interest, it may be permitted. Such grounds have to be non-discriminatory, non-discretionary, and must satisfy the principle of proportionality.

(1) The 2002 Judgments

14.138 In June 2002 the ECJ delivered three judgments on the compatibility of golden shares with European law.[128] While the companies in question operated principally in the energy sector, the judgments have wide implications. Following the many privatizations of the 1980s and 1990s in Europe, many undertakings in key sectors that were formerly in state ownership are now privatized, but nonetheless have a state share in them, usually conferring upon the state shareholder a set of powers capable of deterring potential investors in such companies.

14.139 During 1998 and 1999 the Commission commenced infringement proceedings against Portugal, France, and Belgium, on the grounds that their legislation imposes restrictions on participations or shares following a process of privatization.

---

[124] In French the term is '*actions spécifiques*'; in German it is '*goldene Aktien*'.
[125] 'Spain rules out Endesa "golden share" defence', The Times, 17 August 2006. The share allowed the Government to veto the sale of stakes of 10% or more in the companies concerned. The legislation to remove the golden share had not yet been approved by the Spanish Parliament. Two of the shares expired in 2006, while those in Telefonica and Endesa were to expire in 2007.
[126] 'EU urges Spain not to use Endesa golden share to block E.ON bid', AFX News Ltd, 17 August 2006.
[127] Case C-463/00 *Commission v Spain* [2003] ECR I-4581; Case C-98/01 *Commission v UK* [2003] ECR I-4641.
[128] Case C-367/98 *Commission v Portugal* [2002] ECR I-4731; Case C-483/99 *Commission v France* [2002] ECR I-4781; Case C-503/99 *Commission v Belgium* [2002] ECR I-4809.

This appeared to the Commission to infringe the right to exercise the free movement of capital and freedom of establishment.

14.140 The ECJ decided that the national rules in question constituted per se exceptions to the principle of free movement of capital and consequently to the principle of freedom of establishment. They could be justified only if the objective pursued falls within the ambit of a general or strategic interest and the measures prescribed are based on precise criteria which are known in advance and are open to review by the courts and moreover which cannot be attained by less restrictive measures.

14.141 The judgments do not prohibit the use of golden share arrangements. In some cases, they may be held, subject to two principles set out for their use. The first is that they may no longer be justified only on the grounds that they aid economic performance. The second is that their operation should not be unduly restrictive and should provide legal certainty. But the ECJ did not define what kinds of national interest other than energy supply justify the use of golden shares, leaving loopholes; these may be closed in other rulings on golden shares. In the meantime, these mechanisms can act to shelter corporate managements from market pressures.

(a) The Context: General

14.142 The phenomenon of privatization across the European Union in the 1980s and 1990s has been the source of much comment. In Britain's case, it led to a reduction in the size of the public sector from 12 per cent of GDP in 1979 to 2 per cent in 1997.[129] Other Member States have disposed of telephone companies, airlines, and infrastructure. Between 1990 and 2002, on one calculation, total receipts from privatizations in the EU were about US$675 billion.[130]

14.143 The fact that certain Member States adopted measures to control investment by foreign nationals in their economies prompted the Commission to adopt a Communication in 1997 on certain legal aspects concerning intra-EU investment.[131] This included an interpretation of the relevant Treaty provisions concerning free movement of capital and freedom of establishment, inter alia in the context of procedures for the grant of general authorization or the exercise of a right of veto by public authorities. The analysis contained in that document concluded that discriminatory measures applied exclusively to investors from another EU Member State would be considered incompatible with Articles 73b and 52 EC, while non-discriminatory measures applied to nationals and EU investors alike would be permitted to the extent that they are based upon a set of objective and stable criteria that have been made public. Such criteria have also to be justifiable on the basis

---

[129] 'Special Report on Privatization in Europe', Economist, 29 June 2002, 71.
[130] ibid.
[131] [1997] OJ C220/15.

E. Golden Shares as Barriers

of imperative requirements in the general interest. In all cases, the principle of proportionality has to be respected.

(b) The Context: the Member States Concerned

Portugal In the case of Portugal,[132] the provisions in question were certain laws and regulations concerning privatizations which limit the participation of non-nationals, and which establish a procedure for the grant of prior authorization by the Minister of Finance once the interest of the person acquiring shares in a privatized company exceeds a ceiling of 10 per cent. The principal legal provision was contained in Law No 11/90 that provides in Article 13(3) for limits on foreign holdings in privatized corporations and corresponding methods of control. Penalties for non-compliance include forced sale of shares that exceed the limits set, loss of the voting rights conferred, and nullity of the acquisitions or subscriptions. This provision was the basis for limitations included in many decree-laws on the privatization of certain undertakings. In its submission, the Commission refers to 15 decree-laws providing for a limit on foreign participation ranging from between 5 and 40 per cent in relation to undertakings operating in the banking, insurance, energy, and transport sectors. 14.144

The focus of the Commission action in this case was upon Decree-Laws Nos 380/93 and 65/94 (applicable to the energy sector). Article 1 of Decree-Law No 380/93 provided for prior authorization by the Minister for Financial Affairs for any acquisition of shares representing more than 10 per cent of the voting capital of companies following privatization (or any acquisition which when added to those already held would exceed such a limit). The provision in Decree-Law No 65/90 that attracted the Commission's attention set a ceiling of 25 per cent on the participation by foreign entities in the capital of privatized companies. The Commission argued that Law No 11/90 and the provisions of the two Decree-Laws above were contrary to Articles 52, 56, 58, 73b et seq and 221 EC and to Articles 221 and 231 of the Act of Accession. The latter required the Portuguese Republic to carry out the liberalization of capital movements and invisible transactions according to a timetable. Although the Portuguese Government undertook not to use the possibility of limiting participation by Community investors in future privatizations that Law No 11/90 offered, and claimed that the system established by Decree-Law No 380/93 was applicable without any discrimination based on the nationality of investors, the Commission decided to take action before the ECJ. 14.145

France In the case of France,[133] the Commission noted that Decree No 93-1298 of 1993 vests in the State a 'golden share' in Société Nationale Elf-Aquitaine, a company engaged in supplying France with petroleum products. Through Article 1 14.146

---

[132] Case C-367/98 *Commission v Portugal* [2002] ECR I-4731.
[133] Case C-483/99 *Commission v France* [2002] ECR I-4781.

of this Decree, a golden share is granted to the State in order to protect the national interest. The rights accruing to the State are set out in Article 2 of the Decree. Under this provision, the Minister for Economic Affairs is required, first of all, to approve in advance an acquisition of shares or rights that exceeds established limits on the holding of capital, and secondly the Minister may oppose decisions to transfer shares or use them as security. Finally, two representatives of the State, appointed by decree, are entitled to sit on the board of directors of the company, without voting rights.

14.147 The French Government responded to the Commission's objections by making certain amendments to the above regime in 1999. These were regarded as inadequate by the Commission which then took the case to the ECJ.

14.148 **Belgium** In the case of Belgium,[134] two Royal Decrees were at issue dating from 1994. The first of these, the Royal Decree of 10 June 1994, vested in the State a 'golden share' in Société Nationale de Transport par Canalisations and carried with it the following rights. First, the responsible Minister must be given advance notice of any transfer, use as security, or change in the intended destination of the company's system of lines and conduits that are used or are capable of being used as major infrastructures for the domestic conveyance of energy products. If the Minister considers that such operations adversely affect the national interest in the energy sector, he is entitled to oppose them. Secondly, the Minister may appoint two representatives of the Federal Government to the board of the Company. They may propose to the Minister the annulment of any decision of the board of directors that they regard as contrary to the guidelines for the country's energy policy. This includes government objectives with respect to energy supply.

14.149 The second of the Decrees at issue was the Royal Decree of 16 June 1994 which vested in the State a golden share in Distrigaz, the principal gas transporter and distributor. Through this device the responsible Minister has to be given advance notice of any transfer, use as security, or change in the company's strategic assets, and is entitled to oppose such operations if he considers that they adversely impact upon the national interest in the energy sector. Secondly, the Minister may appoint two representatives of the Federal Government to the board of directors of the company. These representatives may propose to the Minister the annulment of any decision of the board of directors or of the management committee which they regard as contrary to the guidelines for the country's energy policy.

14.150 The Commission argued that the Belgian Government's failure to lay down precise, objective, and permanent criteria for approval of, or opposition to, the operations noted above meant that the Kingdom of Belgium was in breach of its obligations under Articles 43 EC and 56. While the Belgian Government made a number of

---

[134] Case C-503/99 *Commission v Belgium* [2002] ECR I-4809.

E. Golden Shares as Barriers

structural adaptations to the special rights attaching to the golden shares in 1999, these did not in the Commission's view alter the relevant articles in the two Royal Decrees.

(c) The Public Security Argument

14.151 The argument that such golden share arrangements were essential to the fulfilment of public security obligations was advanced in the Belgian case. Any restrictions on freedom of establishment and the free movement of capital which may result from the legislation in question can be justified, it argued, by virtue of (i) the public security exemption laid down in Articles 56 and 73d(1)(b) EC, and (ii) by the overriding requirements of the general interest. These are also proportionate and adequate in relation to the objective pursued by them. An interruption in supplies of natural gas could have a serious effect on public security, given the importance it plays in the economy and essential public services.

14.152 The public security exemption was supported by reference to *Almelo*,[135] with respect to electricity supplies, and *Campus Oil*,[136] with respect to petroleum products. The ECJ accepted that the safeguarding of energy supplies in the event of a crisis fell within the scope of a legitimate public interest.[137] As such, they might justify an obstacle to the free movement of goods. However, the interpretation of public security, as a derogation from the fundamental principle of free movement of capital, has to be strict to ensure that its scope is not determined unilaterally by each Member State without any control by Community institutions. The ECJ noted[138] that it could not be relied upon unless there is 'a genuine and sufficiently serious threat to a fundamental interest of society'.

14.153 In the French case the defence of possible restrictions on the freedom of establishment and the free movement of capital rested on the public security exemption and 'overriding requirements of the general interest'. Specifically, matters of public security justified the right to requisition the crude oil reserves of Société Nationale Elf-Aquitaine located abroad and also the authorization procedures designed to ensure that the central decision-making body of that company remains in France. The availability of supplies of petroleum products in the event of a crisis is guaranteed in this way. In the absence of significant national petroleum reserves, no sectoral measure could be taken to effectively ensure supplies of petroleum products in the event of a crisis.

(d) The Judgments

14.154 The argument of the ECJ was as follows: the EC Treaty prohibits all restrictions on the movement of capital between Member States, and between Member States

---

[135] Case C-393/92 *Gemeente Almelo v Energiebedrijf Ijssellmij NV* [1994] ECR I-1477.
[136] Case 72/83 *Campus Oil Ltd v Minister for Industry and Energy* [1984] ECR 2727.
[137] [2002] ECR I-4809, para 46.
[138] ibid, para 47.

and third countries. Council Directive (EEC) 88/361[139] on the implementation of free movement of capital is designed to define investments in the form of participations constituting movements of capital that are compatible with the provisions of the Treaty.

14.155 With regard to this principle, the ECJ considered whether the 'golden shares' held by each of the three countries meet those requirements, to the extent that they involve:

(1) a prohibition (in Portugal) on the acquisition by nationals of another Member State of more than a given number of shares;

(2) a requirement (in France and Portugal) that prior authorization or notification is to be given where a limit on the number of shares or voting rights held is exceeded;

(3) a right (in France and Belgium) to oppose, *ex post facto*, decisions concerning transfers of shares.

14.156 The ECJ concluded from this analysis that legislation that is liable to impede the acquisition of shares in the undertakings concerned and to dissuade investors in other Member States from investing in the capital of those undertakings may render the free movement of capital illusory, and thus constitutes a restriction on movements of capital. The ECJ then moved on to consider whether these restrictions were permissible.

14.157 The ECJ considered, first, the Portuguese rule providing for the manifestly discriminatory treatment of investors from other Member States. It has the effect of restricting the free movement of capital, and was held to be unlawful.

14.158 Next, the ECJ considered whether the grounds put forward by way of justification for the restrictions in question were acceptable. Such grounds were based on the need to maintain a controlling interest in undertakings operating in areas involving matters of general or strategic interest. In the ECJ's view, the free movement

---

[139] [1998] OJ L178/5. It lists the following movements concerning direct investments and operations in securities that are normally dealt with in the capital market. With respect to the former, this comprises 'establishment and extension of branches or new undertakings belonging solely to the person providing the capital, and the acquisition in full of existing undertakings' and 'participation in new or existing undertakings with a view to establishing or maintaining lasting economic links'. The concept of direct investments is to be understood in its widest sense, according to the explanatory notes at the end of Annex I of the Directive. This means: 'Investments of all kinds by natural persons or commercial, industrial or financial undertakings, and which serve to establish or to maintain lasting and direct links between the person providing the capital and the entrepreneur to whom or the undertaking to which the capital is made available in order to carry on an economic activity'. Moreover, participation by way of direct investment occurs when 'the block of shares held by a natural person or another undertaking or any other holder enables the shareholder, either pursuant to the provisions of natural laws relating to companies limited by shares or otherwise, to participate effectively in the management of the company or in its control'. With respect to transactions in securities on the capital market, operations are defined in the Directive as the 'acquisition by non-residents of domestic securities dealt in on a stock exchange' and 'acquisition by non-residents of domestic securities not dealt in on a stock exchange'.

E. Golden Shares as Barriers

of capital may be restricted only by national rules which fulfil the two-fold criterion of being founded on overriding requirements of the general interest and being proportionate to the objective pursued. In other words, the restriction is permissible where that objective cannot be attained by less restrictive measures and is determined by objective criteria of which the undertakings concerned are aware and which enable them, as appropriate, to contest the decisions adopted by the State.

With respect to the French case, the ECJ noted that although the objective pursued (to guarantee supplies of petroleum products in the event of a crisis) fell within the ambit of a legitimate general interest, the ECJ considered that the measures in question clearly went beyond what is necessary to attain the objective indicated. To the extent that the provisions in question do not indicate the specific, objective circumstances in which prior authorization or a right of opposition *ex post facto* will be granted or refused, they are contrary to the principle of legal certainty. In addition, the ECJ was unable to accept such a lack of precision and such a wide discretionary power, since it constituted a serious impairment of the fundamental principle of the free movement of capital. In July 2002 the French Government announced that it would give up the golden share it had in TotalFinaElf, as required by the ECJ.[140]   **14.159**

In the Belgian case, the ECJ supported the argument based on public security. The ECJ took the view that both the justification put forward for the objective pursued by Belgium (to maintain minimum supplies of gas in the event of a real and serious threat) and the measures prescribed for the attainment of that objective are compatible with the fundamental principles of Community law. No prior approval is required, so the decision-making autonomy of the undertaking is respected. Intervention by the Belgian public authorities in the context of a transfer of installations and the pursuit of management policy is subject to strict time-limits, in accordance with a specific procedure involving a formal statement of reasons that may be the subject of an effective review by the courts. Moreover, the ECJ found that the Commission had not shown that less restrictive measures could have been taken to attain the objective pursued.   **14.160**

The ECJ examined the public security argument in some detail in the Belgian case. The objective of safeguarding energy supplies in the event of a crisis fell undeniably within the scope of a legitimate public interest. The ECJ has in *Campus Oil* recognized that public security considerations may justify an obstacle to the free movement of goods and that this may include the objective of ensuring a minimum supply of petroleum products at all times. The same reasoning applies to the free movement of capital, to the extent that public security is also one of the grounds of justification referred to in Article 73(1)(b) EC.   **14.161**

---

[140] Europe Energy, no 608, 26 July 2002.

14.162 The argument presented in the Portuguese case, that a golden share mechanism can be justified by the need to safeguard the financial interests of the Member State, was rejected by the ECJ. It declared that it is settled case law that such economic grounds (advanced in order to justify a prior authorization procedure) can never serve as a justification for restrictions on the freedom of movement. The ECJ therefore found that the Portuguese measures in question constituted an infringement of the Treaty.

14.163 The ECJ stated in addition that since the legislation at issue involves restrictions on the free movement of capital which are inextricably linked with the obstacles to freedom of establishment to which they gave rise, there was no need for a separate examination of the measures at issue in the light of the Treaty rules on freedom of establishment.

14.164 On the Belgian case, the ECJ stated that even if it were assumed that the protective measures in question may constitute a restriction on freedom of establishment, such a restriction would be justified for the same reasons as those relating to the restriction on the free movement of capital (to secure the objective of guaranteeing energy supplies in the event of a crisis). The Belgian legislation was therefore held to be justified.

(2) The 2003 Judgments

14.165 In May 2003 the ECJ delivered two further judgments on this issue, declaring golden shares in Spain and the UK to be contrary to the free movement of capital. These concerned Repsol (petroleum), Endesa (electricity) and Telefónica (telecoms), and in the UK, the British Airports Authority.

14.166 While all restrictions on the movement of capital between Member States are prohibited under the EC Treaty, the ECJ observed that Member States were justified in having a degree of influence within undertakings that were initially public and subsequently privatized, where those undertakings are active in fields involving the provision of services in the public interest or strategic services. However, such restrictions need to be proportional and so not go beyond what is necessary to attain the objective sought. The ECJ referred to the test for prior administrative approvals set out in the 2002 cases, and assessed the Spanish and UK shares accordingly. It accepted the public security justification for the Spanish shares and endorsed the goal of safeguarding supplies of energy products and the provision of such services in energy and telecoms in the event of a crisis where there is a genuine and sufficiently serious threat to a fundamental social interest.

14.167 There had been a failure to observe the principle of proportionality, however. In particular, the administration has a very broad discretion and it is exercised in an unrestrained manner; investors are not apprised of the specific, objective circumstances in which prior approval will be granted or withheld; and national courts are not provided with precise criteria to review the way in which the authority

F. Conclusions

exercises its discretion. As a result of this decision, and the governments' steps towards compliance, the only Member States with significant industries affected by golden share regimes are Italy and Hungary.

F. Conclusions

The merger control rules discussed in this chapter provide further evidence of the very considerable efforts being made by the Commission to apply competition law in innovative and increasingly strict ways to the context of rapidly consolidating energy markets. The more recent instances of merger control—which have been the focus of this chapter—suggest that much has been learned from the initial wave of mergers in the years up to 2002/03.   14.168

The context remains one that is challenging for the competition authorities, and merger control is of course one instrument that may be brought to bear in support of the liberalization process. It is also one that cannot replace regulation since it deals with incidental concentrations. The use of merger control in future can have little impact on the existing high degree of market concentration in both electricity and gas sectors combined with poor levels of liquidity, which remains a major obstacle. The kind of analysis of mergers that is required by the Commission in energy as in other merger cases is becoming increasingly complex.[141] The most important obstacle remains rooted not in markets but in governments. Member States continue to be attracted to the idea of national champions, as the *E.ON/Endesa* and *E.ON/Ruhrgas* cases illustrate. In other cases, the use of defensive measures by governments is still not excluded, whether golden shares or some alternative measure is used.[142]   14.169

There is plenty of evidence that the concerns about the use of the merger control instrument are acknowledged by the Commission and are being addressed. Examples include the Merger Remedies Study, the review of the Remedies Notice, the policy on assessing non-horizontal mergers, the Sector Review (discussed in Chapter 11), and even the willingness of the Commission to question the operation of the two-thirds rule in the Merger Regulation. Reference can also be made to *ENI/EDP/GDP* in 2005 in which the Commission took a tough line and adopted its first merger prohibition decision in the energy sector (also its first prohibition   14.170

---

[141] There have also been criticisms from the ECJ about the rigour with which the Commission has conducted its competition assessments (see, eg, Case T-464/04 *Impala v Commission*, 13 July 2006). Considerable efforts have been made, however, to increase the role of economic analysis in the preparation of these decisions as one way in which their rigour can be strengthened.

[142] In this context the initial UK approach to a possible takeover by Gazprom of a UK gas company, Centrica, is interesting (a possible prohibition), although it was quickly revised: 'Gazprom warned over Centrica takeover', Financial Times, 2 February 2006.

decision in the merger area since 2002, a year in which it had faced a significant set-back in court due to the annulment of no less than three of its prohibition decisions within a few months).[143] It may also be noted that these are sectors which in the vast majority of Member States have never been open to competition and have long been dominated by incumbent companies. The novelty and the scale of the task cannot therefore be understated.

14.171 In two areas there are respectively causes for concern and for optimism. The first is the continued importance of non-competitive factors in M&A in the electricity and gas sectors. Competition may be central to merger control but it is not the only public policy objective involved. While many of these are legitimate, the overtly political or protectionist aim of establishing a national champion remains a spectre that haunts this particular field of competition law, as several of the above cases demonstrate. The second area of note is the increasing practice of close co-operation between the Commission and NCAs. This is an idea that few would disagree with, but which has developed in a positive way in several cases considered here, including notably the recent *E.ON/MOL* and *DONG/Elsam/E2* cases.

---

[143] *Airtours/First Choice* (Case IV/M.1524) Commission Decision 2000/276/EC, [2000] OJ L93/1; Joined Cases C 12 & 13/03 P *Commission v Tetra Laval BV*, 15 February 2005; *Schneider/Legrand* (Case COMP/M.2283) Commission Decision 2004/275/EC, [2004] OJ L101/1.

15

STATE AID

A. Introduction	15.01	D. Environmental Aid	15.62
B. An Overview of the State Aid Rules	15.04	(1) Promoting Renewable Energy	15.63
C. Liberalization and State Aids	15.10	(a) Germany: *PreussenElektra v*	
(1) Stranded Costs	15.12	*Schleswag* and Overriding	
(a) Commission Response	15.14	Community Interests	15.64
(b) Eligibility of Stranded Costs	15.16	(2) Promoting Biofuels and Wave	
(c) Application of State Aid Rules	15.19	Power	15.73
(d) Financing of Aid to		(3) Climate Change	15.75
Offset Stranded Costs	15.21	E. Aid for Rescue and Restructuring	15.79
(e) Stranded Costs and State Aid	15.24	(1) The *British Energy* Case 2004	15.81
(f) Stranded Costs: Case Studies	15.26	(2) *BNFL* 2006	15.86
(2) State Guarantees: the *EDF* Case	15.56	F. Conclusions	15.90
(3) Public Service Obligations	15.60		

We consider that State aid does not significantly contribute to lasting economic welfare. Experience shows that it rather leads to unfair competition, market distortions, and inefficient allocation of resources.

Philip Lowe, DG of DG Competition, European Commission

A. Introduction

For many years state aid control appeared to have only a minor role to play in the energy sector and especially in the internal market programme. The principal exception was the provision made for 'stranded assets'. This has begun to change. Like the areas of antitrust and merger control, the drivers for change have been partly from the liberalization process in the energy sector and partly from wider changes in thinking about the application of state aid control. Another driver has been the need to accommodate the growing impact of measures taken to promote environmental protection and climate change. As in the other areas of competition law, there is a sense that a stricter approach is now required not only in assessing

15.01

individual cases but in enforcing decisions reached. Moreover, such enforcement is increasingly thought likely to benefit from a greater degree of co-operation with NCAs. A weak point in the enforcement system is that Commission decisions are enforced by Member States under their national procedures, not by Commission departments.

15.02 State aid control is an area that exemplifies the balancing of competing policies that is typical of the energy sector (but not unique to it). The principal task of state aid control is 'to ensure that State intervention does not distort the competitive situation on the market through subsidies and tax exemptions'.[1] However, irrespective of the generally negative view of state aid taken by the Commission, there is a long experience of large amounts of state aid being granted in the energy sector, particularly under the Euratom and now expired ECSC Treaties. Aid has been channelled to the energy sector by means of preferential tariffs and long-term contracts. During the period of market liberalization, there are two kinds of situation in which the grant of state aid has appeared to be justified. The first of these is when aid is deemed to be necessary to counter-balance adverse effects of liberalization. The second is when aid is granted with the objective of supporting the development of renewable and environmentally friendly energy. There are however other areas, such as aid for the rescue and restructuring of failing companies, that require a more careful approach to the balancing of competing policy objectives.

15.03 In this chapter the rules are reviewed, as are the various guidelines for their application. There are no guidelines explicitly addressed to the energy sector but indirectly several are highly relevant: the guidelines on environmental aid and those on rescue and restructuring aid, for example. In some circumstances, the guidelines on regional aid may also be relevant.[2] However, in contrast to antitrust and merger control, there has not yet been a sweeping overhaul of existing rules and practices in the interests of 'modernization' or greater efficiency, although steps in that direction are underway. Indeed, the approach has been deliberately one in which incremental change has been the goal, in part by updating various sets of regulations and guidelines as they

---

[1] European Commission, *XXXIInd Report on Competition Policy* 2002, 19.
[2] Guidelines on national regional aid [1998] OJ C74/9, as amended in [2000] OJ C258/5. These are under revision, with a draft set of guidelines adopted in 2006 for implementation from 1 January 2007: Guidelines on national regional aid for 2007–2013 [2006] OJ C54/13. An example of regional aid in the energy sector is the aid in the form of grants and accelerated depreciation given by Greece to three newly formed natural gas distribution companies in Attica, Thessaloniki, and Thessaly (Case NN 90/2000, [2001] OJ C333/8). The purpose of the aid was to promote the introduction of gas as a mainstream energy source. The aid measures had clear benefits for the whole region and the aid intensity was below the maximum aid intensities allowed under the Greek regional aid map. The Commission noted that the introduction of natural gas in Greece would provide an additional energy source which would enhance competition and result in lower prices for consumers, as well as creating jobs and having environmental benefits.

come up for renewal.[3] In the following sections the diverse energy activities that have been affected by state aid control measures are examined, dealing first with the impact of liberalization; secondly, with environmental protection issues such as renewable energy support measures and climate change; and finally, the role of state aid in rescue and restructuring attempts for energy companies.

B. An Overview of the State Aid Rules

15.04 The rules governing state aid control are set out in Articles 87 to 89 of the EC Treaty. Any aid granted by a Member State or through state resources in any form whatsoever which distorts or threatens to distort competition by favouring certain undertakings or the production of certain goods is prohibited under Article 87(1), in so far as such aid affects trade between Member States. Such aid shall be declared incompatible with the common market. However, three kinds of aid are deemed to be compatible with the common market under Article 87(2). These automatic exemptions are:

- aid that has a social character and is granted to individual consumers, on condition that such aid is granted without discrimination as to the origin of the products concerned;
- aid to remedy damage caused by natural disasters or exceptional occurrences; and
- aid granted to the economy of certain areas of the Federal Republic of Germany affected by the division of Germany, to compensate for the economic disadvantages caused by that division.

15.05 Article 87(3) lists forms of aid from (a) to (e) that may be compatible with the common market. These discretionary exceptions include:

(a) aid to promote the economic development of areas where the standard of living is abnormally low or where there is serious unemployment;
(b) aid to promote the execution of a project of common European interest or to remedy a serious disturbance in the economy of a Member State;
(c) aid to facilitate the development of certain economic activities or certain economic areas, to the extent that such aid does not adversely affect trading conditions in a manner contrary to the common interest;
(d) aid to promote culture and heritage conservation;

---

[3] eg, the new block exemption adopted in October 2006: Commission Press Release IP/06/1453, 'State aid: Commission simplifies procedures for approving regional aid with new block exemption Regulation', 24 October 2006, and the revised draft 'de minimis' rules adopted in December 2006 on the exemption of small subsidies from the notification obligation under the EC Treaty state aid rules.

(e) such other categories of aid as may be specified by decision of the Council acting by a qualified majority on a proposal from the Commission.

Other categories of aid may be specified from time to time by a Council decision on a proposal from the Commission.

15.06 For state support to be classifiable as state aid, it needs to meet the following criteria: it must be selective (it favours certain undertakings or the production of certain goods or services); it must confer a competitive advantage on its beneficiary; it must have an actual or potential effect on trade between Member States; it must distort or threaten to distort competition; and it must involve state resources. The prohibition in Article 87(1) is not confined to any particular form of state aid and, if indeed a particular aid measure is classifiable as state aid, it is not necessarily prohibited (see Article 87(2) and (3)). The Commission has the exclusive competence to decide on the applicability to a particular measure of one of the exemptions in Article 82(3), but has no discretion in the application of the exceptions in Article 87(2).

15.07 The procedure for reviewing state aid is set out in Article 88 and provision for making implementing regulations by the Council is made in Article 89. The oversight requirement imposed upon the Commission under Article 88(1) is extensive. It is required to keep under constant review all systems of aid in the Member States, and to do so in co-operation with them. The Commission has to be informed of any plans to grant or alter aid, in sufficient time to enable it to submit its comments (Article 88(3)). If the Commission decides that the aid is not compatible with the common market, the Member State has to abolish it or it may be referred to the ECJ.

15.08 There have been many consultations about possible improvement in the rules in recent years. In 2005 a State Aid Action Plan was presented by the Commission, which set out a roadmap for a comprehensive reform of state aid control. One of the notable hallmarks of this was to ensure that the design of rules was to be grounded in a rigorous economic analysis, focusing on the market failures that state aid is intended to rectify, and strengthening the transparency and predictability of state aid policy. Further, in April 2006 the Commission published the results of a study into the enforcement of state aid rules at national level.[4] In particular, it addressed the following two issues: the role of national courts in protecting companies against the granting of illegal aid to their competitors; and the execution of the Commission's recovery decisions by Member States. It found a trend towards reliance by companies on state aid rules to defend themselves in national courts against financial burdens imposed on them by the state. This activism was reflected in the number of published state aid judgments by national courts which

---

[4] The final report is available at <http://europa.eu.int/comm/competition/state_aid/others>. It covers only the EU-15 Member States.

had tripled between 1999 and 2005 (from 116 to 357). However, it also found that companies rarely use state aid rules as an instrument to challenge the distortion of competition caused by unlawful subsidies granted to competitors. Private actions remain very unusual. More than 50 per cent of the judgments concern cases in which taxpayers defended themselves against the allegedly discriminatory imposition of a tax burden. In only 6 per cent of cases were national courts asked to decide on the grant of allegedly illegal state aid in actions filed by a competitor against a beneficiary. By the end of 2005 there was no evidence of a single judgment of a national court awarding damages to a competitor. The study also found that the Commission's decisions with respect to the recovery of illegal aid needed to be accelerated by Member States. In some cases the aid-granting authority is also entitled to the recovery and so lacks motivation to claim back the aid it has unlawfully granted.

The expiry of the ECSC Treaty means that the Commission may now take decisions with respect to the compatibility of state aid granted or put into effect without prior Commission approval after the expiry of the ECSC Treaty. The criteria to be applied are guided by the Commission Notice on the determination of the applicable rules for the assessment of unlawful state aid[5] (see paras 8.10–8.26). **15.09**

C. Liberalization and State Aids

Before and during the initial phase of liberalization there was some concern about the immediate effects of the transition from a largely state-controlled, monopolistic system to a market one. The possibility that investments made during the pre-liberalization period would become uneconomic in a liberalized market created some pressure for the establishment of transitional measures in the first Electricity and Gas Directives.[6] The regime established for electricity was set out in Article 24 of the first Electricity Directive but was not included in the current Electricity Directive.[7] The counterpart regime in the first Gas Directive concerned take-or-pay contracts and although it has survived in the current Gas Directive,[8] it has never been put to use. The Article 24 regime did, however, become operational and raised a number of questions with respect to state aids, which the Commission addressed by means of tests in a specially designed methodology. **15.10**

---

[5] [2002] OJ C119/22.
[6] Directive (EC) 96/92 concerning common rules for the internal market in electricity [1997] OJ L27/20; Directive(EC) 98/30 concerning common rules for the internal market in natural gas [1998] OJ L204/1.
[7] Directive (EC) 2003/54 concerning common rules for the internal market in electricity and repealing Directive (EC) 96/92 [2003] OJ L176/37.
[8] Directive (EC) 2003/55 concerning common rules for the internal market in natural gas and repealing Directive (EC) 98/30 [2003] OJ L176/57.

Chapter 15: State Aid

15.11 The stranded costs methodology is of interest since it has been used by the Commission in a considerable number of cases, even though it would appear that applications cannot be made for investments that become uneconomic after 1 July 2004. It has been used in state aid cases involving stranded assets in Hungary and Poland since their accession to the EU in 2004, and is likely to influence Commission thinking in the future. In the sections below the problem of stranded costs is discussed, as is the Commission's response, and the practice established over a range of decisions since liberalization began. Two other issues relevant to the liberalization process are then discussed: the role of state guarantees and the impact of the ECJ ruling in the *Altmark* case.

(1) Stranded Costs

15.12 The device of a transitional regime in the first Electricity Directive represented an attempt to manage a problem familiar in liberalizing electricity markets. The costs of some prior investments, principally in generating plants, may be unrecoverable or 'stranded' in the transition to a competitive pricing regime. Generation from old coal-fired plant, for example, cannot compete with electricity generated from gas-fired power stations constructed as a result of the introduction of competition under the Directive. 'Stranded' costs or assets involve past investments in plant and equipment and power purchases made by utilities to meet estimated customer needs, often required under a public service obligation (PSO), but subsequently stranded as a result of the liberalization process in the markets. New market entrants, which have not been subject to the same PSO to meet customer needs, have no such costs and therefore enjoy an inequitable competitive advantage. Stranded costs impose a significant financial burden on incumbent electricity utilities. Examples of their liabilities include long-term power purchase contracts, investment based on a guaranteed market for output, or investment beyond the scope of normal business.

15.13 Although this was acknowledged to be a temporary problem at the time, it provoked considerable controversy. Part of the EU's mechanism to address this thorny issue was the transitional regime provision in Article 24 of the first Electricity Directive, although the term 'stranded assets'—(or any variation thereon)—is not expressly mentioned in that text. The other part was the development of a set of criteria to assess proposed aid to offset undertakings' stranded costs.

(a) Commission Response

15.14 The Commission and Member States agreed that a methodology for the examination of state aid granted to electricity companies should be prepared and that all of the schemes for financial compensation notified should be assessed according to this methodology. In this way, it was hoped that all financial measures of compensation would be assessed in a coherent and equitable manner. Essentially, such a methodology would provide that aid aimed at compensating stranded costs could be

C. Liberalization and State Aids

authorized by a Member State, on condition that the costs result from 'well identified and quantified historical commitments that can no longer be honoured in the context of liberalization'.[9] In such circumstances, aid could be granted since it would facilitate the transition to a competitive electricity market.

A Communication on the Methodology for Analysing State Aid Linked to Stranded Costs was published by the Commission in July 2001.[10] This replaced a draft memorandum on stranded costs published two years earlier.[11] The Communication (or Notice) was intended to clarify how the Commission intended in the light of Directive (EC) 96/92 to apply the rules of the EC Treaty to state aid of this kind. It is broadly in two parts: the first is concerned with the definition of eligible stranded costs, and the second explains the conditions under which eligible stranded costs may be offset by aid in ways that the Commission would deem compatible with the provisions of Article 87(3)(c) EC. 15.15

(b) Eligibility of Stranded Costs

In the Notice, stranded costs are described as 'commitments or guarantees of operation . . . that it might no longer be possible to honour on account of Directive 96/92/EC'.[12] Liabilities include long-term power purchase contracts, investments undertaken with an implicit or explicit guarantee of sale, or investments undertaken outside the scope of normal activity. The Notice sets out specific criteria that would be applied for possible classification of commitments or guarantees as eligible stranded costs. The criteria are the following: 15.16

(1) Commitments or guarantees of operation must pre-date 19 February 1999, the date of entry into force of Directive (EC) 96/92.[13]
(2) The existence and validity of such commitments or guarantees must be substantiated in terms of the underlying legal and contractual provisions and legislative context in which they were made.
(3) A risk must be created in relation to such commitments and guarantees of operation that they will not be honoured as a result of the application of Directive (EC) 96/92. This applies particularly where the viability of the undertakings

---

[9] ibid 16–17.
[10] European Commission, 'Commission Communication relating to the methodology for analysing State aid linked to stranded costs', 25 July 2001; see Commission Press Release IP/01/1077: 'Commission adopts document on "Methodology for analysing state aid linked to stranded costs" in the electricity sector'. The methodology for stranded costs does not prejudice the application of the guidelines on regional aid, in the regions covered by Art 87(3)(a): [1998] OJ C74/9; it applies independently of whether the undertakings are in public or private ownership.
[11] European Commission, 'Communication relating to the Methodology for analysing State aid linked to stranded costs', 25 July 2001.
[12] ibid 2–3.
[13] ibid, para 3.1. The numbering in this list follows the paragraph numbering in the Commission document. All refernces to 'the Directive' are to the first Electricity Directive.

may be in jeopardy in the absence of aid or any transitional measures (this criterion was further elaborated by the Commission—see para 15.18 below).

(4) The commitments or guarantees must be irrevocable. If, therefore, an undertaking has a possibility of revoking against payment, or of modifying such commitments or guarantees, account will be taken of this in calculating the eligible stranded costs.

(5) Commitments or guarantees that link enterprises belonging to one and the same group cannot usually be eligible as stranded costs.

(6) Stranded costs are economic costs that must correspond to the actual sums invested, paid, or payable because of the commitments or guarantees from which they result. This means that 'flat-rate' calculations will not be accepted unless they can be shown to reflect economic realities.

(7) Stranded costs must be costs net of the income, profits, or added value associated with the commitments or guarantees from which they arise.

(8) Stranded costs must be valued net of any aid that has been paid or is payable in respect of the assets to which they relate. Where a commitment or guarantee of operation corresponds to an investment that is the subject of state aid, the value of the aid must be deducted from any stranded costs resulting from the commitment or guarantee.

(9) Calculation of eligible stranded costs has to take account of the actual change over time in the economic and competitive conditions prevailing on the national and EU electricity markets. This applies whenever stranded costs arise from commitments or guarantees that are difficult to honour on account of the application of the Directive. In cases where stranded costs have arisen because of a foreseeable fall in electricity prices, calculation of the stranded costs must take account of actual movements in electricity prices.

(10) Stranded costs must not include costs that have been depreciated before the transposition of the Electricity Directive into national law. However, provisions or depreciation of assets that have been entered into the balance sheet of the undertaking concerned may be included, where they have the explicit aim of taking account of foreseeable effects of the Directive.

(11) Eligible stranded costs must not exceed the minimum level necessary to allow the undertakings concerned to honour or secure compliance with the commitments or guarantees that have been called into question by the application of the Directive. This means that for long-term contracts of sale or purchase, the stranded costs will be calculated by comparison with the conditions under which in a liberalized market the undertaking would normally have been able to sell or purchase the relevant product. The calculation of stranded costs will have to take into account the most economic solution (in the absence of any aid) from the standpoint of the undertakings concerned. As a result, this may lead to the termination of commitments or guarantees that give rise to

C. Liberalization and State Aids

stranded costs or to the disposal of all or some of the assets that give rise to stranded costs.

(12) Costs that have to be borne by certain undertakings after the date of full market liberalization (the date given is 18 February 2006), are not to constitute eligible stranded costs. However, this is somewhat softened in application. The Commission may take these commitments and guarantees of operation into account and consider them as eligible stranded costs during the next stage of market-opening. In addition, where a failure to honour commitments or guarantees after this date might give rise to major risks concerning protection of the environment, public safety, social protection of workers, or network security, such commitments or guarantees are eligible for treatment as stranded costs. Other stranded costs eligible under this methodology, which may extend beyond 2006, are not affected by the above consideration.

15.17 The criterion in point 12 above is qualified by the declaration that the Commission may agree to classify some costs as eligible stranded costs where the undertakings that have to bear them do so after 18 February 2006, if such costs follow from commitments or guarantees that meet the definitional criteria listed above and are limited to a period not extending beyond 31 December 2010. This applies only to those Member States that open up their market more quickly than the first Electricity Directive required.

15.18 For the provision in point 3 to be operational, the commitments or guarantees that run the risk of not being honoured because of the Directive's application must subsequently become non-economic due to the Directive's effects and must 'significantly affect the competitiveness of the undertaking concerned'.[14] This means that the undertaking must make accounting entries designed to reflect the foreseeable impact of the commitment or guarantee. In addition, when assessing the effects of such commitments or guarantees on the competitiveness or viability of the undertakings concerned, the Commission will do so at what it calls the 'consolidated level'. Eligibility for stranded costs is dependent on the establishment of a cause-and-effect relationship between the entry into force of the Directive and the difficulty that the undertakings concerned may have in honouring or securing compliance with the relevant commitments or guarantees. When the Commission is attempting to establish whether such a cause-and-effect relationship exists, it will take into account any fall in electricity prices or loss of market share experienced by the undertakings concerned. Where commitments or guarantees could not have been honoured irrespective of the Directive entering into force, such commitments or guarantees are not to be eligible as stranded costs.

---

[14] ibid, para 3.3.

(c) Application of State Aid Rules

15.19 In cases where aid is proposed to offset eligible stranded costs, the Commission will have to decide whether the aid in question is compatible with Article 87(3)(c) EC. In doing so, it will seek to ascertain if the aid has satisfied the following criteria:

(1) The aid must be used to offset eligible stranded costs that have been clearly determined and isolated. It may under no circumstances exceed the amount of eligible stranded costs.

(2) The arrangements made for payment of aid must make allowance for future developments in competition—measured by the use of quantifiable factors such as prices, market shares, or other relevant factors indicated by the Member State. The amount of aid paid will vary over time according to the development of competition. The calculation of aid paid over time must also take into account changes in the relevant factors to assess the degree of competition achieved.

(3) The Member State must undertake to deliver an annual report to the Commission, describing developments in the competitive situation in its electricity market and do so by indicating, inter alia, changes observed in the relevant quantifiable factors. The report must also provide details of how the stranded costs taken into account for the relevant year have been calculated, and must specify amounts paid.

(4) The 'degressive' character of aid proposed is to be viewed favourably by the Commission when making its assessment, on the grounds inter alia that this will assist the undertaking concerned to accelerate its preparations for a liberalized market in electricity.

(5) The maximum amount of aid that may be paid to an undertaking to offset stranded costs must be specified in advance. It must take account of productivity gains that may be achieved by the undertaking.

(6) It is also a requirement that the detailed arrangements for calculating and financing aid and the maximum period for which such aid can be granted must be clearly set out in advance. When the aid is notified it should in particular specify how the calculation of stranded costs will take account of changes in the various factors set out in (2) above.

(7) The Member State must undertake in advance not to pay any rescue or restructuring aid to undertakings that are to benefit from aid for stranded costs. The idea is to avoid any accumulation of aid. The thinking behind this is that the payment of compensation linked to investments in stranded assets that offer no prospects of long-term viability will not facilitate the transition to a liberalized electricity market and so cannot qualify for a derogation under Article 87(3)(c) EC.

15.20 A further assessment factor (but not included in the Commission's list of criteria) is the size and level of interconnection of the network concerned and of the structure of the electricity industry. In this context, aid that is to be granted to a small network with

C. Liberalization and State Aids

a low degree of interconnection with the rest of the EU will be viewed more favourably since it will be less likely to give rise to substantial distortions of competition.

(d) Financing of Aid to Offset Stranded Costs

15.21 While the choice of method of financing aid designed to offset stranded costs is a matter left to the Member States, the Commission had to ensure that the method chosen did not give rise to effects that conflict with the objectives of the Electricity Directive or with the Community interest. It defined the latter as taking into account, inter alia, interests relating to consumer protection, free movement of goods and services, and competition. An example of such a conflict would be aid that deterred outside undertakings or new players from entering certain national or regional markets. It would not be acceptable to finance aid to offset stranded costs from levies on electricity in transit between Member States or from levies linked to the distance between producer and consumer.[15]

15.22 Linked to the liberalizing aims of the first Electricity Directive, there was also a concern that any arrangements for financing aid intended to offset stranded costs would result in fair treatment for eligible and non-eligible consumers. The Commission therefore requires that the annual report provide a breakdown by eligible and non-eligible consumers of the sources of finance that are intended to offset the stranded costs.[16] If non-eligible consumers participate in the financing of stranded costs directly through the tariff for electricity purchase, this is to be stated clearly. The contribution to the financing by either eligible or non-eligible customers must not exceed the proportion of stranded costs to be offset that corresponds to the market share accounted for by those customers.

15.23 Finally, the Commission noted that where funds are raised by private undertakings to finance aid mechanisms designed to offset stranded costs, a separation is required between the management of those funds and the normal resources of the undertakings. The investments should not benefit the undertakings that manage them.

(e) Stranded Costs and State Aid

15.24 The overall aim of the Commission in approving state aid corresponding to eligible stranded costs is to facilitate the transition to a competitive electricity market. For several reasons, the Commission takes the view that aid designed to offset stranded costs:

> ... normally qualifies for the derogation under Article 87(3)(c) if it facilitates the development of certain economic activities without adversely affecting trading conditions to an extent contrary to the common interest.[17]

---

[15] [1998] OJ C74/9.
[16] See Albers, M, 'Energy Liberalization and EC Competition Law' in *International Antitrust Law & Policy: Fordham Corporate Law 2001* (2002) 393–421.
[17] ibid 6.

15.25 Among the reasons justifying this view are the following.

- If the distortion to competition that inevitably results is one that is counterbalanced by a contribution made to achieving a Community objective that could not be achieved by market forces alone, then the Commission is prepared to view it favourably.
- In addition, the aid granted for stranded costs enables electricity undertakings to reduce the risks relating to their historic commitments or investments, increasing the likelihood that they will maintain their investments in the long term.
- Without compensation for stranded costs there is a risk that the undertakings concerned might pass on the entire cost of their non-economic commitments or guarantees to their captive customers.
- Aid to compensate for stranded costs in the electricity industry can be justified in relation to other sectors such as telecommunications by the fact that liberalization has not been accompanied by either a speedier technological progress or by increased demand.
- It is also not conceivable to wait until electricity undertakings encounter difficulties before taking a decision on whether to grant them support. Relevant considerations here are environmental protection, security of supply, and the smooth running of the EU economy.

(f) Stranded Costs: Case Studies

15.26 **Austria** The Austrian Government notified two schemes with a transitional regime limited until 31 December 2009. They concerned:

(1) guarantees of operation given to power plants based on the authorization procedure in operation prior to liberalization, and restricted to three hydropower plants in Freudenau, Mittlere Salzach, and Kraftwerksete Obere Drau, with stranded costs estimated at 6.27 billion Schilling (ATS); and

(2) long-term procurement contracts for indigenous lignite for the Voitsberg power plant belonging to Verbundgesellschaft, amounting to estimated stranded costs of ATS 2.43 billion. The mechanism for payments is a levy on power consumption.

15.27 In July 2001 the Commission concluded that the proposed compensation for hydropower plants would comply with its Methodology and might therefore be authorized under Article 87(3)(c) EC. The notified claims for compensation for the lignite plant might benefit from an authorization as a compensation for a service of general economic interest as regards security of supply, under Article 86(2) (and in the light of Articles 3(2) and 8(4) of Directive (EC) 96/92).[18]

---

[18] Commission Press Release IP/01/1079, 'Commission gives green light to "stranded costs" compensation by Spain, Austria and The Netherlands', 27 July 2001; Commission Decision 1999/795/EC, [1999] OJ L319/30.

C. Liberalization and State Aids

Belgium The state aid notified by the Belgian authorities was designed to offset the financial impact of commitments entered into by the electricity generators and distributors or imposed on them when the electricity market was regulated and which were impossible to fulfil once liberalization had begun.[19] It comprised three parts: the dismantling of experimental nuclear sites, a pension scheme for employees in the electricity sector, and the promotion of renewable energy sources and energy conservation. 15.28

The Commission decision explained how the criteria in the Methodology would be applied to the three parts of the measure, but no final decision was taken since the Belgian Government was requested to provide further information, and until it did so no decision could be taken. 15.29

With respect to the first part of the scheme—the dismantling of nuclear sites for which the electricity utilities have been jointly responsible since 1990—it concluded that the compensation proposed to be granted to Electrabel and SPE would be compatible with the criteria set out in points 4.1 to 4.3 of the Methodology. The second part of the scheme, concerning pensions for employees in the electricity industry, was not likely to be compatible however. The funds previously set aside by the two companies were not sufficient to cover the transfer in the financing of their employees' pensions from a pay-as-you-earn scheme to a capitalization scheme, so the State should offset part of the burden. The commitments given by the companies to the employees were non-specific; the arrangement did not appear to be limited in time; the compensation was not modulated according to trends in market prices for electricity and the foreseeable productivity gains of the undertakings concerned. This was incompatible with points 3.12, 4.1, and 4.5 of the Methodology. The third part concerned the promotion of renewable energy sources and rational energy use. This was to be financed by setting a price for electricity end-users higher than the market price. The Commission concluded that this did not involve state aid, in line with the *PreussenElektra* case law. 15.30

The Commission's response was to seek further information from the Belgian authorities about, inter alia, why the part of the measure relating to employees' pensions is deemed to involve a stranded cost that would be eligible under the methodology, how the method of calculating the compensatory amounts for stranded costs was to be justified, and what period was covered by the payment of the compensatory amounts. No response appears to have been received. 15.31

Denmark The Danish Government notified three types of commitments for transitional regimes.[20] They were: 15.32

(1) take-or-pay gas contracts with Dangas, with a stranded cost estimated at 993 million Kroner (DKK);

---

[19] [2002] OJ C222/2.
[20] Commission Decision 1999/798/EC, [1999] OJ L319/47.

(2) closure of 30 or so power plants by 2025, with total stranded costs amounting to DKK 2.75 billion; and

(3) pension obligations of municipal utilities, with stranded costs estimated at DKK 600–700 million.

The mechanism for recovery proposed by the Danish Government was a surcharge on electricity consumption.

15.33 **France** In its submission, the French Government proposed several transitional measures to the Commission.[21] These included:

(1) contracts for electricity purchase when they concern electricity purchase by the 'peak' independent producers, amounting to 250 million Francs (FF) a year until 2012; and

(2) commitments linked to the Superphoenix fast breeder reactor, amounting to FF 12.7 billion.

The Government envisaged a recovery method based on a fund made up of a contribution payable by all users, and based on consumption. In addition, it proposed transitional measures for commitments linked to the financing of the special pension scheme for electricity and gas employees, for which EDF had made neither reserve nor estimate.

15.34 **Greece** Compensation was allowed to the Greek electricity utility, PPC, which covered its costs arising from power stations that were unprofitable in a liberalized market.[22] Prior to liberalization, the costs had been recoverable under a regime in which prices were fixed on an ad hoc basis by the Government. The compensation is to be paid until 2015 and adjusted on an annual basis to the actual amount of PPC's costs subject to a ceiling of €929 million.

15.35 A further element was allowed under the Methodology: compensation that the Government had paid to PPC for water resource management and irrigation work involved in the plant construction, which the Government had imposed on PPC, up to €324 million. An element of compensation by the Government for losses arising from a power sales agreement was not regarded as aid to PPC which was not the ultimate beneficiary of the compensation.

15.36 **Hungary** Like Poland, Hungary had concluded a number of Power Purchase Agreements (PPAs) in the 1990s on very favourable terms with investors to stimulate modernization of its electricity sector. The contracts were entered into by MVM Rt, the fully state-owned monopoly network operator, with electricity generating companies. MVM Rt was obliged to purchase a fixed quantity of electricity at a

---

[21] Commission Decision 1999/792/EC, [1999] OJ L319/6.
[22] Case N 133/01, [2003] OJ C9/6.

C. Liberalization and State Aids

fixed price, which guaranteed it a return on investment to the generators without any risk. The PPAs are scheduled to expire between 2010 and 2020. Since they cover about 80 per cent of the electricity generation market, they constitute a serious potential obstacle to the liberalization of the market.

The Commission takes the view that the compatibility of the PPAs with state aid rules and its Methodology is doubtful.[23] The Commission therefore opened a formal investigation into whether the PPAs are likely to cause undue distortion of competition. **15.37**

The Commission's use of the Methodology in the preliminary stage of this case was extensive. It drew on the criteria in assessing whether the PPAs themselves might constitute state aid to the generators (in addition to another compensation payment granted directly by the Hungarian State to MVM, on the basis of a government decree on stranded costs). While the Hungarian authorities emphasized that the PPAs had the objectives of modernization of the network, adaptation to new environmental objectives, and the preservation of security of supply on the electricity market, the Commission noted that 'the liberalization of the electricity sector has indeed to be achieved in a balanced way that preserves them' (that is, these objectives) that 'are also objectives recognised by the Community'.[24] Precisely for this reason—the need for balance between objectives—and in contrast to other liberalizing sectors, the grant of state aid may be allowed to companies in the electricity sector to achieve a smooth transition to a liberalized market. However, the Methodology constitutes the set of rules and constraints that are appropriate to ensure that a level playing field is the result. The Commission's conclusion was that there were serious doubts that the state aid granted to the electricity generators through the PPAs fulfilled the conditions of the Methodology. **15.38**

The distorting effect of PPAs on competition is considerable. They have the effect of forcing one of the parties to purchase its electricity from the other party, no matter how offers develop from competitors. Indeed, they go so far as to eliminate competition for a certain quantity of supply. In Hungary's case, where the PPAs cover more than 80 per cent of the electricity generated, the limitation has the effect that liberalization has almost no impact on the market for electricity generation. As a result, the balance in the Methodology is altered between the positive and negative effects of state aid in the form of grants for compensation for stranded costs. Indeed, the idea that state aid should be granted in order to compensate in a proportional way for the effects of liberalization is violated by the PPAs, which **15.39**

---

[23] Case NN 49/2005 *Hungarian stranded costs*, [2005] OJ C324/12; Commission Press Release IP/05/1407, 'State aid: Commission opens formal investigation into long term power purchase agreements in Hungary', 10 November 2005.
[24] ibid 13.

Chapter 15: State Aid

undermine liberalization in practice. The Commission also identified concerns about the accounting grant equivalent in relation to points 3.3, 3.4, 3.6, 3.8, and 3.11 of its Methodology. Finally, it noted point 4.1 that the aid may not exceed the amount of eligible stranded costs and point 4.5 where the maximum amount of aid needs to be specified in advance. The Commission's practice is that a maximum should be fixed *ex ante* for the total amount of aid to be granted. There are some difficulties in applying this to PPAs, but a cap on the state aid to be paid for stranded costs compensations should be reflected at least by a cap on the price to be paid under the PPAs. In this case it was doubted whether a cap did in fact exist. In its concluding remarks, the Commission stated that 'PPAs may be by nature incompatible with the Methodology'.[25]

15.40 **Italy** Two cases have arisen involving Italy: the first concerned ENEL and the second AEM Torino. With respect to the former, the Commission adopted a decision on two aspects of state aid for compensation of stranded costs.[26] It covered the costs for power generation plants constructed before 1997 and the costs linked to a 'take-or-pay' contract for the import of LNG from Nigeria, signed by ENEL in 1992, for the part that was used to generate electricity.

15.41 The state aid for the power generation plants covered the period 2000–03. After this period, generators would no longer be entitled to receive compensation for their stranded costs. At most the compensation would be €850 million and would be granted to ENEL and the companies that have inherited ENEL's stranded assets. The second part of the aid covered costs incurred by ENEL because the company was not able to process the gas in Italy, as it had originally planned. It would cover the costs of relocating gas processing outside Italy until 2009. The amount of compensation was set at a maximum of €1,465 million. The compensation was to be granted exclusively for the gas used in the generation of electricity.

15.42 The Commission concluded that the compensation did not involve more than the repayment of initial investments and that a proper mechanism for regularly adapting compensation was introduced to prevent overcompensation, even where competition did not evolve as expected.

15.43 The second case involved AEM Torino, a local utility company that generates, distributes, and sells electricity and heating.[27] The municipality of Turin owns 70 per cent of the company. Italy proposed to grant aid to AEM Torino to compensate for stranded costs in the electricity sector that have arisen from the liberalization process.

---

[25] ibid 18.
[26] Case N 490/2000, [2005] OJ C250/10; European Commission, *Report on Competition Policy 2004*, Vol I, 131–2.
[27] Commission Press Release IP/06/451, 'State aid: Commission opens investigation into Italy's plans to grant aid to AEM Torino for stranded costs', 5 April 2006.

C. Liberalization and State Aids

The amount of the aid is approximately €16 million. In contrast to previous decisions by the Commission based on the Methodology, including the one involving ENEL, this case is the first that concerns a local utility company. The application of the Methodology in this case is as yet unclear since an outstanding issue concerns the repayment of state aid which AEM Torino and other municipal utilities illegally received and have failed to repay. In such circumstances, when assessing the compatibility of new aid, the Commission has to take into account the fact that the beneficiaries may not have complied with earlier Commission decisions that required them to reimburse previous illegal and incompatible aid.[28] The Commission opened an investigation into the case in April 2006.

Luxembourg A scheme proposed by the Government concerned a long-term power supply agreement between RWE and the incumbent distribution company and TSO, Cegedel.[29] The bulk of Cegedel's supply is met by the agreement with RWE, and Cegedel supplied about 70 per cent of the country's power supply. The Government sought approval of a transitional regime until 31 December 2000. The Commission rejected its request on the grounds that the agreement did not include a take-or-pay obligation for Cegedel and allowed for regular adjustments. Faced with a situation in which eligible customers chose to switch suppliers, Cegedel was able to adapt its supplies from RWE. This was a situation characterized by normal commercial risk rather than stranded assets and so the proposed compensation was unjustified. 15.44

Netherlands The Dutch Government notified four transitional measures in two stages. They comprised the following:[30] 15.45

- recovery of the losses on some district heating projects until 2021, amounting to between 1.628 and 2.0 billion Guilder (NLG);
- recovery of extra costs of construction and operation of Demoklec (demonstration coal gasification plant) in Buggenum, with stranded costs amounting to a maximum of NLG 550 million;
- a Protocol agreement concluded between Dutch generators and distributors up to and including 2000, with no estimate of the financial consequences of repeal of the Protocol for the generators; and
- international commitments, or recovery of possible losses from power procurement contracts between SEP, the Dutch electricity utility, and EDF, Preussen-Elektra, and Statkraft, from investment obligations of SEP to Statnett for the NorNed cable, and from a take-or-pay gas contract between SEP and Statoil.

---

[28] Case C-355/95 P *Textilwerke Deggendorg GmbH (TWD) v Commission* [1997] ECR I-2549.
[29] Commission Decision 1999/793/EC, [1999] OJ L319/12.
[30] Commission Press Release IP/01/1079, 'Commission gives green light to "stranded costs" compensation by Spain, Austria and The Netherlands', 27 July 2001; Commission Decision 1999/796/EC, [1999] OJ L319/34.

15.46 In the latter case, the amount of the costs depended on the evolution of gas and electricity prices in the liberalizing market, but was expected to be in the range of NLG 3.1 billion at 7 cents/kWh to NLG 4.6 billion at 5 cents/kWh. Originally, the mechanism for recovery of the stranded costs in each case, except for the Protocol scheme, was through a levy on transport tariffs. Cancellation of the Protocol might lead to a new one being imposed on the parties by the Dutch Minister of Economic Affairs, which he is entitled to do. Initially, the Netherlands had proposed two other transitional schemes, which were subsequently withdrawn. The two schemes concerned:

(1) the delay of privatization of the electricity sector, where express agreement of the Minister is necessary for the sale of shares outside the circle of existing shareholders until the end of 2001; and
(2) the phasing-in of corporation tax to keep pace with the liberalization process.

15.47 The Commission took the view that neither of these proposals could be seen as falling within the scope of Article 24 of the Directive. In June 2001 the Dutch Government withdrew the financing mechanism by means of a levy from its notification to the Commission, clearing the way for Commission approval of the compensation for stranded costs by the State. As a state aid within the meaning of Article 87(1) EC, it was in compliance with the Methodology and could therefore be authorized under Article 87(3)(c).

15.48 **Poland** As with Hungary, PPAs had been signed in the 1990s to attract investment. They were signed between the Polish Power Grid Company and various electricity generators, covering a 20-year period and guaranteeing high prices for them, irrespective of actual market prices. These were to be cancelled by the Government prior to their expiry and as compensation the Government planned to grant a one-off payment aimed at covering their losses resulting from the premature termination.

15.49 The Commission carried out a preliminary assessment and concluded that the scheme was not in line with the Methodology for analyzing state aid in relation to stranded assets.[31] The compensation scheme was not deemed to provide an effective mechanism to adapt the compensation payments to generators to the actual amount of revenue shortfall which they would be faced with on termination of the PPAs. There was also no mechanism in place to factor in the actual evolution of electricity prices. As a result, the risk of granting the generators more than the stranded costs was considerable. Indeed, there appeared to be a significant risk that, if electricity prices did not decrease in Poland, the generator might not face a revenue shortfall at all and therefore not be eligible for compensation for stranded costs.

---

[31] Commission Press Release IP/04/151, 'Commission opens proceeding on a State aid project for compensation of stranded cost in Poland', 3 February 2004; Commission Press Release IP/05/1455, 'State aid: Commission opens investigation into long term power purchase agreements in Poland', 23 November 2005.

Detailed information on the exact amounts of compensation was also not provided by the Polish authorities. In these circumstances, the Commission decided to object to the measure notified within the meaning of the interim mechanism procedure provided for in Annex IV.3 of the Act of Accession. The Commission therefore decided to initiate a formal investigation procedure.

Portugal The Commission raised no objections with respect to the grant of state aid to three Portuguese energy utilities for stranded costs.[32] The costs arose from the cancellation of long-term PPAs. These had been concluded between the state-owned TSO, REN, and the three electricity suppliers prior to liberalization. REN agreed to purchase a guaranteed amount of electricity at a guaranteed price that would cover a number of investment costs. A state-supported refund scheme would replace the PPAs with public compensation payments for stranded costs. **15.50**

The Commission took into account the fact that the investments undertaken by the beneficiaries are very large and are irrevocable. If the losses are not compensated in any manner, given their size, they would place in jeopardy the viability of the undertakings concerned. Information was provided by the Portuguese authorities on the list of costs to be covered by the compensation where a power plant's income was insufficient to cover them. They were deemed by the Commission not to exceed what is necessary to repay the shortfall in investment costs repayment over the asset's lifetime. In addition, the mode of computation of the stranded costs reflected economic costs that correspond to the actual sums invested, taking the actual evolution of prices into account, and was identical to ones used in past cases. **15.51**

Spain The Spanish case concerned two separate schemes,[33] both of which were notified to the Commission. First, there was the Costs of Transition to Competition (CTC) regime, which provided compensation over a maximum of ten years to Spanish electricity generators because of the fall in electricity prices from liberalization. Most of the CTC compensation would accrue to 11 utilities, amounting to 1,693 billion pesetas. The remainder, comprising 295 billion pesetas, was designed to cover a fixed premium of one peseta per kWh of power from indigenous coal. The maximum compensation calculated ex ante was equivalent to approximately €12 billion. The utilities would be able to sell bonds immediately to a group of banks, which would then be paid back over a period of ten years by the utilities. The utilities could pass on the costs to customers via a 4.5 per cent levy on all end-user bills. This method of calculating CTCs was dropped in favour of the 'differences method' in June 2001. **15.52**

---

[32] Commission Press Release IP/04/1123, 'Commission authorises public compensation for stranded costs in Portugal', 22 September 2004.
[33] Commission Decision 1999/797/EC, [1999] OJ L319/41.

15.53 In July 2001 the Commission decided that the component of aid known as the 'technological CTCs' (the premium paid for the generation of electricity from indigenous coal and the two allocations funds) were compatible with Article 87(1) EC and with the Commission's Methodology. Modifications to the Methodology scheme had been made in June 2001 to comply with the Commission's interpretation of the Treaty. The premium for the generation of electricity from indigenous coal did not comply with the Methodology but might benefit from an authorization as a compensation for a service of general economic interest as regards security of supply, under Article 86(2) EC, in the light of Articles 3(2) and 8(4) of the Electricity Directive.

15.54 A second scheme proposed to redistribute the relatively high cost of generation and distribution in the isolated systems by means of a specific levy on the mainland power tariffs and transmission fees. At the time, the operators of the systems in these locations benefited from specific exemptions from the market rules applicable to the mainland power market.

15.55 **UK** In a case submitted by the UK,[34] the Government notified measures designed to compensate for stranded costs related to long-term PPAs in the electricity sector in Northern Ireland. It concerned the PPAs between Northern Ireland Electricity plc (NIE) and the four main independent power producers. The commitments entered into in the PPAs involved stranded capacity, amounting to up to £25 million; excess cost linked to a gas contract between NIE and Premier Power, amounting to up to £25 million; cost of a gas pipeline, amounting to up to £14 million; and flue gas desulphurization, amounting to up to £18 million. The mechanism for recovery of eligible stranded costs proposed by the UK Government was the introduction of a surcharge on the final power consumption, known as 'Franchise Customer Excess Cost'. The Commission found that the resources involved were of private origin, involving no transfer of state resources whatsoever, and therefore, in line with the principles established in the *PreussenElektra* case, did not constitute state aid.

(2) State Guarantees: the *EDF* Case

15.56 For many years EDF, the dominant electricity utility in France, enjoyed a state guarantee, which was unlimited in either amount or duration and which covered all of its commitments. Since the risk of such a company becoming insolvent is almost non-existent, this had a positive impact on its credit rating. As a public enterprise it was not subject to the general law of bankruptcy and with this state guarantee EDF was able to borrow money on more favourable terms. Since the energy sector is in the process of liberalization, the state aid rules had to be applied

---

[34] Case N 661/1999, Commission Decision 1999/791/EC, [1999] OJ L319/1.

C. Liberalization and State Aids

and such unlimited state guarantees could limit the impacts of liberalization. In 2003 the Commission began a formal investigation into this guarantee enjoyed by EDF. At the end of 2003 the French Government agreed to remove the guarantee by the end of 2004 at the latest.[35] The option which the Government chose to achieve this goal was to turn EDF from a public enterprise into a limited company governed by the general corporate law.

In addition to the state guarantee, the Commission had two other sources of concern about EDF's financing. The first centred on the pension scheme for the electricity and gas sector, while the second centred on the non-taxation of a proportion of the accounting reserves created for the renewal of the high-voltage electricity grid. **15.57**

The decision to transform the corporate character of EDF addressed the Commission's concerns with respect to the guarantee. The situation with respect to the pension scheme was less controversial. Pensions for employees in the electricity and gas sector are managed by EDF itself and financed by employees' contributions, with a balancing contribution paid by all of the enterprises in the sector. A reform of this scheme would involve affiliation to the general social security scheme and the transfer of pension rights to a newly created independent pension fund called the National Fund for the Electricity and Gas Industries (CNIEG). Membership of this body is mandatory for all employees and employers in the sector. The Commission reviewed this scheme for possible state aid. The Government gave a formal undertaking that affiliation to the general scheme would be financially neutral. The scheme would pay basic pensions to employees in return for collecting the normal employees' and employers' contributions. The reform conferred an advantage on the sector compared with the existing situation but was nonetheless compatible with the state aid rules since it had the effect of eliminating the entry barrier created by the obligation on any entrant to set aside reserves to finance the pension rights already acquired by employees throughout the sector. The reform was deemed to be proportionate and compatible with the Treaty rules. **15.58**

By contrast, the Commission reached a negative conclusion on a tax concession granted to EDF in 1997, deciding that it constituted an operating aid. A statute, Law No 97-1026 of 10 November 1997, clarified the ownership status of the high-voltage grid with the effect that reserves previously accumulated by EDF free of **15.59**

---

[35] Commission Press Release IP/03/1737, 'Commission secures withdrawal of the unlimited guarantee granted to EDF, thereby encouraging competition in the energy sector', 16 December 2003. See Segura Catalan, MJ, Paroche, E, and Colin-Goguel, A, 'Le Contrôle des aides d'Etat dans la mise en place du marché intérieur de l'électricité: le cas de EDF' (2004) 1 Competition Policy Newsletter 4–7. A separate guarantee granted by France to a € 570 million loan from a syndicate of banks financing the Finnish electricity generator, TVO, is currently under investigation by the Commission: Commission Press Release IP/06/1456, 'State aid: Commission opens inquiry into France's guarantee to Finnish electricity producer TVO', 24 October 2006.

Chapter 15: State Aid

tax from 1987 to 1996 were no longer required and were reallocated. While most of these reserves were subject to corporation tax, a sum of FF 14.119 billion was directly incorporated into EDF's capital without increasing its taxable net assets. This amounted to a tax concession equivalent to €888.89 million. This constituted unjustified operating aid and strengthened EDF's competitive position in relation to its competitors and was therefore incompatible with the common market. The Commission therefore instructed the French Government to recover the amount plus interest that has accrued since 1997 (approximately €1.2 billion). This represents the largest amount that the Commission has ever required an individual company to pay back in an illegal aid case.

(3) Public Service Obligations

15.60 The ECJ ruled in the *Altmark*[36] case that public service compensation is not state aid if it fulfils four conditions.[37] Those conditions are that the public service should be clearly defined; the parameters of the compensation should be objective and established in advance; compensation should not exceed costs; and the company discharging the PSO should be chosen by means of a public procurement procedure or the costs of providing the public service are to be based on the costs of a 'typical undertaking, well run and provided with means of transport so as to be able to meet the necessary public service requirements'. When these conditions are met, there is no state aid and it is therefore not necessary to notify.

15.61 In the energy sector the first application of these criteria was in the CADA case in Ireland.[38] The Commission applied the above criteria and concluded that the arrangements notified by the Irish authorities did not contain any element of state aid. The Commission therefore authorized the measure which would promote investment in new power stations aimed at ensuring security of electricity supply. This case is discussed in more detail at paras 18.102–18.103.

D. Environmental Aid

15.62 The Guidelines on Environmental Aid[39] attempt to balance the promotion of environmental protection with possible negative effects on competition. The centrepiece

---

[36] Case C-280/00 *Altmark Trans GmbH v Nahverkehrsgesellschaft Altmark GmbH* [2003] ECR I-7747.

[37] For a discussion of this case, see Santamato, S and Pesaresi, N, 'Compensation for services of general economic interest: some thoughts on the Altmark ruling' (2004) 1 Competition Policy Newsletter 17–21.

[38] 'State aid N 475/2003—Ireland; Public Service Obligation in respect of new electricity generation capacity for security of supply', C(2003) 4488fin, 16 December 2003.

[39] Community Guidelines on State aid for environmental protection [2001] OJ C37/3.

D. Environmental Aid

of the Commission's policy is the 'polluter pays' principle, which requires that costs of measures to tackle pollution are met by those responsible for the pollution and should be internalized in their production costs. In the Guidelines, environmental protection is defined in such a way as to include energy savings as well as the use of renewable sources of energy. The Commission is required to classify any proposed aid into either investment aid or rules on operating aid.

(1) Promoting Renewable Energy

15.63 In contrast to the role of state aid in the internal market programme, which is in principle at least treated as a transitional issue, the role of aid in promoting renewable energy is one that will be around for the long term. The relationship between renewable energy promotion, state aids, and the internal market programme points to the risks involved in balancing potentially conflicting objectives in energy and environmental policy. In the Commission's view, 'the long-term development of new energy sources, such as the renewable ones, is only instrumental to rendering these new energy sources competitive'.[40] There is real potential for tension between this aim of locating a preferential treatment for renewable energy within a *competitive* framework, and the growing constitutional support for environmental measures from the Treaty of Amsterdam onwards.

(a) Germany: PreussenElektra v Schleswag *and Overriding Community Interests*

15.64 There is some evidence of this tension in a judgment delivered in March 2001 by the ECJ on the existence of aid. It ruled that an obligation to purchase electricity generated from renewable energy sources in Northern Germany did not constitute state aid within the meaning of the Treaty merely because it was imposed by statute.[41] The ruling also had the effect that priority was accorded to environmental goals over those of the internal market.

15.65 The German law adopted in 1990 and twice amended in 1994 and 1998 (the *Stromeinspeisungsgesetz*) requires publicly-quoted electricity supply undertakings to purchase electricity generated within their area of supply from renewable sources, including wind energy, at minimum prices that are higher than the real economic value of that form of energy. The 1998 amendment introduced a mechanism for allocating extra costs due to the fact that a purchase obligation between power suppliers and upstream electricity network operators was established. Schleswag, a regional electricity supply undertaking in the State of Schleswig-Holstein, was required to purchase electricity generated within its area of supply from renewable energy sources, involving an additional cost rising from 5.8 million Deutschmark

---

[40] Schaub, A, 'Competition Policy and Liberalization of Energy Markets', paper presented at the European Utilities Circle 2000 conference, 23 November 2000, 15.
[41] Case C-379/98 *PreussenElektra AG v Schleswag AG* [2001] ECR I-2099.

(DEM) in 1991 to DEM 111.5 million in 1998. Under the mechanisms provided for by the statute, Schleswag applied to PreussenElektra for payment of some amounts that it had already spent in complying with its purchase obligation. PreussenElektra then brought an action for recovery of DEM 500,000, which represented the amount paid to Schleswag in compensation for the additional costs caused by the purchase of wind electricity. PreussenElektra argued that the payment was contrary to EC law since it constituted an amended system of state aid that had not been notified to the Commission (the system established by the 1990 law had been notified to the Commission and duly approved by it). The State court of Kiel asked the ECJ for a ruling on whether the amendment to the statutory system constituted an amendment of aid within the meaning of Community law, and whether the system it established was contrary to the prohibition on quantitative restrictions on trade.

15.66 In its judgment the ECJ ruled that neither the statutory restriction introduced by the 1998 amendment nor the allocation of the financial burden between private supply undertakings and private operators of upstream electricity networks involved a direct or indirect transfer of state resources and was therefore not a state aid within the meaning of Article 87(1) EC. For a measure to constitute state aid, it also had to confer an economic advantage that the undertaking would not normally have received in the course of its business; it had to be selective, affecting the balance between certain firms and their competitors, and it had to have a potential effect on competition and trade between Member States. More importantly in this context, the ECJ stated that the rules were 'capable, at least potentially, of hindering intra-Community trade' but that they are aimed in particular at 'protecting the environment in so far as it contributes to the reduction in emissions of greenhouse gases'.[42] This meant that the aim of these rules was among the priority aims of the Community. The statutory rules were not therefore contrary to the free movement of goods. The ECJ also noted the relevance of two recitals of the first Electricity Directive: first, Recital 28 expressly states that Member States are permitted under Articles 8(3) and 11(3) to give priority to the production of electricity from renewable sources for reasons of environmental protection, and secondly, Recital 39 notes that this Directive constituted only a further phase in electricity liberalization and leaves some obstacles to intra-Community trade in place. In this light, the German legislation was not incompatible with Article 30 EC.

15.67 The impact of this judgment has been much discussed.[43] An early consequence was to influence the Commission's decision on the Spanish and Austrian compensation schemes for stranded assets, discussed above at paras 15.52–15.54 and 15.26–15.27. The Commission was unable to decide whether or not the payments

---

[42] ibid, paras 71 and 73.
[43] eg, Keppenne, J-P, 'National Environmental Policies: Uncharted Waters for EC State Aid Control' (2001) 7/8 *Nederlands Tijdschrift voor Europees recht* 193–9.

D. Environmental Aid

granted to the beneficiaries of the system constituted state resources.[44] The sums involved are transferred from the customers to the beneficiaries through a fund established by the State but over which the State has little control. This is analogous to the effects of the price-fixing mechanism examined by the ECJ in *PreussenElektra*. It is also analogous to the effects of the Austrian compensation scheme for stranded assets. It was not clear whether this analogy was sufficient for the Commission to conclude that the compensation scheme involved no state resources and was therefore not state aid within the meaning of the EC Treaty. The Commission reached its decision in both cases on a different basis.

15.68 Since that time, further attention has been given to the issue of when an aid does indeed exist, a matter further developed in Case C-482/99 *France v Commission (Stardust Marine)*.[45] In that case, it was held that even resources that may eventually be at the state's disposal can be treated as state resources. It also has to be shown that the resources that are used for the benefit of a particular undertaking may be attributed to some form of government decision.

15.69 It has become clear that once an aid is deemed to exist it may be permitted in several ways with the aim of promoting renewable sources of energy. They include: aid compensating for high investment costs; green certificate and other market mechanisms; aid calculated on the basis of external costs avoided; and aid in line with the rules applicable to energy savings. In a Belgian case involving green certificates, the Commission allowed operating aid for renewable electricity under a scheme that gave generators rights to relinquish green certificates for direct tax subsidies.[46]

15.70 There have been a number of other state aid decisions by the Commission in which different Member States have been allowed significant and long-term support for the generation of green electricity. These have included Denmark, the Netherlands, and the UK.[47] In 2006 Austria joined this group when the Commission approved a scheme for 'feed-in' tariffs for electricity from renewable sources and a support tariff for combined heat and power (CHP) installations for public district heating.[48]

15.71 The Austrian scheme is based on the Green Electricity Act 2002, which entered into force in 2003, and provides support for green electricity generation in the form

---

[44] Allibert, B, 'A Methodology for Analysing State Aid Linked to Stranded Costs' (2001) 3 Competition Policy Newsletter 25–7.
[45] [2002] ECR I-4397.
[46] [2002] OJ C292/6.
[47] See, eg, the discussion of two Dutch measures (MEP) in European Commission, *XXXIIIrd Report on Competition Policy 2003*, 102–3.
[48] Commission Press Release IP/06/953, 'State aid: Commission endorses support for green electricity in Austria', 7 July 2006. Austria also benefited from an ECJ ruling which held that Community legislation on public procurement did not prevent a contracting authority from applying an award criterion requiring that a percentage of the electricity supplied be generated from renewable sources (*EVN and Wrenstrom v Austria*, Case C-448/01 [2004] OJ C21/05).

of (1) purchase obligations at fixed prices for electricity from renewable energy sources, and (2) a support tariff for electricity generated in CHP installations for public district heating. The Commission viewed the measure as a form of state aid. The Commission's Guidelines for State Aid for Environmental Protection[49] allow aid for the generation of electricity up to the difference between the market price and the generation cost of this type of electricity. In this case, the feed-in tariffs and the support tariff respected the limits set out in the Guidelines, so the support scheme was deemed to be compatible with the state aid rules and did not threaten to distort competition in the internal market. The decision applied retroactively to the support measures contained in the Act, and provided the basis for continuation of this support under the successor law, the Green Electricity Act 2006.

15.72 The approval was not unconditional, however. The Austrian Government agreed to modify the financing mechanism following criticism by the Commission. This mechanism was designed to ensure that the measures set up under the Act were financed partly by means of a para-fiscal levy paid by final consumers on their electricity consumption. This mechanism could have led to discrimination against imported green electricity, since it had to contribute to financing the national support scheme without being eligible to benefit from it. Since this could lead to a breach of Articles 25 and 90 EC (which prohibit respectively customs duties on imports and exports between Member States and taxes that have the effect of discriminating against products from other Member States), Austria agreed to change the financing mechanism. From 2007 the scheme is to be financed through a lump sum paid per meter. Moreover, for previous years, it agreed to introduce an option to de-tax imported green electricity as long as the claimant is able to provide evidence that the electricity has indeed been generated from green sources.

(2) Promoting Biofuels and Wave Power

15.73 The Commission has authorized various aid schemes in favour of biofuels to replace diesel or petrol for transport, mostly in the form of excise tax reductions. The countries concerned include Austria,[50] the Czech Republic,[51] Estonia,[52] Hungary,[53] Italy,[54] Ireland,[55] Lithuania,[56] the Netherlands,[57] Sweden,[58] and Belgium.[59] The

---

[49] [2001] OJ C37/3.
[50] Case NN/43/2004, [2006] OJ C34/2.
[51] Case N/206/2004, [2005] OJ C103/17 and Case N/223/2005, [2005] OJ C324/28.
[52] Case N/314/2005, [2005] OJ C226/6.
[53] Case N/427/2004, [2005] OJ C133/3.
[54] Case N/582/2004, [2005] OJ C240/21.
[55] Case N/599/2004, [2005] OJ C98/11.
[56] Case N/44/2005, [2005] OJ C329/2.
[57] Case N/570/2005, [2006] OJ C202/9.
[58] Case N/187/2004, [2006] OJ C87/3.
[59] Case N/334/2005, [2006] OJ C34/2.

D. Environmental Aid

justification lies partly in their potential to reduce CO_2 emissions and partly to promote security of supply.

The Commission has also interpreted the requirements on operating and investment aid liberally so as to permit a grant of aid to a UK scheme for wave power.[60] To achieve an acceptable rate of return such projects require relatively high investment and high operating aid. In this case the operating aid complied with the Guidelines for environmental protection, and the split between investment and operating aid caused no undue distortion to the electricity market. The results of the programme could also be widely disseminated. It was compatible directly on the basis of Article 87(3)(c).

15.74

(3) Climate Change

The Commission has assessed aid for the reduction of greenhouse gas emissions in several ways. It has assessed various national schemes and has also intervened with respect to the National Allocation Programmes developed under the Emission Trading Scheme (see paras 17.42–17.50).

15.75

Among the national schemes it has assessed are the following. In the UK, an aid scheme was authorized in connection with the Climate Change Levy (CCL) introduced by the UK Government on non-domestic use of energy in 2001 to meet the Kyoto targets.[61] Energy intensive sectors were offered a rebate of 80 per cent for a period of ten years to adapt to the new context and to improve energy efficiency and cut CO_2 emissions. The agricultural sectors entered into integrated pollution prevention and control agreements. The scheme authorized involved a grant of aid of €687 million over a ten year period, constituting a rebate of 80 per cent of the CCL.

15.76

In an Italian case, the Commission has assessed aid for climate change purposes through alternative energy sources and energy savings in Lazio, Italy.[62] Two projects were involved with the objective of developing the generation and use of alternative energy sources (wind power) and energy savings (by means of CHP generation and district heating). The Commission found both projects to constitute compatible aid, being in line with the Guidelines on state aid to environmental protection, especially points 30 (aid intensity for energy saving), 32 (aid intensity for renewable sources of energy), 36 (eligible investment), and 37 (eligible costs).[63] It has also authorized aid for a Slovenian scheme that grants reductions in CO_2 taxation to operators of CHP installations, non-intensive companies that

15.77

---

[60] Case N/318/2005 *Wave and tidal stream energy demonstration* [2006] OJ C155/6.
[61] Case NN 12/2004, [2005] OJ C262/9.
[62] C 35/2003 ex N 90/2002, [2006] OJ C244/8.
[63] European Commission, Competition Report 2003, 140–1.

participate in the EU Emissions Trading Scheme, and companies that enter into voluntary environmental agreements.[64]

15.78 With respect to the national allocation plans (NAPs), the question arises about the compatibility of these instruments with the requirements of Article 87(1). So far the Commission, after screening all of the NAPs, has not taken any formal state aid decision on a NAP.

E. Aid for Rescue and Restructuring

15.79 The Commission has published detailed rules governing the use of aid to companies in serious difficulty. The most recent of these are the 2004 Guidelines on Rescue and Restructuring Aid,[65] which remain in force until October 2009. They require that rescue aid should:

- take the form of remunerated guarantees and loans;
- be limited to the amount required to keep the enterprise in business;
- be restricted in duration;
- serve to alleviate a social crisis without negative spill-over effects on other Member States.

Restructuring aid may only be granted subject to certain conditions:

- a once-only grant within a ten year period (the 'one last shot' principle);
- a coherent restructuring plan is to be put in place which ensures a return to viability in the foreseeable future; and
- the aid must be limited to the absolute minimum, requiring own investment from private sources and that the aid recipient has to reduce capacity or take other compensatory measures.

The two sets of circumstances are separate but often related. However, the first kind of aid is essentially short-term and enables an assessment of the prospects for a firm that is experiencing difficulty. The second kind of aid is envisaged in cases where a detailed restructuring plan has been designed to help a firm recover.

15.80 The subject of rescue and restructuring aid is a highly sensitive one since this kind of aid is clearly likely to constitute a major distortion of competition and probably of intra-Community trade. It is not always clear what 'in difficulty' means with respect to the firm concerned, and rescue measures are often implemented by

---

[64] Case C 44/2004; Commission Press Release IP/05/1517, 'State aid: Commission closes formal investigation on CO_2 taxation system in Slovenia following changes to legislation', 1 December 2005.
[65] Community Guidelines on State Aid for Rescuing and Restructuring Firms in Difficulty [2004] C 244/2.

E. Aid for Rescue and Restructuring

the Member State prior to approval by the Commission (as in the case below). The Commission's capacity to analyze what are often highly complex business plans under more or less severe time-pressure is also open to question. Ironically, the most recent example of such aid in the energy sector is in what is perhaps the most liberalized of EU energy markets, Great Britain. The case of British Energy and the related case involving BNFL are both reviewed below.

(1) The *British Energy* Case 2004

15.81 A sharp fall in electricity prices in the British electricity market in 2002 led to a collapse in the shares of British Energy, the principal nuclear generator in Britain. A Government rescue aid package followed soon after and this was approved by the Commission on 27 November 2002 (the rescue aid had been granted more than two months earlier).[66] The Commission's approval was conditional on a restructuring of British Energy and the formal notification of this to the Commission. The notification was given to the Commission on 7 March 2003 in accordance with Article 88(3) EC and with the EC Guidelines on restructuring and rescuing firms in difficulty (the 1999 version). The notification was required because the restructuring package involved a number of measures in which the Government undertook to pay for British Energy's liabilities under the existing contracts with BNFL and for certain decommissioning costs and uncontracted nuclear liabilities in so far as the Nuclear Liabilities Fund (NLF) is not able to meet these liabilities through British Energy contributions.

15.82 In July 2003 the Commission commenced a formal investigation procedure into the measures involved in the restructuring. This included the Government's undertakings, the new BNFL contracts, the standstill arrangements, the arrangements between British Energy and the creditors, the introduction of a new trading strategy and some local tax deferrals. A Notice was published under Article 88(2) EC which invited interested third parties to submit comments on the Notice and its preliminary findings.[67] More than 20 interested third parties made submissions.

15.83 On 22 September 2004 the Commission issued the State Aid Approval, stating that the state aid was compatible with the common market and the objectives of the Euratom Treaty.[68] The State Aid Approval states that the Government is allowed to fund the payment of (a) liabilities related to the cost of management of spent nuclear fuel loaded into British Energy AGR power stations prior to the effective

---

[66] Case NN 101/2002, [2003] OJ C39/15. This is described in some detail in the Listing Particulars and Prospectus for the British Energy Group plc and British Energy Holdings plc (November 2004) 353–7. The Commission's decision was challenged by Greenpeace and by DRAX: Case T-121/03 *Greenpeace Ltd and Nexgen Group v Commission* [2003] OJ C184/83; Case T-124/03 *AES Drax Power Ltd v Commission* [2003] OJ C135/59.
[67] [2003] OJ C180/5.
[68] Case C 52/2003 *Aid in favour of British Energy plc* [2005] OJ L142/26.

date (historic spent fuel) up to a specified level; (b) the costs of certain other liabilities set out in the Historic Liabilities Funding Agreement (HLFA); and (c) any shortfall of the NLF as regards the payment of liabilities related to British Energy nuclear assets decommissioning and its uncontracted liabilities.

15.84 The Commission required enhanced additional reports to be submitted to the Commission on an annual basis as soon as specified thresholds are exceeded. These concern expenditure corresponding to (a) the nuclear decommissioning and uncontracted liabilities referred to above; and (b) the costs of certain other liabilities set out in the HLFA. These reports have to demonstrate that the Government payments are restricted to meeting these liabilities, and to show that steps have been taken to limit expenditure to the minimum required to meet those liabilities.

15.85 The Commission imposed three conditions on the grant of the aid. First, a legal separation of nuclear generation, non-nuclear generation and trade businesses was required, preventing cross-subsidization between the businesses. All aid had to be directed to the nuclear generation business only. Secondly, no increase in generation capacity was permitted for a period of six years (although this excludes electricity generated from renewable sources). Thirdly, for a period of six years the company is prohibited from offering prices below the wholesale market prices to its direct business customers (so that the aid cannot be used to subsidize its prices to large users). The overall aim behind the conditions is to ensure that British Energy does not divert the aid it receives from the State to purposes other than funding its nuclear liabilities. Effectively, the conditions establish a ring-fence for the nuclear generation business.

(2) *BNFL* 2006

15.86 Another in-depth investigation was opened by the Commission into the British nuclear energy sector in December 2004.[69] This concerned the establishment of the UK Nuclear Decommissioning Authority (NDA) and the transfer of certain assets and liabilities belonging to British Nuclear Fuels Ltd (BNFL) to the NDA.

15.87 The NDA is a public authority established by the Energy Act 2004.[70] It was created, inter alia, to manage the decommissioning of public sector nuclear assets in the UK. In particular, it is to decommission a number of assets that were previously owned by BNFL, including the Magnox nuclear power plants and the THORP and SMP plants at the Sellafield site (the latter are respectively, a nuclear spent fuel reprocessing plant and a nuclear fuel production plant). All of the assets and liabilities linked to the sites that are to be decommissioned are transferred to the NDA. In the event that assets will not match liabilities, the UK Government will provide

---

[69] [2004] OJ C315/4.
[70] In s 44 of the Act the accumulated losses that have built up in BNFL companies (largely for decommissioning and clean-up purposes) are to be extinguished when the NDA takes over responsibility for decommissioning and clean-up under s 21.

funds for the shortfall. Prior to the transfer of the nuclear plants to the NDA, BNFL was the second electricity generating company in the UK.

15.88 This review resulted in the approval of the measures by the Commission by invoking the polluter-pays principle and applying it to nuclear liabilities.[71] It was stated that operators of nuclear plants should cover the decommissioning costs of their plants. The Commission used several computation methods to determine whether BNFL had completely fulfilled its obligations to cover decommissioning costs. All of these methods reached the conclusion that BNFL had complied with the polluter-pays principle, so the measure did not involve state aid to BNFL.

15.89 Some of the assets that the NDA has taken over will continue to operate commercially until their closure and may not fulfil the polluter-pays principle. In such cases, the state intervention regarding the nuclear liabilities could constitute state aid. Although the Commission authorized a limited derogation from the polluter-pays principle for the NDA, it attached strict conditions for the operation of these assets by the NDA. The derogation was justified on the grounds that the NDA would only operate the power plants for a residual time, and would do so with a view to closing them down as soon as possible for decommissioning. The derogation includes state aid. However, to limit its impact upon competition, the Commission imposed the same conditions on the NDA (with respect to these operations) as it imposed on British Energy in the context of its restructuring plan (see paras 15.84–15.85 above). Among these conditions were:

(1) the requirement of compliance with pricing restrictions when selling its electricity directly to business consumers (the aid was not to be used to undercut wholesale prices); and
(2) with respect to the THORP and SMP plants, which will continue to be operated commercially for a longer period, the Commission insisted that any future contracts they would conclude had to cover all incremental nuclear liabilities generated by the contract.

It is possible to detect in the Commission's decision a slightly less sympathetic view about the application of state aid rules in such cases relative to its earlier decision with respect to British Energy.

F. Conclusions

15.90 The application of state aid control to the energy sector in the context of liberalization has become clearer and more predictable over the past few years, in line

---

[71] The relevant measures in the Energy Act were also found to be in line with the objectives of the Euratom Treaty.

with general state aid policy. The development and implementation of the Methodology for handling stranded costs has contributed to this, as well as the practice evident from the many individual decisions taken under its guidance. However, the case study review in section C reveals at least two problems with the application of this Methodology:

(1) At a general level, this was a very questionable measure for the Commission to adopt, even at the initial stages of liberalization. It allowed incumbents to obtain often very large amounts of assistance from their government authorities in order to compete in a liberalizing environment. The current situation, highlighted in the Commission's Energy Sector Review and in all of the Commission's benchmarking reports, shows that incumbents from the pre-liberalization era remain in a dominant position in most national electricity and gas markets. The benefits which have been made available through the application of this Methodology bear some responsibility for this situation. As the Commission has stated in the Hungarian PPA case, the rules in the Methodology 'aim at ensuring that proper backing can be granted to incumbents in the electricity sector where necessary to allow them to sustain the liberalization process, while at the same time ensuring that the very objective of achieving a free market is met'.[72]

(2) In spite of the transitional problem that the Methodology is designed to address, and therefore the built-in obsolescence of the Methodology itself, it appears to remain of practical relevance at the present time. To a large extent, this is the result of the use of PPAs in some of the new Member States, but not exclusively so (as the stranded costs case with AEM Torino shows). There is a risk that the mechanism helps to tolerate a problem which should not be evident beyond the first years of the liberalization process.

15.91 As is so often the case when attempting to explain the choice of a particular strategy by the Commission in the promotion of competition, the answer is to be found not in the realm of law but in that of politics. It appears that for many Member States the conclusion of a support measure for so-called stranded costs was linked to their support for measures of further liberalization. Without it, the task of securing the agreement of those Member States to a second package of legislative measures in electricity (namely, the Electricity Directive and Regulation 1/2003) in particular would have been more difficult to achieve.

15.92 That said, the Methodology has proved a valuable practical tool in dealing with particular forms of state aid. It has ensured a fair but firm response to those Member States with a rather cavalier attitude to the design of compensation schemes (eg, Belgium, Poland, and initially Spain), to others with a poor or faulty

---

[72] Case NN 49/2005 *Hungarian stranded costs* [2005] OJ C324/12, 13.

F. Conclusions

case (eg, Luxembourg, Italy in *AEM Torino*), and a solid base from which to challenge the eligibility of PPAs for state aid.

The balancing of objectives that the Commission has been so aware of in the Hungarian case above is perhaps more evident in cases that have involved an environmental dimension. The clear anchoring of this objective in the Treaty and the priority given to it in ECJ case law have ensured that the criteria for assessing aid in this area have been given a more formal basis than the Methodology discussed above. The challenges presented by this form of balancing of objectives, between competition and environmental policies, are much more fundamental, however, than those arising from transitional experiences on the road to a liberalized energy market, with as yet unanswered questions emerging with the growing impact of climate change measures. **15.93**

16

SPECIAL AND EXCLUSIVE RIGHTS

A. Introduction	16.01	E. Import and Export of Electricity and Gas	16.46
B. Article 86 and its Context	16.05	(1) Early Enforcement in Energy	16.48
(1) Article 86	16.06	(2) Electricity and Gas Import–Export Monopolies	16.51
(2) The Context	16.09	(a) The Dutch Case	16.56
(3) Winds of Change	16.11	(b) The Italian Case	16.67
C. The Limits of Article 86(3)	16.14	(c) The French Case	16.70
(1) The *Telecoms* Case	16.18	(d) The Spanish Case	16.80
(2) The Issues	16.20	(3) Assessment	16.81
(3) Effects	16.26	(a) Burden of Proof and Article 86 Admissibility	16.84
D. Clarification of Monopoly Rights and their Limits	16.31	(b) Practices Contrary to Article 31	16.85
(1) *Höfner v Macrotron*	16.32	(c) Promoting Adoption of Electricity and Gas Directives	16.86
(2) *ERT*	16.34	F. Conclusions	16.87
(3) *Port of Genoa*	16.37		
(4) The *RTT* case	16.40		
(5) The *Corbeau* case	16.43		

> This privileged access . . . enables the electricity incumbent to maintain its dominant position on the electricity generation and supply markets by preventing market entry of potential competitors.
>
> European Commission (in a letter of formal notice on the grant of exclusive mining rights to the incumbent producer in Greece)[1]

A. Introduction

For several decades the energy markets of Member States were characterized by monopoly structures in electricity and gas activities. The traditional instruments for defending such structures included the use of special and exclusive rights. The Treaty basis for such rights has been primarily Articles 86(1) and 31 EC.   **16.01**

---

[1] *Report on Competition Policy 2004*, Vol I, at point 299.

The impact of the Electricity and Gas Directives[2] has been to usher in a retreat from the use of such defences, and indeed has made them less necessary as industrial structures adapt to a liberalizing market. Nonetheless, the legal basis for such special and exclusive rights remains, even if its potential to bolster anti-competitive practices has been circumscribed by a number of ECJ judgments in recent years. Moreover, the recent debate on Services of General Economic Interest (SGEI), led by the Commission,[3] and the strong commitment to SGEI that is contained in the draft Constitution, show how fundamental the protection of such services (including energy) is in the 'shared values' of the Community.[4]

16.02 Each of the Electricity and Gas Directives envisages that Member States may impose public service obligations (PSOs) on their undertakings (public and private) in the electricity and gas sectors 'in the general economic interest'. This must take full regard of the Treaty provisions but in particular, Article 86. Such obligations may cover a wide range of subjects including security and continuity of supply, quality and price of supplies, and environmental protection. The latter may include requirements on energy efficiency and climate change (see paras 5.09–5.15; 6.06–6.14). Similarly, with respect to distribution undertakings in the electricity and gas sectors, Member States remain able to grant special or exclusive rights to integrated undertakings of a limited size or which serve small isolated electricity systems.[5]

16.03 Moreover, Article 16 EC refers expressly to the kind of services that Article 86 is designed to protect through its special regime. It states that 'given the place occupied by services of general economic interest in the shared values of the Union as well as their role in promoting social and territorial cohesion, the Community and the Member States . . . shall take care that such services operate on the basis of principles and conditions which enable them to fulfil their missions'. The provisions of this article are to be implemented according to a Declaration of the Treaty 'with full respect to the jurisprudence of the Court of Justice, inter alia, as regards the principles of equality of treatment, quality and continuity of service'.

16.04 In this chapter a number of aspects of special and exclusive rights will be considered. First, Article 86 is considered in its context to demonstrate its importance in the energy sector. Secondly, the role of Article 86(3) Directives and decisions is briefly considered in relation to the liberalization programme pursued in the electricity

---

[2] Directive (EC) 2003/54 concerning common rules for the internal market in electricity and repealing Directive (EC) 96/92 [2003] OJ L176/37; Directive (EC) 2003/55 concerning common rules for the internal market in natural gas and repealing Directive (EC) 98/30 [2003] OJ L176/57.
[3] <http://ec.europa.eu/services_general_interest/docs/comm_2004_0326_en01.pdf>.
[4] The Treaty Establishing a Constitution for Europe, Art III-122 builds upon the existing Art 16 EC, and see Art II-96.
[5] Electricity Directive, Art 15(2); Gas Directive, Art 13(2): limited size means fewer than 100,000 connected customers in each case.

B. Article 86 and its Context

and gas sectors in recent years. Thirdly, the various rulings of the courts in relation to monopoly rights are reviewed and, finally, the operation of Article 86 in the electricity and gas sectors is considered.

B. Article 86 and its Context

Historically, monopolies and exclusive/special rights have played a crucial role in the development of the European energy economy. For many years the norm was to have exclusive national monopolies *de jure* or de facto relating to electricity generation, electricity and gas transmission, distribution and supply, and to the import and export of electricity and gas. Such monopolies were vested in undertakings that were more or less controlled by the state. In the case of transmission and distribution of electricity and gas, all Member States except Germany granted undertakings (whether state, private, or mixed in ownership), exclusive or special rights.[6] Even in Germany's case, there were private law agreements between the undertakings that achieved the same effect. Access to networks by third parties was in most Member States not given any special legal protection. The net effect of these arrangements was, as noted by the Commission in its 1988 Working Document, to contribute to the creation of captive markets, and to undermine the creation of a single market in energy.[7] 16.05

(1) Article 86

The legal basis for such monopoly and exclusive rights has been primarily Articles 86(1) and 31 EC, although the preservation of property rights in Article 295 has also played a supporting role. Article 86(1) implicitly recognized the rights of Member States to grant special or exclusive rights to public or private undertakings, while Article 31 requires only the adjustment and not the abolition of state monopolies. It may be noted, however, that Article 86(1) imposes a duty on Member States, in relation to undertakings to which they grant special or exclusive (ie monopoly) rights, not to enact or maintain in force any measures that are contrary to the rules of the EC Treaty, especially in relation to the undertakings that have monopoly or special rights. The latter include the rules relating to discrimination on grounds of nationality (Article 12), and the rules on competition and state aids (Articles 81 to 89 inclusive). 16.06

Article 86(2) provides a potential derogation from the application of all of the Treaty rules for undertakings charged with the operation of services of general economic 16.07

---

[6] The UK became an exception to this from the 1980s onwards but before then its practices fell entirely in the same category.
[7] European Commission, *An Internal Market in Energy*, COM (1988) 4(9).

interest or having the character of a revenue-producing monopoly in so far as the derogation is required in the performance of those services. This provision may be invoked to justify exclusive import and export rights that would otherwise infringe Articles 28, 29 and 31. In the import/export monopoly cases considered at paras 16.51–16.86, the ECJ rejected the Commission's arguments that Article 86(2) did not apply to state measures that were contrary to the Treaty provisions on freedom of movement.

16.08 Finally, in the last part of Article 86, there is a duty imposed on the Commission to ensure that Member States comply with their obligations under Article 86(1). Where necessary, the Commission is required to address 'appropriate directives or decisions' to the Member States, which would require Member States to adjust national measures that the Commission considers to be in conflict with Article 86(1) and (2). The Commission has a wide discretion in relation to the action that it deems to be appropriate and the means that are suitable to achieve that purpose. The power has been used to adopt a number of Directives in economic sectors such as telecommunications, but not electricity or gas, nor has it been used to adopt any decisions with respect to the electricity or gas sectors.

(2) The Context

16.09 Such Treaty provisions were important for the electricity and gas industries—characterized as they were by substantial national monopolies, particularly in transmission, distribution, and supply. The existence of such monopolies was accepted, but the Member States which had granted the exclusive or special rights to the undertakings could not by legal measures protect them in the conduct of their businesses from the full impact of the Treaty rules (including the competition rules). A special exemption from this provision was permitted in the case of undertakings entrusted with the operation of services of general economic interest.

16.10 It is only in the recent past that cases have been brought before the ECJ which required it to rule on the circumstances in which the dominant position created by the grant of an exclusive right could be exercised so as to constitute an abuse of a dominant position,[8] thereby opening up the possibility of challenges to the exclusive right itself.[9] The relevant litigation reflects the general context of liberalization and deregulation in the economic life of the EU.

---

[8] See generally, Buendia Sierra, JL, *Exclusive Rights and State Monopolies under EC Law* (2000).
[9] The first case decided on the Commission's powers under Art 86(3) concerned Commission Directive (EEC) 80/723 on the transparency of financial relations between Member States and public undertakings [1980] OJ L195/35: Joined Cases 188–190/80 *France, Italy and UK v Commission* [1982] ECR 2545. The ECJ interpreted the Commission's duty of surveillance as an extensive one and confirmed the competence of the Commission to act. The scope of the Directive was amended in 1984 to include the energy, water, transport, and telecommunications sectors, which had been excluded from the original draft, analogous to the experience with public procurement legislation.

B. Article 86 and its Context

(3) Winds of Change

16.11 There are two trends that are significant for the promotion of competition. First, the ECJ began to place a more restricted interpretation on the scope of exclusive or special rights granted to undertakings by governments. This has come about largely through judgments of the ECJ on references for preliminary rulings as to the legality of such exclusive or special rights, made by national courts of Member States and arising from legal proceedings brought by undertakings or individuals to challenge such rights. The ECJ had to consider whether the exercise of such rights would in itself lead to a breach of specific rules of the EC Treaty, such as the competition rules in Articles 81 and 82 and those relating to the free movement of goods in Articles 28, 29, 30, and 31. The proceedings were based on Article 86(1). Prior to these judgments there had been a widely accepted view that such exclusive and special rights were presumed to be compatible with EC law. The judgments changed this, and showed a trend to restrict the validity of such rights to those core activities which an undertaking is required to perform in fulfilment of its obligation to provide a service of general economic interest.

16.12 Secondly, progress was made in removing import and export monopolies in electricity and gas. Such rights might seem evidently in breach of the Treaty rules but were unchallenged for decades. The initiation of legal proceedings against Member States was first mooted in 1991, but action was not taken until 1994 and the ECJ delivered its judgments only in 1997. The proceedings, as well as the judgments, did much to change Member State practice in this field, but ultimately require careful assessment of their implications. More recently, the Commission has sent an Article 86(3) letter to Greece concerning the Greek lignite mining and electricity generation and supply markets. Lignite is the cheapest energy source for power generation in Greece and the incumbent electricity generator was granted exclusive rights to extract it without compensation, leading to an infringement of Articles 86(1) and 82 EC.[10]

16.13 During the 1990s the ECJ delivered judgments in a number of cases not involving the energy industry which helped to establish the circumstances in which the exercise of a dominant position created by the grant of a monopoly could in itself be treated as an abuse of a dominant position giving rise to a breach of Article 82. Another judgment helped to clarify the scope of monopolies which might be capable of exemption from the rules of the Treaty and especially Article 86(2). The cases brought before the ECJ were mostly referred by courts of Member States under Article 234 EC. They do not directly concern the electricity and gas sectors but their subject matter is closely related to the kind of special and exclusive rights found in those sectors. In each case the ECJ was required to consider whether

---

[10] *Report on Competition Policy 2004*, Vol I.

an existing special or exclusive right granted by a Member State was compatible with a particular rule or rules of the Treaty. Prior to discussion of the more important of those cases, attention is given here to a case arising from a challenge by several Member States to the Commission's legislation in the telecommunications sector, where the programme of liberalization has been more advanced than in energy. It concerned action by the Commission to put an end to special and exclusive rights, but also the method of enforcement appropriate to achieving this objective.

C. The Limits of Article 86(3)

16.14 The procedure adopted by the Commission to bring about liberalization in the telecommunications sector offers an interesting contrast to its approach in the electricity and gas sectors. Telecommunications policy developed from the late 1980s onwards by relying upon Directives based on both Article 86(3) and Article 95 EC.[11] The relationship between Directives based on the two sets of provisions has been described as one between 'liberalization' and 'harmonization' respectively.[12] The interaction between the two legal bases was a significant feature of liberalization in the telecommunications market. Indeed, as early as its 1987 Green Paper on Telecommunications, the Commission had declared that it 'may use, as appropriate, its mandate under Article 90(3) [now 86(3)] of the Treaty to promote, synchronize and accelerate the on-going transformation'.[13] Despite this, in the energy sector, the Article 86(3) option was only briefly considered and then quickly dropped as a possible route for liberalization.

16.15 It is important to note that the legislative procedures involved in Articles 86(3) and 95 are quite different.

16.16 An important characteristic of Directives and decisions made under Article 86(3) is that they may be adopted by the Commission acting alone without the approval of the Council or the Parliament. The Commission can also deal with sectors on a general rather than a case-by-case basis.

16.17 By contrast, the procedure under Article 95 involves consultation with a very wide range of parties. At that time, Article 95 provided for a co-operation procedure, through which the Council adopted the measure and Parliament was involved to a limited extent. Subsequently, the co-decision procedure applied and measures under Article 95 were adopted jointly by Council and Parliament. However, the key

---

[11] For an overview of developments in this sector from 1987–99, see Larouche, P, *Competition Law and Regulation in European Telecommunications* (2000).
[12] Sauter, W, *Competition Law and Industrial Policy in the EU* (1997) 186 et seq.
[13] *Towards a Dynamic European Economy: Green Paper on the development of the common market for telecommunications services and equipment*, COM (1987) 290 final, 30 June 1987, 186.

C. The Limits of Article 86(3)

feature of Article 95 is that the Council is the motor behind the measure. Under Article 86(3) it is the Commission. Indeed, on the face of it, Article 86(3) is one of the very few instances in the EC Treaty in which a power to make laws of general application is vested in the Commission, with no express requirement to involve either the Council or the Parliament. However, it may be argued that this is not a general legislative power, but in practice one that is limited to the adoption of Directives to spell out pre-existing obligations under other Treaty provisions, in particular Articles 81 and 82, but also the fundamental freedoms, in relation to state measures concerning legal monopolies. In that sense, it is different from, and more specific than, the general power conferred on the Council to adopt harmonization measures under Article 95 or competition law measures under Article 83.[14]

(1) The *Telecoms* Case

In March 1991 the ECJ handed down its judgment in the Telecommunications Terminal Equipment case. The judgment confirmed the right and the duty of the Commission to address to the Member States Directives adopted under Article 86(3) to ensure the application of Treaty rules on free movement of goods and competition under Article 86. The ruling roused considerable interest among all parties involved in the ongoing debate on liberalization in the electricity and gas sectors. **16.18**

The case[15] arose from a Directive issued by the Commission under Article 86(3) as part of its plans to open up access to the EU telecommunications network.[16] The Directive required Member States to withdraw special and exclusive rights[17] granted in respect of the import, supply, installation, and maintenance of telecommunications terminal equipment. The validity of the Directive was challenged by the French Government supported by the Governments of Belgium, Germany, Greece, and Italy.[18] The ECJ was requested to annul some parts of the Directive, including **16.19**

---

[14] Edward, D and Hoskins, M, 'Article 90: Deregulation and EC Law. Reflections arising from the XVI FIDE Conference' (1995) 32 CML Rev 168, 183.
[15] Case C-202/88 *France v Commission* [1991] ECR I-1223.
[16] Commission Directive 88/301/EEC of 16 May 1988 on competition in the markets in telecommunications terminal equipment, [1988] OJ L131/73. A second Directive related primarily to the withdrawal by Member States of special and exclusive rights granted in respect of the supply of telecommunications services, other than voice telephony, and the taking by Member States of measures necessary to ensure that any operator is entitled to supply such services: Commission Directive 90/388/EEC of 28 June 1990 on competition in the markets for telecommunications services, [1990] OJ L192/10.
[17] The Directive defined 'special or exclusive rights' as 'the rights granted by a Member State or a public authority to one or more public or private bodies through any legal, regulatory or administrative instrument reserving them the right to provide a service or undertake an activity' (Art 1).
[18] The aggregate votes of these five Member States would have been sufficient to block the Directive under an Art 95 legislative procedure. Larouche concludes that the Directive 'might not have been enacted with the same content under Art 95 EC, if it is assumed that Member States which went before the ECJ had reservations about the substance of the Directive as well as its legal basis': Larouche, P, *Competition Law and Regulation in European Telecommunications* (2000) 43, n 20.

those parts relating to withdrawal of special or exclusive rights granted by Member States. Although the proceedings commenced in 1988, it was not until 19 March 1991 that the ECJ delivered its judgment. More than a year had passed from the presentation of the Advocate-General's conclusions on the case to the ECJ on 13 February 1990, perhaps indicating the political sensitivity of the case.

(2) The Issues

16.20 There were two issues of importance to be decided by the ECJ. First was whether the Commission should have made use of Article 226 EC[19] rather than Article 86(3) to attain the goal of putting to an end with immediate effect particular national measures. The second was whether the Commission had exceeded its monitoring powers under Article 86(3) by adopting a Directive that required the complete abolition of special and exclusive rights in connection with telecommunications terminal equipment.

16.21 At the time, the answer to the first question was considered a matter of great importance. It would establish what legal powers were available to the Commission to tackle constraints on the establishment of an internal market which arise from the special or exclusive rights granted not only in telecommunications, but also in other sectors such as electricity, gas, and water.

16.22 Traditionally, the transportation and distribution networks in these sectors had been dominated by entities that had been granted special or exclusive rights. The possibility was therefore raised that the Commission could, by means of a Directive issued under Article 86(3), require a Member State to withdraw exclusive rights, and thereby avoid the lengthy process under Article 226 of alleging breaches by individual Member States of EC Treaty obligations. It could also avoid the alternative procedure of requesting the Council to deal with the matter by adopting a Directive under the Article 95 procedure. Under the latter procedure, the Council may adopt 'measures for the approximation of the provisions laid down by law, regulation or administrative action in Member States which have as their object the establishment and functioning of the internal market'.[20] Since it involves consultation with the Parliament and other institutions of the Community such as the Economic and Social Committee, that process is a lengthy one. The decision of the ECJ therefore had considerable importance for the internal market strategy of the Commission.

---

[19] Art 226 states that: 'If the Commission considers that a Member State has failed to fulfil an obligation under this Treaty, it shall deliver a reasoned opinion on the matter after giving the State concerned the opportunity to submit its observations. If the State concerned does not comply with the opinion within the period laid down by the Commission, the latter may bring the matter before the Court of Justice.'
[20] Art 95(1) EC.

C. The Limits of Article 86(3)

The ECJ held, with respect to the first question, that Article 226 was required to be used in cases where a measure existed which was 'clearly and totally contrary to the Treaty'.[21] Article 86(3) gives the Commission power to specify in general terms the obligations arising under Article 86(1) by adopting Directives. The Commission should exercise this power in cases where it defines in concrete terms the obligations imposed on the Member States under the EC Treaty. The ECJ held that 'such a power cannot be used to make a finding that a Member State has failed to fulfil a particular obligation under the Treaty'.[22] In the context of the Directive at issue, 'the Commission merely determined in general terms obligations which are binding on the Member States under the Treaty. The Directive cannot therefore be interpreted as making specific findings that particular Member States failed to fulfil their obligations under the Treaty.'[23]

16.23

In reaching this conclusion, the ECJ did not follow the opinion of the Advocate-General Giuseppe Tesauro,[24] who declared that:

16.24

> The issue of a Directive under Article 90(3) [now Article 86(3)] is not an appropriate way of dealing with a breach, especially in circumstances where, in the pleadings before the Court, the lawyer pleading appearing for the Commission explained the reason for preferring to use the Article 90(3) procedure rather than Article 169 [now Article 226] was that the latter would not have the same direct and immediate effect.

He noted also that a Directive issued under Article 86(3) could not in principle provide for 'repressive' purposes in place of Article 226.

With respect to the second question, the ECJ held that even if Article 86(1) presupposed the existence of undertakings with special or exclusive rights, it did not follow that all such rights were necessarily to be considered incompatible with the EC Treaty. The ECJ held that 'the supervisory power conferred on the Commission includes the possibility of specifying, pursuant to Article 90(3), obligations arising under the Treaty. The extent of that power therefore depends upon the scope of the rules with which compliance is to be ensured.'[25] For the most part, it upheld the content of the Directive, with the notable exception of Article 12. The latter required Member States to take all necessary steps to ensure that national telecommunications monopolies made it possible for their customers to terminate, within a maximum period of notice of one year, leasing or maintenance contracts for terminal equipment which had been the subject of exclusive or special

16.25

---

[21] [1991] ECR I-1223, para 16.
[22] ibid, paras 17–8.
[23] ibid.
[24] The role of the Advocate-General responsible for a case is to summarize the arguments of the parties and to give the ECJ his or her views on the relevant law and the decision which the ECJ should take. The ECJ is not bound to follow these conclusions, but usually does so (see para 2.95).
[25] [1991] ECR I-1223, para 21.

rights at the time of the conclusion of the contracts. The ECJ held that Article 86(3) was not a valid legal basis for such a measure since Article 86 did not govern anti-competitive conduct if such conduct was engaged in by undertakings at their own initiative. It conferred powers solely in relation to state measures and in this case there was no evidence that long-term contracts had been concluded under pressure from the Member States. Anti-competitive conduct of this kind was remediable only on a case-by-case basis and by means of individual decisions adopted under Articles 81 and 82.[26]

(3) Effects

16.26 The initial response of the Commission to the judgment was that its law-making powers under Article 86(3) had been significantly extended or at the very least confirmed. Moreover, the interpretation of Article 28 was wide and potentially useful for the energy sector. Because the holders of the exclusive rights could not satisfy the market demand and since the exclusive import rights could have restricted the trade in products from other Member States, Article 28 was applicable. This included both the products and also the ancillary services necessary for the repair and maintenance of those products. Accordingly, the Commission took two distinct initiatives.

(1) It drafted and informally circulated among Member States Directives based on Article 86(3) to require the removal of import and export monopolies in electricity and gas.
(2) It dispatched letters to several Member States which maintained exclusive import and export rights in electricity and gas. The basis for these infringement actions was Article 31. Its use had so far been very limited with respect to its application to service monopolies. Much earlier, in the *Manghera* case[27] the ECJ had ruled that an exclusive right to import or market manufactured products constituted a form of discrimination prohibited by Article 37(1). However, the application of the article to service monopolies had been limited by the ECJ decision in the *Saatchi* case.[28]

16.27 The first action quickly ran into difficulties. It provoked considerable opposition from the Member States. The unilateral approach by the Commission was also not proposed at a highly propitious moment since the Member States were concluding negotiations on the Treaty of European Union that would increase the consultation process between Community institutions, to allow more input in the legislative process, especially to the Parliament. This approach appeared to

---

[26] Edward, D and Hoskins, M, 'Article 90: Deregulation and EC Law. Reflections arising from the XVI FIDE Conference' (1995) 32 CML Rev 168, 183–4. They see this aspect of the judgment as illustrating the limited nature of the Commission's power under Art 86(3).
[27] Case C-59/75 *Pubblico Ministero v Manghera* [1976] ECR 91.
[28] Case 155/73 *Italy v Saatchi* [1974] ECR 409.

D. Clarification of Monopoly Rights and their Limits

involve action in precisely the opposite direction. Moreover, the legal position was on closer inspection less clear-cut than it seemed.

This element of uncertainty was more apparent in the judgment in a second case in the telecommunications sector, involving a challenge to the validity of the Commission's Telecommunications Services Directive.[29] Significantly, the Directive had included a full explanation by the Commission of the reasons why it was using its powers under Article 86(3) to achieve the objectives of the Directive.[30]   **16.28**

While the second of the Commission's actions (the infringement procedure under Article 226) continued its course, it did so only very slowly and was clearly being used tactically by the Commission—to assist the negotiations on Directives based on Article 95 (see paras 16.51–16.86).   **16.29**

The proposed Directives under Article 86(3) were simply dropped. Arguably, the Commission had learned from the experience of circulating draft Directives based on this article what the limits were of this particular legal instrument in the energy sector. Without a significant level of support from the Member States (or the Parliament) it had little use. Just as important, the provision of a transitional phase to an internal energy market, which all parties considered necessary, was not feasible by this legislative route.   **16.30**

D. Clarification of Monopoly Rights and their Limits

In addition to the Telecoms case, the ECJ clarified the legal position of monopoly rights under Article 86 in a number of cases that are explained and commented on below.   **16.31**

(1) *Höfner v Macrotron*[31]

This case was a reference from the *Oberlandesgericht München* (Higher Regional Court) under Article 234. The ECJ considered whether the grant of an exclusive   **16.32**

---

[29] Joined Cases C 271, 281 & 289/90 *Spain, Belgium, and Italy v Commission* [1992] ECR I-5833, which challenged Commission Directive (EC) 90/388 on competition in the markets for telecommunications services [1990] OJ L192/10.

[30] Recital 33 states that: 'Article 90(3) assigns clearly defined duties and powers to the Commission to monitor relations between Member States and their public undertakings and undertakings to which they have granted special or exclusive rights, particularly as regards the removal of obstacles to freedom to provide services, discrimination between nationals of the Member States and competition. A comprehensive approach is necessary in order to end the infringements that persist in certain Member States and to give clear guidelines to these Member States that are reviewing their legislation so as to avoid further infringement. A Directive within the meaning of Article 90(3) is therefore the most appropriate means of achieving this end.'

[31] Case C-41/90 *Klaus Höfner and Fritz Elser v Macrotron GmbH* [1991] ECR I-1979.

right might inevitably lead to the abuse of a dominant position resulting from the grant of that right. The case arose from the grant of a statutory monopoly by the Federal German Republic to the *Bundesanstalt für Arbeit* (Federal Employment Office), which covered the provision of recruitment and placement services for executive positions throughout Germany. The ECJ was asked, inter alia, by the national court to rule on the question of whether, taking Article 86(2) into account, the monopoly of recruitment of business executives constituted an abuse of a dominant position on the market, contrary to Article 82.

16.33 The ECJ held that 'the simple fact of creating a dominant position . . . by granting an exclusive right . . . is not as such incompatible with Article 82 of the Treaty'. Rather, a Member State would be in breach of its obligations under Article 86(1) in conjunction with Article 82 if the body to which it had granted an exclusive right would, by the mere exercise of its exclusive rights, be led to an abuse of its dominant position.[32] In this case, the Member State had created a situation in which the statutory monopolist (the public employment agency) was manifestly unable to satisfy the demand for its services, but private competitors (Höfner and Elser) were precluded from entering the market by a legal provision that rendered any contract for such services null and void. There was therefore a breach of Article 86(1) coupled with Article 82(b).[33]

(2) *ERT*

16.34 In this case[34] the ECJ examined an exclusive right in conjunction with alleged breaches of the EC Treaty provisions concerning the freedom of movement of goods (Articles 28–30) and the freedom to provide services (Articles 49–55). There was a clear statement in the judgment that exclusive and special rights to provide services are in breach of Article 49.

16.35 The case arose from the grant of exclusive rights to ERT, a Greek national radio and television company, for the organization, transmission, and development of radio and television in the country. In addition to the exclusive right to broadcast its own programmes, ERT had an exclusive right to re-transmit foreign television

---

[32] Recital 29.
[33] The same approach was adopted in Case C-323/93 *La Crespelle* [1994] ECR I-5077, where the Court held: 'The mere creating of a . . . dominant position by the granting of an exclusive right within the meaning of Article 90(1) [now Art 86 (1)] is not as such incompatible with Article 86 [now Art 82] of the Treaty. A Member State contravenes the prohibitions contained in those two provisions only if, in merely exercising the exclusive right granted to it, the undertaking in question cannot avoid abusing its dominant position' (para 18). For a more recent consideration of these issues in the context of an inability to meet demand, see Case C-475/99 *Ambulanz Glockner v Landkreis Sudwestpfalz* [2001] ECR I-8089.
[34] Case C-260/89 *Elliniki Radiophonia Tileorassi AE (ERT) v Dimotiki Etairia Pliroforissis (DEP)* [1991] ECR I-2951.

D. Clarification of Monopoly Rights and their Limits

programmes in Greece. DEP had, together with another individual, established a television transmitter in Salonika, which had begun broadcasting without obtaining a prior consent from ERT as required by Greek law. As a result, ERT had taken steps to restrain DEP from broadcasting. The Greek court referred the case to the ECJ and requested a ruling on whether the exercise of exclusive rights granted to ERT was contrary to any of the rules of the EC Treaty.

The ECJ re-stated its judgment in *Saatchi*[35] to the effect that the EC Treaty does not prevent Member States from conferring exclusive rights to broadcast for non-economic reasons, based on public interest considerations. However, it added that 'the methods of organization and exercise of that monopoly must not run contrary to the rules on free movement of goods and services and the competition rules'.[36] It also examined the operation of the monopoly in relation to the provisions on free movement of goods and the freedom to provide services. With respect to the former, the ECJ ruled that a television monopoly relating to services and not goods could not in itself be contrary to the provisions relating to freedom of movement of goods.[37] With respect to the freedom to provide services, the ECJ held that the grant of the exclusive right to re-transmit foreign television broadcasts was a breach of Article 49 EC unless it was subject to the exemptions contained in Article 55. The latter permits an exemption from the provisions of Article 49 on the grounds specified in Article 46, such as public policy, public security, or public health. 16.36

(3) *Port of Genoa*[38]

The ECJ built on *Höfner* and *ERT* in its interpretation of the circumstances in which the exercise of an exclusive right granted by a Member State could then be an abuse of a dominant position under Article 82. Under Italian law Merci had been granted an exclusive right to handle at the port of Genoa all conventional goods including steel. Gabriella bought some steel from a producer in West Germany and shipped it to Genoa where it wished to unload the cargo. Gabriella was unable to unload the cargo from the boat in part because of strikes by stevedores employed by Merci, although the ship had on board equipment with which it would have been possible to unload the cargo. Gabriella claimed damages against Merci due to the delay in unloading and also claimed the return of money already paid to Merci on the ground that these payments were excessive in view of the 16.37

---

[35] Case 155/73 *Italy v Saatchi* [1974] ECR 409. The judgment did not attempt to identify those instances where the grant of special or exclusive rights could infringe the Treaty rules. By contrast, judgments in subsequent cases have developed the law on this point.
[36] [1991] ECR I-2951, Recital 12.
[37] ibid, Recital 13.
[38] Case C-179/90 *Merci Convenzionale Porto di Genova SpA ('Merci') v Siderurgica Gabriella SpA ('Gabriella')* [1991] ECR I-5889.

service rendered by Merci. The Italian court referred the case to the ECJ, asking it, inter alia, to decide whether the exercise by Merci of its exclusive right to handle cargoes at the port of Genoa constituted an abuse of a dominant position.

16.38 The ECJ held that the creation of a dominant position by the granting of exclusive rights is not in itself incompatible with Article 82.[39] Further, it held that a Member State commits a breach of Article 86(1), in conjunction with Article 82, if the undertaking to which the exclusive rights are granted, is led, by the simple exercise of the exclusive rights granted to it, to exploit its dominant position in an abusive way or where the grant of the exclusive rights is liable to create a situation where the undertaking exploits its dominant position in an abusive manner.[40]

16.39 An important element in the ECJ's judgment is the reaffirmation and extension of its judgment in the *Höfner* case. The extension lay in the words 'or where the granting of the exclusive rights is liable to create a situation where the undertaking is led to exploit its dominant position in an abusive way'. The ECJ also noted in its judgment some observations made before it to the effect that the creation of the exclusive right had led to Merci making charges for services that were not requested and to charging prices that were disproportionate to the work done and refusing to use modern technology. This resulted in increased costs and increases in the time taken to do the work. Conduct of this kind may be relevant in establishing an abuse of a dominant position by an electricity or gas transmission grid or pipeline owner. The significance of this case lies in the fact that it resulted in a successful challenge to the exclusive right. It also developed the definition of 'substantial part of the common market'.

(4) The *RTT* Case

16.40 In this case[41] the ECJ was asked to rule on the abuse of a dominant position that arose as a result of the extension of an existing exclusive right granted by a Member State. Under Belgian law RTT held a monopoly of the provision of public telephone services. Subsequently, the monopoly had been extended by the imposition of a requirement that subscribers to the RTT telephone service could not, without the approval of RTT, attach any apparatus or line to any apparatus which they were entitled to use under their arrangement with RTT. Further, the law required that the apparatus to be attached should be approved by RTT.

---

[39] ibid, Recital 16.
[40] ibid, Recital 17.
[41] Case C-18/88 *Regie des Telegraphes et des Telephones ('RTT') v SA-GB-Inno-BM ('GB')* [1991] ECR I-5973. In this context see also the judgment in Case C-475/99 *Ambulanz Glockner v Landkreis Sudwestpfalz* [2001] ECR I-8089 on the role of the right-holder in determining the conditions of entry of other participants into an ancillary market.

D. *Clarification of Monopoly Rights and their Limits*

16.41 GB was a merchandising company that sold subsidiary telephones to be attached to the RTT telephones in its retailing outlets. It had purchased them with a view to selling them into this market. RTT had asked for an injunction to stop sales of these telephones by GB. In turn, GB asked the ECJ to consider whether this exercise by RTT of its exclusive rights in connection with the sales of the supplementary telephones was an abuse of a dominant position under Article 82.

16.42 The ECJ did not question the legality of RTT's monopoly over the public telephone network. However, it did condemn the legislation that conferred the ancillary rights on RTT. It held that a Member State would be in breach of its obligations under Article 86(1) in conjunction with Article 82, if it granted to an undertaking which already enjoyed a dominant position as a result of a grant of exclusive rights in a particular market an exclusive right to carry on an auxiliary activity, if such auxiliary activity could be carried out by a third party in an adjacent but separate market.[42] There are links between this judgment and the so-called 'essential facilities' doctrine.

(5) The *Corbeau* Case

16.43 This case concerned an exclusive right to collect, transport, and deliver mail in Belgium and was referred to the ECJ by the Tribunel Correctionnel of Liège.[43] It arose from a criminal prosecution brought against Mr Corbeau in respect of an alleged breach by him of the national monopoly of postal services granted to Regie des Postes by Belgian law. Mr Corbeau was alleged to have breached that monopoly by providing a rapid mail delivery service in the city of Liège. This involved the collection of mail from the place of business or residence of the sender and its distribution within the city before midday on the next day. The case had two relevant aspects: (1) the lawfulness of a monopoly over time; and (2) the defence of exclusive rights by reference to PSOs.

16.44 In relation to the first point, at the time when the exclusive rights were granted to the Belgian postal services in 1956 and 1971, commercial demand for specialized rapid courier services did not exist. By the time the case came before the ECJ the market had changed. The question was not therefore whether the exclusive rights had conformed with Article 86(1) when the rights were granted but rather, whether such rights were in conformity with Article 86(1) in the context of the very different market that prevailed in 1993.[44] As a result, the judgment 'places an obligation on the Member States constantly to review legal monopolies in light of changing market conditions'.[45]

---

[42] ibid, Recital 21.
[43] Case C-320/91 [1993] ECR I-2533.
[44] See further Edward, D and Hoskins, M, 'Article 90: Deregulation and EC Law. Reflections arising from the XVI FIDE Conference' (1995) 32 CML Rev 168.
[45] ibid.

16.45 The second aspect of the case concerns the relationship between exclusive rights and PSOs. The ECJ held that the law that granted exclusive rights of collection and distribution of post in Belgium was contrary to Article 86(1) in the sense that it prohibited, with criminal sanctions, an economic operator established in Belgium from operating specific services there, even though such services were distinct from services of general economic interest, met the needs of particular economic operators, and also required certain supplementary services which a traditional postal service does not offer. However, the ECJ added that the monopoly should only be reduced to the extent that the reduction did not put in question the 'economic equilibrium' of the service of general economic interest carried out by Regie des Postes. By this the ECJ meant its service to core customers. In doing so, the ECJ was relying on the exemptions from the Treaty rules which may be granted under Article 86(2) to undertakings that are entrusted[46] with the operation of services of general economic interest, a term not defined in the Treaty itself.[47]

E. Import and Export of Electricity and Gas

16.46 The existence of exclusive rights over imports and exports would seem to be an obvious breach of the EC Treaty rules on the free movement of goods and in particular, of Article 31 EC, which requires that state monopolies of a commercial character (whether operated on a direct or delegated basis) be operated in such a way as to eliminate all discrimination between nationals of Member States. It does not make state monopolies illegal, but requires that they be adjusted to achieve this objective.[48]

---

[46] For the term 'entrusted', see Case 127/73 *BRT v SABAM* [1974] ECR 51 (it can apply to private as well as public undertakings); Case 10/71 *Ministère Public de Luxembourg v Muller* [1971] ECR 723 (the legal measure by which an undertaking is entrusted may take the form of a specific national law); Commission Decision on British Telecommunications (BT), [1982] OJ L360/36 and [1983] 1 CML Rev 457 (UK statute constituting BT was held to have entrusted that body with services of general economic interest for the purposes of Art 86(2)); Commission Decision MAVEWA-ANSEAU, [1982] OJ L167/39 and [1982] 2 CML Rev 193 (the act entrusting the undertaking with a service of general economic interest need not be an act of central government).

[47] But see Art 16 EC and Commission Communication on Services of General Interest in Europe, [2001] OJ C17/4; also, Commission Staff Working Paper, *Report on Public Consultation on the Green Paper on Services of General Interest*, SEC (2004) 326, 15 March 2004. For the term 'service of general economic interest', the jurisprudence of the ECJ has established that services includes goods: see Case 82/71 *Pubblico Ministero v SAIL* [1972] ECR 119 (distribution of milk constituted a service of general economic interest if it was carried out in the interest of the citizens as a whole); Case 10/71 *Ministère Public Luxembourg v Muller* [1971] ECR 723 (an authority responsible for the navigation of an important national waterway may fall within Art 86(2)); Case 155/73 *Italy v Saatchi* [1974] ECR 409 (a television company operating under statutory powers may fall within Art 86(2)); and *Ijsselcentrale* (Case IV/32.732) Commission Decision 91/50/EEC, [1991] OJ L28/32 (generators of electricity and national utility SEP operating under concession agreements were carrying out services of general economic interest).

[48] It may be noted that there is an overlap between the powers contained in Art 31 and those contained in Art 86 which deal with public undertakings and undertakings with exclusive or special rights.

E. Import and Export of Electricity and Gas

The obligation to do so applies to all goods, including those such as electricity and gas that circulate through networks.

16.47 The provisions of Articles 28–30 require the elimination of quantitative restrictions on the import and export of goods between Member States. These obligations apply to all goods and therefore to goods that circulate through networks such as electricity and natural gas. Enforcement of these provisions is a matter for the Commission. Under Article 226, the Commission is required to enforce compliance by Member States of their obligations under the EC Treaty, including Article 31, by first delivering a reasoned opinion on the matter and then, if the Member State still does not comply, by bringing the matter before the ECJ.

(1) Early Enforcement in Energy

16.48 During the 1970s these provisions were applied to adjust state monopolies in the oil industry, and in the 1990s they were applied to electricity and gas networks. This was because state monopolies of import and export of electricity and gas or exclusive rights of transmission and distribution can by their existence frustrate the free circulation of electricity and gas within the EU and thereby frustrate the application of the rules relating to freedom of movement of goods. Prior to 1991 there had only been two challenges to such restrictions in the energy sector under Article 31.[49] They arose concerning the exclusive import of gas granted to Distrigas by the Belgian Government and the exclusive legal monopoly of the French State relating to the import and distribution of petroleum into France (see para 16.50). However, in neither case did the Commission find it necessary to take proceedings against the Member State under Article 226 to secure compliance with Article 31.

16.49 The Belgian case arose from the exclusive import concession held by Distrigas SA under Article 181 of the Act of 8 August 1980. The Commission informed the Belgian Government that the concession was contrary to Article 31. The Belgian Government accepted this opinion and undertook to revoke the concession, noting that the provisions of Article 181 would not be applied while new legislation was being prepared. Subsequently, Article 181 was amended by an Act of 29 July 1983 so as to restrict the exclusive concession to underground storage and to the transportation of natural gas.

16.50 The French case involved the exclusive legal monopoly of the French state in relation to import and distribution of petroleum into France. The Commission's action was directed at the arrangements for the import and distribution of refined petroleum products based on Article 1 of a 1946 law,[50] which reserved to the State

---

[49] *XIIIth Report on Competition Policy 1984*, 121, point 291.
[50] *XIIth Report on Competition Policy 1983*, point 221; Law No 46-628 of 8 April 1946.

exclusive import and marketing rights in relation to petroleum products, among other things. The French Government had relied on that Law to introduce a system of special import permits. In granting such permits the Government stipulated the maximum amount of motor fuel that each permit holder was permitted to sell annually in France, irrespective of whether the product had been imported or refined in France. The Commission complained that this arrangement was contrary to the provisions relating to the free movement of goods. The exclusive rights of monopolies to import or market goods constituted discrimination against exporters from other Member States within the meaning of Article 31(1) so that the special permits scheme ought to be limited to rules laying down objective standards applicable to importers or distributors of oil products.[51] This statement was based on the judgment of the ECJ in the *Manghera* case, which ruled that Article 31 must be interpreted as meaning that as from 31 December 1969 every national monopoly of a commercial character must be adjusted so as to eliminate the exclusive right to import from other Member States.[52]

(2) Electricity and Gas Import–Export Monopolies

16.51 In August 1991 the Commission announced that it intended to take action on the basis of Article 31 under the Article 226 procedure against several Member States on the ground that their legislation provided for import and export monopolies in electricity or gas or both. The countries concerned were Denmark, France, Greece, Ireland, Italy, the Netherlands, Spain, and the UK (with respect to Northern Ireland). Letters were sent in accordance with Article 226, setting a period of two months within which the Member States could submit observations on the Commission's opinion. Most of the Member States concerned indicated a willingness to adapt their legislation to meet the Commission's objections, but in several cases no action was taken within a time-limit. It should be noted that there was a close link between the Commission's actions and the ongoing negotiations concerning the first Directives on common rules for the electricity and gas sectors. This was not accidental and formed part of the Commission's strategy to establish a consensus behind its proposals.[53]

16.52 In January 1994 the Commission referred to the ECJ actions against six Member States for failure to fulfil an obligation in the infringement procedures. In each Member State there were restrictions on the import and export of electricity and,

---

[51] *VIth Report on Competition Policy 1977*, points 268 and 269.
[52] Case 59/75 *Pubblico Ministero v Flavia Manghera* [1976] ECR 91.
[53] Schmidt, SK, 'Commission Activism: Subsuming Telecommunications and Electricity under European Competition Law' [1998] J European Public Policy 169–84. Her conclusions are largely based on extensive interviews conducted with participants in the Community institutions and Member State governments.

E. Import and Export of Electricity and Gas

in the case of France, also of gas. In the Netherlands, final consumers were entitled to import electricity for their own needs, but for voltages exceeding 500V, only the utility Samenwerkende Elektriciteitsproductiebedrijven (SEP) was authorized to import electricity for public distribution. This was provided for in the Electricity Law of 16 November 1989. In Italy all of the activities of import, export, generation, transmission, distribution, and sale of electricity had been entrusted to the Ente Nazionale per l'Energia Elletrica (ENEL) by the nationalization law of 1962, No 1643. Further, undertakings other than ENEL were expressly prohibited from importing, exporting, or trading in electricity or transmitting electricity on behalf of third parties. The restriction was contained in Legislative Decree No 342 of 18 March 1965. Imports and exports of electricity were also subject to the grant of a licence by the Minister of Public Works. In France all activities in the import and export of electricity and gas, as well as generation, transmission, and distribution were nationalized in 1946 and management entrusted to public undertakings of an industrial and commercial nature. As a result, only Electricité de France (EDF) was allowed to carry out import, export, and transmission of electricity. Import and export of gas was entrusted on an exclusive basis to Gaz de France (GDF) under a concession agreement concluded with the State on 27 November 1958 for a period of 75 years. In Spain the national high-voltage electricity system was designated a public service by Law No 49/84 and managed as such by a state company, Red Eléctrica de España (Redesa).

Proceedings against Denmark in relation to its restrictions on gas imports were halted when the Commission was sent a copy of the Danish Government's letter of April 1994 to the state-owned utility, Dangas, which indicated that it would repeal the restriction. Similarly, the case against Ireland was withdrawn from the register before the hearing on the ground that the legislation in question did not expressly prohibit other companies from carrying out the same tasks as the Electricity Supply Board.[54]   **16.53**

The Commission's argument in each of the four remaining cases was that the national rules were liable to restrict trade between Member States and were therefore contrary to Articles 28, 30, and 31 EC. With respect to import rights, the Commission argued that a national import monopoly prevented producers in other Member States from selling electricity and, in the case of France, gas within the territory of the Netherlands, Italy, France, and Spain respectively to customers other than the holders of the monopoly. Moreover, potential customers in one of those Member States were unable freely to choose their source of supply of electricity from other Member States.   **16.54**

---

[54] [1994] OJ C202/9, and Order of the President of 11 September 1995, [1996] OJ C336/23.

16.55 On export rights, the Commission's argument was that holders of such rights tend to reserve national production for the national market, and so place the domestic market at a disadvantage, to the detriment of demand from other Member States.

(a) The Dutch Case

16.56 In its judgment in the case against the Netherlands,[55] the ECJ found that the exclusive import rights were indeed contrary to Article 31 EC, and for that reason it was unnecessary to consider whether they were contrary to Article 28, or whether they might be justified under Article 30.

16.57 It reasoned, first, that it is not necessarily a requirement for illegality that the exclusive rights to import a given product relate to all imports. It is sufficient for these rights to relate to such a proportion that they enable the monopoly to have an appreciable influence on imports, as was shown in an earlier case, *Commission v Greece*.[56] The exclusive rights held by SEP for electricity for public distribution fall within that category.

16.58 Secondly, the ECJ rejected the argument that SEP could not be regarded as a monopoly of a commercial character within the meaning of Article 31. The case law of the Court applies to situations in which the national authorities are in a position to control, direct, or appreciably influence trade between Member States through a body established for that purpose or a delegated monopoly. Exclusive rights give rise to that kind of situation.

16.59 Thirdly, against the contention that only the discriminatory exercise of exclusive rights, not merely the holding of them, is prohibited under Article 31, the ECJ held that the aim of Article 31(1) EC would be met if, in a Member State where a commercial monopoly exists, the free movement of goods from other Member States comparable to those with which the national monopoly is concerned were not ensured. The very existence of exclusive import rights in a Member State impedes free movement since it deprives economic operators in other Member States of the possibility of offering their products to customers of their choice in the Member State concerned. In the Dutch case, all imports had to be incorporated into the plans drawn up by SEP.

16.60 The other key issue in the case concerned the possible justification of these exclusive rights under Article 86(2). The ECJ examined the Commission's main argument that Article 86(2) cannot be relied on to justify state measures that are incompatible with the Treaty rules on the free movement of goods. Taking into account the scope and combined effect of Article 86(1) and (2), the ECJ considered that Article 86(2)

---

[55] Case C-157/94 *Commission v Netherlands* [1997] ECR I-5699.
[56] Case 347/88 *Commission v Hellenic Republic* [1990] ECR I-4747, para 41.

E. Import and Export of Electricity and Gas

could be relied on to justify the grant of exclusive rights by a Member State to an undertaking entrusted with the operation of services of general economic interest. This applied even where such rights were contrary to Article 31, subject to two conditions:

(1) it applied to the extent that performance of the particular tasks assigned to it could only be achieved through the grant of such rights; and
(2) the grant of such rights should not affect the development of trade to such an extent that it would be contrary to the interests of the Community.

16.61 With respect to the first point, the ECJ held that it is not necessary for there to be a threat to the financial balance or economic viability of the undertaking entrusted with the operation of a service of general economic interest. The test is whether it would not be possible for the undertaking to perform the particular tasks entrusted to it in the absence of the rights at issue. The tasks should be defined by reference to the obligations and constraints to which the undertaking is subject. Citing the judgment in *Corbeau*,[57] the ECJ noted that the conditions for the application of Article 86(2) are fulfilled if maintenance of those rights is necessary to permit the holder to perform the tasks of general economic interest assigned to it under economically acceptable conditions. It was beyond doubt that the removal of SEP's exclusive import rights would have radical effects upon the current organization of the electricity supply industry in the Netherlands. Although the Commission, in recognizing this, had outlined in general terms some alternatives in place of the rights at issue, it had not taken into account the particularities of the national electricity system nor of the question whether those alternatives would have enabled SEP to perform the tasks of general economic interest assigned to it in compliance with the obligations and constraints imposed upon it. The burden of proof here lay with the Commission and not with the Member State: the latter did not have to provide positive proof that no other measure could enable those tasks to be performed under the same conditions.

16.62 The ECJ went on to criticize the Commission's responses in the proceedings brought against the Netherlands under Article 226. It was the Commission's task to prove the allegation that the obligation had not been fulfilled and to provide the ECJ with the information required to enable it to determine whether the obligation had not been fulfilled. In the pre-litigation procedure the Netherlands had provided a justification of its position. However, when bringing proceedings before the ECJ, the Commission had specified only the legal considerations and not the factual ones on which the complaint was based. Both were required, even if only in summary form. This, the ECJ argued, had the effect of narrowing the

---

[57] Case C-320/91 [1993] ECR I-2533.

terms of the dispute brought before it. It could base its judgment only on the merits of the pleas in law, since it could not undertake an assessment of the alternatives which a Member State might adopt to ensure an electricity supply which was as inexpensive as possible, and supplied in a socially responsible manner.

16.63 The approach adopted by the Commission (involving failure to produce an economic assessment of the electricity market) was not accepted by the ECJ. Essentially, it was the Commission's job to provide this in an area of industrial activity which is highly regulated and economically complex. Further, on the basis of the above reasons, the ECJ declared itself unable to consider whether the rights granted to SEP went further than was necessary to enable it to perform the tasks of general economic interest assigned to it.

16.64 The second condition which had to be fulfilled for SEP's exclusive import rights to escape the application of the Treaty rules under Article 86(2) was that the development of trade must not be affected to such an extent as would be contrary to the interests of the Community. On this matter, the ECJ noted that the Commission had not provided an explanation which would demonstrate that the development of intra-Community trade in electricity had been and continues to be affected by SEP's exclusive import rights to an extent that is contrary to the interests of the Community. Yet it was the Commission's task to do so, in order to prove the alleged failure to fulfil obligations. It should have provided a definition of the Community interest in relation to which the development of trade had to be assessed. In the absence of a common policy in this area, the Commission was under an obligation to show how the development of direct trade between producers and consumers, in parallel with the development of trade between the major networks, would have been possible, taking into account the existing capacity and the transmission and distribution arrangements. The Commission's application was dismissed.

16.65 As is clear from the above, the question of the admissibility of certain arguments was crucial. It had two aspects which defined the ECJ's later reasoning. To begin with, there had to be debate by the parties on the economic aspects of the action. This had not been done. Secondly, the well-foundedness of the action was preconditioned by its scope: that is, the import and export monopolies. Arguments which extended beyond that scope could not be considered. This meant that a challenge to the existing regimes for transmission and distribution by the Commission was not admissible. If then a Member State were to argue that the abolition of import and export monopolies would require considerable modification of transmission and distribution systems, it could not be countered by the Commission that they also required to be changed. This point about admissibility is relevant to the other cases outlined below.

16.66 It may be noted that, by not examining Articles 28 and 30, the ECJ did not follow the reasoning of Advocate-General Cosmas in his Opinion on the cases delivered

E. Import and Export of Electricity and Gas

on 26 November 1996. He had considered that the exclusive rights infringed Article 28 and were not justifiable on public security grounds under Article 30. It may also be noted that by the time the judgments were delivered the 1989 Electricity Law had been superseded by a new statute on electricity in the Netherlands. If the Commission were to examine the wider, extra-legal context in which the electricity supply arrangements operated, its task would be rather different, although not necessarily any easier.

(b) The Italian Case

16.67 In the linked case C-158/94, the ECJ adopted a similar line of reasoning with respect to the existence of exclusive rights and the interpretation of Article 86(2) as in the Dutch case.[58] However, it also tackled the issue of whether electricity could be classified as goods or services.

16.68 The Italian Government argued that electricity does not fall within the category of 'goods' but is rather a service, and as such does not fall within the scope of Articles 28–31. After all, it is an incorporeal substance that cannot be stored and has no economic existence as such, in the sense that it is not useful in itself but only through its possible applications. In this sense, it resembles a service. The Italian Government made exactly this point in its case: it followed that the import and export of electricity were therefore aspects of management of the electricity network. This argument was (unsurprisingly) rejected by the ECJ. It noted that in the *Almelo* case[59] the ECJ had observed that in Community law and also in the national laws of the Member States, electricity constituted a 'good' within the meaning of Article 28 EC. It also noted that electricity is regarded as a good under the Community's tariff nomenclature (Code CN 27.16) and that it had already been accepted that electricity may fall within the scope of Article 31 in *Costa v ENEL*.[60]

16.69 The Government of Italy had also tried to base its case for electricity as exempt from the rules on the free movement of goods on two earlier cases decided by the ECJ. The judgments were *HM Customs and Excise v Schindler*[61] and *ERT v DEP*.[62] In *Schindler*, the ECJ held that the import of lottery advertisements and tickets into a Member State with a view to the participation by residents of that Member State

---

[58] [1997] ECR I-5789. The ECJ criticized the Commission for failure to take into account the particular features of the national system of electricity supply and especially those imposed by geography. The Commission had also failed to consider whether the alternative means to exclusive rights it proposed would in practice enable the electricity utility, ENEL, to perform the tasks of general economic interest entrusted to it under economically acceptable conditions. Again, it was the task of the Commission to prove that the obligation had not been fulfilled, and this had not been done.
[59] Case C-393/92 *Gemeente Almelo v Energiebedrijf Ijsselmij NV* [1994] ECR I-1477, para 28.
[60] Case 6/64 [1964] ECR 585.
[61] Case C-275/92 [1994] ECR I-1039.
[62] Case C-260/89 [1991] ECR I-2925, paras 5.22–5.23.

in a lottery conducted in another Member State relates to a 'service' within the meaning of Article 49 EC. In *ERT*, it held that the grant to a single undertaking of exclusive rights in relation to television broadcasting and the grant for that purpose of an exclusive right to import, hire, or distribute material and products necessary for that broadcasting does not as such constitute a measure having an effect equivalent to a quantitative restriction within the meaning of Article 28. However, in *Schindler* the ECJ had expressly stated that the import and distribution of the documents and tickets required for the organization of a lottery are not ends in themselves, since their sole purpose was to enable residents of Member States to participate in the lottery. This judgment could not therefore be relied upon in the situation of ENEL, where the services required for the import or export of electricity and its transmission and distribution are only the means to supply users with goods within the meaning of the Treaty. Nor could the Italian Government rely on the *ERT* case. There, it was held that the granting of an exclusive right to import, hire, or distribute materials and products necessary for television broadcasting to an undertaking with a monopoly over television-related services, did not constitute a measure having an effect equivalent to a quantitative restriction provided that no discrimination is created between domestic products and imported ones to the detriment of the latter. There was no support for the argument that the import and export of electricity falls outside the scope of the rules of the Treaty relating to the free movement of goods.

(c) The French Case

16.70 The French case[63] involved arrangements in both the electricity and gas sectors. The exclusive rights in question were based on a concession and not on a statute. The Commission's argument was similar to the previous cases: the national import monopoly enjoyed by EDF and GDF had the effect of preventing producers in other Member States from selling their production to customers in France other than those monopoly holders. It also prevented potential consumers in France from freely choosing their sources of supply for electricity and gas from other Member States. As measures having an effect equivalent to quantitative restrictions on imports, they were contrary to Article 28. They constituted discrimination within the meaning of Article 31 regarding exporters established in the Member States and users established in the Member State concerned. The Commission also argued that the same considerations applied to the exclusive export rights of EDF and GDF. Holders of such rights tend to allocate national production to the national market to the detriment of demand from other Member States. They should therefore be regarded as discriminatory within the meaning of Articles 30 and 31 EC.[64]

---

[63] Case C-159/94 *Commission v France* [1997] ECR I-5815.
[64] See Case C-189/95 *Franzen* [1997] ECR I-5909, for the ECJ's further exposition on Art 31.

E. Import and Export of Electricity and Gas

16.71 In fact, the French Government had already conceded that available national production of both electricity and gas is reserved as a matter of priority to users within French territory. The ECJ concluded therefore that the exclusive export rights of EDF and GDF had the effect—if not the object—of specifically restricting patterns of exports. A difference of treatment was thereby established between domestic trade and export trade, in a way that gave a special advantage to the French domestic market.

16.72 With respect to exclusive import rights, the French Government's objections were not upheld. It had argued that trade in electricity is carried out under largely uniform conditions within the Community but that neither final users nor distributors anywhere enjoy the freedom to choose their suppliers. EDF is therefore not in a more favourable position than operators in other Member States and the import monopoly does not affect the conditions of competition in France, to the detriment of the latter, as compared with those found in other Member States.

16.73 The same argument can be applied to the gas industry, with the caveat that in many cases there is no statutory monopoly on imports. However, referring to the judgment in the *Manghera* case,[65] the ECJ held that the objective of Article 31(1) would not be attained if, in a Member State where a commercial monopoly exists, the free movement of goods from other Member States comparable to those with which the national monopoly is concerned, were not ensured. Exclusive import rights in a Member State do after all deprive economic operators in other Member States of the opportunity to offer their products to consumers of their choice in the Member State concerned. This applies irrespective of the conditions that they encounter in their Member State of origin or in other Member States.

16.74 In the ECJ judgment, the reasoning was similar to that adopted in the Dutch and Italian cases, concluding that the Commission had not proved its case, confining itself only to legal arguments. It was therefore incumbent upon the Commission in proceedings under Article 226 to prove that the obligation had not been fulfilled and to provide the ECJ with sufficient information to enable it to determine whether the obligation had not been fulfilled. This had not been done.

16.75 **Public service element** The ECJ paid special attention to the definition of particular tasks entrusted to EDF and GDF. These included compliance with PSOs and with the implementation of national environmental and regional policies. The elimination of the exclusive rights would, the French Government argued, compromise the performance of some or all of these obligations and make it difficult or impossible to contribute to the above policies. The Commission

---

[65] Case C-59/75 *Public Prosecutor v Manghera* [1976] ECR 91.

challenged the legal basis of the PSOs as insufficient to constitute particular tasks within the meaning of Article 86(2).

16.76 However, the ECJ's decision went against the Commission. An undertaking may be entrusted with the operation of services of general economic interest through the grant of a concession governed by public law[66]—particularly when such concessions have been granted to give effect to the obligations imposed upon undertakings which by statute have been entrusted with the operation of a service of general economic interest, as is the case with EDF and GDF. Moreover, there were clear links between Articles 36 and 37 of the 1946 Law and the concessions granted to the undertakings.

16.77 The ECJ turned to the specific PSOs. For these to fall within the particular tasks entrusted to it, they had to be linked to the subject matter of the service of general economic interest in question. They also had to be designed to make a direct contribution to satisfying that interest. This could not apply to obligations which concerned environmental and regional policy imposed on undertakings entrusted with supplying the country with electricity and gas. Even the French Government had conceded that there was no obligation specific to those undertakings and to their business imposed on EDF and GDF.

16.78 Other PSOs were more defensible. For example, the obligations of supplying all customers, ensuring continuity of supply, and treating customers equally, were each included in terms and conditions annexed to the agreement under which EDF was granted a concession in respect of the general electricity supply network. However, the ECJ ruled differently with respect to the alleged obligation of EDF to seek the most competitive tariffs and the lowest possible costs for the community. Neither the limits laid down in the terms and conditions for the adjustment of tariffs nor those for upward revision were such as to guarantee that the objective of securing the most competitive tariffs and the lowest cost would be attained.

16.79 For GDF the legal basis for its PSOs was unclear in the defence, but the ECJ nonetheless concluded that, on the basis of the texts produced, it was subject to obligations of continuity, supply, and equal treatment as between consumers. As a result, the ECJ held that it was possible to examine the necessity of maintaining EDF's and GDF's exclusive import and export rights but only in relation to the three PSOs which the French Government had proved to exist.

(d) The Spanish Case[67]

16.80 In contrast to the other three decisions, the ECJ found that the Commission had alleged that there was a statutory monopoly but had not proved its existence. The action was dismissed.

---

[66] Case C-393/92 *Gemeente Almelo v Energiebedrijf Ijssellmij NV* [1994] ECR I-1477, para 47.
[67] Case C-160/94 *Commission v Spain* [1997] ECR I-5851.

E. Import and Export of Electricity and Gas

(3) Assessment

16.81 In the cases involving the Netherlands, France, and Italy, the ECJ held that the exclusive import and export rights did indeed impede the free movement of goods and had a direct impact on the conditions regarding both outlets and supplies to operators in other Member States, contravening Article 31. However, the ECJ ruled that the Commission had not proved its case against the restrictions imposed by the Member State concerned.

16.82 These ECJ findings did not follow the Opinion of Advocate-General Darmon[68] in the *Almelo* case, who declared that import monopolies for electricity are justified particularly by considerations of security of supply. Nor do they follow the Opinion of Advocate-General Cosmas, based on Articles 28 and 31, that the import rights did not affect Community trade but the export rights were unjustified. Security of supply arguments played an important role in the Advocate-General's argument, but not in the ECJ judgments.

16.83 There are three positive elements in the judgments that may be noted:[69]

(1) The judgments provided important guidance on matters concerning burden of proof and admissibility in relation to Article 86. This may prove useful to the Commission in any subsequent steps it may take.
(2) The ECJ held that the practices in question were indeed contrary to Article 31 (except in the case involving Spain).
(3) The cases had a beneficial effect on the adoption of the Electricity and Gas Directives.

These three points are elaborated below.

(a) Burden of Proof and Article 86 Admissibility

16.84 In *Commission v Netherlands, Italy and France*,[70] the ECJ held that the exclusive import and export rights did indeed impede the free movement of goods and had a direct impact on the conditions regarding both outlets and supplies to operators in other Member States, contravening Article 31. However, the ECJ ruled that the Commission had not proved the case against the restrictions being imposed by the Member States concerned. The cases raise delicate issues of burden of proof. However, they also settle a key issue. Previous case law has been quite inconsistent as to whether monopolies are *legal* unless shown to be against the Community interest (ie, the Commission must so prove) or monopolies are

---

[68] Case C-393/92 *Gemeente Almelo v Energiebedrijf Ijsselmij NV* [1994] ECR I-1477.
[69] Cameron, P, 'Towards an Internal Market in Energy: The Carrot and Stick Approach' (1998) 23 ELR 579–91.
[70] Joined Cases C 157–159/94 [1997] ECR I-5699.

illegal unless the Member States show them to be in the Community interest. The more complex the area, the more important the burden becomes. Here, it is explicitly stated that the burden of proof falls upon the Member State which invokes Article 86 to show that the conditions are fulfilled.[71] This statement may ease the task of the Commission, not only in energy but also in related fields such as telecommunications. This development is the key to an understanding of how 'conflicts over burdens of proof' can arise: in particular, the burden of proof which falls on the Commission under Article 226 and the burden of proof which falls on the Member State under Article 86. In this case, however, the burden of proof lay on the Commission to show both the infringement and the absence of a basis for an Article 86(2) defence, since this was an infringement action brought under Article 226.

(b) Practices Contrary to Article 31

16.85 Three of the judgments turned on the application of Article 86(2), and clearly the Commission had not prepared itself for the possibility that this would provide a successful defence under Article 31. The supporting arguments presented were deemed insufficient to prove that the Member States' measures affecting imports and exports were restrictive measures not protected by Article 86(2). On the other hand, it is important to note that the ECJ did not endorse the restrictive practices adopted by the Member States concerned. On the contrary, it concluded that they were indeed in breach of Article 31. Instead, it held that the Commission had not proved its case, and by implication left the door open for it to do further research with a view to trying again.

(c) Promoting Adoption of Electricity and Gas Directives

16.86 In the wider context of the internal energy market programme, it may be argued that the ECJ's willingness to consider the actions had important consequences for the debate on the first Electricity Directive in particular.[72] It appears that all parties were eager to reach agreement on a compromise position on that Directive prior to the ECJ's judgments.[73] Above all, the proceedings contributed to the impression among incumbent energy utilities and Member States that the status quo was not sustainable, an impression given already by *Höfner* and other cases mentioned above.

---

[71] ibid, para 94. However, note the contrasting approach adopted in Case C-163/99 *Portugal v Commission* [2001] ECR I-2613.

[72] This is noted also by Blanchard, P, 'French Electricity Sector: ECJ Decision on Monopolies for the Import and Export of Electricity' (1999) 17 J Energy Natural Resources L 265–80.

[73] Schmidt, SK, 'Commission Activism: Subsuming Telecommunications and Electricity under European Competition Law' [1998] J European Public Policy 169–84.

F. Conclusions

16.87 The barriers to import and export of energy in the EU represented a very clear case of incompatibility with the idea of an internal market. Yet it was not until 1991 that a concerted attempt was made to challenge Member States to justify them. The results of the exercise have been very positive, even if the cases brought by the Commission to the ECJ may be assessed less favourably. The procedure adopted led to a considerable debate and to changes in current practices by several Member States before ECJ proceedings began. However, the lack of any real challenge to these exclusive rights for many years should act as a warning against high expectations of change through this route with respect to other exclusive rights that may have less obviously negative effects on the EU economy.

16.88 The exclusive rights on import and export were among the few that were clearly prohibited by Article 31. For other exclusive rights concerning goods and services, the starting point was the presumption of compatibility with Community law.[74] This was reversed by the Court with respect to goods and subsequently with respect to services.

16.89 The *Corbeau* judgment[75] went further and established the principle of the incompatibility of any exclusive right with the competition rules of the EC Treaty, unless it can be shown to be necessary for the achievement of a task of general economic interest. This development in judicial thinking is in line with the priority given to the creation of a single market from 1986 onwards. In this situation, as one author comments:

> The obstacles to the four freedoms have to be justified on a case by case basis, in accordance with the principle of proportionality, on the basis of the exemptions provided for in the Treaty and developed by case law such as the requirements envisaged in Article 36 or the tasks of general interest of Article 90(2) of the EC Treaty.[76]

16.90 For some, the judgments of the ECJ in the cases directly relating to the energy sector proved to be a disappointment.[77] As one observer noted at the time:

> Within the electricity sector, the Commission has proved to be the driving force behind the European integration, whereas the ECJ has tended to take a more

---

[74] Case 155/73 *Italy v Saatchi* [1974] ECR 409.
[75] Case C-320/91 [1993] ECR I-2533.
[76] Ehlermann, CD, 'The Role of the European Commission as regards National Energy Policies' (1994) 12 J Energy Natural Resources L 342, 348. However, note the approaches taken in Joined Cases C 147 & 148/97 *Deutsche Post* [2000] ECR I-825, para 34, and Case 475/99 *Ambulanz Glöckner v Landkreis Südwestpfalz* [2001] ECR I-8089, para 34.
[77] With respect to the judgments in the import and export monopoly cases, they 'seem to herald the end of an era of progressive development towards a more market-oriented economy in the Community': Slot, PJ, 'Note' (1998) 35 CML Rev 1183, 1202.

hesitant and cautious attitude and to pay more regard to the interests of Member States.[78]

This comment is revealing in its assumptions about governance of the EU. The challenge of bringing about liberalization in the energy sector called into question the balance between the various Community institutions. Both the abandonment of the Article 86(3) draft Directives in 1991 and the highly cautious approach adopted by the Commission in the proceedings on import and export monopolies in electricity and gas show an awareness of the delicate nature of its tasks, in the face of strident and persistent opposition on the part of several important Member States and some major industry participants. The absence of a consensus among Member States meant that cases brought before the ECJ carried the direct or indirect effect of bringing pressure on the ECJ to play a law-making role by interpreting Community law in a progressive way with respect to liberalization, when it was clear that such a course had no support among key Member States. The ECJ judgments are only disappointing to the extent that it was expected to play this role—which it refused to do.[79] In the event, the development of ECJ jurisprudence during this period is positive and encouraging but hardly revolutionary. As the judge-rapporteur in the energy import–export monopolies cases commented:

> ... it is unrealistic to assume that a coherent Community policy for each industry can be developed by the Commission pursuing ad hoc cases before the Court of Justice. It follows therefore that there must, to some extent, be Community legislation in this field. Without a legislative framework there will be inequality between the market conditions in each Member State.[80]

16.91 The thesis advanced from the outset of the internal energy market programme, especially by the Commission, that the powers to bring about competition in EU energy markets already existed in the primary law independently of the legislative route under Article 95, is one that *may* be correct. However, it required the slow, consensus-building approach of Article 95, involving all the Community institutions. It may also be correct that the principal ideas contained in the first Electricity

---

[78] Pfrang, E, *Towards Liberalization of the European Electricity Markets* (1999) 122: 'The "velvet revolution", as initiated by the Commission from the late 1980s onwards so as to promote the opening of the electricity sector by applying competition and internal market rules was thus impeded by the ECJ.'

[79] Edward, D and Hoskins, M, 'Article 90: Deregulation and EC Law. Reflections arising from the XVI FIDE Conference' (1995) 32 CML Rev 168, 185–186: 'the Commission and the Council cannot expect the Court of Justice to act as the Community legislator in this field. The role which the Court can play is restricted by limits inherent in the nature of judicial control. Where necessary, the Commission must play its part by proposing legislation to the Council under Art 100A (now Art 95) or by adopting its own legislation under Art 90(3) [now Art 86(3)].'

[80] Edward, D and Hoskins, M, 'Article 90: Deregulation and EC Law. Reflections arising from the XVI FIDE Conference' (1995) 32 CML Rev 168, 181–2.

F. Conclusions

and Gas Directives are implicit in the primary law, but it is also beyond any doubt that the current energy law represented by their successors contains new, pro-market ideas and mechanisms designed for the task of introducing competition into these sectors.

In any case, the elaboration of such detailed rules has to be reviewed by the Council and Parliament. The Article 95 procedure is the available means of ensuring that such a review of proposals for legislation in a sensitive sector takes place. **16.92**

Ultimately the idea that a viable alternative existed to the adoption of Directives under Article 95 is erroneous, at least with respect to this stage of market reform. The early attempt to build a single market in energy on the basis of Directives issued under Article 86(3) was stillborn in the energy sector. Similarly, progress on the basis of Commission decisions taken on a case-by-case basis during this period was encouraging (see paras 13.15–13.30), but it also suggested an uncertain and rather piecemeal strategy, hardly calculated to bring about a level playing field and an internal market in this area. **16.93**

The interplay between Article 86 and the developing secondary rules of the new energy law that characterized this period has continued to be of practical importance (see *VEMW* case, paras 5.132–5.135; 13.59–13.86). The EU's phased approach towards the liberalization of its energy markets appears to offer ample scope for legal challenges as the transitional period to real competition extends further into the future. **16.94**

Part IV

COMPETING OBJECTIVES

17

ENVIRONMENTAL PROTECTION

A. Introduction	17.01	(3) National Measures and State Aid	17.33
B. Renewable Energy	17.05	(a) The Swedish Energy Tax Case	17.35
(1) Combining Internal Market and Renewables Regulation	17.06	(b) The Dutch Energy Tax Exemption	17.38
(2) Trade	17.09	(4) Current Approaches to EU Carbon Taxation	17.39
(3) State Aid	17.10	D. The Emissions Trading Scheme	17.42
(a) The *Q7* Case	17.11	(1) The Scheme	17.43
(b) The German Feed-in Laws	17.14	(2) Implementation	17.46
C. Energy Taxation	17.17	(3) Impacts on Competition and the Internal Energy Market	17.49
(1) The Carbon Tax	17.19		
(2) The Energy Products Directive		E. Conclusions	17.51
(a) Origins	17.22		
(b) What the Energy Products Directive Requires	17.25		

> Environmental protection requirements must be integrated into the definition and implementation of the Community policies and activities.
>
> Article 6 EC

A. Introduction

The commitment of the EC Treaty to a policy on the environment which ensures a high level of environmental protection and an improvement in its quality is clear.[1] The Treaty sets out parameters for that policy and requirements as to its implementation. Under Article 6 EC environmental protection requirements have to be integrated into the definition and implementation of all Community policies and actions referred to in Article 3 EC, in particular with a view to promoting sustainable development. The list of activities includes measures on energy, an internal

17.01

---

[1] Arts 2, 3(1)(l) and 174–6 EC.

market, and the avoidance of distortions to competition. This has been done in relation to both the Electricity and Gas Directives.[2]

17.02 During the period when the Community has been making efforts to establish an internal market in energy, environmental policy has been strongly influenced by the EU's commitments to increase the share of renewable energy and achieve substantial reductions in carbon emissions. The result has been the design and adoption of measures that have actual and potential impacts upon the opening of electricity and gas markets to competition,[3] but are intended to be consistent with such opening. In particular, these are the measures to promote the use of renewable sources of energy under Directive 2001/77 (the Renewables Directive),[4] taxation of energy uses,[5] and the Directive establishing the European Emissions Trading System.[6]

17.03 This chapter is concerned with the interface between the above measures and the introduction of competition into EU energy markets. The authors of the environmental measures could hardly have been unaware of the high price paid in the past by the perceived negative implications of specific environmental proposals for competitiveness.[7] The Community's failure to secure an EU energy tax in the 1990s was only one example of this. As a result, the recent environmental measures have shown a high degree of market sensitivity in both design and implementation. The emissions trading scheme (ETS) is a particularly vivid illustration of this. While in the past the

---

[2] See inter alia Directive (EC) 2003/54 concerning common rules for the internal market in electricity and repealing Directive (EC) 96/92 [2003] OJ L176/37, Recitals 2, 18, 22, 25, and 26; Directive (EC) 2003/55 concerning common rules for the internal market in natural gas and repealing Directive (EC) 98/30 [2003] OJ L176/57, Recitals 27 and 24.

[3] Other measures have been adopted that impact upon the energy sector (and have impacts on the achievement of carbon reduction) but have less evident actual or potential impacts upon competition: eg, the body of energy efficiency legislation comprising Directive (EC) 2003/66 on energy labelling of household electric refrigerators, freezers and their combinations [2003] OJ L170/10; Directive (EC) 2002/91 on the energy performance of buildings [2003] OJ L1/65; Directive (EC) 2005/32 establishing a framework for the setting of ecodesign requirements for energy-using products [2005] OJ L191/29 and Directive (EC) 2006/32 on the promotion of end-use efficiency and energy services [2006] OJ L114/64. Measures concerning environmental impact assessment also have implications for the energy sector, specifically: Directive (EEC) 97/11 on the assessment of the effects of certain public and private projects on the environment [1997] OJ L73/5.

[4] Directive (EC) 2001/77 on the promotion of electricity produced from renewable energy sources in the internal electricity market [2001] OJ L283/33.

[5] Elements of Directive (EC) 2004/8 on the promotion of cogeneration based on a useful heat demand in the internal energy market [2004] OJ L52/50 may also be noted in this respect: 'the development of cogeneration contributes to enhancing competition'; '[i]t is therefore necessary to take measures to ensure that the potential is better exploited within the framework of the internal energy market' (Recitals 2 and 1 respectively).

[6] Directive (EC) 2003/87 establishing a scheme for greenhouse gas emission allowance trading within the European Community and amending Directive (EC) 96/91 [2003] OJ L275/32.

[7] This subject is discussed by Tarasofsky, RG and Cosbey, A, 'Trade, Competitiveness and Climate Change: Exploring the Issues', Chatham House/IISD paper, December 2005, <http://www.chathamhouse.org.uk/sustainabledevelopment>.

overall environmental aims of the EU might have been seen as a source of constraint upon the development of an internal energy market, the declared aim now is to create opportunities for synergy. Nonetheless, the potential for market distortion remains.

The sections of this chapter will address, first, the treatment of competition matters under the Renewables Directive. This will be rather summary in character since the Directive has already been examined in some detail in Chapter 10. Secondly, it addresses the subject of energy taxation as an instrument to improve energy efficiency and for fuel substitution towards products emitting less or no CO_2. In this respect, Directive (EC) 2003/96[8] on energy products taxation is the result of long, and mostly unsuccessful, attempts by the Commission to secure adoption of measures in this field. It is not likely to be the last of such efforts to use the taxation instrument to achieve environmental goals in the energy sector. Finally, the chapter examines some aspects of the ETS introduced in Directive (EC) 2003/87. In all of these cases, the measures provide market-based (or at least market-sensitive) frameworks for environmental measures that are designed to ensure compatibility with the pro-competitive thrust of the single energy market measures. 17.04

B. Renewable Energy

A plethora of mechanisms to support renewable energy sources have been adopted among the Member States. They include green certificates, investment aid, tax exemptions or reductions, tax refunds or direct price support, and have the effect of creating advantages for renewable sources in energy markets. The Renewables Directive does not attempt to harmonize the many support schemes; instead, it attempts to monitor them by means of extensive reporting requirements. As a result, it permits considerable discrepancies among the various schemes to continue, and may create difficulties for an eventual harmonization of the schemes. No attempt at harmonization appears likely in the near future, partly due to the wide differences and trends among the current systems and also due to the possibility that short-term changes 'might potentially disrupt certain markets and make it more difficult for Member States in meeting their targets'.[9] 17.05

---

[8] Directive (EC) 2003/96 restructuring the Community framework for the taxation of energy products and electricity [2003] L283/51.

[9] European Commission, *The Support of Electricity from Renewable Sources*, COM (2005) 627 final, 7 December 2005, 11. The Commission explained elsewhere that '[t]he situation would be very different if wind energy performed across the Community at the level achieved in Denmark, Germany and Spain, if biomass heating was as dynamic everywhere as it is in Finland or if geothermal energy was managed at the level of development being achieved in Sweden and Italy': Commission Communication, *Report in accordance with Article 3 of Directive 2001/77/EC, evaluation of the effect of legislative instruments and other Community policies on the development of the contribution of renewable sources in the EU and proposals for concrete actions*, COM (2004) 366 final, 26 May 2004.

(1) Combining Internal Market and Renewables Regulation

17.06 In spite of this unpromising context, the Commission is optimistic that progress can be made in the context of a competitive market.[10] Suppliers may even be encouraged to innovate by offering 'green' electricity or by giving price reductions to consumers which are able or willing to moderate their electricity demand at peak periods. However, there is some evidence that the differences between national schemes have led to problems in relation to grid management. There have been complaints to the Commission from some suppliers of renewables—and in particular suppliers of wind power—that they have enjoyed only limited access to networks and that the connection agreements they have been offered include terms that are unfair.[11] As small generators and new entrants on the market, they face similar obstacles in gaining network access and are vulnerable to limitations in the forms of unbundling adopted by the utilities concerned.

17.07 In part, this is a complaint that the market has not yet become sufficiently liberalized. Ultimately, if and when the internal energy market develops fully, an independent transmission system operator (TSO) and an independent distribution system operator (DSO) will be required to guarantee grid access to all generators, and will be obliged to develop the network according to a long-term strategy which would take renewable energy into account. However, in some Member States, one or a very few electricity companies are dominant, and are often vertically integrated, contributing to the kind of frustrations behind the above complaints. The uneven progress of the internal market measures may then act to hamper the development of renewable forms of energy. A better exchange of information between TSOs and the introduction of more intra-day trading might improve this situation.

17.08 At the same time, a problem for the TSOs (quite unrelated to any unbundling requirement) arises from the character of renewable sources of energy: they are intermittent sources of supply. The difficulties of predicting wind generation have already been encountered in Denmark, Spain, and the UK. Balancing costs are also affected by the volume of intermittent power that has to be balanced. In these countries, systems are in place for charging for the deviation from the predicted generation of electricity, irrespective of origin, which takes into account renewable sources such as wind power. The timing of 'gate closure'[12] is also affected by this factor. Essentially, systems that are designed with thermal or hydro-electric power in mind have to develop new rules to integrate the intermittent character

---

[10] European Commission, *Report on Progress in Creating the Internal Gas and Electricity Market; Technical Annex to the Report*, SEC (2005), 27.
[11] ibid 101–2.
[12] This means the closing time for electricity markets after which bids from electricity generators are no longer accepted.

B. Renewable Energy

of renewable sources of energy, and take their needs into account. The regulatory challenges that can result are illustrated by the disturbances in the Netherlands and Poland that were created by the influence of wind power on cross-border network connections between Germany and its neighbours.[13]

(2) Trade

The various national support schemes have an impact upon trade within the Community. This potential for distortion was a source of concern in the design of the Directive. For example, Article 5 of the Renewables Directive provides for a certification system, guaranteeing the production source of all electricity put on to the grid. This facilitates the trading of electricity generated from renewable sources, but is designed to avoid difficulties of the kind experienced in the *Outokumpu* case[14] in Finland. The impossibility of differentiating between different sources of electricity generation played havoc with the Finnish internal taxation system, which itself was aimed at increasing the production of renewable energy by means of targeted tax breaks. Another instance of the measures taken in connection with the trade aspects of renewable energy is in Article 3(6) of the Electricity Directive (see paras 5.12, 5.31) which establishes a mandatory disclosure regime that requires consumers to be informed of the contribution that each source of energy makes to the overall energy mix. The aim is to increase the value of green electricity that is generated from renewable sources and promote its role in electricity trade.

17.09

(3) State Aid

As the Renewables Directive recognizes,[15] the rules of Articles 87 and 88 EC apply with respect to public support schemes. The Guidelines on State Aid for Environmental Protection are applicable to such support (see paras 15.62–15.78). In practice, the Commission has interpreted the Guidelines liberally and approved no fewer than 60 state aid schemes between 2001 and 2004 that provided some support for renewable energy schemes.[16] Its decisions appear to have been driven by the consideration that the use of renewables is a priority in the Community and that the beneficial effects of such support schemes are greater than their distorting effects on competition.

17.10

---

[13] Annex 5: Intermittency in production and balancing power: need for an appropriate combination of internal market and renewables regulation, in European Commission, *The Support of Electricity from Renewable Energy Sources*, COM (2005) 627 final, 7 December 2005.
[14] Case C-213/96 [1998] ECR I-1777.
[15] Recital 12.
[16] European Commission, *The Support of Electricity from Renewable Energy Sources*, COM (2005) 627 final, 7 December 2005, 10.

(a) The Q7 Case

17.11 An example of the Commission's treatment of a notified state aid scheme under the above Guidelines is the aid granted by the Netherlands Government to an offshore wind park called Q7 which was notified to the Commission in June 2003,[17] and approved the following month. The Netherlands had committed public support amounting to €230 million in its first five years of operation. This was to be channelled through a mechanism called the VAMIL scheme, which allows investors to apply for depreciation of the full investment costs in the first year.

17.12 In this case, other public support benefits were also to be available. Three are of particular note. First, there is a fiscal measure called the EIA that provides tax relief to companies that invest in energy-saving equipment and sustainable energy, leading to a direct benefit in this case of €49.8 million. This measure of investment support was deemed to be a general measure by the Commission which did not constitute state aid within the meaning of Article 87(1) EC. Secondly, in terms of operating aid, the Q7 project is to benefit from the MEP scheme over a guaranteed period of ten years. This support scheme was authorized by the Commission earlier in 2003.[18] It has a total budget of €2,503 million covering a period of ten years. As one observer comments, the scheme has the potential to operate counter to the principle of universal service, since the price that small consumers will have to pay for electricity of this quality might appear to be disproportionately high.[19] Its operation is also not in line with the polluter-pays principle. A third form of support came in the form of operating aid via a tax reduction granted through the REB, a regulatory energy tax. Initially, this tax gave a zero rating to green energy but it was replaced in 2002 by a reduced tariff, a measure that constituted a state aid but was granted an exemption on the ground that the reduction has the same effect as an agreement relating to a reduction in emissions.[20] The calculation of the eligible investment costs involved a complex mode of assessment, which the Commission appears likely to apply to future projects on electricity generation from renewable sources.

17.13 The forms of public assistance offered by the Netherlands were diverse and the amounts committed to this project very large. In terms of the economics of the project, the reference investment was given as €30 million but the amount of support over a ten-year period is likely to be in excess of €300 million.[21] This underscores

---

[17] Case N 266/2003, [2003] OJ C266/2.
[18] Case N 707/2002 *MEP—Stimulating Renewable Energy*, [2003] OJ C148/11.
[19] Könings, M, 'Wind Energy and the Context of EU State Aid Law' in Roggenkamp, MM and Hammer, U, *European Energy Law Report* I (2004) 73–90, 80.
[20] Case N 652/2002, [2003] OJ C104/9.
[21] Könings, M, 'Wind Energy and the Context of EU State Aid Law' (2004) 90.

B. Renewable Energy

the very liberal approach taken by the Commission under the Guidelines in its balancing of the environmental benefits with potential distortions of competition.

(b) The German Feed-in Laws

17.14 A very different case of balancing the gains from renewable sources of energy with potential market distortions concerned two German laws that provided support for the promotion of electricity from renewable energy sources and from combined heat and power (CHP). The laws—the EEG and the KWKG[22]—were both in force from spring 2000, and gave a clear economic advantage to specific undertakings. They required network operators to connect generators of green electricity to their grids, and to purchase their green electricity at a minimum price set *above* the market price for electricity. Apart from the advantage the laws gave to the generators of green electricity, they had a potential to distort competition.

17.15 The Commission's assessment followed the ruling of the ECJ on a similar purchase obligation in the *PreussenElektra* case in 2001.[23] The ECJ ruled that such an obligation did not imply the use of state resources; the transfers involved were ones that took place between private companies without state involvement (see paras 15.64–15.72). In cases arising under the two German laws, the ECJ conclusions could be extended to apply to all companies—not only private and public network operators and suppliers—that are subject to the purchase and compensation obligation, regardless of the ownership structure. After all, the laws treated private and public companies in exactly the same way, and no transfer of state resources appeared to be involved from the public companies to the beneficiaries. The laws did not therefore have as their aim the use of the resources of the public undertakings to support electricity from renewable sources or CHP. The fact that the grids themselves were for the most part privately owned served to underline this. The laws did not therefore fall within the scope of the definition of state aid in Article 87(1).

17.16 Interestingly, a number of competition concerns were raised during the assessment by various parties.[24] They included the possibility that beneficiaries might be overcompensated, especially generators of wind power. The Commission took the view that it lacked competence to take a position on such matters, since the laws did not constitute state aid and they fell, therefore, within the jurisdiction of the German competition rules.

---

[22] Respectively, *Gesetz über den Vorrang Erneuerbarer Energien* of 29 March 2000 (BGBl.I S.305), *Gesetz zum Schutz der Stromerzeugung aus Kraft-Wärme-Kopplung* of 12 May 2000 (BGBl. I S 703).
[23] Case C-379/98 *PreussenElektra AG v Schleswag AG* [2001] ECR I-2159.
[24] Renner-Loquenz, B and Zuleger, V, 'Commission raises no objections to German feed-in laws for electricity from renewable energy sources and combined heat and power' (2002) 3 Competition Policy Newsletter 67.

C. Energy Taxation

17.17 There have been three distinct strands in Community strategy on energy taxation. The first, and the least successful, was an attempt to introduce an EC carbon tax, soon after the Rio Declaration was signed by the Community and by the Member States.[25] The second was a less ambitious but ultimately more successful effort to harmonize excise duties on, inter alia, mineral oils, which took legislative shape as the Energy Products Directive after six years of negotiation. Finally, there have been various interventions in the many national schemes on energy taxation on state aid grounds that are designed to ensure that market distortions resulting from these measures are kept to a minimum.

17.18 The harmonization of indirect taxes such as excise duties and turnover taxes has long been a goal of the Commission, with a view to ensuring that distortions of competition are eliminated from this source. The justification for measures under Article 93 EC is that such measures of harmonization are required to 'ensure the establishment and the functioning of the internal market'. It has been relevant in the environmental field as Member States have sought to impose levies and other taxes for environmental aims, thereby creating the potential for a highly uneven playing field. However, the Treaty requirement that any such measure proposed by the Commission may only be adopted by the Council under Article 93 'acting unanimously', has acted as a brake on certain Commission proposals, most notably the plan for a Community wide carbon tax. Its failure is instructive about the limits to Community initiatives in the area of energy taxation.

(1) The Carbon Tax

17.19 The Commission published its proposals under the heading, 'Energy: Consequences of the Proposed Carbon/Energy Tax'.[26] The package of measures, of which a carbon/energy tax was a central part, included: (1) a proposal for a Council Directive introducing a tax on carbon dioxide emissions and energy; (2) specific actions for greater penetration for renewable energy sources under the ALTENER programme;

---

[25] The Rio Declaration on Environment and Development was adopted at the 1992 United Nations Conference on Environment and Development and comprised 27 principles setting out the basis on which states and people are to co-operate and further develop 'international law in the field of sustainable development' (Principle 27). States are required to adopt a 'precautionary approach' towards environmental protection, such that where a risk exists of serious or irreversible damage, lack of scientific certainty should not postpone 'cost effective' environmental protection measures (Principle 15). States should endeavour to promote the internalization of environmental costs and the use of economic instruments (Principle 16): see <http://www.unep.org/unep/rio.htm>.

[26] Proposal for a Council Directive introducing a tax on carbon dioxide emissions and energy, 30 June 1992, COM (92) 226 final, [1992] OJ C196/1.

C. Energy Taxation

(3) a Council Directive to limit CO_2 emissions by improving energy efficiency under the SAVE programme; and (4) a call for tender in the frame of the THERMIE programme focusing on the reduction of CO_2 emissions.

The EC's strategy for the limitation of carbon emissions and the improvement of energy efficiency had at its core the introduction of a tax on all energy products, excluding renewables, based 50 per cent on the energy content and 50 per cent according to the carbon content of fuels. The aim was to improve energy efficiency and to favour fuel substitution towards products emitting less or no CO_2. This tax was to be introduced gradually over several years. Neither this nor a modified proposal for a carbon tax met with any success.[27] Following a series of defeats, the Council requested the Commission in March 1996 to propose new measures in the field of taxation of energy products, with a view to reducing greenhouse gases.

17.20

On 12 March 1997 the Commission put forward a proposal to restructure the Community excise duty system on energy products.[28] This proposal did not itself introduce a carbon/energy tax but aimed at establishing a minimum level of taxation on all energy products, as a first step towards the introduction of a new supplement (that is, an energy tax). In terms of EC strategy, the proposal constituted an important change. In the Commission's words, it had 'moved from a Proposal for a CO_2/energy tax with high rates of taxation and a high degree of harmonization, to a more pragmatic approach for an energy products tax that foresees the extension of the existing system of excise duties and a gradual increase in levels of taxation'.[29] In effect, the carbon tax proposal was dead, although it was not formally withdrawn by the Commission until 11 December 2001.

17.21

(2) The Energy Products Directive

(a) Origins

The debate on a carbon tax should not be confused with a separate development involving the imposition of excise duties. The Single European Act of 1986 had imposed an obligation on Member States to harmonize excise duties by 31 December 1992. To achieve this 'internal market' objective, the Council adopted a general Directive covering the movement and control of products subject to excise duties and other indirect taxes levied directly or indirectly on their consumption (except for VAT and taxes established by the EC).[30] A second general Directive made minor amendments

17.22

---

[27] Amended Proposal for a Council Directive introducing a tax on carbon dioxide emissions and energy, COM (95) 172.
[28] Proposal for a Council Directive restructuring the Community framework for the taxation of energy products, COM (97) 30 final.
[29] Commission Communication to the Council and Parliament, 'Preparing for Implementation of the Kyoto Protocol', 19 May 1999, COM (1999) 230, 7.
[30] Directive (EEC) 92/12 [1992] OJ L76/1.

Chapter 17: Environmental Protection

to this Directive, dealing largely with derogations.[31] The recitals underline the internal market orientation of these Directives. In the first Directive, Recitals 5 and 8 state that the establishment and functioning of the internal market require the free movement of goods, including those subject to excise duties, and require that the chargeability of excise duties should be identical in all of the Member States. None of them make any reference to an environmental justification for this harmonization of excise duties.

17.23 Mineral oils were the target of specific measures on structures and rates of excise duty in two further Directives.[32] The first required Member States to impose a harmonized excise duty on mineral oils. Under this regime, hydrocarbons fuels—including leaded and unleaded petrol, heavy fuel oil, gas oil and LPG—were classified according to the Community Customs Tariff. The second required Member States to apply rates of excise duty not less than the minimum prescribed in its provisions. Recitals 7 and 12 of Directive (EEC) 92/81 and Recital 7 of Directive (EEC) 92/82 make it clear that the purpose of the Directives is linked to the achievement of the internal market by the deadline of 1 January 1993. This did not prevent a Member State from subjecting mineral oils to other indirect taxes for specific purposes but that was not a matter for the EC as long as such taxes complied with Directive (EEC) 92/12 (Art 3 (2)).

17.24 Both of the above excise tax measures were replaced by the Energy Products Directive (EPD) in 2003.[33] The EPD is the clear successor to these Directives and the approach to excise taxation they adopted. In the original proposal for the EPD it is clear that it planned to build on the Community's *existing* system of minimum levels of taxation (duty rates) applicable to mineral oils in the 1992 Directives by enlarging the scope of the minimum rate system beyond mineral oils to cover all energy products, including coal, coke, lignite, bitumen, natural gas, and electricity used both domestically and industrially. This would have meant an upward harmonization of tax rates between Member States, which could have restructured the national taxation systems and so achieved objectives in the environment, transport, and energy areas while complying with the single market. It may be noted that although the legal basis for the existing excise duty system dated from 1992 (that is, at roughly the same time as the carbon tax proposal), it was intended to contribute to a tax harmonization objective rooted in the Single European Act and

---

[31] Directive (EEC) 92/108 [1992] OJ L390/124.
[32] Directive (EEC) 92/81 on the harmonization of the structures of excise duties on mineral oils [1992] OJ L316/12 (now repealed and replaced by Directive (EC) 2003/96 [2003] OJ L283/51) and Directive (EEC) 92/82 on the approximation of the rates of excise duties on mineral oils [1992] OJ L316/19 (now repealed and replaced by Directive (EC) 2003/96, ibid).
[33] Directive (EC) 2003/96 restructuring the Community framework for the taxation of energy products and electricity [2003] OJ L283/51.

was not intended as providing the basis for an environmental tax regime. Similarly, the EPD proposal was based on Article 93 EC, concerning the harmonization of indirect taxation in furtherance of internal market goals.

(b) What the Energy Products Directive Requires

The EPD attempts to harmonize energy taxation in the Community. It requires Member States to impose taxation on energy products in line with the regime set out in the Directive. The guiding principle is that energy products are only taxed when they are used as motor or heating fuel and not when they are used as raw materials or for purposes of chemical reduction or in metallurgical processes. On this basis, the Directive sets minimum rates of taxation for motor fuel, motor fuel for industrial or commercial use, heating fuel, and electricity. The levels of taxation applied by the Member States may not be lower than the minimum rates set out in the Directive. **17.25**

This system put in place minimum rates of taxation which for a long time were confined to mineral oils. The EPD extended its scope to include coal, natural gas and electricity, while increasing the existing minimum rates of duty on oils, with a second increase on diesel from 1 January 2010. The new system establishes the minimum rates of taxation applicable to energy products when used as motor or heating fuels and to electricity. Those Member States that did not tax these fuels were required to introduce such taxes. Its aim is therefore to improve the operation of the internal market by reducing distortions of competition between mineral oils and other energy products. This measure is in line with the Community's objectives and the Kyoto Protocol and is aimed to encourage a more efficient use of energy so as to reduce dependence on imported energy products and limit greenhouse gas emissions. In the interests of protecting the environment, it authorizes Member States to grant tax advantages to businesses that take specific measures to reduce their emissions. **17.26**

Main provisions The main provision is that levels of taxation applied by Member States to energy products and electricity listed in Article 2 EPD are not to be less than the minimum levels of taxation prescribed by the Directive.[34] These minimum levels apply to motor fuels, products used as motor fuels, heating fuels, and electricity from 1 January 2004. The 'level of taxation' was defined as the total charge levied in respect of all indirect taxes (except VAT) calculated directly or indirectly on the quantity of energy products and electricity at the time of release for consumption. Differentiated levels of taxation are permitted in specified cases, such as where the differentiation was linked to product quality; when the differentiated rates depend on quantitative consumption levels for electricity and energy **17.27**

---

[34] Art 4 EPD.

products used for heating purposes; for specified uses such as local public passenger transport, waste collection, armed forces and public administration, disabled people and ambulances; and finally, between business and non-business use. The EPD allows exemptions or reductions in the level of taxation, which may be granted directly, by means of a differentiated rate or by refunding all or part of the amount of taxation.

17.28 **Reporting**   There is a reporting requirement imposed on the Commission in Article 7(2) EPD to review the minimum levels of taxation applicable to gas oil and make a proposal for a further period beginning on 1 January 2013. The Council has to decide on this no later than 1 January 2012. Other reporting requirements imposed on the Commission include a periodic examination of the exemptions and reductions and minimum levels of taxation laid down in the EPD.[35] On the basis of these reports, the Council is to take the necessary measures unanimously and after consultation with the European Parliament. Three tests to be included in the reports and the Council deliberations are: the proper functioning of the internal market; the real value of the minimum levels of taxation; and the wider objectives of the Treaty.

17.29 **Exemptions**   Exemptions or reductions in the level of taxation are allowed in whole or in part under Article 15 EPD. This includes a long list of energy products and electricity, eg electricity generated from solar, wind, wave, or geothermal origins or generated from biomass, methane from abandoned coal mines, from fuel cells or hydroelectric installations, or from CHP generation as long as the generators are environmentally friendly. The list also includes natural gas in those Member States in which the share of natural gas in final energy consumption was less than 15 per cent in 2000. This is applicable for a maximum period of ten years after the entry into force of the EPD or until the national share reaches 25 per cent, whichever is the sooner.[36] The UK is allowed to apply the exemptions regime for natural gas separately for Northern Ireland. Member States may also grant refunds to the producer of some or all of the amount of tax paid by the consumer on electricity generated from products specified in the list.

17.30 Further categories of exemption or reductions are provided on specified products made from one or more of certain other products such as biomass.[37] The Commission is required to report to the Council on the fiscal, economic, agricultural, energy, industrial, and environmental aspects of reductions granted under these categories

---

[35] Art 29 EPD.
[36] Art 15(1)(g) EPD. As soon as the national share of natural gas reaches 20% in final energy consumption, the Member State concerned is to 'apply a strictly positive level of taxation', which is to increase on a yearly basis to reach at least the minimum rate at the end of the ten-year period.
[37] Art 16 EPD.

C. Energy Taxation

no later than 31 December 2009. Reductions in the minimum levels of taxation are permitted with respect to energy intensive businesses under certain conditions, and where agreements are concluded with undertakings or associations of undertakings, or where tradable permit schemes or equivalent arrangements are implemented (as long as they lead to the achievement of environmental protection objectives or to improvements in energy efficiency).[38] Certain Member States are granted derogations to continue to apply existing schemes of reductions or exemptions set out in Annex II to the EPD. This authorization does not continue however beyond 31 December 2006 unless the Annex specifies otherwise. In the UK, an exemption was granted for differentiated rates of excise duty for road fuel containing biodiesel and biodiesel used as pure road fuel until 31 March 2007.[39] Further exemptions or reductions may be authorized by the Council, acting unanimously on a proposal from the Commission, if the Member State considers it necessary 'for specific policy considerations'.[40] A procedure is set out for the review and possible approval of such requests. There are also notification requirements on Member States to ensure a flow of data to the Commission.[41] There is a cautionary reminder in Article 26(2) EPD that measures such as tax exemptions, tax reductions, tax differentiation and tax refunds within the meaning of the Directive might constitute state aid; in such cases, notification to the Commission is required under Article 88(3) EC.

EPD and state aid The unanimous agreement required by the EPD measure was only possible once certain guarantees were given to Member States with respect to the operation of state aid controls.[42] Essentially, Member States considered that an energy tax must concentrate on motor fuels and heating fuels. Therefore, the Council and the Commission considered that the new tax system (introduced under the EPD) should exclude from its scope 'other uses' than as motor fuels or as heating fuels.[43] Such other uses of an energy product include dual-use processes, where it is used both as a heating fuel and for purposes other than as motor fuel and heating fuel. While the former would normally be taxable under the EPD, it is difficult in practice to distinguish the two, so they are treated in the same way as products for non-fuel use. This and other uses are included in a list in Article 2(4)(b). 17.31

---

[38] Art 17(1)(b) EPD.
[39] However, Community minimum rates have to be respected and no over-compensation for the extra costs involved in the manufacture of biofuels can take place.
[40] Art 19(1) EPD.
[41] Arts 25 and 26 EPD.
[42] For the debate on this, see the Commission Staff working paper, *State aid aspects in the proposal for a Council directive on energy taxation*, SEC (2002) 1142, 24 October 2002 and Council document 13545/02 Fisc 271 of 28 October 2002.
[43] In line with Commission Decision 2002/676/EC, ECSC on the dual-use exemption which the United Kingdom is planning to implement under the Climate Change Levy and the extended exemption for certain competing processes [2002] OJ L229/15.

The legal certainty given to Member States by placing some politically sensitive sectors explicitly outside the scope of the EPD was decisive in securing unanimous agreement to it.[44] Although the Commission sought to eliminate distortions of competition, it had to balance this goal with the possibility that it might unduly restrict the design of Member States' policy measures.

17.32 **Summary** The EPD restructured the Community framework for the taxation of energy products and electricity. It represented the culmination of six years of efforts to reform excise taxes that began in 1997 following the Commission's failure to introduce a carbon tax. It replaced an earlier set of Directives dating from 1992 applying to excise duties and established a unified framework for the treatment of motor and heating fuels. However, the justification for the EPD was couched in terms of the internal market rather than the achievement of environmental goal.

(3) National Measures and State Aid

17.33 Several Member States have introduced taxes on energy products to encourage a reduction of consumption or on consumption directly, with a view to reducing carbon emissions. In a number of cases a tax relief has been introduced for the most energy-intensive consumers to protect their competitiveness. These exemptions are usually given to manufacturing industry, and have the effect of relieving them of a tax burden which other companies have to carry instead, thereby giving rise to state aid issues.

17.34 The ability of Member States to design tax exemptions as general measures that fall outside the state aid rules has been limited by the ECJ ruling in the *Adria-Wien pipeline* case.[45] The ECJ clarified the criteria for selectivity and ruled that special tax treatments which are aimed at energy intensive companies are always of a selective nature if the service sector is excluded. Those exemptions that do not qualify as general measures must be assessed and approved under the Guidelines on Environmental Aid. The options available under the Guidelines to make such aid compatible with the EC Treaty are designed to maintain an incentive on beneficiaries for reducing the emissions that the tax has targeted. This may be done either by concluding an environmental agreement between the state and the companies concerned or by the adoption of a mechanism that ensures payment of a substantial part of the tax by the companies that receive the tax reduction. The following cases provide illustrations of the kinds of fiscal measures that the Commission is prepared to deem compatible with the Guidelines.

---

[44] Renner-Loquenz, B and Boeshertz, D, 'State aid: key elements for the agreement in the Council on energy taxation' (2003) 3 Competition Policy Newsletter 14–6.
[45] Case C-143/99 *Adria Wien Pipeline GmbH v Finanzlandesdirektion für Karnten* [2001] ECR I-8365.

C. Energy Taxation

(a) The Swedish Energy Tax Case

The Commission carried out an investigation into the energy tax regime in Sweden in 2002–03.[46] Two taxes were involved: a carbon tax and an energy tax, both levied on fossil fuels. The energy tax was also levied on electricity. Exemptions were granted to both taxes for certain categories of energy intensive consumers. Over a ten-year period, manufacturing industry had benefited from a 75 per cent reduction in the carbon tax for fuels used in production processes, and from a full exemption from the energy tax used for heating in production processes.

17.35

In its assessment the Commission accepted the Swedish argument that the carbon and energy taxes (and some related environmental taxes aimed at reducing emissions such as sulphur) complied with state aid rules. The taxes were both levied on fossil fuels used for heating purposes with the same provisions on collection, chargeability, and control that are identical and are presented to taxpayers together for tax collection. They have a behaviour-changing purpose in relation to the consumption of fuels and so could be seen as economic instruments for the achievement of environmental protection, especially carbon reduction. To achieve this purpose, the Government has adjusted the tax levels from time to time. The fact that the two indirect taxes were added together complied with the Guidelines on Environmental Aid (point 5(1)b, second indent) since the undertakings were still required to pay a significant proportion of the taxes. They still had an incentive to reduce consumption.

17.36

The Swedish case was originally concerned with a wide ranging exemption from its electricity tax for its manufacturing industry which then narrowed down to an examination of particular taxes on carbon and energy. The exemptions were treated separately by the Commission. However, the reasoning applied by the Commission to reach its positive conclusion about the compatibility of these exemptions with the Guidelines seems decidedly stretched.

17.37

(b) The Dutch Energy Tax Exemption

A Dutch tax on energy consumption was notified as a fiscal aid measure to the Commission in November 2003.[47] It applied a degressive rate structure for electricity and gas, with the overall goal of achieving carbon emissions reductions and of promoting energy saving. The impact of the EPD meant that an additional tax burden would have to be imposed on a group of energy-intensive business users.

17.38

---

[46] Case NN 3/B/2001, [2003] OJ C189/6. There were two earlier decisions, however, with a narrower focus on a carbon tax reduction: Cases NN 3/A/2001 and NN 4/A/2001—*Sweden*, [2003] OJ C104/10. A different kind of environmental tax exemption granted by the Commission to the UK was tested in the Court of First Instance and upheld: Case T-210/02, *British Aggregates Association v Commission of the European Communities*, 13 September 2006 (Press Release No 74/06).

[47] Koenings, M, 'Energy taxation and state aid: The Netherlands; energy tax exemption for energy intensive end-users' (2004) 1 Competition Policy Newsletter 84–5.

These users were already engaged in a programme of energy use reduction with the public authorities. The solution proposed by the Dutch Government was to propose a tax exemption scheme, which was notified to the Commission as a state aid measure. The Commission applied a number of tests to the scheme, noting that it was to be subject to strict conditions and that only selected undertakings would benefit from the scheme. Since the purpose of the measure was environmental protection, the Guidelines on Environmental Aid were used to make the assessment. Under point 49(b), the Commission may decide that a tax exemption to selected firms on a tax that is to be levied as a result of an EC Directive is compatible with Article 87(1), when the tax exemption is authorized by the Directive in question. The requirements on the necessity and proportionality of the tax exemption were deemed to be fully met.

(4) Current Approaches to EU Carbon Taxation

17.39 The idea of using tax instruments at the Community level to achieve carbon reduction objectives reappears from time to time in Commission discussion documents. For example, in the Green Paper on energy policy (2006) there was a brief reference to 'the Community energy taxation framework' as one of the market-based instruments that could be an efficient tool in designing an energy efficiency policy.[48] A little earlier, in its Green Paper on security of supply in the EU, there was a discussion of energy taxation as a way of steering demand towards better-controlled consumption that is more respectful of the environment. Taxation or para-fiscal levies are advocated as a means of countering the harmful environmental effect of certain forms of energy. The Green Paper noted that the 1997 proposal for changes through increased excise taxes was blocked in the Council, particularly by opposition from Spain. It explicitly noted that the goal of the measure was to harmonize energy taxes upwards.[49] It also advised that: 'In the light of new constraints affecting security of supply, the Commission's tax proposals of 1992 and 1997 could be usefully supplemented by a new proposal designed to steer energy consumption towards more environmentally friendly technologies, which will help to bolster security of supply'.[50] The document is clear in its desire to see a re-examination of the issue of energy taxation, taking into account energy and environmental objectives. A major concern, however, was the connection between this kind of tax policy and EC competitiveness.

17.40 Nevertheless, as far as the state of energy taxation in the Member States is concerned, the section on this in the paper is headed 'Fiscal Disorder', reflecting the

---

[48] European Commission, *Green Paper: A European Strategy for Sustainable, Competitive and Secure Energy*, COM (2006) 105 final, 8 March 2006, 10. For an economist's overview of the issues, see Newbery, DM, 'Why tax energy? Towards a more rational policy' (2005) 26 Energy J 1.

[49] European Commission, *Green Paper: Towards a European strategy for the security of energy supply*, COM (2001) 769, 55.

[50] ibid 57.

tone of the section itself. The frustration of the Commission is expressed in blunt terms and worth quoting at length:

> The unanimity rule stands in the way of any real harmonization of taxation levels. Until such time as the European Union can obtain real harmonization of national taxes on energy, there are unlikely to be any Community taxes introduced in the short term, such as the taxes on pollutant emissions or carbon dioxide. All attempts along these lines so far have failed.[51]

The idea of a carbon tax measure at EC level has not died, however. It was revived following the Lisbon Summit (March 2000), and a study was commissioned into the impacts of energy taxation in the enlarged EU. It was published on 25 July 2005.[52] The main aim was to update the impact assessment of the Commission's 1997 energy tax proposal. Secondary aims were to explore the impacts of (1) environmentally more ambitious tax levels, and (2) the combination of the EU minimum energy tax rates with the EU-wide ETS. In the Commission's view, the results indicate that Member States would benefit from a common energy or carbon tax policy in terms of higher employment and welfare if they used tax revenues to reduce employers' social security contributions. For the achievement of climate change objectives, a common EU carbon tax would be the most cost-efficient approach, although it would have a slightly negative impact on competitiveness in some energy-intensive sectors. Exemptions would only make a small difference to this effect. 17.41

D. The Emissions Trading Scheme

The introduction of emissions trading is the EU's most ambitious effort yet to give companies incentives to invest in low carbon electricity generation and measures to save electricity. In 2003 a Directive was adopted which establishes a Community scheme for greenhouse gas emission allowance trading within the Community.[53] It is based on Article 175(1) EC, as the appropriate legal basis for actions with an environmental aim under Article 174. Its declared goal is to promote reductions of greenhouse gas emissions in a cost-effective and economically efficient manner.[54] In contrast to the Kyoto Protocol, however, it concerns itself 17.42

---

[51] ibid 55.
[52] European Commission, *The Impacts of Energy Taxation in the Enlarged European Union*, 25 July 2005. At the national level the debate is also lively: see, eg, House of Lords Select Committee on Economic Affairs, Second Report of Session 2005–2006, *The Economics of Climate Change* (HL Paper 12-1) vol I, para 140: 'We therefore urge a thorough review of the Climate Change Levy regime, with the aim of moving as fast as possible to replacing it by a carbon tax'.
[53] Directive (EC) 2003/87 establishing a scheme for greenhouse gas emission allowance trading within the Community and amending Council Directive (EC) 96/61 [2003] OJ L275/32.
[54] ibid, Art 1; see discussion in the Commission's Communication to the Council, the European Parliament, the European Economic and Social Committee and the Committee of the Regions, 'Limiting Global Climate Change to 2 degrees Celsius: The way ahead for 2020 and beyond', COM (2007) 2 Final.

with only one of these gases: carbon dioxide or CO_2 (carbon), partly because it is the most harmful and partly because it is easy to monitor. In practice, a number of Member States had already begun such initiatives on an individual basis (for example, the UK, the Netherlands, and Denmark), but a Europe-wide scheme was justified on the grounds that it could accommodate a level playing field and provide a uniform price for allowances traded in the EU. The measure is relevant to the energy sector, and particularly electricity markets, although it is also directed at a wide range of non-energy industries. It has implications for both competition and energy policies, with respect to state aid and market distortion issues. The workings of the ETS have been described in detail elsewhere so they are only summarized here.[55]

(1) The Scheme

17.43

The ETS allows companies operating large installations in industry and the electricity sector to cover their CO_2 emissions by allowances, which they can trade across the EU (and Norway) with each other. It is based on the concept that each Member State allocates permits for a number of site-specific and tradable emission allowances to the approximately 12,000 installations included in the scheme (combustion plants, oil refineries, coke ovens, iron and steel plants, and factories making cement, glass, lime, bricks, ceramics, pulp, and paper). All included installations must hold a permit to perform activities that emit carbon. The permit holders receive a sum of transferable allowances and each allowance is equivalent to one tonne of carbon.

17.44

Member States are obliged to draw up an *ex ante* National Allocation Plan (NAP) which states the total quantity of allowances it intends to allocate to its domestic installations for a given period and how it proposes to allocate them.[56] These NAPs must be published and notified to the Commission, which may reject all or part of the NAP within three months of notification. Experience so far is that only a few NAPs have been accepted unconditionally by the Commission. For the first three years of operation (2005–08) Member States are required to allocate 95 per cent of allowances free of charge. Subsequently, this decreases to 90 per cent for the five years after 2008. The other 5 per cent and subsequently 10 per cent may be auctioned by Member States. Every year a number of allowances equal to total emissions are to be surrendered by the operator of each included installation and

---

[55] See, eg, the collection of writings by the Commission officials closely involved with the design and implementation of the ETS: Delbeke, J, et al, *EU Energy Law, Vol IV, Environmental Law: the EU Greenhouse Gas Emissions Trading Scheme* (2006). For an alternative view, see Grubb, M and Neuhoff, K, 'Allocation and competitiveness in the EU emissions trading scheme: policy overview' (2006) 6 Climate Policy 7–30. For discussion of the wider context, see Freestone, D, and Streck, C, (eds), *Legal Aspects of Implementing the Kyoto Protocol Mechanisms: Making Kyoto Work* (2005).
[56] ETS Directive, Art 9; for the decisions see <http://ec.europa.eu/environment/climat/emission_plans.htm>.

D. The Emissions Trading Scheme

these allowances are then cancelled. Allowances not surrendered are only valid for the periods under which they are issued and are cancelled in the subsequent period. Each company has to comply with its designated CO_2 limit or else it has to purchase credits to 'balance the books'. In rather technical language, the scheme may be described as 'an entity-based domestic cap and trade emissions allowance scheme'.

The Directive obliges the Commission to adopt guidelines on monitoring and reporting of emissions and Member States are obliged to ensure that emissions are monitored according to the guidelines.[57] Companies are to monitor and report emissions from the relevant installations. Reports submitted by operators are subject to independent verification.[58] Member States and the Community must establish and maintain electronic registries to track allowances.[59] At Community level an independent transaction log has to be developed.[60] Sanctions are envisaged in the form of a penalty of €40 for every tonne of emissions that is not covered by an allowance, rising to €100 after 2007. Companies will also have to surrender a compensating amount of allowances in the subsequent year. Finally, a linkage is established by a separate Directive between the ETS and other flexible mechanisms under the Kyoto Protocol, specifically the Clean Development Mechanism and Joint Implementation.[61]   17.45

(2) Implementation

Phase 1 of the ETS came into operation in January 2005. Phase 2 will commence in 2008 and end in 2012. There is as yet no clarity about the form of the ETS beyond this period. It is still very much in the process of development as an instrument of carbon abatement.   17.46

Ex post amendments to the NAPs are not acceptable to the Commission, on the ground that such adaptations could distort competition and market mechanisms, including the price of traded allowances.[62] However, in 2005 the UK proposed to amend its NAP for the allocation of greenhouse gas emissions, and this proposed amendment was rejected by the Commission. The UK subsequently appealed to the CFI which annulled the Commission's decision on the ground that a Member   17.47

---

[57] ibid, Art 14(1) and (2).
[58] ibid, Art 15.
[59] ibid, Art 19.
[60] ibid, Art 20.
[61] Directive (EC) 2004/101 establishing a scheme for greenhouse gas emission allowance trading within the Community, in respect of the Kyoto Protocol's project mechanisms [2004] OJ L338/18; see Commission, COM (2003) 403 final, 23 July 2003. For a different kind of linkage, introduced in the ETS Directive itself, see Art 26 which includes a linkage with Directive (EC) 96/61 concerning integrated pollution prevention and control [1996] OJ L257/26.
[62] Commission Press Release IP/04/862, 'Emissions trading: Commission clears over 5,000 plants to enter emissions market next January', 7 July 2004.

State's right to propose amendments could not be restricted by the Commission.[63] The Court also noted that the Commission had permitted increases in the total quantity of allowances to address gaps which it had identified in the British NAP, a course of action that was inconsistent with its refusal to consider amendments when proposed by the Member State itself.

17.48 Another aspect of implementation is the volatility of carbon allowance prices. In early 2006 these fell sharply, but volatility upwards had been identified earlier, due probably to oil price increases and gas price increases attributable to indexing and substitution effects. Other factors affecting the price movements include the delay in some Member States' allocation procedures, registries coming on stream slowly, the limited number of companies currently taking abatement measures or trading and, last but not least, the fact that the EU's electricity and gas markets do not yet function properly as markets (that is, there is a very limited degree of competition). The latter has been identified as a reason for particular concern by an EU High Level Group on Competitiveness, Energy and Environment. Noting the submissions made to it, it observed that '[i]nsufficiently functioning electricity markets (market dominance, lack of new entry, non-transparency of the market) can reduce the effectiveness of the scheme in terms of providing incentives for abatement, as well as to what extent they will pass through costs'.[64] The interface of the ETS scheme with the efforts to promote competition in EU energy markets, discussed in Parts II and III of this book, is indeed a matter of some concern.[65]

(3) Impacts on Competition and the Internal Energy Market

17.49 One of the obvious ways in which the ETS may distort competition and may interfere with the progress of an internal market, is in the field of state aid. Does the free allocation of tradeable allowances to operators amount to a grant of state aid, in contravention of the EC Treaty? The NAPs are subject to a requirement, under Annex III of the ETS Directive,[66] not to 'discriminate between companies or sectors in such a way as to unduly favour certain undertakings or activities in accordance with the requirements of the Treaty, in particular Articles 87 and 88 EC thereof'. In its Guidance notes, the Commission states that 'the normal State aid rules will apply'. So far, the Commission has not taken any formal state aid decision on a NAP. However, a review of the operation of the ETS and the actions of Member States under the regime has led one author to conclude that 'there is a strong

---

[63] Case T-178/05 *UK v Commission* [2006] 1 CMLR 33.
[64] Ad hoc Group 2 on the EU ETS, Chairman Issues Paper, 5 April 2006, 3.
[65] For a good overview of the internal energy market issues in relation to the ETS, see Sorensen, UL, 'The European Emission Trading Scheme—How Will it Affect the Internal Market in Electricity?' 2005, unpublished LLM dissertation, University of Dundee.
[66] Criterion 5.

series of arguments in support of the view that the free allocation of allowances under the various NAPs involves an element of State aid, which has neither been formally notified to, nor cleared by, the Commission under the EC Treaty'.[67]

17.50 In other ways, there are implications for the internal energy market that are not encouraging. First, the scheme will make carbon-intensive power generation more expensive for consumers while at the same time transferring windfall profits to electricity generators.[68] Secondly, it is left to each Member State to determine the amount of allowances and the allocation method, albeit subject to review by the Commission. Given the long history of national energy policies and favouring of national champions in the EU, it would be very surprising if the allocation of allowances was not influenced by this tradition. Thirdly, there is a lack of guidance to Member States on how to treat new entrants into the scheme. The approach will vary from one State to the next. Finally, there is a risk that uncertainty arising from the ETS will have a negative impact on future investment plans: a 'market wrecker' rather than a market maker, in contradiction to the various efforts being made by the Member States, NRAs, and the Commission itself to promote investments in electricity and gas infrastructure.

E. Conclusions

17.51 The tensions between the objective of enhancing environmental protection on the one hand and avoiding market distortions on the other are evident throughout the sections of this chapter. There is no evidence to suggest that the need for balancing of these objectives will become less difficult. Indeed, given the Community's very strong support for an expanded share of renewable energy in the EU mix and the unfolding of the ETS, there is every reason to expect an increase in the difficulties.

17.52 The Commission's attempts to carry out that balance have led to some surprising outcomes. While it has pressed hard for a Community-wide form of carbon tax (and failed), it has shown a considerable reluctance to take action under the state aid rules against any of the NAPs in spite of evidence of possible incompatibility. It has also shown much willingness to interpret the Guidelines on Environmental

---

[67] Johnston, A, 'Free allocation of allowances under the EU emissions trading scheme: legal issues' (2006) 6 Climate Policy 115–36, 132. However, recent actions by the Commission against Denmark and Sweden indicate that it is aware of the problem: respectively, Commission Press Release IP/06/1274 and IP/06/1525, 28 September 2006 and 8 November 2006 respectively, 'State aid: Commission investigates proposed new Danish CO_2 tax reductions' and 'State aid: Commission investigates proposed new Swedish CO_2 tax reductions'. The proposal was accepted by the Council on 24 July 2006: Council of the European Union Press Release 11554/06 (Presse 215).
[68] Gilbert, R, and Newbery, D, 'Electricity Merger Policy in the Shadow of Regulation' (2006), 25–27.

Aid in ways that are favourable to Member States with ambitious schemes for renewable energy development.

17.53 At the same time, the task of balancing environmental with competition objectives is one that is generated by the different and sometimes inconsistent priorities of the Member States themselves. The efforts made to make the more recent legislative initiatives (the ETS, and renewable energy) market-based are very commendable and make sense: they strive to achieve a potential for greater compatibility between pro-competitive energy and environmental objectives in the medium to long term. However, they fit with more or less difficulty into Member State patterns of balancing policy priorities that are weighted to suit *national* rather than European concerns. These are frequently driven by non-environmental concerns, including the long-standing concern of Member States to achieve a balanced energy mix for reasons of energy security. The technical, practical, and political problems involved in European-wide fiscal measures appear to present even greater challenges.

17.54 Finally, the impact of environmental measures on the energy sector is acquiring a more pervasive *legal* dimension with the development of market-based environmental initiatives that are expressly designed to accommodate (rather than to challenge) the competition orientation in the sector-specific energy law. This is particularly evident with respect to EU measures to address climate change problems and to promote renewable energy. However, they may well cause the industries concerned (particularly steel) to have difficulty in competing in the newly emerging markets such as India and China. Moreover, the present application of the legislation, especially the highly sympathetic interpretation of the Treaty rules on state aids, raises doubts about the ability of such measures to ensure fair competition in the future.

18

ENERGY SECURITY

A. Introduction	18.01	(c) Monitoring	18.55
B. Secondary Legislation	18.07	(d) The Public Service Issue	18.59
(1) The Electricity Directive	18.11	(5) Oil Security	18.60
(a) Public Service Obligations	18.13	(a) Oil Stocks	18.61
(b) Monitoring	18.17	(b) Crisis Management	18.67
(c) Tendering for New Capacity	18.18	(6) Infrastructure	18.68
(d) Reporting	18.21	(a) The TENs Framework	18.71
(e) Safeguard Measures	18.22	(b) Funding	18.75
(2) The Gas Directive	18.23	(c) What the TENs Initiative is Trying to Achieve	18.79
(a) Exemption from TPA	18.24	C. Treaty Provisions	18.81
(b) Derogation and PSOs	18.26	(1) Import and Export	18.83
(c) Upstream Issues	18.28	(a) The *Campus Oil* Case	18.86
(3) Electricity Security	18.29	(b) The Greek Oil Monopolies case	18.94
(a) Implementation	18.32	(2) Services of General Economic Interest	18.99
(b) Network Security	18.35	(a) Grant of Financial Aid	18.101
(c) Supply and Demand Balance	18.40	(b) The *CADA* Case	18.102
(d) Investment	18.42	(3) Euratom	18.104
(e) Reporting	18.43	D. Conclusions	18.107
(4) Gas Security			
(a) Objectives	18.49		
(b) Gas Co-ordination Group	18.53		

Europe's previous overcapacity is becoming history.

Green Paper on Energy Policy[1]

A. Introduction

Energy security has recently moved up the public policy agenda into the first rank of problems to be addressed by governments. We may define 'energy   **18.01**

---

[1] European Commission, *Green Paper: A European Strategy for Sustainable, Competitive and Secure Energy*, COM (2006) 105 final, 8 March 2006, 6.

security'[2] as the ability of the energy industries, primarily in electricity and gas, to provide their respective services throughout the EU to a high standard and at a reasonable cost in a competitive, fully liberalized, pan-European market. This is intended to be a working rather than a comprehensive definition since the focus of this book is on the introduction of competition into the energy markets of the EU, and in this chapter on the impact of energy security on that liberalization process.

18.02 For the continental EU the reasons behind its concerns lie in the negative perceptions about the reliability of non-EU suppliers, especially of gas.[3] For the UK, a Member State which until recently was almost indifferent to the European dimension of energy security, the reasons lie principally in the shift from being a net exporter of oil and gas to becoming a net importer. In general, however, there is a renewed awareness of the risks posed by the long-term trend in the EU towards an increasing degree of dependence on a limited number of non-EU suppliers of fossil fuels.

18.03 A new element in the current debate about energy security in the EU is the idea that a negative relationship might exist between the security objective (however that is defined) and the creation of a more open and competitive internal energy market. This usually expresses itself in two ways: a concern about the reliability and continuity of energy supply (how to avoid a California-style energy crisis), and a concern that a liberalizing environment entails a decline in the investment in major new infrastructure (how to create incentives to invest). The problems are respectively that in a liberalizing market there is a need to ensure a greater degree of network co-ordination at the European level, and that competition alters the basis on which decisions are made about investments, requiring greater certainty about the legal and regulatory frameworks.

18.04 The *legal* issues arising from concerns about energy security have a long history, rooted in the notion that energy is a public service or a service of general economic interest (SGEI). In a number of cases the ECJ and the Commission have had to balance competition concerns with those of supply security, discussed in Section C below. Moreover, this tension is evident in all areas of energy, from gas to oil, from

---

[2] A plethora of definitions are evident in the literature among academics, analysts, industry associations, regulators, and national governments. In the EU 'energy security' is usually understood as 'security of supply'; for the non-EU countries that provide much of EU oil and gas imports, it is rather understood as 'security of demand'. Elements in a general definition would include: regularity and/or continuity, lowest possible cost, access, and physical system security. Distinctions may be drawn between short-term and long-term security: in electricity the former refers to the operational reliability of the system, while the latter refers to the adequacy of power generating capacity and networks. For a variety of perspectives, see the readings in Barton, B, et al (eds), *Energy Security: Managing Risk in a Dynamic Legal and Regulatory Environment* (2004); Kalicki, JH and Goldwyn, DL, (eds), *Energy and Security: Towards a New Foreign Policy Strategy* (2005).

[3] Some parts of the EU are in a very different and more vulnerable situation: Ireland, Malta, and the Baltic States constitute 'energy islands', virtually cut off from the rest of the EU at the present time.

A. Introduction

coal to electricity, and nuclear and renewable sources of energy. However, the tension between security and competition objectives appears in a new light in the current setting of liberalizing energy markets.

In 2006 the Commission's Green Paper on Energy Policy argued that 'liberalized and competitive energy markets help security of supply by sending the right signals to industry participants'.[4] However, it proposed a raft of interventionist measures to improve transparency and predictability. First, a European Energy Supply Observatory could be established to monitor demand and supply patterns on EU energy markets, as well as to identify shortfalls in infrastructure and supply at an early stage and complement the work of the International Energy Agency (IEA) on an EU level. Secondly, a Strategic EU Energy Review could be produced by the Commission, offering an EU framework for national decisions on the energy mix. Thirdly, network security could be improved by the creation of a more formal grouping of TSOs, reporting to the NRAs and the Commission, leading ultimately to a European Centre for Energy Networks, which would have powers to collect, analyze and publish relevant information. Fourthly, a new legislative proposal could be made with respect to gas stocks to ensure a reaction to short-term gas supply disruptions. Fifthly, there could be a publication on a more regular and transparent basis of the state of EU oil stocks. Sixthly, the existing Directives on security of gas and electricity supply should be reviewed to ensure they are able to deal with potential supply disruptions. Finally, it argued that consideration should be given to actions to improve the physical security of infrastructure, such as an assistance mechanism for countries in difficulties following damage to essential infrastructure, and harmonized measures might be taken to protect infrastructure.   **18.05**

This chapter examines the ways in which the energy security objective has been balanced against the competition goal in the various legal and regulatory measures taken to address security problems. It begins with the secondary legislation adopted in recent years when the internal market influence has been strong, emphasizing in particular the electricity and gas sectors. It reviews the various measures taken with respect to oil, which have a longer history in the EU, before examining the specific measures adopted to address infrastructure issues. Next, it examines the Treaty provisions that are relevant to energy security and in particular the various notions of public service and SGEI, which figure in a number of cases. It briefly examines measures arising under the Euratom Treaty with respect   **18.06**

---

[4] European Commission, *Green Paper: A European Strategy for Sustainable, Competitive and Secure Energy*, COM (2006) 105 final, 8 March 2006, 8. Earlier interventions by the Commission in the area of security of supply include the Commission's Communication, *Energy Infrastructure and Security of Supply*, COM (2003) 743 final, 10 December 2003, and the Final Report on the Green Paper, *Towards a European strategy for the security of energy supply*, COM (2002) 321 final.

to the security of nuclear fuel supply, over which there have been concerns, albeit for reasons largely unrelated to liberalization. It concludes that for the moment the concerns about security have not been allowed to undermine the commitment to competition that lies at the heart of the internal energy market programme.

B. Secondary Legislation

18.07 The need to provide specific measures on energy security in the context of a liberalizing market has been considered by the various market players. This is provided principally by two Directives on security of electricity and gas supply, which supplement the framework Directives discussed in Chapters 5 and 6. The main focus in this chapter is on the former Directives, but the latter also provide important and related measures on energy security and are therefore considered first in the sections below.

18.08 The most important (although not the only) concern that the Commission has with energy security is explained in a Note on the security issues arising from the Electricity Directive, in which it is stated: 'The process of market opening in the European Union started at a time with, generally speaking, excess reserve capacity in the system. One of the consequences of market opening and the drive for more efficiency in the sector is a closure of this excess capacity.'[5] While the internal market is likely to deliver the appropriate framework in which energy security can be delivered, by creating a larger market with a variety of suppliers, more flexibility in supply and demand, more effective price signals, efficiency gains inspired by competition, and more innovation, 'additional measures may be necessary to achieve the right social outcome of securing supply at reasonable prices. A disproportionate welfare transfer from consumers to companies in the event of supply scarcity has to be avoided.' The framework for such interventions in the market is provided by the Electricity and Gas Directives, discussed below.

18.09 By contrast, the origins of the two Directives on security of electricity and gas supply are rather different. In principle, they supplement the Electricity and Gas Directives but in practice their adoption was driven by real crisis events more than by the logic of Commission arguments. For the electricity industry, the key events were the following:

- On 14 August 2003 there were black-outs over a very large area of the USA, principally in the North East and Mid West, but affecting major population centres in Canada and leading to several nuclear plants being taken offline in four States.
- On 28 September 2003 the whole of Italy was subject to black-outs for many hours. In the first case the cause was an overload of the grid, while the second happened

---

[5] DG TREN Note, 'Measures to secure electricity supply', 16 January 2004.

B. Secondary Legislation

at a time of minimal consumption. Over 50 million consumers were disconnected for several hours.[6] The lack of co-ordination between transmission system operators (TSOs) in different Member States and neighbouring countries (in particular, Switzerland) needed to be remedied.

- In Norway there was a fall in hydro-electric generation in the winter of 2002–03, following several very dry years. Demand was unable to be met by domestic generation and domestic prices rose sharply in spite of a reversal of the traditional export flow and increase of imports to the limit of the interconnections. Demand was restrained by price variations and no outage resulted.
- On 23 September 2003 a large disruption in transmission lines was experienced in Sweden, leading to the disconnection of 2 million customers. Denmark was affected by this and the previous regional disruption.
- In the UK two local loss-of-supply incidents occurred on 14 August and 5 September 2003. Both resulted from a malfunctioning of equipment on transmission grids, without any connection to excess demand on the system. In each case the outage lasted for less than one hour and affected 400,000 and 200,000 customers respectively.

The events appeared to underline the importance of renewed investment in electricity infrastructure as demand for electricity and the related strain on ageing networks increased. The proposal for a Directive on security of electricity supply was one response to this. However, in the case of gas, a scenario analogous to an electricity 'black-out' is unlikely, and the argument for a special measure is correspondingly weaker.[7] Given the potential for gas storage, and the greater degree of interruptible consumption, the congestion of pipelines is less frequent. The driver behind the proposal for the adoption of additional security of supply measures was linked to the long-term concern about growth of dependence upon external sources of supply and their reliability, but the risks to security that can arise from transit and indeed from damage to essential facilities have since become more widely appreciated.[8]

18.10

---

[6] Vasconcelos, J, 'Lessons that should be drawn from the recent incidents in electricity supply and suggestions for guaranteeing an adequate electricity supply in liberalized markets', 5 October 2003, note by the Council of European Energy Regulators, <www.ceer-eu.org>; the report on the blackout by the UCTE is available at <http://www.ucte.org/pdf/News/20040427_UCTE_IC_Final_report.pdf>. Two reports by Eurelectric provide a thorough analysis of the problems: 'Security of Electricity Supply: Roles, Responsibilities and Experiences within the EU' (January 2006) and 'Power Outages in 2003' (June 2004) <www.eurelectric.org>.

[7] However, see the arguments made by the Commission in its Explanatory Memorandum to the Proposal for a Directive of the European Parliament and the Council concerning measures to safeguard security of natural gas supply; <http://ec.europa.eu/energy/gas/internal_market/oil_gaz/doc/directive_gas_en.pdf>.

[8] With respect to transit, the interruption to the transit of Russian gas through the Ukraine in January 2006 provided a single vivid illustration of transit (and indeed source risk). The severe damage caused by an explosion at the UK Rough field (responsible for a large part of domestic British gas storage) in 2006 underlined the importance of facility risk.

(1) The Electricity Directive

18.11 The Electricity Directive[9] contains a number of provisions that allow Member States to take measures to promote security of supply. Their discretion is considerable but the adoption and exercise of any of these measures has to be justified in terms of their public service character. For that reason the measures adopted have to meet the tests applicable to public service obligations (PSOs) including the requirement that the option adopted is one that is least distortive of competition and the internal market.

18.12 The provisions in the Directive that are most relevant to security of supply are (1) the PSOs in Article 3; (2) the monitoring of security of supply in Article 4; (3) the tendering procedure for new capacity in Article 7; (4) the provision on reporting in Article 28; and (5) the safeguard measures in Article 24. Effectively, they vest responsibility for overall monitoring of security of supply in the TSOs.[10]

(a) Public Service Obligations

18.13 Under Article 3(2) of the Electricity Directive, Member States may impose on undertakings operating in the electricity sector, in the general economic interest, PSOs which 'may relate to security, including security of supply, regularity, quality and price of supplies and environmental protection, including energy efficiency and climate protection'. Such PSOs have to be defined as strictly and narrowly as possible, to be transparent and verifiable. They are not to result in the creation of generation capacity that goes beyond what is necessary to prevent undue interruption of distribution of electricity to final customers. Member States may introduce long-term planning in relation to security of supply.

18.14 Article 3(3) provides further, in relation to security, that Member States shall provide all household customers (at least) with universal service, defined as 'the right to be supplied with electricity of a specified quality within their territory at reasonable, easily and clearly comparable and transparent prices'. To ensure the provision of universal service, Member States may appoint a supplier of last resort.

18.15 Finally, under Article 3(8), Member States are permitted *not* to apply the provisions of the Directive on authorization of new capacity, TPA, and direct lines, if 'their

---

[9] Directive (EC) 2003/54 concerning common rules for the internal market in electricity and repealing Directive (EC) 96/92 [2003] OJ L176/37.

[10] See also Regulation (EC) 1228/2003 of 26 June 2003 on conditions for access to the network for cross-border exchanges in electricity [2003] OJ L176/1, Art 5(1) and (2), and Directive (EC) 2005/89 concerning measures to safeguard security of electricity supply and infrastructure investment [2006] OJ L33/22, Art 4(1) and (2a). In this respect, the efforts to develop a new set of technical rules should be noted. The Florence Forum requested UCTE in 2002 to provide an updated rule-book that takes into account the introduction of competition and the probability that this will lead to less predictability in the EU electricity markets, taking into account the need for the highest standards in system security. Compliance with the new rules is to be enforced with sanctions.

B. Secondary Legislation

application would obstruct the performance, in law or in fact, of the obligations imposed on electricity undertakings in the general economic interest in so far as the development of trade would not be affected to such an extent as would be contrary to the interests of the Community'. It goes on to note that these interests include 'among others, competition with regard to eligible customers in accordance with this Directive and Article 86 of the Treaty'.

Even if the provision in Article 3 is seen as open-ended, permitting Member States a wide discretion, it may be argued that it should be interpreted in relation to the other provisions in the Directive that apply to security of supply, and also in the context of the Electricity Security Directive (discussed below), adopted in 2006. The latter imposes specific obligations on Member States to take measures with respect to security of supply. It is also necessary to take into account the restrictive interpretation placed on the role of PSOs by the Commission in its Note,[11] in which it is argued that the implementation of security of supply obligations must affect the development of trade and competition only in the least possible manner. There must be no alternative solution that is reasonably and economically available. Given the options which are available in the two Directives, a derogation from the Electricity Directive on the ground of security of supply is difficult to justify.[12] The same argument may be applied to the equivalent provision in the Gas Directive.

18.16

(b) Monitoring

Article 4 of the Electricity Directive is also directed at security of supply. It places Member States under an obligation to monitor security of supply issues. This task may be delegated to the regulatory authorities in Article 23(1). This monitoring is to cover the supply/demand balance on the national market, the level of expected future demand and envisaged additional capacity being planned or under construction, and the quality and level of maintenance of the networks, as well as measures to cover peak demand and to deal with shortfalls of one or more suppliers. A report is to be published every two years by the competent authorities, in which they outline the findings that result from the monitoring of these issues as well as any measures taken or envisaged that address them. This report has to be sent to the Commission.

18.17

(c) Tendering for New Capacity

Article 7(1) requires Member States to take measures to provide for the option of a direct tendering procedure or any equivalent procedure for the construction of additional (or reserve) capacity (or energy efficiency and demand-side management measures) if a shortage is foreseen in electricity supply, which the market appears unlikely to resolve, on the basis of the authorization procedure. This option has

18.18

---

[11] DG TREN Interpretation Note, 'Public Service Obligations', 16 January 2004; see paras 5.13–5.15.
[12] This is essentially the argument made by Commission officials in *EU Energy Law*, Vol I, 313–5.

been tried in the Nordic region during the period of extremely low hydropower generation in 2003, and proved very effective. It has also been tried in Ireland and Greece to realize new generation capacity (see paras 18.102 et seq below). However, it is a measure that is clearly an intervention in the market with potentially wide distorting effects, more likely to be apparent in a non-peripheral region than a peripheral one, where the effects of such measures are likely to be limited to the national markets concerned. In the latter two cases, this was underlined by the lack of development of interconnections with other Member States and the small size of the electricity markets concerned.

18.19 **Equivalent measures**   The Electricity Directive is not specific about the timing or the manner of tendering or equivalent measures. In a guidance note provided by the Commission, it lists five distinct measures equivalent to tendering in terms of transparency and non-discrimination that may be taken to achieve the same result.[13] The five measures are:

- *Keeping capacity standby for reserve purposes*. Member States may elect to commit a central body such as a TSO to contract capacity for reserve purposes. While conditions would be attached to the use of the reserve capacity, its existence could potentially distort the investment signal since the reserve capacity might be used before the signal leads to the construction of additional capacity, leading to the possibility that an even larger amount of centralized reserve capacity would be required.
- *Capacity payments*. Member States may decide to reward generators for having capacity available. This does not guarantee that additional capacity will actually be built nor that generators will not abuse their market power in times of scarcity.
- *Capacity requirements*. Suppliers may be obliged to purchase a certain percentage of reserve capacity. This could be tradable capacity and could also be made up of interruptible contracts. Again, there is no guarantee that sufficient capacity will always be available.
- *Reliability contracts*. The TSO is obliged to buy call options from generators. When the options are called, the generators have to pay the difference between the market and the strike price. The income that the generators receive is equal to the strike price. If the generators do not cover the options with capacity, they lose on those when the options are called. In periods of scarcity they do not have an incentive to withhold capacity from the market. The Note proposes that the body best suited to control the central planning element in this measure is the TSO.

---

[13] DG TREN Note, 'Measures to secure electricity supply', 16 January 2004. The Note also envisages the possible use by Member States of long-term contracts between suppliers and generators. However, this option has two disadvantages: eligible customers may switch to suppliers with less expensive contracts, and the contracts might not be long enough to 'dampen' the business cycle.

B. Secondary Legislation

- *Capacity subscriptions.* This option requires each customer to purchase an electronic fuse which potentially limits electricity consumption. The fuses are activated by the TSO in times of scarcity. The fuses vary by size and price, with the result that individual customers pay for reliable supplies and generators can sell fuses only if these are covered by available capacity.

Energy efficiency and demand side management Article 7 of the Electricity Directive also requires Member States to take measures to provide for the option of a direct tendering procedure or any equivalent procedure for energy efficiency and demand-side management measures if a shortage is foreseen in electricity supply, which the market appears unlikely to resolve, on the basis of the authorization procedure. The various options that are available to Member States in this context include: interruptible load; demand-side management, and energy efficiency measures taken by suppliers or at generation plants; and real-time cost information to consumers through metering applications that would allow consumers to adapt their consumption patterns in the event of price increases. **18.20**

(d) Reporting

Under Article 28(1) of the Electricity Directive the Commission is obliged to produce an annual report on various matters including security of supply. This will, in practice, rely heavily on the reports submitted by national regulatory agencies (NRAs) from the Member States on an annual basis. Reporting requirements are also imposed on NRAs and Member States under the Electricity Security Directive that will also be relevant in this context. **18.21**

(e) Safeguard Measures

This measure is carried over from the first Electricity Directive.[14] It allows Member States to take safeguard measures on a temporary basis 'in the event of a sudden crisis in the energy market' and 'where the physical safety or security of persons, apparatus or installations or system integrity is threatened'. The measures taken by the Member State would have to be justified as ones that were the only appropriate ones that would address the crisis situation, and meet the tests of being least restrictive of competition and trade to achieve the objective. **18.22**

(2) The Gas Directive

In the Gas Directive[15] many of the provisions on security of supply are the same as those in the Electricity Directive. The provision on PSOs in Article 3 is one example of this. **18.23**

---

[14] Directive (EC) 96/92 concerning common rules for the internal market in electricity [1997] OJ L27/20.
[15] Directive (EC) 2003/55 concerning common rules for the internal market in natural gas and repealing Directive (EC) 98/30 [2003] OJ L176/57.

Article 5 contains a provision on monitoring that reflects Article 4 of the Electricity Directive (but provides for annual, not bi-annual, reporting). Article 26 on safeguards is similar to that in Article 24 of the Electricity Directive. Article 31(1)(d) contains a reporting requirement on security of gas supply that the Commission must comply with. One key difference is in the treatment of new infrastructure in Article 22, although even here the difference is less significant if one takes the comparable provision (Article 7) of the Electricity Regulation into account.

(a) Exemption from TPA

18.24 Article 22 of the Gas Directive provides for the grant of an exemption from TPA rules to new major gas infrastructure on the ground of security of supply: the proposed investment 'must enhance competition in gas supply and enhance security of supply'. This applies also to 'significant increases of capacity in existing infrastructures and to modifications of such infrastructures which enable the development of new sources of gas supply'. It should be emphasized, however, that Article 22 is for exceptions and entails the application of strict criteria (see paras 6.53–6.58).

18.25 The kind of infrastructure that would fall under this article includes interconnectors between Member States, LNG facilities, and storage facilities. Providing for a diversification of supply routes and sources constitutes an important means of enhancing security of supply.[16] An interconnector as defined in Article 2(17) could contribute to security of supply but any exemption grant is in practice reviewed on a case-by-case basis. In this review, a balancing of the security of supply criterion and the enhancement of competition will have to be made. A similar comment may be made with respect to new LNG facilities, which could be expected to increase the overall supply base of a market and may provide access to new supply sources. Storage facilities are also important instruments for the enhancement of security of supply. However, there are different kinds of storage facility which serve different purposes, depending upon their size and capacity features. Again, there would be a need to take into account the degree to which competition was enhanced by any grant of an exemption from TPA.

(b) Derogation and PSOs

18.26 Security of supply may also constitute a ground for refusing access to the gas network, if security of supply obligations constitute part of, or are defined as, PSOs. Article 21 permits a refusal on the basis of a lack of capacity or where system access would prevent them from fulfilling their PSOs. Duly substantiated reasons must be given for such a refusal. Such a refusal of access in the view of the Commission

---

[16] DG TREN, 'Note on Security of Supply Provisions for Gas', 16 January 2004, 6; also European Commission, *Green Paper: A European Strategy for Sustainable, Competitive and Secure Energy*, COM (2006) 105 final, 8 March 2006, 15.

'should not be authorized beyond what is needed to comply with proportionate and reasonable security of supply standards generally acknowledged across the European gas industry'.[17] A fundamental requirement for such a refusal is that the PSO on security of supply should be clearly defined, transparent, non-discriminatory, and verifiable. The Commission's Note on this subject bluntly states: 'If PSOs on security of supply are not in line with the requirements of Article 3(2), they cannot constitute grounds for refusing access to the system'.[18] Since network access constitutes the heart of the Gas Directive, the criteria for refusal of access to the system on security of supply grounds are likely to be applied in a restrictive manner. The evidence that would need to be provided in support of a derogation would have to demonstrate that there was no reasonable and economically feasible alternative available: in other words, if access were to be granted, it would make it impossible for the PSO to be fulfilled even though that PSO had been imposed on natural gas undertakings. The proportionality test is appropriate here. The requirements and obligations for security of supply cannot be expected to go beyond what is necessary and proportionate. This can be defined in a benchmarking manner against the security of supply requirements in other markets with similar characteristics.

In connection with take-or-pay commitments, derogations may be made on security of supply grounds. Article 27(3)(b) requires the competent authority and the Commission to take into account (among other things) 'the need to fulfil public service obligations and to ensure security of supply' (see paras 6.72–6.98). **18.27**

(c) Upstream Issues

Security of supply considerations may also arise in connection with TPA to upstream pipelines in relation to Article 20 of the Gas Directive. This article states that Member States, in providing for access, are to 'apply the objectives of fair and open access, achieving a competitive market in natural gas and avoiding any abuse of a dominant position, taking into account security and regularity of supplies.' This may be taken into account when designing the regime for access to upstream networks. It may concern specific capacity commitments that may be imposed upon the operator of the upstream pipelines, designed to make capacity available in order to meet demand under certain conditions. For this to be acceptable under the terms of the Directive, it would be important to ensure that such security of supply obligations did not have the effect of depriving the market permanently of a proportion of the upstream pipeline capacity. An offer of gas in such circumstances could be made on interruptible terms with well-defined criteria for interruption.[19] **18.28**

---

[17] DG TREN, 'Note on Security of Supply Provisions for Gas', 16 January 2004, 7.
[18] ibid 7.
[19] ibid 5.

(3) Electricity Security

18.29 In 2006 a Directive[20] was adopted to provide for an enhanced security of electricity supply and to provide some measures aimed at facilitating infrastructure investment. The justification for the Electricity Security Directive was that a competitive single EU electricity market requires transparent and non-discriminatory policies on security of electricity of supply that are compatible with the requirements of such a market, but distortions of competition would result if such policies were absent or contained significant differences between the Member States.[21] A definition of clear roles and responsibilities on the part of the competent authorities as well as the Member States and all market actors was deemed to be 'crucial in safeguarding security of electricity supply and the proper functioning of the internal market'. However, this fixing of responsibilities should avoid the creation of obstacles to new market entrants and the creation of distortions of the internal market in electricity or significant difficulties for market actors. Moreover, while co-operation between national TSOs in network security matters is vital to the development of a well-functioning internal market, it could be further improved. Such a lack of co-ordination is 'detrimental to the development of equal conditions for competition'.[22] These objectives—secure electricity supplies based on fair competition and the creation of a fully operational internal electricity market—could not be sufficiently achieved by the Member States alone, and hence a measure was proposed at Community level.[23]

18.30 The Electricity Security Directive defines security of electricity supply as 'the ability of an electricity system to supply final customers with electricity, as provided for under this Directive'. It aims at safeguarding security to ensure the proper functioning of the internal market for electricity and also to ensure an adequate level of generation capacity, an adequate balance between supply and demand, and an appropriate level of interconnection between Member States for the development of the internal market.[24] It is also intended to establish a framework in which Member States can define transparent, stable, and non-discriminatory policies on supply security for electricity compatible with the requirements of a competitive internal market for electricity.

18.31 The principal obligations imposed on Member States are to ensure a high level of security of electricity supply by (1) taking the necessary measures to facilitate a stable investment climate, (2) defining the roles and responsibilities of competent

---

[20] Directive (EC) 2005/89 concerning measures to safeguard security of electricity supply and infrastructure investment [2006] OJ L33/22.
[21] ibid, Recital 3.
[22] ibid, Recital 7.
[23] ibid, Recital 18.
[24] ibid, Art 1.

B. Secondary Legislation

authorities and all relevant market actors, and (3) publishing information on these matters. The 'competent authorities' are to include regulatory authorities where relevant. These are defined in Article 2(a) of the Electricity Security Directive as the 'regulatory authorities in Member States, as designated in accordance with Article 23 of Directive 2003/54/ EC' (that is, the Electricity Directive). The relevant market actors are to include (but not be limited to) TSOs and distribution system operators (DSOs), electricity generators, suppliers, and final customers.

(a) Implementation

18.32 Implementation of the above obligations is to be carried out by taking into account a set of seven mandatory criteria and a set of four optional criteria.[25] The mandatory criteria are as follows:

(1) the importance of ensuring continuity of electricity supplies;
(2) the importance of a transparent and stable regulatory framework;
(3) the internal market and the possibilities for cross-border co-operation in relation to security of electricity supply;
(4) the need for regular maintenance and, where necessary, renewal of the transmission and distribution networks to maintain the performance of the network;
(5) the importance of ensuring proper implementation of the renewable energy and cogeneration Directives,[26] to the extent that their provisions concern security of electricity supply;
(6) the need to ensure sufficient transmission and generation reserve capacity for stable operation; and
(7) the importance of encouraging the establishment of liquid wholesale markets.

18.33 The four criteria which Member States may take into account when implementing the measures in Article 1 of the Electricity Security Directive are:

(1) the degree of diversity in electricity generation at national or relevant regional level;
(2) the importance of reducing the long-term effects of the growth of electricity demand;
(3) the importance of encouraging energy efficiency and the adoption of new technologies, in particular demand management technologies, renewable energy technologies, and distributed generation; and
(4) the importance of removing administrative barriers to investments in infrastructure and generation capacity.

---

[25] ibid, Art 3(2) and (3) respectively.
[26] Respectively, Directive (EC) 2001/77 on the promotion of electricity produced from renewable energy sources in the internal electricity market [2001] OJ L283/33, as amended by the 2003 Act of Accession, and Directive (EC) 2004/8 on the promotion of cogeneration based on a useful heat demand in the internal energy market [2004] OJ L52/50.

18.34 Any measures taken are required to be non-discriminatory and not to place an unreasonable burden upon the market actors. The latter group includes market entrants and companies with small market shares. In addition, Member States are required to carry out an impact assessment of the proposed measures on the cost of electricity to final customers.[27]

(b) Network Security

18.35 Apart from the above obligations and recommendations to Member States, the body of the Electricity Security Directive is concerned with 'operational network security', 'maintaining balance between supply and demand' and network investment. The first two of these are defined in the Directive. 'Operational network security' means the continuous operation of the transmission system and, where appropriate, the distribution network under foreseeable circumstances.[28] 'Balance between supply and demand' means the satisfaction of foreseeable demands of consumers to use electricity without the need to enforce measures to reduce consumption.

18.36 Under the heading of Operational Network Security, Member States or the competent authorities are required to ensure that TSOs set the minimum operational rules and obligations on network security.[29] They are required to consult with the relevant actors in the countries with which interconnection exists *before* establishing such rules and obligations. Member States may require TSOs to submit such rules and obligations to the competent authority for approval. Member States are also required to ensure that TSOs and, where appropriate, DSOs comply with the minimum operational rules and obligations on network security.

18.37 Member States are obliged to require TSOs to maintain an appropriate level of operational network security. TSOs must therefore maintain an appropriate level of technical transmission reserve capacity for operational network security and co-operate with the TSOs concerned to which they are interconnected. The level of foreseeable circumstances in which security is to be maintained is to be defined in the operational network security rules.

18.38 Information exchange on the operation of networks is required by the Directive. Member States must ensure that interconnected TSOs and, where appropriate, DSOs exchange information in a timely and effective manner in line with the minimum operational requirements. These requirements are to apply to TSOs and DSOs in cases where they are interconnected with system operators outside the EU.

18.39 Three additional sets of requirements or tests are imposed on Member States or TSOs and DSOs. First, Member States or the competent authorities are to ensure

---

[27] Electricity Security Directive, Art 3(4).
[28] ibid, Art 2(c).
[29] ibid, Art 4(1)(a).

B. Secondary Legislation

that TSOs and DSOs impose quality of supply and network security performance objectives, and to ensure that the objectives are met.[30] They are subject to the approval of the Member States or competent authorities and their implementation is to be monitored by them. They are to be objective, transparent, and non-discriminatory and are to be published. Secondly, Member States are obliged not to discriminate between cross-border contracts and national contracts. This arises in the context of measures required to be taken by Member States on safeguards and congestion management in the Electricity Directive (Article 24) and the Electricity Regulation (Article 6) respectively.[31] Finally, when supply has to be curtailed in an emergency situation, Member States are required to ensure that this is based on predefined criteria relating to the management of imbalances by TSOs. Such safeguard measures are to be taken in close consultation with other relevant TSOs, and should respect the relevant bilateral agreements, including agreements on the exchange of information.[32]

(c) Supply and Demand Balance

18.40 The balance between supply and demand is the second specific topic addressed by the Electricity Security Directive. Member States are required to take appropriate measures to maintain a balance between the demand for electricity and the availability of generation capacity. All measures taken are to be published and Member States are required to ensure the 'widest possible dissemination thereof'.[33] Two distinct sets of measures are envisaged:[34] they are to encourage the establishment of a wholesale market framework that provides suitable price signals for generation and consumption; they are to require TSOs to ensure that an appropriate level of generation reserve capacity is available for balancing purposes; and/or adopt equivalent market-based measures. The aim is to ensure a very high degree of transparency for any intervention in the market.

18.41 To deal with problems in this area—maintaining the balance between supply and demand—Member States *may* take additional measures which can include the following:[35] provisions facilitating new generation capacity and the entry of new generation companies to the market; removal of barriers that prevent the use of interruptible contracts; removal of barriers that prevent the conclusion of contracts of varying lengths for both producers and customers; encouragement of the adoption of real-time demand management technologies such as advanced

---

[30] ibid, Art 4(2).
[31] ibid, Art 4(3).
[32] ibid, Art 4(4).
[33] ibid, Art 5(3).
[34] ibid, Art 5(1)(a) and (b). The former subparagraph requires such action to be taken without prejudice to the particular requirements of small isolated systems.
[35] ibid, Art 5(2). These additional measures may be taken without prejudice to Arts 87 and 88 EC.

metering systems; encouragement of energy conservation measures; and tendering procedures or any procedure equivalent in terms of transparency and non-discrimination in accordance with Article 7(1) of the Electricity Directive. Member States have considerable discretion in their choice and specific design of instruments.

(d) Investment

18.42 For investment in networks, Member States are required to establish a regulatory framework that provides investment signals for both the TSOs and DSOs to develop their networks in order to meet foreseeable demand from the market.[36] The regulatory framework has also to facilitate maintenance and where necessary a renewal of their networks. Merchant investments in interconnection may be allowed by Member States. These decisions on investments in interconnection are required to be taken in close co-operation between the relevant TSOs.

(e) Reporting

18.43 The Electricity Security Directive contains extensive reporting requirements, which interface with the requirements of Article 4 of the Electricity Directive.[37] Member States are required to ensure that the report required by Article 4 covers the overall adequacy of the electricity system to supply current and projected demands for electricity. This must include operational network security; the projected balance of supply and demand for the next five-year period; the prospects for security of electricity supply for the period between five and 15 years from the date of the report; and the investment intentions, for the next five or more calendar years, of TSOs and those of any other party of which they are aware, as regards the provision of cross-border interconnection capacity. This report has to be prepared by Member States or the competent authorities in close co-operation with TSOs, which may consult their neighbouring TSOs, if appropriate.

18.44 The section of the above report that relates to interconnection investment intentions has to take into account four elements:[38] the principles of congestion management (as set out in the Electricity Regulation) (see paras 5.90–5.94 and 5.119–5.127); existing and planned transmission lines; expected patterns of generation, supply, cross-border exchanges, and consumption, allowing for demand management measures; and regional, national, and European sustainable development objectives, including those projects that form a part of the Axes for priority projects set out in Annex I to Decision 1229/2003/EC on Trans-European Energy Networks (Guidelines) (see paras 18.68–18.80). Member States are required to ensure that TSOs provide information on their investment intentions or those of any other party that they

---

[36] ibid, Art 6.
[37] ibid, Art 7.
[38] ibid, Art 7(3).

B. Secondary Legislation

are aware of concerning the provision of cross-border interconnection capacity. Member States *may* also require TSOs to provide information on investments related to the construction of internal lines that materially affect the provision of cross-border interconnection.

For the above tasks, Member States or the competent authorities are required to ensure that the necessary means for access to the relevant data are facilitated to the TSOs and/or competent authorities where that is relevant.[39] This also includes provision for the non-disclosure of confidential information. **18.45**

The outcome of this reporting process is that the Commission is to report to the Member States, competent authorities, and the ERGEG (on the basis of the information on short, medium, and long-term factors relevant to security of supply it has received from the competent authorities under Article 4 of the Electricity Directive) on the investments planned and their contribution to the objectives set out in the Electricity Security Directive.[40] **18.46**

A separate reporting requirement falls on the Commission which has to monitor and review the application of the Directive and submit a progress report to the European Parliament and the Council on 24 February 2010.[41] **18.47**

The Electricity Security Directive entered into force on 24 February 2006 but the timetable for transposition is set two years later at 24 February 2008.[42] By 1 December 2007 Member States are to notify the Commission of the text of the provisions of national law which they are to adopt for transposition. **18.48**

(4) Gas Security

(a) Objectives

In 2004 a Directive[43] was adopted to provide for measures to safeguard an adequate level of supply security for gas. The measures were intended to complement existing measures on the internal gas market and contribute to its proper functioning. A minimum common approach to security of supply was thought to be necessary to avoid market distortions and could not be 'sufficiently achieved' in all circumstances by the Member States themselves, especially given the increased interdependency among the Member States on security of gas supply.[44] In particular, the Gas Security Directive had three goals: to establish a common framework in **18.49**

---

[39] ibid, Art 7(4).
[40] This reporting may be combined with the reporting provided for under point (c) of Art 28(1) of the Electricity Directive, and is to be published: ibid, Art 7(5).
[41] ibid, Art 9.
[42] ibid, Art 8.
[43] Directive (EC) 2004/67 concerning measures to safeguard security of natural gas supply [2004] OJ L127/92.
[44] ibid, Recital 19.

which Member States would define 'general, transparent and non-discriminatory security of supply policies compatible with the requirements of a competitive internal gas market';[45] to clarify the general roles and responsibilities of the different market players; and to implement specific non-discriminatory procedures to safeguard security of gas supply.

18.50 The first of these objectives is provided for in Article 3 (Policies for Securing Gas Supply). Each Member State is required to define the roles and responsibilities of the different gas market players in achieving these policies, and to specify minimum security of supply standards that have to be complied with by the players in the Member State. These standards are to be implemented in a non-discriminatory and transparent way and are to be published. There is an obligation imposed on Member States to ensure that the measures referred to 'do not place an unreasonable and disproportionate burden on gas market players and are compatible with the requirements of a competitive internal gas market'. This includes new market entrants and small market players. A list of instruments for enhancing security of gas supply is provided for in an Annex.[46]

18.51 The third objective is attained through Article 4 (Security of Supply for Specific Customers), under which Member States are required to ensure that household customers in their territory are protected 'to an appropriate extent' in the event of defined circumstances. These include: a partial disruption of national gas supplies during a period to be determined by Member States taking into account national circumstances; extremely cold temperatures during a nationally determined peak period; and periods of exceptionally high gas demand during the coldest weather periods statistically occurring every 20 years. These sets of events constitute criteria under Article 4(1) of the Gas Security Directive and are called the 'security of supply standards'. The measures in the Annex are examples of instruments that may be adopted to meet these standards. However, the meaning of the words 'to an appropriate extent' is left to the Member States themselves, as is the choice of measures for delivering the chosen standard of service.

18.52 A number of possible additional steps may be taken by Member States under Article 4. The scope of the above standards may be extended to small and medium-sized

---

[45] ibid, Art 1.
[46] The list of instruments to enhance the security of gas supply is non-exhaustive and includes: working gas in storage capacity; withdrawal capacity in gas storage; provision of pipeline capacity enabling diversification of gas supplies to affected areas; liquid tradable gas markets; system flexibility; development of interruptible demand; use of alternative back-up fuels in industrial and power generation plants; cross-border capacities; co-operation between TSOs of neighbouring Member States for co-ordinated dispatching; co-ordinated dispatching activities between distribution and TSOs; domestic production of gas; production flexibility; import flexibility; diversification of sources of gas supply; long-term contracts, and investments in infrastructure for gas import via re-gasification terminals and pipelines.

B. Secondary Legislation

enterprises and other customers that cannot switch their gas consumption to other energy sources. This includes the provision of measures for the security of a Member State's national electricity system if it depends upon gas supplies. Member States may also take the necessary measures to ensure that gas storage facilities located within their own territory contribute to an appropriate degree towards the achievement of the security of supply standards. This has to take into account the geological conditions of their territory and the economic and technical feasibility of such measures. In cases where an adequate level of interconnection is available, Member States may take the measures appropriate to achieving these standards in co-operation with another Member State, by using gas storage facilities located within that other Member State. These measures are not to impede the proper functioning of the internal gas market, especially with respect to bilateral agreements. Finally, Member States may set or require industry to set indicative minimum targets for a possible future contribution to storage, whether located in or outside the Member State, to security of supply. These targets are to be published. This should not however create any additional investment obligations.[47]

(b) Gas Co-ordination Group

The principal institutional innovation in the Gas Security Directive is the Gas Co-ordination Group (the Group) that is formally established under Article 7 of the Directive. Its aim is to facilitate the co-ordination of security of supply measures at Community level in the event of a major supply disruption. It is composed of representatives of the Member States and representative bodies of the industries concerned as well as relevant consumers, with the Commission as chair. Representatives from Russia and the Ukraine have also been invited to its meetings. The detailed workings of the Group are set out in Article 9. Essentially, the trigger for action is the occurrence of an event that is likely to develop into a 'major supply disruption' for a significant period of time. Such a disruption is defined as a situation where the Community would risk the loss of more than 20 per cent of its gas supply from third countries, and a situation at Community level that is not likely to be adequately managed with national measures.[48] The foreseeable length of such a supply disruption should cover a significant period of time, which the Directive places at a minimum of eight weeks.[49] Alternatively, Member States may indicate to the Chair of the Group that an event or events of magnitude and exceptional character have occurred which they consider to be incapable of adequate management with national measures alone.[50] In either case, the Commission shall convene the Group as soon as possible at its own initiative or at the request of a Member State.

18.53

---

[47] Gas Security Directive, Art 4(6); Recital 7.
[48] ibid, Art 2(2).
[49] ibid, Recital 17.
[50] ibid, Art 9(1).

Prior to the formal transposition date of the Directive, the Group was convened informally at regular intervals, for instance to consider the events arising from the suspension of gas deliveries from Russia to the Ukraine on 1 January 2006, which resulted in a shortfall in gas deliveries to certain EU Member States.[51]

18.54 The Group is also required to examine and, where appropriate, assist the Member States in co-ordinating the measures taken at national level to deal with a major supply disruption.[52] It provides for a three-step approach. The first step is for the Group to take full account of the measures taken by the gas industry as a first response to the major supply disruption and the measures taken by Member States themselves, including any relevant bilateral agreements. A second stage commences if these measures taken at national level prove to be inadequate to deal with the effects of an event, when the Commission may, following consultation with the Group, provide guidance to Member States regarding further measures to assist those Member States that are particularly affected by the major supply disruption.[53] Finally, if these further measures prove to be inadequate, the Commission may submit a proposal to the Council regarding further necessary measures. The Directive is careful to add that any measures at the Community level are to contain provisions which are aimed at ensuring fair and equitable compensation of the undertakings concerned by the measures to be taken.[54]

(c) Monitoring

18.55 The Gas Security Directive provides for an extensive monitoring role by the Commission. This is based on the reporting requirements in Article 5. In addition to the reporting requirements in the Gas Directive (Article 5), through which Member States are required to submit reports to the Commission, they are required to cover four areas in their reporting: the competitive impact of the measures taken pursuant to Articles 3 and 4 on all gas market players; the levels of storage capacity; the extent of long-term gas supply contracts concluded by companies established and registered on their territory,[55] in particular, their remaining duration (based on information supplied by the companies concerned but excluding commercially sensitive information) and the degree of liquidity of the gas market; and

---

[51] Due to a dispute between Russia and the Ukraine on gas deliveries, Gazprom reduced the flow into pipelines crossing Ukraine by the amount that would otherwise have been for Ukrainian use, leaving it at the level Russia is contracted to supply to its other (EU) customers. However, these customers immediately noticed a fall in their gas supply. Russia blamed this on the Ukraine. This was the first interruption in the supply of Russian gas for 40 years.

[52] Gas Security Directive, Art 9(2). The Group should also exchange information on security of gas supply on a regular basis: ibid, Recital 15.

[53] ibid, Art 9(4).

[54] ibid, Art 9(6).

[55] A long-term gas supply contract in the Directive is defined as a gas supply contract with a duration of more than ten years: ibid, Art 2(1).

B. Secondary Legislation

finally, the regulatory frameworks to provide adequate incentives for new investment in exploration and production, storage, LNG, and transport of gas.[56] This information is to feed into the reports that the Commission is required to present under Article 31 of the Gas Directive.

Article 6 of the Gas Security Directive lists five areas in which monitoring is to be carried out by the Commission on the basis of the above reports. These require it to monitor: the degree of new long-term gas supply import contracts from third countries; the existence of adequate liquidity of gas supplies; the level of working gas and of the withdrawal capacity of gas storage; the level of interconnection of the national gas systems of Member States; and the foreseeable gas supply situation in function of demand, supply autonomy, and available supply sources at Community level concerning specific geographic areas in the Community. **18.56**

On the basis of this monitoring, the Commission may conclude that gas supplies in the Community will be insufficient to meet foreseeable gas demand in the long term. If so, it may submit proposals in accordance with the Treaty. By 19 May 2008 the Commission is to submit a review report to the European Parliament and the Council on the experience gained from this monitoring role.[57] By the same date, the Commission is required to report on the effectiveness of the instruments used with respect to Articles 3 and 4 and their effect on the internal gas market and on the evolution of competition on the internal gas market.[58] The Commission may then issue recommendations or present proposals for further measures to enhance security of supply. **18.57**

The Gas Security Directive entered into force on 19 May 2004 but the timetable for transposition was set two years later at 19 May 2006.[59] **18.58**

(d) The Public Service Issue

In the background, the Gas Security Directive had its roots in a greater understanding of the consequences of the development of a liberalizing market. In this context, no single player will necessarily maintain the overall responsibility for short and long-term security of gas supply at the national level. In a competitive market, it is not obvious that gas suppliers will give a strategic priority to security of supply. Security measures can be costly and may therefore be neglected by operators if there is no agreed minimum standard with which they must comply. Yet the internal market is not only about the promotion of consumer choice but also about ensuring that the market provides high levels of public service. In the **18.59**

---

[56] ibid, Art 5(a)–(d). The final subparagraph has to take into account Art 22 of the Gas Directive as far as this is implemented by the Member State.
[57] ibid, Art 6(3).
[58] ibid, Art 10(1).
[59] ibid, Art 8.

Chapter 18: Energy Security

Explanatory Memorandum to the proposal for the Directive, the Commission states that 'security of supply and competition are compatible objectives'.[60] It notes that the first Gas Directive[61] acknowledged the right of Member States to consider security of supply as a public service obligation.

(5) Oil Security

18.60 The measures on oil security of supply have been in place for many years. Their raison d'être has been expressly linked to crisis prevention and management in the light of experiences with oil shortages in the 1970s. However, the first measure to address oil security was the Oil Stocks Directive taken as long ago as 1968.[62] This imposed an obligation on Member States to maintain minimum stocks of crude oil and/or petroleum products. It was amended in 1998 and, in its modified form, is still in force. Two further legislative measures arose from the 1973 oil crisis,[63] and led to the establishment of a crisis mechanism. This was extended later. Basically, the latter measures implement the IEA's regime for oil crisis management.

(a) Oil Stocks

18.61 The Oil Stocks Directive was essentially aimed at requiring Member States to maintain at all times, within the territory of the EU, stocks of petroleum products at a level that corresponds to at least 90 days' average daily internal consumption in the preceding calendar year. The EU bases its calculation of 90 days on domestic consumption of three categories of products for each of its Member States. By contrast, the IEA bases its calculation on the total net oil imports of the preceding year for each participating country concerned.[64] The amendments to the Directive were adopted by the Council of Ministers under Article 103a(1) of the EC Treaty on 14 December 1998. The new provisions entered into force when the Directive was published in the Official Journal on 31 December 1998.[65] It imposed an obligation on Member States to maintain a minimum stock of crude oil and/or petroleum products, and significantly modified the 1968 Directive on compulsory stocks.

---

[60] Explanatory Memorandum, 4.
[61] Directive (EC) 98/30 concerning common rules for the internal market in natural gas [1998] OJ L204/1.
[62] Directive (EEC) 68/414 imposing an obligation on Member States of the EEC to maintain minimum stocks of crude oil and/or petroleum products [1968] OJ L308/14, as amended by Directive (EC) 98/93 [1998] OJ L358/100.
[63] Directive (EEC) 73/238 on measures to mitigate the effects of difficulties in the supply of crude oil and petroleum products [1973] OJ L228/1; Directive (EEC) 77/706 on the setting of a Community target for a reduction in the consumption of primary sources of energy in the event of difficulties in the supply of crude oil and petroleum products [1977] OJ L 292/9.
[64] For a discussion of the EU-IEA linkage in this connection see Willenborg, R, Tonjes, C, and Perlot, W, *Europe's Oil Defences: An Analysis of Europe's oil supply vulnerability and its emergency oil stockholding systems* (Clingendael International Energy Programme, 2004) 31–44.
[65] Oil Stocks Directive, Art 103a(1) provides that such measures may be adopted by means of qualified majority voting.

B. Secondary Legislation

The modifications did not concern matters of principle, but rather technical issues, arising from developments in the security of supply, the oil market, and the internal energy market.

18.62 The background to the revisions is as follows. Since the 1968 Directive was made, the compulsory stockholding systems of the EU had evolved. Originally, Member States were required to maintain oil stocks at a minimum level of 65 days' of internal consumption of the calendar year. In 1972, the minimum stocking requirement was raised from 65 to 90 days' internal consumption by Directive (EEC) 72/425.[66] In 1973 the Council adopted Directive (EEC) 73/238 concerning measures to be taken by the Member States to provide the competent authorities with powers, including drawing on oil stocks, to deal with any disruption of supply. The 1998 Directive continued this process by increasing the level of transparency, easing the rules on stocks being held outside national boundaries, and taking greater account of domestic production, while avoiding market distortions. It also includes a list of stocks that are *excluded* as well as a list of those included.

18.63 There are seven articles common to both the 1968 (as amended) and 1998 Directives:

- Each Member State has to maintain a minimum stock of 90 days' internal consumption for oil/oil products.
- A list is established that excludes maritime bunkers.
- Principles of stocking are established, including the requirement that stocks are to be fully at the disposal of the Member State; that they are to be established in a non-discriminatory manner; and that the Member State may establish a holding body.
- A Member State has to submit data to the EC.
- Provision is made for Member States to hold stocks in product form or in crude oil, with three ways of calculating the split. Three categories of product are permitted: motor spirit and gasoline based aviation fuel; gas oil, diesel oil, kerosene and kerosene type jet fuel; and fuel oils. There is a stock obligation on each category of product.
- A system of supervision is established, including checking and possible sanctions, with the agreement of governments on the products to be counted and those not to be counted when reporting to the EC.
- In the event of security of supply problems, it is possible to draw down stocks on certain conditions.

18.64 Among the changes included in the 1998 Directive are the following. The maximum derogation for Member States with domestic oil production was increased from 15 to 25 per cent from the 90-day consumption requirement. More detailed

---

[66] [1972] OJ L291/154.

provisions were included on bilateral agreements whereby compulsory stocks may be held in another Member State, adding new conditions, but taking into account the cost-effectiveness of this option, the existence of appropriate infrastructure, and the dimension of the internal market. In such cases, there has to be no opposition to a repatriation of the stocks and the host country has an obligation to check. The cost burden resulting from the maintenance of stocks is to be identified by transparent arrangements. The changes had to be introduced by Member States in their laws, regulations, and administrative provisions by 1 January 2000. A three-year transition period was granted to Greece under Article 4 of the Directive. This applied only with respect to the inclusion of bunker supplies for international aviation in the calculation of internal consumption.

18.65 In September 2002 the Commission came forward with proposals to create a central oil storage agency and raise the minimum stock requirement from 90 to 120 days.[67] Also included was a proposal to use stocks in response to price increases or volatile markets. This proposal was defeated on grounds that it would be too expensive and would yield only uncertain results. It may also have led to declining co-operation with the IEA. However, another proposal has been made which would repeal the existing legislation and codify the various amendments into a single law.[68] This process is a very different one from that previously described since a codification exercise does not imply any changes of substance. Indeed, the Directive, if adopted, will fully preserve the content of the acts being codified and therefore does no more than bring them together with only such formal amendments as are required by the codification exercise itself.

18.66 In the context of crisis management it may be noted that strategic stocks offer only a limited solution to risks of disruption to supplies. Such reserves are limited in volume and would not provide a safeguard against a major, sustained disruption to oil supplies. They were used on 2 September 2005 in the context of shortages caused by hurricanes Katrina and Rita in the Gulf of Mexico which led to a reduction

---

[67] Proposal for a Council Decision repealing Council Decision 68/416/EEC on the conclusion and implementation of individual agreements between governments relating to the obligation of Member States to maintain minimum stocks of crude oil and/or petroleum products and Council Decision 77/706/EEC on the setting of a Community target for a reduction in the consumption of primary sources of energy in the event of difficulties in the supply of crude oil and petroleum products [2002] OJ 331E/280; Proposal for a Council Directive repealing Council Directives 68/414/EEC and 98/93/EC imposing an obligation on Member States of the EEC to maintain minimum stocks of crude oil and/or petroleum products, and Council Directive 73/238/EEC on measures to mitigate the effects of difficulties in the supply of crude oil and petroleum products [2002] OJ 331E/279; Proposal for a Directive of the European Parliament and of the Council concerning the alignment of measures with regard to security of supply for petroleum products [2002] OJ 331E/249.

[68] European Commission, Proposal for a Council Directive imposing an obligation on Member States to maintain minimum stocks of crude oil and/or petroleum products, COM (2004) 35 final, 23 January 2004.

B. Secondary Legislation

in refining capacity.[69] Member States currently favour diverse national systems of stockpiling, involving various forms of ownership of management systems. The thrust of the Commission's initiatives is to promote co-operation and co-ordination.

(b) Crisis Management

The separate legal measure of 1973 required Member States to take all necessary measures to provide the competent authorities with the necessary powers in the event of difficulties arising in the supply of crude oil and petroleum products which might appreciably reduce the supply of these products and cause severe disruption. Those powers would allow the authorities to draw on emergency stocks according to the Oil Stocks Directive. It would also allow them to impose specific or broad restrictions on consumption, depending on the estimated shortages, and to give priority to supplies of petroleum products to certain groups of users, and to regulate prices in order to prevent abnormal price rises. The Member States are also required to draw up intervention plans for use in the event of difficulties arising with the supply of crude oil and petroleum products. If difficulties with supply arise in the EC or in one of the Member States, Article 3 mandates the Commission to convene as soon as possible a group of delegates from the Member States, either at its own initiative or at the request of one of the Member States. The group will carry out the necessary consultations to ensure co-ordination of the measures taken or proposed under the powers granted by this Directive. In September 2005 a meeting of the Oil Supply Group, comprising oil experts from the national administrations of the Member States, was convened to review oil stocks levels and to co-ordinate measures if necessary.[70] The Commission intended to request Member States to communicate their plans of action to reduce consumption.

18.67

(6) Infrastructure

The need for additional infrastructure[71] capacity has grown in line with, but not as a result of, the liberalization programme. Its importance in promoting the potential for

18.68

---

[69] For background see Commission Recommendation of 7 December 2005 on the release of security oil stocks following the supply disruption caused by Hurricane Katrina [2005] OJ L326/37.

[70] Commission Press Release IP/05/1114, 'Oil crisis: The European Commission calls on the Member States to pull together', 8 September 2005. The possibility that such gatherings, especially of oil industry personnel, might lead to anti-competitive practices led to the adoption of a Commission Decision providing an exemption from the scope of Art 81(3): *International Energy Agency* (Case IV/30.525) Commission Decision of 21 February 1994 relating to a proceeding under Art 85 EC [1994] OJ L68/35.

[71] The issue of energy infrastructure protection from terrorism is not considered here, but it may be noted that the Commission has addressed this issue in a wider setting in its Communication to the Council and European Parliament, 'Critical Infrastructure Protection in the fight against terrorism', COM(2004)0702 final. It includes energy installations and networks in the category of 'critical infrastructures'.

competition and cohesion was recognized even before the principal internal energy market legislation was in place.[72] It has been the focus of a number of initiatives by the EU, gathered together under the heading of Trans-European Networks (TENs).[73]

18.69 The legal basis of this programme is provided by Articles 154–6 EC.[74] Article 154 sets out the objectives of Community action as:

- contributing to the establishment and development of TENs in the areas of transport, telecommunications, and energy infrastructures;
- aiming at promoting the interconnection and inter-operability of national networks as well as access to such networks; and
- taking account of the need to link island, land-locked, and peripheral regions with the central regions of the Community.

18.70 The overall aim is to provide the 'missing links' in the various sectors to ensure the free movement of persons, goods, services, and capital. Article 155 refers to the means for implementing these objectives, by establishing guidelines—covering objectives, priorities, and the broad lines of measures envisaged. These guidelines seek to identify projects of common interest. Community financial support is available on a limited basis to projects falling within the guidelines: through feasibility studies, loan guarantees, or interest rate subsidies. The Community may also contribute to the financing through the Cohesion Fund, established under Article 161 EC. The potential economic viability of such projects has to be taken into consideration. Measures may also be taken to ensure the inter-operability of networks—especially on technical standardization. Under Article 155(3) co-operation with third countries is permitted to promote projects of mutual interest and ensure the inter-operability of networks. Finally, Article 156 sets out the procedures for carrying out these measures. Approval from the Member State concerned is required for a specific initiative that may affect its territory.

(a) The TENs Framework

18.71 The Guidelines that provide the framework for TENs projects in energy were revised in 2006 to provide for increased co-ordination, exchange of information, and the possible appointment of a European co-ordinator.[75] They presented 42 projects of European interest and integrated the ten Member States from the 2004

---

[72] European Commission, *White Paper: Towards an EU Energy Policy*, COM (1995) 682 final, 13 December 1995; *Green Paper: For a European Union Energy Policy*, January 1995, 38, 104–5; *White Paper on Growth, Competitiveness and Employment*, COM (1993) 700 final, ch 3.

[73] Council Decision 1229/2003/EC of 26 June 2003 laying down a series of guidelines for trans-European energy networks and repealing Decision 1254/96/EC [2003] OJ L176/11; Commission Decision 761/2000/EC of 16 November 2000, [2000] OJ L305/8.

[74] Originally Title XV of the Treaty of Amsterdam, then incorporated into the EC Treaty.

[75] Commission Press Release IP/06/1054, 'Commissioner Piebalgs welcomes the adoption of new guidelines for the Trans-European Energy Networks', 24 July 2006.

B. Secondary Legislation

enlargement into the network. They built on an earlier revision which had identified three new sets of priorities: those arising from the creation of a more open and competitive market in energy; those arising from the growing importance of TENs in diversifying the EU gas supplies; and those arising from their role in ensuring the co-ordinated operation of EU electricity grids and those in the Mediterranean and Black Sea basins.[76]

An important goal of the new Guidelines was the identification of a set of priority projects among the projects of common interest. These are described as 'a restricted number of thematically defined projects of common interest'.[77] The principal criteria for identifying such projects are that they have a significant impact on the competitive operation of the internal market and/or that they strengthen EU security of energy supply.[78] They must also be compatible with sustainable development. One of the three stated objectives is the reinforcing of the security of energy supplies.[79] This may be achieved by strengthening relations with third countries in the energy sector through the Energy Charter Treaty and other co-operation agreements that the EC has concluded with third countries. 18.72

One of the articles is expressly concerned with the effects of the measure on competition. Article 8 requires an effort to be made, when considering projects, to take into account the effects on competition. Any competitive distortion between operators on the markets must be avoided 'in accordance with the provisions of the Treaty'. 18.73

The Guidelines apply not only to networks in electricity and gas but also to equipment and installations that are essential for the system in question to operate properly, including protection, monitoring, and control systems; to reception, storage, and re-gasification facilities for LNG; and to underground storage facilities connected to high pressure gas pipelines.[80] 18.74

(b) Funding

The funding mechanism is set out in a separate instrument.[81] Several financial instruments may be used where appropriate. These include a TENs budget line. 18.75

---

[76] Guidelines, Recitals 2 and 4.
[77] ibid, Recital 7. The second rank concerns projects of common interest and their specifications, which the Commission is empowered to update from time to time according to a committee procedure set out in Art 10. See also European Commission, *Priority Interconnection Plan*, COM (2006) 846 final, 10 January 2007.
[78] ibid, Art 7(3).
[79] ibid, Art 3(a).
[80] ibid, Art 2.
[81] Regulation (EC) 2236/95 of 18 September 1995 laying down general rules for the granting of Community financial aid in the field of trans-European networks [1995] OJ L228/1, as amended by Regulation (EC) 1655/1999 of 19 July 1999 [1999] OJ L197/1; Regulation (EC) 788/2004 of 21 April 2004 [2004] OJ L138/17; Regulation (EC) 807/2004 of 21 April 2004 [2004] OJ L143/46.

Aid has been given for co-financing feasibility studies but may in justified cases be provided for investment by means of interest rate subsidies, contributions to fees for guarantees for loans, or direct grants. Some restrictions apply:

- aid to feasibility studies is limited to a maximum of 50 per cent of the cost;
- the maximum period of interest rate subsidy must not generally exceed five years;
- the total amount of financial support from the TENs budget line must not exceed 20 per cent of the total investment cost; and
- EU financial support should not cause distortions of competition between undertakings in the sector concerned.

18.76 There is a mechanism for granting EU aid on the basis of indicative multi-annual programmes. It allows an EU contribution to the capital risk element of project finance, with the aim of gaining access to the long-term funding available from insurance companies and pension funds for the financing of public infrastructure projects. Applications for TENs financial support must be submitted to the Commission by the governments of the Member States or with their approval. Normally, in the case of energy TENs, the bodies asking for assistance with studies will be the electricity or gas undertakings in the Member States.

18.77 Eligibility for financing is restricted to projects defined as being of common interest by the Community guidelines on TENs. The selection criteria include the socio-economic effects and environmental consequences of the project. Other funds available include structural funds and EIB loans.

18.78 The broader context in which financing is made should be noted. In the Regulation laying down rules for the grant of aid,[82] Recital 16 states that 'Community aid is chiefly intended to overcome any financial obstacles which may arise during the start-up phase of a project'. In the Guidelines themselves, Recital 3 emphasizes that '[a]s a rule the construction and maintenance of energy infrastructure should be subject to market principles . . . Community financial aid for construction and maintenance should therefore remain highly exceptional. These exceptions should be duly justified.'

(c) What the TENs Initiative is Trying to Achieve

18.79 **Promoting integration in infrastructure** Despite the importance of infrastructure to the single market process, a persistent problem has been the apparent lack of co-ordination at national level which has led to missing links in the networks—albeit less so in energy than in transport. To remedy this, the Commission has attempted to build up a co-ordinating role and to promote integration in infrastructure. At a time of growing liberalization, this improvement in infrastructure

---

[82] ibid.

and removal of bottlenecks could have advantages for the security of energy supply. However, in contrast to the transport sector, energy networks are often privately owned. Their operation displays different shortcomings (such as a need to co-ordinate their current expansion and to provide for links with cohesion countries such as Spain, Portugal, Greece, Ireland, and third countries that may otherwise experience congestion in their transmission networks).

Streamlining authorization procedures   Many bottlenecks in the energy sector have nothing to do with financing problems. The fact that only a very modest amount of funding is available through the TENs programme is not decisive in this respect. Often private sector investments are hampered by planning and environmental constraints resulting in limited possibilities for the construction of new energy networks. This is a particular problem for new electricity lines. In this area, the Commission may play a positive role by proposing a common approach to the issue of authorization procedures in the Member States[83] and by co-financing studies investigating and analyzing the alternatives for the implementation of a given project. However, recent evidence suggests that security of gas supply has been well managed with respect to project implementation. By contrast, a lack of electricity generation capacity and interconnection adequacy have led to serious congestion.[84]

18.80

C. Treaty Provisions

A continuing source of constraint—either actual and potential—on actions to promote competition in energy markets in the EU has been the availability of exemptions under Articles 30 and 86(2). The concepts of 'energy security' or 'security of supply' are absent from the EC Treaty, but Article 30 does permit exemptions under restrictions on the free movement of goods if these are necessary to guarantee, inter alia, 'public security'. Moreover, Article 86(2) EC permits a wider derogation by allowing undertakings entrusted with the operation of services of general economic interest a derogation if the application of Treaty rules 'does not obstruct the performance, in law or in fact, of the particular tasks assigned to them'. In the energy sector, these articles may be invoked by Member States on the grounds of security of energy supply, which may amount to a PSO. As the earlier sections of this chapter show, security of supply looms large in the oil and gas sectors due to dependence on non-EU suppliers for a significant proportion

18.81

---

[83] Commission Recommendation 1999/28/EC of 14 December 1998 concerning the improvement of authorisation procedures for trans-European energy networks [1999] OJ L8/27; Commission Draft Report on the Implementation of the Guidelines for TENs in the Period 1996–2001, 14 December 2001, 9.
[84] European Commission, *Report on the Implementation of the Guidelines for Trans-European Energy Networks in the Period 2002–2004*, COM (2006) 443 final.

of consumption; whilst in the electricity sector security of supply derives its significance largely because of the crucial importance of continuity and regularity of supply to certain classes of consumer. These factors distinguish the energy sector from network industries such as most telecommunications services. They have implications for the way in which the energy industries are organized, even in a liberalizing environment, and they provide an incentive for interventions by Member State governments.

18.82 A different set of restrictions which have important implications for security of supply are those on the freedom of capital which derive from 'golden shares' which some Member States retain in companies that have been largely sold into the private sector. The cases that have arisen in connection with such special rights (which are often justified by reference to some form of 'energy security' concept) are discussed at paras 14.137–14.166.

(1) Import and Export

18.83 With respect to import and export of energy, there are obligations under Articles 28 and 29 EC that are subject to exemptions contained in Article 30. Article 28 prohibits quantitative restrictions on imports between Member States and also measures having equivalent effect. Article 29 prohibits restrictions on exports between Member States and all measures with equivalent effect. The prohibition is addressed to Member States.

18.84 Specific grounds for exemption from the prohibitions of quantitative restrictions and measures which have equivalent effect on the import and export of goods include public policy and public security. It is also provided that the exempted prohibitions must not constitute a means of arbitrary discrimination or a disguised restriction on trade between Member States.

18.85 There have been two important cases involving the energy industry in which the exemption of public security under Article 30 was pleaded by a Member State, with different outcomes. The first was *Campus Oil* (1984),[85] and the second was the Greek Oil Monopolies case (1990).[86] This is an area of some sensitivity in relation to the internal market since it raises the prospect of avoidance of some of the effects of liberalization on the ground that countervailing measures are necessary to protect security of supply.

(a) The Campus Oil Case

18.86 In *Campus Oil*, the Irish Government defended a statutory requirement that Irish importers of petroleum products should purchase a percentage of their requirements

---

[85] Case 72/83 *Campus Oil Ltd v Minister for Industry and Energy* [1984] ECR 2727.
[86] Case C-347/88 *Commission v Hellenic Republic* [1990] ECR I-4747.

C. Treaty Provisions

through a national oil refiner. Its defence was based on grounds of public security. The ECJ upheld this defence. The facts were as follows.

The Irish Refining Company (IRC) was the owner of the only refinery in Ireland and was purchased by the Irish National Petroleum Corporation (INPC), owned by the Irish State. The Government sought to acquire the refinery to guarantee the provision of supplies of petroleum products in Ireland, and to do so by keeping refining capacity operational in Ireland, after the owners, four international oil companies, had announced their intention to close the refinery. If it had closed, all suppliers of refined petroleum products would have been obliged to obtain their supplies from abroad. The Irish market depended on them for 80 per cent of its supplies in 1981; without a refinery those supplies would have had to come in future from a single external supplier, the UK. To ensure that the refinery could dispose of its products and preserve its operating capacity, the Fuels (Control of Supplies) Order 1982 was promulgated, requiring any person who imports any of the petroleum products to which it applied to purchase a certain proportion of their requirements from the INPC at a price to be determined by the Minister, who was required to take into account costs incurred by the INPC. Each importer was required to purchase up to a maximum of 35 per cent of its total requirements of petroleum products and 40 per cent of its requirements of each type of petroleum product. **18.87**

Campus Oil was one of several companies trading in petroleum products that were established in Ireland and affected by this Order. They challenged the purchasing requirement under the 1982 Order before the High Court of Ireland, arguing that it constituted a measure having an effect equivalent to a quantitative restriction on imports. The Irish Government maintained that it did not constitute such a restriction but that if it did, it could be justified on the grounds of public policy and public security, for which Article 30 was applicable. The High Court of Ireland referred the two questions on interpretation of EC law to the ECJ for a preliminary ruling. **18.88**

With respect to the first question (applicability of Article 28 to the purchasing requirement of the 1982 Order), the ECJ held that the requirement constituted a measure having equivalent effect to a quantitative restriction on imports, and so fell under the scope of Article 28. The next question was whether an exception from the scope of Articles 28 and 29 was justified under Article 30 or whether such a scheme was capable of being exempt and, if so, under what circumstances. The ECJ took the view that the concept of public security could include the uninterrupted supply of petroleum products, due to their fundamental importance to a country's existence. In a much-quoted passage, the ECJ ruled that: **18.89**

> Petroleum products, because of their exceptional importance as an energy source in the modern economy, are of fundamental importance for a country's existence since not only is its economy but above all its institutions, its essential public services and even the survival of its inhabitants depend upon them. An interruption of supplies of petroleum products, with the resultant dangers for the country's existence, could

Chapter 18: Energy Security

therefore seriously affect the public security that Article 36 [now 30] of the EC Treaty allows States to protect.[87]

18.90 The ECJ noted that recourse to Article 30 EC is not justified if Community rules provide for the necessary measures to ensure protection of the interests set out in that article.[88] National measures that hinder intra-Community trade cannot therefore be justified unless protection of the interests of the Member State concerned is not sufficiently guaranteed by measures taken for that purpose by the Community institutions. However, in this case, the ECJ took the view that a real danger would still occur in the event of a crisis in spite of measures brought out in response to requirements of the IEA and the existence of certain precautionary measures at the Community level,[89] since there was no 'unconditional assurance' that a particular Member State would continue to receive supplies at a level sufficient to meet its minimum needs.[90]

18.91 There was also the issue of whether the obligation to purchase was necessary to ensure that enough of the refinery's production could be marketed to guarantee a minimum supply of petroleum products to the country in the event of a crisis. A crisis may lead either to an interruption or a severe cut in supplies, and the possession of some refining capacity in such situations would allow a Member State to enter into long-term contracts with oil producers that offer better guarantees of supplies in the event of a crisis. The existence of a national refinery also offers a safeguard against the additional risk of interruption of supplies of refined products to which a state with no refinery capacity of its own is exposed. The ECJ set out criteria under which such measures were necessary if the production could not be disposed of at competitive prices on the relevant market.

18.92 As to proportionality, the quantities in question should not exceed the minimum supply requirements without which the public security of the country would be affected. Nor should the minimum supply requirement exceed the level of production necessary to keep the refinery's production capacity available in the event of a crisis and to enable it to continue to refine at all times the crude oil supplies which the state has secured.

18.93 The wider relevance of this judgment is a matter of debate. At the time Ireland was almost totally dependent on imported oil products. As the ECJ noted, these were not substitutable for certain purposes. It is notable that the ECJ emphasized that Article 30 has to be interpreted in such a way that its scope is not extended any further than is necessary to protect the interests it is intended to secure. The measures

---

[87] Case 72/83 *Campus Oil Ltd v Minister for Industry and Energy* [1984] ECR 2727, para 34.
[88] ibid, para 27.
[89] ibid, para 29.
[90] ibid, para 31.

C. Treaty Provisions

taken 'must not create obstacles to imports which are disproportionate to those objectives'.[91] The measures adopted on the basis of Article 30 must not restrict intra-Community trade more than is absolutely necessary.

(b) The Greek Oil Monopolies case

In the second case, *Commission v Hellenic Republic* (Greek Oil Monopolies case),[92] the Government of Greece defended a state monopoly of the import and marketing of refined petroleum products on the grounds of public security because of the geo-political situation of the country. The ECJ held that the state right to import and market up to 25 per cent of domestic petroleum requirements breached the requirement of non-discrimination in Article 31(1) by discriminating against exporters from other Member States.

18.94

The ECJ stated that the exclusive rights guaranteed an outlet for the products of the Greek public sector refineries. They did so at the expense of product exporters established in other Member States. The ECJ also held that the annual procurement programmes and marketing quotas run by the Greek authorities were measures that were capable of hindering intra-Community trade within the meaning of Article 28.

18.95

The defence of public security based on Article 30 was pleaded by the Greek Government but was rejected. The ECJ argued that the Greek Government had failed to produce any evidence that the powers to secure supply were in fact necessary to secure a minimum supply of petroleum products at all times.[93] The public procurement programmes could also not be justified since there were two Greek public sector refineries with a production capacity that exceeded the country's minimum requirements in the event of a crisis. Security of supply could be assured by requiring distribution companies to notify their procurement plans and any amendments to them to the Greek authorities in due time.

18.96

From the two cases above, it can be seen that the *Campus Oil* decision does not allow the conclusion that security of supply will always be considered as an objective falling within the scope of Article 30 if the measure pursuing that objective is not necessary. It is also not possible to apply it directly to import/export, transport, or generation monopolies in the electricity and gas sectors.

18.97

Further, it would be wrong to conclude that the ECJ's decision in *Campus Oil* would be repeated in similar circumstances at the present time.[94] The considerable growth in infrastructure, especially interconnectors between Member States, has

18.98

---

[91] ibid, para 37.
[92] Case C-347/88 *Commission v Hellenic Republic* [1990] ECR I-4747.
[93] ibid, para 60.
[94] See, eg, ibid.

changed, and is still changing, the pattern of energy trade within the EU. The test of 'total or almost total dependence upon imports for petroleum products' as a ground for relying on the public security defence in Article 30 will apply differently in such a context of growing mutual interdependence.

(2) Services of General Economic Interest

18.99 Another EC Treaty provision relevant in the context of exemptions is Article 86(2). With respect to energy, the ECJ has held that security of supply considerations can justify an exemption under Article 86(2). This emerged from the *Almelo* case[95] where a regional distribution company, Ijsselmij, imposed an exclusive purchasing obligation which prohibited local distributors from importing electricity. This clause followed the then model general conditions of supply applicable throughout the Netherlands. The ECJ examined the effect of this clause in relation to Articles 81 and 82 EC. Its conclusion was that the obligation had a restrictive effect on competition, and that it prohibited local distributors from obtaining supplies from other sources. The national market was compartmentalized as a result.

18.100 The security of supply consideration arose in connection with Article 86(2). Ijsselmij had been given the task of ensuring the supply of electricity in its part of the national territory. All customers, whether they were local distributors or end-users, should receive uninterrupted supplies of electricity in sufficient quantities to match demand at any given time. This was a task of general economic interest. The onus of proving that such measures were neither necessary nor proportional and that they had an adverse impact on trade lay with the Commission, although the Member State had to explain in some detail why in the absence of the contested measure the undertaking would not be able to fulfil the tasks entrusted to it.[96]

(a) Grant of Financial Aid

18.101 An issue arose in the *Altmark* case about the grant by Member States of financial aid to undertakings entrusted with services of general economic interest. Essentially, the ECJ set out several conditions which had to be met before compensation for the operation of a service of general economic interest may be granted by Member States without it being classifiable as state aid within the meaning of Article 87(1) EC. The *Altmark* criteria are relevant here since they were applied for the first time to a measure to promote power stations in Ireland that was aimed at ensuring security of electricity supply.[97]

---

[95] Case C-393/92 *Gemeente Almelo v Energiebedrijf Ijsselmij NV* [1994] ECR I-1477. See paras 13.17–13.20.
[96] See also Case C-503/99 *Commission v Belgium* [2002] ECR I-4809, and Case C-463/00 *Commission v Spain* [2003] ECR I-4581, para 82.
[97] 'State aid N 475/2003—Ireland; Public Service Obligation in respect of new electricity generation capacity for security of supply', C(2003) 4488fin, 16 December 2003.

C. Treaty Provisions

(b) The CADA Case

18.102 The Irish Government notified a scheme to ensure the security of electricity supply in Ireland and meet growing electricity demand. In response to a report by the TSO that a capacity deficit would emerge from 2005 onwards, the Commission for Energy Regulation (CER) launched a tender for new capacity. To this effect, it was decided that Capacity and Differences Agreements (CADA) of up to ten years in duration would be granted to generators that were prepared to undertake the construction of this new generation capacity. All electricity generated by CADA could be sold to and bought from the pool market like any other electricity. In that sense, the CADA was a purely financial instrument and not a product delivery contract. However, the dominant utility, ESB, would be responsible for managing the financial instruments and for signing them with the generators and paying the capacity payments as well as receiving any reimbursements. ESB was to be compensated for the difference between the capacity payments and the reimbursements. The funds for this were to be levied from electricity consumers.

18.103 Applying the four *Altmark* criteria to the 'compensation', the Commission concluded that the arrangements notified to it contained no element of state aid. In particular, the Commission found that because of Ireland's island status, the safeguarding of the existence of a 'reserve capacity' which ensures that distributors can supply every consumer with electricity throughout the year constitutes a service of general economic interest. In other words, meeting security of supply by setting up new reserve generation capacity can be considered in itself as a service of general economic interest. However, 'the provision of (or the increase of) normal capacity generation cannot be considered a Service of General Economic Interest'.[98]

(3) Euratom

18.104 The liberalization of EU electricity markets has had an unexpected (if not surprising) effect on security of nuclear fuel supply. Essentially, there has been a significant reduction in inventories in many Member States as part of the efforts to reduce operational costs for utilities.[99] However, in contrast to the situation with oil, there is no mandatory requirement to maintain stocks of nuclear materials. Each utility is free to decide on the appropriate level of stocks and its fuel procurement policy.

18.105 Uranium is almost totally imported into the EU, although a significant part of uranium used comes from historical production such as inventories and from the

---

[98] ibid, para 35; in general, ensuring security of supply 'can be considered as a legitimate objective of general economic interest', but it can be achieved by different means, with very different impacts on competition and trade between Member States (paras 29–30).
[99] Euratom Supply Agency, *Analysis of the Nuclear Fuel Availability at EU Level for a Security of Supply Perspective*, Final Report of the Task Force on Security of Supply, June 2005.

re-enrichment of tails of depleted uranium which result from the enrichment process. The current situation of depleting stocks at the expense of new investment in the fuel supply chain is in contrast to that which prevailed for many decades when a build-up of inventories was typical.

18.106 The Euratom Treaty provides for a monitoring of security of supply by the Euratom Supply Agency (see Chapter 9) under the supervision of the Commission. Under Article 70 of the Euratom Treaty the Commission is empowered to make recommendations to Member States on mineral deposit exploration and development. In the event of a possible supply shortage, Article 72 allows the Agency or the Commission to build up the necessary stocks:

> The Agency may, from material available inside or outside the Community, build up the necessary commercial stocks to facilitate supplies to or normal deliveries by the Community.
>
> The Commission may, where necessary, decide to build up emergency stocks. The method of financing such stocks shall be approved by the Council, acting by a qualified majority on a proposal from the Commission.

While there appears to be no evidence of an imminent shortage, and indeed the method of use of fuel by nuclear power plants provides them with greater autonomy than alternative forms of generation, there is evidence that a combination of liberalizing markets and changing international market conditions are encouraging a review at EU level of the existing emergency mechanisms for supply of nuclear fuel.

D. Conclusions

18.107 The promotion of competition is increasingly having effects on the organization of energy security in the European energy markets. A significant decline in reserve capacity and a growing inter-dependence among Member States are two of the more obvious effects.[100] Another effect is the absence of clarity about who is to take overall responsibility for ensuring security of supply. It is increasingly a task shared de facto by a large number of actors. The provisions of the four Directives

---

[100] Both of these developments have figured largely in debates in the UK on the security of gas supply, as the UK has become more dependent upon the continental European market. The cushion provided by excess capacity built up by state investment in another era ended a long time ago but the debate on market-based alternatives is robust: HM Government, *Energy Review*, Cm 6887 (2006) 77–91; DTI, *Gas Security of Supply: The Effectiveness of Current Gas Security of Supply Arrangements*, October 2006; ILEX Consulting, *Report to the DTI: Strategic Storage and Other Options to Ensure Long-term Gas Security*, April 2006; House of Lords European Union Committee, *Gas: Liberalized Markets and Security of Supply*, HL Paper 105 (2003–04); House of Commons Trade and Industry Committee, *Security of Gas Supply*, HC 632-I (2005–06), and the Responses by Government (HC 833) and Ofgem (HC 992) to this Report; see also Stern, J, 'UK gas security: time to get serious' (2004) 32 Energy Policy 1967–79.

D. Conclusions

on electricity and gas examined in this chapter are essentially an attempt to ensure that all Member States adapt their existing security of supply policies to the new market environment by establishing clear obligations, fixing operational responsibilities, identifying and publishing security criteria, and adapting emergency procedures for all of the participants concerned. The language used, not least in the Recitals, makes it clear that this legal framework is designed to ensure that potential obstacles to the further development of the internal market in these sectors which arise from security issues are removed. Taken together, and in spite of some imperfections, they furnish a new regime for energy security that is explicitly designed to complement the liberalization process rather than act as a brake upon it.

In effecting this change, both market participants and Member State governments are clearly concerned that the new measures may result in the centralizing of additional powers in the Commission. This is reflected in the modest goals of the final versions of the Security of Supply Directives, and the very considerable discretion they leave to Member States with respect to implementation. It is also evident in the lack of teeth given to the single institutional innovation, the Gas Co-ordinating Group, and the Community institutions' refusal to accept the Commission's proposal for a monitoring body, the European Observatory (which subsequently reappeared in the Green Paper 2006). At the same time, this perceived risk of 'centralization' has to be weighed against the risk that diverse national approaches to energy security may become barriers to entry and to cross-border trade, impeding the development of further competition in the electricity and gas markets. It is also clear—not least from the evidence of further short term disruptions in the electricity sector in November 2006 and longer term risks in the gas sector—that some overall co-ordination of EU networks, however minimal, is more necessary in the emerging market-driven system than in the pre-liberalized one, dominated as it was by vertically integrated and often state-owned utilities. In the absence of a clearer mandate, it appears that this role of 'co-ordination for competition' is to be carried out by the Commission, relying heavily on support from the NRAs and the co-operation of the industry. It remains to be seen how reliable this will be as liberalization proceeds. **18.108**

Part V

THE FUTURE OF COMPETITION AND REGULATION IN ENERGY MARKETS

19

CONCLUSIONS

A. Introduction	19.01	E. Other Energy Sources	19.38
B. The Sector-Specific Framework		(1) Oil	19.39
(1) The Regional Setting	19.06	(2) Coal	19.40
(a) Allocation of Authority	19.07	(3) Nuclear Energy	19.41
(b) Sensitivity of Energy	19.10	F. The Market Distorting Effects of Environmental Measures	19.42
(2) The Balancing of Objectives	19.13		
(3) Relationship to the EC Treaty	19.17	G. Dealing with Non-Compliance	19.45
C. The *Support* Role of Competition Law		(1) A Stronger Network of Energy Regulators	19.47
(1) An Interventionist Trend	19.20	(2) Stricter Competition Law Enforcement	19.48
(2) Cautionary Assessments of Instruments	19.23	(3) Regional Focus Not EU-Wide	19.49
(a) Articles 81 and 82	19.24	(4) Improvement of Sector-Specific Legislation	19.50
(b) Merger Control	19.26		
(c) State Aid	19.28	H. A Strategy for Competition in EU Energy Markets	
D. Regulation by Co-operation		(1) The Transition and Beyond	19.51
(1) Who Regulates?	19.30	(2) Saving the Transition	19.53
(2) The Management of Complexity	19.31	(3) Post-Transition	19.57
(3) The Potential for Regulatory Co-operation	19.35		

'The way is certainly both short and steep,
However gradual it looks from here;
Look if you like, but you will have to leap.'

W H Auden, 'Leap Before You Look'

A. Introduction

At the very outset of the EU internal energy market programme, choices were made about its design, and the appropriate instruments to achieve it. Given the political sensitivities about market reform in the electricity and gas sectors, the

19.01

---

* WH Auden, *Leap Before You Look*, in *Collected Shorter Poems* (London: Faber and Faber).

Community institutions and Member States decided to introduce directives under Article 95 in preference to relying upon the existing powers based on EC competition law (see paras 16.14–16.30), and to do so according to a generous timetable that would allow Member States and incumbent utilities to adapt to a 'liberalized' market. Once these choices were made, it became inevitable that the competition authorities would be left to identify and develop a support role in a Community legislative process that was aimed at the introduction of *new, sector-specific* rules aimed at the promotion of competition. Their extensive efforts in this respect were discussed in Part III of this book. However, by 2007 that process appeared to have run its course, and the 'settlement' of roles between competition and sector-specific authorities appeared to be in need of review. Clear and unequivocal evidence of anti-competitive practices combined with a continued segmentation of EU energy markets, and from some quarters instances of national protectionism, combined to suggest that more than a renewed legislative effort is required to bring about genuine competition.

19.01A Sweeping changes have indeed been made over the past decade to Community law as it affects the electricity and gas sectors. A large body of sector-specific legislation has been adopted by the EU with a view to promoting competition in these markets. The principal legal instruments comprise two framework Directives and related regulations. However, they are supplemented by further rule-making on important matters of detail following a complex process of consultation and negotiation with different stakeholders. Among these, the most important are the national regulatory agencies (NRAs) and the industry participants, with the formal initiatives being taken either by the Commission or by the European Regulatory Group for Electricity and Gas (ERGEG), usually following consultation with the Commission. This supplementary rule-making, a kind of 'shadow' legislative process, has resulted in the adoption of important rules in areas such as competition in gas storage, congestion management, network access, and the design and setting of tariffs. Further rules are under discussion.

19.02 This body of pro-market rules is designed to elaborate in a practical way the principles as well as the rules that are set out in the EC Treaty. However, there is also a growing body of decisions on energy from cases arising from the application of the general competition rules that are contained in the Treaty itself. Competition law practice has become increasingly evident and wide-ranging, covering the rules of antitrust, merger control, and state aid control. Moreover, with the evolution of each of these parts of the competition law—the 'modernization' regulation, the new Merger Regulation and an increasingly strict approach to state aid control—it is becoming clear that the electricity and gas sectors are located among the priority areas for enforcement. As this body of law has evolved, so too has the co-operation between the Commission and the national competition authorities (NCAs), becoming significantly closer. For the energy sector, this implies a more vigorous

A. Introduction

enforcement of the competition rules, but also a challenge for co-ordination in enforcement between the NCAs and the specialist regulatory institutions.

In the case of both energy legislation and energy case law the experience of applying the rules is of recent origin. The market opening or liberalization process is one that was deliberately intended to be a gradual one, and enforcement has measured itself against this timetable. However, evidence was already emerging after 2004–05 that suggested that the legal and regulatory framework was in some respects inadequate to bring about the intended introduction of competition, at least on the scale that was envisaged. The benchmarking reports of DG TREN[1] and the results of the Energy Sector Review[2] both provide ample evidence of serious shortcomings in the operation of competition in the markets for electricity and gas. 19.03

Before turning to a detailed, concluding assessment of the legal regime sketched out above, and examined in detail in the previous Parts of this book, it is important to recall that this legal framework has been adopted by Member States acting within the framework of a regional integration entity comprising 27 Member States. The context of nation-states should not be overlooked in any discussion of energy matters in the EU. However, it is certainly true that the drive to introduce competition into these markets for energy, that were subject for many years to various forms of monopoly control, is one that is being carried out in a context quite different from that of a conventional nation-state. The 'project' that the EU is engaged in is in global terms a unique one because of its regional character, as well as its scale. This 'supra-national' factor has a fundamental impact on the approach to the introduction of competition into a highly sensitive economic sector and structures the legal and regulatory framework itself, generating problems and constraining the scope of outcomes. As Chapter 3 has already shown, a vivid illustration of this lies in the design of the regulatory network. All existing experiences to date with energy market liberalization at the national level testify to the decisive role of an independent regulatory authority. At the European level, however, there is no such regulatory body; only a loose network of NRAs with no legal requirement imposed on them to co-operate on cross-border matters and some requirements on TSOs to co-operate in cross-border transactions. The establishment of such a body, better to promote competition in the energy sector, would raise wider matters of principle about Member State powers in relation to Community institutions over an economic sector that is strategic for them, as indeed for any nation-state 19.04

---

[1] Commission of the European Communities, 'Prospects for the internal gas and electricity market', COM (2006) 841 final, and 'Implementation Report', SEC (2006) 1709, an accompanying document to the Communication: <http://ec.europa.eu/energy/energy_policy/doc/10_internal_market_country_reviews_en.pdf>.

[2] Commission of the European Communities, 'Inquiry pursuant to Article 17 of Regulation (EC) No 1/2003 into the European gas and electricity sectors (Final Report)', COM (2006) 851 final: <http://ec.europa.eu/comm/competition/antitrust/others/sector_inquiries/energy/#final>.

(in a way that telecommunications is not, and defence is). At this stage in its development, the EU appears not to be willing to establish a federal-style regulatory agency to address the cross-border issues. As a result, the development of an institutional framework for the regulation of this liberalizing sector appears likely to remain voluntary, a kind of 'regulation by co-operation', in spite of the many shortcomings of such an approach.

19.05 This chapter will provide an assessment of the legal and regulatory framework as it has developed so far, keeping in mind that the internal energy market project is still a work in progress. In particular, it will consider the future role of competition law in the energy markets in the light of the challenges to competition that have been identified. Although the sector-specific framework is treated separately from the competition law aspects, it should be emphasized that the two bodies of rules interact in practice, and that this distinction is made for exposition purposes only.

B. The Sector-Specific Framework

(1) The Regional Setting

19.06 In the context of the EU, the paradigm shift described in Chapter 1 takes a different form than elsewhere, because it has occurred within a regionally integrated organization. The political and legal context for energy market liberalization is quite unlike any context elsewhere, even in a federal constitutional structure such as the USA. Two aspects of this unique setting have important implications for energy market reform.

(a) Allocation of Authority

19.07 There is a complex allocation of authority between the Member States and the EU institutions which results, in this case, in an interplay of regulatory competences over energy.

19.08 It is well known that the debate on innovation in EU governance that culminated in the design of a draft Constitution for the EU has been stilled by the referendum defeats on that document. The appetite for experimenting with new forms of governance to address enlargement or other new challenges facing the EU is absent among the Member States at the present time. In this context, Directives and regulations that have as their aim either liberalization or market integration will be interpreted and applied by Member States and their representatives according to the letter of the law and not by reference to some Community 'spirit'. This context has consequences for energy market reform.

19.09 A paradox has emerged. As Chapters 5 and 6 of this book have emphasized, the sector-specific law is becoming more and more complex, leaving behind the days when the primary measure of liberalization comprised a single Directive for electricity and a counterpart Directive for gas. The measures now comprise a variety of legal

B. The Sector-Specific Framework

instruments such as Directives, regulations, decisions, guidelines, supplemented by non-binding guidance notes and various monitoring reports produced by the Commission on the basis of annual reports submitted to it by 27 NRAs. This is not a sign of bureaucratic zeal so much as an expression *at the European level* of the kind of regulation for competition that is quite normal in a liberalizing market. Indeed, for the sector-specific laws to be effective, and to meet the challenge of liberalizing a region of 27 diverse and currently segmented energy markets, the rules have to become ever more detailed, enforcement has to become ever more vigorous, *and above all it has to become ever more European*. This implies a further transfer of authority to the European institutions, either directly or to surrogate European institutions, such as an association of energy regulators or a similar body.

(b) Sensitivity of Energy

19.10 The energy sector is perhaps the most sensitive economic sector of all in relations between Member States and EU institutions, and one over which the Member States have long sought to retain significant influence.

19.11 Energy is an economic sector which is rightly dear to the hearts and the minds of national policymakers, so the pooling of national sovereignty in energy matters has been done only most reluctantly and in a very limited fashion. For several decades, it is not an exaggeration to say that energy simply did not figure in the EU integration process at all except in terms of a limited co-ordination of nuclear policy and coal restructuring, supplemented by a few measures aimed at improving the security of oil supply. It had de facto an exceptional status. The acceleration of integration that began with the Single European Act of 1986 put an end to the relative insulation of the electricity and gas industries—for good. The energy industries have now joined the mainstream of market-oriented change in Europe. The legal and regulatory framework for government relations with the energy industry is as a result no longer almost exclusively a national one, but to a large extent has become both national and EU in character.

19.12 However, the limits to the changes introduced by the various Directives are clear enough. A number of rights have been explicitly recognized by the Commission as being state rights: eg, the right to decide on the energy mix; and with respect to the development of oil fields, the right to decide on the timing of development and the rate of depletion; and with respect to public service obligations (PSOs), they are enforceable in the jurisdiction that created them, allowing a number to be established over different jurisdictions. Any assessment of the sector-specific legislation must take into account the extent to which it *preserves* as well as limits rights of Member States over energy activities.

(2) The Balancing of Objectives

19.13 The willingness to make concessions with respect to Member State controls over the electricity and gas sectors has only come about because of the prospect of benefits accruing to the individual Member States through the establishment of competitive markets in electricity and gas. For some this required a leap of the imagination, while for others it was another step along a road they were already familiar with. Recently, doubts have surfaced over the priority given to the competition objective. Such doubts have been kindled by a variety of relatively new challenges faced by this liberalization paradigm, principally in the provision of energy security. This has required adaptation of the sector-specific framework to promote new investment in infrastructure and to manage the growing import dependence. As Chapters 5, 6 and 18 show, considerable efforts have been made both to encourage new infrastructure investment through exemption procedures in the Gas Directive and Electricity Regulation and to provide an enhanced legal regime for energy security that is compatible with the overall competition objective by means of two additional Directives that impose specific obligations on Member States to address this subject.

19.14 Prior to the adoption of the Electricity and Gas Directives the Member States had ensured security of supply by the imposition of PSOs, and their right to do so was expressly incorporated into the Directives. This recognition, which enabled Member States to claim, in appropriate circumstances, an exemption under Article 86(2) from (inter alia) the competition rules of the EC Treaty, was an important factor in ensuring the eventual acceptance of the Directives. The object of a secure and continuous supply of energy, especially electricity, is 'an essential public service obligation', and 'probably the most important public service obligation'.[3] The Directives have expressly included provisions to ensure that all the safeguards available to Member States to guarantee security of energy supplies are not undermined by the introduction of competition.

19.15 The adoption of supplementary Directives on security of supply is in line with earlier attempts to incorporate public service considerations in the sector-specific legal framework. The legal provisions for universal service in the Electricity Directive, the consumer protection safeguards in both Electricity and Gas Directives, and the protection of PSOs in both, all contribute to balancing this goal—which is as Article 16 EC states one of the shared values of the Community—with the objective of introducing and promoting competition in the electricity and gas sectors. In practice, the new energy law is based on a balancing of the competition goal with other aims, including those of security and sustainability. With respect to the operation of the market in the energy sector, it implies that some limits on the freedom of market operation are desirable for public policy reasons, a nuance that might be less readily encountered in, say, North American energy markets.

---

[3] Respectively, the quotations are from European Commission, *Green Paper: Towards a strategy for security of energy supplies*, COM (2000) 769 final, 29 November 2000, 55 and the Commission's Communication on Completion of the Internal Market (2001), 21.

B. The Sector-Specific Framework

Indeed, the choice of a sector-specific legal framework with a timetable for gradual implementation was itself an attempt to ensure that the implementation of Treaty rules on competition was conducted on the basis of a specific framework of rules upon which all Member States had agreed, and which incorporated all of the shared values that are in the Treaty. **19.16**

(3) Relationship to the EC Treaty

The programme of secondary legislation introduced from 1997 onwards has transformed the framework of European law as it applied to the energy sector. However, none of this legislation has actually replaced the rules contained in the primary legislation of the EU, either in the EC Treaty or in the jurisprudence of the ECJ. **19.17**

Indeed, throughout this period the Commission has been keen to argue that the internal energy market legislative programme merely defined the application of existing Treaty rules with respect to the energy sector.[4] This could be achieved not only by means of secondary legislation, but also by applying the existing Treaty rules more rigorously on competition matters and, where necessary, by encouraging attempts at clarification from the ECJ on key legal issues. The Commission's strategy has been to pursue both routes whenever possible. From the 1990s onwards, several cases came before the ECJ that were directly or indirectly relevant to the promotion of competition in the electricity and gas industries, especially the former. In addition, a number of cases which could be decided by the Commission on the basis of its powers under the EC Treaty gave it an opportunity to influence the legal and contractual arrangements governing the electricity and gas industries in a way that promoted internal market objectives. However, this *complemented and supported* the ongoing process of developing secondary legislation, rather than replacing it. **19.18**

The long time-frame allowed—over 15 years—for agreement and implementation of this body of EU energy law has been the price required for its adoption by the Member States, many of which have in their history never before countenanced even such modest constraints over their energy industries. **19.19**

---

[4] Ehlermann, CD (former Director-General for Competition, European Commission), 'Establishing the Single Market in Energy' [1991] Oil Gas L Taxation Rev 295–8, 296. This view can be summarized as follows: 'The proposals for Directives presented by the Commission restrict themselves essentially to specifying rights and obligations arising already today from the Treaty in order to ensure the legal safety of all the operators present on the market' (at 13–14); by 'operators' should be understood 'players' (not only transmission network operators). See also remarks by Devlin, B and Levasseur, C, both Commission officials, at a later date: 'parts of both Directives are either directly derived from the competition rules, or are designed to facilitate their application', in Faull, J and Nikpay, A, *The EC Law of Competition* (1st edn, 2000) 735; for an updated review of these developments with particular reference to the UK context, see Cameron, PD, 'The Revival of Nuclear Power; An Analysis of the Legal Implications' (2007) J Environmental Law 1–17.

C. The *Support* Role of Competition Law

(1) An Interventionist Trend

19.20 The principal role of the competition law in energy market reform has been to provide *support* to the development of a sector-specific regime. From the outset the lead role in liberalization has been taken by the latter, and by those who monitored its implementation. The case priorities of the Commission in its application of competition law have been identified and pursued in the light of this supporting role. However, the analyses of the principal cases involving Articles 81 and 82 EC, merger control, and state aids in Chapters 11 to 15 reveal both how wide the scope of that support activity has been and also a trend towards an increasingly strict application of the competition law. In particular, the decision to mount a comprehensive Energy Sector Review in 2005 and initiate action against specific companies as a result of that investigation showed a new determination by the competition authorities to take action against practices that severely limit the operation of competition in the EU energy markets.

19.21 With respect to the evidence of a more interventionist trend, it appears that around 2004 the Commission concluded that a turning point had been reached in the way that it defined its support role for the sector-specific legislation on energy market reform. The adoption of Regulation 1/2003 offered the possibility of an increasingly formal approach to decision-making in antitrust cases rather than the settlement approach so evident in the cases considered in Chapters 12 and 13 (*Marathon* and *GFU*, for example). The Regulation also offered greater opportunities for closer co-operation with the national competition authorities. Moreover, the new Merger Regulation also offered an opportunity to assess the second wave of mergers with a stricter approach than had appeared both possible and appropriate during the first wave of merger activity that followed the adoption of the first electricity and gas Directives. Most importantly of all, however, it was the adoption of two new Directives on electricity and gas in 2004 that registered a new stage in the liberalization programme. With only three years to a complete market opening by 2007, it seemed an appropriate juncture to adopt a more vigorous support role.

19.22 Finally, there is the influence of the consumer, who had been the targeted beneficiary of energy market reform from the outset in the early 1990s. Faced with a high volume of consumer complaints in 2004–05 about energy prices, the Commission has chosen to ratchet up its support for energy market liberalization by the use of competition policy. The next steps will determine whether consumers will benefit from its new, self-proclaimed 'proactive approach' to these markets, and whether competition policy can complement energy policy to achieve a break-through vis-à-vis the remaining barriers in this area.

C. The Support *Role of Competition Law*

(2) Cautionary Assessments of Instruments

In spite of the foregoing, caution should nonetheless be exercised in venturing an assessment of the potential impact of a more intense application of the competition law. There are limits to what may be achieved with competition law instruments. **19.23**

(a) *Articles 81 and 82*

With respect to Articles 81 and 82, each decision is made on a case-by-case basis; fines may be imposed but so far in energy the approach has been to invite the parties to offer concessions in a settlement. If that is replaced by a more formal prohibition approach, the results will remain quite localized. **19.24**

Undoubtedly, some of the interventions of the Commission have made an impact. For example, in upstream markets some principles are now settled. The principle is now established that joint selling of gas by producers is not permitted unless in very exceptional circumstances. Marketing has to be conducted individually by gas producers. The territorial and other restrictions on gas-to-gas supply competition are not in line with EC law, and will be the subject of formal action where they are identified. Even the *Marathon* cases, which could have had stronger outcomes, were an example of what a determined focus on outcomes by the Commission can achieve, and of the added value that the application of the competition law can bring to the ongoing liberalization process. **19.25**

(b) *Merger Control*

The merger control rules discussed in Chapter 14 provide further evidence of the limits of competition law instruments in the liberalization process. If there are no large concentrations being planned or proposed, then the rules do not become operative. Even when they are notified, there are clear limits to the Commission's jurisdiction under the two-thirds rule, as the cases of *E.On/Ruhrgas* and *Gas Natural/Endesa* have illustrated. Moreover, once the market has become concentrated, the merger control instrument can do nothing to make the companies smaller. It can of course prevent large companies from becoming larger if there appear to be valid competition concerns for reaching this conclusion. Even the gas and contract release programmes which represent a real achievement in *E.On/MOL* have limited effects, although they can lead to liquidity improvements and a reduction in market share. **19.26**

It is undeniable that the more recent instances of merger control suggest that much has been learned from the initial wave of mergers in the years up to 2002–03. However, merger control cannot replace regulation since it deals with incidental concentrations. Moreover, the use of merger control in future can have little impact on the existing high degree of market concentration on both electricity and gas sectors combined with poor levels of liquidity which remains a major obstacle. Perhaps the most important obstacle remains rooted not in markets but **19.27** in governments. Some Member States continue to be attracted to the idea of national champions, as the *E.On/Endesa* and *E.On/Ruhrgas* cases illustrate. In other cases, the use of defensive measures by governments is still not excluded, whether golden shares or some alternative measure is used. Competition may be central to merger control but it is not the only public policy objective involved. While many of these are legitimate, the overtly political or protectionist aim of establishing a national champion remains a spectre that haunts this particular field of competition law, as several of the cases in Chapter 14 demonstrate.

(c) State Aid

19.28 The application of state aid control to the energy sector in the context of liberalization has become clearer and more predictable over the past few years, in line with general state aid policy. However, it has undoubtedly occupied a marginal role in the liberalization process so far. The development and implementation of the Methodology for handling stranded costs has contributed to its profile, as well as the practice evident from the many individual decisions taken under its guidance. This instrument has ensured a fair but firm response to the many Member States with compensation schemes for stranded costs in the initial stages of liberalization, and more recently has been applied to challenge the eligibility of power purchase agreements for state aid.

19.29 The role of state aid in a balancing of the competition objective with others has perhaps been more evident in cases that have involved an environmental dimension. The clear anchoring of this objective in the Treaty and the priority given to it in ECJ case law have ensured that the criteria for assessing aid in this area have been given a more formal basis than the Methodology discussed above. The challenges presented by this form of balancing of objectives, between competition and environmental policies, are much more fundamental, however, than those arising from transitional experiences on the road to a liberalized energy market, with as yet unanswered questions emerging with the growing impact of climate change measures particularly the ETS.

D. Regulation by Co-operation

(1) Who Regulates?

19.30 A system of European energy regulation has now begun to emerge. There are several sources for guidance as to how such a system might ultimately develop: the ERGEG and the Council of European Energy Regulators (CEER) are loose associations that could be seen as precursors of a European Energy Regulatory Authority. The minimum powers set out in the respective Directives on electricity and gas provide a legal basis for the mandatory establishment of national

D. Regulation by Co-operation

energy authorities across the EU, and these powers are elaborated in the various regulations and guidelines made under them. However, they are currently weak in areas of co-ordination among regulators, a liability if the EU is to come to grips with the regulatory challenges involved in promoting competition in existing interconnectors and providing certainty to potential investors in new interconnectors. Moreover, the minimum powers the NRAs are required to have under the Directives are probably too few for the tasks they face. The potential for a more demanding role for the ERGEG is evident in its successful preparation of various guidelines for the Commission and its organization of the electricity and gas regional market intitiatives.

(2) The Management of Complexity

A theme in this book has been that as liberalization develops in energy markets the legal and regulatory framework is faced with issues of growing *complexity* that require a highly specialized response. The complexity may arise in issues concerning, for example, congestion management, access to storage of gas, or the inter-TSO compensation mechanism. It is entirely reasonable that issues involving such a detailed grasp of industry operations should be the preserve of the specialist regulators. The current solution to the 'management of complexity' is a combination of discussions in the Forum process and rule-making by 'comitology': the committee procedures for the exercise of powers conferred on the Commission.[5] This mechanism is increasingly used to resolve these and other difficult and complex problems, while allowing the Commission to initiate the necessary measures but also to co-operate with the NRAs in various committees.   19.31

Complexity can also arise from the multiplicity of actors that are involved in the liberalization process. They include the Community institutions, NRAs, NCAs, and other national supervisory bodies, TSOs, market operators, market agents such as producers, suppliers and traders, consumer associations, and the association of EU energy regulators, ERGEG. In this context, co-ordination of and co-operation among the regulators and the regulated is not an option but a necessity. The term 'regulation by co-operation' is therefore not inappropriate as a description of the kind of effort required to develop and enforce the principles, if not necessarily the rules, that apply to the game.[6] As several commentators have noted, the liberalization process has led to an increasingly complex, multi-level form of economic regulation.[7]   19.32

---

[5] See Chalmers, D, et al, *European Union Law* (2006) 159–67.
[6] Vasconcelos, J, 'The Role of Regulation in a Single Energy Market', presentation delivered at the conference on *Launching a Common European Energy Market*, Lisbon, 5–6 June 2000.
[7] Eberlein, B, 'Configurations of Economic Regulation in the European Union: the case of electricity in comparative perspective' in Coen, D and Thatcher, M, (eds), *Current Politics and Economics of Europe* (2000) 407–25; Coen, D and Doyle, C, 'Designing Economic Regulatory Institutions for European Network Industries' in ibid 455–76.

Chapter 19: Conclusions

19.33 In this context there has been a growing demand for EU regulatory solutions. As outlined in Chapters 5 and 6, the number of problems that require a European rather than a national response has grown rapidly, from cross-border tarification and congestion management to interconnector access and access to non-EU gas supplies. There is also a growing awareness among regulators of the advantages of learning from the experiences of regulators in other Member States. Among companies too, there is a growing demand for European solutions to regulatory problems.

19.34 In this context, it is appropriate to consider the solutions available from the Community institutions. The European Commission in particular has not only sought to respond to the demands for regulation but to expand its sphere of action and authority, a phenomenon already seen in telecommunications.[8] Yet there is no evidence to support the idea that Member States would accept the establishment of an EU regulator with the Commission adopting a role analogous to that of the Federal Energy Regulatory Commission in the USA in regulating interstate energy transmission. On the contrary, when raised among the Member States it is clear that the idea that additional powers may be vested in the Commission is not a popular one. This is evident, for example, in the modest goals of the security of supply Directives, proposed by the Commission, and the very considerable discretion they leave to Member States with respect to implementation. It is also evident in the lack of teeth granted to the institutional innovation in gas security, the Gas Co-ordinating Group, and the cautious response to the Commission's proposal for a monitoring body, the so-called European Energy Observatory.

(3) The Potential for Regulatory Co-operation

19.35 What has been accepted by Member States is a significant transfer of powers from Member State governments to NRAs, set up before or as a result of the Directives on electricity and gas. In this area too, there has been a significant increase in complexity of regulation at Member State and Community levels. In every Member State there are sector-specific regulatory authorities as well as NCAs with responsibility for the energy sector. The need for some hierarchy of authority in the face of possible jurisdictional overlap and conflict is clear.[9] If a proper response to the increasingly European aspect of regulatory problems is to be made, some mechanisms for improved co-ordination among the NRAs seems desirable. These are

---

[8] Natalicchi, G, *Wiring Europe: reshaping the European telecommunications regime* (2001) 181–210.
[9] At the Member State level there is already a body of experience in this area. In the UK, for example, the interaction between energy regulation and competition law is subject to concurrent jurisdiction: see Office of Fair Trading/Ofgem, 'Application in the energy sector' (2005); Office of Fair Trading, 'Concurrent Application to Regulated Industries', OFT 409 (1999).

however servants of the Member State governments and responsible to them, not to the Commission. It is true that the CEER, the ERGEG and the Forum concept may be seen as early and potentially dynamic responses to the need for a new form of governance. However, it is also appropriate to point out that at present they act on the European stage as chief co-ordinators rather than as fully-fledged decision-makers.

What is a new and very positive development is the emergence of a multi-level structure of regulatory authorities. The energy sector regulators have to co-ordinate with each other, with their respective governments, and with the Commission, or the EU legal regime for energy will not work. The network of competition authorities that has come into being must, to the extent that it becomes involved in energy matters, co-ordinate with the NRAs and their association, with their respective governments, and with the Commission itself. This complex of regulatory bodies has every incentive to co-operate, comparing notes on solutions to similar problems and discussing common approaches to cross-border issues. The manner of such co-operation and the subjects on which co-operation occurs may still be determined on a pragmatic, case-by-case basis rather than a rule-based system. The alternative is that the new regulatory 'system' will rapidly become a source of regulatory uncertainty. In terms of institutional design, there are few clear divisions of competence among the players, it is complex and untested, and it relies upon voluntary mechanisms to succeed. **19.36**

If optimism about a positive outcome in the EU is justified, that a 'regulatory culture' may indeed develop, and that Member States may let it grow, this is perhaps more soundly based on the parties' awareness that investment in the EU's ageing and increasingly inadequate energy infrastructure will not be forthcoming if the issue of regulatory risk is not squarely addressed. This—and the growing concerns about energy security—should provide a momentum for the co-operation and co-ordination among the various regulatory actors that this model of governance implicitly supports. **19.37**

E. Other Energy Sources

There are significant differences between the provision of legal frameworks for the introduction and operation of competition in electricity and gas markets on the one hand, and on the other hand markets such as those for nuclear energy or coal or oil. The emphasis in this book has been on the former, but Chapters 7, 8, and 9 provided an overview of the relevant features for the markets in the latter category. In the former category, the competition goal is strongly evident and linked to the goal of achieving an internal market. In the latter, the competition objective is usually subordinate to other concerns. This contrast is less marked however when **19.38**

(1) Oil

19.39 The contrast between the expansion of EU oversight and regulatory intervention in the gas sector and the almost laissez-faire approach to the oil sector is pronounced. By and large, these markets are considered open for competition with prices set internationally. The Hydrocarbons Licensing Directive remains a notable exception to this. It is the only instance of a sustained legislative attempt to enforce internal market principles in the exploration and production of oil. The extent to which Member States with commercial petroleum deposits have observed its provisions is considerable, with gains in transparency and potential for new market players as a result. It is also noteworthy that in this area Member States' rights to indigenous resources of petroleum are enthusiastically defended against any attempt to make them the object of a shared competence.[10]

(2) Coal

19.40 The driver for competition in the coal sector has been de facto the state aid controls since a measure of cushioning of the sector from the full blast of market forces has long been considered essential for reasons of social policy. The legal mechanism for achieving this has shifted from being largely the special sector Treaty instrument of the ECSC to the general treaty instrument, namely the EC Treaty. An interesting new source of constraint on the operation of the market mechanism is the security of supply consideration which is explicitly recognized in the Coal Regulation. Nonetheless, the long-term aim of the legal regime for this sector is clearly one of normalization of regulation in line with the EC Treaty rules.

(3) Nuclear Energy

19.41 The key role is played by the *lex specialis*, the Euratom Treaty. There is some debate among scholars and Commission officials about the interrelationship between the Euratom Treaty rules and those of the EC Treaty, but so far there appear to have been no significant tests, although the nuclear sector appears to have benefited from a favourable interpretation of the state aid rules with respect to restructuring. A review of some of the issues that can arise in its application shows the tension between its interventionist or planning side and its market dimension. However, the role it plays with respect to security of supply and de facto the achievement of 'public service' objectives in this sector gives this tension a familiar character in EU energy law and policy.

---

[10] See the Draft Treaty for a Constitution of Europe: <http://europa.eu/constitution/en/lstoc1_en.htm>.

F. The Market Distorting Effects of Environmental Measures

19.42 The development of a low-carbon economy is a challenge that will make significant impacts on the energy sector. While there are early signs of conflicts between the emissions trading legislation and competition law, particularly in the field of state aids, it is mostly in the field of renewable energy promotion that conflicts appear at present.

19.43 It is clear that the EU is still in a transitional phase with respect to the development of renewable energy. The uneven pattern of implementation of the Directive's requirements among the Member States, and very modest progress of some underlines the importance of the monitoring process and the extent to which the EU has to travel to reach a stage in which a Community-wide harmonized regime becomes possible.

19.44 While the market orientation of the Renewable Energy Directive's measures is clear enough,[11] it is equally clear that a principal goal of the legislation has been to limit the impact of competitive forces on this segment of the EU energy market in order to let it grow and take root. Member States have been encouraged to allow a priority access to generators of renewables, to remove administrative obstacles, and to streamline procedures so that investment will flow into this sector. The application of EC law has also been relatively benign, allowing a variety of support schemes to flourish. It may therefore be thought that as renewable energy takes root in many Member States it is appropriate that this approach to enforcement will be reviewed and perhaps replaced with a more constraining application of the Treaty rules on state aid, free movement of goods, and antitrust law in the medium term.

G. Dealing with Non-Compliance

19.45 A key issue that emerges from any study of the sector-specific law on electricity and gas markets at the present time is that of enforcement. The monitoring duties of the Commission and the Sector Inquiry of DG Competition have revealed many areas in which the legal and regulatory framework analyzed in this book is simply failing to work properly.

19.46 In addition to the formal powers that the Commission, the NRAs and the NCAs have, there are specific steps that may be taken to assist in the enforcement of the existing EU legal and regulatory framework. They include the following.

(1) A Stronger Network of Energy Regulators

19.47 The powers which the NRAs currently enjoy are often no more than the minimum set out in the two Directives. The floor should be raised to strengthen those

---

[11] Recital 18.

NRAs that currently have little independence. There should also be greater scope given to them to co-operate with each other on cross-border problems. An illustration of what the regulators can do when they are allowed to co-operate vigorously is provided by the Regional Energy Markets Initiative, which has the potential to achieve a great deal without an additional legislative or regulatory burden on investors. Moreover, a strengthening of regulatory powers is likely to be more acceptable to Member States than any transfer of authority to the Commission.

(2) Stricter Competition Law Enforcement

19.48 This is an option against non-compliance that is already being exercised and which has been discussed in Part III of this book. While the benefits appear to be considerable, the limits to the various competition law mechanisms have been noted earlier in this chapter.

(3) Regional Focus Not EU-Wide

19.49 The focus on the development of regional co-operation in market design in both electricity and gas is one way to gain experience in cross-border co-operation and to establish stepping stones to the more ambitious connections required by a single market. It is one way of putting peer pressure on parties to comply with the requirements of, say, the Electricity Regulation.

(4) Improvement of Sector-Specific Legislation

19.50 The Electricity and Gas Directives require to be strengthened to deal with shortcomings in the areas of unbundling and regulators' powers. Where there is evidence of non-compliance this can be addressed by means of infringement procedures.[12] This possibility has already been provided for in the monitoring and reporting requirements.

H. A Strategy for Competition in EU Energy Markets

(1) The Transition and Beyond

19.51 A striking feature of the internal market programme is the absence of an official vision of the outcome, of what a genuinely competitive EU energy market would look like and how it would be governed. There have been several road maps presented

---

[12] Commission Press Release, 'The Commission takes action against Member States which have still not properly opened up their energy markets', IP/06/1768, 12 December 2006.

H. A Strategy for Competition in EU Energy Markets

by market participants and even by the Commission itself, but there has been no consensus about the end-state that is being sought. It is as if an assumption were being made that the invisible hand of truth will descend into the internal market process and install an orderly form of competition in EU energy markets.

Yet, since the entry into force of the Electricity and Gas Directives, there have been some significant developments which suggest how the direction of this process might unfold. Some of these are negative but others are fairly positive. It is convenient to distinguish two stages in which competition in EU energy markets may proceed in the next few years. The *first* stage mixes some powerful negative elements with a few positive ones and could be described as one of 'saving the transition'. In the face of overwhelming evidence from Commission studies and NRA reports that the current energy law is not working optimally and is being unevenly enforced in the Member States, an extraordinary range of actions are being taken to ensure that the liberalization process continues on course. However, it is far from clear that these will succeed and indeed the outcome will not be known until around 2008–2009. Irrespective of the choice of instruments, the need for action and above all the consequences of failure are clear enough. Assuming that the outcome is a positive one for the internal market process in energy and that competition continues to develop, a *second* stage will begin, which could be called the 'post-transition' phase. This involves the design of the kind of legal, regulatory, and institutional framework that is appropriate to an EU energy market characterized by a significant degree of competition. Features of this phase might include: a high degree of energy inter-dependence among Member States, the development of a substantive common energy policy and the emergence of a European energy grid. It might also include a revival of the draft Constitution with its energy chapter and, beyond the EU, a shift in the current balance away from the energy producing states and back to the consuming countries as was evident in the 1990s. In this second stage, a new structure of governance for the EU energy sector could flourish in which energy regulation and competition law will have distinct roles to play. 19.52

(2) Saving the Transition

The inadequacies of the current state of competition in energy markets need not be recounted here. They are evident from the Commission's Sector Inquiry, but also from the benchmarking reports issued by DG TREN. It is clear that if these are not robustly addressed, there is a risk that the internal energy market programme may stray badly off course. There are several ways of responding to the problems identified, including the introduction of new legislation, the adoption of stricter enforcement procedures, and the launching of antitrust actions under the competition law. There is already evidence that all are being attempted. 19.53

Chapter 19: Conclusions

19.54 Indeed, the sheer volume of measures that are being undertaken or planned by the Commission at the present time[13] shows that it is aware of the scale and the urgency of the task. Further legislation is also envisaged, which will include the launching of measures to tackle the issue of industry structure (ownership unbundling or similar measures). A number of antitrust measures will also figure in this enforcement scenario, raising the question of what role competition law is likely to play after years of providing a support role to the developing body of sector-specific legislation. The probability is that it will remain one of providing support, even if the support is delivered in a more robust form than in the recent past, following the results of the Sector Inquiry. This is in part because of the limited character of competition law instruments. The kind of pro-competitive measures that are required to reshape the industrial structure would be difficult to achieve by the use of antitrust measures (although not impossible if one takes into account the *Marathon* and *GFU* cases), and there is little in past experience to suggest that a majority of Member States would favour such action by the Commission to address structural change in the EU electricity and gas industries. A more vigorous application of competition law can also be expected to lead to legal challenges by incumbents, and recent experience of challenges before the ECJ in other sectors has not been encouraging (see Chapter 14). This suggests that the slow, consensual approach of legislative reform, combined with an assertive enforcement of existing law, that has been tried and tested so far has still some value in securing the consent of Member States to further steps along the road to competition in energy markets.

19.55 A different kind of challenge facing legislators is the need to introduce more of the detailed regulation that is required to make the energy markets work competitively. While the issues of enforcement and further progress are being addressed, the current solution of relying upon the regulators' association, the ERGEG, and the Forum processes, would seem the likely, pragmatic option for dealing with these specialized but highly important matters. In the longer term, however, this would need replacement by a structure that has sounder European foundations.

19.56 Among the sources of optimism that the current phase will result in the acceleration of the introduction of competition are the assertive role of the newly established NRA in Germany, the BundesnetzAgentur, and the steady impact of market reforms there. As the largest and most geographically sensitive energy market in the EU, this is significant. However, another positive development is the recourse of private parties to the courts to enforce their claims against actions that are perceived

---

[13] eg the 26 reasoned opinions sent to 16 Member States on 12 December 2006: Commission Press Release IP/06/1768, 'The Commission takes action against Member States which have still not properly opened up their energy markets'.

to be anti-competitive. Examples of this are the *VEMW* case (see paras 13.59–13.86), the actions in the German courts against the E.On/Ruhrgas merger (see paras 14.41–14.45), and the litigation in the Spanish courts about the Gas Natural/Endesa takeover (see paras 14.46–14.53).

(3) Post-Transition

On the assumption that the transitional process is rescued and achieves its goals, there are several developments that suggest that the medium-term outlook will contain a greater number of positive elements in the mix than at present. In the period after 2008 a European-wide grid can be expected, and inter-dependence in electricity and gas will have increased considerably. The enforcement measures of the previous phase will have had time to work their way through to the markets. The context will be one in which a number of issues can be examined more clearly: **19.57**

Regulation In the light of the experience with ERGEG, it will be clear whether an association of national regulatory bodies can provide the necessary co-ordination of regulation for EU energy markets. At this stage serious consideration may have to be given to the idea of a separate European regulatory agency for the energy sector. Given the increase in energy network inter-dependence, it will be clearer as to just what such a body might be expected to regulate. **19.58**

Competition law The support role of the competition law has always been linked closely to the development of the Electricity and Gas Directives. To the extent that the legislative process becomes more settled (and arguably the legal architecture is already in place), the manner of such support will have to adapt. A more robust approach may be possible and indeed appropriate as the markets reach a 'settled' state of liberalization. **19.59**

Market structure The impact of several years of merger control in the energy sector will be apparent. On the one hand, the structure may prove too concentrated and require further intervention to break up integrated utilities, but on the other hand there will be lessons learned for future approvals in terms of release programmes, divestiture, and such conditions. Above all, the question will be raised very sharply: what kind of structure is compatible with the competition and security goals that the internal energy market is trying to achieve? **19.60**

Relationship between competition and environment The balance between the environmental goals of the Community and the achievement of competition in energy markets can be expected to increase at this stage: the role of state support of renewable energy schemes and the impact of the ETS on the internal market structure will require greater clarity than at present. The start-up period of support will be over and some harmonization of such measures will be required with the pro-competition elements in the new energy law. **19.61**

19.62 This will be the period in which it will be clear enough if the EU version of liberalization of energy markets has indeed delivered on its promises. At the present time it is much too early to provide such an assessment. What is clear however is that the new energy law it has introduced is now firmly established as part of the legal landscape, and the objective of competition in energy markets is one that is being robustly pursued by both this new body of law and an older (but increasingly rejuvenated) body of legal rules, the EC law of competition.

Appendices

1. Electricity Directive (2003/54/EC)   579
2. Electricity Regulation (1228/2003)   603
3. Gas Directive (2003/55/EC)   615
4. Gas Regulation (1775/2005)   641
5. New Annex to Electricity Regulation
   (Commission Decision 2006/770/EC)   653

APPENDIX 1

Directive 2003/54/EC of the European Parliament and of the Council

Of 26 June 2003
concerning common rules for the internal market in electricity and repealing Directive 96/92/EC

THE EUROPEAN PARLIAMENT AND THE COUNCIL OF THE EUROPEAN UNION,

Having regard to the Treaty establishing the European Community, and in particular Article 47(2), Article 55 and Article 95 thereof,

Having regard to the proposals from the Commission,[1]

Having regard to the Opinion of the European Economic and Social Committee,[2]

Having consulted the Committee of the Regions,

Acting in accordance with the procedure laid down in Article 251 of the Treaty,[3]

Whereas:

(1) Directive 96/92/EC of the European Parliament and of the Council of 19 December 1996 concerning common rules for the internal market in electricity[4] has made significant contributions towards the creation of an internal market for electricity.

(2) Experience in implementing this Directive shows the benefits that may result from the internal market in electricity, in terms of efficiency gains, price reductions, higher standards of service and increased competitiveness. However, important shortcomings and possibilities for improving the functioning of the market remain, notably concrete provisions are needed to ensure a level playing field in generation and to reduce the risks of market dominance and predatory behaviour, ensuring non-discriminatory transmission and distribution tariffs, through access to the network on the basis of tariffs published prior to their entry into force, and ensuring that the rights of small and vulnerable customers are protected and that information on energy sources for electricity generation is disclosed, as well as reference to sources, where available, giving information on their environmental impact.

(3) At its meeting in Lisbon on 23 and 24 March 2000, the European Council called for rapid work to be undertaken to complete the internal market in both electricity and gas sectors and to speed up liberalisation in these sectors with a view to achieving a fully operational internal market. The European Parliament, in its Resolution of 6 July 2000 on the Commission's second report on the state of liberalisation of energy markets, requested the Commission to adopt a detailed

---

[1] OJ C 240 E, 28.8.2001, p 60, and OJ C 227 E, 24.9.2002, p 393.

[2] OJ C 36, 8.2.2002, p 10.

[3] Opinion of the European Parliament of 13 March 2002 (OJ C 47 E, 27.2.2003, p 350), Council Common Position of 3 February 2003 (OJ C 50 E, 4.3.2003, p 15) and Decision of the European Parliament of 4 June 2003 (not yet published in the Official Journal).

[4] OJ L 27, 30.1.1997, p 20.

(4) The freedoms which the Treaty guarantees European citizens—free movement of goods, freedom to provide services and freedom of establishment—are only possible in a fully open market, which enables all consumers freely to choose their suppliers and all suppliers freely to deliver to their customers.

(5) The main obstacles in arriving at a fully operational and competitive internal market relate amongst other things to issues of access to the network, tarification issues and different degrees of market opening between Member States.

(6) For competition to function, network access must be non-discriminatory, transparent and fairly priced.

(7) In order to complete the internal electricity market, non-discriminatory access to the network of the transmission or the distribution system operator is of paramount importance. A transmission or distribution system operator may comprise one or more undertakings.

(8) In order to ensure efficient and non-discriminatory network access it is appropriate that the distribution and transmission systems are operated through legally separate entities where vertically integrated undertakings exist. The Commission should assess measures of equivalent effect, developed by Member States to achieve the aim of this requirement, and, where appropriate, submit proposals to amend this Directive. It is also appropriate that the transmission and distribution system operators have effective decision-making rights with respect to assets necessary to maintain, operate and develop networks when the assets in question are owned and operated by vertically integrated undertakings. It is necessary that the independence of the distribution system operators and the transmission system operators be guaranteed especially with regard to generation and supply interests. Independent management structures must therefore be put in place between the distribution system operators and the transmission system operators and any generation/supply companies.

It is important however to distinguish between such legal separation and ownership unbundling. Legal separation does not imply a change of ownership of assets and nothing prevents similar or identical employment conditions applying throughout the whole of the vertically integrated undertakings. However, a non-discriminatory decision-making process should be ensured through organisational measures regarding the independence of the decision-makers responsible.

(9) In the case of small systems the provision of ancillary services may have to be ensured by transmission system operators (TSOs) interconnected with small systems.

(10) While this Directive is not addressing ownership issues it is recalled that in case of an undertaking performing transmission or distribution and which is separated in its legal form from those undertakings performing generation and/or supply activities, the designated system operators may be the same undertaking owning the infrastructure.

(11) To avoid imposing a disproportionate financial and administrative burden on small distribution companies, Member States should be able, where necessary, to exempt such companies from the legal distribution unbundling requirements.

(12) Authorisation procedures should not lead to an administrative burden disproportionate to the size and potential impact of electricity producers.

(13) Further measures should be taken in order to ensure transparent and non discriminatory tariffs for access to networks. Those tariffs should be applicable to all system users on a non discriminatory basis.

(14) In order to facilitate the conclusion of contracts by an electricity undertaking established in a Member State for the supply of electricity to eligible customers in another Member State, Member States and, where appropriate, national regulatory authorities should work towards more homogenous conditions and the same degree of eligibility for the whole of the internal market.

(15) The existence of effective regulation, carried out by one or more national regulatory authorities, is an important factor in guaranteeing non-discriminatory access to the network.

Member States specify the functions, competences and administrative powers of the regulatory authorities. It is important that the regulatory authorities in all Member States share the same minimum set of competences. Those authorities should have the competence to fix or approve the tariffs, or at least, the methodologies underlying the calculation of transmission and distribution tariffs. In order to avoid uncertainty and costly and time consuming disputes, these tariffs should be published prior to their entry into force.

(16) The Commission has indicated its intention to set up a European Regulators Group for Electricity and Gas which would constitute a suitable advisory mechanism for encouraging cooperation and coordination of national regulatory authorities, in order to promote the development of the internal market for electricity and gas, and to contribute to the consistent application, in all Member States, of the provisions set out in this Directive and Directive 2003/55/EC of the European Parliament and of the Council of 26 June 2003 concerning common rules for the internal market in natural gas[5] and in Regulation (EC) No 1228/2003 of the European Parliament and of the Council of 26 June 2003 on conditions for access to the network for cross-border exchanges in electricity.[6]

(17) In order to ensure effective market access for all market players, including new entrants, non discriminatory and cost-reflective balancing mechanisms are necessary. As soon as the electricity market is sufficiently liquid, this should be achieved through the setting up of transparent market-based mechanisms for the supply and purchase of electricity needed in the framework of balancing requirements. In the absence of such a liquid market, national regulatory authorities should play an active role to ensure that balancing tariffs are non discriminatory and cost-reflective. At the same time, appropriate incentives should be provided to balance in-put and off-take of electricity and not to endanger the system.

(18) National regulatory authorities should be able to fix or approve tariffs, or the methodologies underlying the calculation of the tariffs, on the basis of a proposal by the transmission system operator or distribution system operator(s), or on the basis of a proposal agreed between these operator(s) and the users of the network. In carrying out these tasks, national regulatory authorities should ensure that transmission and distribution tariffs are non-discriminatory and cost-reflective, and should take account of the long-term, marginal, avoided network costs from distributed generation and demand-side management measures.

(19) All Community industry and commerce, including small and medium-sized enterprises, and all Community citizens that enjoy the economic benefits of the internal market should also be able to enjoy high levels of consumer protection, and in particular households and, where Member States deem it appropriate, small enterprises should also be able to enjoy public service guarantees, in particular with regard to security of supply and reasonable tariffs, for reasons of fairness, competitiveness and indirectly to create employment.

(20) Electricity customers should be able to choose their supplier freely. Nonetheless a phased approach should be taken to completing the internal market for electricity to enable industry to adjust and ensure that adequate measures and systems are in place to protect the interests of customers and ensure they have a real and effective right to choose their supplier.

(21) Progressive market opening towards full competition should as soon as possible remove differences between Member States. Transparency and certainty in the implementation of this Directive should be ensured.

(22) Nearly all Member States have chosen to ensure competition in the electricity generation market through a transparent authorisation procedure. However, Member States should ensure the possibility to contribute to security of supply through the launching of a tendering procedure or an equivalent procedure in the event that sufficient electricity generation capacity is not

---

[5] See p 57 of this Official Journal.
[6] See p 1 of this Official Journal.

Appendix 1

built on the basis of the authorisation procedure. Member States should have the possibility, in the interests of environmental protection and the promotion of infant new technologies, of tendering for new capacity on the basis of published criteria. New capacity includes inter alia renewables and combined heat and power (CHP).

(23) In the interest of security of supply, the supply/demand balance in individual Member States should be monitored, and monitoring should be followed by a report on the situation at Community level, taking account of interconnection capacity between areas. Such monitoring should be carried out sufficiently early to enable appropriate measures to be taken if security of supply is compromised. The construction and maintenance of the necessary network infrastructure, including interconnection capacity, should contribute to ensuring a stable electricity supply. The maintenance and construction of the necessary network infrastructure, including interconnection capacity and decentralised electricity generation, are important elements in ensuring a stable electricity supply.

(24) Member States should ensure that household customers and, where Member States deem it appropriate, small enterprises, enjoy the right to be supplied with electricity of a specified quality at clearly comparable, transparent and reasonable prices. In order to ensure the maintenance of the high standards of public service in the Community, all measures taken by Member States to achieve the objectives of this Directive should be regularly notified to the Commission. The Commission should regularly publish a report analysing measures taken at national level to achieve public service objectives and comparing their effectiveness, with a view to making recommendations as regards measures to be taken at national level to achieve high public service standards. Member States should take the necessary measures to protect vulnerable customers in the context of the internal electricity market. Such measures can differ according to the particular circumstances in the Member States in question and may include specific measures relating to the payment of electricity bills, or more general measures taken in the social security system. When universal service is also provided to small enterprises, measures to ensure that this universal service is provided may differ according to households and small enterprises.

(25) The Commission has indicated its intention to take initiatives especially as regards the scope of the labelling provision and notably on the manner in which the information on the environmental impact in terms of at least emissions of CO_2 and the radioactive waste resulting from electricity production from different energy sources, could be made available in a transparent, easily accessible and comparable manner throughout the European Union and on the manner in which the measures taken in the Member States to control the accuracy of the information provided by suppliers could be streamlined.

(26) The respect of the public service requirements is a fundamental requirement of this Directive, and it is important that common minimum standards, respected by all Member States, are specified in this Directive, which take into account the objectives of common protection, security of supply, environmental protection and equivalent levels of competition in all Member States. It is important that the public service requirements can be interpreted on a national basis, taking into account national circumstances and subject to the respect of Community law.

(27) Member States may appoint a supplier of last resort. This supplier may be the sales division of a vertically integrated undertaking, that also performs the functions of distribution, provided that it meets the unbundling requirements of this Directive.

(28) Measures implemented by Member States to achieve the objectives of social and economic cohesion may include, in particular, the provision of adequate economic incentives, using, where appropriate, all existing national and Community tools. These tools may include liability mechanisms to guarantee the necessary investment.

(29) To the extent to which measures taken by Member States to fulfil public service obligations constitute State aid under Article 87(1) of the Treaty, there is an obligation according to Article 88(3) of the Treaty to notify them to the Commission.

(30) The requirement to notify the Commission of any refusal to grant authorisation to construct new generation capacity has proven to be an unnecessary administrative burden and should therefore be dispensed with.

(31) Since the objective of the proposed action, namely the creation of a fully operational internal electricity market, in which fair competition prevails, cannot be sufficiently achieved by the Member States and can therefore, by reason of the scale and effects of the action, be better achieved at Community level, the Community may adopt measures in accordance with the principle of subsidiarity as set out in Article 5 of the Treaty. In accordance with the principle of proportionality, as set out in that Article, this Directive does not go beyond what is necessary in order to achieve that objective.

(32) In the light of the experience gained with the operation of Council Directive 90/547/EEC of 29 October 1990 on the transit of electricity through transmission grids,[7] measures should be taken to ensure homogeneous and non-discriminatory access regimes for transmission, including cross-border flows of electricity between Member States. To ensure homogeneity in the treatment of access to the electricity networks, also in the case of transit, that Directive should be repealed.

(33) Given the scope of the amendments that are being made to Directive 96/92/EC, it is desirable, for reasons of clarity and rationalisation, that the provisions in question should be recast.

(34) This Directive respects the fundamental rights, and observes the principles, recognised in particular by the Charter of Fundamental Rights of the European Union,

HAVE ADOPTED THIS DIRECTIVE:

Chapter I. Scope and Definitions

Article 1
Scope

This Directive establishes common rules for the generation, transmission, distribution and supply of electricity. It lays down the rules relating to the organisation and functioning of the electricity sector, access to the market, the criteria and procedures applicable to calls for tenders and the granting of authorisations and the operation of systems.

Article 2
Definitions

For the purposes of this Directive:
1. 'generation' means the production of electricity;
2. 'producer' means a natural or legal person generating electricity;
3. 'transmission' means the transport of electricity on the extra high-voltage and high-voltage interconnected system with a view to its delivery to final customers or to distributors, but not including supply;
4. 'transmission system operator' means a natural or legal person responsible for operating, ensuring the maintenance of and, if necessary, developing the transmission system in a given area and, where applicable, its interconnections with other systems, and for ensuring the long term ability of the system to meet reasonable demands for the transmission of electricity;
5. 'distribution' means the transport of electricity on high-voltage, medium voltage and low voltage distribution systems with a view to its delivery to customers, but not including supply;

---

[7] OJ L 313, 13.11.1990, p 30. Directive as last amended by Commission Directive 98/75/EC (OJ L 276, 13.10.1998, p 9).

Appendix 1

6. 'distribution system operator' means a natural or legal person responsible for operating, ensuring the maintenance of and, if necessary, developing the distribution system in a given area and, where applicable, its interconnections with other systems and for ensuring the long term ability of the system to meet reasonable demands for the distribution of electricity;
7. 'customers' means wholesale and final customers of electricity;
8. 'wholesale customers' means any natural or legal persons who purchase electricity for the purpose of resale inside or outside the system where they are established;
9. 'final customers' means customers purchasing electricity for their own use;
10. 'household customers' means customers purchasing electricity for their own household consumption, excluding commercial or professional activities;
11. 'non-household customers' means any natural or legal persons purchasing electricity which is not for their own household use and shall include producers and wholesale customers;
12. 'eligible customers' means customers who are free to purchase electricity from the supplier of their choice within the meaning of Article 21 of this Directive;
13. 'interconnectors' means equipment used to link electricity systems;
14. 'interconnected system' means a number of transmission and distribution systems linked together by means of one or more interconnectors;
15. 'direct line' means either an electricity line linking an isolated production site with an isolated customer or an electricity line linking an electricity producer and an electricity supply undertaking to supply directly their own premises, subsidiaries and eligible customers;
16. 'economic precedence' means the ranking of sources of electricity supply in accordance with economic criteria;
17. 'ancillary services' means all services necessary for the operation of a transmission or distribution system;
18. 'system users' means any natural or legal persons supplying to, or being supplied by, a transmission or distribution system;
19. 'supply' means the sale, including resale, of electricity to customers;
20. 'integrated electricity undertaking' means a vertically or horizontally integrated undertaking;
21. 'vertically integrated undertaking' means an undertaking or a group of undertakings whose mutual relationships are defined in Article 3(3) of Council Regulation (EEC) No 4064/89 of 21 December 1989 on the control of concentrations between undertakings[8] and where the undertaking/group concerned is performing at least one of the functions of transmission or distribution and at least one of the functions of generation or supply of electricity;
22. 'related undertaking' means affiliated undertakings, within the meaning of Article 41 of the Seventh Council Directive 83/349/EEC of 13 June 1983 based on Article 44(2)(g) [(*)] of the Treaty on consolidated accounts,[9] and/or associated undertakings, within the meaning of Article 33(1) thereof, and/or undertakings which belong to the same shareholders;
23. 'horizontally integrated undertaking' means an undertaking performing at least one of the functions of generation for sale, or transmission, or distribution, or supply of electricity, and another non electricity activity;
24. 'tendering procedure' means the procedure through which planned additional requirements and replacement capacity are covered by supplies from new or existing generating capacity;

---

[8] OJ L 395, 30.12.1989, p 1. Regulation as last amended by Regulation (EC) No 1310/97 (OJ L 180, 9.7.1997, p 1).

[(*)] The title of Directive 83/349/EEC has been adjusted to take account of the renumbering of the Articles of the Treaty establishing the European Community in accordance with Article 12 of the Treaty of Amsterdam; the original reference was to Article 54(3)(g).

[9] OJ L 193, 18.7.1983, p 1. Directive as last amended by Directive 2001/65/EC of the European Parliament and of the Council (OJ L 283, 27.10.2001, p 28).

25. 'long-term planning' means the planning of the need for investment in generation and transmission and distribution capacity on a long term basis, with a view to meeting the demand of the system for electricity and securing supplies to customers;
26. 'small isolated system' means any system with consumption of less than 3 000 GWh in the year 1996, where less than 5% of annual consumption is obtained through interconnection with other systems;
27. 'micro isolated system' means any system with consumption less than 500 GWh in the year 1996, where there is no connection with other systems;
28. 'security' means both security of supply and provision of electricity, and technical safety;
29. 'energy efficiency/demand-side management' means a global or integrated approach aimed at influencing the amount and timing of electricity consumption in order to reduce primary energy consumption and peak loads by giving precedence to investments in energy efficiency measures, or other measures, such as interruptible supply contracts, over investments to increase generation capacity, if the former are the most effective and economical option, taking into account the positive environmental impact of reduced energy consumption and the security of supply and distribution cost aspects related to it;
30. 'renewable energy sources' means renewable non-fossil energy sources (wind, solar, geothermal, wave, tidal, hydropower, biomass, landfill gas, sewage treatment plant gas and biogases);
31. 'distributed generation' means generation plants connected to the distribution system.

CHAPTER II. GENERAL RULES FOR THE ORGANISATION OF THE SECTOR

Article 3

Public service obligations and customer protection

1. Member States shall ensure, on the basis of their institutional organisation and with due regard to the principle of subsidiarity, that, without prejudice to paragraph 2, electricity undertakings are operated in accordance with the principles of this Directive with a view to achieving a competitive, secure and environmentally sustainable market in electricity, and shall not discriminate between these undertakings as regards either rights or obligations.
2. Having full regard to the relevant provisions of the Treaty, in particular Article 86 thereof, Member States may impose on undertakings operating in the electricity sector, in the general economic interest, public service obligations which may relate to security, including security of supply, regularity, quality and price of supplies and environmental protection, including energy efficiency and climate protection. Such obligations shall be clearly defined, transparent, non discriminatory, verifiable and shall guarantee equality of access for EU electricity companies to national consumers. In relation to security of supply, energy efficiency/demand-side management and for the fulfilment of environmental goals, as referred to in this paragraph, Member States may introduce the implementation of long term planning, taking into account the possibility of third parties seeking access to the system.
3. Member States shall ensure that all household customers, and, where Member States deem it appropriate, small enterprises, (namely enterprises with fewer than 50 occupied persons and an annual turnover or balance sheet not exceeding EUR 10 million), enjoy universal service, that is the right to be supplied with electricity of a specified quality within their territory at reasonable, easily and clearly comparable and transparent prices. To ensure the provision of universal service, Member States may appoint a supplier of last resort. Member States shall impose on distribution companies an obligation to connect customers to their grid under terms, conditions and tariffs set in accordance with the procedure laid down in Article 23(2). Nothing in this Directive shall prevent Member States from strengthening the market position of the domestic, small and medium-sized consumers by promoting the possibilities of voluntary aggregation of representation for this class of consumers.

The first subparagraph shall be implemented in a transparent and non-discriminatory way and shall not impede the opening of the market provided for in Article 21.

4. When financial compensation, other forms of compensation and exclusive rights which a Member State grants for the fulfilment of the obligations set out in paragraphs 2 and 3 are provided, this shall be done in a non-discriminatory and transparent way.
5. Member States shall take appropriate measures to protect final customers, and shall in particular ensure that there are adequate safeguards to protect vulnerable customers, including measures to help them avoid disconnection. In this context, Member States may take measures to protect final customers in remote areas. They shall ensure high levels of consumer protection, particularly with respect to transparency regarding contractual terms and conditions, general information and dispute settlement mechanisms. Member States shall ensure that the eligible customer is in fact able to switch to a new supplier. As regards at least household customers, these measures shall include those set out in Annex A.
6. Member States shall ensure that electricity suppliers specify in or with the bills and in promotional materials made available to final customers:
    (a) the contribution of each energy source to the overall fuel mix of the supplier over the preceding year;
    (b) at least the reference to existing reference sources, such as web-pages, where information on the environmental impact, in terms of at least emissions of CO_2 and the radioactive waste resulting from the electricity produced by the overall fuel mix of the supplier over the preceding year is publicly available.

    With respect to electricity obtained via an electricity exchange or imported from an undertaking situated outside the Community, aggregate figures provided by the exchange or the undertaking in question over the preceding year may be used.

    Member States shall take the necessary steps to ensure that the information provided by suppliers to their customers pursuant to this Article is reliable.
7. Member States shall implement appropriate measures to achieve the objectives of social and economic cohesion, environmental protection, which may include energy efficiency/demand-side management measures and means to combat climate change, and security of supply. Such measures may include, in particular, the provision of adequate economic incentives, using, where appropriate, all existing national and Community tools, for the maintenance and construction of the necessary network infrastructure, including interconnection capacity.
8. Member States may decide not to apply the provisions of Articles 6, 7, 20 and 22 insofar as their application would obstruct the performance, in law or in fact, of the obligations imposed on electricity undertakings in the general economic interest and insofar as the development of trade would not be affected to such an extent as would be contrary to the interests of the Community. The interests of the Community include, amongst others, competition with regard to eligible-customers in accordance with this Directive and Article 86 of the Treaty.
9. Member States shall, upon implementation of this Directive, inform the Commission of all measures adopted to fulfil universal service and public service obligations, including consumer protection and environmental protection, and their possible effect on national and international competition, whether or not such measures require a derogation from this Directive. They shall inform the Commission subsequently every two years of any changes to such measures, whether or not they require a derogation from this Directive.

Article 4
Monitoring of security of supply

Member States shall ensure the monitoring of security of supply issues. Where Member States consider it appropriate they may delegate this task to the regulatory authorities referred to in Article 23(1). This monitoring shall, in particular, cover the supply/demand balance on the national market, the level of expected future demand and envisaged additional capacity being planned or under construction, and the quality and level of maintenance of the networks, as well as measures to cover peak demand and to deal with shortfalls of one or more suppliers. The competent authorities shall publish every two years, by 31 July at the latest, a report outlining the findings resulting from the monitoring of these issues, as well as any measures taken or envisaged to address them and shall forward this report to the Commission forthwith.

Article 5
Technical rules

Member States shall ensure that technical safety criteria are defined and that technical rules establishing the minimum technical design and operational requirements for the connection to the system of generating installations, distribution systems, directly connected consumers' equipment, interconnector circuits and direct lines are developed and made public. These technical rules shall ensure the interoperability of systems and shall be objective and non discriminatory. They shall be notified to the Commission in accordance with Article 8 of Directive 98/34/EC of the European Parliament and of the Council of 22 June 1998 laying down a procedure for the provision of information in the field of technical standards and regulations and of rules on Information Society Services.[10]

CHAPTER III. GENERATION

Article 6
Authorisation procedure for new capacity

1. For the construction of new generating capacity, Member States shall adopt an authorisation procedure, which shall be conducted in accordance with objective, transparent and non discriminatory criteria.
2. Member States shall lay down the criteria for the grant of authorisations for the construction of generating capacity in their territory. These criteria may relate to:
   (a) the safety and security of the electricity system, installations and associated equipment;
   (b) protection of public health and safety;
   (c) protection of the environment;
   (d) land use and siting;
   (e) use of public ground;
   (f) energy efficiency;
   (g) the nature of the primary sources;
   (h) characteristics particular to the applicant, such as technical, economic and financial capabilities;
   (i) compliance with measures adopted pursuant to Article 3.
3. Member States shall ensure that authorisation procedures for small and/or distributed generation take into account their limited size and potential impact.
4. The authorisation procedures and criteria shall be made public. Applicants shall be informed of the reasons for any refusal to grant an authorisation. The reasons must be objective, non discriminatory, well founded and duly substantiated. Appeal procedures shall be made available to the applicant.

Article 7
Tendering for new capacity

1. Member States shall ensure the possibility, in the interests of security of supply, of providing for new capacity or energy efficiency/demand-side management measures through a tendering

---

[10] OJ L 204, 21.7.1998, p 37. Directive as amended by Directive 98/48/EC (OJ L 217, 5.8.1998, p 18).

procedure or any procedure equivalent in terms of transparency and non-discrimination, on the basis of published criteria. These procedures can, however, only be launched if on the basis of the authorisation procedure the generating capacity being built or the energy efficiency/demand-side management measures being taken are not sufficient to ensure security of supply.
2. Member States may ensure the possibility, in the interests of environmental protection and the promotion of infant new technologies, of tendering for new capacity on the basis of published criteria. This tender may relate to new capacity or energy efficiency/demand-side management measures. A tendering procedure can, however, only be launched if on the basis of the authorisation procedure the generating capacity being built or the measures being taken are not sufficient to achieve these objectives.
3. Details of the tendering procedure for means of generating capacity and energy efficiency/demand-side management measures shall be published in the *Official Journal of the European Union* at least six months prior to the closing date for tenders.

The tender specifications shall be made available to any interested undertaking established in the territory of a Member State so that it has sufficient time in which to submit a tender.

With a view to ensuring transparency and non-discrimination the tender specifications shall contain a detailed description of the contract specifications and of the procedure to be followed by all tenderers and an exhaustive list of criteria governing the selection of tenderers and the award of the contract, including incentives, such as subsidies, which are covered by the tender. These specifications may also relate to the fields referred to in Article 6(2).

4. In invitations to tender for the requisite generating capacity, consideration must also be given to electricity supply offers with long term guarantees from existing generating units, provided that additional requirements can be met in this way.
5. Member States shall designate an authority or a public body or a private body independent from electricity generation, transmission, distribution and supply activities, which may be a regulatory authority referred to in Article 23(1), to be responsible for the organisation, monitoring and control of the tendering procedure referred to in paragraphs 1 to 4. Where a transmission system operator is fully independent from other activities not relating to the transmission system in ownership terms, the transmission system operator may be designated as the body responsible for organising, monitoring and controlling the tendering procedure. This authority or body shall take all necessary steps to ensure confidentiality of the information contained in the tenders.

Chapter IV. Transmission System Operation

Article 8
Designation of Transmission System Operators

Member States shall designate, or shall require undertakings which own transmission systems to designate, for a period of time to be determined by Member States having regard to considerations of efficiency and economic balance, one or more transmission system operators. Member States shall ensure that transmission system operators act in accordance with Articles 9 to 12.

Article 9
Tasks of Transmission System Operators

Each transmission system operator shall be responsible for:

(a) ensuring the long-term ability of the system to meet reasonable demands for the transmission of electricity;
(b) contributing to security of supply through adequate transmission capacity and system reliability;
(c) managing energy flows on the system, taking into account exchanges with other interconnected systems. To that end, the transmission system operator shall be responsible for ensuring a secure, reliable and efficient electricity system and, in that context, for ensuring the availability of all

necessary ancillary services insofar as this availability is independent from any other transmission system with which its system is interconnected;
(d) providing to the operator of any other system with which its system is interconnected sufficient information to ensure the secure and efficient operation, coordinated development and inter-operability of the interconnected system;
(e) ensuring non-discrimination as between system users or classes of system users, particularly in favour of its related undertakings;
(f) providing system users with the information they need for efficient access to the system.

Article 10
Unbundling of Transmission System Operators

1. Where the transmission system operator is part of a vertically integrated undertaking, it shall be independent at least in terms of its legal form, organisation and decision making from other activities not relating to transmission. These rules shall not create an obligation to separate the ownership of assets of the transmission system from the vertically integrated undertaking.
2. In order to ensure the independence of the transmission system operator referred to in paragraph 1, the following minimum criteria shall apply:
   (a) those persons responsible for the management of the transmission system operator may not participate in company structures of the integrated electricity undertaking responsible, directly or indirectly, for the day-to-day operation of the generation, distribution and supply of electricity;
   (b) appropriate measures must be taken to ensure that the professional interests of the persons responsible for the management of the transmission system operator are taken into account in a manner that ensures that they are capable of acting independently;
   (c) the transmission system operator shall have effective decision-making rights, independent from the integrated electricity undertaking, with respect to assets necessary to operate, maintain or develop the network. This should not prevent the existence of appropriate coordination mechanisms to ensure that the economic and management supervision rights of the parent company in respect of return on assets, regulated indirectly in accordance with Article 23(2), in a subsidiary are protected. In particular, this shall enable the parent company to approve the annual financial plan, or any equivalent instrument, of the transmission system operator and to set global limits on the levels of indebtedness of its subsidiary. It shall not permit the parent company to give instructions regarding day-to-day operations, nor with respect to individual decisions concerning the construction or upgrading of transmission lines, that do not exceed the terms of the approved financial plan, or any equivalent instrument;
   (d) the transmission system operator shall establish a compliance programme, which sets out measures taken to ensure that discriminatory conduct is excluded, and ensure that observance of it is adequately monitored. The programme shall set out the specific obligations of employees to meet this objective. An annual report, setting out the measures taken, shall be submitted by the person or body responsible for monitoring the compliance programme to the regulatory authority referred to in Article 23(1) and shall be published.

Article 11
Dispatching and balancing

1. Without prejudice to the supply of electricity on the basis of contractual obligations, including those which derive from the tendering specifications, the transmission system operator shall, where it has this function, be responsible for dispatching the generating installations in its area and for determining the use of interconnectors with other systems.
2. The dispatching of generating installations and the use of interconnectors shall be determined on the basis of criteria which may be approved by the Member State and which must be objective, published and applied in a non discriminatory manner which ensures the proper functioning of the internal market in electricity. They shall take into account the economic precedence of electricity

from available generating installations or interconnector transfers and the technical constraints on the system.
3. A Member State may require the system operator, when dispatching generating installations, to give priority to generating installations using renewable energy sources or waste or producing combined heat and power.
4. A Member State may, for reasons of security of supply, direct that priority be given to the dispatch of generating installations using indigenous primary energy fuel sources, to an extent not exceeding in any calendar year 15% of the overall primary energy necessary to produce the electricity consumed in the Member State concerned.
5. Member States may require transmission system operators to comply with minimum standards for the maintenance and development of the transmission system, including interconnection capacity.
6. Transmission system operators shall procure the energy they use to cover energy losses and reserve capacity in their system according to transparent, non-discriminatory and market-based procedures, whenever they have this function.
7. Rules adopted by transmission system operators for balancing the electricity system shall be objective, transparent and non-discriminatory, including rules for the charging of system users of their networks for energy imbalance. Terms and conditions, including rules and tariffs, for the provision of such services by transmission system operators shall be established pursuant to a methodology compatible with Article 23(2) in a non-discriminatory and cost-reflective way and shall be published.

Article 12
Confidentiality for Transmission System Operators

Without prejudice to Article 18 or any other legal duty to disclose information, the transmission system operator shall preserve the confidentiality of commercially sensitive information obtained in the course of carrying out its business. Information disclosed regarding its own activities, which may be commercially advantageous, shall be made available in a non-discriminatory manner.

CHAPTER V. DISTRIBUTION SYSTEM OPERATION

Article 13
Designation of Distribution System Operators

Member States shall designate or shall require undertakings that own or are responsible for distribution systems to designate, for a period of time to be determined by Member States having regard to considerations of efficiency and economic balance, one or more distribution system operators. Member States shall ensure that distribution system operators act in accordance with Articles 14 to 16.

Article 14
Tasks of Distribution System Operators

1. The distribution system operator shall maintain a secure, reliable and efficient electricity distribution system in its area with due regard for the environment.
2. In any event, it must not discriminate between system users or classes of system users, particularly in favour of its related undertakings.
3. The distribution system operator shall provide system users with the information they need for efficient access to the system.
4. A Member State may require the distribution system operator, when dispatching generating installations, to give priority to generating installations using renewable energy sources or waste or producing combined heat and power.
5. Distribution system operators shall procure the energy they use to cover energy losses and reserve capacity in their system according to transparent, non-discriminatory and market based procedures,

whenever they have this function. The requirement shall be without prejudice to using electricity acquired under contracts concluded before 1 January 2002.
6. Where distribution system operators are responsible for balancing the electricity distribution system, rules adopted by them for that purpose shall be objective, transparent and non discriminatory, including rules for the charging of system users of their networks for energy imbalance. Terms and conditions, including rules and tariffs, for the provision of such services by distribution system operators shall be established in accordance with Article 23(2) in a non discriminatory and cost-reflective way and shall be published.
7. When planning the development of the distribution network, energy efficiency/demand-side management measures and/or distributed generation that might supplant the need to upgrade to replace electricity capacity shall be considered by the distribution system operator.

Article 15
Unbundling of Distribution System Operators

1. Where the distribution system operator is part of a vertically integrated undertaking, it shall be independent at least in terms of its legal form, organisation and decision making from other activities not relating to distribution. These rules shall not create an obligation to separate the ownership of assets of the distribution system operator from the vertically integrated undertaking.
2. In addition to the requirements of paragraph 1, where the distribution system operator is part of a vertically integrated undertaking, it shall be independent in terms of its organisation and decision making from the other activities not related to distribution. In order to achieve this, the following minimum criteria shall apply:
(a) those persons responsible for the management of the distribution system operator may not participate in company structures of the integrated electricity undertaking responsible, directly or indirectly, for the day-to-day operation of the generation, transmission or supply of electricity;
(b) appropriate measures must be taken to ensure that the professional interests of the persons responsible for the management of the distribution system operator are taken into account in a manner that ensures that they are capable of acting independently;
(c) the distribution system operator shall have effective decision-making rights, independent from the integrated electricity undertaking, with respect to assets necessary to operate, maintain or develop the network. This should not prevent the existence of appropriate coordination mechanisms to ensure that the economic and management supervision rights of the parent company in respect of return on assets, regulated indirectly in accordance with Article 23(2), in a subsidiary are protected. In particular, this shall enable the parent company to approve the annual financial plan, or any equivalent instrument, of the distribution system operator and to set global limits on the levels of indebtedness of its subsidiary. It shall not permit the parent company to give instructions regarding day-to-day operations, nor with respect to individual decisions concerning the construction or upgrading of distribution lines, that do not exceed the terms of the approved financial plan, or any equivalent instrument.
(d) the distribution system operator shall establish a compliance programme, which sets out measures taken to ensure that discriminatory conduct is excluded, and ensure that observance of it is adequately monitored. The programme shall set out the specific obligations of employees to meet this objective. An annual report, setting out the measures taken, shall be submitted by the person or body responsible for monitoring the compliance programme to the regulatory authority referred to in Article 23(1) and published.

Member States may decide not to apply paragraphs 1 and 2 to integrated electricity undertakings serving less than 100 000 connected customers, or serving small isolated systems.

Appendix 1

Article 16
Confidentiality for Distribution System Operators

Without prejudice to Article 18 or any other legal duty to disclose information, the distribution system operator must preserve the confidentiality of commercially sensitive information obtained in the course of carrying out its business, and shall prevent information about its own activities which may be commercially advantageous being disclosed in a discriminatory manner.

Article 17
Combined operator

The rules in Articles 10(1) and 15(1) do not prevent the operation of a combined transmission and distribution system operator, which is independent in terms of its legal form, organisation and decision making from other activities not relating to transmission or distribution system operation and which meets the requirements set out in points (a) to (d). These rules shall not create an obligation to separate the ownership of assets of the combined system from the vertically integrated undertaking:

(a) those persons responsible for the management of the combined system operator may not participate in company structures of the integrated electricity undertaking responsible, directly or indirectly, for the day-to-day operation of the generation, or supply of electricity;

(b) appropriate measures must be taken to ensure that the professional interests of the persons responsible for the management of the combined system operator are taken into account in a manner that ensures that they are capable of acting independently;

(c) the combined system operator shall have effective decision-making rights, independent from the integrated electricity undertaking, with respect to assets necessary to operate, maintain and develop the network. This should not prevent the existence of appropriate coordination mechanisms to ensure that the economic and management supervision rights of the parent company in respect of return on assets, regulated indirectly in accordance with Article 23(2), in a subsidiary are protected. In particular, this shall enable the parent company to approve the annual financial plan, or any equivalent instrument, of the combined system operator and to set global limits on the levels of indebtedness of its subsidiary. It shall not permit the parent company to give instructions regarding day-to-day operations, nor with respect to individual decisions concerning the construction or upgrading of transmission and distribution lines, that do not exceed the terms of the approved financial plan, or any equivalent instrument;

(d) the combined system operator shall establish a compliance programme which sets out measures taken to ensure that discriminatory conduct is excluded, and ensure that observance of it is adequately monitored. The programme shall set out the specific obligations of employees to meet this objective. An annual report, setting out the measures taken, shall be submitted by the person or body responsible for monitoring the compliance programme to the regulatory authority referred to in Article 23(1) and published.

CHAPTER VI. UNBUNDLING AND TRANSPARENCY OF ACCOUNTS

Article 18
Right of access to accounts

1. Member States or any competent authority they designate, including the regulatory authorities referred to in Article 23, shall, insofar as necessary to carry out their functions, have right of access to the accounts of electricity undertakings as set out in Article 19.
2. Member States and any designated competent authority, including the regulatory authorities referred to in Article 23, shall preserve the confidentiality of commercially sensitive information. Member States may provide for the disclosure of such information where this is necessary in order for the competent authorities to carry out their functions.

Article 19
Unbundling of accounts

1. Member States shall take the necessary steps to ensure that the accounts of electricity undertakings are kept in accordance with paragraphs 2 to 3.
2. Electricity undertakings, whatever their system of ownership or legal form, shall draw up, submit to audit and publish their annual accounts in accordance with the rules of national law concerning the annual accounts of limited liability companies adopted pursuant to the Fourth Council Directive 78/660/EC of 25 July 1978 based on Article 44(2)(g) [*] of the Treaty on the annual accounts of certain types of companies.[11]

   Undertakings which are not legally obliged to publish their annual accounts shall keep a copy of these at the disposal of the public in their head office.
3. Electricity undertakings shall, in their internal accounting, keep separate accounts for each of their transmission and distribution activities as they would be required to do if the activities in question were carried out by separate undertakings, with a view to avoiding discrimination, cross subsidisation and distortion of competition. They shall also keep accounts, which may be consolidated, for other electricity activities not relating to transmission or distribution. Until 1 July 2007, they shall keep separate accounts for supply activities for eligible customers and supply activities for non-eligible customers. Revenue from ownership of the transmission/distribution system shall be specified in the accounts. Where appropriate, they shall keep consolidated accounts for other, non-electricity activities. The internal accounts shall include a balance sheet and a profit and loss account for each activity.
4. The audit referred to in paragraph 2 shall, in particular, verify that the obligation to avoid discrimination and cross-subsidies referred to in paragraph 3, is respected.

CHAPTER VII. ORGANISATION OF ACCESS TO THE SYSTEM

Article 20
Third party access

1. Member States shall ensure the implementation of a system of third party access to the transmission and distribution systems based on published tariffs, applicable to all eligible customers and applied objectively and without discrimination between system users. Member States shall ensure that these tariffs, or the methodologies underlying their calculation, are approved prior to their entry into force in accordance with Article 23 and that these tariffs, and the methodologies—where only methodologies are approved—are published prior to their entry into force.
2. The operator of a transmission or distribution system may refuse access where it lacks the necessary capacity. Duly substantiated reasons must be given for such refusal, in particular having regard to Article 3. Member States shall ensure, where appropriate and when refusal of access takes place, that the transmission or distribution system operator provides relevant information on measures that would be necessary to reinforce the network. The party requesting such information may be charged a reasonable fee reflecting the cost of providing such information.

---

[*] The title of Directive 78/660/EEC has been adjusted to take account of the renumbering of the Articles of the Treaty establishing the European Community in accordance with Article 12 of the Treaty of Amsterdam; the original reference was to Article 54(3)(g).

[11] OJ L 222, 14.8.1978, p 11. Directive as last amended by Directive 2001/65/EC of the European Parliament and of the Council (OJ L 283, 27.10.2001, p 28).

Article 21
Market opening and reciprocity

1. Member States shall ensure that the eligible customers are:
   (a) until 1 July 2004, the eligible customers as specified in Article 19(1) to (3) of Directive 96/92/EC. Member States shall publish by 31 January each year the criteria for the definition of these eligible customers;
   (b) from 1 July 2004, at the latest, all non-household customers;
   (c) from 1 July 2007, all customers.
2. To avoid imbalance in the opening of electricity markets:
   (a) contracts for the supply of electricity with an eligible customer in the system of another Member State shall not be prohibited if the customer is considered as eligible in both systems involved;
   (b) in cases where transactions as described in point (a) are refused because of the customer being eligible only in one of the two systems, the Commission may oblige, taking into account the situation in the market and the common interest, the refusing party to execute the requested supply at the request of the Member State where the eligible customer is located.

Article 22
Direct lines

1. Member States shall take the measures necessary to enable:
   (a) all electricity producers and electricity supply undertakings established within their territory to supply their own premises, subsidiaries and eligible customers through a direct line;
   (b) any eligible customer within their territory to be supplied through a direct line by a producer and supply undertakings.
2. Member States shall lay down the criteria for the grant of authorisations for the construction of direct lines in their territory. These criteria must be objective and non discriminatory.
3. The possibility of supplying electricity through a direct line as referred to in paragraph 1 shall not affect the possibility of contracting electricity in accordance with Article 20.
4. Member States may make authorisation to construct a direct line subject either to the refusal of system access on the basis, as appropriate, of Article 20 or to the opening of a dispute settlement procedure under Article 23.
5. Member States may refuse to authorise a direct line if the granting of such an authorisation would obstruct the provisions of Article 3. Duly substantiated reasons must be given for such refusal.

Article 23
Regulatory authorities

1. Member States shall designate one or more competent bodies with the function of regulatory authorities. These authorities shall be wholly independent from the interests of the electricity industry. They shall, through the application of this Article, at least be responsible for ensuring non-discrimination, effective competition and the efficient functioning of the market, monitoring in particular:
   (a) the rules on the management and allocation of interconnection capacity, in conjunction with the regulatory authority or authorities of those Member States with which interconnection exists;
   (b) any mechanisms to deal with congested capacity within the national electricity system;
   (c) the time taken by transmission and distribution undertakings to make connections and repairs;
   (d) the publication of appropriate information by transmission and distribution system operators concerning interconnectors, grid usage and capacity allocation to interested parties, taking into account the need to treat non-aggregated information as commercially confidential;

(e) the effective unbundling of accounts, as referred to in Article 19, to ensure that there are no cross subsidies between generation, transmission, distribution and supply activities;
(f) the terms, conditions and tariffs for connecting new producers of electricity to guarantee that these are objective, transparent and non-discriminatory in particular taking full account of the costs and benefits of the various renewable energy sources technologies, distributed generation and combined heat and power;
(g) the extent to which transmission and distribution system operators fulfil their tasks in accordance with Articles 9 and 14;
(h) the level of transparency and competition.

The authorities established pursuant to this Article shall publish an annual report on the outcome of their monitoring activities referred to in points (a) to (h).

2. The regulatory authorities shall be responsible for fixing or approving, prior to their entry into force, at least the methodologies used to calculate or establish the terms and conditions for:
   (a) connection and access to national networks, including transmission and distribution tariffs. These tariffs, or methodologies, shall allow the necessary investments in the networks to be carried out in a manner allowing these investments to ensure the viability of the networks;
   (b) the provision of balancing services.
3. Notwithstanding paragraph 2, Member States may provide that the regulatory authorities shall submit, for formal decision, to the relevant body in the Member State the tariffs or at least the methodologies referred to in that paragraph as well as the modifications in paragraph 4. The relevant body shall, in such a case, have the power to either approve or reject a draft decision submitted by the regulatory authority. These tariffs or the methodologies or modifications thereto shall be published together with the decision on formal adoption. Any formal rejection of a draft decision shall also be published, including its justification.
4. Regulatory authorities shall have the authority to require transmission and distribution system operators, if necessary, to modify the terms and conditions, tariffs, rules, mechanisms and methodologies referred to in paragraphs 1, 2 and 3, to ensure that they are proportionate and applied in a non-discriminatory manner.
5. Any party having a complaint against a transmission or distribution system operator with respect to the issues mentioned in paragraphs 1, 2 and 4 may refer the complaint to the regulatory authority which, acting as dispute settlement authority, shall issue a decision within two months after receipt of the complaint. This period may be extended by two months where additional information is sought by the regulatory authority. This period may be further extended with the agreement of the complainant. Such a decision shall have binding effect unless and until overruled on appeal.

   Where a complaint concerns connection tariffs for major new generation facilities, the two-month period may be extended by the regulatory authority.
6. Any party who is affected and has a right to complain concerning a decision on methodologies taken pursuant to paragraphs 2, 3 or 4 or, where the regulatory authority has a duty to consult, concerning the proposed methodologies, may, at the latest within two months, or a shorter time period as provided by Member States, following publication of the decision or proposal for a decision, submit a complaint for review. Such a complaint shall not have suspensive effect.
7. Member States shall take measures to ensure that regulatory authorities are able to carry out their duties referred to in paragraphs 1 to 5 in an efficient and expeditious manner.
8. Member States shall create appropriate and efficient mechanisms for regulation, control and transparency so as to avoid any abuse of a dominant position, in particular to the detriment of consumers, and any predatory behaviour. These mechanisms shall take account of the provisions of the Treaty, and in particular Article 82 thereof.

   Until 2010, the relevant authorities of the Member States shall provide, by 31 July of each year, in conformity with competition law, the Commission with a report on market dominance, predatory and anti competitive behaviour. This report shall, in addition, review the changing ownership patterns and any practical measures taken at national level to ensure a sufficient variety of market actors or practical measures taken to enhance interconnection and competition. From 2010 onwards, the relevant authorities shall provide such a report every two years.

9. Member States shall ensure that the appropriate measures are taken, including administrative action or criminal proceedings in conformity with their national law, against the natural or legal persons responsible where confidentiality rules imposed by this Directive have not been respected.
10. In the event of cross border disputes, the deciding regulatory authority shall be the regulatory authority which has jurisdiction in respect of the system operator which refuses use of, or access to, the system.
11. Complaints referred to in paragraphs 5 and 6 shall be without prejudice to the exercise of rights of appeal under Community and national law.
12. National regulatory authorities shall contribute to the development of the internal market and of a level playing field by cooperating with each other and with the Commission in a transparent manner.

Chapter VIII. Final Provisions

Article 24
Safeguard measures

In the event of a sudden crisis in the energy market and where the physical safety or security of persons, apparatus or installations or system integrity is threatened, a Member State may temporarily take the necessary safeguard measures.

Such measures must cause the least possible disturbance in the functioning of the internal market and must not be wider in scope than is strictly necessary to remedy the sudden difficulties which have arisen.

The Member State concerned shall without delay notify these measures to the other Member States, and to the Commission, which may decide that the Member State concerned must amend or abolish such measures, insofar as they distort competition and adversely affect trade in a manner which is at variance with the common interest.

Article 25
Monitoring of imports of electricity

Member States shall inform the Commission every three months of imports of electricity, in terms of physical flows, that have taken place during the previous three months from third countries.

Article 26
Derogations

1. Member States which can demonstrate, after the Directive has been brought into force, that there are substantial problems for the operation of their small isolated systems, may apply for derogations from the relevant provisions of Chapters IV, V, VI, VII, as well as Chapter III, in the case of micro isolated systems, as far as refurbishing, upgrading and expansion of existing capacity are concerned, which may be granted to them by the Commission. The latter shall inform the Member States of those applications prior to taking a decision, taking into account respect for confidentiality. This decision shall be published in the *Official Journal of the European Union*. This Article shall also be applicable to Luxembourg.
2. A Member State which, after the Directive has been brought into force, for reasons of a technical nature has substantial problems in opening its market for certain limited groups of the

non-household customers referred to in Article 21(1)(b) may apply for derogation from this provision, which may be granted to it by the Commission for a period not exceeding 18 months after the date referred to in Article 30(1). In any case, such derogation shall end on the date referred to in Article 21(1)(c).

Article 27
Review Procedure

In the event that the report referred to in Article 28(3) reaches the conclusion whereby, given the effective manner in which network access has been carried out in a Member State — which gives rise to fully effective, non-discriminatory and unhindered network access — the Commission concludes that certain obligations imposed by this Directive on undertakings (including those with respect to legal unbundling for distribution system operators) are not proportionate to the objective pursued, the Member State in question may submit a request to the Commission for exemption from the requirement in question.

The request shall be notified, without delay, by the Member State to the Commission, together with all the relevant information necessary to demonstrate that the conclusion reached in the report on effective network access being ensured will be maintained.

Within three months of its receipt of a notification, the Commission shall adopt an opinion with respect to the request by the Member State concerned, and where appropriate, submit proposals to the European Parliament and to the Council to amend the relevant provisions of the Directive. The Commission may propose, in the proposals to amend the Directive, to exempt the Member State concerned from specific requirements, subject to that Member State implementing equally effective measures as appropriate.

Article 28
Reporting

1. The Commission shall monitor and review the application of this Directive and submit an overall progress report to the European Parliament and the Council before the end of the first year following the entry into force of this Directive, and thereafter on an annual basis. The report shall cover at least:
   (a) the experience gained and progress made in creating a complete and fully operational internal market in electricity and the obstacles that remain in this respect, including aspects of market dominance, concentration in the market, predatory or anti-competitive behaviour and the effect of this in terms of market distortion;
   (b) the extent to which the unbundling and tarification requirements contained in this Directive have been successful in ensuring fair and non-discriminatory access to the Community's electricity system and equivalent levels of competition, as well as the economic, environmental and social consequences of the opening of the electricity market for customers;
   (c) an examination of issues relating to system capacity levels and security of supply of electricity in the Community, and in particular the existing and projected balance between demand and supply, taking into account the physical capacity for exchanges between areas;
   (d) special attention will be given to measures taken in Member States to cover peak demand and to deal with shortfalls of one or more suppliers;
   (e) the implementation of the derogation provided under Article 15(2) with a view to a possible revision of the threshold;
   (f) a general assessment of the progress achieved with regard to bilateral relations with third countries which produce and export or transport electricity, including progress in market integration, the social and environmental consequences of the trade in electricity and access to the networks of such third countries;

(g) the need for possible harmonisation requirements that are not linked to the provisions of this Directive;

(h) the manner in which Member States have implemented in practice the requirements regarding energy labelling contained in Article 3(6), and the manner in which any Commission Recommendations on this issue have been taken into account.

Where appropriate, this report may include recommendations especially as regards the scope and modalities of labelling provisions including eg the way in which reference is made to existing reference sources and the content of these sources, and notably on the manner in which the information on the environmental impact in terms of at least emissions of CO_2 and the radioactive waste resulting from the electricity production from different energy sources could be made available in a transparent, easily accessible and comparable manner throughout the European Union and on the manner in which the measures taken by the Member States to control the accuracy of the information provided by suppliers could be streamlined, and measures to counteract negative effects of market dominance and market concentration.

2. Every two years, the report referred to in paragraph 1 shall also cover an analysis of the different measures taken in the Member States to meet public service obligations, together with an examination of the effectiveness of those measures and, in particular, their effects on competition in the electricity market. Where appropriate, this report may include recommendations as to the measures to be taken at national level to achieve high public service standards, or measures intended to prevent market foreclosure.

3. The Commission shall, no later than 1 January 2006, forward to the European Parliament and Council, a detailed report outlining progress in creating the internal electricity market. The report shall, in particular, consider:
   — the existence of non-discriminatory network access;
   — effective regulation;
   — the development of interconnection infrastructure and the security of supply situation in the Community;
   — the extent to which the full benefits of the opening of markets are accruing to small enterprises and households, notably with respect to public service and universal service standards;
   — the extent to which markets are in practice open to effective competition, including aspects of market dominance, market concentration and predatory or anti-competitive behaviour;
   — the extent to which customers are actually switching suppliers and renegotiating tariffs;
   — price developments, including supply prices, in relation to the degree of the opening of markets;
   — the experience gained in the application of the Directive as far as the effective independence of system operators in vertically integrated undertakings is concerned and whether other measures in addition to functional independence and separation of accounts have been developed which have effects equivalent to legal unbundling.

Where appropriate, the Commission shall submit proposals to the European Parliament and the Council, in particular to guarantee high public service standards.

Where appropriate, the Commission shall submit proposals to the European Parliament and the Council, in particular to ensure full and effective independence of distribution system operators before 1 July 2007. When necessary, these proposals shall, in conformity with competition law, also concern measures to address issues of market dominance, market concentration and predatory or anti-competitive behaviour.

Article 29
Repeals

Directive 90/547/EEC shall be repealed with effect from 1 July 2004.

Directive 96/92/EC shall be repealed from 1 July 2004 without prejudice to the obligations of Member States concerning the deadlines for transposition and application of the said Directive.

References made to the repealed Directive shall be construed as being made to this Directive and should be read in accordance with the correlation table in Annex B.

Article 30
Implementation

1. Member States shall bring into force the laws, regulations and administrative provisions necessary to comply with this Directive not later than 1 July 2004. They shall forthwith inform the Commission thereof.
2. Member States may postpone the implementation of Article 15(1) until 1 July 2007. This shall be without prejudice to the requirements contained in Article 15(2).
3. When Member States adopt these measures, they shall contain a reference to this Directive or shall be accompanied by such reference on the occasion of their official publication. The methods of making such reference shall be laid down by Member States.

Article 31
Entry into force

This Directive shall enter into force on the twentieth day following that of its publication in the *Official Journal of the European Union*.

Article 32
Addressees

This Directive is addressed to the Member States.

Done at Brussels, 26 June 2003.

ANNEX A
Measures on consumer protection

Without prejudice to Community rules on consumer protection, in particular Directives 97/7/EC of the European Parliament and of the Council[12] and Council Directive 93/13/EC,[13] the measures referred to in Article 3 are to ensure that customers:

(a) have a right to a contract with their electricity service provider that specifies:
   — the identity and address of the supplier;
   — the services provided, the service quality levels offered, as well as the time for the initial connection;
   — if offered, the types of maintenance service offered;
   — the means by which up-to-date information on all applicable tariffs and maintenance charges may be obtained;
   — the duration of the contract, the conditions for renewal and termination of services and of the contract, the existence of any right of withdrawal;
   — any compensation and the refund arrangements which apply if contracted service quality levels are not met; and
   — the method of initiating procedures for settlement of disputes in accordance with point (f).

---

[12] OJ L 144, 4.6.1997, p 19.
[13] OJ L 95, 21.4.1993, p 29.

Conditions shall be fair and well known in advance. In any case, this information should be provided prior to the conclusion or confirmation of the contract. Where contracts are concluded through intermediaries, the above information shall also be provided prior to the conclusion of the contract;

(b) are given adequate notice of any intention to modify contractual conditions and are informed about their right of withdrawal when the notice is given. Service providers shall notify their subscribers directly of any increase in charges, at an appropriate time no later than one normal billing period after the increase comes into effect. Member States shall ensure that customers are free to withdraw from contracts if they do not accept the new conditions notified to them by their electricity service provider;

(c) receive transparent information on applicable prices and tariffs and on standard terms and conditions, in respect of access to and use of electricity services;

(d) are offered a wide choice of payment methods. Any difference in terms and conditions shall reflect the costs to the supplier of the different payment systems. General terms and conditions shall be fair and transparent. They shall be given in clear and comprehensible language. Customers shall be protected against unfair or misleading selling methods;

(e) shall not be charged for changing supplier;

(f) benefit from transparent, simple and inexpensive procedures for dealing with their complaints. Such procedures shall enable disputes to be settled fairly and promptly with provision, where warranted, for a system of reimbursement and/or compensation. They should follow, wherever possible, the principles set out in Commission Recommendation 98/257/EC;[14]

(g) when having access to universal service under the provisions adopted by Member States pursuant to Article 3(3), are informed about their rights regarding universal service.

ANNEX B
Correlation table

Directive 96/92/EC	This Directive	
Article 1	Article 1	Scope
Article 2	Article 2	Definitions
Article 3 and 10(1)	Article 3	PSOs and Customer protection
—	Article 4	Monitoring of security of supply
Article 7(2)	Article 5	Technical rules
Article 4 and 5	Article 6	Authorisation procedure for new capacity
Article 4 and 6	Article 7	Tendering for new capacity
Article 7(1)	Article 8	Designation of TSOs
Article 7(3)–(5)	Article 9	Tasks of TSOs
Article 7(6)	Article 10	Unbundling of TSOs
Article 8	Article 11	Dispatching and balancing
Article 9	Article 12	Confidentiality for TSOs
Article 10(2) and (3)	Article 13	Designation of DSOs
Article 11	Article 14	Tasks of DSOs
—	Article 15	Unbundling of DSOs
Article 12	Article 16	Confidentiality for DSOs

---

[14] OJ L 115, 17.4.1998, p 31.

Directive 96/92/EC	This Directive	
—	Article 17	Combined operator
Article 13	Article 18	Right of access to accounts
Article 14	Article 19	Unbundling of accounts
Article 15–18	Article 20	Third Party Access
Article 19	Article 21	Market opening and reciprocity
Article 21	Article 22	Direct lines
Article 20(3)–(4) and 22	Article 23	Regulatory authorities
Article 23	Article 24	Safeguard measures
—	Article 25	Monitoring of imports of electricity
Article 24	Article 26	Derogations
—	Article 27	Review procedure
Article 25 and 26	Article 28	Reporting
—	Article 29	Repeals
Article 27	Article 30	Implementation
Article 28	Article 31	Entry into force
Article 29	Article 32	Addressees
	Annex A	Measures on consumer protection

APPENDIX 2

Regulation (EC) No 1228/2003 of the European Parliament and of the Council

of 26 June 2003

on conditions for access to the network for cross-border exchanges in electricity (Text with EEA relevance)

THE EUROPEAN PARLIAMENT AND THE COUNCIL OF THE EUROPEAN UNION,

Having regard to the Treaty establishing the European Community, and in particular Article 95 thereof,

Having regard to the proposal from the Commission,[1]

Having regard to the Opinion of the European Economic and Social Committee,[2]

Having consulted the Committee of the Regions,

Acting in accordance with the procedure laid down in Article 251 of the Treaty,[3]

Whereas:

(1) Directive 96/92/EC of the European Parliament and of the Council of 19 December 1996 concerning common rules for the internal market in electricity[4] constituted an important step towards the completion of the internal market in electricity.

(2) At its meeting in Lisbon on 23 and 24 March 2000, the European Council called for rapid work to be undertaken to complete the internal market in both the electricity and gas sectors and to speed up liberalisation in these sectors with a view to achieving a fully operational internal market in these areas.

(3) The creation of a real internal electricity market should be promoted through an intensification of trade in electricity, which is currently underdeveloped compared with other sectors of the economy.

(4) Fair, cost-reflective, transparent and directly applicable rules, taking account of a comparison between efficient network operators from structurally comparable areas and supplementing the provisions of Directive 96/92/EC, should be introduced with regard to cross-border tarification and the allocation of available interconnection capacities, in order to ensure effective access to transmission systems for the purpose of cross-border transactions.

(5) In its Conclusions, the Energy Council of 30 May 2000 invited the Commission, Member States and national regulatory authorities and administrations to ensure timely implementation

---

[1] OJ C 240 E, 28.8.2001, p. 72, and OJ C 227 E, 24.9.2002, p. 440.
[2] OJ C 36, 8.2.2002, p. 10.
[3] Opinion of the European Parliament of 13 March 2002 (OJ C 47 E, 27.2.2003, p. 379), Council Common position of 3 February 2003 (OJ C 50 E, 4.3.2003, p. 1) and Decision of the European Parliament of 4 June 2003 (not yet published in the Official Journal).
[4] OJ L 27, 30.1.1997, p. 20.

Appendix 2

of congestion management measures and, in liaison with the European Transmission System Operators (ETSO), rapid introduction of a robust tarification system for the longer term which provides the appropriate cost allocation signals to market participants.

(6) The European Parliament, in its Resolution of 6 July 2000 on the Commission's second report on the state of liberalisation of energy markets, called for conditions for using networks in Member States that do not hamper cross-border trade in electricity and called on the Commission to submit specific proposals geared to overcoming all the existing barriers to intra-Community trade.

(7) It is important that third countries that form part of the European electricity system comply with the rules contained in this Regulation and the guidelines adopted under this Regulation in order to increase the effective functioning of the internal market.

(8) This Regulation should lay down basic principles with regard to tarification and capacity allocation, whilst providing for the adoption of guidelines detailing further relevant principles and methodologies, in order to allow rapid adaptation to changed circumstances.

(9) In an open, competitive market, transmission system operators should be compensated for costs incurred as a result of hosting cross-border flows of electricity on their networks by the operators of the transmission systems from which cross-border flows originate and the systems where those flows end.

(10) Payments and receipts resulting from compensation between transmission system operators should be taken into account when setting national network tariffs.

(11) The actual amount payable for cross-border access to the system can vary considerably, depending on the transmission system operators involved and as a result of differences in the structure of the tarification systems applied in Member States. A certain degree of harmonisation is therefore necessary in order to avoid distortions of trade.

(12) A proper system of long term locational signals would be necessary, based on the principle that the level of the network access charges should reflect the balance between generation and consumption of the region concerned, on the basis of a differentiation of the network access charges on producers and/or consumers.

(13) It would not be appropriate to apply distance-related tariffs, or, provided appropriate locational signals are in place, a specific tariff to be paid only by exporters or importers in addition to the general charge for access to the national network.

(14) The precondition for effective competition in the internal market is non-discriminatory and transparent charges for network use including interconnecting lines in the transmission system. The available capacities of these lines should be set at the maximum levels consistent with the safety standards of secure network operation.

(15) It is important to avoid distortion of competition resulting from different safety, operational and planning standards used by transmission system operators in Member States. Moreover, there should be transparency for market participants concerning available transfer capacities and the security, planning and operational standards that affect the available transfer capacities.

(16) There should be rules on the use of revenues flowing from congestion-management procedures, unless the specific nature of the interconnector concerned justifies an exemption from these rules.

(17) It should be possible to deal with congestion problems in various ways as long as the methods used provide correct economic signals to transmission system operators and market participants and are based on market mechanisms.

(18) To ensure the smooth functioning of the internal market, provision should be made for procedures which allow the adoption of decisions and guidelines with regard to amongst other things tarification and capacity allocation by the Commission whilst ensuring the involvement of Member States' regulatory authorities in this process where appropriate through their European association. Regulatory authorities, together with other relevant authorities in the Member States, have an important role to play in contributing to the proper functioning of the internal electricity market.

(19) The Member States and the competent national authorities should be required to provide relevant information to the Commission. Such information should be treated confidentially by the Commission. Where necessary, the Commission should have an opportunity to request relevant information directly from undertakings concerned, provided that the competent national authorities are informed.

(20) National regulatory authorities should ensure compliance with the rules contained in this Regulation and the guidelines adopted on the basis of this Regulation.

(21) Member States should lay down rules on penalties applicable to infringements of the provisions of this Regulation and ensure that they are implemented. Those penalties must be effective, proportionate and dissuasive.

(22) Since the objective of the proposed action, namely the provision of a harmonised framework for cross-border exchanges of electricity, cannot be achieved by the Member States and can therefore, by reason of the scale and effect of the action, be better achieved at Community level, the Community may adopt measures in accordance with the principle of subsidiarity as set out in Article 5 of the Treaty. In accordance with the principle of proportionality, as set out in that Article, this Regulation does not go beyond what is necessary in order to achieve this objective.

(23) The measures necessary for the implementation of this Regulation should be adopted in accordance with Council Decision 1999/468/EC of 28 June 1999 laying down the procedures for the exercise of implementing powers conferred on the Commission,[5]

HAS ADOPTED THIS REGULATION:

Article 1
Subject-matter and scope

This Regulation aims at setting fair rules for cross-border exchanges in electricity, thus enhancing competition within the internal electricity market, taking into account the specificities of national and regional markets. This will involve the establishment of a compensation mechanism for cross border flows of electricity and the setting of harmonised principles on cross-border transmission charges and the allocation of available capacities of interconnections between national transmission systems.

Article 2
Definitions

1. For the purpose of this Regulation, the definitions contained in Article 2 of Directive 2003/54/EC of the European Parliament and of the Council of 26 June 2003 concerning common rules for the internal market in electricity and repealing Directive 96/92/EC[6] shall apply with the exception of the definition of 'interconnector' which shall be replaced by the following:

   'interconnector' means a transmission line which crosses or spans a border between Member States and which connects the national transmission systems of the Member States;.

2. The following definitions shall also apply:
   (a) 'regulatory authorities' means the regulatory authorities referred to in Article 23(1) of Directive 2003/54/EC;
   (b) 'cross-border flow' means a physical flow of electricity on a transmission network of a Member State that results from the impact of the activity of producers and/or consumers outside of that Member State on its transmission network. If transmission networks of two or more Member States form part, entirely or partly, of a single control block, for the purpose

---

[5] OJ L 184, 17.7.1999, p. 23.
[6] See p. 37 of this Official Journal.

of the inter-transmission system operator (TSO) compensation mechanism referred to in Article 3 only, the control block as a whole shall be considered as forming part of the transmission network of one of the Member States concerned, in order to avoid flows within control blocks being considered as cross-border flows and giving rise to compensation payments under Article 3. The regulatory authorities of the Member States concerned may decide which of the Member States concerned shall be the one of which the control block as a whole shall be considered to form part of;
(c) 'congestion' means a situation in which an interconnection linking national transmission networks, cannot accommodate all physical flows resulting from international trade requested by market participants, because of a lack of capacity of the interconnectors and/or the national transmission systems concerned;
(d) 'declared export' of electricity means the dispatch of electricity in one Member State on the basis of an underlying contractual arrangement to the effect that the simultaneous corresponding take-up ('declared import') of electricity will take place in another Member State or a third country;
(e) 'declared transit' of electricity means a circumstance where a 'declared export' of electricity occurs and where the nominated path for the transaction involves a country in which neither the dispatch nor the simultaneous corresponding take-up of the electricity will take place;
(f) 'declared import' of electricity means the take-up of electricity in a Member State or a third country simultaneously with the dispatch of electricity ('declared export') in another Member State;
(g) 'new interconnector' means an interconnector not completed by the date of entry into force of this Regulation.

Article 3
Inter transmission system operator compensation mechanism

1. Transmission system operators shall receive compensation for costs incurred as a result of hosting cross-border flows of electricity on their networks.
2. The compensation referred to in paragraph 1 shall be paid by the operators of national transmission systems from which cross-border flows originate and the systems where those flows end.
3. Compensation payments shall be made on a regular basis with regard to a given period of time in the past. Ex-post adjustments of compensation paid shall be made where necessary to reflect costs actually incurred.

  The first period of time for which compensation payments shall be made shall be determined in the guidelines referred to in Article 8.
4. Acting in accordance with the procedure referred to in Article 13(2), the Commission shall decide on the amounts of compensation payments payable.
5. The magnitude of cross-border flows hosted and the magnitude of cross-border flows designated as originating and/or ending in national transmission systems shall be determined on the basis of the physical flows of electricity actually measured in a given period of time.
6. The costs incurred as a result of hosting cross-border flows shall be established on the basis of the forward looking long-run average incremental costs, taking into account losses, investment in new infrastructure, and an appropriate proportion of the cost of existing infrastructure, as far as infrastructure is used for the transmission of cross-border flows, in particular taking into account the need to guarantee security of supply. When establishing the costs incurred, recognised standard-costing methodologies shall be used. Benefits that a network incurs as a result of hosting cross-border flows shall be taken into account to reduce the compensation received.

Article 4
Charges for access to networks

1. Charges applied by network-operators for access to networks shall be transparent, take into account the need for network security and reflect actual costs incurred insofar as they correspond

to those of an efficient and structurally comparable network operator and applied in a non discriminatory manner. Those charges shall not be distance-related.
2. Producers and consumers ('load') may be charged for access to networks. The proportion of the total amount of the network charges borne by producers shall, subject to the need to provide appropriate and efficient locational signals, be lower than the proportion borne by consumers. Where appropriate, the level of the tariffs applied to producers and/or consumers shall provide locational signals at European level, and take into account the amount of network losses and congestion caused, and investment costs for infrastructure. This shall not prevent Member States from providing locational signals within their territory or from applying mechanisms to ensure that network access charges borne by consumers ('load') are uniform throughout their territory.
3. When setting the charges for network access the following shall be taken into account:
   — payments and receipts resulting from the inter-transmission system operator compensation mechanism;
   — actual payments made and received as well as payments expected for future periods of time, estimated on the basis of past periods.
4. Providing that appropriate and efficient locational signals are in place, in accordance with paragraph 2, charges for access to networks applied to producers and consumers shall be applied regardless of the countries of destination and, origin, respectively, of the electricity, as specified in the underlying commercial arrangement. This shall be without prejudice to charges on declared exports and declared imports resulting from congestion management referred to in Article 6.
5. There shall be no specific network charge on individual transactions for declared transits of electricity.

Article 5
Provision of information on interconnection capacities

1. Transmission system operators shall put in place coordination and information exchange mechanisms to ensure the security of the networks in the context of congestion management.
2. The safety, operational and planning standards used by transmission system operators shall be made public. The information published shall include a general scheme for the calculation of the total transfer capacity and the transmission reliability margin based upon the electrical and physical features of the network. Such schemes shall be subject to the approval of the regulatory authorities.
3. Transmission system operators shall publish estimates of available transfer capacity for each day, indicating any available transfer capacity already reserved. These publications shall be made at specified intervals before the day of transport and shall include, in any case, week-ahead and month-ahead estimates, as well as a quantitative indication of the expected reliability of the available capacity.

Article 6
General principles of congestion management

1. Network congestion problems shall be addressed with non-discriminatory market based solutions which give efficient economic signals to the market participants and transmission system operators involved. Network congestion problems shall preferentially be solved with non transaction based methods, i.e. methods that do not involve a selection between the contracts of individual market participants.
2. Transaction curtailment procedures shall only be used in emergency situations where the transmission system operator must act in an expeditious manner and redispatching or countertrading is not possible. Any such procedure shall be applied in a non-discriminatory manner.

Except in cases of 'force-majeure', market participants who have been allocated capacity shall be compensated for any curtailment.

3. The maximum capacity of the interconnections and/or the transmission networks affecting cross-border flows shall be made available to market participants, complying with safety standards of secure network operation.
4. Market participants shall inform the transmission system operators concerned a reasonable time ahead of the relevant operational period whether they intend to use allocated capacity. Any allocated capacity that will not be used shall be reattributed to the market, in an open, transparent and non-discriminatory manner.
5. Transmission system operators shall, as far as technically possible, net the capacity requirements of any power flows in opposite direction over the congested interconnection line in order to use this line to its maximum capacity. Having full regard to network security, transactions that relieve the congestion shall never be denied.
6. Any revenues resulting from the allocation of interconnection shall be used for one or more of the following purposes:
    (a) guaranteeing the actual availability of the allocated capacity;
    (b) network investments maintaining or increasing interconnection capacities;
    (c) as an income to be taken into account by regulatory authorities when approving the methodology for calculating network tariffs, and/or in assessing whether tariffs should be modified.

Article 7
New interconnectors

1. New direct current interconnectors may, upon request, be exempted from the provisions of Article 6(6) of this Regulation and Articles 20 and 23(2), (3) and (4) of Directive 2003/54/EC under the following conditions:
    (a) the investment must enhance competition in electricity supply;
    (b) the level of risk attached to the investment is such that the investment would not take place unless an exemption is granted;
    (c) the interconnector must be owned by a natural or legal person which is separate at least in terms of its legal form from the system operators in whose systems that interconnector will be built;
    (d) charges are levied on users of that interconnector;
    (e) since the partial market opening referred to in Article 19 of Directive 96/92/EC, no part of the capital or operating costs of the interconnector has been recovered from any component of charges made for the use of transmission or distribution systems linked by the interconnector;
    (f) the exemption is not to the detriment of competition or the effective functioning of the internal electricity market, or the efficient functioning of the regulated system to which the interconnector is linked.
2. Paragraph 1 shall apply also, in exceptional cases, to alternating current interconnectors provided that the costs and risks of the investment in question are particularly high when compared with the costs and risks normally incurred when connecting two neighbouring national transmission systems by an alternating current interconnector.
3. Paragraph 1 shall apply also to significant increases of capacity in existing interconnectors.
4. (a) The regulatory authority may, on a case by case basis, decide on the exemption referred to in paragraphs 1 and 2. However, Member States may provide that the regulatory authorities shall submit, for formal decision, to the relevant body in the Member State its opinion on the request for an exemption. This opinion shall be published together with the decision.
    (b) (i) The exemption may cover all or part of the capacity of the new interconnector, or of the existing interconnector with significantly increased capacity.
        (ii) In deciding to grant an exemption, consideration shall be given, on a case by case basis, to the need to impose conditions regarding the duration of the exemption and non discriminatory access to the interconnector.
        (iii) When deciding on the conditions in (i) and (ii) account shall, in particular, be taken of the additional capacity to be built, the expected time horizon of the project and national circumstances.

(c) When granting an exemption the relevant authority may approve or fix the rules and/or mechanisms on the management and allocation of capacity.

(d) The exemption decision, including any conditions referred to in (b), shall be duly reasoned and published.

(e) Any exemption decision shall be taken after consultation with other Member States or regulatory authorities concerned.

5. The exemption decision shall be notified, without delay, by the competent authority to the Commission, together with all the information relevant to the decision. This information may be submitted to the Commission in aggregate form, enabling the Commission to reach a well-founded decision.

In particular, the information shall contain:

— the detailed reasons on the basis of which the regulatory authority, or Member State, granted the exemption, including the financial information justifying the need for the exemption;
— the analysis undertaken of the effect on competition and the effective functioning of the internal electricity market resulting from the grant of the exemption;
— the reasons for the time period and the share of the total capacity of the interconnector in question for which the exemption is granted;
— the result of the consultation with the Member States or regulatory authorities concerned;

Within two months after receiving a notification, the Commission may request that the regulatory authority or the Member State concerned amend or withdraw the decision to grant an exemption. The two months period may be extended by one additional month where additional information is sought by the Commission.

If the regulatory authority or Member State concerned does not comply with the request within a period of four weeks, a final decision shall be taken in accordance with the procedure referred to in Article 13(3).

The Commission shall preserve the confidentiality of commercially sensitive information.

Article 8
Guidelines

1. Where appropriate, the Commission shall, acting in accordance with the procedure referred to in Article 13(2), adopt and amend guidelines on the issues listed under paragraph 2 and 3 and relating to the inter-transmission system operator compensation mechanism, in accordance with the principles set out in Articles 3 and 4. When adopting these guidelines for the first time the Commission shall ensure that they cover in a single draft measure at least the issues referred to in paragraph 2 (a) and (d), and paragraph 3.

2. The guidelines shall specify:

(a) details of the procedure for determining which transmission system operators are liable to pay compensation for cross-border flows including as regards the split between the operators of national transmission systems from which cross-border flows originate and the systems where those flows end, in accordance with Article 3(2);

(b) details of the payment procedure to be followed, including the determination of the first period of time for which compensation is to be paid, in accordance with the second subparagraph of Article 3(3);

(c) details of methodologies for determining the cross-border flows hosted for which compensation is to be paid under Article 3, in terms of both quantity and type of flows, and the designation of the magnitudes of such flows as originating and/or ending in transmission systems of individual Member States, in accordance with Article 3(5);

(d) details of the methodology for determining the costs and benefits incurred as a result of hosting cross-border flows, in accordance with Article 3(6);

(e) details of the treatment in the context of the inter-TSO compensation mechanism of electricity flows originating or ending in countries outside the European Economic Area;

(f) the participation of national systems which are interconnected through direct current lines, in accordance with Article 3.
3. The guidelines shall also determine appropriate rules leading to a progressive harmonisation of the underlying principles for the setting of charges applied to producers and consumers (load) under national tariff systems, including the reflection of the inter-TSO compensation mechanism in national network charges and the provision of appropriate and efficient locational signals, in accordance with the principles set out in Article 4.

The guidelines shall make provision for appropriate and efficient harmonised locational signals at European level.

Any harmonisation in this respect shall not prevent Member States from applying mechanisms to ensure that network access charges borne by consumers (load) are comparable throughout their territory.

4. Where appropriate, the Commission shall, acting in accordance with the procedure referred to in Article 13(2), amend the guidelines on the management and allocation of available transfer capacity of interconnections between national systems set out in the Annex, in accordance with the principles set out in Articles 5 and 6, in particular so as to include detailed guidelines on all capacity allocation methodologies applied in practice and to ensure that congestion management mechanisms evolve in a manner compatible with the objectives of the internal market. Where appropriate, in the course of such amendments common rules on minimum safety and operational standards for the use and operation of the network, as referred to in Article 5(2) shall be set.

When adopting or amending guidelines, the Commission shall ensure that they provide the minimum degree of harmonisation required to achieve the aims of this Regulation and do not go beyond what is necessary for that purpose.

When adopting or amending guidelines, the Commission shall indicate what actions it has taken with respect to the conformity of rules in third countries, which form part of the European electricity system, with the guidelines in question.

Article 9
Regulatory authorities

The regulatory authorities, when carrying out their responsibilities, shall ensure compliance with this Regulation and the guidelines adopted pursuant to Article 8. Where appropriate to fulfil the aims of this Regulation they shall cooperate with each other and with the Commission.

Article 10
Provision of information and confidentiality

1. Member States and the regulatory authorities shall, on request, provide to the Commission all information necessary for the purposes of Articles 3(4) and 8.

In particular, for the purposes of Article 3(4) and 3(6), regulatory authorities shall provide on a regular basis information on costs actually incurred by national transmission system operators, as well as data and all relevant information relating to the physical flows in transmission system operators' networks and the cost of the network.

The Commission shall fix a reasonable time limit within which the information is to be provided, taking into account the complexity of the information required and the urgency with which the information is needed.

2. If the Member State or the regulatory authority concerned does not provide this information within the given time-limit pursuant to paragraph 1, the Commission may request all information necessary for the purpose of Article 3(4) and 8 directly from the undertakings concerned.

When sending a request for information to an undertaking, the Commission shall at the same time forward a copy of the request to the regulatory authorities of the Member State in whose territory the seat of the undertaking is situated.

3. In its request for information, the Commission shall state the legal basis of the request, the time limit within which the information is to be provided, the purpose of the request, and also the penalties provided for in Article 12(2) for supplying incorrect, incomplete or misleading information. The Commission shall fix a reasonable time limit taking into account the complexity of the information required and the urgency with which the information is needed.
4. The owners of the undertakings or their representatives and, in the case of legal persons, the persons authorised to represent them by law or by their instrument of incorporation, shall supply the information requested. Lawyers duly authorised to act may supply the information on behalf of their clients, in which case the client shall remain fully responsible if the information supplied is incomplete, incorrect or misleading.
5. Where an undertaking does not provide the information requested within the time-limit fixed by the Commission or supplies incomplete information, the Commission may by decision require the information to be provided. The decision shall specify what information is required and fix an appropriate time-limit within which it is to be supplied. It shall indicate the penalties provided for in Article 12(2). It shall also indicate the right to have the decision reviewed by the Court of Justice of the European Communities.

The Commission shall at the same time send a copy of its decision to the regulatory authorities of the Member State within the territory of which the residence of the person or the seat of the undertaking is situated.

6. Information collected pursuant to this Regulation shall be used only for the purposes of Articles 3(4) and 8.

The Commission shall not disclose information acquired pursuant to this Regulation of the kind covered by the obligation of professional secrecy.

Article 11
Right of Member States to provide for more detailed measures

This Regulation shall be without prejudice to the rights of Member States to maintain or introduce measures that contain more detailed provisions than those set out in this Regulation and the guidelines referred to in Article 8.

Article 12
Penalties

1. Without prejudice to paragraph 2, the Member States shall lay down the rules on penalties applicable to infringements of the provisions of this Regulation and shall take all measures necessary to ensure that they are implemented. The penalties provided for must be effective, proportionate and dissuasive. The Member States shall notify those provisions to the Commission by 1 July 2004 at the latest and shall notify it without delay of any subsequent amendment affecting them.
2. The Commission may by decision impose on undertakings fines not exceeding 1 % of the total turnover in the preceding business year where, intentionally or negligently, they supply incorrect, incomplete or misleading information in response to a request made pursuant to Article 10(3) or fail to supply information within the time-limit fixed by a decision adopted pursuant to the first subparagraph of Article 10(5).

In setting the amount of a fine, regard shall be had to the gravity of the failure to comply with the requirements of the first subparagraph.

3. Penalties provided for pursuant to paragraph 1 and decisions taken pursuant to paragraph 2 shall not be of a criminal law nature.

Article 13
Committee

1. The Commission shall be assisted by a Committee.
2. Where reference is made to this paragraph, Articles 5 and 7 of Decision 1999/468/EC shall apply, having regard to the provisions of Article 8 thereof.

    The period laid down in Article 5(6) of Decision 1999/468/EC shall be set at three months.
3. Where reference is made to this paragraph, Articles 3 and 7 of Decision 1999/468/EC shall apply, having regard to the provisions of Article 8 thereof.
4. The Committee shall adopt its own rules of procedures.

Article 14
Commission Report

The Commission shall monitor the implementation of this Regulation. It shall submit to the European Parliament and the Council no more than three years after the entry into force of this Regulation a report on the experience gained in its application. In particular the report shall examine to what extent the Regulation has been successful in ensuring non-discriminatory and cost-reflective network access conditions for cross border exchanges of electricity in order to contribute to customer choice in a well functioning internal market and to long-term security of supply, as well as to what extent effective locational signals are in place. If necessary, the report shall be accompanied by appropriate proposals and/or recommendations.

Article 15
Entry into force

This Regulation shall enter into force on the twentieth day following that of its publication in the *Official Journal of the European Union*.

It shall apply from 1 July 2004.

This Regulation shall be binding in its entirety and directly applicable in all Member States.

Done at Brussels, 26 June 2003.

ANNEX

Guidelines on the management and allocation of available transfer capacity of interconnections between national systems

General

1. Congestion management method(s) implemented by Member States shall deal with short-run congestion in a market-based, economically efficient manner whilst simultaneously providing signals or incentives for efficient network and generation investment in the right locations.
2. The TSOs, or, where appropriate, Member States, shall provide non-discriminatory and transparent standards, which describe which congestion management methods they will apply under which circumstances. These standards, together with the security standards, shall be described in publicly available documents.
3. Different treatment of the different types of cross-border transactions, whether they are physical bilateral contracts or bids into foreign organised markets, shall be kept to a minimum when designing the rules of specific methods for congestion management. The method for allocating scarce transmission capacity must be transparent. Any differences in how transactions are treated must be shown not to distort or hinder the development of competition.
4. Price signals that result from congestion management systems shall be directional.

5. TSOs shall offer to the market transmission capacity that is as 'firm' as possible. A reasonable fraction of the capacity may be offered to the market under the condition of decreased firmness, but at all times the exact conditions for transport over cross border lines shall be made known to market participants.
6. Considering the fact that the European continental network is a highly meshed network and that the use of interconnection lines has an effect on the power flows on at least two sides of a national border, national Regulators shall ensure that no congestion management procedure with significant effects on power flows in other networks, is devised unilaterally.

Position of long-term contracts

1. Priority access rights to an interconnection capacity shall not be assigned to those contracts which breach Articles 81 and 82 of the EC Treaty.
2. Existing long-term contracts shall have no pre-emption rights when they come up for renewal.

Provision of information

1. TSOs shall implement appropriate coordination and information-exchange mechanisms to guarantee security of the network.
2. TSOs shall publish all relevant data concerning the cross-border total transfer capacities. In addition to the winter and summer ATC values, estimates of transfer capacity for each day shall be published by the TSOs at several time intervals before the day of transport. At least accurate week-ahead estimates shall be made available to the market and the TSOs should also endeavour to provide month-ahead information. A description of the firmness of the data shall be included.
3. The TSOs shall publish a general scheme for calculation of the total transfer capacity and the transmission reliability margin based upon the electrical and physical realities of the network. Such a scheme shall be subject to approval by the regulators of the Member States concerned. The safety standards and the operational and planning standards shall form an integral part of the information that TSOs shall publish in publicly available documents.

Principles governing methods for congestion management

1. Network congestion problems shall preferentially be solved with non-transaction based methods, i.e. methods that do not involve a selection between the contracts of individual market participants.
2. Cross-border coordinated redispatching or counter trading may be used jointly by the TSOs concerned. The costs that TSOs incur in counter-trading and redispatching must, however, be at an efficient level.
3. The possible merits of a combination of market splitting, or other market based mechanisms, for solving 'permanent' congestion and counter-trading for solving temporary congestion shall be immediately explored as a more enduring approach to congestion management.

Guidelines for explicit auctions

1. The auction system must be designed in such a way that all available capacity is being offered to the market. This may be done by organising a composite auction in which capacities are auctioned for differing durations and with different characteristics (e.g. with respect to the expected reliability of the available capacity in question).
2. Total interconnection capacity shall be offered in a series of auctions, which, for instance, might be held on a yearly, monthly, weekly, daily or intra-daily basis, according to the needs of the markets involved. Each of these auctions shall allocate a prescribed fraction of the available transfer capacity plus any remaining capacity that was not allocated in previous auctions.
3. The explicit auction procedures shall be prepared in close collaboration between the national regulatory authority and the TSO concerned and designed in such a way as to allow bidders to participate also in the daily sessions of any organised market (i.e. power exchange) in the countries involved.

Appendix 2

4. The power flows in both directions over congested tie lines shall in principle be netted in order to maximise the transport capacity in the direction of the congestion. However, the procedure for netting of flows shall comply with safe operation of the power system.
5. In order to offer as much capacity to the market as possible, the financial risks related to the netting of flows, shall be attributed to those parties causing those risks to materialise.
6. Any auction procedure adopted shall be capable of sending directional price signals to market participants. Transport in a direction against the dominant power flow relieves the congestion thus resulting in additional transport capacity over the congested tie line.
7. In order not to risk creating or aggravating problems related to any dominant position of market participant(s), capping of the amount of capacity that can be bought/possessed/used by any single market participant in an auction shall be seriously considered by the competent regulatory authorities in the design of any auction mechanisms.
8. To promote the creation of liquid electricity markets, capacity bought at an auction shall be freely tradeable until the TSO is notified that the capacity bought will be used.

APPENDIX 3

Directive 2003/55/EC of the European Parliament and of the Council

of 26 June 2003
concerning common rules for the internal market in natural gas and repealing Directive 98/30/EC

THE EUROPEAN PARLIAMENT AND THE COUNCIL OF THE EUROPEAN UNION,

Having regard to the Treaty establishing the European Community, and in particular Article 47(2), Article 55 and Article 95 thereof,

Having regard to the proposals from the Commission, [1]

Having regard to the Opinion of the European Economic and Social Committee,[2]

Having consulted the Committee of the Regions,

Acting in accordance with the procedure laid down in Article 251 of the Treaty, [3]

Whereas:

(1) Directive 98/30/EC of the European Parliament and of the Council of 22 June 1998 concerning common rules for the internal market in natural gas [4] has made significant contributions towards the creation of an internal market for gas.

(2) Experience in implementing this Directive shows the benefits that may result from the internal market in gas, in terms of efficiency gains, price reductions, higher standards of service and increased competitiveness. However, significant shortcomings and possibilities for improving the functioning of the market remain, notably concrete provisions are needed to ensure a level playing field and to reduce the risks of market dominance and predatory behaviour, ensuring non-discriminatory transmission and distribution tariffs, through access to the network on the basis of tariffs published prior to their entry into force, and ensuring that the rights of small and vulnerable customers are protected.

(3) At its meeting in Lisbon on 23 and 24 March 2000, the European Council called for rapid work to be undertaken to complete the internal market in both electricity and gas sectors and to speed up liberalisation in these sectors with a view to achieving a fully operational internal market. The European Parliament, in its Resolution of 6 July 2000 on the Commission's second report on the state of liberalisation of energy markets, requested the Commission to adopt a detailed timetable for the achievement of accurately defined objectives with a view to gradually but completely liberalising the energy market.

---

[1] OJ C 240 E, 28.8.2001, p. 60 and OJ C 227 E, 24.9.2002, p. 393.
[2] OJ C 36, 8.2.2002, p. 10.
[3] Opinion of the European Parliament of 13 March 2002 (OJ C 47 E, 27.2.2003, p. 367), Council Common Position of 3 February 2003 (OJ C 50 E, 4.3.2003, p. 36) and Decision of the European Parliament of 4 June 2003 (not yet published in the Official Journal).
[4] OJ L 204, 21.7.1998, p. 1.

(4) The freedoms which the Treaty guarantees European citizens — free movement of goods, freedom to provide services and freedom of establishment — are only possible in a fully open market, which enables all consumers freely to choose their suppliers and all suppliers freely to deliver to their customers.
(5) In view of the anticipated increase in dependency as regards natural gas consumption, consideration should be given to initiatives and measures to encourage reciprocal arrangements for access to third-country networks and market integration.
(6) The main obstacles in arriving at a fully operational and competitive internal market relate to, amongst other things, issues of access to the network, access to storage, tarification issues, interoperability between systems and different degrees of market opening between Member States.
(7) For competition to function, network access must be non-discriminatory, transparent and fairly priced.
(8) In order to complete the internal gas market, non-discriminatory access to the network of the transmission and distribution system operators is of paramount importance. A transmission or distribution system operator may consist of one or more undertakings.
(9) In case of a gas undertaking performing transmission, distribution, storage or liquefied natural gas (LNG) activities and which is separate in its legal form from those undertakings performing production and/or supply activities, the designated system operators may be the same undertaking owning the infrastructure.
(10) In order to ensure efficient and non-discriminatory network access it is appropriate that the transmission and distribution systems are operated through legally separate entities where vertically integrated undertakings exist. The Commission should assess measures of equivalent effect, developed by Member States to achieve the aim of this requirement, and, where appropriate, submit proposals to amend this Directive.

It is also appropriate that the transmission and distribution system operators have effective decision making rights with respect to assets necessary to maintain and operate and develop networks when the assets in question are owned and operated by vertically integrated undertakings.

It is important however to distinguish between such legal separation and ownership unbundling. Legal separation implies neither a change of ownership of assets and nothing prevents similar or identical employment conditions applying throughout the whole of the vertically integrated undertakings. However, a non-discriminatory decision-making process should be ensured through organisational measures regarding the independence of the decision-makers responsible.
(11) To avoid imposing a disproportionate financial and administrative burden on small distribution companies, Member States should be able, where necessary, to exempt such companies from the legal distribution unbundling requirements.
(12) In order to facilitate the conclusion of contracts by a gas undertaking established in a Member State for the supply of gas to eligible customers in another Member State, Member States and, where appropriate, national regulatory authorities should work towards more homogenous conditions and the same degree of eligibility for the whole of the internal market.
(13) The existence of effective regulation, carried out by one or more national regulatory authorities, is an important factor in guaranteeing non-discriminatory access to the network. Member States specify the functions, competences and administrative powers of the regulatory authorities. It is important that the regulatory authorities in all Member States share the same minimum set of competences. Those authorities should have the competence to fix or approve the tariffs, or at least, the methodologies underlying the calculation of transmission and distribution tariffs and tariffs for access to liquefied natural gas (LNG) facilities. In order to avoid uncertainty and costly and time consuming disputes, these tariffs should be published prior to their entry into force.
(14) The Commission has indicated its intention to set up a European Regulators Group for Electricity and Gas which would constitute a suitable advisory mechanism for encouraging

cooperation and coordination of national regulatory authorities, in order to promote the development of the internal market for electricity and gas, and to contribute to the consistent application, in all Member States, of the provisions set out in this Directive and Directive 2003/54/EC of the European Parliament and of the Council of 26 June 2003 concerning common rules for the internal market in electricity [5] and in Regulation (EC) No 1228/2003 of the European Parliament and of the Council of 26 June 2003 on conditions for access to the network for cross-border exchanges in electricity. [6]

(15) In order to ensure effective market access for all market players including new entrants, non discriminatory and cost-reflective balancing mechanisms are necessary. As soon as the gas market is sufficiently liquid, this should be achieved through the setting up of transparent market-based mechanisms for the supply and purchase of gas needed in the framework of balancing requirements. In the absence of such a liquid market, national regulatory authorities should play an active role to ensure that balancing tariffs are non-discriminatory and cost-reflective. At the same time, appropriate incentives should be provided to balance in-put and off-take of gas and not to endanger the system.

(16) National regulatory authorities should be able to fix or approve tariffs, or the methodologies underlying the calculation of the tariffs, on the basis of a proposal by the transmission system operator or distribution system operator(s) or LNG system operator, or on the basis of a proposal agreed between these operator(s) and the users of the network. In carrying out these tasks, national regulatory authorities should ensure that transmission and distribution tariffs are non-discriminatory and cost-reflective, and should take account of the long-term, marginal, avoided network costs from demand-side management measures.

(17) The benefits resulting from the internal market should be available to all Community industry and commerce, including small and medium-sized enterprises, and to all Community citizens as quickly as possible, for reasons of fairness, competitiveness, and indirectly, to create employment as a result of the efficiency gains that will be enjoyed by enterprises.

(18) Gas customers should be able to choose their supplier freely. Nonetheless a phased approach should be taken to completing the internal market for gas, coupled with a specific deadline, to enable industry to adjust and ensure that adequate measures and systems are in place to protect the interests of customers and ensure they have a real and effective right to choose their supplier.

(19) Progressive opening of markets towards full competition should as soon as possible remove differences between Member States. Transparency and certainty in the implementation of this Directive should be ensured.

(20) Directive 98/30/EC contributes to access to storage as part of the gas system. In the light of the experience gained in implementing the internal market, additional measures should be taken to clarify the provisions for access to storage and ancillary services.

(21) Storage facilities are essential means, amongst other things of implementing public service obligations such as security of supply. This should not lead to distortion of competition or discrimination in the access to storage.

(22) Further measures should be taken in order to ensure transparent and non discriminatory tariffs for access to transportation. Those tariffs should be applicable to all users on a non discriminatory basis. Where a storage facility, linepack or ancillary service operates in a sufficiently competitive market, access could be allowed on the basis of transparent and non-discriminatory market-based mechanisms.

(23) In the interest of security of supply, the supply/demand balance in individual Member States should be monitored, and monitoring should be followed by a report on the situation at Community level, taking account of interconnection capacity between areas. Such monitoring

---

[5] See p. 37 of this Official Journal.
[6] See p. 1 of this Official Journal.

should be carried out sufficiently early to enable appropriate measures to be taken if security of supply is compromised. The construction and maintenance of the necessary network infrastructure, including interconnection capacity, should contribute to ensuring a stable gas supply.

(24) Member States should ensure that, taking into account the necessary quality requirements, biogas and gas from biomass or other types of gas are granted non-discriminatory access to the gas system, provided such access is permanently compatible with the relevant technical rules and safety standards. These rules and standards should ensure, that these gases can technically and safely be injected into, and transported through the natural gas system and should also address the chemical characteristics of these gases.

(25) Long-term contracts will continue to be an important part of the gas supply of Member States and should be maintained as an option for gas supply undertakings in so far as they do not undermine the objectives of this Directive and are compatible with the Treaty, including competition rules. It is therefore necessary to take them into account in the planning of supply and transportation capacity of gas undertakings.

(26) In order to ensure the maintenance of high standards of public service in the Community, all measures taken by Member States to achieve the objectives of this Directive should be regularly notified to the Commission. The Commission should regularly publish a report analysing measures taken at national level to achieve public service objectives and comparing their effectiveness, with a view to making recommendations as regards measures to be taken at national level to achieve high public service standards.

Member States should ensure that when they are connected to the gas system customers are informed about their rights to be supplied with natural gas of a specified quality at reasonable prices. Measures taken by Member States to protect final customers may differ according to households and small and medium sized enterprises.

(27) The respect of the public service requirements is a fundamental requirement of this Directive, and it is important that common minimum standards, respected by all Member States, are specified in this Directive, which take into account the objectives of consumer protection, security of supply, environmental protection and equivalent levels of competition in all Member States. It is important that the public service requirements can be interpreted on a national basis, taking into account national circumstances and subject to the observance of Community law.

(28) Measures implemented by Member States to achieve the objectives of social and economic cohesion may include, in particular, the provision of adequate economic incentives, using, where appropriate, all existing national and Community tools. These tools may include liability mechanisms to guarantee the necessary investment.

(29) To the extent to which measures taken by Member States to fulfil public service obligations constitute State aid under Article 87(1) of the Treaty, there is an obligation according to Article 88(3) of the Treaty to notify them to the Commission.

(30) Since the objective of the proposed action, namely the creation of a fully operational internal gas market, in which fair competition prevails, cannot be sufficiently achieved by the Member States and can therefore, by reason of the scale and effects of the action, be better achieved at Community level, the Community may adopt measures in accordance with the principle of subsidiarity and proportionality as set out in Article 5 of the Treaty. In accordance with the principle of proportionality, as set out in that Article, this Directive does not go beyond what is necessary in order to achieve that objective.

(31) In the light of the experience gained with the operation of Council Directive 91/296/EEC of 31 May 1991 on the transit of natural gas through grids,[7] measures should be taken to ensure

---

[7] OJ L 147, 12.6.1991, p. 37. Directive as last amended by Commission Directive 95/49/EC (OJ L 233, 30.9.1995, p. 86).

homogeneous and non-discriminatory access regimes for transmission, including cross-border flows of gas between Member States. To ensure homogeneity in the treatment of access to the gas networks, also in the case of transit, that Directive should be repealed, without prejudice to the continuity of contracts concluded under the said Directive. The repeal of Directive 91/296/EEC should not prevent long-term contracts being concluded in the future.

(32) Given the scope of the amendments that are being made to Directive 98/30/EC, it is desirable, for reasons of clarity and rationalisation, that the provisions in question should be recast.

(33) This Directive respects the fundamental rights, and observes the principles, recognised in particular by the Charter of Fundamental Rights of the European Union.

(34) The measures necessary for the implementation of this Directive should be adopted in accordance with Council Decision 1999/468/EC of 28 June 1999 laying down the procedures for the exercise of implementing powers conferred on the Commission, [8]

HAVE ADOPTED THIS DIRECTIVE:

Chapter I. Scope and Definitions

Article 1
Scope

1. This Directive establishes common rules for the transmission, distribution, supply and storage of natural gas. It lays down the rules relating to the organisation and functioning of the natural gas sector, access to the market, the criteria and procedures applicable to the granting of authorisations for transmission, distribution, supply and storage of natural gas and the operation of systems.
2. The rules established by this Directive for natural gas, including liquefied natural gas (LNG), shall also apply to biogas and gas from biomass or other types of gas in so far as such gases can technically and safely be injected into, and transported through, the natural gas system.

Article 2
Definitions

For the purposes of this Directive:

1. 'natural gas undertaking' means any natural or legal person carrying out at least one of the following functions: production, transmission, distribution, supply, purchase or storage of natural gas, including LNG, which is responsible for the commercial, technical and/or maintenance tasks related to those functions, but shall not include final customers;
2. 'upstream pipeline network' means any pipeline or network of pipelines operated and/or constructed as part of an oil or gas production project, or used to convey natural gas from one or more such projects to a processing plant or terminal or final coastal landing terminal;
3. 'transmission' means the transport of natural gas through a high pressure pipeline network other than an upstream pipeline network with a view to its delivery to customers, but not including supply;
4. 'transmission system operator' means a natural or legal person who carries out the function of transmission and is responsible for operating, ensuring the maintenance of, and, if necessary, developing the transmission system in a given area and, where applicable, its interconnections with other systems, and for ensuring the long-term ability of the system to meet reasonable demands for the transportation of gas;

---

[8] OJ L 184, 17.7.1999, p. 23.

5. 'distribution' means the transport of natural gas through local or regional pipeline networks with a view to its delivery to customers, but not including supply;
6. 'distribution system operator' means a natural or legal person who carries out the function of distribution and is responsible for operating, ensuring the maintenance of, and, if necessary, developing the distribution system in a given area and, where applicable, its interconnections with other systems, and for ensuring the long-term ability of the system to meet reasonable demands for the distribution of gas;
7. 'supply' means the sale, including resale, of natural gas, including LNG, to customers;
8. 'supply undertaking' means any natural or legal person who carries out the function of supply;
9. 'storage facility' means a facility used for the stocking of natural gas and owned and/or operated by a natural gas undertaking, including the part of LNG facilities used for storage but excluding the portion used for production operations, and excluding facilities reserved exclusively for transmission system operators in carrying out their functions;
10. 'storage system operator' means a natural or legal person who carries out the function of storage and is responsible for operating a storage facility;
11. 'LNG facility' means a terminal which is used for the liquefaction of natural gas or the importation, offloading, and re-gaseification of LNG, and shall include ancillary services and temporary storage necessary for the re-gaseification process and subsequent delivery to the transmission system, but shall not include any part of LNG terminals used for storage;
12. 'LNG system operator' means a natural or legal person who carries out the function of liquefaction of natural gas, or the importation, offloading, and re-gaseification of LNG and is responsible for operating a LNG facility;
13. 'system' means any transmission networks, distribution networks, LNG facilities and/or storage facilities owned and/or operated by a natural gas undertaking, including linepack and its facilities supplying ancillary services and those of related undertakings necessary for providing access to transmission, distribution and LNG;
14. 'ancillary services' means all services necessary for access to and the operation of transmission and/or distribution networks and/or LNG facilities and/or storage facilities including load balancing and blending, but excluding facilities reserved exclusively for transmission system operators carrying out their functions;
15. 'linepack' means the storage of gas by compression in gas transmission and distribution systems, but excluding facilities reserved for transmission system operators carrying out their functions;
16. 'interconnected system' means a number of systems which are linked with each other;
17. 'interconnector' means a transmission line which crosses or spans a border between Member States for the sole purpose of connecting the national transmission systems of these Member States;
18. 'direct line' means a natural gas pipeline complementary to the interconnected system;
19. 'integrated natural gas undertaking' means a vertically or horizontally integrated undertaking;
20. 'vertically integrated undertaking' means a natural gas undertaking or a group of undertakings whose mutual relationships are defined in Article 3(3) of Council Regulation (EEC) No 4064/89 of 21 December 1989 on the control of concentrations between undertakings [9] and where the undertaking/group concerned is performing at least one of the functions of transmission, distribution, LNG or storage, and at least one of the functions of production or supply of natural gas;
21. 'horizontally integrated undertaking' means an undertaking performing at least one of the functions of production, transmission, distribution, supply or storage of natural gas, and a non-gas activity;

---

[9] OJ L 395, 30.12.1989, p. 1. Regulation as last amended by Regulation (EC) No 1310/97 (OJ L 180, 9.7.1997, p. 1).

22. 'related undertakings' means affiliated undertakings, within the meaning of Article 41 of the Seventh Council Directive 83/349/EEC of 13 June 1983 based on the Article 44(2)(g)[10] of the Treaty on consolidated accounts, [11] and/or associated undertakings, within the meaning of Article 33(1) thereof, and/or undertakings which belong to the same shareholders;
23. 'system users' means any natural or legal persons supplying to, or being supplied by, the system;
24. 'customers' means wholesale and final customers of natural gas and natural gas undertakings which purchase natural gas;
25. 'household customers' means customers purchasing natural gas for their own household consumption;
26. 'non-household customers' means customers purchasing natural gas which is not for their own household use;
27. 'final customers' means customers purchasing natural gas for their own use;
28. 'eligible customers' means customers who are free to purchase gas from the supplier of their choice, within the meaning of Article 23 of this Directive;
29. 'wholesale customers' means any natural or legal persons other than transmission system operators and distribution system operators who purchase natural gas for the purpose of resale inside or outside the system where they are established;
30. 'long-term planning' means the planning of supply and transportation capacity of natural gas undertakings on a long-term basis with a view to meeting the demand for natural gas of the system, diversification of sources and securing supplies to customers;
31. 'emergent market' means a Member State in which the first commercial supply of its first long-term natural gas supply contract was made not more than 10 years earlier;
32. 'security' means both security of supply of natural gas and technical safety;
33. 'new infrastructure' means an infrastructure not completed by the entry into force of this Directive.

CHAPTER II. GENERAL RULES FOR THE ORGANISATION OF THE SECTOR

Article 3
Public service obligations and customer protection

1. Member States shall ensure, on the basis of their institutional organisation and with due regard to the principle of subsidiarity, that, without prejudice to paragraph 2, natural gas undertakings are operated in accordance with the principles of this Directive with a view to achieving a competitive, secure and environmentally sustainable market in natural gas, and shall not discriminate between these undertakings as regards either rights or obligations.
2. Having full regard to the relevant provisions of the Treaty, in particular Article 86 thereof, Member States may impose on undertakings operating in the gas sector, in the general economic interest, public service obligations which may relate to security, including security of supply, regularity, quality and price of supplies, and environmental protection, including energy efficiency and climate protection. Such obligations shall be clearly defined, transparent, non discriminatory, verifiable and shall guarantee equality of access for EU gas companies to national consumers. In relation to security of supply, energy efficiency/demand-side management and for the fulfilment of environmental goals, as referred to in this paragraph, Member States may introduce

---

[10] The title of Directive 83/349/EEC has been adjusted to take account of the renumbering of the Articles of the Treaty establishing the European Community in accordance with Article 12 of the Treaty of Amsterdam; the original reference was to Article 54(3)(g).
[11] OJ L 193, 18.7.1983, p. 1. Directive as last amended by Directive 2001/65/EC of the European Parliament and of the Council (OJ L 283, 27.10.2001, p. 28).

the implementation of long term planning, taking into account the possibility of third parties seeking access to the system.
3. Member States shall take appropriate measures to protect final customers and to ensure high levels of consumer protection, and shall, in particular, ensure that there are adequate safeguards to protect vulnerable customers, including appropriate measures to help them avoid disconnection. In this context, they may take appropriate measures to protect customers in remote areas who are connected to the gas system. Member States may appoint a supplier of last resort for customers connected to the gas network. They shall ensure high levels of consumer protection, particularly with respect to transparency regarding general contractual terms and conditions, general information and dispute settlement mechanisms. Member States shall ensure that the eligible customer is effectively able to switch to a new supplier. As regards at least household customers these measures shall include those set out in Annex A.
4. Member States shall implement appropriate measures to achieve the objectives of social and economic cohesion, environmental protection, which may include means to combat climate change, and security of supply. Such measures may include, in particular, the provision of adequate economic incentives, using, where appropriate, all existing national and Community tools, for the maintenance and construction of necessary network infrastructure, including interconnection capacity.
5. Member States may decide not to apply the provisions of Article 4 with respect to distribution insofar as their application would obstruct, in law or in fact, the performance of the obligations imposed on natural gas undertakings in the general economic interest and insofar as the development of trade would not be affected to such an extent as would be contrary to the interests of the Community. The interests of the Community include, inter alia, competition with regard to eligible customers in accordance with this Directive and Article 86 of the Treaty.
6. Member States shall, upon implementation of this Directive, inform the Commission of all measures adopted to fulfil public service obligations, including consumer and environmental protection, and their possible effect on national and international competition, whether or not such measures require a derogation from the provisions of this Directive. They shall notify the Commission subsequently every two years of any changes to such measures, whether or not they require a derogation from this Directive.

Article 4
Authorisation procedure

1. In circumstances where an authorisation (e.g. licence, permission, concession, consent or approval) is required for the construction or operation of natural gas facilities, the Member States or any competent authority they designate shall grant authorisations to build and/or operate such facilities, pipelines and associated equipment on their territory, in accordance with paragraphs 2 to 4. Member States or any competent authority they designate may also grant authorisations on the same basis for the supply of natural gas and for wholesale customers.
2. Where Member States have a system of authorisation, they shall lay down objective and non discriminatory criteria which shall be met by an undertaking applying for an authorisation to build and/or operate natural gas facilities or applying for an authorisation to supply natural gas. The non discriminatory criteria and procedures for the granting of authorisations shall be made public.
3. Member States shall ensure that the reasons for any refusal to grant an authorisation are objective and non discriminatory and are given to the applicant. Reasons for such refusals shall be forwarded to the Commission for information. Member States shall establish a procedure enabling the applicant to appeal against such refusals.
4. For the development of newly supplied areas and efficient operation generally, and without prejudice to Article 24, Member States may decline to grant a further authorisation to build and operate distribution pipeline systems in any particular area once such pipeline systems have been or are proposed to be built in that area and if existing or proposed capacity is not saturated.

Article 5
Monitoring of security of supply

Member States shall ensure the monitoring of security of supply issues. Where Member States consider it appropriate, they may delegate this task to the regulatory authorities referred to in Article 25(1). This monitoring shall, in particular, cover the supply/demand balance on the national market, the level of expected future demand and available supplies, envisaged additional capacity being planned or under construction, and the quality and level of maintenance of the networks, as well as measures to cover peak demand and to deal with shortfalls of one or more suppliers. The competent authorities shall publish, by 31 July each year at the latest a report outlining the findings resulting from the monitoring of these issues, as well as any measures taken or envisaged to address them and shall forward this report to the Commission forthwith.

Article 6
Technical rules

Member States shall ensure that technical safety criteria are defined and that technical rules establishing the minimum technical design and operational requirements for the connection to the system of LNG facilities, storage facilities, other transmission or distribution systems, and direct lines, are developed and made public. These technical rules shall ensure the interoperability of systems and shall be objective and non-discriminatory. They shall be notified to the Commission in accordance with Article 8 of Directive 98/34/EC of the European Parliament and of the Council of 22 June 1998 laying down a procedure for the provision of information in the field of technical standards and regulations and of rules on Information Society Services.[12]

CHAPTER III. TRANSMISSION, STORAGE AND LNG

Article 7
Designation of system operators

Member States shall designate or shall require natural gas undertakings which own transmission, storage or LNG facilities to designate, for a period of time to be determined by Member States having regard to considerations of efficiency and economic balance, one or more system operators. Member States shall take the measures necessary to ensure that transmission, storage and LNG system operators act in accordance with Articles 8 to 10.

Article 8
Tasks of system operators

1. Each transmission, storage and/or LNG system operator shall:
   (a) operate, maintain and develop under economic conditions secure, reliable and efficient transmission, storage and/or LNG facilities, with due regard to the environment;
   (b) refrain from discriminating between system users or classes of system users, particularly in favour of its related undertakings;
   (c) provide any other transmission system operator, any other storage system operator, any other LNG system operator and/or any distribution system operator, sufficient information to ensure that the transport and storage of natural gas may take place in a manner compatible with the secure and efficient operation of the interconnected system;

---

[12] OJ L 204, 21.7.1998, p. 37. Directive as amended by Directive 98/48/EC (OJ L 217, 5.8.1998, p. 18).

(d) provide system users with the information they need for efficient access to the system.
2. Rules adopted by transmission system operators for balancing the gas transmission system shall be objective, transparent and non-discriminatory, including rules for the charging of system users of their networks for energy imbalance. Terms and conditions, including rules and tariffs, for the provision of such services by transmission system operators shall be established pursuant to a methodology compatible with Article 25(2) in a non-discriminatory and cost-reflective way and shall be published.
3. Member States may require transmission system operators to comply with minimum requirements for the maintenance and development of the transmission system, including interconnection capacity.
4. Transmission system operators shall procure the energy they use for the carrying out of their functions according to transparent, non-discriminatory and market based procedures.

Article 9
Unbundling of transmission system operators

1. Where the transmission system operator is part of a vertically integrated undertaking, it shall be independent at least in terms of its legal form, organisation and decision making from other activities not relating to transmission. These rules shall not create an obligation to separate the ownership of assets of the transmission system from the vertically integrated undertaking.
2. In order to ensure the independence of the transmission system operator referred to in paragraph 1, the following minimum criteria shall apply:
   (a) those persons responsible for the management of the transmission system operator may not participate in company structures of the integrated natural gas undertaking responsible, directly or indirectly, for the day-to-day operation of the production, distribution and supply of natural gas;
   (b) appropriate measures must be taken to ensure that the professional interests of persons responsible for the management of the transmission system operator are taken into account in a manner that ensures that they are capable of acting independently;
   (c) the transmission system operator shall have effective decision-making rights, independent from the integrated gas undertaking, with respect to assets necessary to operate, maintain or develop the network. This should not prevent the existence of appropriate coordination mechanisms to ensure that the economic and management supervision rights of the parent company in respect of return on assets regulated indirectly in accordance with Article 25(2) in a subsidiary are protected. In particular, this shall enable the parent company to approve the annual financial plan, or any equivalent instrument, of the transmission system operator and to set global limits on the levels of indebtedness of its subsidiary. It shall not permit the parent company to give instructions regarding day-to-day operations, nor with respect to individual decisions concerning the construction or upgrading of transmission lines, that do not exceed the terms of the approved financial plan, or any equivalent instrument;
   (d) the transmission system operator shall establish a compliance programme, which sets out measures taken to ensure that discriminatory conduct is excluded, and ensure that observance of it is adequately monitored. The programme shall set out the specific obligations of employees to meet this objective. An annual report, setting out the measures taken, shall be submitted by the person or body responsible for monitoring the compliance programme to the regulatory authority referred to in Article 25(1) and shall be published.

Article 10
Confidentiality for transmission system operators

1. Without prejudice to Article 16 or any other legal duty to disclose information, each transmission, storage and/or LNG system operator shall preserve the confidentiality of commercially sensitive information obtained in the course of carrying out its business, and shall prevent information about its own activities which may be commercially advantageous from being disclosed in a discriminatory manner.

2. Transmission system operators shall not, in the context of sales or purchases of natural gas by related undertakings, abuse commercially sensitive information obtained from third parties in the context of providing or negotiating access to the system.

CHAPTER IV. DISTRIBUTION AND SUPPLY

Article 11
Designation of distribution system operators

Member States shall designate, or shall require undertakings which own or are responsible for distribution systems to designate, for a period of time to be determined by Member States, having regard to considerations of efficiency and economic balance, one or more distribution system operators and shall ensure that those operators act in accordance with Articles 12 to 14.

Article 12
Tasks of distribution system operators

1. Each distribution system operator shall operate, maintain and develop under economic conditions a secure, reliable and efficient system, with due regard for the environment.
2. In any event, the distribution system operator shall not discriminate between system users or classes of system users, particularly in favour of its related undertakings.
3. Each distribution system operator shall provide any other distribution system operator, and/or any transmission, and/or LNG system operator, and/or storage system operator with sufficient information to ensure that the transport and storage of natural gas takes place in a manner compatible with the secure and efficient operation of the interconnected system.
4. Each distribution system operator shall provide system users with the information they need for efficient access to the system.
5. Where distribution system operators are responsible for balancing the gas distribution system, rules adopted by them for that purpose shall be objective, transparent and non-discriminatory, including rules for the charging of system users for energy imbalance. Terms and conditions, including rules and tariffs, for the provision of such services by system operators shall be established pursuant to a methodology compatible with Article 25(2) in a non-discriminatory and cost-reflective way and shall be published.

Article 13
Unbundling of distribution system operators

1. Where the distribution system operator is part of a vertically integrated undertaking, it shall be independent at least in terms of its legal form, organisation and decision making from other activities not relating to distribution. These rules shall not create an obligation to separate the ownership of assets of the distribution system from the vertically integrated undertaking.
2. In addition to the requirements of paragraph 1, where the distribution system operator is part of a vertically integrated undertaking, it shall be independent in terms of its organisation and decision making from the other activities not related to distribution. In order to achieve this, the following minimum criteria shall apply:
    (a) those persons responsible for the management of the distribution system operator may not participate in company structures of the integrated natural gas undertaking responsible, directly or indirectly, for the day-to-day operation of the production, transmission and supply of natural gas;
    (b) appropriate measures must be taken to ensure that the professional interests of persons responsible for the management of the distribution system operator are taken into account in a manner that ensures that they are capable of acting independently;
    (c) the distribution system operator shall have effective decision-making rights, independent from the integrated gas undertaking, with respect to assets necessary to operate, maintain or

develop the network. This should not prevent the existence of appropriate coordination mechanisms to ensure that the economic and management supervision rights of the parent company in respect of return on assets, regulated indirectly in accordance with Article 25(2), in a subsidiary are protected. In particular, this shall enable the parent company to approve the annual financial plan, or any equivalent instrument, of the distribution system operator and to set global limits on the levels of indebtedness of its subsidiary. It shall not permit the parent company to give instructions regarding day-to-day operations, nor with respect to individual decisions concerning the construction or upgrading of distribution lines, that do not exceed the terms of the approved financial plan, or any equivalent instrument;

(d) the distribution system operator shall establish a compliance programme, which sets out measures taken to ensure that discriminatory conduct is excluded, and ensure that observance of it is adequately monitored. The programme shall set out the specific obligations of employees to meet this objective. An annual report, setting out the measures taken, shall be submitted by the person or body responsible for monitoring the compliance programme to the regulatory authority referred to in Article 25(1) and shall be published.

Member States may decide not to apply paragraphs 1 and 2 to integrated natural gas undertakings serving less than 100 000 connected customers.

Article 14
Confidentiality for distribution system operators

1. Without prejudice to Article 16 or any other legal duty to disclose information, each distribution system operator shall preserve the confidentiality of commercially sensitive information obtained in the course of carrying out its business, and shall prevent information about its own activities which may be commercially advantageous from being disclosed in a discriminatory manner.
2. Distribution system operators shall not, in the context of sales or purchases of natural gas by related undertakings, abuse commercially sensitive information obtained from third parties in the context of providing or negotiating access to the system.

Article 15
Combined operator

The rules in Articles 9(1) and Article 13(1) shall not prevent the operation of a combined transmission, LNG, storage and distribution system operator, which is independent in terms of its legal form, organisation and decision making from other activities not relating to transmission LNG, storage and distribution system operations and which meets the requirements set out in points (a) to (d). These rules shall not create an obligation to separate the ownership of assets of the combined system from the vertically integrated undertaking:

(a) those persons responsible for the management of the combined system operator may not participate in company structures of the integrated natural gas undertaking responsible, directly or indirectly, for the day-to-day operation of the production and supply of natural gas;
(b) appropriate measures must be taken to ensure that the professional interests of persons responsible for the management of the combined system operator are taken into account in a manner that ensures that they are capable of acting independently;
(c) the combined system operator shall have effective decision-making rights, independent from the integrated gas undertaking, with respect to assets necessary to operate, maintain or develop the network. This should not prevent the existence of appropriate coordination mechanisms to ensure that the economic and management supervision rights of the parent company in respect of return on assets, regulated indirectly in accordance with Article 25(2) in a subsidiary are protected. In particular, this shall enable the parent company to approve the annual financial plan, or any equivalent instrument, of the combined system operator and to set global limits on the levels of indebtedness of its subsidiary. It shall not permit the parent company to give instructions regarding day-to-day operations, nor with respect to individual decisions concerning the

construction or upgrading of transmission and distribution lines, that do not exceed the terms of the approved financial plan, or any equivalent instrument;
(d) the combined system operator shall establish a compliance programme, which sets out measures taken to ensure that discriminatory conduct is excluded, and ensure that observance of it is adequately monitored. The programme shall set out the specific obligations of employees to meet this objective. An annual report, setting out the measures taken, shall be submitted by the person or body responsible for monitoring the compliance programme to the regulatory authority referred to in Article 25(1) and shall be published.

Chapter V. Unbundling and Transparency of Accounts

Article 16
Right of access to accounts

1. Member States or any competent authority they designate, including the regulatory authorities referred to in Article 25(1) and the dispute settlement authorities referred to in Article 20(3), shall, insofar as necessary to carry out their functions, have right of access to the accounts of natural gas undertakings as set out in Article 17.
2. Member States and any designated competent authority, including the regulatory authorities referred to in Article 25(1) and the dispute settlement authorities, shall preserve the confidentiality of commercially sensitive information. Member States may provide for the disclosure of such information where this is necessary in order for the competent authorities to carry out their functions.

Article 17
Unbundling of accounts

1. Member States shall take the necessary steps to ensure that the accounts of natural gas undertakings are kept in accordance with paragraphs 2 to 5. Where undertakings benefit from a derogation from this provision on the basis of Article 28(2) and (4), they shall at least keep their internal accounts in accordance with this Article.
2. Natural gas undertakings, whatever their system of ownership or legal form, shall draw up, submit to audit and publish their annual accounts in accordance with the rules of national law concerning the annual accounts of limited liability companies adopted pursuant to the Fourth Council Directive 78/660/EEC of 25 July 1978 based on Article 44(2)(g) [13] of the Treaty on the annual accounts of certain types of companies[14]. Undertakings which are not legally obliged to publish their annual accounts shall keep a copy of these at the disposal of the public at their head office.
3. Natural gas undertakings shall, in their internal accounting, keep separate accounts for each of their transmission, distribution, LNG and storage activities as they would be required to do if the activities in question were carried out by separate undertakings, with a view to avoiding discrimination, cross-subsidisation and distortion of competition. They shall also keep accounts, which may be consolidated, for other gas activities not relating to transmission, distribution, LNG and storage. Until 1 July 2007, they shall keep separate accounts for supply activities for eligible customers and supply activities for non-eligible customers. Revenue from ownership of the transmission/distribution network shall be specified in the accounts. Where appropriate, they shall keep consolidated accounts for other, non-gas activities. The internal accounts shall include a balance sheet and a profit and loss account for each activity.

---

[13] The title of Directive 78/660/EEC has been adjusted to take account of the renumbering of the Articles of the Treaty establishing the European Community in accordance with Article 12 of the Treaty of Amsterdam; the original reference was to Article 54(3)(g).
[14] OJ L 222, 14.8.1978, p. 11. Directive as last amended by Directive 2001/65/EC of the European Parliament and of the Council (OJ L 283, 27.10.2001, p. 28).

4. The audit, referred to in paragraph 2, shall, in particular, verify that the obligation to avoid discrimination and cross-subsidies referred to in paragraph 3, is respected.
5. Undertakings shall specify in their internal accounting the rules for the allocation of assets and liabilities, expenditure and income as well as for depreciation, without prejudice to nationally applicable accounting rules, which they follow in drawing up the separate accounts referred to in paragraph 3. These internal rules may be amended only in exceptional cases. Such amendments shall be mentioned and duly substantiated.
6. The annual accounts shall indicate in notes any transaction of a certain size conducted with related undertakings.

Chapter VI. Organisation of Access to the System

Article 18
Third party access

1. Member States shall ensure the implementation of a system of third party access to the transmission and distribution system, and LNG facilities based on published tariffs, applicable to all eligible customers, including supply undertakings, and applied objectively and without discrimination between system users. Member States shall ensure that these tariffs, or the methodologies underlying their calculation shall be approved prior to their entry into force by a regulatory authority referred to in Article 25(1) and that these tariffs — and the methodologies, where only methodologies are approved — are published prior to their entry into force.
2. Transmission system operators shall, if necessary for the purpose of carrying out their functions including in relation to cross-border transmission, have access to the network of other transmission system operators.
3. The provisions of this Directive shall not prevent the conclusion of long-term contracts in so far as they comply with Community competition rules.

Article 19
Access to storage

1. For the organisation of access to storage facilities and linepack when technically and/or economically necessary for providing efficient access to the system for the supply of customers, as well as for the organisation of access to ancillary services, Member States may choose either or both of the procedures referred to in paragraphs 3 and 4. These procedures shall operate in accordance with objective, transparent and non-discriminatory criteria.
2. The provisions of paragraph 1 shall not apply to ancillary services and temporary storage that are related to LNG facilities and are necessary for the re-gaseification process and subsequent delivery to the transmission system.
3. In the case of negotiated access, Member States shall take the necessary measures for natural gas undertakings and eligible customers either inside or outside the territory covered by the interconnected system to be able to negotiate access to storage and linepack, when technically and/or economically necessary for providing efficient access to the system, as well as for the organisation of access to other ancillary services. The parties shall be obliged to negotiate access to storage, linepack and other ancillary services in good faith.

Contracts for access to storage, linepack and other ancillary services shall be negotiated with the relevant storage system operator or natural gas undertakings. Member States shall require storage system operators and natural gas undertakings to publish their main commercial conditions for the use of storage, linepack and other ancillary services within the first six months following implementation of this Directive and on an annual basis every year thereafter.

4. In the case of regulated access Member States shall take the necessary measures to give natural gas undertakings and eligible customers either inside or outside the territory covered by the

interconnected system a right to access to storage, linepack and other ancillary services, on the basis of published tariffs and/or other terms and obligations for use of that storage and linepack, when technically and/or economically necessary for providing efficient access to the system, as well as for the organisation of access to other ancillary services. This right of access for eligible customers may be given by enabling them to enter into supply contracts with competing natural gas undertakings other than the owner and/or operator of the system or a related undertaking.

Article 20
Access to upstream pipeline networks

1. Member States shall take the necessary measures to ensure that natural gas undertakings and eligible customers, wherever they are located, are able to obtain access to upstream pipeline networks, including facilities supplying technical services incidental to such access, in accordance with this Article, except for the parts of such networks and facilities which are used for local production operations at the site of a field where the gas is produced. The measures shall be notified to the Commission in accordance with the provisions of Article 33.
2. The access referred to in paragraph 1 shall be provided in a manner determined by the Member State in accordance with the relevant legal instruments. Member States shall apply the objectives of fair and open access, achieving a competitive market in natural gas and avoiding any abuse of a dominant position, taking into account security and regularity of supplies, capacity which is or can reasonably be made available, and environmental protection. The following may be taken into account:
   (a) the need to refuse access where there is an incompatibility of technical specifications which cannot be reasonably overcome;
   (b) the need to avoid difficulties which cannot be reasonably overcome and could prejudice the efficient, current and planned future production of hydrocarbons, including that from fields of marginal economic viability;
   (c) the need to respect the duly substantiated reasonable needs of the owner or operator of the upstream pipeline network for the transport and processing of gas and the interests of all other users of the upstream pipeline network or relevant processing or handling facilities who may be affected; and
   (d) the need to apply their laws and administrative procedures, in conformity with Community law, for the grant of authorisation for production or upstream development.
3. Member States shall ensure that they have in place dispute settlement arrangements, including an authority independent of the parties with access to all relevant information, to enable disputes relating to access to upstream pipeline networks to be settled expeditiously, taking into account the criteria in paragraph 2 and the number of parties which may be involved in negotiating access to such networks.
4. In the event of cross border disputes, the dispute settlement arrangements for the Member State having jurisdiction over the upstream pipeline network which refuses access shall be applied. Where, in cross border disputes, more than one Member State covers the network concerned, the Member States concerned shall consult with a view to ensuring that the provisions of this Directive are applied consistently.

Article 21
Refusal of access

1. Natural gas undertakings may refuse access to the system on the basis of lack of capacity or where the access to the system would prevent them from carrying out the public service obligations referred to in Article 3(2) which are assigned to them or on the basis of serious economic and financial difficulties with take-or-pay contracts having regard to the criteria and procedures set out in Article 27 and the alternative chosen by the Member State in accordance with paragraph 1 of that Article. Duly substantiated reasons shall be given for such a refusal.

2. Member States may take the measures necessary to ensure that the natural gas undertaking refusing access to the system on the basis of lack of capacity or a lack of connection makes the necessary enhancements as far as it is economic to do so or when a potential customer is willing to pay for them. In circumstances where Member States apply Article 4(4), Member States shall take such measures.

Article 22
New infrastructure

1. Major new gas infrastructures, i.e. interconnectors between Member States, LNG and storage facilities, may, upon request, be exempted from the provisions of Articles 18, 19, 20, and 25(2), (3) and (4) under the following conditions:
   (a) the investment must enhance competition in gas supply and enhance security of supply;
   (b) the level of risk attached to the investment is such that the investment would not take place unless an exemption was granted;
   (c) the infrastructure must be owned by a natural or legal person which is separate at least in terms of its legal form from the system operators in whose systems that infrastructure will be built;
   (d) charges are levied on users of that infrastructure;
   (e) the exemption is not detrimental to competition or the effective functioning of the internal gas market, or the efficient functioning of the regulated system to which the infrastructure is connected.
2. Paragraph 1 shall apply also to significant increases of capacity in existing infrastructures and to modifications of such infrastructures which enable the development of new sources of gas supply.
3. (a) The regulatory authority referred to in Article 25 may, on a case by case basis, decide on the exemption referred to in paragraphs 1 and 2. However, Member States may provide that the regulatory authorities shall submit, for formal decision, to the relevant body in the Member State its opinion on the request for an exemption. This opinion shall be published together with the decision.
   (b) (i) The exemption may cover all or parts of, respectively, the new infrastructure, the existing infrastructure with significantly increased capacity or the modification of the existing infrastructure.
   (ii) In deciding to grant an exemption consideration shall be given, on a case by case basis, to the need to impose conditions regarding the duration of the exemption and non-discriminatory access to the interconnector.
   (iii) When deciding on the conditions in this subparagraph account shall, in particular, be taken of the duration of contracts, additional capacity to be built or the modification of existing capacity, the time horizon of the project and national circumstances.
   (c) When granting an exemption the relevant authority may decide upon the rules and mechanisms for management and allocation of capacity insofar as this does not prevent the implementation of long term contracts.
   (d) The exemption decision, including any conditions referred to in (b), shall be duly reasoned and published.
   (e) In the case of an interconnector any exemption decision shall be taken after consultation with the other Member States or regulatory authorities concerned.
4. The exemption decision shall be notified, without delay, by the competent authority to the Commission, together with all the relevant information with respect to the decision. This information may be submitted to the Commission in aggregate form, enabling the Commission to reach a well-founded decision.

In particular, the information shall contain:
(a) the detailed reasons on the basis of which the regulatory authority, or Member State, granted the exemption, including the financial information justifying the need for the exemption;
(b) the analysis undertaken of the effect on competition and the effective functioning of the internal gas market resulting from the grant of the exemption;

(c) the reasons for the time period and the share of the total capacity of the gas infrastructure in question for which the exemption is granted;
(d) in case the exemption relates to an interconnector, the result of the consultation with the Member States concerned or regulatory authorities;
(e) the contribution of the infrastructure to the diversification of gas supply.

Within two months after receiving a notification, the Commission may request that the regulatory authority or the Member State concerned amend or withdraw the decision to grant an exemption. The two month period may be extended by one additional month where additional information is sought by the Commission.

If the regulatory authority or Member State concerned does not comply with the request within a period of four weeks, a final decision shall be taken in accordance with the procedure referred to in Article 30(2).

The Commission shall preserve the confidentiality of commercially sensitive information.

Article 23
Market opening and reciprocity

1. Member States shall ensure that the eligible customers are:
    (a) until 1 July 2004, the eligible customers as specified in Article 18 of Directive 98/30/EC. Member States shall publish by 31 January each year the criteria for the definition of these eligible customers;
    (b) from 1 July 2004, at the latest, all non-household customers;
    (c) from 1 July 2007, all customers.
2. To avoid imbalance in the opening of gas markets:
    (a) contracts for the supply with an eligible customer in the system of another Member State shall not be prohibited if the customer is eligible in both systems involved;
    (b) in cases where transactions as described in point (a) are refused because the customer is eligible in only one of the two systems, the Commission may, taking into account the situation in the market and the common interest, oblige the refusing party to execute the requested supply, at the request of one of the Member States of the two systems.

Article 24
Direct lines

1. Member States shall take the necessary measures to enable:
    (a) natural gas undertakings established within their territory to supply the eligible customers through a direct line;
    (b) any such eligible customer within their territory to be supplied through a direct line by natural gas undertakings.
2. In circumstances where an authorisation (e.g. licence, permission, concession, consent or approval) is required for the construction or operation of direct lines, the Member States or any competent authority they designate shall lay down the criteria for the grant of authorisations for the construction or operation of such lines in their territory. These criteria shall be objective, transparent and non-discriminatory.
3. Member States may make authorisations to construct a direct line subject either to the refusal of system access on the basis of Article 21 or to the opening of a dispute settlement procedure under Article 25.

Article 25
Regulatory authorities

1. Member States shall designate one or more competent bodies with the function of regulatory authorities. These authorities shall be wholly independent of the interests of the gas industry.

They shall, through the application of this Article, at least be responsible for ensuring non-discrimination, effective competition and the efficient functioning of the market, monitoring in particular:
(a) the rules on the management and allocation of interconnection capacity, in conjunction with the regulatory authority or authorities of those Member States with which interconnection exists;
(b) any mechanisms to deal with congested capacity within the national gas system;
(c) the time taken by transmission and distribution system operators to make connections and repairs;
(d) the publication of appropriate information by transmission and distribution system operators concerning interconnectors, grid usage and capacity allocation to interested parties, taking into account the need to treat non-aggregated information as commercially confidential;
(e) the effective unbundling of accounts as referred to in Article 17, to ensure there are no cross subsidies between transmission, distribution, storage, LNG and supply activities;
(f) the access conditions to storage, linepack and to other ancillary services as provided for in Article 19;
(g) the extent to which transmission and distribution system operators fulfil their tasks in accordance with Articles 8 and 12;
(h) the level of transparency and competition.

The authorities established pursuant to this Article shall publish an annual report on the outcome of their monitoring activities referred to in points (a) to (h).

2. The regulatory authorities shall be responsible for fixing or approving prior to their entry into force, at least the methodologies used to calculate or establish the terms and conditions for:
(a) connection and access to national networks, including transmission and distribution tariffs. These tariffs, or methodologies, shall allow the necessary investments in the networks to be carried out in a manner allowing these investments to ensure the viability of the networks;
(b) the provision of balancing services.

3. Notwithstanding paragraph 2, Member States may provide that the regulatory authorities shall submit, for formal decision, to the relevant body in the Member State the tariffs or at least the methodologies referred to in that paragraph as well as the modifications in paragraph 4. The relevant body shall, in such a case, have the power to either approve or reject a draft decision submitted by the regulatory authority. These tariffs or the methodologies or modifications thereto shall be published together with the decision on formal adoption. Any formal rejection of a draft decision shall also be published, including its justification.

4. Regulatory authorities shall have the authority to require transmission, LNG and distribution system operators, if necessary, to modify the terms and conditions, including tariffs and methodologies referred to in paragraphs 1, 2 and 3, to ensure that they are proportionate and applied in a non-discriminatory manner.

5. Any party having a complaint against a transmission, LNG or distribution system operator with respect to the issues mentioned in paragraphs 1, 2 and 4 and in Article 19 may refer the complaint to the regulatory authority which, acting as dispute settlement authority, shall issue a decision within two months after receipt of the complaint. This period may be extended by two months where additional information is sought by the regulatory authorities. This period may be extended with the agreement of the complainant. Such a decision shall have binding effect unless and until overruled on appeal.

6. Any party having a complaint against a transmission, LNG or distribution system operator with respect to the issues mentioned in paragraphs 1, 2 and 4 and in Article 19 may refer the complaint to the regulatory authority which, acting as dispute settlement authority, shall issue a decision within two months after receipt of the complaint. This period may be extended by two months where additional information is sought by the regulatory authorities. This period may be

extended with the agreement of the complainant. Such a decision shall have binding effect unless and until overruled on appeal.
7. Member States shall take measures to ensure that regulatory authorities are able to carry out their duties referred to in paragraphs 1 to 5 in an efficient and expeditious manner.
8. Member States shall create appropriate and efficient mechanisms for regulation, control and transparency so as to avoid any abuse of a dominant position, in particular to the detriment of consumers, and any predatory behaviour. These mechanisms shall take account of the provisions of the Treaty, and in particular Article 82 thereof.
9. Member States shall ensure that the appropriate measures are taken, including administrative action or criminal proceedings in conformity with their national law, against the natural or legal persons responsible where confidentiality rules imposed by this Directive have not been respected.
10. In the event of cross border disputes, the deciding regulatory authority shall be the regulatory authority which has jurisdiction in respect of the system operator, which refuses use of, or access to, the system.
11. Complaints referred to in paragraphs 5 and 6 shall be without prejudice to the exercise of rights of appeal under Community and national law.
12. National regulatory authorities shall contribute to the development of the internal market and of a level playing field by cooperating with each other and with the Commission in a transparent manner.

Chapter VII. Final Provisions

Article 26
Safeguard measures

1. In the event of a sudden crisis in the energy market or where the physical safety or security of persons, apparatus or installations or system integrity is threatened, a Member State may temporarily take the necessary safeguard measures.
2. Such measures shall cause the least possible disturbance to the functioning of the internal market and shall not be wider in scope than is strictly necessary to remedy the sudden difficulties which have arisen.
3. The Member State concerned shall without delay notify these measures to the other Member States, and to the Commission, which may decide that the Member State concerned must amend or abolish such measures, insofar as they distort competition and adversely affect trade in a manner which is at variance with the common interest.

Article 27
Derogations in relation to take-or-pay commitments

1. If a natural gas undertaking encounters, or considers it would encounter, serious economic and financial difficulties because of its take-or-pay commitments accepted in one or more gas-purchase contracts, an application for a temporary derogation from Article 18 may be sent to the Member State concerned or the designated competent authority. Applications shall, according to the choice of Member States, be presented on a case-by-case basis either before or after refusal of access to the system. Member States may also give the natural gas undertaking the choice of presenting an application either before or after refusal of access to the system. Where a natural gas undertaking has refused access, the application shall be presented without delay. The applications shall be accompanied by all relevant information on the nature and extent of the problem and on the efforts undertaken by the natural gas undertaking to solve the problem.

If alternative solutions are not reasonably available, and taking into account the provisions of paragraph 3, the Member State or the designated competent authority may decide to grant a derogation.

Appendix 3

2. The Member State, or the designated competent authority, shall notify the Commission without delay of its decision to grant a derogation, together with all the relevant information with respect to the derogation. This information may be submitted to the Commission in an aggregated form, enabling the Commission to reach a well-founded decision. Within eight weeks of its receipt of this notification, the Commission may request that the Member State or the designated competent authority concerned amend or withdraw the decision to grant a derogation.

If the Member State or the designated competent authority concerned does not comply with this request within a period of four weeks, a final decision shall be taken expeditiously in accordance with the procedure referred to in Article 30(2).

The Commission shall preserve the confidentiality of commercially sensitive information.

3. When deciding on the derogations referred to in paragraph 1, the Member State, or the designated competent authority, and the Commission shall take into account, in particular, the following criteria:
   (a) the objective of achieving a competitive gas market;
   (b) the need to fulfil public service obligations and to ensure security of supply;
   (c) the position of the natural gas undertaking in the gas market and the actual state of competition in this market;
   (d) the seriousness of the economic and financial difficulties encountered by natural gas undertakings and transmission undertakings or eligible customers;
   (e) the dates of signature and terms of the contract or contracts in question, including the extent to which they allow for market changes;
   (f) the efforts made to find a solution to the problem;
   (g) the extent to which, when accepting the take-or-pay commitments in question, the undertaking could reasonably have foreseen, having regard to the provisions of this Directive, that serious difficulties were likely to arise;
   (h) the level of connection of the system with other systems and the degree of interoperability of these systems; and
   (i) the effects the granting of a derogation would have on the correct application of this Directive as regards the smooth functioning of the internal natural gas market.

A decision on a request for a derogation concerning take or pay contracts concluded before the entry into force of this Directive should not lead to a situation in which it is impossible to find economically viable alternative outlets. Serious difficulties shall in any case be deemed not to exist when the sales of natural gas do not fall below the level of minimum offtake guarantees contained in gas purchase take or pay contracts or in so far as the relevant gas purchase take-or-pay contract can be adapted or the natural gas undertaking is able to find alternative outlets.

4. Natural gas undertakings which have not been granted a derogation as referred to in paragraph 1 shall not refuse, or shall no longer refuse, access to the system because of take-or-pay commitments accepted in a gas purchase contract. Member States shall ensure that the relevant provisions of Chapter VI namely Articles 18 to 25 are complied with.
5. Any derogation granted under the above provisions shall be duly substantiated. The Commission shall publish the decision in the *Official Journal of the European Union*.
6. The Commission shall, within five years of the entry into force of this Directive, submit a review report on the experience gained from the application of this Article, so as to allow the European Parliament and the Council to consider, in due course, the need to adjust it.

Article 28
Emergent and isolated markets

1. Member States not directly connected to the interconnected system of any other Member State and having only one main external supplier may derogate from Articles 4, 9, 2 3 and/or 24 of

this Directive. A supply undertaking having a market share of more than 75 % shall be considered to be a main supplier. This derogation shall automatically expire from the moment when at least one of these conditions no longer applies. Any such derogation shall be notified to the Commission.

2. A Member State, qualifying as an emergent market, which because of the implementation of this Directive would experience substantial problems may derogate from Articles 4, 7, 8(1) and (2), 9, 11, 12(5), 13, 17, 18, 23(1) and/or 24 of this Directive. This derogation shall automatically expire from the moment when the Member State no longer qualifies as an emergent market. Any such derogation shall be notified to the Commission.

3. On the date at which the derogation referred to in paragraph 2 expires, the definition of eligible customers shall result in an opening of the market equal to at least 33 % of the total annual gas consumption of the national gas market. Two years thereafter, Article 23(1)(b) shall apply, and three years thereafter, Article 23(1)(c). Until Article 23(1)(b) applies the Member State referred to in paragraph 2 may decide not to apply Article 18 as far as ancillary services and temporary storage for the re-gaseification process and its subsequent delivery to the transmission system are concerned.

4. Where implementation of this Directive would cause substantial problems in a geographically limited area of a Member State, in particular concerning the development of the transmission and major distribution infrastructure, and with a view to encouraging investments, the Member State may apply to the Commission for a temporary derogation from Article 4, Article 7, Article 8(1) and (2), Article 9, Article 11, Article 12(5), Article 13, Article 17, Article 18, Article 23(1) and/or Article 24 for developments within this area.

5. The Commission may grant the derogation referred to in paragraph 4, taking into account, in particular, the following criteria:
   — the need for infrastructure investments, which would not be economic to operate in a competitive market environment,
   — the level and pay-back prospects of investments required,
   — the size and maturity of the gas system in the area concerned,
   — the prospects for the gas market concerned,
   — the geographical size and characteristics of the area or region concerned, and socioeconomic and demographic factors.
   (a) For gas infrastructure other than distribution infrastructure a derogation may be granted only if no gas infrastructure has been established in this area, or has been so established for less than 10 years. The temporary derogation may not exceed 10 years from the time gas is first supplied in the area.
   (b) For distribution infrastructure a derogation may be granted for a time period which may not exceed 20 years for the distribution infrastructure from the time gas is first supplied through the said system in the area.

6. Luxembourg may benefit from a derogation from Articles 8(3) and 9 for a period of five years from 1 July 2004. Such a derogation shall be reviewed before the end of the five year period and any decision to renew the derogation for another five years shall be taken in accordance with the procedure referred to in Article 30(2). Any such derogation shall be notified to the Commission.

7. The Commission shall inform the Member States of applications made under paragraph 4 prior to taking a decision pursuant to paragraph 5, taking into account respect for confidentiality. This decision, as well as the derogations referred to in paragraphs 1 and 2, shall be published in the *Official Journal of the European Union*.

8. Greece may derogate from Articles 4, 11, 12, 13, 18, 23 and/or 24 of this Directive for the geographical areas and time periods specified in the licences issued by it, prior to 15 March 2002 and in accordance with Directive 98/30/EC, for the development and exclusive exploitation of distribution networks in certain geographical areas.

Article 29
Review Procedure

In the event that the report referred to in Article 31(3) reaches the conclusion whereby, given the effective manner in which network access has been carried out in a Member State — which gives rise to fully effective, non-discriminatory and unhindered network access —, the Commission concludes that certain obligations imposed by this Directive on undertakings (including those with respect to legal unbundling for distribution system operators) are not proportionate to the objective pursued, the Member State in question may submit a request to the Commission for exemption from the requirement in question.

The request shall be notified, without delay, by the Member State to the Commission, together with all the relevant information necessary to demonstrate that the conclusion reached in the report on effective network access being ensured will be maintained.

Within three months of its receipt of a notification, the Commission shall adopt an opinion with respect to the request by the Member State concerned, and where appropriate, submit proposals to the European Parliament and to the Council to amend the relevant provisions of the Directive. The Commission may propose, in the proposals to amend the Directive, to exempt the Member State concerned from specific requirements subject to that Member State implementing equally effective measures as appropriate.

Article 30
Committee

1. The Commission shall be assisted by a Committee.
2. Where reference is made to this paragraph, Articles 3 and 7 of Decision 1999/468/EC shall apply, having regard to the provisions of Article 8 thereof.
3. The Committee shall adopt its rules of procedure.

Article 31
Reporting

1. The Commission shall monitor and review the application of this Directive and submit an overall progress report to the European Parliament and the Council before the end of the first year following the entry into force of this Directive, and thereafter on an annual basis. The report shall cover at least:
    (a) the experience gained and progress made in creating a complete and fully operational internal market in natural gas and the obstacles that remain in this respect including aspects of market dominance, concentration in the market, predatory or anti-competitive behaviour;
    (b) the derogations granted under this Directive, including implementation of the derogation provided for in Article 13(2) with a view to a possible revision of the threshold;
    (c) the extent to which the unbundling and tarification requirements contained in this Directive have been successful in ensuring fair and non-discriminatory access to the Community's gas system and equivalent levels of competition, as well as the economic, environmental and social consequences of the opening of the gas market for customers;
    (d) an examination of issues relating to system capacity levels and security of supply of natural gas in the Community, and in particular the existing and projected balance between demand and supply, taking into account the physical capacity for exchanges between areas and the development of storage (including the question of the proportionality of market regulation in this field);
    (e) special attention will be given to the measures taken in Member States to cover peak demand and to deal with shortfalls of one or more suppliers;
    (f) a general assessment of the progress achieved with regard to bilateral relations with third countries which produce and export or transport natural gas, including progress in market integration, trade and access to the networks of such third countries;

(g) the need for possible harmonisation requirements which are not linked to the provisions of this Directive.

Where appropriate, this report may include recommendations and measures to counteract negative effects of market dominance and market concentration.

2. Every two years, the report referred to in paragraph 1 shall also cover an analysis of the different measures taken in Member States to meet public service obligations, together with an examination of the effectiveness of those measures, and in particular their effects on competition in the gas market. Where appropriate, the report may include recommendations as to the measures to be taken at national level to achieve high public service standards or measures intended to prevent market foreclosure.

3. The Commission shall, no later than 1 January 2006, forward to the European Parliament and Council, a detailed report outlining progress in creating the internal gas market. The report shall, in particular, consider:
   — the existence of non-discriminatory network access;
   — effective regulation;
   — the development of interconnection infrastructure, the conditions of transit, and the security of supply situation in the Community;
   — the extent to which the full benefits of the opening of the market are accruing to small enterprises and households, notably with respect to public service standards;
   — the extent to which markets are in practice open to effective competition, including aspects of market dominance, market concentration and predatory or anti-competitive behaviour;
   — the extent to which customers are actually switching suppliers and renegotiating tariffs;
   — price developments, including supply prices, in relation to the degree of the opening of markets;
   — whether effective and non-discriminatory third party access to gas storage exists when technically and/or economically necessary for providing efficient access to the system;
   — the experience gained in the application of the Directive as far as the effective independence of system operators in vertically integrated undertakings is concerned and whether other measures in addition to functional independence and separation of accounts have been developed which have effects equivalent to legal unbundling.

Where appropriate, the Commission shall submit proposals to the European Parliament and the Council, in particular to guarantee high public service standards.

Where appropriate, the Commission shall submit proposals to the European Parliament and the Council, in particular to ensure full and effective independence of distribution system operators before 1 July 2007. When necessary, these proposals shall, in conformity with competition law, also concern measures to address issues of market dominance, market concentration and predatory or anti-competitive behaviour.

Article 32
Repeals

1. Directive 91/296/EEC shall be repealed with effect from 1 July 2004, without prejudice to contracts concluded pursuant to Article 3(1) of Directive 91/296/EEC, which shall continue to be valid and to be implemented under the terms of the said Directive.
2. Directive 98/30/EC shall be repealed from 1 July 2004, without prejudice to the obligations of Member States concerning the deadlines for transposition and application of the said Directive. References made to the repealed Directive shall be construed as being made to this Directive and should be read in accordance with the correlation table in Annex B.

Article 33
Implementation

1. Member States shall bring into force the laws, regulations and administrative provisions necessary to comply with this Directive not later than 1 July 2004. They shall forthwith inform the Commission thereof.

2. Member States may postpone the implementation of Article 13(1) until 1 July 2007. This shall be without prejudice to the requirements contained in Article 13(2).
3. When Member States adopt these measures, they shall contain a reference to this Directive or shall be accompanied by such reference on the occasion of their official publication. The methods of making such reference shall be laid down by Member States.

Article 34
Entry into force

This Directive shall enter into force on the twentieth day following that of its publication in the *Official Journal of the European Union*.

Article 35
Addressees

This Directive is addressed to the Member States.

Done at Brussels, 26 June 2003.

ANNEX A
Measures on consumer protection

Without prejudice to Community rules on consumer protection, in particular Directives 97/7/EC of the European Parliament and of the Council [15] and Council Directive 93/13/EC [16], the measures referred to in Article 3 are to ensure that customers:

(a) have a right to a contract with their gas service provider that specifies:
   — the identity and address of the supplier;
   — the services provided, the service quality levels offered, as well as the time for the initial connection;
   — if offered, the types of maintenance service offered;
   — the means by which up to date information on all applicable tariffs and maintenance charges may be obtained;
   — the duration of the contract, the conditions for renewal and termination of services and of the contract, the existence of any right of withdrawal;
   — any compensation and the refund arrangements which apply if contracted service quality levels are not met; and
   — the method of initiating procedures for settlement of disputes in accordance with point (f).

Conditions shall be fair and well known in advance. In any case, this information should be provided prior to the conclusion or confirmation of the contract. Where contracts are concluded through intermediaries, the above information shall also be provided prior to the conclusion of the contract:

(b) are given adequate notice of any intention to modify contractual conditions and are informed about their right of withdrawal when the notice is given. Service providers shall notify their subscribers directly of any increase in charges, at an appropriate time no later than one normal billing period after the increase comes into effect. Member States shall ensure that customers are free to withdraw from contracts if they do not accept the new conditions, notified to them by their gas service provider;

(c) receive transparent information on applicable prices and tariffs and on standard terms and conditions, in respect of access to and use of gas services;

---

[15] OJ L 144, 4 6 1997, p 19.
[16] OJ L 95, 21.4.1993, p 29.

(d) are offered a wide choice of payment methods. Any difference in terms and conditions shall reflect the costs to the supplier of the different payment systems. General terms and conditions shall be fair and transparent. They shall be given in clear and comprehensible language. Customers shall be protected against unfair or misleading selling methods;
(e) shall not be charged for changing supplier;
(f) benefit from transparent, simple and inexpensive procedures for dealing with their complaints. Such procedures shall enable disputes to be settled fairly and promptly with provision, where warranted, for a system of reimbursement and/or compensation. They should follow, wherever possible, the principles set out in Commission Recommendation 98/257/EC; [17]
(g) connected to the gas system are informed about their rights to be supplied, under the national legislation applicable, with natural gas of a specified quality at reasonable prices.

ANNEX B

Correlation table

Directive 98/30/EC	This Directive	
Article 1	Article 1	Scope
Article 2	Article 2	Definitions
Article 3	Article 3	PSOs and Customer protection
Article 4	Article 4	Authorisation procedure
—	Article 5	Monitoring of security of supply
Article 5	Article 6	Technical rules
Article 6	Article 7	Designation of TSOs
Article 7	Article 8	Tasks of TSOs
—	Article 9	Unbundling of TSOs
Article 8	Article 10	Confidentiality for TSOs
Article 9(1)	Article 11	Designation of DSOs
Article 10	Article 12	Tasks of DSOs
—	Article 13	Unbundling of DSOs
Article 11	Article 14	Confidentiality for DSOs
—	Article 15	Combined operator
Article 12	Article 16	Right of access to accounts
Article 13	Article 17	Unbundling of accounts
Article 14-16	Article 18	Third Party Access
—	Article 19	Access to storage
Article 23	Article 20	Access to upstream pipeline networks
Article 17	Article 21	Refusal of access
—	Article 22	New infrastructure
Article 18 and 19	Article 23	Market opening and reciprocity
Article 20	Article 24	Direct lines
Article 21(2)–(3) and 22	Article 25	Regulatory authorities
Article 24	Article 26	Safeguard measures
Article 25	Article 27	Derogations in relation to take-or-pay commitments
Article 26	Article 28	Emergent and Isolated Markets
—	Article 29	Review procedure
—	Article 30	Committee

---

[17] OJ L 115, 17.4.1998, p 31.

Appendix 3

Correlation table (*cont.*)

Directive 98/30/EC	This Directive	
Article 27 and 28	Article 31	Reporting
—	Article 32	Repeals
Article 29	Article 33	Implementation
Article 30	Article 34	Entry into force
Article 31	Article 35	Addressees
	Annex A	Measures on consumer protection

APPENDIX 4

Regulation (EC) no 1775/2005 of the European Parliament and of the Council

of 28 September 2005

on conditions for access to the natural gas transmission networks
(Text with EEA relevance)

THE EUROPEAN PARLIAMENT AND THE COUNCIL OF THE EUROPEAN UNION,

Having regard to the Treaty establishing the European Community, and in particular Article 95 thereof,

Having regard to the proposal from the Commission,

Having regard to the opinion of the European Economic and Social Committee, [1]

Following consultation of the Committee of the Regions,

Acting in accordance with the procedure laid down in Article 251 of the Treaty, [2]

Whereas:

(1) Directive 2003/55/EC of the European Parliament and of the Council of 26 June 2003 concerning common rules for the internal market in natural gas [3] has made a significant contribution towards the creation of an internal market for gas. It is now necessary to provide for structural changes in the regulatory framework to tackle remaining barriers to the completion of the internal market in particular regarding the trade of gas. Additional technical rules are necessary, in particular regarding third party access services, principles of capacity allocation mechanisms, congestion management procedures and transparency requirements.

(2) Experience gained in the implementation and monitoring of a first set of Guidelines for Good Practice, adopted by the European Gas Regulatory Forum (the Forum) in 2002, demonstrates that in order to ensure the full implementation of the rules set out in the Guidelines in all Member States, and in order to provide a minimum guarantee of equal market access conditions in practice, it is necessary to provide for them to become legally enforceable.

(3) A second set of common rules entitled 'the Second Guidelines for Good Practice' was adopted at the meeting of the Forum on 24-25 September 2003 and the purpose of this Regulation is to lay down, on the basis of those Guidelines, basic principles and rules regarding network access and third party access services, congestion management, transparency, balancing and the trading of capacity rights.

(4) Article 15 of Directive 2003/55/EC allows for a combined transmission and distribution system operator. Therefore, the rules set out in this Regulation do not require modification of the organisation of national transmission and distribution systems that are consistent with the relevant provisions of Directive 2003/55/EC and in particular Article 15 thereof.

---

[1] OJ C 241, 28.9.2004, p 31.
[2] Opinion of the European Parliament of 20 April 2004 (OJ C 104 E, 30.4.2004, p 306), Council common position of 12 November 2004 (OJ C 25 E, 1.2.2005, p 44), position of the European Parliament of 8 March 2005 (not yet published in the Official Journal) and Council Decision of 12 July 2005.
[3] OJ L 176, 15.7.2003, p 57.

(5) High pressure pipelines linking up local distributors to the gas network which are not primarily used in the context of local distribution are included in the scope of this Regulation.

(6) It is necessary to specify the criteria according to which tariffs for access to the network are determined, in order to ensure that they fully comply with the principle of non-discrimination and the needs of a well-functioning internal market and take fully into account the need for system integrity and reflect actual costs incurred, insofar as such costs correspond to those of an efficient and structurally comparable network operator and are transparent, whilst including appropriate return on investments, and where appropriate taking account of the benchmarking of tariffs by the regulatory authorities.

(7) In calculating tariffs for access to networks it is important to take account of actual costs incurred, insofar as such costs correspond to those of an efficient and structurally comparable network operator and are transparent, as well as of the need to provide appropriate return on investments and incentives to construct new infrastructure. In this respect, and in particular if effective pipeline-to-pipeline competition exists, the benchmarking of tariffs by the regulatory authorities will be a relevant consideration.

(8) The use of market-based arrangements, such as auctions, to determine tariffs has to be compatible with the provisions laid down in Directive 2003/55/EC.

(9) A common minimum set of third party access services is necessary to provide a common minimum standard of access in practice throughout the Community, to ensure that third party access services are sufficiently compatible and to allow the benefits accruing from a well-functioning internal market for gas to be exploited.

(10) References to harmonised transportation contracts in the context of non-discriminatory access to the network of transmission system operators do not mean that the terms and conditions of the transportation contracts of a particular system operator in a Member State must be the same as those of another transmission system operator in that Member State or in another Member State, unless minimum requirements are set which must be met by all transportation contracts.

(11) The management of contractual congestion of networks is an important issue in completing the internal gas market. It is necessary to develop common rules which balance the need to free up unused capacity in accordance with the 'use-it-or-lose-it' principle with the rights of the holders of the capacity to use it when necessary, while at the same time enhancing liquidity of capacity.

(12) Although physical congestion of networks is rarely a problem at present in the Community, it may become one in the future. It is important therefore to provide the basic principle for the allocation of congested capacity in such circumstances.

(13) For network users to gain effective access to gas networks they need information in particular on technical requirements and available capacity to enable them to exploit business opportunities occurring within the framework of the internal market. Common minimum standards on such transparency requirements are necessary. The publication of such information may be done by different means, including electronic means.

(14) Non-discriminatory and transparent balancing systems for gas, operated by transmission system operators, are important mechanisms, particularly for new market entrants which may have more difficulty balancing their overall sales portfolio than companies already established within a relevant market. It is therefore necessary to lay down rules to ensure that transmission system operators operate such mechanisms in a manner compatible with non-discriminatory, transparent and effective access conditions to the network.

(15) The trading of primary capacity rights is an important part of developing a competitive market and creating liquidity. This Regulation should therefore lay down basic rules on that issue.

(16) It is necessary to ensure that undertakings acquiring capacity rights are able to sell them to other licensed undertakings in order to ensure an appropriate level of liquidity on the capacity market. This approach, however, does not preclude a system where capacity unused for a given period, determined at national level, is made re-available to the market on a firm basis.

(17) National regulatory authorities should ensure compliance with the rules contained in this Regulation and the guidelines adopted pursuant to it.

(18) In the Guidelines annexed to this Regulation, specific detailed implementing rules are defined on the basis of the second Guidelines for Good Practice. Where appropriate, these rules will evolve over time, taking into account the differences of national gas systems.

(19) When proposing to amend the Guidelines laid down in the Annex to this Regulation, the Commission should ensure prior consultation of all relevant parties concerned with the Guidelines, represented by the professional organisations, and of the Member States within the Forum and should request the input of the European Regulators Group for Electricity and Gas.

(20) The Member States and the competent national authorities should be required to provide relevant information to the Commission. Such information should be treated confidentially by the Commission.

(21) This Regulation and the guidelines adopted in accordance with it are without prejudice to the application of the Community rules on competition.

(22) The measures necessary for the implementation of this Regulation should be adopted in accordance with Council Decision 1999/468/EC of 28 June 1999 laying down the procedures for the exercise of implementing powers conferred on the Commission. [4]

(23) Since the objective of this Regulation, namely the setting of fair rules for access conditions to natural gas transmission systems, cannot be sufficiently achieved by the Member States and can therefore, by reason of the scale and effects of the action, be better achieved at Community level, the Community may adopt measures in accordance with the principle of subsidiarity, as set out in Article 5 of the Treaty. In accordance with the principle of proportionality, as set out in that Article, this Regulation does not go beyond what is necessary in order to achieve that objective,

HAVE ADOPTED THIS REGULATION:

Article 1
Subject matter and scope

1. This Regulation aims at setting non-discriminatory rules for access conditions to natural gas transmission systems taking into account the specificities of national and regional markets with a view to ensuring the proper functioning of the internal gas market.

   This objective shall include the setting of harmonised principles for tariffs, or the methodologies underlying their calculation, for access to the network, the establishment of third party access services and harmonised principles for capacity allocation and congestion management, the determination of transparency requirements, balancing rules and imbalance charges and facilitating capacity trading.

2. Member States may establish an entity or body set up in compliance with Directive 2003/55/EC for the purpose of carrying out one or more functions typically attributed to the transmission system operator, which shall be subject to the requirements of this Regulation.

Article 2
Definitions

1. For the purpose of this Regulation, the following definitions shall apply:
   1. 'transmission' means the transport of natural gas through a network, which mainly contains high pressure pipelines, other than an upstream pipeline network and other than the part of high pressure pipelines primarily used in the context of local distribution of natural gas, with a view to its delivery to customers, but not including supply;
   2. 'transportation contract' means a contract which the transmission system operator has concluded with a network user with a view to carrying out transmission;

---

[4] OJ L 184, 17.7.1999, p 23.

3. 'capacity' means the maximum flow, expressed in normal cubic meters per time unit or in energy unit per time unit, to which the network user is entitled in accordance with the provisions of the transportation contract;
4. 'unused capacity' means firm capacity which a network user has acquired under a transportation contract but which that user has not nominated by the deadline specified in the contract;
5. 'congestion management' means management of the capacity portfolio of the transmission system operator with a view to optimal and maximum use of the technical capacity and the timely detection of future congestion and saturation points;
6. 'secondary market' means the market of the capacity traded otherwise than on the primary market;
7. 'nomination' means the prior reporting by the network user to the transmission system operator of the actual flow that he wishes to inject into or withdraw from the system;
8. 're-nomination' means the subsequent reporting of a corrected nomination;
9. 'system integrity' means any situation in respect of a transmission network including necessary transmission facilities in which the pressure and the quality of the natural gas remain within the minimum and maximum limits laid down by the transmission system operator, so that the transmission of natural gas is guaranteed from a technical standpoint;
10. 'balancing period' means the period within which the offtake of an amount of natural gas, expressed in units of energy, must be offset by every network user by means of the injection of the same amount of natural gas into the transmission network in accordance with the transportation contract or the network code;
11. 'network user' means a customer or a potential customer of a transmission system operator, and transmission system operators themselves in so far as it is necessary for them to carry out their functions in relation to transmission;
12. 'interruptible services' means services offered by the transmission system operator in relation to interruptible capacity;
13. 'interruptible capacity' means gas transmission capacity that can be interrupted by the transmission system operator according to the conditions stipulated in the transportation contract;
14. 'long-term services' means services offered by the transmission system operator with a duration of one year or more;
15. 'short-term services' means services offered by the transmission system operator with a duration of less than one year;
16. 'firm capacity' means gas transmission capacity contractually guaranteed as uninterruptible by the transmission system operator;
17. 'firm services' means services offered by the transmission system operator in relation to firm capacity;
18. 'technical capacity' means the maximum firm capacity that the transmission system operator can offer to the network users, taking account of system integrity and the operational requirements of the transmission network;
19. 'contracted capacity' means capacity that the transmission system operator has allocated to a network user by means of a transportation contract;
20. 'available capacity' means the part of the technical capacity that is not allocated and is still available to the system at that moment;
21. 'contractual congestion' means a situation where the level of firm capacity demand exceeds the technical capacity;
22. 'primary market' means the market of the capacity traded directly by the transmission system operator;
23. 'physical congestion' means a situation where the level of demand for actual deliveries exceeds the technical capacity at some point in time.
2. The definitions contained in Article 2 of Directive 2003/55/EC, which are relevant for the application of this Regulation, shall also apply with the exception of the definition of transmission in point 3 of that Article.

Article 3
Tariffs for access to networks

1. Tariffs, or the methodologies used to calculate them, applied by transmission system operators and approved by the regulatory authorities pursuant to Article 25(2) of Directive 2003/55/EC, as well as tariffs published pursuant to Article 18(1) of that Directive, shall be transparent, take into account the need for system integrity and its improvement and reflect actual costs incurred, insofar as such costs correspond to those of an efficient and structurally comparable network operator and are transparent, whilst including appropriate return on investments, and where appropriate taking account of the benchmarking of tariffs by the regulatory authorities. Tariffs, or the methodologies used to calculate them, shall be applied in a non-discriminatory manner.

   Member States may decide that tariffs may also be determined through market-based arrangements, such as auctions, provided that such arrangements and the revenues arising therefrom are approved by the regulatory authority.

   Tariffs, or the methodologies used to calculate them, shall facilitate efficient gas trade and competition, while at the same time avoiding cross-subsidies between network users and providing incentives for investment and maintaining or creating interoperability for transmission networks.

2. Tariffs for network access shall not restrict market liquidity nor distort trade across borders of different transmission systems. Where differences in tariff structures or balancing mechanisms would hamper trade across transmission systems, and notwithstanding Article 25(2) of Directive 2003/55/EC, transmission system operators shall, in close cooperation with the relevant national authorities, actively pursue convergence of tariff structures and charging principles including in relation to balancing.

Article 4
Third party access services

1. Transmission system operators shall:
   (a) ensure that they offer services on a non-discriminatory basis to all network users. In particular, where a transmission system operator offers the same service to different customers, it shall do so under equivalent contractual terms and conditions, either using harmonised transportation contracts or a common network code approved by the competent authority in accordance with the procedure laid down in Article 25 of Directive 2003/55/EC;
   (b) provide both firm and interruptible third party access services. The price of interruptible capacity shall reflect the probability of interruption;
   (c) offer to network users both long and short-term services.
2. Transportation contracts signed with non-standard start dates or with a shorter duration than a standard annual transportation contract shall not result in arbitrarily higher or lower tariffs not reflecting the market value of the service, in accordance with the principles laid down in Article 3(1).
3. Where appropriate, third party access services may be granted subject to appropriate guarantees from network users with respect to the creditworthiness of such users. Such guarantees must not constitute any undue market entry barriers and must be non-discriminatory, transparent and proportionate.

Article 5
Principles of capacity allocation mechanisms and congestion management procedures

1. The maximum capacity at all relevant points referred to in Article 6(3) shall be made available to market participants, taking into account system integrity and efficient network operation.
2. Transmission system operators shall implement and publish non-discriminatory and transparent capacity allocation mechanisms, which shall:
   (a) provide appropriate economic signals for efficient and maximum use of technical capacity and facilitate investment in new infrastructure;

(b) be compatible with the market mechanisms including spot markets and trading hubs, while being flexible and capable of adapting to evolving market circumstances;
(c) be compatible with the network access systems of the Member States.
3. When transmission system operators conclude new transportation contracts or renegotiate existing transportation contracts, these contracts shall take into account the following principles:
   (a) in the event of contractual congestion, the transmission system operator shall offer unused capacity on the primary market at least on a day-ahead and interruptible basis;
   (b) network users who wish to re-sell or sublet their unused contracted capacity on the secondary market shall be entitled to do so. Member States may require notification or information of the transmission system operator by network users.
4. When capacity contracted under existing transportation contracts remains unused and contractual congestion occurs, transmission system operators shall apply paragraph 3 unless this would infringe the requirements of the existing transportation contracts. Where this would infringe the existing transportation contracts, transmission system operators shall, following consultation with the competent authorities, submit a request to the network user for the use on the secondary market of unused capacity in accordance with paragraph 3.
5. In the event that physical congestion exists, non-discriminatory, transparent capacity allocation mechanisms shall be applied by the transmission system operator or, as appropriate, the regulatory authorities.

Article 6
Transparency requirements

1. Transmission system operators shall make public detailed information regarding the services they offer and the relevant conditions applied, together with the technical information necessary for network users to gain effective network access.
2. In order to ensure transparent, objective and non-discriminatory tariffs and facilitate efficient utilisation of the gas network, transmission system operators or relevant national authorities shall publish reasonably and sufficiently detailed information on tariff derivation, methodology and structure.
3. For the services provided, each transmission system operator shall make public information on technical, contracted and available capacities on a numerical basis for all relevant points including entry and exit points on a regular and rolling basis and in a user-friendly standardised manner.
4. The relevant points of a transmission system on which the information must be made public shall be approved by the competent authorities after consultation with network users.
5. Where a transmission system operator considers that it is not entitled for confidentiality reasons to make public all the data required, it shall seek the authorisation of the competent authorities to limit publication with respect to the point or points in question.

   The competent authorities shall grant or refuse the authorisation on a case by case basis, taking into account in particular the need to respect legitimate commercial confidentiality and the objective of creating a competitive internal gas market. If the authorisation is granted, available capacity shall be published without indicating the numerical data that would contravene confidentiality.

   No such authorisation as referred to in this paragraph shall be granted where three or more network users have contracted capacity at the same point.
6. Transmission system operators shall always disclose the information required by this Regulation in a meaningful, quantifiably clear and easily accessible way and on a non-discriminatory basis.

Article 7
Balancing rules and imbalance charges

1. Balancing rules shall be designed in a fair, non-discriminatory and transparent manner and shall be based on objective criteria. Balancing rules shall reflect genuine system needs taking into account the resources available to the transmission system operator.

2. In the case of non-market based balancing systems, tolerance levels shall be designed in a way that either reflects seasonality or results in a tolerance level higher than that resulting from seasonality, and that reflects the actual technical capabilities of the transmission system. Tolerance levels shall reflect genuine system needs taking into account the resources available to the transmission system operator.
3. Imbalance charges shall be cost-reflective to the extent possible, whilst providing appropriate incentives on network users to balance their input and offtake of gas. They shall avoid cross-subsidisation between network users and shall not hamper the entry of new market entrants.

   Any calculation methodology for imbalance charges as well as the final tariffs shall be made public by the competent authorities or the transmission system operator as appropriate.
4. Transmission system operators may impose penalty charges on network users whose input into and offtake from the transmission system is not in balance according to the balancing rules referred to in paragraph 1.
5. Penalty charges which exceed the actual balancing costs incurred, insofar as such costs correspond to those of an efficient and structurally comparable network operator and are transparent, shall be taken into account when calculating tariffs in a way that does not reduce the interest in balancing and shall be approved by the competent authorities.
6. In order to enable network users to take timely corrective action, transmission system operators shall provide sufficient, well-timed and reliable on-line based information on the balancing status of network users. The level of information provided shall reflect the level of information available to the transmission system operator. Where they exist, charges for the provision of such information shall be approved by the competent authorities and shall be made public by the transmission system operator.
7. Member States shall ensure that transmission system operators endeavour to harmonise balancing regimes and streamline structures and levels of balancing charges in order to facilitate gas trade.

Article 8
Trading of capacity rights

Each transmission system operator shall take reasonable steps to allow capacity rights to be freely tradable and to facilitate such trade. Each such operator shall develop harmonised transportation contracts and procedures on the primary market to facilitate secondary trade of capacity and recognise the transfer of primary capacity rights where notified by network users. The harmonised transportation contracts and procedures shall be notified to the regulatory authorities.

Article 9
Guidelines

1. Where appropriate, Guidelines providing the minimum degree of harmonisation required to achieve the aim of this Regulation shall specify:
   (a) details of third party access services including the character, duration and other requirements of these services, in accordance with Article 4;
   (b) details of the principles underlying capacity allocation mechanisms and on the application of congestion management procedures in the event of contractual congestion, in accordance with Article 5;
   (c) details on the definition of the technical information necessary for network users to gain effective access to the system and the definition of all relevant points for transparency requirements, including the information to be published at all relevant points and the time schedule according to which this information shall be published, in accordance with Article 6.
2. Guidelines on the issues listed in paragraph 1 are laid down in the Annex. They may be amended by the Commission; this shall be done in accordance with the procedure referred to in Article 14(2).
3. The application and amendment of Guidelines adopted pursuant to this Regulation shall reflect differences between national gas systems, and shall therefore not require uniform detailed terms

and conditions of third party access at Community level. They may, however, set minimum requirements to be met to achieve non-discriminatory and transparent network access conditions necessary for an internal gas market, which may then be applied in the light of differences between national gas systems.

Article 10
Regulatory authorities

When carrying out their responsibilities under this Regulation, the regulatory authorities of the Member States established under Article 25 of Directive 2003/55/EC shall ensure compliance with this Regulation and the Guidelines adopted pursuant to Article 9 of this Regulation.

Where appropriate they shall cooperate with each other and with the Commission.

Article 11
Provision of information

Member States and the regulatory authorities shall, on request, provide to the Commission all information necessary for the purposes of Article 9.

The Commission shall fix a reasonable time limit within which the information is to be provided, taking into account the complexity of the information required and the urgency with which the information is needed.

Article 12
Right of Member States to provide for more detailed measures

This Regulation shall be without prejudice to the rights of Member States to maintain or introduce measures that contain more detailed provisions than those set out in this Regulation and the Guidelines referred to in Article 9.

Article 13
Penalties

1. The Member States shall lay down the rules on penalties applicable to infringements of the provisions of this Regulation and shall take all measures necessary to ensure that they are implemented. The penalties provided for must be effective, proportionate and dissuasive. The Member States shall notify those provisions to the Commission by 1 July 2006 at the latest and shall notify it without delay of any subsequent amendment affecting them.
2. Penalties provided for pursuant to paragraph 1 shall not be of a criminal law nature.

Article 14
Committee procedure

1. The Commission shall be assisted by the Committee set up by Article 30 of Directive 2003/55/EC.
2. Where reference is made to this paragraph, Articles 5 and 7 of Decision 1999/468/EC shall apply, having regard to the provisions of Article 8 thereof.

    The period laid down in Article 5(6) of Decision 1999/468/EC shall be set at three months.
3. The Committee shall adopt its Rules of Procedure.

Article 15
Commission report

The Commission shall monitor the implementation of this Regulation. In its report under Article 31(3) of Directive 2003/55/EC, the Commission shall also report on the experience gained in the application of this Regulation. In particular the report shall examine to what extent the Regulation has been successful in ensuring non-discriminatory and cost-reflective network access conditions for gas transmission networks in order to contribute to customer choice in a well functioning internal market and to long-term security of supply. If necessary, the report shall be accompanied by appropriate proposals and/or recommendations.

Article 16
Derogations and exemptions

This Regulation shall not apply to:

(a) natural gas transmission systems situated in Member States for the duration of derogations granted under Article 28 of Directive 2003/55/EC; Member States which have been granted derogations under Article 28 of Directive 2003/55/EC may apply to the Commission for a temporary derogation from the application of this Regulation, for a period of up to two years from the date at which the derogation referred to in this point expires;

(b) interconnectors between Member States and significant increases of capacity in existing infrastructures and modifications of such infrastructures which enable the development of new sources of gas supply as referred to in Article 22(1) and (2) of Directive 2003/55/EC which are exempted from the provisions of Articles 18, 19, 20 and 25(2), (3) and (4) of that Directive as long as they are exempted from the provisions referred to in this subparagraph; or

(c) natural gas transmission systems which have been granted derogations under Article 27 of Directive 2003/55/EC.

Article 17
Entry into force

This Regulation shall enter into force on the 20th day following its publication in the *Official Journal of the European Union*.

It shall apply from 1 July 2006 with the exception of the second sentence of Article 9(2), which shall apply from 1 January 2007.

This Regulation shall be binding in its entirety and directly applicable in all Member States.

Done at Strasbourg, 28 September 2005.

ANNEX

Guidelines on

1. Third party access services,
2. Principles underlying the capacity allocation mechanisms, congestion management procedures and their application in the event of contractual congestion, and
3. Definition of the technical information necessary for network users to gain effective access to the system, the definition of all relevant points for transparency requirements and the information to be published at all relevant points and the time schedule according to which this information shall be published

1. Third party access services
   (1) Transmission system operators shall offer firm and interruptible services down to a minimum period of one day.
   (2) Harmonised transportation contracts and common network codes shall be designed in a manner that facilitates trading and re-utilisation of capacity contracted by network users without hampering capacity release.
   (3) Transmission system operators shall develop network codes and harmonised contracts following proper consultation with network users.
   (4) Transmission system operators shall implement standardised nomination and re-nomination procedures. They shall develop information systems and electronic communication means to

provide adequate data to network users and to simplify transactions, such as nominations, capacity contracting and transfer of capacity rights between network users.

(5) Transmission system operators shall harmonise formalised request procedures and response times according to best industry practice with the aim of minimising response times. They shall provide for on-line screen based capacity booking and confirmation systems and nomination and re-nomination procedures no later than 1 July 2006 after consultation with the relevant network users.

(6) Transmission system operators shall not separately charge network users for information requests and transactions associated with their transportation contracts and which are carried out according to standard rules and procedures.

(7) Information requests that require extraordinary or excessive expenses such as feasibility studies may be charged separately, provided the charges can be duly substantiated.

(8) Transmission system operators shall cooperate with other transmission system operators in coordinating the maintenance of their respective networks in order to minimise any disruption of transmission services to network users and transmission system operators in other areas and in order to ensure equal benefits with respect to security of supply including in relation to transit.

(9) Transmission system operators shall publish at least once a year, by a predetermined deadline, all planned maintenance periods that might affect network users' rights from transportation contracts and corresponding operational information with adequate advance notice. This shall include publishing on a prompt and non-discriminatory basis any changes to planned maintenance periods and notification of unplanned maintenance, as soon as that information becomes available to the transmission system operator. During maintenance periods, transmission system operators shall publish regularly updated information on the details of and expected duration and effect of the maintenance.

(10) Transmission system operators shall maintain and make available to the competent authority upon request a daily log of the actual maintenance and flow disruptions that have occurred. Information shall also be made available on request to those affected by any disruption.

2. **Principles underlying capacity allocation mechanisms, congestion management procedures and their application in the event of contractual congestion**

2.1. *Principles underlying capacity allocation mechanisms and congestion management procedures*

(1) Capacity allocation mechanisms and congestion management procedures shall facilitate the development of competition and liquid trading of capacity and shall be compatible with market mechanisms including spot markets and trading hubs. They shall be flexible and capable of adapting to evolving market circumstances.

(2) These mechanisms and procedures shall take into account the integrity of the system concerned as well as security of supply.

(3) These mechanisms and procedures shall neither hamper the entry of new market participants nor create undue barriers to market entry. They shall not prevent market participants, including new market entrants and companies with a small market share, from competing effectively.

(4) These mechanisms and procedures shall provide appropriate economic signals for efficient and maximum use of technical capacity and facilitate investment in new infrastructure.

(5) Network users shall be advised about the type of circumstance that could affect the availability of contracted capacity. Information on interruption should reflect the level of information available to the transmission system operator.

(6) Should difficulties in meeting contractual delivery obligations arise due to system integrity reasons, transmission system operators should notify network users and seek a non-discriminatory solution without delay.

Transmission system operators shall consult network users regarding procedures prior to their implementation and agree them with the regulatory authority.

2.2. *Congestion management procedures in the event of contractual congestion*

(1) In the event that contracted capacity goes unused, transmission system operators shall make this capacity available on the primary market on an interruptible basis via contracts of differing duration, as long as this capacity is not offered by the relevant network user on the secondary market at a reasonable price.

(2) Revenues from released interruptible capacity shall be split according to rules laid down or approved by the relevant regulatory authority. These rules shall be compatible with the requirement of an effective and efficient use of the system.

(3) A reasonable price for released interruptible capacity may be determined by the relevant regulatory authorities taking into account the specific circumstances prevailing.

(4) Where appropriate, transmission system operators shall make reasonable endeavours to offer at least parts of the unused capacity to the market as firm capacity.

3. **Definition of the technical information necessary for network users to gain effective access to the system, the definition of all relevant points for transparency requirements and the information to be published at all relevant points and the time schedule according to which this information shall be published**

3.1. *Definition of the technical information necessary for network users to gain effective access to the system*

Transmission system operators shall publish at least the following information about their systems and services:

(a) a detailed and comprehensive description of the different services offered and their charges;

(b) the different types of transportation contracts available for these services and, as applicable, the network code and/or the standard conditions outlining the rights and responsibilities of all network users including harmonised transportation contracts and other relevant documents;

(c) the harmonised procedures applied when using the transmission system, including the definition of key terms;

(d) provisions on capacity allocation, congestion management and anti-hoarding and re-utilisation procedures;

(e) the rules applicable for capacity trade on the secondary market vis-à-vis the transmission system operator;

(f) if applicable, the flexibility and tolerance levels included in transportation and other services without separate charge, as well as any flexibility offered in addition to this and the corresponding charges;

(g) a detailed description of the gas system of the transmission system operator indicating all relevant points interconnecting its system with that of other transmission system operators and/or gas infrastructure such as liquefied natural gas (LNG) and infrastructure necessary for providing ancillary services as defined by Article 2(14) of Directive 2003/55/EC;

(h) information on gas quality and pressure requirements;

(i) the rules applicable for connection to the system operated by the transmission system operator;

(j) any information, in a timely manner, on proposed and/or actual changes to the services or conditions, including the items listed in points (a) to (i).

3.2. *Definition of all relevant points for transparency requirements*

Relevant points shall include at least:

(a) all entry points to a network operated by a transmission system operator;

(b) the most important exit points and exit zones covering at least 50 % of total exit capacity of the network of a given transmission system operator, including all exit points or exit zones covering more than 2 % of total exit capacity of the network;
(c) all points connecting different networks of transmission system operators;
(d) all points connecting the network of a transmission system operator with an LNG terminal;
(e) all essential points within the network of a given transmission system operator including points connecting to gas hubs. All points are considered essential which, based on experience, are likely to experience physical congestion;
(f) all points connecting the network of a given transmission system operator to infrastructure necessary for providing ancillary services as defined by Article 2(14) of Directive 2003/55/EC.

3.3. *Information to be published at all relevant points and the time schedule according to which this information should be published*

(1) At all relevant points, transmission system operators shall publish the following information about the capacity situation down to daily periods on the Internet on a regular/rolling basis and in a user-friendly standardised manner:
   (a) the maximum technical capacity for flows in both directions,
   (b) the total contracted and interruptible capacity,
   (c) the available capacity.
(2) For all relevant points, transmission system operators shall publish available capacities for a period of at least 18 months ahead and shall update this information at least every month or more frequently, if new information becomes available.
(3) Transmission system operators shall publish daily updates of availability of short-term services (day-ahead and week-ahead) based, *inter alia,* on nominations, prevailing contractual commitments and regular long-term forecasts of available capacities on an annual basis for up to 10 years for all relevant points.
(4) Transmission system operators shall publish historical maximum and minimum monthly capacity utilisation rates and annual average flows at all relevant points for the past three years on a rolling basis.
(5) Transmission system operators shall keep a daily log of actual aggregated flows for at least three months.
(6) Transmission system operators shall keep effective records of all capacity contracts and all other relevant information in relation to calculating and providing access to available capacities, to which relevant national authorities shall have access to fulfil their duties.
(7) Transmission system operators shall provide user-friendly instruments for calculating tariffs for the services available and for verifying on-line the capacity available.
(8) Where transmission system operators are unable to publish information in accordance with paragraphs 1, 3 and 7, they shall consult with their relevant national authorities and set up an Action Plan for implementation as soon as possible, but not later than 31 December 2006.

APPENDIX 5

Commission Decision

of 9 November 2006

amending the Annex to Regulation (EC) No 1228/2003 on conditions for access to the network for cross-border exchanges in electricity

(Text with EEA relevance)

(2006/770/EC)

THE COMMISSION OF THE EUROPEAN COMMUNITIES,

Having regard to the Treaty establishing the European Community,

Having regard to Regulation (EC) No 1228/2003 of the European Parliament and of the Council of 26 June 2003 on conditions for access to the network for cross-border exchanges in electricity,[1] and in particular Article 8(4) thereof,

Whereas:

(1) Regulation (EC) No 1228/2003 set up guidelines on the management and allocation of available transfer capacity of interconnections between national systems.

(2) Efficient methods of congestion management should be introduced in these guidelines for cross-border electricity interconnection capacities in order to ensure effective access to transmission systems for the purpose of cross-border transactions.

(3) The measures provided for in this Decision are in accordance with the opinion of the Committee referred to Article 13(2) of Regulation (EC) No 1228/2003,

HAS DECIDED AS FOLLOWS:

Article 1

The Annex to Regulation (EC) No 1228/2003 is replaced by the Annex to this Decision.

Article 2

This Decision shall enter into force on the twentieth day following that of its publication in the *Official Journal of the European Union*.

Done at Brussels, 9 November 2006.

---

[1] OJ L 176, 15.7.2003, p 1.

Appendix 5

ANNEX

Guidelines on the management and allocation of available transfer capacity of interconnections between national systems

1. **General Provisions**
1.1. TSOs shall endeavour to accept all commercial transactions, including those involving cross-border-trade.
1.2. When there is no congestion, there shall be no restriction of access to the interconnection. Where this is usually the case, there need be no permanent general allocation procedure for access to a cross-border transmission service.
1.3. Where scheduled commercial transactions are not compatible with secure network operation, the TSOs shall alleviate congestion in compliance with the requirements of grid operational security while endeavouring to ensure that any associated costs remain at an economically efficient level. Curative redispatching or countertrading shall be envisaged in case lower cost measures cannot be applied.
1.4. If structural congestion appears, appropriate congestion management rules and arrangements defined and agreed upon in advance shall be implemented immediately by the TSOs. The Congestion management methods shall ensure that the physical power flows associated with all allocated transmission capacity comply with network security standards.
1.5. The methods adopted for congestion management shall give efficient economic signals to market participants and TSOs, promote competition and be suitable for regional and communitywide application.
1.6. No transaction-based distinction may be applied in congestion management. A particular request for transmission service shall be denied only when the following conditions are jointly fulfilled:
    (a) the incremental physical power flows resulting from the acceptance of this request imply that secure operation of the power system may no longer be guaranteed, and
    (b) the value in monetary amount attached to this request in the congestion management procedure is lower than all other requests intended to be accepted for the same service and conditions.
1.7. When defining appropriate network areas in and between which congestion management is to apply, TSOs shall be guided by the principles of cost-effectiveness and minimisation of negative impacts on the Internal Electricity Market. Specifically, TSOs may not limit interconnection capacity in order to solve congestion inside their own control area, except for the above mentioned reasons and reasons of operational security[2]. If such a situation occurs, this shall be described and transparently presented to all the users by the TSOs. Such a situation may be tolerated only until a long-term solution is found. The methodology and projects for achieving the long-term solution shall be described and transparently presented to all the users by the TSOs.
1.8. When balancing the network inside the control area through operational measures in the network and through redispatching, the TSO shall take into account the effect of these measures on neighbouring control areas.
1.9. By not later than 1 January 2008, mechanisms for the intra-day congestion management of interconnector capacity shall be established in a coordinated way and under secure operational conditions, in order to maximise opportunities for trade and to provide for cross-border balancing.
1.10. The national Regulatory Authorities shall regularly evaluate the congestion management methods, paying particular attention to compliance with the principles and rules established

---

[2] Operational security means 'keeping the transmission system within agreed security limits'.

in the present Regulation and Guidelines and with the terms and conditions set by the Regulatory Authorities themselves under these principles and rules. Such evaluation shall include consultation of all market players and dedicated studies.

2. **Congestion management methods**

2.1. Congestion management methods shall be market-based in order to facilitate efficient cross-border trade. For this purpose, capacity shall be allocated only by means of explicit (capacity) or implicit (capacity and energy) auctions. Both methods may coexist on the same interconnection. For intra-day trade continuous trading may be used.

2.2. Depending on competition conditions, the congestion management mechanisms may need to allow for both long- and short-term transmission capacity allocation.

2.3. Each capacity allocation procedure shall allocate a prescribed fraction of the available interconnection capacity plus any remaining capacity not previously allocated and any capacity released by capacity holders from previous allocations.

2.4. TSOs shall optimise the degree to which capacity is firm, taking into account the obligations and rights of the TSOs involved and the obligations and rights of market participants, in order to facilitate effective and efficient competition. A reasonable fraction of capacity may be offered to the market at a reduced degree of firmness, but the exact conditions for transport over cross-border lines shall at all times be made known to market participants.

2.5. The access rights for long- and medium-term allocations shall be firm transmission capacity rights. They shall be subject to the use-it-or-lose-it or use-it-or-sell-it principles at the time of nomination.

2.6. TSOs shall define an appropriate structure for the allocation of capacity between different timeframes. This may include an option for reserving a minimum percentage of interconnection capacity for daily or intra-daily allocation. This allocation structure shall be subject to review by the respective Regulatory Authorities. In drawing up their proposals, the TSOs shall take into account:
   (a) the characteristics of the markets,
   (b) the operational conditions, such as the implications of netting firmly declared schedules,
   (c) the level of harmonisation of the percentages and timeframes adopted for the different capacity allocation mechanisms in place.

2.7. Capacity allocation may not discriminate between market participants that wish to use their rights to make use of bilateral supply contracts or to bid into power exchanges. The highest value bids, whether implicit or explicit in a given timeframe, shall be successful.

2.8. In regions where forward financial electricity markets are well developed and have shown their efficiency, all interconnection capacity may be allocated through implicit auctioning.

2.9. Other than in the case of new interconnectors which benefit from an exemption under Article 7 of the Regulation, establishing reserve prices in capacity allocation methods shall not be allowed.

2.10. In principle, all potential market participants shall be permitted to participate in the allocation process without restriction. To avoid creating or aggravating problems related to the potential use of dominant position of any market player, the relevant Regulatory and/or Competition Authorities, where appropriate, may impose restrictions in general or on an individual company on account of market dominance.

2.11. Market participants shall firmly nominate their use of the capacity to the TSOs by a defined deadline for each timeframe. The deadline shall be set such that TSOs are able to reassign unused capacity for reallocation in the next relevant timeframe—including intra-day sessions.

2.12. Capacity shall be freely tradable on a secondary basis, provided that the TSO is informed sufficiently in advance. Where a TSO refuses any secondary trade (transaction), this must be clearly and transparently communicated and explained to all the market participants by that TSO and notified to the Regulatory Authority.

2.13. The financial consequences of failure to honour obligations associated with the allocation of capacity shall be attributed to those who are responsible for such a failure. Where market participants fail to use the capacity that they have committed to use, or, in the case of explicitly auctioned capacity, fail to trade on a secondary basis or give the capacity back in due time, they shall lose the rights to such capacity and pay a cost-reflective charge. Any cost-reflective charges for the non-use of capacity shall be justified and proportionate. Likewise, if a TSO does not fulfil its obligation, it shall be liable to compensate the market participant for the loss of capacity rights. No consequential losses shall be taken into account for this purpose. The key concepts and methods for the determination of liabilities that accrue upon failure to honour obligations shall be set out in advance in respect of the financial consequences, and shall be subject to review by the relevant national Regulatory Authority or Authorities.

3. **Coordination**

3.1. Capacity allocation at an interconnection shall be coordinated and implemented using common allocation procedures by the TSOs involved. In cases where commercial exchanges between two countries (TSOs) are expected to significantly affect physical flow conditions in any third country (TSO), congestion management methods shall be coordinated between all the TSOs so affected through a common congestion management procedure. National Regulatory Authorities and TSOs shall ensure that no congestion management procedure with significant effects on physical electric power flows in other networks is devised unilaterally.

3.2. A common coordinated congestion management method and procedure for the allocation of capacity to the market at least yearly, monthly and day-ahead shall be applied by not later than 1 January 2007 between countries in the following regions:
   (a) Northern Europe (ie Denmark, Sweden, Finland, Germany and Poland),
   (b) North-West Europe (ie Benelux, Germany and France),
   (c) Italy (ie Italy, France, Germany, Austria, Slovenia and Greece),
   (d) Central Eastern Europe (ie Germany, Poland, Czech Republic, Slovakia, Hungary, Austria and Slovenia),
   (e) South-West Europe (ie Spain, Portugal and France),
   (f) UK, Ireland and France,
   (g) Baltic states (ie Estonia, Latvia and Lithuania).

   At an interconnection involving countries belonging to more than one region, the congestion management method applied may differ in order to ensure the compatibility with the methods applied in the other regions to which these countries belong. In this case the relevant TSOs shall propose the method which shall be subject to review by the relevant Regulatory Authorities.

3.3. The regions referred to in 2.8. may allocate all interconnection capacity through day-ahead allocation.

3.4. Compatible congestion management procedures shall be defined in all these seven regions with a view to forming a truly integrated Internal European Electricity Market. Market parties shall not be confronted with incompatible regional systems.

3.5. With a view to promoting fair and efficient competition and cross-border trade, coordination between TSOs within the regions set out in 3.2. above shall include all the steps from capacity calculation and optimisation of allocation to secure operation of the network, with clear assignments of responsibility. Such coordination shall include, in particular:
   (a) Use of a common transmission model dealing efficiently with interdependent physical loop-flows and having regard to discrepancies between physical and commercial flows,
   (b) Allocation and nomination of capacity to deal efficiently with interdependent physical loop-flows,
   (c) Identical obligations on capacity holders to provide information on their intended use of the capacity, ie nomination of capacity (for explicit auctions),
   (d) Identical timeframes and closing times,

(e) Identical structure for the allocation of capacity among different timeframes (eg 1 day, 3 hours, 1 week, etc.) and in terms of blocks of capacity sold (amount of power in MW, MWh, etc.),
(f) Consistent contractual framework with market participants,
(g) Verification of flows to comply with the network security requirements for operational planning and for realtime operation,
(h) Accounting and settlement of congestion management actions.

3.6. Coordination shall also include the exchange of information between TSOs. The nature, time and frequency of information exchange shall be compatible with the activities in 3.5 and the functioning of the electricity markets. This information exchange shall in particular enable the TSOs to make the best possible forecast of the global grid situation in order to assess the flows in their network and the available interconnection capacities. Any TSO collecting information on behalf of other TSOs shall give back to the participating TSO the results of the collection of data.

4. **Timetable for market operations**

4.1. The allocation of the available transmission capacity shall take place sufficiently in advance. Prior to each allocation, the involved TSOs shall jointly publish the capacity to be allocated, taking into account where appropriate the capacity released from any firm transmission rights and, where relevant, associated netted nominations, along with any time periods during which the capacity will be reduced or not available (for the purpose of maintenance, for example).

4.2. Having full regard to network security, the nomination of transmission rights shall take place sufficiently in advance, before the day-ahead sessions of all the relevant organised markets and before the publication of the capacity to be allocated under the day-ahead or intra-day allocation mechanism. Nominations of transmission rights in the opposite direction shall be netted in order to make efficient use of the interconnection.

4.3. Successive intra-day allocations of available transmission capacity for day D shall take place on days D-1 and D, after the issuing of the indicated or actual day-ahead production schedules.

4.4. When preparing day-ahead grid operation, the TSOs shall exchange information with neighbouring TSOs, including their forecast grid topology, the availability and forecasted production of generation units, and load flows in order to optimise the use of the overall network through operational measures in compliance with the rules for secure grid operation.

5. **Transparency**

5.1. TSOs shall publish all relevant data related to network availability, network access and network use, including a report on where and why congestion exists, the methods applied for managing the congestion and the plans for its future management.

5.2. TSOs shall publish a general description of the congestion management method applied under different circumstances for maximising the capacity available to the market, and a general scheme for the calculation of the interconnection capacity for the different timeframes, based upon the electrical and physical realities of the network. Such a scheme shall be subject to review by the Regulatory Authorities of the Member States concerned.

5.3. The congestion management and capacity allocation procedures in use, together with the times and procedures for applying for capacity, a description of the products offered and the obligations and rights of both the TSOs and the party obtaining the capacity, including the liabilities that accrue upon failure to honour obligations, shall be described in detail and made transparently available to all potential network users by TSOs.

5.4. The operational and planning security standards shall form an integral part of the information that TSOs publish in an open and public document. This document shall also be subject to review of national Regulatory Authorities.

5.5. TSOs shall publish all relevant data concerning cross-border trade on the basis of the best possible forecast. In order to fulfil this obligation the market participants concerned shall provide the TSOs with the relevant data. The way in which such information is published shall be subject to review by Regulatory Authorities. TSOs shall publish at least:

(a) annually: information on the long-term evolution of the transmission infrastructure and its impact on cross-border transmission capacity;

(b) monthly: month- and year-ahead forecasts of the transmission capacity available to the market, taking into account all relevant information available to the TSO at the time of the forecast calculation (eg impact of summer and winter seasons on the capacity of lines, maintenance on the grid, availability of production units, etc.);

(c) weekly: week-ahead forecasts of the transmission capacity available to the market, taking into account all relevant information available to the TSOs at the time of calculation of the forecast, such as the weather forecast, planned maintenance works of the grid, availability of production units, etc.;

(d) daily: day-ahead and intra-day transmission capacity available to the market for each market time unit, taking into account all netted day-ahead nominations, day-ahead production schedules, demand forecasts and planned maintenance works of the grid;

(e) total capacity already allocated, by market time unit, and all relevant conditions under which this capacity may be used (eg auction clearing price, obligations on how to use the capacity, etc.), so as to identify any remaining capacity;

(f) allocated capacity as soon as possible after each allocation, as well as an indication of prices paid;

(g) total capacity used, by market time unit, immediately after nomination;

(h) as closely as possible to real time: aggregated realised commercial and physical flows, by market time unit, including a description of the effects of any corrective actions taken by the TSOs (such as curtailment) for solving network or system problems;

(i) ex-ante information on planned outages and ex-post information for the previous day on planned and unplanned outages of generation units larger than 100 MW.

5.6. All relevant information shall be available for the market in due time for the negotiation of all transactions (such as the time of negotiation of annual supply contracts for industrial customers or the time when bids have to be sent into organised markets).

5.7. The TSO shall publish the relevant information on forecast demand and on generation according to the timeframes referred to in 5.5 and 5.6. The TSO shall also publish the relevant information necessary for the cross-border balancing market.

5.8. When forecasts are published, the ex post realised values for the forecast information shall also be published in the time period following that to which the forecast applies or at the latest on the following day (D+1).

5.9. All information published by the TSOs shall be made freely available in an easily accessible form. All data shall also be accessible through adequate and standardised means of information exchange, to be defined in close cooperation with market parties. The data shall include information on past time periods with a minimum of two years, so that new market entrants may also have access to such data.

5.10. TSOs shall exchange regularly a set of sufficiently accurate network and load flow data in order to enable load flow calculations for each TSO in their relevant area. The same set of data shall be made available to the Regulatory Authorities and to the European Commission upon request. The Regulatory Authorities and the European Commission shall ensure the confidential treatment of this set of data, by themselves and by any consultant carrying out analytical work for them on the basis of these data.

6. **Use of congestion income**

6.1. Congestion management procedures associated with a pre-specified timeframe may generate revenue only in the event of congestion which arises for that timeframe, except in the case of new interconnectors which benefit from an exemption under Article 7 of the Regulation. The procedure for the distribution of these revenues shall be subject to review by the Regulatory

New Annex to Electricity Regulation

Authorities and shall neither distort the allocation process in favour of any party requesting capacity or energy nor provide a disincentive to reduce congestion.

6.2. National Regulatory Authorities shall be transparent regarding the use of revenues resulting from the allocation of interconnection capacity.

6.3. The congestion income shall be shared among the TSOs involved according to criteria agreed between the TSOs involved and reviewed by the respective Regulatory Authorities.

6.4. TSOs shall clearly establish beforehand the use they will make of any congestion income they may obtain and report on the actual use of this income. Regulatory Authorities shall verify that this use complies with the present Regulation and Guidelines and that the total amount of congestion income resulting from the allocation of interconnection capacity is devoted to one or more of the three purposes described in Article 6(6) of Regulation.

6.5. On an annual basis, and by 31 July each year, the Regulatory Authorities shall publish a report setting out the amount of revenue collected for the 12-month period up to 30 June of the same year and the use made of the revenues in question, together with verification that this use complies with the present Regulation and Guidelines and that the total amount of congestion income is devoted to one or more of the three prescribed purposes.

6.6. The use of congestion income for investment to maintain or increase interconnection capacity shall preferably be assigned to specific predefined projects which contribute to relieving the existing associated congestion and which may also be implemented within a reasonable time, particularly as regards the authorisation process.

SELECT BIBLIOGRAPHY

BOOKS

Ariño Ortiz, GO, *Principios de Derecho Público Económico* (Comares Editorial, 1999)
Arnull, A, *The European Court of Justice* (2nd edn, Oxford University Press, 2006)
Barton, B, Redgwell, C, Ronne, A, and Zillman, DN, (eds), *Energy Security: Managing Risk in a Dynamic Legal and Regulatory Environment* (Oxford University Press, 2004)
Bellamy, CW and Child, GD, *European Community Law of Competition* (5th edn, Roth, PM, (ed), Sweet and Maxwell, 2001)
Buendia Sierra, JL, *Exclusive Rights and State Monopolies under EC Law* (Oxford University Press, 1999)
Cameron, PD, (ed), *Legal Aspects of EU Energy Regulation: Implementing the New Directives on Electricity and Gas across Europe* (Oxford University Press, 2005)
——, *Competition in Energy Markets: Law and Regulation in the European Union* (Oxford University Press, 2002)
——, *Property Rights and Sovereign Rights: the Case of North Sea Oil* (Academic Press, 1983)
—— and Zillman, D, (eds), *Kyoto: From Principles to Practice* (Kluwer Law International, 2002)
Chalmers, D, Hadjiemmanuil, C, Monti, G, and Tomkins, A, *European Union Law* (Cambridge University Press, 2006)
Cowgill, A and Cowgill, A, *The European Constitution in Perspective: Analysis and Review of The Treaty Establishing a Constitution for Europe* (British Management Data Foundation, 2004)
Daintith, T and Hancher, L, *Energy Strategy in Europe: The Legal Framework* (Walter de Gruyter, 1986)
—— and Williams, S, *The Legal Integration of Energy Markets* (Walter de Gruyter, 1987)
De Jong, J, Weeda, E, Westerwoudt, T and Correlje, A, *Dertig Jaar Nederlands Energiebelied* (Clingendael International Energy Programme, 2005)
Delbeke, J et al, *EU Energy Law, Vol IV: Environmental Law: the EU Greenhouse Gas Emissions Trading Scheme* (Claeys & Casteels, 2006)
Ehlermann, CD and Gosling, L, (eds), *Regulating Communications Markets* (Hart Publishing, 2000)
Faull, J and Nikpay, A, *EC Competition Law* (2nd edn, Oxford University Press, 2007)
—— and ——, *EC Competition Law* (Oxford University Press, 1999)
Freestone, D and Streck, C, (eds), 'Legal Aspects of Implementing the Kyoto Protocol Mechanisms: Making Kyoto Work' (Oxford University Press, 2005)
Giddens, A, *The Third Way: the Renewal of Social Democracy* (Polity Press, 1998)
——, *The Third Way and its Critics* (Polity Press, 2000)
Goyder, DG, *EC Competition Law* (4th edn, Oxford University Press, 2003)
Grunwald, J, *Das Energierecht der Europäischen Gemeinschaften* (De Gruyter Recht: Berlin, 2003)
Hayes-Renshaw, F and Wallace, H, *The Council of Ministers* (2nd edn, Palgrave, 2006)
Helm, D, (ed), *Climate Change Policy* (Oxford University Press, 2005)
——, *Energy, the State, and the Market: British Energy Policy since 1979* (2nd edn, Oxford University Press, 2004)
Horbach, NLJT, *Contemporary Developments in Nuclear Energy Law: Harmonising Legislation in CEEC/NIS* (Kluwer Law International, 1999)

Select Bibliography

Jensen, JT, *The Development of a Global LNG Market: Is it likely? If so, when?* (Oxford Institute of Energy Studies, 2004)

Jones, CW, *EU Energy Law, Vol I: The Internal Energy Market* (2nd edn, Claeys & Casteels, 2006)

Kahn, AE, *The Economics of Regulation: Principles and Institutions* (MIT Press, 1998)

Kalicki, JH and Goldwyn, DL, (eds), *Energy and Security: Towards a New Foreign Policy Strategy* (Woodrow Wilson Center Press/The Johns Hopkins University Press, 2005)

Kapteyn, PJG and VerLoren van Themaat, P, *Introduction to the Law of the European Communities: From Maastricht to Amsterdam* (3rd edn, Gormley, L, (ed), Kluwer, 1998)

Kuhn, T, *The Structure of Scientific Revolutions* (University of Chicago Press, 1970)

Larouche, P, *Competition Law and Regulation in European Telecommunications* (Hart Publishing, 2000)

McCahery, J, Bratton, WW, Picciotto, S, and Scott, C, *International Regulatory Competition and Coordination: Perspectives on Economic Regulation in Europe and the US* (Oxford University Press, 1996)

Natalicchi, G, *Wiring Europe: reshaping the European telecommunications regime* (Rowman and Littlefield, 2001)

Navarro, E, Font, A, Folguera, J, and Briones, J, *Merger Control in the EU: Law, Economics and Practice* (2nd edn, Oxford University Press, 2005)

Newbery, DM, *Privatization, Restructuring, and Regulation of Network Utilities* (MIT Press, 1999)

OECD/IEA, *Electricity Market Reform: An IEA Handbook* (OECD, 1999)

——, *Lessons from Liberalised Electricity Markets* (OECD, 2005)

——, *Regulatory Reform in Argentina's Natural Gas Sector* (OECD, 1999)

——, *Regulatory Reform in Mexico's Natural Gas Sector* (OECD, 1996)

Ogus, A, *Legal Form and Economic Theory* (Oxford University Press, 1994)

Ohmae, K, *The End of the Nation State: The Rise of Regional Economies* (Harper-Collins, 1996)

Patterson, W, *Transforming Electricity* (Earthscan/RIIA, 1999)

Pfrang, E, *Towards Liberalisation of the European Energy Markets* (Peter Lang, 1999)

Prechal, S, *Directives in Community Law: A Study of Directives and their Enforcement in National Courts* (2nd edn, Oxford University Press, 2005)

Prosser, T, *Law and the Regulators* (Oxford University Press, 1997)

——, *The Limits of Competition Law: Markets and Public Services* (Oxford University Press, 2005)

Roggenkamp, MM and Boisseleau, F, *The Regulation of Power Exchanges* (Intersentia, 2005)

Sassen, S, *Losing Control? Sovereignty in an Age of Globalization* (Columbia University Press, 1996)

Sauter, W, *Competition Law and Industrial Policy in the EU* (Oxford University Press, 1997)

Sidak, G, and Spulber, D, *Deregulatory Takings and the Regulatory Contract: the Competitive Transformation of Network Industries in the US* (Cambridge University Press, 1998)

Stiglitz, J, *Globalization and its Discontents* (WW Norton, 2003)

——, *Making Globalization Work* (Allen Lane, 2006)

Weatherill, S, *Law and Integration in the European Union* (Oxford University Press, 1995)

Zaccour, G, (ed), *Deregulation of Electric Utilities* (Kluwer Law International, 1998)

ARTICLES AND CHAPTERS IN BOOKS

Albers, M, 'The New EU Directives on Energy Liberalization from a Competition Point of View' in Cameron, PD, (ed), *Legal Aspects of EU Energy Regulation: Implementing the New Directives on Electricity and Gas Across Europe* (Oxford University Press, 2005) 41–58

——, 'Horizontal Restraints on Competition' in Jones, CW, *EU Energy Law, Vol II: EU Competition Law and Energy Markets* (Claeys & Castells, 2005) 113–71

Cameron, PD, 'Joint Convention on the Safety of Spent Fuel Management and on the Safety of Radioactive Waste Management' in Horbach, NLT, (ed), *Contemporary Developments in Nuclear Energy Law: Harmonising Legislation in CEEC/NIS* (Kluwer Law International, 1999) 117–28

——, 'Completing the Internal Market in Energy: An Introduction to the New Legislation' in Cameron, PD, (ed), *Legal Aspects of EU Energy Regulation: Implementing the New Directives on Electricity and Gas across Europe* (Oxford University Press, 2005) 7–39

Coen, D and Doyle, C, 'Designing Economic Regulatory Institutions for European Network Industries' in Coen, D and Thatcher, M, (eds), *Current Politics and Economics of Europe* (Nova Science Publishers, 2000) 455–76

Daintith, T, 'Regulation: Legal Form and Economic Theory' in *International Encyclopaedia of Comparative Law, Vol XVII: State and Economy* (Brill, 1981) Ch 10

Devlin, B and Levasseur, C, 'Energy' in Faull, J and Nikpay, A, (eds), *The EC Law of Competition* (1st edn, Oxford University Press, 2000)

Eberlein, B, 'Configurations of Economic Regulation in the European Union: the case of electricity in comparative perspective' in Coen, D and Thatcher, M, (eds), *Current Politics and Economics of Europe* (Nova Science Publishers, 2000) 407–25

——, 'Regulation by Cooperation: The "Third Way" in Making Rules for the Internal Energy Market' in Cameron, PD, (ed), *Legal Aspects of EU Energy Regulation: Implementing the New Directives on Electricity and Gas across Europe* (Oxford University Press, 2005) 59–88.

Fingleton, J, 'The Role of Economics in Merger Review' in Robinson, C, (ed), *Regulating Utilities and Promoting Competition: Lessons for the Future* (Edward Elgar, 2006) 161–83

Flynn, L, 'Access to the Postal Networks: the Situation after Bronner' in Geradin, G and Humpe, C, *Postal Services, Liberalisation and EC Competition Law* (Kluwer Law International, 2002) 181–204

Garayar, E, 'National Approaches to Implementation: Spain' in Cameron, PD, (ed), *Legal Aspects of EU Energy Regulation: Implementing the New Directives on Electricity and Gas across Europe* (Oxford University Press, 2005) 315–44

Grunwald, J, 'The Rôle of Euratom' in Cameron, PD, Hancher, L, and Kuhne, W, (eds), *Nuclear Energy Law After Chernobyl* (Graeme and Trotman, 1988) 33–48

Koenings, M, 'Wind Energy and the Context of EU State Aid Law' in Roggenkamp, MM and Hammer, U, *European Energy Law Report I* (Intersentia, 2004) 73–90

Maresceau, M, 'Association, Partnership, Pre-Accession and Accession' in Maresceau, M, (ed), *Enlarging the EU: Relations between Central and Eastern Europe* (Longman, 1997) 12

Nocera, F and Roggenkamp, MM, 'Energy Law in Italy' in Roggenkamp, MM, Ronne, A, Redgwell, C, and Del Guayo, I, *Energy Law in Europe: National, EU and International Law and Institutions* (Oxford University Press, 2001) 569–627

Nyssens, H, and Schnichels, D, 'Energy' in Faull, J and Nikpay, A, *The EC Law of Competition* (2nd edn, Oxford University Press, 2006)

Pritzsche, K and Klauer, S, 'National Approaches to Implementation: Germany' in Cameron, PD, *Legal Aspects of EU Energy Regulation: Implementing the New Directives on Electricity and Gas across Europe* (Oxford University Press, 2005) 145–71

Protasio, M and Pinto Correia, C, 'National Approaches to Implementation: Portugal', in Cameron, PD, *Legal Aspects of EU Energy Regulation: Implementing the New Directives on Electricity and Gas across Europe* (Oxford University Press, 2005) 287–313

Schwarze, J, 'European Energy Policy in Community Law', in Mestmaeker EJ, (ed), *Natural Gas in the Internal Market* (Kluwer Law International, 1992) 155

Sharpe, T, 'Trying to Make Sense of Abuse of a Dominant Position' in Robinson, C, *Regulating Utilities and Promoting Competition: Lessons for the Future* (Edward Elgar, 2006) 138–55

Steiner, J, 'Subsidiarity under the Maastricht Treaty' in O'Keeffe, D, (ed), *Legal Issues of the Maastricht Treaty* (Kluwer Law International,1994) 49

Temple-Lang, J, 'Decentralised Application of Community Competition Law' in Rivas, J and Horspool, M, (eds), *Modernisation and Decentralisation of EC Competition Law* (Kluwer Law International, 2000) 13–29

Tesauro, G, 'Modernisation and Decentralisation of EC Competition Law' in Rivas, J and Horspool, M, (eds), *Modernisation and Decentralisation of EC Competition Law* (Kluwer Law International, 2000) 1–12

Toth, A, 'A Legal Analysis of Subsidiarity' in O'Keeffe, D, (ed), *Legal Issues of the Maastricht Treaty* (Kluwer Law International, 1994) 37

Usher, J, 'The Commission and the Law' in Edwards, G and Spence, D, (eds), *The European Commission* (Cartermill, 1994) 212

Vasconcelos, J, 'Co-operation between Energy Regulators in the European Union' in Henry, C, Matheu, M, and Jeunemaitre, A, (eds), *Regulation of Network Utilities* (Oxford University Press, 2001) 284–89

ARTICLES AND PAPERS

Ad hoc Group 2 EU Emissions Trading Scheme: Chairman Issues Paper, 5 April 2006, 3

Albers, M, 'Energy Liberalization and EC Competition Law' in International Antitrust Law & Policy: Fordham Corporate Law 2001 (2002) 393–421

Allen, D, 'The Euratom Treaty, Chapter IV: New Hope or False Dawn?' (1983) 20 CML Rev 473

Bamberger, CS, Linehan, J, and Waelde, T, 'Energy Charter Treaty in 2000: in a New Phase' (2000) 18 J Energy Natural Resources L 331–52

Bartok, C, Moonen, S, Lahbabi, P, Paolicchi, A, and De la Mano, M, 'A Combination of gas release programmes and ownership unbundling as remedy to a problematic energy merger: E.ON/MOL' (2006) 1 Competition Policy Newsletter 73–83

Blanchard, P, 'French Electricity Sector: ECJ Decision on Monopolies for the Import and Export of Electricity' (1999) 17 J Energy Natural Resources L 265–80

Böge, U, 'Merger Control and Regulation of the Energy Sector: Contradiction or Complement?', paper presented at the Second Annual EU Energy Law and Policy Workshop, European University Institute, Florence, 25 September 2003 (author's copy)

Börner, AR, 'Negotiated Third Party Access in Germany: Electricity and Gas' (2001) 19 J Energy Natural Resources L 32

Bouquet, A, 'The Euratom provisions on nuclear supply and ownership' (2000) 68 Nuclear Law Bulletin 1–32

Brice, A, 'A Methodology for Analysing State Aid Linked to Stranded Costs' (2001) 3 Competition Policy Newsletter 25–7.

Brinkhorst, L, 'Subsidiarity and EC Environmental Policy' (1993) 8 European Environmental L Rev 20

Brothwood, M, 'The EU Gas Directive and Take or Pay Contracts' [1998] Oil Gas L Taxation Rev 318

Cameron, PD, 'The Rules of Engagement: Developing Cross-Border Petroleum Deposits in the North Sea and the Caribbean' (2006) 55 ICLQ 559–86

——, 'The Consumer and the Internal Market in Energy: Who Benefits?' (2006) 31 ELR 114–24

——, 'The Internal Market in Energy: Harnessing the New Regulatory Regime' (2005) 30 European L Rev 631–48

——, 'Het Verdrag inzake het Energiehandvest: een beoordeling na zes jaar' (2001) SEW 139–48

——, 'Towards an Internal Market in Energy: The Carrot and Stick Approach' (1998) 23 ELR 579–91

——, 'The Revival of Nuclear Power: An Analysis of the Legal Implications' (2007) J Environmental Law (forthcoming)

CEER Working Paper, 'Key Interactions and potential trade distortions between electricity markets', September 2004

Codognet, M-K, Glachant, JM, Leveque, F, and Plagnet, M-A, 'Mergers and Acquisitions in the European Electricity Sector—Cases and Patterns' (Cerna, 2003) <http://www.cerna.ensmp.fr/Documents/FL-MA-MAsEu.pdf>

Conte, G, Loriot, G, Rouxel, F-X, and Tretton, W, 'EDP/ENI/GDP: the Commission prohibits a merger between gas and electricity national incumbents' (2005) 1 Competition Policy Newsletter 84–7

Cultrera, C, 'Les décisions GDF: La Commission est formelle: les clauses de restriction territoriale dans les contrats de gaz violent l'article 81' (2005) 1 Competition Policy Newsletter 45–8

Dashwood, A, 'The Constitution of the European Union after Nice: law-making procedures' (2001) 26 ELR 215–38, 218

De Bauw, R, 'Legal Implementation of Energy Policy', paper presented to EU Colloquium, Florence, Italy, September, 1982.

De Burca, G, 'The Constitutional Challenge of New Governance in the European Union' (2003) 28 ELR 814–39

De Esteban, F, 'The Future of Nuclear Energy in the European Union, Background Paper', 23 May 2002

Delcourt, C, 'The acquis communautaire: Has the concept had its day?' (2000) 38 CML Rev 829

Dinnage, J, 'Competition in Gas Supply: The Competition Man Cometh' (1998) 16 J Energy Natural Resources L 249–85

Doherty, B, 'Just What are Essential Facilities?' (2001) 38 CML Rev 397–436

Edward, D, 'The Modernisation of Competition Law: Some Reflections', paper presented at Workshop on the Modernisation of Competition law, European University Institute, Florence, 2000

——, and Hoskins, M, 'Article 90: Deregulation and EC Law. Reflections arising from the XVI FIDE Conference' (1995) CML Rev 168, 183

EFET, 'Open Letter on Gas VV', 8 August 2000

——, 'Present Rules of Auctions of Virtual Power Plant Capacity in France will not lead to Effective Opening of the Market', 12 July 2001

Ehlermann, CD, 'Establishing the Single Market in Energy' (1991) Oil Gas L Taxation Rev 295–8, 296

——, 'The Role of the European Commission as regards National Energy Policies' (1994) 12 J Energy Natural Resources L 342, 348

ERGEG, 'Discussion Paper: the Creation of Regional Electricity Markets', June 2005

Estrategia, 'Revolution in the European Energy Market', 22 March 2006

European Council, 'Presidency Conclusions', 23/24 March 2006

Fernandez Salas, M, 'Long-term supply agreements in the context of gas market liberalization: Commission closes investigation of Gas Natural' (2000) 2 Competition Policy Newsletter 55

——, Klotz, R, Moonen, S, and Schnichels, D, 'Access to gas pipelines: lessons learnt from the Marathon case' (2004) 2 Competition Policy Newsletter 41–3

Fountoukakos, K, 'Judicial Review and Merger Control: The CFI's Expedited Procedure' (2002) 3 Competition Policy Newsletter 7–12

Gialdino, C, 'Some Reflections on the Acquis Communautaire' (1995) 32 CML Rev 1089

Gilbert, R and Newbery, D, 'Electricity Merger Policy in the Shadow of Regulation', EPRG 06/27:<http://www.electricitypolicy.org.uk/pubs/wp/eprg0628.pdf>

Green, N, 'The Implementation of Treaty Policies: the energy dilemma' (1983) 8 ELR 186, 189

Grubb, M and Neuhoff, K, 'Allocation and competitiveness in the EU emissions trading scheme: policy overview' (2006) 6 Climate Policy 7–30

Gunst, A, 'Impact of European Law on the Validity and Tenure of National Support Schemes for Power Generation from Renewable Energy Sources' (2005) 23 J Energy and Natural Resources L 95–119

Helm, D, 'The Assessment: the New Energy Paradigm' (2005) 21 Oxford Rev of Economic Policy 1–18

—— and Yarrow, G, 'Regulation and Utilities' (1988) 4 Oxford Rev of Economic Policy vii

Hogan, WF, 'Making Markets in Power' (London, 2000) <http://ksghome.harvard.edu/~.whogan.cbg.ksg/index.htm>

Keppenne, JP, 'National Environmental Policies: Uncharted Waters for EC State Aid Control' (2001) 7/8 Nederlands Tijdschrift voor Europees recht 193–9

Koenings, M, 'Energy taxation and state aid: The Netherlands; energy tax exemption for energy intensive end-users' (2004) 1 Competition Policy Newsletter 84–5

Lapuerta, C, Pfaffenberger, W, and Pfeifenberger, J, 'Netzzugang in Deutschland: ein Laendervergleich (Tiel I & II)', Energiewirtschaft, March/April 1999

Lowther, J, 'State aids and free movement issues for renewables' (2001) 13(3) Environmental Law & Management 103–4

Johnston, A, 'Free allocation of allowances under the EU emissions trading scheme: legal issues' (2006) 6 Climate Policy 115–36, 132

Lenaerts, K, 'The Principle of Subsidiarity and the Environment in the European Union: Keeping the Balance of Federalism' (1994) 17 Fordham Intl LJ 846

Lennartz, R and Bouquet, A, 'The Legal Framework of the EAEC Common Supply Policy in Nuclear Materials in the Light of the "ENU" and "KLE" Cases' (1996) 27 Energy in Europe 21–7, 22

Lindroos, M, Schnichels, D, and Svane, LP, 'Liberalisation of European Gas Markets—Commission settles GFU case with Norwegian gas producers' (2002) 3 Competition Policy Newsletter 50–2

Lowe, P, 'Anti-Trust Reform in Europe: A Year In Practice', paper delivered at International Bar Association/European Commission Conference, Brussels, 11 March 2005, 4

——, 'EC Merger Regulation: Is there really a new approach?', presentation at EC Competition Day, 19 June 2006

Monti, M, 'Applying EU competition law to the newly liberalised energy markets', World Forum on Energy Regulation, Rome, 6 October 2003

Newbery, DM, 'Why tax energy? Towards a more rational policy' (2005) 26 Energy J 1

Nyssens, H, Cultrera, C, and Schnichels, D, 'The territorial restrictions case in the gas sector: a state of play' (2004) 1 Competition Policy Newsletter 48–51

Select Bibliography

—— and Osbourne, I, 'Profit splitting mechanisms in a liberalised gas market: the devil lies in the detail' (2005) 2 Competition Policy Newsletter 5–28

Pedersen, TT, Smidt, C, and Christiansen, PK, 'Topics in Merger Control—Experiences from a Recent Merger in the Danish Electricity Sector' (2004) 27 World Competition 595–612

Pierce Jr, RJ, 'The Antitrust Implications of Energy Restructuring' [1998] Natural Resources & Environment 269

Piper, J, 'State Aid to the European Union coal industry' (194) 23 Energy in Europe 22

Renner-Loquenz, B and Boeshertz, D, 'State aid: key elements for the agreement in the Council on energy taxation' (2003) 3 Competition Policy Newsletter 14–6

—— and Zuleger, V, 'Commission raises no objections to German feed-in laws for electricity from renewable energy sources and combined heat and power' (2002) 3 Competition Policy Newsletter 67

Rushbrooke, G, 'Clarification or Complication: The New Energy Title in the Draft Constitution for Europe', in 22 En N L (2004), 373–387

Ryan, SA, 'The revised system of case referral under the Merger Regulation: experiences to date' (2005) 3 Competition Policy Newsletter 38–42

Santamato, S and Pesaresi, N, 'Compensation for services of general economic interest: some thoughts on the Altmark ruling' (2004) 1 Competition Policy Newsletter 17–21

Schaub, A, 'Competition Policy and Liberalization of Energy Markets', paper presented at the European Utilities Circle 2000 conference, 23 November 2000

Schmidt, SK, 'Commission Activism: Subsuming Telecommunications and Electricity under European Competition Law' [1998] J European Public Policy 169–84

Schnichels, D and Valli, F, 'Vertical and horizontal restraints in the European gas sector—lessons learnt from the DONG/DUC case' (2003) 2 Competition Policy Newsletter 60–3

Segura Catalan, MJ, Paroche, E, and Colin-Goguel, A, 'Le Contrôle des aides d'Etat dans la mise en place du marché interieur de l'électricité: le cas de EDF' (2004) 1 Competition Policy Newsletter 4–7

Slot, PJ, 'Note' (1998) 35 CML Rev 1183, 1202

Sorensen, UL, 'The European Emission Trading Scheme—How Will it Affect the Internal Market in Electricity?, unpublished LLM dissertation, University of Dundee

Stern, J, 'UK gas security: time to get serious' (2004) 32 Energy Policy 1967–79

Stevens, P, 'Pipelines or Pipe Dreams? Lessons from the history of Arab Transit Pipelines' (2000) 54 Middle East J 224–41

Stiglitz, J, 'Globalization and its Discontents' (2003) WW Norton ——, 'making Globalization work' (2006) Allen Lane

Stothers, C, 'Refusal to Supply as Abuse of a Dominant Position: Essential Facilities in the European Union' [2001] ECLR 256–62

——, 'The Role of the Essential Facilities Doctrine in the Regulated Sectors in the United Kingdom' (2001/02) 12 Utilities L Rev 5

Talus, K, 'First Experience under the Exemption Regime of EC Regulation 1228/2003 on Conditions for Access to the Network of Cross-Border Exchanges in Electricity' (2005) 23 J Energy Natural Resources L 266–81

——, and Wälde, TW, 'Electricity Interconnectors—A Serious Challenge for EC Competition Law', 1 *Competition and Regulation in Network Industries* (2006) 353–388

Tarasofsky, RG and Cosbey, A, in 'Trade, Competitiveness and Climate Change: Exploring the Issues', a Chatham House/IISD paper, December 2005 <http://www.chathamhouse.org.uk/sustainabledevelopment>

Select Bibliography

Temple-Lang, J, 'Defining Legitimate Competition: companies' duties to supply competitors and access to essential facilities' (1994) 18 Fordham Intl LJ 437

Tradacete, A, 'Role of EC Competition Policy in the Liberalization of EU Energy Markets', April 2000

Trischmann, H, 'LNG into Europe: regulation—American style?' [2004] IELTR 233–43

Vasconcelos, J, 'Lessons that should be drawn from the recent incidents in electricity supply and suggestions for guaranteeing an adequate electricity supply in liberalised markets', 5 October 2003, note by the Council of European Energy Regulators; the report on the blackout by the UCTE is available at <http://www.ucte.org/pdf/News/20040427_UCTE_IC_Final_report.pdf>

——, 'The Rôle of Regulation in a Single Energy Market', presentation delivered at the conference on 'Launching a Common European Energy Market', Lisbon, 5–6 June 2000

——, 'Towards the internal energy market: how to bridge a regulatory gap and build a regulatory framework' [2005] European Rev of Energy Markets 81–103

REPORTS

Barquin, J et al, 'Brief Academic Opinion of Economics Professors and Scholars on the Project of Acquisition of Endesa by Gas Natural', 26 October 2005

Brattle Group, 'DTe Implementation of the Gas Act', December 2000

——, 'Methodologies for Establishing National and Cross-Border Systems of Pricing of Access to the Gas System in Europe', report for the European Commission, February 2000

—— and University of Cambridge, 'Factors Affecting Geographic Market Definition and Merger Control for the Dutch Electricity Sector', June 2006

British Energy Group plc, 'Offer for Sale', 2005

Cameron, PD, 'Stabilization in Investment Contracts and Changes of Rules in Host Countries: Tools for Oil and Gas Investors', Association of International Petroleum Negotiators, Texas, 2006

CEER, 'Practical Steps for Developing a Competitive European Gas Market', October 2000

Centre for European Policy Studies, 'Rethinking the EU Regulatory Strategy for the Internal Energy Market', 2004

Clingendael Institute, 'The paradigm change in international natural gas markets and the impact on regulation', report presented to International Gas Union Conference, 2006

Consentec and Frontier Economics, 'Analysis of Cross-Border Congestion Management Methods for the EU Internal Electricity Market', June 2004

De Jong, J, 'The "Regional Approach" in Establishing the Internal EU Electricity Market', Clingendael International Energy Programme, 2004

DG Energy and Transport Working Paper, 'Strategy Paper: Medium Term Vision for the Internal Electricity Market', 1 March 2004

DTI, 'Gas Security of Supply: The Effectiveness of Current Gas Security of Supply Arrangements', October 2006.

EFET, 'The Past and Future of European Energy Trading', 22 June 2005

ERGEG, 'Annual Report 2005', 7

——, 'Public Guidelines on ERGEG's Consultation Practices', 10 August 2004

Eurelectric, 'A Quantitative Assessment of Direct Support Schemes for Renewables', January 2004

Select Bibliography

——, 'Report on Regulatory Models in a Liberalised European Electricity Market', 2004
——, 'Report on Public Service Obligations', February 2004
Euratom Supply Agency, 'Analysis of the Nuclear Fuel Availability at EU Level for a Security of Supply Perspective, Final Report of the Task Force on Security of Supply', June 2005
——, 'Annual Report 2005'
European Commission, 'Communication to the Council, First orientation for a common energy policy', 18 December 1968
——, 'Sixth Report on Competition Policy', 1976
——, 'Development of an Energy Strategy for the Community', COM (1981) 540 final
——, 'XIIth Report on Competition Policy', 1982
——, 'XIIIth Report on Competition Policy', 1983
——, 'Towards a Dynamic European Economy: Green Paper on the development of the common market for telecommunications services and equipment', COM (1987) 290 final
——, 'The Internal Energy Market', COM (1988) 238 final
——, 'Security of Supply, the Internal Market and Energy Policy, Working Paper of the Commission of the EC', 1990, SEC (90) 1248
——, 'XXth Report on Competition Policy', 1990
——, 'White Paper on Growth, Competitiveness and Employment', COM (1993) 700 final
——, 'Strengthening the Mediterranean Policy of the European Union: Establishing a Euro-Mediterranean Partnership', COM (1994) 427
——, 'Green Paper: For a European Union Energy Policy', January 1995
——, 'Towards an EU Energy Policy (the White Paper)', COM (1995) 682 final
——, 'Communication on the Euro-Mediterranean Partnership in the Energy Sector', COM (1996) 149 final, 3 April 1996
——, 'Report on Competition Policy', 1996
——, 'An Overall View of Energy Policy and Actions', COM (1997) 167
——, 'Energy for the Future: Renewable Sources of Energy', COM (1997) 599 final
——, 'Communication to the Council and Parliament, Preparing for Implementation of the Kyoto Protocol', COM (1999) 230
——, 'White Paper on Modernisation of the Rules Implementing Articles 85 and 86 of the EC Treaty', COM (1999) 101
——, 'Second Report to the Council and the European Parliament on Harmonisation Requirements', SEC (1999) 470
——, 'Annual Competition Law Report 2000'
——, 'Next Steps Towards Completion of the Internal Market in Gas: draft strategy Paper for discussion', 2000
——, 'Towards a European Strategy for the Security of Energy Supply (the Green Paper)', COM (2000) 769 final
——, 'Communication on Completing the Internal Market in Energy', COM (2001) 125 final
——, 'Enhancing Euro-Mediterranean Co-operation on Transport and Energy, Euromed Report, Issue No 26', 22 March 2001
——, 'Communication on European Energy Infrastructure', COM (2001) 775
——, 'Communication on Services of General Interest in Europe' [2001] OJ C17/4
——, 'Proposal for a Regulation of the European Parliament and Council on Conditions for Access to the Network for Cross-Border Exchanges in Electricity in the Internal Electricity Market', 2001

——, 'Staff working paper: State aid aspects in the proposal for a Council directive on energy taxation', SEC (2002)
——, 'Communication from the Commission to the Council and the European Parliament: Nuclear Safety in the European Union', COM (2002) 605 final
——, 'Final Report on the Green Paper: Towards a European strategy for the security of energy supply', COM (2002) 321 final
——, 'XXXIInd Report on Competition Policy', 2002
——, 'XXXIIIrd Report on Competition Policy', 2003
——, 'Communication, Energy Infrastructure and Security of Supply', COM (2003) 743 final
——, 'Second Commission Benchmarking Report', SEC (2003) 448
——, 'Staff Working Paper: Report on Public Consultation on the Green Paper on Services of General Interest', SEC (2004) 326
——, 'Communication of 26 May 2004, Report in accordance with Article 3 of Directive 2001/77/EC, evaluation of the effect of legislative instruments and other Community policies on the development of the contribution of renewable sources in the EU and proposals for concrete actions', COM (2004) 366 final
——, 'White Paper on Services of General Interest', COM (2004) 374 final
——, 'Critical Infrastructure Protection in the fight against terrorism', COM (2004) 702 final
——, 'XXXIVth Report on Competition Policy', 2004
——, 'Implementing the Community Lisbon Programme—A Strategy for the simplification of the regulatory environment', COM (2005) 535 final
——, 'Report on Progress in Creating the Internal Gas and Electricity Market', SEC (2005)
——, 'Report on Progress in Creating the Internal Gas and Electricity Market: Technical Annex to the Report', SEC (2005)
——, 'Communication to the Spring European Council—Working together for growth and jobs—A new start for the Lisbon Agenda', COM (2005) 24
——, 'On energy efficiency or doing more with less', COM (2005) 265 final
——, 'XXXVth Report on Competition Policy', 2005
——, 'Communication from the Commission to the Council and the European Parliament: Report on progress in creating the internal gas and electricity market', COM (2005) 568 final
——, 'The Support of Electricity from Renewable Energy Sources', COM (2005) 627 final
——, 'Merger Remedies Study', October 2005
——, 'Competition DG, Energy Sector Inquiry—Issues Paper', 15 November 2005
——, 'Energy: Competitiveness, Security and Sustainability, March 2006', COM (2006)
——, 'Green Paper: A European Strategy for Sustainable, Competitive and Secure Energy', COM (2006) 105 final
——, 'Commission Staff Working Document on the decision C-17 of 7 June 2005 of the Court of Justice of the European Communities: Preferential Access to Transport Networks under the Electricity and Gas Internal Market Directives', SEC (2006) 547
——, 'Study on Unbundling of Electricity and Gas Transmission and Distribution System Operators', March 2006
——, 'Preliminary Report: sector inquiry under Art 17 Regulation 1/2003 on the gas and electricity markets', 16 February 2006
——, 'Prospects for the internal gas and electricity market', COM (2006) 841 final
——, 'Implementation Report', SEC (2006) 1709

——, 'Sustainable power generation from fossil fuels: aiming for near-zero emissions from coal after 2020', COM (2006) 843 final
——, 'Nuclear Illustrative Programme', COM (2006) 844 final
——, 'Biofuels Progress Report', COM (2006) 845 final
——, 'Priority Interconnection Plan', COM (2006) 846 final
——, 'Renewable Energy Road Map: Renewable energies in the 21st century; building a more sustainable future', COM (2006) 848 final
——, 'Green Paper Follow-up Action; Report on Progress in Renewable Electricity', COM (2006) 849 final
——, 'Inquiry pursuant to Article 17 of Regulation (EC) No 1/2003 into the European gas and electricity sectors (Final Report)', COM (2006) 851 final
——, 'An Energy Policy for Europe', COM (2007) 1 final
——, 'Limiting Global Climate Change to 2 degrees Celsius: The way ahead for 2020 and beyond', COM (2007) 2 final
HM Government, 'Energy Review', Cm 6887 (2006)
House of Commons Trade and Industry Committee, 'Security of Gas Supply, HC 632–I (2005–06), and the Responses by Government (HC 833) and Ofgem (HC 992) to this Report'
House of Lords European Union Committee, 'Gas: Liberalised Markets and Security of Supply', HL Paper 105, 2003–04
House of Lords Select Committee on Economic Affairs, Second Report of Session 2005–2006: 'The Economics of Climate Change', HL Paper 12–1, vol I
IEA Clean Coal Centre, 'Profiles: Coal in an Enlarged European Union', June 2004
ILEX Consulting, 'Report to the DTI: Strategic Storage and Other Options to Ensure Long-term Gas Security', April 2006
International Exchanges of Electricity, 'Rules proposed by the European Transmission System Operators', 23 March 1999
International Nuclear Law Association Working Group on International Nuclear Trade, 'Legal Certainty in International Nuclear Trade', 2001
Kroes, N, 'Towards an Efficient and Integrated European Energy Market—First Findings and Next Steps', 16 February 2006
Nagy, M, Wagner, R, and MacCormick, N, 'Contribution to the European Convention: The Future of the Euratom Treaty in the Framework of the European Constitution', CONV 563/03, 18 February 2003
Netherlands Competition Authority, 'Consultation Document on Mergers on the Energy Markets in the Netherlands and a Possible North-West European Market', June 2006
Nordic competition authorities, 'A Powerful Competition Policy: Towards a more coherent competition policy in the Nordic market for electric power', 1/2003, June 2003
Office of Fair Trading (UK), 'Concurrent Application to Regulated Industries', OFT 409, 1999
——, 'Application in the Energy Sector: Understanding competition law', 2005
—— and Ofgem (UK), 'Application in the energy sector', 2005
Report of the Conference of the Representatives of the Governments of the Member States, 22 February 2000, CONFER 4711/00
Secretariat of the Intergovernmental Conference, 'Rapport des Chefs de Délégations aux Ministères des Affaires Étrangères (the Spaak Report)', Brussels, 21 April 1956
Willenborg, R, Tonjes, C, and Perlot, W, 'Europe's Oil Defences: An Analysis of Europe's oil supply vulnerability and its emergency oil stockholding systems', Clingendael International Energy Programme, 2004

INDEX

abuse of dominant position 11.09, 13.02
   case law 16.40–2
   prohibitions on under EEC Treaty 2.28
abuse of market power
   potential for in electricity industry 1.65
access
   entry-exit regime 13.123–6
   Gas Directive continues special regime
      for upstream pipeline networks 6.47
   general principles for upstream pipeline
      networks 6.49
   handling requests for 13.114
      BEB to improve 13.116
      Gasunie to improve 13.115
      GDF to improve 13.117
      Ruhrgas to improve 13.117
   interconnection capacity for wholesale
      exporters and importers 5.47
   offshore installations 6.21
   pipeline facilities 6.21
   provisions in Electricity Directive 5.44
   refusal of 5.46
   refusal to interconnectors 13.88
   transit pipelines 6.61
accounts
   unbundling of 5.58
acquis communautaire
   development for energy 2.61
   for energy 2.08
   widening of in relation to energy 2.160
acquisitions
   DONG acquires Energi E2 and Elsam 14.89–92
   proposal by EnBW to acquire ENI and share
      of GVS 14.76–8
   proposal by E.ON to acquire MOL 14.79–84
Advocate-General
   role of 2.95
agriculture
   excluded from competition rules of EU 2.10
Algeria
   gas supply 1.67
   import of gas from 12.59
Almelo *see* Gemeente Almelo
annulment
   ECJ proceedings 2.99

appeals
   ECJ may hear from CFI 2.102
area gas boards 1.27
Assembly of the European Communities
   original name of European Parliament 2.85
auctions
   capacity 5.91, 14.135
   design of in contract release programmes 14.130
   mechanism of in energy release
      programmes 14.125
   remedy in merger proceedings 14.111–2
Austria
   import of gas from Russia 12.49
   merger proposals 14.72–3
   regulation 3.07
   stranded costs 15.26–7
authorization
   application for electricity generation 5.20
   construction of direct lines 6.66
   distributed generation 5.21
   establishment of criteria for electricity
      generation 5.19
   exemptions to provisions of Gas Directive 6.11
   small generation 5.21
   streamlining procedures by TENs 18.80
   terminals for Hackberry LNG 6.59–60
   under Gas Directive 6.15

balancing
   assistance offered by BEB 13.111
   assistance offered by Gasunie 13.110
   energy security with competition 18.06
   free system offered by Thyssengas 13.109
   issues of ETS 17.51–3
   objectives in energy sector 19.13
   services offered by GDF 13.113
   services offered by Ruhrgas 13.112
   supply and demand under Electricity
      Security Directive 18.40–1
balancing rules 6.129
BEB
   balancing assistance offered by 13.111
   entry-exit regime 13.125
   monitoring of 13.133
   to improve handling access requests 13.116

Index

BEB (*cont.*)
  transparency on availability of capacity 13.106
  undertakings on congestion management 13.120
Belgium
  anti-competitive activity of Distrigas 13.11
  golden shares and 14.139
  merger proposals 14.54–5
  practical implementation of unbundling in 5.41
  privatization 14.148–50
  stranded costs 15.28–31
biofuels
  state aid to promote 15.73
block exemptions 12.36
  competition 11.08
  none to be granted in respect of infrastructure 6.57
Bord Gáis Eireann 12.11
Brazil
  energy crisis in 1.54
Britannia gas field 12.12
British Energy Group Plc
  capacity conditions for restructuring aid 9.34
  conditions for restructuring aid to 9.32
  monitoring restructuring aid 9.35
  Rescue and Restructuring Aid for 15.81–5
  restructuring aid to 9.30
  restructuring plan for 9.31
  ring fencing requirements for restructuring aid 9.33
British Gas Corporation 1.27
British Nuclear Fuels Ltd
  state aid and 15.86–9
brown coal
  production of 8.03
budget
  European Parliament's control of 2.90
Bundeskartellamt *see* **German Federal Cartel Office**
burden of proof
  import-export monopolies 16.84

Canada
  energy supply failures in 18.09
capacity
  auctions 5.91, 14.135
  availability for market participants 5.93
  available to upstream pipeline networks 6.51
  excess 1.46
  power stations 1.64
  securing on transit pipelines 6.62
  tendering for new for promotion of new technologies 5.23
  tendering for new in interests of environmental protection 5.23
  tendering procedure for new 5.22
  transparency on availability of 13.104–8

capacity allocation 13.49
  compatibility with competition law 13.51
  information on 5.58
  method of 13.50
  principles of 6.125
  procedure for 5.124
capacity reservation
  case law on 13.59–86
  compatibility with competition law 13.54
  competition issues 13.47
  Dutch/German Interconnector 13.59–62
  long-term 13.52
  Skagerrak Cable 13.53
  UK/Belgium Interconnector 13.57–8
  UK/French Interconnector 13.55–6
capacity rights
  trade in 6.130, 13.118
  trading
  TSOs must allow to be freely tradable 6.131
carbon allowance
  volatility of prices 17.48
carbon emissions
  limitation of 17.20
carbon taxation 17.19
  at European level 17.41
  proposals to introduce 17.39
Central Electricity Generating Board (CEGB) 1.27
central oil storage agency
  European Commission proposals to create 18.65
Chernobyl accident 9.02
climate change
  state aid for 15.77
Climate Change Levy 15.76
climate protection
  obligations under Gas Directive 6.08
co-decision procedure
  applied to all internal market legislation 2.54
  between Council of Ministers and European Parliament 2.81
  European Parliament with Council of Ministers 2.87
  Hydrocarbons Licensing Directive subject to 7.23
co-operation procedure
  introduction of 2.41, 2.86
  operation of 2.42
coal
  decline in consumption of 8.03
  early importance of in ECSC countries 2.16
  European law relating to 4.01
coal industry
  drive for competition in 8.27
  regulation of 19.40
  state aids 8.10

Index

coal industry (cont.)
  success of ECSC in managing contraction of 8.09
  transfer of control to supranational authority 2.14
coal production
  decline of 8.03
Coal Regulation 2002
  conditions for state aid in 8.21
  decisions taken under 8.22
  decisions with respect or Member States whose coal industries were subject to ECSC 8.24
  main aims of 8.18
  provisions on state aid 8.19
  restructuring under 8.23
coal sector
  economic and social factors in decline of 8.04
  ETS may work to advantage of 8.03
  legal framework governing 8.01
  under EC Treaty 8.02
Commission Decisions
  provisions on undertakings 11.15
Commissioners
  appointment of 2.65
  number of 2.65
  requirement for independence of 2.66
  support for 2.67
Committee of Permanent Representatives (Coreper) 2.71
  role in decision-making process 2.82
Committee of the Regions 2.71
Committees
  European Parliament 2.91
common market
  forms of state aid compatible with 15.05
  objectives of ECSC 8.06
  provisions in EEC Treaty establishing 2.23
common supply policy
  of ESA 9.17
Community law
  importance of preliminary rulings in development of 2.105
  supremacy of 2.107
companies
  aid for those in serious difficulty 15.79
compatibility
  problems of 1.50, 1.55
compensation
  calculation of amounts payable by TSOs 5.109
  for costs of carrying out PSOs is not state aid 5.14
  inter-TSO mechanism under Electricity Regulation 5.84
  mechanisms for TSOs under Electricity Regulation 5.81
compensation schemes
  state aid and design of 15.92
competence
  co-ordination of existing 2.58
  Euratom primary source of for European Commission 9.14
  Member States' wish to retain over energy 2.57
  parallel under Regulation on the Implementation of the Rules on Competition 11.19
  where EU does not have exclusive 2.48
competition 4.02
  achieving 6.94
  advantages if 1.06
  as concept in EC Treaty 1.08
  background of in energy markets 1.02
  balancing energy security with 18.06
  block exemptions 11.08
  capacity hoarding and 13.47
  central to merger control 14.171
  constraints in gas supply 1.69
  contribution of merger control to in energy markets 14.06
  definition of 1.05
  distortion 4.03, 11.09
    arising from PSOs 5.13
    by Rescue and Restructuring Aid 15.80
  distribution networks 13.02
  doubts about objectives of 1.97
  drive for in coal industry 8.27
  effects of mergers on 14.11
  European law on gas sector to stimulate 6.148
  exemption to provisions in EC Treaty 11.08
  impact of ETS on 17.49
  implication of environmental policy for in energy market 17.03
  importance of ownership in 1.93
  issues in respect of TENs 18.73
  issues relating to energy security 18.03
  issues under Euratom 9.16
  long-term contracts 13.02
  need for transmission pricing if to be effective 13.31
  negative consequences for development of by M&A 14.02
  network for 11.11
  nuclear energy 9.01
  objective of 1.01
  objectives of ECSC 8.08
  objectives of Electricity Regulation 5.81
  obstacles on 1.62
  open-ended framework 1.48
  powers to bring about exist in primary law 16.91

675

competition (*cont.*)
   prerequisites for introduction of into gas and electricity markets 1.75
   problems of introducing into network-bound energy sector 1.49
   promotion of and energy security 18.107
   promotion of in energy 1.21
   provisions in EC Treaty 11.07
   provisions in Energy Charter Treaty 2.157
   regulation for 1.47, 1.76
   requirements of ECSC 8.07
   role of Regulation on the Implementation of the Rules on Competition in reform 11.10
   role of state aid in balancing objectives in energy sector 19.29
   strategy of European Commission 11.02
   transmission management 13.02
   treatment of under Renewables Directive 17.04
competition authorities 3.07
   demarcation of competence with NRAs in UK 3.51
   relationship with NRAs 3.48
   variation in structure of 3.44
Competition Directorate
   lead institution in energy review of under Regulation on the Implementation of the Rules on Competition 11.41
competition law
   application of 11.06
   application of in energy sector 11.01
   application of in liberalized energy markets 1.53
   caution required in assessing impact of on energy sector 19.23
   changes to 8.12
   compatibility of capacity allocation with 13.51
   compatibility of capacity reservation with 13.54
   complementary role to Electricity and Gas Directives 13.01
   decisions made on case-by-case basis 19.24
   energy industry exempt from national 1.28
   enforcement of 11.05, 19.48
   flexibility of in calculation of transmission pricing 13.45
   in respect of downstream markets 13.139
   incompatibility of long-term gas contracts with 13.08
   incompatibility of Verbändevereinbarung with 13.38
   increasing reach of 2.178
   investigations into infringements of by energy sector 11.44
   merger control under 19.26
   new approach to application of 11.04
   on-site inspections into compliance with by energy sector 11.45
   overhaul of 11.66
   relationship to sector regulation 3.49
   remedies 11.60
   role of in energy sector 19.20
   second generation of Directives on 11.03
   set out in EC Treaty 4.04
   supremacy of EC 11.13
   to be reviewed by European Council and Parliament 16.92
competition policy 2.58
   developing new direction of 11.67
   EC Treaty and 1.09
   gas sector 12.03
Completing the Internal Market 2.38
compliance
   lack of by Greece with unbundling requirements in Electricity Directive 5.78
   programme under Electricity Directive 5.40
concentration of undertakings
   appraisal of 14.33
   competence of EEA in respect of 14.27
   criteria for appraisal of 14.13
   decisions of European Commission on 14.56
   definition in terms of product and geographical dimensions 14.29
   economic analysis of 14.31
   financial power and 14.34
   market definition of 14.28
   Member States may ask for referral 14.21
   Merger Regulation application to 14.12
   notification of 14.14
   operation of remedies for 14.16
   parties to concentration can trigger re-allocation 14.24
   powers of European Commission to inspect 14.17
   protection of legitimate interests 14.38
   re-allocation 14.23
   relevant geographic markets 14.30
   relevant product markets 14.30
   remedies proposed for 14.15
   security of energy supply and 14.39
   substantive test for 14.32
   thresholds for competence over by European Commission 14.20
concession regime
   establishment of 1.94
confidentiality
   information supplied under Electricity Regulation 5.112
conflict of interests
   natural monopolies 1.84

Index

congestion management 5.58, 13.119–21
  common co-ordinated method 5.124
  common rules required for 6.126
  methods for 5.120–1
  new guidelines in respect of 5.119
  provisions under Electricity Regulation 5.115
  role of TSOs in 5.90
  use of income from 5.126
    discretion in 5.127
  use of revenues from 5.94
connection
  level of 6.91
constitution
  energy provisions in draft 2.59
  European Union 2.56
consultation
  by European Commission 2.71
  under Art 95 EC Treaty 16.17
consumer protection
  extent of under Electricity Directive 5.11
  household customers under Gas Security Directive 18.51
  provisions of Gas Directive 6.10
  under Electricity Directive 5.08
    scope of 5.09
consumers
  access to under contract release programmes 14.133
  role of in energy sector reform 19.22
consumers associations
  Germany 13.40
consumption
  balance of charges between electricity generation and 5.88
contract release programmes
  access to customers under 14.133
  access to storage under 14.132
  access to transmission 14.131
  auction design 14.130
  duration of 14.126
  flexibility of 14.127
  gas delivery points 14.128
  monitoring 14.134
  remedy in merger proceedings 14.113
  reviewing 14.134
  security of supply 14.129
  use of 14.115
contracts
  applications for derogations 6.76
  criteria for derogations 6.82
  date of signature 6.85
    relevance of 6.86
  decisions on derogations 6.79
  duration of 6.73

  granting of derogations 6.77
  priorities for derogations 6.83
  results of refusal of derogations 6.80
  review of derogations 6.81
  scope for derogations 6.84
  ship-or-pay 6.96
    complementary to take-or-pay contracts 6.97
    no grounds for derogations on basis of 6.98
  take-or-pay clauses 6.72
    acceptance of 6.92
  take-or-pay derogations 6.75
  terms of 6.85
  transitional regime for 6.74
  transportation 6.123
  withdrawal of derogations 6.78
Corrib gas field 12.12
Council of European Energy Regulators (CEER) 3.02
  composition of 3.25
Council of Ministers
  changes to voting procedures of 2.39
  co-decision procedure with European Parliament 2.81
  competition law to be reviewed by 16.92
  composition of 2.77
  decision making role of 2.69, 2.78
  power of co-decision with European Parliament 2.87
  relationship between European Commission and 2.76
countervailing purchasing power 12.11
Court of First Instance (CFI)
  composition of 2.109
  ECJ may hear appeals from 2.102
  establishment of 2.108
courts
  role of in reviewing powers of NRAs 3.08, 3.53
cross-border trading
  development of guidelines on by ERGEG 3.38
  NRA functions 5.63
  rules for cross-border flows under Electricity Regulation 5.80, 5.85
  under Electricity Directive 5.05
customer contracts
  termination of 14.119
customer release 14.119
Czech Republic
  brown coal production in 8.03
  hard coal production in 8.03
  reliance on nuclear energy 9.02

damages
  actions in ECJ 2.101
Danish Competition Authority
  monitoring by 12.28

677

Danish Underground Consortium (DUC)
  12.15, 12.21–3
  commitments offered by 12.19
  gas supply agreement with DONG 12.16
  joint marketing with DONG 12.17
Dansk Olie og Naturgas (DONG) 12.14, 12.21–3
  acquisition of Elsam and Energi E2 by 14.89–92
  exclusive supply to 12.15
  gas supply agreement with DUC 12.16
  joint marketing with DUC 12.17
  undertakings given by 12.24–7
date of signature
  contracts 6.85
    relevance of 6.86
decisions
  scope of 2.113
decommissioning
  establishment of NDF 9.37
  no provisions for under Euratom 9.15
delivery
  dependence of electricity and gas on fixed
    networks to 1.60
demand side management
  energy security 18.20
Denmark
  accession to EU 2.45
  energy supply failures in 18.09
  joint marketing arrangements 12.14
  stranded costs 15.32
derogations
  applications for in respect of take-or-pay
    contracts 6.76
  criteria for on take-or-pay contracts 6.82
  decisions on take-or-pay contracts 6.79
  effects of granting on internal market 6.95
  Electricity Regulation
    importance for Slovenia 5.138
    justification for Slovenia 5.137
    Slovenia 5.136
  emergent markets 6.103
  for investment risk 6.104
    application of criteria for 6.107
    criteria for 6.106
    procedure for 6.105
    test for 6.108
  from Electricity Directive 5.70
    scope of 5.71
    unbundling 5.72
  from Gas Directive 6.69
  from Gas Regulations 6.144
  from parts of Electricity Directive by
    Estonia 5.49
  granting in respect of take-or-pay contracts 6.77
  isolated markets 6.103

  no grounds for on basis of ship-or-pay
    contracts 6.98
  possibilities of from Gas Directive 6.71
  potential beneficiaries of for investment risk 6.109
  priorities for on take-or-pay contracts 6.83
  result of refusal on take-or-pay contracts 6.80
  review of on take-or-pay contracts 6.81
  rules relating to from Gas Directive 6.70
  scope for on take-or-pay contracts 6.84
  take-or-pay contracts 6.75
    as last resort 6.93
  withdrawal in respect of take-or-pay contracts 6.78
destination clauses 12.33
  as vertical agreements 12.36
  deletion of imposed on ENI 12.45
  ENI to refrain from introducing into new
    gas supply contracts 12.46
  Gazprom 12.42
  investigations into gas supply contracts 12.34
  Nigeria NLG 12.39
  Norway 12.38
  origins of 12.35
  possibility of use by Sonatrach in
    contracts 12.58
  procedure adopted by European Commission
    against 12.37
  publication of formal decision by European
    Commission on 12.57
developing countries
  energy markets in 1.54
direct effect
  definition of 2.106
direct lines 5.51
  authorization of 6.66
  definition of 5.53, 6.67
  facilitation of construction under Gas
    Directive 6.65
  supply through 5.52
  where may be used 5.54
Direct Supply to Business (DSB) 9.31
**Directive on Insider Dealing and Market
  Manipulation 2003**
  transparency obligations under 11.63
**Directive on Markets in Financial
  Instruments 2004**
  transparency obligations under 11.63
Directive on the Promotion of Biofuels 2003
  commitment of EU to 10.03
Directive on the Promotion of Cogeneration 2003
  commitment of EU to 10.03
directives
  scope of 2.111
Director General of Fair Trading 3.51
Directorates-General 2.67

Index

dispute resolution
  by NRAs 5.64
    jurisdictional aspects 5.65
  in relation to upstream pipeline networks 6.52
  mechanism under Energy Charter Treaty 2.149
  more formal decisions to be taken 12.62
  persuasion to reach settlement 12.61
  provisions of Energy Charter Treaty 2.138
  transit 2.147
distributed generation
  authorization for 5.21
distribution
  case law on exclusive rights of 2.30
  common rules for gas 6.04
  definition of 5.34
  electricity
    market definition 11.24
  provisions under Gas Directive 6.26
distribution networks
  competition issues relating to 13.02
  creation of non-discriminatory access rights to 1.91
distribution system operators (DSOs)
  designation of under Gas Directive 6.27
  priorities of 5.37
  renewable energy and 10.29
  requirements for under Electricity Directive 5.35
  responsibilities of 5.36
  responsibilities of under Gas Directive 6.28
Distrigas
  anti-competitive activity of 13.11
  merger with Tractebel 14.88
diversification
  energy sources 9.19
divestiture
  effectiveness of remedy 14.120
  remedy in merger proceedings 14.107
dominant position
  abuse of 11.09, 13.02
  arising from mergers 14.09
  created by grant of special and exclusive rights 16.10
  definition of under Merger Regulation 14.10
  prohibitions on abuse of under EEC Treaty 2.28
downstream market segment
  competition law in respect of 13.139
  gas supply 1.69
  market definition 11.30
Dutch/German Interconnector 13.59–62

EC law
  harmonization 16.15
  liberalization 16.15
EC Treaty
  application of to internal energy market 19.18
  basis for special and exclusive rights in 16.01

coal sector under 8.02
competition as concept in 1.08
competition law set out in 4.04
competition policy in 1.09
competition provisions in 11.07
consultation process under Art 95 of 16.17
development of environmental policy in 17.01
differences from ECSC 8.12
duty imposed on European Commission to ensure Member States comply with Art 86 of 16.08
energy sector and 2.09
energy security provisions of 18.81
exemptions to competition provisions 11.08
extension of European Commission's Investigatory powers under 11.17
import-export monopolies
  practices contrary to Art 31 of 16.85
incompatibility of exclusive rights with competition rules of 16.89
key differences with Euratom 9.06
legislative procedures in Art 83(3) of 16.16
legislative procedures in Art 95 of 16.16
monopoly rights under Art 86 of 16.31
powers of European Commission under 2.70
restrictions on exclusive purchasing agreements under 13.19
role of European Commission as guardian of 2.74
Economic and Social Committee 2.71
economic difficulties 6.87
economic integration
  Europe 1.31
economy
  factors influencing energy 1.22
ECS
  proposed merger with Sibelga 14.54–5
EDF Trading 12.20, 12.24
EDP
  proposed merger with ENI 14.93–7
EEC Treaty 1957
  obligations on essential services under 2.27
  prohibition on state aids under 2.29
  prohibitions on abuse of dominant position under 2.28
  prohibitions on quantitative restrictions on imports and exports in 2.24
  provisions establishing common market in 2.23
  public service obligations under 2.26
  requirements on Member States to adjust state monopolies in 2.25
  scope of 2.22
EFTA Surveillance Authority
  co-operation with European Commission 2.119
  investigation into Norwegian gas sales by 2.126
  responsibilities of 2.121

Index

elections
  European Parliament 2.84
Électricité de France (EDF) 1.27
  proposal to merge with EnBW 14.68
  proposal to merge with Louis Dreyfus 14.66–7
  state guarantees to 15.56–9
electricity
  characteristics of 1.63
  convergence with gas 15.85–8
  European law relating to 4.01
  findings of Energy Sector Inquiry
    market concentration 11.49
    market integration 11.51
    price formation 11.53
    transparency 11.52
    vertical foreclosure 11.50
  fluctuation in demand 1.63
  high cost of outages 1.63
  how European Commission decides scope of geographic market 11.35
  import-export monopolies 16.51–74
  joint marketing 12.30
  lack of storage potential 1.63
  long-term contracts 13.13
    case law 13.25–30
    duration of 13.21
    market foreclosure 13.24
    Scottish Nuclear Ltd 13.22–3
    Netherlands 13.14
    network access 13.15
  progress of internal market 5.140
  regional approach to internal market 5.141
  relevant geographic market for 11.34
  technical specifications 1.63
  trading in 3.26
  transformation of 1.63
Electricity and Gas Forum 2.130
electricity companies
  use of stranded costs methodology in determining state aid for 15.14
Electricity Council 1.27
Electricity Directive 2003
  access provisions in 5.44
  activities of NRAs under 5.58
  aims of 5.06
  choice of payment methods under 5.11
  common rules under 5.07
  comparisons with Gas Directive 6.12
  competition law and 13.01
  compliance programme under 5.40
  concept of universal service under 5.10
  consumer protection under 5.08
    scope of 5.09
  cross-border trade under 5.05
  derogation of Estonia from parts of 5.49
  derogations from 5.70
    scope of 5.71
    unbundling 5.72
  ECJ ruling on preferential access in relation to 5.133
  electricity generation under 5.18
  energy security measure in 18.07–8, 18.11–2
  enforcement mechanisms of 5.69
  extension and reinforcement of role of NRAs under 5.04
  extent of consumer protection under 5.11
  general responsibilities of NRAs under 5.57
  harmonization provisions of 5.56
  information on generation characteristics under 5.12
  interpretation of provisions on unbundling 5.43
  lack of compliance by Greece with unbundling requirements in 5.78
  lack of provision for incentive-based regulation under 5.60
  legal unbundling under 5.39
  main features of 5.02
  minimum functions and competences of NRAs set out under 5.56
  monitoring and review of operation of 5.73
  network access provisions of 5.03
  once only progress report on 5.76
  practical unbundling under 5.41
  principle EU legislation applicable to electricity industry 5.01
  provisions on market opening 5.48
  PSOs under 16.02
  public service guarantees under 5.11
  public service obligations 5.08
    scope of 5.09
  regulatory role of 3.62
  report on 5.74
    contents of 5.75
  reporting requirements on imports 5.77
  reporting requirements under 5.59
  requirements for DSOs for 5.35
  security of supply under 5.11
  types of unbundling envisaged by 5.38
  unbundling provisions of 5.02
electricity generation
  applications for authorization of 5.20
  balance of charges between consumption and 5.88
  common rules for 5.07
  establishment of criteria for authorization of 5.19
  market definition 11.24
  under Electricity Directive 5.18

Index

electricity generators
  supply to own premises 5.51
electricity industry
  characteristics of 1.10
  common technical model of 1.13
  decision-making in 1.15
  differences between gas industry and in respect of liberalization 1.43
  EU legal regime for 2.02
  importance of special and exclusive rights 16.09
  mergers in 14.57
  network access provisions of Electricity Directive 5.03
  potential for abuse of market power in 1.65
  principal EU legislation applicable to 5.01
  regulatory characteristics 1.14
  review of under Regulation on the Implementation of the Rules on Competition 11.39
  shortcomings of 1.16
  single regulator for 1.81
  transmission 1.16
  unbundling provisions of Electricity Directive 5.02
  vertically-integrated systems 1.36
electricity markets
  definition of 11.24
  early experiments in liberalization 1.41
  non-uniform opening of 1.92
  prerequisites for introduction of competition into 1.75
electricity networks
  access to in Germany 13.34
electricity origin
  guarantees of 10.21
Electricity Regulation 2003
  aims of 5.79
  amendment of guidelines under 5.117
  comitology of guidelines under 5.118
  compensation mechanism for TSOs under 5.81
  competition objectives of 5.81
  conditions to be met for exemptions under 5.97
  confidentiality of information supplied under 5.112
  congestion management provisions under 5.115
  decisions on exemptions under 5.99
  entry into force 5.139
  guidelines produced under 5.113
  harmonization of charges under 5.89
  information on safety and security required from TSOs under 5.108
  information required from TSOs on interconnection capacities under 5.107
  information requirements on TSOs under 5.106
  infringements of 5.128
  inter-TSO compensation mechanism under 5.84
  main guidelines produced under 5.114
  monitoring of implementation by European Commission 5.131
  NRAs charged with ensuring compliance with 5.130
  penalties for infringement 5.129
  progression towards harmonization under 5.116
  provisions for charges by TSOs under 5.82
  provisions for exemption for new interconnectors under 5.96
  requesting exemptions under 5.98
  rules for cross-border flows of electricity under 5.80, 5.85
  Slovenian derogation from 5.136
    importance of 5.138
    justification for 5.137
Electricity Security Directive 2005
  background to 18.29
  criteria for implementation 18.33–4
  definition of electricity supply under 18.30
  entry into force 18.48
  implementation 18.32
  investment provisions under 18.42
  network security under 18.35–9
  obligations under 18.31
  outcome of reporting process 18.46
  reporting requirements under 18.43–5
  role of European Commission on reporting to Member States 18.47
  supply and demand balance under 18.40–1
electricity suppliers
  supply to own premises 5.51
electricity supply
  adjustments in relation to demand 11.28
  common rules for 5.07
  definition under Electricity Security Directive 18.30
  dependence on fixed networks to transport and deliver 1.60
  lack of import dependence in Europe 1.66
  market definition 11.24
  poor interconnections in Europe 1.66
Electricity Supply Board (ESB) 12.11
  commitments offered by 12.32
  joint marketing with Statoil 12.31
electricity transmission
  market definition 11.24
eligible customers
  distinction between non-eligible customers and in respect of gas supply 11.31
Elsam
  acquisition of by DONG 14.89–92

Index

emergency measures
  energy crises 2.32
emergent markets 6.99
  derogations for 6.103
  problems experienced by 6.102
emissions trading scheme (ETS) 17.03
  balancing issues of 17.52–3
  difficulties of 17.51
  effect on internal market 17.49
  impact on competition 17.49
  implementation 17.46
  introduction of 17.42
  may work to advantage of coal sector 8.03
  monitoring and reporting 17.45
  NAPs 17.44
  negative impact of 17.50
  obligations on Member States 17.44
  operation of 17.43
Empresa Nacional de Uranio (ENU) 9.19
  case relating to ESA assistance 9.21
    appeal 9.22
EnBW
  proposal to acquire ENI and share of GVS 14.76–8
  proposal to merge with EDF 14.68
  proposal to merge with Hidrocantábrico 14.69–71
Endesa
  investigation into long-term contracts of 13.12
  proposed merger with Gas Natural 14.46–53
Energi E2
  acquisition of by DONG 14.89–92
EnergieAllianz
  proposal to merge with Verbund 14.72–3
Energiebedrijf Ijssellmij NV 13.15
  European Commission prohibits long-term contract of 13.16
energy
  acquis communautaire for 2.08
  attempt to put end to special status of in EU 2.01
  beginning of market-based approach 1.24
  co-ordination of regulation 3.06
  creation of internal market by EU in 2.01
  crises in 1.24, 1.32
  deregulation of 1.25
  differences between legal frameworks in 19.38
  economic factors influencing 1.22
  emergency of EU law on 2.06
  EU integration and 1.31
  EU legal order for 2.03
  government involvement in 1.10
  government relationships in 1.17
  historical factors affecting 1.23
  Hydrocarbons Licensing Directive early example of pan-European co-operation on 7.24
  ideological factors influencing 1.22
  jurisprudence of ECJ 2.93
  market definition 11.21
  Member States' wish to retain competence over 2.57
  nationalization in 1.23
  new legal order for 2.174
  new paradigm of 1.20
  objectives of Euro-Mediterranean Association Agreements 2.169
  original proposals to include separate chapter on in Treaty on European Union 2.52
  origins of EU law on 2.05
  paradigm of 1.12
  pre-liberalization 1.11
  privatization 1.25
  promotion of competition in 1.21
  provisions in draft constitution 2.59
  references to in Treaty on European Union 2.51
  regulation 1.19, 3.04
  restructuring of 1.18
  scope of EU law on 2.04
  state monopolies
    adjustment of 16.48–50
  tensions over competing policies 2.175
  widening of *acquis communautaire* 2.160
energy *acquis*
  development of 2.61
Energy Charter Treaty 1994
  co-operation in transit under 2.145
  competition provisions of 2.157
  contracting parties to facilitate transit of energy 2.143
  developmental character of 2.153
  dispute resolution mechanism of 2.149
  dispute resolution under 2.138
  east-west exchange provisions of 2.156
  freedom of transit under 2.144
  future credibility of 2.159
  in line with WTO rules on trade in goods 2.141
  investment provisions of 2.134
  legal composition of 2.155
  legal protection offered by 2.139
  limitations on transit provisions 2.152
  main obligations of 2.158
  negotiations for 2.154
  objectives of 2.131
  obligations on transit states under 2.151
  post-investment provisions of 2.135

682

Index

Energy Charter Treaty 1994 (cont.)
  pre-investment phase 2.136
  provision for constructing new transit facilities under 2.150
  provisions on transit of energy 2.142
  requirements on transit state under 2.146
  rights and obligations created by 2.133
  scope of 2.132
  subjects trade in energy to GATT 2.140
  supplementary treaty negotiations 2.137
  transit disputes 2.147

Energy Community Regulatory Board 2.129

Energy Community Treaty 2005
  institutions of 2.129
  main provisions of 2.128
  signatory states 2.127

Energy Council 2.44

energy crises
  Brazil 1.54
  emergency measures taken during 2.32

energy efficiency
  energy security 18.20
  obligations under Gas Directive 6.08

Energy Experts' Group 2.71

energy industry
  exempt from national competition law 1.28
  globalization 1.37
  link between governments and 1.26
  post-1945 nationalization 1.27
  public service obligations on 1.28
  reasons for mergers in 14.58
  unbundling 1.85
    by law 1.86
    functional separation 1.87
    separation for accounting purposes 1.88
  West Germany 1.29

energy law
  development of body of pro-competitive 2.173
  developments in 16.94
  time frame for implementation 19.19

energy markets
  application of competition law in liberalized 1.53
  background to introduction of competition into 1.02
  contribution of merger control to competition in 14.06
  distortions due to intervention 1.34
  early abortive attempts to create single market 16.93
  EU programme for reform 1.07
  faith in new paradigm of 1.99
  government interventions 1.33
    negative effects 1.35
  implication of environmental proposals for competition in 17.03
  new governance of 3.61
  no one model of liberalization in 1.42
  objective of competition in 1.01
  obstacles to internal market in 2.44
  progress of competition in 1.02
  remaining questions on 1.98
  unbundling 1.36

Energy Markets Authority of Finland 5.103

energy network
  interconnector capacity vital to pan-European 13.48

energy paradigm
  changing 1.04

energy policy
  balancing interests and priorities 2.176
  beginnings of European 2.31
  identification of common objectives 2.33
  impact of collapse of Soviet Union on European 2.07
  increasing inter-dependence of EU Member States 2.177
  increasing reach of 2.178
  influence of environmental policy on 17.02
  legislative role of European Parliament on 2.83
  long term view 2.179
  making of 2.60
  new approaches to European 2.32
  no mention of in founding documents 2.57
  relationship with other policies 2.62
  reluctance of Member States to cede control to EU 2.13
  renewable energy 10.01

energy products
  excise duty on 17.21
  introduction of taxes on by Member States 17.33

Energy Products Directive 1992
  exemptions under 17.29–30
  extended scope of 17.26
  framework for taxation of energy 17.32
  framework for taxation under 17.32
  main provisions 17.27
  objectives of 17.24
  origins of 17.22
  reporting requirements under 17.28
  requirements of 17.25
  state aid and 17.31

energy release programmes
  auction mechanism 14.125
  duration of 14.123
  effectiveness of remedy 14.121
  price and costs 14.124
  remedy in merger proceedings 14.108–11
  use of 14.115
  volume to be released 14.122

Index

energy sector
  announcement of review of under Regulation on the Implementation of the Rules on Competition 11.40
  application of competition law in 11.01
  application of rules on 19.03
  application of state aid control in 15.90
  balancing of objectives in 19.13
  caution required in assessing impact of competition law on 19.23
  changes in 19.01A, 19.12
  choice of sector-specific legal framework for 19.16
  complex relationships within 1.56
  EC Treaty and 2.09
  effect of EEA on 2.123
  effect of environmental policy on 2.43
  effect of subsidiarity on 2.49
  effects of Single European Act on 2.36
  EFTA and 2.117
  emergence of system of European regulation for 19.30
  emerging trends of state aid in 19.28
  European Commission initiates study of 2.44
  impact of intervention on 19.25
  importance of 19.11
    to EU 2.11
    to special and exclusive rights 16.04
  improvement of sector-specific legislation 19.50
  increasing body of rules on 19.02
  increasing complexity of regulation 19.31–4
  interventionist role of state in 1.30
  interventionist trend in 19.21
  investigations into infringements of competition law by 11.44
  investment behaviour 1.56
  legal dimensions of environmental protection on 17.54
  legal framework adopted for 19.04–5
  merger control in 14.04
  monopolies in historical context of 16.05
  on-site inspections into compliance with competition law by 11.45
  paradigm shift in 1.59
  potential for regulatory co-operation in 19.35–7
  pre-liberalization paradigm 1.58
  problems of compatibility 1.50, 1.55
  problems of introducing competition into network-bound 1.49
  problems solving in 1.57
  regional co-operation 19.49
  regulation 1.56
    non-compliance 19.45–6
  remedies to address competition concerns relating to merger proposals 14.104–19
  resistance to integration 2.35
  review of under Regulation on the Implementation of the Rules on Competition 11.38
  role of competition law in 19.20
  role of consumers in reform of 19.22
  role of European Commission in liberalizing 2.64
  role of state aid in balancing competition objectives in 19.29
  scale of review of under Regulation on the Implementation of the Rules on Competition 11.42
  second phase of review of under Regulation on the Implementation of the Rules on Competition 11.43
  secondary legislation on 19.17
  sensitivity of 1.03, 19.10
  strategic importance of 1.03
  sustainable development 1.50
Energy Sector Inquiry 6.62, 11.38–45
  content of 11.47
  context of 11.47
  electricity
    market concentration 11.49
    market integration 11.51
    price formation 11.53
    transparency 11.52
    vertical foreclosure 11.50
  gas
    LNG not included in 11.59
    market concentration 11.54
    market integration 11.56
    price information 11.58
    transparency 11.57
    vertical foreclosure 11.55
  Issues Paper on 11.46
  policy-making and 11.47
  preliminary report on 11.48
energy security 4.02
  adoption of supplementary Directives on 19.15
  balancing with competition 18.06
  capacity on transit pipelines 6.62
  case law on 18.82
  competition issues 18.03
  concentration of undertakings and 14.39
  definition of 18.01
  demand side management 18.20
  derogations for PSOs on grounds of 18.26–7
  discretion of European Commission on 18.108
  electricity 18.29–48
  energy efficiency 18.20
  examples of failures 18.09

Index

energy security (*cont.*)
  exemptions from TPA rules on grounds
      of 18.24–5
  factors leading to 1.45
  gas
      upstream issues 18.28
  Gas Directive 18.23–8
  import and export 18.83–4
  imports
      case law 18.86–98
  increasing concerns over 2.160
  information on required from TSOs under
      Electricity Regulation 5.108
  infrastructure 18.68
  legal issues 18.04
  liberalization on 18.05
  measures in Electricity Directive 18.07–8, 18.11–2
  measures in Gas Directive 18.07–8
  monitoring 18.17
  need for investment in 18.10
  nuclear fuel 18.104–6
  prior to adoption of Directives 19.14
  promotion of competition and 18.107
  provision of 'missing links' 18.70
  provisions of EC Treaty 18.81
  PSOs 18.13–6
  reasons for fears 18.02
  reporting 18.21
  safeguard measures 18.22
  secondary legislation 18.07–10
  services of general economic interest 18.99–100
      state aid 18.101–3
  supply
      contract release programmes 14.129
      ensuring 6.88
      monitoring 5.16
      nuclear energy 9.11
      obligations under Gas Directive 6.08
      PSOs relating to 6.18
      under Electricity Directive 5.11
      under Gas Directive 6.17
  tendering
      equivalent measures 18.19
      new capacity 18.18
  TENs and 18.68
  under Euratom 18.106
energy sources
  diversification 9.19
energy supply
  examples of failures 18.09
  interconnectors and 18.25
energy taxes
  attempts to introduce 17.17
  investigation into regime in Netherlands 17.38–9

investigation into regime in Sweden 17.35–7
state of in Member States 17.40
enforcement
  Gas Regulations 6.142
  mechanisms of Electricity Directive 5.69
  regulation 4.03
enrichment services
  contracts for supply of 9.28
  supplies from FSU 9.18
Ente Nazionale Idrocarburi (ENI)
  contract for transportation of natural
      gas with GDF 12.56
  European Commission investigation
      into contracts with GDF 12.55
  proposal by EnBW to acquire 14.76–8
  proposed merger with EDP and GDP 14.93–7
Ente Nazionale per l'Energia Elletrica (ENEL)
  contract for swap of LNG with GDF 12.56
  European Commission investigation into
      contracts with GDF 12.55
Enterprise Energy Ireland Ltd 12.11
environmental aid
  guidelines on 15.62
environmental policy 2.58
  development of in EC Treaty 17.01
  effect on energy sector 2.43
  implication of for competition in
      energy market 17.03
  increasing reach of 2.178
  influence on energy policy 17.02
  renewable energy 10.01
  requirements of TSO in 5.31
environmental protection
  legal dimensions on energy sector 17.54
  market distorting effects of 19.42–4
  obligations under Gas Directive 6.08
  tendering for new capacity in interests of 5.23
environmental sustainability 4.02
E.ON
  proposals to acquire MOL 14.79–84
  proposed merger with Ruhrgas 14.41–5
  undertakings given on acquisition
      of MOL 14.117
  undertakings given on acquisition
      of Ruhrgas 14.116
equipment
  guidelines in relation to TENs 18.74
equivalent measures
  tendering
      energy security 18.19
essential facilities
  doctrine of 13.98
  criticism of 13.99
  never applied by courts 13.100

essential services
  obligations on under EEC Treaty 2.27
Estlink Interconnector 5.100
Estonia
  derogation from parts of Electricity Directive 5.49
  electricity generation in 5.104
  interconnector between national grids of Finland and 5.100, 5.105
Estonian Energy Markets Inspectorate (ENI) 5.102
  deletion of destination clause imposed on 12.45
  to refrain from introducing destination clauses into new gas supply contracts 12.46
  undertakings given by 12.48
  undertakings given to 12.44
EU law
  applicable to electricity industry 5.01
Euratom Supply Agency (ESA)
  appeal against bar on imports of nuclear materials 9.27
  case relating to assistance to ENU 8.21
  appeal 9.22
  common supply policy of 9.17
  establishment under Euratom 9.13
  market share 9.18
  may bar imports of nuclear materials 9.26
Euro-Mediterranean Association Agreements
  energy objectives of 2.169
  establishment of 2.168
  possible model for regional co-operation 2.171
  priority areas under 2.172
  scope of 2.170
Europe 3.26
  beginnings of energy policy in 2.31
  economic integration 1.31
  gas markets 1.68
  impact of collapse of Soviet Union on energy policy 2.07
  lack of import dependence in relation to electricity supply in 1.66
  natural gas 1.67
  new approaches to energy policy in 2.32
  poor interconnection in electricity supply in 1.66
  privatization across 14.142
European Atomic Energy Community Treaty 1957 (Euratom)
  limit on operation of 2.21
  narrow jurisdiction of 2.20
  objectives of 2.17
  origins of 2.18
  overview of work of 9.38
  second instrument of integration of energy sector 2.17
  state aids under 9.29
European Coal and Steel Community Treaty 1951 (ECSC)
  case law relating to state aids under 8.25
  changes to merger control under 8.16
  common market objectives of 8.06
  competition requirements of 8.07
  competition objectives of 8.08
  decisions under Coal Regulation with respect or Member States whose coal industries were subject to 8.24
  differences from EC Treaty 8.12
  earliest Community interest in energy matters in 2.15
  expiry of 8.10
  general aims of 8.05
  joint ventures under 8.14
  legal framework established by 8.01
  main objectives of 2.15
  market share provisions under 8.14
  merger control under 8.13
  principles of market economy in 8.06
  procedural changes under 8.15
  restructuring aid under 8.26
  success of in managing contraction of coal and steel industry 8.09
  transfer of assets of 8.11
European Commission
  approach to M&A 14.60
  co-operation between NCAs and 11.16
  co-operation with EFTA Surveillance Authority 2.119
  collection of information by 11.18
  commitments on TPA obtained by 13.135
  Communication on stranded costs methodology 15.15
  competition strategy of 11.02
  composition of 2.65
  conclusion of investigations into export restrictions by 12.54
  conclusion of investigations into gas export restrictions by 12.54
  consultation by 2.71
  decision of on concentrations 14.56
  decisions by relating to new infrastructure and interconnectors 6.55
  discretion of on energy security 18.108
  duty imposed on to ensure Member States comply with Art 86 EC Treaty 16.08
  electricity
    how scope of geographic market is determined by 11.35

European Commission (*cont.*)
  Euratom primary source of
    competence for 9.14
  executive function of 2.72
  expansion of role of 2.75
  extension of Investigatory powers of 11.17
  gas
    how scope of geographic market is determined
      by 11.33
  guidelines made under Gas Regulations may only
    be amended by 6.135
  information to be provided to under Gas
    Regulations 6.136
  initiates study of EU energy sector 2.44
  investigation into contracts entered into by GDF
    with ENI and ENEL 12.55
  investigation into Norwegian gas sales by 2.126
  law-making powers 2.73
  legislative role 2.69
  limitation on exemptions from Gas Directive's
    access provisions on storage 6.42
  monitoring of implementation of Electricity
    Regulation by 5.131
  must explain policies to European Parliament 2.89
  powers of under Merger Regulation 14.18
  powers to inspect concentrations 14.17
  powers under EC Treaty 2.70
  principle functions of 2.68
  priorities of 2.63
  procedure adopted by against destination
    clauses 12.37
  prohibits long-term contract of Ijssellmij 13.16
  proposals to create a central oil
    storage agency 18.65
  publication of formal decisions on destination
    clauses 12.57
  regulatory function of 2.73
  relationship between Council of
    Ministers and 2.76
  relationship with NRAs 3.56
  report by into operation of Renewables
    Directive 10.12
  report by on implementation of Renewables
    Directive 10.33
  required under Renewables Directive to present
    report on support mechanisms 10.11
  requirements on under Renewables Directive to
    conduct evaluations in respect of support
    schemes 10.10
  role of 2.65
    as guardian of EC Treaty 2.74
    in determining state aid 15.09
    in liberalizing energy sector 2.64
    in regulation 3.09
    on reporting to Member States on Electricity
      Reporting Directive 18.47
  secondary legislation making by 2.73
  thresholds for competence over
    concentrations 14.20
European Competition Network
  (ECN) 3.02, 11.03
  constitution of 11.06
  role of 11.20
European Court of Justice (ECJ)
  actions for damages 2.101
  annulment proceedings 2.99
  citizens activating procedure for preliminary
    rulings 2.104
  composition of 2.94
  emergence of energy jurisprudence from 2.93
  enforcement of Gas Directive by 6.114
  failure to act 2.100
  failure to fulfil obligations 2.98
  importance of preliminary rulings in development
    of Community law 2.105
  jurisdiction 2.97
  may hear appeals from CFI 2.102
  preliminary rulings 2.103
  procedure 2.96
  restricted interpretation of special and exclusive
    rights by 16.11
  rulings
    on exclusive purchasing obligations 13.18
    on exclusive rights 16.90
    on golden shares 14.137–41
    on preferential access 5.132, 5.134–5
    in relation to Electricity Directive 5.133
European Economic Area (EEA) 2.115
  competence of in respect of
    concentrations 14.27
  co-operation with EFTA 2.120
  effect on energy sector 2.123
  EFTA and 2.116
  judicial enforcement of 2.124
  management of 2.120
  rights and obligations under 2.117
  scope of 2.116
European Emissions Trading System 17.02
European energy regulator
  goal of 3.10
European Federation of Energy Traders (EFET) 3.26
European Free Trade Association (EFTA)
  co-operation with EEA 2.120
  court of 2.122
  dynamic nature of 2.118
  EEA and 2.116
  energy sector and 2.117
  institutions of 2.119

European law
  second generation of Directives on competition 11.03
European Parliament
  adoption of resolutions by 2.92
  co-decision procedure with Council of Ministers 2.81
  committees of 2.91
  competition law to be reviewed by 16.92
  elections to 2.84
  enhanced role of 2.53
  enhancement of role of 2.81
  European Commission must explain policies to 2.89
  evolution of 2.85
  financial control of 2.90
  legislative role in energy policy 2.83
  number of Members 2.84
  originally called Assembly of the European Communities 2.85
  power of co-decision with Council of Ministers 2.87
  procedures for measures presented to 2.88
European Regulatory Group for Electricity and Gas (ERGEG) 3.02
  advisory role of 5.66
  changes brought about by 19.01A
  co-operative function of 5.68
  consultation procedures established by 3.13
  development of guidelines on cross-border trade 3.38
  development of guidelines on gas 3.39
  relationship with Forums 3.37
European Transmission System Operators (ETSO)
  composition of 3.22
  creation of 3.21
  proposals of 3.23
  unbundling role of 3.24
European Union
  agriculture excluded from competition rules of 2.10
  allocation of authority 19.07
  approach adopted by in creating internal market 3.59
  changes to nuclear policy with enlargement 9.20
  constitution for 2.56
  creation of internal market in energy by 2.01
  creation of legal regime for gas and electricity by 2.02
  emergency of energy law 2.06
  energy and integration within 1.31
  enlargement of 2.40, 2.45
  entry barriers 1.90
  expansion of 19.06
  identification of common objectives in energy policy 2.33
  impact of enlargement 2.160
  importance of energy sector to 2.11
  innovation in governance of 19.08
  legal order for energy 2.03
  nuclear policy 9.02
  origins of energy law 2.05
  PCA concluded between Russian Federation and 2.163
  principle objectives of 2.164
  policy on nuclear energy 9.03
  policy on renewable energy 10.01
  programme for reform of energy markets 1.07
  relations with former Soviet Union 2.161
  relations with Russia 2.165
  role of in managing relationships of NRAs 3.54
  scope of law on energy 2.04
  sector-specific law in 19.09
  small amount of oil production in 7.01
  Treaty of Nice preparing for further enlargement of 2.55
  uranium mine in 9.02
excise duty
  energy products 17.21
  mineral oils 17.23
exclusive purchasing agreements
  interpretation of 13.20
  restrictions under EC Treaty 13.19
exclusive purchasing obligations
  ECJ ruling on 13.18
  prohibition of imposed by Almelo 13.17
exclusive rights
  case law 2.30, 16.37–9
  incompatibility of with competition rules of EC Treaty 16.89
  of GFU 12.06
  postal service
    case law 16.43–5
    rulings of ECJ on 16.90
exclusive supply agreements
  case law on 13.13
  special circumstances 13.14
exemptions
  decisions taken on since adoption of Gas Directive 6.58
export restrictions
  gas
    conclusion of European Commissions investigations into 12.54
exporters
  wholesale 5.47

Index

exports
  energy security and 18.83–4
  prohibitions on quantitative restrictions on in EEC Treaty 2.24
Exxon
  proposal to merge with Mobil 14.74–5

failure to act
  ECJ proceedings on 2.100
Federal Energy Regulatory Agency (FERC) 6.59
feed-in schemes
  state aids 10.37
financial difficulties 6.87
Finland
  electricity generation in 5.104
  exclusion form Hydrocarbons Licensing Directive 7.08
  interconnector between national grids of Estonia and 5.100, 5.105
  tax incentives in 10.18
fixed networks
  dependence of electricity and gas on to transport and deliver 1.60
Florence Regulatory Forum on Electricity 3.02
  agreements reached by 3.15
  composition of 3.20
  development of 3.14
  exchange of information by 3.27
  initial role of 3.18
  legal status of 3.17
  matters discussed by 3.19
  regulation by co-operation by 3.16
  regulatory input from 3.13
  relationship with ERGEG 3.37
fluctuation
  demand of electricity 1.63
force majeure 5.92
foreign nationals
  control of investment by 14.143
former Soviet Union (FSU)
  relations with EU 2.161
  supply of enrichment services from 9.18
France
  dismantling of oil products monopolies in 7.01
  golden shares and 14.139
  import-export monopolies 16.70–4
  merger proposals 14.66–7, 14.98
  monopolies in oil markets 12.01
  nationalization 1.27
  notification under Hydrocarbons Licensing Directive 7.11
  privatization 14.146–7
  state guarantees to EDF 15.56–9
  stranded costs 15.33
  tendering procedures in 10.17
free movement of capital
  ECJ ruling that golden shares may be contrary to 14.165–7
freedom of movement of goods
  case law 16.34–6
freedom of transit
  under provisions of Energy Charter Treaty 2.144

gas
  convergence with electricity 14.85–8
  European law relating to 4.01
  export restrictions 12.54
  findings of Energy Sector Inquiry
    market concentration 11.54
    market integration 11.56
    price information 11.58
    transparency 11.57
    vertical foreclosure 11.55
  findings of Energy Sector Inquiry did not include LNG 11.59
  import from Algeria 12.59
  import-export monopolies 16.51–74
  joint marketing of 12.29
  long-term contracts 13.04
    guidelines on long-term contracts from FCO 13.09
    incompatibility of with competition law 13.08
    investigation into Endesa 13.12
    investigation into Gas Natural 13.12
    limits on duration of 13.10
    problems of 13.05
    report by German FCO on 13.07
    role of 13.06
  preparation for internal market in by Madrid Forum 3.34
  price obligations under Gas Directive 6.08
  product market 11.30
  relevant geographical markets 11.36
  sale of in Norway 2.125
  upstream issues
    energy security 18.28
Gas Co-ordination Group
  establishment under Gas Security Directive 18.53
  role of 18.54
gas companies
  European Commission initiates proceedings against Norwegian 12.07
gas conversion 13.130
Gas Council 1.27
gas delivery points
  contract release programmes 14.128

689

Index

Gas Directive 1998 (First Gas Directive)
   experiences gained from in relation to storage 6.41
Gas Directive 2003
   access to storage facilities under 6.29
   aims of 6.03
   applications for exemptions from application of on grounds of PSOs 6.14
   attention paid to LNG in 6.35
   authorization under 6.15
   common rules established by 6.04
   comparisons with Electricity Directive 6.12
   competition law and 13.01
   compliance provision in respect of unbundling under 6.37
   consumer protection provisions of 6.10
   contents of report on 6.111
   contents of second one-off report on 6.113
   continues special access regime for upstream pipeline networks 6.47
   decisions taken on exemptions since adoption of 6.58
   derogations from 6.69
   designation of DSOs under 6.27
   designation of TSOs under 6.23
   energy security 18.23–8
   energy security measure in 18.07–8
   enforcement by ECJ 6.114
   European Commission's limitation on exemption from access provisions on storage in 6.42
   exemptions from application of on grounds of PSOs 6.13
   exemptions to authorization provisions of 6.11
   exemptions under 6.16
   facilitation of construction of direct lines under 6.65
   general duties under 6.25
   guidelines on TPA under 6.43
   limitation on exemptions relating to storage under 6.42
   main PSOs provisions under 6.07
   possibilities of derogations from 6.71
   provisions for NRAs in 6.68
   provisions on distribution under 6.26
   provisions on supply under 6.26
   PSOs under 16.02
   public service provisions under 6.05
   regulation of TPA under 6.39
   report on may contain recommendations 6.112
   reporting requirements 6.110
   responsibilities of DSOs under 6.28
   role of Member States in designating TSOs under 6.24
   rules relating to derogations from 6.70
   scope of 6.02
   scope of PSOs under 6.06
   security of supply under 6.17
   specific obligations of 6.08
   storage capacity and 6.46
   technical rules 6.19
   TPA provisions under 6.38
      in relation to storage under 6.40
   unbundling provisions in 6.36
Gas Directives
   regulatory role of 3.62
gas industry
   characteristics of 1.10
   differences between electricity industry and in respect of liberalization 1.43
   EU legal regime for 2.02
   importance of special and exclusive rights 16.09
   mergers in 14.57
   single regulator for 1.81
gas markets
   definition of geographic market 11.32
   early experiments in liberalization 1.41
   European 1.68
   Germany
      TPA 13.40
   how European Commission decides on scope of geographic market 11.33
   joint selling not permitted 12.63
   non-uniform opening of 1.92
   position of undertaking in 6.89
   prerequisites for introduction of competition into 1.75
   progress of integration 6.149
   responsibilities or participants under Gas Security Directive 18.50
Gas Natural
   investigation into long-term contracts of 13.12
   proposed merger with Endesa 14.46–53
gas networks
   access to in Germany 13.34
   pressure levels 6.20
gas production
   horizontal arrangements 12.13
   joint ventures 12.04
Gas Regulations 2005
   adoption of Guidelines envisaged by 6.132
   aims of 6.115
   based on guidelines of Madrid Forum 6.116
   competition law and 6.146
   derogations from 6.144
   enforcement of 6.142
   entry into force of 6.147
   guidelines under may only be amended by European Commission 6.135

Index

Gas Regulations 2005 (*cont.*)
   information to be provided to European
      Commission under 6.136
   monitoring of implementation of 6.145
   role of NRAs in ensuring compliance with 6.143
   significance of guidelines under 6.134
   specific goals of 6.117
   transparency requirements 6.128
gas release programmes 13.129
gas reserves
   Norway 2.125
Gas Sales Consortium (GFU) 2.125
   exclusive rights of 12.06
   investigations into joint selling arrangements 12.05
   proceedings against 12.08
   settlement of case 12.08
gas sector
   competition policy on 12.03
   European law on to stimulate competition 6.148
   international character of 12.02
   main legislation pertaining to 6.01
Gas Security Directive 2004
   entry into force 18.58
   establishment of Gas Co-ordination
      Group under 18.53
   monitoring under 18.55–7
   protection of household customers under 18.51
   provisions of 18.49
   public service issues 18.59
   responsibilities of market participants under 18.50
   scope of 18.52
gas storage
   market definition 11.30
gas supply
   characteristics of 1.67
   common rules for 6.04
   constraints on competition 1.69
   dependence on fixed networks to transport and
      deliver 1.60
   distinctions between eligible and non-eligible
      customers 11.31
   downstream market segment 1.69
   efforts to ensure no further reduction 12.43
   from Russia 12.42
   gas chain 1.67
   geopolitics of 1.67
   interruption to 9.02
   market definition 11.30
   PSOs relating to security of 6.18
   quality obligations under Gas Directive 6.08
   safety 1.67
   security obligations under Gas Directive 6.08
   security of under Gas Directive 6.17
   size of provider 1.67
   storage factors 1.67
   upstream market segment 1.70
   market definition 11.30
gas supply agreements
   similarity to reduction clauses 12.21
gas supply contracts
   destination clauses in 12.45–7
   investigations into destination clauses 12.34
gas trading
   market definition 11.30
Gas Transmission Infrastructure (GTI)
   diversity of 3.33
Gas VV Agreement
   Germany 13.40–4
Gasunie
   balancing assistance offered by 13.110
   entry-exit regime 13.124
   investigations into contracts with Gazprom 12.53
   monitoring of 13.132
   to improve handling access requests 13.115
   transparency on availability of capacity 13.105
Gaz de France (GDF) 1.27
   balancing services offered by 13.113
   contract for swap of LNG with ENEL 12.56
   contract for transportation of natural gas
      with ENI 12.56
   European Commission investigation into
      contracts with ENI and ENEL 12.55
   gas conversion by 13.130
   gas release programme of 13.129
   monitoring of 13.134
   proposed merger with Suez 14.98
   system of tariff zones introduced by 13.128
   to improve handling access requests 13.117
   transparency on availability of capacity 13.108
   undertakings on congestion management 13.121
Gazprom
   destination clauses and 12.42
   investigations into contracts with Gasunie 12.53
   undertakings given by 12.52
GDP
   proposed merger with ENI 14.93–7
Gemeente Almelo 13.15
   prohibition of exclusive purchasing obligation
      imposed by 13.17
**General Agreement on Tariffs and
   Trade (GATT)** 1.38
   provisions of Energy Charter Treaty subjects trade
      in energy to 2.140
generating capacity
   impact of liberalization on 1.51
   new 1.46
generation characteristics
   information on under Electricity Directive 5.12

Index

geographic market
  electricity 11.34
    how European Commission decides on scope of 11.35
  gas 11.36
    definition of 11.32
    how European Commission decides scope of 11.33
geopolitics
  gas supply 1.67
German Federal Cartel Office (FCO)
  Guidelines on long-term contracts from 13.09
  report by into gas supply contracts 13.07
Germany
  access to gas and electricity networks in 13.34
  brown coal production in 8.03
  calculation of transmission pricing in 13.33
  gas imports into 12.51
  gas markets
    TPA 13.40
  Gas VV Agreement 13.40–4
  hard coal production in 8.03
  merger proposals 14.41–5, 14.62–5, 14.68, 14.76–84
  regulation 3.07
  state aid
    renewable energy 17.14–6
  Verbändevereinbarung 13.34–9
globalization
  debate on nation-state and 1.39
  development of 1.38
  energy industry 1.37
  progress of 1.40
golden share
  case law on 14.154–64
  ECJ judgments on 14.137–41
  ECJ ruling that may be contrary to free movement of capital 14.165–7
  public security arguments 14.151–3
governments
  link between energy industry and 1.26
Greece
  accession to EU 2.45
  brown coal production in 8.03
  dismantling of oil products monopolies in 7.01
  energy security
    imports
      case law 18.94–8
  lack of compliance by with unbundling requirements in Electricity Directive 5.78
  monopolies in oil markets 12.01
  potential benefit of derogations for investment risk 6.109
  regulation 3.07

stranded costs 15.34–5
green certificate system
  secondary market developed by 10.16
  support schemes 10.15
green electricity
  state aid to support generation of 15.70–2
  trading 10.21
Green Paper on Energy Policy 18.05
greenhouse gas emissions
  state aid for reduction of 15.75
grid access
  renewable energy
    new generators 10.31
grid systems
  legal framework in respect of renewable energy 10.30
  renewable energy and 10.28
grid usage
  information on 5.58
guarantees
  electricity origin 10.21
  origins 10.23
  origins under Renewables Directive 10.26
  renewable energy generators 10.22
  TPA 6.124
guidelines
  amendment of under Electricity Regulation 5.117
  comitology of under Electricity Regulation 5.118
  definition of 6.133
  made under Gas Regulations may only be amended by European Commission 6.135
  main matters under Electricity Regulation 5.114
  new in respect of congestion management 5.119
  produced under Electricity Regulation 5.113
  renewable energy 10.35
  significance of under Gas Regulations 6.134
  to be adopted under Gas Regulations 6.132
Guidelines for Good TPA for Storage System Operators 3.39, 6.137
  basis of 6.138
  main provisions of 6.140
  monitoring operation of 6.141
  scope of 6.139
Gulf Co-operation Council (GCC) 2.34
GVS
  proposal by EnBW to acquire share of 14.76–8

Hackberry LNG Terminal LLC
  authorization of terminals for 6.59–60
hard coal
  production of 8.03
harmonization
  attempts on indirect taxation 17.18
  charges under Electricity Regulation 5.89

Index

harmonization (cont.)
  progression towards under Electricity
      Regulation 5.116
  provisions of Electricity Directive 5.56
  qualified majority needed for 2.40
  reliance on Directives 16.15
health
  provisions in Euratom 9.08
Hidrocantábrico
  proposal to merge with EnBW 14.69–71
High-Level Energy Group 2.71
horizontal arrangements
  gas production 12.13
horizontal demarcation
  definition of 1.69
household customers
  protection of under Gas Security
      Directive 18.51
Hungary
  brown coal production in 8.03
  hard coal production in 8.03
  practical implementation of unbundling in 5.41
  reliance on nuclear energy 9.02
  stranded costs 15.36–9
hydrocarbons
  liberalization of licensing 7.25
Hydrocarbons Licensing Directive 1994
  application for licences under 7.09
  background to 7.03
  criteria for determining applications for
      licences under 7.12
  directed at oil sector 7.02
  early example of pan-European co-operation
      on energy 7.24
  establishment of common rules under 7.06
  exclusion of Finland and Luxembourg
      from 7.08
  exemptions to 7.21
  geographical limitations 7.18
  implementation 7.22
  in relation to upstream pipeline networks 6.51
  in respect of natural gas production 6.21
  issue of sovereignty under 7.07
  links with public procurement legislation 7.20
  main objectives of 7.04
  monitoring of EU entities in third
      countries under 7.19
  monitoring of licencees under 7.17
  notifications under 7.11
  permitted procedures under 7.10
  provisions for state licence holders under 7.16
  results of 7.26
  scope of 7.05
  state participation in 7.13

state protection of financial interests under 7.14
states' ability to impose conditions and
    requirements relating to 7.15
subject to co-decision procedure 7.23
Iceland
  co-operation with EEA 2.116
ideology
  factors influencing energy 1.22
Ijssellmij *see* Energiebedrijf Ijssellmij NV
imbalance charges 6.129
import dependence
  lack of in Europe in relation to
      electricity supply 1.66
import-export monopolies
  burden of proof 16.84
  case law 16.81–3
  compromises on 16.86
  early prohibition of 16.88
  electricity 16.51–74
  gas 15.51–74
  incompatibility with internal market 16.87
  practices contrary to Art 31 EC Treaty 16.85
  public service element 16.75–9
  Spain 16.80
importers
  wholesale 5.47
imports
  electricity
      market definition 11.24
  energy security 18.83–4
      case law 18.86–98
  gas 12.49, 12.51
      from Algeria 12.59
  prohibitions on quantitative restrictions
      on in EEC Treaty 2.24
  reporting requirements of Electricity
      Directive 5.77
incentive-based regulation
  lack of provision for in Electricity Directive 5.60
independent regulator 1.79
indigenous primary fuel sources
  priority given to 5.32
indirect taxes
  attempts to harmonize 17.18
information
  capacity allocation 5.58
  confidentiality of supplied under Electricity
      Regulation 5.112
  failure of NRAs to provide 5.110
  grid usage 5.58
  interconnection 5.58
  on safety and security required from TSOs under
      Electricity Regulation 5.108

Index

information (cont.)
  required from TSOs on interconnection capacities under Electricity Regulation 5.107
  requirements on TSOs under Electricity Regulation 5.106
  to be provided to European Commission under Gas Regulations 6.136
  undertakings by NRAs to supply 5.111
information exchange
  Florence Regulatory Forum on Electricity 3.27
infrastructure
  energy security 18.68
  high costs of 1.61
  no block exemptions to be granted in respect of 6.57
  power of NRAs to choose specific rules for specific pieces of 6.56
  release 14.118
infringement
  Electricity Regulation 5.128
inspections
  on-site into compliance with competition law by energy sector 11.45
installations
  guidelines in relation to TENs 18.74
integration
  energy and EU attempts at 1.31
  energy sector resistance to 2.35
inter-operability
  degree of 6.91
interconnection
  access to 13.48
    for wholesale exporters and importers 5.47
  allocation of capacity 5.58
  functions of TSOs in 5.30
  information on 5.58
    from TSOs on under Electricity Regulation 5.107
  poor for electricity supply in Europe 1.66
  release 14.118
interconnectors
  between national grids of Finland and Estonia 5.100, 5.105
  energy supply and 18.25
  exemptions for new 5.95
  insufficient for market integration 13.46
  market definition 11.27
  provisions for exemption for new under Electricity Regulation 5.96
  refusal of TPA 13.87–95
    case law 13.96–7, 13.101–3
Internal Energy Market programme
  changes made to by Treaty on European Union 2.47

internal market
  application of EC Treaty to 19.18
  approach adopted by EU in creating 3.59
  co-decision procedure applied to all legislation on 2.54
  commitment to 2.37
  creation of in energy by EU 2.01
  effect of ETS on 17.49
  effects of granting derogations on 6.95
  gas
    preparation for by Madrid Forum 3.34
  incompatibility of import-export monopolies with 16.87
  natural monopolies no barrier to creation of 1.95
  obstacles to in energy 2.44
  progress of electricity 5.140
  regional approach to 5.141
  renewable energy and 17.06
  state monopolies not perceived as obstacle to establishment of 2.12
intervention
  distortions due to 1.34
  energy markets 1.33
  impact of on energy sector 19.25
  role of state in energy sector 1.30
  trend in energy sector 19.21
intra-day trading opportunities
  wholesale markets
    electricity 11.29
investigations
  into Norwegian gas sales by EFTA Surveillance Authority and European Commission 2.126
  under Regulation on the Implementation of the Rules on Competition 11.12
investment
  control of by foreign nationals 14.143
  derogations for risk to 6.104
    application of criteria for 6.107
    criteria for 6.106
    procedure for 6.105
    test for 6.108
  impact of liberalization on 1.51
  provisions of Energy Charter Treaty 2.134
  provisions under Electricity Security Directive 18.42
investment disputes
  provisions of Energy Charter Treaty 2.138
invitation to tender 5.25
Ireland
  accession to EU 2.45
  energy security
    imports
      case law 18.86–93
  joint marketing arrangements 12.11

Index

Ireland (*cont.*)
  notification under Hydrocarbons Licensing
      Directive 7.11
  tendering procedures in 10.17
isolated markets 6.99
  derogations for 6.103
  lack of system connection 6.101
Issues Paper
  on Energy Sector Inquiry 11.46
Italy
  energy supply failures in 18.09
  import-export monopolies 16.67–9
  notification under Hydrocarbons Licensing
      Directive 7.11
  practical implementation of unbundling in 5.41
  regulation 3.07
  stranded costs 15.40–3
IVO
  merger with Neste 14.88

joint marketing
  Denmark 12.14
  DONG with DUC 12.17
  electricity 12.30
  Ireland 12.11
joint production
  under Regulation on Categories of Specialization
      Agreements 12.18
joint selling
  investigations into by GFU 12.05
  not permitted in gas market 12.63
joint ventures
  gas producers 12.04
  under ECSC 8.14
jurisprudence
  energy 2.93

Kernkraftwerke Lippe-Ems (KLE)
  case relating to source of uranium 9.23
    appeal 9.25
  diversification of sources of supply by 9.24
Latin America
  energy markets in 1.54
legislation
  institutions making 2.110
  subsidiarity and 2.48
liberalization
  application of competition law in energy
      markets 1.53
  conditions for 1.90
  differences between gas and electricity industries
      in respect of 1.43
  early experiments in electricity markets 1.41
  early experiments in gas markets 1.41

  energy security and 18.05
  hydrocarbons licensing 7.25
  importance of merger control to 14.169
  importance of storage in relation to 6.34
  long-term contracts to promote 13.03
  no one model in energy markets 1.42
  non-uniformity of 1.92
  potential impact of NRAs on 3.46
  reliance on Directives 16.15
  renewable energy issues 17.07
  role of European Commission in respect of
      energy sector 2.64
  state aid and 15.10, 15.91
  structural actions for 11.64
  support for 12.60
  TPA and 13.140
  transition to 1.51
  transitional period 1.52
licencees
  monitoring of under provisions of Hydrocarbons
      Licensing Directive 7.17
licences
  applications for under Hydrocarbons Licensing
      Directive 7.09
  criteria for determining applications for
      licences under Hydrocarbons Licensing
      Directive 7.12
licensing regime
  establishment of 1.94
  liberalization of hydrocarbons 7.25
Liechtenstein
  co-operation with EEA 2.116
lignite
  production of 8.03
liquidity
  aim to improve 14.114
liquefied natural gas (LNG)
  attention paid to in Gas Directive 6.35
  capacity 1.73
  increased supplies of 1.72
  not included in Energy Sector Review 11.59
  TPA rules 1.74
  US experience with authorization of terminals 6.59
Lisbon Agenda 1.07
Lithuania
  reliance on nuclear energy 9.02
LNG system operators
  general duties of under Gas Directive 6.25
LNG terminals
  capital intensiveness of 1.73
  managed access 6.59
  US experience with authorization of 6.59
local production operations
  storage facilities used in connection with 6.44

Index

long-term contracts
  competition issues relating to 13.02
  electricity 13.13
    case law 13.25–30
    duration of 13.21
      market foreclosure 13.24
      Scottish Nuclear Ltd 13.22–3
    Netherlands 13.14
    network access 13.15
  gas 13.04
    Guidelines on long-term contracts from FCO 13.09
    incompatibility of with competition law 13.08
    investigation into Endesa 13.12
    investigation into Gas Natural 13.12
    limits on duration of 13.10
    problems of 13.05
    report by German FCO on 13.07
    role of 13.06
  to promote liberalization 13.03
Louis Dreyfus
  proposal to merge with EDF 14.66–7
low-carbon economy
  advent of 1.59
Luxembourg
  exclusion form Hydrocarbons Licensing Directive 7.08
  potential benefit of derogations for investment risk 6.109
  stranded costs 15.44
Madrid Regulatory Forum on Gas 3.02
  agreements reached by 3.15
  broad aims of 3.29
  composition of 3.30
  development of 3.14
  establishment of 3.28
  formation of group of TSOs by 3.33
  Gas Regulation based on guidelines of 6.116
  legal status of 3.17
  limitations of 3.36
  preparation for internal market in gas by 3.34
  regulation by co-operation by 3.16
  regulatory input from 3.13
  relationship with ERGEG 3.37
  similarity to Florence Forum 3.31
  successes of 3.32
  vulnerability of 3.35
Malta
  tax incentives in 10.18
managed access
  LNG terminals 6.59
Marathon 12.11
market concentration
  electricity

    findings of Energy Sector Inquiry on 11.49
  gas
    findings of Energy Sector Inquiry on 11.54
    remedies for 11.61
market conditions
  ambiguity of 6.90
market definition
  electricity 11.24
  energy 11.21
  interconnectors 11.27
  variations in 11.23
market distortion
  effects of environmental protection 19.42–4
market economy
  declaration that Russia is 2.166
  principles of in ECSC 8.06
market foreclosure
  contract duration and 13.24
market integration
  electricity
    findings of Energy Sector Inquiry on 11.51
  gas
    findings of Energy Sector Inquiry 11.56
  geographic factors 11.37
  insufficient interconnectors for 13.46
market opening
  provisions in Electricity Directive 5.48
  schedule for 6.63
  transitional mechanisms 5.50, 6.64
market share
  ESA 9.18
  provisions under ECSC 8.14
markets
  creation of 1.96
Member States
  duty imposed on European Commission to ensure compliance with Art 86 EC Treaty 16.08
  increasing inter-dependence of 2.177
  introduction of taxes on energy products by 17.33
  limitation on tax exemptions by 17.34
  may use referral system in respect of concentrations 14.22
  number of votes 2.79
  obligations under ETS 17.44
  regulation in 3.07
  regulatory authority in 3.01
  reluctance of to cede control of energy policy to EU 2.13
  role of in designating TSOs under Gas Directive 6.24
  state of energy taxes in 17.40
  variation of functioning of NRAs in 3.57
  wish to retain competence over energy 2.57

Index

merger control 14.03
  addressing concerns over 14.170
  changes to under ECSC 8.16
  competition central to 14.171
  contribution of to competition in energy markets 14.06
  energy sector 14.04
  importance of to liberalization process 14.169
  legal regime for under Merger Regulation 14.07
  progress of 14.168
  recent instances of 19.27
  under competition law 19.26
  under ECSC 8.13
merger proceedings
  auctions as remedy in 14.111–2
  contract release programmes as remedy in 14.113
  divestiture as remedy in 14.107
  energy release programmes as remedy in 14.108–11
merger proposals
  Austria 14.72–3
  Belgium 14.54–5
  France 14.66–7, 14.98
  Germany 14.41–5, 14.62–5, 14.68, 14.76–84
  Netherlands 14.74–5
  notification of 14.61
  Portugal 14.93–7
  remedies to meet competition concerns 14.99–103
    energy sector 14.104–19
  Spain 14.46–53, 14.69–71
  two-thirds rule and 14.40
Merger Regulation 1989
  criticism of 14.05
Merger Regulation 2004
  action on market concentration under 11.61
  application to concentrations 14.12
  changes under 8.16
  definition of dominant position under 14.10
  introduction of 14.08
  jurisdiction under 8.13
  legal regime for merger control under 14.07
  limited jurisdiction of 14.36–7
  powers of European Commission under 14.18
  referral system under 14.19
mergers and acquisitions (M&A)
  cross-border 14.01
  disincentives to 14.59
  dominant position arising from mergers 14.09
  effects of mergers on competition 14.11
  electricity and gas sector 14.57
  European Commission's approach to 14.60
  jurisdiction over mergers 14.35
  negative consequences for development of competition 14.02

  political intervention in 14.136
mineral oils
  excise duty on 17.23
Ministerial Council
  Energy Community Treaty 2.129
Mobil
  proposal to merge with Exxon 14.74–5
MOL
  proposals by E.ON to acquire 14.79–84
  undertakings given on acquisition by E.ON 14.117
monitoring 13.131–4
monopolies 4.03
  dismantling oil products in France and Greece 7.01
  historical context of in energy sector 16.05
monopoly rights
  case law 16.32–3
  under Art 86 EC Treaty 16.31
Most Favoured Nation treatment 2.135

nation-state
  globalization and debate on 1.39
national allocation plans (NAPs) 15.78
  amendments to 17.47
  ETS 17.44
national competition authorities (NCAs)
  co-operation between European Commission and 11.16
  competence of 13.01
  compulsory functions of 11.14
  enforcement role of 11.06
  freedom in application of national law 11.13
  referral system and 14.26
national indicative targets
  under Renewables Directive 10.07
national regulatory authorities (NRAs) 3.02
  activities of under Electricity Directive 5.58
  applications for exemptions in respect of new infrastructure 6.54
  changes brought about by 19.01A
  charged with ensuring compliance with Electricity Regulation 5.130
  co-ordination among 3.52
  competence of 3.05, 13.01
  consultation procedures established by 3.13
  cross-border functions of 5.63
  demarcation of competence with competition authorities in UK 3.51
  development of role of 3.45
  dispute resolution role of 5.64
    jurisdictional aspects 5.65
  enforcement role of 19.47
  enhancement of legal status of 5.55
  extension and reinforcement of role of under Electricity Directive 5.04

national regulatory authorities (NRAs) *(cont.)*
  failure of to provide required
    information 5.110
  general responsibilities under Electricity
    Directive 5.57
  independence required of 3.07
  minimum functions and competences set out
    under Electricity Directive 5.56
  potential impact of 3.46
  power of to choose specific rules for specific
    pieces of infrastructure 6.56
  provisions of Gas Directive on 6.68
  relationship with competition authorities 3.48
  relationship with European Commission 3.56
  role in ensuring compliance with Gas
    Regulations 6.143
  role of courts in reviewing powers of 3.08, 3.53
  role of EU in managing relationships 3.54
  scope of 3.03
  tariff supervision role of 5.61
    limitations on 5.62
  undertakings to supply information 5.111
  variation in functioning in Member States 3.57
  variation in structure of 3.44
national treatment 2.135
nationalization
  energy 1.23
    post-1945 1.27
  France 1.27
natural gas
  common rules for transmission of 6.05
  definition of transmission in respect of 6.22
  Europe 1.67
  introduction of 1.23
natural gas production
  Hydrocarbons Licensing Directive in
    respect of 6.21
natural monopolies
  no barrier to creation of internal market 1.95
  pipeline network 12.02
  potential conflict of interests 1.84
Neste
  merger with IVO 14.88
Netherlands
  import-export monopolies 16.56–66
  investigation into energy taxes
    regime in 17.38–9
  long-term contracts
    electricity 13.14
  merger proposals 14.74–5
  notification under Hydrocarbons Licensing
    Directive 7.11
  practical implementation of unbundling in 5.41
  regulation 3.07

state aid
  renewable energy 17.11–3
  stranded costs 15.45–7
network access
  barriers to 3.13
  charges by TSOs for 5.86
    setting 5.87
  costs 6.119
  electricity
    long-term contracts 13.15
  provisions of Electricity Directive 5.03
  tariffs for 6.118
    set through market-based arrangements 6.120
network security
  under Electricity Security Directive 18.35–9
networks
  competition 11.11
  non-discriminatory TPA to 5.45
new capacity
  tendering
    energy security 18.18
new generators
  renewable energy
    grid access 10.31
new infrastructure
  applications to NRAs for exemptions for 6.54
  TPA and 6.53
new interconnectors
  applications to NRAs for exemptions for 6.54
  TPA and 6.53
new producers 5.58
new suppliers
  remedies for 11.65
new technologies
  tendering for new capacity for
    promotion of 5.23
Nigeria NLG
  destination clauses and 12.39
  undertakings given by 12.41
non-eligible customers
  distinction between eligible customers and in
    respect of gas
  supply 11.31
non-governmental organizations (NGOs)
  support for globalization 1.38
Nordic Link 5.101
Nordpool 5.103
Norsk Hydro 2.125
  commitments from in respect of destination
    clauses 12.38
  commitments made by 12.09
  undertakings given by 12.10
Norway
  co-operation with EEA 2.116

Index

Norway (cont.)
  destination clauses 12.38
  energy supply failures in 18.09
  European Commission initiates proceedings against gas companies in 12.07
  gas sales in 2.125
  gas supply from 1.67
  joint selling arrangements in 12.05
  notification under Hydrocarbons Licensing Directive 7.11
nuclear accidents
  trans-boundary potential of 9.02
Nuclear Decommissioning Authority (NDA)
  state aid and 15.86–9
Nuclear Decommissioning Fund (NDF)
  establishment of 9.37
nuclear energy
  alternative to imported oil 9.05
  EU policy on 9.03
  European law relating to 4.01
  failure by Member States to agree on common policy for 2.19
  issues of competition in 9.01
  need for adaptation of EU legal order for 9.39
  objectives of Euratom in relation to 2.17
  regulation of 19.41
  state aids 9.01
  states' reliance on 9.02
nuclear fuel
  energy security 18.104–6
nuclear materials
  appeal against EAS barring imports of 9.27
  EAS may bar imports of 9.26
nuclear policy
  changes to with enlargement of EU 9.20
  EU 9.02
nuclear power
  security of supply 9.11
nuclear power stations
  construction of 1.24
nuclear reactors 9.02

obligations
  ECJ decisions on failure to fulfil 2.98
offshore installations
  access to 6.21
Ofgem 3.51
oil
  nuclear energy as alternative to imported 9.05
oil industry
  attempt to impose common rules relating to 7.01
  internal market programme has little impact on 7.01
  regulation of 19.39

security of supply 1.24
oil markets
  monopolies in 12.01
oil prices
  fall in 2.34
oil production
  small in European Union 7.01
oil products
  dismantling of monopolies in France and Greece 7.01
oil reserves
  Norway 2.125
oil sector
  Hydrocarbons Licensing Directive directed at 7.02
Oil Stocks Directive 1968
  background to 18.60
  main provisions of 18.63
  requirements under 18.61
  revisions of 18.62
Oil Stocks Directive 1998
  changes made by 18.64
oil supply
  crises in 1.32
  crisis management 18.66–7
  reliability of 1.32
OMV
  constraints on 12.49
  undertakings given by 12.50
opinions
  scope of 2.114
Organization for Economic Co-operation and Development (OECD)
  globalization and 1.38
Organization of Arab Petroleum Exporting Countries (OAPEC) 2.34
Organization of Petroleum Exporting Countries (OPEC) 1.32, 2.34
origins
  guarantee of 10.23
  under Renewables Directive 10.26
outages
  high cost of electricity 1.63
overriding community interests
  state aid and 15.64–9
own premises
  electricity supply to 5.51
ownership
  importance of in competition 1.93

Partnership and Co-operation Agreements (PCA) 2.167
  concluded between EU and Russian Federation 2.163
  principle objectives of 2.164

699

Index

Partnership and Co-operation Agreements (PCA) (*cont.*)
  development of 2.161
  main provisions of 2.162
payment methods
  choice of under Electricity Directive 5.11
Pego project 13.25
Permanent High Level Group
  Energy Community Treaty 2.129
Permanent Partnership Council (PPC) 2.165
pipeline facilities
  access to 6.21
pipeline networks
  importance of storage in operations of 6.30
  natural monopoly in 12.02
planning
  obligations under Gas Directive 6.08
Poland
  brown coal production in 8.03
  hard coal production in 8.03
  notification under Hydrocarbons Licensing Directive 7.11
  stranded costs 15.48–9
political intervention
  M&A 14.136
polluter-pays principle 15.88
Portugal
  accession to EU 2.40, 2.45
  golden shares and 14.139
  merger proposals 14.93–7
  privatization 14.144–5
  procedural requirements in 3.50
  stranded costs 15.50–1
post-investment
  provisions of Energy Charter Treaty 2.135
postal service
  exclusive rights
    case law 16.43–5
power exchanges
  trading on 3.26
power generators
  impact of liberalization on 1.51
power stations
  capacity 1.64
pre-investment
  provisions of Energy Charter Treaty 2.136
preferential access
  ECJ ruling on 5.132, 5.134–5
  in relation to Electricity Directive 5.133
preliminary rulings
  citizens activating procedure for 2.104
  ECJ 2.103
  importance of in development of Community law 2.105

pressure levels
  gas networks 6.20
price
  obligations under Gas Directive 6.08
price formation
  electricity
    findings of Energy Sector Inquiry on 11.53
price information
  gas
    findings of Energy Sector Inquiry on 11.58
private monopolies
  United States 1.29
privatization 1.25
  across Europe 14.142
  Belgium 14.148–50
  France 14.146–7
  generation of state finances from 1.44
  Portugal 14.144–5
procurement
  by TSOs
    for reserve capacity 5.33
    to cover losses 5.33
product market
  definition 11.22
  electricity
    balancing powers 11.28
  gas 11.30
profit splitting mechanisms 12.40
public control *see* **nationalization**
public procurement 2.58
  under Hydrocarbons Licensing Directive 7.20
public security
  arguments relating to golden shares 14.151–3
public service compensation
  not state aid if fulfilling certain conditions 15.60–1
public service guarantees
  under Electricity Directive 5.11
public service obligations (PSOs) 16.02
  applications for exemptions from application of Gas Directive on grounds of 6.14
  compensation for costs of carrying out is not state aid 5.14
  concerns over distortions of competition arising from 5.13
  derogations
    in respect of energy security 18.26–8
  energy industry 1.28
  energy security 18.13–6
  exemptions from application of Gas Directive on grounds of 6.13
  main provisions under Gas Directive 6.07
  need for clear definition of 6.09
  need to fulfil 6.88
  provisions under Gas Directive 6.05

Index

public service obligations (PSOs) (cont.)
   security of gas supply 6.18
   under EEC Treaty 2.26
   under Electricity Directive 5.08
     scope of 5.09
   under Gas Directive
     scope of 6.06

qualified majority voting
   adoption of acts by 2.79
   in harmonization votes 2.40
   increase in legislative decisions subject to 2.50
   justification for 2.80
   need for 2.39
quality
   regulation 1.78
quantitative restrictions
   prohibitions on imports and exports in EEC Treaty 2.24
radiation standards
   under Euratom 9.09
radioactive waste
   no provisions for under Euratom 9.15
re-allocation
   concentration of undertakings 14.23
   parties to concentration can trigger 14.24
recommendations
   scope of 2.114
reduction clauses 12.20
   defence of 12.22
   similarity to gas supply agreements 12.21
referral system
   Member States may as to use in respect of concentrations 14.21
   NCAs and 14.26
   operation of 14.25
   under Merger Regulation 14.19
regional co-operation
   energy sector 19.49
   Euro-Mediterranean Association Agreements possible model for 2.171
regional electricity boards 1.27
Regional Energy Markets Initiative 3.40
regional markets
   concept of 3.41
   definition of 3.42
   support of Member States' governments for 3.43
regional policy 2.58
regulation
   Austria 3.07
   basis of European 3.03
   case for supranational form of 3.11
   co-ordination of 3.06
   coal industry 19.40
   competition, for 1.47, 1.76
   conduct 1.78
   development of jurisprudence 3.07
   emergence of system of European for energy sector 19.30
   emergency of multi-level structure of 3.60
   emerging structure 3.12
   energy sector 3.04
     non-compliance 19.45–6
   enforcement 4.03
   extension and reinforcement of role of NRAs under Electricity Directive 5.04
   Germany 3.07
   Greece 3.07
   increasing complexity of in energy sector 19.31–4
   independent regulator 1.79
   Italy 3.07
   key relationships in 3.47
   lack of consistency in 3.58
   Member States 3.07
   Netherlands 3.07
   nuclear energy 19.41
   oil industry 19.39
   organization of 1.80
   potential for increased co-operation in energy sector 19.35–7
   procedures for 1.82
   quality of 1.78, 3.55
   relationship of competition law to sector 3.49
   renewable energy 17.06
   requirement for 3.01
   role of European Commission in 3.09
   safety 1.78
   single regulator to monitor gas and electricity industries 1.81
   Spain 3.07
   stranded investments 1.78
   structure of 1.77, 1.83
Regulation on Categories of Specialization Agreements 2000
   joint gas production under 12.18
Regulation on the Implementation of the Rules on Competition 2003
   announcement of review of energy sector under 11.40
   Competition Directorate lead institution in energy review of under 11.41
   investigations under 11.12
   parallel competences under 11.19
   review of electricity industry under 11.39
   review of energy sector under 11.38
   role of in reform of competition law 11.10
   scale of review of energy sector under 11.42
   second phase of review of under 11.43

Index

regulations
  scope of 2.112
regulatory authority
  emerging network of 3.02
  established in Member States 3.01
Regulatory Committee
  role of 5.67
relevant markets
  attempts to define 11.21
  geographical definition of 11.32
remedies
  divestiture
    effectiveness of 14.120
  energy release programmes
    effectiveness of 14.121
  to meet competition concerns over proposed
    mergers 14.99–103
    energy sector 14.104–19
renewable energy
  challenges to support schemes for 10.34
  commitment to 17.02
  DSOs and 10.29
  EU policy on 10.01
  European law relating to 4.01
  grid system issues 10.28
  guarantees to generators 10.22
  guidelines on 10.35
  internal market and regulation 17.06
  legal framework in respect of grid
    systems 10.30
  liberalization issues 17.07
  market distorting effects of 19.43
  new generators
    grid access 10.31
  problems relating to TSOs 17.08
  role of state aid in promoting 15.63
  state aid 10.36, 17.10
    Germany 17.14–6
    Netherlands 17.12, 17.11, 17.13
  support for 17.05
  support schemes for 10.02
  trade aspects 17.09
  TSOs and 10.29
renewable energy sources
  definition of 10.05
Renewables Directive 2001
  administrative barriers 10.27
  Commission required to present report on
    support mechanisms 10.11
  commitment of EU to 10.03
  definition of renewable sources under 10.05
  guarantees of origins under 10.26
  implementation of 10.38
  main aims of 10.04

market orientation of 10.40
national indicative targets under 10.07
oversight tasks in 10.24
progress of 10.39
provision for support schemes under 10.09
report by European Commission on
  implementation of 10.33
report by European Commission into
  operation of 10.12
reporting requirements 10.08, 10.25, 10.32
requirements on Commission to conduct
  evaluations in respect of support 10.10
scope of 10.06
treatment of competition under 17.04
Renewables Obligation 2002
  adoption in UK 10.20
  certificates under 10.21
repairs 5.58
reporting requirements
  contents of report on Gas Directive 6.111
  energy security 18.21
  outcome of process under Electricity
    Directive 18.46
  report on Gas Directive may contain
    recommendations 6.112
  under Electricity Directive 5.59
  under Electricity Security Directive 18.43–5
  under Gas Directive 6.110
  under Renewables Directive 10.08, 10.25, 10.32
Rescue and Restructuring Aid 15.79
  British Energy 15.81–5
  distortion of competition and 15.80
Research Fund for Coal and Steel 8.11
reserve capacity
  procurement by TSOs for 5.33
Resolution on Renewable Energies 2005
  adoption of 10.19
resolutions
  adoption by European Parliament 2.92
restructuring
  British Energy 9.30–5
restructuring aid
  under ECSC 8.26
retail markets
  electricity 11.26
Ruhrgas
  balancing services offered by 13.112
  entry-exit regime 13.126
  monitoring of 13.134
  proposed merger with E.ON 14.41–5
  system of tariff zones introduced by 13.127
  to improve handling access requests 13.117
  transparency on availability of capacity 13.107
  undertakings given by 12.52

Index

Ruhrgas (*cont.*)
    on acquisition by E.ON 14.116
    on congestion management 13.120
Russia
    declaration that is market economy 2.166
    gas imported into Austria from 12.49
    gas imported into Germany from 12.51
    gas supply from 1.67, 12.42
    PCA concluded between EU and 2.163
        principle objectives of 2.164
    relations with EU 2.165

safety
    gas supply 1.67
    information on required from TSOs under Electricity Regulation 5.108
    provisions under Euratom 9.10
    regulation 1.78
Saga Petroleum 2.125
Scottish Nuclear Ltd
    long-term contracts
        electricity
            duration of 13.22–3
secondary legislation
    energy sector 19.17
    function of European Commission 2.73
secondary trade
    refusal of by TSOs 5.123
security of supply *see* energy security
services of general economic interest 5.15
    energy security 18.99–100
        state aid 18.101–3
    review of 5.14
    special and exclusive rights for 16.07
ship-or-pay contracts 6.96
    complementary to take-or-pay contracts 6.97
    no grounds for derogations on basis of 6.98
Sibelga
    proposed merger with ECS 14.54–5
Single European Act 1986
    effects on energy sector 2.36
single market
    early abortive attempts to create in energy 16.93
single market rules 2.58
Skagerrak Cable 13.53
Slovakia
    brown coal production in 8.03
    reliance on nuclear energy 9.02
Slovenia
    brown coal production in 8.03
    derogation from Electricity Regulation 5.136
        importance of 5.138
        justification for 5.137
    reliance on nuclear energy 9.02

small generation
    authorization for 5.21
Sonatrach
    possibility of use of destination clauses in contracts 12.58
source of supply
    diversification of 9.24
    uranium 9.23
South-East Asia
    energy markets in 1.54
sovereignty
    issue under Hydrocarbons Licensing Directive 7.07
Soviet Union
    impact of collapse of on European energy policy 2.07
Spain
    accession to EU 2.40, 2.45
    brown coal production in 8.03
    hard coal production in 8.03
    import-export monopolies 16.80
    investigation into long-term contracts of Endesa 13.12
    investigation into long-term contracts of Gas Natural 13.12
    merger proposals 14.46–53, 14.69–71
    regulation 3.07
    stranded costs 15.52–4
special and exclusive rights
    case law on 16.13
    changes in practice 16.12
    dominant position created by grant of 16.10
    EC Treaty basis for 16.01
    importance for electricity and gas industries 16.09
    importance of to energy sector 16.04
    legal basis for 16.06
    protection of 16.03
    restricted interpretation of by ECJ 16.11
    services of general economic interest 16.07
state aid
    application of control in energy sector 15.90
    application of rules on 15.19
    assessment factors 15.20
    balancing of objectives and 15.93
    case law relating to under ECSC 8.25
    coal industry 8.10
    compensation for costs of carrying out PSOs is not 5.14
    conditions for under Coal Regulation 8.21
    control of 15.01
        objectives of 15.02
    controls on 8.17
    definition of 15.06

Index

state aid (*cont.*)
  design of compensation schemes and 15.92
  emerging trends in energy sector 19.28
  energy security
    services of general economic interest 18.101–3
  feed-in schemes 10.37
  for climate change 15.77
  for reduction of greenhouse gas emissions 15.75
  forms of compatible with common market 15.05
  liberalization and 15.10, 15.91
  Nuclear Decommissioning Authority
    and 15.86, 15.88–9
  nuclear energy 9.01
  overriding community interests and 15.64–9
  overview of 15.04
  possible improvement to rules 15.08
  procedure for reviewing 15.07
  prohibition on under EEC Treaty 2.29
  provisions in Coal Regulation 8.19
  public service compensation not if fulfilling
    certain conditions 15.60–1
  renewable energy 10.36, 17.10
    Germany 17.14–6
    Netherlands 17.11–3
  restrictions on for TENs 18.77
  role of European Commission in
    determining 15.09
  role of in balancing competition objectives in
    energy sector 19.29
  role of in promoting renewable energy 15.63
  rules on 15.03
  stranded costs and 15.24–5
  stranded costs methodology and 15.11
  TENs 18.76, 18.78
  to promote biofuels 15.73
  to support generation of green electricity 15.70–2
  under Energy Products Directive 17.31
  under Euratom 9.29
  use of stranded costs methodology in determining
    for electricity
  companies 15.14
  wave power and 15.74
state finances
  generation of from privatization 1.44
state guarantees
  EDF 15.56–9
state monopolies
  adjustment of 16.48–50
  not perceived as obstacle to establishment of
    internal market 2.12
  requirements on Member States to adjust in
    EEC Treaty 2.25
  suppliers 1.23
state ownership *see* **nationalization**

Statoil 2.125, 12.11
  commitments made by 12.09, 12.32
    in respect of destination clauses 12.38
  joint marketing with ESB 12.31
steel industry
  success of ECSC in managing contraction of 8.09
  transfer of control to supranational authority 2.14
storage
  access to 6.32
    under contract release programmes 14.132
    under Gas Directive 6.29
  common rules for gas 6.04
  dependence on 6.31
  European Commission's limitation on exemption
    from access provisions on Gas Directive 6.42
  experiences gained from First Gas Directive 6.41
  facilities used in connection with local production
    operations 6.44
  gas supply 1.67
  general duties of under Gas Directive 6.25
  importance of in operations of pipeline
    networks 6.30
  importance of in relation to market
    liberalization 6.34
  lack of potential of electricity 1.63
  limitation on exemptions relating to under Gas
    Directive 6.42
  tariffs for 6.45
  TPA in relation to under Gas Directive 6.40
  variation of provision of facilities 6.33
storage capacity
  Gas Directive and 6.46
stranded asset problem 1.49
stranded costs
  Austria 15.26–7
  Belgium 15.28–31
  classification of 15.17
  competitiveness and 15.18
  definition of 15.12
  Denmark 15.32
  eligibility of 15.16
  France 15.33
  Greece 15.34–5
  Hungary 15.36–9
  Italy 15.40–3
  Luxembourg 15.44
  Netherlands 15.45–7
  offsetting 15.21–3
  Poland 15.48–9
  Portugal 15.50–1
  Spain 15.52–4
  state aid and 15.24–5
  transitional provisions on 15.13
  UK 15.55

stranded costs methodology
    European Commission Communication on 15.15
    state aid and 15.11
    use of in determining state aid for electricity
        companies 15.14
stranded investments 1.78
subsidiarity
    effect on energy sector 2.49
    introduction of notion of 2.47
    legislation and 2.48
Suez
    proposed merger with Gaz de France 14.98
supply
    case law on exclusive rights of 2.30
    provisions under Gas Directive 6.26
supply and demand balance
    under Electricity Security Directive 18.40–1
support schemes
    advantages of 10.14
    challenges to in respect or renewable
        energy 10.34
    Commission required under Renewables Directive
        to present report on 10.11
    green certificate system 10.15
    provision for under Renewables Directive 10.09
    renewable energy 10.02
    requirements on Commission under Renewables
        Directive to conduct evaluations on 10.10
    tax incentives 10.18
    tendering procedures 10.17
    types of 10.13
sustainable development
    energy sector 1.50
swap agreements
    contract for swap of LNG between GDF and
        ENEL 12.56
Sweden
    energy supply failures in 18.09
    investigation into energy taxes
        regime in 17.35–7
Synergen power plant 12.31
system connection
    lack of 6.101
take-or-pay clauses
    contracts 6.72
        acceptance of 6.92
        derogations 6.75, 6.77
            criteria for 6.82
            decisions on 6.79
            priorities for 6.83
            refusal of derogations 6.80
            review of 6.81
            scope for 6.84
            withdrawal of 6.78

tariff supervision
    by NRAs 5.61
    limitations on 5.62
tariff zones 13.127–8
tax
    framework for under Energy Products
        Directive 17.32
    introduction of on energy products by
        Member States 17.33
    limitation on exemptions by Member States 17.34
tax harmonization 2.58
tax incentives
    support schemes 10.18
technical rules 5.17
    under Gas Directive 6.19
technical specifications
    electricity 1.63
telecommunications policy 16.14
Telecommunications Terminal Equipment
    case 16.18–25
    effects of 16.26–30
tendering
    control of procedure 5.26
    details of procedure 5.24
    equivalent measures
        energy security 18.19
    invitations for 5.25
    new capacity
        energy security 18.18
        for promotion of new technologies 5.23
        in interests of environmental protection 5.23
    procedure for 5.22
termination of customer contracts 14.119
territorial sales restrictions see destination clauses
third countries
    monitoring of EU entities in under Hydrocarbons
        Licensing Directive 7.19
third party access (TPA)
    assessment of progress 13.135
    commitments on obtained by European
        Commission 13.135
    elements of 13.136
    exemptions from on grounds of energy
        security 18.24–5
    gas markets
        Germany 13.40
    guidelines on under Gas Directive 6.43
    in relation to storage under Gas Directive 6.40
    liberalization and 13.140
    new infrastructure 6.53
    new interconnectors 6.53
    non-discriminatory to networks 5.45
    progress on 13.137
    provisions under Gas Directive 6.38

third party access (TPA) (*cont.*)
  refusal of by interconnectors 13.88–95
    case law 13.96–7, 13.101–3
  regulation of under Gas Directive 6.39
  rules relating to LNG 1.74
  services offered by TSOs to 6.122
  subject to guarantees 6.124
  transparency requirements 6.128
Thyssengas
  commitments on trading of capacity rights 13.118
  entry-exit regime 13.123
  free balancing system offered by 13.109
  monitoring of 13.131
  transparency on availability of capacity 13.104
  undertakings on congestion management 13.119
Tractebel
  merger with Distrigaz 14.88
trading
  capacity rights 6.130, 13.118
  electricity 3.26
  renewable energy 17.09
Trans European Networks (TENs) 2.58
  competition issues 18.73
  energy security and 18.68
  funding 18.75
  guidelines for 18.71
    on equipment 18.74
    on installations 18.74
  legal basis for 18.69
  objectives of 18.79
  priority projects 18.72
  restrictions on state aid for 18.77
  state aid and 18.76, 18.78
  streamlining authorization procedures 18.80
Trans Tunisian Pipeline Co 13.87
Trans-Austrian Gas (TAG) pipeline 12.42
transaction curtailment procedure
  limited by TSOs 5.92
transformation
  electricity 1.63
transit
  contracting parties to Energy Charter Treaty to facilitate 2.143
  co-operation in under Energy Charter Treaty 2.145
  disputes over 2.147
  enforcement of 2.148
  limitations on provisions of Energy Charter Treaty 2.152
  provisions on Energy Charter Treaty on 2.142, 2.150
  requirements on transit state under Energy Charter Treaty 2.146

transit pipelines
  access to 6.61
  securing capacity on 6.62
transit states
  obligations under Energy Charter Treaty 2.151
transmission
  access to under contract release programmes 14.131
  case law on exclusive rights of 2.30
  definition of 5.27
    in respect of natural gas 6.22
  general duties of under Gas Directive 6.25
transmission capacity rights
  firm 5.122
transmission management
  competition issues relating to 13.02
transmission networks
  creation of non-discriminatory access rights to 1.91
transmission of electricity
  common rules for 5.07
  market definition 11.24
transmission of gas
  common rules for 6.05
transmission pricing
  case law relating to 13.33
  flexibility of competition law in calculation 13.45
  need for if competition to be effective 13.31
transmission systems operators (TSOs) 3.03
  appointment of 5.28
  calculation of amounts of compensation payable by 5.109
  capacity availability and 5.93
  charges for network access 5.86
    setting 5.87
  compensation mechanism under Electricity Regulation 5.81
  congestion management by 5.90
  designation of under Gas Directive 6.23
  firm transmission capacity rights for 5.122
  formation of group by Madrid Forum 3.33
  guidelines contained in 5.83
  information on safety and security required from under Electricity Regulation 5.108
  information required from on interconnection capacities under Electricity Regulation 5.107
  information requirements on under Electricity Regulation 5.106
  inter-TSO compensation mechanism under Electricity Regulation 5.84
  interconnection functions of 5.30
  limited transaction curtailment procedure by 5.92
  must allow capacity rights to be freely tradable 6.131

Index

transmission systems operators (TSOs) (*cont.*)
  problems relating to renewable energy 17.08
  procurement of reserve capacity 5.33
  procurement to cover losses 5.33
  provisions for charges under Electricity Regulation 5.82
  refusal of secondary trade by 5.123
  renewable energy and 10.29
  requirements for legal unbundling of 5.42
  requirements of in relation to environmental policy 5.31
  responsibilities of 5.29
  role of Member States in designating under Gas Directive 6.24
  TPA services offered by 6.122
  transparency requirements 5.125, 6.128
transparency
  electricity
    findings of Energy Sector Inquiry on 11.52
  gas
    findings of Energy Sector Inquiry on 11.57
  obligations
    under Directive on Insider Dealing and Market Manipulation 11.63
    under Directive on Markets in Financial Instruments 11.63
    under Gas Regulations 6.128
  regulatory action 11.62
transport
  dependence of electricity and gas on fixed networks to 1.60
transportation contracts 6.123
transportation networks
  unbundling 1.89
transportation of natural gas
  contract for transportation of between GDF and ENI 12.56
Treaty Establishing the European Atomic Energy Community 1957 (Euratom)
  absence of provisions for decommissioning under 9.15
  competition issues under 9.16
  energy security under 18.106
  establishment of ESA under 9.13
  health provisions of 9.08
  institutional features 9.12
  key differences with EC Treaty 9.06
  no provisions for radioactive waste under 9.15
  objectives of 9.07
  primary source of competence for European Commission 9.14
  purpose of 9.04
  radiation standards under 9.09
  safety provisions under 9.10

Treaty of Nice 2001
  establishment of Research Fund for Coal and Steel under 8.11
  preparing for further enlargement of European Union 2.55
Treaty on European Union 1992
  changes made to Internal Energy Market programme by 2.47
  effects of 2.46
  enhanced role of European Parliament under 2.53
  original proposals to include separate chapter on in 2.52
  references to energy in 2.51
Treaty Secretariat
  Energy Community Treaty 2.129
two-thirds rule
  merger proposals and 14.40

UK/Belgium Interconnector 13.57–8
UK/French Interconnector 13.55–6
unbundling
  accounts 5.58
  compliance provisions in respect of under Gas Directive 6.37
  derogation from Electricity Directive provisions 5.72
  energy industry 1.85
    by law 1.86
    functional separation 1.87
    separation for accounting purposes 1.88
  energy markets 1.36
  interpretation of provisions on in Electricity Directive 5.43
  lack of compliance by Greece with requirements in Electricity Directive 5.78
  legal under Electricity Directive 5.39
  practical considerations under Electricity Directive 5.41
  practical implementation
    Belgium 5.41
    Hungary 5.41
    Italy 5.41
    Netherlands 5.41
  provisions in Gas Directive 6.36
  provisions of Electricity Directive 5.02
  requirements of legal of TSOs 5.42
  role of ETSO 3.24
  transportation networks 1.89
  types of envisaged by Electricity Directive 5.38
undertakings
  provisions in Commission Decisions on 11.15
uneven market development 6.100
unfair pricing
  test for 13.32

Union for the Co-ordination of the Transmission of Electricity (UCTE)
    Operational Handbook of 3.24
United Kingdom
    accession to EU 2.45
    energy supply failures in 18.09
    notification under Hydrocarbons Licensing Directive 7.11
    stranded costs 15.55
United States
    energy supply failures in 18.09
    experience with authorization of LNG terminals 6.59
    private monopolies 1.29
universal service
    concept of under Electricity Directive 5.10
unused capacity 6.127
upstream market
    gas supply 1.70
    market definition 11.30
upstream pipeline networks
    capacity available to 6.51
    considerations when making rules for 6.50
    dispute resolution in relation to 6.52
    Gas Directive continues special access regime for 6.47
    general principles for access to 6.49
    Hydrocarbons Licensing Directive in relation to 6.51
    sensitive issue of 6.48
uranium
    contracts for enrichment of 9.28
    source of 9.23
uranium mine
    European Union 9.02
Uruguay Round 1.38

VEBA
    proposal to merge with VIAG 14.62–5
Verbändevereinbarung
    balancing mechanism of 13.37
    incompatibility of with competition law 13.38
    principles for calculation of prices under 13.34
    problems arising from 13.36
    second framework agreement under 13.35
Verbund
    proposal to merge with EnergieAllianz 14.72–3
vertical agreements
    destination clauses as 12.36
vertical demarcation
    definition of 1.69
vertical foreclosure
    electricity
        findings of Energy Sector Inquiry on 11.50
    gas
        findings of Energy Sector Inquiry on 11.55
VIAG
    proposal to merge with VEBA 14.62–5
voting
    changes to procedures of Council of Ministers 2.39
    increase in legislative decisions subject to qualified majority 2.50

wave power
    state aid and 15.74
West Germany
    energy industry 1.29
White Paper on the Internal Market 2.37
wholesale exporters 5.47
wholesale importers 5.47
wholesale markets
    electricity 11.25
        intra-day trading opportunities 11.29
Wingas 12.20, 12.24
World Trade Organization (WTO)
    creation of 1.38
    Energy Charter Treaty in line with rules on trade in goods 2.141